Chambers
Crossword
Completer

An alternate letter word list

Compiled by
J. C. P. Schwarz

Foreword by
Don Manley

Chambers

© 1987 W & R Chambers Ltd Edinburgh

British Library Cataloguing in Publication Data

Schwarz, J. C. P.
   Chambers crossword completer: an alternate letter
   word-list.
   1. Crossword puzzles—Glossaries, vocabularies, etc.
   etc.
   I. Title
   793.73'2   GV1507.C7

   ISBN 0-550-19015-5

Printed in Great Britain at the University Press, Cambridge.

Foreword

Most cryptic crosswords have answers with alternate letters 'checked' by crossing answers. The other letters are 'unchecked'. This means that you may find yourself with a diagram entry like this:

> a – a – e –   where the answer could be   azalea,
>
> or like this:
>
> – a – a – e   where the answer could be   parade.

These are only two of the possibilities.

Until now there has been no 'alternate letter dictionary' to help the solver to explore the different alternatives – or indeed to help the crossword setter to complete filling up the grid with words. *Chambers Crossword Completer* helps to change all that, using as a database all the words in *Chambers 20th Century Dictionary*. (Phrases, and most plural forms and variant verb endings, are not included, for reasons of space, but you can't have everything!)

Entries, ranging from 4-letter words to 15-letter ones, are arranged by length and then alphabetically according to the alternate letters. These letters are shown in bold for the first word in the group of words for which they are relevant.

For quick and easy reference, the *Crossword Completer* is divided into two sections. The first lists the words according to the alphabetical order of the *odd* letters (e.g. **ab**ac, ... **ab**ba and so on to **zoogeographical** and **zoophytological**); the second section lists them according to the *even* letters (e.g. b**ab**a ... b**ar**b and so on to s**ys**t**em**i**sa**t**io**n and C**ze**c**ho**s**lo**v**ak**i**an**).

You may have to solve a few clues of course, but there is no harm in having your inspiration prompted from time to time!

Don Manley
Oxford 1987

Words arranged according to
ODD LETTERS

For words arranged according to EVEN LETTERS see pages 335-667.

abac	alga	atop	bray	brit	booh	batt	craw	calx
Adam	Argo	avow	buat	buik	book	beta	Crax	cell
Adar	ache	axon	baba	bake	boom	bête	cyan	celt
adaw	achy	adry	babe	bike	boon	bete	czar	cill
afar	agha	aery	Babi	boko	boor	beth	caba	cola
agar	ashy	afro	babu	buke	boot	bite	cube	cold
ajar	Abib	airn	baby	byke	brod	bito	coca	cole
Ajax	abid	airt	boba	bald	brog	bitt	coch	coll
alae	acid	airy	buba	bale	broo	both	cock	colt
alar	adit	'Arry	bubo	balk	brow	bott	coco	cull
alas	agin	aura	bach	ball	buoy	butt	cade	culm
alay	agio	awry	back	balm	bapu	byte	cadi	cult
amah	akin	aesc	beck	Balt	barb	baud	cede	Cama
anal	alit	also	bice	balu	bard	bauk	cedi	came
anan	amid	apse	bock	bell	bare	baur	cide	camp
anas	amie	arse	buck	belt	bark	blub	coda	coma
apay	amir	acta	bade	bile	barm	blue	code	comb
Arab	amis	aitu	bede	bilk	barn	blur	chef	come
arak	anil	alto	bide	bill	barp	Blut	cher	comp
Aran	aria	anta	bode	bold	bere	bouk	chew	coms
arar	arid	ante	body	bole	berg	houn	chez	cyma
asar	aril	anti	bael	boll	berk	bout	clef	cyme
atap	avid	arty	Beeb	bolt	berm	Brum	cleg	cane
aval	axil	Asti	beef	bulb	bird	brut	clem	cang
away	axis	auto	been	bulk	birk	bevy	clew	cann
ayah	ankh	abut	beer	bull	birl	bawd	coed	can't
azan	able	ague	beet	bema	Biro®	bawl	cree	cant
abba	ably	alum	bhel	Bimm	birr	bawn	crew	cany
abbé	ally	anus	bien	boma	bora	bawr	café	cent
albe	amla	aqua	bier	bomb	bord	bowl	caff	cond
ambo	aula	arum	bleb	bumf	bore	bowr	coff	cone
arba	auld	arvo	bled	bump	born	Bixa	coft	conk
ance	axle	abye	blee	banc	bort	baye	cuff	conn
arch	acme	amyl	blet	band	burd	bayt	cage	cony
arco	alma	aryl	blew	bane	burg	boyg	cagy	cunt
asci	alme	azym	bley	bang	burk	buzz	coho	choc
aide	alms	adze	Boer	bank	burl	ceas	cain	chop
abed	ammo	Baal	bred	bant	burn	cell	cell	chou
abet	army	baas	hree	bend	burp	chai	chad	chow
Acer	aîné	bead	bren	béne	burr	chal	chid	cion
Ades	ain't	beak	brer	beni	bury	cham	chik	clod
aged	Ainu	beam	brew	benj	byre	chap	chin	clog
agee	anna	bean	baff	bent	base	char	chip	clop
agen	anno	bear	baft	bind	bash	chat	chit	clot
ahem	aunt	beat	biff	bine	bask	chaw	chiv	clou
ajee	awny	beau	buff	bing	bass	chay	Clio	clow
akee	aeon	bias	bufo	bink	bast	ciao	clip	cloy
alee	agog	blab	bego	bint	best	clad	cuif	coof
alew	agon	blad	biga	bona	bise	clag	cuit	cook
amen	ahoy	blae	bigg	bond	bish	clam	cake	cool
anew	alod	blah	bogy	bone	bisk	clan	caky	coom
apex	aloe	blat	baht	bony	bosh	clap	coke	coon
area	alow	blay	buhl	buna	bosk	clat	calf	coop
ared	amok	boar	bail	bund	bos'n	claw	calk	co-op
aret	anoa	boat	bait	bung	boss	clay	call	coot
arew	anon	brad	bein	bunk	bush	coal	calm	croc
aver	anow	brae	blin	bunt	busk	coat	calp	crop
Aves	apod	brag	blip	biog	buss	coax		crow
awed	arow	bran	boil	blob	bust	crab		capa
axel	atóc	bras	Brie	bloc	busy	crag		cape
axes	atok	braw	brig	blot	bate	cram		capo
affy	atom		brim	blow	bath	cran		caps
alfa			brio	boob	bats	crap		cope

Copt	clue	deep	duma	disc	ecce	expo	fled	fink
copy	coup	deer	dumb	dish	ecco	**eard**	flee	Finn
card	cour	deev	dump	disk	eech	earl	fleg	fino
care	crud	dieb	**Dane**	diss	etch	earn	flew	fond
cark	crue	died	dang	dose	**Edda**	ecru	flex	fone
carl	crux	dies	dank	doss	eddo	eery	fley	font
carp	**cave**	diet	dant	dost	eddy	eorl	foen	fund
carr	cavy	Dieu	dene	dush	**Eden**	euro	foes	fung
cart	cive	doen	dent	dusk	eger	eyra	free	funk
cere	cove	doer	ceny	dust	emeu	eyre	fret	**feo**d
cert	**cawk**	does	dine	**data**	enew	eyry	fuel	floe
ciré	cowl	dree	ding	date	épée	**ease**	**faff**	flog
cirl	cowp	drew	dink	dita	eten	east	fife	flop
cord	**coxa**	drey	dint	dite	even	easy	fuff	flow
core	coxy	duel	Doña	ditt	ever	else	**fegs**	food
corf	**coze**	duet	dona	dote	evet	Erse	figo	fool
cork	cozy	dyed	done	doth	ewer	erst	fogy	foot
corm	**D-day**	dyer	dong	doty	exes	esse	**fehm**	frog
corn	dead	**daff**	don't	duty	eyed	**eath**	föhn	from
curb	deaf	daft	dune	**daub**	eyes	Esth	**faik**	frow
curd	deal	deft	dung	daud	**edge**	**elul**	fail	**fard**
cure	dean	defy	dunk	deus	edgy	etui	fain	fare
curé	dear	doff	dunt	douc	eggy	exul	fair	farl
curl	deaw	duff	dyne	doup	ergo	**eevn**	faix	farm
curn	**dhak**	**dago**	**dhow**	dour	euge	envy	feis	faro
curr	dhal	digs	doob	dout	eugh	**emys**	flip	fart
curt	dial	doge	dook	drub	**eche**	**feal**	flit	fere
casa	Dian	dogy	dool	drug	echo	fear	flix	ferm
case	doab	**dahl**	doom	drum	echt	feat	foil	fern
cash	doat	**Dáil**	door	Druz	epha	fiat	foin	fire
cask	drab	dais	drop	**Davy**	ethe	flab	frig	firk
cast	drad	deid	drow	deva	**edit**	flag	fris	firm
cess	drag	deil	**dopa**	diva	egis	flak	frit	firn
cist	dram	doit	dope	dive	emir	flam	friz	fora
cose	drap	drib	dopy	divi	emit	flan	**fake**	ford
cosh	drat	drip	dupe	dove	epic	flap	fike	fore
coss	draw	**dika**	**Dard**	**dawd**	eric	flat	fiky	fork
cost	dray	dike	dare	dawk	evil	flaw	fyke	form
cosy	duad	duke	darg	dawn	exit	flax	**fa-la**	fort
cush	dual	dyke	dari	dawt	**ekka**	flay	fall	furl
cusk	duan	**dale**	dark	dewy	EOKA	foal	falx	furr
cusp	duar	dali	darn	dowd	Esky®	foam	fell	fury
cuss	dwam	dalt	dart	dowf	**eale**	frab	felt	fyrd
cyst	dyad	dele	dere	dowl	eild	frae	file	**fash**
cate	**debt**	delf	derm	down	**egma**	frap	fill	fast
cite	**dace**	deli	dern	dowp	elmy	frau	film	fess
cito	deck	dell	derv	dows	emma	fray	fils	fisc
cits	dice	dill	dire	**dixi**	Emmy	**face**	fold	fish
city	dich	dole	dirk	dixy	**eine**	fact	folk	fisk
cote	dick	doll	dirl	doxy	erne	feck	full	fist
coth	dict	dolt	dirt	**daze**	esne	fico	fyle	foss
cott	dock	dule	Dora	doze	etna	foci	**fame**	fusc
cute	duce	dull	dorm	dozy	eyne	fuck	feme	fuse
cyte	duck	duly	dorp	**ecad**	**ebon**	**fade**	fume	fuss
cauk	duct	**dame**	dorr	Edam	enow	fado	fumy	fust
caul	**Dada**	damn	dort	egad	epos	fady	**fand**	**fate**
caum	dado	damp	dory	egal	Eros	Fido	fane	fête
caup	dido	deme	dura	élan	Eton	**feed**	fang	fett
chub	dodo	demo	dure	élan	euoi	feel	fank	fitt
chug	dude	demy	durn	eoan	evoe	feer	fend	**faun**
chum	**deed**	dime	duro	état	exon	feet	fent	feud
chut	deem	dome	**dash**	exam	eyot	fief	find	flub
club	deen	domy	desk	eyas	**espy**	flea	fine	flue

flux	grey	ginn	glum	**ha**ik	hone	haul	**impi**	jure
foud	**gaff**	gone	glut	hail	hong	haut	I-spy	jury
foul	gift	gong	gouk	hain	honk	houf	**inro**	**jas**p
four	goff	gonk	gout	hair	hung	hour	**into**	jasy
five	guff	gunk	grub	ha'it	hunk	hout	iota	jess
fawn	**ga**ga	Günz	grue	heil	hunt	**have**	**idyl**	jest
fowl	gage	gyny	grum	heir	hood	hive	ivy'd	Jesu
foxy	gogo	**gao**l	grum	hoik	**hoo**d	Hova	**jean**	jism
faze	**gaid**	glob	**gave**	huia	hoof	hove	jeat	josh
fizz	gain	glow	give	**haji**	hook	**hawk**	**jibe**	joss
fozy	gair	good	gyve	hajj	hoop	hawm	jobe	just
fuze	gait	goof	**gawd**	**haka**	hoot	hawm	juba	**jat**o
fuzz	geit	gook	gawk	hake	**hep**t	hewn	jube	jeté
geal	glia	gool	gawp	hike	hipt	howe	**jack**	jota
gean	glib	goon	gowd	hyke	hope	howf	jock	jute
gear	glid	goop	gowf	**hale**	hype	howk	joco	**jaup**
geat	glim	goor	gowk	half	hypo	howl	**jade**	jouk
ghat	glit	grog	gowl	hall	**hard**	**hiya**	judo	jour
glad	grid	grot	gown	halm	hare	hwyl	judy	**Java**
glam	grig	grow	**gaze**	halo	hark	**haze**	**jeel**	jive
G-man	grim	**gape**	gazy	halt	harl	hazy	jeep	Jove
gnar	grin	gapó	gizz	held	harm	hizz	jeer	**jowl**
gnat	grip	**garb**	**haa**f	hele	harn	**igad**	joey	**jazy**
gnaw	gris	gare	haar	he'll	haro	imam	J-pen	jazz
goad	grit	gart	head	hell	harp	**Igbo**	**jeff**	**khan**
goaf	guid	germ	heal	helm	hart	inby	jiff	khat
goal	**gajo**	gird	heap	help	herb	**Inca**	**juga**	knag
goat	**gala**	girl	hear	hila	herd	inch	**Jehu**	knap
grab	gale	girn	heat	hild	here	itch	john	knar
Graf	gall	giro	hoar	hill	herl	**ibex**	**jail**	koan
gram	geld	girr	hoax	hilt	herm	iced	Jain	ksar
gran	gelt	girt	**hebe**	hold	hern	icer	joln	kyat
grat	gila	gore	hobo	hole	hero	idca	**juju**	**kibe**
gray	gild	gorm	**hac**k	Herr	Herr	idée	**jake**	**keck**
guan	gill	gory	hech	Holi	hers	idem	joke	kick
guar	gilt	gurl	heck	holm	hery	Ides	joky	**kade**
gyal	gold	gurn	hick	holp	hire	ilea	juke	kadi
gaby	gole	guru	hock	hols	hore	ilex	**jell**	kudu
gibe	golf	gyre	huck	holt	horn	item	jill	**keek**
gobo	golp	**gash**	**ha**de	holy	hors	**info**	jilt	keel
goby	gula	gasp	hadj	hula	hurl	**ibid**	jole	keen
go-by	gule	gast	hide	hule	hurt	ibis	joll	keep
gybe	gulf	gest	**haem**	hulk	**hash**	ilia	jolt	kier
geck	gull	gism	haet	hull	hask	inia	July	knee
gade	gulp	gist	heed	hyle	hasp	irid	**jamb**	knew
gadi	guly	gosh	heel	**ham**e	hast	iris	jimp	**koff**
gude	**gamb**	Goss	hied	heme	hesp	Isis	jomo	**kago**
gaed	game	gush	hoed	hemp	hest	iwis	jump	**kohl**
Gael	gamp	gust	hoer	home	hjsh	ixia	**jane**	**kaid**
Geëz	gamy	**gate**	hued	homo	hisn	**icky**	jann	kaie
ghee	gimp	geta	huer	homy	hiss	ilka	jink	kaif
gied	gump	gite	**haff**	huma	hist	inky	jinn	kail
gien	gymp	Goth	haft	humf	hose	**idle**	jinx	kaim
gled	**gane**	gyte	heft	hump	hoss	idly	June	kain
glee	gang	**gaud**	hi-fi	hymn	host	illy	junk	keir
gleg	gant	Gaul	huff	**hand**	hush	inly	Juno	knit
glei	gena	gaum	**hagg**	hang	husk	isle	jynx	kris
glen	gene	gaun	high	hank	huso	**iamb**	**jook**	**kaka**
gley	gens	gaup	hogg	hend	huss	ismy	**jape**	kaki
goel	gent	gaur	hogh	hent	**hate**	**iynx**	**jark**	kike
goer	genu	geum	huge	hind	hath	**icon**	jarl	kuku
gree	ging	glue	hugy	hing	hete	idol	jerk	**kale**
grew	gink	glug	**ha-ha**	hint	hote	ikon	jura	kali

kell	kyte	lehr	lung	loun	mein	myna	mate	Noël
kelp	khud	laic	lunt	loup	moil	meow	maté	noes
kelt	knub	laid	lyne	lour	moit	mood	math	nife
kild	knur	laik	lynx	lout	muid	mooi	matt	niff
kill	knut	lain	lion	lava	muil	mool	maty	naga
kiln	kava	lair	loof	lave	muir	moon	mete	nigh
kilo	kiwi	leir	look	leva	make	moop	mite	Naia
kilp	kayo	loid	loom	leve	mako	moor	mitt	naïf
kilt	Keys	loin	loon	levy	mike	moot	mity	naik
kola	lead	luit	loop	live	moke	muon	mote	nail
kolo	leaf	lake	loor	love	moko	mara	moth	nain
kyle	leak	lakh	loos	lawk	male	marc	mott	Nair
Kama	leal	laky	loot	lawn	mali	mard	mute	neif
kame	leam	leke	Lyon	lewd	mall	mare	mutt	noil
kami	lean	like	Lapp	lowe	malm	marg	myth	Naja
kemb	leap	Loki	lope	lown	malt	mark	maud	Nike
kemp	lear	luke	lard	lowt	meld	marl	maul	nuke
kana	leat	la-la	lare	laze	mell	marm	maun	nala
kang	liar	lill	lark	lazy	melt	Mars	moue	nill
kans	Lias	lilo	larn	lezz	mild	mart	moup	nole
kant	load	lilt	lere	ma'am	mile	merc	meve	noll
kent	loaf	lily	lira	maar	milk	mere	move	null
kina	loam	loll	lire	mead	mill	meri	movy	name
kind	loan	lull	lirk	meal	milo	merk	mewl	nemn
kine	lyam	lulu	lord	mean	milt	merl	mews	noma
king	lobe	lama	lore	meat	mold	Mira	mowa	nome
kink	lobi	lamb	lorn	moan	mole	mire	mown	numb
kino	lace	lamé	lory	moat	moll	mirk	maxi	nana
kond	lack	lame	lure	M-way	molt	Mirv	mixt	nene
konk	lacy	lamp	lurk	myal	moly	miry	mixy	nine
kynd	lice	leme	Lyra	mace	mule	mora	moxa	none
kyne	lich	lima	lyre	mack	mull	more	maya	nong
kaon	lick	limb	lase	mica	mama	morn	moyl	no-no
khor	loch	lime	lash	mice	memo	Moro	maze	non-U
knob	loci	limn	lass	mick	mime	mort	mazy	naos
knop	lock	limp	last	mico	mome	mure	meze	neon
knot	loco	limy	less	mock	mumm	murk	moze	nook
know	luce	loma	lest	much	mump	murl	naam	noon
kook	luck	lome	lisp	muck	mana	mase	naan	noop
Kroo	lade	lump	list	made	mand	mash	neal	nape
kepi	lady	lyme	lose	Mede	mane	mask	neap	Nipa
kept	lido	lana	losh	midi	many	mass	near	nope
kipe	lode	land	löss	mode	mend	mast	neat	nard
kipp	ludo	lane	loss	modi	mene	masu	nyas	nare
kart	laer	lang	lost	mods	meng	mesa	nabk	nark
kerb	leek	lank	lush	meed	ment	mese	nabs	nary
kerf	leer	lant	lusk	meek	menu	mesh	nach	nirl
kern	lees	lanx	lust	meer	mina	mess	neck	norm
kiri	leet	lend	lyse	meet	mind	mise	nice	Norn
kirk	lied	leng	late	mien	mine	miso	nick	nurl
kirn	lief	leno	lath	miff	ming	miss	nock	nurr
kora	lien	lens	Lett	muff	mini	mist	nide	nesh
Kurd	lier	lent	lite	mage	mink	mose	nidi	ness
kest	lieu	lind	lith	magg	mino	moss	node	nest
kish	lues	line	lota	Magi	mint	most	nodi	nisi
kiss	left	ling	lote	mags	minx	Musa	nude	nose
kist	life	link	loth	Moho	miny	muse	need	nosh
koss	lift	linn	loto	mohr	mona	mush	neem	nosy
kati	loft	llno	lute	maid	mong	musk	neep	Nato
keta	luff	lint	lutz	maik	monk	muss	ne'er	nete
kite	loge	lone	lyte	mail	mono	must	nief	nett
kith	logo	long	laud	maim	mony			note
koto	luge	lune	loud	main				not-l

nott	omit	**paca**	pall	plop	pest	real	rail	rook
nuts	otic	pace	palm	plot	pisé	ream	rain	room
neuk	**oaky**	pack	palp	plow	pish	rean	rait	roon
neum	**ogle**	paco	paly	ploy	piss	reap	reif	roop
noul	oily	pact	pela	pood	posé	rear	reik	root
noun	olla	pacy	Pele	poof	pose	rial	rein	ryot
noup	only	pech	pelf	pooh	posh	road	reis	**rape**
nous	orle	peck	pell	pook	poss	roam	roil	rapt
nout	oulk	pica	pelt	pool	post	roan	roin	repp
nave	owly	pice	pila	poon	posy	roar	ruin	reps
navy	**oint**	pick	pile	poop	push	ryal	**raja**	ripe
névé	oons	Pict	pili	poor	puss	**rabi**	**rake**	ripp
nova	oont	pock	pill	poot	**pate**	robe	raki	ript
news	**oboe**	poco	pole	proa	pâté	rube	reke	rope
newt	obol	puce	polk	prod	path	ruby	roke	ropy
nowl	odor	puck	poll	prof	pita	**raca**	roky	rype
nown	**Ogpu**	**peek**	polo	prog	pith	race	rukh	**rare**
nowt	olpe	peel	polt	prom	pity	rach	ryke	rore
nowy	oops	peen	poly	proo	pote	rack	**rale**	rort
next	**oary**	peep	pule	prop	pott	racy	rely	rory
nixy	ogre	peer	pulk	pros	putt	reck	rile	**rase**
naze	okra	phew	pull	prow	**paua**	rice	rill	rash
Nazi	orra	pied	pulp	pyot	paul	rich	role	rasp
odal	ourn	pier	pulu	**papa**	phut	rick	roll	rast
ogam	ours	piet	puly	pape	pium	ricy	rule	rest
okay	owre	plea	**pimp**	pepo	plug	roch	ruly	rise
opah	**oast**	pleb	pome	pipa	plum	rock	**Rama**	risk
opal	odso	pled	pomp	pipe	plus	ruck	rami	risp
oral	onst	poem	puma	pipi	pouf	**rade**	ramp	Riss
oval	oose	poet	pump	pipy	pouk	redd	rams	Rosa
ombu	oosy	pree	pumy	pope	pour	rede	rima	rose
orby	oust	prep	**pand**	pupa	pout	re-do	rime	rosé
once	**oath**	prex	pane	**Pará**	pruh	ride	rimu	rosy
Orca	oats	prey	pang	para	**pave**	rode	rimy	rusa
ouch	onto	puer	pant	pard	Pavo	rudd	roma	ruse
odds	otto	pyet	pend	pare	**pawa**	rude	Rome	rusé
oldy	**onus**	**puff**	pene	park	pawk	**reed**	romp	rush
obey	opus	**page**	peni	parr	pawl	reef	rume	rusk
odea	ovum	pegh	penk	part	pawn	reek	rump	Russ
ogee	**odyl**	pugh	pent	père	pown	reel	**rana**	rust
Olea	onyx	**paid**	piña	peri	**pixy**	reen	rand	**rata**
oleo	oryx	paik	pine	perk	**pays**	rhea	rang	rate
omen	**ooze**	pail	ping	perm	Pnyx	riel	rani	rath
omer	oozy	pain	pink	pern	prys	riem	rank	rats
oner	ouzo	pair	pint	pert	**pize**	roed	rant	rete
open	**peag**	pais	piny	Peru	pozz	rued	rend	rite
oven	peak	pein	pond	perv	**quad**	**raff**	rent	ritt
over	peal	phiz	pone	pirl	quag	raft	reny	rota
owed	pean	plié	pong	pirn	quat	reft	rind	rote
ower	pear	plim	pons	pore	quay	rife	rine	rotl
oxen	peat	prig	pony	pork	**qadi**	riff	ring	Ruta
oxer	plan	prim	puna	porn	**quep**	rift	rink	ruth
oyer	plap	puir	punk	port	quey	ruff	rone	**raun**
oyes	plat	**puja**	punt	pory	**quid**	ryfe	rong	rhus
oyez	play	**Paki**	puny	pure	quim	**raga**	ront	roué
orfe	prad	peke	pyne	purl	quin	rag'd	rund	roul
orgy	pram	pika	**peon**	purr	quip	rage	rune	roum
obia	prat	pike	phoh	pyre	quit	ragg	rung	roup
obit	prau	poke	phon	pyro	quiz	ragi	runt	rout
odic	pray	poky	phot	**pash**	**quod**	rigg	rynd	roux
Odin	pyat	puke	pion	pass	quop	**Rahu**	**riot**	**rave**
olid	**peba**	**pale**	pioy	past	**read**	**raid**	rood	riva
olio		Pali	plod	peso	reak	raik	roof	rive

rivo	swan	syen	Sikh	shot	siss	**Saxe**	ta'en	toke
rove	swap	**safe**	soke	show	sist	sext	teed	toko
ryve	swat	sift	sukh	slob	so-so	sexy	teel	tyke
rawn	sway	sofa	syke	sloe	soss	**says**	teem	**tala**
rowt	**Saba**	Sofi	**sale**	slog	suss	scye	teen	talc
raze	sibb	soft	salp	slop	**sate**	Skye	teer	tale
razz	sybo	Sufi	salt	slot	sati	skyr	Thea	talk
scab	**sack**	**saga**	seld	slow	seta	soya	thee	tall
scad	sech	sage	sele	smog	sett	stye	them	tela
scam	sect	sago	self	snob	site	Styx	then	teld
scan	sice	sego	sell	snod	sith	**size**	thew	tell
scar	sich	sigh	sild	snog	**saul**	sizy	they	telt
scat	sick	sign	sile	snot	saut	**taal**	tied	tile
scaw	sock	**so-ho**	silk	snow	scud	T-bar	tier	till
seal	such	**saic**	sill	sook	scug	tead	toed	tilt
seam	suck	said	silo	soom	scul	teak	tree	tola
sean	syce	sail	silt	soon	scum	teal	tref	told
sear	**sida**	saim	sola	soop	scup	team	trek	tole
seat	side	sain	sold	soot	scur	Tean	tret	toll
shad	soda	sair	sole	spot	scut	tear	trew	tolt
shag	sudd	seif	soli	stoa	shul	teat	trey	tolu
shah	suds	seil	solo	stob	shun	thae	trez	tule
sham	**seed**	shim	sols	stop	shut	Thai	twee	**tame**
shan	seek	shin	sulk	stot	Sium	than	**teff**	tamp
shat	seel	ship	**same**	stow	skua	thar	tiff	teme
shaw	seem	shir	samp	swob	skug	that	tift	temp
shay	seen	shit	semé	swop	slub	thaw	toff	tems
sial	seep	shiv	semi	swot	slue	tiar	toft	time
skat	seer	ski'd	sima	soph	slug	toad	**tegg**	tomb
skaw	shea	skid	simp	sype	slum	trad	tige	tome
slab	shed	skim	soma	**sard**	slur	tram	toga	tump
slae	she'd	skin	some	sari	slut	trap	toge	tymp
slag	she's	skio	sumo	sark	smug	tray	**taha**	**tana**
slam	shet	skip	sump	scry	smur	tsar	tahr	tane
slap	shew	skis	**sand**	sera	smut	tuan	tehr	T'ang
slat	sien	skit	sane	Serb	snub	twae	toho	tang
Slav	skeg	slid	sang	sere	snug	twal	Tshi	tanh
slaw	skeo	slim	sank	serf	souk	'twas	**tail**	tank
slay	skep	slip	sans	serk	soul	twat	tait	tend
snab	sker	slit	send	serr	soum	tway	teil	tene
snag	skew	smir	sens	Shri	soup	tzar	thig	tent
snap	sled	smit	sent	sire	sour	**tabu**	thin	tind
snar	slee	snib	sind	siri	sous	to-be	thir	tine
soak	slew	snig	sine	skry	sout	toby	this	ting
soap	sley	snip	sing	sora	spud	tuba	toil	tink
soar	smee	soil	sinh	sorb	spue	tube	trie	tint
spae	smew	spic	sink	sord	spun	**tace**	trig	tiny
Spam®	sneb	spie	sone	sore	spur	tach	trim	tone
span	sned	spik	song	sori	stub	tack	trin	tong
spar	spec	spin	sung	sorn	stud	taco	trio	tony
spat	sped	spit	sunk	sort	stum	tact	trip	tuna
spaw	spet	spiv	sunn	spry	stun	tice	twig	tund
spay	spew	stie	sync	sura	swum	tich	twin	tune
stab	sted	stir	synd	surd	**save**	tick	twit	tuny
stag	stem	suit	syne	sure	Siva	toco	**taka**	tynd
stap	sten	swig	**scog**	surf	**sawn**	tuck	take	tyne
star	step	swim	scot	**sash**	sewn	**tedy**	taky	**thon**
staw	stet	swiz	scow	sass	shwa	tide	tika	Thor
stay	stew	**soja**	shod	sese	sowf	tidy	tike	thou
swab	stey	**sake**	shoe	sess	sowl	to-do	tiki	took
swad	sued	saki	shog		sowm	tody		tool
swag	suet	sika	shoo		sown	tyde		toom
swam	swee	sike	shop		sowp	**tael**		toon

toot	tote	urva	vest	whin	wipe	yuca	you'd
trod	tuts	V-day	visa	whip	ward	yuck	youk
trog	tutu	veal	vise	whir	ware	yede	your
tron	tyte	vial	visé	whit	wark	yode	yeve
trot	taut	voar	veto	whiz	warm	ybet	yawl
trow	thud	vibe	vita	writ	warn	yeed	yawn
troy	thug	vibs	vite	wake	warp	ylem	yawp
tapa	thus	vice	vote	weka	wart	yaff	yaws
tape	touk	vade	vaut	woke	wary	yuft	yawy
tapu	toun	Veda	viva	wald	we're	yegg	yowe
tipi	tour	vide	vive	wale	were	yoga	yowl
tipt	tout	veer	vivo	wali	wert	yogh	yo-yo
tope	true	vied	vizy	walk	wire	yogi	zeal
topi	trug	view	Waac	wall	wiry	yuga	zebu
Tupi	taws	vlei	Waaf	waly	word	yo-ho	zobo
type	tawt	vagi	weak	weld	wore	ywis	zobu
typo	town	vega	weal	welk	work	ylke	zack
tara	towt	vehm	wean	well	worm	yoke	zoea
tare	towy	vail	wear	we'll	worn	yuke	zein
tarn	taxa	vain	wham	welt	wort	yuky	zoic
taro	taxi	vair	whap	wild	Würm	yald	zila
tart	text	veil	what	wile	wase	yale	Zulu
terf	tizz	vein	woad	wili	wash	yeld	zimb
term	toze	void	wrap	will	wasp	yelk	zyme
tern	tuzz	vril	wick	wilt	wast	yell	zany
thro	udal	vale	wock	wily	west	yelp	Zend
thru	unau	vali	wadd	wold	wise	yelt	zinc
tire	upas	vela	wade	wolf	wish	yill	zing
tirl	Ural	veld	wadi	wull	wisp	yold	zona
tiro	urao	vele	wady	wame	wist	yolk	zone
tirr	utas	vell	wide	wemb	wost	yule	Zuñi
torc	umbo	vild	weed	wimp	wate	Yama	Zion
tore	unbe	vile	week	womb	wats	yang	zoom
tori	upby	vill	weel	wand	watt	yank	zoon
torn	unce	vola	weem	wane	wite	yond	zupa
torr	unci	vole	ween	wang	with	yoni	zarf
tort	unco	volt	weep	wank	wots	yont	zero
Tory	unde	vuln	weet	want	wyte	yunx	zurf
turd	undo	vamp	whee	wany	wauk	ygoe	zest
turf	urdé	vane	when	wend	waul	yoop	zati
Turk	Urdu	vang	whe'r	went	waur	yapp	zeta
turm	urdy	vant	whet	wind	wave	ympe	'zbud
turn	ulex	vena	whew	wine	wavy	ympt	Zeus
tyre	urea	vend	whey	wing	we've	yard	
tyro	used	vent	wiel	wink	wive	yare	
tash	user	vina	wren	winn	wove	yarn	
task	uvea	vine	Wafd	wino	wawe	yarr	
tass	upgo	vino	waff	win't	wawl	yerd	
test	urge	vint	waft	winy	wowf	yerk	
tose	Unio	viny	weft	wont	waxy	yird	
tosh	unit	viol	wife	won't	wexe	yirk	
toss	uric	vara	wage	wynd	Xian	yore	
tost	Urim	vare	waid	whoa	Xmas	york	
tush	utis	vary	waif	whom	X-ray	yurt	
tusk	ugli	Vera	wail	whop	Xema	yesk	
ta-ta	ugly	verb	wain	whot	Xosa	yest	
tate	ulna	vers	wait	whow	xyst	yate	
tath	upon	vert	weid	wood	yead	yeti	
tatt	umph	very	weil	woof	yeah	yett	
tatu	upsy	virl	weir	wool	yean	yite	
tête	Ursa	vasa	whid	woon	year	yaud	
tite	unto	vase	whig	woot	yuan	yaup	
titi	urus	vast	whim	wept	yack	yeuk	

abaca	ambos	avens	anise	arles	agoge	aerie	Anura	bwazi
abaya	abbot	adept	arise	atlas	agone	agree	adunc	black
Agama	ambit	agent	aside	ablet	alone	aurae	agued	blank
anana	abbey	aleft	avine	aglet	alowe	ayrie	abune	brack
araba	ambry	alert	avise	allot	amove	arrah	abuse	brank
asana	aecia	ament	avize	ablow	anode	aurei	acute	be-all
aband	abcee	anent	axile	aglow	apode	April	alure	brail
afald	ancle	apert	aging	allow	arose	aural	amuse	brawl
aland	ancon	arett	a-wing	agley	atoke	abram	azure	blain
apaid	arcus	avert	ahigh	allay	atone	abrim	aguti	brain
apayd	ascus	aiery	anigh	alley	avoué	abrin	amuck	brawn
award	accoy	apery	apish	alloy	awoke	agrin	ahull	beano
abase	aldea	arefy	arish	armed	azote	apron	azurn	bravo
abate	Ardea	awful	acini	almug	aloof	atrip	adult	blaes
adage	ardeb	affix	alibi	almah	among	airer	adust	brass
agape	Asdic	algid	amici	almeh	azoth	Abrus	azury	braws
agate	aided	algae	ariel	armil	acock	après	abuzz	beast
agave	addle	angle	axial	aumil	awork	arras	anvil	beaut
agaze	ardri	argue	apism	ad-man	aboil	arris	arval	blast
alate	ard-ri	aygre	axiom	admin	afoul	afrit	advew	boart
amate	addio	aggri	alien	amman	atoll	amrit	aswim	boast
amaze	add-to	algal	align	ammon	acorn	arrêt	ajwan	bract
apace	audio	Algol	anion	atman	adorn	arrow	alway	brast
apage	adder	angel	apian	armor	adown	abray	asway	beaux
avale	aider	argal	Arian	admit	apoop	array	auxin	beady
awake	alder	argil	Asian	armet	amour	aisle	adyta	beamy
aware	aidos	argol	avian	admix	abort	assai	avyze	braky
awave	audit	algum	avion	awmry	about	adsum	azyme	braxy
alang	addax	algin	amigo	amnia	adopt	arson	abysm	bobac
abash	arena	argan	aviso	apnea	afoot	aesir	Aryan	Babee
awash	Avena	argon	abies	awned	aloft	apsis	abyss	bible
abaci	acerb	aggro	adios	aînée	amort	arses	azygy	bobak
acari	ahead	Anglo	alias	annal	aport	arsis	Anzac	Babel
agami	amend	agger	amiss	annul	ayont	asses	aizle	babul
Amati	an-end	anger	Aries	awner	a'body	absit	Anzus	bubal
aback	aread	auger	agist	Alnus	agony	asset	brava	baboo
abask	aredd	augur	ahint	annat	anomy	assot	bwana	bebop
alack	abele	aegis	ariot	arnut	atomy	absey	beard	Bibby
avail	agene	argus	atilt	annex	atony	assay	bland	bobby
alarm	akene	angst	adieu	annoy	atopy	antic	blaud	bubby
again	aleye	argot	amity	aunty	alpha	artic	board	bacca
amain	amene	aught	atimy	agora	aspic	attic	braid	bocca
awarn	anele	aggry	alkyd	aloha	ample	Aztec	brand	becke
adays	arede	angry	ackee	Anona	apple	antae	beare	boche
amass	arere	aphid	ankle	aroba	appui	antre	blade	bacon
aways	arête	ashen	alkyl	aroma	ampul	aitch	blame	bacco
abaft	aleph	abhor	anker	A-bomb	appal	artal	blare	bucko
adapt	Adeni	aphis	asker	azoic	aspen	artel	blasé	buchu
agast	apeak	agila	ankus	abord	appro	astun	blate	bucku
apart	apeek	anima	askew	acold	asper	attap	blaze	baccy
avant	a-week	ahind	ad-lib	agood	Ampex®	actor	brace	bedad
avast	areal	abide	aulic	ahold	amply	after	brake	bided
await	aweel	afire	allod	aloed	appay	altar	brame	badge
alary	abeam	agile	aglee	aloud	apply	alter	brave	bedye
Araby	adeem	Alice	all-be	A-road	appuy	antar	braze	bodge
ataxy	aweto	alike	allée	aroid	aorta	aster	buaze	bodle
albee	aheap	aline	Allah	avoid	atria	astir	bhang	budge
amble	ayelp	alive	allel	axoid	Afric	attar	beach	bedel
album	abear	amice	allyl	abode	auric	altos	beath	bedim
Alban	afear	amide	all-in	above	acred	aptly	blash	bidet
amban	ameer	amine	all-to	adobe	acrid	abuna	brach	bedew
amber	anear	anile	all-up	adore	adrad	alula	brash	baddy
arbor	arear	anime	allis	afore	adred		bravi	badly

biddy	build	belly	booze	burnt	bitty	coarb	chary	check
buddy	baize	bilgy	broke	burst	bothy	chard	clary	cheek
bield	beige	billy	brose	borax	butty	cease	coaly	cleck
bleed	blite	bulgy	boong	bardy	blurb	ceaze	crapy	cleek
blend	blive	bulky	booth	barky	bluid	chace	crazy	clerk
bread	bribe	bully	broch	barmy	bound	chafe	cobia	creak
breed	bride	bemad	brogh	beray	bourd	chape	cobra	creek
by-end	brine	bemud	broth	berry	blude	chare	cabob	creel
brede	brize	bombe	block	birsy	bouge	chase	cubeb	cream
breme	brief	bombé	brock	burly	boule	chave	caboc	clean
brere	ba'ing	bumph	brook	burry	bouse	clame	cubic	credo
breve	being	bumbo	broil	basta	brûlé	clave	cable	cheap
beech	bring	bumpy	brool	basic	brume	coate	cabré	cheep
bleak	blini	bania	bloom	based	brute	crake	coble	cleep
break	blink	Binca®	broom	basse	bluff	crame	cabal	creep
bream	brick	benne	blown	baste	bourg	crane	cibol	cheer
breem	brink	binge	brown	besee	blush	crape	Cobol	clear
bleep	brisk	bonce	boots	basal	bough	crare	cabin	chess
blear	brill	bonie	biont	basil	brush	crate	Cuban	cress
breer	bairn	bonne	bloat	besom	baulk	crave	caber	cheat
beefs	blimp	bonze	boost	bosom	blunk	craze	cabas	chert
bless	briar	bunce	blowy	basan	bourn	chaff	Cebus	chest
bleat	brier	bunje	booby	basin	Bruin	clang	cubit	cleat
blent	bliss	bandh	boody	bason	blunt	craig	cabby	cleft
blest	blist	bench	booky	bison	blurt	clash	cobby	crept
brent	built	bunch	booty	boson	boult	coach	cubby	crest
beefy	buist	benni	boozy	bosun	bruit	crash	cocoa	chevy
beery	blimy	banal	biped	basso	brunt	coati	cycad	chewy
buffa	briny	banco	bipod	basto	brust	chack	cache	Cufic
bifid	blitz	banjo	bepat	bases	bluey	chalk	cycle	cuffo
buffe	bajra	bingo	barca	basis	bousy	chank	cacti	caged
befog	bajri	bongo	burka	buses	bevue	chark	cocci	cogie
buffi	bajan	bunco	burqa	beset	bevel	clack	cecum	cogue
buffo	bijou	bunko	bursa	besit	bavin	clank	cacao	cigar
befit	baked	boner	berob	besot	bever	crack	cocco	cagot
baffy	bekah	banns	baric	bussu	bevvy	crank	cyclo	ci-gît
bigha	baken	bonus	barbe	bosky	bivvy	crawl	cocky	cagey
begad	baker	Banat	barge	bossy	bowed	charm	cadge	ciggy
bigae	balsa	benet	barré	busby	bowne	chasm	cadre	cohoe
bogie	belga	Bantu	barre	bushy	bowse	claim	codon	cohog
bogle	bulla	bandy	barye	busky	bewig	chain	cedar	chica
bugle	balk'd	bendy	birle	busty	bowel	chaco	cider	china
bagel	belee	benty	birse	batta	bower	champ	cyder	cnida
begem	belie	bonny	borde	Butea	bowes	clamp	cedis	chimb
begum	belle	bungy	boree	betid	bewet	clasp	cadet	climb
began	bilge	bunjy	borne	bathe	bowat	cramp	codex	caird
begin	bulge	bunny	borné	bitte	bowet	chair	caddy	child
begun	bulse	bunty	burke	botte	bawdy	charr	cadgy	cried
begar	belah	biota	burse	butte	byway	chaos	cuddy	chide
bogus	belch	blond	berth	batch	buxom	chaps	caeca	chile
begat	baloo	blood	birch	bitch	boxen	claes	cheka	chime
beget	bilbo	boord	birth	botch	boxer	class	chela	chine
begot	baler	broad	burgh	butch	bayle	craps	crena	chive
bight	balas	brond	beryl	batik	buy-in	crass	creed	clime
bigot	bolas	brood	borel	betel	boyar	chaft	caese	cline
baggy	bolus	biome	baron	botel	buyer	chant	chère	clipe
biggy	below	bloke	boron	butyl	bayou	chart	clepe	crime
bogey	bylaw	blore	buran	baton	boyau	claut	cleve	crine
boggy	bolix	boose	burin	béton	bezel	coact	crême	crise
buggy	balky		borgo	biter	bazar	coapt	crêpe	chief
bohea	bally		burro	batts	buzzy	coast	crewe	cliff
Bahai	balmy		borer	batty	chara	craft	ctene	cling
blind	belay		beret	betty	chaya		Czech	chich

Column 1: crith, cuish, **ceili**, chili, **chick**, chink, chirk, click, clink, crick, **chiel**, chill, chirl, **chirm**, **cairn**, Chian, coign, **chiao**, chino, **chimp**, chirp, crimp, crisp, **chirr**, crier, **chips**, cries, **chirt**, clift, clipt, **chivy**, **cokes**, **calla**, calpa, cella, cilia, colza, **colic**, **calid**, **calve**, **calif**, **culch**, **celom**, **colin**, colon, **cello**, **color**, **culet**, **calix**, calyx, culex, cylix, **calmy**, coley, colly, cully, **comma**, **comic**, cumec, **combe**, **camel**, comal

Column 2: **caman**, cumin, **cameo**, combo, commo, compo, **cimar**, comer, cymar, **camas**, camis, camus, combs, comus, **comet**, compt, **cimex**, **campy**, comby, **comfy**, Cymry, **canna**, conga, conia, **conic**, cynic, **canid**, **canoe**, cense, congé, conne, conte, **caneh**, cinch, conch, **canal**, **canon**, cañon, **canto**, cento, congo, conto, Canis, **canst**, **candy**, canny, canty, coney, conky, **clomb**, coomb, cromb, **chord**, cloud, cooed, crowd, **chode**, choke, chore, chose, cloke, clone, close

Column 3: clote, clove, cloye, cloze, cooee, crome, crone, crore, croze, **cloff**, **cloth**, **choli**, **chock**, chook, cloak, clock, clonk, croak, crock, cronk, crook, **ceorl**, **choom**, cloam, **clown**, croon, crown, **chomp**, cloop, croup, **choir**, clour, **cross**, **chout**, cloot, clout, co-opt, coost, Croat, croft, crost, crout, **choux**, **choky**, cooey, cooky, cooly, coomy, crony, **copra**, cuppa, **cupid**, **caple**, copse, **cippi**, **capul**, cupel, capon, caper, coper, capot, caput

Column 4: **copsy**, **carta**, ceria, circa, curia, **Carib**, carob, **cored**, carse, carte, carve, cerge, cerne, corbe, corse, curie, curse, curve, **curch**, **cardi**, cirri, corgi, **carol**, coral, **carom**, **cargo**, corno, corso, curio, **corer**, curer, **Ceres**, circs, corps, **carat**, caret, curat, curst, **cornu**, **carex**, **cardy**, carny, carry, carvy, certy, corky, corny, curdy, curly, curny, curry, curvy, **costa**, **cosec**, cusec, **caste**, coste, **casco**, cisco, **cissy**, cushy, **cotta**, **cutie**

Column 5: **catch**, cutch, **cetyl**, cital, **cut-in**, cutin, cyton, **cutto**, cater, **cates**, cutis, **catty**, cutey, cutty, **chufa**, **Chubb**, courb, crumb, cauld, could, courd, **cause**, chuse, chute, coudé, coupe, coupé, coure, crude, cruse, cruve, **chuff**, **clung**, **couch**, cough, couth, crush, chuck, chunk, cluck, clunk, cruck, **churl**, cruel, **churn**, **chump**, clump, crump, **churr**, cruor, **clubs**, **count**, court, cruet, crust, **crudy**, crusy, **civic**, coved, cavie, cuvée, **cavel**

Column 6: cavil, civil, **coven**, covin, **cover**, civet, covet, covey, **cowed**, **cower**, **cowry**, **coxal**, **cowan**, **crwth**, **caxon**, **chynd**, **chyle**, **coypu**, **coyly**, **cozen**, Diana, drama, **deare**, **deave**, **drake**, **drape**, **drave**, **dwale**, **draff**, **dwarf**, **death**, **D-mark**, drank, **do-all**, drail, drawl, **dwalm**, dwaum, drawn, **dearn**, drain, **diazo**, Draco, **dealt**, diact, **draft**, drant, **deary**, deawy, diary, **Debye**, **de-bag**, debug, **debel**, **debar**, **debit**, début, **debby**, dobby

Column 7: **dacha**, Decca®, dicta, **decad**, **decal**, ducal, **decko**, **décor**, dicer, **ducks**, **dicht**, docht, ducat, **decay**, decoy, decry, dicey, dicky, duchy, ducky, **dodge**, **dedal**, **dados**, dodos, **didst**, **daddy**, doddy, dodgy, **dread**, **deere**, deeve, drere, **doeth**, **dwell**, **dream**, **drear**, **dregs**, dress, **doest**, drent, drest, duett, dwelt, **deedy**, **defer**, **daffy**, **dagga**, dogma, **dogie**, **degum**, **doggo**, **dight**, digit, doggy, **dried**, **daine**, de-ice, drive, dwine, **doing**, dying, **drink**

Column 8: **drill**, **deism**, **deign**, djinn, **drier**, **daint**, deist, doilt, drift, **daily**, dairy, daisy, deify, deity, doily, drily, **dekko**, **daker**, diker, **dikey**, dykey, **delta**, dolia, dulia, **dalle**, delve, dolce, dulse, **delph**, **dilli**, **Dalek**, **dildo**, **delft**, **dally**, delay, dilly, Dolby®, dolly, dully, **dumka**, **demob**, **demic**, **domed**, **damme**, **domal**, **daman**, demon, **damar**, demur, dimer, **demos**, **demit**, dempt, **dampy**, dimly, dumky, dummy, dumpy, **donga**, Donna, **dinic**, **dance**

Column 9: dense, dinge, donee, donné, donne, dunce, **donah**, dunch, dunsh, **denim**, **danio**, dingo, dunno, **dinar**, diner, donor, **Donat**, Donet, donut, **dandy**, denay, dingy, dinky, dungy, dunny, **diota**, **dhole**, diode, doole, drôle, drome, drone, drove, **dhobi**, dhoti, **drook**, drouk, **dholl**, droil, **droll**, **drool**, **doorn**, drown, **dsobo**, dsomo, duomo, **droop**, **dooms**, dross, **droit**, **doomy**, drony, **duple**, **depth**, **dipso**, **doper**, duper, **depot**, **dippy**, dopey, **duply**, **duppy**, **darga**

derma	daunt	elbow	eliad	egret	frate	freer	felon	float
durra	doubt	embow	edile	early	flaff	fleet	folio	flout
daric	dauby	embox	elide	easle	flash	freet	filar	front
Doric	Douay	embay	élite	ensue	frati	freit	filer	frost
dared	drusy	emcee	esile	easel	flank	faery	Felis	flory
dorad	druxy	elchi	evite	eisel	flask	fiery	filet	footy
darre	dovie	excel	exile	eusol	frack	fifth	felly	frory
dirge	devel	escot	exine	elsin	frank	fifer	filly	frowy
dirke	devil	Eddic	eying	eosin	flail	fifty	filmy	farad
doree	divan	ended	erick	ensew	frail	fuffy	folly	fired
dorse	diver	endue	Elian	ensky	flamm	fugie	fully	farce
daraf	dover	eldin	exies	essay	fraim	fugle	famed	farle
derth	Dives	end-on	edict	entia	flawn	fugue	femme	farse
darzi	davit	eider	evict	extra	flair	fugal	femal	force
dural	divot	elder	exist	estoc	fiars	Fagin	femur	forge
durum	duvet	endew	edify	eathe	frass	Fagus	fomes	forme
dares	divvy	endow	enjoy	ettle	feast	fagot	fumet	forte
Doras	downa	edema	eikon	Eytie	fract	fight	fonda	furze
Doris	dowed	enema	eskar	extol	flaky	fogey	fence	firth
dorts	dowie	emend	esker	eaten	flamy	foggy	finch	forth
durst	dowle	exeme	Eolic	ettin	flary	fuggy	Fanti	furth
darky	dowse	elemi	Eblis	estro	flawy	fehme	fundi	farci
deray	dowel	Eyeti	éclat	estop	flaxy	fried	fungi	fermi
derby	dewan	exeem	elmen	eater	foamy	faine	fanal	feral
dirty	diwan	emeer	emmer	enter	fable	flite	final	forel
dormy	dowar	evens	emmet	ester	fibre	trize	fanon	fural
dorty	dower	egest	emmew	entry	fiber	fling	fango	furol
durgy	dowdy	eject	enmew	Eruca	fubby	faith	finer	forum
duroy	downy	elect	Ernie	educe	fubsy	frith	fenks	furan
desse	dowry	erect	ennui	elude	facia	flick	finis	fordo
disme	dixie	event	éloge	elute	faced	flisk	finks	forgo
doseh	dryad	evert	elope	emule	fiche	frisk	fonds	firer
disco	doyen	ewest	emote	emure	fecal	frill	fancy	furor
dishy	dryer	exeat	emove	enure	focal	feign	fanny	first
dusky	daynt	exert	epode	étude	facer	flimp	fendy	farcy
dusty	dryly	elegy	erode	exude	feces	flier	fenny	ferly
dated	dazed	emery	erose	equal	focus	friar	finny	ferny
ditch	dozed	enemy	evoke	equip	fucus	frier	fonly	ferry
dutch	dizen	every	exode	Equus	facet	flies	funky	firry
datal	dozen	elfin	emong	educt	fecht	fries	funny	foray
dital	dozer	enfix	epoch	eruct	fecit	faint	flora	forby
dotal	dizzy	edged	enorm	erupt	fichu	feint	flota	forky
datum	eland	eagle	eloin	exult	fidge	flint	fiord	forty
ditto	elate	eagre	elops	envoi	fudge	flirt	fjord	furry
dater	enate	eigne	E-boat	eeven	faddy	flitt	flood	furzy
deter	erase	ergon	epopt	elvan	frena	foist	frond	festa
doter	étage	eager	ebony	erven	field	frist	f-hole	fossa
ditty	étape	eggar	elogy	elver	fiend	flote	flote	fesse
dotty	evade	egger	epoxy	eaves	freed	frore	frore	fosse
douma	e-la-mi	eight	eupad	elves	fremd	froze	froze	fusee
doura	enarm	ergot	elpee	envoy	feeze	feoff	feoff	fasci
Druid	Erato	ethic	expel	etwee	fiere	flong	flong	fasti
daube	Elaps	ephod	empty	etyma	fleme	flosh	flosh	fusil
deuce	enact	evhoe	eared	Egypt	flesh	frock	frock	Fusus
douce	epact	ephah	erred	Enzed	fresh	fella	flown	fishy
douse	exact	ethal	eerie	franc	fleck	folia	frorn	fisty
drupe	exalt	ethyl	eyrie	fa'ard	freak	folic	frown	fussy
druse	erbia	ephor	earth	fraud	fleam	filed	floor	fusty
Druze	embed	ether	enrol	feare	foehn	false	flour	fetwa
dough	embog	ethos	error	flake	Freon®	fille	floss	fated
drunk	embar	ewhow	épris	flame	fuero	folie	foots	fetid
douar	ember	erica	Eurus	flare	fleer	F-clef	filch	fitte
dault	embus	eniac	earst	frame		filth		fytte

5 f□t□h

fetch	fuzee	gadge	grill	genii	gyppy	giust	Hodge	holly
fitch	fezes	gadje	guimp	genal	gypsy	grunt	hadji	hulky
fatal	fizzy	gadso	grits	genom	garda	g-suit	hydro	hully
fetal	fuzzy	godso	gaitt	Genro	garbe	gaucy	Hades	hamza
futon	grama	Gadus	geist	genip	garre	gaudy	hadst	humic
fatso	guana	godet	glift	goner	gerbe	gaumy	hedgy	humid
fit-up	guava	giddy	glint	gents	gerle	gauzy	hyena	homme
fetor	gland	godly	grift	genus	gerne	gluey	heeze	humph
fetus	grand	gleed	grist	genet	gorge	gouty	hiems	hamal
fatly	guard	greed	guilt	genty	gorse	gavel	heedy	hemal
fatty	geare	gyeld	gaily	gundy	gurge	given	hefte	he-man
fitly	glacé	geese	grimy	gungy	garth	giver	hefty	human
fauna	geese	glebe	grisy	gunny	gerah	gowan	huffy	hymen
faurd	glade	glede	glitz	gynny	girth	gawcy	hogan	homer
fluid	glare	grebe	galea	groma	garni	gawky	hogen	humor
found	glaze	grece	gelid	geoid	goral	gawsy	hight	humus
Fauve	grace	grège	golpe	goold	gyral	gryde	hollo	hammy
fluke	grade	grese	G-clef	geode	giron	ho-hum	hullo	hempy
flume	grame	greve	gulag	globe	gyron	hoise	haler	homey
flute	grape	Guelf	galah	glode	Garbo	hying	hilar	humpy
foulé	grate	gleek	gulch	glove	gyrus	Haikh	halos	henna
fluff	grave	Greek	gulph	gloze	Gerry	haith	hilus	hance
flung	graze	gleam	golem	gnome	girly	heigh	helot	Hanse
faugh	graff	glean	galop	goose	gormy	haick	helix	hence
flush	gnash	green	gular	grone	gorsy	hoick	hilly	henge
fouth	graph	grein	gilts	grope	gurly	heist	holey	hinge
frush	ghazi	grego	gally	grove	gurry	hoist	heald	hynde
flunk	glaik	grees	gelly	go-off	gusla	haiku	heard	hanch
Fluon®	gnarl	ghest	gilly	groof	gesse	haily	hoard	hunch
flump	graal	gleet	gilpy	grouf	geste	hairy	heame	Hindi
frump	grail	glent	goldy	glogg	gosse	guyot	heare	hanap
feuar	glaum	great	golly	ghoul	gusle	grypt	heave	honor
fluor	gnawn	greet	gulfy	growl	gusli	guyse	heath	hunks
flurr	grain	guest	gully	gloom	gesso	gayal	heaps	Hindu
fault	guaco	Gueux	gamba	groom	gismo	ghyll	Hyads	handy
fouat	guano	gleby	gamma	groan	gusto	goyim	heart	hanky
fouet	graip	goety	gemma	groin	gases	geyan	heast	henny
fount	grasp	gaffe	gumma	grown	gaspy	gayer	hiant	henry
fruit	glair	gofer	gamic	good-o	gassy	glyph	hoast	hinny
frust	glaur	gigue	gimme	group	gushy	hejra	heady	honey
fluey	gnarr	gigot	gemel	gloss	gotta	hijra	heapy	honky
fluky	glans	grind	gamin	gross	gutta	hajji	heavy	hunky
fluty	glass	guild	gombo	ghost	gated	hakam	hoary	haoma
fovea	grass	glide	gumbo	gloat	get-up	hakim	hable	hoo-ha
favor	ghast	glike	gamut	glout	gutsy	hokum	heben	hooka
fever	ghaut	grice	gemot	groat	gutty	hiker	habit	H-bomb
fiver	graft	gride	gammy	grout	Gouda	hokku	hobby	hoord
favus	grant	grike	gemmy	globy	Goura	halfa	hubby	hyoid
fives	Glaux	grime	gummy	glory	glued	halma	hocus	hoove
fowth	glady	gripe	ganja	goody	gourd	halva	Hecat	hooch
fixed	glary	grise	genoa	gooey	gauge	holla	hecht	hoosh
foxed	glazy	grize	gonia	goofy	gauje	hylic	hodja	hoo-oo
fixer	goary	guide	gonna	gooly	gauze	halo'd	hydra	hooey
fayne	goaty	guile	genic	goopy	glume	halse	hedge	hooky
flype	grapy	guise	gonad	goosy	gouge	halve		hooly
flyte	gravy	gliff	genie	gopak	grume	helve		hypha
foyle	gable	grief	genre	gippo	gruff	hyleg		hippo
foyne	gibel	griff	gunge	gyppo	gruel	hilch		hepar
fry-up	gebur	going	gynae	gaper	gluon	halal		hyper
flyer	giber	grith	ganch	gappy	gluer	hilum		haply
foyer	gibus	glisk		gippy	gauss	hallo		happy
fryer	gabby	glial		gipsy	gault	hello		hippy
fly-by	gecko			guppy	gaunt	hillo		hoppy

5 l□m□e

herma	haugh	indol	issue	jumar	krang	kilty	kevel	laded
hurra	heuch	indew	imshi	james	kyang	kyley	keyed	ladle
hired	heugh	index	issei	jambu	khadi	kamme	kayle	ledge
heroe	hough	ileac	inset	jammy	khaki	kembo	kayoe	lodge
herse	houri	idea'd	imshy	jemmy	knack	kimbo	kayak	ledum
herye	haulm	ideal	intra	jimmy	knarl	Khmer	kazoo	laden
horde	hault	I-beam	ictic	jimpy	kraal	kamis	liana	Ladin
horme	haunt	ileum	istle	jumby	krans	kempt	llama	loden
horse	hevea	inerm	ixtle	jumpy	kvass	kanga	liard	ledgy
harsh	havoc	ileus	ictal	junta	kraft	kynde	leare	leese
horal	hovel	inept	intil	Jonah	krait	kenaf	lease	leeze
haram	haven	inert	intro	jinni	kraut	kaneh	leave	liege
harem	hoven	infra	inter	jingo	kranz	kinin	leaze	lieve
harim	haver	infer	ictus	junco	kabab	kendo	liane	leech
heron	hiver	infix	inula	junto	kabob	ken-no	loave	lie-in
hirer	hover	ingle	inure	Janus	kebab	kanzu	liang	leear
hards	haves	ingan	inurn	jinns	kebob	kandy	leach	loess
harns	hives	ingot	Inuit	janty	koban	kinky	leash	leery
here's	hewed	ichor	inust	jenny	kacha	khoja	loach	luffa
hurds	hawse	iliac	Invar®	jonty	kecks	krona	loath	lefte
horst	howbe	Isiac	inwit	junky	kedge	knowe	learn	lifer
hurst	howre	Iliad	idyll	japan	kidge	krone	llano	lefty
hyrax	howff	ivied	Iyyar	jupon	Kodak®	kloof	leant	lofty
hardy	hewgh	imide	izzet	jarta	kidel	kiosk	leapt	logia
harpy	howso	icing	jebel	jerid	kudos	knock	least	logic
harry	how-to	Irish	jiber	jarul	kydst	knoll	liart	legge
herby	hewer	idiom	jabot	jural	kudzu	known	loast	ligge
herry	howdy	ilium	Jacob	joram	kedgy	knosp	lyart	ligne
horny	hexad	Ilian	jocko	jorum	kiddy	knout	leady	logie
horsy	hayle	inion	jaded	juror	kheda	Kuo-yü	leafy	legal
hurly	huzza	iaido	judge	jurat	kwela	kooky	leaky	lagan
hurry	hazel	idiot	jodel	jerky	knead	kappa	leany	ligan
hertz	hazer	Idist	judas	jerry	kneed	koppa	leary	logan
hasta	huzzy	icily	jeely	jaspé	keeve	kopje	leavy	lager
hosta	Itala	Injun	Jaffa	Jesse	kieve	kapok	loamy	leger
Hasid	izard	inkle	jiffy	jésus	kreng	kaput	labda	liger
hosed	image	icker	jugal	Jesus	keech	karma	labia	Luger
haste	inane	inker	jugum	jasey	karma	kurta	labra	Logos
hosen	irade	illth	jäger	jeton	kneel	kerne	libra	legit
hyson	irate	Islam	jagir	jotun	knell	kerve	lubra	light
hashy	imari	igloo	jigot	jetty	knelt	kurre	lobed	leggy
hasty	Iraqi	idler	jaggy	jutty	Kufic	Kyrie	label	lahar
hushy	imaum	Iblis	jehad	jeune	Kafir	karri	libel	laika
husky	inarm	inlet	jihad	joule	kefir	Karen	labor	laird
hussy	igapo	islet	Jaina	jougs	kight	Koran	liber	lying
hutia	imago	in-law	juice	jaunt	knife	Karoo	lobar	laigh
hithe	idant	inlay	joint	joust	knive	karat	labis	laith
hythe	inapt	iambi	joist	javel	Koine	karst	lobus	lairy
hatch	imbed	immit	juicy	Javan	kaiak	kasba	lobby	laity
hitch	imbue	immew	jokol	jawed	krill	kisan	laced	lakin
hotch	inbye	immix	joker	jewel	kokra	kesar	lucid	liken
hutch	imbar	ionic	jakes	jawan	kukri	kithe	lucre	likin
hotel	incog	inner	jokey	jowar	kokum	kythe	lycée	laker
hoten	in-car	Idola	jelab	Jewry	kylie	ketch	lichi	liker
hater	incur	inorb	jello	joyed	kyloe	kutch	local	lilac
hotly	incus	in-off	jalap	jazzy	kalif	katti	locum	lolog
Hausa	incut	irony	julep	Kaaba	kulak	Kotys	locus	laldy
hauld	itchy	ivory	jelly	kaama	kulan	kotow	luces	lolly
hound	Indra	impel	jolly	khaya	kylin	kitty	lacet	lamia
hause	Indic	impot	jolty	koala	kylix	kaugh	licht	lemma
haute	iodic	input	jambe	knave	kelpy	kauri	licit	Lemna
house	indue	imply	jambo	kiang	kelty	knurl	lacey	limma
houff	indri	ihram	jumbo	klang	kiley	knurr	lucky	lumme

lymph	lurid	lauch	mucid	moiré	mince	merge	mashy	moust
leman	large	laugh	macle	moire	Minié	merle	massy	mousy
lemon	Lerne	leuch	miche	meith	monte	morne	masty	moved
limen	larch	leugh	Maçon	mains	maneh	morné	meshy	movie
lumen	lurch	lough	mucin	meint	month	morse	messy	mover
limbo	Lurgi	louis	macho	moist	munch	murre	missy	mavis
lemur	loral	loury	micro	muist	mynah	marah	misty	mowra
limes	lorel	lousy	mucro	meiny	manul	march	mosey	mowed
limit	larum	lavra	macer	mujik	monal	marsh	mossy	mower
limax	loran	lived	mucor	major	minim	mirth	mushy	mixed
lammy	largo	livid	mucus	makar	mango	morph	musky	maxim
limey	Larus	levee	macaw	maker	manto	myrrh	mussy	mixen
lummy	liras	livre	micky	Malta	mungo	merel	musty	mix-in
lumpy	loris	level	mucky	malva	Munro	meril	matza	mix-up
linga	Lurex	levin	media	Melia	manor	moral	motza	mixer
longa	lardy	liven	medic	molla	minar	morel	metic	maybe
linac	larky	laver	Médoc	mulga	miner	mural	meted	moyle
lined	lordy	lever	madid	malic	minor	moron	moted	Mayan
lance	lorry	liver	madge	melic	moner	morro	muted	mayor
lande	lurry	livor	medle	mêlée	manes	maror	matte	mayst
longe	lisle	lover	midge	mille	Manis	marls	metre	meynt
lunge	los'te	lavas	modii	milch	manus	mores	mitre	Muzak®
lanch	losel	levis	medal	mulch	minus	Morus	motte	mizen
linch	lysol	lives	modal	mulsh	monas	merit	metif	mezzo
lunch	losen	lovat	model	molal	manet	morat	motif	mazer
lynch	lysin	lovey	madam	melon	mangy	mpret	match	mazut
lungi	lasso	lownd	modem	molto	manky	murex	mutch	muzzy
linen	laser	lowne	mid-on	malar	manly	mardy	metal	neafe
linin	loser	lowse	mudir	miler	manty	marly	metol	nyaff
lento	lysis	lower	Midas	milor	mingy	mercy	motel	neath
lingo	lassu	lawks	modus	molar	minty	merry	matin	Naafi
liner	lossy	lewis	midst	mulct	money	mirky	moten	ngaio
loner	lushy	lawny	Medau	malax	moola	mirly	muton	nubia
lunar	lusty	lowly	madly	Malay	myoma	moray	matlo	nabob
lenes	lytta	luxes	middy	malty	myoid	murky	matzo	noble
lenis	lated	laxly	muddy	milky	moose	murly	metro	nebek
lanky	lathe	loyal	mieve	molly	moove	murry	motto	nebel
lingy	Lethe	lay-up	mneme	muley	myope	massa	mater	nobby
linny	lithe	layer	Mafia	miltz	M-roof	Musca	meter	nobly
linty	litre	lay-by	mufti	mamba	mooch	musha	miter	nubby
L-dopa	lythe	lozen	miffy	mamma	Maori	mesic	motor	nucha
loofa	latch	lazar	mifty	momma	mhorr	music	maths	nache
loord	letch	lezzy	magma	mimic	mools	mused	meths	nacre
loose	lotah	meal'd	magic	mambo	myops	massé	métis	niche
looby	lathi	mear'd	Magog	mimer	moody	mesne	motet	nicol
loony	laten	meane	mogul	Mimus	mooly	musse	matey	nudge
loopy	Latin	meare	maggs	Momus	moony	musth	Mitty	nidal
lepra	litho	mease	magus	mumps	moory	Masai	motey	nodal
lepta	lotto	miaul	magot	mammy	moped	Musci	mothy	nadir
lepid	let-up	myall	might	mommy	maple	Musak	motty	nidor
lipid	later	miasm	moggy	mummy	mop-up	mesal	maund	nidus
lapje	liter	means	muggy	mania	mopus	mesel	mould	nodus
lapse	luter	meant	mahua	manna	moppy	mason	mound	neddy
lapel	lotos	miaow	mahwa	manta	mopsy	meson	mauve	noddy
lupin	lotus	mealy	mahoe	Mensa	maqui	mesto	meuse	neeld
leper	latex	meany	Mahdi	Munda	maria	misdo	mouse	naeve
lapis	lathy	meaty	mohel	manic	Mirza	misgo	mvule	neele
lupus	laura	moble	mohur	maned	moria	maser	mouch	neese
lippy	laund	mebos	Moira	monad	morra	miser	mouth	neeze
larva	lound	mobby	maile	mange	murra	muser	mourn	niece
Lerna	loupe	Mecca	maire	manse	murva	muset	mouls	nieve
loric	loure	Mocha	maise	menge	marid	musit	moult	naevi
lyric	louse	mucic	maize	mense	marle		mount	needs

needy	neper	ngwee	olent	oboli	plash	piend	pride	pilau
niffy	nepit	newel	overt	ovolo	poach	plead	prime	pilaw
nifty	nappy	Nowel	onely	odour	plack	pseud	prise	pilow
nugae	nippy	newly	offal	ouphe	plank	peece	prize	phlox
Negro	nerka	newsy	offer	orpin	prank	peepe	prief	Pulex
nagor	noria	noway	orgia	ocrea	pearl	peeve	plink	palay
Niger	Norma	nixie	orgic	oared	plasm	phene	prick	pally
negus	Norna	noxal	orgue	oorie	praam	phese	prink	palmy
night	narre	nexus	organ	ourie	psalm	piece	phial	palsy
naggy	nerve	Nayar	ought	owrie	plain	prese	prial	poley
nahal	Norse	noyes	oshac	omrah	prawn	preve	prism	polly
nihil	nurse	noyau	ochre	orris	piano	preif	primo	pulpy
nohow	north	nizam	ogham	ossia	peart	plesh	priep	pampa
naira	naras	nazir	ocher	o'erby	plait	paean	primp	pombe
naiad	nares	omasa	other	ousel	plant	paeon	plier	pumie
naive	narky	orate	ochry	owsen	plast	pheon	prier	Pomak
neive	nervy	Osage	Oriya	oases	prahu	pleon	prior	pommy
noise	nirly	ovate	ouija	oasis	peaky	preen	plies	panda
neigh	nosed	obang	ogive	onset	peaty	piezo	pries	panga
Naias	nisse	orang	olive	ostia	peavy	pheer	paint	penna
noils	Neski	orach	opine	optic	platy	plebs	point	pinna
neist	nisei	okapi	ovine	octad	praty	press	print	pinta
noint	Nasik	orant	oxide	outed	pzazz	P-Celt	poilu	punka
noisy	nasal	oracy	owing	outré	pubic	piert	pricy	panic
naked	Nisan	otary	oribi	octal	pubes	P-Kelt	primy	Punic
naker	noser	ovary	oriel	oaten	pubis	pleat	privy	paned
nalla	nisus	orbed	odism	often	pacha	prent	pi-jaw	pance
nulla	nasty	ombre	odium	ortho	Picea	prest	pakka	panne
nylon	nosey	oobit	opium	outdo	picra	peeoy	pukka	pence
nelis	nitid	orbit	onion	outgo	pucka	peery	piked	penie
Nilot	noted	oubit	Orion	ottar	paced	piety	poked	penne
nelly	nltre	ox-bot	osier	otter	pecke	poesy	pekoe	ponce
nomic	natch	ox-bow	obiit	outer	picul	predy	pikul	punce
named	notch	owche	odist	oxter	pecan	prexy	pokal	pinch
nomad	natal	orcin	ovist	octet	pacer	puffy	pekan	punch
nymph	notal	Oscan	objet	outby	Picus	pagod	Pekin	panel
nimbi	notum	occur	oakum	ovule	Pecht	pagle	piker	penal
no-man	niton	oncer	oaken	orval	picot	pogge	poker	panim
nomen	noter	Oscar	oaker	oaves	pacey	pagri	puker	piñon
numen	nates	oncus	ocker	Oryza	picky	pugil	palea	panto
namer	Notus	oucht	onkus	odyle	pocky	pygal	palla	pinko
nomos	natty	oidia	oflag	ouzel	padma	pagan	pelma	pinto
nempt	netty	oldie	omlah	playa	podia	pager	pelta	pongo
nanna	nitry	olden	orlop	plaza	pudic	Peght	pilea	punto
nance	nitty	order	oxlip	poaka	padle	pight	polka	pin-up
nonce	nutty	on-dit	ogler	plaid	padre	peggy	pulka	pants
ninth	nould	oddly	oiler	peace	podge	piggy	pilch	penes
ninon	neume	omega	owler	peare	pudge	pigmy	palki	penis
Nones	noule	opera	owlet	pease	pi-dog	puggy	palpi	panax
nonet	nouns	oleic	ollav	peaze	pedal	pygmy	palpi	pandy
nandu	naunt	ogee'd	ogmic	phage	podal	pshaw	pilei	pansy
nancy	novae	oread	ohmic	phare	pedro	paisa	pilum	penny
nanny	naval	obese	osmic	phase	pudor	plica	pylon	piney
ninny	navel	ox-eye	oomph	place	podex	prima	polio	pinky
nonny	nevel	obeah	ormer	plage	paddy	plied	pulmo	pinny
Nantz	nival	obeli	ounce	plane	poddy	poind	polyp	poney
Niobe	novel	ozeki	owner	plate	podgy	pried	piler	ponty
no-one	novum	odeum	ornis	poake	puddy	paire	polar	punty
noose	never	oleum	oundy	prase	pudgy	paise	puler	Phoca
nooky	navew	ocean	ovoid	prate	pietà	peise	palas	pooja
nappe	navvy	odeon	ohone	phang	presa	peize	pilus	psora
nopal	nawab	olein	ozone	prang	piel'd	poise	palet	proud
napoo	nowed	one-er	on-off	peach		price	pilot	pyoid

phone	perse	putid	powin	quiet	ricin	raine	rente	rishi
pioye	Porte	patte	power	quilt	recto	raise	rinse	resin
poove	purée	patté	pewit	quint	recap	reive	ronde	risen
probe	purge	petre	pawaw	quirt	racer	rhime	ronne	rosin
proke	purse	patch	pawky	quist	recur	rhine	ronte	riser
prole	parch	pitch	powny	quipu	ricer	ruing	renig	risus
prone	perch	potch	pixie	qanat	richt	Reich	ranch	reset
prore	porch	putti	pixel	quota	ricey	reign	runch	resit
prose	pardi	petal	pyxis	quoad	rocky	rhino	renal	roset
prove	parki	paten	phyla	quote	redia	reins	renin	rosit
proof	Parsi	patin	payed	quoif	re-did	reist	run-in	raspy
plong	parti	piton	paysd	quoth	ridge	roist	run-on	resay
prong	perai	potin	payee	quonk	radii	rainy	rondo	resty
pooch	pirai	put-in	peyse	quoll	radon	reify	roneo	risky
paoli	parol	put-on	phyle	quoin	redan	roily	run-up	rushy
plonk	peril	patio	poyse	Q-boat	radio	rejig	renew	rusty
proll	poral	potto	pryse	quoit	rodeo	re-jig	randy	rated
proul	pyral	putto	psych	Qoran	redip	rajah	rangy	rathe
prowl	purim	put-up	psyop	Qurân	radar	rakee	renay	retie
pro-am	purin	pater	payer	quyte	rider	raker	reney	ratch
proem	porno	petar	pryer	reata	rudas	roker	rindy	retch
proyn	parer	peter	poynt	riata	radix	relic	runny	rotch
paolo	porer	petit	pizza	reame	redox	rille	runty	ratel
photo	Paris	patly	puzel	reate	reddy	Ralph	Rioja	rotal
Provo	Pyrus	patsy	pozzy	reave	redly	ruler	roosa	ratan
pious	perst	patty	quayd	roate	ridgy	relet	rhomb	rutin
props	perdu	petty	quake	reach	ruddy	relax	rhone	ratio
psoas	Pyrex®	pithy	quaff	roach	reede	rally	roose	retro
poort	pardy	potty	quash	realm	reeve	relay	roost	rater
peony	parky	putty	quasi	rearm	rieve	Riley	roofy	rotor
phony	parly	plumb	quack	react	reech	rumba	rooky	ratty
piony	parry	pound	quark	reast	rheum	Romic	roomy	retry
poovy	party	pause	quail	riant	reest	rimed	roopy	ritzy
prosy	perdy	plume	qualm	roast	reedy	ramee	rooty	rutty
proxy	perky	pouke	quair	ready	reeky	ramie	rupia	rhumb
poppa	porgy	poule	quant	reamy	rifle	rimae	rapid	round
piped	porky	poupe	quart	roary	ruffe	rymme	roped	reuse
pupae	porty	pruce	quaky	Rubia	refel	ramal	raphe	rouge
papal	purpy	prude	qibla	rabic	refer	romal	rupee	roule
pipal	pursy	prune	queme	rebec	refit	rumal	repel	rouse
pipul	purty	pluff	queue	rabid	regma	reman	ripen	route
pupal	pasha	plush	quell	rebid	raged	roman	repro	rough
pupil	pasta	pouch	quean	rigid	ragde	rumen	raper	routh
pop-up	passé	pluck	queen	ruble	rigid	Romeo	riper	roust
paper	paste	plunk	quern	rabbi	Ruman	rumbo	roper	roupy
piper	piste	Pluto	queyn	rebel	rogue	rimer	ryper	rived
pipit	posse	plump	queer	robin	regal	rumor	repot	revie
papaw	pusle	poulp	Q-Celt	rubin	Rigel	ramus	repay	revue
pappy	Pasch	poult	Q-Kelt	rebus	Rigil	remit	reply	ravel
peppy	Pesah	poupt	quest	Ribes	rigol	remex	roque	revel
pippy	pashm	prunt	query	Rubus	rager	Rumex	roric	rival
poppy	paseo	plumy	quina	rabat	regar	rammy	rorid	rivel
popsy	poser	paved	quine	rebut	regur	renga	rorie	raven
puppy	posit	pavid	quire	robot	rigor	runic	roral	ravin
pique	paspy	pavan	quite	rybat	Roger	runed	rural	riven
Parca	pasty	paven	quiff	ribby	right	rance	rerun	raver
parka	pesky	pavin	quich	recta	raggy	ranee	rorty	river
Perca	pisky	paver	qui-hi	rache	roguy	range	Rasta	rover
porta	pushy	pavis	quick	recce	rugby	ranke	rusma	revet
parge	pussy	pivot	quirk	recti	ruggy	renne	rased	rivet
parle	pitta	pownd	quill	recal	raird		rosed	rownd
parse	pated	powre	quipo	recal	reird		rasse	rowme
perce		powan	quits	racon	raile			rewth

rowth	soare	small	soapy	stedd	steep	Saiva	**saick**	spiky
rowel	space	snail	spacy	steed	sweep	Shiva	shirk	spiny
rowan	spade	snarl	stagy	stend	**shear**	spica	skink	spiry
rowen	spake	spall	swaly	scene	sheer	spina	slick	stimy
rower	spale	spaul	**sabra**	shere	skeer	stipa	slink	stivy
rawly	spane	spawl	**sable**	siege	smear	**stilb**	smirk	**spitz**
rowdy	spare	stall	sabre	sieve	sneer	**shied**	snick	**sajou**
rhyta	spate	swayl	sybbe	skene	spear	skied	spick	**sakia**
rayed	stade	shalm	syboe	stede	speer	spied	spink	**Sakta**
rayle	stage	shawm	**subah**	stele	speir	stied	stick	**Sakai**
rayne	stake	smalm	**Sabal**	steme	stear	**saice**	stink	**Sakti**
rhyme	stale	smarm	sibyl	stere	steer	saine	stirk	**Sikel**
royne	stane	spasm	sybil	suede	swear	seine	swink	**soken**
rayah	stare	swarm	**sebum**	swede	sweer	seise	**shiel**	**saker**
riyal	state	sdayn	**sabin**	**sheaf**	sweir	seize	shill	syker
royal	stave	sharn	**Saber**	shelf	**specs**	shine	skill	**sekos**
rayon	suave	slain	sober	skelf	speos	shire	skirl	**Salpa**
royst	swage	spain	suber	swerf	**sceat**	shite	spial	selva
razed	swale	spawn	**sabot**	**sieth**	scent	shive	spiel	silva
razee	sware	stain	Sebat	**sheik**	sheet	skite	spill	sol-fa
razor	coaff	starn	**sybow**	sleek	shent	skive	still	sylva
rozet	scarf	swain	**sacra**	smeek	sient	slice	swill	**salic**
rozit	staff	**shako**	**socle**	sneak	skeet	slide	swirl	**salad**
scala	swarf	spado	sucre	speak	sleet	'slife	**seism**	silo'd
scapa	**slang**	**scalp**	sycee	speck	slept	slime	**scion**	solid
shama	spang	scamp	**shchi**	spelk	smelt	slipe	**skimp**	**salle**
shaya	staig	scarp	succi	steak	speat	slive	stirp	salse
scald	stang	scaup	**Sicel**	steek	spelt	smile	**shier**	salue
scand	swang	sharp	**Sican**	sheal	spent	smite	shirr	salve
scaud	**scath**	stamp	**secco**	sheel	stent	snide	skier	selle
shand	shash	swamp	**socks**	she'll	stept	snipe	skirr	solde
shard	slash	**scaur**	**Sudra**	shell	sweat	spice	smirr	solve
skald	smash	spaer	**sodic**	she'ol	sweet	spide	**snips**	selah
slaid	snash	stair	**sided**	smell	swelt	spike	spies	solah
spald	snath	starr	**sedge**	snell	swept	spile	sties	sylph
spard	staph	**shaps**	sidle	speel	**seedy**	spine	Swiss	**salmi**
spayd	stash	swats	**sedum**	spell	seely	spire	swits	soldi
etaid	swash	**scant**	Sodom	steal	seepy	spite	**saint**	sulci
stal'd	swath	scart	**sedan**	steel	spewy	stile	saist	**salal**
stand	**scapi**	scatt	Sudan	steil	stewy	stime	shift	**sclim**
sward	spahi	shaft	**Seder**	stell	suety	stipe	shirt	sklim
scale	swami	shakt	sider	sweal	**softa**	stire	skint	solum
scape	**shack**	shalt	sudor	sweel	**Sufic**	stive	skirt	**salon**
scare	shank	shan't	**sedes**	swell	**sofar**	suite	slipt	silen
seame	shark	skart	**sadhu**	skelm	**Sufis**	swine	snift	solan
seare	slack	slant	**sadly**	sperm	**softy**	swipe	snirt	solen
sease	smack	smalt	sedgy	steam	**sigla**	swire	spilt	Solon
seaze	**smaik**	smart	soddy	steem	sigma	**skiff**	spirt	**Salmo**
shade	snack	spalt	sudsy	sdein	**segue**	sniff	stilt	salvo
shake	snark	spart	**scena**	sigil	**segol**	spiff	stint	soldo
shale	spank	start	Sheba	sheen	sigil	stiff	suint	**salep**
shame	spark	swapt	Shema	shewn	**sagum**	**sling**	swift	salop
shape	stack	swart	sheva	skean	**segno**	sting	**saily**	**siler**
share	stalk	**snafu**	stela	skein	**segar**	suing	seity	solar
shave	stank	**scaly**	**scend**	spean	soger	swing	shily	soler
skate	stark	scary	seeld	stean	sugar	**saith**	shiny	**solus**
slade	swack	seamy	shend	steen	**sight**	Shiah	skiey	**salet**
slake	swank	shady	sherd	stein	**soggy**	slish	skivy	splat
slane	**scail**	shaky	snead	stern	**schwa**	smith	slily	split
slate	scall	shaly	speed	sheep	**sahib**	stich	slimy	**salix**
slave	shall	slaty	speld	skelp	**schul**	swish	snipy	silex
snake	shawl	snaky	spend	sleep	**schmo**	swith	soily	**sally**
snare	skail	snary	stead	sneap	**saiga**	sci-fi	spicy	salty

silky	stood	sloom	smoky	strig	sasse	sculk	sower	twain
silly	sword	spoom	snowy	sirih	sushi	shuck	Sawny	tea-ho
silty	scone	storm	sooty	surah	sisal	skulk	sexed	tramp
splay	scope	scorn	stogy	serai	sasin	skunk	sixth	trass
sulky	score	shoon	stony	strak	sassy	slunk	Saxon	T-cart
sully	shone	shorn	story	seral	sesey	snuck	sixer	toast
samba	shope	shown	sepia	soral	sissy	spunk	sixty	tract
summa	shore	septa	sopha	sorel	Sitta	stunk	sayid	trait
sumac	shote	spoon	sopra	sural	sutra	scull	styed	trant
semée	shove	stonn	sapid	scram	sated	skull	sayne	tuart
semie	slope	swoln	sepad	scrim	setae	stull	skyre	teary
sumph	slove	sworn	Sophi	scrum	sithe	stulm	skyte	thawy
sampi	smoke	swoon	sepal	serum	sythe	spurn	slype	toady
samel	smore	swoun	sapan	strum	Satan	scudo	soyle	tabla
samen	smote	smoko	sapor	sarin	satin	sculp	spyre	tibia
semen	snoke	scoop	super	scran	seton	slump	style	tabid
sambo	snore	scoup	sappy	serin	sit-in	slurp	styme	tubed
simar	soole	scowp	sepoy	seron	set-to	stump	styre	table
symar	soote	sloop	Sophy	siren	Sotho	sault	styli	tubae
semis	spode	snoop	soppy	skran	set-up	saunt	spyal	tubal
samfu	spoke	stoep	sarsa	syren	satyr	scuft	sayon	tabun
samey	spore	stomp	sarza	servo	sitar	shunt	seyen	taboo
Sammy	stoae	stoop	serra	sorbo	sauba	sluit	say-so	tabor
sansa	stoke	stoup	sorda	sordo	sauna	souct	stylo	tubar
senna	stole	swoop	sorra	sorgo	scuba	spurt	sayer	tuber
senza	stone	scour	stria	scrap	scuta	squat	shyer	tabes
Sunna	stope	shoer	surra	scrip	sputa	squit	skyer	Tibet
Sinic	store	smoor	Surya	sirup	stupa	stunt	slyer	Tobit
sonic	stove	spoor	scrab	strap	slubb	sturt	styes	tabby
synod	swone	stoor	scrub	strep	slurb	squaw	sayst	tubby
sense	swore	stour	shrub	strip	squab	saucy	shyly	ticca
since	scoff	Scops	sérac	strop	squib	saury	skyey	tache
singe	skoff	Scots	seric	syrup	slued	soupy	slyly	Tyche
sonce	spoof	shoes	siroc	saros	sound	spumy	sized	tical
sonde	scoog	slops	shred	sarus	squad	study	sizel	Tacan
sonne	scoug	smous	sprad	sorus	squid	saved	sizar	tacet
sonse	stong	scoot	spred	scrat	sauce	savin	sizer	tacit
synch	slosh	scout	sprod	sprat	sauté	seven	thana	tacky
Sunni	sloth	'sfoot	strad	sprit	scuse	Sivan	tiara	techy
sanko	sooth	shoat	strid	strut	scute	saver	teade	tichy
sun-up	sposh	shoot	saree	surat	sluse	savor	tease	todde
Señor	shoji	short	sarge	scraw	souce	sever	teaze	tidal
sonar	stoai	shott	scrae	screw	souse	siver	thane	Tudor
sinus	Suomi	shout	scree	scrow	spule	syver	toaze	teddy
sinew	shock	sloot	serge	serow	spume	savey	trace	tiddy
sandy	shook	smolt	serre	shrew	stupe	savoy	trade	today
senvy	smock	smoot	serve	shrow	sture	savvy	trape	toddy
sinky	snoek	smout	soree	straw	scuff	sawed	twang	theca
sonny	snook	smowt	spree	strew	scurf	sewed	teach	thema
sonsy	spook	snoot	sprue	strow	snuff	sowed	trash	theta
sunny	stock	snort	strae	sorex	stuff	sownd	tuath	trefa
scopa	stonk	snout	surge	sarky	slung	sowle	track	trema
shola	stook	sport	serif	scray	stung	sowne	traik	theic
Shona	stork	spout	scrag	serry	swung	sowse	twank	teend
stola	scowl	stoat	scrog	sorry	sauch	sowff	trail	they'd
stoma	shoal	stoit	shrug	spray	saugh	sowth	T-rail	tread
stoic	shool	stout	sprag	stray	shush	sewel	trawl	trend
scold	skoal	swopt	sprig	stroy	slush	sewen	thaim	tweed
shoed	snool	Sioux	sprog	surfy	snush	sewin	train	teene
sloid	spoil	showy	sprug	surgy	sough	sawer		theme
sloyd	spool	slopy	strag	surly	south	sewer		there
snood	stool			sessa	scudi	sowar		these
stond								thete

'twere	thilk	Timon	trode	thrae	titer	tryer	urine	**untin**
thelf	think	timon	troke	three	tutor	twyer	urite	**utter**
teeth	trick	toman	trone	throe	**tatts**	**tryst**	utile	**untax**
theek	twink	**tempo**	trope	torse	**tatou**	**thymy**	**umiak**	**uvula**
treck	**thill**	timbó	**thong**	torte	**tatow**	**tazza**	**urial**	usure
tweak	thiol	**tamer**	**Thoth**	turme	**tatty**	**tazze**	**union**	U-tube
tweel	thirl	timer	tooth	turme	titty	tozie	**Uniat**	usual
therm	trial	tumor	troth	**Torah**	totty	**tizzy**	**unify**	U-turn
thegn	trill	**tamis**	torch	torch	tutty	ukase	**unity**	**usurp**
tie-in	twill	Times	**tholi**	tarsi	**thuja**	urate	**upjet**	**uhuru**
treen	'twill	timps	**trock**	terai	Thuya	usage	**unked**	urubu
'tween	twirl	tempt	**thowl**	torii	Tsuga	**urali**	unkid	**usury**
tie-up	**tuism**	**tammy**	troll	Turki	**thumb**	urari	**unket**	**unwed**
twerp	**Teian**	tommy	**thorn**	**tarok**	**tauld**	**unarm**	**unled**	**unwon**
their	**Taino**	tummy	**thorp**	terek	**taube**	**unapt**	unlid	**unwet**
tweer	**twirp**	tumpy	tromp	torsk	taupe	**umbra**	upled	unwit
thews	**trier**	**tanga**	troop	**thrum**	Thule	**unbed**	**uhlan**	**ulyie**
tress	trior	tanka	two-up	**toran**	touse	unbid	**unlet**	**ulzie**
trews	twier	tanna	**thous**	**torso**	touze	**umbre**	unlit	**unzip**
theft	**Trias**	tenia	toots	turbo	truce	upbye	unlaw	**vraic**
treat	tries	tinea	**thoft**	Turco	**teuch**	**unbag**	**unlay**	**viand**
tweet	**taint**	tonga	troat	**thrip**	teugh	Uzbeg	uplay	**veale**
theow	trist	**tonic**	trout	teras	touch	**Uzbek**	**ulmin**	**Vlach**
teeny	twilt	tunic	**tappa**	terts	tough	**umbel**	unman	**vealy**
thewy	twist	**tined**	Typha	tiros	truth	**urban**	urman	**vibes**
tafia	'twixt	toned	**topic**	torus	**truck**	**umber**	**Ulmus**	**vibex**
tuffe	**twiny**	tuned	typic	turps	trunk	unbar	**unmew**	**vacua**
taffy	**taken**	tyned	**tepid**	**tarot**	**trull**	up-bow	**usnea**	**vocal**
toffy	takin	**tenné**	**tepee**	**thraw**	**thump**	**uncle**	**urned**	**vicar**
tufty	token	tense	topee	threw	trump	**uncap**	**ulnae**	**voces**
toga'd	**taker**	tenue	**tophi**	throw	**truss**	**ulcer**	**urnal**	**Vichy**
toged	**Tokay**	tinge	**topck**	**tardy**	**taunt**	**uncus**	**ulnar**	**Vedda**
togue	**talma**	tonne	tupek	tarry	trust	**uncut**	**U-boat**	vodka
tigon	talpa	tynde	tupik	tarty	**tousy**	**undid**	U-bolt	**Vedic**
tiger	Tilia	**tench**	**typal**	terry	**truly**	**undée**	**upped**	**video**
tight	**telic**	tenth	**tapen**	turfy	**taver**	undue	**unpeg**	**veena**
tehee	**tell'd**	tanti	**typto**	**tesla**	**tawie**	urdee	**unpen**	**V-neck**
taiga	tiled	**tonal**	**tip-up**	testa	**tawse**	**undug**	unpin	**veery**
taira	**telae**	**tenon**	top-up	**tasse**	**towse**	**undam**	**upper**	viewy
teind	tilde	**tango**	**taper**	taste	**towze**	**udder**	**umpty**	**vifda**
third	tulle	tondo	tapir	teste	**tewel**	under	unpay	**vigia**
triad	**tilth**	**ton-up**	toper	**Tisri**	towel	**ulema**	**Ugric**	**vague**
tried	**taluk**	**tenor**	**tapis**	**tasar**	**tawer**	urena	**unred**	**vogie**
trild	**talon**	tuner	topos	'tisn't	tower	up-end	unrid	**vogue**
thine	**tulip**	**tongs**	**tapet**	**tasty**	**tewit**	**uneth**	**unrig**	**vagal**
toise	**talar**	tonus	**tippy**	testy	**tawny**	**uteri**	**uprun**	vigil
tribe	tiler	**tenet**	tipsy	toshy	towny	**ureal**	**unrip**	**vegan**
trice	tyler	tinct	**topaz**	tossy	towsy	uveal	U-trap	**vigor**
tride	**tales**	**tangy**	**toque**	tusky	**toxic**	**uredo**	**unsod**	**vagus**
trike	talus	tansy	tuque	**tetra**	**taxed**	**urent**	**upsee**	**vuggy**
trine	telos	tenty	**terra**	**tatie**	**Texel**	usen't	**urson**	**vehme**
tripe	**telex**	tinny	**throb**	tithe	**taxon**	**unfed**	**Ursus**	**voilà**
trite	**tally**	tinty	**taroc**	title	Texan	**unfit**	**unset**	**vairé**
twice	**telly**	toney	toric	titre	toxin	**unfix**	upset	voice
twine	**timed**	tunny	**thrid**	tutee	taxer	**ungod**	**unsew**	voile
twire	timid	**trona**	tired	**titch**	taxor	**ungum**	**unsex**	**vying**
twite	tumid	**Troic**	tyred	**tutti**	taxis	**urger**	**unsay**	**V-sign**
thief	**Tempe**	tronc	**targe**	**total**	Taxus	**unget**	upsey	vails
thing	temse	**thou'd**	tarre	**totem**	texas	**ungot**	**ultra**	**vairy**
tying	**tempi**	troad	terce	**titan**	**tayra**	uh-huh	**untie**	veily
taish	**tamal**	T-bone	terfe	**titup**	**thyme**	**usher**	uptie	veiny
thigh	Tamil	thole	terne	**Tatar**	**try-on**	**unhat**	**uptak**	**vakil**
thick	**tamin**	those	terse	tater	**toyer**	**unite**	**until**	**villa**

volta	varix	wicky	whist	wroot	yeard	yours
volva	vardy	wedge	wrist	woody	ysame	yourt
vulva	verry	wodge	whiny	woofy	yearn	yeven
valid	vespa	width	whity	woozy	yeast	yewen
valse	vesta	widen	whizz	wootz	yrapt	yawey
value	vista	Woden	waked	wiper	yobbo	yawny
valve	visie	wader	waken	wired	yabby	Yezdi
vilde	visne	widow	woken	world	yacca	zabra
volae	vasal	waddy	waker	warre	yucca	zebra
volte	vison	widdy	walla	worse	yacht	zebub
volve	visto	wield	welke	wersh	yucky	zebec
villi	visor	weeke	wolve	worth	yodle	zibet
velum	visit	weete	Wolof	wirer	yodel	zocco
vulgo	vasty	where	welch	works	yield	zoeae
velar	vitta	whelk	welsh	warst	yfere	zoeal
volar	vatic	wreak	waler	worst	yrent	zygal
vales	vetch	wreck	welkt	wurst	yogic	zigan
valet	vital	wheal	wally	warby	yogin	zygon
veldt	voter	wheel	walty	warty	yager	zoism
volet	Vitis	whelm	welly	wordy	Yahve	zoist
vomer	vitex	wheen	willy	wormy	Yahwe	zilch
vomit	vaute	whelp	waltz	worry	yahoo	zamia
Vinca	vouge	whear	wamed	waste	yrivd	zimbi
vaned	vouch	wheat	woman	washy	ylike	zombi
venae	vault	wheft	women	waspy	yoick	zambo
venge	vaunt	wrest	wamus	wispy	yojan	zanja
venue	voulu	waefu'	Wimpy®	withe	yakka	zonda
venal	vivda	weedy	womby	watch	yokel	zoned
vinal	vivid	weeny	winna	witch	yokul	zante
vinyl	viver	weepy	wonga	witan	Yakut	zanze
venom	vives	wefte	waned	water	yukky	zinke
venin	vivat	woful	wanle	withy	yclad	zonae
viner	vowed	wafer	wanze	witty	ycled	zonal
venus	vawte	wagon	wince	would	yulan	zinco
vinew	vowel	wigan	winge	wound	yolky	zincy
veney	vexed	wages	winze	wauff	yamen	zingy
viola	vixen	wight	wench	wrung	yummy	zinky
V-bomb	vexer	wahoo	winch	waugh	yince	zooea
viold	vezir	weird	winds	waulk	yonks	zooid
vroom	vizir	waide	waney	waved	ycond	zhomo
vrouw	vizor	waive	wanly	woven	ybore	zooks
vapid	weamb	weise	wanty	waver	Y-moth	zloty
vapor	weald	weize	wenny	wives	ymolt	zupan
viper	weave	while	windy	wavey	ytost	zoppo
varna	whale	whine	winey	waxen	yapok	zappy
virga	whare	white	wingy	woxen	yapon	zippy
varec	wrate	write	wonky	waxer	yupon	zerda
virid	wharf	whiff	wooed	wryly	yippy	zoril
varve	whang	wring	woold	wizen	yarfa	zorro
verge	wrath	weigh	whole	wazir	yarta	zesty
verse	whack	which	whore	X-rays	yerba	zowie
verve	wrack	whish	whose	xebec	ydrad	zizel
virge	wrawl	whilk	wroke	xylic	ydred	
viral	whaup	whisk	wrote	xylol	yarto	
varan	whaur	wrick	wrong	xylyl	Yorks	
verso	wrapt	whirl	woosh	xylem	yesty	
vireo	wrast	whirr	wroth	xenon	yauld	
Virgo	weary	whiss	whorl	Xhosa	you're	
varus	weber	waift	whoso	X-body	you've	
virus	webby	waist	whoop	xeric	young	
verst	wacke	whift	wooer	Xeres	youth	
vertu	wecht	whipt	whoot	Xyris	you'll	
virtu	wacky		whort	Xerox®	yourn	

Agadah	abbacy	adduct	avenue	at-home	alkane	arnica	arolla
agapae	albedo	addeem	acetyl	achene	askant	apnoea	abound
anabas	aubade	addled	aye-aye	aching	Atkins	aunter	agoing
ananas	ambler	Andrew	affrap	aphony	acknow	alnage	amount
anarak	albugo	aldrin	affray	ashine	askari	Aeneid	anoint
atabal	ambage	aedile	affect	Athena	arkose	agnail	aroint
ataman	albeit	audile	affyde	Athene	arkite	auntie	around
avatar	Albany	addend	affeer	a'thing	afloat	annuli	aroynt
anarch	albino	aidant	affied	athrob	all-day	agname	agorot
awatch	Albion	aiding	affret	awhape	allice	Annona	aboard
abased	albert	Aldine	affair	adhere	anlace	awning	adoors
abated	ambery	Andine	aefald	ashery	allude	amnion	Anoura
acater	anbury	ardent	affine	ashore	allied	agnise	avoure
acates	auburn	addoom	affirm	a'where	allies	adnate	avowry
agazed	abbess	aldern	afford	aghast	all-red	agnate	ahorse
alated	ambush	aldose	afflux	alidad	asleep	Arnaut	arouse
anadem	albata	aidful	afghan	animal	allege	annexe	abouts
Aranea	albite	ardour	arghan	apical	anlage	aboral	agouta
atabeg	arbute	acetal	Augean	avital	Aglaia	Adonai	agouti
atabek	arbour	alegar	angico	akimbo	all-hid	ajowan	Acorus
awaked	ascian	apeman	alglet	apiece	aslake	amoral	amomum
awaken	aucuba	agency	angled	abided	allele	anodal	amoove
awayes	accede	alerce	angler	aliped	aflame	anorak	anonym
azalea	arcade	amerce	arguer	apices	aplomb	apodal	azodye
apache	Arcady	aperçu	argufy	arisen	ablins	atokal	appeal
apathy	accrew	areach	algoid	alight	ailing	atonal	appear
abatis	arched	agenda	Anguis	anight	allons	avowal	alpaca
acacia	archer	amende	Angola	aright	aslant	azonal	aspect
acarid	accoil	amends	argala	acidic	abloom	amoeba	aspick
adagio	Alcaic	A-level	argali	adipic	aslope	amorce	alpeen
Adamic	Archie	apexes	argyle	afield	allure	avouch	appaid
agamic	archil	abeigh	Argyll	aridly	ablush	adorer	appair
agamid	arctic	alegge	angina	arilli	ablate	amoret	ampule
agaric	ancile	avenge	argand	avidly	ablaut	apogee	alpine
alalia	archly	a-weigh	argent	axilla	Allium	apozem	Alpini
Arabic	ancome	acedia	Aegypt	alisma	all-out	atoner	Alpino
arabin	accend	acetic	angary	azione	alleys	avocet	append
Arabis	accent	alevin	angora	apiary	ablaze	avoset	arpent
aralia	Ancona	alexia	Asgard	aviary	asmear	avowed	aspine
ataxia	arcana	alexic	augury	ahimsa	armada	avoyer	ampere
ataxic	arcane	alexin	argosy	amidst	armlet	awoken	apport
ananke	arcing	amelia	august	arioso	almain	anough	aspire
afawld	ascend	anemia	algate	arista	armpit	Adonia	asport
arable	ascent	anemic	argute	aristo	aumail	Adonic	appose
availe	accloy	anetic	augite	aviate	awmrie	Adonis	aspout
avaunt	anchor	avenir	Argive	acinus	aemule	Aeolic	appayd
abator	archon	anerly	achkan	adieus	Almany	agogic	asquat
acajou	accept	areola	ash-can	adieux	almond	agonic	acquit
amadou	accord	areole	ashlar	anicut	admire	alogia	abroad
amatol	ancora	ageing	ash-pan	animus	almery	anodic	adread
amazon	access	apedom	ashram	abject	armory	anomic	aerial
analog	accost	afeard	aphids	adjoin	armure	anomie	air-car
araise	accuse	aweary	ash-key	abjure	aumbry	anoxia	air-gap
arayse	accite	ageism	ashler	adjure	admass	anoxic	air-gas
abattu	accrue	ageist	awheel	adjust	almost	aporia	airman
acanth	aecium	apepsy	achage	ack-ack	acmite	atocia	air-sac
anatta	alcove	a-per-se	Alhagi	aikido	almous	atomic	airway
anatto	Andean	averse	aphtha	ankled	armful	atonic	aortal
avanti	abdabs	Alecto	ash-bin	anklet	armour	atopic	arrear
abacus	abduce	amenta	ash-pit	auklet	awmous	azonic	atrial
acarus	abduct	aneath	ashake	alkali	anneal	azotic	aerobe
alarum	addict	aseity	awhile	Ankole	annual	abolla	arroba
asarum	adduce	Avesta	ashame	aikona	Aonian	apollo	arrack

arrect	absent	autism	beaker	by-blow	boding	bugler	Briard
awrack	arsine	aptote	beamer	Babism	bedrop	buglet	briery
abrade	assent	astute	bearer	Babist	bedash	begift	bhisti
arride	alsoon	antrum	beaten	buccal	bedust	baggit	blintz
afreet	absorb	artful	beater	backed	bedaub	bagnio	brigue
agreed	absurd	astrut	beaver	backer	bedbug	baguio	bajada
air-bed	adsorb	auteur	biased	backet	bedaze	bagwig	bejade
air-sea	assart	active	bladed	becket	beegah	beguin	bajree
'Arriet	assert	aoudad	blamed	bicker	beenah	biggie	bejant
Azrael	assort	abuser	blazer	bucker	bye-law	biggin	bijoux
adrift	assure	acumen	blazes	bucket	bleach	bigwig	bukshi
aurify	assess	aludel	boatel	bocage	blench	begild	baking
abrégé	assist	amulet	boater	buckie	breach	boggle	bikini
agrégé	ansate	amused	bracer	becall	breech	bigamy	bakery
Auriga	assets	amuser	brayer	becalm	bieldy	begone	bekiss
abraid	assott	abulia	brazen	buckle	begone	begunk	Balaam
adroit	actual	Anubis	beachy	became	beeves	bogong	ballad
afraid	assize	anuria	blashy	become	brevet	bugong	ballan
aortic	astral	Aquila	brashy	beckon	brewer	bygone	ballat
airily	astray	alumna	Baalim	biceps	brewis	begird	balsam
Abroma	attrap	alumni	beanie	becurl	bleaky	begirt	beldam
afront	antick	aburst	brazil	bicarb	breeks	bog-ore	Belial
airing	attach	aguise	blanky	buckra	beetle	bagful	bilian
arrant	attack	aguish	branks	back-up	bregma	big-bud	bulbar
awrong	aether	avulse	branky	badman	blenny	bug-out	Bulgar
abrupt	anthem	acuity	beadle	bedlam	brenne	bogeys	Baluch
Atropa	anther	aguize	beagle	bedpan	brehon	behead	belace
air-arm	antler	advice	bragly	bedral	breton	belace	bolide
aurora	astrex	abvolt	branle	bodrag	bleary	bahada	baleen
across	Altaic	advene	brawly	bedeck	breare	behalf	balker
afresh	Altair	advent	Brahma	beduck	breast	beheld	balled
agrise	antlia	alvine	Brahmi	bodach	breese	behold	ballet
aorist	attain	adverb	baaing	bodice	breath	behind	belied
arrest	astely	advert	Beaune	bedide	baetyl	bohunk	belief
arrish	asthma	advise	brainy	bedyde	bye-bye	behoof	belted
aurist	autumn	atweel	branny	badger	breeze	behest	bilker
aerate	acting	atween	brawny	bedded	breezy	behote	billed
amrita	anting	atwain	beacon	bedder	befoam	behave	billet
aurate	astone	aswing	blazon	bed-key	buffer	behove	bolden
air-bus	astony	aswoon	bravos	bedyed	buffet	behowl	bolled
air-gun	attend	adward	braird	bidden	biffin	Bairam	bollen
atrium	attent	aswarm	blaise	bidder	boffin	bridal	bolter
aureus	attone	aswirl	braise	bodger	baffle	boffin	bulbed
aurous	attune	ayword	brassy	bodied	befall	bailee	bulger
arrive	action	atwixt	beauty	bodies	befell	bailer	bulker
acrawl	ant-cow	always	beat-up	budded	befoul	bailey	buller
arrowy	astoop	anyway	blague	budger	bifold	baiter	bullet
arroyo	author	anyone	blaize	budget	befana	beigel	beluga
agrize	acture	anyhow	braize	bodega	befool	blimey	bolshy
agryze	afters	adytum	bablah	Buddha	before	boiled	Baltic
aisled	altern	amylum	bobcat	baddie	biform	boiler	Belgic
answer	artery	asylum	bibber	bed-sit	by-form	briber	billie
Auster	astare	Aizoon	bobbed	beduin	beflum	bridge	bollix
assign	astart	bharal	bobbin	bodgie	befoul	blight	bulbil
abseil	astern	Bharat	bobwig	bodkin	bagman	blithe	belike
arshin	astert	biaxal	babble	budgie	beggar	bright	baldly
assail	attire	blanch	bobble	bedell	begnaw	bailie	boldly
assoil	attorn	blanco	bubble	boddle	bogoak	bridie	belamy
Aussie	artist	branch	bubbly	bodily	bagged	blinks	bulimy
Austin	attask	braide	bebung	buddle	begged	bricky	Belone
alsike	attest	brandy	baboon	bedung	bigger	brisky	belong
assume		beaded		bident	bogies	bailli	by-lane
awsome		beaked		biding	bugged	bridle	byline
					bugger	briony	
						Briton	

balboa	bunjee	broker	borsch	burbot	bishop	bathos	bow-boy
ballot	bunker	brolga	Bursch	burgoo	bisson	batoon	bowpot
ballow	Bunsen	brough	boride	burrow	bosbok	betook	bowwow
bellow	bunted	broché	barbed	burton	boston	betrod	bewept
billon	bunter	bionic	barbel	byroom	busboy	bettor	bawdry
billow	benign	biopic	barber	barish	besort	bittor	beware
belfry	bunchy	biotic	barbet	barite	bistre	bottom	bowery
bolero	bandit	biotin	barded	baryta	bistro	button	byword
balata	ben-oil	boodle	bargee	berate	Basuto	bêtise	bywork
belate	benzil	boogie	barken	borate	Basutu	betoss	box-car
belaud	bonnie	bookie	barker	buriti	boshta	batata	box-day
bulbul	bonxie	bromic	barley	barful	basque	battue	baxter
belive	bungie	boodle	barney	barium	besmut	bittur	box-bed
belove	bunjie	brolly	barred	barque	bestud	Beulah	boxing
bylive	bunnia	bloomy	barrel	burn-up	bisque	brumal	boxful
billy-o	bunyip	broomy	barren	bashaw	bust-up	brutal	beyond
bemean	bangle	browny	barret	bespat	byssus	brumby	bryony
bemoan	bingle	booboo	barter	bestad	bateau	bounce	buying
bombax	bundle	boo-hoo	Berber	bestar	batman	bouncy	Bayard
bemock	bungle	biopsy	berret	bismar	betray	brunch	boyish
Bembex	bename	blouse	birken	bus-bar	bothan	bluidy	boyaux
bomber	benumb	blowse	birler	busman	betide	bouget	buy-out
bum-bee	by-name	blowsy	bordel	byssal	bather	boules	bazaar
bummed	banana	booksy	border	bisect	batler	brunet	bezoar
bummer	boning	broose	boreen	beside	batlet	bludge	buzzer
bumper	bandog	browse	borrel	basher	batted	bluggy	bezzle
bemoil	benzol	browst	burden	basket	battel	blunge	bezant
bumkin	bonbon	blotto	burgee	basnet	batten	bouche	bizone
bumalc	bunion	blotty	burger	basset	batter	bought	byzant
bumble	binary	blow-up	burhel	baster	beteem	brushy	bazazz
bummle	banish	brogue	buried	beseem	bethel	bludie	bezazz
Bimana	bonism	blowze	burler	beseen	betted	bougie	bizazz
bamboo	bonist	blowzy	burned	besped	better	bauble	chadar
bemire	Banate	bronze	burner	bister	bitted	bouclé	chagan
bemuse	binate	bronzy	burnet	bosker	bitten	boulle	chalan
bemete	bonito	brouze	burrel	bosket	bitter	bluing	charas
bemaul	bang-up	by-play	bereft	bossed	bother	bourne	cravat
Bombyx	ben-nut	bo-peep	barege	bushed	bo-tree	bouton	clambe
bandar	bonduc	bopper	borage	bushel	butler	beurré	crabby
banian	bunkum	bepuff	bertha	busied	butted	bluish	crambo
banjax	benzyl	bepelt	berthe	busked	butter	bourse	chance
Bannat	baobab	by-plot	burkha	busker	bitchy	bruise	chancy
bantam	biogas	bypass	bardic	busket	botchy	bounty	clatch
banyan	brogan	by-past	barrio	busted	betoil	Brutus	cranch
banzai	blotch	bepity	berlin	bustee	betrim	bovine	cratch
benzal	broach	bypath	birdie	buster	bittie	bovate	chafer
bonsai	bronco	barkan	birkie	besigh	bothie	bivium	chalet
banded	brooch	barman	burdie	bosche	betake	bewray	chapel
banged	blonde	barrat	byrnie	besoin	battle	bow-man	chared
banger	bloody	Berean	barely	bespit	Betula	bow-oar	charet
banker	boorde	bordar	barfly	bestir	botfly	bow-saw	chaser
banket	broody	boreal	birsle	buskin	bottle	bawbee	claret
banner	biogen	Boreas	burble	basalt	buttle	bawler	claver
banter	blowed	bureau	bireme	basely	betime	bawley	claves
bended	blower	burial	barony	busily	by-time	beweep	clawed
bender	boomer	burlap	borane	bustle	bating	bowget	clayey
bennet	booted	Burman	boring	bosomy	betony	bow-leg	coatee
binder	bootee	bursae	barrow	basing	biting	bowler	coaxer
bonded	Boötes	bursal	barton	besing	botany	bowser	crases
bonder	boozed	bursar	baryon	besung	botone	bowyer	crater
bonnet	boozer	byrlaw	borrow	busing	butane	bewail	craven
bonzer	boozey	byroad	borzoi	bespot	but-end	bowfin	craver
bungee	broken	barock		bestow	butene	bawble	crayer

crazed	**cabbie**	caesar	chequy	critic	culler	coming	cantle
chaffy	cabrie	Ceefax®	cherub	**chinks**	cullet	**cameos**	**cinema**
chaufe	cabrit	chenar	cherup	chinky	culmen	camion	conima
chauff	cobric	coeval	**cleave**	cricky	culter	come-on	**canine**
change	cuboid	credal	**caftan**	**chicle**	culver	common	caning
charge	**cabala**	Cretan	**coffee**	chicly	**calefy**	commot	conine
claggy	cobalt	**clench**	coffer	chield	**caligo**	compot	**candor**
craggy	cobble	cleuch	**coffin**	chilli	colugo	camera	cannon
cha-cha	Cybele	coerce	cuffin	chilly	**calcic**	**camera**	cannot
coachy	**cabana**	creach	**cafila**	criblé	calkin	comarb	canton
Charis	**Cabiri**	**chenet**	coffle	**client**	callid	comart	cantor
Chasid	coburg	cheven	cuffle	coigne	Celtic	**camash**	cantos
clavie	**cubism**	chewet	**cafard**	criant	collie	camass	canyon
clavis	cubist	clever	Caffre	**chibol**	cullis	camese	censor
crania	**cobnut**	crenel	**Cognac**	chicon	cultic	camise	centos
crasis	**coccal**	crewel	**cogged**	chigoe	**calmly**	comose	cineol
cyanic	**cicada**	**cierge**	cogger	chikor	coldly	cymose	condom
cyanin	**cachet**	clergy	cygnet	chiton	**calami**	**comate**	condor
chalky	cocked	cleugh	**ciggie**	**chippy**	column	comity	congou
chapka	cocker	creagh	coggie	chirpy	**colony**	**campus**	convoy
cranky	cocket	**cleché**	coggly	crimpy	**callow**	comous	**canapé**
czapka	cycler	crèche	coggle	crispy	collop	cymous	canopy
cradle	**coccid**	**chemic**	coggly	**chigre**	**caliph**	**cancan**	Cynips
craple	Cochin	chenix	**cogent**	**chiasm**	**celery**	Cantab	**canard**
crawly	cyclic	chesil	**cagoul**	cuisse	colure	cantar	canary
chacma	**cackle**	chevin	**cahier**	**chintz**	**calash**	canvas	cendré
chasmy	cecils	cleric	**co-heir**	chitty	**call-up**	cental	**centre**
clammy	cicala	clevis	**cohune**	clifty	callus	confab	**centry**
chaunt	cicely	credit	**cahoot**	crista	calque	con-man	contra
cranny	cicely	cretic	**cohere**	**caique**	cilium	cuneal	**canful**
chador	**cachou**	cretin	cohorn	chiaus	coleus	**canuck**	cangue
Charon	cacoon	cyesis	cohort	clique	colour	conics	cantus
chaton	cocoon	**checky**	**caimac**	cliquy	cultus	**cañada**	census
clamor	cuckoo	cheeky	caiman	Cnicus	**combat**	**cancel**	centum
craton	**cicero**	creaky	chinar	coitus	comsat	cancer	cinque
crayon	**cocksy**	creeky	chital	**chivvy**	cymbal	canker	concur
chappy	**cecity**	**creole**	climax	**cojoin**	**comedo**	canned	consul
crampy	cicuta	**chemmy**	cnidae	**cajole**	comedy	cannel	**choral**
charry	**cactus**	creamy	coital	**caking**	**camber**	canner	clonal
chaise	coccus	**creant**	crinal	**calcar**	camlet	canter	crotal
chasse	cock-up	**coelom**	**chinch**	calpac	camper	censer	**choice**
chassé	cyclus	cremor	clinch	celiac	cimier	center	cloaca
classy	**coccyx**	crepon	**childe**	cellae	combed	cinder	crotch
clause	**cadeau**	cresol	**chided**	cellar	comber	conder	crouch
coarse	caduac	**creepy**	chider	collar	commer	confer	**cloddy**
chaeta	**cadger**	**cheero**	chimer	Colmar	compel	congee	cloudy
chanty	codded	cheers	Chinee	**colobi**	cumber	conger	**choked**
charta	codger	cheery	chisel	**calico**	cummer	conjee	choker
chaste	cudgel	cherry	coiner	cilice	**camsho**	conker	chokey
chatta	**codify**	cheese	crikey	cultch	**comfit**	conned	choler
chatty	**caddie**	cheesy	cripes	**calced**	commie	conner	chorea
clarty	caddis	crease	crises	calces	commis	convex	choree
coaita	codlin	creasy	cuiter	calker	commit	convey	chosen
crafty	cuddie	creese	**cliffy**	caller	commix	cunner	closed
crants	cedula	creesh	**clingy**	callet	cummin	**canthi**	closer
claque	coddle	cressy	cringe	calmed	cymoid	concha	closet
cratur	cuddle	cueist	**chicha**	calver	Cymric	conchy	cloven
cabman	cuddly	**cherty**	chichi	calves	**cample**	**candid**	clover
cubica	**cadent**	chesty	chi-rho	calxes	comble	candie	cloyed
cobber	**cedarn**	create	**cliché**	celled	comely	confit	cooker
cobweb	cidery	cuesta	**chitin**	collet	comply	confix	cooler
cubbed	**codist**	**caecum**	clinic	colter	cumuli	conoid	cooper
cubage	**caecal**	cheque	crisis	Culdee	**cement**	**candle**	coosen

cooser
cronet
crowed
chough
cloggy
clough
cloche
clothe
Clotho
cloths
croche
cholic
chopin
choria
choric
clonic
cookie
coolie
coosin
croaky
clodly
coolly
cooing
croton
choppy
croppy
croupe
croupy
chowri
chowry
choose
choosy
chouse
crosse
crouse
Cloots
clotty
coolth
coonty
croüte
chorus
clonus
cloqué
crocus
capias
captan
cupman
copeck
capped
capper
cipher
copied
copier
copped
copper
cupped
cupper
cypher
caplin
capric
capsid
coppin
Coptic

cupric
cup-tie
cyprid
cypris
copple
copula
cupola
cupule
coping
captor
capita
capote
copita
cippus
cop-out
cupful
cyprus
coquet
carfax
carman
carnal
carpal
carrat
cercal
cereal
circar
corban
corral
cursal
curtal
caribe
carack
caract
Carica
curacy
corody
carder
careen
career
caries
carnet
carney
carpel
carper
carpet
carrel
cartel
carter
carved
carvel
carven
carver
cermet
certes
corbel
corded
corked
corker
cornea
corned
cornel
corner
cornet

corset
Cortes
cortex
corvée
corves
corvet
curfew
curiet
curled
curler
curlew
curney
curpel
cursed
curser
curved
curvet
carafe
cerris
certie
cervix
corbie
corkir
corrie
corvid
currie
circle
curdle
curtly
curule
carème
chroma
chrome
chromo
corymb
caranx
carina
caring
corona
carbon
carboy
carfox
carlot
carrot
carton
ceroon
cordon
curios
cursor
Carapa
ceriph
curara
curare
curari
caress
cerise
ceruse
chrism
Christ
corpse
curtsy
cerate
cerite

curate
carpus
cercus
Cereus
cerium
circus
cirque
cirrus
corium
cormus
cornua
Cornus
corpus
corvus
curium
cursus
corozo
coryza
casbah
cashaw
casual
costal
co-star
cushat
cosech
cashew
casket
casted
caster
cisted
cosher
cosier
cosmea
cosset
coster
cusped
cussed
cusser
casein
cassia
cassis
cistic
cosmic
cossie
cuspid
cystic
cystid
castle
cosily
costly
casing
casino
cosine
castor
cosmos
custom
custos
casern
cesura
cesure
casque
cesium
cestui

cestus
cistus
costus
cuscus
Cathar
cat-lap
catnap
coteau
cottar
cotwal
cytode
catnep
cither
cotted
cotter
cutler
cutlet
cutter
cut-off
catcht
catchy
cutcha
catkin
catnip
citric
citrin
cytoid
catalo
cattle
citole
cotyle
cuttle
catena
cetane
cation
citron
cotton
cuttoe
citess
cotise
cytase
cytisi
catgut
catsup
citrus
Cottus
cut-out
caudal
causal
chukar
coucal
cougar
crural
chubby
crumbs
crumby
church
clunch
clutch
crunch
crutch
cruddy
caudex

cauker
caules
causen
causer
causey
cautel
cauter
Clupea
coulée
couped
coupee
couper
couter
cruces
crumen
cruset
cruxes
chuffy
caught
couché
couthy
caulis
clusia
cousin
coutil
crusie
chukka
chunky
caudle
couple
cruels
chummy
crummy
chukor
coupon
clumps
clumpy
crumpy
clumsy
course
cruise
county
deathy
drachm
crusty
caucus
cruive
caveat
caviar
civics
cavier
cave-in
caving
covent
coving
covyne
cavern
cavort
covary
covert
cavass
civism
cavity
cowman

cowpat
cawker
cowled
cow-pea
cowage
cowrie
cawing
cowboy
cowpox
coward
cowish
Caxton
cayman
chylde
crying
Ceylon
chypre
cayuse
coyish
coyote
crypto
cozier
cizers
drabby
diarch
deaden
deader
deafen
dealer
deaner
diadem
diaper
doater
dragée
draped
draper
drapet
drawee
drawer
drazel
draffy
dearie
deasil
deawie
diacid
diapir
dualin
dyadic
deadly
deafly
dearly
doable
drably
dually
dyable
dharma
dharna
draunt
deacon
dialog
diatom

diaxon
dragon
drappy
dearth
drafts
diamyl
dabbed
dabber
debted
debtee
dibbed
dibber
dobber
dubbed
debris
dobbie
dobbin
dubbin
dabble
debile
dibble
debunk
debtor
debark
debase
debosh
debate
dybbuk
decoct
decade
decide
decode
dacker
decked
decker
decree
decrew
dicker
dickey
docken
docker
docket
ducker
dacoit
deceit
decoke
deckle
docile
decamp
décime
decane
decani
decant
decent
dicing
doctor
decarb
decare
decern
Dectra
decury
dicast
dacite

Docete · dictum · dactyl · dodman · deduce · deduct · dadoes · didder · dodded · dodder · dodgem · dodger · dodoes · dudder · dudeen · dodkin · duddie · daddle · diddle · dedans · dudish · dudism · daedal · deejay · dreich · drench · deemed · deepen · diesel · dieses · dieter · djebel · dzeren · dredge · dreggy · deepie · diesis · deeply · duello · dreamt · dreamy · duenna · dyeing · daemon · dièdre · dreary · duetto · dueful · defeat · defray · deface · defect · defied · defier · deflex · differ · doffer · duffel · duffer · daftie · daftly · deffly · defile

deftly · duffle · defame · defend · define · deform · defast · defuse · defoul · defuze · degras · dog-ear · dagoba · dagger · dagoes · degree · digged · digger · dog-bee · dogged · dogger · dog-hep · dog-leg · dégagé · dog-hip · daggle · digamy · dog-end · dugong · diglot · dogfox · dog-ape · degust · digest · dogate · dégoût · dugout · dahlia · dehorn · dehort · daiker · daimen · de-icer · doiled · doited · drivel · driven · driver · duikep · daimio · deific · deixis · doitit · daidle · djinni · drippy · driest · dainty · drifty · deject · diktat · dakoit · dik-dik

dukery · dikast · Delian · dollar · dolman · delice · delict · deluce · delude · delver · delves · dolmen · dulcet · deluge · delphs · Dalila · dolent · dallop · dildoe · dollop · delate · delete · dilate · dilute · dolium · dolour · dammar · demean · démodé · dammed · dammer · damned · dampen · damper · damsel · dimmed · dimmer · dumper · damage · dammit · demain · domain · damply · dimble · dimple · dimply · dumbly · dumple · demand · dement · domino · damson · demark · demure · demise · demiss · demist · dumose · demote · dimity · domett · dim-out

dumdum · dumous · denial · dental · donnat · denude · dynode · dancer · dander · danger · Daniel · denied · denier · dennet · dentel · dinged · dinger · dinges · dingey · dinned · dinner · donkey · donned · donnée · donzel · dunder · Dunker · dunned · dinghy · dentil · dentin · donsie · dunlin · dandle · dangle · dindle · dingle · dinnle · dynamo · danton · donjon · donnot · dun-cow · Dunlop · denary · donary · Danish · dynast · Danite · denote · donate · dunite · dioxan · doodad · doodah · droich · dooket

doomed · droger · drongo · dioxin · doolie · dromic · drosky · dhooly · doodle · drolly · droome · Diodon · doocot · dromoi · dromon · dromos · droopy · dropsy · drossy · drowse · drowsy · dhooti · drogue · dipsas · depict · dipody · dapper · diplex · dip-net · dipped · dipper · dopper · duplet · duplex · dipole · daphne · depend · depone · dopant · doping · deploy · diploe · diplon · Dipnoi · dupion · depart · deport · dupery · depose · depute · deputy · Dardan · derham · dermal · dirham · Dorcas · Dorian · dorsal · durbar

durgan · Durham · durian · direct · deride · dirndl · dorado · darken · darkey · darned · darnel · darner · darred · darter · dirhem · dormer · dorsel · dorser · dorter · dirige · Dardic · darkie · derail · dermic · dermis · derris · dormie · durrie · dargle · darkle · darkly · dartle · dernly · dor-fly · daring · durant · during · durion · dartre · dorise · Dorism · duress · derate · dirdum · dor-bug · dorsum · durdum · derive · desman · disbar · dismal · disman · dismay · distal · dossal · dosi-do · dasher · dished · dispel · dossel · dosser · dusken · duster

design · dosage · dassie · desmid · distil · dossil · desalt · disple · desine · desyne · despot · descry · desert · desire · desorb · disarm · dysury · desist · disuse · disbud · discus · diseur · dust-up · disown · dittay · detach · detect · dither · ditted · dotted · dutied · dotage · detail · detain · dittit · dottle · detent · détenu · ditone · dotant · doting · datary · datura · detort · dotard · detest · dotish · detour · dative · dauber · dauner · deuced · doucet · drupel · drudge · douche · dought · doughy · dautie

double · doubly · drumly · douane · deuton · dhurra · device · divide · devvel · devoid · devoir · devall · Divali · divine · diving · divers · divert · devest · devise · divest · dovish · devote · devour · devout · dyvour · dewlap · dowlas · dawner · downed · downer · dowser · dowset · dawtie · Downie® · dawdle · Dewali · dewily · Diwali · dewani · dew-bow · dawbry · dawish · dewitt · dexter · day-bed · doyley · duyker · day-fly · day-old · dry-fly · drying · day-boy · dry-rot · dryish · dizain · dazzle · dozing · elance · enarch · eparch · exarch · elanet · elater

E-layer	excite	effere	epigon	espial	eisell	enwomb	fibrin
enamel	encave	effort	epizoa	expect	ensile	enwind	fibula
erased	endear	enfire	émigré	espada	Essene	emydes	facial
eraser	eddied	enform	Erinys	espied	ensure	eryngo	fecial
examen	eddoes	effuse	enjoin	expugn	exsert	etymic	façade
eyalet	Eddaic	elfish	enjamb	esprit	ensate	etypic	facies
Elaeis	eidola	effete	Eskimo	empale	ersatz	etymon	fucked
egally	end-all	efflux	Eolian	expand	ensoul	elytra	fucker
enable	eident	engram	eyliad	expend	essive	enzian	fucoid
epaule	elding	eaglet	enlace	employ	entrap	Eozoic	facile
enamor	ending	eggler	enlock	euphon	estray	eczema	facula
etalon	endart	erg-ten	eel-set	empare	entice	enzyme	feckly
elapse	endure	eughen	eulogy	empery	either	enzone	fecula
écarté	eadish	ewghen	éclair	empire	entrée	evzone	fickle
embace	eddish	engagé	esloin	expert	entrez	Eozoon	fo'c'sle
embody	eldest	engage	enlink	expire	eothen	fracas	facing
emblem	endoss	engild	ellops	expiry	esteem	flabby	fecund
embail	endite	engulf	enlard	export	eatage	flambé	factor
emblic	endive	edging	eclose	empusa	eatche	fiancé	fictor
emboil	evejar	engine	enlist	empuse	eltchi	fiasco	facete
ecbole	egence	egg-box	eolith	expose	entail	flanch	factum
embale	egency	eggnog	enlevé ·	exposé	entoil	franco	fuck-up
emball	elench	engaol	ermine	ear-cap	eathly	fratch	fidget
embalm	éperdu	eggery	emmesh	earlap	extold	feared	fodder
emboly	eleven	engird	enmesh	earwax	entame	flamed	fade-in
embank	eyelet	engirt	enmity	enrobe	entomb	flamen	faddle
embark	emerge	engore	emmove	eirack	eating	flaser	fiddle
embase	energy	eighth	enmove	enrace	extant	flawed	fiddly
emboss	Edenic	eighty	ennead	enrich	extend	flaxen	fuddle
embost	Egeria	ergate	Etnean	earner	extent	flayed	fading
embusy	emesis	eggcup	esnecy	étrier	extine	flayer	fedora
embrue	emetic	englut	eunuch	enrage	ectopy	framer	fade-up
erbium	emetin	ephebe	eonism	enragé	ectype	frater	fadeur
embryo	eremic	ephebi	ennuyé	earthy	eatery	flange	faecal
eschar	eyelid	ethics	enodal	earwig	entera	flashy	foeman
encode	eye-pit	echoed	euouae	eureka	entire	flavin	foetal
escudo	Eyetie	echoer	evovae	eerily	extern	frazil	fierce
excide	evenly	echoes	Elodea	enroll	extirp	featly	fleece
elchee	eterne	echoic	eloper	earing	extort	flatly	fleech
eschew	exeunt	ethnic	epopee	enrank	eftest	fiaunt	fleecy
etcher	eyeing	enhalo	eroded	enring	extasy	flaune	flench
exceed	elevon	exhale	exogen	errand	entité	flaunt	fletch
encage	erenow	exhume	eloign	errant	entity	fraena	french
eucain	exempt	ethane	enough	erring	estate	flacon	fresco
encalm	epeira	ethene	epocha	earbob	estrum	flagon	faeces
encamp	exedra	ethyne	Elohim	enroot	eutaxy	fragor	feeder
excamb	egesta	Ethiop	enosis	enrapt	emulge	frappé	feeler
Eocene	ejecta	exhort	epodic	egress	emunge	fiacre	flewed
escroc	émeute	epical	erotic	éprise	écurie	fratry	foemen
escrol	Erebus	Evipan®	exodic	errata	epulis	fraise	fledge
escrow	exequy	eriach	exomis	earful	eluant	fealty	fledgy
escape	eyeful	evince	exotic	enseal	equine	feague	flèche
except	enerve	epimer	étoile	enseam	elutor	flatus	fleshy
encore	efface	exited	exopod	ensear	équipe	franzy	faerie
escarp	effect	eringo	egoism	exsect	épuisé	Fabian	féerie
escort	enface	elicit	egoist	eassel	evulse	fabled	flemit
euchre	ewftes	elixir	egoity	easter	eluate	fabler	foetid
encase	effigy	exilic	econut	ensued	equate	fibbed	fremit
encash	effeir	edible	évolué	ensign	equity	fibber	freaky
encyst	enfold	enisle	exodus	eassil	envier	fibred	feeble
excess	effing	evilly	evolve	elshin	elvish	fabric	feebly
excise	enfant	enigma	eponym	essoin	enwrap	fibril	freely
excuse		editor	exonym	easily	enwall		frenne

flexor	feints	Fenian	frothy	ferric	fetich	fixate	grassy
foetor	feisty	fenman	fiorin	fervid	fat-hen	fixity	graith
fleury	flinty	fingan	florid	firkin	father	fixive	Granth
flense	frieze	finial	florin	forbid	fatted	fly-man	graste
freest	frizzy	finjan	frolic	fordid	fatten	Flysch	giaour
fiesta	fikery	finnac	frowie	formic	fatter	flying	gradus
freety	fikish	finnan	footle	fornix	fetter	frying	glaive
freity	fallal	fin-ray	foozle	forpit	fitted	fezzed	gib-cat
fretty	fellah	fontal	frorne	forrit	fitter	fezzes	gubbah
foetus	filial	fungal	flow-on	fortis	fother	fizzed	gabber
frenum	foliar	fanged	floppy	ferula	fitché	fizzen	gabled
freeze	fulham	fan-jet	floury	ferule	fitchy	fizzer	gablet
frenzy	fullam	fanned	footra	firmly	fettle	fizgig	gibber
Fifish	fullan	fannel	floosy	furole	futile	fizzle	gibbet
fogman	fulmar	fanner	flossy	farand	fathom	fuzzle	giblet
fogram	falces	Fantee	flouse	farina	future	ghazal	gobbet
fagged	fallen	fenced	floush	ferine	fetish	glance	goblet
figged	falser	fencer	froise	firing	fitful	grande	goblin
fogged	falter	fender	frowst	forane	fit-out	geared	gabble
fogger	feller	fennec	frowsy	forint	faucal	ghazel	gobble
fag-end	felter	fennel	floaty	furane	faunae	glazen	gobang
faggot	filler	finder	frosty	firlot	faunal	glazer	gobony
fog-bow	fillet	fineer	floozy	forgot	feudal	goatee	gabion
fog-dog	filter	finger	frowzy	forhoo	frugal	graben	gibbon
fegary	folder	finned	fipple	forhow	fauces	graced	gabbro
figure	fuller	finner	faquir	formol	faucet	grated	go-cart
fogash	filthy	funded	ferial	furrow	flugel	grater	goddam
fugato	fall-in	funnel	firman	furore	flukey	graved	gadded
Führer	falsie	Finnic	forbad	forest	fluter	gravel	gadder
fehmic	fillip	funkia	forçat	ferity	fouter	graven	gadget
Friday	filmic	finsko	forgat	far-out	frutex	graver	Gadhel
flitch	fulfil	fangle	formal	fureur	fluffy	graves	gidgee
faikes	fulgid	fankle	format	furfur	flushy	grazer	gidjee
failed	fulvid	finale	forrad	forbye	fought	grange	godded
foiled	feline	finely	forray	festal	foully	glacis	god-den
fridge	felony	fondle	forsay	fiscal	fluent	goalie	gadgie
fringe	filing	fondly	furcal	fasces	fautor	gradin	gadoid
fringy	falcon	fining	foreby	fasten	frumpy	Gräfin	godwit
flight	fallow	fandom	fardel	faster	feutre	gratis	gadfly
fricht	felloe	fanion	farden	fester	flurry	gravid	guddle
fright	fellow	fantod	farmer	fisher	foutra	guanin	godson
frigid	filfot	fantom	ferrel	fishes	foutre	gladly	godown
flisky	follow	finery	ferret	fossed	foussa	gnarly	go-down
friska	fulgor	finish	forced	foster	faulty	graile	greece
frisky	fylfot	funest	forcer	fusser	fluate	grakle	greedy
faible	filtre	finite	forfex	fustet	fourth	graple	gee-gee
faille	filose	fondue	forger	fascia	fruity	grayle	geezer
fainly	folksy	fundus	forget	fascio	frusta	gramme	Gheber
fairly	folium	fungus	forked	fisgig	foul-up	Grammy	gleyed
foible	fumado	feodal	forker	fistic	foveae	goanna	Gueber
frilly	fumage	florae	formed	fossil	foveal	graine	greige
friand	family	floral	former	fusain	favism	grainy	Gaelic
friend	female	flocci	forpet	fustic	favose	granny	greyly
faitor	fimble	Fronde	forren	fastly	favour	geason	gleamy
foison	fumble	floret	furder	fissle	favous	glamor	greeny
frigot	famine	flotel	furred	fusile	fawner	grappa	guenon
frijol	foment	flowed	far-off	fossor	fewmet	gharri	Guelph
fripon	femora	flower	forage	fusion	fewter	gharry	Ghebre
frivol	famish	footed	forego	fustoc	fowler	glairy	Guebre
friary	famous	footer	forthy	fescue	fox-bat	glaury	ghesse
flimsy	fumous	froren	forwhy	fat-cat	fixing	glassy	gneiss
faints	fantad	frozen	furphy		foxing		grease
fainty	fan-tan	froggy	farcin	fetial	fixure		

greasy
greese
ghetto
gleety
Greats
greete
Gnetum
greave
guffaw
gaffer
gifted
goffer
gigman
gagged
gagger
giglet
goglet
gag-bit
Giggit
gaggle
giggle
giggly
gigolo
goggle
goggly
guggle
giglot
guitar
glitch
griece
gainer
gaited
gaiter
glider
Glires
goidel
goiter
grices
griper
grivet
guider
guiled
guiler
guinea
guiser
griffe
gringo
geisha
gainly
glibly
grille
grimly
griple
grisly
glioma
grison
guidon
grippe
grippy
guimpe
goitre
gri-gri
griesy

grilse
gaiety
gritty
guilty
Griqua
grieve
glitzy
go-kart
gilgai
golias
gollan
gollar
Gullah
gelada
gallet
galley
gelded
gelder
gelled
gilded
gilden
gilder
gillet
gilpey
golden
golfer
gulden
guller
gullet
gulley
gylden
galage
Galago
Gallic
Gallio
gilgie
gillie
galant
galena
galiot
gallon
gallop
gallow
galoot
gollop
galère
galore
galosh
gelosy
golosh
galuth
gallus
gilcup
galaxy
gemmae
gemman
gimbal
gimmal
gymmal
gambet
gammer
gemmed
gemmen

gimlet
gimmer
gummed
gambir
gambit
gymnic
gomoku
gamble
gamely
gamine
gaming
gemini
geminy
gemony
gambol
gammon
gimmor
Gemara
gombro
gamash
gamesy
gamete
gomuti
gomuto
genial
gingal
gunman
gunyah
gander
ganger
gannet
gender
genned
gennet
gentes
ginger
ginned
ginnel
ginner
gunnel
gunner
gunsel
gunter
gynney
ginkgo
gung-ho
gun-shy
ganoid
ganoin
gingko
gangly
gentle
gently
gingle
genome
gentoo
gonion
gantry
genera
gentry
Ganesa
gunite
gangue

genius
geneva
global
gnomae
grouch
gaoler
globed
gloved
glover
glower
goober
gooley
gooney
gooses
goosey
grocer
gromet
groper
groser
groset
grovel
grower
George
groggy
geodic
globin
gloria
gnomic
gnosis
goodly
google
googly
grooly
growly
gloomy
ground
groyne
gnomon
good-oh
googol
gooroo
groupy
glossa
glossy
grouse
ghosty
groats
grotto
grotty
grouty
growth
groove
groovy
Geomys
gipsen
gopher
gypped
gyppie
gaping
gopura
gypsum
gardai
garial

garjan
garran
german
gurrah
garuda
garden
garget
garner
garnet
garred
garret
garter
germen
girded
girder
girnel
gorged
gorget
gurlet
gurnet
garage
Gurkha
garlic
garvie
gerbil
germin
girkin
girlie
girnie
gorgio
garble
gargle
girdle
gorily
gurgle
goramy
gurami
gerent
gerund
goring
gyrant
garçon
garron
garrot
gorgon
garish
gyrose
gyrate
gurjun
gyrous
garrya
gas-bag
gas-jar
gasman
gas-tap
gas-tar
gossan
guslar
gas-jet
gasket
gasper
gassed
Goshen

goslet
gospel
gusher
gusset
gasify
gaskin
gas-lit
gestic
gossib
gossip
gashly
gascon
go-slow
gâteau
guttae
gather
getter
gotten
gutted
gutter
Gothic
guttle
gating
gitana
gitano
get-out
grubby
gaunch
grutch
gourde
gourds
gourdy
gaufer
gauger
glutei
gluten
grudge
gauche
gaucho
gaucie
glumly
grumly
glumps
glumpy
grumph
grumpy
gaufre
gru-gru
gluish
giusto
gousty
goutte
gaupus
gavial
gavage
giving
govern
gewgaw
gowf-ba'
gowfer
gowned
gowpen
gowany

gawpus
geyser
guyler
glycin
grysie
gay-you
glycol
gryfon
gayest
goyish
gryesy
gozzan
gazebo
gizzen
guzzle
gazump
gazoon
headed
header
healer
hearer
heated
heater
heaved
heaven
heaver
hoaxer
Hyades
heathy
hearie
heaume
hyaena
head-on
hearse
hearsy
hoarse
health
hearth
hearty
heaste
hiatus
hobday
hub-cap
Hebrew
hoboes
Hebrid
hubris
hybrid
hybris
habile
hobble
hebona
haboob
hobjob
hobnob
hubbub
hackee
hocker
hockey
hachis
hectic
hackle
hackly

heckle
huckle
hector
Hecate
hiccup
hodman
hadden
hedger
hidden
hidder
hodden
hudden
hidage
haddie
hydria
hydric
heddle
hoddle
huddle
hiding
hydyne
hadron
Hedera
hadith
huddup
haemal
heehaw
Hielan'
hiemal
hyetal
heeled
heeler
haemin
heezie
hieing
haffet
haffit
hog-rat
hagden
hagged
haglet
higher
hogged
hogger
hogget
hog-pen
hugged
haggis
hoggin
hogtie
haggle
higgle
highly
hugely
hagdon
hegira
highth
hagbut
high-up
haikai
hainch
hair-do
hained

haired
heifer
hoiden
hoised
height
hoicks
hairst
haiduk
haique
hijrah
hijack
hejira
Hyksos
hallal
hallan
halvah
heliac
halide
halfen
haloed
haloes
halsed
halser
halter
halver
halves
heller
helmed
helmet
helped
helper
hilled
holden
holder
holler
holpen
haloid
holmia
holmic
holily
holing
halloa
halloo
hallow
holloa
hollow
Hilary
holism
holist
hylism
hylist
halite
hallux
helium
hold-up
hammal
hammam
hamzah
Humean
Humian
hymnal
humect
hamlet

hammer
hamper
hemmed
hempen
hummed
hummel
hummer
humped
hymned
humefy
humify
homage
humlie
hymnic
hamble
homely
homily
humble
humbly
homing
hominy
humane
hombre
humeri
hamose
Humism
Humist
hamate
hamite
humite
humpty
hamous
humbug
haptic
hippic
hummum
hummus
humour
humous
hangar
hanjar
handed
hander
hanged
hanger
hanker
hansel
henner
hen-pen
hinder
hinged
honied
hunger
hunker
hunter
hand-in
hankie
hen-bit
honkie
Hunnic
handle
hantle
hansom
Hindoo

hungry
honest
hang-up
hen-run
honour
hookah
hootch
hooded
hoofed
hooked
hooker
hookey
hooley
hooper
hooter
hooven
hoover
hooves
hoop-la
hoodoo
hoopoe
hook-up
hep-cat
heptad
hyphae
hyphal
happed
happen
hipped
hopped
hopper
hyphen
hop-off
haptic
hippic
hypnic
hypoid
hop-fly
hopple
hopdog
Hypnos
hypate
hippus
hypnum
harman
hartal
herbal
Herbar
hereat
hermae
hurrah
hurray
hereby
harden
hareem
harken
harmel
harper
harten
herden
Hermes
heroes
herpes

Herren
hersed
hirsel
horkey
horned
horner
hornet
hurden
hurler
hurley
hurter
harmin
herdic
herein
hermit
hernia
heroic
heroin
Hornie
horrid
hardly
hareld
herald
hirple
hirsle
hurdle
hurtle
hiring
harbor
harlot
harrow
hereof
hereon
heriot
heroon
horror
horson
Herero
horary
harass
harish
heresy
hereto
hard-up
hassar
Hesvan
hussar
haslet
hasten
Hesper
hosier
hostel
hushed
husher
husked
husker
Hassid
hispid
histie
hussif
hassle
hustle
hyssop

hostry
hetman
hit-man
hatpeg
hatred
hatted
hatter
hether
hither
hitter
hotbed
hotter
hutted
hitchy
hatpin
hot-air
hottie
hatbox
hotpot
hatful
houdah
houdan
haunch
hauler
housel
haught
hourly
haüyne
haulst
Havana
having
have-on
haw-haw
howdah
hawked
hawker
hawkey
hawser
howe'er
howker
howled
howler
howlet
hawkie
hawkit
howdie
hewing
hexact
hexane
hexene
hexing
hexose
heyday
haysel
hoyden
haying
haybox
haymow
huzza'd
hazily
hazing
huzoor
hazard

Idaean
inarch
isabel
Iranic
isatin
Isatis
italic
imagos
imbibe
imbody
imbrex
imbase
imbosk
imboss
imbrue
incubi
incede
inched
incage
inclip
ischia
in-calf
incult
income
incony
incept
incase
incest
incise
incuse
incite
incave
incavo
Indian
indaba
indict
induce
induct
iodide
indeed
indign
indigo
indris
indole
indult
indene
indent
induna
iodine
indoor
indart
iodise
iodism
indite
iodate
indium
iodous
ice-bag
ice-cap

iceman
ice-pan
ipecac
ibexes
ideaed
ilexes
Iberis
irenic
icebox
ideate
ice-run
ireful
ice-axe
in-foal
infect
infeft
infall
infelt
infill
infold
infula
infame
infamy
infant
inflow
infare
infere
infirm
inform
infest
infuse
influx
ingram
ingoes
ingulf
ingénu
ingine
ingest
ingate
ingrum
inhale
inhume
inhoop
inhere
iridal
idiocy
ibices
ibidem
ilices
irides
irised
irises
iridic
iritic
iritis
icicle
inisle
inject
in-joke
injure
injury
ink-bag
ink-cap

ink-sac
inkpot
illiad
inlace
inlock
illude
inlier
ill-off
inlaid
illume
inland
island
ill-got
illipe
illupi
ill-use
iolite
in-laws
iambic
immane
immune
immure
immask
immesh
inmost
inmate
iambus
Ionian
Innuit
ignomy
inning
ionone
ignaro
ignore
ionise
Ionism
Ionist
ignite
innate
ionium
isobar
ironer
isohel
isomer
iconic
ironic
Isodia
Idolon
isogon
isopod
Idoist
Idolum
impact
impede
implex
impugn
impair
impala
impale
impend
impone
impark
imparl

impart	inward	juicer	jurist	kiblah	kalpak	kronor	leader
import	in-word	jailor	jarful	kebbie	killas	Kronos	leafed
impure	inwork	jojoba	jerque	kabuki	kelter	knotty	leaker
impish	inworn	jujube	Jashar	kabala	killer	kopeck	leaned
impose	inwith	jejune	Jasher	kabele	kilted	kipper	leaped
impost	inwove	Julian	jasper	Kabyle	kilter	kephir	leaper
impute	inyala	jillet	jessed	kebele	kalmia	keppit	leaser
impave	ivy-tod	jolter	jestee	kibble	kalpis	koppie	leaved
impawn	izzard	jalopy	jester	kobold	keloid	kaputt	leaven
inroad	Jeames	jamjar	josher	kobang	kelpie	kurgan	leaves
irrupt	jibbah	jampan	josser	kibosh	Keltic	kirsch	loaded
inrush	jubbah	jimjam	jaspis	kybosh	keltie	kermes	loaden
inseam	jabber	jumbal	jessie	kibitz	kelvin	kernel	loader
inspan	jibbed	jambee	Jesuit	kabaya	kiltie	kersey	loafer
instal	jibber	jamber	joskin	kicker	kalong	kirbeh	loaves
instar	jobbed	jammed	jostle	Kuchen	kelson	kurvey	leachy
insect	jobber	jumped	justle	keckle	kilerg	karait	loathe
inside	jabble	jumper	justly	kecksy	kalium	karmic	loathy
inseem	job-lot	jumbie	joseph	kick-up	killut	kermis	lead-in
instep	jabers	jimply	jetsam	keddah	Kultur	kirkin'	lea-rig
issuer	jabiru	jumble	jitney	kedger	kamees	korkir	leanly
lastic	jubate	jumbly	jitter	kidded	kemper	karaka	liable
inship	jackal	jymold	jotted	kidder	kimmer	kirtle	learnt
instil	jacket	jemima	jotter	kidney	kümmel	koruna	leasow
insole	jockey	jiminy	jutted	kiddle	kamsin	Karroo	llanos
insula	jacana	jambok	jataka	kid-fox	kamala	korora	liaise
insult	jacent	jampot	jötunn	kamela	kamela	kaross	lealty
itself	jocund	jumart	jetsom	kamila	kamila	karate	lean-to
insane	jocose	jambul	jetson	keeker	kemple	karite	league
insert	Jacque	Janian	jetton	keeled	kimono	kasbah	labial
insure	Judean	jingal	jaunce	keeler	kumara	Kisleu	lablab
insist	Judica	janker	jounce	keener	kumari	Kislev	Libyan
insoul	judder	jantee	jaunse	keeper	kumiss	kismet	libido
in-tray	judogi	jennet	jaunty	klepht	kantar	kisser	labret
intact	Judaic	jinnee	jovial	keelie	kunkar	kosher	lebbek
intoed	judoka	jinxed	Jovian	kie-kie	Kanuck	kiss-me	libber
iatric	jadery	junker	jowled	kierie	kanten	kosmos	libken
intuit	jadish	junket	jowler	keenly	kenned	kit-bag	lobbed
intake	jaeger	junkie	jawing	Kneipe	kennel	kit-car	lubber
intima	jeerer	jangle	jawbox	kreese	kenner	Kitcat	lubric
intime	jeelie	jangly	jawari	kaftan	kennet	kotwal	labile
intomb	jaguar	jingle	jowari	kufiah	kanaka	kitsch	lobule
intend	jigsaw	jingly	Jewess	Kaffer	kindle	kitten	lobuli
intent	jagged	jungle	Jewish	keffel	kindly	kutcha	libant
intine	jagger	jungli	joyful	Kaffir	kingle	kettle	lobing
intone	jigged	jungly	joyous	kafila	kingly	kittle	lobose
intern	jigger	junior	jezail	kufiya	kinkle	kittly	libate
intire	jogged	juncus	keasar	kagool	kinema	ketone	lobate
intuse	jogger	jupati	khalat	kagoul	kinone	kation	labium
intown	jugged	jarrah	knawel	k'thibh	kincob	kittul	labour
inulin	jaghir	Jordan	kraken	kaikai	kinase	koulan	labrum
iguana	jigjig	jarvey	khanga	khilat	kunkur	knubby	Labrus
invade	jarred	jereed	kiaugh	knitch	konfyt	Keuper	labrys
invoke	joggle	jerker	knaggy	kaiser	koolah	knurly	lochan
invent	juggle	jersey	kwacha	knives	knobby	khurta	laches
invert	jig-jog	jerbil	khalif	krises	knower	kavass	lacker
invest	jugate	jerkin	kharif	keight	kronen	kowhai	lackey
invis'd	jugful	jirble	knacky	knight	kroner	kowtow	lecher
invite	jug-jug	jurant	klaxon	knicks	kaolin	key-way	lichee
inwrap	Jahveh	jargon	kia-ora	kakapo	kookie	key-pin	lichen
inwick	johnny	jarool	krantz	keksye	khodja	laager	licker
inwall	jailer	jerboa	khanum	kikuyu	kgotla	leaded	locker
inwind	joiner		keblah	kalian	koodoo	leaden	locket

locoed	lagged	lumbar	lungie	liquid	lather	levity	micher
lucken	laggen	lum-hat	lunyie	liquor	latten	law-day	mickey
lychee	lagger	lambda	lankly	lariat	latter	lawman	mocker
lactic	legged	lammer	lingle	larnax	lethee	low-tar	muchel
lochia	legger	limbec	lonely	larvae	letted	lawyer	mucker
luckie	leglen	limbed	longly	larval	letter	low-key	mucoid
locale	leglet	limber	lunula	lurdan	lither	Lowrie	mackle
locule	liggen	limmer	lunule	lorica	litten	lowsit	macula
loculi	ligger	limner	lining	larder	litter	lewdly	macule
lucuma	logged	limpet	lentor	largen	lotted	lawing	mickle
lucumo	logger	lumber	lenvoy	larker	lutten	lowing	muchly
lacing	lugged	lumpen	lingot	lurden	let-off	lowboy	muckle
lacuna	lugger	lumper	long-on	lurker	litchi	lowery	macron
lucent	laggin	lambie	lunary	lorcha	latria	lowest	micron
Lucina	leglin	lammie	lanose	laroid	Lettic	lawful	mucosa
lector	lignin	limpid	lanate	lordly	lithia	luxury	micate
lictor	loggia	lamely	length	larine	lithic	laxism	mucate
lucern	loggie	lament	lenity	larynx	lutein	laxist	mock-up
locust	luggie	lamina	lunate	loring	lately	laxity	mucluc
Lycosa	ligula	lemans	langue	lardon	little	luxate	mucous
locate	ligule	lemony	langur	loriot	latent	lay-day	macoya
lacmus	legume	liming	line-up	lyrism	litany	layman	madcap
lock-up	lagena	loment	lingua	lyrist	luting	lay-off	madman
lyceum	lag-end	lumina	link-up	lorate	latron	laying	madras
lac-dye	lagune	lumine	loofah	lyrate	lotion	lay-out	medial
Lydian	legend	lummox	lionel	larrup	lettre	lay-bye	median
la-di-da	ligand	lamish	lionet	lascar	latest	lay-bys	medlar
ladder	luging	Limbus	looker	Lusiad	latish	lazily	midday
ladies	lagoon	limous	looped	lasher	lutist	lozell	midway
ledden	legion	landau	looper	lasket	let-out	Luzula	mud-cat
ledger	logion	lineal	loosen	laster	litmus	lizard	medick
lidded	loglog	linear	looten	lessee	lituus	luzern	medico
lidger	ligure	lingam	looter	lessen	launce	meatal	madden
lodger	legist	linhay	looves	lesser	launch	mealer	madder
ladify	legate	longan	Leonid	lisper	lauder	meawes	medley
ladyfy	legato	lunacy	look-in	lisses	laurel	meazel	midden
laddie	ligate	lancer	loonie	listed	louden	moaner	midget
lading	lights	lances	lionly	listel	loupen	moated	mid-leg
Ladino	lignum	lancet	lipide	listen	louses	meathe	mid-sea
leeway	leg-bye	landed	lapped	lister	louver	mealie	madefy
lienal	laical	lander	lappel	lusher	lounge	meanie	mid-off
lieder	leiger	lanner	lapper	luster	laughy	mia-mia	modify
liefer	loiter	lender	lappet	lassie	louche	meanly	mid-age
lieger	luiten	lenger	lapsed	lastly	leucin	measle	mid-air
liever	laidly	lenses	lepped	lushly	loupit	measly	midrib
laesie	leipoa	lenten	lipped	losing	loudly	miasma	mud-pie
Leerie	laisse	linden	lippen	lysine	louvre	miasms	mid-sky
Liebig	likely	lingel	lopped	lassos	Laurus	meadow	meddle
luetic	liking	linger	lopper	lesion	lavabo	meagre	middle
leetle	lakish	linnet	luppen	lesson	laveer	meatus	module
lierne	lallan	linsey	lappie	lessor	lavage	mob-cap	moduli
lifter	lilied	lintel	lipoid	levied	lovage	mob-law	modulo
lofter	loller	linter	lippie	Lisbon	live-in	mobbed	muddle
leftie	Loligo	longer	lipoma	lissom	lavolt	mobled	madame
lifull	laldie	lunged	lupine	lustra	lively	mobbie	medina
lyfull	lalang	lynxes	lapdog	lustre	lovely	mobble	modena
leglan	lollop	lenify	lepton	lash-up	levant	mobile	modern
leg-man	Lilium	lanugo	lipase	Latian	living	machan	Medise
loggat	Lolium	linage	Lapith	lethal	loving	Micmac	Medism
log-jam	Lammas	lynage	Laputa	luteal	livery	macaco	medusa
log-man	lampad	lentic	lapful	let-a-be	lavish	mocock	modest
log-saw	lampas	lentil	lapsus	lateen	levite	mocuck	modish
legacy		lintie	loquat	lathee		macled	modist
				lathen			

medium	moiety	mimbar	manche	Maoist	merell	musher	metred
medius	Majlis	mammee	Manchu	moorva	merely	musked	mither
mid-gut	Mejlis	mammer	munshi	mapped	morale	muskeg	mitten
modius	make-do	mammet	mandir	mapper	morall	musket	mothed
maenad	mikado	member	mantic	mopped	morula	mussel	mother
meeken	making	mommet	mantid	mopper	myrtle	mustee	motley
meered	mikron	mummed	mantis	moppet	merome	muster	motser
mnemic	make-up	mummer	menhir	mopoke	marina	mashie	mutter
myelin	mukluk	mumper	minnie	mopish	marine	masjid	metage
meekly	malmag	memoir	mundic	maquis	merino	maslin	matric
meetly	mellay	mummia	muntin	margay	murena	massif	matrix
muesli	mollah	mumble	manuka	Marian	murine	mastic	metric
mnemon	mullah	moment	mangle	marram	marmot	mesail	mythic
myelon	malice	mammon	manila	mercat	maroon	misaim	mettle
Maffia	Molech	Memnon	mantle	merman	marrow	misdid	motile
muffin	moloch	memory	mingle	morgay	merlon	misfit	mottle
muffle	malady	mimosa	minima	mornay	mirror	mishit	mutely
muflon	melody	man-day	mañana	morsal	morion	missis	mutule
Magian	miladi	mangal	manent	mortal	Mormon	mosaic	matins
magmas	milady	maniac	meninx	mortar	morrow	mossie	mutant
magyar	mallee	manoao	mining	murlan	Merops	muscid	mutine
moggan	mallet	manual	mandom	murram	marish	Muslim	mutiny
magnes	malted	menial	manioc	murray	Marist	muslin	matlow
magnet	melder	mensal	mentor	myriad	merism	mystic	matron
maguey	melted	mental	minion	maraca	morass	mascle	matzoh
mugger	milden	minbar	minnow	Myrica	morish	masula	meteor
megohm	mildew	Minoan	mongol	marcel	Morisk	mistle	method
magpie	milieu	Minyan	mantra	marked	morose	mostly	motion
megrim	milken	Monday	manure	marker	miriti	muscle	motmot
magilp	milker	monial	monera	market	maraud	muskle	motto'd
megilp	milled	menace	montre	marled	mark-up	myself	mutton
mygale	miller	monact	minish	marred	marque	mishmi	mythos
maggot	millet	Munich	'mongst	martel	marrum	Mishna	metope
magnox	milsey	monody	monism	marten	morbus	musang	mature
mignon	milter	mangel	monist	marvel	morgue	musing	Mithra
Magism	mulled	manger	monosy	mercer	murmur	mascon	motory
megass	muller	mangey	manati	merger	Myrtus	mascot	mutism
mighty	mullet	manned	manito	moreen	martyr	musmon	motett
magnum	mulley	manner	minute	morgen	mescal	musrol	mutate
mugful	Malaga	manred	moneth	morned	mesial	Masora	mutuum
mug-ewe	malign	mantel	munite	morsel	mesian	Messrs	mythus
mahmal	milage	mender	mancus	murder	messan	misère	motive
mihrab	maltha	meneer	manful	murken	mishap	misery	methyl
Mohock	maleic	menged	manqué	murren	mislay	misuse	moutan
mahsir	malkin	menses	mantua	murrey	missal	misust	maundy
mohair	mollie	minced	Mensur	mirage	missay	masque	mouldy
mahzor	mildly	mincer	mentum	murage	moshav	mess-up	maumet
Mahoun	melano	minded	minium	marshy	muscae	miscue	Mauser
mahout	moline	Mindel	monaul	morpho	muscat	missus	mouser
mohawk	mallow	minder	moolah	murphy	masher	mosque	mousey
maidan	mellow	minged	mooned	murrha	masked	museum	mouter
Moirai	melton	minter	mooner	margin	masker	musive	mought
maiden	malgre	minuet	mooter	marlin	masted	matzah	mouthy
mailed	milord	monger	myogen	martin	master	met-man	mauvin
mailer	malist	monied	miosis	merkin	mestee	mitral	moujik
maimed	molest	monies	Moonie	merlin	misken	mutual	moulin
meiney	mulish	monkey	muonic	morbid	misled	matico	mousie
moider	malate	montem	myopia	morkin	missee	motuca	mousle
moiler	Milvus	minify	myopic	morris	missel	mutuca	mousmé
meinie	mulmul	munify	myosin	murlin	misses	matted	maunna
mainly	multum	manage	myosis	murrin	misset	matter	maugre
mainor	mammae	manège	myotic	marble	mister	métier	mousse
maigre	mammal	ménage	Maoism	marbly	Moslem		mounty

miurus	nebbuk	nailed	narras	notion	ovator	oneyre	objure
muu-muu	nobbut	nailer	nerval	natura	Onagra	obeism	oikist
movies	nectar	naiant	norlan'	nature	omasum	oleate	oak-nut
moving	nickar	nekton	normal	nitery	opaque	omenta	oilcan
mawmet	nuchal	nallah	norman	notary	ox-bird	owelty	oil-gas
mewses	nacket	nilgai	Norway	notate	orbita	obelus	oil-man
mawkin	necked	nilgau	nurhag	nutate	orbity	Olenus	owl-car
mowing	niched	nullah	narked	netful	orchat	one-two	o'clock
mawpus	nicher	nelies	nerved	notour	orchel.	off-day	oillet
maxima	nickel	nilled	nerver	not-out	orcein	office	oblige
myxoma	nicker	nelson	nirled	native	orchid	olfact	oology
maxixe	nochel	Nilote	nurser	nitryl	orchil	off-key	oil-rig
mayday	nocket	Nemean	nereid	neural	orchis	offset	oilily
mayhap	nuclei	numbat	nirlie	nougat	occult	onfall	ollamh
may-dew	nocake	numdah	nirlit	nounal	oscule	offend	oblong
mayhem	nicely	numnah	Nordic	nautch	occamy	offing	ogling
mayfly	nucule	nomade	neroli	noulde	oncome	Oxford	on-lend
maying	Nicene	nimbed	nursle	nausea	orcine	oafish	on-line
mayest	nocent	nimmed	narine	neuter	oscine	offish	oolong
moyity	nicety	nimmer	nerine	naught	occupy	offcut	oulong
may-bug	nickum	numbed	nardoo	nought	oecist	offput	oxland
mizzen	noctua	number	narrow	nautic	oncost	orgeat	oilery
mezail	nidget	nympho	Norroy	nousle	oocyte	orgies	owlery
mozzie	nodded	nim-oil	Nernst	neuron	odd-man	ouglie	oblast
muzhik	nodder	namely	Nerita	Novial	ogdoad	oughly	owlish
mazily	nidify	nimble	nerite	novice	ordeal	oogamy	oblate
mizzle	noddle	nimbly	norite	navaid	oodles	oogeny	oolite
mizzly	nodule	naming	Nerium	novena	ordain	orgone	oilnut
muzzle	nudely	numina	nosean	Nivôse	oedema	oxgang	oomiac
mazuma	niding	Nimrod	no-side	novity	ondine	orgasm	oomiak
mazard	nid-nod	nomism	Nissen	new-sad	onding	oxgate	oompah
mazout	nodose	nimbus	Naskhi	newell	odd-job	oxhead	ormolu
mezuza	nudism	nonage	Neskhi	new-old	odds-on	ochrea	osmund
near-by	nudist	non-ego	nastic	Nowell	obdure	ochrey	osmose
nuance	nudity	nankin	nestle	newton	ordure	ochone	osmate
neaped	nodous	nuncio	nosily	newish	oddish	ochery	osmium
nearer	need-be	nuncle	nosing	nowise	oldest	Ophism	osmous
neaten	needer	nonane	nasion	noways	oldish	ophite	Ormazd
neaffe	noesis	nandoo	Nesiot	nix-nie	oddity	obi-man	Ormuzd
neanic	noetic	nincom	Nestor	nextly	oidium	obital	omnify
niacin	needle	non-com	nostoc	nay-say	one-man	ogival	ornery
nearly	needly	non-con	nostos	noyade	one-way	ooidal	ornate
neatly	nielli	nonary	nasard	noyous	overby	origan	omnium
nyanza	niello	nanism	nasute	nuzzer	owerby	ovisac	oroide
nebeck	naevus	ninety	nosh-up	Nazify	oreide	obiter	oboist
nobody	niffer	nincum	notice	nozzle	overdo	oliver	obolus
nabbed	nefast	niobic	natter	nuzzle	obeyer	olivet	orphan
nabber	nuggar	nookie	nether	Nazism	O-level	orifex	osprey
nebbed	nagged	noodle	netted	omasal	omelet	oniric	oppugn
neb-neb	nagger	Nuphar	nutlet	onager	omened	origin	Orphic
nibbed	nigger	napped	nutmeg	opaled	oneyer	Osiris	orpine
nebris	nugget	napper	nutted	orange	opener	otitis	oppose
nebula	noggin	nephew	nutter	otalgy	ox-eyed	oriole	oar-lap
nebulé	niggle	nipped	notify	orache	one-off	oniony	ocreae
nebule	niggly	nipper	nitric	ogamic	overgo	orient	o'erlay
nebuly	nighly	nipter	nitwit	oxalic	obeche	orison	oorial
nibble	nagana	napkin	nut-oil	oxalis	olefin	ovibos	ourebi
no-ball	nig-nog	napalm	nutria	Ozalid®	orexis	osiery	oarage
nobble	nagari	nipple	nettle	oracle	ocelli	obiism	ourali
nubble	negate	napron	natant	orally	openly	otiose	orrery
nubbly	nights	Nippon	nutant	ovally	overly	opiate	ourari
nubile	nighty	napery	nation	ozaena	Oberon	odious	ogress
nebish	naiads	narial	natron	orator	ocelot	object	ogrish

onrush	obtuse	phalli	peddle	phenol	prized	polder	pampas
Ossian	out-ask	prawle	piddle	pie-dog	prizer	polled	pomace
onside	octett	Phasma	puddle	plexor	priefe	pollen	pumice
ouster	ostium	plasma	puddly	pye-dog	plight	poller	pomade
oyster	outgun	plaint	padang	preppy	painim	pollex	pamper
ossify	outjut	peacod	pedant	pheere	paidle	puller	pommel
obsign	output	pea-pod	Podunk	pleura	paigle	pullet	pompey
ossein	outrun	peason	pudent	poetry	primly	pulley	pummel
oxslip	outsum	pharos	podsol	pheese	prismy	pulper	pumped
obsess	octave	pearst	podzol	pierst	pliant	pulsed	pumper
osteal	octavo	praise	Podura	please	puisne	pulver	pimple
Ostiak	ottava	planta	pedate	prease	puisny	pllaff	pimply
ostial	outbye	plaste	podite	plenty	phizog	pelage	pomelo
Ostyak	ocular	peanut	padauk	presto	poison	phlegm	pumelo
outbar	ovular	plague	padouk	pretty	prison	pulkha	piment
outeat	oeuvre	plaguy	podium	peepul	pliers	pallia	Pomona
outgas	opulus	plaque	pieman	plenum	priory	pallid	pompom
outlaw	obvert	piazza	Pleiad	plexus	plissé	peloid	pompon
outlay	ouvert	public	prefab	preeve	priest	pelvic	pomroy
outman	onward	pebble	prepay	phenyl	prissy	pelvis	pomato
obtect	oxygen	pebbly	pre-tax	prewyn	painty	pull-in	pandar
optics	oxymel	pachak	plebby	pheeze	plinth	pulpit	penial
outact	onycha	pochay	pierce	puffed	pointe	pulvil	penman
ostler	oozily	packer	pleach	puffer	paid-up	palely	pennae
Ostmen	plagal	packet	pleuch	puffin	primus	palolo	pennal
Ostrea	planar	pecker	preace	piffle	prieve	pilula	pen-pal
outher	platan	pecten	preach	poffle	pajock	pilule	pentad
outjet	pearce	picked	pseudo	pig-man	pakeha	palama	pineal
outler	plaice	picker	peeled	pig-rat	pyknic	paling	pin-man
outlet	planch	picket	peeler	pagoda	poking	Poland	pinnae
outred	prance	pocked	peeper	pegged	Pakhto	poling	pontal
outset	pranck	pocket	peeved	peg-leg	Pakhtu	polony	punkah
outage	pea-hen	pucker	peever	pig-bed	paleae	puling	panick
obtain	peaked	pacify	peewee	pigged	pallae	pylons	Punica
outbid	peavey	pectic	piecen	piglet	pallah	pallor	panada
outfit	phased	pectin	piecer	pigpen	Pallas	pillow	pander
outhit	phases	picnic	prefer	piggie	Palmae	pull on	pangen
outlie	placed	picric	premed	piggin	palmar	pulton	panter
outsit	placer	pycnic	preses	paging	palpal	polype	panzer
outvie	placet	pickle	preife	pigsny	pelham	polypi	pencel
outwin	planer	picene	peenge	peg-box	pillar	polyps	penned
outwit	planet	picine	pledge	peg-top	pillau	paltry	penner
oxtail	plated	pycnon	pleugh	pigeon	pole-ax	pelory	pensée
outfly	platen	Pecora	peerie	pogrom	pollan	peltry	pensel
optima	plater	picoté	peewit	pug-dog	pulsar	palish	pincer
optime	player	pactum	phenic	pygarg	pultan	pilose	pinder
obtend	prater	pick-up	pierid	pigsty	pulwar	polish	pinger
obtund	prayed	pad-nag	Pieris	pig-nut	palace	pilose...	pinked
octane	prayer	pad-saw	poetic	plicae	Polack	pelite	pin-leg
Octans	piaffe	Paduan	précis	primal	police	pelota	pinned
octant	peachy	pedlar	prefix	ptisan	policy	polite	pinner
optant	plashy	podial	prelim	paiock	palkee	polity	pinnet
ostent	poachy	padded	premia	peinct	palled	palpus	ponder
outing	phaeic	padder	pteria	prince	pallet	Phleum	pongee
octroi	phasic	pedder	pterin	pained	palmed	pileum	pontes
octuor	phasis	podded	Pteris	paired	palmer	pile-up	punier
option	phatic	podley	pyemia	poised	palter	pileus	punned
outbox	placid	pudden	paella	poiser	pellet	pilous	punner
outfox	placit	pudder	pueblo	priced	pelmet	Pollux	punnet
outtop	pratie	pudsey	pneuma	pricey	pelter	pull-up	puntee
octopi	praxis	pidgin	paeony	primer	pelves	pulque	punter
outcry	pranky	paddle	pieing	priser	phloem	pultun	pangfu'
obtest	pearly	pedalo	pyeing	privet	pilfer	poleyn	poncho

punchy	proper	popery	pirnit	passer	putted	pluffy	quasar
pandit	proser	papish	porgie	pastel	puttee	pouffe	quaich
pencil	protea	papism	purlin	paster	putten	plunge	quatch
pen-nib	proved	papist	purpie	pester	putter	plushy	Quaker
pensil	proven	popish	peruke	Pisces	put-off	pouchy	quaver
pinkie	prover	pupate	parkly	pissed	potage	plug-in	quagga
pinnie	pyoner	pappus	parole	posnet	patchy	poukit	quaggy
pinxit	proofs	pepful	partly	posset	pitchy	pourie	quaigh
Pinyin	plongd	peplum	pertly	poster	potche	pyuria	quango
pongid	plonge	peplus	portly	pushed	pathic	plucky	qualmy
pontic	plough	pop-gun	purely	pusher	patois	plummy	quaint
pontie	proign	papaya	purfle	pussel	pot-lid	pruina	quahog
pontil	phobia	pop-eye	purfly	pashim	putois	pruine	quaere
pundit	phobic	piquet	purple	passim	putrid	pluton	quarry
penile	phonic	Parcae	purply	pastil	puttie	plumpy	quanta
penult	photic	pardal	Pyrola	pastis	Pythia	poulpe	quarte
pingle	pookit	pariah	paramo	pistil	Pythic	poudre	quarto
pinole	profit	parial	Paraná	possie	Pitaka	pousse	quartz
pintle	prolix	Parian	parang	postie	pattle	Plutus	queach
punily	prosit	parlay	parent	postil	pettle	pavage	quelch
panama	psoric	parral	paring	pestle	pot-ale	pavane	quench
ponent	ptosis	partan	perone	poshly	pottle	paving	quetch
panton	people	perfay	pirancda	pesant	puteli	pavone	Q-fever
pennon	poodle	portal	Purana	posing	patent	pavior	quelea
pinion	poorly	portas	purine	pastor	patina	pavise	queued
ponton	Progne	purdah	pyrene	pistol	patine	pawpaw	quethe
panary	proine	piracy	pardon	piston	potent	powwaw	queint
pantry	proyne	parade	parrot	pastry	pathos	pawnce	queasy
penury	phonon	parody	parson	Pashto	patrol	pawnee	queest
pinery	photon	parcel	parton	Pashtu	patron	pawner	queazy
panisc	proton	parded	period	peseta	petrol	pewter	quidam
panisk	prompt	parget	Pernod®	Pushto	pithos	powder	quince
punish	plotty	parkee	perron	Pushtu	pot-boy	powney	quitch
pineta	pronto	parker	person	passus	potion	powter	quited
pinite	propyl	parley	paraph	poseur	putlog	pownie	quiver
puncta	protyl	parpen	pyrope	possum	python	powwow	quiche
puncto	Papuan	parrel	parure	pesewa	patera	paxwax	quight
panful	Popian	parsec	parish	peshwa	petara	pay-day	quinic
pantun	poplar	Parsee	perish	Pathan	petard	psywar	quinie
penful	papacy	parser	peruse	pitman	petary	pay-off	quirky
pen-gun	pepper	parted	phrase	pit-pat	pitara	psyche	quinoa
pensum	pipped	parter	phrasy	pit-saw	pituri	psycho	quinol
pent-up	popped	percen	porism	pot-hat	puture	paynim	quinsy
phocae	popper	perfet	porose	pot-man	potash	physic	quinta
pholas	poppet	porker	purism	puteal	potass	physio	quinte
phonal	pupped	porter	purist	putsch	petite	ptyxis	qui-hye
poojah	puppet	purger	parity	patted	potato	payola	quinze
poonac	pipage	purler	pirate	pattée	potful	paying	qintar
phoebe	papain	purser	purity	patten	pot-gun	plying	quoter
phoney	pepsin	pursew	pyrite	patter	put-put	prying	quotes
phooey	peptic	purvey	perdue	pether	pausal	pay-box	quotha
piolet	pipkin	purify	persue	petrel	plural	phyton	quokka
pioned	pippin	parage	porous	petted	paunce	poyson	quooke
pioner	poplin	pardie	pursue	petter	paunch	peyote	quoist
pioney	papula	parkin	piraya	pitied	pounce	pay-out	quorum
pioted	papule	partim	pascal	pitier	pauper	phylum	quotum
plover	popple	parvis	pasear	pitted	pauser	puzzel	riancy
pooped	popply	perdie	postal	pitten	plumed	pizzle	reader
Pooter	piping	pereia	Pesach	pitter	pouder	puzzle	reamer
proker	peplos	perkin	pesade	poteen	poufed	pezant	reaper
proleg	popjoy	permit	posada	pother	pourer	pazazz	rearer
proler	papery	Persic	passed	potted	pouter	Peziza	reaver
propel	papyri	pirnie	passée	potter	pruner	pizazz	roamer

roarer
rhaphe
realia
roadie
roarie
re-ally
really
rearly
reason
realty
reasty
Rialto
ribibe
reback
rebeck
rabbet
rabies
ribbed
robbed
robber
rubbed
rubber
rubbet
rubied
rebuff
rubefy
rubify
rabbin
rabbit
reboil
rubbit
rubric
rebuke
rabble
ribald
robalo
rubble
rubbly
rebind
riband
robing
rubine
ribbon
rebore
reborn
rebury
ribose
robust
rabato
rebate
rebato
rebite
rubato
ribaud
racial
reckan
rectal
ric-rac
rictal
rococo
recede
racked
racker

racket
recked
richen
riches
ricker
rochet
rocker
rocket
rachis
rechie
recoil
Riccia
racily
recall
recule
richly
rickle
rickly
ruckle
raceme
racing
recant
recent
racoon
reckon
rector
recept
recipe
record
racism
racist
recast
recess
recuse
recite
race-up
recoup
rectum
rectus
rictus
ruckus
radial
radian
red-cap
red-hat
rediae
red-mad
red-man
redraw
rodman
redact
reduce
redden
redder
redeem
redleg
redrew
ridded
ridden
ridged
ridgel
rudder

reduit
ridgil
raddle
radula
reddle
riddle
ruddle
rudely
radome
re-done
rident
riding
rodent
roding
red-box
red-dog
red-hot
redtop
rudery
radish
rudish
radium
radius
red-bud
red-gum
redwud
redowa
redeye
reeded
reeden
reeder
roofer
reeler
reeved
riever
roemer
re-echo
reechy
Raetia
re-edit
reekie
rhexis
ruelle
rheumy
rueing
reebok
rhetor
reesty
rhesus
rueful
regive
reface
refect
rafter
reflet
reflex
refuel
rifler
ruffed
refuge
raffia
ruffin
rafale
raffle

refill
rifely
riffle
ruffle
refine
refund
reflow
refoot
reform
refuse
refute
reflux
rufous
rag-bag
raglan
ragman
rag-tag
reggae
regnal
ragged
raggee
reglet
regret
rigged
rigger
rugged
rugger
regain
riglin
raggle
raguly
regale
regula
rigoll
régime
raging
regent
regina
region
regard
regest
rugose
righto
rugate
ragout
regius
rigour
rig-out
rugous
regive
rehear
reheat
reheel
rehash
raiyat
rhinal
raider
railer
raiser
raited
reiter
reiver
ruined

ruiner
raisin
rhizic
railly
reject
rejoin
Rajput
raking
rakery
rakish
reload
relict
reluct
relide
relied
relief
relier
rillet
rolled
roller
relaid
relume
relent
reline
Roland
ruling
roll-on
relish
relate
Rallus
roll-up
relive
rallye
ramcat
rameal
ramean
remead
remade
remede
remedy
remuda
ram-jet
rammed
rammer
ramper
rimmed
romper
rummer
Rumper
ramify
romage
remain
remeid
Romaic
rumkin
remake
ramble
ramuli
remble
rumble
rumple
remand
remind

Romany
rumina
ramrod
ramson
remark
remora
Ramism
Ramist
ramose
remise
remiss
rimose
Romish
ramate
remote
ramous
remoud
rimous
rum-bud
rumour
rumpus
remove
randan
rental
runway
rancel
random
ranger
ranked
ranker
ransel
ranter
ranzel
render
renied
rennet
rentor
rinded
ringed
ringer
rinser
rondel
runlet
runnel
runner
runnet
runted
run-off
renege
rancho
rancid
randie
rennin
runrig
rankle
rankly
ranula
rundle
runkle
rename
ranine
rancor
random

randon
ransom
renvoi
renvoy
rondos
ronyon
renown
rhombi
reopen
Rhodes
rioter
roofed
roofer
roomed
roomer
rooted
rooter
rhodic
rhotic
rookie
roopit
rootle
riotry
repeal
repeat
replan
replay
riprap
rip-saw
rupiah
ropack
ripeck
rypeck
rapier
rapped
rappee
rappel
rapper
repped
ripped
ripper
rip-off
repugn
Raphia
raphis
repaid
repair
repulp
ripely
ripple
ripply
ropily
rapine
raping
repand
repent
repine
repone
roping
raptor
Rippon
report
repure

ropery
rapist
repass
repast
repose
repost
repute
replum
roquet
requit
reread
rorter
rarefy
rerail
rarely
raring
rarity
rascal
reseat
réseau
roseal
resect
rosace
Reseda
reside
rasher
rasper
raster
reskew
restem
rester
risker
rosier
rosser
roster
rushen
rusher
russel
russet
rusted
resign
resaid
reship
roscid
russia
rustic
Russki
Russky
rashly
resale
resell
resile
resold
resole
result
rosily
rosula
rustle
résumé
resume
resent
rising
rosiny

rusine	retrod	**raylet**	sealed	swathe	starry	**sacral**	Shebat
rasure	**re-type**	rhymed	sealer	swathy	stayre	siccan	she-oak
resorb	**retard**	rhymer	seamer	**sea-air**	**sparse**	siccar	stelae
resort	retire	**rhythm**	sea-mew	sea-fir	**scaith**	social	stelar
rosary	retort	**rhyton**	sea-pen	sea-pie	scanty	socman	**snebbe**
rosery	returf	**rizzar**	seared	sea-pig	scarth	**secede**	**sheuch**
rostra	return	**rizzer**	seated	sharia	scatty	**sachem**	sketch
rustre	rotary	rozzer	shaded	shavie	Shakta	sachet	sleech
resist	**retuse**	**razzia**	shaked	sialic	Shakti	sacred	smeech
re-site	**ratite**	**razzle**	shaken	Slavic	shanty	seckel	speccy
rosety	rotate	**rizzor**	shaker	spadix	skaith	secret	speech
rescue	**retour**	**razure**	shamed	sparid	skarth	sicken	spence
reskue	rotgut	rizard	shamer	stadia	smalto	sicker	spetch
risqué	**Rouman**	**scalae**	shaped	stasis	smarty	soccer	stench
risque	**rhumba**	scalar	shapen	static	snaste	socker	**speedo**
ruscus	**raunch**	scarab	shaper	stay-in	Sparta	socket	speedy
ratbag	rounce	sea-bat	sharer	Sparta	sparth	succès	steady
rattan	rouncy	sea-cap	shaved	**sparke**	stacte	sucked	stedde
rat-tat	**rouser**	sea-cat	shaven	stalko	staith	sucken	steddy
retial	router	sea-ear	shaver	stalky	swarth	sucker	steedy
retral	**raunge**	sea-fan	skater	swanky	swarty	sucket	**saeter**
ritual	reurge	sea-law	slated	**shalli**	**scapus**	**socage**	seeded
rottan	**raught**	seaman	slater	'snails	Scarus	**sickie**	seeder
rather	rought	sea-mat	slaver	snaily	sea-bun	**sickle**	seeker
ratted	roughy	sea-maw	slavey	snarly	shaduf	suck-in	seemer
ratten	**raucid**	Seanad	slayer	spalle	shamus	sickly	shekel
ratter	roupit	sea-pay	snarer	spauld	slap-up	suckle	shewel
retree	**raucle**	searat	soaked	stable	statua	**secant**	sieger
retted	rouble	seaway	soaken	stably	statue	second	skewed
ritter	**roucou**	shaman	soaker	staple	status	secund	skewer
rother	**reveal**	spayad	spaced	suable	**Shaiva**	**saccos**	sleded
rotted	**review**	stalag	spacer	status	starve	sector	slewed
rotten	revved	statal	spacey	**shammy**	swarve	succor	soever
rotter	**ravage**	swaraj	spahee	smalmy	**sea-owl**	**secern**	spewer
rutted	rivage	**scabby**	sparer	smarmy	**snazzy**	secure	stereo
rutter	**revoke**	shabby	staged	**sdaine**	stanza	**secesh**	steven
ratify	**revile**	slabby	stager	shanny	stanze	**sacque**	stewed
rotche	revolt	scatch	stagey	sharny	stanzo	sacrum	stewer
ratlin	**revamp**	sea-ice	stamen	stayne	**sabbat**	succus	sweven
rat-pit	raving	sealch	stapes	swanny	Sabean	**seduce**	**sheafy**
retail	roving	séance	starer	**scazon**	Sabian	**sadden**	shelfy
retain	**reverb**	searce	stated	sea-boy	subman	sadder	**sheugh**
retrim	revere	search	stater	sea-cob	subway	sedged	skeigh
retake	revers	smatch	staved	sea-cow	**subact**	sodden	sledge
rattle	revert	snatch	staves	sea-dog	**sobbed**	sodger	sleigh
retell	revery	stance	stawed	sea-fog	subbed	sudden	Swerga
retold	rivery	stanch	stayed	sea-fox	subdew	sudder	**seethe**
rotolo	**ravish**	stanck	stayer	sea-god	subfeu	**saddhu**	**scenic**
rotula	revest	starch	swayed	sea-hog	sublet	**sodaic**	sheria
rutile	revise	swatch	swayer	season	sub-sea	sodain	sherif
retama	**rave-up**	**shandy**	**sea-egg**	shadow	subset	**saddle**	specie
rythme	rêveur	stadda	sealgh	shalot	**sobeit**	sedile	step-in
ratine	**revive**	swaddy	shaggy	shamoy	submit	**sodomy**	steric
rating	**rewrap**	swardy	slaggy	slalom	subtil	**sedent**	**sheikh**
retene	**rawing**	**scaled**	slangy	stator	**sobole**	siding	sleeky
retina	rewind	scaler	snaggy	**scampi**	subtle	**side-on**	sneaky
retund	**row-dow**	scamel	sparge	sea-ape	subtly	**sudary**	specks
rotund	**reward**	scarer	Svarga	swampy	Sabine	**sadism**	specky
ration	rewire	scarey	Swarga	**scarre**	**suborn**	sadist	**seemly**
ratoon	reword	seabed	scathe	scarry	suburb	**sedate**	sheila
ratton	rework	Seabee	snathe	scaury	**sebate**	sudate	shelly
retook	**rawish**	sea-eel	spathe	shairn	subito	**sodium**	skeely
retool			swashy	sparre	**subdue**	seesaw	skelly
				sparry			

6 s□o□c

smelly	sheave	schizo	slight	stilty	solemn	semmit	sunbed
snelly	shelve	shikar	smight	stinty	salina	simkin	sunder
steale	shelvy	smilax	smithy	saique	saline	summit	sun-dew
stealt	sleave	spinal	spight	ski-run	Selene	sumpit	sunken
steeld	sleeve	spinar	stithy	slip-up	silane	samely	sunket
steely	steeve	spiral	swishy	skivvy	silene	sample	sunned
smegma	sterve	spital	seisin	spivvy	silent	semble	sunset
steamy	swerve	Suidae	seizin	stieve	sklent	semple	syndet
stemma	sleazy	smirch	skivie	sejant	soland	simile	sanify
stemme	sleezy	snitch	spiric	sakieh	solano	simple	senega
scerne	sneeze	stitch	spirit	sakkos	so-long	simply	sancho
seeing	sneezy	switch	stimie	Sukkot	splent	sememe	sandhi
sheeny	sifter	shindy	slinky	salaam	spline	simony	santir
sienna	soften	smiddy	smirky	Salian	splint	samfoo	sennit
steane	suffer	sailed	sticky	sallad	sallow	Samiot	sonsie
sweeny	soffit	sailer	scilla	sallal	salmon	Samson	sunkie
sterol	softie	seiner	shield	silvae	saloon	'simmon	sunlit
sheepy	suffix	seised	skilly	silvan	saloop	simoom	syndic
sherpa	safely	seizer	slimly	soldan	salvor	simoon	sanely
sleepy	siffle	shined	stifle	sol-fa'd	'sblood	summon	senile
steepy	softly	shiner	stilly	sollar	seldom	symbol	single
steppe	safari	shiver	swirly	sulcal	salary	samara	singly
sweepy	Sofism	skiver	shimmy	sultan	sclera	sempre	sonant
shears	Sufism	slicer	stigma	sylvan	sclere	simorg	santon
sheart	safety	slided	stigme	select	splore	simurg	Senhor
sheers	sag-bag	slider	swimmy	silica	sultry	sombre	senior
sherry	saggar	slived	scient	solace	silica	samite	sensor
sierra	seggar	sliven	shinne	splice	splash	Semite	sindon
skeary	signal	sliver	shinny	salade	splosh	somite	sunbow
skeery	sagged	smiler	skiing	solidi	salute	sambur	sun-dog
skerry	sagger	smilet	skinny	sallee	sclate	Somnus	sungod
smeary	sigher	smiter	soigné	sallet	sklate	sandal	senary
sneery	signer	sniper	spinny	salted	solito	sangar	Sencdora
speary	signet	snivel	sailor	salter	solute	sanjak	sentry
sperre	sogged	soiled	sciroc	salued	saltus	sanpan	soneri
steard	sagoin	soirée	shivoo	salve'd	Seljuk	santal	sundra
steare	saguin	spiced	ski-bob	salver	soleus	sendal	sundri
steery	sagely	spicer	slip-on	seller	sulcus	sontag	sundry
sweard	sagene	spider	spigot	selves	sulfur	sundae	sanity
sweert	seghol	spiked	suitor	silken	saliva	Sunday	senate
sweirt	signor	spined	shippo	siller	sclave	sungar	sonata
she-ass	sugary	spinel	skimpy	siloed	solive	sunhat	sannup
sneesh	sphear	spinet	slippy	silver	salewd	sunray	santur
speiss	sahiba	spirea	snippy	solder	sambar	suntan	send-up
sperse	schlep	spired	stirps	soller	Samian	syntan	sensum
sperst	sphaer	stilet	sbirri	solver	sampan	syntax	sinful
sceatt	schtik	stipel	sbirro	spleen	simial	Seneca	sinewy
'sdeath	schuit	stipes	shirra	sullen	simian	sonics	Scogan
sheath	schelm	stived	smirry	salify	simpai	sanded	scopae
sheety	schema	stiver	stirra	sclaff	summar	sander	shofar
Shelta	scheme	suited	stirre	silage	summat	sanies	shoran
shelty	sphene	suivez	saidst	sulpha	sumach	sended	Siouan
siesta	sphinx	swiper	shiest	salmis	samiel	sender	slogan
sleety	schmoe	swipes	Shiism	salvia	samlet	sennet	Slovak
sleuth	school	swipey	shiksa	selkie	Samoed	sensed	storax
smeath	schorl	swivel	slimsy	silkie	semper	singed	slobby
smeeth	sphere	sniffy	shifty	solein	semsem	singer	snobby
sneath	sphery	spiffy	Shiite	sylvia	simmer	sinker	sconce
suetty	schism	stingo	Shinto	saluki	simnel	sinned	scorch
svelte	schist	stingy	shinty	saltly	simper	sinner	scotch
sweaty	schuss	swinge	shirty	solely	summed	sinnet	slouch
sweety	schout	saithe	snifty	salame	summer	sinter	smooch
step-up	schuyt	seiche	spilth	salami	semeia	sonnet	smouch

shoddy	stownd	Sapium	street	sprang	strewn	smutch	square
scolex	swound	sepium	surbed	sprent	strown	source	squire
scorer	swoune	septum	surbet	spring	scraye	stucco	squirm
scoter	swowne	supawn	surfer	sprint	syrlye	spuddy	squirr
shoder	swownd	sequel	surrey	sprong	scruze	sturdy	squirt
shorer	spot-on	sequin	survew	sprung	sashay	saucer	sourse
shovel	stolon	screak	survey	strand	sestet	sauger	squash
shover	shoppy	scream	syrtes	strene	sister	saurel	squish
showed	sloppy	serdab	scruff	Strine	system	souled	smutty
shower	stoope	serial	shrift	string	siskin	souper	scutum
sloken	stoury	serrae	shroff	strond	suslik	soused	sputum
sloven	stowre	serran	strafe	strong	seseli	souses	scurvy
smoked	scorse	serras	straff	strung	sesame	souter	squawk
smoker	scouse	serval	strife	strunt	sasine	squier	spulye
snorer	smouse	sircar	strift	syrinx	seston	stumer	sovran
spoken	spouse	sirdar	sorage	sartor	sissoo	scuffy	savvey
stogey	swoosh	Sirian	striga	scroop	sistra	scurfy	Sèvres
stoker	Scotty	sirkar	sorgho	sermon	Sathan	snuffy	soviet
stokes	scouth	sirrah	sarnie	seroon	satrap	squiff	savage
stoled	scowth	spread	serail	sordor	sittar	stuffy	savant
stolen	shorty	streak	serein	sorrow	shtick	saulge	savine
stoned	smooth	stream	shreik	strook	sateen	sludge	saving
stonen	snooty	striae	sordid	scrape	settee	sludgy	sevens
stoner	snorty	stroam	sortie	script	setter	smudge	savory
storer	snotty	surtax	spraid	serape	sithen	smudgy	severe
storey	snouty	Syriac	sprain	seraph	sithes	snudge	severy
stover	sports	Syrian	spruit	seriph	sitrep	spunge	savate
stower	sporty	scribe	straik	stripe	sitter	spurge	savour
spoffy	spotty	scrobe	strain	stripy	sotted	stuggy	sawder
shough	spouty	strobe	strait	syrupy	sutler	slushy	sawney
slough	stouth	sprack	syrtis	serosa	suttee	sought	saw-set
smoggy	shogun	spruce	scrike	sprush	set-off	saulie	sawyer
sponge	snooze	strack	shrike	strass	shtchi	Sauria	sowter
spongy	sappan	strich	shrake	stress	Sothic	shut-in	sewage
stodge	septal	strict	strike	Syrism	settle	squail	sawpit
stodgy	sapped	struck	stroke	scruto	situla	studio	saw-fly
stooge	sapper	scryde	scroll	sprite	sutile	stupid	sawing
stop-go	sephen	spredd	shrill	strata	suttle	shucks	sewing
storge	septet	stride	sorell	strath	satiny	spunky	sowans
sloshy	sipped	strode	sorely	Sûreté	set-tos	sculle	sowens
soothe	sipper	sardel	spryly	surety	sitcom	smugly	sowing
sposhy	sippet	sarney	stroll	sargus	satara	snugly	siwash
scoria	sopped	sarsen	surely	serous	satire	souple	sowsse
Scotia	supped	screed	scrimp	shroud	satori	sourly	sow-bug
Scotic	supper	screen	scrump	Sirius	Saturn	squall	sextan
skolia	sapego	scried	shrimp	sprout	satyra	squill	sexual
stogie	Sappho	scryer	skrimp	stroud	suture	scummy	six-day
stolid	sepsis	series	skrump	stroup	setose	slummy	sextet
Suomic	septic	server	stramp	strout	shtetl	squama	sexfid
snooks	sophia	shreek	stroma	scrive	set-out	squame	saxony
spooky	sophic	shriek	stromb	shrive	sative	spurne	sexpot
stocky	sapele	sirree	struma	shrove	scutal	squint	sexton
shoaly	sipple	skreen	sarong	strive	Soudan	squiny	sexism
should	supple	skryer	scrine	strove	soutar	stupor	sexist
slowly	supply	sorbet	scrunt	scrawl	squeak	sculpt	saxaul
smoile	supine	sordes	scryne	scrawm	squeal	slumpy	six-gun
smoyle	sap-rot	sorner	serang	screwy	slubby	stumpy	skyman
spollt	siphon	sorrel	serene	scrowl	snubbe	scurry	skyway
sloomy	syphon	sorter	shrank	shrewd	snubby	skurry	stylar
stormy	superb	sortes	shrine	shrowd	stubby	slurry	styrax
spoony	sapota	spryer	shrink	sprawl	scutch	smurry	stylet
stonne	sopite	streek	shrunk	strawn	sluice	souari	scyphi
stound	sapful	streel	sirene	strawy	sluicy	spurry	scythe

sayyid	tebbad	trendy	tiglon	twisty	tymbal	tinier	though
stymie	tib-cat	teehee	tigery	tail-up	tympan	tinker	troggs
Scylla	tibiae	teepee	tights	thin'un	tamber	tinned	trough
saying	tibial	tee-tee	togate	trisul	tamper	tinner	toothy
spying	tabbed	teeter	tchick	thieve	temper	tinsel	troche
sayest	tabled	Thebes	tahsil	tailye	timber	tinsey	trophi
shyest	tablet	theses	tahina	takahe	tumefy	tinter	trophy
shyish	tabret	thewed	tahini	take-in	tumphy	Tunker	toorie
skyish	tubber	thewes	T-shirt	taking	tombic	tunnel	tropic
slyest	tabefy	teethe	taipan	token'd	tomtit	tangie	two-bit
slyish	tubage	taenia	tribal	take-up	tamale	tankia	troika
stylus	tabula	Themis	tricar	tallat	tarnely	tannic	tootle
sazhen	tubule	thesis	trinal	tele-ad	temple	tannin	troely
syzygy	tubing	thetic	trilby	tellar·	timely	tan-pit	trolly
sizzle	tabard	tie-pin	taisch	tulban	tumble	tenail	troule
sozzle	Tibert	tie-wig	triact	tulwar	tumuli	tennis	two-ply
sozzly	Tyburn	tmesis	twitch	teledu	tumult	tentie	thorny
sizing	Tebeth	trémie	triode	Toledo	tamanu	tenuis	tholoi
tea-bag	tubate	trepid	tailed	talker	tamine	tinnie	tholos
thanah	tabour	trevis	taiver	tallet	taming	tonsil	thoron
tiara'd	tubful	Thecla	thibet	talweg	timing	tangle	too-too
trapan	tic-tac	they'll	thivel	teller	tampon	tangly	trogon
tsamba	tacked	treble	toiled	tiller	tomboc	tingle	thorpe
thatch	tacker	trebly	toiler	tilted	tomboy	tingly	trompe
trance	tacket	teeing	toilet	tilter	tompon	tinkle	troppo
teamed	teckel	theine	trimer	toller	tom-tom	tinkly	troupe
teamer	ticked	tweeny	trivet	tolsel	tamara	to-name	tooart
tearer	ticken	tie-rod	twicer	tolsey	tamari	toneme	Taoism
teasel	ticker	trek-ox	twined	tolter	timbre	tenant	Taoist
teaser	ticket	tremor	twiner	tolzey	tamise	tonant	tootsy
tea-set	tickey	theirs	thingy	telega	timist	tuning	trouse
teated	tocher	theory	triage	Telugu	tomato	Tannoy®	tsotsi
teazel	tucker	they're	twiggy	talkie	Tammuz	tendon	trouty
thaler	tucket	teensy	twinge	til-oil	timous	tenson	tholus
thawer	tactic	theism	twight	toluic	tomium	tensor	trotyl
tracer	tocsin	theist	trifid	talcky	tumour	tenzon	tip-cat
traded	tuck-in	tressy	trivia	talant	tum-tum	tinpot	top-hat
trader	tackle	tsetse	twilit	talent	tannah	tonsor	topman
trapes	tickle	teenty	thicky	tiling	tan-vat	Tantra	Tupian
travel	tickly	theave	tricky	toling	teniae	tendre	tapped
Tuareg	tycoon	they've	taigle	talbot	tincal	tenure	tapper
twangy	tuchun	twelve	thible	talion	tin-can	tundra	tappet
trashy	tedded	toffee	thinly	tallot	tindal	tanist	tipped
Thalia	tedder	tuffet	trifle	tallow	tinman	tonish	tipper
tragic	tidied	tufted	trigly	telson	tonnag	tenuto	tippet
travis	tidbit	tufter	trillo	tol-lol	tenace	tonite	Tophet
teagle	tiddle	tiffin	trimly	toluol	tan-bed	tangun	topped
teazle	tiddly	to-fall	triple	Tulipa	tandem	tenour	topper
thalli	tidily	tofore	triply	telary	tanged	tinful	tepefy
trauma	toddle	Tagday	tuille	tilery	tanked	tongue	tip-off
thanna	tedium	tagrag	twilly	telesm	tanker	tundun	typify
tranny	Theban	taguan	twirly	T-cloth	tanned	Tungus	tappit
trayne	thecae	tagged	triune	T-plate	tanner	Thorah	Tupaia
tea-pot	thecal	tagger	tailor	tylote	tanrec	thorax	tipple
teapoy	thenar	tegmen	toison	talcum	tended	trocar	tipula
trappy	tietac	togaed	tricot	Talmud	tender	Trojan	topple
tea-urn	toecap	tugged	trigon	Tellus	tenner	Troyan	tupelo
thairm	toe-rag	tugger	tripod	tam-tam	tenrec	two-way	typing
transe	trepan	tegula	tripos	timbal	tented	troade	tiptoe
twaite	thence	toggle	triton	tombac	tenter	thowel	tiptop
teacup	thetch	tag-end	thirst	tombak	tenues	tooter	Typhon
Teague	tierce		thirty	tom-cat	tinded	trover	tapist
tragus	trench		triste	tomial	tinder	trowel	typist

tapeta	turbid	tasset	thumby	thyrsi	uncurl	urging	unkept
tapeti	turbit	tasted	tauten	toyish	upcurl	upgrow	unkiss
tophus	turgid	taster	toupee	thymus	uncase	ungird	unlead
typhus	Turkic	testee	toupet	try-out	upcast	ungirt	unleal
tarmac	turkis	tester	tourer	usance	uncate	ungord	unload
tarnal	turnip	testes	touser	unawed	uncowl	Utgard	uplead
tarpan	tartly	tosher	touter	usager	undeaf	upgush	uplean
tarras	termly	tossed	trudge	uracil	undear	unglue	upleap
tarsal	thrall	tossen	taught	Uralic	undraw	ungyve	unlace
tartan	thrill	tosser	touché	Urania	updrag	ungown	unlich
tartar	Torula	tusked	touchy	uranic	updraw	upgaze	unlock
Tarzan	turtle	tusker	truthy	uranin	undeck	unhead	uplock
tergal	tarand	tusseh	taupie	undeck	undock	unheal	unlade
ternal	thrang	tusser	tauric	unable	undies	upheap	uglify
terrae	threne	tusche	tautit	usable	undoer	unhair	uplift
Terran	throne	tassie	thulia	uraeus	undyed	unhele	ullage
terras	throng	testis	toutie	Uranus	unduly	unhelm	unlaid
thread	tiring	tussis	tousle	uranyl	undine	unholy	unlike
threap	torana	tystie	touzle	umbral	undone	upheld	uglily
threat	to-rend	tussle	truant	unbear	undern	uphild	unlime
throat	to-rent	tisane	tautog	unbias	undate	uphill	ulling
turban	tyrant	teston	Teuton	upbear	update	uphold	unline
Tyrian	tyring	Tishri	truism	upbeat	uneven	unhand	unlink
thrice	tar-box	tissue	trusty	upbray	uneyed	unhang	upland
turaco	tarpon	toss-up	Taurus	umbles	ureter	unhung	up-line
teredo	tarrow	tetrad	tavern	umbrel	unedge	uphand	uplook
tirade	termor	titian	tavert	unbred	uremia	uphang	unlord
tarcel	terror	to-tear	towbar	umbril	uremic	unhood	unlash
target	torpor	tutman	thwack	upboil	uresis	unhook	unless
tarred	turbot	tutsan	towhee	unbelt	uretic	unhoop	unlost
tarsel	turgor	tatler	townee	unbolt	unease	uphroe	umlaut
tercel	turion	tatter	tow-net	unbend	uneasy	unhurt	unlive
tercet	teraph	tether	towser	unbent	uberty	unhurl	unlove
termer	thrips	tetter	towage	unbind	uneath	unhasp	unmade
Termes	torero	titfer	tawpie	unbone	used-up	unhusk	unmeek
terret	T-cross	tithed	tawtie	upbind	useful	uphaud	unmeet
threep	thrash	tither	tewhit	urbane	uterus	unhive	unmake
tiroes	thresh	titled	townie	unboot	upblow	unhewn	upmake
torret	thrist	titler	townly	umbery	unfact	unital	unmoor
torsel	thrush	ti-tree	tawing	unbare	unfeed	urinal	unmard
tureen	thrust	titter	towing	unbark	unfree	uniped	unmiry
turfed	terata	tother	Tswana	unborn	unfair	unisex	unmask
turfen	terete	totter	towmon	unbury	unfelt	united	upmost
turkey	Targum	tetchy	tu-whoo	unbusy	unfold	uniter	utmost
turned	tarsus	tattie	tawdry	unbitt	upfill	ulitis	unmown
turner	tergum	tettix	tawery	uncial	unfine	unific	unnail
turret	torque	titbit	tewart	unclad	unfool	ukiyo-e	urning
turves	Turdus	tottie	thwart	uncock	unfirm	ulicon	ulnare
tyroes	turn-up	tutrix	toward	unclew	unform	ulikon	unnest
tariff	thrave	titoki	towery	uncage	unfurl	unipod	urnful
terefa	thrive	tattle	tuxedo	uncoil	upfurl	unison	unowed
thrift	throve	titely	taxied	upcoil	ungear	ubiety	up-over
Torify	thrawn	tittle	toxoid	urchin	unglad	Uniate	ulosis
Toryfy	throwe	titule	taxing	uncolt	ungual	ubique	urosis
tarsia	thrown	tatami	toyman	upcome	ungues	unique	utopia
terbic	Tuscan	tetany	thyine	uncini	upgrew	unjust	uropod
tercio	tuskar	tattoo	toying	unclog	ungain	upkeep	unpray
territ	tussah	titupy	trying	uncool	unguis	unknit	unpack
tertia	tussal	tittup	thymol	uncape	ungild	upknit	unpick
tirrit	tisick	tut-tut	Trygon	uncope	ungilt	unkent	unpaid
toroid	tasker	Tethys	tuyere	uncart	ungula	unkind	unpent
torpid	taslet	tetryl	twyere	uncord	upgang	unking	upping
torrid	tassel	toucan	thyrse	uncork	urgent	unknot	unprop

unpope	unsure	unyoke	Vulpes	vinous	vistal	whacko	wafter
umpire	unshut	Veadar	vilify	venewe	visual	whacky	waffle
uppish	unsoul	viable	volage	violer	vesica	weakly	wifely
uppity	unspun	viator	vildly	violet	vesper	whally	wafery
unplug	unsewn	Vibram®	vilely	violin	vessel	wraxle	wigwag
Ugrian	unsown	vibrio	volume	voodoo	vested	whatna	wigwam
unread	unteam	vibist	valine	Vipera	visaed	weapon	wagged
unreal	unthaw	vacked	Volans	vapour	viséed	whatso	wigged
uprear	uptear	victim	volant	varsal	visier	wrasse	waggle
uproar	untack	vocule	vellon	verbal	visage	wealth	waggly
unrobe	untuck	vacant	Volvox	vernal	viscid	wraith	wiggle
unrude	urtica	vicuña	Velcro®	versal	viscin	wharve	wiggly
unreel	untidy	vector	velure	vorpal	visile	webbed	woggle
unrein	untied	victor	volary	varech	Vishnu	wabain	waggon
unrake	untrim	vicary	volery	varied	vision	wabble	wigeon
unroll	uptake	vacate	valise	varier	vestry	wobble	Wahabi
unrule	untile	vacuum	volost	varlet	visite	wobbly	wahine
unruly	untold	vidual	valeta	varved	viscum	waboom	weirdo
uproll	up-till	vidame	valuta	varvel	viscus	wicked	wailer
unrent	uptilt	Vedism	velate	verdet	visive	wicken	waiter
unroof	ultima	Vedist	veleta	verger	vittae	wicker	waiver
unroot	ultimo	viewer	volute	verier	vetoes	wicket	whiles
uproot	untame	vielle	valgus	vermes	vetted	wadmal	whiner
unripe	untomb	viewly	Valium®	verrel	voteen	wadded	whiten
unrope	untent	voguey	vallum	verrey	vetchy	wadset	whites
unrest	untune	vagile	valour	versed	vitric	wedded	whitey
uprest	ultion	vagina	vellum	verser	vitals	wedged	writer
uprise	untrod	vagrom	velour	verset	vittle	widget	whiffy
uprist	ustion	vagary	villus	vertex	votary	waddie	whinge
uprose	untorn	vegete	vulgus	vervel	vatful	wedgie	weight
uprush	unturf	vigour	vomica	verven	votive	waddle	whisht
uprate	unturn	vehmic	vamper	vervet	vaunce	wedeln	wright
unseal	uptorn	vihara	vimana	virger	voulge	widely	writhe
unseam	upturn	veiled	vamose	vortex	vaudoo	wading	whisky
unseat	untrue	veined	vomito	verify	voudou	wadmol	whilly
unspar	uptown	voiced	vandal	virago	vaulty	whenas	whimmy
upstay	uvulae	voicer	venial	vorago	verdit	whence	whinny
upsway	uvular	voided	Venice	verdit	vivace	wrench	whilom
upside	unused	voidee	vanned	Verein	vivres	wretch	whippy
ulster	usurer	voider	vanner	vermil	vivify	wieldy	whirry
unseel	unvail	vainly	vendee	vermin	vively	weeded	whilst
unseen	unveil	Vaisya	vender	vermis	vivary	weeder	whimsy
unshed	unweal	vakeel	veneer	versin	vivers	weeper	wristy
unsped	unwrap	viking	venger	virgin	vaward	weeten	wakiki
unstep	upwaft	vakass	vennel	verily	vowess	weever	waking
unsafe	unwell	vallar	vented	virile	vexing	wee-wee	wallah
unsoft	unwill	valval	venter	Varuna	voyage	wheyey	walker
unsaid	upwell	valvar	vendis	virent	voyeur	wheugh	walled
unship	unwind	villan	ventil	vorant	vizier	wrethe	waller
unsuit	unwont	villar	venule	verdoy	vizzie	weepie	wallet
unself	upwind	vulcan	vendor	virion	vizsla	weevil	welder
unsold	unwept	vulgar	ven'son	verism	vizard	whelky	welter
ugsome	unware	vulval	venery	verist	weaken	wreake	wilder
unsent	unwary	vulvar	venire	virose	weanel	weekly	willed
unsung	unwire	veloce	ventre	verity	wearer	wheely	willer
upsend	unwork	valley	vinery	versus	weasel	wheare	willet
ursine	unworn	valued	vintry	vertue	weaved	wherry	willey
unshod	upward	valuer	vanish	virous	weaver	wreath	wolfer
unshoe	usward	valved	venose	virtue	weazen	waeful	wolver
unshot	unwise	vellet	vanity	vassal	whaler	woeful	wolves
unstop	unwish	velvet	venite	vestal	whaten	wheeze	walk-in
unstow	unwist	volley	vendue	vestas	woaded	wheezy	welkin
upshot		vulned	venous	vista'd	wrathy	wafted	wellie

wilily	wooded	wisher	yabber	zebeck
walk-on	wooden	wisket	yabbie	zabeta
wallop	woofed	wash-in	yacker	zodiac
wallow	woofer	wisely	yucker	zoetic
weldor	woosel	wistly	yodler	zaffer
willow	wroken	wesand	Y-level	zufolo
Wilton	woodie	wisent	yaffle	zaffre
walise	wholly	wisdom	yagger	zigzag
walnut	woolly	wastry	yogism	zygoma
walrus	wooing	wisard	Yahveh	zygose
wilful	whoosh	wash-up	Yahweh	zygote
wombat	woodsy	withal	yo-ho-ho	zillah
wampee	wroath	wether	yshend	zelant
wamble	woobut	wetted	yah-boo	zeloso
wambly	wapper	wither	ypight	zimmer
wimble	wiping	witted	yoicks	zombie
wimple	wapiti	witter	yojana	zymoid
woman'd	warman	wotted	yakker	zymome
womera	warran	wuther	yoking	zymase
wammus	warray	within	yelper	zymite
wampum	worral	wattle	yolked	Zuñian
wampus	warded	wet-fly	yblent	zander
wangan	warden	wet-rot	Y-alloy	zinced
windac	warder	wittol	yellow	zingel
windas	warmed	watery	yclept	zinked
wander	warmer	woundy	yplast	zonked
wanker	warner	waucht	yammer	zendik
wanned	warped	waught	yum-yum	zinnia
wannel	warper	woubit	Yankee	zonoid
wanted	warred	wou-wou	yanker	zincky
wanter	warren	waurst	yonder	zonula
wended	warrey	waving	yonker	zonule
wincer	warted	wavery	yankie	zenana
wincey	worded	wivern	yeoman	zoning
winded	worked	wyvern	yeomen	zonary
winder	worker	wowser	ybound	zenith
winged	wormed	wow-wow	yoo-hoo	zonate
winger	wormer	wax-red	yaourt	zooeae
winker	worrel	wax-end	yapock	zooeal
winner	worsen	waxing	yapper	zoonal
winsey	worser	waylay	yippee	zoonic
winter	wurley	why-not	Yoruba	zoozoo
wonder	worthy	weyard	Y-track	zlotys
wonted	work-in	way-out	yorker	zipper
wunner	worrit	wizier	yarpha	zephyr
Wendic	warble	wuzzle	ywrake	zareba
wandle	warily	wezand	ywroke	zariba
wangle	warmly	wizard	yarely	zereba
wankle	warsle	xoanon	ybrent	zeriba
windle	wirily	xyloid	yarrow	zarnec
winkle	wortle	xyloma	yes-man	zorino
winnle	wiring	xylene	yester	zircon
wintle	wardog	xylose	yatter	zarape
waning	war-god	xenial	yttria	zeroth
woning	war-cry	xenium	yttric	zoster
wanion	warmth	Xhosan	youthy	zither
wanton	warm-up	xeroma	you-all	zounds
window	washed	xyster	yaupon	zeugma
winnow	washen	xystos	yawper	Zouave
winery	washer	xystus	yowley	
wintry	wastel	ynambu	Yezidi	
wangun	waster	yearly	zealot	
wind-up	wester	yeasty	Zabian	

atalaya	amatory	auction	aheight	alforja	acharné	aliases
Aramaic	anagogy	alcalde	Amerind	afforce	Acheron	arietta
anatase	analogy	archlet	adenine	alférez	adherer	abiotic
apanage	anatomy	accompt	alepine	aefauld	athirst	Asiatic
atamans	anagram	accinge	alewife	aggrace	ash-tray	ariette
adamant	atabrin	asconce	alerion	aggrade	aphasia	aviette
agaçant	acantha	arcanum	atelier	aggrate	aphasic	agister
amarant	atactic	ancones	acetify	algebra	aphesis	agistor
ataraxy	adapted	arctoid	amenity	aggress	aphetic	aviator
anarchy	abactor	anchovy	areolae	augment	aphotic	Avicula
acaudal	adapter	alcorza	Ameslan	anglice	Achates	azimuth
Abaddon	adaptor	ascarid	areolar	anguine	ashiver	aliquot
abandon	abattis	accurse	adermin	angling	agitate	adjudge
alameda	abature	Alcoran	Avernus	anguish	alidade	abjoint
araneid	analyse	ascaris	adenoma	Anglian	alizare	adjoint
academe	analyze	accurst	adenoid	anglist	animate	adjunct
araceae	analyst	accused	aneroid	anglify	abigail	abjurer
Araneae	ambs-ace	accusal	apehood	angrily	agitato	adjourn
acaleph	arblast	accuser	acerose	angekok	Arimasp	awkward
amateur	ambient	ascesis	acetone	angelic	alicant	asklent
anapest	ambages	ascetic	acetose	angular	amiable	alkalis
academy	ambling	ascites	ale-pole	angelus	amiably	ack-emma
amalgam	aiblins	accrual	anemone	alginic	abidden	askance
abashed	albumen	account	awesome	anginal	amildar	alkanet
ataghan	albumin	accourt	ale-hoof	angioma	aniseed	Alkoran
arachis	albinos	ascaunt	agelong	argyria	aliment	askesis
Acarida	ambones	archway	acerous	augural	agilely	all-hail
Acarina	ambroid	accoyed	acetous	augurer	atingle	axle-box
amanita	ambered	accoyld	alecost	angerly	apishly	alledge
acarine	auberge	alcayde	averred	algesia	aniline	allseed
Adamite	albergo	alchymy	aneurin	auguste	asinine	allheal
amative	arboret	alcázar	atebrin	algesis	axinite	all-seer
apatite	Abbasid	audible	apepsia	augitic	abiding	ailment
arabise	ambassy	audibly	asepsis	algates	animism	alleged
avarice	ambatch	adducer	amentia	Angevin	Apician	allegro
amazing	arbiter	address	aseptic	ashrama	Arician	awlbird
awaking	arbutus	aidless	Avestic	athwart	Azilian	all-tlme
abaxial	ambltty	addrest	abetted	adhibit	asinico	allying
adaxial	archaic	audient	averted	aphides	animist	aclinic
Arabism	arcuate	andvile	aventre	athleta	ability	allonge
atavism	acclaim	ard-righ	amental	achieve	acidify	ailanto
Acadian	arc-lamp	abdomen	amentum	athlete	acidity	aplenty
acarian	accoast	addenda	Avestan	Achaean	agility	all-good
Arabian	accablé	aidance	abetter	ash-heap	anility	all-work
adagios	aecidia	andante	abettor	awheels	aridity	aileron
Ananias	ascidia	ardency	alertly	aphagia	avidity	allergy
Arabist	arcaded	android	ale-bush	aphthae	axillae	aplasia
anaemia	accidie	arduous	asexual	atheise	axillar	atlases
anaemic	acceder	andiron	affear'd	athrill	arillus	ailette
alarmed	Alcides	auditor	aufgabe	atheism	axially	ablator
acapnia	accrete	acetate	affable	Achaian	anionic	all-star
alannah	ancress	amenage	affably	atheist	Asianic	ally-tor
against	archeus	ames-ace	affiche	aphelia	avionic	ally-taw
araroba	ancient	anelace	A-effect	aphelic	aliened	alluvia
acaroid	alchemy	average	affaire	aphylly	alienee	all-over
agamoid	archery	apetaly	affying	ashamed	aliunde	allowed
abalone	arch-foe	acerbic	afflict	aphonia	alienor	alleyed
alamode	alcohol	alembic	alfalfa	aphonic	adipose	allayer
anagoge	accoied	amender	awfully	athanor	aciform	armband
apagoge	alcaide	ageless	affined	ash-hole	aviform	Asmoday
acatour	archive	aweless	affoord	atheous	alimony	aimless
agamous	ascribe	alength	affront	adharma	aripple	armless
alamort	arcking	avenger	alfaquí	Amharic	abiosis	alms-fee

armiger	amorism	Aspasia	aureole	althaea	asteria	anxious
Almaine	atomism	apposer	air-lock	astrand	altered	auxesis
armoire	aeolian	ampassy	airport	abthane	asterid	auxetic
armilla	aeonian	amputee	agrapha	actuate	alterne	amylase
alms-man	amorino	ampoule	atropia	amtrack	Astarte	anyways
ammonia	agogics	appuyed	atropin	attract	apteral	amygdal
almanac	agonist	asphyxy	apropos	actuary	Antares	amylene
ammonal	amorist	acquest	Atropos	astable	anthrax	anywhen
almoner	atomist	acquire	atrophy	autobus	apteryx	anytime
almonry	aboulia	acquite	auroral	attaboy	autarky	anywise
armhole	apoplex	asquint	air-drop	antacid	altesse	azymite
Armoric	anosmia	air-raid	air-trap	anticke	artiste	acyclic
almirah	acorned	airward	air-crew	article	artisan	abysmal
admiral	amorosa	acreage	atresia	attaché	aptotic	amyloid
admirer	apocope	air-base	agrised	autocue	astatic	anyroad
ammeter	axolotl	air-lane	arrased	autocar	astatki	azygous
armoury	amoroso	airwave	agraste	Actaeon	astound	azymous
annicut	amorous	arriage	aerosol	Aetnean	autovac	anybody
awnless	apodous	aureate	aurated	ant-bear	altezza	abyssal
alnager	atokous	abroach	airstop	actress	abusage	alyssum
annuity	azotous	air-bath	acroter	aptness	adulate	asylums
annelid	apology	air-mail	aerator	artless	ajutage	anziani
annular	arousal	air-rail	aground	antient	asudden	Bharati
annulus	arouser	abreact	air-pump	attuent	asunder	bradawl
annulet	anoesis	abreast	agravic	antefix	azurean	bravado
agnamed	aloetic	already	arrival	antigen	azulejo	blatant
agnomen	anoetic	aerobic	apraxia	ant-eggs	acutely	blabbed
Arnaout	adopted	aerobus	abraxas	ant-bird	aquafer	brabble
amnesia	apostle	acrobat	assuage	antliae	aquifer	bramble
amnesic	apostil	auricle	asswage	astride	ague-fit	bean-bag
amnesty	avoutry	African	abstain	attrite	ahungry	blaubok
annatta	anonyma	aurochs	apsidal	attuite	acushla	blabber
agnatic	acolyte	apricot	apsides	Althing	alumina	brambly
annatto	anodyne	abridge	assiege	ant-hill	abusive	braccia
arnotto	acolyth	acridin	Auslese	asteism	alunite	braccio
annates	applaud	arreede	austere	ant-lion	amusive	bear-cat
annoyed	appease	arriéré	arsheen	astrict	azurine	branchy
avocado	appeach	air-bell	abscess	attaint	azurite	bearded
anomaly	asprawl	air-cell	assagai	attrist	amusing	braided
apogamy	asphalt	arriero	assegai	astelic	alumish	branded
amoebic	aspidia	airless	abscind	antilog	alumium	bladder
amoebae	aspread	agraffe	arshine	astylar	abusion	boarder
acouchy	adpress	acrogen	auspice	artsman	Aquilon	brander
apogeal	appress	alright	absciss	attempt	alumnae	blandly
apogean	applied	airship	absolve	automat	alumnus	by-and-by
alonely	appuied	airtime	assumed	actinia	anurous	brasero
anorexy	apprise	'Arryish	arsenic	antenna	aqueous	braless
aloofly	appoint	airsick	absence	actinic	aquaria	beavery
abought	amplify	arraign	absinth	actinal	aquatic	bravely
alongst	ampulla	air-miss	arsenal	antonym	abutted	bravery
amongst	appulse	airlift	abscond	autonym	abuttal	beaufin
another	Appalto	aureity	alsoone	actinon	abutter	beaufet
aconite	amphora	aurelia	Austric	anthoid	aquavit	boat-fly
adonise	approve	acrylic	assured	astroid	alveary	bragged
agonise	approof	aurally	austral	asthore	advance	brangle
anodise	alphorn	Ahriman	also-ran	art-song	alveole	beached
atomise	asprout	Aaronic	assurer	artwork	alveoli	blather
azotise	asperge	arrange	Alsatia	althorn	adverse	brachet
abolish	asperse	adrenal	ansated	aftmost	advised	Baalite
amorini	apparel	acronym	assault	Anthony	adviser	beading
alodial	apperil	aureola	assever	autopsy	advisor	beaming
asocial	aspirin	abrooke	assayer	antique	akvavit	bearing
alodium	apparat	airhole	assizer	apteria	anxiety	beating

biasing	babbler	bedtick	bifilar	brindle	ballant	bolster
boating	bubalis	bodikin	buffoon	build-up	ballast	Boletus
bracing	Bubalus	bedeman	beghard	blinder	balsamy	bulrush
beamish	bibelot	bedsore	boggard	builder	biliary	beloved
bearish	bubinga	bedrock	bogland	blindly	bullary	bolivar
beauish	bubonic	bedwork	baggage	buirdly	bilobed	Baldwin
boarish	baboosh	bed-roll	bugbane	boilery	bilobar	billy-oh
biaxial	bibcock	bedroom	bagwash	bribery	bullbat	bombard
Baalism	baby-sit	badious	boggart	brimful	bell-boy	bumbaze
brasier	babassu	bedpost	beggary	briefly	Baluchi	bummalo
brazier	baccara	bedropt	bugaboo	bringer	bulldog	bombast
beamily	baclava	bederal	bighead	blither	baladin	bemedal
beatify	baccare	bedouin	bogbean	blighty	believe	bambino
blacken	baccate	bedevil	bugbear	bailiff	balneal	bumpkin
bracken	backare	bedawin	bigness	baiting	baleful	bimanal
blanket	becharm	bedazed	biggest	boiling	Bologna	bummock
bracket	bicycle	bedizen	buggery	briming	bolshie	bum-boat
blankly	back-end	brewage	bagpipe	brinish	bellhop	bemired
Braille	buck-eye	beefalo	begrime	British	belcher	bemouth
beagler	buckeen	blewart	beguile	brinjal	bellied	bemazed
brawler	Bacchic	blesbok	beguine	beinked	bullied	bandana
beadman	backhoe	breccia	big-time	blinked	balding	bandage
boatman	bacchii	blended	bagging	brickle	balking	bondage
Brahman	Bacchus	breaded	begging	bricken	balling	beneath
Brahmin	buccina	breadth	bugging	brisken	belting	bone-ash
brained	backing	bleeder	bygoing	blinker	belying	Bengali
brawned	bucking	blender	biggish	brisket	billing	bunraku
braunch	buckish	breeder	bogyism	briskly	bolting	bone-bed
beatnik	bycoket	breveté	baggily	bridled	bulging	band-box
bran-new	bucolic	brewery	boggler	baillie	baldish	binocle
blarney	backlog	beet-fly	bogy-man	bridler	bullish	bone-dry
bravoes	bacilli	beef-ham	begonia	brimmed	ballium	benzene
blawort	buckler	brecham	beginne	brimmer	Belgian	banteng
bran-pie	becloud	beechen	bigener	bairnly	billion	bonkers
biassed	backpay	blether	bygones	bricole	bullion	bandeau
bransle	buckram	beehive	bug-word	bridoon	bilies	bindery
brassie	bécasse	bee-kite	begloom	briared	bulkily	benefic
brasset	bucksom	brewing	bighorn	briered	bell-jar	baneful
bran-tub	backset	blemish	bog-moss	britska	bulimia	benefit
blasted	backsaw	brevier	bugloss	bhistee	bilimbi	benight
beastie	buck-saw	blewits	bugwort	blintze	bellman	benthic
brantle	backsey	brevity	begorra	bristle	billman	bunched
brattle	bycatch	break-in	begored	brittle	bulimus	banshee
blaster	because	bee-skep	bagarre	Bristol	balance	bencher
blatter	bedward	break-up	bog-iron	built-in	Balanus	benthos
boaster	bedwarf	breaker	bagasse	built-up	baloney	bandied
beastly	badmash	bleakly	bigoted	blister	boloney	benzine
bravura	budmash	bee-glue	bigotry	bristly	Bellona	bonfire
bobtail	bedfast	beesome	bagfuls	brisure	biltong	banding
babuche	budgero	bee-moth	bug-eyed	briquet	bullock	banging
Bobadil	badness	bleeper	Bahadur	britzka	balloon	banking
babudom	budless	bleared	behight	bejewel	bellows	banting
bebeeru	bodeful	blessed	Bahaite	beknave	bilboes	bending
bobbery	bedight	bheesty	Bahaism	bukshee	bilious	binding
bobbing	bedridd	beeftea	Bahaist	beknown	bulbous	bonding
babyish	bedrite	bletted	behoove	belgard	balcony	bunting
bobbish	bedside	breathe	behaved	bollard	billowy	bandits
Babiism	bedtime	breathy	brigand	ballade	bull-pen	bonnily
babuism	bedding	beeswax	brigade	beldame	bull-pup	bangled
babbitt	bidding	beffana	brioche	Beltane	baldric	bungler
biblist	bodying	buffalo	blinded	bullace	balista	bendlet
bubukle	budding	bifocal	brinded	bullate	balls-up	Benelux
bobsled	baddish	baffler	builded	bulwark	belated	banally

benamed	bionics	baracan	barbule	bestrew	bethump	bivouac
bondman	boozily	barocco	bordure	bostryx	bathyal	bow-hand
benempt	blocked	borscht	borough	bus-stop	bruhaha	bowlder
bynempt	brocked	bird-dog	bergylt	boshter	boutade	bowhead
bonanza	brodkin	boredom	borazon	bush-tit	Bauhaus	bowbent
benzoic	blocker	Bursera	bastard	basqued	bourbon	bowshot
bandore	brocket	bur-reed	bustard	bascule	blubber	bowline
benzole	brockit	burweed	beshame	bismuth	bluecap	bawling
bandook	bootleg	Burmese	beslave	bestuck	bouncer	bowling
bannock	broiler	berserk	bespake	biscuit	bounded	bawdily
bundook	booklet	bar-bell	boscage	bit-part	bounden	bawdkin
benzoyl	bookman	borrell	bus-fare	bateaux	bourdon	bywoner
bone-oil	bloomer	burrell	bestain	batable	blunder	bewhore
benzoin	brommer	burgeon	bass-bar	betided	boulder	bawcock
bonjour	brownie	burgess	basoche	bottega	bounder	bewitch
bonsoir	boobook	bargest	bush-cat	betread	bourder	box-calf
bandrol	blow-out	berceau	basidia	butt-end	blue-eye	box-haul
banksia	biology	burghal	besides	beteeme	bluffer	box-seat
benison	blowsed	burrhel	bespeed	between	bluffly	box-kite
bonasus	bloosme	barchan	bestead	bittern	bludger	boxwood
boneset	booksie	barkhan	beseeke	battels	blunger	boxroom
band-saw	blossom	birchen	besiege	bitters	brushed	box-coat
banquet	blouson	burthen	beseech	butment	bauchle	box-tree
biodata	biontic	burgher	bespeak	battery	brush-up	box-iron
brocard	bloated	berried	besmear	butlery	blucher	boxfuls
brocade	blotted	berline	bashful	buttery	blusher	buyable
brocage	bloater	bornite	bastide	betight	brusher	Brython
brokage	blotter	barring	beshine	botcher	blushet	bay-line
bromate	booster	birding	bespice	butcher	bauxite	bay-tine
buoyage	blowzed	birling	byssine	bottine	brucine	bayonet
biomass	bronzed	burning	bashing	batting	brucite	boyhood
buoyant	bronzen	burying	basting	betting	blueing	boycott
bloubok	Buphaga	burnish	busking	by-thing	bousing	Bryozoa
bronchi	biplane	birlinn	bussing	bethink	brutish	buzzard
broncho	byplace	barrico	busying	battill	bruxism	bazzazz
blotchy	bepearl	barrier	bestick	betwixt	brutify	bezzazz
blooded	bipedal	berries	ba'spiel	betaken	bourkha	bizzazz
broaden	baptise	barmkin	bestial	betoken	bruckle	bez-tine
broider	baptism	barilla	bestill	bottled	blunker	buzzing
brooder	baptist	burglar	busgirl	battler	bouilli	bizonal
blow-dry	bepaint	byreman	bastion	bottler	bourlaw	bazooka
broadly	bipolar	boronia	bushido	bathmic	Brummie	bezique
book-end	beprose	Byronic	besaint	bitumed	brummer	bizarre
booze-up	bequest	baronet	bashlyk	batsman	bausond	buzz-saw
biogeny	bergama	barbola	basilar	bitumen	boudoir	buzz-wig
brokery	barmaid	barwood	bustler	betimes	brumous	chalaza
bookful	barbate	burdock	basbleu	botanic	brusque	chamade
blowfly	barrace	bar-room	bosomed	bitonal	baudric	charade
blowgun	barrage	burnous	baseman	bothole	blurred	clavate
brought	bereave	burn-out	bushman	betroth	bourrée	cranage
brothel	burgage	baroque	basenji	bittock	blue-rot	cyanate
brochan	burdash	bar-iron	basinet	buttock	bruiser	chapati
biophor	biryani	bortsch	byssoid	bittour	bluette	charact
brother	barrack	biretta	beshone	buttons	bluster	clamant
biocide	bargain	barytic	bespoke	bottony	boulter	coal-bed
biotite	bureaus	bursted	bestorm	buttony	bluntly	crabbed
bromide	bureaux	burette	bassoon	butyric	bouquet	chambré
bromine	Barbary	borstal	besport	botargo	brulyie	chamber
booking	Barnaby	baryton	bespout	batiste	brulzie	clabber
booming	bursary	bursten	bistort	bathtub	bevvied	clamber
boozing	byrlady	burst-up	bestrid	betitle	bivalve	coal-box
bookish	bark-bed	burster	bistred	battuta	bivious	chancre
boorish	boracic	barytes	beshrew	bethumb	buvette	chancel

7 c□□c

chancer	charlie	crassly	cacumen	clerisy	coherer	criollo
claucht	challan	chaotic	coconut	cleeked	chikara	Chislev
Chaldee	crawler	clastic	cockney	check-up	chicane	chimley
czardom	Chablis	chatted	coccoid	checker	climate	crimmer
chaddar	challis	chaetae	cuckold	cleekit	coinage	Chianti
chalder	chamlet	chantie	cycloid	clerkly	crinate	chignon
csárdás	chaplet	chattel	cyclone	creamer	Chicago	chimney
czardas	charley	coastal	cyclops	cleanse	chicano	cricoid
co-agent	chasmic	chasten	cockpit	creance	cuirass	crinoid
chapeau	charmed	chanter	cacique	clean-up	climbed	crinose
château	chasmed	chantor	cockshy	cleaner	cribbed	chibouk
cramesy	clammed	chapter	cocotte	chesnut	cribble	chinook
chaffer	crammed	charter	cedrate	cleanly	climber	chicory
chamfer	coalman	chatter	cadrans	cremona	coin-box	chipped
cragged	charmer	clatter	caducei	cheloid	childed	clipped
changer	claimer	coal-tar	codicil	ctenoid	chidden	clippie
charger	crammer	coaster	codices	coelome	childer	crimple
clanger	chained	coal-tit	Cedrela	coehorn	chindit	cripple
clangor	chaunce	chantey	cudweed	cheroot	childly	crispin
coal-gas	chaunge	chantry	Cadmean	creepie	chimera	chipper
claught	crannog	chauvin	cudbear	cheapen	Cairene	chirper
Cyathea	craunch	cabbala	caddice	cheeper	chimere	clipper
coachee	channel	cabbage	cedrine	creeper	Chinese	crimper
clachan	charnel	cab-rank	codeine	cheaply	Chilean	crisper
coacher	clapnet	cob-wall	codding	chevron	clivers	crisply
cyathus	crab-nut	cabbagy	codling	cheerio	crivens	chirrup
czarina	chalone	cubicle	caddish	cheerer	cliffed	chiasma
chalice	cladode	cubical	codfish	clearer	chiffon	caisson
chamise	cracowe	Cebidae	cadmium	cheerly	chiefer	crimson
coalise	chabouk	cubless	cedilla	clearly	chiefly	cuisser
Coalite®	coal-oil	cob-pipe	codilla	Chelsea	chiefry	clifted
cyanide	crab-oil	cabling	codille	cheesed	cringle	cuittle
cyanine	clamour	cubbing	cadenza	chessel	chigger	chitter
cyanise	chamois	cubbish	cadence	cresset	cringer	clitter
cyanite	chanoyu	Cabeiri	cadency	creeshy	clichéd	critter
ceasing	champac	cobbler	cedared	creatic	cain-hen	crittur
charing	chapped	cabinet	cidaris	chested	chikhor	chintzy
chasing	clapped	cubhood	cadaver	crested	chip-hat	cliquey
coating	cramped	caboose	caddyss	cheetah	chiliad	chinwag
craving	chappie	cobloaf	chelate	cheater	Cainite	cajoler
clayish	charpie	cab-tout	cremate	creator	caitive	cajeput
coaxial	champak	ciboria	crenate	caestus	crimine	cajuput
cranial	crampon	Cabiric	cue-ball	caesura	crinite	Ciliata
charism	clamper	cabaret	creedal	caerule	cuisine	collard
cranium	clapper	cubital	Cheddar	cleruch	caitiff	ciliate
czarism	clasper	cubitus	crewels	coequal	ceiling	collage
clarion	clay-pit	cob-swan	clement	chequer	chiding	collate
chamiso	coal-pit	cockade	credent	cherubs	coining	calpack
clavier	crampet	cacodyl	chéchia	cleaved	ceilidh	callant
chariot	crampit	cockeye	Czechic	chervil	crimini	calmant
czarist	charpoy	cachexy	coeliac	Chesvan	Chilian	Calvary
charily	charqui	cacoepy	chemise	cleaver	coition	ciliary
charity	charred	Cocagne	crevice	caffila	Chinkie	calibre
clarify	chagrin	cocaine	cieling	coffret	crinkle	colibri
clarity	classic	coctile	cherish	cognate	chicken	Caliban
crazily	Chassid	coction	chewink	cage-cup	clicker	caliber
clarkia	classed	cyclist	caesium	cognise	clinker	coluber
cracked	clausal	cockily	chemism	cogging	clicket	colobus
crackle	chanson	cochlea	cretism	cogence	cricket	call-box
crankle	coarsen	cichlid	chekist	cogency	crickey	call-boy
clacker	chassis	cockled	chemist	cagoule	crinkly	culicid
cracker	classis	cackler	Cheviot	cohabit	chilled	caliche
crackly		cacolet	co-exist	cohibit	chillum	calycle

calyces	collude	comb-out	conject	consort	close-up	croquis
culices	culture	comfort	connect	contort	crop-ear	croquet
cylices	calculi	comport	consent	Canopic	choreus	cap-case
colicky	Calmuck	compost	content	Canopus	closely	caprate
celadon	coloury	compony	contest	cinerea	clovery	cup-mark
caldera	caliver	comique	context	conaria	cookery	cupgall
college	calyxes	Camorra	convent	centric	coopery	captain
colleen	caloyer	cambric	convert	cantred	cropful	capable
collect	campana	cambrel	cankery	centred	clogged	capuche
culvert	command	cameral	cannery	congree	clogger	copy-cat
collied	compage	cumarin	cindery	congrue	clothed	cepheid
cullied	compare	comfrey	congery	cantref	clothes	cuphead
calcine	comrade	comitia	conifer	central	crochet	Cepheus
calcite	Campari	cometic	conchie	control	choc-ice	cypress
collide	cembalo	comital	canthus	centrum	choline	coppery
calling	cymbalo	compter	candida	cantrip	chopine	cop-shop
colling	compass	commune	cantina	concrew	chorine	copaiba
culling	compact	commute	candied	canasta	closing	copaiva
coldish	compart	compute	centime	cunette	cloying	caprice
coltish	compast	combust	concise	conster	coolish	caprine
calcium	company	cumquat	confide	conatus	chorion	capsize
cultism	camp-bed	cantata	confine	cannula	crosier	captive
cullion	comical	cantate	coniine	contund	crozier	coppice
collier	Comecon	centage	connive	censure	chorist	cuprite
Celsius	cimices	concave	convive	conduce	clocked	cyprine
Collins	commend	connate	canning	confuse	crooked	capping
cellist	compend	cuneate	canting	confute	chookie	copying
cultist	commère	cannach	conning	conjure	chocker	c-spring
calcify	compere	contain	cunning	consume	clocker	cupping
calumba	compete	centavo	confirm	contuse	croaker	copyism
Columba	compear	centaur	cantion	censual	crocket	Capsian
celomic	compeer	canvass	condign	conquer	crowned	caption
calomel	comment	cineast	consign	canfuls	crooner	cyprian
columel	cumbent	contact	cantico	concuss	crowner	copyist
calamus	camphor	cenacle	candies	conduct	crownet	Cypriot
chlamys	cumshaw	conacre	consist	conduit	choenix	caprify
calumet	combine	conical	convict	consult	choroid	Capella
calumny	compile	cynical	cannily	century	cookout	cupola'd
colonic	cambial	conidia	canakin	concupy	cropped	capelin
colonel	cambism	Canidae	canikin	conjury	croupon	cipolin
calando	cambium	cantdog	canella	condyle	chopper	copular
Calanus	Comtism	candela	cantlet	chorale	cropper	cupolar
calends	campion	contend	conflux	cromack	crouper	cupular
colloid	Comtian	concede	canonic	coolant	crossed	copilot
callous	cambist	convene	centner	choc-bar	cloison	caproic
calipee	Comtist	conteck	canonry	clobber	chooser	copious
calypso	camaieu	conceal	canzona	clotbur	Croesus	cup-moss
caloric	cimelia	congeal	concord	crow-bar	choosey	cuprous
chloric	complin	conseil	canzone	cloacae	crossly	copepod
calorie	cumulus	canteen	cineole	cloacal	clotted	cap-à-pie
chloral	camelot	concern	condole	coon-can	clouted	caporal
caldron	complot	condemn	condone	clodded	chortle	caperer
caltrap	complex	contemn	connote	clouded	Clootie	Cyperus
caltrop	camelry	confess	console	crowded	chondre	capital
culprit	cam-wood	conkers	convoke	chondre	crottle	Capitol
celesta	camboge	candent	canzoni	croodle	crow-toe	capitan
celeste	commode	conceit	candock	crowdie	croûton	capstan
calotte	commove	concent	conform	chondri	clotter	capsule
culotte	componé	concept	conjoin	chordal	crofter	capture
colitis	compose	concert	candour	chobdar	choctaw	cupfuls
cole-tit	compote	confect	contour	chowder	choltry	coquito
Calluna	come-off	confest	consols	crowder	closure	cariama
cellule	commons	congest	concoct	cholera	cloture	Circaea

curtana	carbide	coronet	casuals	catcher	chuddah	coulter
carcake	carbine	carioca	cistern	catbird	clued-up	counter
carcase	carline	córdoba	costean	cat-like	chuddar	country
carnage	carmine	corpora	coshery	citrine	chunder	courtly
cartage	cervine	curiosa	costive	cottise	clupeid	coupure
cirrate	cordite	cariole	Cushite	catling	crubeen	couture
cordage	cornice	carnose	casting	cutling	couvert	couguar
cordate	corsive	cirrose	cosmism	catfish	cautery	caviare
corkage	cortile	corrode	cession	cattish	crudely	civvies
cornage	corvine	carlock	cushion	Cataian	chuffed	cavalla
corrade	cursive	cork-oak	cassino	cottier	crushed	covelet
corsage	carking	cardoon	cashier	catmint	couchee	cavally
curtate	carping	cartoon	casuist	catskin	couthie	cavalry
curtaxe	carving	cargoes	cosmist	cutikin	cougher	civilly
curvate	cording	carious	castled	catalpa	crusher	caveman
car-wash	corking	cereous	case-law	cotylae	Cluniac	covered
currach	curling	cirrous	caseman	catalog	cauline	cover-up
curragh	cursing	corious	cestoid	catelog	crucial	coveted
carpark	curving	curious	cissoid	Catalan	Couéism	cuvette
carrack	carlish	car-coat	cystoid	cotyles	caution	cavetto
cure-all	Cornish	carport	cassone	cotinga	crucian	cowhand
curtail	currish	carroty	cestode	catenae	crusian	cowbane
certain	car-sick	corrody	custode	cathood	courier	cowhage
curtain	cerrial	cursory	cast-off	cottoid	Couéist	cow-calf
corsair	cordial	Corypha	cassock	cathode	crucify	cowherd
carcass	Carlism	coryphe	castock	cat-hole	crudity	cow-weed
corcass	carrion	corn-pit	custock	cot-folk	chuckie	cowbell
carract	carrier	corn-rig	caseous	cutworm	chuckle	cowheel
currant	currier	chrisom	castory	cottown	crunkle	cowshed
curable	Carlist	cerasin	custody	citrous	caulker	cowbird
corn-bin	cornist	ceresin	cesspit	catboat	chukker	cowhide
Carabus	certify	Christy	caserne	cottony	courlan	cowling
caribou	curvity	curtsey	castral	catapan	coupler	cowfish
curaçoa	coralla	carotid	costrel	cat's-paw	cruller	cowlick
corn-cob	corella	curette	custrel	coterie	cruells	cowgirl
caroche	corolla	carotin	costume	catarrh	couplet	cowslip
coracle	circled	curator	cithara	cateran	club-law	cowpoke
caracal	cork-leg	caritas	cotland	caterer	chumley	cow-tree
caracol	circler	carauna	citrate	catasta	cruelly	cowitch
caracul	Carolus	curcuma	cottage	cytisus	cruelty	cow-dung
curaçao	Corylus	carouse	cat-walk	cothurn	clubman	coxcomb
carices	circlet	cornute	cutback	catsuit	chunnel	caymans
Corydon	corslet	cornual	catcall	catawba	chunner	cry-baby
cariere	corn-law	cornuto	cattalo	cutaway	chutney	clypeal
cortège	caramba	carduus	cutlass	cat-eyed	coulomb	clypeus
carrell	ceramic	circuit	cattabu	Catayan	caulome	coyness
corbeil	chromic	corrupt	coteaux	citizen	couloir	cryogen
corneal	caramel	circusy	citable	caudate	crumple	chymify
Circean	caromel	caravel	Cetacea	courage	crupper	cayenne
carve-up	cerumen	co-rival	cuticle	couvade	crumpet	chymous
carrect	ceramet	caravan	catechu	crusade	caudron	cryptic
Corbett	cork-mat	corn-van	citadel	chupati	churrus	cryptal
cornett	caranna	caraway	co-tidal	crusado	cruisie	crystal
correct	chronic	cartway	cathead	courant	counsel	crypton
current	corsned	carry-on	cat's-eye	chubbed	courser	clyster
cardecu	coronae	cascara	cithern	clubbed	cruiser	cozener
corbeau	Corinth	cassava	cittern	crumble	caustic	cazique
corn-fed	coronal	costard	cat's-ear	clumber	counted	deaf-aid
careful	chronon	custard	cattery	crumbly	crustae	diabase
cornfly	coranto	cascade	cutlery	council	crustal	diapase
cardiac	coroner	costate	catched	churchy	chunter	drayage
carried	coronas	cuspate	catchen	crunchy	cluster	drabble
curried	coronis	Cossack	catchup	cruddle	clutter	drabber

drag-bar	dobhash	decapod	defiant	dwindle	dilutee	donship
draw-bar	débâcle	decuple	defacer	drip-dry	delator	dun-bird
drabbet	Debrett	decuria	deficit	deiseal	dilater	Dunciad
draw-boy	dubiety	decorum	deflect	drive-in	dilator	dentine
diarchy	debrief	Docetic	daffing	dyingly	diluter	dancing
duarchy	dabbing	Docetae	defying	daisied	dilutor	denying
dyarchy	dibbing	docquet	defiler	deified	delouse	dinning
dvandva	dubbing	decayed	defence	deicide	deliver	donning
diandry	dabbler	decrypt	defense	driving	delayed	dunning
dead-end	dibbler	doddard	defunct	deifier	delayer	dankish
dead-eye	dubious	didicoi	defrock	doitkin	demeane	donnish
dialect	dibasic	didicoy	difform	drinker	dum-palm	dun-fish
deanery	debased	dudgeon	defrost	driblet	domical	dunnish
drapery	debaser	Dodgems	deforce	deiform	domicil	Dunkirk
dwarfed	dibutyl	doddery	defaste	dripped	demoded	donnism
dragged	dabster	dodgery	diffuse	deictic	dimness	Dantist
draggle	debater	duddery	default	deistic	demigod	dentist
draught	debitor	Dadaism	degrade	drip-tip	demaine	dandify
drachma	debauch	Dadaist	dogbane	drifter	damming	dandily
deathly	debouch	didakai	dogeate	drizzle	damning	density
diarise	decease	didakei	dogvane	drizzly	dimming	Dansker
dealing	deciare	diddler	digraph	dejecta	dampish	dangler
doating	declare	dedimus	dogdays	dejeune	dimmish	danelaw
drawing	dictate	daddock	dogcart	dukedom	dumpish	dynamic
deasiul	dockage	die-hard	dog-head	dakoiti	dumaist	dentoid
diarial	ducdame	daedale	dog's-ear	dika-oil	damnify	dunnock
dualism	declaim	dieback	digress	deltaic	dimpled	dingoes
diarian	declass	die-cast	doggess	dullard	demonic	dinmont
drapier	duck-ant	dietary	dog-belt	deleble	dominie	dendron
dialist	docible	dyeable	doggery	delible	démenti	dynasty
diarist	decibel	Dresden	dogship	deluded	demonry	dinette
dualist	dice-box	dreader	digging	dolldom	damfool	donator
duality	decidua	dreadly	dogging	deluder	dimeric	denture
dialled	decided	deedful	dogfish	dulness	dambrod	dinky-di
dialler	decadal	deep-fet	doggish	diluent	demerge	denizen
drabler	decider	deep-fry	dogsick	doleful	demerse	Dionaea
drawler	decoder	dredger	dog-tick	delight	dimorph	diorama
dead-men	decreed	diethyl	dignify	Delphic	demirep	deodand
drag-man	dickens	dietine	dignity	delphin	demerit	deodate
drayman	duchess	dyeline	dogskin	dolphin	demesne	dioxane
drainer	decreet	drevill	digamma	dallied	damosel	Dioecia
drag-net	decagon	dietist	Digynia	dollied	domatia	droichy
draw-net	decried	deedily	digonal	delaine	demotic	drosera
dearnly	deceive	doe-skin	dagwood	dulcite	dimeter	duodena
diamond	decline	duelled	dogwood	dilling	demount	diocese
Diasone	dockise	dwelled	doggone	dollish	demayne	doomful
deasoil	ductile	dueller	doghole	doltish	damozel	dropfly
dragoon	decking	dweller	dog-rose	dullish	donnard	drought
diabolo	docking	deerlet	daglock	dallier	dentate	drogher
drappie	ducking	dreamed	dogtown	dollier	dunnage	droshky
dead-pan	decrial	dreamer	dogbolt	dulcify	donnart	diorite
dead-pay	diction	dye-wood	dog-crab	Dalilah	donnert	dioxide
diagrid	decrier	die-work	doggrel	Delilah	dentary	D-notice
diadrom	dacoity	dye-work	dogtrot	dilemma	dingbat	dooming
diagram	deckled	diedral	digital	delimit	donnerd	dronish
dead-set	decolor	deep-sea	Dogstar	delenda	Dantean	diorism
drastic	ducally	dressed	degauss	deltoid	dungeon	drookit
dratted	decimal	dresser	diglyph	dulcose	danseur	droukit
draftee	decuman	dyester	dehisce	delapse	donkeys	doodler
drafter	decanal	die-away	dribble	deliria	données	droplet
draft-ox	decency	doe-eyed	djibbah	dulosis	donnert	door-man
dialyse	dichord	defraud	dribber	dulotic	densely	doormat
dialyze	decrown	deflate	dribbly	dilated	duncery	drowned

dvornik	darkish	dissent	discuss	dovekie	day-coal	embroil
drowner	dervish	distent	disgust	devalue	dry-foot	embloom
drop-net	derrick	dishful	disrupt	devolve	daystar	embrown
dromond	dornick	dislimb	disavow	divulge	dry-cure	embargo
duotone	deraign	desmine	distyle	develop	dry-eyed	embased
drop-out	dernier	despise	detrain	devilet	dizzard	embaste
duopoly	darbies	despite	detract	dovelet	dazedly	embosom
dropped	dirtily	destine	dittany	devilry	dizzily	embassy
dropple	duramen	discide	datable	diviner	dazzler	embathe
dropper	dirempt	dislike	Dyticus	devious	dozenth	embound
deontic	derange	dashing	dutiful	diverge	emanate	embrute
dioptre	durance	dishing	ditcher	diverse	étalage	embowed
diopter	dariole	distich	dotting	divorce	exarate	embowel
drouthy	dortour	duskish	dottled	devisee	emanant	embower
droguet	dirt-pie	dislink	détente	devisal	épatant	embayld
doorway	dart-sac	distill	détenue	divisim	ébauche	embryon
deprave	duresse	dislimn	detinue	deviser	eparchy	embryos
dupable	dastard	dossier	duteous	devisor	exarchy	enchafe
dépêche	disband	dismiss	dataria	divisor	étagère	enchase
Diptera	discard	destiny	deterge	devoted	evangel	enclave
deplete	dismayd	duskily	dottrel	devotee	edaphic	escuage
depress	discage	dustily	detrude	dyvoury	elative	euclase
deprive	discase	disally	datival	dew-fall	evasive	exclave
dip-pipe	disease	display	drubbed	downa-do	examine	encharm
dipping	disfame	dustman	drumble	dewlapt	evanish	exclaim
dopping	dispace	dyspnea	druidic	down-bed	epaxial	enchain
depaint	disrate	desmoid	daunder	dowable	etacism	enclasp
dappled	distaff	despond	douleia	downbow	elation	enchant
dipolar	disbark	discoid	douceur	dowager	enation	etchant
diploma	dismask	discord	daubery	dawning	erasion	encraty
diploid	dispark	disload	doucely	dowdily	evasion	excudit
dapsone	disrank	dishome	drugged	dawdler	edacity	excreta
deplore	dismayl	dispone	drudger	dew-claw	egality	excrete
diphone	disdain	dispose	drugger	dawn-man	epaulet	encheer
dipnoan	distain	disrobe	drugget	dewanny	enarmed	escheat
diplont	despair	disyoke	dauphin	dowlney	epagoge	excheat
dip-trap	descant	despoil	doughty	dew-pond	enamour	eccrine
deposal	discant	disform	doucine	dawcock	example	escribe
deposer	dismast	disgown	dourine	dew-worm	epacrid	eucaine
deposit	dispart	dishorn	daubing	dew-drop	etaerio	eucrite
deplume	distant	disjoin	Drusian	dewfull	epacris	etching
diptych	disable	disport	drucken	dextral	elastic	escalop
dorlach	dust-bin	dispost	drunken	dextran	exalted	escolar
dorhawk	disobey	disroot	drumlin	dextrin	elastin	encomia
darrain	disedge	distort	doubler	dry-wash	enactor	encloud
darrayn	dysodil	dyslogy	doublet	daymark	exacter	enclose
dormant	dos-à-dos	dasypod	double-u	dry-salt	exactor	escroll
durmast	descend	dust-pan	drummed	dryades	exactly	escapee
dirt-bed	dispend	Dasypus	drummer	dry-cell	erasure	escaper
durable	distend	dash-pot	diurnal	day-peep	evacuee	excurse
durably	disleaf	dysuria	dhurrie	dryness	embraid	excerpt
derider	disleal	dysuric	doubted	drybeat	emblaze	excusal
dareful	dishelm	deserve	daunton	dry-shod	embrace	excited
dernful	discern	dish-rag	doubter	daytime	embrave	exciton
direful	discerp	desirer	duumvir	day-girl	emblema	exciter
dureful	descent	destroy	Deutzia	dry-fist	embread	excitor
darshan	dessert	disturb	deviate	day-lily	embrewe	exclude
dirtied	discept	dasyure	deviant	daysman	ebbless	encrust
dormice	disgest	discure	dovecot	doyenne	embogue	each-way
darling	disject	diseuse	divider	daylong	ebb-tide	endgame
darning	disnest	disjune	devoice	day-book	ecbolic	endlang
darting	disseat	dispute	devling	day-work	embolic	endways
Dorking	dissect	distune	doveish	dry-dock	embolus	endless

endogen	eyebolt	engloom	epidote	erotism	espouse	essayed
end-ship	exempla	engross	epigone	emotion	empower	enstyle
endwise	exemple	egg-cosy	episode	erosion	empayre	essoyne
eddying	eye-spot	engorge	epitome	Etonian	enquire	eustyle
eidolon	epeirid	eagerly	epigoni	exomion	esquire	essayer
endemic	exedrae	eightvo	epizoan	ebonist	enquiry	estrade
endlong	eye-drop	ergates	epizoon	egotist	ebriate	entrail
endmost	eyebrow	ephebic	epigons	elogist	earbash	entrain
endorse	emersed	ephebos	epigram	Elohist	earmark	entrant
endarch	erepsin	ephebus	ekistic	exodist	errable	extract
enderon	Eleatic	exhibit	eristic	enounce	earache	extrait
endiron	erected	ethical	emitted	ecology	earldom	estuary
endurer	edental	echidna	epistle	economy	earless	eatable
elderly	electro	ephedra	edictal	enomoty	earnest	enticer
end-user	ejector	exhedra	evictor	étourdi	ebriety	estrepe
ecdysis	elector	echoise	epicure	ego-trip	enraged	extreme
eidetic	erecter	echoing	Erinyes	elocute	earthen	entreat
endowed	erector	echoism	epigyny	evolute	ear-shot	estreat
endower	eventer	echoist	enjoyer	ecotype	earthly	extreat
endozoa	erectly	echelon	ellwand	emplace	errhine	entwine
enemata	execute	exhumer	eelfare	emplane	earning	estoile
ewe-lamb	elfland	enhance	eulogia	expiate	earring	estrich
emerald	enframe	ethanol	ellagic	empeach	earpick	entrism
elevate	effable	echinus	eclogue	explain	earlier	entrist
eye-bath	enflesh	ethmoid	enlight	explant	earplug	entwist
eyelash	elf-shot	ethiops	eilding	empyema	earflap	entomic
eye-wash	enfiled	échappé	erl-king	empress	eirenic	entente
eyeball	effulge	etheric	eelworm	express	enrange	extense
elegant	enfelon	exhaust	eelpout	empight	étrenne	extinct
elenchi	effendi	emicate	eclipse	emptied	Euronet	entrold
éperdue	elfhood	emirate	ellipse	empaire	ear-bone	entropy
exegete	enfeoff	epilate	enlarge	emprise	ear-hole	eutropy
ewe-neck	elf-bolt	evirate	enliven	espying	ebriose	ectopia
eye-beam	efforce	evitate	esloyne	emption	earlock	ectopic
elevens	enforce	epitaph	ermelin	emptier	euripus	entopic
eyeless	England	epicarp	ermined	empties	Etruria	ectypal
element	enguard	epitaxy	ennoble	enprint	eardrum	enteric
Everest	egg-case	epicede	eanling	expulse	eardrop	Euterpe
energic	engrace	epicene	evocate	expanse	erratic	externe
energid	engrave	epigene	exocarp	expense	erratum	enteral
epergne	engraff	epigeal	exogamy	expunge	Euratom	enthral
exergue	engrail	epigean	écorché	empanel	enround	enteron
Erewhon	engrain	eminent	exordia	expunct	enrough	enterer
eye-shot	engrasp	evident	erotema	explode	enriven	ectasis
elegiac	eggmass	exigent	eroteme	explore	enslave	entasis
eyeliad	engraft	epithem	exoderm	exploit	ensnare	entotic
elegise	ergodic	epithet	erodent	euphony	ensnarl	extatic
emetine	Euglena	edified	esotery	euphory	enstamp	entêtée
eremite	egghead	edifice	emonges	eupepsy	ecstasy	entitle
evening	egg-cell	erinite	emongst	emporia	eustacy	enthuse
emeriti	engaged	elitism	epochal	empiric	eustasy	extrude
ewe-milk	Engager	epicism	erotica	expired	enshell	entrust
eye-wink	egg-bird	edition	exotica	emperce	eastern	estival
E-region	erg-nine	elision	ebonise	euphroe	ensteep	estover
etesian	English	edifier	ebonite	expurge	ensweep	eutexia
elegist	engulph	épicier	ecocide	esparto	easeful	ecthyma
eye-flap	egg-plum	elitist	egotise	emperor	exscind	entayle
eternal	egg-flip	epicist	emotive	exposed	easting	ectozoa
eye-hole	Eugenia	exility	epoxide	exposal	ensuing	entozoa
eyesore	eugenic	etiolin	erosive	exposer	eastlin	educate
erelong	eugenol	epizoic	egotism	empathy	epsilon	emulate
eyehook	enginer	ericoid	elogium	expound	essence	epurate
emerods	englobe		erodium	emplume	easy-osy	exudate

exurbia	flaring	fuchsia	flea-pit	feigned	filmish	fennish
equable	flaying	focused	fleuron	faience	fullish	fineish
exurban	foaming	fucused	fleerer	friande	falsism	Finnish
equably	framing	focuses	Fuehrer	frijole	falsies	fancier
Equidae	fraying	fucuses	fleuret	faitour	falsify	funnies
elusive	Flavian	faceted	freesia	flipper	falsity	funnily
erudite	franion	facture	fretsaw	fripper	filemot	finikin
exuviae	flacker	factual	fretted	friarly	Falange	fangled
eluvial	flanker	fadable	fletton	Friesic	Felinae	fondler
exuvial	flacket	fidibus	fleetly	frisson	felonry	fontlet
eluvium	flasket	fadedly	flexure	fainted	foliole	finally
elusion	frankly	fidgety	freeway	flitted	foliose	finance
elution	flatlet	fadaise	freezer	fritted	fulsome	fin-toed
écuelle	frailly	faddish	fifteen	flitter	fulgour	fungoid
equally	frailty	faddism	fifthly	foister	fulvous	finnock
equinia	flannel	fideism	fifties	fritter	fall-out	fungous
equinal	fraenum	faddist	foggage	faintly	felwort	funeral
equinox	flannen	fuddled	fog-bank	failure	fold-out	findram
emulous	flaunty	fiddler	fog-lamp	frisure	full-out	finesse
elusory	flavone	fuddler	fogydom	friture	felspar	finnsko
equerry	flavour	fiddley	fig-leaf	flivver	Filaria	fanatic
épuisée	featous	fade-out	fog-bell	fairway	fulcrum	fenitar
emulsin	flapped	fedarie	fogless	friezed	filasse	froward
emulsor	frappée	federal	figment	frizzed	falcula	flotage
eductor	frampal	fedayee	faggery	frizzle	folkway	flowage
equator	flapper	fee-farm	figgery	frizzly	filazer	footage
eevning	frantic	free-arm	fig-bird	falbala	fumbler	flotant
envying	flatted	freebie	fagging	falcade	famulus	feodary
envelop	fracted	flea-bag	figging	falcate	feminal	footbar
envenom	flatten	fleeced	fogyish	faldage	fimbria	frogbit
envious	feaster	fleecer	fogyism	fellate	Fumaria	footboy
environ	flatter	Frenchy	fuguist	filiate	femoral	floccus
envault	Fraktur	fielded	foggily	foliage	fumette	flooded
enwheel	feature	freedom	fugally	foliate	femiter	fronded
Elysium	frazzle	fielder	foghorn	fullage	fomites	Floréal
Elysian	fibbery	fretful	figwort	folk-art	fenland	floreat
elytral	fubbery	fledged	figured	fallacy	fanfare	flowery
elytrum	febrile	freight	fig-tree	Félibre	finback	foolery
elytron	fabling	fleshed	figural	filabeg	finnack	feoffee
enzymic	fibbing	freshen	fagotto	filibeg	fantail	foodful
Elzevir	fabliau	flesher	fighter	felucca	fantasm	feoffer
frabbit	fabular	fresher	fahlerz	filacer	funfair	feoffor
flaccid	fibular	freshet	fahlore	Filices	fantast	flogged
fiancée	fibroma	fleshly	frigate	Felidae	fondant	frogged
flat-cap	fibroid	freshly	friable	filmdom	fantasy	froughy
fratchy	fibrose	flexile	fribble	fulness	finable	flowing
flag-day	fibroin	feeding	Frisbee	filbert	funèbre	fooling
flare-up	fibrous	feeling	flip-dog	fulgent	funicle	footing
frame-up	Fabergé	fleeing	flinder	fullest	finical	foolish
flâneur	fibster	Fleming	fair-day	falsely	finicky	florist
fratery	factive	freeing	friseur	full-fed	fanteeg	foot-jaw
fearful	fictile	Flemish	fritfly	falafel	fannell	frocked
flaffer	fictive	flexion	fringed	felafel	finless	foozler
flamfew	fucking	fierily	frigger	fall-guy	finagle	froglet
flagged	faction	flecked	flighty	filcher	finched	footman
flanged	fiction	freckle	failing	full-hot	fancied	footmen
flaught	faculae	flecker	fairing	felsite	fanzine	frogman
fraught	facular	freckly	foiling	fulmine	fen-fire	flounce
feather	faculty	fuelled	fairish	falling	fanning	frounce
flasher	faceman	fueller	fairily	felting	fencing	footpad
flavine	façonné	feedlot	flicker	filling	finding	floored
fragile	face-off	freeman	frisker	folding	funding	floorer
flaming	factory	freemen	frisket	falsish	funning	footrot

floosie	fernery	farmost	fat-face	fluoric	Glaucus	grasper
flotsam	ferrety	furrowy	futhark	foudrie	grandma	grampus
frowsty	forgery	firepan	fetiche	fourses	grandpa	gnarred
fronted	furmety	firepot	fat-head	Flustra	gladded	glairin
frosted	firefly	forepaw	fatness	fructed	grandad	grassum
floatel	forager	fir-tree	fitness	fruited	guarded	glassen
frontal	foregut	foreran	fattest	fouetté	grandee	grasser
foot-ton	farthel	forerun	fitment	frustum	grandam	grantee
fronton	farther	Fortran	fateful	fluster	gladden	grafter
floater	further	foresee	fatigue	flutter	gladdon	granter
floruit	Formica	foresaw	fitchée	fruiter	graddan	grantor
footway	farcied	foresay	futchel	feu-duty	grandly	ghastly
floozie	ferried	foretop	fitchet	foveate	go-ahead	giantly
foppery	ferrite	firstly	fitchew	five-bar	goateed	giantry
fopling	fertile	farruca	fatling	foveola	glareal	granule
foppish	forgive	formula	fatting	foveole	gradely	gravure
fermata	forpine	furcula	fitting	fivepin	grapery	guayule
forlana	furtive	ferrule	fattish	fevered	gravely	gradual
furlana	farcing	fortune	fitlier	fewness	goat-fig	glaived
farrand	farding	ferrugo	fatuity	fawning	gladful	gabbard
forward	farming	forever	fettler	fowling	granfer	gabnash
fardage	firring	faraway	fatally	fox-tail	grayfly	gabbart
ferrate	forging	forayer	Fatimid	fixable	goat-god	giblets
forbade	forming	fusible	futhorc	fixedly	granger	gabfest
forgave	furring	fast-day	fetlock	foxship	gnathic	gubbins
formate	furbish	fish-day	futhork	foxhole	graphic	gabelle
forsake	furnish	fisheye	futtock	fox-trap	gnathal	Gobelin
furcate	fermium	Fastens	fatuous	fox-trot	Graphis	gabbler
furnace	fermion	fashery	fat-lute	fixture	gracile	gobbler
fire-arm	foreign	fishery	foulard	fox-hunt	gradine	gibbose
forearm	farrier	fish-fag	fougade	fox-evil	granite	gibbous
forwarn	furrier	fishful	four-ale	flybane	guanine	goburra
farrago	forties	fistful	foumart	fly-half	gearing	godward
forzato	farcify	fish-god	feudary	flyable	glaring	gadwall
forfair	fortify	fishgig	f-number	flyleaf	glazing	goddamn
furfair	furmity	fascine	fluidic	flybelt	grating	Gadidae
farrant	forelie	festive	fluidal	flyting	graving	godhead
formant	forsloe	fissile	foulder	fly-kick	grazing	godsend
firebug	foreleg	fissive	founder	fly-flap	goatish	gudgeon
fire-bar	fortlet	fasting	foundry	flyblow	guarish	goddess
firebox	forslow	fishing	fourgon	fly-slow	gharial	godless
forecar	forelay	fastish	flushed	fayence	glacial	godship
faradic	fireman	fossick	flusher	flybook	gradino	godlike
firedog	foramen	fascial	foughty	flyboat	glacier	gadding
faraday	foreman	fascism	flutina	fly-trap	glazier	gadling
foreday	foremen	fashion	fluxive	flyover	grazier	godling
fore-end	fire-new	fission	feuding	flyaway	gladius	giddily
forfend	fir-wood	fushion	fluting	fizzgig	gratify	godlily
forlend	fir-cone	fustian	faucial	fizzing	gravity	gadsman
forlese	forbode	fascist	fluvial	fuzzily	grackle	gude-man
fur-seal	forbore	fishify	Fauvism	guaraná	glaiket	godhood
farceur	fordone	fussily	fluxion	gradate	glaikit	gadroon
forbear	forgone	fist-law	faunist	gramash	gnarled	godroon
farness	forlore	fish-net	Fauvist	Guaraní	Grallae	gude-son
forceps	furlong	fish-oil	feudist	guarani	grammar	godetia
ferment	forsook	festoon	flutist	guanaco	grained	gregale
fervent	fern-owl	fuscous	frutify	gramary	grannie	grenade
forfeit	forlorn	fuss-pot	flunkey	granary	grapnel	guerdon
forhent	forworn	fusarol	flummox	grabbed	grannam	guereza
forlent	furioso	fistula	fluence	grabble	grainer	Guelfic
fornent	fervour	fissure	fluency	grab-bag	glamour	gleeful
forwent	ferrous	fish-way	four-oar	grabber	grapple	greyhen
farmery	furious		frumple	gearbox	graupel	Grecise

greyish	glimmer	gallows	gin-fizz	giocoso	gas-well	grummet
gremial	grinned	galopin	ganglia	globous	gashful	glucose
Grecism	Guignol	galipot	gantlet	geogony	gustful	grumose
Grecian	gripped	galatea	gunplay	geology	Gasthof	grumous
gherkin	glimpse	gelatin	gondola	groupie	gasahol	glue-pot
grey-lag	gripple	gummata	gun-lock	grouper	gasohol	glutted
gremlin	gripper	gemmate	gunroom	grogram	gas-fire	gruntle
gleeman	goitred	gambado	gunboat	Glossic	gas-lime	glutton
greenth	griesie	gymnast	gunport	glossal	gas-pipe	grutten
gleaner	gainsay	game-bag	genappe	good-son	gasping	gaulter
greenly	griesly	gemsbok	genipap	glosser	gas-ring	grunter
glenoid	gristle	gombeen	generic	grouser	gassing	gauntly
glebous	glisten	gemmery	gangrel	grossly	gosling	gauntry
gregory	glister	gumshoe	general	glottic	gushing	gavotte
grecque	glitter	gummite	genista	gnostic	gaskins	gowland
ghessed	grifter	gemming	geneses	glottal	gaseity	gownboy
greisen	gritter	gumming	genesis	glottis	gossipy	gownman
greaser	gristly	gampish	genetic	ghostly	Gosplan	gowaned
guesser	guipure	gimmick	genette	globule	gas-coke	grysbok
greisly	griever	gambier	genital	gopuram	gas-coal	gayness
greeted	Gaikwar	gambist	genitor	garland	gossoon	grysely
greaten	grizzle	gamelan	Genevan	gormand	gaseous	glyphic
guesten	grizzly	gambler	gangway	gurnard	gastric	gryphon
greater	goliard	Geminid	genizah	garbage	gisarme	gwyniad
greatly	golland	gamboge	globate	germane	gas-trap	glycine
geebung	galeate	gammock	good-bye	germain	gesture	gaysome
greaves	gallate	gumboil	grow-bag	gardant	gas-buoy	glycose
Gaekwar	Goliath	gummous	gnocchi	gyrocar	guttate	guy-rope
gaffing	gallant	gumboot	grouchy	gerbera	gytrash	goyisch
gagging	galabea	gambrel	geordie	gorsedd	gittern	gryesly
goggled	galabia	gomeral	geoidal	garment	gutless	glyptic
giggler	gold-bug	gomeril	good-dcn	giraffe	gutcher	gizzard
goggler	golf-bag	gumdrop	good-day	garpike	göthite	gazeful
G-agents	galoche	gametic	good-e'en	girding	getting	gazelle
gagster	giltcup	gametal	gooleys	garfish	G-string	guzzler
gahnite	gelidly	gemmule	grosert ·	garnish	gutting	gazooka
Gehenna	goldeye	gunnage	geodesy	girlish	Gothick	gazette
guisard	galleon	gunwale	geogeny	Gordian	gateleg	heal-all
grimace	gulleys	gingall	goosery	Gordius	gateman	huanaco
guidage	gilbert	gang-bye	grocery	gorilla	gateway	hoarder
gribble	gallery	gonidia	georgic	girdled	getaway	heathen
grieced	gullery	gonadic	gloried	garbler	goulash	heather
griddle	gall-fly	gonidic	glowing	girdler	glutaei	hyacine
gliadin	gullied	gunnera	glozing	gyrally	gourami	hyaline
glidder	Gallice	Genoese	growing	gyronny	grubbed	hyalite
grinder	gallise	ginseng	gnomish	girlond	grubble	heading
guilder	galling	genteel	goodish	garvock	grumble	healing
guildry	gelding	gingery	Grobian	gorcock	grubber	heaping
grisely	gelling	ginnery	Grotian	garboil	grumbly	hearing
gainful	gilding	gunnery	Grolier	gorsoon	gouache	heating
griffin	golfing	gingham	goolies	gorcrow	Gruyère	heaving
griffon	goldish	ginshop	glorify	girasol	gluteal	heavier
ghilgai	gullish	gunship	goofily	girosol	gluteus	headily
guichet	gallium	gunshot	Goorkha	garotte	gaudery	heavily
gwiniad	gilion	gentile	grockle	gestate	goutfly	hoarily
gliding	gullies	genuine	growler	gas-mask	gruffly	hearken
griping	galliot	gunfire	goodman	gas-tank	gaudgie	headman
guiding	galilee	ganging	grommet	goshawk	glucina	hyaloid
grimily	galumph	ginning	groined	gas-main	gauging	headrig
griskin	galanga	gunning	grown-up	Gestapo	Gaulish	hoarsen
grilled	Galenic	gingili	good-now	gas-lamp	grunion	headset
grisled	gall-nut	gentian	globoid	gestalt	gaudily	hearsay
ghillie	galloon	Günzian	globose	gestant	gourmet	hearted

hearten	huff-cap	holy-ale	hallyon	hangman	hepster	herdman
healthy	huffish	hallali	hummaum	hanuman	hipster	horn-nut
heartly	hafnium	hold-all	hymnary	hen-toed	hypoxia	heronry
headway	huffily	hollaho	humidor	hand-off	hypoxic	hardoke
hoatzin	hafflin	helibus	humidly	hen-coop	harmala	herbose
Hebraic	Haggada	halibut	himself	handout	herbage	hormone
hobnail	haggard	holibut	humogen	hangout	hersall	hordock
habdabs	hogward	hell-box	homager	hanaper	herbary	harpoon
hobodom	hog-mane	Halacha	hem-line	hundred	hirable	harbour
hobbish	hogwash	helical	hemming	handsel	hornbug	herbous
Hobbism	hogback	half-cap	humming	hunt's-up	hurl-bat	harmost
hoboism	hag-seed	helices	hymning	handset	herdboy	harmony
Hobbian	hag-weed	hell-cat	hymnist	handsaw	hyraces	hard-pan
Hobbist	hog-weed	Helodea	homolog	honesty	haricot	harn-pan
hobbler	hygiene	halidom	homelyn	henotic	hirudin	hard-run
hob-a-nob	hog-deer	holydam	hamular	Honiton	herself	heretic
hebenon	Highers	half-day	hamulus	honeyed	Hordeum	hirstie
habitué	highest	holiday	humbles	hoop-ash	hordein	heritor
habitat	hoggery	halberd	hominid	hoosgow	harness	hirsute
hectare	high-fed	Hellene	hymenal	hoodlum	herdess	herb-tea
hackbut	high-hat	Hulsean	homonym	hoodman	harvest	hard-won
Hock-day	hag-ride	halvers	humanly	hoolock	horrent	horizon
hackery	hogging	halbert	hemiola	hook-pin	hartely	husband
hacking	hugging	helpful	hemione	hoof-rot	harmful	hastate
hack-log	hagfish	halogen	hammock	hop-yard	hornful	hostage
hackler	haggish	halling	hemlock	heptane	hurtful	hushaby
heckler	highish	halting	hommock	hip-bath	hard-got	Hasidic
hacklet	hoggish	helping	hummock	hopsack	harshen	has-been
hackney	hog-fish	hilding	hymnody	hop-oast	hership	hostess
hickory	hoggish	holding	Homeric	hop-head	hard-hit	hosiery
hocused	Hygeian	hulking	Homerid	hapless	harshly	hospice
hack-saw	hog-skin	hylding	humeral	hip-belt	harried	hostile
hicatee	hog-plum	hellish	humoral	hopeful	hurried	Hussite
hachure	haggler	holmium	humdrum	hypogea	harmine	huswife
hiccupy	higgler	hallian	humerus	hip-shot	heroine	hissing
hydrate	high-low	hallion	Hamitic	hopbind	heroise	hosting
hydrant	highman	hellier	hamster	hopbine	hircine	husking
hydride	highmen	hyloist	Hamburg	hoplite	harling	hashish
hedging	hoghood	Halakah	Homburg	hop-vine	herling	hessian
hidling	hog-nose	halflin	humbuzz	happing	herring	hastily
hidlins	hagdown	heliman	Hansard	hipping	hirling	huskily
hidalga	hugeous	hillmen	hennaed	hopping	horning	hostler
huddled	hagbolt	halimot	henbane	hippish	horsing	hustler
hidalgo	high-set	hellova	Hungary	haptics	hurling	hoseman
hedonic	high-top	helcoid	handbag	happily	hardish	hosanna
hydroid	highway	half-one	handcar	hop-flea	hornish	hose-net
hadrome	huitain	hillock	hangdog	hip-knob	hernial	histoid
haddock	haircut	holm-oak	henpeck	ha'pence	heroism	histone
hideous	heirdom	helipad	hunkers	ha'penny	hornito	hassock
hydrous	hair-eel	half-pay	hennery	haploid	harrier	history
hideout	heiress	holesom	handful	hypnoid	hurdies	histrio
hydroxy	heigh-ho	hilltop	hand-gun	hip-bone	harpist	Heshvan
hederal	haining	holster	hind-gut	hop-pole	herbist	hatband
hydatid	hair-net	halitus	hen-wife	hypnone	hornist	hatrack
Hieland	hair-oil	helotry	hanging	hip-roof	hardily	hetmans
hoe-cake	heinous	helluva	hinging	hip-lock	horrify	hatable
Hielant	hairpin	halavah	hunting	hip-gout	Harijan	hetaera
hueless	heister	half-wit	Hunnish	hop-tree	hare-lip	hothead
heedful	Heimweh	halfway	handlly	hap'orth	harslet	hatless
heeling	hijinks	hallway	handjar	hypural	herblet	hotness
hoedown	halyard	helixes	handled	heparin	hornlet	hutment
haemony	holland	halcyon	hindleg	hyperon	horn-mad	
heel-tap	half-ape		handler	hepatic		

hateful	imagery	inditer	inglobe	immerge	imprint	intoner
hatchel	irately	indexer	ingrown	immerse	impulse	introld
hatcher	imagine	indexes	ingroup	immoral	impinge	introit
hitcher	isatine	ikebana	ingesta	ismatic	impanel	icteric
hatchet	imagism	Iceland	ingowes	innyard	implode	interne
hotshot	itacism	iterate	Ishmael	ignoble	implore	inthral
hetaira	Icarian	icepack	ichabod	ignobly	improve	interim
Hittite	idalian	ice-fall	inhabit	ionomer	impious	icterus
hatting	Iranian	inexact	inhibit	innings	imperil	ictuses
hitting	Italian	iterant	ichthic	igneous	impasse	intrude
hutting	imagist	iceberg	ichthys	innerve	impaste	intrust
hottish	Italiot	ice-fern	ichnite	ignorer	impasto	inulase
hattock	inanity	ice-belt	inhaler	innards	imposer	Iguvine
hotfoot	isagoge	ice-show	inhuman	igniter	imputer	invader
Hotspur	inaptly	ice-bird	inherce	isobare	impetus	invoice
hot-trod	iracund	itemise	inherit	isobase	impound	inveigh
hatfuls	inboard	ice-fish	in-house	isolate	impavid	invalid
haulage	imbrast	ice-pick	inhaust	isobath	inquere	involve
hautboy	imbiber	ice-rink	imitate	isogamy	inquest	invenit
heureka	inbreed	ice-hill	irisate	isomere	inquire	invious
hauberk	inbreak	Iberian	imitant	isogeny	inquiet	inverse
hauteur	inbeing	irenics	Isiacal	isochor	inquiry	inviter
haughty	inbring	ice-blue	Irideae	ivoried	inqilab	invexed
housing	in-built	ice-floe	irideal	iconise	Israeli	inweave
heurism	imbrown	ideally	iciness	idolise	ivresse	inwards
haulier	imburse	ice-cold	Irisher	ironise	inscape	inwoven
haunted	inburst	ice-worm	Irishry	isoline	insnare	idyllic
haunter	imbosom	ice-boat	iridise	ironing	instate	ivy-bush
hive-bee	imbathe	ice-foot	initial	idolism	install	joannes
havened	imbrute	ice-spar	iridial	idolist	instant	jealous
have-not	imbower	ice-free	iridium	ironist	issuant	jobless
haveour	inchase	inearth	iridian	ivorist	Insecta	jobbery
haviour	Inclasp	Isegrim	idiotic	ipomoea	insecty	jibbing
haverel	incubus	inertia	idiotcy	isodoma	insider	jobbing
hawkbit	incudes	identic	injoint	Isopoda	instead	jubilee
howbeit	incline	ileitis	injelly	Iron-ore	inshell	jib-boom
hawking	ischial	ineptly	injunct	isotone	inspect	jib-door
howling	ischium	inertly	injurer	isotope	insofar	jackass
hawkish	incense	ice-cube	ilkaday	Isodont	insigne	Jacobin
hawbuck	inconie	inflame	ink-feed	isokont	insight	jacobus
however	inconnu	inflate	in-kneed	isonomy	inspire	jackdaw
howdy-do	inclose	infract	inkwell	isotopy	inswing	jacchus
hexadic	inchpin	infidel	inkling	iron-pan	instill	jocular
hexagon	incurve	infield	irksome	isogram	insulse	jackman
hexapla	incised	inflect	inkhorn	isotron	insulin	jacamar
hexapod	incisor	inflict	ill-fame	isoetes	insular	jacinth
hexarch	inciter	infulae	illicit	isotype	insanie	jaconet
hayband	include	infanta	illness	isohyet	insinew	jackpot
hayward	incrust	infante	illegal	implate	inshore	Jacuzzi®
hey-pass	indrawn	infancy	inlying	inphase	insooth	Jeddart
hayseed	indraft	inforce	ill-will	impeach	insipid	jadedly
haywire	indicia	inferno	Islamic	impearl	insurer	Judaean
hayrick	indican	infarct	isleman	implant	insculp	jadeite
hay-bote	inducer	infuser	illapse	impresa	inspyre	Judaise
haycock	indices	infaust	ill-bred	implead	intrant	Judaism
hayfork	indwell	ingrate	ill-used	implete	intreat	Judaist
hayloft	indwelt	ingrain	idlesse	imprese	integer	judoist
heyduck	indulge	ingraft	ill-luck	impregn	intwine	j'adoube
huzzaed	indoors	ingress	ill-turn	impress	in-thing	jeepers
hazelly	in-depth	ingoing	inlayer	imprest	intwist	jeering
igarapé	indorse	ingulph	Ismaili	impiety	intimae	Juglans
imamate	ioduret	ingénue	iambist	implied	isthmus	jaggery
in-and-in	indusia	ingener	immense	impaint	intense	jaghire

jagging	Jenkins	Jezebel	knitted	knowing	leafbud	Lockist
jigging	jangler	jazzily	knittle	knock-on	leap-day	luckily
jogging	jingler	jazzman	knitter	knock-up	llanero	lock-jaw
jugging	jinglet	khanate	kajawah	knocker	loathed	locular
jiggish	junkman	khaddar	kakodyl	kroo-man	leather	loculus
juggins	jannock	knavery	kikumon	knotted	loather	locally
jigajig	juniper	khalifa	kellaut	knotter	loathly	lace-man
jigajog	janitor	kyanise	kilobar	kippage	leading	lockman
joggled	jonquil	kyanite	kilobit	kip-shop	leafing	locoman
juggler	janizar	knavish	killcow	kip-skin	leaning	lacinia
jugular	jeopard	klavier	killdee	kurbash	leaping	laconic
jog-trot	jeofail	knacker	kiln-dry	kursaal	leasing	Lychnic
jugfuls	jookery	knapped	kolkhoz	Kurhaus	leaving	lacunae
Johnian	jap-silk	knapple	Kallima	Kartell	loading	licence
johnnie	Japonic	knapper	killing	kermess	loafing	license
Jehovah	Jupiter	knarred	killick	kirmess	loaning	lacunal
joinder	jury-box	khamsin	killjoy	kerygma	leaflet	lacunar
joinery	Jericho	Kabbala	kalends	kerogen	learned	lychnis
joining	juridic	kebbock	killock	Karaite	learner	lock-nut
Jainism	jarring	kibitka	kiloton	kernite	leasowe	lucency
jointed	jerking	kebbuck	Kalmuck	Karling	lead-out	lactose
jointer	Jersian	kibbutz	kamichi	karting	Liassic	lich-owl
jointly	jurally	kachcha	kamseen	kirking	liaison	lockout
jejunum	jarkman	kuchcha	Kommers	kernish	leaguer	lycopod
ju-jitsu	juryman	kacheri	kemping	Kurdish	libbard	Lacerta
juke-box	jurymen	kick-off	kimboed	karakul	lubbard	lucarne
jellaba	jargoon	kidding	kampong	kirtled	labiate	lucerne
jellied	jerquer	kidling	kamerad	keramic	librate	lockram
jellify	jarfuls	Kaddish	kumquat	kirimon	library	locusta
jollify	jessant	kiddier	Kannada	Koranic	lubfish	lichtly
jollily	jessamy	kiddies	kingcup	Karenni	Librium®	licitly
jollity	jaspery	kid-skin	kingdom	keratin	labella	Lactuca
jalapic	jestful	keelage	kinless	kirkton	lobelia	lecture
jalapin	jasmine	knee-cap	kinchin	Kashmir	lobular	lecturn
jaloppy	jussive	kneader	kinship	kestrel	lobulus	lacquer
jalouse	justice	knevell	king-hit	kithara	lobelet	lace-ups
jamdani	jesting	khediva	kenning	kitschy	labroid	lyceums
jampani	justify	khedive	Kentish	katydid	labrose	lacquey
jamadar	Jethart	keeling	Kennick	kitteny	lobworm	lichway
jemadar	jitters	keeping	Kantism	kitchen	lobiped	ladybug
jemidar	jittery	kneeled	Kantian	ketchup	liberal	ladycow
jambeau	jotting	kremlin	Kantist	kitling	labarum	lidless
jambeux	jutting	kneeler	kindler	kathode	liberty	laddery
Jamaica	jetfoil	keelman	kinglet	kit-boat	lobster	ladyfly
jambiya	joukery	keepnet	kinsman	ketosis	lac-lake	ludship
jamming	journal	knee-pan	kinfolk	Kotytto	lactase	Luddite
jumping	journey	keelson	king-pin	knubble	lactate	lyddite
jambier	jauntee	knees-up	kindred	khutbah	lockage	lodging
jumpily	jauntie	Knesset	king-rod	knubbly	lack-all	ladyish
jump-jet	javelin	koftgar	kenosis	koumiss	lucidly	ladyism
jumelle	juvenal	kufiyah	kinesis	knuckle	Lycaena	Luddism
jumbler	jawfall	kagoule	kenotic	knurled	lacteal	ladykin
jambone	Jew's-ear	Kuh-horn	kinetic	key-desk	lectern	ladanum
jump-off	jewfish	klipdas	know-all	keyless	lechery	ladrone
jambool	jewelry	Krishna	knobbed	key-seat	lockful	leeward
jim-crow	jawbone	kainite	knobble	key-ring	lucifer	laetare
jumbuck	jawhole	Krilium®	khotbah	key-cold	lucigen	lee-gage
juncate	jaw-foot	klinker	khotbeh	keyhole	lacking	lee-lane
January	jaywalk	knicker	knobber	keynote	licking	lie-abed
jankers	Joycean	keitloa	knobbly	krypsis	lochial	liefest
Janeite	joyless	krimmer	kroo-boy	krypton	lection	lievest
jinjili	joy-ride	kail-pat	know-how	leafage	Lockian	leechee
Jungian	joyance	kail-pot	kaoline	leakage	Locrian	leering

lie-down	Lakshmi	lantana	lioncel	losable	leuchen	meander
lifeful	lakelet	laniard	Lyomeri	listeth	leughen	moanful
leftism	lollard	lanyard	lioness	listful	laugher	meat-fly
leftist	Lallans	lindane	loosely	lustful	lauwine	myalgia
loftily	lullaby	lineage	loofful	lasagna	leucine	myalgic
left-off	lalling	lineate	lyophil	lasagne	leucite	Moabite
lift-off	lemmata	linkage	leonine	lashing	louring	meaning
laggard	Limnaea	linsang	lionise	lasting	loudish	myalism
lignage	Lymnaea	long-ago	looking	lisping	loutish	measled
luggage	lombard	laniary	looning	listing	lousily	measles
lugsail	lamb-ale	longbow	looping	luskish	leucoma	miasmic
legible	limbate	linkboy	lionism	lustick	louvred	miasmal
legibly	lumbang	linocut	Laotian	lesbian	livable	meal-man
logical	lumbago	linseed	loobily	lustily	lovable	meat-man
log-head	lambast	lantern	lookout	lashkar	live-box	miasmas
log-reel	limacel	Linnean	look-see	lassoed	love-day	meacock
legless	limaçon	lyncean	lip-read	lissome	levying	meadowy
leg-rest	limaces	lengest	lip-deep	lassock	lavolta	meat-pie
log-chip	lum-head	lenient	lipless	lassoes	live-oak	meat-tea
log-ship	limbeck	longest	lapping	lustral	livered	meat-tub
leg-show	lampern	luncher	lapwing	lustrum	lovered	measure
lignite	lambent	linchet	lipping	lustres	leveret	mobbing
logline	lambert	lynchet	lopping	lispund	loverly	mobbish
lagging	lamp-fly	landing	Lappish	lithate	levitic	mobsman
Lagting	lamiger	lending	lapilli	latices	levator	mobster
legging	lymphad	longing	lupulin	lethean	lawland	mace-ale
logging	lamming	lunging	leprose	lettern	lowland	macramé
lugeing	lamping	longish	leptome	lathery	low-paid	mockage
lugging	lemming	lentisk	lapwork	lithely	law-calf	macrami
leggism	limning	lentigo	leprous	littery	low-bell	Meccano®
lignify	limping	long-leg	leprosy	lottery	low-gear	mockado
leg-slip	lumping	lanolin	Laputan	latchet	lawless	machair
ligular	lompish	ländler	liquate	lethied	lowness	macabre
legally	lumpish	lunular	liqueur	latrine	low-life	macadam
legumin	Lamaism	land-law	liquefy	lattice	low-rise	machete
Logania	lampion	landman	larvate	lithite	law-list	mochell
logwood	Lemnian	lineman	lurdane	lathing	lowlily	muchell
legwork	Lamaist	linkman	loricae	letting	law-book	mockery
log-book	lumpily	lentoid	lyrical	lotting	low-born	mucigen
log-roll	lambkin	long-off	Laridae	Lettish	low-down	macchie
legroom	lumpkin	long-oil	luridly	lithium	low-cost	machine
lugworm	lamella	lentous	lorrell	Latvian	low-bred	miching
leghorn	limulus	line-out	lernean	luthier	low-brow	mocking
ligroin	lomenta	Londony	largess	Latakia	lewdsby	miction
leg-spin	laminae	long-pig	larceny	littlin	lawsuit	micella
leg-iron	liminal	langrel	largely	latence	lexical	mycelia
lighted	lumenal	land-rat	larchen	Latiner	lexicon	maculae
legatee	luminal	lunatic	lurcher	latency	laxness	micelle
legitim	laminar	lunated	lording	lithoid	loxygen	Mechlin
lighten	lampoon	lunette	lurking	let-down	laxator	macular
legator	lamboys	Landtag	largish	luteous	layback	meconic
lighter	limbous	linctus	larkish	lateral	laytime	meconin
lightly	Lemuria	land-tax	larmier	literal	loyally	microbe
leg-pull	lemures	lengthy	lordkin	Lythrum	loyalty	microhm
lairage	lamprey	lingula	lorimer	Lateran	laylock	macaque
lying-in	limosis	langued	lorgnon	liturgy	layered	machree
leidger	limited	languid	loriner	litotes	layette	mycosis
lyingly	lameter	lingual	lardoon	latitat	layaway	mycotic
laithfu'	lamiter	languor	lyrated	lettuce	lazy-bed	mycetes
laicise	limiter	languet	lorette	launder	lozenge	Macrura
leister	lymiter	leopard	lyra-way	lounder	lozengy	machzor
leisure	limites	leotard	lastage	laundry	lazaret	madrasa
likable	langaha	lion-cub	Lusiads	lounger	meal-ark	mud-lava

7 m□d□a

Midgard	meeting	mainour	molerat	Monodon	manhole	moorlog
midland	meerkat	Meissen	malarky	minuend	mannose	moonlit
mediate	moellon	meiosis	melisma	man-week	man-cook	moorman
Midrash	myeloma	myiasis	Molasse	manteel	menfolk	mootman
mud-bath	myeloid	meiotic	molossi	montero	minnock	Mjölnir
mudlark	maestro	moisten	malison	man-year	monsoon	myosote
mudpack	muezzin	maintop	milk-sop	mynheer	man-hour	myology
mediant	maffick	maister	malmsey	manrent	mangoes	moor-pan
mediacy	maffled	moistly	militia	manteau	man-body	myogram
medical	muffled	mail-van	mulatta	mongery	maniple	moonset
modicum	mafflin	majorat	mulcted	monkery	Minerva	mooktar
mudscow	muffler	majesty	mulatto	mindful	Minorca	myotube
mid-week	mafioso	makable	militar	monofil	monarda	mappery
mid-term	mofette	mukhtar	mollusc	manager	menorah	mapwise
mid-year	magmata	mallard	multure	manihoc	monarch	mapping
madness	mug-lamb	maleate	mollusk	menthol	mandrel	mopping
maddest	magnate	maltase	mulmull	manchoo	mandril	mappist
middest	migrate	mileage	Malayan	muncher	mineral	Marsala
mid-Lent	migrant	miliary	mammate	manchet	mongrel	mermaid
Midwest	megabar	milk-bar	mammary	Manihot	mantram	mirbane
midship	megabit	malacia	mimical	monthly	moneron	muriate
madeira	magical	malicho	mimicry	mandira	mantrap	myrbane
muddied	Megaera	milk-cow	mummery	mandioc	manurer	murlain
midwife	magneto	melodic	mummied	mankind	minaret	murrain
midwive	megafog	milldam	mumming	manlike	mini-sub	marcato
midriff	mugshot	mylodon	mumpish	mannite	menisci	Marrano
madding	mugging	Maltese	mimmick	man-size	mono-ski	mormaor
madling	muggish	mill-eye	mummify	manning	monosis	mordant
mud-fish	muggins	mullein	mamilla	mending	minutia	marybud
muddily	magnify	malleus	mamelon	mincing	manatee	mirable
medulla	magsman	milreis	mumbler	munting	minette	marabou
mud-flap	magenta	milieux	mimulus	mannish	minster	miracle
meddler	mugwort	mildewy	momenta	monkish	monitor	moriche
modular	maggoty	malefic	memento	minnick	monster	morocco
muddler	megarad	malaise	mim-mou'd	mondial	manitou	murices
modulus	megaron	mellite	mammoth	mansion	monture	Muridae
medalet	megasse	millime	mammock	mention	mensual	mirador
mud-flat	megaton	milvine	mummock	munnion	Mantuan	muraena
modally	mightst	malting	membral	mundify	manhunt	murgeon
Madonna	mugwump	melting	mu-meson	muntjac	minever	marrels
madroña	mugfuls	milking	mimesis	muntjak	miniver	margent
Modiola	Mohican	milling	mimetic	manakin	minivet	mar-text
mud-cone	mahseer	meltith	mandala	manikin	man-o'-war	mordent
mud-hole	Mohegan	million	mansard	minikin	monaxon	morceau
mud-hook	Mahdism	mullion	mandate	moniker	moneyed	mercery
madzoon	Mahdist	milkily	man-made	manilla	moneyer	mirific
midnoon	mahonia	mollify	miniate	monilia	moorage	morphia
madroño	mah-jong	milk-leg	mintage	manille	moon-bow	morrhua
mid-hour	mahatma	melilot	montage	mangler	Miocene	morphic
madwort	Mahound	maltman	montane	mingler	moon-eye	myrrhic
midmost	mail-bag	milkman	mundane	mantlet	Mooress	marshal
mud-boat	mail-box	molimen	manjack	minimal	Moorery	myrrhol
mudwort	mail-car	melanic	man-days	minimum	moon-god	Märchen
madoqua	moineau	mélange	montant	Manxman	moorhen	marcher
mudiria	mail-gig	melanin	minibus	mint-man	moocher	markhor
mad-bred	moither	Malines	minicab	monomer	mooring	murther
medusae	mailing	maltose	monacid	minimus	mooting	marches
modiste	maiming	mullock	manacle	manumit	moonish	merchet
medusan	maidish	milfoil	monocle	mandola	moorish	morphew
modesty	maidism	Miltown	minicar	mandora	moor-ill	married
mud-lump	maillot	mellowy	monocot	mineola	muonium	marline
meercat	mailman	malaria	monadic	mangold	Moonies	marmite
mueddin	moidore	milk-run	monodic	manhood	moodily	moraine

morrice	martyry	mistime	miserly	metopic	mazeful	nigrify
mortice	mascara	mastiff	musk-sac	metopon	muzzily	nigella
mortise	mastaba	mashing	misuser	Mithras	muzzler	niggler
murrine	mislaid	meshing	mash-tub	métisse	mazurka	negroid
marking	missaid	missing	musette	mitosis	Mozarab	Negroes
marling	mustard	misting	mash-tun	mitotic	mozetta	nighted
marring	massage	mastich	mess-tin	motivic	mezuzah	nightie
merling	message	Messiah	misstep	mitzvah	nearest	nightly
morling	misdate	missish	meshuga	métayer	Noachic	Nahuatl
morning	misease	Mosaism	misrule	metazoa	naartje	no-hoper
moreish	misfare	mission	mistune	mousaka	nabbing	nail-bed
murkish	misgave	mestizo	misluck	mauvais	nebbich	naiades
martini	mismade	mistico	mesquin	maunder	nebbish	naïveté
martial	mismake	Messias	masquer	moulder	niblick	nailery
Marxism	mismate	misdiet	mesquit	mousery	nobbily	naïvely
Martian	misname	messily	missuit	maulgre	nebulae	naïvety
Marxian	misrate	mistily	masculy	mouthed	nebular	neither
mersion	mistake	mushily	mash-vat	mauther	nibbler	nailing
morrion	mustang	muskily	Mesozoa	moucher	nobbler	noisily
murrion	miscall	mystify	methane	mouther	nictate	noisome
marrier	misfall	mascled	matrass	mousing	nectary	nail-rod
Marxist	mista'en	meseled	metcast	Maurist	nucleal	nainsel'
mercify	miscast	muscled	mutable	mouillé	Nicaean	nakedly
merrily	mishapt	Moselle	mutably	maudlin	nuclein	niks-nie
mortify	musk-bag	mashlam	matador	mouflon	nucleon	nylghau
murkily	musk-cod	mashlim	matweed	mousmee	nuclear	nulling
marbled	musical	mashlum	moth-eat	mourner	nucleus	nullify
morello	musk-cat	mashlin	mattery	mounted	nacrite	nullity
marbler	Mustela	Musales	mothery	mountie	nuclide	nelumbo
morular	misdeed	mesally	mutagen	moulten	necking	Nilotic
marplot	mislead	misplay	matched	mounter	niceish	nummary
martlet	misread	mishmee	matcher	movable	nacelle	namable
morally	missend	musimon	matrice	movably	necklet	nomadic
Morglay	miswend	masonic	mythise	mawseed	necrose	name-day
maremma	misdeal	mesonic	matting	mawther	nacrous	nimiety
marimba	misfell	Mishnic	methink	mawkish	nocuous	nymphic
markman	mistell	Mishnah	mythism	maw-worm	nacarat	nymphae
Maranta	misdeem	misknow	mattins	mowburn	necktie	nymphal
Moringa	misseem	masonry	metrics	Mexican	noctuid	nymphet
myringa	misterm	Massora	metrist	mixed-up	noctule	nymphly
moronic	misween	mastoid	mythist	mixedly	nocturn	numbing
morendo	masseur	mistold	Matilda	maxwell	nodical	numbles
mariner	mishear	misword	mettled	mixtion	nodding	nimonic
merinos	meseems	muscoid	mottled	maxilla	noduled	nominee
margosa	missent	misdone	Mytilus	maximal	nodular	nominal
marmose	miswent	misgone	matelot	maximum	nodated	nimious
morwong	mastery	misyoke	metally	mixture	ne'erday	numeric
Marconi	mistery	muscose	metamer	May-game	needful	nomarch
merfolk	mystery	mistook	mutanda	Mayfair	Noetian	nemoral
Mormops	mast-fed	misform	metonic	May-lady	needily	nombril
marrowy	mastful	Mas-John	matinée	mayweed	needler	numeral
marl-pit	mistful	Mes-John	matinee	may-bird	naevoid	nemesia
Moresco	museful	misborn	matinal	May-time	naebody	name-son
Morisco	moss-hag	misjoin	metonym	may-lily	no-fines	nemesis
morassy	mestiza	misdoer	mattoid	May-lord	niggard	nematic
Maratha	massive	miscopy	mottoed	maypole	nagmaal	non-term
Marathi	misfile	Muscovy	matzoth	May-morn	Negress	nankeen
marital	misfire	musk-pod	mattock	mayoral	neglect	non-hero
marquee	misgive	Masorah	matzoon	mayster	niggery	nunnery
morsure	mislike	mesarch	matross	may-duke	nuggety	nonaged
marquis	mislive	mistral	mottoes	mazzard	négligé	nonagon
mercury	missile	musk-rat	Methody	mizmaze	nogging	nunship
murexes	missive	misdraw	muttony	Mazdean	Negrito	ninthly

nandine	nervule	nourish	oscular	overjoy	ochroid	osmosis
nundine	nervure	nautili	obconic	overlie	ochrous	ommatea
nunnish	nurture	nautics	orcinol	overlap	ophitic	osmotic
non-skid	nosebag	nauplii	Oscines	ocellar	Ophiura	omniana
non-slip	nest-egg	neuroma	occiput	ocellus	origane	omnibus
nonplus	nascent	neurone	occlude	overlay	oxidase	omniety
nunhood	nashgab	neutral	oddball	overman	oxidate	omnific
non-come	nosegay	neutron	oddness	oceanic	origami	omneity
nine-pin	nastily	noursle	oldness	oceanid	oxidant	oenomel
non-drip	nose-led	neuston	oddment	overnet	olivary	Odonata
non-user	Nasalis	navvied	odd-like	oceloid	Oniscus	obovate
nonette	nasally	novalia	old-time	onefold	olivine	odorate
nunatak	nose-rag	novella	on-drive	operose	orifice	odorant
nonetto	nostril	novelle	oodlins	onerous	ovicide	obolary
non-stop	nostrum	novelty	oddsman	overpay	oxidise	ovoidal
nonsuch	nitrate	niveous	ordinee	overply	opinion	oropesa
nonsuit	nutcase	navarch	ordinal	oneiric	Osirian	orogeny
nun-buoy	netball	navarin	ordinar	overred	Ovidian	oporice
Neogaea	nut-gall	navarho	Oedipal	overran	oligist	ozonise
neonate	notable	navette	Oedipus	overrun	oriency	otolith
neo-Nazi	notably	new-laid	orderer	oversea	oviform	oxonium
noonday	notedly	Newgate	orderly	oversee	ominous	Oxonian
Neogene	nut-meal	new-made	ondatra	overset	olitory	obovoid
Niobean	notaeum	newsboy	oldster	oversew	osiered	oloroso
neoteny	nathemo	nowhere	odd-even	oversow	omicron	odorous
niobite	nattery	newness	operand	orectic	omitted	orology
nooning	notched	newsman	operate	omental	opiated	otology
neolith	notchel	newcome	over-age	omentum	omitter	odoured
niobium	nitride	newborn	overawe	onestep	obitual	opossum
Neozoic	nitrile	new-mown	overall	overtop	oviduct	odontic
neology	nitrite	noxious	overarm	oven-tit	oak-gall	orotund
noology	nut-pine	nayward	oregano	overtax	oak-mast	otocyst
napless	netting	noyance	open-air	overtly	oak-fern	oppidan
napping	nithing	nayword	operant	overuse	oakling	Orphean
nipping	nothing	noysome	overact	one-eyed	oak-wood	oppress
nuptial	nutting	Naziism	overbid	offhand	oak-tree	Orpheus
nephric	net-fish	oxalate	overbuy	off-ward	oak-lump	Orphism
nephron	nit-pick	ouabain	overdue	offtake	oil-cake	orphrey
naphtha	natrium	otalgia	overdye	offscum	oil-bath	opposer
nepotic	Nitrian	ocarina	oreades	officer	oil-palm	oophyte
Neptune	nattily	opaline	open-end	offpeak	orleans	ocreate
nirvana	nitrify	otarine	oreweed	offbeat	oil-seed	o'ergang
norland	notelet	odalisk	overeye	off-line	oil-well	oarweed
norward	net-play	onanism	oneself	offside	oil-belt	ourself
narrate	notanda	orarium	oneness	ooftish	obligee	oarless
nervate	net-cord	orarian	overeat	offence	obligor	oar-fish
nor'-east	network	orarion	overfed	offense	oil-bird	ogreish
nor'-west	nut-hook	oration	overfar	ox-fence	oil-silk	oarsman
nursery	nitrous	ovarian	overfly	offload	oil-mill	o'erword
nuraghe	notepad	ovation	overget	off-come	oilskin	o'ercome
nuraghi	natured	otaries	one-shot	offered	oolakan	oar-lock
narwhal	niterie	onanist	overhit	od-force	oulakan	oersted
norther	nut-tree	opacity	obelise	offerer	owl-moth	ossuary
narthex	natural	odaller	olefine	off-duty	oblique	ossicle
nargile	notitia	opacous	one-time	orgiast	obloquy	onstead
nervine	netsuke	oratory	Owenite	ongoing	oil-tree	obscene
nargily	no-trump	oratrix	opening	oogonia	oolitic	ossific
nartjie	noumena	oxblood	obelisk	organza	owl-eyed	od's-life
norimon	nousell	orbital	Owenism	organic	osmiate	oustiti
Neronic	nouveau	orbiter	obelion	organum	oomiack	osselet
Norfolk	naughty	orchard	Owenian	organon	osmunda	opsonic
nervous	neurine	oscheal	Owenist	Ophidia	Osmanli	opsonin
neritic	nourice	osculum	obesity	oghamic	osmious	onshore

oospore	outlive	out-over	peaking	plaster	pedlary	poetess
od's-bobs	outride	out-owre	plating	platter	pedicab	precess
osseous	outside	outhyre	prating	praetor	pedicle	precept
obsequy	outsize	oculate	praying	Psalter	pedicel	prefect
observe	outwing	ovulate	planish	peartly	pidgeon	preheat
oestral	ostrich	opuscle	phaeism	planula	padrero	prelect
oestrum	outwith	opulent	pianism	plaguey	pedrero	present
oestrus	outwick	oculist	plagium	planury	podagra	pretext
osseter	orthian	oeuvres	pianino	play-way	padding	prevent
obscure	outlier	opuntia	pianist	planxty	podding	preyful
ostraca	ortolan	obviate	piarist	pharynx	pudding	pledgee
ostraka	outflow	ouvrage	pravity	pébrine	padella	pledger
outland	outplay	Orvieto	prankle	publish	podalic	pledgor
outward	optimal	ouvrier	placket	pebbled	paddler	pledget
oatcake	optimum	obvious	phallic	pabulum	peddler	pie-shop
ostiate	Ottoman	obverse	pearled	pabular	piddler	poe-bird
outdare	osteoma	onwards	pearlin	pibroch	puddler	Peelite
outdate	osteoid	oxy-salt	phallin	puberal	pudenda	poetise
outface	ostiole	oxy-acid	prawlin	puberty	pudency	precise
outgate	outcome	onychia	pearler	pubises	padrone	premise
outname	outgone	odylism	phallus	pochard	padroni	preside
outpace	outmode	Ogygian	playlet	pockard	paddock	previse
outrace	outmove	oxytone	pyaemia	package	padlock	puerile
outrage	outrope	olycook	plasmic	pickaxe	piddock	peeling
outtake	outsole	olykoek	ptarmic	picrate	puddock	peevish
out-half	outvote	onymous	pyaemic	peccant	pad-tree	piedish
outlash	outlook	Olympia	phasmid	peccary	podesta	plenish
outback	outwork	Olympic	plasmid	pacable	pedesis	prejink
outrank	outworn	Olympus	peatman	picador	pedetic	predial
outtalk	outroop	odyssey	plasmin	pickeer	piebald	pietism
outwalk	outdoor	odzooks	planned	pickery	prefard	premium
outfall	outgoer	placard	praunce	puckery	prepaid	Pierian
outhaul	outpour	placate	planner	pacific	pyebald	pterion
outsail	outroar	platane	plainly	pack-ice	peerage	plenipo
out-wall	outsoar	Pharaoh	Pianola®	pectise	phenate	premier
outcast	outfoot	peasant	phacoid	picrite	pierage	prelims
outlast	outmost	play-act	placoid	pycnite	Pleiade	premiss
outpart	outport	phalanx	plafond	packing	predate	pietist
ostiary	outpost	peatary	play-off	pecking	preface	plenist
October	outroot	peat-bed	peacock	picking	prefade	predict
optical	octapla	prabble	pea-fowl	peckish	prelate	preview
octadic	octopod	peat-bog	platoon	Pictish	prepare	plebify
outedge	octuple	play-box	pea-soup	puckish	presage	phellem
outweed	outspan	playboy	pea-coat	pachisi	prepack	pre-empt
oatmeal	octopus	peascod	play-pen	paction	prevail	paeonic
outsell	outbred	prancke	pea-crab	pickled	peekabo	pfennig
outtell	outbrag	prancer	prairie	pucelle	Pleiads	pleroma
outwell	outcrop	placcat	pea-iron	pickler	precast	plerome
outleap	orthros	plaided	Prakrit	packman	plenary	premove
outpeep	outgrow	plaudit	praiser	picamar	prelacy	precook
outweep	outpray	play-day	praeses	pickmaw	prelaty	predoom
outpeer	out-tray	placebo	plastic	pectose	pierced	preform
outwear	octette	plateau	practic	puccoon	piercer	pleopod
outness	outstep	peatery	plaited	piccolo	preachy	pleurae
outjest	outstay	playful	plastid	pochoir	pleaded	pleural
outwent	obtrude	piaffer	platted	piceous	pleader	preoral
octofid	outdure	peat-hag	piastre	pockpit	prebend	pleuron
octagon	outgush	peacher	prattle	pack-rat	prehend	pierrot
outshot	outrush	poacher	phantom	picotee	pretend	pleased
outwind	outburn	plashet	phaeton	picture	precede	preasse
outgive	outturn	placita	plaiter	picquet	prevene	press-up
outhire	outjump	platina	plantar	packway	preterm	pleaser
outline	octaval	praline	planter	pedrail	peeress	plessor

presser	pegasus	pajocke	polymer	pomatum	panging	peonage
plectra	pightle	pyjama'd	polenta	poniard	panning	phonate
P-Celtic	pig-jump	pajamas	Polonia	pancake	panting	probate
P-Keltic	pig-eyed	pyjamas	polynia	pannage	pending	proface
peep-toe	Pahlavi	pokeful	polynya	pen-case	penning	profane
plectre	Pehlevi	pikelet	polonie	pen-name	pinking	prolate
Prestel®	plicate	pikeman	Pilsner	pennate	pinning	pronate
paenula	primage	pakfong	pili-nut	pentane	punning	propage
plexure	primate	paktong	palooka	pincase	pinfish	propale
prelude	prisage	pollard	pallone	pinnace	pinkish	propane
prepuce	private	palmate	pellock	pinnate	pannick	prorate
presume	paisano	palpate	pollock	pondage	pennill	probang
prequel	poinado	peltate	palm-oil	pontage	Pandion	pronaoi
prerupt	privado	pileate	pilcorn	Panjabi	Peneian	proball
pteryla	primacy	pillage	pultoon	pindari	pension	pronaos
pie-eyed	primary	pole-axe	pulpous	Punjabi	pannier	provant
prenzie	privacy	poll-axe	pull-out	pinball	panties	Pooh-Bah
prezzie	pliable	pulsate	pillory	pintail	pennies	Phoebus
pretzel	pribble	pellach	pillowy	pintado	paneity	poor-box
pheazar	pliably	pellack	Pelopid	pendant	pontify	plodded
puff-box	paiocke	pollack	polypod	pennant	punalua	prodded
po-faced	princox	peltast	polypes	pentact	pantler	plodder
piffero	poinder	polyact	polypus	pangamy	pingler	proudly
puffery	primero	palmary	peloria	panacea	Pan-Slav	proverb
puffing	primeur	palabra	peloric	panocha	penally	proceed
puffily	primely	pill-bug	pyloric	panache	penalty	propend
piffler	pailful	pill-box	pilgrim	panicle	penance	proteid
pigwash	painful	polacca	puldron	pinocle	pandora	protend
Pugwash	prigger	polacre	pelorus	Panicum	penfold	provend
pigtail	peishwa	pelican	Polaris	panicky	pinfold	phoneme
pageant	prithee	palm-cat	pylorus	Panadol®	pinnoed	propene
page-boy	primine	polecat	pilcrow	pinhead	pandore	protégé
pigfeed	pairing	paludic	palfrey	pangene	pannose	phone-in
pig-herd	priming	paludal	pelisse	pentene	pentode	protean
pig-lead	pairial	paladin	pelitic	pink-eye	pentose	protein
pigweed	pridian	pollent	politic	Pandean	pinhole	pioneer
pigmean	privily	pilfery	palette	pandect	pinnock	proneur
pygmean	privity	palmful	palatal	pendent	pantoum	process
pig-deer	pliskie	pelagic	paletot	pungent	pontoon	profess
pigmeat	prickle	polygam	poll-tax	puniest	pandoor	proteus
pigment	pricker	polygon	pollute	ponceau	pandour	prowess
piggery	pricket	phlegmy	pulture	Panagia	pint-pot	project
puggery	prickly	pilcher	palaver	punt-gun	panoply	protect
pegging	paillon	palsied	palmyra	penthia	Pan-Arab	protest
pigging	paisley	palling	Polyzoa	pinched	pangram	prowest
pigling	primmed	pelting	pompano	punch-up	pinetum	plovery
pugging	psionic	polling	pemican	panther	punctum	poovery
pig-fish	pliancy	pulvini	pommele	pincher	Pinxter	progeny
piggish	pair-oar	pallial	pampean	puncher	punster	pronely
puggish	priapic	pallium	pampero	ponchos	penates	plotful
pug-mill	Priapus	pilion	pompelo	panchax	pandura	proffer
piggies	poitrel	palmiet	pompion	pansied	pinnula	pronged
pig-lily	primsie	palmist	pumpion	pennied	pinguid	prothyl
pigskin	poisson	poloist	pompier	pantile	pinnule	prophet
pigsnie	painted	pollicy	pumpkin	pantine	pin-tuck	phocine
paginal	pointed	pulpify	pimpled	pennine	penguin	plosive
pigsney	philtre	pulpily	pimento	pensile	pinguin	profile
pygmoid	pointel	Palilia	pompoon	pensive	panfuls	promise
pug-nose	painter	pilular	pompous	pentice	pin-dust	propine
pug-moth	philter	polemic	pomfret	pentise	pin-eyed	provide
pigboat	pointer	palamae	pomeroy	pin-fire	prosaic	provine
puggree	printer	pollman	pi-meson	pontile	proband	pioning
pig-iron	primula	Pullman	pontiff	pontiff	provand	prosing

7 p□u□d

proving	pap-meat	Perseid	perkily	paritor	pissoir	patrial
poorish	peppery	portend	parella	arotis	passout	Pittism
peonism	pipeful	Purbeck	purfled	pyrites	push-pin	pythium
phobism	pop-shop	peraeon	pyralid	phratry	piss-pot	Pythian
photism	paprika	Perseus	parelle	Purpura	posited	patrico
protium	poppied	porpess	parulis	perturb	positon	puttier
plosion	pepsine	portess	Pyralis	parture	Pushtoo	patriot
proviso	peptide	parpent	partlet	perdure	pasture	petrify
proximo	peptise	percept	perplex	perfume	posaune	pettily
phonics	pipping	perfect	parsley	perfuse	poseuse	pithily
photics	popping	perpent	pyramid	perjure	posture	patella
pionies	pupping	pervert	portman	permute	pustule	patulin
phobist	pupfish	porrect	pyramis	pertuse	Pasquil	potamic
protist	Paphian	portent	piranha	purpure	Pasquin	putamen
probity	peptics	parvenu	phrenic	pursual	pesaunt	patamar
prodigy	pipe-key	parafle	Puranic	pursuer	post-war	petunia
prosily	papilla	porifer	paronym	percuss	pottage	patined
prop-jet	papulae	piragua	parsnep	parquet	pot-bank	patonce
plonker	papilio	perigee	parsnip	pursuit	patball	potencé
problem	papular	pirogue	pardner	perfumy	pitfall	potence
proller	popular	peregal	partner	perjury	petrary	patency
prouler	papules	paragon	phrensy	periwig	patible	potency
prowler	papally	perigon	pergola	parkway	potable	petiole
poor-law	pupunha	pyrogen	persona	pyrexia	potiche	pothole
prommer	papoose	pyrrhic	percoid	pyrexic	pot-herb	petcock
Phoenix	pappose	parched	purpose	parazoa	pithead	pothook
pronota	peptone	perched	partook	passade	pot-head	putlock
promote	pop-song	percher	parboil	passage	pattern	puttock
propone	popcorn	porthos	perform	postage	potheen	pit-coal
propose	pappous	pareira	purloin	passado	patrero	patroon
provoke	pap-boat	partita	parlour	passant	patness	put-down
prolong	puparia	pereira	parlous	pessary	patient	petrous
poon-oil	piperic	parried	perlous	piscary	pothery	piteous
pronoun	poperin	pardine	portous	post-bag	pottery	pit-pony
provost	papyrus	partite	percoct	post-bus	putrefy	pitapat
prosody	pipette	parvise	periost	post-box	pithful	paterae
plopped	Papaver	percine	purport	post-day	pitiful	pitarah
propped	popover	perlite	parroty	pastern	patagia	Patarin
prosper	pop-eyed	porcine	pork-pie	posteen	patched	potoroo
program	piquant	purline	pyropus	postern	pitched	pit-prop
piously	pargana	parking	parapet	paste-up	putchuk	pit-brow
prootic	pardale	parsing	Perspex®	possess	patch-up	potassa
plotted	parpane	parting	perique	pestful	pot-shop	petasus
plottie	partake	purging	parerga	pushful	patcher	pit-stop
pooftah	percale	purling	para-red	postfix	pitcher	pot-luck
proctal	percase	purring	portray	paschal	potcher	potfuls
plotter	pertake	parkish	parasol	piscina	pith-hat	pathway
plouter	pervade	perjink	perusal	passive	pot-shot	poulard
plowter	portage	partial	phrasal	pastime	pituita	plumage
poofter	portate	Parsism	parison	piscine	puttied	plumate
proctor	pertain	Persism	peruser	pismire	Petrine	plusage
procure	perhaps	pereion	phraser	passing	pittite	plumbic
produce	parfait	Permian	paresis	posting	pituite	plumbum
profuse	periapt	Persian	porosis	pushing	patting	plumber
product	persant	portion	pyrosis	passion	petting	pounced
propyla	parable	persico	paratha	Peshito	pitting	plumcot
protyle	paracme	porrigo	paretic	peskily	pitying	pouncet
Procyon	parodic	portico	parotic	passkey	potting	paunchy
papable	parados	perrier	piratic	passman	putting	pouldre
popadum	peridot	persist	pyretic	postman	pettish	poundal
popedom	paradox	purlieu	pyritic	pesante	patrick	plunder
pop-weed	parpend	purview	parotid	pistole	pit-mirk	poulder
pipless	perpend	perfidy	puritan	push-off	pot-sick	pounder

pluteal	psychic	Quichua	reallot	reclaim	radicle	re-edify
pluteus	prythee	quinine	roadman	recycle	radical	ruellia
prudent	poy-bird	quiting	road-map	recheck	radicel	rheumed
plumery	pay-bill	quickie	Réaumur	rock-cod	reducer	rye-wolf
prudery	physics	quicken	readmit	rock-elm	radices	rye-roll
plugged	pay-dirt	quickly	Rhamnus	rickets	red-head	rye-corn
plugger	pay-list	quilled	reannex	rackett	red-seed	riempie
plunger	ptyalin	quillai	readopt	recheat	redneck	re-enter
pouched	pay-slip	quiblin	read-out	rackety	redsear	re-entry
pouther	pay-load	quillon	reapply	rickety	redness	roebuck
plug-hat	plywood	quillet	Rhaetia	rockery	redress	re-equip
paughty	pay-roll	quinnat	Rhaetic	reclimb	rodless	reflate
Pauline	pazzazz	quinone	realtie	receive	reddest	reframe
pausing	pizzazz	quiesce	reactor	recline	red-heat	refrain
pouring	puzzler	quintic	re-alter	recuile	ruddied	refract
pouting	quayage	quilted	Realtor®	racking	redrive	refresh
pruning	quahaug	quitted	roaster	rocking	rodlike	reflect
prudish	quamash	quintal	roadway	ruching	redding	refugia
pluvial	quavery	quittal	ribband	rachial	redwing	refugee
Paulian	quaffer	quieten	rebrace	rection	ridding	rifling
prurigo	Quashee	quintan	ribcage	ruction	ridging	raffish
plumist	Quashie	quieter	reboant	rockier	reddish	ruffian
paucity	quaking	quilter	ribible	receipt	redfish	ruffled
plucked	qualify	quitter	Rebecca	rectify	ruddier	raffler
plucker	quality	quittor	rubicon	rockily	ruddily	riffler
plunker	quackle	quietus	rub-a-dub	rocklay	redskin	ruffler
plummet	quannet	quintet	rabidly	racemic	raddled	raftman
plumose	quadric	quietly	ribless	racemed	radulae	refined
plumous	quarrel	quizzed	robbery	recense	radular	refiner
plumpie	quadrat	quizzer	rubbery	Ricinus	riddler	referee
plumpen	quassia	quizzes	rebuild	recency	rodsman	refusal
plumper	quantic	quondam	riblike	reclose	redwood	refuser
plumply	quartic	quodlin	ribbing	rock-oil	red-book	refutal
prussic	quantal	quoiter	robbing	raccoon	ruddock	refuter
poursue	quantum	reawake	rubbing	racloir	red-cowl	refound
poussin	quartan	readapt	rubying	recross	redpoll	regmata
poursew	quarter	rhatany	rubbish	rectory	redcoat	riggald
prunted	quartet	road-bed	rabbity	recurve	red-root	regrade
pouftah	quartzy	rhabdom	rebuker	rectrix	ridered	regrate
poufter	Qaddish	rear-dos	rubella	ricksha	ruderal	rag-fair
poulter	Quercus	rhabdus	rabbler	ricotta	rudesby	regnant
poultry	queachy	reamend	rabanna	recital	ridotto	regrant
plumula	queechy	road-end	robinia	reciter	rodster	rag-baby
plumule	quechua	reagent	rubeola	rock-tar	redound	Rigsdag
pavlova	queried	realgar	rib-bone	recluse	redoubt	rigidly
paviour	queuing	reached	rabboni	recoure	rodeway	Rigveda
poverty	querist	road-hog	ribwork	racquet	re-enact	ragweed
pivoted	queller	reacher	rebloom	recount	reed-bed	regrede
pivotal	queynie	rhachis	rubdown	recruit	re-endow	regress
pivoter	queenly	rhaphis	rubious	rocquet	rye-peck	ragment
pew-rent	queerly	realise	ribwort	recover	roe-deer	regreet
powdery	quetsch	rearise	ribbony	recower	re-elect	raggedy
pawkily	Q-Celtic	reading	ruby-red	raceway	re-erect	raggery
powered	Q-Keltic	reaming	rebirth	recoyle	reeding	roguery
pyxidia	quester	roading	rebuses	Radiata	reefing	rageful
pyxides	questor	roaring	robotic	red-hand	reeking	regrind
pixy-led	quetzal	realism	rabatte	radiale	reeling	ragtime
paxiuba	quinate	realign	ribston	radiate	Rhemish	ragging
paysage	quinary	readier	rebater	red-tape	Rhenish	rigging
poynant	quibble	realist	rebound	radiant	rhenium	rigling
payable	quinche	readily	rybauld	redraft	Raetian	roguing
pay-desk	quiddle	reality	rechate	ridable	re-exist	rugging
payment	quiddit	reallie	réclame	reduced	Rhemist	riggish

7 r□v□r

roguish	relievo	Romansh	riotise	ropeway	resiner	rattlin
regalia	rilievo	Romanes	riotize	repryve	roseola	rattler
raguled	relight	remanet	rioting	requere	respond	rotunda
regulae	rallied	rameous	roofing	request	rescore	retinae
regular	ralline	remerge	rooting	require	restore	retinue
regulus	relying	remorse	rookish	requite	rissole	retinal
regally	rolling	remarry	rhodium	requiem	restock	retinol
regimen	rellish	remercy	Rhodian	rarebit	rose-red	rat-hole
regence	rollick	rematch	roomily	reredos	rustred	retired
reginal	rullion	ramstam	rootlet	rurally	reserve	retiree
regency	rallier	remould	rooinek	rorqual	resurge	retiral
rag-book	rollmop	remount	rhodora	rescale	rostral	rat-trap
ragwork	rollock	romaunt	rhodous	reshape	rastrum	Ratitae
rag-doll	rullock	removed	riotous	restage	rostrum	rotator
rag-wool	roll-out	removal	roof-top	restate	Rasores	rat-a-tat
ragworm	relapse	remover	rooster	roseate	respray	retouch
rug-gown	relique	rundale	replace	restaff	rosette	rhubarb
regroup	rulesse	ransack	replant	resiant	risotto	roulade
ragbolt	related	ringbit	reptant	restart	rosetty	rousant
ragwort	roll-top	Ranidae	ropable	réseaux	rescued	raunchy
regorge	relater	rent-day	rapidly	rose-bud	resound	rounded
regatta	relator	ringent	replete	risible	rescuer	roundle
right-oh	reliver	rondeau	ripieno	rose-bug	restyle	roundel
righten	relaxin	renague	repress	rose-bay	retrace	round-up
righter	relayed	renegue	replevy	rosacea	retrate	rounder
rightly	rampage	röntgen	replica	rose-cut	rat-tail	roundly
rag-bush	rummage	reneger	replied	residua	retrain	rouleau
rag-dust	rampant	ringgit	raphide	residue	retract	roughie
rehouse	rampart	rancher	Rappite	resider	retrait	routhie
ruinate	remnant	Rankine	reprime	rest-day	retiary	roughen
rein-arm	Rommany	ranking	reprise	rosiere	ratable	rougher
railbus	remodel	renying	reprive	respeak	retable	roughly
rainbow	Ramadan	ringing	reprize	respell	ratably	reunite
rail-car	romneya	rinsing	reptile	respect	reticle	routine
raiment	rump-end	running	riptide	russety	retread	rouming
rhizine	rimless	runtish	rapping	restful	Ruthene	rousing
railing	rump-fed	runnion	ripping	riskful	ratteen	routing
raising	remiges	rondino	replier	rose-hip	rathest	reunion
raiting	rum-shop	rentier	rippier	rescind	retreat	reunify
ruining	romaika	rundled	Rappist	reseize	rattery	raucous
roinish	rampike	ringlet	repaint	respire	rettery	routous
railman	rampire	rundlet	repoint	respite	ratafia	reutter
rhizoid	ramming	runflat	reprint	restive	ruthful	rouster
rhizome	rimming	ringman	repulse	restiff	rotifer	riviera
ruinous	rammish	run-down	rippler	rasping	rotchie	rivière
reissue	rompish	rancour	ripplet	resting	ratchet	ravager
reinter	rummish	ring-taw	repiner	rusting	retsina	revving
roister	rampick	rondure	rip-cord	Rissian	retried	revying
railway	rampion	renewal	reprove	Roscian	ratline	revalue
rejudge	remains	renewer	reproof	Russian	rut-time	revolve
rejoice	rummily	ringway	raploch	Roscius	ratling	ravelin
Rajpoot	ramakin	runaway	rape-oil	riskily	ratting	reviler
rejourn	ramekin	renayed	rapport	Russify	retting	rivulet
Riksdag	Ramilie	rootage	repaper	rustily	rotting	revelry
rakshas	remblai	rhombic	repique	rosaker	rutting	rivalry
rokelay	rambler	rhomboi	roper-in	rosalia	rattish	ravined
rake-off	ramular	rhombos	reposed	rosella	ruttish	revenge
release	rumbler	rhombus	riposte	rusalka	ratfink	revenue
reliant	ramulus	rhonchi	reposal	resolve	rethink	ravioli
rulable	ramenta	root-cap	reposit	roselle	retrial	rivered
roll-bar	Romanic	reorder	reputed	rosolio	retaken	reverie
relâche	remanié	rookery	rapture	rustler	retaker	reverse
relieve	romance	roomful	rupture	rosined	rat-flea	reversi

reverso
reverer
riveret
revisal
reviser
revisor
revisit
riveted
riveter
rêveuse
revival
reviver
revivor
rowable
rawhead
rawness
rawhide
rewrite
reweigh
rowdily
rawbone
rewrote
rowlock
rowboat
row-port
reynard
rayless
rhytina
roynish
rhymist
royalet
royally
royalty
Reynold
royster
rizzart
rozelle
sea-card
sea-maid
sea-sand
seaward
scalade
scavage
sea-dace
sea-gate
sea-hare
sea-kale
sea-lane
sea-ware
sea-wave
soakage
sea-calf
sea-tang
siamang
sladang
sea-path
sea-bank
sea-hawk
sea-lark
seamark
sea-wall
scalado
smarago

sea-haar
sea-bass
sea-pass
sealant
sea-salt
statant
scabbed
slabbed
stabbed
swabbed
scabble
scamble
shabble
shamble
snabble
sjambok
slabber
stabber
swabber
soapbox
spancel
snatchy
starchy
sraddha
scaldic
Scandic
skaldic
sharded
swarded
staddle
swaddle
scandal
Slavdom
stardom
standen
stand-in
so-and-so
stand-to
stand-up
scalder
slander
stander
Scandix
shandry
staidly
stand-by
sea-reed
seaweed
scalene
siamese
siameze
spa-well
sea-term
sea-bean
shake-up
sea-bear
sea-legs
starets
sea-beat
sea-beet
sealery
shapely
slavery

sparely
stagery
stalely
stately
suavely
slavish
staretz
scarfed
scaffie
snaffle
staffer
shagged
snagged
swagged
spangle
swaggie
spadger
sparger
stagger
swagger
spangly
spathic
slashed
spathed
smash-up
slasher
slather
smasher
swasher
stamina
stasima
sea-bird
sea-wind
sea-like
sea-line
sea-mile
sea-pike
seaside
sea-wife
stabile
statice
stative
suasive
scaling
sea-king
sealing
searing
seating
sea-wing
shading
shaking
shaping
sharing
shaving
skating
slating
snaring
soaking
soaring
spacing
sparing
staging
staring

staying
swaling
swaying
sea-fish
slavish
snakish
Spanish
Swahili
sea-pink
sea-risk
seasick
spacial
spaniel
spatial
staniel
Slavism
stadium
statism
sea-lion
Shavian
station
suasion
scabies
statics
sea-girt
shariat
statist
sea-view
scarify
sea-lily
shadily
shakily
snakily
soapily
stagily
suavity
shanked
stacked
stalked
shackle
sparkle
slacken
starken
sharker
slacker
smacker
spanker
stalker
swanker
stacket
slackly
starkly
swankey
scaglia
scailed
snarled
stalled
star-led
sea-blue
sea-slug
shallon
scallop

shallop
snarl-up
snarler
stabler
stapler
scarlet
shallot
starlet
starlit
swallet
shallow
swallow
spasmic
shammed
slammed
stammel
spaeman
star-man
swagman
star-map
shammer
slammer
stammer
swarmer
stannic
scanned
spanned
stained
Shawnee
slàinte
starnie
staunch
stannel
scanner
spanner
spawner
stainer
stamnos
span-new
sea-food
sea-lord
sea-road
sialoid
sparoid
scatole
sea-dove
skatole
sea-wolf
shadoof
sea-loch
sea-cock
sea-cook
sea-folk
sea-coal
sea-fowl
sea-foam
sea-room
sea-worm
sea-born
sea-gown
sea-worn
sea-moss
spadoes

sea-boat
seaport
sea-tost
shadowy
suasory
scarped
slapped
snapped
swapped
scapple
stapple
scalpel
sharpen
shampoo
scalper
scamper
scarper
scauper
sharper
slapper
snapper
stamper
swamper
swapper
sharply
scabrid
scarred
sparred
staired
starred
spairge
sparrer
sea-fret
sea-crow
sparrow
sebific
seam-set
shastra
spastic
shafted
slanted
slatted
scantle
smartie
sparthe
spattee
staithe
startle
shaitan
smarten
Spartan
start-up
scatter
sea-star
shafter
shaster
shatter
slatter
smatter
spatter
starter
swatter
scantly
slantly

smartly
startly
swarthy
scapula
spatula
statued
seasure
spatule
stature
statute
sea-duck
seagull
sea-turn
sea-dust
starved
scarves
seal-wax
stanyel
sublate
Sabbath
subtack
sebacic
subacid
subadar
subedar
subedit
sub-head
subtend
Sabaean
subdean
subzero
subject
subtext
subvert
sibship
sublime
subside
subtile
sibling
sobbing
subbing
Sabaism
submiss
subsist
subsidy
sabella
soboles
subplot
subunit
sebundy
subzone
Sabaoth
subsoil
subjoin
subaqua
saburra
suberic
subarid
suberin
soberly
sybotic
subatom

sabaton	sacculi	seether	stewpan	swerver	spheric	slither
subfusc	succubi	Shemite	steep-to	sheaves	sphered	swisher
subdued	succuss	sterile	steep-up	shelves	spheral	swither
subduce	side-box	syenite	sleeper	sneezer	Saharan	stichos
subsume	seducer	sheriff	steeper	sofa-bed	scherzo	Saivite
subfusk	sidecar	seeding	stepper	suffete	schisma	spilite
subdual	sadness	seeling	sweeper	suffice	schmuck	stibine
subduer	sodaine	seeming	skew-put	sifting	spiraea	suicide
subduct	sodding	stewing	stewpot	softish	spicate	sailing
subtype	saddish	Swedish	sleepry	Sufiism	spinage	seining
saccate	sedilia	special	steeply	saffian	spinate	seizing
sackage	saddler	sferics	stearic	safrole	spinach	shining
soccage	sudamen	species	sheared	saffron	shikari	skiving
sociate	sudanic	sheriat	speared	suffuse	spirant	slicing
succade	sideral	seedily	sweered	saggard	skiable	sliding
sucrase	sudoral	specify	sierran	sigmate	stibble	smiling
sectary	sad-iron	speckle	stearin	saguaro	spit-box	sniping
sick-bed	sideway	sleeken	shearer	signary	ship-boy	soiling
sackbut	sad-eyed	sneak-up	sneerer	signeur	switchy	spiling
sick-bay	steward	sleeker	steerer	segment	spindle	suiting
secodcr	seepage	sneaker	swearer	suggest	stiddie	swinish
secreta	shebang	speaker	sherris	sighful	swindge	saimiri
succeed	scenary	sleekit	sheerly	sagging	swindle	stibial
secrete	seedbed	steekit	spersed	sighing	shindig	Saivism
sockeye	seeable	sleekly	stemson	sogging	slidden	stibium
sacless	sueable	seed-lac	stepson	Signior	shidder	suidian
success	stembok	shellac	Stetson	signify	slidder	ski-lift
secrecy	sherbet	shelled	scepsis	soggily	spindly	slimily
society	seedbox	spelled	skepsis	sagaman	spin-dry	spicily
sackful	stencil	stealed	skeptic	Signora	Sciaena	spikily
sectile	stew-can	steeled	spectra	sigmoid	stipend	spirity
siclike	spencer	stelled	sceptic	Signore	spireme	shicksa
sacking	sketchy	swelled	skeptic	signory	shiness	sticked
sacring	sleechy	stealth	smectic	sugared	saidest	swinked
sucking	stenchy	skellum	scented	sage-tea	shivery	stickle
sickish	sledded	seedlip	sheeted	sagitta	snidely	slicken
section	sleided	sheller	stetted	sighted	spicery	snick-up
suction	speeded	smeller	sweated	sighter	spidery	stickup
sucrier	steaded	speeler	swelted	sagathy	swinery	shicker
sacrist	smeddum	speller	sceptre	sightly	skiffle	shirker
sacrify	speldin	stealer	sheathe	sagouin	sniffle	skinker
siccity	speed-up	stellar	sheltie	spheare	shipful	slicker
sacella	shedder	sweller	spectre	schnaps	skilful	slinker
sickled	skelder	Szekler	sperthe	sahibah	skinful	smicker
seculum	slender	sterlet	sweetie	sphaere	stiffen	snicker
secular	speeder	spermic	sweeten	schnell	sniffer	sticker
suckler	spelder	steamed	shelter	schlepp	stiffly	stinker
sick-man	spender	stemmed	skeeter	schmelz	stir-fry	smicket
seconde	Sienese	steamie	skelter	schlich	stinged	stickit
Seconal®	stelene	steamer	smelter	schtick	shingle	slickly
secondo	shereef	sterned	specter	scholia	sniggle	smickly
succose	shebeen	sternal	spelter	scholar	swingle	skid-lid
sucrose	spelean	sternum	stentor	schemer	smidgen	skilled
Succoth	she-bear	shea-nut	sweater	sphenic	smidgin	spilled
succour	siemens	stepney	swelter	sthenic	slinger	stifled
succous	scenery	sternly	sceptry	schoole	snigger	sciolto
succory	skepful	steroid	sheathy	schlock	stinger	shiplap
securer	sdeigne	seed-oil	sweetly	schmock	swigger	spieler
sycosis	stengah	stepped	sweltry	schnook	swinger	spiller
succuba	skegger	steeple	specula	schnorr	shingly	stifler
succumb	sledger	stemple	scedule	schloss	swing-by	stiller
saccule	sleight	stempel	sheaved	schmoes	stichic	swiller
seclude	seethed	steepen	sleaved	schappe	stichoi	skillet
			sleeved			

skimmia	skittle	salices	salt-pan	sambuca	sundial	snowcap
seismic	smittle	salicet	salt-pit	samovar	sensism	Scotchy
skimmed	snirtle	salt-cat	siliqua	someway	sonties	slouchy
slimmed	spirtle	solicit	Salique	somewhy	sensist	snodded
seismal	spittle	splodge	silique	Samoyed	sunnily	snooded
shipman	shittah	solidum	splurge	Sinhala	sun-clad	spondee
shipmen	shittim	solidus	scleral	sunward	singlet	spondyl
shimmer	spitten	solidly	Silurus	sinkage	sunglow	stooden
skimmer	Stilton	splodgy	splurgy	sinuate	sandman	scolder
slimmer	shifter	self-end	silesia	sondage	songman	scowder
swimmer	skirter	salfern	splashy	sun-bath	sonance	smolder
skinned	skitter	saltern	splatch	sundari	synonym	sworder
science	slitter	silvern	splotch	sun-dawn	sonancy	snoddit
soignée	snifter	silvery	saluter	sun-lamp	Senhora	Slovene
spignel	spitter	salient	Solpuga	syncarp	sinuose	stonern
skinner	stilter	solvent	salival	sunfast	syncope	smoke-ho
spinner	stinter	Sillery	seltzer	syngamy	send-off	showery
spinnet	swifter	silvery	summand	sand-bed	sun-roof	snow-fed
spinney	saintly	spleeny	summary	sandbag	sundown	shopful
spiroid	swiftly	self-fed	someday	sand-bar	santour	scoffer
spinode	spicula	salt-fat	sumless	sand-box	sanious	spoofer
spinose	seizure	saligot	summery	sand-boy	sinuous	snow-fly
spin-off	soilure	silphia	samshoo	sanicle	sensory	shogged
ski-bobs	spicule	sylphid	somehow	sinical	syntony	shoogle
spinous	spinule	sulphur	Samnite	Senecan	sinopia	showghe
spinout	stipule	silk-hat	sampire	senecio	synapse	Scoggin
shipped	stimuli	salchow	summing	synodic	synapte	shotgun
skipped	ship-way	sallied	somnial	synodal	sinopis	sloe-gin
slipped	slipway	sullied	semeion	sincere	sand-pit	spongin
snipped	swizzle	saltire	symbion	sondeli	sunspot	stop-gap
stipple	Switzer	sylvine	summist	sun-deck	sangria	slogger
swipple	sejeant	sylvite	simpkin	sand-eel	suntrap	sponger
shippen	sojourn	salting	semilog	sun-beam	synergy	stodger
shippon	saksaul	salving	sampler	Sinaean	Senussi	sloughy
skidpan	Saktism	saltish	similar	sun-bear	synesis	sloshed
shipper	Sikhism	selfish	similor	sanders	sanctum	shophar
skipper	sokeman	selfism	simpler	sinless	senator	smother
slipper	Sukkoth	salpian	simular	sonless	Sanctus	soother
snipper	sakeret	Sylvian	simplex	sunless	sensual	soothly
Scirpus	sakiyeh	saltier	seminal	sun-beat	sunburn	scoriac
stirpes	sultana	soldier	seminar	sintery	singult	stonied
shilpit	salband	selfist	Samiote	songful	sun-cult	storied
skippet	sol-faed	soloist	shmoose	sand-fly	sunsuit	scoriae
snippet	saltate	salpinx	someone	Sankhya	synovia	Scotice
sciarid	salvage	salsify	symbole	sand-hog	sinewed	snow-ice
shirred	selvage	saltily	simious	sonship	synaxis	scoring
stirred	solvate	silkily	summons	song-hit	sinsyne	shoeing
stirrah	sulcate	sillily	semiped	sun-bird	sun-myth	shoring
stirrup	sulfate	sulkily	simarre	sensile	stomata	showing
stirrer	sullage	salamon	simurgh	Sonnite	scopate	sloping
Sciurus	syllabi	silk-man	samurai	sunlike	storage	slowing
skirret	saltato	Solomon	samisen	Sunnite	stowage	smoking
scissel	soldado	selenic	sumatra	sunrise	stomach	snoring
scissil	saltant	splenic	sematic	sunwise	saouari	sooping
scissor	salsafy	silence	Semitic	sanding	swobbed	stoping
sciatic	salable	solanum	somatic	sending	Scomber	stoving
Shiitic	soluble	silenus	somitic	sensing	slobber	stowing
sainted	salt-box	Salsola	somital	singing	swobber	Scotish
shifted	salably	sell-off	symptom	sinking	show-box	slowish
skirted	silicic	sillock	semitar	sinning	snow-box	snowish
spitted	silicle	salvoes	simitar	sunning	shop-boy	Suomish
stilted	salicin	sell-out	sumpter	sun-fish	showbiz	Scotism
stinted	silicon	sallowy	symitar	sun-disk	stoical	spodium

Scotian	smouser	seppuku	spryest	strumae	sorites	set-line
skolion	sponsor	sequela	surfeit	surfman	stratus	sittine
stovies	shotted	sequent	surgent	scrimpy	serpula	setting
Scotist	snouted	sequoia	servery	scrummy	scrouge	sitting
scorify	spotted	serfage	sorcery	scrumpy	scrauch	sotting
Scotify	Scottie	seriate	streety	seringa	scraugh	sottish
showily	shoe-tie	serrate	surgery	Sirenia	shroudy	settled
smokily	shortie	sirname	sarkful	syringa	shrived	situlae
snowily	shottle	sorbate	sarafan	saronic	strived	settler
sootily	smoothe	spreaze	scruffy	sirenic	shrivel	settlor
stonily	shorten	striate	strigae	springe	shriven	satanic
shocked	shotten	surbase	strigil	strange	strivon	Satanas
snorkel	stouten	surbate	Striges	surance	shriver	satinet
slocken	scooter	surface	shright	syringe	striver	set-down
shocker	scouter	surname	spright	scranch	screwed	sitdown
snooker	shooter	sirgang	scraggy	scrunch	strawed	sit-upon
stonker	shouter	spreagh	scroggy	sarangi	strewed	satiric
stooker	slotter	serkali	spriggy	shrinal	strowed	satyric
spoiled	snorter	sarcasm	syrphid	Surinam	scrowle	satyrid
stoolie	snotter	Syriasm	sorghum	sarsnet	'strewth	sutured
swollen	sporter	surpass	sorehon	scranny	strawen	satyral
scollop	spotter	servant	Syrphus	scrunty	screwer	sutural
spoiler	spouter	skreaky	serried	springy	strewer	satisfy
spooler	stoiter	streaky	sardine	stringy	strower	satsuma
shopman	stotter	streamy	service	sarcoma	scrawly	sausage
showman	swotter	strobic	servile	sarcoid	scrawny	scutage
snowman	shortly	scribal	Servite	sarcode	sprawly	scutate
swooned	stoutly	soroban	sordine	scrooge	sprayed	soutane
scorner	scopula	scriber	surmise	strooke	strayed	sfumato
spooney	sporule	scrubby	survive	sirloin	scroyle	squeaky
scotoma	snoozle	shrubby	sarking	surloin	spray-on	slubbed
show-off	snoozer	soroche	scrying	sarcous	sprayer	snubbed
stop-off	septate	Saracen	serving	serious	strayer	stubbed
scotomy	soprani	sericin	sorning	surcoat	sprayey	scumble
scooped	suppawn	sericon	sorting	surtout	sustain	stubble
shopped	sapsago	sirocco	surfing	Sarapic	sassaby	stumble
slopped	soprano	soredia	surging	Serapic	suspend	scumber
stooped	saphead	spredde	scraich	striped	suspens	slubber
stopped	supreme	strodle	scraigh	scrapie	sestett	slumber
swopped	supremo	strudel	screich	scruple	suspect	snubber
stopple	sapless	serfdom	screigh	strophe	sestina	slumbry
shoe-peg	sapient	sarsden	serfish	scraper	sessile	squabby
scorpio	septett	stridor	skreigh	Sarapis	sestine	stubbly
scooper	Sapphic	shreddy	Sorbish	seraphs	Sistine	stumbly
scorper	septime	seriema	sordini	Serapis	suspire	stucco'd
shopper	sapling	screeve	Serbian	stripes	sossing	soupçon
snooper	sapping	scriene	Servian	scrappy	session	squacco
stooper	sipping	scrieve	Sorbian	strappy	systole	stuccos
stopper	sopping	seruewe	serpigo	stripey	sistrum	scudded
swopper	supping	servewe	sordino	stroppy	systyle	studded
shot-put	sophism	shrieve	sorrier	sororal	satiate	scuddle
scourge	sophist	spreeze	sardius	serosae	setuale	studdle
scourie	soppily	survewe	spraint	sorosis	situate	souldan
scourse	sapajou	screech	straint	stretta	setback	studden
scowrie	sapples	scriech	surview	soritic	setwall	scudder
sporran	saponin	shriech	sorrily	scratch	sitfast	shudder
scourer	sap-wood	skriech	surdity	scritch	satrapy	sounder
scowrer	saprobe	skriegh	surlily	shritch	Sotadic	soundly
spoorer	suppose	surreal	stroken	stretch	setness	squaddy
sponsal	sepiost	surgeon	striker	scrotal	sithens	shut-eye
spousal	support	sarment	stroker	scrotum	satiety	squeeze
sponson	Siporex	serpent	surplus	stratum	sutlery	student
scorser	septuor	sorbent	shrilly	stretto	satchel	stupent

squeezy	spun-out	sixteen	tram-car	travois	tactics	trekked
stupefy	sculpin	sexless	thatcht	tea-cosy	tachist	trekker
stuffed	skulpin	sextett	trap-cut	trapped	tackled	treille
scuffle	scupper	sixthly	twaddle	traipse	tackler	tie-clip
shuffle	stumper	sextile	twaddly	trample	tickler	toeclip
snuffle	slurred	sixaine	tuatera	tramper	technic	trellis
souffle	spurred	sixties	tea-lead	trapper	tuck-out	thermic
soufflé	squared	Saxonic	trapeze	tear-pit	tectrix	thermae
soulful	scurril	sixfold	tea-leaf	tea-tree	tacitly	thermal
snuffer	spurrer	sexfoil	trade-in	tea-tray	tactual	thermos
stuffer	squarer	saxhorn	traject	transom	tachyon	Thermit®
squiffy	spurrey	six-foot	transit	transit	tedding	theroid
snugged	squirmy	sextuor	tranect	toasted	tidying	toe-hold
smuggle	sour-sop	scybala	tracery	twattle	tiddled	trefoil
snuggle	squashy	skyward	tragedy	toaster	tiddler	tremolo
slugger	squishy	scytale	traffic	tractor	toddler	theoric
smudger	smutted	stylate	tearful	traitor	tiddley	theorem
scuchin	stunted	skyjack	trayful	tranter	tidings	theorbo
souther	scuttle	skylark	trangle	tractus	tadpole	theurgy
studied	shuttle	skysail	twangle	traduce	tedious	tressed
soubise	skuttle	sayable	trangam	tragule	tide-rip	tressel
spuriae	spurtle	styrene	tear-gas	thalweg	tedesca	treason
souming	squitch	shyness	trachea	tramway	tedesco	theatre
souring	saunter	slyness	teachie	to-brake	tide-way	trestle
sousing	scutter	scythed	teach-in	tubfast	themata	trental
sourish	shunter	scyther	tea-shop	tobacco	trehala	treetop
saurian	shutter	scyphus	teacher	to-break	Thebaic	theater
saucier	sputter	skyline	tsarina	tableau	Thebaid	treater
studier	stutter	stylise	toadied	tubeful	teenage	tweeter
saucily	squatty	stylite	tea-time	tabbied	thecate	teentsy
spunkie	spur-way	sky-high	teaming	tabling	trepang	tiffany
stuck-up	squawky	stylish	tearing	tubbing	tietack	taffeta
shucker	spulyie	sky-sign	teasing	tubbish	toe-nail	taffety
skulker	snuzzle	Stygian	thawing	tubfish	trenail	tiffing
squalid	spulzie	stylist	tracing	toby-jug	therapy	tufting
squelch	save-all	skyclad	trading	tabulae	tremble	toffish
souslik	savable	sky-blue	tea-dish	tabular	treybit	tag-tail
scudler	Sivaite	styloid	tsarism	tubular	treacle	taggers
sculler	Sivaism	spy-hole	thalian	tabanid	tiercel	tigress
skudler	saveloy	shy-cock	Tsabian	Tabanus	treacly	toggery
squalor	savanna	Shylock	tsarist	tabinet	treadle	tegmina
squally	seventh	skyborn	tracked	tabloid	treddle	tigrine
scummed	seventy	sky-bred	thankee	tabooed	tweedle	tagging
stummed	saviour	smytrie	trankum	taborin	treader	tugging
squamae	several	stypsis	thanker	taborer	Tuesday	tigrish
stummel	savarin	styptic	tracker	tabaret	thereof	tegulae
scummer	savoury	shyster	traikit	taboret	tie-beam	Tagalog
skummer	saw-gate	seysure	twankay	Tabasco®	therein	tegular
slummer	saw-edge	sizable	thallic	tabetic	thereon	tigroid
shunned	saw-kerf	syzgial	trailer	Tibetan	thereto	tug-boat
stunned	saw-fish	sozzled	trawler	to-brusd	tieless	tigerly
squinch	saw-bill	sizzler	thallus	tubfuls	thereat	togated
sputnik	saw-mill	tuatara	trammel	toccata	thereby	tighten
scunner	sow-skin	tiaraed	thammuz	tuck-box	twelfth	tagetes
spurner	sawn-off	twafald	trained	tackety	teemful	tightly
stunner	saw-wort	tea-cake	trainee	tactful	treague	T-shaped
Sturnus	sowarry	thanage	trannie	tactile	thether	toheroa
squinny	saw-buck	thalami	thannah	tacking	theriac	tailard
sauroid	sawdust	travail	trainer	ticking	taeniae	tribade
sourock	six-pack	tear-bag	tea-rose	tachism	trenise	tsigane
sautoir	sextans	traybit	twasome	tactism	teeming	tridarn
spumous	sextant	tranced	tea-room	tychism	taedium	tribady
shut-out	sex-cell	tranche	tea-gown	taction	treviss	trigamy

trinary	twirler	take-out	Tampico	tanagra	thonder	to-pinch
tzigany	triblet	tallage	Tamilic	tanager	twoness	toponym
thimble	triglot	tillage	Tamulic	tonight	thonged	top-knot
triable	triolet	tollage	templed	tinchel	thought	tapioca
tribble	triplet	toll-bar	time-lag	tanghin	trophic	tiptoed
triacid	triplex	tallboy	templar	tenthly	toothed	typhoid
twiscar	trimmed	til-seed	tumbler	tan-ride	trochee	top-hole
twitchy	triumph	toluene	tumular	tensile	trochal	top-soil
triadic	thiamin	tallent	tumulus	tensive	thother	taproom
trindle	trimmer	taleful	templet	tontine	trochus	typhoon
twiddle	trismus	tulchan	temenos	tanking	thorite	typhous
thirdly	tzimmes	telpher	tombola	tanling	two-line	tap-bolt
twiddly	thinned	tile-hat	tempore	tanning	two-time	taproot
tail-end	twinned	tallied	tomfool	tenting	tooling	top-boot
Trilene®	trionym	tillite	tombolo	tinging	Thomism	top-coat
trireme	thinner	talking	tambour	tinning	thorium	topmost
triseme	triones	telling	timeous	tinting	tropism	topspin
toisech	Tritoma	tilling	time-out	tunning	Thomist	tapered
triceps	twifold	tilting	timbrel	tonnish	tropist	toparch
taivert	trilobe	tolling	tumbrel	tun-dish	toolkit	taperer
trident	tritone	tallith	tamarin	tension	troelie	tapetal
trisect	trizone	Tullian	tom-trot	tentigo	troolie	tapetum
tripery	tripoli	tallies	tamasha	tondino	trollop	tapster
tritely	triform	telamon	tumesce	tenpins	troller	tipster
triffid	tricorn	tollman	tempter	tantivy	trolley	tapstry
toilful	trifoly	taloned	timothy	tensity	trommel	topfull
tail-fly	trilogy	talcose	tempura	tenuity	thorned	T-square
tringle	tripody	tall-oil	tantara	tangled	trounce	tequila
twiggen	tripped	talcous	tankard	tangler	two-inch	tartana
thigger	tripple	teleost	tanyard	tingler	twofold	tar-sand
trigger	tripper	tallowy	Tynwald	tinkler	twosome	turband
twigger	trippet	taliped	tankage	tonemic	two-tone	tartane
thiggit	triarch	tylopod	tannage	tinamou	two-four	tartare
thither	trigram	talipes	tannate	tenoner	two-foot	ternate
trishaw	thiasus	talipat	teniate	tenancy	trooper	terrace
tailing	tripsis	talipot	tentage	tangoed	trouper	threave
T'ai-p'ing	twin-set	talaria	tInware	tenfold	tootsie	tornade
toiling	thirsty	tile-red	tonnage	tenioid	trotted	torsade
twining	triatic	telergy	tunnage	tan-ooze	two-step	terrain
trilith	tainted	telesis	tan-bark	tinfoil	trotter	tornado
trivial	twisted	tyloses	tin-tack	tung-oil	trouter	turbant
twibill	twitted	tylosis	tone-arm	tenuous	two-eyed	Tartary
tritium	thistle	Telstar	tent-bed	ten-foot	taplash	ternary
trivium	twitten	talaunt	tenable	tantony	topsail	thready
tuition	twinter	tilbury	tunable	tent-peg	tip-cart	throaty
trinity	twister	tally-ho	tunably	tent-pin	topmast	turbary
trickle	twitter	talayot	tunicle	Tantric	topiary	terebra
twinkle	thistly	tympana	tunicin	tendril	type-bar	turacin
trinkum	trisula	timbale	tank-car	tangram	topical	turndun
thicken	tribune	timpani	tanadar	tantrum	typical	term-day
thick'un	tribute	timpano	tonnell	tendron	topless	tarweed
thinker	triduum	tympano	tangelo	tonetic	tap-shoe	terpene
tricker	triduan	Tammany	tangent	tongued	tappice	terrene
thicket	thieves	tympany	tiniest	tonsure	top-line	turpeth
trinket	triaxon	tamable	tonneau	tinfuls	topside	tar-heel
thickly	tuilyie	timidly	tannery	tintype	tapping	tar-seal
trickly	tailzie	tumidly	tensely	two-hand	tipping	terreen
tricksy	tuilzie	tempera	tindery	two-pair	topping	torpedo
trilled	takable	tempest	tendenz	two-part	tipsify	Turkess
twilled	takahea	time-gun	tankful	trouble	tipsily	torment
taillie	tektite	tamping	tentful	toolbag	tippler	torrent
thiller	tokamak	tampion	tuneful	toolbox	tapsman	turgent
trifler	take-off	tompion		trodden	topsman	tersely

torpefy	turmoil	Titania	towline	upbrast	undight	unheedy
torrefy	turn-out	tutania	townish	umbrere	undried	uphoist
turnery	tar-spot	tetanic	towmond	upbreak	undoing	unhuman
terefah	tortrix	titanic	towrope	unbless	undying	unhinge
thrifty	tirasse	tutenag	towmont	unblent	undeify	unhandy
torchon	thristy	tetanal	towered	unblest	uddered	uphoord
torcher	thrutch	tetanus	to-worne	unbegun	underdo	unhoped
tormina	thretty	Totanus	tow-iron	unbeget	undergo	U-shaped
tarried	torqued	tetrode	towards	unbegot	undated	unhappy
tardive	Tartufe	titmose	tax-cart	unblind	undrunk	unhired
tartine	torture	tutwork	taxable	unbuild	ukelele	unhorse
tergite	tarbush	Tataric	taxably	upbuild	useless	unherst
termite	through	to-torne	taxicab	unbeing	urethra	unhardy
terrine	thrived	tittupy	toxical	upbring	urethan	unhasty
torsive	thriven	trucage	textile	Umbrian	uredine	unhitch
tortile	thriver	tsunami	taxing	unbuilt	uterine	unhouse
tortive	throw-in	touraco	taximan	unbaked	uredium	uricase
turbine	thrower	thumbed	text-man	umbonal	uberous	urinate
turdine	thruway	truncal	tax-free	umbones	uneared	urinant
turfite	testate	trundle	texture	umbrose	unearth	unitary
tarring	toshach	thunder	textual	unbroke	utensil	urinary
turfing	testacy	taurean	trysail	unblock	uneaten	unidea'd
turning	test-bed	trumeau	thyself	unblown	uveitis	unideal
tarnish	tessera	truffle	toyshop	upblown	unequal	ulichon
tartish	tassell	thuggee	thymine	umbrous	unfaded	unified
turbith	testern	trudgen	thyroid	umbered	unflesh	unitise
Turkish	tushery	trudger	twyfold	unburnt	unfaith	unitive
termini	test-fly	touched	thylose	upburst	unfiled	utilise
tertial	tussive	toughie	toysome	unbosom	unfilde	uniting
terbium	tasking	toughen	toylsom	unbated	unfamed	unition
Toryism	tasting	toucher	trypsin	unbound	unfumed	unifier
ternion	testing	teuchat	thyrsus	upbound	unfunny	unicity
tersion	tossing	toughly	tryptic	unbowed	unfrock	utility
tertian	tastily	taurine	tryster	uncharm	unfired	uniform
torsion	testify	thulite	unaware	unchain	unfitly	unicorn
tarrier	testily	touring	unaided	unclasp	unfeued	urinous
tarsier	tossily	tousing	urachus	upcoast	unfound	unjaded
terrier	tussore	trucial	unalike	unchary	upflung	unjoint
Tarsius	tussock	thulium	unalive	uncheck	unflush	unkempt
tertius	testoon	tourism	uralite	unclean	unfixed	unknown
turkies	tosspot	tourist	uranide	unclear	unfazed	unleash
tardily	testril	thurify	uranite	upcheer	unguard	unlearn
terrify	testudo	trunked	unaking	upclimb	upgrade	unlucky
turnkey	titrate	truckle	uranism	unchild	ungodly	unladen
torulin	titlark	trucker	uranium	unction	unguent	uplying
turtler	tetract	Trullan	Uralian	unclipt	upgoing	unlimed
torulus	tutress	Thummim	Uranian	uncinus	unguled	unlined
tartlet	totient	trueman	unalist	uncanny	ungulae	unloose
thrilly	tattery	tourney	unasked	uncloud	urgence	unlaste
thrombi	tottery	truancy	udaller	unclose	urgency	unlatch
turfman	titmice	thumper	uraemia	upclose	unglove	unloved
Turkman	tatting	trumpet	uraemic	uncloak	ungrown	unmeant
thrummy	tithing	trussed	unaimed	uncrown	upgrown	upmaker
throned	titling	trusser	unarmed	uncross	ungored	unmanly
tyranne	totting	toustie	up-along	ulcered	ungirth	unmoral
threnos	Titoism	trustee	uranous	uncured	ungyved	unmarry
tyrones	Titoist	taunter	unaired	uncurse	ungazed	unmated
tyranny	tattily	truster	uva-ursi	upcatch	unheard	unmeted
turbond	tattler	taverna	unacted	uncouth	unhoard	unmould
turnoff	titular	towpath	unaptly	uncivil	uphoard	unmount
turn-off	tutelar	tow-head	upbraid	uncover	upheave	unmoved
torgoch	totally	town-end	umbrage	updrawn	unheart	unmixed
tarrock	totemic	thwaite	unbrace	undress	unhable	unneath

unnoble	unroyal	unstrip	unwhipt	V-necked	velated	verdant
unnamed	unstaid	unscrew	unwaked	vagrant	voluted	vernant
ulnaria	upstand	unsated	unweldy	vaguely	volutin	versant
unnerve	unscale	unsound	unwoman	voguish	valvula	varices
unnoted	unshale	unslung	unwooed	veganic	valvule	verbena
urnfuls	unshape	unstuck	unwiped	vaginae	velouté	vermeil
unorder	unstate	unsaved	unwarie	vaginal	vulture	vermell
Urodela	upspake	unsewed	unworth	V-agents	vulturn	varment
urodele	upstage	unsexed	unwares	vaginas	velours	veriest
uromere	upstare	unsized	upwards	vegetal	vilayet	variety
urolith	upstate	untrace	unwitch	vehicle	vampire	versine
uxorial	unstack	unteach	unwater	vihuela	vamping	varying
utopism	unsnarl	up-train	unwitty	V-shaped	vampish	versing
utopian	upswarm	uptrain	unwound	vyingly	vamoose	varnish
utopist	unslain	untread	upwound	Vaishya	vomited	vermian
unoiled	upstair	uptrend	unwrung	veiling	ventana	version
unowned	unsmart	uptight	unwived	veining	vanward	vertigo
urosome	upstart	untried	unwoven	voicing	vantage	vernier
ufology	upsides	untride	unwayed	voiding	vendace	varmint
urology	unspeak	untwine	unyoked	vaivode	vendage	verdict
unoften	upspeak	untylng	unzoned	voivode	ventage	varsity
unplace	unshell	unthink	vialful	veinous	vintage	vermily
unplait	unspell	untwist	vialled	voiture	vanadic	verminy
umpteen	unsteel	untaken	viaduct	voltaic	Vendean	versify
unpaged	upswell	untiled	vibrate	valuate	venefic	verglas
unpaint	unshewn	untamed	vibrato	valvate	vinegar	virelay
uppiled	upsweep	up-tempo	vibrant	village	ventige	veranda
unpanel	unswear	untoned	vibices	voltage	vanning	viranda
unpinkt	upspear	untuned	vacuate	volvate	venting	Veronal®
unpaper	unshent	untenty	viciate	vulgate	vendiss	virando
unpared	unspent	untired	vocable	vulvate	vanilla	Varanus
unpurse	unsweel	utterer	vaccine	villain	Vinalia	variola
unperch	unswept	upthrow	vacking	viliaco	venally	variole
unposed	upswept	utterly	vacuist	viliago	venomed	verbose
unplumb	unsight	untruth	vacuity	volcano	vintner	various
unplume	unspied	untruss	vocalic	valiant	Ventôse	verismo
unpaved	unspide	untrust	vocular	vallary	ventose	virosis
unqueen	unsling	untruly	vocally	villany	vent-peg	viretot
unquiet	upswing	untaxed	vicomte	volable	vine-rod	verruca
unquote	unstick	ululate	vacance	voluble	ventral	verruga
unreave	unsaint	ululant	vicinal	volubil	venerer	vareuse
unready	unspilt	usucapt	vacancy	volubly	vanessa	verdure
unraced	unsolid	ukulele	vacuole	validly	vinasse	versute
utricle	upsilon	usuress	vacuous	villein	venison	virgule
unreeve	unsense	unurged	vicious	velvety	venatic	virtual
unruffe	unsinew	usuring	victory	veliger	vingt-un	vistaed
unright	unsonsy	usually	victrix	vulpine	venator	vassail
upright	unsunny	usurous	viceroy	volpino	vincula	vessail
upraise	upstood	usurped	vacatur	volumed	venture	visible
unraked	unsmote	usurper	victual	velamen	venturi	visibly
unruled	unsoote	unusual	viduage	valonea	vinewed	vesicae
unrimed	unspoke	unvocal	Vidicon®	valonia	Vandyke	vesicle
unroost	upspoke	unvaile	viduity	valance	violate	vesical
uprisal	unstock	unvoice	vedalia	valence	violent	viscera
unrisen	unshorn	upvalue	vidimus	volante	violist	Vosgean
uprisen	unshown	unvisor	Vedanta	valency	violone	visaged
unround	unsworn	unvital	videnda	villose	vapidly	vespine
uprouse	unshoot	unvexed	Veddoid	villous	vapoury	vestige
unrough	unshout	unweave	viduous	Volapük	vaquero	vesting
unravel	upshoot	unweary	vedette	velaria	variate	Vosgian
unriven	unsured	umwhile	vidette	velaric	virgate	vastity
upriver	upsurge	unwrite	veering	vervain	vespoid
unrivet	unstrap	upwhirl	viewing	volatic	variant	viscose

viscous	whaling	wheeled	waiting	wildish	whoobub	Wormian
visnomy	wearish	wheelie	whining	wolfish	whomble	Würmian
visored	wearily	wheeler	whiting	wolvish	woodcut	warrior
vestral	whacked	whemmle	writing	Wolfian	woolded	worrier
visitee	whacker	wheenge	whitish	willies	woolder	wurlies
visiter	whatnot	waesome	wrinkle	wolfkin	woomera	wordily
visitor	wrapped	woesome	whicker	welcome	woosell	warbler
vascula	whample	woeworn	whisker	well-off	woolfat	wire-man
vesture	wrapper	wheeple	whisket	Walloon	wronger	workman
vis-à-vis	whaisle	wherret	whiskey	walk-out	wrought	warlord
vitiate	whatsis	wheeson	wrinkly	wildoat	wrongly	warwolf
vitrage	whatsit	wheesht	wrizled	willowy	whorish	werwolf
vittate	whatten	whey-tub	whirler	wall-rue	wholism	war-song
vitrail	wealthy	whetted	whitlow	wolfram	woozily	warlock
vitrain	wharves	wreathe	waivode	well-set	whorled	war-worn
vitraux	whaizle	wrestle	woiwode	well-won	woolled	work-out
Vatican	webbing	wheaten	whipped	walkway	woollen	worn-out
vitreum	wabbler	whetter	whimple	welaway	whommle	war-drum
Vitrina	wobbler	wrester	whimper	waltzer	woodman	wardrop
vitrine	web-toed	wreaths	whipper	wameful	woolman	warison
vetting	webworm	wren-tit	whisper	wampish	wood-oil	work-shy
vitriol	web-foot	wreathy	whippet	womanly	wood-owl	worsted
vitrics	wabster	wheezle	whirred	wimbrel	wool-oil	waratah
vitrify	webster	waftage	whirret	wantage	whoopee	wiretap
vitelli	wych-elm	weftage	whitret	windage	whooper	worktop
vitular	wadmaal	wafting	Whitsun	wind-bag	whopper	wire-way
vitally	wide-boy	wofully	whip-saw	wine-bag	woolsey	wastage
vitamin	widgeon	wafture	whimsey	wind-egg	wood-tin	wassail
veteran	wadsett	wagtail	waisted	wanness	wood-tar	wash-day
vettura	wide-gab	wigless	whirtle	wintery	whoever	western
vetiver	wadding	waggery	whistle	wine-fat	wood-wax	wastery
vouchee	wedding	wiggery	whittle	wanigan	wappend	wishful
voucher	wedging	wagging	written	wind-gun	warrand	wistful
vaurien	widener	wigging	whip-top	wencher	warfare	wosbird
Vaudois	wedlock	waggish	waister	wanting	war-game	washing
vaudoux	wadmoll	wiggler	whittaw	wincing	wordage	wasting
vaulted	widower	wagoner	whizzed	winding	warpath	westing
vaunted	wheedle	wagerer	whizzer	winking	warrant	wishing
vaulter	wielder	wightly	wakeful	winning	work-bag	waspish
vaunter	weekday	Wahabee	wakeman	wannish	work-box	wistiti
vividly	weekend	wainage	wakened	Wendish	worlded	westlin
vivific	whereof	whipcat	wakener	wennish	work-day	wash-out
vivency	wherein	weirdie	wallaba	wannion	worldly	wash-pot
vivaria	whereon	whidder	welfare	windily	warhead	wastrel
Viverra	whereso	weirdly	wild-ass	wing-led	wormery	wash-tub
vowelly	whereto	write-in	wallaby	wangler	workful	wetland
vexedly	whene'er	write-up	wild-cat	winglet	wart-hog	wattage
vexilla	where'er	whitely	wild-dog	wanhope	warship	wetback
vixenly	waeness	whiffle	wolf-dog	windore	worship	witwall
voyager	whereas	wailful	wall-eye	winsome	wergild	wotteth
vizored	whereat	whiffer	willest	Wenlock	worried	wet-cell
weasand	weedery	whiffet	well-fed	windock	warlike	wetness
weazand	whereby	wringed	wileful	winnock	wartime	withers
Wealden	whether	wriggle	welcher	wondred	warding	witless
whate'er	weeding	whinger	welsher	windrow	warling	witness
whalery	weeping	wringer	walking	wine-sap	warming	wottest
whangee	weeting	weighed	walling	Windsor	warning	Watteau
wrangle	wheyish	weigh-in	welding	wine-vat	warping	wet-shod
whangam	weevily	writhen	welling	want-wit	warring	witchen
weather	whelked	weigher	wilding	woorara	wording	watcher
wearied	wreaked	whither	willing	wood-ash	working	wotcher
wearing	wreaker	weighty	wolfing	woorali	wordish	watchet
weaving	wrecker	wailing	wolving	wood-ant	Wardian	wetting

witling	yeading	ziganka	zootype
witting	yibbles	zygosis	zaptiah
wotting	yachter	zygotic	zaptieh
wettish	Yiddish	Zairean	Ziphius
wittily	yielder	Zoilean	zareeba
wattled	yeggman	zoisite	zorgite
witloof	yoghurt	Zoilism	zarnich
wet-dock	Yahvist	Zoilist	zorille
wet-look	Yahwist	zakuska	zorillo
without	yakhdan	zakuski	Zostera
watered	ycleap'd	Zolaism	zestful
waterer	ycleepe	zillion	zithern
wourali	yplight	zimocca	zetetic
would-be	yelling	zymogen	zeuxite
wounder	yelping	zamarra	Zeuxian
wauling	yslaked	zamarro	Zezidee
whummle	yelloch	zymosis	Zizania
wavelet	yellowy	zymotic	
waverer	ycleped	zemstvo	
waveson	yolk-sac	zamouse	
wawling	yamulka	Zincala	
wax-palm	yanking	Zingana	
waxwing	ymolten	Zingara	
wax-bill	yapster	Zingane	
wax-moth	yardage	Zingare	
waxwork	yardang	Zincali	
wax-doll	yard-arm	Zingani	
wax-tree	Yoruban	Zingari	
wayward	Yorkish	Zincalo	
weyward	Yorkist	Zingano	
wayfare	ywroken	Zingaro	
waymark	yardman	zanjero	
wryneck	yestern	zincite	
wayless	ypsilon	zincing	
wryness	yashmak	zinking	
wayment	yu-stone	zanyism	
wrythen	yatagan	Zantiot	
wayside	yttrium	zincify	
way-bill	youngth	zinkify	
wrybill	youngly	zincked	
waygone	youthly	zanella	
wayworn	younker	zonular	
way-post	yawning	zonulet	
whyever	yowling	zincoid	
wizened	yew-tree	zincode	
X-factor	Yezidee	zincous	
xylogen	zealant	Zonurus	
xylonic	zealful	zonated	
xylenol	zoarium	zoogamy	
Xylopia	zealous	zootaxy	
xanthic	zebrass	zooecia	
xanthin	zebrine	zoogeny	
Xenopus	zabtieh	zoopery	
Xenurus	zebroid	zeolite	
Xiphias	zebrula	zoolite	
xiphoid	zebrule	zoonite	
xerafin	zoccolo	zoolith	
xerarch	zedoary	Zionism	
xerasia	Zadkiel	Zionist	
xerosis	zoeform	zoogony	
xerotic	ziffius	zoology	
xerotes	zuffolo	zoonomy	
yealdon	Zygaena	zootomy	

agar-agar	anatropy	ascender	ale-berry	aiguille	abidance	alkaline
amadavat	alacrity	arcanely	avenging	Anguilla	agitated	alkalise
Aramaean	abattoir	accentor	anechoic	aggrieve	animated	ankylose
avadavat	acanthin	arcanist	amethyst	angekkok	alizarin	acknowne
anasarca	alastrim	archness	American	angelica	amicable	ankerite
apanaged	awanting	anchoret	alewives	algology	amicably	alliance
anabasis	adaption	accepter	adenitis	argemone	animally	ad-libber
anabatic	acanthus	arch-poet	aperitif	argument	apically	allocate
ataraxia	adaptive	acceptor	aperient	Algonkin	avifauna	allodial
ataraxic	arapunga	accuracy	areolate	arginine	agitator	allodium
abatable	analyser	accorder	abetment	alginate	animator	allogamy
arapaima	analyses	accursed	averment	argonaut	akinesia	allegory
anapaest	analysis	ascorbic	agedness	aegrotat	akinesis	alligate
Aramaism	analytic	accurate	adenoids	aeglogue	anisette	all-fired
amaranth	ambiance	accustom	ale-house	Algerian	acid-head	all-fives
Atalanta	albacore	ancestor	adespota	algaroba	alighted	all-giver
amaracus	albicore	ancestry	awearied	auger-bit	arillode	all-night
anarchal	ambience	alcatras	aberrant	aegirine	axiology	all-risks
anarchic	ambulant	accoutre	aleurone	algerine	arillary	all-clear
analcime	arbalest	Arcturus	averring	algorism	axillary	alleluia
analcite	arbalist	archwise	aneurism	aegirite	arillate	aglimmer
amandine	ambulate	addicted	aneurysm	argyrite	amidmost	Atlantes
acaudate	Albanian	abdicant	aberrate	Augustan	avionics	Atlantic
Araldite®	albiness	abducent	aversely	Argestes	alienage	Atlantis
Araneida	albinism	adducent	aversion	augustly	alienism	all-round
acalepha	ambrosia	abductor	aversive	argutely	alienist	all-fours
acalephe	arboreal	adductor	agential	angstrom	Arianise	allspice
academia	amberoid	abdicate	a-weather	aphicide	Arianism	allopath
academic	arborist	audacity	aventail	aphidian	aridness	aularian
apatetic	amberite	audience	ale-stake	ash-leach	alienate	allergen
amazedly	arboreta	aldehyde	abetting	athletic	Adiantum	allergic
analecta	alburnum	ardently	axe-stone	ashy-grey	amiantus	alluring
analects	amberous	addendum	aleatory	aphthous	acidosis	allerion
araceous	arborous	androgen	aperture	aphelian	amitosis	aplastic
araneous	Abbaside	Abderian	aseptate	ash-blond	amitotic	allusion
arachnid	asbestic	alderman	adequacy	ash-plant	aniconic	aplustre
anathema	asbestos	addorsed	adequate	atheling	agitprop	allosaur
anaphora	abbatial	Alderney	acervate	aphelion	apiarian	allusive
anaphase	arbitral	alder-fly	affiance	aphanite	acierage	aglitter
acaridan	ambition	Anderson	afflated	achenial	apiarist	allotted
Adamical	albitise	abeyance	affrayed	Athenian	aviarist	axle-tree
Agamidae	arboured	abeyancy	afflatus	athanasy	acierate	ablation
Aranidae	ambivert	Arenaria	affected	aphonous	amissing	ablution
Adamitic	Archaean	amenable	affecter	Achernar	agiotage	ablative
Aganippe	archaise	amenably	alfresco	abhorred	aviatrix	alluvial
agalloch	archaism	Alemaine	affeered	abhorrer	aviation	alluvion
availing	archaist	areca-nut	affright	atheroma	aristate	alluvium
anableps	archaeus	acerbate	affinity	adherent	acicular	alley-taw
anaglyph	Accadian	acerbity	affronté	Atherina	aliquant	alleyway
alarming	Arcadian	ayenbite	affirmer	atherine	abjectly	allaying
alarmist	ascidian	acescent	afferent	aphorise	adjacent	alley-tor
anaconda	archduke	amelcorn	afforest	aphorism	adjuring	alms-deed
araponga	accident	Aberdeen	affusion	aphorist	adjuster	alms-dish
anabolic	arcading	anecdote	affluent	aphasiac	adjustor	Asmodeus
anagogic	aecidium	alebench	alguacil	adhesion	adjutage	alms-folk
analogic	ascidium		alguazil	adhesive	adjutant	Armagnac
anatomic	accredit		arguable	athetoid	adjuvant	Almagest
apagogic	alchemic		arguably	ash-stand	Akkadian	almighty
analogon	alcahest		algicide	aphetise	ark-shell	armchair
analogue	archival		algidity	athetise	alkahest	atmology
abampere	arc-light		aigrette		alkalies	atmolyse
acarpous	accolade		Anglican		alkalify	armament
anaerobe	archlute		anguiped		alkaloid	ammoniac

Armenian	apolline	appetite	agronomy	assemblé	antlered	Asterias
Arminian	Apollyon	asphyxia	airiness	assembly	ants'-eggs	attorney
Armenoid	Anoplura	applying	aeronaut	assuming	anthelia	altarage
arm-in-arm	apoplexy	appuying	airwoman	Ausonian	anthelix	autarchy
admonish	acosmism	acquaint	air-cover	arsenide	anthemia	asteroid
ammonite	acosmist	arquebus	air-power	absentee	anthesis	autarkic
ammonium	acoemeti	acquiral	aureoled	assenter	asthenia	alterant
armorial	acorn-cup	acquired	air-to-air	absinthe	asthenic	attiring
armorist	apodosis	airwards	airborne	absently	artefact	anterior
admitted	apologia	aerially	air-house	absonant	artifact	anteroom
armature	apologue	aerobics	airspace	assonant	artifice	attercop
armoured	apospory	aerobomb	agraphia	assentor	antefixa	asterisk
armourer	apograph	abricock	agraphic	arsonist	astigmia	asterism
armozeen	anourous	apricock	abruptly	arsenate	autogamy	alterity
armozine	acoustic	airscrew	atropine	arsenite	autogeny	apterium
annealer	aboiteau	auricled	agraphon	arsonite	autogiro	apterous
annually	anorthic	auricula	atropism	assonate	autogyro	aftereye
abnegate	abortion	apricate	atropous	aasvogel	anti-hero	antistat
Annelida	adoption	atrocity	agrarian	Assyrian	autoharp	Artesian
annulled	amortise	abridger	aurorean	Austrian	altrices	attested
annalise	apostasy	Airedale	air-brick	abstract	astringe	attester
annalist	apostate	abradant	aircraft	abstrict	antliate	artistic
annulose	abortive	acridine	air-drain	absorbed	antilogy	autistic
Annulata	adoptive	aerodyne	air-brake	absorber	autology	autosome
annulate	Apocynum	aerodart	airdrome	asserter	antelope	attestor
amniotic	alphabet	acridity	airframe	assorted	Antilope	antisera
abnormal	appearer	air-bends	airgraph	assorter	autolyse	artistry
amnesiac	applause	aerofoil	air-brush	absurdly	autumnal	altitude
agnostic	appraise	aeriform	air-drawn	anserine	attemper	aptitude
adnation	aspidium	auriform	aerostat	assertor	antimony	attitude
agnation	apple-pie	aerogram	agrestal	adscript	antimask	antithel
annotate	arpeggio	arrogant	arrestee	abstruse	automata	astutely
announce	apprizer	abrogate	arrester	assisted	automate	autotomy
annexion	Amphibia	arrogate	acrostic	assassin	astomous	astatine
annexure	amphipod	airshaft	agrestic	assessor	actiniae	antitype
apogaeic	appliqué	Ayrshire	après-ski	Alsatian	actinian	autotype
aromatic	ampullae	airliner	arrasene	assotted	antennae	artfully
adorable	appalled	airtight	abrasion	aesculin	antennal	altruism
adorably	appanage	aortitis	arrestor	Aesculus	antennas	altruist
avowable	appendix	adroitly	abrasive	assaying	actinide	actively
abomasum	alpinism	airfield	airstrip	astragal	antinode	antevert
abomasus	alpinist	Aprilian	aeration	ant-eater	attender	activism
amoeboid	amphorae	aurelian	acrotism	actually	actinoid	activist
aboideau	approval	aerology	arraught	actuator	antinomy	activate
alopecia	approach	agrology	air-built	antibody	autonomy	activity
anoretic	approver	acrolein	airburst	Autobahn	actinism	adularia
anorexia	asphodel	airplane	aardvark	autocrat	astonish	amusable
anorexic	amphoric	air-plant	aardwolf	antecede	antenati	adulator
avowedly	asperger	Aprilish	answerer	autocade	autunite	aquacade
amoretti	asperges	acrolith	absterge	articled	actinium	ague-cake
amoretto	amperage	aerolite	assiento	attached	although	aduncate
apophyge	apparent	aerolith	Ansafone®	attacker	Anthozoa	aduncity
apothegm	aspirant	acromial	assignat	autacoid	antrorse	aguacate
alogical	aspiring	atremble	assignee	autocarp	antipode	aduncous
atomical	asperate	acrimony	assignor	Atticise	autopsia	aqueduct
aborigen	asperity	agrémens	arsehole	Atticism	autoptic	abundant
agonised	aspirate	agrément	aesthete	anticous	antipole	amuletic
atomiser	asperous	agrimony	aestival	anticize	antiphon	amusedly
aborigin	appestat	atrament	abscissa	auto-da-fé	antipope	aculeate
aconitic	apposite	acromion	abscisse	autodyne	antepast	amusette
apomixis	appetent	apron-man	absolver	antedate	ante-post	abutilon
apositia	appetise	aeronomy	absolute	antidote	alternat	aluminum
aconitum	amputate		assemble		arterial	aqualung

aquiline	brandish	blastoid	Buccinum	bedarken	beflower	brisling
abutment	brake-van	boattail	bacillar	bedesman	befitted	brimless
aquanaut	beam-ends	blastula	bucellas	bedstead	bog-Latin	bailment
aquarian	beavered	blastema	becalmed	bedstraw	beggarly	brimming
alum-root	bracelet	blasting	back-lill	bed-staff	baguette	beinness
aquarist	brazenly	boasting	baculine	bodywork	bagpiper	blimpish
aquarium	brazenry	brattish	buckling	badly-off	bagpipes	Briarean
Aquarius	blameful	boastful	backlash	bedazzle	beguiler	bailsman
aguishly	Beaufort	bearward	baculite	bee-eater	bigamist	blissful
avulsion	boarfish	beauxite	bacillus	bleacher	bigamous	bristled
abutting	bragging	Babeeism	becoming	breeched	beginner	bristols
aquatint	braggart	babyfood	backmost	breeches	Bignonia	blistery
adultery	brachial	bobwheel	Baconian	beefcake	bughouse	briguing
alveated	biathlon	babyhood	biconvex	bleeding	begorrah	britzska
advocaat	boat-hook	bob-white	backpack	blending	begirded	blizzard
advocacy	Baathism	biblical	Bactrian	breeding	begetter	bejabers
Arvicola	Baathist	bobbinet	by-corner	breadnut	begotten	Bajocian
·dvocate	beatific	Babbitry	backroom	breveted	begrudge	bijwoner
advanced	beak-iron	babbling	back-rope	bien-être	bogey-man	bejesuit
alveolar	blackcap	bobolink	backside	bretesse	bogeyism	Bakelite®
alveolus	black-cat	bubaline	buckshee	brethren	beheadal	bakemeat
advising	blackleg	babeldom	backspin	beech-oil	beholden	balsamic
advisory	black-neb	babelish	bicuspid	Blenheim	beholder	Bulgaric
advoutry	bean-king	babelism	buckskin	breviary	Bohemian	balladry
advowson	blacking	bibulous	backstop	breviate	behemoth	bilabial
auxiliar	blackboy	babushka	buckshot	break-jaw	behappen	bull-beef
adynamia	black-fox	baby-talk	backveld	breakage	behovely	bellbind
adynamic	blacktop	bibation	backward	breaking	bailable	bell-buoy
amygdala	blackish	bobstays	backword	break-vow	bail-ball	billbook
amygdale	brackish	babouche	backwork	break-out	bail-bond	bell-bird
amygdule	blankety	bobby-pin	backwash	beetling	blimbing	bilobate
apyretic	blackout	baccarat	buck-wash	bdellium	britches	belabour
apyrexia	boat-load	bechance	backyard	bregmata	bail-dock	ballcock
anything	beagling	béchamel	badlands	biennial	brindled	bull-calf
anywhere	bratling	backache	bedwards	Blennius	blindage	bald-coot
atypical	brawling	buckaroo	bedeafen	Brezonek	blinding	bellcote
Aryanise	beamless	buckbean	bedmaker	bee-house	building	bale-dock
asystole	bran-mash	backband	beddable	breloque	blind-gut	bile-duct
bearable	biannual	backbond	bed-table	beer-pump	brideman	baladine
bearably	brainpan	backbone	biddable	bee-bread	brine-pan	bulldoze
beatable	brainish	backbite	bedabble	beetroot	bride-bed	believer
blamable	blazoner	backchat	bud-scale	breasted	brine-pit	belleter
blamably	blazonry	back-comb	bedrench	brewster	bride-ale	billeted
bravados	beanpole	buckcart	budgeree	bheestie	brief-bag	balletic
blah-blah	beau-pere	back-door	budgeted	breaskit	brim-full	bulletin
boatbill	boatrace	backdrop	badgerly	blessing	briefing	balneary
bearbine	bead-roll	back-date	budgerow	Boeotian	baitfish	bilberry
blabbing	baasskap	backdown	bedeguar	brettice	bridging	balled-up
branched	beadsman	bacteria	bedaggle	breathed	bringing	billfold
brancher	bear's-ear	bacteric	Buddhism	breather	blighted	bullfrog
bratchet	Bradshaw	bachelor	Buddhist	bleating	blighter	bale-fire
branchia	brassica	backfall	bed-linen	beeswing	brighten	ball-game
brancard	bearskin	backfill	bedright	beef-wood	blithely	bald-head
braccate	brassily	backfire	buddleia	breezily	brightly	billhead
boat-deck	biassing	bacchiac	bodiless	bifacial	brickbat	bolt-head
brandied	boat-song	bacchian	bed-plate	buff-coat	brinkman	bulkhead
brand-new	brassard	back-hair	bedimmed	bifocals	brick-red	bullhead
boarding	brassart	bacchant	bodement	befuddle	brick-tea	bolthole
braiding	bracteal	backhand	bidental	buffered	blinking	billhook
bladdery	brattice	buckhorn	badinage	befringe	bricking	bull-hoof
blandish	bractlet	bacchius	bedcover	befriend	brick-nog	bull-horn
Braidism	beautify	beck-iron	bedsocks	befallen	blinkard	billiard
brandise	blast-off	bick-iron	badmouth	baffling	briskish	ballista

balkline	bungalow	bandster	block-tin	bereaved	barkless	bestiary
balanced	bank-bill	bangster	blocking	bereaven	bergmehl	Basilian
balancer	bonibell	banister	blockish	burganet	barometz	basilica
bilander	bank-book	beniseed	brookite	barbaric	baronial	basaltic
bylander	bone-cave	bonassus	booklice	byrlakin	baronage	base-line
baldness	Benedick	bénitier	bootlace	barnacle	bareness	baselard
Balinese	Benedict	bang-tail	bootlick	Barbados	baroness	baseless
boldness	bunodont	binaural	blowlamp	barrator	burinist	bashless
balmoral	bone-dust	banausic	bookland	bergamot	Byronism	basilisk
balconet	bandelet	bung-vent	booklore	barratry	borrowed	basement
ballonet	bannered	bindweed	bioblast	bargaist	borrower	baseness
balloted	banneret	bentwood	bioplasm	bareback	burgonet	business
ballotee	banterer	bendwise	bioplast	bird-bolt	bargoose	busyness
bellower	bonneted	bandyman	bookless	barebone	burnouse	basanite
billowed	bunkered	bandying	bootlast	beriberi	bar-graph	basinful
ballocks	banderol	boneyard	bootless	birdbath	burgrave	bestowal
bollocks	bannerol	bunny-hug	browless	burschen	barostat	bespoken
bellpull	bontebok	buoyance	blooming	birdcage	Burnsian	bestower
bellpush	bandeaux	buoyancy	bloomers	borachio	burnside	bistoury
baldpate	benefact	brocaded	bloomery	birdcall	birdseed	bespread
baldrick	benefice	brocatel	bookmark	borecole	bardship	bestreak
belfried	boniface	browbeat	book-mate	boracite	birdshot	biserial
bull-ring	band-fish	blowball	Brownian	barndoor	Burnsite	bestride
ball-room	benignly	bloncket	browning	bargeman	bird's-eye	bestrode
bell-rope	benthoal	blotched	brownish	barterer	burnt-ear	bescreen
bolt-rope	bonehead	broacher	Brownism	bird-eyed	barathea	by-street
baluster	bank-high	bronchia	Brownist	bordered	borstall	besprent
bullshit	bung-hole	broccoli	bionomic	borderer	baritone	bush-rope
bull's-eye	Banthine®	bioscope	biomorph	berberis	barytone	bescrawl
belittle	bunching	bookcase	book-oath	bargello	Bermudas	bestrewn
bell-tent	bun-fight	bronchus	blowpipe	bordello	burgundy	bestrown
bulrushy	bone-idle	blood-tax	book post	barberry	barouche	bestsell
beloving	banditry	broadway	biograph	Burberry	berrying	besetter
bellwort	banditti	book-debt	bookrest	berceuse	biriyani	besotted
boll-worm	bindi-eye	blood-red	blossomy	barbette	barnyard	besmutch
ballyrag	bone-lace	blood-wit	browsing	barrette	Biscayan	besouled
billy-can	bantling	bloodily	bookshop	burletta	bastardy	besought
bullyrag	bundling	blood-hot	boob-tube	barbecue	beslaver	basquine
bully-off	bungling	broidery	boottree	Bordeaux	bostangi	bushveld
bellying	buntline	broadish	bloating	bergfall	biscacha	basswood
bullying	boneless	blowdown	blotting	barefoot	bistable	bisexual
ballyhoo	banality	biogenic	brow-tine	barogram	beshadow	betrayal
belly-god	binomial	brodekin	bookwork	baregine	bush-baby	betrayer
billyboy	bone-meal	bromelia	bookworm	berghaan	bush-buck	battalia
bully-boy	benumbed	brokenly	boobyish	birthday	busybody	bittacle
bullyism	bondmaid	biometry	boobyism	borehole	baseball	bathcube
bellyful	bone-mill	booked-up	bronzify	barchane	base-born	betacism
bemoaner	boniness	brougham	bronzing	birthdom	bisector	Bethesda
bummaree	bank-note	brouhaha	bronzite	bar-chart	basicity	batteler
bimbashi	buncombe	blowhole	bepraise	barghest	basidial	bettered
bemuddle	bonhomie	boot-hook	buplever	barbican	basidium	bathetic
bemuffle	banjoist	biophore	bepommel	barbital	by-speech	bitterly
bum-clock	benzoate	brochure	Baphomet	bartisan	besieger	batching
bimanous	bonspiel	boothose	bepepper	bartizan	Bessemer	botching
bomb-site	bona-roba	biocidal	biparous	barbicel	boss-eyed	butching
by-motive	bongrace	bootikin	bepester	bursitis	beseemly	bitchery
bombycid	bankroll	bromidic	beplumed	bird-lice	basketry	botchery
bondager	banxring	boom-iron	bepowder	beryllia	besognio	butcher's
bone-ache	bankrupt	boot-jack	bequeath	Bartlemy	boschbok	butchery
benjamin	bank-rate	brockram	barracan	bird-lime	besmirch	battle-ax
bankable	bandsman	blockade	barranca	bardling	bassinet	batology
binnacle	banksman	brooklet	barranco	burbling	buskined	butylene
bandanna	bondsman	blockage	barbated	burglary	bastille	bateless

botulism	bountree	chapelry	clay-marl	crab-wood	cyclopic	Chelifer
bateleur	bourtree	châteaux	claymore	crabwise	cyclosis	cheliped
betel-nut	blurting	coal-flap	charmful	crab-yaws	cacholot	clerihew
batement	boulting	coal-face	chainsaw	caboceer	coco-palm	Caecilia
bathmism	blustery	chauffer	charneco	caboched	cocoplum	chenille
botanise	bluntish	cram-full	chainlet	cabochon	cucurbit	cheville
botanist	blueweed	chaffing	chaunter	cable-car	cicerone	credible
batwoman	bluewing	chaffron	crannied	cableway	ciceroni	credibly
bottomed	bevelled	chaffery	chauntry	cobwebby	cicisbei	creditor
bathorse	beveller	coalfish	clannish	cubiform	cicisbeo	caesious
bathrobe	bivalent	cragfast	cyanogen	cuboidal	cockshot	crepitus
bethrall	beverage	crawfish	cyanosed	cabriole	cocksure	check-key
bathroom	bevatron	crayfish	chalonic	caballed	cockshut	check-off
buttress	bawd-born	clanging	cyanosis	caballer	cockspur	cheekily
butyrate	bi-weekly	clangour	cyanotic	cobaltic	coco-tree	creakily
betatron	bewigged	coachman	chaconne	cobbling	cicatrix	clecking
Batavian	bewailed	coach-way	cramoisy	cobblery	cocktail	clerkdom
bethwack	bewilder	crashpad	clapping	cabalism	cactuses	clerkess
batswing	bowelled	coal-hole	clasping	cabalist	cachucha	clerkish
bothyman	bowsprit	clashing	champion	cabin-boy	Cocculus	Chellean
botryoid	bewetted	coaching	clay-pipe	caboodle	coco-wood	creolian
botryose	box-wagon	crashing	champart	Cabirian	coccyges	creamery
brutally	Bixaceae	coach-box	champers	ciborium	caducean	cream-bun
Brumaire	box-pleat	coachdog	Coalport	cub-drawn	caducity	cream-nut
blueback	box-cloth	cyathium	chairman	caboshed	caduceus	cleanser
blue-buck	box-lobby	chamisal	coatrack	cabotage	caducous	cleaning
bluebell	bayadère	chaliced	chair-bed	cab-stand	codified	clean-cut
bluebird	bayberry	chapiter	charring	cibation	codifier	Cherokee
bluecoat	bryology	Charites	chay-root	cubature	cod-piece	Chelonia
blue-chip	boyishly	clarinet	clansman	cocoa-fat	cadenced	coelomic
bouncily	bizcacha	claviger	classman	cyclamen	code-name	coenobia
bouncing	bozzetto	caatinga	class-war	Cockayne	ciderkin	cremorne
bounding	bezonian	coamings	cragsman	cachalot	cider-and	cretonne
boundary	clamancy	Chasidic	clarsach	ciclaton	cedar-nut	creeping
baudekin	clavated	clavicle	chausses	cockatoo	cider-cup	clearway
Brunella	chapatti	charisma	classify	cocoanut	cadastre	clearage
brunette	clawback	Craniata	clanship	cockboat	crepance	cheerily
bouffant	clambake	czaritza	clap-sill	cockbird	chevalet	chevrony
bluefish	coalball	crackjaw	clausula	Coca-Cola®	crenated	clearing
blue-grey	clay-bank	cracknel	coarsely	cock-crow	clematis	cheerful
bludgeon	chapbook	chalkpit	chat-show	cacodoxy	chelator	clear-cut
bourgeon	charcoal	crankily	claustra	cycle-car	cremator	chessman
bluegown	cratches	clanking	coarsish	cycleway	crevasse	creasote
boughten	clay-cold	cracking	chasseur	cockerel	chee-chee	creosote
brush-off	Chancery	clack-box	claptrap	cockeyed	crescent	creutzer
blushing	coat-card	crackpot	chaptrel	cachexia	coercion	creatrix
brushing	Chaldean	crackers	crab-tree	cache-pot	coercive	co-extend
boughpot	Claudian	charlock	chantage	cacafogo	crescive	creatine
blushful	chandler	charlady	chastely	Coccidae	creodont	creation
bauxitic	Chaldaic	chaplain	craftily	cyclical	clemence	C-section
boutique	cladding	crablike	chatting	coccidia	clemency	cheatery
bruilzie	chaldron	cradling	coasting	Cocaigne	credence	creature
baubling	chawdron	crawling	coaction	cochlear	credenda	chestful
bouillon	clapdish	chapless	co-author	cockloft	cheverel	chestnut
blueness	coal-dust	clawless	chartism	cacology	cheveril	creative
bluenose	clarence	coatless	chartist	cichloid	cleverly	caesural
bouzouki	co-agency	clammily	chastise	cucumber	cheveron	chemurgy
boutonné	coalesce	clay-mill	chastity	cacomixl	cleveite	cleruchy
baudrick	clavecin	charming	coactive	cicinnus	credenza	cherubic
Baudrons	crane-fly	claimant	cyanuret	cuckoldy	Cheshvan	cherubim
blurring	cravenly	clamming	chasuble	cyclopes	chechako	cherubin
Brussels	czarevna	coal-mine	claqueur	Cecropia	chemical	cleavage
bruising	chaperon	cramming	coagulum	cyclonic	clerical	cleaving

cleavers	criminal	culicine	colossal	complain	conceder	canonise
cheewink	critical	calidity	cole-seed	cameline	conferee	canonist
coenzyme	cuitikin	Caladium	calfskin	compline	congener	caninity
coffered	chiliasm	cul-de-sac	coliseum	cameleon	convener	cantonal
caffeine	chiliast	calvered	colossus	camelish	convexed	cantoned
caffeism	clinique	colleger	calisaya	combless	conveyer	canzonet
cagebird	critique	culverin	culottes	cumulose	converge	consoler
cog-wheel	chick-pea	calceate	calc-tuff	cimolite	centesis	cantoris
cageling	clicking	coliform	calf-time	complete	cancelli	canoodle
cogently	clinking	call-girl	colotomy	cumulate	convexly	consommé
caginess	chinkara	calthrop	colation	camomile	canoeing	confound
cagyness	caillach	cultivar	calotype	ciminite	convenor	conjoint
cognosce	chilily	calliper	colature	Campodea	conveyor	contorno
cognomen	chilling	cultigen	calcular	commoner	cunjevoi	concolor
cognovit	chinless	calcific	cellular	commoney	contempt	cannonry
cogitate	chipmuck	Calliope	cultural	composed	canoeist	centoist
cagework	chipmunk	colliery	colluder	composer	condense	Congoese
coherent	cliental	call-loan	coloured	commonly	converse	convolve
cohesion	clitoral	calf-lick	cultured	compound	conceity	canopied
cohesive	clitoris	calfless	calculus	Comsomol	concerto	canephor
caimacam	chirpily	calf-love	coltwood	Cambrian	concetti	conspire
Chinaman	chipping	Columban	cold-work	comprint	concetto	cinereal
climatal	chirping	columnal	cole-wort	compress	confetti	conarial
chicaner	clipping	columnar	Calixtin	comprise	conceive	conurban
clinamen	crispate	columned	cullysim	cumbrous	conferva	contract
crinated	chirrupy	Columbic	cullying	camisade	conserve	centrode
climatic	cribrose	calamine	commando	camisado	coniform	congreet
cnidaria	cribrate	calamint	combated	camisole	conchoid	cancroid
chinampa	chiastic	calamary	compages	camp-shot	Cinchona	cant-rail
chimaera	chip-shot	calamite	campaign	camisard	canthook	centroid
chiragra	chiasmus	calamity	campagna	campsite	canthari	contrail
chivalry	coistrel	calendar	cum-savvy	comether	conchate	conurbia
cribbled	coistril	colonial	come-back	camstane	cannibal	Cinerama®
cribbage	cristate	calender	comedian	camstone	conoidal	cancrine
climbing	cliquish	colander	co-meddle	cemetery	convince	centring
cribbing	cliquism	cylinder	comedown	cometary	confider	confront
chitchat	crivvens	calendry	commence	comatose	confined	cinerary
coincide	cribwork	culinary	commerce	cymatium	confiner	confrère
clincher	cajolery	calmness	compesce	communal	conniver	contrary
chin-chin	cokernut	coldness	cumbered	commuter	consider	Canarese
clip-clop	cakewalk	colonise	cumberer	computer	cannikin	centrism
chiccory	cellarer	colonist	commerge	comb-wise	conoidic	centrist
childbed	cellaret	call-note	camp-fire	cinnabar	canaille	congress
children	ciliated	collogue	camshoch	contango	candidly	contrast
childing	collagen	colloque	cam-wheel	cannabic	canticle	contrist
childish	collared	colloquy	camshaft	cannabin	canticoy	concrete
chimeric	colza-oil	Calippic	camphane	cannabis	canaigre	contrate
criteria	culpable	colophon	camphene	cinnamic	centiare	contrite
clitella	culpably	calipers	camphine	cuneatic	congiary	canorous
cribella	chloasma	calyptra	camphire	cinnamon	canticum	conarium
Cricetus	Calvados	calipash	compital	centaury	continua	Congreve
crimeful	collator	celeriac	combined	concause	continue	contrive
chiefdom	collapse	chloride	compiler	cineaste	continuo	canaster
chiefery	celibacy	chlorine	combings	cunabula	conglobe	canister
coiffure	calibred	colorant	cymbidia	cenobite	conflict	cynosure
chiefess	call-bird	calorist	compleat	Canicula	conclude	canstick
chiefest	calabash	celerity	complect	cynicism	contline	canities
coiffeur	celibate	chlorate	complice	Canadian	canalise	constant
cringing	calicoes	chlorite	complied	conidial	conflate	conation
clithral	calycled	cultrate	complier	conidium	conclave	cenotaph
clip-hook	calycoid	chlorous	camellia	conveyal	cane-mill	cincture
co-inhere	calycule	calcspar	cameloid	cankered	cynanche	constate
clinical	calycine	cole-slaw	cameloid	centered	canoness	construe

conative	cloak-bag	cephalic	corn-beef	cursitor	curarise	cast-iron
cannulae	croakily	copybook	cerebric	curlicue	chrismal	cuspidor
conjugal	croaking	capybara	corn-ball	corn-kist	curbside	case-load
consular	crockery	capuchin	carabine	Carolean	cerastes	ciselure
conjunct	cromlech	capacity	corybant	cartload	christen	ciseleur
confused	choultry	cupidity	cerebrum	cerulean	Christie	casement
conjurer	cloyless	copperas	carucage	carolled	Christly	cashmere
consumer	chow-mein	cupreous	coracoid	caroller	cork-sole	costmary
cinquain	cookmaid	copyhold	corn-cake	cornloft	ceresine	casemate
centuple	cloyment	capsizal	caracole	cerulein	christom	cosiness
conjuror	crown-cap	capricci	caracara	Cyrillic	corn-snow	Casanova
consumpt	crown-saw	cyprides	corn-cure	Carolina	curassow	customed
conquest	crownlet	caprifig	corocore	Caroline	cerusite	customer
convulse	cooingly	capsicin	corocoro	circling	cork-tree	cesspool
cingulum	clowning	capriole	card-case	cornland	ceratoid	cost-plus
cony-wool	crooning	Cypriote	carucate	carillon	curatrix	Cesarean
condylar	crowning	capsicum	cervelat	careless	carotene	castrate
Cenozoic	clownery	captious	cornetcy	cordless	curatory	castrati
coolabah	clownish	Cyprinus	currency	coreless	curative	castrato
choragic	coolness	capellet	carpeted	curbless	carousal	case-shot
chorally	cromorna	cupelled	cornered	cureless	circular	cislunar
choragus	cromorne	cupolaed	corselet	corallum	carburet	costumed
crotalum	crocoite	capeline	corseted	corn-mill	carousel	costumer
Crotalus	croupade	copulate	curveted	cerement	carouser	cistvaen
crow-bill	croupier	cupulate	cursedly	ceremony	cornuted	case-work
cook-book	clodpole	caponier	cargeese	coramine	curculio	case-worm
crotched	clodpoll	caponise	cornetto	ceramist	corduroy	cuss-word
crotchet	clotpoll	cup-coral	corvette	chromate	circussy	Cathaian
choicely	chopping	cupboard	cardecue	chromite	circuity	Cathayan
choo-choo	cropping	caproate	carneous	corn-moth	cernuous	cottaged
chop-chop	clodpate	Copepoda	Cerberus	chromium	card-vote	cottager
chow-chow	croupous	caper-tea	corneous	coranach	cordwain	cut-water
clop-clop	choirman	capitula	corn-flag	coronach	corkwing	citrange
chondral	choirboy	capitano	coraggio	coronoid	cord-wood	cottabus
cloudlet	choy-root	capstone	card-game	Cyrenaic	corkwood	Cuthbert
cloudage	cookroom	capitate	co-regent	caruncle	careworn	cetacean
chondrin	crossbar	capsular	cork-heel	coronary	cornworm	catacomb
cloudily	crossway	caprylic	carl-hemp	curtness	carry-all	catechol
clodding	cropsick	coquetry	cornhusk	carinate	carrying	catheter
clouding	chop-suey	coquette	cardigan	coronate	currying	cathexis
cloddish	cloister	coquilla	cardinal	coronium	carrycot	cathedra
Chordata	crosslet	carraway	carnival	corundum	carry-out	cathetus
chordate	cross-rib	Circaean	cervical	Caryocar	castaway	citreous
chondrus	cross-tie	curtal-ax	cortical	cordovan	cascabel	cat's-foot
closeted	cross-ply	carnauba	Corvidae	corporal	Castanea	category
clovered	crousely	carcanet	Corvinae	corporas	costated	catch-pit
choleric	cloysome	curvated	curvital	cartouch	casually	catch-all
choregic	coon-song	caryatic	carritch	cursores	casualty	catchfly
croceate	crossing	caryatid	carnifex	carbolic	casebook	catching
choregus	cookshop	cercaria	circiter	carbonic	cash-book	cutchery
clotebur	crossbow	carnally	cordiner	cargoose	cosecant	cathisma
chorioid	cross-row	curbable	corniced	carbonyl	cosherer	cetology
chorisis	crossish	carcajou	cortices	carboxyl	cosseted	cytology
cootikin	cross-bun	cardamom	carriage	carapace	cosmesis	cotyloid
choliamb	crosscut	cardamon	corniche	coryphee	cosmetic	Catiline
choriamb	Croatian	cariacou	cardioid	carap-oil	cassette	coteline
	clotting	carjacou	carditis	corn-pone	cost-free	cotilon
	crofting	cornacre	cornific	cornpipe	caschrom	catalase
	co-option	curranty	carriole	carap-nut	cosmical	catalyse
	co-optive	carbaryl	cornicle	cart-road	cuspidal	catalyst
	chorused	cerebral	curricle	corn-rent	Cushitic	cat's-meat
	cap-paper	corn-baby	corridor	curarine	cystitis	catamite
	Capparis	Caribbee	cortisol	curb-roof	cushiony	Catonian

co-tenant	crucifer	cavesson	draffish	dead-shot	decolour	deep-felt
catenary	churinga	cavitied	dwarfish	drag-shot	dochmiac	deer-hair
cutinise	crucifix	cavatina	draw-gear	dram-shop	December	deer-horn
catenate	caudicle	coveting	dragging	draft-bar	decemvir	djellaba
cathodal	caudillo	covetise	draughty	draw-tube	duckmole	deer-lick
cathodic	caulicle	covetous	dead-head	diastole	document	deep-laid
catholic	cousinly	cow-leech	dead-heat	diastyle	docimasy	duelling
chthonic	coutille	cowberry	death-cap	diastema	decimate	dwelling
cathouse	crucible	cow-wheat	death-ray	diactine	dochmius	deedless
cot-house	cousinry	cow-pilot	drachmae	diastase	decanter	duellist
catapult	coulisse	cow-plant	drachmai	dianthus	decently	dreamily
cataract	cruciate	cowhouse	drachmas	dead-wall	dicentra	dreaming
ceterach	cautious	co-worker	death-bed	draw-well	doctoral	dreamery
cut-price	chuckies	cowardly	dead-hand	dead-wind	dicrotic	deepmost
catering	caulking	cowardry	diaphone	dead-wood	doctorly	dreamful
cateress	club-line	cowgrass	drag-hunt	dead-work	dice-play	deer-neck
cytisine	coupling	coxalgia	death-cup	dialyser	Decapoda	deepness
cytosine	churlish	coxiness	deathful	dialyses	decipher	daemonic
cat-stick	clueless	coxswain	diapiric	dialysis	duck-pond	dye-works
cat's-tail	crummack	cly-faker	deadlock	dialytic	dichroic	dye-house
catatony	crummock	clypeate	dead-lift	dobber-in	doctrine	deer-park
citation	chummage	cryogeny	diallage	dabchick	decurion	deep-read
citatory	club-moss	chymical	deadline	dobchick	doctress	drearily
cotquean	churning	cryolite	dearling	debelled	decorate	drearing
cothurni	churn-owl	cryonics	dialling	dabbling	decorous	deemster
cutpurse	crumpled	cayenned	dragline	debility	dicastic	dressage
cetywall	clumping	cryostat	diaglyph	debonair	decision	deerskin
Cotswold	clubroom	coyishly	diablery	debarred	duck-shot	dress-tie
caudated	clubroot	coystrel	dead-meat	debasing	decisory	duelsome
crusader	club-rush	coystril	drammach	débutant	decisive	dressing
coumaric	clumsily	cryotron	drammock	dubitate	duck-tail	die-stock
coumarin	coursing	chyluria	deaf-mute	débouché	ducatoon	dyestuff
causally	court-day	cozenage	drainage	deceased	Docetism	duettino
clubable	courtier	diabasic	deadness	declared	Docetist	duettist
chupatti	courtlet	dramatic	deafness	declarer	declutch	diestrus
courante	crustily	drawable	dearness	dichasia	duckweed	dielytra
clubbing	courting	Dracaena	diagnose	dictator	dactylar	defrayal
clubbish	clustery	diapason	drabness	déclassé	dactylic	defiance
clubbism	countess	diapause	dearnful	duckbill	Dactylis	deflater
clubbist	courtesy	diamanté	diaconal	dice-coal	decrying	defrayed
crutched	crustate	dead-beat	diagonal	dicyclic	dockyard	defrayer
churchly	count-out	drawback	dianodal	dicacity	didrachm	deflator
couscous	chutzpah	drabbler	dragoman	decidual	didactic	defector
cauldron	cave-bear	dead-bolt	dragonet	dock-dues	dedicant	defecate
causeway	cavicorn	dead-born	diadochi	decadent	dedicate	deflexed
crumenal	civilian	drabbish	diabolic	decedent	didactyl	defreeze
caudexes	cavalier	dealbate	dialogic	decretal	doddered	defilade
causeyed	cavilled	diarchal	diatomic	docketed	dodderer	defaming
causerie	caviller	diarchic	diatonic	decrepit	diddicoi	defenced
clupeoid	covalent	dead-cart	draconic	decrease	dedalian	defended
cruzeiro	civilise	dead-deal	dragonné	duchesse	didymium	defender
club-face	civilist	Diandria	deaconry	decagram	didymous	daftness
club-foot	civility	diazepam	dialogue	decigram	Dodonian	deftness
chugging	covenant	deadener	dead-pull	deck-game	didapper	definite
club-head	Coventry	diabetes	diaspora	deck-hand	diddycoy	deflower
crush-hat	covinous	diademed	diaspore	duck-hawk	daedalic	daffodil
couchant	caverned	diameter	diatribe	declinal	drencher	deferral
couching	coverlet	diabetic	diarrhea	deceiver	deep-dyed	diffract
coughing	coverage	diapente	dead-rope	deck-load	dreadful	deferred
crushing	coverlid	drabette	diagraph	dockland	diereses	deferrer
crumhorn	coverall	dead-fall	dragsman	duckling	diegesis	deformed
club-haul	covertly	dead-fire	dragster	ductless	dieresis	deformer
caudices	covering	dealfish	deanship	docility	dietetic	deferent

deforest	drilling	delaying	demiurge	dioramic	diplogen	disvalue
diffused	dripping	dolly-mop	demi-volt	doorbell	diplopia	disabled
diffuser	drift-way	dolly-tub	demi-wolf	Dioscuri	dipnoous	dust-ball
defluent	drift-ice	damnable	dungaree	dioecism	departer	disabuse
dog-watch	drift-net	damnably	dentalia	door-case	deportee	dust-bath
degraded	driftage	demeanor	dentaria	diocesan	depurant	dust-bowl
dog-eared	driftpin	demobbed	dunnakin	duodenal	depurate	dust-coat
dog-faced	daintily	dumb-bell	deniable	Diogenic	dip-stick	dust-cart
dog-Latin	daiquiri	democrat	deniably	duodenum	deputise	dysodile
dogmatic	dairyman	domicile	Denebola	drop-goal	dormancy	dysodyle
diggable	dairying	dumb-cane	dung-cart	droughty	darraign	disadorn
dog-daisy	deifying	dummerer	ding-dong	dromical	dermatic	disbench
dog's-body	dejected	demagogy	denudate	dioritic	dorsally	dispeace
dog'sbane	dukeling	domainal	dentelle	drop-kick	darraine	dispence
dog-leech	Dukhobor	demijohn	duncedom	drooking	directly	dishevel
doggerel	dukeship	demology	danseuse	drouking	déraciné	dissever
doggedly	dollared	demi-lune	dancette	doorknob	director	disherit
dogberry	dalmatic	dumpling	dancetté	drolling	Doricism	dysgenic
dog-weary	dalmahoy	demolish	dancetty	drollery	doridoid	dyslexia
degrease	delibate	demoniac	dung-fork	drollish	dirigent	dyslexic
dog-cheap	delubrum	Demonian	danegeld	doornail	dirigism	dysmelia
dog-wheat	delicacy	domanial	danegelt	drowning	derogate	dysmelic
dog-whelk	dolichos	demander	dung-heap	duologue	derailer	dispense
dog-tired	delicate	demented	dane-hole	doom-palm	dormient	disperse
diggings	dull-eyed	domineer	dene-hole	droopily	durukuli	disseise
dog-fight	delegacy	dominoes	dung-hill	dropping	derelict	dyspepsy
dog-sleep	diligent	dementia	dun-diver	doorpost	darkling	diskette
dog's-meat	delegate	dominant	denticle	drop-ripe	darkmans	disleave
digamist	Delphian	dominion	don't-know	doomsday	diriment	disserve
digamous	dollhood	dampness	danelagh	doomsman	dart-moth	disseize
digynian	dulcimer	demoness	dangling	door's-man	daring-do	designer
dog's-nose	Dulcinea	demonise	dynamics	diopside	deranged	disagree
digynous	dulciana	demonism	dungmere	doomster	daringly	dysphagy
doggoned	dulcitol	demonist	dynamism	doorstep	darkness	dust-hole
do-gooder	dolomite	diminish	dynamist	dropsied	der-doing	disthene
dog-house	dullness	dumbness	dynamite	door-sill	dormouse	dyschroa
dog-louse	doldrums	dominate	dankness	drop-shot	dirt-road	despisal
dogtooth	doloroso	dumfound	doneness	deontics	dark-room	discinct
dog-trick	dolerite	damboard	dandriff	dioptric	dartrous	distinct
dog-grass	delirium	demersal	dandruff	dioptase	darksome	despiser
digester	dolorous	demurral	dinarchy	drop-wort	derision	dissight
dogeship	dalesman	demersed	dendroid	dropwise	derisory	distichs
digitise	dolesome	demurred	Dinornis	Dionysia	derisive	dispirit
digitate	delusion	demurrer	dendrite	door-yard	derating	disciple
doggy-bag	delusory	demurely	denarius	depraved	deration	displace
dahabieh	delusive	demerara	dynastic	dipsades	duration	displode
dihybrid	dule-tree	dimerise	dinosaur	dip-slope	derivate	desilver
dihedral	dilatant	dimerism	donation	depilate	dirtying	dosology
dihydric	delation	dimerous	dynatron	dopamine	Darbyite	disclaim
dyhydric	deletion	demister	denature	deponent	despatch	displume
dihedron	dilation	dempster	donatary	dipteral	dispatch	displant
dehorner	dilution	damaskin	donatory	dipteran	distance	disallow
dehorter	deletory	damassin	donatism	dapperly	dastardy	disclose
dribbler	dilatory	demyship	Donatist	dipteros	discandy	disclost
dribblet	deletive	domestic	denotate	diphenyl	diseased	disflesh
driveway	dilative	demissly	donative	dipchick	disgavel	dustless
drip-feed	diluvial	dumb-show	denounce	deprival	dyspathy	desolate
deisheal	diluvian	dumosity	do-naught	deprived	desyatin	dyspneal
deicidal	diluvion	dimetric	do-nought	dip-slope	dishabit	disannex
deifical	delivery	demotion	dandy-hen	depilate	dismally	disinter
dricksie	diluvium	demotist	dinky-die	deponent	distally	dyspnoea
drinking	dilly-bag	domatium	dandyish	diplomat	disfavor	dyspneic
daidling	dallying	dimethyl	dandyism	diploidy	distaste	desinent

disendow	disjunct	druggist	dowel-pin	epanodos	encomium	ebenezer
disenrol	dissuade	drumhead	downland	examplar	encroach	exegesis
disunion	disputer	daughter	down-line	Erastian	encloser	exegetic
disinure	disquiet	dauphine	dowel-rod	exanthem	enclothe	eleventh
duskness	dispunge	dough-boy	downmost	enacting	enchoric	evenfall
disunite	disburse	doughnut	dewiness	exacting	escapade	exergual
disunity	disguise	drunkard	dowfness	enaction	escapado	emergent
disannul	dispurse	doubling	dewpoint	exaction	encipher	emerging
despotat	Dasyurus	doubloon	downpipe	enacture	exceptor	energise
disloyal	desk-work	drummock	downpour	enactive	escapism	eyeshade
disposal	dutiable	drumming	downrush	evacuant	escapist	erewhile
disvouch	databank	dourness	downtime	evacuate	encircle	eye-rhyme
disbowel	database	doum-palm	down-trod	evaluate	escarole	elephant
discover	detached	doubting	downturn	embraced	escargot	erethism
dismoded	detector	doubtful	down-town	embracer	eucaryon	emetical
disponee	dithecal	duumviri	downwind	emblazon	eucaryot	eremital
disponer	ditherer	duumvirs	downward	embrasor	encarpus	eye-piece
disposed	dotterel	deviance	dowdyish	embodied	excursus	eyeliner
disposer	ditheism	deviancy	dowdyism	embalmer	encysted	eyesight
disgorge	ditheist	deviator	doxology	embolden	excuse-me	eremitic
dislodge	duty-free	dive-bomb	dextrine	embolism	excision	elegiast
disloign	Dutchman	dovecote	dextrose	embanker	excusive	ébéniste
disponge	Dutchmen	dividual	dextrous	embarked	excitant	emeritus
despotic	ditch-dog	dividend	day-level	embarred	exciting	eyeglass
dystopia	detrital	dividing	day-shift	emborder	excluded	evermore
discount	detailed	dividivi	daylight	embossed	excavate	eternise
disjoint	detainee	dove-eyed	day-sight	embosser	endeared	evenness
dismount	detainer	divagate	dry-bible	embussed	end-paper	eternity
disbosom	detritus	devilled	dry-clean	embusqué	endocarp	eye-tooth
dishonor	ditokous	devilkin	dry-plate	embitter	endodyne	exemplar
dishorse	date-line	dovelike	day-to-day	embattle	endoderm	exemplum
dishouse	dateless	Davy-lamp	day-woman	embryons	Erdgeist	execrate
dissolve	datolite	deviling	dey-woman	embezzle	endogamy	evensong
disapply	detonate	divalent	dry-goods	enchased	endogeny	emersion
disarray	duty-paid	devildom	dry-point	encharge	eldritch	eversion
dispread	date-palm	deviltry	daybreak	exchange	endeixis	eventual
describe	date-plum	deviless	daydream	encradle	endemial	eventide
destruct	deterred	devilish	dry-stane	eschalot	endamage	electret
disfrock	daturine	devilism	dry-stone	excubant	eudemony	electric
disgrace	dethrone	Devonian	dry-stove	encyclic	endemism	erectile
distract	dytiscid	divan-bed	dry-nurse	eucyclic	endanger	eyestalk
district	Dytiscus	divinify	dazzling	ecclesia	Eldorado	eventing
disgrade	date-tree	divinely	doziness	encaenia	endorsed	egestion
descried	dotation	divinise	dizzying	encrinal	endorsee	ejection
deserter	detoxify	divinity	erasable	eccrisis	endorser	election
deserved	ditty-bag	divorcee	evadable	eccritic	endermic	electron
destrier	ditty-box	divorcer	enarched	enclisis	enduring	erection
discreet	drumbeat	diversly	ecaudate	enclitic	elder-gun	evection
disorbed	drubbing	division	evanesce	encrinic	endosarc	exertion
disorder	Druidess	divisive	elaterin	eucritic	endozoic	Edentata
distrain	druidism	dovetail	elatedly	enceinte	endozoon	edentate
distrait	deuce-ace	devotion	evangely	escalade	elegance	electrum
disproof	douzeper	devourer	elaphine	escalado	elegancy	eventful
distress	drupelet	devoutly	examinee	excelled	elevated	egestive
distrust	diuresis	downbeat	examiner	esculent	elevator	ejective
discrete	diuretic	down-come	evasible	escallop	eye-water	elective
desirous	deucedly	downcast	étatisme	escalope	elevator	erective
disprove	deuteron	dewy-eyed	emaciate	eucalypt	eye-salve	exertive
discrown	drumfire	dew-berry	eradiate	encolure	elenctic	exequial
disprize	drumfish	downfall	edacious	escalate	exercise	executer
disaster	drugging	downflow	enallage	encolour	elenchus	exequies
disusage	drudgery	downhill	enaunter	encumber	emendals	executor
dust-shot	drudgism	down-haul	epagogic	encomion	emendate	executry

enervate	egg-fruit	exigency	elkhound	ecostate	emptysis	essonite	
emery-bag	engirdle	epicedia	enkernel	eloquent	emptying	ensconce	
everyday	eight-day	epidemic	eukaryon	evolvent	Esquimau	exserted	
Everyman	eight-oar	epimeric	eukaryot	euonymin	enquirer	enshrine	
everyway	eighteen	episemon	ex-libris	euonymus	ebriated	enshroud	
everyone	eighties	erigeron	eulachon	emphases	Eurobond	eastward	
efficacy	ergatoid	epilepsy	éolienne	emphasis	enridged	elsewise	
effecter	eighthly	epigeous	eulogise	emphatic	earth-bag	essaying	
effector	ergotise	epithema	eulogist	expiable	earthwax	essayish	
effierce	ergotism	Epiphany	eclogite	expiator	earth-fed	essayist	
enfierce	engouled	epiphyte	eklogite	especial	earth-pea	entrance	
enfeeble	egg-purse	eligible	eulogium	empacket	ear-shell	estrange	
enfreeze	edgewise	eligibly	enlumine	expected	earphone	entrails	
effigies	edgeways	exigible	eclampsy	expecter	earth-hog	extrados	
elf-child	ethnarch	elicitor	eel-spear	expedite	earth-nut	enthalpy	
elf-shoot	enhearse	eximious	ellipses	empierce	earpiece	entr'acte	
enfilade	ethicise	Ewigkeit	ecliptic	empyesis	earnings	estacade	
effulged	ethicism	epiploic	ellipsis	espiègle	earwiggy	eutectic	
enflower	ethicist	epiploon	elliptic	espresso	earliest	enticing	
enfrosen	exhedrae	epiblast	eolipile	explicit	enrolled	ectoderm	
elflocks	enhydros	etiolate	eelwrack	empoison	enroller	entoderm	
efferent	echogram	ebionise	enlarged	empolder	Euromart	entrench	
elf-arrow	ethnical	ebionism	enlarger	espalier	errantly	entremes	
enforest	ethology	evilness	eelgrass	expelled	erringly	esteemed	
enfested	ethylene	Ebionite	eclestic	expellee	errantry	extremer	
effusion	exhalant	epifocal	eclosion	expander	eeriness	enthetic	
effusive	echoless	episodal	eolithic	expender	European	esthetic	
enfetter	ethylate	epigones	eglatere	expunger	europium	Eutheria	
effetely	ephemera	epidotic	Emmental	exponent	Etrurian	entrepot	
effluvia	exhumate	epilogic	Emmanuel	expandor	errorist	entresol	
effluent	enhunger	epinosic	emmarble	employed	Etruscan	entreaty	
egg-dance	echinoid	epipolic	eumerism	employee	Eurasian	ectogeny	
engraved	Echinops	episodic	enmossed	employer	écraseur	entailer	
engraven	echinate	epitomic	enneadic	exploded	eurythmy	estridge	
engraver	Ethiopic	epitonic	enneagon	exploder	earmuffs	extolled	
engramma	Eohippus	epilogue	egomania	explorer	enraunge	entellus	
edgebone	ethercap	epicotyl	exogamic	euphonia	enravish	estimate	
Eugubine	ethereal	episperm	exorable	euphonic	enslaved	Estonian	
eagle-ray	etherial	epispore	exorcise	euphoria	enslaver	entender	
eagle-owl	exhorter	emigrant	exorcism	euphoric	enswathe	extended	
ergogram	etherion	epigraph	exorcist	empeople	ecstasis	extender	
engaging	etherise	editress	exordial	eupepsia	ecstatic	estancia	
eggshell	etherism	emigrate	exordium	eupeptic	eustatic	entangle	
egg-whisk	etherist	epitrite	erogenic	empyreal	Eusebian	extensor	
egg-timer	Ephesian	emissile	erotesis	empyrean	easy-care	eutrophy	
engrieve	epigaeal	emission	erotetic	exporter	easterly	ectropic	
egg-slice	epigaean	emissary	esoteric	empurple	ensheath	eutropic	
egg-plant	exitance	emissive	exoteric	expertly	ensiform	eftsoons	
edgeless	epigamic	ekistics	emongest	expirant	ensigncy	extrorse	
egg-glass	epitasis	epistler	elongate	expiring	ensphere	estopped	
eugenics	epically	epistyle	exophagy	emperise	essoiner	estoppel	
engender	evitable	emitting	erotical	emperish	enshield	entoptic	
engineer	epilator	existent	exoplasm	euphrasy	ensilage	ettercap	
enginery	epinasty	emiction	exosmose	emporium	eastland	external	
edginess	epicalyx	eviction	enormity	exposure	eastling	externat	
eugenism	episcope	emictory	enormous	empathic	eastlins	esterify	
eugenist	episcopy	epidural	ecologic	eupatrid	ensample	enthrall	
egg-bound	evincive	exiguity	economic	empatron	ensemble	entirely	
egg-tooth	evil-doer	exiguous	epopoeia	espousal	easement	entering	
engroove	eminence	epicycle	exospore	espouser	eastmost	enthrone	
egg-apple	eminency	edifying	ecofreak	euphuise	epsomite	exterior	
egg-spoon	evidence	enjoiner	exocrine	euphuism	easiness	enterate	
engorged	exigence	enkindle	egoistic	euphuist	Essenism	entirety	

ectosarc	flambeau	flattery	frescoer	figurant	fellatio	fall-trap
extruder	flatboat	fracture	frescoes	figurine	fellable	folk-tale
eutaxite	flambéed	flattish	fiercely	figurist	filially	full-tilt
ectozoan	flax-bush	flautist	fuel-cell	figurate	filmable	full-time
entozoal	flanched	feastful	free-cost	fagoting	faltboat	felstone
ectozoic	flax-comb	featured	free-city	fighting	foldboat	folk-tune
entozoic	francium	featuous	freedman	fugitive	fall-back	filatory
ectozoon	fraudful	flatuous	Freudian	fahlband	full-cock	filature
entozoon	frame-saw	flag-worm	field-dew	Frimaire	filicide	fulgural
educable	flamenco	flatware	fielding	fribbler	felicity	fumigant
educator	flamelet	flat-worm	fiendish	flincher	falderal	fumigate
emulator	flânerie	flatwise	frenetic	fail-dike	fulgency	familial
ecumenic	flagella	flatways	free-fall	fainéant	filleted	familiar
enuresis	feateous	febrific	feed-head	flim-flam	full-eyed	fameless
enuretic	flat-foot	fibrilla	freshman	flip-flap	folderol	familism
emulgent	foalfoot	fabliaux	fresh-new	flip-flop	faldetta	Familist
evulgate	flatfish	fabulise	flesh-fly	flinging	falsetto	femality
educible	flagging	fabulist	freehold	frigging	full-face	fomenter
eludible	flathead	fabulous	free-hand	flichter	folk-free	feminine
esurient	flashily	fibrosis	flesh-pot	flighted	filiform	feminise
exuviate	flashing	fibrotic	freshish	frighten	file-fish	feminism
equalled	feathery	faburden	fresh-run	faithful	feldgrau	feminist
equalise	flash-gun	February	flexible	frigidly	filagree	feminity
equality	flamingo	face-ache	flexibly	friskily	filigree	femerall
eburnean	feasible	facially	fremitus	frisking	filmgoer	fumarole
equinity	feasibly	face-card	freckled	friskful	filthily	fumosity
epulotic	flatiron	fucoidal	freakish	fair-lead	filching	femetary
equipped	Fraxinus	factious	freakful	frillies	falchion	fumatory
equipage	flapjack	face-lift	freak-out	frilling	fillibeg	fumitory
emulsify	frabjous	facilely	freeload	friended	filliped	famously
emulsoid	frank-fee	feculent	fuelling	friendly	felsitic	fontanel
emulsion	franklin	faceless	feeblish	feigning	fallible	fandango
evulsion	Frankish	feckless	freeness	fainness	fallibly	fontange
emulsive	frailtee	focalise	feed-pump	fairness	follicle	fantasia
equitant	fräulein	facility	feed-pipe	frijoles	filmland	fundable
exultant	flax-lily	factotum	free-port	flippant	folkland	fanfaron
eduction	flatling	focusing	fee-grief	flipping	folklore	funebral
equation	flatlong	fuchsine	free-reed	frippery	filament	finochio
eruption	fearless	fuchsite	fleering	Friesian	folkmoot	fine-draw
eructate	flawless	facetiae	free-soil	flip-side	filander	fingered
eruptive	foamless	fade-away	fleasome	fail-safe	fellness	finnesko
equivoke	frailish	fiducial	free-shot	flimsily	fullness	fen-berry
enviable	flammule	fade-down	Flextime®	Friesish	felinity	fin-whale
enviably	flax-mill	fidgeted	fleeting	flintify	falconer	funkhole
enveigle	fragment	fodderer	fretting	flintily	falconet	fanlight
envelope	flatmate	fiddious	flexural	fainting	follower	fencible
elvanite	flaunter	fedelini	frequent	flirting	fellowly	fanciful
environs	flatness	fiddling	flexuose	flitting	follow-on	fantigue
envassal	frampler	fuddling	flexuous	fritting	falconry	fondling
envisage	flagpole	fadeless	free-will	friction	filioque	fangless
envision	frampold	fidelity	fretwork	flittern	follow-up	finalise
enwallow	flapping	federacy	frenzied	faintish	full-page	finalism
euxenite	flat-race	federary	freezing	flirtish	full-pelt	finalist
eryngium	flagrant	federate	freeze-up	flix-weed	Filipina	fineless
erythema	fragrant	fedayeen	fiftieth	fairydom	Filipino	fundless
etypical	flax-seed	foedarie	fiftyish	fairyism	filarial	finality
Erysimum	flagship	feed-back	Fagaceae	fakement	folkrock	fineness
epyllion	fearsome	flea-bane	fugacity	fakirism	filtrate	fondness
Epyornis	feast-day	freeborn	fugleman	falcated	fulcrate	funereal
Egyptian	feasting	flea-bite	fughetta	foliaged	feldspar	Fanariot
Enzedder	flatting	frescade	figuline	foliated	feldsher	funerary
enzootic	feast-won	fletcher	fog-smoke	full-aged	full-sail	finesser
Fragaria	fraction	frescoed	fogbound	fellahin	folk-song	finished

finisher	foot-race	fervency	foremast	furcular	Fascists	foulmart
fenestra	footrule	ferreted	foremost	furfural	fashious	fluently
fine-spun	flooring	ferreter	Faringee	furfuran	fusileer	foulness
finitude	foot-rope	fire-eyed	forinsec	fortuned	fusilier	faubourg
finitely	flourish	fire-edge	Feringhi	forjudge	fuselage	foul-play
fine-tune	footrest	fore-edge	forensic	farouche	fusel-oil	four-part
function	foolscap	forcedly	furuncle	furfurol	fish-meal	frumpish
funguses	footstep	forkedly	forename	fortuity	fastness	fluoride
Funtumia	frowster	formerly	forenoon	forswear	fishpond	flurried
fancying	frog-spit	furbelow	farinose	fireweed	fusarole	fluorine
frowards	footslog	forweary	firmness	farewell	fostress	fluorite
florally	footsore	farceuse	fire-opal	fire-walk	fish-stew	foursome
football	frontman	fornenst	furlough	forewent	fishskin	faustian
fool-born	frontier	furmenty	forhooie	forewind	fish-tail	fruit-bat
foot-bath	frontlet	ferreous	forborne	forewing	fistulae	fourteen
floccule	floatage	forceful	fordoing	forswink	fistular	fructify
flocculi	frontage	fire-flag	forgoing	forswunk	fissured	fruitage
floscule	frottage	forefeel	far-forth	firewood	fastuous	fountain
food-card	frostily	forefeet	forsooth	firework	fishwife	faultily
floccose	floatant	forefelt	forepeak	fireworm	fish-weir	fourthly
floodway	floating	forefoot	foreplan	firmware	fat-faced	fruit-fly
frondage	frosting	foregoer	foreplay	foreward	feticide	frustule
floodlit	frontoon	foregone	forspeak	forewarn	fattener	fruiting
flooding	frotteur	forehead	far-spent	foreword	fatherly	fruition
frondent	footwear	forkhead	forspend	formwork	fatigued	flustery
frondose	footwork	farm-hand	forspent	forswore	fatigate	fruitery
frondeur	footworn	farthing	forepart	forsworn	fetching	fructose
florence	fippence	forehand	fire-plug	forswatt	fitliest	faultful
flowered	forwards	forehent	foreread	ferryman	futilely	fountful
flowerer	forzando	forthink	fore-rank	ferrying	fettling	fruit-bud
floweret	forrader	fire-hook	fire-risk	farmyard	fatalism	fruitful
fromenty	forsaken	farthest	fortress	fortyish	fatalist	fruitive
footfall	furcated	fire-hose	fernshaw	farcy-bud	fatality	fluework
frou-frou	formalin	furthest	festally	futility	fivefold
frogfish	fern-ally	farcical	forestal	fishable	fattrels	fivepins
footgear	fordable	forcipes	forestay	fastback	futurism	feverfew
flogging	forhaile	forgiven	fireside	fishball	futurist	feverish
froggery	formally	ferriage	foreside	fuss-ball	futurity	feverous
foothill	forfairn	ferritic	fern-seed	fish-bone	fitfully	favoured
foothold	forwaste	fervidly	fire-step	fishcake	feudally	favourer
froth-fly	firebrat	forcible	foreseen	fish-dive	frugally	favourer
frothily	forebear	forcibly	foreshew	Fosseway	fougasse	fowl-pest
frothery	fire-back	farriery	forested	fastener	four-ball	fewtrils
florigen	forebode	furriery	forester	fosterer	faulchin	fox-earth
floridly	fore-body	formiate	fireship	fossette	fluidics	foxberry
flotilla	fire-ball	fortieth	foresaid	fish-farm	fluidify	fox-shark
flock-bed	fire-bomb	foreking	foresail	fusiform	founding	foxglove
frocking	furibund	foreknow	foreship	fish-guts	fluidise	foxiness
footling	fire-bird	fire-lock	foreskin	fish-glue	fluidity	foxhound
foozling	fire-bote	forelock	foreshow	Fasching	four-eyes	fox-grape
frogling	forebitt	forslack	foreslow	fish-hook	fauteuil	fox-brush
foodless	fire-clay	forelift	forestry	fish-hawk	fauvette	fixation
footmuff	forecast	forelimb	first-day	festival	frumenty	fixature
footmark	feracity	far-flung	fire-tube	fistical	fourfold	fixative
flounder	ferocity	foreland	first-aid	fissiped	four-foot	fly-maker
frowning	furacity	forelend	fork-tail	fascicle	foul-fish	flypaper
footnote	foredeck	forelent	foretell	fasciola	foughten	fly-sheet
footpace	firedamp	fireless	foretold	fasciole	flushing	flywheel
footpage	foredoom	firmless	foretime	Fascismo	flush-box	fayalite
floppily	faradise	formless	feretory	fistiana	frutices	fly-blown
foot-pump	faradism	foremean	farm-toun	fasciate	four-leaf	fly-under
footpost	foredate	foramina	formulae	Fascista	fluellin	fly-spray
footpath	forgeman	fire-mark	formular	Fascisti	flummery	fly-tying

fuzz-ball	graining	guéridon	gliomata	Golgotha	gentilic	geophagy
foziness	gladness	Greekdom	grinning	galapago	gangliar	geophone
Ghanaian	grasping	Greekish	glibness	gold-rush	ginglymi	geophyte
gravamen	goalpost	gleaming	grimness	gelastic	gangland	gloxinia
gradatim	glabrate	green-bag	Guicowar	gulosity	gangling	gloriole
gradable	glabrous	greenlet	grimoire	gold-size	gantline	gloriosa
gram-atom	glassman	guernsey	gripping	gilt-tail	gin-sling	glorious
guaranty	goadsman	greenfly	goitrous	gelatine	gunflint	good-lack
guaiacum	goadster	gleaning	gripsack	gelation	ganglion	goodlier
gramarye	glassify	greening	glissade	galluses	gantlope	glowlamp
grabbing	goatskin	greenery	gainsaid	gallumph	Ganymede	growling
glaucoma	grass-oil	greenish	guiltily	galowses	gunsmith	growlery
glancing	glassily	greyness	glittery	gulfweed	gynandry	ghoulish
gear-case	gladsome	gneissic	grievous	gull-wing	goneness	gloomily
Graecise	glassine	greasily	grizzled	giltwood	ginhouse	gloaming
Graecism	grassing	gleesome	grizzler	gold-wire	gentrice	glooming
glaucous	grass-box	greesing	Gujarati	gall-wasp	gentrify	gloomful
granddad	Glassite	gressing	Gujerati	gold-wasp	generale	grounded
guardian	glassful	guessing	goliardy	gillyvor	gangrene	grounden
guardage	goat's-rue	greeting	galeated	gollywog	generant	grounder
glandule	grattoir	gift-book	gallabea	gymnasia	generate	groaning
gladding	graithly	giftedly	gallabia	gymnasic	generous	groining
guardant	grafting	gefuffle	galvanic	gemma-cup	gangsman	geognost
grandson	giantess	giff-gaff	gullable	game-bird	Genesiac	geognosy
glanders	giantism	gaff-sail	gillaroo	game-cock	gangster	goodness
grandeur	ghastful	gift-shop	galbanum	gambeson	ganister	groanful
grave-wax	granular	gift-wrap	galabeah	gemmeous	gongster	geologer
gramercy	graduand	gig-lamps	galabiah	gymkhana	genetics	geogonic
glabella	graduate	gaggling	galabieh	gumphion	gunstick	geologic
gravelly	gratuity	giggling	galabiya	gimmicky	gunstock	geoponic
glareous	goatweed	goggling	galactic	gemology	genetrix	gnomonic
graceful	gable-end	gigantic	golf-ball	gameness	genitrix	groupage
grateful	Gobiidae	gag-tooth	golf-club	geminate	genitals	grouping
Graafian	gabeller	go-getter	gall-duct	geminous	gunstone	groupist
goat-fish	gabbling	gigawatt	gold-dust	gammoner	genotype	glossily
graffiti	Gobelins	guidance	gelidity	gambogic	geniture	glosseme
graffito	gibingly	gainable	gold-ends	gummosis	genitive	glossina
graphics	gabioned	guidable	goldenly	gimcrack	geniuses	grog-shop
grapheme	gabbroic	glibbery	galleass	gambroon	Genevese	glossary
goatherd	gabbroid	guimbard	gold-foil	gamester	Genovese	goodsire
guacharo	gibbsite	grinding	goldfish	gamesome	geomancy	grossart
gnathite	Geckones	gliddery	gilt-head	gematria	globated	goodtime
graphite	godwards	grindery	Gallican	gemstone	geotaxis	grouting
graphium	gadabout	Griselda	gallivat	gumption	globally	globular
gravitas	gude-dame	Goidelic	gullible	gunlayer	geocarpy	globulet
glacises	Gadhelic	gridelin	gallipot	gunmaker	geolatry	globulin
granitic	gadgetry	grisette	golliwog	genially	grosbeak	goodwife
gladiole	godchild	griseous	galliard	gendarme	goofball	goodwill
gladioli	God-given	guileful	galliass	gonfalon	gaol-bird	gromwell
gradient	god-smith	gliffing	Galilean	gonfanon	groschen	glow-worm
graviton	gadzooks	griefful	gold-leaf	gang-bang	good-dame	goodyear
gracioso	godspeed	gairfowl	gold-lace	genocide	goose-cap	glory-pea
glaciate	Gadarene	grisgris	gall-less	gonocyte	geometer	geomyoid
gladiate	gudesire	goings-on	goldless	gonadial	good-even	glorying
gracious	god-awful	gainings	gold-mine	gonidial	goose-egg	glorybox
goal-kick	Gnetales	gridiron	galangal	gonidium	geodesic	gypseous
gralloch	grey-coat	gridlock	galenoid	gunmetal	geodetic	gapingly
gnatling	greedily	grillade	Galenism	gingelly	goosegob	gapeseed
goal-line	grey-eyed	grillage	Galenist	gingerly	goosegog	gapeworm
goatling	greffier	grilling	galenite	gannetry	geometry	gypsydom
grayling	grey-fish	gaillard	Galloway	gingival	Georgian	gypsyism
goat-moth	greegree	gainless	Golconda	Ganoidei	groo-groo	garganey
grainage	guerilla	glimmery	galloper	gunfight	groggery	Germanic

germaine	gasolene	glyptics	habitans	Haggadic	hell-bent	half-pike
geriatry	gasoline	gazpacho	habitant	huggable	half-boot	half-pint
germ-cell	gas-plant	gazogene	hebetant	hog's-back	hell-born	heliport
gyrodyne	gospodar	gazement	hebetate	high-bred	hylobate	holy-rood
gardener	gas-poker	gazetted	hubbuboo	highball	half-blue	hilarity
garreted	gas-works	headache	hobbyism	highbrow	Halachah	helmsman
gardenia	gas-motor	headachy	hobbyist	high-born	half-cock	hillside
gorgerin	gastraea	healable	hiccatee	hog-score	Halachic	half-step
gor-belly	gastrula	headband	hackbolt	hoggerel	helicoid	Holostei
gorgeous	gas-stove	head-boom	hock-cart	hygienic	half-calf	holistic
garefowl	gestural	heavenly	hacienda	Huguenot	Holocene	helistop
garaging	gossypol	headfast	hectical	hagberry	halicore	half-tide
girlhood	guttated	headgear	hectorer	higher-up	hylicism	helotage
germinal	gatherer	hoarhead	hiccough	hog-reeve	hylicist	half-time
gyroidal	gatefold	heath-hen	hectorly	high-gear	half-dead	half-tint
Garcinia	gate-fine	headhunt	hocussed	hogshead	holydame	half-tone
garlicky	gateless	heathery	huckster	highjack	half-done	halation
gerbille	gate-post	heaviest	hocusing	Hegelian	half-door	holotype
garrison	guttural	hyacinth	hock-tide	higgling	hall-door	half-term
gorblimy	gate-vein	headlamp	hecatomb	highland	hull-down	helotism
garbling	glutaeal	headland	hiccuped	high-lone	halteres	halitous
girtline	glucagon	headline	hickwall	hegemony	helmeted	half-text
gormless	glutaeus	headlong	hack-work	highmost	Hellenic	halluces
Garamond	grumbler	headless	hideaway	highness	Helvetic	hellward
gerontic	grubbing	headmark	hydranth	hugeness	half-face	half-year
Girondin	glutelin	headmost	hedgepig	highroad	hillfolk	holly-oak
geraniol	glumella	headnote	hydremia	hog-frame	hell-fire	holozoic
geranium	goujeers	headrace	hiddenly	high-rise	hill-fort	humpback
Gorgonia	gruffish	headrail	hedgehog	hightail	hold-fast	home-bred
gargoyle	grudging	headring	hedge-hop	high-test	hologram	home-brew
gurgoyle	glucinum	headroom	hedgerow	hair-ball	hell-gate	home-born
garboard	grub-kick	headrope	hidy-hole	hairbell	hell-hole	hempbush
garrotte	Gaullism	headrest	hidlings	hair-band	hula-hula	homicide
geropiga	Gaullist	headsman	hidalgas	hair-grip	hula-hoop	humidify
gyrostat	gaumless	headship	hidalgos	heighten	half-hour	homodont
garishly	gourmand	hoarsely	hedonics	heich-how	hellicat	homodyne
girasole	glumness	healsome	hedonism	hairline	hollidam	humidity
garotted	grumness	heatspot	hedonist	heirloom	halliard	himseems
garotter	grumphie	hoastman	hydrogen	hairless	helminth	home-felt
gyration	grumpily	heartlet	hydromel	heirless	hell-kite	home-farm
gyratory	glumpish	heartpea	hadronic	hair-seal	half-loaf	home-fire
Gurmukhi	gaussian	hoactzin	hidrosis	huissier	half-life	homogamy
gurdwara	gruesome	heartily	hidrotic	heirship	halfling	homogeny
gardyloo	gauntlet	heart-rot	hydropic	hailshot	helmless	home-life
gas-water	gauntree	head-tire	hydroski	hoistman	helpless	homology
gossamer	gruntled	hiatuses	Hydrozoa	hoistway	helpmeet	homaloid
gustable	glutting	headword	hydropsy	hair-tail	half-moon	homelike
gas-meter	gluttony	headwork	Hydromys	hoisting	hall-moot	homelily
gesneria	grunting	Hyblaean	hydroxyl	hair-work	hallmark	homeland
gasifier	goutweed	hobdayed	hydatoid	hair-worm	half-mast	humbling
gasiform	goutwort	Hebraise	had-I-wist	hair-wave	halimote	homeless
gasogene	gaudy-day	Hebraism	hielaman	hijacker	helpmate	homilist
gas-shell	giveaway	Hebraist	hierarch	hoky-poky	haleness	hamulate
Gasthaus	gavelman	hobbling	haematic	heliacal	holiness	humility
gas-fired	gavelock	habanera	haematin	hollands	half-note	Himalaya
gaslight	governor	hebdomad	hieratic	Helladic	haliotis	home-made
gas-tight	gownsman	hobnobby	heel-ball	hallaloo	heliosis	hymeneal
gas-field	glyceric	hibernal	heedless	holla-hoa	hollowly	hymenean
gossipry	glycerin	hub-brake	hierurgy	half-beak	heliodor	hymenial
gas-globe	glycerol	Hibiscus	Haggadah	half-back	Heliozoa	hominoid
gasalier	glyceryl	habitual	Hogmanay	holdback	halfpace	humanoid
gaselier	glycogen	habitude	hag-taper	half-bred	holoptic	homuncle
gasolier	glyconic	hebetude	hog-maned	hell-bred		humanely

homonymy	handling	hyphenic	here-from	hardware	hatguard	isagogic
humanise	hand-loom	hapteron	hard-fern	hornwork	hautbois	inaurate
humanism	handless	hopped-up	Hereford	hornworm	houseman	inaction
humanist	hand-list	hypogeal	harigals	hornwort	heuretic	inactive
humanity	hen-flesh	hypogean	horngeld	herewith	house-fly	imbecile
hymenium	handmade	hypogaea	hardhead	harrying	houseboy	imbrices
hemiolia	handmaid	hypogene	hardhack	hurrying	house-dog	imborder
hemiolic	hand-mill	hypogyny	hurcheon	Hertzian	housetop	imbitter
hemiopia	hindmost	hypogeum	harridan	hastated	houseful	incubate
hemiopic	hangnail	hypalgia	heroical	Hispanic	hausfrau	incubous
homeosis	hangnest	hip-flask	harpings	hush-boat	hour-hand	incident
hummocky	handover	hopeless	horrific	Hasidism	hauriant	ischemia
hemionus	hangover	hopingly	heroicly	Hasidist	haurient	ischemic
hemp-palm	hung-over	haploidy	horrible	hastener	hourlong	increase
hamartia	hen-court	hypnosis	horribly	hosteler	housling	increate
humoresk	hen-house	hypnotic	horridly	hesperid	haunting	inclined
humorist	hen-roost	hip-joint	hirrient	Hesperis	hout-tout	inchmeal
humorous	handplay	Hyperion	hara-kiri	hysteria	havocked	incoming
homesick	hand-pick	Hepatica	hari-kari	hysteric	havildar	itch-mite
hampster	hanepoot	hypothec	horologe	has-beens	havelock	incenser
hemp-seed	hand-post	hipsters	horology	hostelry	hoveller	incensor
homespun	henequen	hepatise	heraldic	hasheesh	hivelike	incentre
homotony	henequin	hepatite	hardline	Hesperus	hiveless	inconnue
himation	handrail	hippuric	hireling	hush-hush	hive-nest	incloser
homotype	hungrily	Hippuris	hurdling	hospital	have-nots	inchoate
homotypy	honorary	haqueton	heraldry	hastings	hover-car	inceptor
hematite	huntress	hereaway	harmless	hustings	hover-bed	incurred
humstrum	huntsman	hard-a-lee	herbless	Hassidic	hover-fly	incurved
home-town	honestly	herbaged	hornless	histioid	hover-bus	incorpse
humoured	handsome	harmalin	hurtless	hospitia	hiveward	incision
Hamburgh	hand-sewn	herbaria	Huronian	hustling	hawkbell	incisure
homeward	honoured	hireable	heronsew	hospodar	hawk-eyed	incisive
homework	honourer	hardbeam	hardness	histogen	hawthorn	incitant
hamewith	hen-hussy	hornbeak	hereness	historic	Hawaiian	inch-tape
hangable	Hinduise	hornbeam	harangue	hassocky	hawfinch	included
hen-padle	Hinduism	hardback	hormonal	hosepipe	hawk-moth	ischuria
hen-party	hind-wing	hark-back	harmonic	hose-reel	howitzer	incivism
hung beef	handwork	hartbees	hormonic	histrion	hawkweed	itchweed
handball	hindward	herb-beer	harlotry	hesitant	how-d'ye-do	inch-worm
hand-ball	handyman	hardbake	harmosty	hesitate	hexagram	Indiaman
handbell	honey-bee	harebell	hornpipe	hateable	hexaglot	indebted
handbill	honey-dew	hornbill	Hereroes	Hatteria	hexylene	induciae
handbook	honey-ant	herd-book	horn-rims	hetaeria	hexaplar	indictee
hangbird	honeying	hornbook	hare's-ear	hitherto	Hexapoda	indocile
handclap	honeypot	Heraclid	harp-seal	hotted-up	hexapody	indecent
handcuff	honeybun	hyracoid	herdsman	hatchway	haymaker	indicant
hand-cart	hyoscine	hardcore	hernshaw	hitchily	hay-de-guy	inductor
hinderer	hoosegow	heredity	harassed	hatching	hey-de-guy	indicate
hungerly	hoolican	Harleian	harasser	hotchpot	hayfield	indrench
hanger-on	hooligan	horsecar	haruspex	hatchery	hey-go-mad	iodoform
handfuls	hoodless	horseman	hardship	hot-short	haystack	indigene
hind-foot	hoofless	horseway	heroship	hatchety	huzzaing	indigent
hangfire	hoof-mark	hardened	herisson	hetairai	hazelnut	indigest
handfast	huon-pine	hardener	Horatian	hetairia	haziness	indagate
handgrip	hoot-toot	herbelet	hardtack	hotelier	hazardry	indulger
henchman	hoodwink	hermetic	heritage	hat-plant	inarable	indolent
hindhead	hook-worm	herpetic	heritrix	hateless	in-and-out	induline
henchmen	heptarch	horsefly	horntail	hothouse	isabella	indented
hand-held	hipparch	herseems	hereupon	hot-brain	imaginal	indenter
handhold	heptagon	horse-boy	harrumph	haterent	imaginer	indirect
hand-horn	hypobole	hardface	hereunto	hatbrush	imagines	indurate
handicap	hypocist	hornfels	herdwick	hot-press	Italiote	iodyrite
hand-line	hypoderm	hare-foot	hardwood	hatstand	inasmuch	indusial

industry
indusium
induviae
induvial
indexing
iterance
ice-water
ice-yacht
ice-ledge
ideogram
Isengrim
ice-sheet
irenical
inedited
ice-field
inedible
irenicon
ice-skate
ideology
iceblink
ice-plant
idealess
idealise
idealism
idealist
ideality
ice-lolly
ice-bound
ice-house
ice-apron
inexpert
ice-cream
ice-craft
ice-front
inerrant
inessive
inertial
identify
ice-stone
ideation
identity
ideative
irefully
inequity
inflamed
inflamer
inflated
infra-red
inflator
inflatus
infecund
infector
inficete
inflexed
infefted
infringe
in-flight
infilter
infamise
infamous
infantry
infinite
infinity

infernal
informal
inferred
informed
informer
infirmly
inferior
infusion
infusory
infusive
influent
inguinal
ingenium
ingrowth
ingroove
inhearse
inholder
inhalant
inhumane
inhumate
inherent
ichorous
inhesion
imitancy
irisated
imitable
imitator
iriscope
Irishman
Irishism
inimical
initiate
idiolect
idiotish
idiotism
iniquity
injector
injurant
inkiness
inkstand
inkstone
ill-faced
ill-fated
ill-faurd
ill-deedy
ill-being
idlehood
ill-timed
ill-blood
illumine
Islamise
Islamism
Islamite
inlander
islander
idleness
illinium
ill-spent
illiquid
ill-treat
Illyrian
islesman
ill-usage

illision
illusion
illusory
illusive
illation
inlaying
immobile
immodest
immolate
immoment
Immanuel
immanely
immantle
immingle
immanent
imminent
immunise
ilmenite
immanity
immunity
immortal
immersed
immitted
immature
iambuses
innocent
Ionicise
innuendo
ianthine
ignominy
ignorant
Ignatian
innately
ignition
ignitron
innative
innovate
idolater
isobaric
isogamic
isolable
isolator
idolatry
ironbark
iron-clad
iron-clay
isomeric
isometry
iron-gray
iron-grey
isocheim
isochime
isochore
isothere
isotherm
isochasm
ironical
idoliser
inositol
isodicon
isocline
isogloss
isopleth

iron-mail
iron-mole
iron-mine
inornate
isogonal
isopodan
isogonic
isonomic
isotonic
isotopic
isodomon
isomorph
isodomum
isologue
isospory
isocracy
isocryme
isobront
isoprene
isotropy
idocrase
iron-sick
Ironside
iron-sand
Isoptera
isostasy
inoculum
ironwood
ironware
ironwork
ivory-nut
impocket
impudent
impleach
impledge
impresse
impugner
implicit
imprimis
imprison
impolicy
impelled
impeller
impolder
impolite
impannel
imponent
impanate
impunity
implorer
improper
improver
imperial
imparter
importer
impurely
impurple
imparity
impurity
imperium
impasted
imposter
impishly

imposing
impasto'd
impostor
impetigo
impotent
implunge
impluvia
implying
inquirer
irrigate
irrision
irrisory
irritant
irritate
instance
instancy
issuance
inswathe
instable
issuable
issuably
insucken
insecure
insignia
insphere
instinct
inspired
inspirer
inspirit
inscient
insulter
insolent
insulant
insolate
insulate
insomuch
insomnia
insanely
Ibsenism
Ibsenite
insanity
insconce
inscribe
instruct
inserted
inserter
inscroll
inshrine
insurant
instress
insculpt
intrados
intubate
iotacism
intrench
intrepid
integral
intaglio
iatrical
intrince
intuited
intrigue
Intelsat

isthmian
intimacy
intimism
intimist
intimate
intimity
intended
intender
intently
intoning
intonate
intromit
introrse
interlay
internal
interval
interwar
interact
internee
interred
interrex
intersex
intorted
intarsia
intarsio
intermit
intermix
intertie
icterine
intercom
interior
Interpol
interess
interest
intercut
intitule
intruder
inurbane
inundant
inundate
inustion
inveagle
inviable
invecked
invected
invocate
inveigle
involute
inventor
inverted
inverter
invertin
invertor
invasion
investor
invasive
inviting
inwardly
idyllian
idyllist
jealouse
jealousy
jabberer

jibbings
jubilant
jubilate
jibingly
jib-crane
Jebusite
jobation
jackaroo
jickajog
Jacobean
Jacobian
jackboot
Jacobite
jacketed
jackeroo
jockette
jack-fool
jack-high
jaculate
jocundly
jack-pine
jocorous
jocosely
jocosity
jack-tree
jacquard
judicial
jodphurs
Judaical
Judaiser
judgment
Jiffybag
jiggered
jaggedly
joggling
juggling
jugglery
jugulate
Jugoslav
johannes
Jehovist
jail-bird
join-hand
joint-fir
joint-oil
jointure
jejunely
jejunity
jokingly
jokesome
jillaroo
julienne
jolthead
jelutong
jalousie
jelly-pan
jampanee
jambeaux
jumped-up
Jamaican
jambiyah
jimpness
jambolan

jamboree	Javanese	knife-boy	king-size	leap-frog	lock-gate	Ladinity
jumboise	Jew's-harp	knightly	kinetics	leaching	lychgate	lodesman
jimcrack	jewelled	knickers	kingwood	loathing	lacrimal	lodestar
Jamesian	jeweller	kail-runt	knowable	leathern	lactific	ladyship
jump-seat	jowing-in	knitting	klondike	leathery	lace-leaf	lee-gauge
jingbang	jaw-tooth	knitwear	klondyke	leachate	Lucullan	liegeman
junketed	Jewishly	kailyard	kromesky	leach-tub	Lucullic	liegedom
janiform	joy-wheel	kok-sagyz	knot-hole	loathful	lackland	leechdom
Januform	joy-rider	kaka-beak	kaoliang	leavings	luculent	lee-board
jangling	joy-stick	kaka-bill	knocking	leaf-like	localise	lientery
jingling	joyfully	kakemono	knockout	lead-line	localism	liftable
jongleur	joyously	kala-azar	knotless	load-line	luckless	lifeboat
Junonian	krameria	killadar	knotting	leadless	locality	lifebelt
jingoish	khalifah	killcrop	knotweed	leafless	loculate	left-bank
jingoism	khalifat	killdeer	knotwork	learning	lack-love	life-buoy
jingoist	knackery	kilogram	kephalic	leanness	locomote	lifehold
junk-ring	knackish	kiln-hole	kipperer	leaf-roll	laciniae	left-hand
junk-shop	knapping	keloidal	kyphosis	leadsman	Laconian	lifelike
Jonathan	Klansman	kalamdan	kyphotic	leaf-scar	licensed	life-line
janitrix	knapscal	kalumpit	kirn-baby	loadstar	licensee	lifelong
junction	knapsack	kalendar	korfball	loan-word	licenser	lifeless
juncture	knapweed	kolinsky	kernelly	leap-year	licensor	left-over
junk-yard	Kabbalah	kalinite	kyrielle	Labiatae	lacunars	life-peer
janizary	kabeljou	killogie	kurveyor	labially	lacunary	lift-pump
jeopardy	kibitzer	kyllosis	kerchief	Labrador	lecanora	life-rent
Japhetic	kickable	kalyptra	kirn-milk	labdanum	laconism	lifespan
japonica	kachahri	Kolarian	kurtosis	libeccio	lacunose	lifesome
japanned	kickback	kalotype	kerb-side	lubberly	lacunate	life-size
japanner	kickdown	Kalevala	Kuroshio	libretti	lacrosse	lifetime
Japanese	keckling	kilovolt	kerosene	libretto	licorice	left-wing
Japanesy	kickshaw	kilowatt	kerosine	lobe-foot	lacerant	leftward
jeroboam	kedgeree	kaliyuga	keratoid	Labridae	lectress	life-work
jordeloo	kidology	kamacyte	keratose	lubrical	lacerate	log-cabin
jerrican	kid-glove	Kamadeva	kirktown	labelled	locksman	log-canoe
jirkinet	keelboat	kamikaze	kirkward	libelled	locustae	logician
jeremiad	kvetcher	Komsomol	kirkyard	libeller	lockstep	logicise
Jeremiah	knee-deep	komissar	kiss-curl	lobeline	lecithin	ligneous
jurymast	knee-high	komitaji	Kushitic	lobulate	lecythis	logogram
jararaca	klephtic	kangaroo	kistvaen	labellum	location	lug-chair
jararaka	kneehole	kinkajou	kottabos	loblolly	locution	Lagthing
Jurassic	keeshond	king-bolt	kitschly	liberate	locutory	lignitic
juristic	keelhaul	king-bird	katakana	laburnum	Lecythus	liguloid
jarosite	khedival	king-crab	kite-mark	lobotomy	locative	legalise
juratory	knee-jerk	king-crow	kourbash	libation	lecturer	legalism
jerquing	kreplach	kinsfolk	krumhorn	lobation	loco-weed	legalist
jerrycan	keenness	kingfish	kauri-gum	libatory	lichwake	log-glass
jestbook	keepsake	kinghood	khuskhus	laboured	lace-wing	legality
justicer	keepsaky	kink-host	kouskous	labourer	lacrymal	ligulate
Jesuitic	knee-stop	kantikoy	knurling	lobbying	lucky-bag	log-slate
Jesuitry	kreasote	kinakina	key-plate	lobbyist	lucky-dip	ligament
jostling	kreosote	kinglike	keyboard	lackaday	ladybird	legendry
justness	kreutzer	kindlily	key-fruit	lichanos	lodicula	legioned
jetliner	kreatine	kindling	keystone	lace-boot	lodicule	logboard
jettison	kefuffle	kingling	klystron	lacebark	laddered	log-house
jet-black	koftgari	kindless	keybugle	lucidity	ladleful	leg-break
jetplane	kaffiyeh	kingless	leasable	lichened	ladified	legering
jet-drive	keffiyeh	kindness	loanable	Lachesis	ladyfied	legerity
jaundice	kuffiyeh	kenspeck	leaf-base	lichenin	lady-fern	logistic
jiu-jitsu	koftwork	kingpost	loaf-cake	licker-in	lady-help	legatine
jauntily	kohlrabi	Kanarese	leaf-curl	lacteous	ladyhood	lighting .
jaunting	kaimakam	kings-man	leadenly	locofoco	ladylike	legation
jovially	khilafat	kinesics	lease-rod	lockfast	lady-love	ligation
juvenile	knife-box	kingship	leaf-fall	lichgate	lodgment	logotype

legatary	limerick	landlord	linkwork	larboard	lathyrus	live-well
ligature	lemuroid	landless	lungwort	liripoop	Laurasia	liveware
lightish	lemurine	lunulate	longwise	liripipe	laudable	live-wire
lightful	lampreys	langlauf	long-wave	lordship	laudably	law-maker
log-juice	lambskin	linoleum	longways	larkspur	laudanum	lawyerly
leg-guard	lamasery	land-mine	loo-table	lyra-viol	launcher	law-agent
lah-di-dah	lime-tree	liniment	loosener	lyra-wise	louvered	law-giver
laid-back	lime-twig	landmark	looker-in	lorry-hop	laureate	low-lived
loiterer	limiting	landmass	looker-on	listener	lounging	low-slung
leisured	limation	long-nine	loose-box	luscious	laughter	lewdness
likeable	limitary	lankness	lyophobe	lustique	louchely	law-court
likeness	Limousin	Leninism	loophole	lasslorn	laughing	lowering
lekythos	lima-wood	Leninist	lyophile	listless	laughful	Lewisian
likewake	lime-wood	loneness	lion-like	lustless	leucitic	lewdster
lykewake	limewash	longness	loop-line	losingly	loudness	lewisson
likewalk	lumpy-jaw	Leninite	lop-eared	lushness	Leucojum	lewisite
lukewarm	Linnaean	Londoner	lapsable	lassoing	louis-d'or	lawfully
likewise	lentando	land-poor	lipsalve	lispound	leviable	luxmeter
Lollardy	lineated	lunarian	lapidify	lustrine	liveable	lexigram
lollipop	lineally	landrace	lapidary	lustring	live-axle	luxurist
Lilliput	linearly	langrage	lapidate	lustrate	loveable	luxation
lallygag	land-army	landrail	lepidote	lustrous	live-bait	laxative
lollygag	longboat	land-roll	lappeted	lysozyme	live-born	lixivial
limnaeid	lung-book	lunarist	lipogram	lethargy	lovebird	lixivium
lampasse	land-crab	Landsmål	lop-sided	litharge	lividity	layabout
lambaste	landdros	landsman	lapelled	Lothario	love-drug	lay-shaft
Limaceae	lancegay	Langshan	lupuline	lutecium	love-feat	loyalist
limacine	longeval	linesman	lipgloss	Lutheran	lavaform	layering
lambdoid	lenience	long-stay	lipomata	lettered	love-game	lay-stall
lambency	leniency	langspel	lap-board	letterer	levigate	lazy-jack
lumberer	lancelet	lingster	Lupercal	littered	love-knot	lazulite
limnetic	lanceted	linkster	leporine	latterly	Lovelace	lozenged
lumberly	lanneret	lintseed	lopgrass	litherly	lovelock	laziness
lumpenly	lingerer	land-ship	liparite	litigant	levelled	Lazarist
lumpfish	lynx-eyed	landskip	liposome	litigate	leveller	lazurite
lamphole	lingerie	landslip	Laputian	latchkey	livelily	meat-ball
lymphoma	lungeing	lantskip	lipstick	let-alone	lovelily	mean-born
lamp-hour	longeron	longship	lapstone	Lettland	livelong	meatless
lammiger	landfall	long-slip	liquable	littling	lovelorn	miasmata
limpidly	landfill	lonesome	liquesce	latently	levulose	miasmous
limekiln	long-firm	longsome	liquidly	lateness	loveless	meanness
lamellae	land-fish	long-stop	loquitur	Latinise	lava-lava	meal-poke
lamellar	line-fish	long-spun	liquored	Latinism	lavement	meagrely
lamblike	lung-fish	linstock	lernaean	Latinist	lavender	meat-safe
lambling	landgirl	lengthen	larnakes	lutanist	Levanter	meal-tide
limbless	long-head	long-togs	larvated	lutenist	lovingly	meal-tree
limbmeal	lynch-law	long-tail	lyre-bird	Latinate	love-nest	meal-time
lemon-dab	linchpin	lenition	lyricism	Latinity	laverock	meantime
lemonade	long-hair	lunation	loricate	littoral	liveried	mean-tone
lamented	longhand	Linotype®	larcener	luteolin	leverage	measured
lamantin	luncheon	lincture	larderer	literacy	live-rail	measurer
luminant	land-herd	long-term	largesse	liturgic	liver-rot	meatuses
laminary	lanthorn	lenitive	lyriform	literary	liverish	meal-worm
luminary	longhorn	lingular	larrigan	literose	levirate	mealy-bug
lameness	long-haul	language	larrikin	laterite	love-seat	mobocrat
liminess	lenticel	languish	lorikeet	literate	lovesick	mobilise
luminist	lenticle	linguist	lordling	literati	love-suit	mobility
laminate	landlady	longueur	lordless	literato	lavishly	mechanic
limonite	long-life	Landwehr	laryngal	Lutetian	lovesome	moccasin
lomentum	long-legs	longwall	larynges	latitude	love-song	mockable
luminous	lent-lily	landwind	larynxes	latitant	lavation	mocuddum
lamppost	land-line	landward	lordosis	lutetium	lavatory	mackerel
lemurian	lanoline	lindworm	lordotic	latewake	levitate	muck-heap

macahuba
mackinaw
machismo
micellar
mycelial
muckluck
mucilage
mycology
muculent
maculose
maculate
mycelium
muchness
meconate
meconium
microbar
microbic
microdot
microlux
muck-rake
macaroni
macaroon
macarise
macarism
macerate
macarize
mocassin
mucosity
mycetoma
macrural
micrurgy
muck-worm
madrasah
medially
mediator
Medicean
mid-ocean
medicaid
medicine
medicare
medicate
medieval
modified
modifier
midships
madrigal
midwifed
midwived
midwives
midnight
Medjidie
midfield
medullae
medullar
medalled
modelled
modeller
medallic
meddling
middling
mud-clerk
modalism
modalist

modality
modulate
madwoman
modiolar
mediocre
madhouse
modiolus
mad-apple
mudirieh
madbrain
mid-brain
modernly
maderise
moderate
moderato
medusoid
modestly
modishly
mudstone
meditate
mud-puppy
mud-guard
modiwort
muddying
maenadic
Maecenas
myelitis
Maeonian
meekness
meetness
mnemonic
maestoso
maffling
mofussil
Magdalen
magmatic
migraine
migrator
megabyte
magician
megadyne
magnesia
magnetic
magneton
mug-sheep
magnific
megalith
magnolia
mug-house
megapode
magister
mageship
magot-pie
mightily
mightest
mightful
megavolt
megawatt
magazine
Mahratta
Mahadeva
mahogany
Mahdiism

Mahdiist
mah-jongg
mahzorim
Moharram
Muharram
Muharrem
maharaja
maharani
mailable
mail-boat
mainboom
mail-clad
mail-cart
mail-drag
main-deck
main-door
maidenly
maidhood
maiolica
mainland
mellitic
mainline
maidless
mainmast
meionite
maid-pale
muir-poot
muir-pout
mainstay
mainsail
moistify
maintain
moisture
maieutic
mainyard
majolica
majority
majestic
makeable
makebate
mokaddam
makeless
makomako
makimono
malvasia
molybdic
molecule
molecast
maledict
melodics
mule-deer
mylodont
melodeon
melodion
malt-dust
melodise
melodist
malodour
meltdown
milleped
mole-eyed
mallecho
malvesie
moltenly

mulberry
malleate
multeity
malefice
male-fern
milkfish
maligner
malignly
mill-girl
Malagash
Malagasy
mole-hill
mill-hand
milch-cow
millibar
milliner
milliped
Mulciber
multiped
mellitic
multifid
multifil
multiple
multiply
millième
milliard
milliare
milliary
malt-kiln
milk-loaf
milklike
milkless
melilite
molality
milkmaid
malt-mill
melamine
malamute
malemute
malander
malinger
melanoma
melanism
mildness
Molinism
Molinist
melanite
melinite
mylonite
melanous
miltonia
Miltonic
mellowly
millpond
malapert
malarial
malarian
maltreat
millrace
malgrado
malarkey
molarity
Milesian

maltster
molasses
molester
moleskin
mulishly
molossus
malstick
milk-tree
muleteer
mill-tail
militant
military
militate
Mollusca
multurer
milk-weed
milk-walk
milkwood
maltworm
milk-warm
milkwort
mill-work
moldwarp
malaxage
malaxate
Mammalia
mem-sahib
mimicked
mimicker
membered
mamselle
mammetry
Memphian
Memphite
mammifer
mammilla
mamillae
mamillar
mameluco
Mameluke
mumbling
momently
momentum
memorial
membrane
memorise
mimester
mimetite
mummying
Mandaean
maniacal
mancando
man-eater
mangabey
manna-dew
menhaden
mandarin
manganic
manganin
monoacid
montaria
manually
mentally

mandator
manna-ash
mandamus
manubria
monachal
monocrat
Manichee
monicker
menacing
manicure
mind-cure
mongcorn
monocarp
mungcorn
minacity
Monachus
monodont
monadism
monodist
mannered
mantelet
many-eyed
mince-pie
Monoecia
mannerly
minneola
monteith
manteaux
menseful
man-of-war
manifold
maniform
manifest
monk-fish
monogram
monogamy
managing
monogeny
monogony
monogyny
monoglot
mon-khmer
manshift
man-child
monohull
monkhood
mandioca
man-sized
Mandingo
mannikin
manciple
mandible
mantilla
monticle
mannitol
mantissa
monsieur
menology
monology
mantling
mingling
maneless
mindless

monolith
monomial
miniment
monument
muniment
mint-mark
monomark
minimise
minimism
minimist
meninges
monandry
mangonel
manpower
mandolin
Mongolic
menfolks
mandorla
man-hours
mongoose
mungoose
monopode
minipill
monopoly
menopome
manorial
manurial
menarche
Monarcho
monarchy
monorail
mandrake
mandrill
manuring
many-root
minoress
minorite
minority
mangrove
monk-seal
minister
miniskis
monastic
monistic
ministry
meniscus
minutiae
minstrel
minutely
monotint
monotone
monotony
monition
munition
monotype
minatory
monetary
monitory
monetise
menstrua
Minotaur
monitive
mensural

monaural	myriadth	marbling	muscatel	massicot	miswrite	mutandum
mensuren	mersalyl	mortling	mustache	masticot	masurium	mutinous
manfully	mortbell	moralise	mescalin	Messidor	misproud	matronal
mansuete	moribund	moralism	moshavim	mestizos	misprize	motional
Menevian	marabout	moralist	muscadin	missilry	misusage	meteoric
mansworn	Moraceae	morality	mesially	misbirth	mesotron	methodic
monaxial	marocain	Merulius	mascaron	mystique	misstate	matronly
monoxide	mericarp	mortmain	massacre	mass-john	muscular	metaphor
money-bag	merycism	Merimake	miscarry	mess-john	misguide	metopism
money-box	muricate	Maronian	mismarry	misplead	meshugga	metopryl
monazite	meridian	marinade	misfaith	Musulman	meshugge	material
myomancy	mire-drum	Marinism	moss-back	mashloch	messuage	maternal
mootable	mark-down	Marinist	mass-bell	misplace	misjudge	motor-car
moonbeam	mergence	miriness	musk-ball	misology	musquash	motorial
moor-band	marketed	marinate	mass-book	mossland	mesquite	motorman
moorcock	marketer	Maronite	Musaceae	muscling	misquote	motorway
mooncalf	murderer	meringue	musician	misallot	mosquito	matériel
moon-eyed	murrelet	marjoram	musicker	mastless	mostwhat	Mithraea
myogenic	marcella	marmoset	music-pen	mesolite	mesh-work	motor-jet
moon-face	markedly	marooner	musicale	mishmash	Mesozoic	Mithraic
moon-fish	martello	mirrored	moss-crop	messmate	mutually	motorail
moorfowl	martenot	moreover	music-box	Mishnaic	methadon	maturely
moot-hall	morceaux	myriopod	mesocarp	musingly	methanol	matgrass
moot-hill	muriform	mirepoix	musk-cavy	misandry	metabola	maturity
myositic	marigram	mar-sport	musk-duck	misentry	moth-ball	motorise
myositis	mortgage	more-pork	musk-deer	masoolah	matachin	motorist
Mjöllnir	marigold	mariposa	mesoderm	Massorah	muticous	maturate
moorland	maraging	maroquin	misteach	misdoubt	matadore	maturity
moonless	merogony	margrave	masseter	misnomer	mittened	motor-bus
myoblast	marchman	marksman	meseemed	massoola	mutterer	motorium
myosotis	marsh-gas	meresman	miscegen	miscount	mathesis	matutine
moor-pout	marshman	meristem	misfeign	misdoing	motherly	mutation
myograph	morphean	mort-safe	mesmeric	mispoint	matfelon	mutatory
moonrise	mort-head	marasmic	Moslemin	mastodon	mitigant	mutative
moonseed	murphies	masterly	misdealt	misspeak	mitigate	Mathurin
moonshee	merchild	myristic	musk-pear	mutchkin	mitzvoth
moonsail	morpheme	morosely	misbegot	misapply	mote-hill	motivate
moonshot	merchant	merosome	mismetre	misspell	matching	motivity
moon-type	morphine	mirksome	musketry	misspell	matchbox	metewand
moonwort	murrhine	murksome	masseuse	misspend	metrical	métayage
moody-mad	myrrhine	morosity	moss-flow	misspent	mythical	methylic
mopehawk	marchesa	marasmus	misogamy	musk-plum	matrices	methysis
mephitic	marchese	Moresque	misogyny	misarray	matrixes	meteyard
mephitis	mirthful	maritage	masthead	misdread	métairie	metazoan
Mephisto	Morpheus	Marattia	mischief	mistreat	metritis	metazoic
mopingly	marginal	maritime	moss-hagg	mistrial	methinks	metazoon
mopboard	marzipan	marathon	misthink	miscreed	mittimus	moulding
mopishly	morainal	moratory	misshood	misorder	metalled	mouse-ear
mapstick	margined	marauder	misshape	misgraff	motelier	mouterer
mopstick	Marsilea	murmurer	mestizas	misgraft	metallic	mousekin
muqaddam	martinet	mercuric	Muscidae	mesaraic	mytiloid	mauveine
maquette	marriage	mortuary	mystical	misprint	mottling	maumetry
moquette	mornings	marquess	misgiven	mess-room	mateless	mouse-dun
mordancy	Marsilia	marquise	misliker	mushroom	matelote	moufflon
muriated	morainic	Moravian	mistimed	Miserere	motility	mouthful
mariachi	morbific	maravedi	muslined	misprise	mutilate	moulinet
margaric	mortific	merryman	muslinet	mistress	metamere	meunière
margarin	morbidly	marrying	moslings	mistrust	matamata	mourning
muriatic	morbilli	mismatch	misdight	mistryst	mutineer	mournful
mortally	mirliton	mesdames	mislight	moss-rose	mutinied	mounseer
martagon	myrmidon	mismated	mastitis	musk-rose	metanoia	moussaka
Mercator	merciful	mistaken	miscible	Masorete	metonymy	mountain
myriapod	moraller	muscadel	mistitle	Masoreth	muteness	moulting

mountant	neck-beef	night-man	nonsense	narcissi	nut-brown	newsroom
mounting	neck-band	night-fly	ninefold	nursling	natation	newly-wed
moveable	neck-bone	negation	nine-foot	Neronian	notation	next-door
moveably	nucleide	negatron	nanogram	narcoses	nutation	nextness
movables	nickelic	night-dog	nine-hole	narcosis	natatory	naythles
moveless	nucleole	night-foe	non-thing	narcotic	no-trumps	Nazarean
movement	nucleoli	night-ape	nuncheon	narrowly	natively	Nazarene
movingly	nucleary	negatory	non-white	Neritina	nativism	Nazarite
maverick	nuclease	nugatory	nundinal	nervular	nativist	Nazirite
mawmetry	nucleate	negative	nine-inch	nurtural	nativity	orangery
mawbound	nacreous	night-owl	non-rigid	nurturer	naumachy	Orangism
mowburnt	neck-gear	nihilism	non-elect	nastalik	noumenal	omadhaun
maxi-coat	Noctilio	nihilist	non-claim	nose-band	nauseant	opalised
myxedema	nucellar	nihility	nine-mile	nose-cone	noumenon	ovaritis
maxillae	necklace	nohowish	non-union	nose-dive	nauseate	ovariole
maximise	neckline	nuisance	non-entry	nascence	nauseous	odalique
maximist	nucellus	nail-bomb	non-moral	nascency	nautical	oragious
myxomata	nocently	noisette	nenuphar	nisberry	neuritic	ovarious
mixy-maxy	nickname	noiseful	nonuplet	nose-herb	neuritis	oratorio
Mayology	niceness	nail-file	ninepins	nescient	nautilus	oratress
may-bloom	necrosis	nail-head	nonesuch	nose-leaf	nauplius	oracular
may-apple	necrotic	nail-hole	non-stock	nosology	neuronal	opaquely
mayoress	necropsy	nainsell	nineteen	nestling	neuroses	ombrella
may-queen	nicotian	naissant	nineties	nasalise	neurosis	Oxbridge
Mazdaism	nicotine	nainsook	nonjuror	noseless	neurotic	Orbilius
Mazdeism	nocturne	nullness	non-quota	nasality	neutrino	Orcadian
mozzetta	noctuary	nolition	non-event	noselite	navy-blue	occident
mizzling	neckwear	naloxone	nancy-boy	neshness	navicula	oncidium
mazement	neckweed	nameable	Neogaean	nosiness	navicert	orchella
maziness	nicky-tam	name-drop	neonatal	nose-ring	navigate	orchitic
mazarine	nudicaul	nomadise	neopagan	nuthatch	novellae	orchitls
mezereon	nodalise	nomadism	neo-Latin	not-pated	noveldom	orchilla
mezereum	nodulose	numberer	neotenic	notebook	navalism	occulted
mezuzahs	nodality	nomogram	neoteric	note-case	navy-list	oncology
mezuzoth	nodulous	nomogeny	noometry	nattered	novelise	occultly
near-beer	nudeness	nymphean	neophyte	nutmeggy	novelish	osculant
Nearctic	nidering	Nymphaea	neoplasm	not being	novelism	osculate
near-gaun	nidorous	nymphish	neologic	notified	novelist	oncoming
Noachian	nodosity	numskull	neoprene	notifier	November	Occamism
near-hand	nudities	nomology	noontide	natiform	novenary	Occamist
neat-herd	nidation	nameless	neomycin	Notogaea	never-was	oscinine
nearness	nodation	nominate	napiform	nutshell	novercal	once-over
neatness	nudation	numinous	napoleon	notching	navarchy	occupied
nearside	nieveful	name-part	nepenthe	Nethinim	noverint	occupier
near-silk	need-fire	numeracy	nepionic	nutrient	Novatian	occupant
neaptide	naething	Nemertea	Naperian	nathless	novation	occupate
nubecula	nielloed	nomarchy	nephroid	noteless	navvying	occurred
nobleman	needless	numerary	nephrite	natality	navy-yard	occasion
noblemen	niellist	numerate	naphthol	notandum	newscast	oscitant
noblesse	needment	nemorous	nepotist	national	nowadays	oscitate
nubiform	Niflheim	numerous	normalcy	notional	nowhence	occlusal
nebbishe	nifnaff	nomistic	normally	nitrogen	newsgirl	occlusor
nibbling	nigh-hand	namesake	narrator	nut-house	nowt-herd	ordnance
Nibelung	negligee	Nematoda	naricorn	nitroxyl	newshawk	old-timer
nebulise	Negrillo	nematode	Norseman	notarial	new-risen	ordainer
nobility	Negritos	nematoid	Norweyan	nutarian	newelled	ordalian
nubility	niggling	name-tape	nervelet	notornis	new-blown	ordalium
nebulium	nighness	nummular	nerve-end	naturing	newcomer	ordinand
nebulous	negroism	nimbused	Northman	naturism	new-model	ordinant
nobelium	niger-oil	nimbuses	narghile	naturist	Newtonic	ordinary
nubilous	nightcap	non-party	northing	nit-grass	new-found	ordinate
neckatee	night-hag	non-metal	northern	notarise	newspeak	old-world
nectared	nightjar	nine-eyes	nargileh	nut-grass	newsreel	Oedipean

8 o☐d☐q

oldsquaw	overhair	overrank	off-sorts	oologist	opsimath	outflash
obduracy	overhale	overripe	off-break	obligate	opsonium	outflush
ordering	overhold	overrash	offering	oil-shale	on-stream	obtemper
obdurate	overhand	overrate	offprint	oil-fired	obstruct	outsmart
ordurous	overhang	overseas	off-drive	owl-light	observer	optimise
opera-hat	overhent	oversman	off-stage	oil-field	oestrous	optimism
overarch	overhung	overstay	orgulous	oil-gland	ossarium	optimist
operatic	obeahism	oversway	oogamous	owl-glass	onsetter	optimate
openable	overhaul	overside	oogonial	oilcloth	obscurer	Ottamite
operable	one-piece	oleaster	organdie	oiliness	outdance	Ottomite
operator	one-liner	overseen	organise	onlooker	outmarch	octantal
overbear	one-sided	overseer	organism	obliquid	outmatch	octonary
overbeat	obedient	overstep	organist	owl-train	outrance	ostinato
overboil	olefiant	oversail	organity	oil-press	outwatch	ox-tongue
overbold	overjump	overskip	oogonium	oilstone	outwards	optional
overbulk	overkeep	overslip	orgasmic	oblation	outdated	outvoice
overblow	overknee	overspin	orgastic	oblivion	outtaken	outmoded
overbook	overkill	overswim	ophidian	ohmmeter	oathable	outpower
overbrow	overkind	oversell	ochidore	ommateum	ostracod	outroper
oven-bird	overking	oversold	ochreate	osnaburg	ostracon	outvoter
overburn	overleaf	obeisant	ochreous	omniform	ostrakon	orthotic
overbusy	overleap	overshoe	ocherous	oenology	outlawry	outbound
overbite	overload	overshot	Ochotona	ointment	outcaste	outgoing
Oleaceae	overlade	oversoul	Ophitism	ornament	outvalue	outpoint
overclad	overlier	oversize	ophiuran	oenophil	optician	orthodox
overcoat	oreology	overteem	ophiurid	ornithic	oiticica	orthopod
opercula	overlaid	overtoil	oligarch	ornately	obtected	orthoepy
overcall	overlain	overtrip	opinable	omnivore	outscold	outboard
overcome	overland	overtake	olibanum	opopanax	outscorn	outdoors
overcloy	overlong	overtalk	origanum	otoscope	outreach	outhouse
over-cool	overlook	overtime	Olivetan	odometer	ostreger	outworth
overcrop	overlard	overtone	oximeter	orogenic	outremer	outspeak
overcrow	overlord	ore-stare	olive-oil	odometry	outreign	octapody
open-cast	ocellate	overtire	orichalc	omophagy	outweigh	Octopoda
overcast	owerloup	overture	oliphant	ozoniser	out-Herod	octuplet
over-club	overlive	overturn	original	omoplate	outvenom	outsport
overdraw	overmuch	overtask	opificer	odograph	outlearn	outbreak
overdoer	overmast	overview	oxidiser	odontoid	outweary	outbreed
overdone	Oceanian	overveil	opinicus	odontona	ontogeny	outdrink
open-door	overneat	overwear	oeillade	odontist	outshine	octaroon
overdose	overnice	overween	orielled	omohyoid	outthink	octoroon
overdust	oleander	overwent	orillion	omphalic	outshoot	oat-grass
open-eyed	overname	overwind	oriental	omphalos	outrival	outcross
omelette	openness	overwing	oriented	ox-pecker	obtainer	outwrest
operetta	oceanaut	ovenwood	obi-woman	oppugner	oft-times	obturate
overfeed	one-to-one	ovenware	oviposit	oppilate	outrider	outbrave
overfree	one-horse	overword	osier-bed	orpiment	outsider	outdrive
overfall	open-plan	overwore	omission	opponent	outsized	outfrown
overfill	overplay	overwork	otiosity	oophoron	outfight	outprize
overfold	overpeer	overworn	omissive	opposing	outnight	obtusely
overfull	overpage	overwash	omitting	opposite	outright	obtusity
overfine	overpart	overwise	ouistiti	owrecome	outsight	outstrip
overfond	overpass	overyear	oviducal	oerlikon	osteitis	outstand
overflow	overpast	offwards	odiously	ourology	outfield	outstare
overfire	overpost	official	obituary	owreword	orthicon	optative
overfish	overplus	off-shake	objector	Ossianic	outskirt	obtruder
overgall	overread	offshoot	oak-egger	obstacle	outsleep	outguard
overgang	one-track	offshore	oak-apple	obsidian	ontology	outburst
overgrow	overrack	off-white	oil-gauge	ossified	optology	ottavino
overgive	override	offsider	oil-paint	oosphere	outflank	outswear
overhead	overruff	offender	oulachon	orseille	outfling	outdwell
overhear	overrake	off-and-on	obligant	orsellic	outglare	outswell
overheat	overrule	off-board	obliging	obsolete	outclass	outswing

outlying	poaching	prattler	pick-me-up	pseudery	pleasant	princess
oculated	Pharisee	plantage	pecan-nut	plebeian	pleasing	prie-dieu
ocularly	platinic	Plantago	pectoral	presence	pressing	poinding
opuscula	pea-rifle	plantain	Picariae	pretence	peep-show	price-tag
opuscule	placidly	plantule	picarian	piecener	press-box	primeval
opulence	plagiary	phantomy	picaroon	precepit	pression	prize-man
Orvietan	pianiste	playtime	pacation	premedic	pleasure	prideful
obvolute	placitum	pea-stone	picotite	preterit	pressure	prigging
onwardly	platinum	plaiting	pictural	predella	pressful	priggery
ox-warble	pratique	planting	pichurim	preceese	prentice	priggish
onychite	plank-bed	platting	picayune	prepense	prettify	priggism
onychium	planking	Phaethon	paduasoy	preserve	prestige	peishwah
oxytocin	pranking	plant-pot	podiatry	pyengadu	prettily	plighted
oxymoron	plankton	plastron	pudibund	pledgeor	plectron	plighter
Olympiad	prankish	plastery	pedicled	preggers	plectrum	philibeg
Olympian	prankful	psaltery	pedicure	phengite	prehuman	pricking
olympics	peak-load	phantasm	pudicity	pier-head	plexuses	phialled
Odyssean	pearlies	phantasy	podagral	peep-hole	presumer	painless
ooziness	phalloid	practise	pedigree	plethora	prejudge	prismoid
phalange	pea-plant	practive	pedagogy	psephism	preludio	primming
placable	pearling	piacular	podagric	psephite	precurse	phinnock
placably	pearl-ash	planulae	Podogona	Pieridae	peesweep	peignoir
playable	phallism	planular	puddingy	poetical	peetweet	pliantly
platanna	planless	planuria	pedalier	precinct	pre-exist	phisnomy
Platanus	pearlite	plaguily	pedalled	Pierides	pterylae	poignant
playback	pearl-eye	platysma	pedaller	premised	phenylic	primness
play-bill	pharmacy	platypus	pedology	premises	pterygia	Philomel
peat-bank	psalmody	piazzian	podology	presidia	puffball	poisoner
platband	pearmain	publican	paddling	presidio	puff-bird	prisoner
playbook	peat-moor	publicly	peddling	pyelitic	piffling	phimosis
planched	play-mare	pebbling	piddling	pyelitis	puff-puff	psllosis
planchet	peat-moss	pabulous	puddling	première	pygmaean	psilotic
prancing	psalmist	pubertal	pad-cloth	precious	pig-faced	ptilosis
plaidman	playmate	pub-crawl	pediment	previous	pug-faced	philomot
praedial	psammite	pabouche	pudendal	pre-elect	puggaree	Psilotum
prandial	plainant	peccancy	pedantic	preclude	pygidial	Priapean
play-debt	plaining	packaged	peduncle	phelloid	pygidium	priapism
plaiding	planning	pachalic	pedantry	pie-plant	pagehood	paitrick
pear-drop	plainish	peccable	pudendum	peerless	pugilism	primrose
plaudite	plainful	po'chaise	pedipalp	psellism	pugilist	primrosy
placeman	platonic	pickback	paderero	preamble	paganise	prioress
plateman	peacocky	pickerel	pederero	Piedmont	paganish	priorate
platelet	pea-soupy	picketed	Podargus	plein-air	paganism	priority
planetic	pear-push	picketer	padishah	pfenning	paginate	plimsole
pease-cod	prairial	pocketed	pedestal	pregnant	pig-woman	plimsoll
peaberry	pea-green	pochette	pedately	piedness	pug-nosed	priestly
plateasm	peat-reek	pacifier	Paddyism	pleonasm	pegboard	puissant
pianette	prairied	packfong	prenasal	pleonast	pigeonry	painting
placenta	playroom	pacifism	prenatal	prehnite	Pegasean	pointing
peaceful	piassaba	pacifist	Pleiades	phenogam	pigswill	printing
plateaux	plaister	puckfist	prepared	premolar	pig's-wash	pristine
plateful	peatship	pectinal	preparer	phenolic	primatal	paint-box
poaceous	playsuit	pectines	presager	pteropod	philabeg	painture
praefect	playsome	Puccinia	poematic	premorse	plicated	print-out
pratfall	praising	picnicky	prelatic	preorder	Primates	print-run
platform	piassava	pack-load	peekaboo	pre-print	primatic	pairwise
play-goer	plausive	peculiar	predator	piecrust	primally	pyjamaed
plangent	pea-straw	picklock	plenarty	pleurisy	prizable	pejorate
playgirl	plastral	pucelage	presbyte	pressfat	philamot	pikadell
pea-chick	plastics	peculate	preacher	pressman	pair-bond	pike-head
peat-hagg	practice	peculium	piercing	press-bed	princock	Pekinese
peat-hole	pear-tree	pack-mule	prescind	poetship	princely	pokerish
plashing	plantlet	pockmark	pleading	pheasant	Pliocene	pokeweed

8 p□□a

polyarch	polliwog	pilosity	pinacoid	pansophy	proseman	photopic
palmated	pulpitry	palatial	pinochle	pangolin	protégée	propolis
pileated	palliate	politick	pine-cone	Panionic	phonemic	prosodic
pillager	pulpitum	politico	panic-buy	pantofle	phoner-in	protonic
palladic	pulvinus	politics	ponderal	pinpoint	phonetic	pro-forma
pelmatic	pelology	palm-tree	pendency	pundonor	progeria	profound
polyacid	polemics	palstaff	penneech	penn'orth	pyogenic	propound
pulza-oil	Polymnia	pilotage	penneeck	panoptic	properly	promotor
palpable	pall-mall	politely	pungence	punt-pole	provedor	protocol
palpably	pell-mell	palatine	pungency	ping-pong	propense	protozoa
polka-dot	pulpmill	palstave	pince-nez	pancreas	protease	photopsy
polyaxon	palamino	polluted	pink-eyed	pin-prick	protense	prologue
pulsator	palimony	polluter	ponderer	pencraft	property	pronotum
pellagra	palomino	pellucid	pandemia	panorama	proofing	prorogue
Polabian	polymery	polyuria	pandemic	pentroof	plougher	prospect
palebuck	polemise	palm-wine	Pentelic	pinkroot	phosgene	prompted
pull-back	polemist	pulpwood	panderly	panislam	proggins	prompter
pale-dead	palamate	pilework	ponceaux	puntsman	prong-hoe	promptly
paludine	polymath	pile-worm	pang-full	pinaster	prophecy	plopping
paludism	Polonian	pilewort	pinafore	Pinkster	prophyll	propping
paludose	palinode	pill-worm	panegyry	punisher	prothyle	phosphor
paludous	palinody	pillwort	pin-wheel	pony-skin	prophase	piou-piou
pale-eyed	Polander	palewise	pinch-hit	punctual	prophesy	pooh-pooh
palleted	pulingly	pollywig	penchant	penstock	Phocidae	protract
palterer	paleness	pollywog	pinching	pine-tree	prodigal	protrude
pilferer	polonise	polyzoan	pancheon	pony-tail	proximal	prodrome
Pilsener	polonism	polyzoic	panchion	punctule	procinct	prodromi
pulsejet	polonium	polyzoon	Pantheon	penitent	province	prop-root
Palmerin	pillowed	pomwater	puncheon	punition	profiler	progress
palmette	pullover	pumicate	pinchgut	puncture	profiter	poor-rate
palmetto	pulmones	Pompeian	pannikel	punitory	promisee	poor's-box
pale-face	pulsojet	pamperer	Pan-pipes	punctate	promiser	prostyle
poltfoot	pulmonic	pimiento	pantiled	punitive	provided	plotting
paliform	pilhorse	pommetty	pen-wiper	pendular	provider	poortith
piliform	polyonym	pump-head	pinniped	pinguefy	pyonings	prostate
Pelagian	palm-play	pamphlet	pontifex	pendulum	prohibit	procurer
polygala	polypide	pump-hood	penlight	pondweed	prolific	producer
polygamy	polypody	pemmican	panmixia	pine-wood	prolixly	profuser
polygene	polypoid	pomology	panmixis	pine-wool	proviant	promulge
polygeny	polypine	pomander	pannikin	penny-fee	proditor	poorwill
polygony	polyphon	pembroke	pontific	penny-pig	promisor	poon-wood
polygyny	polypary	pump-room	pannicle	penny-dog	providor	propylic
phlegmon	polypite	pump-well	pendicle	pholades	provisor	propylon
polyglot	polypous	pentarch	punditry	profaner	Protista	pappadom
pilchard	Polaroid	pindaree	pinakoid	prolamin	poor-john	poppadum
pollical	paltrily	pin-maker	punaluan	protasis	plonking	pipeclay
pulvinar	pelerine	pinnated	panelled	protatic	proclaim	pupa-case
palmiped	poltroon	Punjabee	pond-life	probable	prowling	pepperer
pollices	pelorism	pangamic	penology	probably	plotless	puppetry
pulpited	polarise	Panhagia	pond-lily	provable	proclive	pipe-fish
pulpiter	polarity	pentadic	pingling	provably	proemial	popehood
pulsidge	palisade	Pindaric	pangless	Phocaena	phorminx	poplitic
palmitic	palisado	pantable	penalise	procaine	phormium	pop-visit
palmitin	pilaster	pentacle	penumbra	ptomaine	poorness	papillae
pollinia	polished	pinnacle	penoncel	pronator	pronotal	papillar
pollinic	polisher	pintable	penknife	prolapse	proposal	populace
polliwig	pollster	pantalon	pinkness	prosaism	photogen	pupilage
pulsific	Pelasgic	pentagon	puniness	prosaist	promoter	pipelike
pulvilio	polyseme	pintados	pentosan	Phoebean	proposer	pipeline
pallidly	polysemy	Pandanus	penwoman	plodding	provoker	popeling
pellicle	polysome	panacean	pandowdy	prodding	prolonge	papillon
pulville	polysomy	panicked	pennoned	proudish	photo-fit	papilla
pulvilli	palestra	panicled	pin-money	prometal	photopia	pupilary

papalise	parochin	perthite	pardoner	pyrexial	post-obit	petalody
papalism	pork-chop	pyrrhous	parroted	peroxide	pastorly	petalled
papalist	pericope	partisan	parroter	pyroxyle	pishogue	petaloid
papulose	pericarp	partizan	purposed	pyroxene	post-paid	pithlike
pipeless	peracute	Percidae	parsonic	paroxysm	push-pull	petaline
populism	peridial	parritch	percolin	party-man	postpone	petulant
populist	parodied	porridge	periodic	parrying	passport	pot-plant
populate	paradigm	perlitic	periotic	partyism	post-road	pathless
pupilate	pyridine	partible	parpoint	parazoan	pastrami	petalism
papulous	paradrop	particle	parrotry	pirozhki	poshteen	pithless
populous	periderm	persicot	porpoise	parazoon	post-time	pitiless
popinjay	paradise	portière	portoise	pastance	positing	patulous
pappoose	parodist	Parsiism	perspire	piss-a-bed	position	petalous
puppodum	peridote	perviate	peripety	pashalik	positron	putamina
pap-spoon	peridium	partitur	periplus	passable	positive	patentee
paper-day	paradoxy	pervious	paraquat	passably	post-town	potently
puparial	parietal	pirlicue	paroquet	piscator	pastural	patentor
pipe-rack	Parmesan	portigue	parbreak	paspalum	postural	petuntse
papering	perdendo	purlicue	pirarucu	push-bike	pustular	pétanque
peperino	parcener	parakeet	portrait	push-ball	posturer	petuntze
piperine	pargeted	parallax	parergon	pass-book	password	patronal
paper-boy	pargeter	parallel	portress	Postcode	pussy-cat	petiolar
pop-group	purse-net	perilled	perorate	postcard	Puseyism	petrosal
puparium	parhelia	paralogy	Parisian	push-cart	Puseyite	pathogen
Pepysian	parhelic	purslain	pyrostat	postdate	pittance	petioled
papisher	paroemia	parklike	parishen	passer-by	potlatch	petronel
pipe-stem	porterly	parkland	perished	Passeres	phthalic	petrolic
papistic	purveyor	perilune	perisher	paste-eel	phthalin	pythonic
popeship	parterre	porkling	poristic	pesterer	pitiable	pot-bound
popishly	perverse	portland	puristic	postface	pitiably	pothouse
papistry	porpesse	purblind	piroshki	post-free	pithball	pot-roast
pipe-tree	portesse	purfling	Pyrosoma	pisiform	petechia	paternal
pupation	perfecti	purslane	pyrosome	pasch-egg	poticary	peter-man
pop-music	perfecto	purulent	parasang	post-hole	pot-metal	pityroid
pipe-wine	permeate	paralyse	part-song	post-horn	patience	Patarine
pipework	perseity	parclose	phrasing	piscinae	pattened	paterero
pipewort	porteous	portlast	perisarc	pasticci	patterer	putashes
puppy fat	purseful	purplish	parasite	pastiche	potterer	potassic
poppy-oil	perceive	pyrolyse	porosity	postiche	pathetic	pot-stick
puppy-dog	purified	perilous	part-time	passible	pettedly	pith-tree
puppydom	purifier	parament	pyritise	passibly	pot-belly	potatoes
puppyish	paraffin	paramese	pyritous	pastille	putter-on	pot-still
puppyism	parafoil	paramour	persuade	possible	pita-flax	potstone
piquancy	paraffle	parental	perfumed	possibly	patagial	petition
parlance	Porifera	perineal	perfumer	Poseidon	patagium	potation
pernancy	port-fire	peroneal	perjured	Peshitta	putchock	petitory
portance	pyriform	Pyrenean	perjurer	Peshitto	patchily	potatory
parlando	paragram	paranoea	pertused	postlude	pita-hemp	putative
partaken	Paraguay	paranoia	Portugee	posology	patching	pot-au-feu
partaker	perigeal	paranoic	parousia	passless	pitching	pitty-pat
pardalis	perigean	paranoid	purpuric	pisolite	patch-box	puttying
perradii	Phrygian	pyrenoid	purpurin	post-mill	patchery	plumaged
phreatic	paragoge	paronymy	pursuant	pashmina	petchary	plurally
portable	porogamy	pertness	pursuing	passment	potsherd	poulaine
pirrauru	perigone	poriness	perruque	postmark	pit-viper	plumbago
perianth	perigyny	pureness	Peruvian	puss-moth	petrific	plumbing
periagua	Parthian	paranete	paravail	posingly	phthisic	plumb-bob
portague	porthole	perineum	paravane	poshness	phthisis	plumbery
periblem	perching	peroneus	paravant	post-nati	putridly	plumbism
pure-bred	Porphyra	Pareoean	port-wine	pastoral	pettifog	plumbate
parabola	porphyry	personal	port-winy	Passover	patriate	plumbite
parabole	porthors	portolan	parkward	pistolet	patellae	plumbous
parabema	purchase	perforce	partwork	push-over	patellar	plum-cake

pound-day
pound-net
plum-duff
poundage
pauldron
pouldron
prudence
plumelet
prunella
prunelle
prunello
pauseful
plugging
plunging
pouchful
plumiped
plurisie
pruritic
prurient
pluviose
pluvious
pruritus
pluckily
pruinose
plutonic
plumpish
Paul's-man
Prussian
Prussify
plussage
poultice
plum-tree
plumulae
plumular
plug-ugly
pavilion
pavement
pavonian
pavonine
pivot-man
pivoting
pewterer
powdered
pew-chair
powsowdy
powerful
pawnshop
pyxidium
pax-board
pax-brede
pixy-ring
phylarch
prytanea
physalia
physalis
physeter
phyletic
psychics
pay-sheet
psychoid
pay-phone
psychism
psychist

physical
physicky
paynimry
physique
phyllode
phyllody
phylloid
phyllome
phyllary
ptyalise
ptyalism
phyllite
pryingly
phytosis
Plymouth
pizzeria
puzzling
pezizoid
quandang
quandong
quandary
quaverer
quakerly
quackery
quailing
qualming
quagmire
quagmiry
qualmish
quaintly
quatorze
quarried
quarrier
quadriga
quatrain
quadrans
quadrant
quadroon
quadrate
quayside
quaestor
quartier
quantify
quartile
quantong
quart-pot
quartern
quantise
quantity
quartett
quencher
Quebecer
quenelle
queueing
Quechuan
queen-bee
queenlet
queening
queendom
queenite
queerdom
queerish
queerity

queasily
questant
questing
question
querying
quibbler
quincunx
quiddler
quiddany
quiddity
quivered
Quichuan
Quirinal
Quirites
Quirinus
quickset
quirkish
quillman
quill-pen
quillaia
quill-nib
quillaja
quilling
quisling
quidnunc
quixotry
quippish
quit-rent
quipster
quietude
quintain
quintile
quieting
quilting
quitting
quietism
quietist
quintett
quietive
quizzify
quizzing
quizzery
qalamdan
quotable
quotably
quotient
rear-arch
reawaken
readable
readably
road-book
reascend
reascent
reaedify
rhabdoid
reagency
reaffirm
rhaphide
reaching
realiser
readiest
readjust

rear-lamp
rearmice
rearmost
realness
reasoned
reasoner
reappear
rear-rank
rearrest
roadsman
rhapsode
rhapsody
roadside
reanswer
roadster
reassign
reassume
roadshow
reabsorb
reassert
reassure
reassess
Rhaetian
reattach
reattain
realtime
readvise
rearward
ready-mix
rubicund
rabidity
rubidium
rabbeted
rubaiyat
rubrical
rabbiter
rubbishy
rabbinic
rabbitry
rubellan
rebelled
rebeller
rabbling
rebeldom
rebellow
ribaldry
ribbonry
rib-roast
reburial
roborant
rib-grass
roburite
robustly
ribosome
rebuttal
robotics
rebutted
rebutter
ruby-tail

ribstone
rubstone
rebutton
ribaudry
rockaway
recharge
rectally
rock-alum
rice-beer
race-ball
rice-bird
rock-bird
ricochet
rock-cake
rock-cook
race-card
rock-cork
receding
rock-dove
racketed
racketer
rocketer
Roccella
Rochelle
recreant
rocketry
richesse
recreate
ricketty
rock-fall
rock-fish
racegoer
rice-glue
racahout
rock-hewn
receival
rachides
received
receiver
reclined
recliner
rachitic
rachitis
rectitic
rectitis
rachilla
rocaille
récollet
rich-left
reckling
rockling
rock-lark
reckless
recommit
rice-milk
racemise
racemism
racemose
racemate
racemize
recanter
reconvey
recently

recentre
raciness
richness
rectoral
reckoner
reclothe
recaptor
receptor
race-path
ricercar
recorder
recurred
recurved
rack-rail
rack-rent
rectress
rock-rose
rickshaw
rucksack
recessed
rock-salt
recusant
recision
rice-soup
recourse
Racovian
recovery
rockweed
rock-wood
rackwork
rock-work
rickyard
radiance
radiancy
riddance
radiated
red-faced
red-water
radialia
radially
rideable
radiator
radicule
ridicule
radicant
reducing
redactor
radicate
ridgeway
reddenda
reddendo
redeemer
red-belly
red-shank
redshare
redshire
red-shirt
redshort
red-light
ruddiest
redolent
riddling

ridgling
redeless
radulate
rudiment
Rodentia
rudeness
redeploy
redbrick
redirect
radar-gun
redargue
redesign
redistil
red-start
redouble
redivide
ruddying
rhematic
re-embody
reed-band
reef-band
reed-bird
re-embark
rheocord
re-emerge
re-engage
reef-knot
rheology
reedling
Riesling
re-enlist
rye-flour
reed-mace
rhetoric
re-expand
reed-pipe
re-export
rye-bread
reed-rand
reed-rond
rye-grass
rheostat
reed-stop
rye-straw
roentgen
rheotome
roestone
ruefully
reed-wren
Rh-factor
rifleman
raftered
reflexed
rifle-pit
reflexly
refreeze
refigure
refugium
refringe
refelled
ruffling
refunder
refining

refinery	raisable	rillmark	remittal	renounce	repenter	resigner
rifeness	ruinable	roll-neck	remitted	renovate	repining	rosoglio
raft-port	rain-band	role-play	remittee	renowned	ripeness	rose-hued
referral	rain-bird	relapsed	remitter	renowner	ropiness	rest-home
referred	rainbowy	relapser	remotely	ring-walk	reproval	rustical
reformed	raincoat	roly-poly	remittor	ring-wall	reproach	rispings
reformer	railcard	relation	remotion	renewing	Raptores	rose-knot
riff-raff	reindeer	relative	rambutan	ringwork	reprover	resalgar
referent	raindrop	relevant	rum-punch	ringworm	repeople	risaldar
raft-rope	reinette	relaxant	rumourer	ringwise	riparial	rose-leaf
raftsman	rainfall	relaxing	Romeward	renaying	riparian	reselect
refusnik	reinfund	rallying	Ramayana	rhodanic	repartee	resolved
refusion	reinform	rampancy	rondavel	rhopalic	reporter	resolver
refluent	reinfuse	rummager	rondache	rood-beam	repurify	roselike
rag-paper	railhead	rampauge	rentable	root-beer	rope-ripe	rush-like
regrater	rein-hand	rump-bone	rinsable	rhomboid	reperuse	resplend
Ragnarök	rhinitis	Ramadhan	runnable	rhonchal	rephrase	rustling
regrator	reillume	remedial	rent-a-mob	root-crop	rape-seed	restless
regicide	raillery	remediat	roncador	reoccupy	rope's-end	roseless
rigidify	railless	remedied	ring-bolt	rhonchus	reposure	rustless
rigadoon	rainless	remodify	ringbone	reordain	repetend	resalute
rigidise	reinless	rumbelow	ring-bark	reopener	reputing	resolute
rigidity	re-ignite	ramified	runabout	Rhodesia	raptured	risoluto
raggedly	rhizobia	remigial	ring-dial	rootedly	repoussé	rosulate
ruggedly	raisonné	remigate	ring-dyke	reoffend	rope-walk	resemble
ragwheel	Rhinodon	ram's-horn	ring-dove	root-fast	ropework	rosemary
ragtimer	rhizopod	rum-shrub	renderer	root-hair	repaying	Russniak
regainer	rhizopus	rum-ti-tum	renverse	roothold	replying	resenter
regalian	reimport	Ramilies	renverst	Rhodites	rope-yarn	resinify
reguline	reimpose	Ramillie	rondeaux	reorient	roquette	rosin-oil
regalism	railroad	rambling	runner-up	root-knot	requital	resonant
regalist	reinsman	rumbling	rent-free	rood-loft	required	rashness
regulise	reinsert	ramulose	raniform	roof-like	requirer	resinise
rugulose	reinsure	rumpless	reniform	roofless	requited	rosiness
regality	rain-tree	ramulous	renegade	rootless	requiter	resinata
regelate	roisting	remember	renegado	room-mate	rere-arch	resinate
regolith	reinvest	Romanian	reneguer	roof-rack	rarefied	resonate
regulate	rain-wash	Rumanian	renegate	roomsome	ruralise	rosinate
regiment	rejecter	Romansch	runagate	rood-tree	ruralism	resinous
ragingly	rejector	Rumansch	ranchman	roof-tree	ruralist	restorer
ragwoman	rejigger	Rumonsch	ringhals	ryotwari	rurality	Responsa
regional	rejoicer	reminder	rinkhals	rapparee	reremice	response
rag-money	rajaship	romancer	ranching	repealer	rareness	resupine
regrowth	rakehell	romantic	ranchero	repeated	rerevise	rose-pink
regarder	rakshasa	remanent	rinsings	repeater	rereward	rasorial
rigorism	rekindle	ruminant	rinsible	replacer	Rastaman	rosarian
rigorist	rakishly	Romanise	runcible	raphania	research	restrict
rigorous	reliance	Romanish	rindless	ropeable	resiance	reserved
register	releasee	Romanism	ringless	Raphanus	rascally	resorter
rugosely	releaser	Romanist	renumber	republic	resubmit	resurvey
registry	reliable	ruminate	rankness	rape-cake	rose-bush	resorcin
rugosity	reliably	ramentum	renforce	rapacity	rose-bowl	restrain
regather	rollable	rump-post	ransomer	rapidity	Rosaceae	restring
ragstone	releasor	ramequin	randomly	replevin	rose-comb	rush-ring
righting	roll-call	remarked	ranarian	reprisal	rest-cure	rest-room
rogation	relucent	remarker	ring-road	raphides	residual	rose-root
rogatory	relocate	rim-brake	rent-roll	repairer	resident	rescript
rightist	reliever	remarqué	ranarium	repriefe	rose-drop	rose-rash
rightful	religion	remurmur	ringside	Reptilia	rosy-drop	rostrate
reheater	relegate	rumorous	ringster	reprieve	residuum	rosarium
rehearse	Rallidae	rampsman	ring-tail	repelled	rispetto	resistor
rehoboam	ruleless	remissly	ring-time	repeller	rosefish	resetter
rehandle	relumine	Rome-scot	renitent	rippling	resigned	rose-tree

rosetted
resettle
resource
rescuing
rosewood
rateable
rateably
retrally
ritually
retraitt
rutabaga
ratsbane
Rutaceae
reticule
reticent
retrench
ruthenic
rottenly
ratified
ratifier
retiform
Rotifera
rat-rhyme
retailer
retainer
retrieve
retaking
reteller
rattline
rattling
rutilant
riteless
ruthless
retinula
rotundly
rotenone
retinite
ritenuto
rational
retroact
ratooner
retrofit
retrorse
rataplan
Rotarian
retiracy
retarded
retarder
retorted
retorter
ritornel
roturier
retiring
ratproof
rathripe
rotgrass
rat's-tail
rot-stone
rotation
rotatory
rotative
rat-guard
retrying

rhubarby
reusable
rout-cake
roundlet
rounding
round-top
round-arm
roundure
roundish
roulette
rouleaux
rough-hew
roughage
rough-dry
roughish
rout-seat
revealer
reviewal
reviewer
reveille
ravelled
revelled
reveller
revolted
revolter
revolver
rivalled
rivelled
reviling
rivaless
rivalise
revolute
rivality
revenger
revenued
revanche
ravingly
rovingly
ravening
revenant
ravenous
rove-over
reversal
riverman
river-rat
riverway
reversed
reverser
reverted
river-bed
reversis
riverain
reverend
reverent
riverine
river-god
river-hog
reverist
ravisher
revision
revestry
revisory
revetted

rivetted
riveting
revivify
row-barge
rowndell
rowdedow
rowelled
rawboned
rewarder
rowdydow
rowdyish
rowdyism
rhythmal
rhythmed
rhythmic
rhythmus
Rhytisma
royalise
royalism
royalist
rhyolite
roysting
razmataz
scalawag
soakaway
seawards
scarabee
scavager
seafarer
sea-water
staragen
sea-marge
Scalaria
shamanic
scalable
sea-eagle
seamanly
shakable
shapable
sparable
statable
stalagma
sway-back
scambler
snap-brim
seat-belt
shabbily
soap-ball
stay-bolt
slap-bang
stabbing
swabbing
scabbard
shag-bark
slabbery
soap-bark
shadbush
searcher
snatcher
stanchel
stancher
starched

starcher
scarcely
shauchle
shauchly
stanchly
seascape
sea-acorn
scarcity
staccato
shanghai
sea-scout
Scandian
Shandean
shaddock
sea-adder
spandrel
swaddler
stand-off
spandril
scalding
scaldini
scaldino
scandent
standing
standard
slap-dash
soap-dish
standish
star-dust
scandium
stay-down
shake-bag
shake-rag
shareman
space-bar
spaceman
spademan
sea-beach
sea-perch
sea-level
slaverer
snake-eel
stake-net
stamened
scavenge
Swadeshi
sea-devil
shale-oil
snake-oil
snake-pit
spageric
stapelia
sea-jelly
snake-fly
statedly
slave-ant
sea-lemon
stage-box
seaberry
sea-beast
sea-heath
shake-out
shameful
share-out

spadeful
slate-axe
staffage
scarf-pin
scaffold
scarfing
scarfish
starfish
shanghai
spangled
spangler
spanglet
shaggily
slangily
slanging
staggard
slangish
star-gaze
stag-head
scaphoid
smash-hit
seashell
staphyle
scathing
slashing
smashing
stag-hunt
swashing
stanhope
sea-chart
seashore
staghorn
swanherd
sea-chest
spathose
sea-shrub
spar-hawk
Scaridae
Sparidae
staminal
statical
sea-piece
shamisen
spadices
spavined
sea-fight
spagiric
spadille
spadillo
suasible
shamiana
stasimon
Spaniard
Scabiosa
Shafiite
scabious
scarious
spacious
slapjack
slack-jaw
snack-bar
spark-gap
sparkler

sparklet
shark-oil
sharking
smacking
spanking
stacking
stalking
swanking
starkers
sparkish
Stahlian
stallman
stay-lace
stall-fed
sea-cliff
smallage
stallage
starlike
swanlike
small-ale
seaplane
shawling
snap-link
snarling
span-long
sparling
stabling
stalling
starling
swayling
scallion
sea-floor
shalloon
smallpox
stallion
small-arm
snailery
scarless
seamless
seatless
smallish
soapless
spanless
stablish
Stahlism
starless
stayless
sea-blite
scarmoge
smalmily
smarmily
scammony
shamming
slamming
swarming
swan-mark
swan-neck
sea-snail
sea-snake
scanning
spanning
spawning
stagnant

staining
swaining
sea-onion
sea-snipe
stannary
swannery
searness
star-nose
swainish
stagnate
stannate
stannite
stannous
seasonal
sea-woman
sea-loach
sea-power
sea-rover
seasoned
seasoner
shadower
spadones
sea-robin
Slavonia
Slavonic
sea-holly
seaborne
sea-going
sea-hound
sea-mount
seaboard
sea-coast
sea-horse
sea-mouse
sea-boots
starosta
starosty
stampede
stampedo
sharp-set
spalpeen
snappily
scamping
scarping
sharping
slapping
snapping
stamping
swapping
shampoo'd
seal-pipe
scampish
sharpish
snappish
scalprum
sharp-cut
star-pav'd
sea-bream
stairway
star-read
sea-orach
sea-wrack
shabrack

shamrock	Shaktism	subimago	succinct	saddlery	speeding	stealing
sea-brief	soap-test	subsolar	succinic	sedulity	spelding	steeling
sea-green	startish	subtotal	sacristy	sodalite	spending	sterling
shagreen	scantity	subzonal	succinum	sodality	steading	swealing
seacraft	smaltite	subsonic	Sicilian	sedulous	speed-cop	swelling
starrily	startful	subtonic	Siculian	sodamide	speedful	steelbow
seadrome	scapular	subtopia	sicklied	sediment	step-down	stellion
scarring	spatular	subpoena	so-called	sudamina	scelerat	swelldom
sea-front	statured	subcosta	Sicelain	sodomise	scene-man	swell-mob
seal-ring	sea-lungs	subequal	suchlike	Sodomite	skeletal	seedless
seam-rent	seaquake	saburral	sicklily	Sudanese	skene-dhu	seemless
seat-rent	seacunny	suburban	suckling	side-note	she-devil	stemless
sparring	statuary	subtribe	Siceliot	side-post	stereome	swellish
starring	sea-purse	suberect	sucklers	side-path	skeleton	stellate
shagroon	starving	subtract	sackless	sidereal	suedette	shellful
soap-root	Shaivism	subtrude	sick-list	side-road	siege-gun	spellful
spadroon	Shaivite	subbreed	sacellum	sederunt	stem-form	steam-car
span-roof	spaewife	suborder	sycamine	siderite	seed-fish	sperm-oil
stair-rod	sea-swine	suborner	sycamore	sudarium	shelf-ful	steamily
sea-grape	slag-wool	suburbia	sycomore	sudorous	Spergula	steaming
sea-grass	soap-work	sobering	Sicanian	sidesman	sledging	stemming
sea-froth	soapwort	subprior	Socinian	side-step	seething	spermary
scabrous	stalwart	soberise	seconder	sadistic	stephane	stemmata
sea-trout	starwort	suberise	secondly	side-slip	shepherd	spermous
swagsman	sealyham	suberose	sickness	side-show	scenical	steam-tug
soap-suds	scaly-leg	subtrist	suchness	sedately	Shekinah	sternway
seamster	spagyric	suberate	syconium	sedation	specimen	sternage
slaister	sea-nymph	sybarite	sectoral	sedition	specific	skean-dhu
sealskin	stanzaic	suberous	Suctoria	sudation	spelikin	steaning
staysail	subbasal	subgroup	sack-race	sudatory	syenitic	steening
swan-skin	sabbatic	sebesten	sucurujú	sedative	sterigma	steining
spansule	Sobranje	sabotier	securely	Sadducee	speciate	steenbok
sparsely	Sobranyo	sob-stuff	security	side-view	specious	sternson
swan-song	subacrid	sabotage	secesher	sidewalk	sneaksby	seedness
scansion	subucula	substage	sack-tree	side-wind	speckled	Siennese
snapshot	subacute	substyle	secateur	sideward	sneakily	sternite
starspot	submerge	sob-story	saccular	sidewise	sleeking	stenosed
swagshop	sublease	sybotism	succubae	sideways	sneaking	stenosis
swan-shot	submerse	saboteur	succubas	spelaean	speaking	stenotic
swap-shop	subtense	subhuman	saccules	seecatch	sheikdom	stegodon
sparsity	subverse	sublunar	secluded	scenario	sneakish	sweep-saw
star-trap	sabre-cut	subduple	sacculus	Sheraton	sneak-cup	sheep-ked
sea-stick	subgenus	subovate	succubus	skew-back	seed-leaf	sheep-pen
sea-stock	subserve	suboxide	suchwise	stembuck	shell-lac	steepled
sea-otter	subagent	sacraria	sad-faced	skewbald	seed-lobe	sweep-net
soap-tree	subahdar	Socratic	sidearms	spekboom	shell-ice	sheep-dip
startled	subshrub	sociable	side-band	seed-coat	skelloch	sleepily
startler	subsizar	sociably	side-comb	sketcher	stenlock	skelping
svastika	sublimed	socially	seducing	swelchie	seemlier	sleeping
swastika	subtilly	sectator	seductor	seedcake	steel-pen	sneaping
scantily	subtitle	sack-coat	side-door	seed-corn	stellify	stepping
shafting	sobriety	secodont	side-dish	speedway	shell-egg	stewpond
shantung	subtilty	societal	side-drum	shelduck	stealthy	sweeping
slanting	sibilant	sickener	suddenly	steadied	seed-like	seed-plot
starting	subfloor	socketed	suddenty	steadier	seedling	sheepdog
stay-tape	sabulose	suckener	side-face	speldrin	shealing	sheep-pox
scattery	subclass	suckered	side-kick	speedily	sheeling	sheep-rot
sea-storm	subtlist	secretin	sidelock	spendall	sheiling	sleepery
shattery	sibilate	sacredly	soda-lake	steadily	shelling	sheepish
slattern	subtlety	secretly	soda-lime	stepdame	shetland	steepish
slattery	subulate	sickerly	side-line	sheading	smelling	sheep-run
star-turn	sabulous	sick-flag	sideling	shedding	spelling	steepe-up
seas-tost	sibilous	sackfuls	sidelong	sledding	sperling	shearman

smear-dab	sufferer	spheroid	slipform	swilling	scirrhus	sellable
spearman	softhead	spherule	spit-fire	skillion	snip-snap	solvable
shear-leg	suffixal	Schizaea	sail-fish	stillion	spinster	syllable
steerage	soffioni	schizoid	stiffish	ski-slope	swimsuit	sol-faing
smearily	softling	schizont	skiagram	saikless	scissile	sol-faism
shearing	sufflate	shikaree	sting-ray	sailless	swissing	sol-faist
sneering	safeness	shiralee	shingled	sciolism	scission	sillabub
stearine	softness	shivaree	shingler	sciolist	slipshod	syllabub
steering	suffrage	spicated	shingles	shipless	slip-shoe	syllabus
swearing	saffrony	spirated	sniggler	skilless	slipslop	self-born
shear-hog	soft-soap	sailable	stingily	skinless	scissors	salt-bush
stearate	Sufistic	seizable	skin-game	soilless	scissure	selictar
seedsman	soft-sell	spiracle	stinging	stirless	Swiftian	silicide
sneeshan	soft-shoe	spirally	swinging	Seidlitz	sciatica	selected
speisade	soft-slow	suitable	smidgeon	sciolous	ski-stick	silicify
sneeshin	softwood	suitably	swingism	swill-tub	shift-key	salt-cake
seed-shop	software	Shivaism	skinhead	skim-milk	skittles	silicula
sceattas	sigmatic	Shivaite	slightly	shipment	swiftlet	silicule
scent-bag	signally	sail-boat	swishing	skimming	shirt-pin	salicine
sceptral	sage-cock	stibbler	slithery	slimming	shiftily	salicane
spectral	sagacity	shin-bone	smithers	swimming	shifting	silicone
sweet-bay	signeted	stilbene	smithery	shimmery	shirting	selector
sceptred	segreant	stilbite	scimitar	seismism	skirting	solecise
sheathed	signieur	sticcado	suicidal	skirmish	slitting	solecism
shea-tree	signless	snitcher	scilicet	slimmest	spitting	solecist
sweetpea	segolate	spitcher	spinifex	slimmish	stilting	salacity
sheet-tin	sagamore	stitched	Spirifer	shipmate	stinting	saliceta
sweet-oil	sageness	stitcher	spirited	stigmata	saintdom	salt-cote
seed-time	sagenite	switchel	stipites	scienced	skiatron	silicate
steatoma	saginate	scincoid	spilikin	scienter	spittoon	solicity
scenting	Signoria	spit-curl	spilitic	spinnies	ship-tire	silicium
sheeting	sago-palm	slip-case	spirilla	skinning	saintess	solidify
smelting	signpost	suit-case	spiritus	spinning	saintish	salading
stetting	sugaring	spiccato	skipjack	seignior	saintism	seladang
sweating	sugar-gum	sticcato	stickjack	seignory	skittish	solidare
sweeting	sigisbeo	slip-dock	stick-lac	spinnery	stiltish	solidary
scent-box	sagittal	skin-deep	spicknel	slimness	spintext	solidish
sweet-sop	sightsee	swindler	stickler	stibnite	spicular	solidism
sheltery	schläger	sliddery	stickily	seigneur	stipular	solidist
smeltery	schnapps	shireman	skinking	spinneys	stipuled	solidate
sweetish	schmaltz	seine-net	slicking	scirocco	spiculum	solidity
spectate	schedule	spikelet	sticking	slip-over	stimulus	salience
steatite	schiedam	sciaenid	stinking	slivovic	stievely	saliency
scentful	schleppy	slime-pit	slip-knot	sailorly	spivvery	solvency
spectrum	sphygmic	Spigelia	stink-pot	stippled	swimwear	solderer
stentour	Sphagnum	spike-oil	stinkard	stippler	skin-wool	solleret
specular	sphygmus	shigella	stickful	slippage	ship-worm	selvedge
saeculum	Sahelian	snivelly	ship-load	skimpily	slipware	solfeggi
speculum	schiller	spice-box	spillway	shipping	sail-yard	silverly
steevely	scholion	swine-pox	shielder	skimping	shipyard	sullenly
shelving	schellum	seicento	sail-loft	skipping	Sikelian	salified
steeving	scholium	spinette	spillage	slipping	Sikeliot	salt-foot
swerving	schimmel	stiletto	stillage	snipping	sukiyaki	self-heal
stepwise	scheming	swine-sty	saibling	soil-pipe	silladar	sulphide
seedy-toe	schemata	smileful	shieling	slippery	saltando	sylphide
sleazily	sphinges	spiteful	shilling	snippety	sulcated	self-help
sneezing	sphenoid	stived-up	skilling	sciuroid	silvatic	sulphone
safranin	sphingid	sniffler	skirling	sliprail	sultanic	sylphine
softback	schooled	sainfoin	slimline	sciurine	syllabic	selfhood
soft-boil	schooner	stiff-bit	spilling	shirring	sylvatic	sulphury
softball	schmooze	sniffily	stifling	stirring	saleable	sylphish
soft-core	schapska	sniffing	stilling	sail-room	saleably	self-hate
softener	spherics	spiffing	suilline	suitress	salvable	sulphate

sulphite	sclerous	semilune	syntagma	syncline	sanatory	shoddily
silphium	solarium	semolina	syncarpy	sand-lark	sanitary	scolding
salvific	Salesian	simpling	Santalum	songless	sanitise	shop-door
Salvinia	salesman	simulant	sand-bank	senility	sanctity	snowdrop
sylviine	sales-tax	samplery	songbook	sand-mole	sanitate	sword-arm
salpicon	seldseen	similise	sonobuoy	Senonian	sanative	scordato
soldiery	splasher	simplism	songbird	son-in-law	singular	sword-cut
salt-junk	self-sown	simplist	sand-bath	synanthy	sun-cured	show-down
salt-lick	solstice	simulate	Sanscrit	synonymy	sanguify	slow-down
self-left	solitude	semi-mute	synechia	saneness	sanguine	stowdown
self-life	splatter	simoniac	synectic	syncopal	sunburnt	shoreman
salt-lake	split-new	semi-nude	sinecure	santonin	Scnoussi	stone-rag
self-like	splitted	semantic	sand-cast	sinfonia	sensuism	stone-raw
saltless	splitter	semuncia	sinicise	syncopic	sensuist	scoleces
selfless	splutter	Seminole	Sinicism	syntonic	sunburst	sloe-eyed
self-lost	splotchy	semantra	synedria	syntonin	sensuous	snow-eyes
self-love	silktail	seminary	sand-dune	sand-peep	synovial	storeyed
self-made	solation	sameness	sanidine	synaphea	sandwich	scolecid
shlemiel	solution	simonist	sand-dart	synopses	sand-worm	stone-oil
solemnly	salutary	seminate	sentence	Sinophil	sandwort	stone-pit
salt-mine	solitary	semi-opal	sundered	synapsis	sand-wasp	slovenly
splenial	solatium	summoner	sunderer	synaptic	sandyish	stone-fly
selenide	solutive	semiotic	sanserif	synopsis	sannyasi	smoke-box
silenced	Seleucid	symbolic	syndesis	synoptic	stomatal	stone-bow
silencer	salivary	sympodia	syndetic	sand-pump	stowaway	slovenry
solander	salivate	symposia	syntexis	sand-pipe	stomachy	smoke-dry
splinter	self-will	Sumerian	sunbeamy	sinapism	sporadic	Scopelus
solenoid	salework	simaruba	singeing	sinopite	stomatic	shore-due
splendid	salt-work	somerset	sonnetry	Sangraal	smokable	scot-free
silently	salt-wort	sombrely	senseful	Sangreal	storable	shot-free
solanine	silkworm	semi-ring	sand-flag	sun-crack	stovaine	snow-flea
splendor	sally-man	sombrero	sand-flea	Sangrado	show-boat	snowfall
saltness	sallying	samarium	sand-heap	sengreen	slowback	scoffing
selfness	sullying	sombrous	sun-shade	sun-dried	shoe-bill	slow-foot
soleness	silly-how	semester	sand-hill	sundries	shop-bell	spoofery
salinity	sympathy	sempster	sand-hole	sentry-go	show-bill	scomfish
selenate	semi-axis	semi-soft	sink-hole	synarchy	snowball	sloughed
selenite	somebody	Semitics	sunn-hemp	Sangrail	swobbing	spongoid
selenium	semibull	sometime	sunshine	synergic	smrbrd	spongily
selenous	semicoma	semitone	sunshiny	synergid	snow-boot	stodgily
splenium	somedeal	Semitise	syndical	syndrome	slobbery	shogging
splenius	somedele	Semitism	sandiver	sonorant	snobbery	shop-girl
salmonet	semi-dome	Semitist	sentinel	sun-print	snow-bird	showgirl
salmonid	simperer	somatism	sindings	sunproof	sloebush	soothsay
selcouth	summerly	somatist	syndings	sun-drops	snobbish	shot-hole
salopian	symmetry	semitaur	sennight	syngraph	snobbism	soothing
self-pity	somegate	Samaveda	sunlight	sun-dress	stop-bath	shoehorn
salariat	symphile	somewhat	Sinaitic	Señorita	slop-bowl	smothery
Silurian	symphily	somewhen	sinuitis	sonority	stop-cock	slothful
salaried	Symphyla	somewise	sensible	senarius	stoccado	soothful
sclereid	symphony	someways	sensibly	sonorous	scorched	Scotican
scleroid	samphire	Samoyede	sensilla	sand-star	scorcher	sporidia
siluroid	sumphish	samizdat	sentient	sinister	sloucher	stolidly
sultrily	sumpitan	sandarac	sun-visor	songster	snow-cold	spoliate
sclerema	samnitis	sunwards	sinciput	sinusoid	shot-clog	scorious
scleroma	somnific	sangaree	Sanskrit	singsong	snow-capt	stotious
sale-room	symbiont	sin-eater	sanglier	sand-shoe	show-card	stockman
sclerose	summitry	sinuated	Sinology	synastry	showcase	stockade
silurist	semplice	sun-baked	song-like	sand-trap	stoicism	spookily
solarise	symploce	sunbathe	sandling	sanctify	stoccata	stockily
solarism	simplify	santalin	singling	sonatina	sword-law	shocking
solarist	sampling	syngamic	sun-blind	sunstone	swordman	smocking
sclerite	semblant	singable	sun-blink	sanction	spondaic	

stocking
shock-dog
stock-pot
spookery
spookish
stockish
stockist
shoe-lace
shoulder
smoulder
spoilage
snowlike
Scotland
scowling
shoaling
slobland
snobling
snowline
stowlins
smouldry
shoeless
shouldst
snowless
sootless
spotless
stopless
spoilful
stormily
spooming
storming
stormful
spoon-fed
shoe-nail
spoonily
scorning
swooning
scoinson
slowness
scornful
spoonful
Scolopax
stop-over
Scopolia
scotopia
scotopic
slogorne
Sporozoa
scoop-net
stoppage
slop-pail
slowpoke
sloppily
scooping
shopping
slopping
stooping
stopping
swopping
scorpion
scoopful
Scorpius
scourger
scouring

showroom
shoe-rose
shofroth
Scotsman
shop-sign
spousage
sponsing
shoe-shop
slop-shop
snow-shoe
sponsion
scout-law
Scottice
scouther
scowther
shoe-tree
short-leg
shouther
sloetree
smoothen
smoother
Scottify
shortage
short-oil
short-rib
smoothie
smoothly
snottily
sportily
spottily
scouting
shooting
shotting
shouting
snorting
sporting
spotting
Storting
swotting
scontion
spontoon
snottery
Scottish
shortish
stoutish
shoot-out
shortcut
snootful
sportful
sportive
shogunal
sporular
spot-weld
shopworn
slopwork
slow-worm
storying
show-yard
Scolytus
sforzato
smorzato
septaria
sapucaia

sapidity
sapience
suppeago
sopheric
sopherim
septette
sept-foil
sapphire
sapphism
sapphist
septimal
sophical
syphilis
supplial
sepalody
supplied
supplier
sepaloid
sepaline
supplant
sepalous
septleva
sepiment
saponify
supinely
saponite
supinate
Sapindus
siphonal
supposal
sapropel
siphonet
supposed
supposer
supposes
siphonic
superman
supernal
supertax
superadd
sap-green
superhet
super-jet
super-ego
superbly
superior
soporose
suppress
separate
superate
saporous
soporous
sapi-utan
septuple
sequelae
sequence
sortance
Syriarch
screamer
serrated
spreader
streaked
streaker

streamer
striated
surbased
surbated
surfaced
surfacer
spreathe
Sarmatia
Sarmatic
sarrasin
sarrazin
seriatim
serranid
siriasis
sortable
sargasso
Serranus
serratus
striatum
surf-boat
scrubbed
scrubber
scrabble
scribble
scribbly
strobila
strobile
strobili
saraband
scribing
surf-bird
scribism
strabism
surucucu
sprocket
stricken
soricoid
sprackle
sprucely
strickle
strictly
soricine
sericite
suricate
soredial
surf-duck
shredded
shredder
stridden
shraddha
shred-pie
straddle
striddle
stroddle
strident
stradiot
soredium
shrieval
surveyal
sarcenet
sarsenet
screeder

screener
screever
shrieker
shrieved
sorcerer
streeted
screechy
spreethe
sardelle
sergeant
serjeant
surveyor
surcease
sarmenta
sirvente
surgeful
surrebut
scrofula
serafile
sure-fire
surf-fish
scragged
shrugged
spragged
sprigged
scroggie
seraglio
scraggly
scriggle
scriggly
straggle
straggly
struggle
scrag-end
strigine
Strigops
strigose
strigate
sorehead
serfhood
sore-hawk
surgical
surmisal
survival
strained
strainer
straiten
surmiser
straicht
straight
sordidly
straitly
servient
servitor
sorbitol
survivor
sorriest
striking
stroking
surplice
scrolled
stroller
serology

strelitz
streltzi
scrimped
shrimper
strammel
strummed
strummel
strumpet
scramble
scrimply
sortment
scrimure
stramash
strumose
stromata
strombus
strumous
sirenian
springal
syrenian
serenade
scrannel
shrinker
shrunken
springer
sprinter
stranded
stranger
stringed
stringer
stronger
syringes
syrinxes
scrunchy
strontia
serenely
sprangle
springle
sprinkle
strangle
strinkle
strongly
sereness
soreness
spryness
sureness
serenata
serenity
strength
surroyal
Sarcodes
sermoner
sermonet
sorrowed
sorrower
sarcodic
sardonic
sermonic
Sorbonne
surmount
surround
sardonyx
scrap-man

Strepyan
scrapped
scrupler
shrapnel
strapped
strapper
stripped
stripper
stropped
seraphic
seraphim
seraphin
strap-oil
strophic
scraping
strepent
striping
Strephon
Serapeum
Sartrian
sororial
sororise
surprise
sororate
sorority
stressed
serfship
serosity
strutted
strutter
stratify
Saratoga
strategy
scratchy
stretchy
sark-tail
Struthio
scrattle
sprattle
spritely
scrutiny
serotine
sorption
serotype
stratose
stratous
serpulae
surquedy
scrouger
shrouded
sprouted
scrounge
straunge
straucht
straught
surculus
stravaig
shriving
striving
screw-cap
straw-hat
scrawler
sprawler

scrowdge	slug-a-bed	smuggler	sculpsit	saw-edged	thatcher	trappean
strewage	squeaker	skua-gull	stumpily	saw-shark	trauchle	trampler
shrewdly	squealer	smudgily	sculptor	saw-blade	tear-duct	trapping
screwing	soutache	spur-gall	sourpuss	sewellel	twaddler	teaspoon
strewing	sauba-ant	squiggle	scuppaug	saw-bones	T-bandage	Trappist
strowing	stubbled	squiggly	spur-rial	saw-tones	tear-drop	tranquil
screwtop	stumbler	snugging	spur-ryal	saw-horse	trap-door	tea-bread
shrewish	squab-pie	sturgeon	scurrier	saw-tooth	teaseled	tea-break
shrew-run	soul-bell	sluggard	spurrier	sewer-gas	teaseler	tram-road
straying	squabble	snuggery	squireen	sewer-rat	trade-off	trap-rock
sorryish	stud-bolt	sluggish	squirrel	sow-bread	trapezia	toad-rush
spray-gun	slubbing	southpaw	squirter	sowarree	tsarevna	transact
Sassanid	snubbing	southsay	squirage	sewerage	thanedom	transect
sash-cord	stubbing	souchong	scurrile	saw-frame	teaberry	transude
sash-door	stud-book	southing	squarely	sewering	traverse	teamster
sesterce	slumbery	southron	squirely	sow-drunk	trabeate	transfer
systemed	stubborn	slughorn	slurring	sawdusty	travesty	transmew
systemic	snubbish	southern	spurring	sexually	tradeful	toad-spit
sisterly	squabash	scutiger	squaring	Saxicola	toadflax	transfix
suspense	scutcher	squailer	squarson	sixscore	trap-fall	tranship
sestette	stuccoed	stupidly	squarish	Saxicava	toad-fish	transmit
sestetto	stuccoer	sauciest	squiress	sixpence	twanging	transume
syssitia	sour-cold	saucisse	stuprate	sixpenny	tracheae	tram-stop
sesamoid	sound-bar	spurious	soul-scat	sextette	tracheal	transept
sassolin	sturdied	studious	soul-sick	sixtieth	trash-can	transire
systolic	sturdily	shucking	squasher	sexology	tracheid	twattler
sesspool	scudding	skulking	stunsail	Saxondom	trashily	tractrix
sastruga	sounding	stunkard	soul-scot	Saxonise	trachoma	tractile
sasarara	sourdine	skull-cap	soul-shot	Saxonism	teaching	toasting
siserary	studding	squaller	stuntman	Saxonist	trashery	traction
susurrus	sound-bow	squilgee	scuttler	sexiness	tea-chest	tractate
sash-tool	sound-box	squelchy	squatted	saxonite	trachyte	tractive
Sathanas	squadron	spuilzie	squatter	sextolet	tragical	traducer
satrapal	shuddery	sculling	stultify	saxatile	tea-fight	team-work
situated	Stundism	spurling	smuttily	sextuple	traditor	teamwise
satrapic	Stundist	scullion	squattle	skywards	tsaritsa	toadying
satiable	shut-down	scullery	shunting	scybalum	trackman	toadyish
sitz-bath	sauceman	shunless	shutting	skyscape	trackway	toadyism
set-screw	saucepan	soulless	sluttery	Scythian	trackage	tubicole
Sotadean	sour-eyed	spurless	sputtery	say-piece	thanking	table-mat
sithence	squeegee	slummock	sluttish	sky-diver	tracking	table-top
sitter-in	squeezer	squamula	Saururae	skylight	thankful	tableaux
setter-on	souvenir	squamule	scurvily	sky-pilot	trail-net	table-cut
setter-up	scutella	scumming	squawman	spyglass	trawl-net	tableful
satelles	souterly	slumming	squawker	sayonara	thalloid	tube-foot
sitology	Sauterne	stumming	studwork	spy-money	tea-plant	tubiform
settling	sauce-box	squamose	studying	slyboots	thalline	taboggan
sateless	souped-up	Squamata	spun-yarn	sizeable	tram-line	toboggan
satanism	souse-tub	squamate	sovranty	syzygial	trawling	toboggin
satanist	scuffler	squamous	sovietic	syzygies	tearless	tabbinet
satanity	shuffler	squander	savagely	sizzling	thawless	Tebilise
Saturday	snuffler	squinter	savagery	siziness	tea-cloth	tubeless
soterial	squiffer	stub-nail	savegard	suzerain	thallium	tabulate
sutorial	stuffily	sturnoid	savannah	tearaway	thallous	tubulate
sutorian	snuffing	shunning	seven-day	thanadar	team-mate	tubulous
Saturnia	stuffing	spurning	savingly	thataway	traumata	to-broken
saturnic	snuffbox	stunning	suversed	tea-caddy	train-oil	tabooing
saturant	snuffers	sturnine	severely	thalamic	training	taberdar
satirise	stud-farm	smugness	severity	tea-table	thatness	tubercle
satirist	scumfish	snugness	savorous	tea-party	tragopan	tuberose
satyress	slugfest	sourness	savoured	thalamus	tea-towel	Taborite
satyrisk	spur-gear	sauropod	savourly	trap-ball	tea-board	tuberous
saturate	smuggled	stumpage	Savoyard	thatched	tea-house	tabashir

tabouret
tabourin
to-bruise
tube-well
tube-worm
tabby-cat
tabbying
tuckahoe
tacked-on
tacahout
tactical
tachisme
tachiste
tocology
tackling
tickling
tactless
ticklish
tuck-mill
technics
tectonic
Tychonic
tacksman
tick-shop
tuck-shop
tick-tack
tick-tick
tick-tock
tucotuco
tucutuco
taciturn
tac-au-tac
tadvance
tide-gate
tide-lock
toddling
tideless
tidemill
tidemark
tidiness
tide-race
tides-man
tedesche
tedeschi
tedisome
tidivate
tide-wave
toddy-cat
toe-dance
teen-aged
teenager
thematic
trematic
trevally
thebaine
trembler
Theaceae
theocrat
treacher
trencher
tree-calf
theodicy
treadler

treading
Tremella
therefor
trecento
thereout
tree-frog
tree-fern
theogony
teething
trephine
tee-shirt
thetical
theriaca
toe-piece
taenioid
tredille
taeniate
trekking
theology
tree-lily
tree-line
teemless
thewless
treeless
thermion
tree-moss
thermite
treenail
theonomy
teetotal
theropod
teetotum
thespian
trespass
tie-break
thearchy
theurgic
theorise
theorist
trewsman
theistic
treeship
theosoph
treasure
treasury
tressure
theatral
theatric
Theatine
treating
trey-tine
treatise
twelvemo
tweezers
taffetas
tafferel
taffrail
taghairm
teguexin
tug-of-war
taglioni
tegument
tiger-cat

tigerish
tigerism
tiger-nut
tiger-eye
tightwad
together
tightish
trimaran
thio-acid
tribasic
twin-axis
tribally
tridacna
trivalve
tailback
tail-boom
twin-born
tail-coat
twitcher
twiddler
thirding
Triodion
triadist
tripedal
tripeman
toiseach
toileted
trimeter
trimeric
trisemic
trilemma
toiletry
toilette
thingamy
thigging
tail-gate
trichoid
twichild
trichome
trichina
triphone
trip-hook
trichord
trichite
tritical
toilinet
twilight
tritiate
Triticum
thickset
tricklet
twinkler
trickily
triskele
thinking
tricking
trickery
thickish
trickish
thickety
trial-day
thirlage
triploid

trifling
trilling
triplane
tripling
twinling
trillion
triglyph
tailless
toilless
trialism
trialist
triality
trillium
triumvir
thiamine
trimming
triangle
thinning
twinning
thinness
thinnest
thinnish
thisness
trigness
trimness
triunity
trifocal
trigonal
tripodal
trizonal
trilobed
triforia
trigonic
trisomic
tritonia
tricorne
tricolor
triapsal
trippler
trippant
tripping
tail-pipe
trippery
tail-race
tribrach
triarchy
tail-rope
trigraph
thirster
tailskid
tail-spin
Triassic
twinship
thio-salt
toilsome
twigsome
thin-spun
thin-sown
tric-trac
triptych
tristich
thirteen
triptane

twisting
twitting
tainture
twittery
triptote
tristful
triethyl
tribunal
tributer
Trimurti
thieving
thievery
thievish
toil-worn
trip-wire
triaxial
trioxide
Trigynia
tricycle
take-away
takeable
take-down
tokology
takamaka
takingly
tokenism
take-over
talkable
tellable
tillable
tollable
tilt-boat
talk-back
toll-bait
toll-call
telecine
telecast
tolldish
toll-free
telefilm
talkfest
tilefish
telegram
telegony
tollgate
tile-hung
Talpidae
talliate
talukdar
telemark
talented
tallness
tolbooth
Tylopoda
talapoin
thlipsis
tulipant
telepath
telergic
tolerant
tolerate
talesman
talisman

telestic
teleseme
talk-show
tell-tale
telltale
telethon
teletron
Teletype®
teletext
tellural
Talmudic
telluric
teleview
televise
tallyman
tallying
tilt-yard
tympanal
tympanic
tameable
tympanum
time-ball
time-bill
time-bomb
time-card
timidity
tumidity
tamperer
tempered
temperer
timbered
tumefied
time-fuse
tomogram
tomahawk
Tamilian
tomalley
temulent
tumbling
tump-line
tumulary
tameless
timeless
tombless
template
timoneer
tamanoir
tameness
Timonise
Timonism
Timonist
tamandua
tomentum
temporal
tom-noddy
tamboura
tamarack
tamarind
timariot
tomorrow
tamarisk
temerity
temerous

timorous
tumorous
tomatoes
tempting
time-unit
timously
time-work
time-worn
tommy-bar
tommy-rot
tommy-gun
time-zone
tendance
tantalic
teniasis
tan-balls
tannable
tentacle
tuneable
tantalum
tantalus
tenebrae
tenebrio
tunicked
ten-score
tenacity
tonicity
Tunicata
tunicate
tone-deaf
tangency
tendence
tendency
tenpence
tenderer
tenderly
tinselly
tunbelly
tenpenny
tin-terne
tinselry
tuna-fish
Tineidae
tonsilar
tontiner
tangible
tangibly
tenaille
tensible
tanaiste
tenuious
tinnitus
tangling
tinkling
tinglish
tintless
toneless
tuneless
tin-plate
tonalite
tonality
tenement
tinsmith

tenon-saw
tenantry
tininess
tenendum
ten-pound
tandoori
tangoist
tent-pole
tenurial
tenoroon
tent-rope
Tantrism
Tantrist
tenorist
tenorite
tungsten
tungstic
tonishly
tanistry
tenesmus
tank-trap
tung-tree
tenotomy
tinstone
tint-tool
tincture
tonsured
Tunguses
Tungusic
tonguing
tent-work
tentwise
thoraces
two-faced
thoracic
troparia
teocalli
troubled
troubler
trombone
two-score
trot-cozy
two-edged
twopence
thole-pin
twopenny
trochlea
trophied
trochaic
trochoid
trochisk
trophesy
trochite
toothful
trothful
tropical
two-piece
two-sided
two-timer
two-digit
trolling
trotline
toodle-oo

trollopy
thowless
troilism
troilite
thornset
trouncer
thorough
two-horse
troopial
troupial
toolroom
tool-shed
Taoistic
thousand
trossers
trousers
troutlet
trottoir
trotting
trouting
trout-rod
troutful
trouvère
trouveur
tap-dance
tap-water
topmaker
type-body
tapacolo
tapaculo
typecast
tapadera
tapadero
tepidity
tuppence
top-level
tuppenny
top-heavy
type face
typified
typifier
type-high
top-shell
top-liner
topology
typology
tapeline
tapeless
toponymy
Typhoean
top-notch
typhonic
tap-house
toplofty
Typhoeus
toparchy
tapiroid
tapering
top-dress
tephrite
top-proud
tapestry
tape-tied

tipstaff
top-stone
tapeworm
tipsy-key
topazine
tequilla
tarlatan
Tyrtaean
tar-paper
tartaned
tar-water
terraced
threaden
threader
threaten
throated
turbaned
tartaric
Tartarie
terrapin
terraria
threapit
tornadic
tartarly
tarragon
toreador
Tartarus
terrazzo
turnback
throbbed
terebene
turf-clad
turncoat
turncock
thridace
torn-down
turn-down
Tarpeian
three-man
three-way
targeted
tercelet
turreted
threepit
turmeric
terrella
terzetta
terzetto
tarted-up
tara-fern
tarwhine
Tyrrhene
torchère
terminal
torminal
toroidal
turbinal
Tarsipes
terminer
tirrivee
turbined
turbines

tarsioid
terrific
tirrivie
terrible
terribly
torpidly
tortilla
turbidly
turgidly
tertiary
terminus
tortious
Tyrolean
thriller
Terylene®
tireling
turtling
thraldom
termless
tireless
torulose
tyreless
Tyrolese
thrum-cap
thrummed
thrummer
thrombin
thrombus
tarantas
Tironian
Turanian
threnode
threnody
thronged
tyrannic
tyrannis
tartness
turbocar
turbofan
Turcoman
Turkoman
turbo-jet
turnover
turlough
tarboosh
tarboush
tortoise
thripses
teraphim
turnpike
thrapple
thropple
tar-brush
tartrate
thrasher
threshel
thresher
thrissel
thruster
turnskin
turnspit
thristle
throstle

turnsole
tiresome
tyrosine
teratoid
throttle
teratoma
term-time
teru-tero
teratism
torcular
torturer
Tartuffe
Targumic
toreutic
torquate
tortuous
thriving
throwing
thraward
thrawart
throw-out
tarrying
tastable
testable
testator
testamur
testatum
test-case
tesserae
tesseral
tasselly
tessella
taste-bud
tasteful
testicle
tuskless
tussocky
testrill
test-tube
tasswage
taskwork
tetrarch
tetracid
tetradic
tetrapla
tithable
tetragon
tetrapod
tetraxon
titubant
titubate
tattered
titterer
tottered
totterer
tithe-pig
tetchily
totalled
tutelage
tattling
tutelary
totalise
totality

totemism
totemist
Titanian
tetanoid
tetanise
Titaness
Titanism
titanate
titanite
titanium
titanous
tctronal
tattooed
tattooer
titmouse
Tatarian
tutorial
tutorage
tutoring
tutoress
tutorise
tutorism
tityre-tu
totitive
titivate
toucanet
true-bred
thumbpot
true-born
truncate
thundery
trumeaux
truffled
trudging
thuggery
thuggism
truchman
teuchter
touchily
touching
touch-box
toughish
truthful
thurifer
thurible
touristy
truckman
truckage
trucking
trunking
trunkful
true-love
trunnion
tournure
truantry
tautness
thusness
trueness
tautomer
Teutonic
tautonym
thumping
trumpery

Teucrian
tau-cross
Thursday
truistic
trussing
trustier
tau-staff
trustily
taunting
trusting
trustful
truquage
truqueur
thuswise
taverner
tovarish
thwacker
towelled
townland
townling
tow-plane
thwarted
thwarter
tawdrily
thwartly
towardly
towering
townsman
township
townskip
town-talk
taxiarch
tax-payer
textbook
text-book
Taxaceae
toxicant
toxocara
toxicity
Taxodium
toxaemia
toxaemic
text-hand
taxonomy
taxation
taxative
textural
textured
textuary
thyreoid
tryingly
toywoman
thyloses
thylosis
thyroxin
try-house
thyrsoid
toyishly
unabated
unawares
upadaisy
unanchor
up-anchor

8 u□a□e

unaneled	unbeseem	undimmed	unfreeze	unhacked	unlocked	urologic
unargued	unbishop	undinted	unfairly	unhedged	uplocked	urostege
unaching	unbathed	undoomed	unfriend	unhidden	unlidded	urostyle
Upanisad	unbitted	undrossy	unfilial	unheeded	unlading	unplaced
unarisen	unbutton	undipped	unfallen	unhailed	uplifted	unpraise
uralitic	unbought	under-jaw	unfelled	unhaired	uplifter	unpacked
uranitic	unchancy	underlap	unfilled	unhalsed	unlikely	unpacker
unallied	uncharge	underlay	unfilmed	unhelmed	unlimber	unpicked
unadored	unchaste	underman	unfolded	unhelped	unlineal	unpreach
unatoned	unclench	underpay	unfolder	unholpen	unlinked	unpeeled
unavowed	unchewed	undersay	upfollow	upholder	uplander	unpeered
unafraid	uncreate	underact	unfanned	unholily	ugliness	unpoetic
upas-tree	unciform	underfed	unfenced	unhallow	unlooked	unpretty
unartful	uncoined	underlet	unfunded	unhomely	unloosen	unpained
unactive	uncalled	undersea	unfooted	unhanged	unlopped	unpaired
unamused	unculled	underset	unfrozen	unhinged	unlorded	unpoised
umbrated	uncombed	under-age	unformal	unhunted	unlordly	unpriced
unbeaten	uncomely	underbid	unforced	unhonest	unlisted	unprized
unbiased	uncommon	underdid	unforged	unhooded	unlively	unpliant
unblamed	uncandid	underlie	unformed	unheppen	upmaking	unpoison
unbraced	uncinate	underlip	unfurred	unharmed	unmelted	unprison
umbratic	uncloudy	underpin	unforbid	unheroic	unmilked	unpriest
unbacked	unchosen	underwit	unforgot	ushering	unmilled	umptieth
unbuckle	unclosed	undersky	unfasten	usheress	unmanned	unpolled
unbedded	uncloven	under-boy	unfished	unhatted	unminded	unpulled
unbidden	uncooked	underdog	unfetter	unhoused	unmantle	unpolish
unbodied	unclothe	undertow	unfitted	urinator	unmarked	unpolite
unbudded	urceolus	underarm	unfeudal	univalve	unmarred	unpanged
unboding	uncipher	underuse	unfought	unimbued	up-market	unpannel
unbreech	uncurbed	udderful	unfaulty	unitedly	unmasked	unpenned
umble-pie	uncurled	underbuy	unfixity	universe	unmasker	unpinked
umbrella	upcurved	undercut	ungeared	unifilar	unmissed	unpinned
umbrello	uncaring	underfur	unglazed	utiliser	un-mosaic	unproper
umbrette	ulcerate	underrun	ungraced	unionise	unmoving	unproved
unbaited	ulcerous	undashed	ungraded	unionism	unmuzzle	unproven
unbridle	uncashed	undesert	ungifted	unionist	uintaite	unpeople
umbriere	uncostly	undouble	unguided	unilobar	unneeded	unpurged
unbelief	unchurch	undivine	ungainly	unipolar	urnfield	umpirage
unbelted	unclutch	undevout	unguilty	unisonal	unnerved	unperson
unbolted	uncaused	undazzle	ungalled	univocal	unnethes	unposted
unbanded	uncaught	unelated	ungilded	unilobed	unnetted	uppishly
unbanked	upcaught	unending	Ungulata	unironed	unnative	unpathed
unbended	uncouple	ureteral	ungulate	unicolor	uroscopy	unpitied
unbonnet	unctuous	ureteric	ungummed	uninured	urodelan	unpruned
unbenign	uncowled	unevenly	ungenial	uniquely	udometer	umquhile
unbundle	uncoyned	urethrae	ungentle	ubiquity	unobeyed	unreaped
urbanely	undraped	urethral	ungently	uniaxial	unopened	upreared
urbanise	undubbed	urethane	urgently	unicycle	Ulothrix	unreally
umbonate	undecked	unedited	ungloved	unifying	urochord	unreason
urbanite	undocked	uredines	unground	unjustly	utopiast	unribbed
urbanity	undecent	uteritis	upgrowth	unjoyful	uxorious	unrubbed
unbloody	undeeded	unespied	ungirded	unjoyous		unracked
unblowed	undreamt	unearned	ungorged	unknight		unrecked
unbooked	undefied	unerring	ungotten	unkenned		utriculi
unbroken	undriven	uneasily	upgather	unkennel		unridden
unbarbed	undulled	uneathes	ungauged	unkindly		unriddle
unbarked	undulant	usefully	ungiving	unkingly		unrifled
unbarred	undulose	unenvied	ungowned	unkissed		unruffle
unburden	undulate	unfeared	upheaval	unleased		unrigged
unburied	undulous	unflawed	unhealed	unloaded		unraised
unburned	undammed	unframed	unheated	unloader		unreined
unbereft	undamned	unfabled	unhearse	unlearnt		upraised
unburrow	undamped	unfading	unhealth	unlicked		unringed

uprootal	unsolder	untenant	unworked	vaginate	valeting	vandyked
unroofed	unsolved	untapped	unwormed	vagaries	volitant	vineyard
unrooted	unsolemn	unthread	unworthy	vagarish	volition	violable
uprooter	Ursuline	untarred	unwarely	vigorous	volution	violably
unripped	unseldom	unturned	unwarily	vegetant	velatura	violator
unrepaid	unsummed	upturned	upwardly	vegetate	volitate	violence
unrepair	unsensed	unthrift	unwashed	vegetive	volitive	vapidity
uprising	unsunned	unturbid	unwasted	vehmique	valvular	vapulate
unrotted	unspoken	unthrone	unwisely	vehement	Volsungs	viperine
unrotten	unspoilt	untiring	unwisdom	voidance	volvulus	vaporise
unrouged	unsmooth	uttering	unwetted	voidable	Valkyrie	viperish
unrhymed	unsapped	ulterior	unwatery	voice-box	vampiric	vaporous
unstarch	upstream	upthrust	unyeaned	vainesse	vamplate	viperous
unscaled	unstruck	utterest	vraicker	voiceful	vambrace	vapoured
unsealed	unsorted	untasted	viameter	veilless	vomerine	vapourer
unseamed	upstroke	untested	viaticum	vainness	vomiting	variance
unseated	unsprung	untether	vibrancy	voidness	vomitory	verdancy
unshaded	unstring	untitled	vibrator	valiance	vomitive	vartabed
unshaked	unstrung	untaught	vibrissa	valiancy	vintager	verbatim
unshaken	upsprang	untruism	vibronic	villager	Vandalic	variable
unshamed	upspring	untrusty	viburnum	villagio	venially	variably
unshaped	upsprung	untoward	vice-dean	villatic	ventaile	verbally
unshapen	unshroud	unusable	vaccinal	volcanic	ventayle	vernally
unshared	unsashed	unusably	vaccinia	vulcanic	vindaloo	viricide
unshaved	upsetter	uvularly	vice-king	Valhalla	vine-clad	verecund
unshaven	unsettle	unuseful	vocalion	valuable	vanadate	varactor
unslaked	unsating	uvulitis	vocalise	valuably	vanadium	varicose
unsoaped	unsluice	usurious	vocalism	vulgarly	vanadous	veracity
unspared	unsouled	usurping	vocalist	villainy	veneerer	voracity
unstated	unsoured	usufruct	vocality	valuator	vendeuse	viridian
unstayed	unstuffy	unviable	vicinage	villadom	vendetta	viridite
unswayed	unsought	unviewed	vacantly	voltaism	vengeful	viridity
unswathe	unsexual	unveiled	vicenary	Volscian	vine-gall	varietal
unstable	unthatch	unveiler	vicinity	velocity	vinegary	verse-man
unseason	ultrared	unvoiced	vacuolar	validate	vent-hole	vergency
unshadow	unthawed	unvulgar	victoria	validity	vendible	verderer
upstairs	untraced	unvalued	vicarial	valvelet	vendibly	verselet
unsubtle	untraded	unvented	vicarage	velveret	vincible	vortexes
unsocial	ultraism	unvaried	vicaress	velveted	vine-leaf	variedly
unsecret	ultraist	unversed	victress	volleyed	vinology	varletry
unsicker	untucked	unvirtue	vicarate	vulsella	vanillin	vertebra
unsocket	untackle	unvizard	vacation	velleity	vinolent	varletto
unsucked	urticant	unweaned	vocation	vilified	vaneless	verified
unsodden	urticate	unweapon	vocative	vilifier	venality	verifier
unsaddle	untidily	unwebbed	Vichyite	villiago	venomous	variform
unsteady	up-to-date	unwedded	Vedantic	vulvitis	vine-prop	virogene
ulstered	untilled	unwieldy	videndum	velskoen	vent-pipe	vertical
unseeded	uptilted	unweeded	videotex	volplane	vent-plug	virginal
unseemly	Ustilago	unweened	viewable	velamina	venereal	vortical
unseeing	ultimacy	unwifely	viewdata	volumist	venerean	verditer
unsued-to	untemper	unwigged	viewless	valanced	venerate	vermined
unsifted	untombed	unwalled	Viennese	vildness	Venusian	vertices
unsafely	untimely	unwilled	vee-joint	vileness	vanisher	vortices
unsafety	ultimata	unwilful	vagrancy	vallonia	venosity	verbiage
unsigned	ultimate	unwanted	vagabond	Vellozia	vinosity	verticil
unsphere	Ultonian	unwinged	vigneron	vilipend	Venetian	Virginia
unstitch	untanned	unwonted	vignette	valerian	Venutian	vernicle
unsailed	untended	unwooded	vigilant	valorise	venation	versicle
unsained	untender	unwarded	vagility	valarise	vanitory	virginly
unseized	untented	unwarmed	vaginula	valorous	venturer	verligte
unsoiled	untinged	unwarned	vaginule	velarium	vanguard	virology
unsuited	untinned	unwarped	vaginant	volutoid	vanquish	virulent
unsalted	untangle	unworded	veganism	volatile	vinculum	verbless

virilism	vitellin	weakness	wagon-bed	whistler	wallowed	wingspan
virility	vituline	whatness	wagonage	whittret	wallower	wind-sock
virement	vitalise	weaponed	wagon-lit	wristlet	welcomer	wind-side
veranda'd	vitalism	wrapover	wagon-box	whip-tail	willowed	wind-sail
verandah	vitalist	weaponry	wagonful	wrist-pin	wolf-pack	wine-skin
veronica	voteless	wrappage	waggoner	whim-wham	well-read	wing-shot
variolar	vitality	wrapping	wagmoire	Whitweek	well-room	windward
vermouth	vitellus	wealsman	wage-work	whipworm	Wellsian	wood-acid
variorum	votaress	wobegone	Wahabism	whinyard	well-seen	wool-ball
veristic	votarist	webwheel	Wahabite	whizz-kid	wolf-skin	woodbind
varistor	vitative	wabbling	wait-a-bit	whizzing	wallsend	woodbine
verities	vauncing	wobbling	writable	wakeless	well-to-do	wood-born
veratrin	voussoir	wickered	whimbrel	wakening	wall-tree	wood-chat
veratrum	vaultage	wickedly	whipbird	wakerife	wilfully	wood-coal
verrucae	vauntage	wide-body	whinchat	walk-away	wild-wood	woodcock
verrugas	vaulting	wide-eyed	whipcord	welladay	wall-wort	wool-clip
verjuice	vaunting	waddling	whitecap	wellaway	wallwort	wool-comb
verdured	vauntery	wideness	white-wax	Walhalla	well-worn	wool-card
vargueño	vauntful	Wodenism	white-leg	walkable	well-wish	wool-dyed
verquere	vivacity	wide-open	whitener	weldable	Walkyrie	woolding
verquire	vividity	widow-man	write-off	wallaroo	willyard	whomever
virtuosa	vivifier	Wedgwood	white-ale	well-boat	willyart	whosever
virtuose	vivipary	wretched	white-fly	wild-boar	waltzing	wood-evil
virtuosi	vivarium	wheedler	white-ant	well-bred	wambling	woodenly
virtuoso	vivisect	whenever	Whiteboy	well-born	womanise	whole-hog
vertuous	vavasory	wherever	white-hot	wild-born	womanish	whoredom
virtuous	vavasour	wye-level	white-pot	well-curb	winnable	whoreson
viscacha	vowelled	wherefor	while-ere	well-deck	wingbeat	woolfell
visually	vowelise	whereout	white-arm	well-doer	windburn	wrongful
vassalry	vexillum	whey-face	white-out	wall-eyed	wind-cone	wrongous
vesicula	vexingly	weephole	white-eye	wildered	wine-cask	whoa-ho-ho
vesicant	vixenish	weeviled	whiffler	walker-on	wing-case	wood-hole
vesicate	vexation	weevilly	whiffing	Wolffian	wingding	wood-ibis
vesperal	vexatory	wreckage	wriggler	well-far'd	wandered	whorl-bat
visceral	voyageur	wrecking	wringing	wildfire	wanderer	woodlice
vasiform	vizcacha	wreakful	Whiggery	wallfish	wintered	woollies
Visigoth	vizirial	wreckful	Whiggish	wolf-fish	wondered	woodland
Vespidae	vizarded	wheelman	Whiggism	wild-fowl	wonderer	wood-lark
vestigia	vizirate	wheeling	writhled	wall-game	wingedly	woodless
vespiary	wearable	weedless	weighage	well-head	winterly	wood-meal
vestiary	whale-man	weetless	weighing	Welshman	wanderoo	woodmice
vestment	weakener	wheel-cut	whip-hand	well-hole	windfall	wool-mill
vastness	weak-eyed	wherries	writhing	well-hung	wind-gall	wood-mite
visional	weaseler	wheat-ear	weigh-out	waldhorn	winchman	wood-note
visioned	weazened	wheatear	whiniard	williwaw	wanthill	wood-opal
visioner	whatever	wheat-eel	whipjack	well-knit	wangling	wool-pack
visnomie	whale-oil	wreathed	wrinkled	wall-knot	windlass	wood-pile
viscount	weaselly	wreathen	whisking	wildlife	windless	wood-pulp
visitant	wharf-rat	wreather	whiskery	wild-land	wine-list	whooping
visiting	wharfage	wrestler	whirl-bat	wolfling	wingless	whopping
vascular	wharfing	wrest-pin	whirling	wall-less	wontless	woodruff
vestural	weakfish	wheat-fly	whitling	weldless	windmill	wood-roof
vestured	wrangler	whetting	wait-list	well-made	wanwordy	wood-rush
vesturer	wrathily	waesucks	whiplash	walk-mill	windowed	woodsman
vasculum	wrathful	woefully	whinnied	weldment	winnowed	woolsack
Vesuvian	wear-iron	wheezily	whipping	wall-moss	winnower	woodshed
vitiable	weariful	wheezing	whispery	well-nigh	wantonly	wood-sage
vitiator	whacking	wifehood	whirring	wildness	wanworth	wood-skin
Vitaceae	wrackful	wife-like	waitress	wiliness	wine-palm	wood-tick
vaticide	what-like	wifeless	whipster	wolf-note	windpipe	who-dun-it
viticide	weakling	wig-maker	Whigship	wall-newt	wind-rode	wood-wren
vitreous	weanling	wage-fund	whimsily	walk-over	windrose	woodwale
vitiligo	wraxling	wig-block	wainscot	walloper	wondrous	woodwind

wood-wool	war-proof	water-ram	xanthein	zoetrope	zeppelin
woodward	workroom	water-rat	xanthoma	zigzaggy	zopilote
woodwork	wire-rope	water-tap	xanthene	zygodont	zerumbet
wood-worm	wardress	waterway	xanthine	zygaenid	zirconia
woolward	worm-seed	water-yam	Xanthura	ziggurat	zirconic
woolwork	wardship	water-ice	xanthate	Zigeuner	zaratite
wood-wasp	worksome	water-bed	xanthium	zugzwang	zarzuela
woodwose	workshop	water-hen	xanthous	Zwieback	zastruga
warragal	worm-tube	water-jet	Xantippe	zoiatria	Zizyphus
workaday	workwear	waterage	xenolith	zikkurat	
war-dance	wartweed	water-ski	xenophya	Zelanian	
warfarer	werewolf	water-fly	xenurine	zylonite	
warfarin	wormwood	watering	xenotime	Zalophus	
warhable	wartwort	water-boa	xeransis	zombiism	
workable	wirework	water-box	xerantic	zamindar	
warranty	wire-worm	water-cow	xeraphim	zemindar	
workboat	wirewove	water-dog	year-book	zambomba	
wordbook	worky-day	water-god	yeanling	zampogna	
workbook	worrying	waterlog	yearling	zomboruk	
wire-bird	worrycow	Waterloo	yearlong	zingiber	
ward-corn	wurtzite	water-lot	yearning	Zantippe	
worm-cast	wash-away	water-pot	yachting	Zentippe	
wire-draw	wistaria	water-pox	Ygdrasil	Zantiote	
world-old	washable	waterish	yodeller	zinckify	
warrener	wiseacre	water-bug	yielding	zincking	
wardenry	wash-ball	water-bus	yoghourt	zoneless	
war-weary	wishbone	wet-nurse	Yugoslav	zenithal	
warmed-up	wash-bowl	withwind	yokelish	zonation	
workfolk	wash-dirt	woundily	yoke-mate	zoomancy	
worm-gear	Wesleyan	wounding	yoke-toed	zoolater	
weregild	wisteria	wauk-mill	yeldrock	zoopathy	
work-girl	westerly	waukrife	yeldring	zoolatry	
wire-heel	washed-up	waveband	yoldring	zooscopy	
worthies	wasteful	waveform	yuletide	zooecium	
wire-hair	wise-like	wivehood	yglaunst	zooperal	
worm-hole	wiseling	wavelike	yongthly	zoogenic	
worthily	westmost	waveless	yeomanly	zoometry	
war-whoop	wiseness	waviness	yeomanry	Zoophaga	
worthful	washroom	wavering	ybounden	zoophile	
warrigal	westward	waverous	yardland	zoothome	
warrison	wish-wash	wax-paper	yarmulka	zoochore	
wirricow	withdraw	waxberry	yarmulke	zoochory	
worricow	withdrew	wax-light	yardwand	Zoophyta	
workload	withered	wax-cloth	ypsiloid	zoophyte	
warbling	watchman	waxiness	yestreen	zeolitic	
warplane	watch-key	wayfarer	yataghan	zoolitic	
wire-line	witch-elm	waylayer	yttrious	zoonitic	
word-lore	withheld	way-maker	ytterbia	zoogloea	
wareless	withhold	way-leave	youngish	zooblast	
wartless	witching	waywiser	youthful	zoonoses	
wireless	watch-box	way-going	yourself	zoonomia	
wordless	watch-dog	way-board	zealless	zoonomic	
workless	witchery	waygoose	zealotry	zoonosis	
wariment	watchful	waybread	Zoanthus	zootomic	
ward-mote	watch-out	way-train	zabaione	zootoxin	
work-mate	watt-hour	wizardly	zebrinny	zoomorph	
wariness	wattling	wizardry	zibeline	zoosperm	
warmness	witeless	xylocarp	zuchetta	zoospore	
wiriness	wittolly	xyloidin	zuchetto	zoograft	
work-over	water-bag	xylology	zecchine	zootrope	
war-horse	water-gap	Xylonite®	zecchino	Zionward	
wardrobe	water-gas	xenogamy	zucchini	zoocytia	
ward-room	waterman	xanthian	zodiacal	zootypic	

avalanche
alabamine
atacamite
agalactia
ataractic
alabaster
Amarantus
anarchise
anarchial
anarchism
anarchist
araucaria
abandoned
abandonee
anandrous
awareness
abasement
abatement
amazement
acalephan
asafetida
awakening
academist
Agamemnon
Agapemone
arabesque
analectic
analeptic
analgesia
analgesic
abashless
abashment
Arachnida
anathemas
arachnoid
anaphoric
anacharis
apathetic
acaridean
amazingly
acaricide
Adamitism
acaridian
arabinose
acariasis
anabiosis
anabiotic
atavistic
alack-a-day
available
availably
anaglypta
anaplasty
alarmedly
alarm-bell
anamnesis
amazon-ant
amazonite
analogise
anatomise
aragonite
amatorial
anabolism

amatorian
amazonian
Anatolian
analogist
anatomist
ayatollah
analogous
acarology
anaerobic
anabranch
amaurosis
anacruses
anacrusis
amaurotic
amassable
amassment
Adansonia
adaptable
apartheid
apartness
apartment
acanthine
abactinal
acanthoid
acanthous
ananthous
anastasis
anastatic
anaptyxis
Ayahuasco
amaryllid
amaryllis
arblaster
ambiguity
ambagious
ambiguous
aubrietia
ambulacra
ambulance
ambulator
album-leaf
albinoism
albinotic
ambrosial
ambrosian
ambrotype
albertite
aubergine
amber-fish
albarello
alburnous
arboreous
ambergris
arboretum
ambassage
ambuscade
ambuscado
albescent
albespine
asbestine
asbestous
albespyne
arbitrage

arbitrate
arbitrary
arbitress
abbotship
albatross
ambitious
amblyopia
archangel
arcuation
archaiser
archducal
archduchy
accedence
accidence
arch-druid
archeress
arch-enemy
asclepiad
accretive
accretion
asclepias
Asclepios
Asclepius
alchemist
anciently
ancientry
archetype
arch-fiend
arch-felon
alcoholic
Archibald
acclimate
archimage
Arctiidae
architect
archivist
acclivity
archilowe
acclivous
archivolt
ancillary
accompany
ascendant
ascendent
ascensive
ascending
arc-en-ciel
accension
ascension
accentual
Arctogaea
anchorage
anchoress
anchor-ice
anchorite
auctorial
Alcyonium
anchorman
archology
archontic
acceptant
acceptive
ancipital

ascorbate
ascertain
accordant
Ascaridae
ascarides
according
accordion
accessary
accusable
accession
arch-stone
ascospore
accessory
ancestral
ascetical
ascitical
accoutred
anchylose
Aldebaran
abdicable
adducible
addictive
adductive
abduction
addiction
adduction
audacious
addlement
addressed
addressee
addresser
addressor
abdominal
andantino
andromeda
audiophil
andrology
audiology
audiogram
arduously
androgyny
audiphone
adderwort
andesitic
auditress
auditoria
Aceraceae
alewashed
acetamide
arenation
Alemannic
Ametabola
apetalous
asepalous
acetabula
alembroth
acescence
acescency
amendable
amendment
anecdotal
avengeful
Americana

aperiodic
aperitive
americium
Aretinian
acellular
areolated
areometer
adenomata
adenoidal
awesomely
ale-conner
anemology
anemogram
Areopagus
ademption
Averroism
Averroist
aberrance
aberrancy
ale-draper
Aleuritis
area-sneak
areostyle
avertable
avertible
avertedly
alertness
apertness
aventaile
awestrike
azeotrope
aleatoric
awe-struck
asexually
acetylene
affianced
afflation
affective
affecting
affection
affidavit
affricate
afflicted
affiliate
awfulness
affronted
affrontée
affirmant
affluxion
affluence
aggravate
algebraic
argy-bargy
aggregate
anglesite
anglewise
angle-worm
aggressor
augmented
augmenter
augmentor
anguipede
angriness

anguished
anglicise
anglicism
anglicist
anguiform
aggrieved
angel-cake
angelical
argillite
angel-fish
angel-food
angelhood
angulated
argentine
argentite
Algonkian
Argentino
Algonquin
angiomata
anglophil
angiogram
angerless
augurship
algarroba
auger-hole
auger-worm
algarrobo
algorithm
Augustine
Angostura
argus-eyed
ashlaring
Ashtaroth
aphidical
anhydride
anhydrite
anhydrous
ashlering
achaenium
athletics
atheistic
Achillean
ash-blonde
aphyllous
ashamedly
athematic
Athenaeum
ashen-grey
Ashtoreth
atheology
athrocyte
abhorrent
abhorring
adherence
aphoriser
apheresis
arhythmia
arhythmic
athetesis
athetosis
Acheulean
Acheulian
ash-bucket

avisandum
avizandum
agitative
alizarine
animalise
animating
animalism
animatism
agitation
animation
animalist
animality
adiabatic
alinement
avisement
alimental
avizefull
apishness
aliphatic
abidingly
acidified
asininity
aciniform
animistic
arillated
axiomatic
alienable
alignment
amianthus
alienator
amino-acid
adipocere
aniconism
aniconist
adiposity
animosity
apivorous
adiaphora
amissible
amidships
Aristides
agistment
Aristarch
aciculate
acidulate
apiculate
azimuthal
acidulous
alicyclic
adjective
abjection
adjacency
adjoining
adjunctly
adjutancy
adjuvancy
awkwardly
ankle-jack
ankle-boot
ankylosed
alkalosis
ankylosis
all-father

ad-libbing
allocable
allicholy
allocarpy
all-seeing
axle-guard
allograph
allegiant
allegedly
allegoric
alligator
alleluiah
allemande
allomorph
Atlantean
ailanthus
all-ending
allantoic
allantoid
allantois
allenarly
aplanatic
alloplasm
arle-penny
allophone
allopathy
Aylesbury
allotment
allotting
allotrope
allotropy
ablatival
all-ruling
alleviate
allowable
allowably
allowedly
allowance
auld-warld
allayment
admeasure
alms-drink
armadillo
aimlessly
armigeral
alms-house
armillary
atmolysis
atmometer
adminicle
almandine
almond-oil
admonitor
Axminster
admirable
admirably
Armorican
Admiralty
admissive
armistice
admission
admitting
asmoulder

alms-woman
admixture
annualise
annealing
abnegator
annuitant
annulment
annulling
annulated
abnormity
abnormous
adnascent
agnatical
annotator
announcer
annexment
annoyance
Anonaceae
aromatise
amoralism
atonalism
adoration
avocation
amoralist
atonality
anomalous
apogamous
amoebaean
avoidable
abondance
avoidance
aforehand
aforesaid
aloneness
abodement
atonement
aforetime
anorectic
aloofness
alongside
apothecia
anopheles
apophyses
apophysis
apophatic
abominate
adoringly
atoningly
aborigine
aconitine
aeolipile
agonising
abolition
atomicity
atonicity
agonistic
apodictic
apomictic
atomistic
agonistes
aeolipyle
acock-bill
adornment

abounding
amornings
apoenzyme
apocopate
apologise
apologist
amorosity
amorously
amorphism
amorphous
apocrypha
amourette
acoustics
aloeswood
about-face
about-ship
anorthite
apostolic
apostille
adoptious
avouterer
apostatic
about-turn
acoluthic
akoluthos
anonymity
anonymous
applauder
appealing
appraisal
appraiser
asphaltic
asphaltum
aspectual
aspidioid
apple-jack
apple-cart
apple-tart
apprehend
ampleness
apple-wife
Asplenium
apple-john
apple-tree
adpressed
applicate
applicant
appliable
amplified
apprizing
amphibian
amplifier
appliance
Amphipoda
amphibole
amphiboly
amphigory
appointed
appointee
appointor
amplitude
amphioxus
appellate

appellant
appalling
Appaloosa
appendage
appendant
appanaged
aspen-like
alpenhorn
approbate
Aepyornis
amplosome
ampholyte
alpargata
ampersand
amperzand
appertain
asparagus
aspersive
aspergill
apportion
aspersion
apparency
aspersoir
aspersory
apparitor
aspirator
apparatus
appetible
appetence
appetency
appetiser
amputator
arquebuse
acquiesce
acquitted
acquittal
arrearage
Afro-Asian
aerialist
aeriality
air-cavity
air-jacket
aerobiont
acrobatic
arracacha
auricular
Africaner
atrocious
aerodrome
agreeable
agreeably
agreement
airy-fairy
aerograph
arrogance
arrogancy
abrogator
air-minded
arraigner
Afrikaans
Afrikaner
agrologic
April-fish

aerolitic
aeromancy
aerometer
aeromotor
aerometry
Aaronical
air-engine
Adrenalin®
acronymic
agronomic
apriorism
apriorist
apriority
air-pocket
air-cooled
agriology
airworthy
aeroplane
atrophied
abruption
air-splint
acropolis
aerophone
acrophony
acropetal
aerophyte
air-bridge
aurorally
aerospace
aeroshell
acrospire
arrestive
agrestial
auriscope
aerotrain
air-strike
acroteria
aerotaxis
air-bubble
arrivance
arrivancy
arrivisme
arriviste
arrow-head
arrow-shot
arrowroot
arrayment
Ausländer
assuasive
assuaging
abstainer
associate
assiduity
apsidiole
assiduous
austerely
austenite
austerity
assuetude
aesthesia
aesthesis
aesthetic
Anschluss

aestivate	authentic	astronomy	antitypal	advisedly	blackjack
auspicate	autoflare	anthocyan	anti-trust	advoutrer	blackball
assailant	artificer	autophagy	antitoxic	auxiliary	blackmail
abstinent	antefixal	antipodal	antitoxin	auxometer	blackhead
abseiling	antefixes	antipodes	autotoxin	anxiously	blacklead
abscissae	autograph	autopoint	astounded	aryballos	blackness
abscissas	autograft	autopilot	anthurium	amygdalin	blankness
abscisses	autogamic	antiphony	Arthurian	Amygdalus	Blackfeet
assoilzie	antigenic	autophoby	antiviral	asyndetic	blackbird
Ausgleich	antihelix	autophony	activator	asyndeton	blackfish
assumable	aitchbone	antipapal	Antrycide	asynergia	blacklist
assumably	ant-thrush	autopista	adulation	arytenoid	blackwood
assumedly	attainder	antipasto	adulatory	abysmally	blackcock
assembler	attuitive	antipathy	aquaboard	asymmetry	Blackfoot
assumpsit	altricial	antiquate	adumbrate	amyloidal	blackbuck
arseniate	attrition	antiquark	aquabatic	asymptote	beadledom
arsenical	attuition	antiquary	avuncular	Aizoaceae	Brahmanic
assentive	attribute	antiquely	aduncated	bravadoes	Brahminic
assonance	antiknock	antiquity	abundance	blatantly	Brahminee
arsenious	artillary	afterward	abundancy	brambling	braincase
absconder	antelucan	aftercare	aquadrome	bear-berry	brainwave
adsorbate	Autolycus	aftergame	acuteness	blaeberry	brainwash
assurable	attollent	altercate	amusement	branchery	brain-dead
assuredly	autolysis	alternate	aculeated	branchiae	brainless
absorbent	autolytic	aftermath	ahungered	branching	béarnaise
adsorbent	autolatry	after-damp	acuminate	branchial	brainsick
assurgent	antimonic	alternant	aluminate	branchlet	blaspheme
assertive	artemisia	alterable	abusively	board-game	blasphemy
absorbing	asthmatic	anthracic	amusingly	brand-name	bead-proof
assertion	automatic	autarchic	aluminise	boardwalk	beanstalk
absurdity	automaton	after-life	aluminium	brandreth	boatswain
assurance	altimeter	aftertime	aluminous	beardless	brassière
assertory	attempter	altarwise	anucleate	blandness	boar-spear
assistant	attenuate	autarkist	aquilegia	brandling	bear's-foot
assaulter	attendant	after-clap	aquaplane	boardroom	brasserie
arsy-versy	attenuant	afterglow	ague-proof	board-foot	bracteate
assayable	antennary	afterings	aqua-regia	bladdered	boat-train
astraddle	antinodal	altar-tomb	aquariist	brandered	boastless
attrahent	attentive	afterword	aquarelle	brand-iron	bractless
astrakhan	attention	arteriole	aquariums	blameless	blastment
actualise	antinomic	afternoon	alum-shale	brakeless	beautiful
actuarial	autonomic	aftermost	alum-slate	brazeless	beastlike
actuation	antenatal	anthropic	alum-stone	Boanerges	blast-pipe
actualist	antennule	arthropod	aquatinta	brake-shoe	brattling
actuality	anti-novel	after-crop	adulthood	brakes-man	blastular
Astrantia	Actinozoa	arthrosis	adulterer	blade-bone	beastings
attractor	astrolabe	Antarctic	aqua-vitae	beaver-rat	beasthood
autoclave	anthocarp	arthritic	adviceful	beanfeast	blast-hole
autocracy	astronaut	arteritis	advection	brangling	bracteole
autocycle	astrofell	arthritis	advocator	beach-ball	beauteous
anticline	authoress	autoroute	advantage	beachhead	bratwurst
antichlor	astrophel	autos-da-fé	adventive	Brachyura	bobtailed
articular	authorise	antispast	Adventist	boarhound	babacoote
artichoke	authoring	antiscian	adventure	bead-house	bibacious
antechoir	authorish	altissimo	alveolate	boathouse	bebeerine
astichous	authorial	autosomal	adversary	beau-ideal	bob-cherry
astucious	authorism	autoscopy	advertent	beaminess	Babbitism
autocross	actionist	antiserum	adversely	beamingly	biblicism
anticivic	authority	antitrade	advertise	Brazilian	biblicist
antidotal	astrodome	autotelic	adverbial	beatitude	bobbin-net
anthelion	aetiology	autotimer	adversity	blackband	bubble-car
anthemion	anthology	autotroph	advisable	blackgame	bubble-gum
artlessly	astrology	antitypic	advisably	black-wash	bobsleigh

baboonery	bedlamite	breathing	Briticise	ballerine	belly-flop
baboonish	bedlamism	breathily	bailiwick	believing	billycock
babirussa	bed-jacket	beestings	Briticism	billeting	bully-rook
bobbysock	body-curer	biestings	brinjarry	bolletrie	billy-goat
bacharach	budgetary	Bretwalda	brickyard	bulletrie	bully-tree
beccaccia	badger-dog	Beelzebub	brickwall	bilge-pump	bombardon
buccaneer	budgeting	buffaloes	briskness	bald-faced	bombasine
beccafico	bedfellow	buffeting	brick-kiln	bold-faced	bombazine
buccanier	bodyguard	bifoliate	brick-clay	bullfight	bemoaning
buckboard	bedridden	befalling	brickwork	balefully	bum-baylie
back-bench	badminton	bifurcate	brick-dust	bullfinch	bummaloti
back-block	bed-sitter	bifarious	brilliant	bell-glass	bombastic
backbiter	bedelship	befortune	bain-marie	Bolognese	bomb-happy
back-crawl	bed-closet	buff-stick	bairn-team	balthasar	bombilate
back-chain	bedimming	befitting	baignoire	Bolshevik	bombinate
bicyclist	bidentate	buff-wheel	bairnlike	balthazar	bumpiness
back-cloth	bedropped	beggardom	bairn-time	balminess	bomb-ketch
backcross	bedspread	beggar-man	Britoness	bulginess	bumble-bee
bucketful	bodyshell	bugle-band	brier-wood	bulkiness	Bumbledom
bacterise	bedazzled	bugle-call	brier-root	balkingly	bimonthly
bucketing	bedizened	beglerbeg	blissless	bullishly	bemonster
bacterial	bretasche	big-headed	britschka	billionth	bumpology
bacterium	beemaster	bugle-horn	brimstone	Baltimore	bamboozle
bacterian	beef-broth	beguinage	brimstony	bellibone	bombproof
bacteroid	bleachers	bogginess	bristling	bellicose	bump-start
backfisch	bleachery	beggingly	briquette	baldi-coot	bombshell
back-green	bleaching	bagpiping	bakeapple	billiards	bumptious
bacchante	breeching	beginning	bakeboard	ballistic	bank-agent
bacchanal	breed-bate	bigeneric	baksheesh	balalaika	bengaline
buckhound	breadline	bog-spavin	bakehouse	belemnite	bungaloid
bacciform	breadroom	begetting	bakhshish	bilimbing	bandalore
bacillary	bread-corn	bagatelle	bakestone	baldmoney	band-brake
bucolical	breadroot	bog-butter	balaam-box	belomancy	bone-black
Baculites	bread-tree	bug-hunter	balladeer	bell-metal	baneberry
bicameral	breveting	beheading	baldachin	bolometer	binocular
biconcave	beekeeper	beholding	Balsamina	bolometry	benedight
Bucentaur	brevetted	buhrstone	Balaamite	belamoure	benne-seed
backplate	beefeater	behoveful	Balkanise	Belonidae	bantering
back pedal	beech-mast	bahuvrihi	balzarine	bull-nosed	bandelier
backpiece	beech-fern	behaviour	Bulgarian	balanitis	banderole
bicipital	Brechtian	brigandry	balladist	bilingual	bone-earth
backstage	beech-wood	brigadier	billabong	ballot-box	beneficed
back-slang	beer-house	Britannia	Bellatrix	balconied	banefully
backspaul	brew-house	Britannic	ballasted	balloting	benefited
backstall	beeriness	bric-à-brac	baldaquin	billowing	bent-grass
backstays	breakback	blindless	beleaguer	Baltoslav	benignant
backspeer	breakfast	blindness	bilharzia	biliously	benignity
backspeir	breakable	blind-side	billboard	ball-point	benighted
backsight	breakneck	blindfish	bull-board	bell-punch	benighten
backslide	bleakness	blindfold	bilabiate	ball-proof	benighter
backshish	break-wind	blind-coal	bilobular	baldpated	bench-mark
buckshish	breakdown	blindworm	Balaclava	bilirubin	benthonic
backsword	break-even	bridemaid	balection	ballsed-up	bench-hole
buck's-horn	breakaway	bridecake	bolection	bull-trout	benni-seed
backtrack	bee-flower	baisemain	bilocular	bolstered	bonnibell
bucktooth	beer-money	bridewell	bile-ducts	bilateral	bonniness
buckthorn	bregmatic	bridesman	ball-dress	biliteral	bendingly
buckwheat	bee-orchis	brief-case	bull-dance	bell-tower	benzidine
buck-wagon	blear-eyed	briefless	bulldozer	boliviano	bandicoot
backwoods	blessedly	beingless	belvedere	bullwhack	binominal
backwards	beefsteak	beingness	bilge-keel	belly-band	boning-rod
backwater	breastpin	blighting	bald-eagle	bellyache	bandobast
bedraggle	breathful	Britisher	ballerina	bully-beef	bandolero

bandoleer	bloodlust	Barbadian	burrstone	beslubber	brushwood
bandoline	brokerage	barbarian	barnstorm	besmutted	blush-rose
bentonite	boomerang	barbarity	bird's-foot	bushwhack	brushwork
benzoline	bromeliad	barracker	bird-table	batrachia	brutishly
bandolier	biogenous	barnacled	burnt-cork	battalion	brutified
bonhommie	booked-out	byrlaw-man	barathrum	bethankit	Brummagem
bonhomous	biometric	bargainer	byrewoman	bath-brick	Brunonian
bundobust	boot-faced	bar-magnet	bystander	butadiene	boutonnée
bank-paper	brotherly	barcarole	bastardly	butlerage	blueprint
binervate	boorishly	bird-alone	bespangle	butterbur	brusquely
bandstand	boodie-rat	barracoon	bashawism	butter-box	bluestone
bond-slave	blockhead	Barbadoes	bescatter	buttercup	bluntness
bangsring	brookweed	barbarous	bespatter	butter-fat	bountiful
band-stone	block-ship	barbastel	baseboard	butterfly	bounteous
bondstone	brooklime	barracuda	bushcraft	butterine	blutwurst
bank-stock	block-book	barmbrack	bisection	battening	bevel-gear
banjulele	block-coal	bark-bound	basically	bettering	bevelment
banausian	booklouse	bard-craft	basecourt	bitterish	bevelling
binturong	broomrape	berg-cedar	besteaded	butternut	bivalence
banqueted	bloomless	barm-cloth	basketful	bitter-pit	bivalency
banquette	bookmaker	barrelage	beseeched	butter-pat	bavardage
Bantustan	bootmaker	barret-cap	beseecher	butcherly	bivariate
banqueter	broom-corn	bartender	bas-relief	bathhouse	bivariant
bone-weary	brownness	barrelful	beseeming	batmizvah	bow-backed
band-wheel	bionomics	Barmecide	besieging	battle-axe	bow-legged
bandwagon	biologist	berberine	bespeckle	battle-cry	bowler-hat
bond-woman	bromoform	berkelium	busheller	bottleful	bow-window
bandy-ball	bookplate	berserker	bushel-man	bottle-gas	bawdiness
bunny-girl	biosphere	berserkly	basifugal	bottle-imp	bewailing
biohazard	biography	barrelled	bashfully	betumbled	bowelling
bioparent	bookstand	bargepole	bush-fruit	botanical	bower-bird
bootblack	boom-slang	burdenous	basifixed	betrodden	bowstring
brow-bound	bookstall	barkeeper	boschveld	bethought	bowstrung
blotching	bookshelf	burlesque	bastinade	betrothed	box-camera
bronchial	bookstore	barperson	bastinado	betrothal	boxwallah
broadband	biostable	barefaced	boskiness	batholite	boxkeeper
blond-lace	bioethics	barograph	bossiness	batholith	box-office
blood-bath	book-token	baragouin	bushiness	Bathonian	box-girder
broadtail	book-tally	birth-rate	bismillah	battology	buxomness
blood-rain	blowtorch	birthmark	bastioned	butt-shaft	Brythonic
broadways	blowvalve	birthwort	besainted	bath-salts	bay-antler
broadcast	booby-trap	borghetto	basmizvah	bethumbed	bayoneted
boondocks	beplaster	barricade	bisulcate	bytownite	Bryophyta
blood-feud	Buprestis	barricado	basilical	butty-gang	bryophyte
broad-leaf	baptismal	barminess	basilican	bathylite	boyfriend
broad-bean	baptistry	burliness	basilicon	bathylith	bezoardic
bloodless	bipinnate	burnisher	besom-head	bathybius	buzzingly
broadness	by-product	birlieman	bush-metal	brutalise	Byzantine
bloodheat	bipartite	barbitone	basin-wide	brutality	bez-antler
bloodshed	bipyramid	bursiform	basinfuls	bourasque	char-à-banc
bloodshot	by-passage	barrister	beslobber	blue-black	charabanc
blood-bird	bepatched	barmizvah	bishopdom	blubbered	Characeae
blood-wite	bird-alane	beryllium	bishopess	blueberry	Crataegus
broadside	burd-alane	Bartlemew	bishopric	boundless	chabazite
broadwise	bergamask	bird-louse	bespotted	blunderer	cyanamide
by-ordinar	bargander	barometer	baseplate	boulevard	clavation
bloodwood	berg-adder	barometry	basipetal	bruteness	crab-apple
blood-worm	bergander	baronetcy	biserrate	bluffness	chaparral
broadloom	barbarise	bergomask	bestrewed	bluegrass	character
bloodroot	Barnabite	barrow-boy	besetment	blue-green	clapboard
broad-brim	Bernadine	borrowing	besetting	bourgeois	coal-black
broiderer	bursarial	bird's-nest	besitting	blushless	coal-brass
blood-dust	barbarism	baroscope	besotting	brush-fire	chaw-bacon

crabbedly	claviform	classable	caballing	cock-robin	caecilian
clapbread	clavicorn	classible	cabin-crew	Ciceronic	clericity
chambered	clavicula	classical	cab-runner	cockswain	chemicked
chamberer	coadjutor	Chassidic	cubby-hole	cockscomb	cherimoya
cranberry	crankcase	crab-sidle	cyclamate	cocus-wood	cretinoid
coarctate	crack-hemp	clam-shell	Cactaceae	cocksfoot	cteniform
chanceful	clankless	classless	cockateel	cockshoot	cretinous
chancroid	crankness	crassness	Cockaigne	cicatrice	chemistry
chancrous	crackling	classific	cockatiel	cicatrise	chemitype
clay-court	clackdish	crabstick	cocoa-nibs	cacotopia	chemitypy
Chaldaean	cracksman	clausulae	cachaemia	coccygeal	checkmate
coat-dress	crack-rope	clausular	cachaemic	coccygian	check-rein
chandlery	crackdown	class-book	cocoa-wood	cockyolly	clerkless
chaldaism	challenge	classroom	ciclatoun	cuddeehih	clerkship
châtelain	chapleted	Chassepot	cock-a-hoop	cudgelled	clerk-like
claret-cup	charlotte	claustral	cock-broth	cudgeller	clerkling
clarendon	charlatan	claustrum	cacodemon	codifying	check-till
chavender	crab-louse	chaussure	coco-de-mer	caddie-car	checklist
chameleon	claimable	coat-style	cache-sexe	caddis-fly	cheek-bone
ceaseless	crammable	crab's-eyes	cacoethes	cod-fisher	checkroom
chapeless	charmless	coastward	cachectic	cadential	checkered
cease-fire	coal-miner	chaetodon	cacafuego	code-named	clew-lines
czarevich	charmeuse	chantress	cockfight	cedar-bird	creolised
claret-jug	coal-mouse	chartless	cockhorse	cedarwood	cream-laid
chaperone	chain-gang	craftless	cochineal	cadastral	cream-cake
craterous	chain-mail	Chartreux	cockiness	cadetship	cream-wove
chase-port	chain-gear	coastline	cocainise	cadaveric	cleanness
clay-eater	chainless	coastwise	cocainism	Caesarean	cleansing
crab-eater	chain-shot	Chantilly	coccidium	chelaship	cheong-sam
chamfrain	chain-pier	craftsman	cyclicism	cheralite	chernozem
crab-faced	chainwork	chastened	cocainist	Caesarism	Coelomata
coalfield	chain-bolt	chastener	cyclicity	Caesarian	coenosarc
chauffeur	chain-rule	chartroom	cactiform	chelation	coelomate
chaffless	chain-pump	chaetopod	cochleate	cremation	cremocarp
chaffinch	Charolais	chartered	cucullate	crenation	cheloidal
coat-frock	chatoyant	charterer	cockle-bur	chevalier	coenobite
chamfered	Ceanothus	chatterer	Cichlidae	Caesarist	crepoline
coal-fired	chamomile	clatterer	cockle-hat	crematory	coenobium
chafferer	Cracovian	chanteuse	cocklaird	cremaster	chelonian
changeful	coal-owner	clavulate	cacuminal	crenature	Caenozoic
chargeful	clamorous	coadunate	cockmatch	cheechako	chemostat
charge-man	clamourer	coagulant	Cicindela	coercible	coelostat
crash-land	cyanotype	crapulent	cockneyfy	coercibly	cheap-jack
clathrate	coal-plate	chalumeau	cyclorama	crescendo	cheapness
cha-cha-cha	cramp-bark	crapulous	cuckoo-bud	credendum	cee-spring
coachwhip	coal-plant	charwoman	cycloidal	cleverish	coemption
coach-hire	champlevé	Charybdis	cuckoldom	crewelist	cheapener
crash-dive	champagne	Chalybean	cuckoldly	crenelled	creep-hole
coach-road	cramp-ring	chalybite	cuckoldry	coeternal	creepered
coachwork	cramp-fish	cabbalism	cyclopean	clerecole	cherry-bob
coach-horn	champaign	cabbalist	cocoonery	clemently	cheerless
coal-house	cramp-bone	cubically	cuckoo-fly	chevelure	clearness
charivari	clampdown	cebadilla	coccolite	clergyman	clearwing
chariness	cramp-iron	cable-laid	coccolith	chechacho	clear-skin
craziness	champerty	Cobdenite	cyclolith	chechaquo	chevroned
coaxingly	chair-days	Cobdenism	Cichorium	clericate	clearance
clarified	chairlift	cablegram	cyclopian	crepitate	clearcole
cyaniding	chagrined	cabriolet	cacholong	clericals	cherry-pie
Chasidism	chaprassi	cobriform	cyclotron	crepitant	cherry-pit
coalition	cranreuch	caballero	cyclopses	chelicera	chevrette
clarifier	coatstand	caballine	cock-padle	cherished	clear-eyed
coaxially	classmate	cobaltite	cacophony	Ctesiphon	clepsydra
clarionet	clay-slate		cockroach	cretinism	caen-stone

cheese-vat	clitellum	caldarium	columbine	cellulose	cumulated
creatable	cribellum	collation	columbite	calculous	complexus
creatress	clitellar	cellarist	columbium	calavance	complexly
crestless	cribellar	cellarman	Columbian	Calixtine	Camembert
chest-note	cliff-face	colcannon	columnist	collyrium	camanachd
chest-tone	cliffhang	caliatour	columella	combatant	Comintern
cleithral	chieftain	cellarous	calamanco	come-and-go	cementite
creatural	chiefless	culpatory	call-money	commander	Cominform
crenulate	chiefship	calibrate	celomatic	compander	comings-in
caerulean	chiefling	celebrate	cole-mouse	compandor	commonage
chemurgic	coiffeuse	celebrant	colonnade	campanero	cameo-part
cleruchia	criminate	calabrese	celandine	comradely	commorant
cherubims	ceilinged	colubriad	colonelcy	companied	component
credulity	chiliagon	colubrine	calandria	campanile	composite
coequally	criticise	celebrity	cylindric	combative	come-o'-will
credulous	criticism	calaboose	calendrer	combating	commotion
chequered	clinician	calibered	calendula	campanili	compotier
cleavable	cuisinier	calf-bound	calenture	companion	commodity
coffee-bug	chirimoya	Culicidae	ciliolate	campanist	cameo-rôle
coffee-cup	chitinous	colocynth	collocate	cembalist	commodore
coffer-dam	criminous	calycinal	colloidal	cymbalist	comforter
coffee-pot	chiliarch	cilicious	colcothar	compacted	composure
coffinite	clip-joint	Colocasia	collodion	compactor	cymophane
cafeteria	chickadee	cold-drawn	cultorist	compactly	Cambridge
cognation	chickweed	calfdozer	callosity	Campanula	comprador
cognisant	chickling	cullender	caliology	camp-chair	Camorrism
cognitive	chinkapin	called-for	callously	Cimicidae	Camorrist
cognition	chickaree	colleague	colloquia	comically	camarilla
cigarillo	cricketer	collegial	collotype	compendia	cameraman
cigar-tree	cailleach	collegium	caliphate	commendam	cumbrance
cigarette	cailliach	collegian	colophony	campeador	comprisal
cogitable	chillness	culver-key	chloracne	competent	camera-shy
cohabitee	clientage	cul-de-four	calorific	Commelina	camerated
coheiress	clientèle	calcedony	colorific	Cimmerian	combretum
coherence	clianthus	calceated	Chlorella	campesino	camp-stool
coherency	cairngorm	collected	chlorosis	compelled	camass-rat
coheritor	chipolata	collector	chloritic	commensal	camsteary
cohesible	Crinoidea	cold-frame	chlorotic	commenter	comptable
China-ware	crinoidal	cole-garth	cultrated	commentor	comptible
chicanery	crinoline	colchicum	calmstane	camp-fever	comitadji
climatise	chinovnik	coldhouse	colosseum	cymagraph	camstairy
chicaning	Chilopoda	colligate	Celestine	cymograph	comptroll
Chinatown	Cainozoic	collimate	celestial	camphoric	comitatus
chinaroot	chirology	culminate	calmstone	camsheugh	communard
chiragric	chironomy	cultivate	calf's-foot	combinate	commutate
chivalric	chiropody	culminant	cold-short	comminate	computant
climactic	chibouque	collinear	coltsfoot	commingle	communise
climature	clinoaxis	callipers	colostomy	combining	communing
chipboard	crispness	Calvinism	colostric	cymbidium	communism
clip-board	crippling	Celticism	colostrum	cambiform	communion
chilblain	crispated	collision	calculate	cymbiform	communist
climbable	clinquant	calvities	colourant	commissar	computist
climb-down	chinstrap	Calvinist	calculary	committed	community
chincapin	Cointreau®	callidity	colourful	committee	camouflet
chincough	chihuahua	cullionly	colouring	committal	commutual
childless	calcarate	calcicole	cellulite	cambistry	cantabank
childness	cellarage	Callippic	collusion	comfiture	Cingalese
childlike	calcaneal	calligram	colluvies	comminute	concavely
child-wife	calcaneum	calcifuge	colourist	camelback	contangos
childhood	calcanean	celsitude	culturist	compliant	contadina
crimeless	calcarine	columbate	colourman	complying	cantabile
criterion	calmative	columbary	celluloid	complaint	contadine
chiselled	collative	chlamydes	calculose	completed	contadini

contagium	confestly	conundrum	cunctator	chokebore	crossroad
connation	cannelure	cannonade	construer	clove-hook	crossword
contagion	confervae	centonate	construct	close-down	crosswort
contadino	conserver	connotate	cannulate	crop-eared	crow's-foot
concavity	Coniferae	consolate	conjugate	clove-tree	crossbred
container	canefruit	convocate	consulage	choke-full	crosstree
cantaloup	cynegetic	consonant	consulate	cholecyst	cloistral
Centaurus	cinchonic	concordat	contumacy	crowfoots	crossette
canvasser	cantharid	Cantonese	contumely	cloth-yard	cross-ruff
contactor	cantharis	Congolese	concubine	cloth-hall	crossover
connature	cantharus	cannoneer	conducive	crocheted	cross-eyed
cant-board	conchitis	condolent	contusive	chop-house	clout-nail
cane-brake	candidate	connotive	conjuring	cookhouse	clout-shoe
cane-chair	confidant	cantorial	consuming	cool-house	clouterly
conscient	candidacy	censorial	centurial	chorizont	chorusing
conscribe	condiddle	censorian	connubial	crosiered	croquette
conscript	cantilena	cannonier	centurion	chorister	cephalate
canicular	centipede	centonist	Confucian	crookback	capsaicin
conically	confiteor	conformal	confusion	chowkidar	captaincy
cynically	canniness	conformer	contusion	crookedly	captainry
conscious	cantiness	conjoined	concurred	clockwise	cephalous
cony-catch	condiment	consonous	conqueror	clock-golf	capacious
cancerate	confident	contoured	consultee	clockwork	copacetic
centenary	connivent	concourse	conductor	cloakroom	capacitor
contender	conticent	consortia	consulter	chock-full	co-present
conger-eel	continent	consorted	consultor	chop-logic	ciphering
canceleer	concisely	contorted	centumvir	crop-marks	coppering
connexive	cunningly	concocter	concyclic	crown-land	copperish
centering	confiding	concoctor	condyloma	crown-bark	cipher-key
congenial	confining	consorter	condyloid	crown-gall	copsewood
connexion	convivial	convolute	candytuft	crown-head	cuphearer
cancelier	concision	Cynipidae	crotaline	crownless	Cupressus
centenier	condition	canopying	crotalism	clownship	captivate
congeries	conciliar	can-opener	cholaemia	crownwork	capriccio
convexity	confirmed	canephora	cholaemic	crown-post	cup-lichen
concerned	confirmee	canephore	Cro-Magnon	chocolate	captivity
condemned	confirmer	conspirer	crow-berry	crocodile	cyprinoid
contemned	confirmor	concreate	cropbound	chorology	caprifole
contemner	consigned	centre-bit	crotchety	clodpated	capriform
contemnor	consignee	centrical	choiceful	crow-quill	Capricorn
cancerous	consigner	congruent	cloacalin	choir-girl	capillary
cankerous	consignor	centreing	cloacinal	crossband	capelline
contemper	cincinnus	congruity	cloudland	cross-fade	cupelling
conferred	condignly	contralti	cloudless	croustade	cipollino
conferrer	cuneiform	contralto	chondrite	crossjack	co-polymer
confessed	concierge	centrally	chondrify	cross-talk	cupolated
condenser	centigram	cineramic	clogdance	crosswalk	caponiere
confessor	continued	confronté	chondroid	crossfall	coping-saw
consensus	configure	cinereous	chondrule	croissant	coprolite
conceited	confiture	congruous	choleraic	cross-head	coprology
concerted	continual	cineraria	cooperage	crossbeam	copiously
congested	continuum	confrérie	cooperate	crossness	copyright
connected	continuer	cinerator	co-operate	crow-steps	co-portion
contented	canal-rays	contriver	chokedamp	crow's-nest	copartner
contested	concluded	canescent	co-operant	crosswind	caparison
concentre	candle-end	cane-sugar	cooperant	crossbite	caper-bush
concenter	canal-cell	Cynosurus	choke-pear	crossfire	copes-mate
connecter	confluent	cane-trash	closeness	crosswise	cope-stone
connector	Candlemas	constrain	closeting	crossfish	capotaine
convector	candle-nut	constable	coopering	crossbill	copataine
converter	canal-boat	constrict	cholelith	cross-sill	copatriot
convertor	cinematic	constancy	clove-pink	crow's-bill	capitella
concertos	canonical	cinctured	close-knit	cloisonné	capitulum

capitular
capitally
capotasto
capsulate
capsulary
capsulise
caprylate
coquetted
carbamate
coriander
Cornaceae
carrageen
carbamide
cardamine
carnalise
curvative
carnalism
curialism
carnation
cercarian
circadian
corrasion
curtation
curvation
caryatids
carnalist
cerealist
curialist
carnality
certainly
certainty
currajong
currawong
carvacrol
Cordaites
carnahuba
curvature
cardboard
cerebrate
corn-brake
cornbrash
Carabidae
corn-bread
Caribbean
corybants
cork-borer
corn-borer
corncrake
cere-cloth
ceraceous
Corydalis
careenage
correlate
carpet-bed
carpet-bag
corner-boy
Carmelite
cartelise
carpeting
corseting
curveting
careerism
carnelian

Cartesian
cerberian
cornelian
Cordelier
corsetier
careerist
cornetist
corbelled
corbeille
corner-man
curvesome
carpet-rod
curvetted
carpenter
corrector
correctly
currently
cornemuse
cornfield
carefully
corn-flour
cerograph
cord-grass
Coregonus
cirrhopod
cart-horse
Corchorus
cirrhosis
cart-house
corf-house
cartilage
circinate
corticate
curtilage
cardiacal
card-index
cirripede
corkiness
curdiness
curliness
corrigent
cursively
carpingly
currishly
certified
certifier
cardialgy
cordially
carcinoma
Carnivora
corticoid
carnivore
cortisone
cirriform
cordiform
corniform
curviform
corbicula
curricula
certitude
corollary
coral-reef
coralline

corallite
corolline
carolling
coral-fish
Corallian
coralloid
coral-rock
ceruleous
coral-root
coral-wort
coral-tree
corsleted
chromidia
ceromancy
carambola
carambole
corymbose
chromatic
chromatin
chronicle
chronical
carangoid
coronated
coroneted
carbonade
carbonate
carronade
cartonage
corporate
Carbonari
carbonado
cormorant
corposant
cartouche
corporeal
cornopean
corrodent
carbonise
carnotite
corrosive
cursorial
corrosion
carnosity
corporify
curiosity
cursorily
cartology
cordotomy
cartogram
caryopsis
curiously
coryphaei
coryphene
card-punch
carap-wood
curl-paper
carap-nuts
cartridge
coruscate
cornstalk
cart's-tail
card-sharp
coruscant

cerussite
caressing
Cerastium
Christian
chrysalid
corn-salad
chrysalis
Christmas
chrysanth
cornstone
curbstone
cork-screw
corn-shuck
curettage
cart-track
card-table
ceratodus
curstness
caretaker
ceratitis
carburate
circulate
corrugate
cartulary
carbuncle
corpuscle
corpulent
carfuffle
curfuffle
carburise
curcumine
corrupter
circuitry
corruptly
co-rivalry
caravaned
caravance
caravaner
cartwheel
carrytale
Carlylese
curry-leaf
Carlylean
cordyline
Carlylism
curry-comb
Cispadane
Cassandra
Cistaceae
cassareep
castanets
Casuarina
cassaripe
casualise
casualism
caseation
cassation
Castalian
cessation
case-bound
caste-mark
coshering
cosseting

castellum
castellan
casserole
co-sphered
castigate
cuspidate
cassimere
cystidean
costively
Castilian
coseismic
coseismal
cushioned
cushionet
cespitose
cuspidore
cystiform
cashierer
casuistic
casuistry
case-knife
Cisalpine
casemaker
casemated
cosmorama
cassonade
cystocarp
cosmonaut
cassowary
customary
Cystoidea
cystocele
castoreum
cosmogeny
customise
cystolith
custodial
custodian
custodier
cassocked
cassoulet
castor-oil
cosmogony
cosmology
cystotomy
cosmotron
cosmocrat
castrated
cesarevna
cask-stand
cast-steel
case-study
custumary
costumier
catharise
Catharism
Catharist
citharist
cat-hammed
catharsis
cathartic
cataclasm
catechise

catechism
catechist
coticular
cuticular
cetaceous
cataclysm
Cytherean
cotter-pin
cathedral
cathectic
cut-leaved
catafalco
citigrade
catchable
catchweed
catchment
catchword
catchpole
catchpoll
cut-throat
catch-crop
cutcherry
cat-rigged
cat-witted
cat-silver
cytokinin
cotyledon
catalogue
cataloger
cotillion
cattleman
catalepsy
catalyser
catalysis
cytolysis
catalytic
côtelette
catalexis
catamenia
catamaran
catamount
cat-and-dog
cotangent
co-tenancy
cutaneous
cottonade
cotton-gin
chthonian
cataplasm
cytoplasm
cataplexy
catoptric
cataphyll
caterwaul
catarrhal
catarhine
cityscape
catatonia
catatonic
cytotoxic
cytotoxin
cothurnus
cutty-sark

citizenry
causative
Caucasian
causation
causality
clubbable
chubb-lock
courbaril
crumb-tray
church-ale
churching
churchism
councilor
churchman
churchway
cauld-rife
cauterant
Clupeidae
causeless
crudeness
cauterise
cauterism
cautelous
chub-faced
courgette
crushable
crush-room
cough-drop
couchette
clubhouse
cousinage
caulinary
crucified
crucifier
cautioner
cautionry
cauliform
cruciform
chuckling
chuck-full
cruelness
churn-milk
crumpling
churr-worm
chuprassy
caumstane
caumstone
cruiseway
court-card
court-hand
courtyard
countable
Crustacea
countless
crustless
court-leet
countship
courtship
courtlike
courtling
court-fool
court-roll
count-down

courteous
clustered
courtesan
crustated
courtezan
couturier
clubwoman
civically
cevadilla
cave-earth
cavalcade
cavaliero
covellite
cavilling
covalency
civilised
civiliser
cavendish
covin-tree
covariant
coverslip
cavernous
coverture
covetable
cevitamic
cowfeeder
cowdie-gum
cowardice
cowl-staff
coxcombic
coxcombry
ceylanite
cly-faking
cryogenic
chymistry
cryometer
Ceylonese
ceylonite
cryoscope
cryoscopy
cryptical
cryptadia
cryptogam
cryptonym
dead-alive
dramatise
dramatics
dramatist
diamagnet
dramaturg
drabbling
drag-chain
dratchell
diandrous
dead-drunk
draperied
deadening
deafening
diapering
dianetics®
draperies
diametric
diametral

dialectic
dialectal
diazeuxis
draughter
draught-ox
deathward
death-rate
death-mask
diaphragm
death-damp
death-bell
death-cell
deathless
death-fire
deathlike
diachylum
diachylon
death-blow
deathsman
death-song
death-roll
dray-horse
death-trap
diathermy
diaphysis
diathesis
diathetic
drag-hound
dead-house
death-duty
Dravidian
dualistic
diallagic
diablerie
dead-level
dharmsala
dead-march
drainable
drain-pipe
drain-tile
drawn-work
drain-trap
diagnoses
diagnosis
diaconate
dragomans
diamonded
deaconess
dragoness
dragonfly
diabolise
dialogise
dialogite
diatomite
dragonise
dragonish
diabolism
diacodium
draconism
dragonism
diacodion
draconian
dialogist

diabology
dianoetic
dracontic
dial-plate
draw-plate
dead-point
diarrheic
diarrheal
diarrhoea
diatropic
diaereses
diaeresis
diacritic
diatretum
draw-sheet
diastolic
draftsman
diactinic
diactinal
diastasic
diastasis
diastatic
dead-water
diapyesis
diapyetic
de-bagging
debelling
debenture
dubiosity
dubiously
Dobermann
debarrass
debarment
debarring
debatable
dubitable
dubitably
debutante
dib-stones
dubitancy
debauched
debauchee
debaucher
debruised
declarant
dichasial
dichasium
dictation
declaimer
dictatory
dictatrix
déclassée
dictature
duck-board
decubitus
deck-chair
dock-cress
decoctive
decoction
decachord
dicacious
deck-cargo
decocture

deciduate
decidable
decidedly
decadence
decadency
deciduous
decrement
decretive
decreeing
docketing
decretist
decretory
Decagynia
decagonal
decoherer
deck-house
dacoitage
declinate
declinant
deceitful
diclinism
declivity
ductility
declivous
diclinous
decollate
décolleté
decalogue
decillion
decalcify
decalitre
decilitre
decumbent
decemviri
decemvirs
decomplex
decimally
decompose
Decameron
decametre
decimetre
decimator
decantate
decennary
decongest
decennial
decennium
Decandria
decontrol
doctorand
doctorate
dichogamy
doctoress
doctorial
dicrotism
dicrotous
dichotomy
decapodal
decapodan
deceptive
deception
deceptory
decurrent

decursive
dichroite
dichroism
decursion
dichromic
dichromat
doctrinal
decorated
decorator
decussate
decastere
declstere
duck's-meat
dicastery
decastich
decession
Dicksonia
duck's-foot
dachshund
decastyle
Dicotylae
decathlon
decaudate
decoupage
dictyogen
dicky-bird
dactylist
decoy-duck
didrachma
deducible
dodecagon
deductive
deduction
didactics
dedicated
dedicatee
dedicator
doddering
doddipoll
Dadaistic
Didelphia
didelphic
Didelphys
Dodonaean
Didynamia
doddypoll
drepanium
Daedalian
dietarian
diet-bread
deerberry
deep-drawn
dreadless
diet-drink
dieselise
dietetics
dae-nettle
deer-fence
dredge-box
deer-hound
dietician
dietitian
die-sinker

djellabah	dog-legged	delighted	damp-proof	drop-drill	deprogram
dreamland	doggerman	delphinia	demipique	dromedare	departing
dreamless	dog-kennel	Delphinus	demarcate	dromedary	depurator
dreamhole	dog-letter	dolphinet	demurrage	duodenary	departure
dreamboat	dogshores	doliness	dimorphic	drone-pipe	deposable
deer-mouse	dignitary	doltishly	demurring	duodecimo	depositor
dyer's-weed	dogginess	dulcified	demersion	drove-road	depasture
dyer's-weld	doggishly	dalliance	demisable	diosgenin	diphthong
dress-form	dignified	Dulcitone	damascene	deoxidate	dip-switch
dress-coat	dog-violet	dulcitude	damaskeen	droningly	diphysite
dress-suit	do-goodery	dolomitic	demissive	dronishly	darraigne
deep-toned	do-goodism	delineate	demission	deoxidise	Dardanian
defrauder	dog-collar	delundung	dimissory	dioristic	dermatoid
defraying	degarnish	Daltonism	damasquin	doodlebug	dart-board
defeatism	dogaressa	Daltonian	demitasse	drollness	dirt-cheap
deflation	degustate	delapsion	demiurgic	doorn-boom	directive
defeatist	digestive	deliquium	demiurgus	deodorant	direction
defiantly	digestion	deliriant	dentalium	deodorise	directory
defeature	digastric	dolorific	dentation	door-plate	directrix
deficient	digitalin	delirious	dune-buggy	drop-press	Dorididae
defective	Digitalis	doleritic	Dinoceras	dropsical	dare-devil
defection	dog's-tooth	Delftware	dance-band	door-stead	dor-beetle
defecator	digitiser	dilatable	dance-hall	drop-scene	direfully
defaecate	digitated	dilatancy	denseness	door-stone	dirigible
dufferdom	dahabeeah	dilatator	dandelion	drop-scone	dirigisme
different	dahabiyah	deliverer	donkey-man	drop-stone	dirigiste
dufferism	dahabiyeh	deliverly	dungeoner	dioestrus	dark-house
deflexion	dehydrate	dill-water	dangerous	dioptrate	dirtiness
deflected	dehiscent	dolly-shop	Dantesque	dioptrics	derring-do
deflector	deiparous	Domdaniel	dannebrog	doomwatch	derringer
deflexure	drivelled	damnation	dinner-set	Dionysiac	dartingly
diffident	driveller	dimyarian	dancettee	Dionysian	dormitive
difficult	dyingness	demeanour	dance-tune	depravity	Darwinism
defalcate	dziggetai	damnatory	denigrate	depictive	Darwinian
defoliate	drink-hail	demobbing	dandiacal	depiction	dormition
defoliant	drinkable	democracy	dinginess	depicture	dorsiflex
diffluent	deinosaur	Damoclean	denyingly	deprecate	dormitory
defendant	Deinornis	domiciled	dandified	depredate	duralumin
definable	drip-stone	dumb-cluck	dentition	deprehend	darklings
definably	drift-land	dimidiate	dentiform	depletive	derisible
defensive	drift-sail	demi-deify	dandiprat	depletion	dirt-track
deflorate	deistical	demi-devil	dentistry	dipterist	derivable
defroster	drift-weed	dumbfound	dynamical	dipterous	derivably
deferable	driftless	demagogic	dynamiter	depletory	disparage
deferment	drift-wood	demagogue	dynamotor	depressed	disparate
deferring	drift-bolt	demi-gorge	dining-car	depressor	discalced
deformity	deid-thraw	dumminess	Dinantian	dip-sector	discandie
deference	dairymaid	dumpiness	Dundreary	dope-fiend	dastardly
diffusely	dairy-farm	dumpishly	dendritic	depthless	dismayful
diffusive	dejection	demulcent	denitrate	depth-bomb	dismality
defluxion	dejectory	demulsify	denotable	duplicand	disparity
diffusion	dika-bread	demi-lance	Dunstable	duplicate	disjaskit
defaulter	Dekabrist	demi-monde	do-nothing	dip-circle	dishallow
dog-paddle	dulcamara	dementate	denitrify	duplicity	disdained
dog-eat-dog	delta-wing	demandant	denouncer	dapple-bay	disfavour
dogmatise	Dalmatian	dominical	dandy-cart	depilator	dispauper
degrading	Dalradian	Dominican	dandy-cock	dependant	dismantle
dogmatism	dulocracy	demanding	dandy-roll	dependent	distantly
dogmatics	delicious	dimension	dandyprat	depending	dashboard
dogmatist	deludable	dominance	dandyfunk	dupondius	dust-brand
dog-salmon	dolefully	dominancy	door-cheek	diplomate	disoblige
dogmatory	delegable	dominator	dioecious	diplomacy	dust-brush
degree-day	diligence	dumb-piano	Dioscorea	Diplozoon	desecrate

desiccate	doss-house	despoiler	dittander	dividuous	dry-fisted
desiccant	destinate	discommon	detractor	dove-house	dayspring
disaccord	dissipate	discolour	détraquée	devaluate	Dryasdust
dish-cloth	duskiness	dishonour	duty-bound	divulgate	dizygotic
dish-clout	dustiness	dosiology	detective	devil's-bit	dizziness
dish-cover	dissident	discourse	detection	devilment	emanative
dust-cover	distingué	distorted	dithelete	divellent	emanation
dust-devil	dashingly	disposure	dithelism	devilship	evagation
disregard	distichal	dissolute	dithecous	divulsive	exaration
desperate	duskishly	disappear	dutifully	devilling	emanatist
desperado	dissimile	desipient	dottiness	devil-fish	Elaeagnus
disrepair	distilled	dustproof	detriment	divulsion	emanatory
dissemble	distiller	desirable	detrition	developed	eparchate
dismember	dismissal	describer	dottipoll	developer	exarchate
dissembly	destitute	desirably	datum-line	devil-crab	exarchist
descended	disfigure	disgracer	detention	davenport	Ecardines
descender	displease	discredit	detonator	devonport	erasement
disbelief	desulphur	disorient	ditrochee	divinator	elaterite
disrelish	desalting	disprofit	dittology	deviously	elaterium
dysgenics	desultory	dispraise	duteously	divergent	enamelled
dispelled	desolater	descrying	detergent	diversely	enameller
discernor	desolator	deserving	determent	divertive	evangelic
dispeople	disillude	disarming	deterrent	divorcive	eradicate
destemper	displayed	desertion	determine	diverging	evaginate
distemper	displayer	distraint	detersive	diverting	examinate
dyspepsia	disembark	disbranch	deterring	diversion	exanimate
dispensed	disemploy	dystrophy	detersion	diversify	examinant
dispersal	disembody	dyscrasia	detorsion	diversity	evasively
disseisin	dose-meter	disprison	detortion	devastate	examining
dispenser	dosimeter	disproved	dethroner	devisable	evanition
disperser	dosimetry	disproval	date-shell	divisible	emaciated
disseisor	disimmure	disproven	date sugar	divisibly	epaulette
dyslectic	disengage	destroyed	detrusion	dove's-foot	état-major
dyspeptic	disentail	destroyer	dithyramb	devotedly	epaenetic
dystectic	disenable	disesteem	druidical	devitrify	epainetic
dissected	dyspnoeic	dust-sheet	deuterate	devouring	elaborate
dissector	dyspnoeal	dust-storm	doucepere	dewlapped	evaporato
dissenter	disinfect	disattire	douceness	downgrade	enamorado
desuetude	disinfest	disattune	douzepers	down-going	elaeolite
disrepute	disinvest	dish-towel	deuterium	down-gyved	enamoured
disseizin	dysentery	despumate	drug-fiend	dowdiness	exanthema
disseizor	disanchor	disputant	dough-ball	downiness	exactness
dish-faced	disanoint	disturbed	Doukhobor	down-lying	exactress
disaffect	desinence	discumber	doughtily	down-quilt	enactment
disaffirm	disentomb	disturber	drunkenly	dowerless	exactment
designate	disinhume	disburden	double-axe	downright	elastomer
designful	despotate	dissuader	double-bar	downstage	elastance
designing	dislocate	dissunder	doubleton	downstair	ejaculate
dysphagia	dissonant	dishumour	double-you	downswing	evacuator
dysphagic	disgodded	disguised	drum-major	down-train	embraceor
dysthymia	dispondee	disbursal	diurnally	down-throw	embracery
dysthymic	discoidal	disguiser	drumstick	downwards	embrangle
dysphonia	discovert	discursus	drug-store	Dixieland	embracive
dysphonic	disforest	disgusted	doubtable	dexterity	embracing
dyschroia	dishonest	dislustre	dauntless	dexterous	embrasure
disthrone	discovery	disrupter	doubtless	dextrally	embrazure
dysphoria	discomfit	disruptor	diuturnal	dextrorse	embedment
dysphoric	disbodied	dispurvey	duumviral	dry-waller	embodying
discharge	disposing	disavouch	deviation	day-labour	emblemata
dischurch	dissocial	disavowal	deviatory	drysalter	emblemise
dysphasia	desmodium	dash-wheel	deviceful	day-school	embreathe
dysthesia	despotism	dish-water	dividable	day-nettle	emballing
dysthetic	dystopian	dusty-foot	dividedly	day-return	embalming

embellish	euchology	endurance	electrode	ethically	epinician
embrocate	enclosure	eiderdown	electoral	echidnine	epinicion
embroider	exclosure	eider-duck	executant	enhydrite	epinikian
embroglio	exceptant	ecdysiast	executive	ephedrine	epinikion
emblossom	escapable	endosteal	execution	enhydrous	edibility
embarrass	excipient	endosperm	executory	ethnicism	epiclesis
Ember-days	exceptive	endosteum	executrix	ethnicity	enigmatic
Ember-week	excepting	endoscope	exequatur	exhalable	eriometer
embarking	exception	endosmose	edelweiss	ethologic	ebionitic
embarring	escopette	endospore	everywhen	echolalia	epidosite
embargoed	escortage	endoscopy	everybody	ephemerid	epilogise
embargoes	excoriate	endowment	efficient	ephemerae	epitomise
emboscata	encurtain	Ebenaceae	effective	ephemeral	editorial
embassade	excurrent	epedaphic	effectual	ephemeron	episodial
embassage	excursive	elevation	enfreedom	ephemeris	epilobium
embussing	excursion	edematose	exfoliate	enhancive	epipolism
embattled	eucaryote	edematous	effulgent	echinated	epitomist
elbow-room	excerptor	elevatory	effulging	ethmoidal	epizootic
embayment	excisable	elegantly	efference	ethnocide	epirrhema
embryonic	excusable	exerciser	effluvial	Ethiopian	epigraphy
embryonal	excusably	emendable	effluvium	ethnology	epicritic
embryo-sac	excessive	emendator	effluxion	etherical	eristical
embryotic	exciseman	événement	effluence	ephoralty	epistolic
embezzler	excitable	exegetics	Englander	ethereous	epistoler
esclandre	excitancy	exegetist	engravery	exhausted	epistolet
exchanger	encourage	ewe-necked	engraving	exhauster	edictally
Encratite	excaudate	elevenses	engrained	Ericaceae	epistemic
Encratism	exclusive	elemental	engrainer	epitaphic	existence
Eucharist	exclusion	everglade	engrenage	epitapher	epistasis
enchanted	exclusory	evergreen	eagle-hawk	epitaxial	epistatic
enchanter	encaustic	energumen	eaglewood	emication	epistaxis
excrement	encounter	emergence	egg-beater	epilation	Epicurean
excretive	excavator	emergency	eagle-eyed	evitation	epicurise
exceeding	encrypted	energetic	ergograph	epigaeous	epicurism
ecclesial	endearing	eye-shadow	Englisher	epinastic	etiquette
excretion	endeavour	ewe-cheese	Englishry	evincible	epicyclic
excretory	eudialyte	erethitic	Englified	evincibly	epigynous
encheason	endoblast	elegiacal	ergometer	episcopal	enjoyable
escheator	endecagon	eremitism	ergonomic	exilement	enjoyably
exchequer	endocrine	eye-glance	engine-man	epicedial	enjoyment
enchilada	end-reader	epeolatry	eigentone	epicedium	enkindled
escribano	eudaemony	eternally	engendure	epicedian	eukaryote
Euclidean	endlessly	esemplasy	egg-powder	epidermic	eel-basket
encrinite	eidograph	exemplary	engrossed	epidermal	ex-librism
encrimson	endogamic	eye-splice	engrosser	epidermis	ex-librist
exculpate	endogenic	exemption	engarland	eviternal	eclectics
Excalibur	endeictic	exemplify	eagerness	epileptic	enlighten
excellent	endolymph	eye-opener	engiscope	epicentre	eclampsia
excelling	endemical	execrable	engyscope	eminently	eclamptic
encolpium	endamoeba	execrably	eightieth	evidently	eglantine
encolpion	eudemonia	Epeiridae	eightsman	epizeuxis	ealdorman
excelsior	eudemonic	eyebright	ergataner	epiphragm	ellipsoid
eucalypti	endomorph	eversible	eightfold	epiphanic	enlivener
euchloric	endomixis	eventuate	eightsome	epiphyses	Eumycetes
escalator	endungeon	eyestrain	eight-foil	epiphysis	eumelanin
encompass	endenizen	electuary	eight-hour	epithesis	Eumenides
encomiast	endoplasm	eleutheri	eight-foot	epiphytic	Emmenthal
excambium	endophagy	electress	engoûment	epithetic	emmetrope
excambion	endophyte	erectness	ethnarchy	epiphytal	eunuchism
encanthis	endurable	ejectment	enhearten	epitheton	eunuchoid
eccentric	endurably	electrise	ephialtes	eliminate	egomaniac
excentric	endorphin	eye-string	exhibiter	eliminant	evocative
enchorial	eldership	electrify	exhibitor	edificial	evocation

exoration	emplecton	erroneous	ectogenic	enumerate	fraternal
exogamous	explicate	ebriosity	extricate	exuberate	framework
evocatory	emptiness	ear-cockle	extrinsic	exuberant	flap-eared
exorciser	emptional	enrapture	entelechy	educement	flame-tree
exonerate	expellant	Euraquilo	extolment	ecumenism	flay-flint
elopement	expellent	egression	extolling	ecumenics	fearfully
esoterism	expulsive	erratical	estimable	emulgence	Franglais
exodermal	expelling	eurytherm	estimably	elucidate	frangible
exodermis	expulsion	écritoire	entamoeba	elusively	flaughter
erogenous	emphlysis	eurhythmy	estaminet	eruditely	flash-back
exogenous	empennage	ecstasied	extempore	erudition	feathered
elongated	exponible	ecstasise	ectomorph	esurience	flash-bulb
ecophobia	expansile	enstatite	estimator	esuriency	flashcube
esophagus	expansive	Euskarian	extenuate	eruciform	flagitate
egotheism	expensive	exsiccate	extendant	enucleate	flakiness
eroticism	expansion	easy-chair	extensile	equalness	fragilely
exoticism	empanoply	exsiccant	extensive	ebullient	flamingos
eroticist	espionage	exsection	extension	equalling	flamingly
emotional	euphorbia	exsuccous	extensity	equaliser	flaringly
egotistic	euphonise	Eastender	extrovert	eburneous	foamingly
Elohistic	explosive	easterner	eutrophic	emulously	fragility
emolliate	exploring	ensheathe	ectropium	equipment	frankness
emollient	euphonium	enshelter	entropium	equipoise	Frankenia
exosmosis	explosion	easy-going	ectropion	equipping	frailness
exosmotic	exploiter	eastlings	entropion	elutriate	flatlings
eloinment	expurgate	essential	Esthonian	equisetic	flammable
economise	expirable	ensorcell	eutropous	equisetum	flaunting
exopodite	empirical	exsertile	estoppage	equitable	flannelly
economics	expertise	ex-service	ectoplasm	equitably	flavorous
ecologist	esperance	exsertion	estopping	exultance	flagrance
economist	Esperanto	elsewhere	entoptics	exultancy	fragrancy
ecosphere	empyreuma	erstwhile	ectophyte	equivocal	flagrancy
exosphere	expiscate	eastwards	entophyte	equivalve	fragrancy
exosporal	expositor	essayette	entertake	equivoque	flagstaff
écossaise	exposture	estrapade	extirpate	ervalenta	flagstick
erostrate	expatiate	euthanasy	entertain	enveloped	flagstone
exostosis	empathise	extravert	enterable	enviously	feast rite
emolument	expounder	eutrapely	Euterpean	envermeil	fractious
evolutive	emphysema	estranged	extermine	eavesdrip	flatterer
elocution	Esquimaux	estranger	extorsive	eavesdrop	flatulent
evolution	exquisite	estuarine	extortive	envoyship	featurely
eloquence	Eurocracy	extradite	extortion	enwreathe	flax-wench
elocutory	earnestly	estuarial	enteritis	Edwardian	flag-waver
evolvable	egregious	estuarian	estate-car	erythrina	Fabianism
eponymous	earthward	entrammel	ectotherm	erythrite	Fabianist
ecosystem	earth-bath	entrapper	entourage	erythrism	fabaceous
esplanade	earthfall	extractor	En-Tout-Cas®	erythemal	fibreless
emphasise	earthfast	ectoblast	extrusive	etymology	fabricate
expiation	earthling	entoblast	extrusion	enzymatic	fabricant
explainer	earthflax	establish	extrusory	flambeaux	febricity
expiatory	earthwolf	ectocrine	eutaxitic	flaccidly	febrility
emplastic	earthwork	Eutychian	enthymeme	fratchety	fibrillae
emplaster	earthworm	eutectoid	educative	franchise	fibrillar
expectant	earthborn	entremets	emulative	flanching	fibriform
expecting	earth-bred	extremely	exudative	fratching	fibrinous
expedient	earth-star	entrechat	education	francolin	febricula
euphemise	earliness	extremism	emulation	fraudster	febricule
expletive	ebrillade	euthenics	epulation	flare-path	febrifuge
euphemism	enrolment	euthenist	epuration	flame-leaf	fibromata
expletory	enrolling	extremist	exudation	flameless	fibroline
expressly	errand-boy	extremity	educatory	flabellum	fibrolite
empaestic	eirenicon	entrecôte	enunciate	flagellum	fibrocyte
emplectum	enranckle	estafette	emunctory	flageolet	face-cloth

face-guard	free-liver	friarbird	full-orbed	fungibles	footprint
facsimile	freemason	faintness	fulsomely	fungiform	foolproof
factitive	free-rider	flirt-gill	falconine	financial	foot-pound
factional	free-range	flintlock	following	financier	floorhead
fictional	fleurette	fritterer	Fallopian	fining-pot	flourishy
feculence	free-space	fairyland	fellow-man	fungoidal	footstalk
feculency	freesheet	fairy-tale	foliolose	finnochio	foot-stall
focimeter	freestone	fairylike	fulgorous	fungosity	footstool
fecundate	feedstock	fairy-ring	filoplume	fin-footed	food-stuff
facundity	feedstuff	fairyhood	filtrable	finessing	frontward
fecundity	free-style	fallalery	folk-right	finishing	front-page
factorage	free-trade	falcation	Falernian	font-stone	front-rank
factorise	fleetness	fellation	full-scale	fenestral	frost-nail
factoring	fleet-foot	filiation	feldspath	fanatical	frontways
factorial	frequence	foliation	full-speed	fen-sucked	floatable
factotums	frequency	foliature	filoselle	fancy-sick	frontless
face-plate	free-wheel	full-blast	full-split	fancywork	frostless
face-saver	freewoman	Félibrige	faldstool	fancy-free	frontager
facetious	freewomen	full-blood	full-timer	frowardly	front-line
fiduciary	feed-water	full-blown	falculate	flotation	frontwise
fadedness	freezable	full-bound	fulgurate	footboard	frostbite
fidgeting	frenzical	folk-craft	fulgurant	floccular	frostwork
foddering	freeze-dry	full-cream	fulgurite	floscular	foppishly
faddiness	fifteenth	felicific	fulgurous	flocculus	fire-alarm
fiddle-bow	fifteener	Filicales	folk-weave	footcloth	forwander
fuddle-cap	fife-major	filaceous	fumigator	floodgate	forwarder
federarie	fogramite	full-dress	Fomalhaut	floodmark	forwardly
fee-faw-fum	fogramity	folk-dance	femineity	floodtide	firmament
free-board	fagaceous	false-card	fimbriate	flowerage	foreanent
free-bench	fugacious	filter-bed	fumatoria	flower-bed	forgather
freebooty	fig-pecker	falseness	fanfarade	flower-bud	formalise
fleeching	fogginess	faltering	Finlander	flowering	formative
frescoing	fog-signal	filleting	fundament	flowerpot	fortalice
frescoist	faggoting	Folketing	fandangle	floreated	forsaking
Frenchify	figurable	falsehood	fantasied	frog-eater	formalism
fieldward	figurante	falsework	fantasise	feoffment	formation
fieldfare	fight-back	filter-tip	Fenianism	footfault	furcation
fiend-like	fightback	fulgently	fantasist	frothless	formalist
fieldsman	fagottist	full-faced	fantailed	froth-fomy	formality
fieldwork	fricative	full-front	fanfarona	fool-happy	forjaskit
free-diver	frigatoon	filigrane	fantasque	foolhardy	fire-arrow
foederati	fricassee	filigrain	fantastic	flophouse	firebrand
fretfully	fribbling	filigreed	fantastry	Florideae	fore-brace
fledgling	fribblish	full-grown	funebrial	floridean	fore-brain
freighter	friedcake	fill-horse	finocchio	flowingly	fire-blast
fleshless	feiseanna	fulminate	finicking	foolishly	foreboder
freshness	fainéance	fulminant	funicular	floridity	fire-break
flesh-meat	fainéancy	fillipeen	funiculus	frolicked	firebrick
fleshment	fair-faced	filminess	finically	floriform	forecabin
fleshling	faithless	falsified	fine-drawn	floristic	fore-caddy
flesh-tint	frightful	filliping	finger-end	floriated	firecrest
freshener	frithgild	falsifier	fenceless	floristry	foreclose
fleshings	flightily	fulfilled	fingering	fioritura	forecloth
flesh-hood	frithborh	fulfiller	funnelled	fioriture	feracious
flesh-hook	faith-cube	falciform	funnel-net	frockless	ferocious
fleshworm	foiningly	fulminous	fingertip	frock-coat	furacious
fieriness	frigidity	fillister	find-fault	footlight	fore-cited
feelingly	feignedly	folkloric	fenugreek	foot-loose	fork-chuck
flexitime	friending	folk-music	fan-shaped	frogmarch	forecourt
foeticide	frivolity	falangism	fanciless	flowmeter	fire-drake
fleckless	frivolous	falangist	funkiness	frogmouth	fire-drill
freckling	flippancy	felonious	funniness	flouncing	force-land
free-lance	fripperer	foliolate	fungicide	footplate	forgeable

fardel-bag	farandine	forewomen	fattening	faveolate	gracility
force-feed	forensics	fire-water	fatefully	fivepence	gravidity
farmeress	forenamed	forky-tail	fatigable	fivepenny	gladiolus
forceless	farandole	forsythia	fatiguing	fever-heat	granitoid
forcemeat	far-sought	forty-five	fattiness	favourite	gladiator
forgetful	furiosity	ferry-boat	fittingly	fawningly	graticule
forgetive	forlornly	fish-creel	fatuitous	fixedness	gratitude
far-seeing	fervorous	fosterage	fat-witted	fox-hunter	gear-lever
ferreting	ferrogram	fasten-e'en	fetlocked	flyweight	grammatic
forjeskit	furiously	fesse-wise	fatiscent	fly-fisher	goalmouth
forcepses	forgotten	fastening	fetishism	fly-bitten	glamorise
fermented	ferrotype	fostering	fetishist	frying-pan	glamorous
fire-eater	farm-place	fisherman	fettucine	fuzziness	graspable
forfeiter	fireplace	foster-son	fettucini	gradation	graspless
forgetter	forepoint	fish-guano	feudalise	guaranies	glaireous
fervently	fireproof	fish-garth	feudalism	guacamole	gear-ratio
force-pump	fire-power	fascinate	feudalist	guanazolo	grassland
firefloat	forereach	festinate	frugalist	guarantee	glassware
forefront	fire-robed	fustigate	feudality	guarantor	glass-gall
fireguard	forestage	fissipede	frugality	grandpapa	goat's-hair
fire-grate	foreslack	fishiness	feudatory	guard-rail	glasslike
forage-cap	forestall	tussiness	foul-brood	guardable	gear-stick
foregleam	forestair	fustiness	four-by-two	grandaddy	gear-shift
foregoing	farmstead	festively	faulchion	guardedly	grass-plot
forthwith	forespend	fossilise	Fourcroya	guard-cell	glass-rope
forthcome	forespeak	fastigium	fluidness	grandness	grass-moth
fore-horse	foresteal	festivity	foundress	guardless	glasswork
furtherer	foreshewn	tissility	foundling	guard-ship	grasshook
farmhouse	forest-fly	fossicker	flûte-à-bec	grandsire	glass-soap
firehouse	foresight	fascicled	flute-bird	guard-ring	glasswort
forficate	forestine	fashioner	flugelman	glandular	glass-crab
formicate	fire-stick	festivous	flukeworm	guardsman	grass-tree
fornicate	foreskirt	festilogy	four-flush	grandiose	grantable
fortilage	firestone	fascistic	flushness	guard-book	ghastness
formicant	foreshore	fasciated	four-horse	guard-room	giantship
formicary	foreshock	fascicule	four-hours	glandered	gianthood
forbiddal	forest-oak	fisticuff	fluxional	grand-aunt	giant-rude
forbidden	fire-storm	fasciculi	fruticose	graveyard	granulate
forkiness	foreshown	fustilugs	faunistic	grapeseed	gratulate
fertilely	forasmuch	fish-joint	fluviatic	graceless	gratulant
furtively	first-hand	fusillade	fourpence	grapeless	granulary
furnished	first-rate	fish-louse	fourpenny	graveless	granulite
furbisher	foreteach	fossorial	flurrying	graveness	gradually
furnisher	fernticle	fusionism	fluorspar	grapeshot	granuloma
fortified	foreteeth	fusionist	fluoresce	grapevine	granulose
fertilise	first-time	festology	fluorosis	gravelled	granulous
forgiving	firstling	fish-plate	fourscore	glabellae	graduated
fortifier	forethink	fish-spear	fluctuate	glabellar	graduator
fertility	foretoken	fish-slice	flustrate	gravel-pit	graywacke
fervidity	foretooth	fish-scrap	fructuate	grapetree	gear-wheel
foreigner	first-born	fish-sauce	fruit-cake	Gradgrind	gravy-boat
fire-irons	first-foot	fossulate	frustrate	graphical	gibberish
Forficula	foretaste	fistulose	fluctuant	graphemic	gabionade
fortitude	formulate	fistulous	fructuary	gnathonic	gabionage
furniture	fortunate	fish-woman	Fructidor	graphitic	Gibeonite
forejudge	formulary	fishyback	faultless	gravitate	gibbosity
foreknown	formulise	fat-tailed	fruitless	Gramineae	gibbously
firelight	fortunize	feticidal	fruitwood	glaringly	gabardine
feralised	furfurole	fetichism	fructuous	gratingly	gaberdine
foraminal	furfurous	fetichist	fruit-tree	gratified	go-between
forenight	fore-wheel	fatidical	fruiterer	granitise	godparent
fortnight	foreweigh	fetidness	four-wheel	granitite	godfather
Feringhee	forewoman	fat-headed	five-a-side	gratifier	goddamned

gadgeteer	guitarist	goldfinny	gin-palace	goose-girl	gerfalcon
godlessly	grimalkin	gold-fever	genialise	geodetics	gyrfalcon
giddiness	grisaille	gelignite	goniatite	geodesist	germander
godliness	guildhall	gill-house	geniality	goose-club	garlandry
god-gifted	guide-rail	gallinazo	genealogy	grovelled	germanely
God-a-mercy	guideless	galliwasp	gangboard	groveller	gargarise
godmother	guileless	gallivant	gonococci	goosefoot	Germanise
gadrooned	guinea-hen	gallingly	genocidal	grotesque	Germanish
Gnetaceae	guideship	gallicise	gingerade	geometric	gargarism
Gregarina	Ghibeline	Gallisise	gynaeceum	geometrid	Germanism
gregarine	guideline	gallicism	ganderism	goose-step	germanium
grenadine	guide-rope	galli-crow	gynoecium	glomerule	Germanist
gregarian	guide-book	gallinule	genteelly	glomeruli	geriatric
grenadier	guide-post	gold-laced	gynaecoid	good-faced	garibaldi
greybeard	guinea-pig	golf-links	gingerous	gaol-fever	gore-blood
gier-eagle	griefless	gall-midge	genuflect	grosgrain	garreteer
grey-goose	grief-shot	golomynka	genuinely	georgette	gardening
glengarry	gainfully	goldminer	gentilise	geophilic	garderobe
grewhound	goings-out	galengale	gentilish	geophytic	garmented
greyhound	going-over	galingale	gentilism	goodiness	giraffine
gaelicise	griminess	Galenical	gentility	goofiness	girthline
gmelinite	glidingly	galantine	gannister	glowingly	germinate
gaelicism	gripingly	gallonage	gangliate	gropingly	germinant
Greekless	guilloche	gallopade	gentleman	glorified	garnishee
Greekling	guillemot	galiongee	gentlemen	goodliest	garnisher
Glenlivet	grill-room	gallophil	ginglymus	groomsman	garnishry
greenhand	glissando	galloping	ganglions	groundage	girlishly
greensand	gritstone	gallooned	gunpowder	ground-ash	germicide
greengage	gainsayer	gallowses	Gongorism	good-night	garniture
greenback	guiltless	gold-plate	gondolier	ground-hog	gorilline
greenweed	grist-mill	galdragon	Gongorist	grounding	gorillian
greenness	grievance	goldsmith	guncotton	ground-ivy	gorblimey
Greenwich	Gujarathi	goldspink	gangplank	groundman	germ-layer
greenwood	Gujerathi	goldsinny	gonophore	ground-nut	gyromancy
green-bone	galravage	goldsinny	gynophore	ground-oak	gerundive
greenroom	gilravage	gall-stone	generable	groundsel	gerundial
greenhorn	goliardic	goldstone	generical	geognosis	Girondism
green-eyed	gallabeah	gully-hole	gonorrhea	geologise	Girondist
glenoidal	gallabiya	gally-crow	generalia	geoponics	girandola
Gregorian	galvanise	gemmative	generally	gnomonics	girandole
guerrilla	gallabiah	gymnasial	generator	geologist	gorgoneia
guessable	gallabieh	gymnasium	gong-stick	globosity	gorgonise
grease-gun	galvanism	gammadion	Genesitic	geosphere	gorgonian
gneissoid	galvanist	gammation	genetical	geotropic	garrotted
gneissose	gallantly	gemmation	genitalia	geography	garrotter
guesswork	gallantry	gymnasien	genotypic	good-speed	gyroplane
Gaeltacht	gold-brick	gimmalled	genitival	grossness	germ-plasm
greatness	galabiyah	gummatous	gunrunner	grossular	gyroscope
guestwise	goldcrest	gymnastic	geomancer	glossator	garotting
gee-string	galactose	gama-grass	goosander	glossitis	garrulity
guest-rope	gold-cloth	gumshield	globalise	good-sized	garrulous
guest-room	gala-dress	gomphosis	geocarpic	gnostical	gyrovague
greatcoat	gelidness	gumminess	geomantic	glottides	garryowen
great-aunt	golden-eye	gimmickry	geotactic	ghost-like	gas-carbon
greywacke	gilt-edged	gemel-ring	gaol-break	ghost-word	gossamery
goffering	galleried	gaminerie	good-cheap	ghost-moth	gestative
gigmanity	gelsemine	gammoning	grouchily	geostatic	goslarite
gigahertz	Gelsemium	gambogian	glomerate	globulite	gustative
goggle-box	Galwegian	gummosity	goose-herd	globulous	gestation
gigantean	golden-rod	gambolled	goose-neck	goodyears	gustation
gigantism	goldfield	gymnosoph	goose-wing	Geomyidae	gestatory
go-getting	gillflirt	gemmology	globe-fish	glory-hole	gustatory
gris-amber	goldfinch	gumptious	goose-fish	gypsywort	gas-mantle

gaspereau	glutinous	heart-beat	hedge-bote	high-grown	hellenise
gospelise	gruelling	healthful	hedge-born	hag-ridden	Hellenism
gospeller	glucoside	heartling	hodograph	hog-ringer	helvetium
gas-helmet	gruppetto	heart-sick	hydriodic	haggishly	Helvetian
gas-retort	grub-stake	healthily	heddle-eye	hoggishly	Hellenist
gas-heater	grub-screw	heartikin	hodometer	hygristor	hellebore
gaspiness	gauntness	heart-bond	hodometry	highlight	halieutic
gustiness	goustrous	heartwood	hydrovane	highlands	half-faced
gaspingly	glueyness	heartsome	hadrosaur	high-level	holograph
gushingly	gavelkind	heart-sore	hydronaut	hegemonic	half-hardy
gossiping	givenness	heart-free	hydrocele	hygrodeik	hell-hated
gas-filled	governall	hearth-rug	hydroxide	hygrophil	half-hitch
gas-fitter	governess	hearth-tax	hideosity	hagiology	hellhound
gas-liquor	governing	heartburn	hydrosoma	hygrology	hilliness
gasometer	gowpenful	head-water	hydrosome	hugeously	haltingly
gasometry	gawkiness	Hebraical	hydrofoil	hygrostat	hellishly
gas-engine	gawkihood	hobnailed	hydrozoan	high-place	half-light
Gasconade	gowdspink	Hebraiser	hydrozoon	high-proof	half-miler
gas-holder	geyserite	Hebrewess	hydrology	high-speed	holing-axe
Gasconism	glyceride	Hebrewism	hideously	high-toned	holloware
gas-cooker	glycerine	Hobbesian	hydroptic	high-taper	Hallowe'en
gas-cooled	glycocoll	Hebridean	hydrostat	high-viced	Hallowmas
gas-bottle	Glyptodon	hybridise	hydropult	heir-at-law	heliozoic
gastraeum	gaze-hound	hybridism	hydrolyse	hair-brush	heliozoan
gastropod	gazetteer	Hebridian	hydrolyte	haircloth	heliology
gastritis	gazetting	hybridity	hedyphane	hair-drier	heliostat
gas-escape	headboard	Hobbinoll	hederated	hair-dryer	heliotype
gas-burner	headchair	hybridous	hodoscope	hair-grass	half-plate
gossypine	headcloth	hubristic	hydathode	hairiness	half-price
Gossypium	head-dress	habilable	hidey-hole	heinously	halophile
Gothamite	haanepoot	hob-and-nob	hierarchy	hair-piece	halophily
guttation	headframe	hobjobber	hieratica	hair-space	helipilot
Gothamist	hoar-frost	hobgoblin	haematite	hair-slide	halfpence
gatecrash	heath-bird	hibernate	Hieracium	hair-shirt	halfpenny
gathering	heathenry	habergeon	haematoma	hailstone	holophote
gettering	heathcock	haberdine	haematoid	hail-storm	half-pound
gutter-man	heath-fowl	hibernise	haecceity	hairst-rig	halophyte
gate-house	hoarhound	Hibernian	heedfully	hair-spray	holophyte
gutsiness	headiness	habituate	heediness	hairstyle	hylophyte
gothicise	heaviness	habitable	hierology	hair-waver	Haloragis
Gothicism	hoariness	habitably	hyetology	Hollander	hilarious
gate-money	healingly	hobbyless	hierogram	half-board	Holarctic
get-at-able	hyalinise	huckaback	hierocrat	hell-black	half-round
gate-tower	hearkener	hackamore	haemostat	half-breed	half-royal
gutbucket	headlight	hackberry	hierodule	half-baked	hallstand
glutamate	headliner	hecogenin	haemocyte	hill-billy	Hallstatt
glutamine	Hyaenidae	hackneyed	heel-piece	half-blood	half-shell
grumbling	hyalonema	hectorism	huffiness	hell-broth	half-shift
Grundyism	headpiece	hectogram	huffishly	halobiont	half-sword
gourd-worm	headphone	huckstery	hagiarchy	Hylobates	holystone
gaugeable	headreach	hocussing	haggardly	half-bound	heliscoop
gaudeamus	headshake	hiccuping	Haggadist	Helicidae	halothane
glutenous	headstall	hacqueton	high-blest	half-cheek	half-track
gauze-tree	heapstead	hodmandod	high-blown	holocrine	half-timer
gauleiter	headstick	hydrangea	high-chair	helically	holotypic
gruffness	headstone	hydrazine	high-class	half-close	holstered
grudgeful	hoar-stone	hydration	high-dried	half-crown	halitosis
gaucherie	headstock	hydraulic	hygienics	half-caste	half-title
gauchesco	heartland	hydraemia	hygienist	holy-cruel	half-truth
gaudiness	heartache	hide-bound	high-flier	holocaust	hellwards
gauziness	heartseed	hiddenite	high-flown	helidrome	holly-fern
goutiness	heart-dear	hedgebill	high-flyer	half-dozen	Hollywood
glucinium	heartless	hodiernal	high-grade	holderbat	hollyhock

hylozoism	homestall	honeyless	hypergamy	hardiness	hornyhead
hylozoist	homestead	honey-bird	Hypericum	hermitess	herryment
ham-handed	hemistich	honey-blob	hyperbola	horniness	hercynite
Himyarite	hamstring	honeycomb	hyperbole	horsiness	Hercynian
hamfatter	homotonic	handywork	hyperopia	hardiment	husbandly
homebound	hemitrope	honky-tonk	hypercube	herriment	husbandry
humectate	homotypic	honeymoon	hypostyle	harbinger	histamine
homecraft	homotypal	hunky-dory	Hepaticae	herringer	Hesychasm
humectant	hem-stitch	hoolachan	hepatical	horrified	Hesychast
homicidal	hamstrung	hoof-bound	hypotonic	herbicide	Hesperian
humective	home-truth	hooped-pot	hepatitis	herbivora	hysterics
home-comer	homotaxic	hood-mould	hypotaxis	hardihood	hosteller
home-croft	homotaxis	hootnanny	hippurite	herbivore	hesternal
humidness	humbugged	hook-nosed	hypoxemia	herniated	hysteroid
hamadryad	hamburger	hoofprint	hypoxemic	horologic	hospitage
hammering	humbugger	hoop-snake	hermandad	horologer	hospitale
hammerkop	homousian	haphazard	harmaline	hardliner	hastiness
hummeller	homewards	heptarchy	hortative	horn-maker	huskiness
himseemed	hen-paddle	hop-garden	herbarium	hard-metal	hostilely
hammerman	hen-paidle	Hipparion	herbarian	horometry	hissingly
homoeosis	Hungarian	heptaglot	hortation	heronshaw	histidine
hammer-toe	hand-brake	heptapody	herbalist	hirundine	Hassidism
home-guard	hind-brain	hypoblast	hereabout	hardnosed	hospitium
homograph	hindberry	hope-chest	hortatory	harangued	hispidity
homograft	hand-clasp	hypocrite	harmattan	haranguer	hostility
homogamic	handcraft	hypocrisy	hereafter	hariolate	hostlesse
home-grown	hinder-end	hop-scotch	hardboard	hercogamy	hyson-skin
hemihedry	hungerful	hypocotyl	Heraclean	herkogamy	histogeny
humdinger	hankering	hypocaust	hard-cured	harmonica	hessonite
ham-fisted	Hunterian	hypoderma	hard-drawn	harmonise	historism
humiliate	hanselled	hyphenate	harm-doing	Harmonite	historian
humiliant	Hanseatic	hyphenise	Hirudinea	harrowing	historify
humble-bee	hand-glass	happening	horseback	harmonium	histology
homologue	hunchback	hyphenism	horsetail	Harrovian	histogram
humble-pie	hendiadys	haplessly	horsehair	harmonics	hesitance
humblesse	handiness	hopefully	horseless	harmonist	hesitancy
homiletic	hintingly	hypogaeal	horsemeat	herborist	hesitator
Himalayan	handiwork	hypogaeum	horseshoe	hircosity	hetmanate
homemaker	hen-witted	hypogaean	horsewhip	harpooner	hit-parade
Hamamelis	handlebar	hypogeous	horsehide	harmotome	hotheaded
homomorph	hansom-cab	hip-girdle	hermetics	harbourer	Hitlerite
Hominidae	hand-organ	happiness	horsemint	herb-Paris	hetaerism
humanness	hand-press	hop-picker	hordeolum	hard-paste	Hitlerism
humankind	hand-punch	hippiatry	horseplay	herb-Peter	hetaerist
humanlike	hand-paper	hypallage	herpetoid	hard-ruled	Hitlerist
homonymic	hundredth	hypomania	horse-pond	hare-stane	hottentot
homuncule	hundreder	hypomanic	horse-foot	hardshell	Hottentot
homunculi	hundredor	hypinosis	harvester	harp-shell	hatefully
homeopath	honorific	hyponasty	Herpestes	harassing	hatchback
homeomery	hindrance	hippodame	harlequin	haruspicy	hatchment
hymnodist	hen-driver	hypnoidal	harmfully	hornstone	hitch-hike
hummocked	handstand	hypnogeny	hurtfully	horoscope	hatchling
hymnology	handshake	hypnotise	herb-grace	hartshorn	hut-circle
hemiopsia	handstaff	hypnotism	hardgrass	hare's-foot	hetairism
homoplasy	hindsight	hypnotist	harigalds	horoscopy	hetairist
Hemiptera	handspike	hip-pocket	herd-groom	heritable	hot-and-hot
Homoptera	hone-stone	hop-pocket	harshness	heritably	hit-and-run
homophile	hand-screw	hypnotoid	horehound	heretical	Huttonian
homopolar	handsturn	haplology	hermitage	heritress	heterodox
homophone	handtowel	hippology	hurricane	harquebus	hit-or-miss
homophony	hind-wheel	hoplology	hurricano	hereunder	heteronym
Homeridae	honey-cart	hypnology	hurriedly	Herculean	heteropod
home-ruler	honey-bear	hippocras	hardihead	hornwrack	heterosis

hour-angle	inaudibly	incursion	idealiser	ichnolite	Ismailian
hound-fish	imageable	incurvity	ice-anchor	ichnology	immolator
housemaid	imageless	incurious	ice-hockey	inherence	immanacle
hause-bane	inaugural	incorrupt	irenology	inherency	immensely
house-mate	inanimate	incessant	inebriate	inharmony	immensity
house-carl	imaginary	inclusive	inebriant	inheritor	immanence
house-leek	italicise	incaution	inerrable	Iridaceae	imminence
houseless	imagining	inclusion	inerrably	imitative	immanency
house-line	italicism	indraught	inebriety	imitation	imminency
housewife	inanition	Indianise	inerrancy	irisation	immersion
houselled	imaginist	Indianist	identical	idioblast	immorally
house-flag	inability	indubious	ineptness	itinerate	immission
household	imagistic	indocible	inertness	itinerant	immutable
house-bote	isallobar	inducible	identikit	itineracy	immutably
hause-lock	inamorata	inductile	inequable	itinerary	ismatical
housework	inamorato	inductive	inerudite	idiograph	immitting
house-room	isagogics	indiction	ice-bucket	isinglass	immatured
house-boat	inaptness	induction	inflative	initially	immovable
house-coat	imbrangle	indecency	inflation	initiator	immovably
housefuls	inbreathe	indecorum	infracted	idiomatic	innocuity
house-duty	imbricate	indicator	infractor	Isidorian	innocence
hour-glass	imbalance	indweller	infective	iridotomy	innocency
Houyhnhnm	inbrought	indignant	infection	idioplasm	innocuous
haughtily	imbroglio	indignify	infielder	idiophone	innuendos
heuristic	inburning	indignity	inflexion	idiopathy	innkeeper
hourplate	in-between	indigence	inflexure	idiotical	innholder
haustella	ischaemia	indigency	infilling	idioticon	ionopause
haustoria	ischaemic	indigotin	infantile	injection	innervate
have-at-him	incubuses	indagator	infantine	injurious	ignorable
havocking	incubator	indelible	inflowing	injustice	ignoramus
hive-honey	incidence	indelibly	infuriate	inkholder	ignorance
hovel-post	incremate	indulgent	informant	irksomely	innermost
haversack	inclement	indolence	infirmary	ink-bottle	ignescent
haversine	increment	indolency	inferable	ink-eraser	ignitable
haverings	increaser	indemnify	infertile	ill-manned	ignitible
hoverport	incognita	indemnity	inferring	ill-haired	innovator
hivewards	incognito	Indention	infirmity	ill-nature	innoxious
hawsepipe	ischiadic	indenture	inference	illiberal	isogamete
hawsehole	itchiness	iodophile	infortune	illicitly	isobathic
hawkishly	inclining	Indirubin	infuscate	ill-headed	isolative
hawk-nosed	ischiatic	indusiate	infusible	ill-temper	isolation
howtowdie	inculcate	indispose	infusoria	ill-versed	isogamous
howsoever	inculpate	induviate	infatuate	illegible	isotactic
hawksbill	incumbent	indexical	influxion	illegibly	iron-bound
hexachord	incommode	indexless	influenza	illogical	iso-octane
Hexagynia	incunable	index-link	influence	illegally	isosceles
hexagonal	incentive	Icelandic	ingrained	ill-wisher	iron-cased
hexameter	incondite	Icelander	ingle-side	ill-omened	isomerise
Hexandria	incensory	iterative	ingle-nook	illuminer	isomerism
hexaploid	inclosure	iteration	ingenuity	Islamitic	isogenous
hexastich	incapable	inelastic	ingenious	illimited	isomerous
hexastyle	incapably	inexactly	ingenuous	ill-boding	isometric
Hexateuch	incipient	ice-action	ingrowing	ill-gotten	inorganic
haymaking	inceptive	inelegant	ingestive	ill-judged	isochimal
hoydenish	inception	isenergic	ingestion	ill-humour	isochrone
hoydenism	incarnate	ineffable	ingluvial	idle-wheel	isochoric
hey-presto	incurvate	ineffably	ingluvies	idle-worms	isotheral
hazardize	incurable	ideograph	inhabitor	immediate	inopinate
hazardous	incurably	irenicism	inhibitor	immediacy	isoniazid
irascible	incorrect	idealless	ichneumon	immodesty	isoclinic
irascibly	incurrent	ideologic	ichthyoid	immigrate	isoclinal
inaidable	incursive	idealogue	inhalator	immigrant	iron-miner
inaudible	incurring	ideologue	inhumanly	Ismailism	iron-mould

isopolity	imperfect	inspector	introduce	Iguanidae	judicable
inodorous	impartial	inspheare	interlard	Iguanodon	judicious
isodomous	imperious	instigate	interface	invective	judicator
isologous	imperator	inswinger	interlace	invidious	judge-made
isonomous	importune	instilled	interpage	inveigler	judgement
isopodous	imposable	inscience	intervale	involucre	judgeship
iconology	impassive	institute	interdash	involucel	Judaistic
Isokontae	impassion	insultant	interbank	invalidly	Judas-kiss
isodontal	impastoed	insoluble	icterical	involuted	Judas-hole
isokontan	impostume	insolubly	Icteridae	inventive	Judas-tree
iconostas	imposture	inselberg	intercede	Irvingite	jeeringly
isocrymal	impetrate	insolvent	interfere	Irvingism	jaghirdar
inotropic	imputable	insulting	intervene	invention	jigamaree
isotropic	imputably	insulsity	interleaf	inventory	Jagannath
isopropyl	impeticos	insolence	interdeal	inviolate	jiggumbob
isocratic	impatiens	insulance	intervein	invertase	John-apple
iron-sided	impatient	insularly	intercept	invariant	Johannean
Ironsides	in-patient	insulator	interject	Inverness	Johannine
ironsmith	impotence	insomniac	interment	inversely	Johnny-raw
ironstone	impotency	insensate	intersect	inversive	jail-break
isosteric	impetuous	insinuate	intersert	inversion	jaileress
isostatic	impetuses	insincere	interwind	invisible	juiceless
inoculate	impounder	insipidly	interdine	invisibly	jail-fever
Iroquoian	imprudent	insipient	interline	inwreathe	jailhouse
ivory-gate	inpouring	insurable	interring	inwrought	juiciness
ivory-palm	impluvium	inscriber	interlink	inworking	joint-heir
isocyclic	impavidly	insurgent	intorsion	ivy-leaved	jointless
ivory-tree	inpayment	in-service	intortion	jeannette	jointness
isohyetal	inquinate	insertion	interdict	jealously	jointress
impeacher	inquiline	insurance	internist	job-master	joint-worm
impeccant	inquiring	insistent	interview	jabbering	juke-joint
impacable	inquietly	insisture	intercity	jobcentre	jokesmith
impactite	irreality	insatiate	interflow	jubilance	jillflirt
impaction	irradiate	insatiety	interplay	jubilancy	jolliness
impedance	irradiant	integrand	interknit	jaborandi	jolliment
impudence	Israelite	integrate	interfold	jobernowl	joltingly
imprecate	irrigable	integrant	interlope	Jebusitic	jelliform
impresari	irregular	integrity	internode	Jack-a-Lent	jalousied
impleader	iriguous	intricate	interpone	jactation	jollyhead
implement	irrigator	intrigant	interpose	jackalled	jellybean
imprecise	irrelated	intricacy	interzone	Jacobinic	jellyfish
impletion	irruptive	intuitive	interlock	jack-block	jollyboat
implexion	irruption	intuition	interwork	Jacobitic	jam-packed
implicate	inrushing	intrinsic	interjoin	jockeyism	jemminess
impliedly	irritable	intriguer	interbred	jack-fruit	jumpiness
impellent	irritably	intellect	intercrop	jack-knife	jambolana
impulsive	irritancy	intumesce	inter-arts	jocularly	jump-start
impelling	irritator	intensate	interpret	jaculator	Juncaceae
impulsion	installed	intendant	intergrow	joculator	Juneberry
impulsory	inshallah	intenable	interfuse	jocundity	junkerdom
impolitic	inspanned	intenible	interlude	jack-plane	jenneting
impendent	instanter	intensely	intermure	jacaranda	junketing
impingent	instantly	intensive	interrupt	Jack-slave	Jansenism
impending	itsy-bitsy	intentive	intestate	jack-staff	junkerism
impinging	insectary	intension	intestacy	jack-stays	Jansenist
implodent	insectile	intention	intestine	jack-snipe	Junoesque
implosive	insection	intensify	intrusive	jacksmith	jingo-ring
improvise	insect-net	intensity	intrusion	jockstrap	juniority
improving	inside-car	intonator	inumbrate	jack-straw	Juniperus
implosion	insidious	introject	inunction	jack-sauce	janissary
improbity	issueless	introvert	inurement	jockteleg	janitress
impromptu	insheathe	iatrogeny	inusitate	Jacquerie	jenny-wren
important	inshelter	introitus	inutility	judiciary	jeoparder

japanning	knapskull	king's-evil	loaf-sugar	lacunaria	logarithm
Japaneses	kabeljouw	king-sized	loadstone	licensure	legislate
jequirity	kibbutzim	kinetical	leaf-trace	lectorate	logistics
jerfalcon	kickshaws	Kunstlied	leastways	laccolite	light-ball
Jordanian	kick-start	kinswoman	leastwise	laccolith	logothete
juridical	kidnapped	knotgrass	labialise	loco-plant	light-year
jerkiness	kidnapper	knowingly	labdacism	locuplete	lightless
jarringly	kidney-ore	kaolinise	labialism	lickpenny	lightness
jargoneer	kiddywink	kaolinite	librarian	luck-penny	lightship
jargonise	knee-cords	knock-knee	libration	lace-paper	lightning
jargonist	knee-drill	knock-down	libratory	lacerable	light-mill
Jerusalem	klendusic	knocker-up	libecchio	lacertine	lightsome
jurywoman	kieserite	knowledge	lobectomy	lacertian	light-foot
jurywomen	klephtism	knob-stick	lobscouse	lachrymal	light-dues
jerry-shop	knee-holly	Keplerian	libidinal	lacertine	leg-puller
jessamine	khedivate	kurrajong	lubricate	lacerated	loin-cloth
joss-block	keelivine	karabiner	lubricant	Lycosidae	lairdship
jesserant	khedivial	kermesite	lubricous	locksmith	loitering
jasperise	knee-joint	kirbigrip	libellant	lacquerer	Leicester
jasperous	knee-swell	kerbstone	labelling	lacrymary	leitmotif
joss-house	keelyvine	keratosis	libelling	lacrymose	leitmotiv
jaspidean	Kshatriya	keratitis	labelloid	lodiculae	leisurely
jestingly	knife-edge	kerfuffle	libellous	ludicrous	lake-basin
justified	kaiserdom	kirkyaird	lobulated	lodge-gate	Lollardry
Jesuitism	knifeless	kirby-grip	libertine	lodgement	Liliaceae
justiciar	knife-rest	kathakali	liberally	lodgepole	lallation
justifier	kaiserism	katharsis	labyrinth	ladlefuls	lollingly
joss-stick	knightage	katabolic	laborious	lady's-maid	loll-shrob
jettatura	Kniphofia	katabasis	liberator	lodestone	lily-white
jitterbug	knickered	katabatic	Labourite	lady-smock	lampadary
jet-setter	Kainozoic	kittenish	labourism	liegeless	Lombardic
jut-window	klinostat	kitchener	labourist	liege-lord	Lemnaceae
jettiness	kallyaird	kittiwake	lucrative	leeringly	lampadist
juttingly	kilocycle	kettleful	lactation	lienteric	lamp-black
jet-driven	kiln-dried	kauri-pine	luctation	laevulose	limaceous
jetstream	kilderkin	krummhorn	lack-beard	life-blood	lumbering
jaundiced	kilohertz	Keynesian	lucubrate	life-cycle	lumberman
journeyed	Kelticism	kryometer	lack-brain	life-force	lumber-pie
journeyer	kallitype	keystroke	lock-chain	lifeguard	lambently
joviality	kilolitre	loaf-bread	lucidness	loftiness	lamp-glass
juvenilia	kalamkari	lease-band	lickerish	life-saver	lyme-grass
jawbation	kilometre	leaseback	lichenism	life-sized	lymphatic
jaw-fallen	kymograph	lease-lend	lichenist	life-table	lime-hound
jewel-case	Komintern	leavening	lichenoid	life-weary	lyme-hound
jewel-weed	Kominform	loaferish	lichenose	leftwards	lumpiness
jewellery	king-apple	leasehold	lecherous	lignaloes	limpingly
jewelling	kent-bugle	leavenous	lichenous	logically	lumpishly
jewelfish	kingcraft	lean-faced	lace-frame	logograph	lambitive
jawboning	king-cobra	leaf-green	luciferin	logogriph	limpidity
Jew's-pitch	kink-cough	loathsome	lockhouse	legginess	lamaistic
Jew's-stone	kingdomed	lyam-hound	lacrimary	laggingly	lime-juice
Jew's-trump	kennelled	leafiness	luckie-dad	lignified	lamellate
juxtapose	kennel-man	leakiness	luckiness	lagrimoso	lamplight
jaywalker	kinsfolks	loaminess	lacrimose	lagniappe	limelight
joylessly	kink-hoast	liability	locellate	logomachy	lamelloid
joy-riding	kentledge	leaf-metal	Lucullean	lagomorph	lamellose
jazziness	kintledge	leaf-mould	Lucullian	legendary	laminable
knaveship	king-maker	learnable	lack-linen	legendist	lemon-weed
khalifate	kinematic	learnedly	localiser	legionary	luminaire
knavishly	konimeter	leaf-nosed	lack-Latin	logaoedic	lamenting
knackered	koniology	lead-paint	locomotor	Liguorian	luminance
krakowiak	king's-hood	leaf-stalk	laciniate	log-roller	lemon-sole
knapscull	koniscope	loan-shark	laconical	leger-line	Laminaria

luminesce	lentiform	lapidific	late-comer	leucocyte	lazy-tongs
limonitic	longicorn	lapideous	litter-bug	leviathan	meandrian
laminated	longitude	lip-reader	litter-bin	love-apple	meandrous
lamington	lend-lease	lippening	letter-box	love-arrow	meandered
laminator	landloper	Lippizana	latter-day	livraison	meat-eater
laminitis	lunulated	lippitude	litheness	live-birth	moanfully
lampooner	long-lived	lupulinic	letter-gae	love-charm	mealiness
limnology	linen-fold	leprosery	lettering	love-child	meatiness
lumbrical	Langobard	leprosity	Lutherism	lividness	meaningly
lumbricus	Longobard	lap-roller	Lutherist	love-feast	miasmatic
lampshade	lineolate	leptosome	lithesome	levigable	meadow-rue
lamp-shell	Londonese	lophodont	latter-wit	love-juice	meat-plate
lump-sugar	Londonise	liposomal	latifondi	lavaliere	meat-paste
limestone	Londonish	lapstreak	litigable	lovelight	means-test
lamb's-wool	Londonism	liquation	litigious	levelling	measuring
lamaserai	Londonian	loquacity	luteinise	level-coil	meanwhile
limitable	landowner	liquefied	lithiasis	love-maker	mob-handed
limitedly	langouste	liquefier	lithistid	love-match	mobocracy
limitless	land-plane	liquidate	littleane	loving-cup	Maccabean
limburger	land-pilot	liquified	lithoidal	Levantine	mechanise
limousine	langridge	liquidise	latrociny	loverless	mechanism
limewater	land-reeve	liquidity	lithopone	liver-wing	mactation
land-agent	long-range	liquorice	lithotome	liveryman	mechanics
lineament	Land-rover®	liquorish	luteolous	liverwort	mechanist
lineation	landscape	lardalite	lithology	love-shaft	micaceous
lineality	land-shark	Largactil®	lithotomy	livestock	macedoine
linearity	Landsmaal	lyrically	lithocyst	love-story	muckender
landaulet	landslide	luridness	Lotophagi	levitical	mocker-nut
landamman	Landsting	largeness	liturgics	Leviticus	machinate
longaeval	langspiel	larcenist	liturgist	love-token	muckiness
long-chain	lunisolar	larcenous	laterally	lowlander	machinery
long-coats	longshore	larghetto	literally	low-necked	mockingly
long-cloth	lintstock	larkiness	literatim	lawlessly	machinist
long-drawn	line-storm	larvicide	literator	low-minded	mycologic
landdamne	land-scrip	larvikite	literatus	lowlihead	machmeter
landdrost	Landsturm	largition	Lotus-land	lowliness	Mycenaean
long-dated	long-sixes	larviform	latescent	law-giving	macintosh
lance-jack	lengthful	larum-bell	lutescent	lowrie-tod	microcard
lingering	lengthily	laryngeal	latitancy	lawn-mower	microwave
longevity	linctuses	lorgnette	lathyrism	low-loader	mucronate
lintelled	lingulate	lark's-heel	Lauraceae	lawmonger	microwatt
lanterloo	languidly	lardy-cake	laudative	low-downer	microchip
lanceolar	languaged	last-ditch	laudation	lawn-party	microlite
lance-wood	lingually	Listerise	Laurasian	lower-case	microwire
longevous	languette	Listerism	leucaemia	lower-deck	microlith
long-eared	land-value	Listerian	leukaemia	lowermost	microbial
leniently	lintwhite	lustfully	laudatory	law-writer	microfilm
long-faced	landwards	lysigenic	laundress	lexically	macrobian
long-field	land-yacht	lush-house	launderer	loxodrome	microbian
line-fence	look-alike	lustihead	laurelled	loxodromy	macrodome
land-flood	lioncelle	lustiness	lousewort	luxuriate	microsome
land-force	loose-leaf	lastingly	lounge-bar	luxuriant	microtome
landgrave	looseness	lispingly	laughable	luxurious	microtone
line-grove	lyomerous	lustihood	laughably	lixiviate	macrocosm
lung-grown	lion-heart	lassitude	laughsome	lixivious	microcosm
lunch-time	lyophobic	lysimeter	Leuciscus	layperson	microform
lanthanum	lyophilic	lessoning	lousiness	lay-figure	macrocopy
lunch-hour	Laodicean	lysergide	louringly	layer-cake	macrology
long-house	loop-light	laserwort	loutishly	lazzarone	microcopy
lancinate	look-round	lethargic	loudmouth	lazzaroni	micrology
lankiness	lion-tamer	latration	leuco-base	lazy-bones	microtomy
longingly	Laplander	lethality	leucotome	lazar-like	microgram
lanciform	lipectomy	laticlave	leucotomy	lazaretto	micropsia

macroaxis	midinette	mainbrace	malt-house	mill-wheel	Manichean
macrocyte	mad-doctor	mail-coach	milk-house	milk-white	monactine
microcyte	modernise	maid-child	multipara	melt-water	monocline
micropyle	modernish	maidenish	multi-wall	malaxator	monachism
mycophagy	modernist	mainframe	millipede	mollymawk	Munichism
Mecoptera	modernity	mainliner	multipede	Malaysian	monachist
mycorhiza	madarosis	mail-order	milkiness	Malayalam	monocular
muck-raker	moderator	mail-plane	millinery	mammalian	manically
Mucorales	midi-skirt	mainprise	meltingly	mammalogy	monochord
macaronic	midstream	mainsheet	Malpighia	mimicking	minacious
macaronis	meditated	mail-train	mollified	mumchance	monecious
macerator	midsummer	moistness	mollifier	Memphitic	municipal
mica-slate	Maeonides	maistring	mollities	mumpishly	monocoque
muck-sweat	mnemonist	maieutics	multiplet	mummified	mind-curer
mycotoxin	Mnemosyne	majorship	multiplex	memoirism	monoceros
Mycetozoa	maelstrom	major-domo	mullioned	memoirist	monodrama
micturate	muffettee	majorette	millionth	mammiform	monadical
macrurous	muffin-cap	majuscule	multifoil	mummiform	monodical
macaw-palm	muffineer	mekometer	multiform	mamillate	minidress
macaw-tree	miffiness	make-peace	multitude	mamillary	mini-dress
machzorim	mafficker	make-ready	multihull	momentany	menadione
mediately	muffin-man	makeshift	milk-molar	momentary	monkey-bag
Midrashlm	magdalene	mallander	melomania	momentous	menseless
mediatise	Magyarise	Malvaceae	melomanic	mammonite	mincemeat
mediative	mugearite	Meliaceae	melampode	mammonish	mongering
mediation	Magianism	maltalent	milometer	mammonism	monkeyish
mediatory	magnalium	mill-board	malingery	Memnonian	mannerism
mediatrix	Magyarism	molybdate	malengine	mammonist	Mendelism
madrassah	migration	Meliboean	melanuria	memorable	monkeyism
mediaeval	migratory	Malebolge	melanuric	memorably	monoecism
medicable	megacycle	molybdous	melanosis	memoranda	Mendelian
medically	magically	malachite	melanotic	memorlter	Mindelian
medicinal	megacurie	molochise	mylonitic	mumpsimus	mannerist
mediciner	megadeath	molecular	meliorate	mimetical	monkey-jar
medicated	magnesite	malicious	Melpomene	mum-budget	mangetout
medaewart	magnetise	melocoton	meliorism	mummy-case	monkey-pot
maddening	magnetite	melodrama	Miltonism	manganate	monkey-run
madrepore	magnesium	melodrame	Miltonian	mandatary	mannequin
medresseh	magnetism	melodious	meliorist	manhandle	manoeuvre
mid-season	magnesian	maladroit	meliority	manganese	mine-field
mid-heaven	magnetics	millenary	malformed	mundanely	mindfully
modifying	magnetist	malleable	mill-owner	manzanita	manifesto
muddiness	magnetron	mallender	millocrat	mandarine	monograph
midwifery	megafarad	millepede	malvoisie	manganite	monogamic
maddingly	megagauss	mallee-hen	milk-punch	monoamine	Monogynia
midwifing	megahertz	millerite	melaphyre	Mondayish	menagerie
midwiving	magnified	Millerian	malarious	mentalism	monthling
mid-wicket	magnifico	malleolar	melismata	Montanism	Manchuria
mud-minnow	magnifier	malleolus	milk-shake	mentation	Menshevik
mydriasis	magnitude	millennia	mole-spade	miniation	mancipate
mydriatic	megajoule	millepore	molestful	mentalist	mendicant
mid-winter	maggot-pie	mallemuck	milk-sugar	Montanist	mandiocca
medullate	megaphone	milken-way	Molossian	mendacity	man-minded
middle-age	magistery	malt-floor	Melastoma	mentality	manginess
medullary	megascope	milk-float	milestone	mundanity	manliness
madeleine	megaspore	milk-fever	millstone	manganous	minginess
medalling	magistral	milk-gland	Malathion®	mandatory	mincingly
modelling	mug-hunter	malignant	militancy	Manhattan	menticide
medallion	Mahometan	malagueña	milk-tooth	miniature	mandilion
modillion	maharajah	malignity	mill-tooth	manubrial	mendicity
medallist	maharanee	mylohyoid	militaria	manubrium	Monsignor
middleman	maharishi	malt-horse	molluscan	monobasic	mansionry
modulator	mahlstick	mill-horse	milk-vetch	monocracy	manticora

manticore	miniskirt	margarine	mirligoes	music-rack	muskiness
monticule	meniscoid	margarite	meroistic	music-hall	mussiness
mint-julep	monkshood	marialite	marijuana	misoclere	misdirect
monologic	minkstone	marmarise	moraliser	music-demy	massively
monologue	Monastral	morganite	myrtle-wax	musicking	missilery
monolater	mint-sauce	mortalise	myriorama	masochism	missingly
monolatry	minuscule	mordacity	marmoreal	masochist	mystified
man-slayer	monostyle	mortality	marrowfat	musically	misgiving
mine-layer	Minitrack®	murrained	Mormonite	music-roll	misliking
monomachy	monotreme	Myriapoda	marooning	music-room	mosaicism
monomania	monitress	merganser	mirroring	musaceous	Muslimism
menominee	minute-gun	mercaptan	marrowish	misadvise	mysticism
monomeric	monatomic	mordantly	Mormonism	misregard	mystifier
manometer	minuteman	mirabilia	marrow-men	masterate	mosaicist
monometer	monotonic	mirabelle	Mariology	misbehave	mispickel
meningeal	Monotropa	myrobalan	Maryology	misrelate	Messianic
Monandria	minutiose	mirabilis	marrowsky	masterdom	missioner
mandoline	monotroch	mortcloth	Meropidae	misleader	mislippen
Mennonite	monstrous	moraceous	meropidan	miscegene	mistigris
Mongolise	monotypic	muricated	mare's-tail	misbeseem	messieurs
monzonite	man-at-arms	mercenary	mare's-nest	misdemean	misplease
mentorial	menstrual	market-day	mareschal	musketeer	misallege
mongolism	menstruum	marketeer	marischal	misdesert	misallied
Monroeism	manducate	murderess	Myristica	masterful	muscle-man
Mongolian	mundungus	mercerise	mire-snipe	messenger	mistletoe
monsoonal	Mancunian	marketing	Marasmius	mesmerise	musk-melon
mine-owner	Manxwoman	marcelled	marlstone	miscegine	misemploy
mongoloid	monoxylon	martelled	merestone	musteline	mesomorph
mangouste	monaxonic	marvelled	mort-stone	misbelief	misintend
mongooses	moneyless	market-man	maritally	mastering	mesentery
mangostan	money-wise	myrmecoid	moratoria	mesmerism	masonried
monophase	money-bill	murderous	murmuring	Moslemism	misoneism
monoplane	mandylion	merpeople	marsupial	mysteries	misoneist
monophagy	moneywort	mirifical	mercurial	mesmerist	misinform
Menippean	myomantic	marigraph	marsupium	misreckon	muscovado
maniplies	moon-blind	mortgagee	mercurous	master-key	mastoidal
manyplies	moot-court	mortgager	murmurous	musselled	Massorete
moniplies	mooseyard	mortgagor	marquetry	misdeemed	misgovern
monyplies	moon-faced	marihuana	mark-white	misbecome	Muscovite
manipular	moon-glade	marshland	merrymake	musketoon	muscovite
monoptote	moothouse	marchpane	martyrdom	misreport	Muscovian
monophony	moodiness	mirthless	mercy-seat	mistemper	miscolour
monopsony	moon-knife	march-dike	martyrise	misleared	muscology
menopause	myoglobin	marshalcy	merozoite	misfeasor	museology
manor-seat	moonlight	morphemic	mismanage	misbestow	misgotten
menorrhea	moon-loved	marshwort	moss-agate	musefully	moss-plant
monarchic	myologist	murtherer	mishandle	musk-gland	musk-plant
monorchid	moonquake	morphosis	mistaught	mesogloea	musk-pouch
monarchal	moonraker	morphetic	mustachio	moss-grown	mesophyte
minorship	myography	morphotic	muscadine	mischance	mesophyll
man-orchis	moonscape	march-dyke	muscarine	mischancy	miscreate
monorhine	moonshine	marginate	misfaring	misshaped	miscreant
monergism	moonshiny	merciable	missaying	misshapen	miserable
mongrelly	moonstone	merciless	mistaking	mischarge	miserably
manurance	mepacrine	merriness	mescalism	moschatel	miscredit
monorhyme	mop-headed	murkiness	massagist	masthouse	mispraise
many-sided	mappemond	merriment	mashallah	masticate	misprised
monk's-seam	mephitism	mortified	misfallen	mussitate	Masoretic
mane-sheet	maquisard	mortician	mystagogy	massiness	misgrowth
monastery	marmalade	mortifier	mishappen	messiness	misesteem
monostich	mermaiden	morbidity	mishanter	mistiness	musk-sheep
mono-skier	Myrtaceae	martially	mesoblast	mossiness	misassign
mini-skirt	marcasite	Martinmas	music-case	mushiness	musk-shrew

misguided	metonymic	moveables	necessity	night-work	ninepenny
misguider	matronage	mowdiwart	nicotiana	night-fowl	non-usager
misguggle	methought	mawkishly	nachtmaal	night-soil	nine-score
masculine	mutton-ham	mowdiwort	nicotinic	nightgown	ninetieth
Mussulman	matronise	maxi-dress	Noctuidae	nightspot	nunataker
Mussulmen	meteorite	mixedness	nocturnal	night-crow	nuncupate
musculous	methodise	myxoedema	neckverse	night-rule	non-juring
misaunter	meteorism	maxillary	niddering	nuisancer	nanny-goat
misavised	methodism	maxillula	nodulated	nail-brush	neo-Nazism
massymore	meteorist	maximally	niderling	noiseless	neoterise
mutualise	methodist	maxi-skirt	neesberry	neighbour	neoterism
mutualism	motionist	myxovirus	needfully	noisiness	neoterist
mutuality	motion-man	moygashel	neediness	noisomely	neoteinia
mitraille	meteoroid	may-beetle	needleful	nakedness	neoteinic
mattamore	metronome	mayflower	needle-gun	nullipara	neotenous
methadone	meteorous	mayorship	nielloing	nullified	neophobia
metabolic	mythopoet	mayoralty	niellated	nullifier	neophytic
metabasis	mythology	mezzanine	needle-tin	nelumbium	Neolithic
metabatic	metaphase	muzziness	needy-hood	Nilometer	Neopilina
motocross	metaplasm	muzzle-bag	niftiness	no-meaning	noodledom
matterful	moth-proof	mizzonite	niff-naffy	nomocracy	Neo-Gothic
mothering	motorcade	mezzotint	nefandous	name-child	neologise
muttering	maturable	Mozarabic	nefarious	nomograph	neologism
mother-lye	motorable	Mozartian	niggardly	nymphical	Neocomian
metheglin	Mithraeum	no-account	négociant	nymphaeum	neologian
mitre-wort	motor-ship	neat-house	niggerdom	nymph-like	neonomian
moth-eaten	motor-bike	neat-stall	niggerish	nymphalid	neologist
mother-wit	Mithraism	near-white	niggerism	numble-pie	noosphere
mitigable	Mithraist	nubeculae	neglecter	nominable	neodymium
mutagenic	maternity	nobleness	nigricant	nominally	nephalism
mitigator	motor-boat	nobbiness	negligent	nominator	nephalist
matchable	metestick	nebblsher	Nigritian	name-plate	nepheline
matchless	mutoscope	nobiliary	Negrillos	nemophila	nephelite
match-play	motettist	nebuliser	negritude	numerable	Napierian
match-cord	matutinal	Nabataean	nigritude	numerably	nipperkin
matchwood	Mathurine	nectareal	negroidal	numerical	nip-cheese
matchlock	methylate	nectarean	negrohead	nomertean	happiness
metricate	methylene	nectarine	negrophil	nemertine	nippingly
matricide	methystic	nectarial	nigrosine	numeraire	nepenthes
metricise	mouldwarp	nictation	negro-corn	nemertian	Nipponese
mythicise	mouldable	nectarous	nightward	numerally	nephology
mythicism	mound-bird	nyctalops	negotiate	numerator	nephogram
metrician	mould-loft	neck-cloth	nightmare	numbskull	nephralgy
metrifier	maunderer	nickeline	night-hawk	nomothete	nephrosis
metricist	mouse-tail	nickelise	night-walk	nummulary	nephratic
mythicist	mouse-deer	nickelled	nightfall	nummuline	nephritic
matriliny	mouse-hole	nucleolar	night-rail	nummulite	nephritis
mitriform	mouse-trap	nucleolus	night-cart	nonpareil	neptunium
matrimony	mouse-hunt	nickelous	nightmary	nunnation	Neptunian
matriarch	mouth-made	nucleated	night-bell	nonparous	Neptunist
matricula	mouthwash	nictitate	night-gear	non-access	narrative
Mytilidae	mouth-harp	Nickie-ben	nightwear	non-member	normalise
metalline	mouthable	noctiluca	nightless	nonce-word	normative
metallise	mouthless	nicompoop	night-rest	non-person	narration
metalling	mouthfuls	nick-nacky	night-bird	nun's-flesh	nervation
metallist	moudiwart	necrotise	nightfire	nine-holes	normality
metalloid	Mauritius	niccolite	night-line	non-linear	narratory
metal-work	moudiwort	necrology	night-side	nonillion	nor'-easter
matelassé	mournival	necrotomy	night-tide	non-smoker	nervature
mutilated	mausoleum	nocuously	night-time	nanometre	nursemaid
mutilator	mausolean	neck-piece	night-club	nonentity	nurse-tend
metameric	maulstick	necessary	night-robe	non-voting	nerve-cell
mutinying	moustache	nickstick	nightlong	ninepence	nerveless

nurselike	Notonecta	ovalbumin	opercular	overperch	officiant
nurseling	nutjobber	orangeade	overcloud	overpitch	office-boy
Norwegian	natrolite	opal-glass	overcrowd	overpower	olfactive
nor'-wester	nitro-silk	Orangeism	oleaceous	overreach	olfaction
northland	notionist	Orangeman	overcarry	overreact	officinal
northward	notaphily	orang-utan	overcatch	overroast	officious
north-east	notepaper	orange-tip	overcount	oven-ready	olfactory
north-west	notoriety	odalisque	overcover	overrider	offseason
narghilly	nature-god	onanistic	overdraft	overruler	off-centre
northmost	naturally	oratorial	overdress	olecranal	off-chance
northerly	nut-wrench	oratorian	overdight	olecranon	off-the-peg
nerviness	notorious	oratories	overdrive	overripen	offensive
narcissus	Nithsdale	oraculous	okey-dokey	oleo-resin	off-colour
narcotine	Nototrema	orbicular	overdated	overstand	offspring
narcotise	no-trumper	ombudsman	over-exact	overshade	offerable
narrowing	nut-butter	obbligato	open-ended	overstare	Oxfordian
narcotism	neuralgia	oubliette	obeseness	overstate	offertory
narcotist	neuralgic	ombrophil	overexert	overstaff	obfuscate
nervously	naumachia	orchestra	one-legged	overstain	off-stream
Neritidae	neuration	orchestic	Olenellus	overspend	off-street
nurturant	naughtily	oncogenic	ore-rested	open-steek	off-putter
nostalgia	nourisher	Orchideae	open-field	overswell	orgiastic
nostalgic	neurility	orchidist	overflown	oversleep	orgillous
nystagmic	nouriture	oscillate	overflush	oversteer	organical
nystagmus	nauplioid	occulting	overglaze	overswear	organ-pipe
nose-bleed	neuropath	occultism	overgraze	overspent	organzine
naseberry	neuroglia	occultist	oleograph	oversight	organelle
nose-flute	neurology	oecumenic	overgrain	overshine	organised
nastiness	neurotomy	oncometer	overgrass	Odelsting	organiser
nescience	neurogram	obconical	overgreen	overstink	oogenesis
Nestorian	neutrally	occupying	overgreat	overspill	oogenetic
nostology	neutretto	occupance	overgoing	overshirt	oughtness
nose-piece	noviciate	occupancy	overgloom	overskirt	ophiology
nose-wheel	Novocaine®	occipital	overgrown	obeisance	ochlocrat
nitratine	navicular	obcordate	overgorge	overscore	otherness
nitration	novodamus	occurrent	overhaile	overstock	otherwise
notabilia	navigable	occurring	olephilic	overshoot	Ophiuchus
notochord	navigator	oscitancy	overhappy	overstrew	Ophiurida
notedness	novelties	occludent	overhaste	overstuff	ophiuroid
Notodonta	navelwort	occlusive	overhasty	overstunk	oligarchy
Notre-Dame	noveliser	occlusion	obeliscal	overstudy	oxidation
not-headed	novelette	odd-man-out	overinked	oversexed	oviparity
natheless	novennial	oddfellow	obedience	oversized	oviparous
netheless	nevermore	ordinance	overissue	overtrade	olive-yard
nutmegged	novitiate	Oudenarde	overladen	overtrain	olivenite
nutpecker	newsagent	odd-jobber	overlying	overtrick	Origenism
net-veined	newfangle	odd-jobman	overlusty	overtaken	Oliverian
nathemore	newmarket	orderless	ocellated	overtimer	Origenist
nut-weevil	new-fallen	order-book	overmerry	overthrow	oviferous
notifying	news-flash	one-handed	overmatch	overtrump	ovigerous
Notogaeic	newshound	ore-raught	overmount	overtrust	originate
Notogaean	newsiness	operative	oceanides	overtower	orificial
notchback	nowhither	operating	overnight	overvalue	opinioned
nattiness	Newtonian	operation	operosely	overweary	Oriolidae
nuttiness	newsprint	overalled	operosity	overwhelm	oriflamme
nutriment	newspaper	open-armed	onerously	overwrest	orientate
net-winged	new-create	overboard	overpress	overwrite	onion-skin
nitrified	news-stand	overbuild	overpoise	overweigh	onion-eyed
nutritive	news-sheet	overblown	overprize	overwatch	Oligocene
nitriding	news-value	overbound	overpaint	overwound	ovibovine
nutrition	newswoman	open-chain	overprint	offhanded	oligopoly
nitwitted	noxiously	overcheck	overproud	offsaddle	onirology
net-player	Nazaritic	operculum	overproof	officiate	ominously

omissible	oppressor	out-of-work	outgrowth	peace-pipe	Planorbis
omittance	oppugnant	Octogynia	octastich	peacetime	phacoidal
oviductal	opponency	ontogenic	octastyle	place-kick	placoderm
objective	Orpington	octagonal	octostyle	planetoid	phacolite
objection	opportune	octahedra	outstrain	piacevole	piano-wire
objectify	opposable	outlinear	outstrike	plate-room	Platonise
objurgate	ourselves	outrigger	outnumber	pease-soup	phacolith
Ockhamism	oar-footed	outgiving	obtrusive	played-out	Platonism
Ockhamist	obreption	outwitted	obtruding	plane-tree	Platonist
oakenshaw	orris-root	outfitter	obtrusion	prayer-rug	pea-souper
Orleanism	ouroscopy	ontologic	outrunner	placentae	phagocyte
Orleanist	oarswoman	octillion	outlustre	placental	Prakritic
oil-tanker	onslaught	octameter	ovulation	playfully	peat-spade
owl-parrot	obsecrate	optometer	obumbrate	play-going	peat-stack
on-licence	ossicular	optimates	opusculum	plangency	plausible
oil-beetle	oyster-bed	optometry	opulently	playgroup	plausibly
owle-glass	obscenely	oftenness	obviation	peach-palm	praesidia
oil-engine	obscenity	obtundent	obvolvent	peach-blow	play-spell
onlooking	obstetric	ostensive	obvoluted	peach-wood	praiseful
oil-colour	ossifraga	octennial	obvention	peach-tree	peat-smoke
obliquely	ossifrage	obtention	obviously	playhouse	plaustral
obliquity	ossifying	out-and-out	obversely	pharisaic	plantable
oil-burner	obsignate	ostensory	obversion	pratingly	practical
oblivious	oast-house	ortanique	Orwellian	prayingly	practicum
osmometer	obstinate	Octandria	oxy-halide	planisher	plantless
ommatidia	obstinacy	octonarii	oxygenate	platinise	psaltress
osmeteria	obsolesce	ostiolate	oxygenise	placidity	plant-lice
omnibuses	opsomania	osteopath	oxygenous	platinoid	plant-like
oenomania	opsimathy	osteoderm	onychitis	platinous	plantling
oenomancy	obsequent	orthopedy	oxy-iodide	placitory	plaything
oenometer	obsequial	osteogeny	ouzel-cock	pianistic	plant-lore
oenanthic	obsequies	outtongue	phalangid	platitude	psalteria
oenophile	observant	orthotics	phalangal	plackless	plastered
oenophily	obstruent	orthotist	phalanger	pranksome	plasterer
ownerless	oestrogen	outworker	phalanges	prankster	phantasma
ownership	observing	outbounds	placation	pearl-sago	practised
Oenothera	obsessive	orthotone	planarian	pearl-edge	phantasim
ornithoid	obsession	osteotome	planation	pearl-wort	practiser
obnoxious	onsetting	Ostrogoth	Phanariot	pearl-spar	phantasms
Orobanche	obscurant	orthodoxy	pea-jacket	pearl-gray	planuloid
obovately	obscurely	osteology	pharaonic	pearl-grey	plague-pit
ozonation	obscurity	osteotomy	phalarope	pearlitic	plaquette
opobalsam	outlander	orthoepic	placatory	pearl-eyed	play-world
onomastic	outwardly	outrooper	play-actor	plasmodia	pharyngal
opodeldoc	ostracise	outpourer	peasantry	psalmodic	pharynges
ozocerite	outparish	outdoorsy	phalanxes	Phasmidae	pharynxes
ozokerite	ostracism	orthoptic	praecoces	ptarmigan	publisher
ovotestis	Ostracion	out-porter	peat-creel	psalm-book	publicise
omophagia	outbacker	orthoaxis	plaid-neuk	plasmatic	publicist
omophagic	outhauler	octapodic	plate-mark	pragmatic	publicity
orologist	outlaunch	octopodes	plate-rack	psammitic	pubescent
otologist	Ostracoda	outspread	plate-rail	psalm-tune	pickaback
odorously	outmantle	outspring	planetary	plain-darn	pickapack
ororotund	Octobrist	outspoken	peaceable	plainness	packaging
odourless	optically	octaploid	peaceably	plaintful	piccadill
otorrhoea	octachord	octoploid	pease-meal	phaenogam	pictarnie
orography	outredden	optophone	peaseweep	plaintive	peccantly
odontalgy	ostleress	octopuses	peaceless	plaintiff	pack-cinch
orphanage	ottrelite	outerware	phaseless	plainsman	pack-cloth
omphacite	outrelief	outcrafty	placeless	praenomen	pack-drill
orphanism	on-the-spot	outermost	placement	plainsong	pocketful
orpharion	out-sentry	obturator	prayerful	plain-cook	picketing
omphaloid	out-of-date	outtravel	plate-ship	plainwork	pocketing

pickeerer	prelation	phengites	precocity	pignorate	philomath
pacifical	prelatist	pre-shrink	prepollex	pigeon-pea	Philomela
Puck-hairy	plenarily	plethoric	Pteropoda	page-proof	philopena
pack-horse	predacity	peel-house	pheromone	pogo-stick	Philomene
pectinate	prepacked	predicate	paedology	pygostyle	poison-gas
pectineal	prehallux	predicant	phenology	piggyback	poison-ivy
pycnidium	precatory	predikant	poenology	piggy-bank	poison-nut
picnicked	predatory	predigest	pyelogram	philander	poison-oak
picnicker	prefatory	predilect	phenotype	privateer	poisonous
pactional	poetaster	president	preoption	philately	prisonous
peculator	poetastry	precisely	puerperal	plicately	philology
pacemaker	prelature	peevishly	preordain	privately	prison-van
pockmanky	premature	pieridine	preorally	privatise	philogyny
pecuniary	presbyope	poeticise	poetresse	privative	priorship
pecunious	presbyopy	precipice	pleuritic	primatial	primrosed
pecan-tree	presbyter	precisive	Pierrette	plication	pair-royal
pectolite	prescient	presidial	pleuritis	privation	priestess
pictorial	prescribe	poeticism	press-gang	primality	puissance
pictogram	preaching	presidium	press-mark	primarily	priest-rid
pick-purse	prescript	Pteridium	peep-sight	peirastic	puissaunt
packstaff	preachify	puerilism	pleaseman	plicature	point-lace
packsheet	preachily	Phenician	pleasance	primaeval	paintable
pick-thank	preschool	precisian	press-book	poinciana	printable
pack-train	prescious	precision	press-work	princedom	Psittacus
pack-twine	prescutum	prefixion	press-room	princekin	pointedly
pick-tooth	preoccupy	prevision	pleasurer	princelet	paintress
pachyderm	pleadable	puerility	press-stud	principia	pointless
pad-saddle	pre-adamic	plexiform	pier-table	principle	printless
pedicular	pseudonym	pietistic	plentiful	principal	print-shop
Pediculus	pseudopod	prebiotic	prettyish	princesse	pointillé
puddening	pseudaxis	predictor	prettyism	priceless	pointsman
pedigreed	piece-rate	paediatry	plenteous	prideless	painterly
pedagogic	paederast	plenilune	peel-tower	primeness	point-duty
pedagogue	preverbal	plenitude	prejudice	prize-ring	primuline
podagrous	pretended	poeticule	prelusive	price-list	pokeberry
podginess	prebendal	précieuse	prenubile	prize-list	Pekingese
pudginess	pretender	prefigure	presuming	prize-crew	pike-perch
paddle-box	piecemeal	phellogen	preludial	paideutic	poker-face
pedalling	pieceless	pre-employ	preputial	painfully	poker-work
pedal-bone	precedent	pneumonia	prelusion	plightful	pikestaff
pademelon	preselect	pneumonic	prelusory	pair-horse	Pakistani
padymelon	predefine	pneumatic	precurrer	philhorse	pillar-box
pedometer	preterite	pre-emptor	precursor	primipara	polyarchy
pedantise	preceding	pre-engage	pre-exilic	privilege	polyandry
pedantism	predesign	pregnable	pterygial	priciness	palmately
pudendous	preterist	pregnance	pterygium	primitiae	polianite
Pedipalpi	pretermit	pregnancy	pterygoid	primitive	polyamide
pedatifid	pre-vernal	pleonaste	puff-adder	primitial	pulsatile
paddy-bird	predevote	premosaic	pifferari	primitias	pulsative
pre-cancel	piece-work	phenolate	pifferaro	philippic	polyaxial
prelatess	preferred	pterosaur	puffiness	Philister	palladium
prevalent	preferrer	piepowder	puffingly	prickling	pelmanism
phenacite	prehensor	phenomena	puff-paste	prickwood	Palladian
phenakite	paedeutic	Pleiocene	pegmatite	prick-song	palmarian
precative	presentee	prepotent	pugnacity	prick-spur	palmation
predative	precentor	pleiomery	pageantry	phillabeg	palpation
prelatise	preceptor	preconise	pigsconce	phillibeg	pulsation
prelatish	prelector	premonish	pignerate	phialling	pillarist
prefacial	presenter	precocial	pigheaded	Phillyrea	palladous
prelatial	preventer	phelonion	pigmented	paillasse	pulsatory
phenakism	presently	premotion	pigmental	paillette	Pellagrin
prelatism	preserver	prenotion	piggishly	prismatic	pulpboard
predation	pier-glass	prerosion	pug-engine	poignancy	polybasic

phlebitis	palempore	pumiceous	penthouse	penetrate	properdin
palace-car	polymeric	pomoerium	pine-house	punctuate	proceeder
Pulicidae	polemarch	pommelled	panchayat	penetrant	provender
police-dog	polymorph	pummelled	pinnipede	pin-stripe	proneness
pole-clipt	polymasty	pimpernel	pannikell	panatella	phonetism
policeman	polymathy	pemphigus	penniless	punctilio	Pooterism
palm-civet	palankeen	pompholyx	pinkiness	penstemon	prooemium
Paludrine	polonaise	pomposity	punkiness	penitence	prooemion
paludinal	palanquin	pompously	pensively	penitency	phonemics
pilferage	Pulmonata	pome-water	pantingly	punctured	phonetics
pulse-rate	pulmonate	pump-water	penninite	punctated	phonetist
pulse-wave	pulmonary	pantagamy	pontifice	punctator	procerlty
pulseless	pillow-cup	Punjaubee	pantiling	pandurate	propelled
palletise	pilloried	pentarchy	pensility	pendulate	propeller
pelletise	pillorise	panhandle	pencilled	pinnulate	proteinic
polverine	polyonymy	pantaleon	penciller	pen-pusher	provedore
pulverine	polyphase	pantalets	pendicler	penduline	prose-poem
pulverise	polyphagy	pentamery	pontianac	penguinry	processed
pilfering	polypidom	pinnately	pontianak	pendulous	professed
pelletify	polyploid	pentangle	pensioner	pennyland	prowessed
pulverous	polyphone	Pindarise	pantihose	penny-bank	processor
palpebral	polyphony	pin-making	pencil-ore	pentylene	professor
pollen-sac	Polyporus	pennalism	penniform	penny-rent	prolepses
palaestra	polyposis	Pindarism	panniered	penny-wise	prolepsis
polyester	polyptych	pandation	panoistic	penny-post	proleptic
palafitte	pilgrimer	Pindarist	penultima	pennywort	protected
palsgrave	pelorised	pinnacled	panelling	propagate	progestin
polygraph	polarised	pintailed	panellist	prosaical	projector
Polygamia	polariser	Pantaloon	Pan-Slavic	protandry	prorector
polygamic	palfreyed	pentapody	pontlevis	profanely	prosector
Polygynia	palm-sugar	pentalpha	penumbral	prolately	protector
polygenic	Pelasgian	pineapple	pen-and-ink	promachos	protester
polygonal	pulpstone	pentagram	peninsula	probative	protestor
polygonum	palustral	pennatula	pentosane	prolamine	procedure
polyglott	polystyle	panicking	pennoncel	prolative	prosecute
polyhedra	pilot-jack	piña-cloth	penholder	protamine	proselyte
palm-honey	palatable	panic-bolt	pontoneer	phonation	proof-mark
palmhouse	palatably	ponderate	pantoffle	probation	proof-read
palmitate	political	panderess	pantoufle	prolation	proofless
palpitate	politicly	panderism	pansophic	pronation	proof-text
pollinate	polythene	pandemian	pantomime	proration	proffered
pulvinate	pilotless	Pan-German	pentoxide	procacity	profferer
palpitant	pilot-fish	panderous	panlogism	profanity	ploughboy
palmipede	pilot-flag	ponderous	pontonier	phonatory	ploughing
pulpiteer	polytonal	Pentecost	pancosmic	probatory	ploughman
pulpiness	pilot-boat	Pinkerton	pontooner	prolapsus	ploughmen
peltingly	polytypic	pendently	peneplane	prolactin	pronghorn
pollinium	politique	pungently	peneplain	propagule	prongbuck
pallidity	Politburo	pansexual	panoplied	procaryon	prothalli
pulvilled	pullulate	pine-finch	panspermy	prokaryon	prothorax
pulvillio	pollutant	pinafored	Pan-Arabic	procaryot	prothesis
pulvillar	pollutive	panegoism	pen-friend	prokaryot	prophetic
pulvillus	pollution	panegyric	pendragon	proscribe	prothetic
pillicock	polyvinyl	punch-card	panoramic	proscript	poorhouse
pelviform	palaverer	punch-ball	pantryman	proudness	proximate
pelitory	pole-vault	pinchbeck	penurious	proud-pied	profiteer
palliasse	polywater	pantheism	pancratic	Ptolemaic	phoniness
palmistry	polyzoary	pantheist	pen-driver	promenade	prosiness
pulvinule	polyzonal	pinchfist	pond-snail	proletary	procident
palillogy	polyzooid	panthenol	punishing	proveably	prominent
polemical	pompadour	pinchcock	penistone	proseucha	provident
poll-money	pomace-fly	punch-bowl	pint-stoup	proseuche	prolicide
palampore	pomaceous	punch-prop	pint-sized	Provençal	profiting

promising	phosphide	paper-reed	porterage	Persicise	paranymph
prosimian	phosphine	paper-file	porcelain	partition	parenesis
provision	phosphite	paper-girl	parcenary	perdition	phrenesis
profilist	prompting	paper-mill	permeable	partially	phrenetic
prolixity	plot-proof	paper-clip	permeably	persimmon	phrenitic
proximity	prompture	piperonal	persevere	portioned	perinatal
proditory	procreate	paper-coal	porteress	persienne	phrenitis
provisory	procreant	paper-pulp	porbeagle	portioner	parsonage
promissor	propriety	paparazzo	porrenger	porticoed	percolate
psoriasis	prodromic	pipestone	paroemiac	perciform	perforate
protistic	programme	pipe-track	pargeting	paroicous	periodate
psoriatic	prodromal	papeterie	paroemial	porticoes	personage
poodle-dog	prodromus	poppy-head	Parseeism	parsimony	personate
profluent	pyorrhoea	poppy-seed	parhelion	pereiopod	corporate
proclitic	proustite	puppyhood	parcelled	permitted	portolano
proembryo	Proustian	poppycock	permeance	permitter	perforans
phonmeter	phossy-jaw	piquantly	parge-work	partitura	perforant
prognoses	poor's-roll	parrakeet	peraeopod	parfleche	parrot-cry
prognosis	prostrate	permanent	Pernettya	Pyralidae	purposely
proenzyme	proptosis	pargasite	percental	paralogia	personise
prorogate	prostatic	percaline	perfecter	perilling	purposive
photocall	proctitis	pervasive	perfector	paralalia	pardoning
provocant	procuracy	portatile	perverter	perilymph	parsonish
proboscis	promuscis	portative	perfectly	purulence	purdonium
protonema	procuress	purgative	persecute	purulency	personify
photogene	profusely	partaking	perpetual	paralyser	parrot-jaw
photocell	profusion	perradial	perfervid	paralysis	performer
propodeum	prolusion	pervasion	parleyvoo	pyrolysis	personnel
propodeon	pronuclei	purgation	perceiver	paralytic	part-owner
proponent	prolusory	perradius	perfervor	pyrolytic	purloiner
photogeny	propylaea	permalloy	paraffine	pyrolater	parroquet
prolonger	propylene	purgatory	purifying	pyrolatry	periplast
photophil	propylite	Parnassus	paraffiny	paralexia	parapodia
phonolite	prozymite	periaktos	portfolio	paramecia	periphery
prologise	pipe-dream	parabrake	poriferal	paramedic	pyrophone
promotive	pepper-box	parabolic	poriferan	pyramidic	periproct
protogine	puppeteer	parabolas	paragraph	pyramidal	peripetia
protoxide	peppering	peribolos	paragogic	pyramidon	parapeted
provoking	poppering	peribolus	paragogue	pyramides	peripatus
prosodial	Popperian	pure-blood	peregrine	pyromania	paraquito
promotion	pop-record	parabasis	porogamic	pyromancy	partridge
prosodian	pepper-pot	periclase	pyrogenic	poromeric	portreeve
prosodist	popliteal	pericrany	paregoric	paramorph	portrayal
pronounce	pop-singer	pericycle	parchedly	perimorph	portrayer
protozoic	pepticity	paraclete	parchment	paramatta	parasceve
phonopore	papillate	Periclean	Pyrrhonic	parameter	perisperm
protozoan	pupillage	parochine	perchance	perimeter	parischan
protozoon	pupillate	pericline	Parthenon	pyrometer	perishing
phonology	papillary	parochial	porphyria	perimetry	periscian
photocopy	pupillary	pyracanth	percheron	pyrometry	phraseman
phonogram	pipe-light	parecious	porphyrio	paramount	periscope
photogram	papilloma	paracusis	parrhesia	parentage	peristome
photopsia	papillose	parachute	purchaser	perennate	poroscope
proconsul	papillote	parodical	perthitic	paranoeic	pyroscope
provostry	papillous	parodying	porthouse	perinaeal	poroscopy
phonotype	popularly	peridinia	pervicacy	perinaeum	parasitic
phototype	papillule	peridrome	perkiness	Pyrenaean	peristyle
prototype	pipe-layer	paradisic	pertinent	paranoiac	piratical
phonotypy	pipe-organ	paradisal	porwiggle	pyreneite	pyritical
phototypy	peptonise	peridotic	porringer	parenting	part-timer
protogyny	pipsqueak	paradoxal	purringly	perennial	paratonic
phosphate	paper-case	pyridoxin	parricide	perennity	puritanic
phosphene	paperback	paradoxer	partitive		pyrethrum

pyrethrin	pastiness	pituitary	pluralist	powerless	quadratic
parotitis	pestilent	pettiness	Poujadist	power-dive	quaeritur
parataxis	passively	pithiness	plurality	power-loom	quadratus
portulaca	pushingly	pottingar	plumbless	powerboat	quaesitum
permutate	pesticide	pottinger	plumb-line	pixie-hood	quantical
pertusate	passivism	pityingly	pourboire	pixilated	quartzite
perturbed	pessimism	pettishly	plumbeous	pixy-stool	quartzose
pursuable	postilion	petrified	plumb-rule	phylarchy	quartered
perturber	passivist	patricide	pounce-bag	prytaneum	quarterly
persuader	pessimist	pethidine	pounce-box	paysagist	quartette
purpureal	passivity	Petrinism	pound-cake	pay-packet	quartetto
perfumery	postiller	patrician	plumdamas	paymaster	quenching
perfusive	passioned	putridity	plunderer	pay-office	quercetum
porcupine	passional	pettitoes	pauperess	psychical	Quebecker
perfusion	pisciform	petticoat	pauseless	psychogas	Québecois
pertusion	posticous	patrimony	plumeless	psychoses	queue-jump
parbuckle	pisolitic	patriarch	plume-bird	psychosis	querimony
pursuance	post-nasal	pituitrin	pauperise	psychotic	queen-cake
pergunnah	post-natal	patriotic	pauperism	physicism	queen's-arm
perjurous	pastorale	patristic	prunellos	physician	queenless
percussed	pastorate	pot-liquor	plume-moth	physicist	queenship
pertussal	pistoleer	patellate	prudently	physicked	queen-like
percussor	pistolled	pétillant	plus-fours	physic-nut	queen-size
pertussis	pestology	petulance	prudhomme	phyllopod	queenhood
parqueted	piston-rod	petulancy	pouchfuls	phylogeny	queen-post
pirouette	postponer	pottle-pot	pluripara	phytogeny	quebracho
parquetry	push-start	potometer	pausingly	phycology	queerness
Portuguee	pasturage	potentate	poutingly	phytology	questrist
paravaunt	postulate	potential	prudishly	phytotomy	querulous
parkwards	pustulate	patinated	Paulinism	phytotron	quibbling
pyroxylic	postulant	patronage	Paulician	phycocyan	quit-claim
pyroxylin	pustulant	petiolate	Paulinian	pay-gravel	quiverful
pyroxenic	posturist	petrolage	Paulinist	pizzicato	quiverish
parhypate	pasquiler	petroleum	prurience	puzzledom	quinidine
party-call	pustulous	patroness	pruriency	puzzle-peg	quirister
party-wall	post-woman	pythoness	pousowdie	pozzolana	quicksand
party-line	pussyfoot	pathogeny	Plutonism	puzzolana	quickbeam
party-jury	phthalate	patronise	plutonium	qualamdan	quickness
pistareen	phthalein	pothollng	Plutonian	Quakerdom	quick-fire
pascament	pot-hanger	patrolled	Plutonist	quarenden	quicklime
pistachio	pot-waller	petrolled	paulownia	quarender	quickener
piscatory	pot-barley	patroller	plutology	Quakeress	quick-born
piscatrix	pot-valour	pot-boiler	plutonomy	quavering	quickstep
push-chair	pit-sawyer	patrolman	plutocrat	Quakerish	quick-eyed
push-cycle	petechiae	pathology	plumpness	Quakerism	quillwort
pass-check	petechial	patrology	pourpoint	quakiness	quinoline
passement	pothecary	petrology	prussiate	quakingly	quixotism
passenger	putrefied	pot-pourri	plum-stone	qualified	quinquina
passepied	pottering	piteously	poussette	qualitied	quiescent
passerine	pithecoid	petiolule	poult-foot	qualifier	quietness
posterior	putter-out	petersham	poulterer	Quasimodo	quittance
posterity	patiently	paternity	plumulate	quail-call	quietsome
pesterous	pitifully	patercove	plumulose	quail-pipe	quintroon
possessed	pitch-dark	peter-boat	Pavlovian	qualmless	quintuple
possessor	patchable	potassium	pivotally	quadrifid	quintette
passers-by	patchocke	potato-pit	powder-box	quadrigae	quintetto
post-entry	pitchpine	potato-rot	pew-fellow	quarrying	quizzical
pushfully	pitchpipe	petaurine	pawkiness	quadrille	quotative
post-horse	patchwork	petaurist	powellise	quadruman	quotation
post-haste	pitchfork	pot-hunter	powellite	quarryman	quotidian
pesthouse	pitch-tree	pluralise	Powellism	quadruped	quotition
posthouse	patchouli	pluralism	pew-holder	quadruple	road-agent
pasticcio	patchouly	Poujadism	pew-opener	quarry-sap	roadblock

road-borne	rubineous	rocambole	red-tapism	re-enforce	refounder
road-craft	Ribbonism	recomfort	radiation	reed-grass	refluence
readdress	ribbon-man	racing-bit	red-tapist	rye-whisky	regrating
rear-dorse	reblossom	racing-car	radiality	reediness	rigmarole
rear-guard	rebaptise	reconvene	radiatory	reelingly	regicidal
reachable	rebaptism	raconteur	red-carpet	re-edifier	rigidness
rhachides	rubescent	reconnect	radial-ply	reed-knife	rug-headed
rhaphides	rabatment	reconvert	red-haired	rheologic	reguerdon
reachless	rabatting	reconcile	red-rattle	rheumatic	regretful
rearhorse	rebutting	recondite	radiantly	rheometer	rogueship
rhachitis	ribattuta	reconfirm	reductase	rheumatiz	regretted
roadhouse	ribaudred	recension	redecraft	rye-coffee	rigwiddie
reanimate	rybaudrye	Ricinulei	reductant	reed-organ	roguishly
readiness	Richardia	rock-'n'-roll	reducible	rhetorise	rag-picker
roaringly	réchauffé	reconquer	reductive	reef-point	regularly
realising	rectangle	rectorate	redaction	re-entrant	regulator
realistic	Rechabite	rectoress	reduction	rheotrope	regiminal
rear-light	racialism	reckoning	radicular	rheotaxis	regionary
realmless	raciation	rectorial	ridiculer	re-educate	rigwoodie
road-maker	ructation	rock-plant	radically	reflation	regardant
road-metal	racialist	recipient	radicated	refracted	regardful
rearmouse	reclaimer	receptive	ridgeback	refractor	regarding
reasoning	raccahout	recaption	reddendum	ruff-a-duff	registrar
rearousal	rock-brake	reception	red-legged	refection	right-hand
rhapontic	rock-borer	rack-punch	ridge-tile	refectory	rightward
reappoint	rock-basin	rice-paper	redeeming	refreshen	right-bank
rhamphoid	rock-bound	rock-pipit	rudbeckia	refresher	rightable
reapparel	rockcress	rock-perch	red-heeled	rifle-shot	rightless
reacquire	rock-drill	recapture	ridge-bone	rifle-bird	rightness
rearrange	recherché	ricercata	ridge-pole	reflexive	right-wing
rhapsodic	racketeer	ricercare	ridge-rope	raftering	right-down
roadstead	rocketeer	rectrices	redresser	reflexion	righteous
road-sense	recrement	recurrent	red-letter	reflected	rehearing
reassurer	racketing	recursive	ruddiness	reflecter	rehearsal
reactuate	ricketily	recording	redding-up	reflector	rehearser
road-train	recreance	recurring	rodfisher	raffinate	rehousing
roast-beef	recreancy	recursion	red-plague	raffishly	ruination
roast-meat	rice-field	Ricardian	raddleman	ruffianly	rail-borne
reactance	rice-flour	rickstand	reddleman	raffinose	reimburse
readvance	rock-flour	rock-snake	ruddleman	refulgent	rain-bound
ready-made	rice-grain	rock-shaft	redolence	refelling	rainbowed
Rubiaceae	rock-guano	recessive	riddlings	Rafflesia	raincheck
reboation	rice-grass	rickstick	redolency	refinedly	rain-cloud
rubicelle	recognise	recession	redeliver	reflowing	reiterate
rabidness	race-going	rock-solid	redundant	reformade	reiterant
robber-fly	racehorse	recusance	redingote	reformado	raiseable
rubberise	reclinate	racetrack	riding-rod	referable	Rhineodon
rabbeting	recoinage	rock-tripe	radionics	referring	Rhinewine
rabbinate	rockiness	reclusely	red-looked	refurbish	rail-fence
rubricate	rectified	reclusive	red-polled	refurnish	reinforce
rubbishly	reclining	reclusion	radiology	reformism	rain-gauge
rabbinite	rachidial	reclusory	radiogram	reformist	reinhabit
rabbinism	rachidian	recruital	redbreast	refortify	Reichsrat
rubrician	rectifier	recruiter	riderless	referenda	Reichstag
rabbinist	rectitude	recoveree	redescend	reference	rhipidate
rebukable	recalment	recoverer	redstreak	refusable	raininess
rebukeful	recollect	recoveror	redoubted	rufescent	railingly
rubellite	recalesce	rice-water	redevelop	refashion	rhipidium
rebelling	recompact	rockwater	redivivus	refusenik	rhipidion
rebellion	recommend	redhanded	re-examine	refutable	rain-maker
rib-plough	recumbent	radiately	rheochord	refutably	rail-motor
robe-maker	recombine	radialise	re-elevate	refitment	rhizocaul
	recompose	radiative	rue-leaved	refitting	rhizocarp

9 r□u□d

rhizoidal	remercied	rhopalism	repercuss	rusticate	reticence
rhinolith	remarqued	rhotacism	repassage	riskiness	reticency
rhizobium	remissive	roof-board	reposedly	rushiness	rutaceous
Rhizopoda	remission	root-bound	repossess	rustiness	retreaded
rhinology	remissory	rhonchial	reposeful	restively	ratherest
ruinously	remitment	root-cause	rope-soled	raspingly	ratheripe
rain-print	remittent	Rhodesian	repositor	rusticise	rattening
rainproof	remitting	root-eater	repasture	rusticial	ratherish
reinstate	remoulade	roof-guard	reputable	Rosminian	ruthenium
reinstall	rum-runner	root-house	reputably	rusticity	Ruthenian
reinspect	rum-butter	roominess	reputedly	restiform	ratifying
reinspire	removable	rhodolite	repotting	restitute	ruthfully
rain-stone	removably	rhodonite	rope-trick	resultant	rotiferal
rainstorm	Romewards	rhodopsin	rapturise	resoluble	rotograph
reinsurer	ransacker	riotously	rapturist	resilient	retaining
raintight	rentaller	roof-plate	rapturous	resolvent	retribute
roisterer	rune-craft	root-prune	ropeworks	resultful	retrieval
reinvolve	ring-canal	rootstock	repayable	rushlight	retriever
rain-water	ring-cross	rood-tower	repayment	resulting	retaliate
rejection	ring-dance	repeating	Roquefort	resumable	rattlebag
rajahship	rennet-bag	reptation	requester	resembler	rutilated
rejoinder	rendering	Ripuarian	requisite	risk-money	rotundate
rejoicing	ranterism	republish	requiring	rose-noble	retentive
rakehelly	ranzelman	repechage	requicken	rosin-weed	retention
rakeshame	renversed	rapacious	rerebrace	resentful	rotundity
roll-about	ring-fence	repudiate	reradiate	resentive	retinulae
reluctate	ring-gauge	rapidness	reredorse	resonance	retinular
reluctant	ranshakle	rapid-fire	reredosse	Rosinante	retinitis
relieving	rancheria	rope-dance	raree-show	resinosis	rationale
relegable	runcinate	reprehend	rare-earth	resonator	retrodden
religiose	ranginess	represent	rarefying	responder	retrocede
religious	rantingly	replenish	ruralness	resinous	retroject
relenting	ringingly	repletion	reremouse	Russophil	retrovert
relapsing	runningly	ripienist	Ruritania	Raskolnik	retroflex
reliquary	rendition	repressor	Rastafari	responsum	retroussé
reliquiae	rancidity	repugnant	rascaldom	responser	rat-poison
rulership	rantipole	rope-house	ressaldar	responsor	rotaplane
relatival	renfierst	reprimand	rosmarine	rust-proof	ratepayer
relevance	ringleted	replicate	rascalism	resorbent	retardate
relevancy	ring-money	rippingly	rascality	resurgent	retardant
relay-race	ranunculi	reptilian	rascaille	resurrect	retiredly
rampantly	randomise	repairman	raspatory	reserpine	ritornell
remeasure	rancorous	reptiloid	rose-apple	reservist	rotor-ship
remediate	ring-ousel	reprieval	resnatron	restraint	retortive
remedying	rencontre	repellant	restarter	restringe	retorsion
ramfeezle	ring-ouzel	repellent	raspberry	reservoir	retortion
ramifying	rank-rider	repulsive	resection	rostrated	rotatable
remigrate	ringstand	repelling	rosaceous	resistant	retoucher
remainder	ring-shake	repulsion	rose-cross	resistent	rotavirus
rumminess	ring-snake	rope-maker	residuary	resistive	rotavator
rompingly	rune-stave	repentant	residence	rosa-solis	rotovator
rompishly	ring-small	reprobate	residency	rose-topaz	retexture
rampicked	ringsider	reprobacy	residuous	rescuable	Roumanian
Ramillies	renascent	reprocess	rose-elder	reshuffle	Roumansch
remontant	renitency	reproving	rostering	rose-water	rhumb-line
remindful	renouncer	raptorial	russeting	rusty-back	rounceval
romancing	renovator	reproduce	rostellum	ritualise	roundhand
remanence	renewable	reportage	rostellar	ritualism	Roundhead
remanency	rhodanate	reparable	respecter	retiarius	roundness
reminisce	rhodamine	reparably	restfully	ritualist	round-fish
romaniser	rhodanise	reporting	rush-grown	retracted	roundelay
ruminator	rhoeadine	repertory	rasp-house	retractor	roundsman
Rome-penny	rhotacise	reperusal	rest-house	reticulum	round-worm

roundarch	rivetting	slabberer	stapedial	smasheroo	smallness
round-trip	rivet-hole	shadberry	shakerism	spaghetti	small-debt
round-eyed	revivable	soapberry	stapedius	staghound	starlight
rousement	revivably	searching	spagerist	staminate	small-time
route-step	rowdiness	stanching	statelily	sea-girdle	snail-like
roughcast	rewritten	stanchion	slate-club	stamineal	snail-fish
rough-neck	rowel-head	snatchily	stage-play	scaliness	spauld-ill
rough-hewn	rowelling	starchily	sharesman	seaminess	snail-slow
roughness	rowel-spur	star-crost	spadesman	shadiness	stable-man
rough-shod	rowan-tree	standgale	statesman	shakiness	scagliola
rough-draw	row-dow-dow	scald-head	snakewood	slatiness	small-bore
routineer	rewardful	staidness	statehood	snakiness	small-coal
rousingly	rewarding	stand-pipe	spade-bone	soapiness	scalloped
routinism	rix-dollar	scald-fish	scale-work	staginess	small-arms
routinist	Roxburghe	star-drift	slave-fork	suasively	scallawag
Rauwolfia	Rhynchota	stag-dance	spadework	sea-ginger	scallywag
raucously	rhymeless	scaldings	stateroom	soakingly	swallower
routously	rhyme-word	slanderer	shake-down	soaringly	shallowly
roussette	rhymester	scald-crow	slave-born	sparingly	spasmodic
revealing	rhythmise	stander-by	stage-door	staringly	slammakin
revocable	rhythmics	space-band	scale-moss	sea-fisher	stay-maker
revocably	rhythmist	stage-hand	scapegoat	slavishly	stammerer
revictual	rhyolitic	stage-name	snakeroot	scarified	spasmatic
rivalless	roysterer	stalemate	spade-foot	stabilise	spawn-cake
ravelment	ray-fungus	shamefast	shageared	Stagirite	seannachy
rivalship	Rozinante	shakeable	shade-tree	Stalinism	stainless
revulsive	razor-back	shapeable	snare-drum	stasidion	sea-anchor
ravelling	razorable	scare-head	share-crop	scarifier	staunchly
revelling	razor-edge	snakeweed	scarecrow	spagirist	stagnancy
revolting	razor-fish	scale-leaf	slate-gray	stability	star-nosed
revolving	razor-bill	scale-beam	slate-grey	suability	stannator
rivalling	razor-clam	scale-fern	sea-nettle	spadillio	sea-robber
revulsion	sea-canary	scaleless	sea-lentil	spatially	Slavophil
revalenta	seawardly	scapeless	sea-beaten	shamianah	scapolite
revel-rout	shamateur	shadeless	sea-letter	stational	Slavonise
revelator	sea-tangle	shameless	slave-hunt	stationer	sea-roving
revengive	sea-margin	shapeless	snake-cult	staminoid	seasoning
revenging	sea-ranger	slakeless	space-suit	staminode	shadowing
raven-bone	Spatangus	spaceless	scaff-raff	staminody	sialolith
raven-duck	shanachie	spareless	scarfwise	stadia-rod	statolith
river-sand	sea-bather	spareness	scarf-ring	statistic	Slavonian
river-bank	star-anise	staleness	scarfskin	star-jelly	sea-rocket
river-jack	seafaring	stateless	staffroom	stackyard	scatology
river-wall	shamanism	scapement	staff-tree	slack-bake	skatology
reverable	swarajism	statement	staff-duty	slackness	sialogram
river-head	shamanist	soar-eagle	shanghai'd	sparkless	slavocrat
riverweed	swarajist	scavenger	star-grass	stalkless	sea-sorrow
riverless	sea-walled	slave-ship	Shangri-la	starkness	scazontic
reversely	spanaemia	spaceship	spangling	sparkling	sea-bottle
revertive	spanaemic	snakebird	slangular	sharkskin	sea-bottom
riverlike	sea-salmon	scalelike	swan-goose	spark-plug	seaworthy
riverside	scaraboid	scare-line	staggered	shank-bone	statocyst
river-tide	star-apple	shale-mine	staggerer	slack-rope	swampland
reversing	sea-parrot	snakebite	swaggerer	spark-coil	sea-spider
reversion	spadassin	snakelike	slaughter	stack-room	scalpless
river-flat	stalactic	snakewise	star-gazer	stalk-eyed	sharpness
reverence	sea-satyre	space-time	scatheful	small-hand	sharp-shod
river-boat	sea-lawyer	spare-time	Staphylea	small-talk	stamp-mill
revisable	starboard	stateside	sea-change	stable-boy	seal-point
ravishing	scambling	statewide	snaphance	stall-feed	sharpener
rivet-head	shambling	shaveling	swashwork	sea-sleeve	scarpines
revetment	shambolic	slavering	scaphopod	Stahlhelm	shampooed
revetting	swag-belly	scale-fish	slap-happy	shawlless	stamp-note

star-proof
scalp-lock
scamp-work
shampooer
snapper-up
stag-party
scarpetti
scarpetto
scaup-duck
stamp-duty
sharp-eyed
sea-squill
sea-squirt
staircase
sea-breach
sea-orache
stairhead
sea-breeze
stair-well
sea-dragon
sea-urchin
stairwise
sea-orange
stair-work
stairfoot
sea-island
slab-sided
sparsedly
star-shell
slaistery
starshine
seat-stick
slapstick
slabstone
soapstone
star-stone
swans-down
swansdown
Scansores
sea-strand
swart-back
slantways
smart-weed
scantness
shaftless
smartness
swartness
slantwise
sparteine
scantling
startling
startlish
smart-alec
shantyman
spartanly
scattered
shattered
scart-free
sparterie
scatterer
smatterer
slant-eyed
spatulate

scapulary
statutory
sea-turtle
statuette
star-wheel
stalworth
soapworks
scaly-bark
seamy-side
Stagyrite
spagyrist
subcaudal
subwarden
subjacent
sabbatine
sabbatise
submarine
sabbatism
Sabianism
sublation
subfamily
subsacral
subvassal
subcantor
suboctave
subscribe
subaction
subscript
subocular
sebaceous
sabadilla
subeditor
subtenant
subdeacon
subgenera
submerged
sublethal
subsecive
sabre-wing
subaerial
subregion
subseries
subsellia
subneural
submersed
sublessee
subversal
sublessor
subjected
submental
submentum
subletter
subverter
suboffice
subagency
subahdary
subahship
subphylum
sublimate
subniveal
subnivean
sublinear
sublimely

subtilely
subtilety
sobbingly
subdivide
sublimise
subsidise
subtilise
subliming
subtilist
sublimity
subtility
submicron
submissly
submitted
sob-sister
submitter
sobriquet
subaltern
Sibylline
subalpine
Sabellian
Sibyllist
sibilance
sibilancy
subclause
subentire
subincise
subungual
subrogate
subtopian
subsoiler
subnormal
subpoena'd
subdolous
subcostal
se-baptist
soberness
subursine
subbranch
subtropic
subarctic
sybaritic
subastral
substrata
substrate
substract
substylar
subatomic
substance
substruct
subjugate
sublunate
sublunary
subduable
subduedly
subsultus
sacrament
siccative
socialise
socialite
sociative
Socratise
sectarial

sacrarium
socialism
sectarian
socialist
sociality
sick-berth
sackcloth
secretage
secretary
societary
sachemdom
succeeder
secretive
sickening
socketing
secretion
secretory
successor
succentor
saccharic
Saccharum
saccharin
sick-house
succinate
sacrilege
sickishly
sacrifice
succinite
sectility
sectional
sacciform
sacristan
siciliana
sick-leave
siciliano
sickleman
secularly
secondary
second-day
secundine
sick-nurse
sociopath
succotash
sectorial
suctorial
sociology
sociogram
succourer
sycophant
securable
secernent
securance
securitan
secession
sick-tired
secateurs
succulent
seclusive
succubine
seclusion
succubous
succursal
sideboard

side-bones
side-burns
side-chain
seductive
seduction
sedgeland
sedge-bird
sedge-wren
side-issue
saddle-bag
saddle-bar
saddle-bow
sidelight
saddle-lap
saddle-pin
sudaminal
sodomitic
sedentary
sudorific
siderosis
sideritic
sideswipe
soda-scone
side-track
side-table
seditious
Sadducean
Sadducism
side-wheel
sidewards
soda-water
skedaddle
stewardry
scenarise
steradian
scenarist
stewartry
shewbread
stepbairn
speechful
stepchild
sketchily
speechify
sterculia
seed-coral
stercoral
sheldrake
speed-ball
steadfast
spendable
speedwell
speedless
steadiest
speldring
steadying
seed-drill
step-dance
speed-boat
slenderly
speedster
shelduck
scelerate
shebeener

stevedore
sieve-tube
shelf-mark
seed-field
shelf-life
shelfroom
step-fault
sleighing
Shechinah
seediness
spewiness
seemingly
specified
sterilise
sherifian
sterility
specially
specialty
sneak-raid
speak-easy
speakable
sheikhdom
sleekness
speckless
sneck-draw
shell-sand
steelyard
steel-ware
shellback
shellbark
shell-marl
spellable
spellican
shell-heap
shell-less
smell-less
seemliest
seemlihed
spellbind
shellfire
shell-like
shell-lime
shellfish
spellikin
steel-clad
steel-blue
stellular
shell-hole
speal-bone
shellwork
steelwork
steel-wool
spelldown
Stellaria
smell-trap
steel-trap
steel-gray
steel-grey
stellated
shellduck
steam-haul
sperm-cell
steamship

steam-pipe	skeesicks	signatory	scholarly	snivelled	spiritual
steam-dome	sneeshing	sage-apple	schematic	spider-leg	spirituel
steam-coal	step-stone	sigmatron	sphenodon	sniveller	stink-ball
steamboat	sweet-gale	signature	sphendone	spider-man	slinkweed
steam-port	sweet-talk	signboard	sphincter	sciaenoid	slickness
spermaria	swept-back	sagebrush	school-age	swinehood	stink-bird
steam-trap	skew-table	sagacious	schoolbag	seine-boat	slinkskin
spermatia	spectacle	segregate	schoolboy	shire-moot	stink-bomb
spermatic	sceptical	signeurie	school-day	slide-rule	stink-wood
spermatid	sheet-bend	segmented	schoolery	spice-bush	stinkhorn
sternward	sheet-lead	segmental	schooling	spike-rush	shickered
stern-fast	sweetmeal	suggester	schnorkel	spider-web	stink-trap
sternebra	scentless	sage-green	schoolman	stiff-neck	shield-bug
sternness	sweetness	sogginess	schnorrer	stiffness	still-head
steenkirk	sweetmeat	sighingly	schnozzle	skinflick	skill-less
steinbock	sheathing	signified	spherical	skinflint	stillness
sternmost	sheat-fish	signifier	spherular	skilfully	still-life
sternport	sweetfish	significs	schistose	stiffener	spillikin
stern-post	sweet-flag	sigillate	schistous	sail-fluke	shillelah
stegnosis	sweetener	sigillary	schizopod	ship-fever	shield-may
stegnotic	sweetwood	sagenitic	spiration	skiagraph	still-room
sternitic	sweet-corn	segholate	spirality	sling-back	still-born
stenopaic	sweetwort	sigmoidal	stirabout	swing-back	shielduck
stegosaur	sheltered	Signorina	spiraster	stingless	still-hunt
stegodont	sweltered	signorial	spiracula	sling-shot	spillover
stegomyia	sheet-iron	sagapenum	sailboard	shingling	swimmable
stenotype	shelterer	sugar-cane	shipboard	sniggling	seismical
stenotypy	steatosis	sugar-palm	slip-board	swingeing	sciamachy
shemozzle	steatitic	sugar-bean	sail-broad	swingling	skiamachy
sheep-wash	spectator	sugarless	sail-borne	swing-wing	ship-money
sheepwalk	speculate	sugar-beet	soil-bound	sting-fish	Stigmaria
sweepback	sleeve-dog	sugar-mite	slip-coach	swing-door	swimmeret
seed-pearl	sleeve-nut	sugar-pine	stitchery	swingboat	stigmatic
seed-plant	skew-whiff	sugar-mill	stitching	stingaree	sciential
sheep's-bit	sneeze-box	sugar-plum	switching	swingtree	scientism
sheep-scab	safranine	sugar-ally	switchman	sniggerer	scientist
sheep's-eye	softening	sugar-loaf	ship-canal	sting-bull	spinnaker
sleepless	suffering	sugar-cube	sail-cloth	stichidia	seigniory
steepness	safeguard	sugar-lump	ski-school	slightish	seignoral
sheepmeat	soft-grass	sagittate	spindling	sticheron	spinneret
sheep-lice	soft-goods	sagittary	swindling	stipitate	sgian-dubh
sheep-tick	siftingly	sight-read	spin-drier	soi-disant	sailor-hat
sheepskin	sufficing	sightseer	spindrift	spicilege	slivovica
sheepfold	Sufiistic	sightless	skin-diver	sliminess	spilosite
sheep-cote	safflower	sight-line	spin-dryer	soiliness	sailoring
sheep-hook	soft-nosed	sight-sing	spikenard	spiciness	skijoring
steep-down	suffocate	sight-hole	spice-cake	spikiness	Spinozism
spearhead	soft-pedal	schiavone	spike-nail	spininess	Spinozist
sweirness	soft-paste	schnapper	swineherd	spiritful	spinosity
spear-side	suffragan	schmaltzy	swivel-eye	spirit-gum	slivovitz
shearling	saffroned	schnauzer	shineless	shiningly	slivowitz
steerling	soft-shell	sphacelus	smileless	slidingly	sailor-man
spearfish	sofa-table	scheduled	snideness	smilingly	ship-owner
spearmint	safety-net	scheelite	spineless	swinishly	Spirogyra
steersman	safety-pin	sphaerite	spireless	ski-kiting	shimozzle
speerings	suffusion	schlemiel	slide-rest	spiriting	sailplane
speirings	signal-box	schlemihl	swivel-gun	spiritism	stippling
spear-wood	signalise	sphygmoid	spirewise	spiritist	slippered
swear-word	sigmatism	sphagnous	shivering	spirillum	ship-pound
spearwort	sigmation	schlieren	snipe-fish	spirillar	Sciaridae
shear-hulk	signalled	scholiast	spike-fish	spiniform	Sciuridae
sheer-hulk	signaller	schilling	swine-fish	spiritoso	scirrhoid
seed-stalk	signalman	scholarch	Spigelian	spiritous	scirrhous

shipshape	selachian	salimeter	semi-angle	symbolist	synoecise
skiascopy	selection	self-moved	summarise	symbolled	sonneting
sciosophy	salicylic	shlimazel	summative	semiology	sundering
scissorer	select-man	salangane	semi-Arian	symbology	synoecism
shirt-band	salacious	splendent	summation	someplace	sanbenito
shirt-tail	siliceous	splintery	simpatico	semaphore	sonnetist
sciatical	silicious	splendour	summarist	semiplume	sincerity
stiltedly	solacious	selenious	summarily	semi-rigid	sunbeamed
stintedly	silicosis	selenitic	semibreve	Samaritan	sun-helmet
shiftless	silicotic	splenetic	semi-bajan	sumpsimus	Sanhedrim
shirtless	salicetum	solenette	semicolon	somascope	Sanhedrin
skirtless	solicitor	splenitis	simpering	semestral	sinlessly
stintless	solidness	Sellotape®	summering	Semi-Saxon	sun-beaten
swiftness	self-drive	saloon-bar	sommelier	sumptuary	songfully
skin-tight	self-doubt	saloon-car	symmetric	something	sangfroid
saintship	spleenful	salmon-fly	symmetral	sometimes	sand-grain
stilt-bird	silver-fir	salmon-fry	summerset	semitonic	sand-glass
saintlike	silver-fox	syllogise	Simmental	sumptuous	sand-grass
saintling	solfeggio	sallowish	semifinal	symptosis	synagogue
Shintoism	silverise	syllogism	semifluid	symptotic	synagogal
Shintoist	silvering	saloonist	semigrand	semivowel	synchrony
scintilla	soldering	salmonoid	symphonic	somewhere	synchysis
sainthood	spleenish	sole-plate	symphysis	somewhile	syntheses
shift-work	solferino	sale-price	symphytic	Samoyedic	synthesis
saintfoin	sallee-man	solipsism	Symphytum	sink-a-pace	synthetic
swift-foot	syllepses	solipsist	sempitern	sandarach	syndicate
shirt-stud	syllepsis	self-pious	summing-up	Sinhalese	sandiness
spiculate	Salientia	salopette	symbiosis	sinuately	sunniness
spinulate	sylleptic	saltpetre	semeiotic	sennachie	sentiment
stimulate	saliently	siliquose	symbiotic	sunbather	Sinningia
stipulate	self-faced	Siluridae	simulcast	sin-eating	singingly
stimulant	Solifugae	salt-rheum	semblable	sensation	sensitise
stipulary	salifying	sclereide	semblably	sinuation	sensitive
spinulose	silk-gland	sclerosed	simulacra	sandalled	sunrising
spinulous	salt-glaze	sclerosis	simulacre	sun-parlor	sensilium
shipwreck	silk-grass	sclerotia	simplices	suntanned	sons-in-law
sojourner	sylph-like	sclerotic	semblance	sing-along	sentience
sokemanry	sulphonic	sclerotal	semi-lunar	syngamous	sentiency
solfatara	sulphuric	saleratus	similarly	sans-appel	synoicous
self-aware	salt-horse	scleritis	simpliste	syntactic	single-end
sultanate	sulphuret	sales-talk	simulated	syndactyl	Sinologue
syllabary	sulphatic	self-slain	simpleton	sand-blast	synclinal
sultaness	self-image	saleslady	simulator	sand-break	singleton
sulcalise	Sylviidae	splashing	semilatus	sand-blind	sunflower
syllabise	saltiness	salesgirl	semi-metal	sand-crack	sand-mason
sylvanite	silkiness	splashily	semanteme	songcraft	synanthic
syllabism	silliness	siltstone	semuncial	song-cycle	synangium
saltation	sulkiness	salt-spoon	semantics	synectics	synonymic
salvation	saltishly	seldshown	seminally	synodical	syncopate
siltation	selfishly	self-study	simonious	synedrial	santolina
solvation	sylvinite	Solutrean	semantron	synedrium	santonica
sulcation	Sylviinae	spluttery	simon-pure	synedrion	Senhorita
syllabics	salpiform	solitaire	somnolent	synodsman	Sanforise
syllabify	soldierly	splitting	symposiac	sand-dance	sensorial
syllabled	soliloquy	Solutrian	Simeonite	sand-devil	sensorium
saltatory	solemness	self-trust	symbolise	sonnetary	seniority
salvatory	solemnise	spleuchan	sympodial	sentencer	sinuosity
salvarsan	solemnify	Seljukian	symposial	sinoekete	sun-lounge
self-abuse	solemnity	self-wrong	symbolism	synoecete	sun-downer
self-begot	Salomonic	salt-works	sympodium	sonneteer	sun-bonnet
salubrity	Solomonic	salt-water	symposium	senseless	syntonous
self-borne	salt-money	sallyport	semiotics	sincerely	sinuously
selective	salt-marsh	splay-foot	symbolics	sonnetise	syncoptic

synaptase	spot-check	spokesman	stockless	sponsible	supremely
synapheia	sconcheon	smoke-bomb	stock-whip	shoeshine	septemfid
sand-pride	slouch-hat	scolecoid	stockpile	sponsalia	supremity
Sinophile	scorching	stokehold	stockfish	snowstorm	septennia
Sinophily	slouching	stone-cold	stock-list	shorthand	sapiently
sandpaper	stoically	stoke-hole	stockinet	shortcake	septemvir
sandpiper	Scotchman	stonework	stock-dove	short-wave	sapphired
sun-spurge	sword-hand	stone-coal	stock-lock	shortfall	sappiness
sentry-box	sword-cane	smoke-room	stockwork	snort-mast	soppiness
sun-bright	sword-rack	storeroom	stock-room	shootable	syphilise
synergism	sword-tail	shore-boat	shoal-mark	sportable	septicity
synergist	sword-bean	stonewort	spoil-bark	short-term	syphiloma
syndromic	swordless	shore-crab	stoolball	shortness	syphiloid
syneresis	sword-belt	smoke-tree	spoil-heap	sportless	septimole
syncretic	swordlike	stonecrop	shoalness	spoutless	septiform
sand-snake	swordfish	score-draw	shouldest	stoutness	sophistic
senescent	sword-bill	smoke-bush	spotlight	scouthery	sophister
seneschal	snowdrift	snowflake	shoalwise	short-life	sophistry
songsmith	spondulix	sootflake	spoil-five	short-time	suppliant
singspiel	swordplay	snowfield	spoilsman	smoothing	supplicat
sandstone	swordsman	snowfleck	storm-sail	Storthing	sepulchre
sand-storm	sword-knot	snowflick	stormless	smoothish	supplying
sand-spout	score-card	snow-finch	storm-beat	short-list	sepulture
sinistral	shoreward	shop-floor	storm-belt	short-slip	sapan-wood
sand-screw	stone-hard	shop-front	storm-bird	sportsman	Saponaria
sinusitis	spore-case	shotfirer	storm-wind	sportance	supinator
sanctuary	stoneware	snow-guard	shoemaker	shortener	siphonage
sand-table	smoke-jack	sponge-bag	showmanly	spout-hole	siphonate
sunstroke	stone-hawk	snow-goose	storm-cone	shortgown	saprolite
sanitaria	smoke-ball	spongiose	storm-cock	short-horn	sepiolite
sunstruck	smoke-sail	spongeous	slow-march	sloethorn	supposing
sensually	stonewall	spongious	storm-drum	short-coat	saprozoic
sunburned	store-farm	sloggorne	slow-match	stouthrie	sophomore
synovitis	stone-cast	soothfast	slot-meter	short-stop	sapi-outan
sinewless	shore-weed	sloth-bear	storm-stay	shot-tower	supporter
sand-yacht	stone-dead	soothlich	spoonways	scopulate	supermart
syncytial	stone-deaf	shophroth	spoon-bait	shogunate	supersalt
syncytium	stone-cell	smothered	spoon-feed	sporulate	separable
sannyasin	shoreless	sloghorne	spoonmeat	spodumene	superable
synizesis	smokeless	smotherer	spoonwise	snow-white	separably
sporangia	stoneless	slow-hound	spoonbill	shopwoman	superably
stomachic	shovelful	sporidesm	stownlins	stop-watch	supersede
stomached	showerful	showiness	stornelli	snow-water	supervene
stomachal	store-ship	smokiness	stornello	scolytoid	superheat
stomacher	shovel-hat	snowiness	spoon-food	story-book	soporific
sloganise	stonechat	sootiness	spoon-hook	storyette	superfine
Slovakish	stoneshot	stoniness	scoundrel	sforzando	superhive
Slovakian	scolecite	slopingly	scotomata	smorzando	supervise
shopboard	shoreline	Scotified	sporocarp	Sephardic	superbity
shoeblack	shore-side	sporidial	sporogeny	Sephardim	superplus
showbread	slopewise	sporidium	scorodite	septarium	superflux
snow-break	spokewise	scorifier	sporocyst	septarian	supernova
snow-blind	stone-pine	'sbodikins	show-place	septation	supercold
snow-blink	stove-pipe	stolidity	snow-plant	sopranino	superpose
slop-built	showering	scoliosis	slow-paced	sopranist	supercool
scombroid	stonefish	scoliotic	Scorpaena	sapraemia	separatum
snow-broth	stone-mill	Scotistic	showpiece	sapraemic	separator
snow-berry	Slovenian	storiated	stop-press	sapidless	superstar
slop-basin	stone-lily	storiette	scorpioid	sapodilla	superfuse
scorbutic	sooterkin	spoliator	shot-proof	septenary	suppurate
snow-bound	shovelled	stockyard	slop-pouch	supremacy	siphuncle
shoe-brush	shoveller	smock-race	snowscape	September	sapsucker
slowcoach	shoresman	shock-head	soopstake	sapheaded	septuplet

sequacity	streetage	servitude	Sarcodina	serpulite	sitzkrieg
sequester	street-boy	stroke-oar	sermonise	shrouding	settle-bed
sarbacane	street-car	strikeout	sorrowing	sprouting	satellite
seriately	surrender	strike-pay	sermonish	strouding	satanical
serialise	surrendry	surpliced	sartorial	surmullet	satin-bird
stream-ice	sorceress	scrollery	sardonian	surculose	satinwood
screaming	surgeless	shrilling	sartorian	scrivener	satin-spar
spreading	streetful	strolling	Serbonian	straw-yard	satinetta
streaking	sore-eagle	scroll-saw	sartorius	screwball	satinette
streaming	screecher	scrimmage	Sorbonist	screw-nail	sitiology
surfacing	serrefile	scrummage	sarcology	strawless	saturable
serialism	screeding	skrimmage	seriously	strewment	satirical
Syriacism	screening	scrum-half	sarcoptic	screw-pile	satyrical
Syrianism	screeving	stramaçon	Sarcoptes	screw-pine	Satyridae
Sarmatian	shrieking	scrimshaw	scrap-yard	screw-wise	saturnine
seriation	surveying	shrimping	scrippage	shrew-mice	saturnism
serration	surveille	strumming	strap-game	scrawling	Saturnian
sortation	surreined	scrimply	strap-hang	sprawling	saturnist
striation	sergeancy	scrambler	strappado	straw-rope	suturally
serialist	serjeancy	shrimp-net	strip-leaf	screw-worm	Satyrinae
seriality	serjeanty	stromatic	scrap-heap	straw-worm	saturated
streakily	surgeoncy	strumatic	strapless	screw-down	saturator
streamlet	shriek-owl	strumitis	scrape-gut	screw-bolt	satisfied
serranoid	surrejoin	stramazon	seraphine	straw-stem	satisfier
sorb-apple	sorcerous	springald	strip-mine	strayling	Soudanese
sarcastic	surfeited	shrinkage	scrapping	sassarara	squeakery
stream-tin	sarmentum	strongarm	strapping	sussarara	squeaking
surmaster	surfeiter	spring-bed	stripling	Sassanian	squealing
servantry	serpentry	string-bag	stripping	sustained	squeamish
serrature	streetway	springbok	stropping	sustainer	squeakily
striature	shroffage	spring-box	seraphims	saskatoon	scumbling
scrubland	strifeful	strong-box	seraphins	sassafras	squibbing
surf-board	sgraffiti	serenader	scrappily	systaltic	squabbish
scribable	sgraffito	syringeal	scrap-book	Sassenach	squabbler
shrubless	serigraph	stringent	strap-work	sisserary	slumbrous
shrubbery	spragging	strongest	strapwort	suspended	slumberer
scrub-bird	sprigging	strangely	scriptory	suspendor	scuncheon
scrubbing	strigging	spring-gun	scrap-iron	systemise	scutcheon
strobilae	scraggily	springing	scripture	sistering	scutching
scrabbler	straggler	sprinting	surprised	suspensor	sour-crout
scribbler	struggler	stringing	surprisal	sestertia	soul-curer
strobilus	sprightly	strongish	surpriser	suspected	sound-wave
scrub-fowl	scrog-bush	strontium	strossers	susceptor	soundless
Soricidae	scrog-buss	springily	stressful	sostenuto	soundness
sprechery	Syrphidae	strenuity	seraskier	sash-frame	sound-film
spruce-fir	surcharge	stringily	spritsail	suscitate	scuddaler
strictish	sortilege	sprinkler	scrutable	sustinent	sound-hole
spreckled	sorriness	strangler	soritical	suspicion	squadrone
strychnia	surliness	strangles	spriteful	sessional	sound-post
Saracenic	servilely	springlet	strategic	sisal-hemp	sound-body
strychnic	sortilegy	strongman	stratagem	sassolite	sour-dough
surf-canoe	surcingle	strenuous	stretched	Sisyphean	spulebane
sericeous	straining	Stringops	scratcher	susurrant	saucer-eye
sericitic	surmising	string-pea	stretcher	sasquatch	souteneur
stricture	surviving	serinette	scrutoire	satiation	saucerful
structure	surficial	string-tie	strutting	situation	stupefied
sorediate	servilism	strangury	stratonic	setaceous	sousewife
shredless	Sardinian	strongyle	serotonin	satedness	squeezing
shredding	sortition	sarcomata	scrutator	sutteeism	stupefier
stridling	servility	surrogate	serrulate	setter-off	scutellum
scroddled	spraickle	sarcocarp	surquedry	setter-out	scutellar
stridence	serricorn	sermoneer	scrounger	sottishly	Sauternes
stridency	serviette	sorrowful	sprauchle	sottisier	spulebone

sauce-boat	soupspoon	styptical	tradition	Tubularia	treachour
sou'-wester	squatness	sizarship	thankless	tabularly	theaceous
studentry	squatting	tea-garden	trackless	tubulated	tierceron
smug-faced	shuttered	thanatism	trackroad	tubulator	treadling
shuffling	saunterer	thanatist	track-boat	Tabanidae	treadmill
snuffling	sputterer	travailed	trawl-line	tubercled	thereness
snuff-dish	stutterer	thanatoid	trawl-fish	tubercule	Thelemite
snuff-mill	spur-whang	thalassic	traumatic	tabasheer	therewith
soulfully	spur-wheel	tea-taster	train-band	tabescent	thereinto
stuff-gown	squawking	tway-blade	trainable	tube-skirt	thereunto
snuff-mull	sovietise	trancedly	twa-lofted	tabbyhood	therefore
sluggabed	sovietism	thatching	traipsing	toccatina	tregetour
slung-shot	savagedom	tray-cloth	trampling	Tocharish	thereupon
smuggling	Sivaistic	twaddling	trampolin	Tocharian	therefrom
stud-groom	seventeen	tradename	trappings	ticket-day	thereaway
sour-gourd	seventhly	tragelaph	twalpenny	tactfully	twelfthly
southland	seventies	trademark	translate	tackiness	theogonic
southward	sovenance	traceable	trap-stair	tactician	trepidant
south-east	sevenfold	traceably	transcend	tactilist	theriacal
south-west	severable	traceless	tear-shell	tacticity	thegither
Southdown	sovereign	tradeless	tear-sheet	tactility	taeniasis
Southroun	severally	thaneship	transient	tectiform	treillage
southmost	severalty	traceried	transvest	tacamahac	theologic
slughorne	severance	teaseling	transship	technical	theologue
stud-horse	savourily	trapesing	transpire	technique	theologer
southerly	sow-gelder	tsarevich	trap-stick	tycoonate	tree-lined
studiedly	sexvalent	trapezial	transumpt	tycoonery	trellised
sauciness	sexualise	trapezium	transenna	tectorial	thermical
sourishly	sexualism	tragedian	transonic	tectonics	theomachy
squailing	sexualist	trapezius	toad-stone	tachogram	Thermidor
stupidity	sexuality	teaselled	transmove	tectrices	thermally
scutiform	sextantal	travelled	transpose	tacitness	theomania
saucisson	sixteenth	teaseller	toadstool	tactually	theomancy
skunk-bird	sixteenmo	traveller	transform	tachylite	thermotic
squalidly	sixteener	tradesman	transport	tachylyte	tie-and-dye
squelcher	Saxifraga	thanehood	transfuse	tediosity	'tween-deck
squalling	saxifrage	trapezoid	transhume	Tod-lowrie	theandric
squamella	sex-change	traversed	transmute	tediously	tremolant
scummings	sex-linked	traverser	toast-rack	tide-table	treponema
squamosal	sex-kitten	trabeated	tractable	tide-water	tremolite
Sturnidae	sexennial	tea-kettle	traitress	toddy-palm	tree-onion
squint-eye	sextoness	travertin	twattling	teddy-bear	trefoiled
squinting	six-footer	toad-eater	trattoria	toe-ragger	therology
squinancy	sex-appeal	trabecula	traitorly	theralite	theophagy
snub-nosed	saxophone	tearfully	tractator	therapist	theophany
Sauropoda	sextuplet	tear-gland	teacupful	trepanned	theopathy
stuporous	skyjacker	toad-grass	traguline	trepanner	tee-square
soup-plate	scybalous	twangling	traducing	Trematoda	thearchic
stump-work	say-master	Thargelia	Traducian	trematoid	theorbist
sculpture	spymaster	Tracheata	tablature	trematode	theurgist
squireage	styleless	tracheate	tubicolar	thenabout	tredrille
squiredom	style-book	tracheary	tubectomy	thesaurus	theorique
squirting	soya-flour	teachable	tableland	therapsid	theoriser
square-leg	scytheman	teachless	table-maid	tremblant	theoretic
squiralty	Scyphozoa	tracheide	table-ware	trembling	tree-snake
souari-nut	stylishly	tea-things	table-talk	Theobroma	theosophy
squarrose	sky-diving	Trachinus	table-leaf	trenchand	tressured
scurriour	styliform	trashtrie	table-beer	trenchard	treasurer
squirarch	stylistic	trachytic	tablewise	trenchant	tree-shrew
soubrette	stylobate	trachitis	table-book	theocracy	Thersitic
spur-rowel	sky-rocket	twalhours	table-work	theocrasy	treatable
spur-royal	sky-colour	teasingly	tubbiness	treachery	twentieth
squashily	sky-troops	traditive	tabellion	tiercelet	treatment

twentyish	tri-weekly	triangled	tellingly	timenoguy	tendinous
theatrics	tribesman	trionymal	toluidine	tomentose	tan-liquor
theotokos	twice-told	Triandria	Telamones	tomentous	tent-maker
theftbote	twice-born	trilobate	telemeter	tamponade	tonometer
theftuous	trimerous	trifocals	telemetry	tamponage	tuning-key
theftboot	trihedral	tailoress	teleosaur	temporary	tuning-peg
twenty-two	trihedron	Trilobita	tallow-dip	temporise	tuning-pin
tree-trunk	toilet-set	trilobite	tallowish	tambourin	tentorial
tremulate	tridented	tailoring	tol-lolish	timeously	tonsorial
tremulant	tridental	trinomial	teleology	timepiece	tentorium
trebuchet	trimester	trifolium	teleonomy	timorsome	tenuously
tremulous	trisector	triforium	Teleostei	timescale	tin-opener
Teeswater	thin-faced	twiforked	talbotype	time-sheet	tenor-clef
tie-dyeing	thief-like	triformed	telophase	tumescent	tungstate
thelytoky	thingness	twiformed	telepheme	tombstone	tunesmith
tufaceous	thingummy	tricolour	tulip-wood	temptable	tinguaite
tegmental	thinghood	trigonous	telephone	timetable	Tungusian
tegmentum	tritheism	tribology	telephoto	temptress	tonguelet
tug-of-love	tritheist	tailplane	telephony	tommy-shop	tank-wagon
tuggingly	trichinae	twin-plane	tulip-root	tantarara	tunny-fish
tegularly	trichroic	tailpiece	telephony	tantalate	two-handed
tegulated	thigh-bone	trierarch	tulip-tree	Tantalean	two-hander
tiger-tail	trichrome	tricrotic	telepathy	tonga-bean	troparion
tiger's-eye	trichosis	thirstful	tolerable	tonka-bean	two-masted
tiger-lily	trichitic	thirstily	tolerably	tantalise	two-parted
tiger-wood	Tripitaka	twin-screw	tularemia	tantalite	two-master
tiger-wolf	triticale	twistable	tularemic	tentative	troubling
tiger-moth	trilinear	thirtieth	tolerance	ting-a-ling	troublous
tight-lace	twiningly	taintless	tolerator	tantalism	trot-cosey
tightness	trilithic	thirtyish	telestich	Tantalian	two-headed
tightener	trilithon	triatomic	telescope	tentation	two-leafed
tight-knit	triticism	taint-worm	tile-stone	tentacled	two-legged
tight-rope	trivially	triptyque	telescopy	tanka-boat	two-decker
tahsildar	tuitional	trieteric	tellurate	tentacula	trowelled
trivalent	think-tank	twitterer	telluride	tenebrism	troweller
trifacial	thinkable	tribunate	tellurise	tenebrist	twoseater
triradial	thickhead	triturate	tellurite	tenebrity	two-leaved
trihadism	thickness	tributary	tellurium	tenebrose	thoughted
tribalism	trickling	tribunite	tellurian	tint-block	thoughten
trisagion	twinkling	tripudium	tellurion	tenebrous	toothwash
tribalist	thick-lips	tricuspid	Talmudist	tenaculum	toothache
trigamist	thickskin	triquetra	tellurous	tent-cloth	Trochidae
trigamous	triskelia	tridymite	televisor	tenacious	trochlear
tridactyl	thick-knee	trigynian	tallyshop	tunicated	toothless
trivalved	thickener	tricyclic	timpanist	tinder-box	trothless
tail-board	tricksome	tricycler	tympanist	tenseness	troth-ring
thin-belly	thick-sown	trigynous	timocracy	tangerine	toothpick
twin-birth	thicketed	trihydric	time-clock	tenderise	trochilic
triactine	trickster	trihybrid	timidness	tendering	trochilus
twitching	trinketer	Tokharish	tumidness	tinkering	toothcomb
triecious	trinketry	Tokharian	temperate	tinselled	toothsome
third-hand	thick-eyed	take-leave	tampering	tunnelled	toothwort
third-rate	trialogue	taking-off	tempering	tunneller	toolhouse
twiddling	tail-light	teknonymy	timbering	tunnel-net	two-timing
thirdsman	trial-fire	Tiliaceae	timber-man	tunefully	two-lipped
twice-laid	triploidy	talkative	tumefying	tanagrine	Thomistic
tail-ender	triclinic	tollbooth	tomograph	tanghinin	tropistic
tribeless	tuillette	telegraph	tim-whisky	tintiness	two-fisted
triteness	triumphal	talegalla	tumble-bug	tonnishly	trollopee
trimethyl	triumpher	telegenic	tumble-car	tensility	toodle-pip
tripe-shop	triumviri	toll-house	time-limit	tan-pickle	toolmaker
tripewife	triumviry	talliable	temulence	tenaillon	thornback
tricerion	triennial	talking-to	temulency	tonsilar	thornless

trouncing	tipstaffs	torch-lily	thrasonic	tetterous	Teutonism
thorntree	tipstaves	torch-song	threshold	tithe-free	Teutonist
thorn-bush	typewrite	terminate	turnstone	tittivate	tautology
tholobate	tipsy-cake	turbinate	turn-screw	tattiness	trump-card
two-forked	terramara	termitary	turntable	totting-up	trumped-up
two-roomed	terramare	terpineol	teratogen	titillate	truepenny
tropology	turnagain	tardiness	throttler	tittlebat	trumpeted
two-footed	termagant	tarriness	turbulent	totalling	trumpeter
two-bottle	turmagant	turfiness	throughly	titularly	truss-beam
thorow-wax	Tartarean	turnip-fly	turquoise	totaliser	trust-deed
troop-ship	tervalent	tarnished	torturing	Totaninae	trustless
taoiseach	ternately	tarnisher	Tartufish	tetroxide	trustiest
trousseau	threatful	terrified	Tartufism	tutiorism	truculent
trousered	tarsalgia	terminism	Tartufian	tattooist	thwacking
trout-farm	terza-rima	terminist	toreutics	tutiorist	town-crier
troutless	tartarise	torpidity	Targumist	tutworker	tow-headed
troutling	torbanite	torridity	torturous	tutorship	townhouse
twostroke	terracing	tortility	torquated	thumb-mark	tawniness
two-storey	terrarium	turbidity	tire-woman	thumb-tack	towel-rack
two-by-four	tarnation	turgidity	throw-down	thumbnail	towel-rail
tap-dancer	Tartarian	tarriance	throwster	thumbless	towelling
Typhaceae	throatily	torsional	throw-away	thumbling	towing-net
topmaking	tarpaulin	terricole	Taraxacum	thumb-ring	towerless
topiarian	Tarragona	torminous	testament	thumbkins	thwarting
topiarist	tornadoes	territory	Tasmanian	thumb-knot	townscape
top-hamper	turnabout	turnip-top	testation	thumb-hole	townsfolk
top-sawyer	tirra-lyra	torpitude	testatrix	truncheon	toxically
topically	terebrate	turpitude	test-drive	T-junction	taxed-cart
typically	terebrant	thrillant	tasteless	truncated	taxidermy
topectomy	terebrant	thralldom	tasselled	thundrous	taximeter
tepidness	throbless	thrilling	tessellae	thunderer	taxonomic
typifying	throbbing	torulosis	tessellar	truceless	taxonomer
tape-grass	terebinth	thrumming	taste-bulb	Trubenise®	textorial
type-genus	turf-drain	thrombose	task-force	touch-back	toxaphene
tip-cheese	tiredness	thrum-eyed	task-group	touch-mark	toxophily
Tupaiidae	teredines	tarantara	testiness	touchable	texturise
tap-cinder	three-card	tarantass	testified	touchless	textually
tipsiness	three-pair	threnodic	testifier	toughness	thylacine
topping-up	three-part	tyranness	testimony	truthless	thyratron
toppingly	three-deck	throngful	tessitura	touch-line	Thysanura
tappit-hen	targeteer	tyrannise	test-match	truthlike	thymidine
tephigram	terseness	tarantism	tasimeter	toughener	thyristor
tip-tilted	threeness	Terentian	Tisiphone	touchwood	thyroxine
Tipulidae	terrenely	tyrannous	test-paper	touch-hole	twyforked
topologic	turret-gun	threnetic	tusk-shell	touch-tone	twyformed
top-flight	turkey-hen	tarantula	tetrarchy	touch-down	thymocyte
typhlitic	torrefied	tarboggin	tête-à-tête	touch-type	Thyestean
typhlitis	three-pile	Turcophil	tetradite	tauriform	unabashed
typomania	Turnerian	terrorise	titration	touristic	unadapted
type-metal	threefold	terrorism	tetralogy	trunk-call	unaccused
toponymic	threesome	terrorist	tetrapody	trunk-mail	unaidable
toponymal	three-four	turcopole	tetragram	truck-farm	up-and-down
tip-and-run	torpedoer	turboprop	tête-bêche	truck-shop	up-and-over
typhoidal	torpedoes	turn-penny	titubancy	trunk-line	unamerced
tiptoeing	three-foot	tortricid	title-page	truckling	unamended
tuptowing	tormented	tortrices	tithe-barn	trunkfish	unavenged
Typhonian	tormentil	turnround	title-deed	truck-load	unashamed
top-booted	tormentum	turf-spade	title-leaf	trunk-road	unamiable
taperness	tormentor	thrust-hoe	titleless	trunk-hose	uraniscus
taperwise	turgently	turnstile	tittering	trunk-work	Upanishad
tephroite	thriftier	thrashing	tottering	tournedos	uralitise
tephritic	thriftily	threshing	title-role	tourneyer	uraninite
top-drawer	toruffled	thrusting	title-poem	Teutonise	unanimity

9 u□m□n

unanimous	unbruised	undrained	underwood	unfranked	unhasting
unallayed	unblunted	undebased	underdone	unfocused	unhatched
unalloyed	unchanged	undecided	undernote	unfadable	unhatting
unadmired	uncharged	undeceive	undertone	unfledged	unhaunted
unavoided	unceasing	undecimal	under-roof	unfleshed	univalent
uvarovite	uncharity	undecayed	underfong	unfleshly	urinative
unadorned	uncharmed	undreaded	undersong	unfeeling	Unitarian
uranology	unclaimed	undreamed	undercook	unfuelled	urination
unadopted	unchained	undressed	undertook	unfreeman	uniparous
unapplied	uncharnel	undefaced	underwork	unfretted	unincited
unapparel	up-Channel	undefiled	undercool	unfigured	unindexed
unassumed	unclassed	undefined	undersoil	unfailing	uniserial
unassured	uncharted	undignify	undergown	unfeigned	universal
unassayed	uncleship	undyingly	underdoer	unfolding	unisexual
unactable	unchecked	undrilled	undercoat	upfilling	unifiable
unaptness	uncleaned	undeluded	underfoot	unfrocked	unitively
upaithric	uncleanly	undelight	undermost	unfloored	uliginous
unaltered	uncheered	undulancy	underbred	unfurnish	uninjured
unattired	uncleared	undiluted	undergrad	unfortune	unillumed
unamusing	upcheered	undulated	underprop	unfitness	uniplanar
unadvised	unclearly	undelayed	underdraw	unfitting	Unionidae
unanxious	uncreated	undamaged	underhung	unfounded	unionised
unbearded	unclipped	undrowned	underbush	unguarded	unisonant
unbraided	uncombine	underhand	undesired	ungravely	Uriconian
upbraider	uncongeal	underlaid	undeserve	ungodlike	uniformed
umbratile	unconcern	underpaid	undutiful	ungodlily	uniformly
unbearing	unconfine	underrate	unduteous	unguessed	unicolour
unbiassed	uncannily	undertake	undaunted	ungainful	unisonous
unblended	uncanonic	underlain	undoubted	unguiform	urinology
unblessed	unconform	underpass	undivided	ungallant	unimpeded
unbaffled	uncandour	undercast	undawning	ungenteel	unimposed
unbeguile	uncinated	underfeed	undazzled	ungenuine	uninsured
unblinded	urceolate	underself	unexalted	upgrowing	uninvited
unbridged	unclouded	underdeck	unexcited	ungroomed	unjealous
un-British	uncrowded	underseal	unendowed	unglossed	unjointed
unbridled	unclogged	undersell	uselessly	unghostly	unknelled
unbuilt-on	unclothed	underkeep	unelected	ungirthed	unkindled
unbrizzed	uncrowned	underpeep	uneffaced	ungarbled	unknowing
unbcknown	uncropped	underbear	unengaged	upgushing	unloading
umbellate	uncrossed	underwear	un-English	ungrudged	unlearned
umbilical	uncapable	udderless	unethical	unheard-of	unluckily
umbilicus	uncertain	underfelt	Uredineae	upheaping	unlocated
unbelieve	uncurtain	undervest	uredinial	unhearsed	uplifting
unbalance	uncurable	undershot	uredinium	unhealthy	unlogical
umbellule	uncurrent	undergird	uredinous	unheedful	unlighted
unbeloved	up-current	underbite	uterotomy	unheeding	uplighted
unbending	uncareful	underfire	unemptied	unheedily	unlikable
unbinding	uncurling	underline	unexpired	unhelpful	unlimited
unblooded	uncordial	undermine	unexposed	upholding	uplandish
upbrought	uncurdled	under-ripe	unearthed	upholster	unlosable
unbookish	uncurious	underside	unearthly	unhumbled	unlivable
unblotted	unchrisom	undertime	unessence	unhandily	unlived-in
unbaptise	uncorrupt	underking	unessayed	unhandled	unmeaning
unburthen	uncessant	underling	uneatable	unhopeful	ulmaceous
umber-bird	uncrudded	underwing	unextinct	unhappily	unmakable
upburning	uncouthly	undersign	unentered	unharness	unmanacle
unbasedly	uncoupled	undertint	unequable	unharmful	unmindful
unbespeak	uncounted	underclub	unequally	unhurtful	unmanaged
unbashful	uncourtly	underclad	unenvying	ushership	unmanlike
unbosomer	up-country	underplot	unenvious	unhurried	unmingled
unbounded	uncivilly	underflow	unfearful	unharming	unmanured
upbounden	uncovered	underclay	unfraught	unharbour	unmoneyed
unbrushed	up-draught	underplay	unfearing	usherette	unmolteyed

unmarried	unpoliced	unrounded	unstriped	ululation	vicennial
unmerited	unpalsied	unrevoked	unshrived	usucapion	vacuolate
unmusical	unpolitic	unrevised	unshriven	unushered	victoress
unmasking	unpiloted	unroyally	unsuspect	usualness	victorine
unmatched	unpennied	unrazored	unsisting	usurpedly	vectorial
unmatured	unpeopled	unswaddle	unsatiate	unuttered	Victorian
unmotived	unprovoke	unshapely	unsatable	unusually	viciosity
unmoulded	unpropped	unscathed	upsetting	unveiling	vacuously
unmourned	unpopular	unsparing	upsitting	unvoicing	viciously
unmounted	unpapered	unstaying	unsettled	unvarying	vice-queen
unmovable	upper-case	upstaring	unsounded	unvisited	vicariate
unmovably	unperfect	unshackle	unsoundly	unwearied	vice-regal
unmovedly	unpervert	unscanned	unsnuffed	unweeting	vicarship
unmixedly	up-perched	unstained	unstuffed	unwreaked	vicereine
unmuzzled	unpartial	unstamped	unstudied	unwreathe	vicarious
uintahite	unperplex	unscarred	unshunned	unweighed	vicesimal
unneedful	uppermost	unsubject	unsquared	unwriting	videlicet
urn-shaped	unpursued	unsubdued	unshutter	unwrinkle	vade-mecum
unnamable	unpotable	unsuccess	unsevered	unwhipped	videotape
unnerving	unpitiful	unsickled	unsavoury	unwritten	viewiness
unnoticed	unpitying	unsecular	unsayable	unwakened	veeringly
unnatural	up-putting	unsecured	unscythed	unwilling	viewpoint
urolagnia	unplumbed	unseduced	unsizable	upwelling	viewphone
unordered	unplugged	ups-a-daisy	uitlander	unwelcome	vee-gutter
unorderly	unplucked	upsy-daisy	ultra-high	unwomanly	vagueness
urodelous	unpayable	unsaddled	unthanked	unwinding	vignetter
udometric	unqualify	unseeable	untracked	unwinking	vigilance
unoffered	unquelled	unsued-for	untrained	unwrought	vigilante
urochrome	unqueened	unsterile	urticaria	upwrought	vaginulae
Urochorda	unqueenly	unseeming	untressed	unworldly	vaginated
uxoricide	unquietly	unscented	untreated	unworried	vaginitis
ufologist	unreached	unsheathe	untoiling	unwarlike	vagarious
urologist	unrealise	unslept-in	uptrilled	unworking	vigesimal
unopposed	unrealism	unsighing	untrimmed	unwishful	vegetable
ulotrichy	unreadily	unsighted	untainted	unwasting	vegetably
urography	unreality	unsightly	untwisted	unwishing	vegetated
unobvious	unrebuked	unskilful	untamable	unwatched	vehicular
uropygial	unrebated	unsmiling	untamably	unwitting	vehemence
uropygium	utricular	unsuiting	untumbled	unwittily	vehemency
unplanked	utriculus	unskilled	untimeous	unwatered	voiceless
unplained	unridable	unspilled	untempted	unwounded	voice-over
unplanned	unreduced	unstifled	ultimatum	unzealous	vainglory
unpraised	unredrest	unstilled	untenable	vraicking	Vaishnava
unplaited	unriddler	unskimmed	untunable	viaticals	voisinage
unplanted	unruffled	unskinned	untunably	viability	veilleuse
unplagued	unrefined	unstinted	untuneful	viatorial	veinstone
unpacking	unrefuted	unsmitten	untangled	vibraharp	veinstuff
unprepare	uprightly	unsaintly	untrodden	vibratile	voiturier
unpierced	Ukrainian	unsalable	untypical	vibrative	vikingism
unpledged	unrelated	unsolaced	untirable	vibration	villanage
unprecise	unrelaxed	unsolidly	utterable	vibratory	villagery
unpredict	unrumpled	unsullied	utterless	vibracula	volcanise
umpteenth	unremoved	unselfish	utterness	vibrissae	vulcanise
unpleased	unrenewed	unsaluted	unthrifty	vacuation	vulcanite
unpressed	uprooting	unsinewed	unturning	vocabular	vulgarise
unpleated	unripping	unshocked	upturning	vaccinate	volcanism
unpliable	unripened	unstocked	utterance	victimise	vulcanism
unpliably	Utraquism	unspoiled	uttermost	vaccinial	vulgarism
unpainful	Utraquist	unstopped	untutored	vaccinium	valuation
up-pricked	unrestful	unstopper	upthunder	vacillate	volcanian
unpainted	unresting	unscoured	untouched	vacillant	vulcanian
unpointed	unrosined	unspotted	untrussed	vocalness	vulgarian
unprinted	unreserve	unserious	untrusser	vocaliser	volcanist

vulcanist	vengement	varvelled	vesicular	wrangling	wheat-corn
vulgarity	veneering	vervelled	vasectomy	wrathless	wheat-crop
villanous	vindemial	vermeille	viscerate	weathered	wofulness
volcanoes	vengeance	vertebrae	visagiste	weatherly	wafer-cake
valvassor	venefical	vertebral	vestiment	weariless	waghalter
valiantly	ventilate	verifying	vestigial	weariness	Wagnerite
volucrine	vindicate	viragoish	vestigium	wearisome	Wagnerism
validness	ventifact	verminate	vastidity	weak-kneed	Wagnerian
velodrome	vendition	varnisher	viscidity	wrapround	Wagnerist
villenage	ventiduct	versified	vastitude	whatsoe'er	waggishly
volte-face	ventosity	verbicide	vestibule	wealthily	wagons-lit
vulnerate	venerable	vermicide	vestiture	wobbegong	wagon-load
vulnerary	venerably	virginium	vasomotor	web-footed	wagon-roof
velveteen	ventricle	vorticism	visionary	wych-hazel	wagon-lock
valueless	ventrally	Vergilian	visioning	wackiness	wagenboom
valveless	venireman	vermilion	visionist	Wyclifite	wagonette
velveting	venereous	Virgilian	viscosity	wide-awake	wager-boat
vulsellae	venerator	Virginian	viscounty	wide-angle	wages-fund
vulsellum	vanishing	versifier	visor-mask	Wednesday	Wahabite
Valdenses	vine-stock	vorticist	vestryman	wedgewise	Wahabiism
vallecula	vanity-bag	verticity	visitable	wadsetter	Wehrmacht
vilifying	vanity-box	virginity	visitress	widow-wail	writative
volageous	venatical	versional	visitator	widow-bird	whipcordy
vellicate	vingt-et-un	versioner	vitiation	widowhood	weirdness
voltigeur	venturing	vorticose	vaticinal	wrenching	waiterage
vulpicide	venturous	vermiform	vitecetum	whencever	white-face
vulpinite	Violaceae	versiform	vetchling	wieldable	whiteware
voltinism	violative	verminous	vitrified	wieldless	whitewash
vulpinism	violation	vertiport	vitriolic	wheedling	write-back
villiform	violently	verdigris	vitriform	week-ender	Whitehall
vulviform	violin-bow	vermicule	vitellary	whereness	whitebass
voluminal	violinist	vermituge	vitelline	wherewith	white-hass
voltmeter	voodooism	virulence	vitaliser	whereinto	whitebait
volumeter	voodooist	virulency	vitiosity	whereunto	white-salt
voluntary	vapidness	Varanidae	vitascope	wherefore	white-lady
volunteer	vaporable	Varangian	vetturini	woebegone	White-head
valentine	Viperidae	véronique	Vitruvian	whereupon	whiteboam
villosity	vaporific	variolate	vetturino	wherefrom	white-seam
velarised	vaporiser	verbosely	vouchsafe	whey-faced	white-bear
volksraad	vaporetto	variolite	vivianite	weel-faird	whiteness
Volkslied	vapouring	verbosity	vivacious	weel-faur'd	writeress
veldskoen	vapourish	varioloid	vividness	weed-grown	white-rent
volitient	Verbascum	variolous	vivamente	weediness	white-lime
vol-au-vent	variative	variously	vivandier	weepingly	waitering
veloutine	verbalise	virescent	viverrine	weetingly	whitening
vulturine	vernalise	variscite	vow-fellow	weedicide	whitewing
vulturish	versatile	veritable	vowelless	weevilled	whitefish
vulturism	verbalism	veritably	vexedness	wreakless	whitewood
vulturous	variation	veratrine	vexillary	wheelbase	write-down
Valkyriur	verbarian	Varityper®	vexatious	wheel-race	whifflery
vampirise	vernation	virgulate	voyeurism	wheel-lock	whiffling
vampirism	verbalist	verjuiced	vizierate	wheelwork	whip-graft
vimineous	verbality	virtually	vizierial	wheel-spin	whingeing
vambraced	vernality	verrucose	vizirship	weeknight	wriggling
vandalise	verdantly	verdurous	wyandotte	wherryman	wring-bolt
vintaging	varicella	verrucous	whale-calf	whet-slate	weigh-bank
vandalism	veracious	virtuosic	whale-back	whetstone	weighable
veniality	voracious	vassalage	weasel-cat	wheat-meal	weighting
vantbrace	veridical	vassaless	whale-head	wheat-germ	weightily
vant-brass	variegate	vistaless	whale-line	wheat-bird	whichever
vinaceous	verberate	visualise	weaseller	wrestling	whininess
vengeable	varletess	visualist	whalebone	wheat-moth	wailingly
vengeably	varieties	visuality	whale-boat	wheat-worm	waitingly

whiningly	wild-geese	window-box	war-wasted	waste-book	water-vine
whiskered	Weltgeist	winsomely	warrantee	washed-out	water-mill
whirligig	wild-goose	wantonise	warranter	wishfully	waterlily
whirlwind	well-given	wincopipe	warrantor	wistfully	water-flea
whirl-bone	wild-honey	winnowing	word-blind	wase-goose	water-flag
whirlpool	wolf-hound	window-tax	wordbound	wash-house	water-flow
whillywha	well-house	wine-press	wart-cress	washiness	water-core
whinnying	willingly	wine-party	wiredrawn	washing-up	water-hole
whipper-in	wolfishly	wind-shak'd	worldwide	waspishly	water-mole
whimperer	wolvishly	wing-snail	worldling	wash-stand	water-pore
whisperer	well-known	wing-shell	worseness	wasp-stung	water-vole
whip-round	well-lined	windswept	wernerite	westwards	water-cock
whip-snake	well-meant	wind-swift	Wernerian	witwanton	water-work
whipstaff	wild-olive	wine-stone	worm-eaten	withdrawn	water-cool
whipstall	walloping	wind-tight	worcester	witherite	water-fowl
whimsical	wallowing	wang-tooth	workfolks	withering	water-worn
whinstone	willowish	wine-vault	worm-fence	wuthering	water-polo
whip-stock	Waltonian	windwards	workforce	witnesser	water-poet
waistband	well-oiled	woodblock	worm-fever	witlessly	water-drop
wristband	wall-plate	wood-borer	wire-guard	watch-case	water-cure
waist-deep	wallpaper	woodcraft	wire-grass	witch-meal	water-buck
waistbelt	wall-space	woodchuck	worm-grass	watch-fire	water-bull
wrist-shot	wolfsbane	wholesale	wire-gauze	witch-wife	water-jump
waistline	well-smack	woomerang	worthless	watch-bill	water-pump
whistling	well-spent	whore's-egg	worm-holed	witch-knot	water-butt
waist-high	wolf's-claw	whole-meal	workhorse	watchword	withstand
waistboat	wolf's-foot	wholeness	warehouse	witchetty	withstood
waistcoat	well-set-up	wholefood	workhouse	withhault	withywind
wrist-drop	well-timed	wholesome	wordiness	wittiness	woundable
whittawer	wolf-tooth	wood-fibre	worriment	wittingly	woundless
whizz-bang	wild-water	wood-flour	warningly	witticism	woundwort
wakefully	welly-boot	wrongness	worrisome	wattmeter	waulk-mill
wake-robin	wallydrag	wrong-doer	warble-fly	wit-monger	whunstane
wellanear	womankind	wrong-foot	workmanly	withouten	wavefront
welfarism	womenkind	wrought-up	warmonger	water-gage	waveguide
welfarist	woman-like	whoa-ho-hoa	warlockry	Watergate	wavellite
well-aimed	womanhood	wood-honey	workplace	water-gate	wavemeter
walkabout	womenfolk	wood-horse	workpiece	water-rate	waveshape
wall-board	woman-born	woodhouse	wire-photo	water-wave	wax-flower
well-being	woman-post	woodiness	wardrober	water-bath	wax-insect
well-built	woman-body	wooziness	wordsmith	water-cask	waxworker
well-borer	womaniser	whorishly	wire-sewed	watermark	way-warden
wall-cress	wink-a-peep	wholistic	work-table	waterfall	waywardly
Walachian	wind-break	woodlouse	worm-wheel	water-gall	wayfaring
well-drain	wine-berry	woodmouse	work-woman	water-rail	wry-necked
well-doing	wind-bound	wood-nymph	wassailer	water-main	wayzgoose
Willesden	wind-chart	whosoever	wassailry	water-cart	X-particle
wolverene	wind-chest	wood-paper	west-about	water-head	xylograph
willemite	winter-bud	wood-reeve	wash-board	water-weed	xyloidine
wolverine	wonderful	wood-stamp	wash-basin	water-leaf	xylometer
wulfenite	winterise	wood-sugar	westbound	water-deck	Xylophaga
weltering	wandering	wood-spite	wisecrack	water-cell	xylophage
wildering	wondering	wood-stone	wash-cloth	water-seal	xylophone
wylie-coat	wonderous	wood-shock	wasteland	water-fern	xenocryst
Waldenses	wine-glass	wood-screw	waste-gate	water-deer	xenograft
well-famed	wind-gauge	whodunnit	wasteness	water-lens	Xanthippe
well-found	wanchancy	wood-waxen	wasterful	waterless	Xanthoura
waldflute	wind-hover	wapper-jaw	waste-pipe	watershed	xenomania
wall-fruit	windiness	wapentake	wasterife	water-shot	xenomenia
well-faurt	windingly	wapenshaw	westering	water-bird	xenophile
waldgrave	winkingly	wapinshaw	washerman	water-line	xenophobe
wild-grape	winningly	warfaring	wasserman	water-pipe	xenophoby
wildgrave	window-bar	warranted	westerner	waterside	Xenarthra

Xiphiidae
xiphoidal
Xiphosura
xerochasy
Xyridales
xeroderma
xeromorph
xerophagy
xerophily
xerophyte
yravished
year-round
yacht-club
yachtsman
Yiddisher
yieldable
Yggdrasil
yo-heave-ho
yohimbine
Yajurveda
yoke-devil
yoke-stalk
yakety-yak
yakity-yak
yellow-boy
yellow-dog
yellowish
yammering
Yankeedom
Yankeeism
yird-house
Yorkshire
yardstick
yesterday
yestereve
yattering
ytterbium
youngness
youngthly
youngling
youngster
young-eyed
youthhead
youthhood
youthsome
yawningly
zealotism
zealously
Zwanziger
zebra-wood
zibelline
zucchetto
Zechstein
zoechrome
zoetropic
zigzagged
zygaenine
zygaenoid
zygomatic
zygantrum
zygophyte
zygosperm
zygospore

Zwinglian
zeitgeist
zoiatrics
zelotypia
zymogenic
zymologic
zymolysis
zymolitic
zamindari
zemindari
zemindary
zamboorak
zumbooruk
zinc-bloom
zinc-colic
zinkenite
zante-wood
Zanzibari
Zonuridae
zinc-white
zoogamete
zoogamous
zoolatria
zoomantic
zooscopic
zootechny
zooperist
zoogenous
zoometric
zoophobia
zoothecia
zoophagan
zootheism
zoophilia
zoophoric
zoophorus
zoophytic
zoolithic
zoobiotic
zoogloeic
zooplasty
zoologist
zoonomist
zootomist
zoogonous
zoomorphy
zoosporic
zoography
zootrophy
zoocytium
Zapodidae
Ziphiidae
zapateado
zapotilla
zircalloy
Zernebock
zirconium
zero-rated
zestfully
Zeuglodon
zeugmatic

asarabacca
alabandine
alabandite
anacardium
acatalepsy
acanaceous
anapaestic
adamantean
adamantine
amarantine
anabaptise
anabaptism
anabaptist
agapanthus
Amaranthus
anarchical
academical
amazedness
arabesqued
amateurish
amateurism
alang-alang
amalgamate
arachnidan
anaphylaxy
anachronic
Araliaceae
Adamitical
avaricious
availingly
anaglyphic
anaglyptic
anaclastic
anaplastic
alarm-radio
alarm-clock
alarmingly
anamnestic
araeometer
araeometry
acarophily
anagogical
analogical
anatomical
apagogical
amatorious
Amazon-like
anamorphic
asafoetida
araeostyle
anacolutha
analphabet
anadromous
anatropous
anacrustic
avant-garde
anaptyctic
anastigmat
anastomose
anastrophe
avanturine
anarthrous
adaptation

adaptative
adaptively
amanuenses
amanuensis
analysable
analytical
anadyomene
ambidexter
abbreviate
Albigenses
ambagitory
ambulacral
ambulacrum
arbalester
arbalister
ambulation
ambulatory
albuminoid
albumenise
albuminise
albuminate
albuminous
Ambarvalia
aubergiste
ambassador
ambuscados
albescence
ambushment
ambisonics
asbestosis
arbitrable
arbitrator
ambivalent
abbey-laird
abbey-piece
Amblyopsis
Amblystoma
archaicism
archaistic
arcubalist
archbishop
accubation
arch-chimic
archdeacon
accidental
accidented
accrescent
arc-welding
archer-fish
alchemical
accredited
archeology
archegonia
ance-errand
archetypal
arch-flamen
alcoholise
alcoholism
ascribable
auctioneer
auctionary
architrave
ascription

accelerant
accelerate
accultural
ascomycete
accomplice
accomplish
accumulate
accomptant
ascendance
ascendancy
ascendable
ascendence
ascendency
ascendible
arcaneness
accentuate
Arctogaean
Alcyonaria
Arctogaeic
anchoretic
anchor-hold
arctophile
anchoritic
anchorless
aeciospore
anchor-ring
archonship
archontate
acceptance
acceptancy
acceptable
acceptably
arch-priest
arch-pirate
ancipitous
accordance
accordancy
ascariasis
accordable
accurately
accostable
accessible
accessibly
accusement
accustomed
ancestress
accusation
accusative
asceticism
accoucheur
accoutring
accountant
accounting
anchylosed
anchylosis
audibility
abdication
aide-de-camp
addle-pated
Andalusian
aedileship
andalusite
abdominous

androecium
audiometer
androgenic
audiophile
androphore
audiograph
aldermanic
aldermanly
aldermanry
adderstone
adder's-wort
additament
additional
auditorium
additively
alexanders
aceraceous
arenaceous
avenaceous
ametabolic
adelantado
arefaction
acetabular
acetabulum
amerciable
amercement
Aberdonian
anecdotage
amendatory
anecdotist
aberdevine
ateleiosis
adenectomy
areography
avengement
avengeress
acephalous
Amerindian
ameliorate
areolation
anemometer
anemometry
anemophily
anemograph
Areopagite
age-bracket
Averrhoism
Averrhoist
aneurismal
aneurysmal
aberration
averseness
asepticise
asepticism
azeotropic
aventurine
asexuality
adequately
adequative
acervation
affability
affectedly
affeerment

affricated
affrighted
affrighten
afflicting
affliction
afflictive
affiliable
Aufklärung
affinitive
affronting
affrontive
affirmance
affirmable
affettuoso
affluently
aggrandise
angwantibo
algebraist
aggression
aggressive
anguifauna
Anguillula
angel-water
algolagnia
algologist
angelology
angularity
argumentum
Algonquian
argonautic
anglomania
Anglo-Saxon
anglophobe
anglophone
angiosperm
Anglo-Irish
algophobia
argyrodite
auger-shell
Angaraland
augustness
arguteness
agglutinin
ashlar-work
adhibition
aphidicide
Ashkenazim
achievable
aphaeresis
anhelation
Athanasian
achromatic
achromatin
aphrodisia
athermancy
abhorrence
abhorrency
Acherontic
anharmonic
aphoristic
adhesively
Achitophel
animalcula

animalcule
agitatedly
animatedly
acinaceous
Arimaspian
animadvert
amiability
alineation
alimentary
abiogenist
arithmetic
Ahithophel
acidimeter
acidimetry
aficionado
acidifying
axiologist
Alismaceae
axiomatics
alienation
axinomancy
anisotropy
amido-group
amino-group
adiaphoron
aristocrat
Asiaticism
aristology
Aristippus
Avicularia
Aviculidae
abiturient
apiculture
aviculture
adjectival
adjacently
abjectness
adjudicate
adjudgment
abjunction
adjunction
adjunctive
abjuration
adjuration
adjuratory
adjustable
adjustment
awkwardish
alkalinity
ankylosaur
alliaceous
All-Hallows
able-bodied
allochiria
aplacental
allycholly
allocation
allocution
allegeance
allegiance
allegretto
allogamous
allegorise

allegorist
allegation
alligation
all-firedly
aplanatism
all-rounder
allophonic
allopathic
all-dreaded
allergenic
allurement
alluringly
arles-penny
Allosaurus
allusively
allotropic
alliterate
all-purpose
alleviator
all-overish
almacantar
almucantar
Armageddon
armigerous
atmologist
ammoniacal
ammoniated
ammoniacum
almond-eyed
administer
almond-tree
admonition
ammunition
admonitory
admonitive
armipotent
admiringly
admiration
admirative
atmosphere
admissible
admittance
admittable
admittedly
armour-clad
armourless
abnegation
annihilate
annularity
annalistic
annulation
annunciate
annuntiate
abnormally
annotation
annexation
annoyingly
anonaceous
apocarpous
apolaustic
apocalypse
amoebiform
avouchable

avouchment
above-named
aposematic
apodeictic
adolescent
above-board
apopemptic
azobenzene
alongshore
apothecial
apothecary
apothecium
apophthegm
anopheline
apochromat
apotheoses
apotheosis
abominable
abominably
abominator
agonisedly
aboriginal
apolitical
aborigines
agonistics
apoplectic
Apollonian
acorn-shell
apologetic
apomorphia
aeolotropy
acolouthic
acolouthos
akolouthos
aposporous
apocryphal
apotropaic
apocryphon
apotropous
ahorseback
acoustical
aborticide
apostolate
apostrophe
apostatise
abortively
acotyledon
appearance
appealable
appeasable
applauding
alphabetic
alphameric
alphametic
applausive
aspectable
Ampicillin®
aspidistra
appreciate
apple-woman
apprentice
arpeggione
arpeggiate

amphimacer
applicable
applicably
applicator
amphiscian
Amphineura
amphimixis
amphibious
amphibolic
amphibrach
Amphitryon
Amphictyon
ampliation
ampliative
appointive
amplifying
ampelopsis
appendices
appendixes
alpenstock
approvance
approvable
amphoteric
approximal
Alphonsine
apperceive
asparagine
aspergilla
apparelled
apparently
aspiringly
apparition
aspiration
aspiratory
appositely
apposition
appositive
ampussy-and
appetising
amputation
appetition
appetitive
asphyxiant
asphyxiate
acquainted
acquirable
acquitment
acquitting
acroamatic
air-marshal
airmanship
abreaction
aerobiosis
aerobiotic
acrobatics
aerobatics
acrobatism
auriculate
Africander
Africanoid
Africanise
Africanism
Africanist

aprication
abridgment
arrière-ban
aeroengine
acriflavin
air-officer
auriferous
aerography
aerogramme
arrogantly
arragonite
acrogenous
aeruginous
abrogation
arrogation
abrogative
Abraham-man
arraigning
adroitness
Afrikander
air-bladder
aerologist
agrologist
acromegaly
atramental
aerometric
acronychal
aerenchyma
agronomial
aeronomist
agronomist
acronymous
apron-stage
aeronautic
air-cooling
air-hostess
aureomycin
abruptness
acrophobia
acrophonic
aerophobia
aerophobic
air-traffic
afrormosia
air-grating
aerostatic
arrestable
arrestment
aerotactic
aerotropic
acroterial
acroterion
acroterium
amritattva
air-cushion
arrow-grass
arrhythmia
arrhythmic
assibilate
associable
answerable
answerably
abstergent

austenitic	attraction	automatons	after-light	adulterous
abstemious	attractive	automation	afterbirth	advice-boat
answerless	actability	automatism	arthralgia	arvicoline
abstersion	ante-bellum	automatist	arthralgic	advocation
abstersive	antibiosis	astomatous	altar-cloth	advocatory
abstention	antibiotic	automotive	after-image	adventurer
assafetida	antechapel	attendance	attirement	adversaria
assignable	autocratic	attendancy	attornment	advertence
assignment	attachable	attenuated	arthromere	advertency
aesthetics	attackable	attenuator	afterworld	advertiser
Anschauung	arty-crafty	ante-Nicene	anteriorly	advisement
assailable	antecedent	actinolite	astarboard	advisorate
abstinence	anticlimax	antinomian	Arthropoda	advisatory
abstinency	anticlinal	autonomics	anthropoid	anxiolytic
auspicious	autecology	attendment	aftergrass	amylaceous
assailment	Articulata	attunement	asterisked	aryballoid
assoilment	articulate	autonomist	altar-stone	arytaenoid
abscission	attachment	autonomous	alteration	asynartete
arse-licker	anticipant	astonished	alterative	asynchrony
absolvitor	anticipate	anthomania	after-guard	amygdaloid
absolutely	Antichrist	actionable	antistatic	anywhither
absolution	artocarpus	astrolatry	attestable	asymmetric
absolutory	antecessor	Antiochian	antisocial	asymptotic
absolutism	Antichthon	Antiochene	artistical	Abyssinian
absolutist	autochthon	anthophore	anti-Semite	asyntactic
assemblage	anticivism	authorless	altisonant	asystolism
assimilate	autodidact	astrologer	autoscopic	bragadisme
assumingly	antidromic	astronomer	antisepsis	Bramah-lock
assumption	anthelices	astrologic	antiseptic	blancmange
assumptive	antheridia	astronomic	autostrada	branchiate
assentator	antler-moth	Anthonomus	antitragus	branchless
assentient	autoerotic	authorship	antitheses	branch-work
assonantal	anthemwise	autoplasty	antithesis	board-wages
absorbable	artificial	antipodean	antithetic	brandy-ball
assertable	antifreeze	autoptical	antitheism	brandering
abstracted	autography	antepenult	antitheist	beard-grass
abstracter	astigmatic	antiphonal	autotheism	bladder-nut
abstractly	autogamous	antiphoner	autotheist	brandy-snap
abstractor	antagonise	antiphonic	altitonant	brazen-face
absorbency	antagonism	antiproton	astuteness	beam-engine
assurgency	antagonist	antipathic	astounding	brake-wheel
absorbedly	autogenous	antiquated	Arthuriana	brake-block
Australian	altogether	alternance	artfulness	brazenness
Australorp	anti-heroic	afterwards	altruistic	beaver-tree
australite	attainable	asteriated	activeness	blamefully
assortment	astringent	alternatim	activation	beaver-wood
austringer	attainment	altar-rails	altazimuth	braggingly
absurdness	auto-immune	afterpains	Ahuramazda	beach-la-mar
abstrusely	Aethiopian	alternator	aquabatics	brachyaxis
absorption	astriction	aftertaste	abundantly	brachydome
adsorption	attainture	anthracoid	aquafortis	brachylogy
absorptive	astrictive	anthracene	acuminated	brachiopod
assistance	antilogous	anthracite	anucleated	brachyural
assessable	antilopine	apterygial	Adullamite	beatifical
assessment	autumnally	Apterygota	aquamanale	brazil-wood
assythment	automobile	aftershaft	aquamanile	Beaujolais
auscultate	attempered	autarchist	aquamarine	blackfaced
asseverate	antimonial	aftershave	aquaplaner	blackwater
assay-piece	antimonide	asteroidal	adulterant	blackberry
astragalus	antimonate	autarkical	adulterine	blackheart
actualités	antimonite	afterpiece	adulteress	Blackshirt
antiaditis	antimasque	altarpiece	adulterise	blackthorn
attractant	anti-matter	Asteroidea	adulterate	blackamoor

blacksmith	back-garden	beetlehead	bridle-rein	bell-turret
blackboard	backhanded	beetmister	bairn's-part	bolstering
blanketing	backhander	biennially	blissfully	balbutient
black-bully	bacchanals	bleary-eyed	blister-fly	biliverdin
blackguard	buccinator	bleariness	blistering	boll-weevil
bear-leader	buck-jumper	breastbone	boisterous	bell-wether
beadlehood	becomingly	breast-deep	blitzkrieg	belly-dance
beadleship	Buchmanism	breast-feed	blizzardly	belly-laugh
Brahmanism	Buchmanite	breast-high	bijouterie	bombardier
Brahminism	backmarker	breast-knot	baking-soda	bumbailiff
brainchild	back-number	bressummer	Bollandist	bumpkinish
braininess	Bucephalus	breastrail	bellarmine	bumble-foot
brawniness	backpacker	breastwork	belladonna	bumfreezer
brainstorm	buck-rabbit	breathless	bellamoure	bimestrial
blasphemer	bichromate	brent-goose	bull-beeves	bimetallic
blanquette	backspauld	breath-test	bull-beggar	bomb-vessel
boat-racing	backstairs	beeswinged	balibuntal	Bombycidae
brassiness	backsheesh	beef-witted	bill-broker	bank-cheque
beadswoman	backstitch	breezeless	bulk-buying	band-clutch
beautician	backslider	breeziness	bel-accoyle	benedicite
bratticing	backstroke	buffalo-nut	bilocation	Benedictus
blastocyst	bacitracin	buff-jerkin	bilge-water	banderilla
blastoderm	backvelder	bufflehead	believable	banker-mark
beautifier	backworker	bafflingly	balderdash	Benzedrine
Blastoidea	backwardly	buffoonery	billet-doux	beneficial
blastomere	bedraggled	bifurcated	ballet-girl	beneficent
brant-goose	budgerigar	beforehand	billet-head	benefactor
blastopore	badderlock	beforetime	bullet-head	benefiting
beauty-spot	bed-wetting	baggage-car	ballerinas	benignancy
boastfully	bedchamber	big-bellied	balneology	benighting
bradyseism	Buddhistic	bigamously	beliefless	bond-holder
baby-farmer	Bedlington	big-mouthed	belletrist	Benthamism
biblically	by-drinking	bogtrotter	bullet-tree	Benthamite
bobbin-lace	bedellship	bagassosis	balneation	bunchiness
bibliology	bedclothes	behind-door	ball-flower	bunch-grass
bibliomane	bidentated	behind-hand	bell-flower	bantingism
bibliopegy	bedpresser	brigandage	bald-headed	bunglingly
bibliophil	bedevilled	brigandine	bull-headed	benumbment
bibliopole	bed-swerver	brigantine	bellhanger	bandmaster
bibliopoly	beef-brewis	blind-alley	bolshevise	benzocaine
baby-jumper	beefburger	blind-drunk	bolshevism	benzpyrene
bubbly-jock	beer-barrel	bride's-cake	bolshevist	bankruptcy
babblement	beer-bottle	bridesmaid	belshazzar	boneshaker
Babylonian	brecciated	bridegroom	bullionist	bone-spavin
Babylonish	breechless	bridgehead	ballistics	banishment
babblative	breadberry	bridgeless	ballistite	bondswoman
baby-minder	bread-board	Bridgerama	bolometric	band-string
bubonocele	breadfruit	blitheness	bull-necked	bonesetter
baby-ribbon	bread-crumb	brightness	belongings	bond-timber
babiroussa	bread-stick	blithering	bilinguist	binaurally
baby-sitter	breadstuff	blithesome	balconette	banqueteer
baby-walker	beer-engine	brightsome	ballooning	banqueting
bobbysoxer	beekeeping	Britishism	balloonist	benevolent
beccaficos	brevetting	bailieship	billposter	brocatelle
back-blocks	by-election	bricklayer	bull-roarer	brow-antler
buck-basket	beer-garden	brickmaker	Balbriggan	blow-by-blow
backbiting	blethering	brick-earth	bell-ringer	bookbinder
bêche-de-mer	beech-drops	brickfield	Belgravian	bioscience
bucketfuls	blepharism	brilliance	bell-shaped	bronchitic
bacterioid	breakwater	brilliancy	balustered	bronchitis
back-friend	bierkeller	bridle-hand	bell-siller	bronchiole
backgammon	break-front	bridle-path	balustrade	bioecology
background	beetle-eyed	bridle-road	belittling	boot-closer

broad-based
broad-gauge
blood-wagon
bloody-eyed
Brobdignag
boondoggle
broadsheet
broadpiece
blood-sized
blonde-lace
blood-plate
broadcloth
broodingly
broodiness
blood-royal
brood-pouch
blood-money
bloodhound
blood-horse
broidering
broad-arrow
blood-group
bloodstock
bloodstain
bloodstone
blood-guilt
broadsword
broken-down
biogenesis
biogenetic
biomedical
brokenness
biometrics
brome-grass
book-holder
biochemist
book-hunter
brother-man
biophysics
biorhythms
bookkeeper
block-chain
blockhouse
bootlicker
bootlegger
bootlessly
Bloomsbury
bookmaking
bootmaking
bookmarker
book-muslin
broomstick
broomstaff
Brownshirt
brownstone
biopoiesis
biological
biomorphic
biographer
biographic
bookseller
blossoming
blottesque

brontosaur
biodynamic
booby-prize
bronze-wing
bipedalism
baptistery
bipolarity
bipinnaria
baphometic
bipartisan
bipetalous
bequeathal
biquintile
bureaucrat
barracking
bar-parlour
barcarolle
barracoota
barracouta
barratrous
bursarship
barramunda
barramundi
burramundi
barebacked
bark-beetle
beribboned
bird-cherry
barley-bree
barrel-bulk
barley-broo
barleycorn
Berkeleian
barrelfuls
Barmecidal
borderland
borderline
borderless
barbellate
burnet-moth
barrenness
barge-board
burdensome
barber-shop
barkentine
burnettise
barbed-wire
barrenwort
barefooted
bareheaded
birthnight
birthright
birthplace
Bartholmew
bird-hipped
bur-thistle
bartisaned
barring-out
burnishing
barmitsvah
barbituric
barmitzvah
barelegged

burglarise
barometric
baronetage
baronetess
bardolatry
burrow-duck
barrow-tram
bird-pepper
bordraging
barysphere
bird-spider
bird-skiing
Bergsonian
Bergsonism
bird-strike
birostrate
burr-walnut
bird-witted
bastard-bar
bastardise
bastardism
byssaceous
bashawship
baseballer
basketball
basketfuls
basket-hilt
beseeching
basset-horn
Boswellian
bushelling
Boswellise
Boswellism
bissextile
basketwork
bass-fiddle
bush-harrow
bastinaded
bestialise
bestialism
bestiality
byssinosis
basmitsvah
basmitzvah
bisulphide
bisulphate
besom-rider
base-minded
bushmaster
bishop-bird
bestowment
bassoonist
bescribble
bestridden
bestraddle
baserunner
bushranger
besprinkle
bestraught
bestseller
bush-shrike
besottedly
batrachian

butter-bean
butter-boat
butter-bake
butter-bump
Battenberg
butter-bird
butterdock
butter-dish
butter-fish
bitter-king
bitterling
butter-milk
betterment
bettermost
betterness
bitterness
betweenity
bitter-root
bitter-spar
butlership
bothersome
butter-tree
butter-wife
bitterwood
butterwort
buttery-bar
bitchiness
butchering
bathing-box
bathing-hut
batmitsvah
batmitzvah
Betulaceae
battledoor
battledore
Betelgeuse
Betelgeuze
bottle-feed
bottle-fish
batologist
bottle-head
battlement
bottle-neck
bottle-nose
battleship
bottle-tree
bituminise
bituminate
bituminous
bathmizvah
bitonality
button-ball
button-bush
bathometer
buttoned-up
bottom-fish
button-hold
button-hole
button-hook
batholitic
batfowling
bottom-land
bottomless

button-wood
bathyscape
bathyscaph
bathymeter
bathymetry
botryoidal
bathylitic
bluebreast
blue-bonnet
Bourbonism
Bourbonist
bluebottle
blue-cheese
blue-collar
bounciness
blundering
brushwheel
blushingly
bousingken
Bourignian
brutifying
bluejacket
bouillotte
blue-pencil
brusquerie
bountihood
blue-tongue
bluethroat
blustering
blusterous
bluey-green
bivalvular
bivouacked
beweltered
bewildered
bowdlerise
bowdlerism
bow-fronted
bowerwoman
bowerwomen
bewitching
bewitchery
bawdy-house
bryologist
boyishness
bizarrerie
charabancs
chaparajos
clarabella
chaparejos
chamaeleon
coat-armour
Chamaerops
Charadrius
charactery
coal-bunker
Chambertin
chambering
chamberpot
Chamber-lye
Chalcidian
chalcedony
coal-cellar

chancellor	chalkiness	coactivity	cicatrices	coelomatic
chanceless	crankiness	coagulable	cicatrixes	chemonasty
Chaucerian	chalkboard	coagulator	cocktailed	Ctenophora
Chaucerism	crackbrain	crapulence	cacotrophy	ctenophore
coal-cutter	crack-tryst	chalumeaux	cacotopian	coenobitic
chandlerly	chalkstone	craquelure	cockyleeky	cheapskate
chaud-mellé	chaplaincy	chauvinism	codicology	creepingly
chandelier	chaplainry	chauvinist	cudgelling	creepmouse
chaudfroid	challenger	chalybeate	cudgel-play	caespitose
châtelaine	Charleston	cabbage-fly	caddis-case	cherry-bean
cranesbill	chaulmugra	cobwebbery	cod-fishing	cherry-coal
coalescent	cradlewalk	cobalt-blue	cod-fishery	cheirology
Clarenceux	chasmogamy	cabalistic	codlin-moth	cheironomy
crake-berry	charmingly	cybernetic	cuddlesome	cheeriness
czarevitch	clamminess	cub-hunting	code-number	cherry-plum
cravenness	coalmaster	cocoa-beans	cider-press	chevrotain
coacervate	chain-cable	cactaceous	cadaverous	clear-story
chauffeuse	channelled	cock-a-bondy	codswallop	cheerfully
chapfallen	chain-smoke	cockalorum	coelacanth	cheesecake
chaffingly	chauntress	cockatrice	coetaneous	chessylite
changeable	chain-drive	cockchafer	cretaceous	cheese-mite
changeably	clannishly	cacodaemom	Caesarship	cheesiness
chargeable	chain-store	Cecidomyia	cheechalko	chersonese
chargeably	chatoyance	cockernony	crescented	chessboard
charge-hand	coat-of-arms	cacography	crescentic	creatinine
craigfluke	cyanometer	cacogenics	coercively	creational
changeling	Charollais	cack-handed	chevesaile	chest-voice
changeless	clapped-out	cyclically	crewellery	creaturely
chargeless	champignon	coccineous	crenellate	creatively
cragginess	clay-pigeon	cachinnate	cleverness	creativity
change-over	clasp-knife	cochleated	co-eternity	crenulated
clay-ground	coal porter	cucullated	crêpe-soled	cheque-book
clangorous	clappering	Cochlearia	credential	crepuscule
coal-heaver	clapperboy	cucumiform	clementine	cherubical
cyathiform	chairwoman	cacuminous	clerestory	cherubimic
coach-wheel	claircolle	cacomistle	crewelwork	coequality
claw-hammer	chair-organ	coconut-shy	clergiable	coffee-bean
coat-hanger	chasse-café	coconut-oil	clergyable	coffer-fish
coach-horse	chaise-cart	cockneydom	clew-garnet	coffee-mill
coach-house	classicism	cockneyish	chevisance	caffeinism
crash-proof	classicist	cockneyism	chemically	coffee-room
coach-stand	Chassidism	cycloramic	creditable	coffee-tree
coach-built	classified	cycloidian	creditably	coffin-bone
charitable	classifier	cuckoldise	chelicerae	coffin-nail
charitably	chaiseless	cyclometer	chemisette	coffin-ship
clarichord	coarseness	cyclopedia	chewing-gum	cognisance
clavichord	clanswoman	cyclopedic	cretinised	cognisable
craniology	crab-stones	cyclothyme	chemicking	cognisably
coati-mondi	crassitude	cuckoo-pint	cherimoyer	cognominal
charioteer	coastwards	cyclograph	chemiatric	cogitation
craniotomy	Chartreuse	cyclo-cross	co-existent	cogitative
clavicular	chartulary	cuckoo-spit	check-taker	cohabitant
coati-mundi	chaptalise	cyclostyle	checklaton	cohibition
clarifying	chasteness	cyclostome	check-clerk	cohibitive
charity-boy	craftiness	cock-paddle	cheek-pouch	coherently
coadjacent	charthouse	cock-paidle	cheek-tooth	cohesively
coadjutrix	Chaetopoda	cacophonic	cream-faced	chinachina
coadjutant	chattering	cucurbital	cream-slice	climatical
clack-valve	chatterbox	Ciceronian	creaminess	chitarrone
crankshaft	coaptation	cicisbeism	cleansable	chivalrous
chank-shell	craft-guild	cocksiness	crew-necked	cuirassier
crank-sided	coastguard	cockteaser	cleromancy	chip-basket
crackajack	Chautauqua	cecutiency	chemotaxis	crib-biting

coincident	chirurgeon	cellophane®	compaction	comanchero
chinchilla	chirurgery	ciliophora	compacture	commonable
childbirth	cliquiness	coleorhiza	campanular	compotator
Childermas	cajolement	colportage	companying	commonalty
child-proof	collatable	Coleoptera	comicality	componency
childishly	collar-beam	colporteur	comédienne	composedly
child-study	collar-bone	colloquial	comedietta	cameo-shell
chimerical	cellar-book	collocutor	cummerbund	Compositae
chiselling	collateral	colloquise	commercial	compositor
chief-baron	collarette	colloquist	compendium	commodious
chiff-chaff	calcareous	colloquium	competence	compounder
chiffonier	cellar-flap	calyptrate	competency	commonness
ca'ing-whale	collar-stud	chlorodyne	competitor	commonweal
cringeling	collar-work	chloridise	compelling	compradore
cringingly	celebrated	chloridate	cumberless	camerlengo
clinginess	calibrator	calorifier	cumberment	comprehend
clingstone	celebrator	chloroform	compearant	camerlingo
clish-clash	Colubridae	cultriform	cumbersome	Camorrista
clinically	calico-bush	chloralism	commeasure	compromise
criminally	calyciform	chlorinise	compensate	Cameronian
critically	culiciform	chlorinate	campestral	compressed
chiliarchy	cold-chisel	chlorophyl	commentary	compressor
chiliastic	calico-tree	chloroquin	commentate	cameration
click-clack	calico-wood	coloration	Camberwell	cumbrously
chickenpox	Caledonian	coloratura	camphorate	comestible
chicken-run	cul-de-lampe	calescence	come-hither	comstocker
clinkstone	Collembola	calc-sinter	compilator	camsteerie
cricketing	calves'-foot	colostrous	commingled	cymotrichy
chilliness	calceiform	calotypist	Commiphora	cometology
chionodoxa	colleagued	colatitude	commitment	Camptonite
clientship	collegiate	calculated	commission	comitative
chimney-can	calceolate	cellulated	commissary	comeupance
chimney-pot	culvertage	calculable	commissure	come-upance
chimney-top	Colbertine	calculably	committing	communally
chiromancy	collecting	colourable	commixtion	commutable
crinoidean	collection	colourably	commixture	computable
clinometer	collective	culturable	compliance	commutator
clinometry	calefactor	culturally	compliancy	computator
crinolette	caliginous	calculator	compliable	comburgess
crinolined	calf-ground	colour-fast	complicacy	communique
cnidoblast	colchicine	cellulitis	complected	camouflage
chirognomy	calcinable	colourless	complacent	compulsion
chironomer	cultivable	cellulosic	complicant	compulsory
chironomic	collimator	calculuses	complicate	compulsive
chironomid	cultivator	colour-wash	complicity	combustion
Chironomus	calciferol	colour-ways	cumuliform	combustive
chirograph	calliature	combatable	complainer	cinnabaric
Chiroptera	colliquant	come-at-able	complement	canvas-back
crippledom	colliquate	comparable	compliment	connascent
chimpanzee	columnated	comparably	comeliness	convalesce
chirpiness	chlamydate	comparator	complanate	contadinas
crispbread	calumniate	commandeer	camel-corps	cannabinol
crispation	calumnious	commandant	camelopard	contagious
crispature	calamander	commanding	complotted	cinnamonic
chinquapin	calamitous	commandery	completely	cantaloupe
cribriform	calendarer	campaigner	completion	centaurian
cribration	colonnaded	compatible	cumulation	cantatrice
crio-sphinx	colonially	compatibly	completory	contactual
criss-cross	cylindroid	comparison	completive	confabular
cristiform	cylindrite	compatriot	cumulative	connatural
clistogamy	Celtomania	compass-saw	compluvium	canvas-work
chittagong	colposcope	compassing	complexion	cony-burrow
chittering	colposcopy	compassion	complexity	conscience

conacreism	contention	conviction	contraband	consumable
cine-camera	convection	consistory	canary-bird	conjurator
convenance	convention	convictism	contrabass	conjunctly
conveyance	conjecture	convictive	contribute	confusedly
convenable	consectary	continuant	contracted	consumedly
conveyable	contexture	contiguity	contractor	cinque-foil
candelabra	concettism	continuate	centricity	conducible
canterbury	concettist	continuity	contrecoup	consummate
cannel-coal	convertite	contiguous	contradict	cinque-pace
candescent	conceitful	continuous	congruence	Cantuarian
cinder-cone	conceptive	candle-bomb	congruency	concurrent
condescend	congestive	conglobate	centrifuge	concurring
contendent	connective	candle-coal	centrefold	conquering
contending	convective	canaliculi	cancriform	conqueress
confederal	consequent	concluding	congregant	consulship
conference	confervoid	candle-doup	congregate	convulsant
congeneric	conservant	confluence	centre-half	concussion
congenetic	canker-worm	candle-fish	contrahent	convulsion
cankeredly	coniferous	conclusion	controlled	consubsist
Cinderella	conchiform	conclusory	controller	concussive
convexedly	conchoidal	conclusive	contraltos	convulsive
convergent	conchology	candle-tree	centralise	consuetude
converging	cinchonine	conflation	centralism	consultant
centesimal	cinchonise	conclavist	centralist	consulting
congenital	cinchonism	candlewick	centrality	conduction
candelilla	connivance	candle-wood	contraplex	consultory
convenient	connivancy	canonicals	contraprop	conductive
cancelling	cannibally	canonicity	centre-rail	consultive
cannelloni	confinable	canonistic	contrarily	centumviri
cancellate	confidante	consonance	cinerarium	candy-floss
cancellous	cone-in-cone	consonancy	canary-seed	crotalaria
conferment	convincing	consolable	centrosome	chota-hazri
centennial	confiscate	cannonball	concretely	Crotalidae
concerning	confidence	concordial	contritely	cholagogic
contemning	confidency	concordant	cineration	cholagogue
convexness	connivence	condolence	concretion	crotcheted
cinder-path	connivency	canzonetta	contrition	cuomceiled
conferring	continence	canzonette	concretism	cloacaline
cancer-root	continency	cannon-game	concretist	choiceness
consecrate	cantilever	consociate	concretive	crouch-ware
consensual	centimeter	censorious	canorously	cloudberry
conversely	centimetre	cantonment	contravene	chondritic
conversant	contingent	conformist	controvert	cloudiness
concession	conoidical	conformity	canary-wood	co-ordinate
confession	consimilar	confounded	cancrizans	coordinate
conversion	concipient	conjointly	canescence	crop-duster
condensery	consilient	censorship	constraint	cloud-built
condensate	centilitre	cannon-shot	constringe	cloudburst
concessive	conciliary	concoction	constantan	cooperator
conceptual	conciliate	contortion	Constantia	co-operator
contextual	centillion	consortism	constantly	closed-door
conventual	cantillate	consortium	constipate	chokeberry
concentred	confirmand	concoctive	cunctation	clove-hitch
concentric	confirming	contortive	cunctatory	cloverleaf
concertina	consignify	convoluted	constitute	choreology
concertino	cancionero	conspectus	constative	closet-play
contestant	candidness	canophilia	cunctative	close-stool
contesting	cincinnate	canophobia	Conjugatae	chopfallen
convertend	concinnity	cynophobia	conjugated	crow-flower
conception	concinnous	canephorus	censurable	clogginess
confection	centigrade	conspiracy	censurably	cloth-eared
congestion	consistent	conspirant	confutable	cool-headed
connection	conniption	centre-back	conjugally	clodhopper

clothes-peg
clothes-pin
crocheting
cooling-off
clomiphene
choliambic
choriambic
clockmaker
clock-radio
crowkeeper
chock-tight
crook-kneed
chockstone
crown-jewel
crown-agent
crown-wheel
crown-piece
crown-glass
crown-green
crown-graft
clownishly
Crocodilia
Crocodilus
crocoisite
croupiness
choir-organ
cross-match
crosspatch
cross-ratio
crossbench
cloistered
cloisterer
cross-refer
cross-check
crosspiece
crosslight
chopsticks
cross-birth
cross-claim
crossroads
crossbones
crossbower
cross-armed
crossbreed
crow-shrike
cloistress
cross-staff
cross-stone
caoutchouc
clostridia
clottiness
co-optation
co-optative
chorus-girl
cephalagra
cephalitis
cephalopod
capability
capacitate
cupidinous
capodastro
co-presence
copperhead

capreolate
copper-nose
copperskin
copper-work
copper-worm
copyholder
capsizable
cypripedia
copying-ink
Cyprinidae
capricious
captiously
capillaire
copulation
copulatory
copulative
cup-and-ball
cup-and-ring
capnomancy
coprolalia
coprophagy
coprolitic
caper-sauce
Capernaite
Cyperaceae
coparcener
Copernican
copartnery
capernoity
copesettic
capitolian
capitoline
capitulant
capitulary
capitalise
capitalism
capitalist
capitulate
capitellum
copy-typing
copy-typist
capitation
cappuccino
copywriter
coquelicot
coquetting
coquettish
coquimbite
Cortaderia
coriaceous
curvaceous
carragheen
caryatidal
caryatides
caryatidic
curvacious
carnallite
carmagnole
carnassial
Circassian
currant-bun
corn-brandy
cerebritis

cerebellar
curability
cerebellum
carabineer
carabinier
corybantes
corybantic
care-crazed
Caricaceae
corncockle
cork-carpet
card-castle
cork-cutter
corn-cutter
caricatura
caricature
corn-dealer
coradicate
corn-dodger
corn-dollie
corydaline
curfew-bell
corselette
corregidor
corsetière
corbelling
carpellary
carpet-moth
cursedness
correspond
curled-pate
circensian
cornel-tree
curvetting
correction
correption
correctory
corrective
cornerwise
cornflakes
corn-factor
cornflower
cerography
coregonine
cork-heeled
card-holder
carphology
carthamine
cirrhipede
Cirrhopoda
Carthusian
cornhusker
corticated
cardinally
corrigenda
Cirripedia
cardiogram
corking-pin
corrigible
cardiology
cardialgia
cordillera
cordialise

cordiality
carcinogen
carcinosis
cirrigrade
certiorari
cordierite
corbiculae
curricular
corniculum
curriculum
certifying
cork-jacket
corn-kister
coral-berry
Carolinian
coral-snake
carelessly
co-relation
co-relative
chrome-alum
ceramicist
chromidium
chromogram
corn-maiden
corn-miller
caramelise
ceremonial
coromandel
ceruminous
curb-market
chromosome
chromatics
chromatype
chromotype
chrematist
chronicler
chronicity
chronogram
Cerinthian
Corinthian
chronology
chronotron
coronation
caruncular
cartomancy
corporally
corporator
carbon-copy
cariogenic
corporeity
cartophile
cartophily
carpophore
cormophyte
corrodible
corrosible
carbonnade
cartonnage
cartoonist
corroboree
coryphaeus
carapacial
corn-popper

cornstarch
corpse-gate
Christhood
corn-spirit
Christiana
chrysalids
Christlike
Christless
chrysolite
Christmasy
chrysophan
chrysotile
curb-trader
carotenoid
carotinoid
corn-thrips
curateship
corrugated
circulable
circularly
circulator
corrugator
carbuncled
corpuscule
circumcise
circumduce
circumduct
corpulence
corpulency
circumflex
circumfuse
curmudgeon
circummure
cornucopia
circumpose
curmurring
circuiteer
corruption
circuitous
corruptive
circumvent
caravaneer
caravanned
caravaner
caravaning
curb-vendor
corn-weevil
cordwainer
cartwright
corn-whisky
carrying-on
custard-pie
cascarilla
casualness
case-bottle
cash-credit
Cistercian
cosmetical
costean-pit
costeaning
cussedness
cashew-nuts
Cassegrain

Cisleithan	catenation	churn-staff	dramaturge	deaspirate
case-harden	cotton-boll	coulometer	dramaturgy	diatribist
cuspidated	cathode-ray	coulometry	drawbridge	drag-racing
cosmically	citronella	clumpiness	drabbiness	diarrhoeal
castigator	catholicon	counselled	dealbation	diarrhoeic
cassia-bark	catholicos	counsellor	dearbought	diagraphic
casting-net	cotton-mill	clumsiness	Drawcansir	diatropism
cessionary	cottonseed	court-baron	diazeuctic	dead-stroke
Cassiopeia	cotton-tree	crustacean	diagenesis	draw-string
cashiering	cottontail	causticity	diagenetic	diastaltic
cash-keeper	cottonweed	courtierly	diapedesis	diastemata
costliness	cotton-wood	count-wheel	diapedetic	draft-horse
casemented	cotton-wool	crustiness	diabetical	deactivate
co-sentient	cotton-worm	court-house	Diadelphia	dead-weight
cosmoramic	catapultic	counteract	dealership	dialysable
customable	cataphonic	courtcraft	dialectics	Dibranchia
cosmolatry	cataphract	clustering	drakestone	dabblingly
cystoscope	catoptrics	counter-spy	dead-finish	debilitate
cystoscopy	cat-cracker	court-dress	dwarfishly	debonnaire
cestoidean	catarrhine	cluster-cup	dead-ground	debonairly
cassolette	catarrhous	courtesied	draught-bar	debentured
customised	catastasis	cruet-stand	draughtman	debasement
custom-made	cat-burglar	crustation	draught-net	debasingly
cosmogonic	cutty-stool	court-guide	death-watch	debateable
cosmopolis	citizeness	court-sword	death-adder	debatingly
cosmodrome	citizenise	countryman	death-agony	dubitation
cismontane	courageful	country-box	death's-head	dubitative
cispontine	courageous	couturière	death-throe	debauchery
Cestracion	coumarilic	Cavicornia	death-knell	debouchure
castration	crumb-cloth	cavalierly	diaphanous	declarable
costus-root	chubbiness	cavalryman	death-token	declarator
cassumunar	crumb-brush	covenanted	diachronic	declaredly
case-worker	church-goer	covenantee	death-wound	dictaphone
catabolism	councilman	covenanter	diathermal	declaimant
cat's-cradle	councillor	covenantor	diathermic	declaiming
catechesis	churchless	covariance	drawing-pen	dictatress
catechetic	church-rate	covetingly	drawing-pin	declassify
catechiser	church-text	cavitation	diaskeuast	decrassify
catacumbal	couscousou	covetously	diallagoid	deck-bridge
cytochrome	churchward	cowcatcher	dead-lights	duck-billed
catechumen	churchyard	cow-parsley	drawlingly	docibility
catafalque	causewayed	cow-parsnip	deadliness	decoctible
categorial	caulescent	cow-chervil	dead-letter	dickcissel
categories	chuffiness	cowdie-pine	dharmshala	decadently
categorise	club-footed	cowrie-pine	deaf-mutism	decreeable
categorist	club-headed	coweringly	diagnostic	decrescent
catch-basin	crushingly	cowardship	dead-nettle	Dickensian
catchpenny	couch-grass	cowpuncher	diagonally	declension
catch-drain	Clusiaceae	coxcomical	diagometer	decagramme
cote-hardie	Cruciferae	cryoconite	dragon-fish	decigramme
cottierism	cousinhood	Clydesdale	dragonhead	decagynian
cuttle-bone	cauliflory	clypeiform	deaconhood	decagynous
catalectic	cautionary	cryogenics	diabolical	decahedral
cotyliform	cousinship	cryometric	draconites	decahedron
cuttlefish	cautiously	cryophorus	diaconicon	deceivable
cataloguer	cauliculus	coyishness	dragonlike	deceivably
cattle-grid	crucifying	cryoscopic	dragonnade	declinable
cytologist	chuck-wagon	cryptogram	dragon-root	declinator
catalogize	chucker-out	cryptogamy	deaconship	dictionary
cataleptic	couplement	cryptology	diacoustic	decollated
catamenial	churlishly	dramatical	dragon-tree	deckle-edge
Cotingidae	clubmaster	diacaustic	Dracontium	duck-legged
catenarian	churn-drill	diamantine	dray-plough	decalogist

decolonise	didynamian	defunctive	dilacerate	dominative
decolorant	didynamous	deflowerer	delicately	dumfounder
decolorise	Didunculus	daffodilly	dolichurus	demurrable
decelerate	didascalic	difformity	dolcemente	dimorphism
decolorate	die-casting	deferrable	diligently	dimorphous
dochmiacal	deep-browed	deformable	delegation	demoralise
decumbence	dreadlocks	deformedly	deligation	demureness
decumbency	dreadfully	deforciant	delightful	demirepdom
Decemberly	dietetical	diffusedly	delphinoid	damasceene
decemviral	dielectric	diffusible	dolphin-fly	dame-school
docimology	deep-freeze	degradable	delphinium	domestical
decimalise	deer-forest	dog-fancier	deltiology	dumbstruck
decimalism	dregginess	dogmatiser	dulciloquy	demoticist
decimalist	die-sinking	digladiate	dilemmatic	dumb-waiter
decampment	dreikanter	dog-parsley	delaminate	dumpy-level
documental	dreamwhile	doggedness	dolomitise	dung-beetle
decomposer	dreamingly	daguerrean	delimitate	denudation
decompound	dreaminess	degreasant	delineable	dunderfunk
Decembrist	dream-world	degression	delineator	dinner-gown
decompress	drearihead	digression	delinquent	dunderhead
decamerous	drearihood	degressive	dildo-glass	dinner-hour
dock-master	dreariment	digressive	dilapidate	dinnerless
docimastic	dreariness	digger-wasp	deliquesce	dinner-pail
decimation	deep-rooted	dog's-fennel	deliration	donkey-pump
dicynodont	drearisome	dog-biscuit	dolorously	dunderpate
decennoval	deep-seated	dignifying	dolesomely	dinner-time
decandrian	dressmaker	daggle-tail	delusional	dance-music
decinormal	dress-shirt	degeneracy	doll's-house	donkey-work
decandrous	deep-sinker	degenerate	delusively	denigrator
doctor-fish	dress-goods	digoneutic	dilettante	denegation
Dictograph	dyer's-broom	digestedly	dilettanti	dung-hunter
doctorship	dressguard	digestible	diluteness	densimeter
dice-player	defeasance	digitiform	dilatorily	densimetry
decapodous	defrayable	dog's-tongue	dilatation	dentifrice
decipher	defeasible	digitorium	dull-witted	dynamicist
deceptible	defrayment	digitately	dilly-dally	dynamogeny
deceptious	deflagrate	digitation	delayingly	denominate
decapitate	deficience	dehydrater	demobilise	dynamistic
deck-quoits	deficiency	dehydrator	democratic	dynamitard
decurrency	defectible	dehumidify	demi-cannon	dinanderie
dichroitic	defacement	dehumanise	damp-course	dining-hall
dichromism	defacingly	dehiscence	demi-ditone	denunciate
dichromate	defecation	drivelling	demography	dining-room
decoration	difference	driving-box	damageable	dendrobium
decorative	differency	drink-money	demagogism	dendriform
decorously	deflection	drill-press	Demogorgon	dendrogram
decussated	deflective	Deinoceras	demoiselle	dendroidal
decisively	diffidence	daintiness	damping-off	dendrology
decathlete	difficulty	daisy-wheel	dumbledore	Dendrophis
deck-tennis	defalcator	daisy-chain	dimplement	dynastical
Docetistic	defoliator	dejectedly	demolisher	Dinosauria
decivilise	defilement	dijudicate	demolition	denotement
decryption	defamation	dika-butter	demoniacal	denaturant
didactical	defamatory	dukkeripen	demandable	denaturise
deductible	defendable	dollarless	diminuendo	donatistic
deducement	defensible	dollarship	dementedly	denotation
dedication	defensibly	dull-browed	demonology	denotative
dedicatory	definement	deliberate	dominantly	dénouement
dedicative	definitude	delibation	diminished	duniwassal
didgeridoo	definitely	delectable	diminution	dandy-fever
didelphian	definition	delectably	domination	dandy-horse
didelphine	defunction	dilucidate	demonetise	Donnybrook
didelphous	definitive	Dolichotis	diminutive	dandy-brush

denization
duodecimal
duodenitis
diothelism
dyothelism
diothelete
diothelite
dyothelete
dyothelite
drop-hammer
diophysite
dyophysite
deoxidiser
door-keeper
drop-letter
drosometer
drosophila
deodoriser
deoppilate
droopingly
droopiness
drossiness
drowsiness
door-to-door
dioptrical
deontology
diorthosis
diorthotic
depravedly
dupability
deprecable
deprecator
depredator
depreciate
dapperling
dapperness
depressant
depressing
depression
depressive
deprivable
duplicator
dapple-grey
depolarise
dopplerite
depilation
depilatory
dependable
dependably
dependence
dependency
diplomatic
dipsomania
deplorable
deplorably
deployment
Diplodocus
depopulate
department
deportment
depuration
depuratory
depurative

deposition
depositary
depository
depositive
diphtheria
diphtheric
dipetalous
deputation
diphyodont
diphyletic
dermatitis
dermatogen
dermatosis
Dermaptera
durability
directness
deracinate
Directoire
directress
deridingly
dirt-eating
derogately
derogation
derogatory
derogative
dorsifixed
dérailleur
derailment
dorsigrade
diremption
Dermoptera
dirt-rotten
derisively
durational
derivation
derivative
disparager
disparates
dispatcher
diseaseful
dissatisfy
déshabillé
dishabille
disbarment
disharmony
disgarnish
dismalness
disdainful
despairing
despairful
dispassion
disnatured
disability
desecrater
desecrator
desiccator
diseconomy
disadvance
desiderata
desiderate
desiderium
desperados
dissembler

descendant
descendent
descending
dissevered
disherison
disheritor
disbelieve
dispelling
dispermous
discerning
disrespect
dishearten
dispersoid
distensile
dispersant
descension
dispersion
dissension
distension
dispensary
dispersive
distensive
dissecting
dissenting
disjection
dissection
distention
disfeature
dissertate
dissective
disservice
disc-floret
disc-flower
designable
designator
designedly
designless
designment
dissheathe
dysthymiac
dysphemism
discharger
disc-harrow
dissipated
despicable
despicably
dispisable
dislikable
dissipable
distinctly
dissidence
despiteful
despiteous
dislikeful
dispiteous
distinguée
distichous
dissimilar
dispirited
dissilient
discipline
distilland
distilling

distillery
distillate
discission
dismission
dismissory
dismissive
dessiatine
disc-jockey
dust-jacket
displeased
disyllabic
disyllable
disulphide
disulphate
disclaimer
displenish
desalinate
disglorify
displosion
disclosure
desolately
desolation
desolatory
disimagine
disembowel
disembosom
disembogue
disembroil
disimprove
disengaged
disinherit
dysenteric
disenvelop
disenthral
disinthral
disenchain
disenchant
disinhibit
disentitle
disenviron
disincline
disenclose
disinclose
disenslave
disanimate
disendowed
disennoble
disinvolve
disentrain
disentwine
dissonance
dissonancy
disloyally
disposable
disloyalty
disconcert
dispondaic
despondent
disponding
discordant
discordful
discoverer
disposedly

dishonesty
discomfort
discophile
Discophora
despotical
dispositor
dissociate
discommode
discommend
disconnect
discounsel
discounter
disjointed
discobolus
discompose
discourser
discourage
disworship
disconsent
dispossess
discontent
distortion
distortive
dissoluble
dissolvent
dissolving
disapparel
desipience
disepalous
disc-plough
disappoint
disapprove
disarrange
disorganic
distribute
distracted
destructor
disordered
deservedly
discreetly
disorderly
disprofess
dispraiser
distrainee
distrainer
distrainor
desertless
desireless
distringas
disgruntle
dysgraphia
dysgraphic
dystrophia
dystrophic
discrepant
distressed
dyscrasite
dysprosium
discretely
desorption
discretion
discretive
distraught

desirously	detergence	devotional	enamouring	euchlorine
distrouble	detergency	devourment	exasperate	escalation
disprovide	determiner	devoutness	enarration	escalatory
destroying	dethroning	down-and-out	elasticise	encampment
desistance	detestable	down-at-heel	elasticate	encincture
desistence	detestably	down-easter	elasticity	encroacher
disespouse	detruncate	dew-retting	enantiosis	encloister
disastrous	detoxicant	downfallen	exactitude	encephalic
disutility	detoxicate	dawdlingly	exaltation	encephalin
disputable	drug-addict	dowel-joint	evacuation	encephalon
disputably	drupaceous	down-market	evaluation	exceptious
disturbant	drumbledor	Dewar-flask	evacuative	escapology
disjunctor	drudgingly	dower-house	evaluative	escapeless
disquieten	dough-baked	downstairs	emblazoner	escapement
disquietly	doughfaced	downstream	emblazonry	eccoprotic
Dasyuridae	daughterly	downstroke	eubacteria	encircling
discutient	dauphiness	downwardly	embodiment	escarpment
disqualify	doughiness	dexterwise	emblematic	eucaryotic
desquamate	double-bass	doxography	emblements	excerpting
disfurnish	double-chin	dextrogyre	emboldener	excerption
disculpate	double-dyed	dextrality	embalmment	excursuses
disguising	double-eyed	dextrously	embolismal	encasement
discursion	double-flat	drysaltery	embolismic	encashment
discussion	double-gild	day-scholar	embankment	encystment
dissuasion	double-hung	day-release	embonpoint	excusatory
discursory	doubleness	day-wearied	embroidery	escutcheon
dissuasory	double-park	day-boarder	embrowning	excitement
discursist	doubletree	daydreamer	embarkment	excitation
discursive	double-take	day-tripper	embargoing	excitatory
discussive	double-talk	dry-cupping	ember-goose	excitative
dissuasive	diurnalist	dazzlement	embassador	encourager
disburthen	deutoplasm	dazzlingly	embasement	excruciate
disgusting	doulocracy	epanaphora	embossment	excavation
disruption	doubtingly	emasculate	embittered	ecchymosed
disgustful	doubtfully	emancipist	embitterer	ecchymosis
disruptive	diuturnity	emancipate	embouchure	ecchymotic
disavaunce	duumvirate	ecardinate	elbow-chair	encryption
disownment	dive-bomber	exacerbate	embowelled	endearment
dish-washer	devocalise	evanescent	embryogeny	endocrinal
dessyatine	dove-colour	enamelling	embryology	endocrinic
detracting	dive-dapper	enamellist	embryulcia	endocritic
detraction	divagation	elatedness	embryonate	endodermal
detractory	developing	evangeliar	embryotomy	endodermic
detractive	devalorise	evangelise	escharotic	endodermis
detachable	devilishly	evangelism	enchanting	eudaemonia
detectable	devolution	evangelist	encyclical	eudaemonic
date-coding	diving-bell	emarginate	escadrille	endogamous
detachedly	devanagari	exaggerate	excrescent	endogenous
detectible	divineness	edaphology	excrementa	endemicity
detachment	divineress	eradicated	ecclesiast	endamoebae
ditheletic	diving-suit	eradicable	escheatage	eudemonics
ditheistic	divination	examinable	excogitate	endomorphy
ditch-water	divinatory	eradicator	encrinital	endangerer
Dutchwoman	divaricate	examinator	encrinitic	endopodite
Dutchwomen	divergence	emaciation	encoignure	endopleura
ditriglyph	divergency	eradiation	escritoire	endophytic
detainment	divertible	edaciously	exculpable	endermatic
dithionate	devastator	epaulement	excellence	endorsable
datum-level	devastivit	eyas-musket	excellency	end-product
datum-plane	divestible	evaporable	escalloped	elderberry
datamation	divestment	elaborator	escallonia	endermical
detonation	divisional	evaporator	eucalyptol	endorhizal
ditrochean	devitalise	epagomenal	eucalyptus	enduringly

endoscopic	everyplace	exhalation	enigmatist	economiser
endosmosis	emery-cloth	ephemerist	ebionitism	exopoditic
endosmotic	emery-board	euhemerise	episodical	ecospecies
end-stopped	effaceable	euhemerism	epitomical	exospheric
eye-catcher	efficacity	euhemerist	epidotised	exosporous
emerald-cut	efficience	ephemerous	epitomiser	eloquently
elecampane	efficiency	exhumation	editorship	evolvement
emendation	effectible	ethambutol	epizootics	eponychium
emendatory	effectless	echinoderm	epiloguise	emphatical
epexegesis	effacement	Echinoidea	eriophorum	emplastron
epexegetic	enfacement	Etheostoma	epispastic	emplastrum
eyelet-hole	effectuate	echopraxia	epigrapher	expectance
exegetical	effleurage	echopraxis	epigraphic	expectancy
eye-legible	effigurate	ethereally	emigration	especially
eleventhly	effulgence	exheredate	emigratory	expectedly
elementary	enfoldment	enharmonic	emissivity	expedience
eye-service	effeminacy	euharmonic	ekistician	expediency
eye-servant	effeminise	exhaust-gas	epistolary	espadrille
Everglades	effeminate	exhaustion	epistolise	expedition
emergently	effloresce	exhaustive	epistolist	expeditate
energetics	effrontery	ericaceous	epistemics	expeditive
Erewhonian	effervesce	epitaphian	epistrophe	expressman
even-handed	enforcedly	epitaphist	episternal	expressway
erethismic	effortless	epicanthic	episternum	expressage
erethistic	enfestered	epigastric	evil-worker	expression
emetically	effusively	epicanthus	epicycloid	expressure
eremitical	effeteness	evincement	edifyingly	expressive
eye-witness	egg-capsule	episcopacy	enjoinment	expugnable
ever-living	ergodicity	episcopant	enjambment	explicable
even-minded	Euglenales	episcopise	enkephalin	explicator
eternalise	eagle-stone	episcopate	eukaryotic	explicitly
eternalist	engagement	eviscerate	enlacement	empoisoned
eye-spotted	engagingly	Eriocaulon	eulogistic	expendable
epeirogeny	egg-binding	episematic	eglandular	expansible
execration	Englishman	epideictic	elliptical	expansibly
execratory	Englishism	epigenesis	enlargedly	empanelled
execrative	engulfment	epigenetic	enlistment	expunction
Eleusinian	eigenvalue	epimeletic	enlevement	employable
eventually	egg-and-dart	epidemical	Emmentaler	euphorbium
epenthesis	ergonomics	epidermoid	emmenology	ecphonesis
epenthetic	ergonomist	eviternity	emmetropia	euphonical
electrical	engine-room	eminential	emmetropic	euphoriant
erectility	engendrure	epicentral	Enneandria	euphonious
edentulous	engrossing	evidential	enneagonal	employment
electrogen	ergophobia	epithelial	enneastyle	exprobrate
electromer	engarrison	epithelium	exorbitant	exploitage
electronic	ergosterol	epithemata	exorbitate	exploitive
electorial	eightscore	epiphonema	exogenetic	exportable
electoress	eightpence	epithermal	exoterical	expurgator
electorate	eighteenmo	epiphytism	egocentric	ecphractic
exenterate	eightpenny	eliminable	eloignment	emphractic
electively	eighteenth	eliminator	elongation	empiricism
electivity	ergatogyne	epilimnion	exophagous	empiricist
executancy	engouement	epidiorite	exothermal	emparadise
executable	exhibition	epididymis	exothermic	experience
executress	exhibitory	edibleness	exobiology	experiment
enervating	exhibitive	epiblastic	éboulement	expertness
enervation	enhydritic	epiplastra	emollition	Euphrosyne
enervative	ethnically	epiglottic	enormously	expiration
emery-paper	ethologist	epiglottis	erotomania	expiratory
emery-wheel	ethylamine	etiolation	erotogenic	exposition
everything	exhilarant	evil-minded	ecological	expository
everywhere	exhilarate	enigmatise	economical	expositive

expatiator	extraction	exulcerate	feateously	factorship
empathetic	extractive	exuberance	flat-footed	face-powder
expatriate	extra-mural	exuberancy	flagginess	face-saving
euphuistic	enticeable	enumerator	frangipane	face-to-face
empoverish	enticement	erubescent	frangipani	factuality
Eurocratic	enticingly	erubescite	fraughtage	faceworker
ebracteate	ectodermal	ecumenical	flashlight	fiducially
enrichment	ectodermic	egurgitate	flashiness	fiddle-back
Euroclydon	entremesse	elucidator	flash-point	fiddlehead
Eurafrican	entreasure	exuviation	flash-board	fadelessly
enragement	entreating	ebullience	flash-house	fiddlewood
enregiment	entreative	ebulliency	feather-bed	federalise
enregister	ectogenous	ebullition	feathering	federalism
earth-table	extricable	equanimity	Fraxinella	federalist
earth-shine	entailment	equanimous	flamingoes	federation
earth-light	entoilment	eburnation	Flamingant	federative
earth-plate	ecthlipsis	equipotent	flaminical	fuddy-duddy
earth-smoke	entamoebae	elutriator	flagitious	flea-beetle
eard-hunger	entomology	emulsifier	frabjously	freebooter
eard-hungry	entombment	equestrian	fearlessly	flea-bitten
earthiness	extemporal	exultantly	fragmental	fleeceless
earthbound	ectomorphy	exultingly	fragmented	fleechment
earth-board	estimation	eruptional	flaunching	fierceness
earth-house	estimative	equatorial	flannelled	flea-circus
earthquake	extendable	equitation	fearnought	fleece-wool
ear-witness	extenuator	eructation	flavouring	fieldwards
earlierise	extendedly	exultation	flapperish	fieldpiece
ear-kissing	extendible	equivocate	fratricide	freedwoman
Euromarket	extensible	equivalent	flagrantly	freedwomen
errand-girl	estanciero	environics	fragrantly	fieldmouse
eurypterid	extinction	enwrapment	fearsomely	fieldboots
Eurypterus	extincture	enwrapping	frantic-mad	fieldstone
enraptured	extinctive	erythritic	fractional	free-diving
ear-trumpet	extinguish	erysipelas	flattering	foederatus
éprouvette	Eatanswill	elytriform	flatulence	fremescent
ear-bussing	estipulate	Egyptology	flatulency	frenetical
Eurovision	entophytal	enzymology	flag-waving	free-fooder
eurhythmic	ectophytic	eczematous	fibreglass	free-footed
Eustachian	entophytic	framboesia	fibreboard	free-for-all
exsiccator	externally	flabbiness	fabricator	free-fisher
eisteddfod	extirpable	flag-basket	fibrillary	fledgeling
easselgate	extirpator	flamboyant	fibrillose	freight-car
easterling	enterocele	flaccidity	fibrillate	freightage
eastermost	enthralled	fianchetto	fibrillous	feed-heater
Eastertide	enthraldom	franchiser	fibrinogen	flesh-eater
Eastertime	enterolith	flanconade	febrifugal	freshwater
easselward	enthronise	francophil	fabulosity	freeholder
exsufflate	entireness	Franciscan	fabulously	fresh-blown
ensignship	exteriorly	flap-dragon	fibrositis	free-handed
enschedule	enterprise	fraudulent	fibroblast	fleshiness
eosinophil	enterotomy	flapdoodle	factitious	flesh-wound
ensanguine	estatesman	fraudfully	fictitious	fresherdom
exsanguine	enthusiasm	frame-maker	factionary	flesh-brush
essayistic	enthusiast	Fratercula	factionist	flesh-broth
euthanasia	Euthyneura	flavescent	fictionist	foeticidal
entrancing	Entryphone®	flake-white	factiously	flexihours
eutrapelia	emulatress	flagellant	facileness	fee-fi-fo-fum
extraneity	equability	flabellate	fickleness	freakiness
extraneous	exurbanite	Flagellata	fecklessly	freakishly
estrangelo	enunciable	flagellate	facilities	freeloader
entrapment	enunciator	fraternise	facilitate	free-labour
extra-solar	edulcorant	fraternity	facinorous	freelancer
extractant	edulcorate	frame-house	factorable	feebleness

free-minded	fairy-cycle	famishment	frowningly	formidable
freemartin	foliaceous	fumatorium	floppiness	formidably
fleur-de-lis	fallacious	famousness	foot-racing	fornicator
fleur-de-lys	full-bodied	fontanelle	floorcloth	forbidding
fleeringly	filibuster	fantastico	floorboard	forcing-pit
free-school	full-bottom	finicality	flourished	far-sighted
free-soiler	full-cocked	funiculate	frog's-march	fertiliser
free-select	Filicineae	fingerbowl	frog's-mouth	fervidness
free-spoken	filicinean	fingerhold	frontwards	fortissimo
free-trader	full-circle	fingerhole	front-bench	forkit-tail
fleetingly	file-cutter	fingerling	frost-smoke	fortifying
frequenter	felicitate	fingerless	floatingly	formlessly
frequently	felicitous	fingermark	floutingly	foraminous
free-verser	false-faced	fingernail	frostiness	fire-master
fifty-pence	filterable	fingerpost	frostbound	forinsecal
fifty-fifty	fuliginous	finger's-end	float-board	firing-step
figurehead	full-handed	fund-holder	float-stone	fore-notice
figuration	filchingly	fontinalis	floatation	furuncular
figurative	filthiness	fungicidal	foot-warmer	foreordain
fugitation	fulmineous	fancifully	fore-and-aft	fire-office
fugitively	falling-off	fonticulus	farrandine	forfoughen
Fahrenheit	falsidical	fantoccini	ferrandine	ferronière
fricandeau	fulfilling	Finno-Ugric	forwarding	ferro-alloy
fricasseed	fulfilment	fan-cricket	forsakenly	ferroprint
fair-boding	faldistory	fen-cricket	fore-advise	furrow-weed
friability	follicular	fenestella	fire-bucket	fire-policy
flindersia	falsifying	fine-spoken	foreboding	fire-plough
fringillid	file-leader	fenestrate	fire-blight	fore-quoted
fringeless	full-length	fanaticise	fire-basket	fire-raiser
fair-ground	folklorist	fanaticism	forechosen	forerunner
fair-headed	folk-memory	fine-tuning	forecasted	foreshadow
flight-deck	fellmonger	finiteness	forecaster	forest-bred
frightened	fallow-chat	functional	forecastle	forest-born
fair-haired	falcon-eyed	fool-begged	forecourse	foreshewed
flightless	fellow-heir	footbridge	fore-damned	foreseeing
frithsoken	fallowness	Froebelian	fer-de-lance	fire-shovel
frightsome	fellowship	footballer	far-fetched	foreshowed
frithstool	felspathic	Froebelism	forfeuchen	fire-screen
faithfully	filariasis	flocculent	fervescent	forest-tree
fritillary	full-rigged	flocculate	fire-escape	fernticled
frigidness	fell-runner	flosculous	fire-engine	ferntickle
flick-knife	filtration	foot-candle	fortepiano	first-thing
friskingly	folk-speech	floodwater	forcedness	first-aider
friskiness	full-sailed	floodlight	forkedness	fork-tailed
fair-leader	full-summed	flower-bell	forbearant	first-night
fair-minded	folksiness	florescent	forbearing	foreteller
friendlily	full-voiced	flower-girl	forgetting	first-floor
friendless	fell-walker	flower-head	forfeiture	first-class
friendship	full-winged	flowerless	forgettery	first-fruit
frigorific	fimicolous	flower-show	fermentive	foretaught
foisonless	fumigation	florentine	forcefully	fortuitism
flippantly	fumigatory	foot-guards	forefinger	fortuitist
flimsiness	familiarly	frothiness	forefather	fortuitous
fair-spoken	fumblingly	frog-hopper	foreground	fire-walker
faint-heart	femaleness	florilegia	foregather	fire-warden
flint-heart	familistic	florideous	forthright	forty-niner
flint-glass	feminality	frolicking	fore-hammer	ferry-house
flirtingly	feminility	floridness	forehanded	fustanella
flintiness	femininely	frolicsome	forthgoing	fuss-budget
flirtation	femininism	floristics	forcipated	fusibility
fairy-beads	femininity	floribunda	formicaria	fish-carver
fairy-money	feministic	flock-paper	farcically	foster-home
fairy-stone	fimbriated	foot-licker	forgivable	fosterling

Fescennine
fesse-point
Fastens-eve
fesseewise
fish-finger
fish-farmer
fish-gutter
fast-handed
fascinator
fishing-rod
fastigiate
fastidious
fossicking
fashionist
fustianise
fustianist
fasciation
fascicular
fasciculus
fish-kettle
fish-ladder
fishmonger
fish-manure
fusionless
festoonery
fish-trowel
fatherhood
fetterlock
fatherland
fatherless
fetterless
fathership
fatiguable
fitting-out
fatalistic
fathomable
fathometer
fathom-line
fathomless
fat-brained
futurology
futureless
futuristic
futurition
fatiscence
fettuccine
fitfulness
fourchette
founderous
foundation
flugelhorn
flute-mouth
four-figure
fluffiness
four-footed
four-handed
four-inched
four-in-hand
fluvialist
fluxionary
fluxionist
Fourierism
fluviatile

flunkeydom
flunkeyish
flunkeyism
four-leafed
four-leaved
feuilleton
four-legged
four-letter
fluentness
four-o-clock
four-parted
four-poster
fluoridise
fluoridate
fluorinate
fluorotype
foudroyant
four-seater
foul-spoken
fourscorth
four-stroke
foursquare
frustrated
fourteener
fourteenth
fruit-knife
faultiness
fruitarian
fruiteress
fourth-rate
fruitfully
five-finger
five-parted
feverishly
five-square
favourable
favourably
favourless
fowling-net
fowl-plague
fox-terrier
fox-hunting
fly-catcher
fly-fishing
fly-flapper
faying-face
flyposting
fly-by-night
fizzenless
granadilla
guaranteed
glauberite
glance-coal
glancingly
glauconite
granddaddy
grandmamma
glandiform
grandchild
grand-niece
glandulous
grand-uncle
guard-house

glanderous
grandstand
grand-ducal
grave-maker
gravelling
graveolent
grape-louse
grapefruit
Gravettian
grapestone
gravestone
gracefully
gratefully
gravel-walk
grangerise
Grangerism
graphology
Gnaphalium
graphemics
glad-hander
gnashingly
graphitoid
graphitise
gravimeter
gravimetry
gramineous
gramicidin
glaciology
glacialist
gratillity
gradienter
graciosity
glaciation
gladiatory
graciously
gratifying
goal-keeper
graplement
grammarian
grammatist
gramophone
gramophony
granophyre
Glagolitic
graspingly
glass-faced
glass-paper
goatsucker
goat's-beard
goat's-thorn
grass-widow
goat-sallow
glass-cloth
gladsomely
glass-snake
grass-snake
glassiness
grassiness
glass-coach
glasshouse
grass-roots
grasswrack
grass-green

grass-grown
glassfulls
graptolite
goal-tender
grant-in-aid
ghastfully
granulater
granularly
granulator
granulitic
gradualism
gradualist
graduality
graduation
gratuitous
Glaswegian
goat-willow
Gibberella
gabblement
gubernator
gabbroitic
God-fearing
gadolinite
gadolinium
gadrooning
giddy-paced
grenadilla
gregarious
grey-coated
greediness
glendoveer
glebe-house
grey-headed
grey-haired
gleemaiden
greenheart
greenshank
greenfinch
greencloth
greenhouse
green-drake
greenstuff
greenstone
greensward
Greco-Roman
gneissitic
guessingly
greasiness
greisenise
gressorial
greasewood
great-niece
guest-night
great-uncle
guest-house
grey-wether
giftedness
gaff-rigged
goggle-eyed
gigglesome
gag-toothed
grindstone
gripe-water

guinea-corn
guinea-fowl
Ghibelline
guilefully
guinea-worm
griffinish
griffinism
gaingiving
grith-stool
grisliness
grimlooked
guillotine
glimmering
gliomatous
gainstrive
gainsaying
guilty-like
grittiness
guiltiness
glistering
glitterand
glittering
grievingly
grievously
gilravager
goliardery
goliathise
gallabiyah
galravitch
galvaniser
gold-beater
gold-beetle
golf-course
gold-digger
gold-end-man
goloe-shoes
gelder-rose
golden-seal
Gilbertian
Gilbertine
galley-worm
galley-west
galleryite
galliambic
goldilocks
galimatias
gallomania
gallophobe
gallophile
galloglass
gallows-lee
goloptious
goluptious
gillravage
gelatinoid
gelatinise
gelatinate
gelatinous
gold-thread
gold-washer
gemmaceous
gymnasiast
game-dealer

gimlet-eyed
gombeen-man
gambit-pawn
gamekeeper
gemologist
gemination
gambolling
gymnosophy
gymnosperm
gametangia
gamotropic
gem-cutting
genialness
genealogic
gonococcal
gonococcic
gonococcus
geniculate
gensdarmes
genteelish
genteelism
gander-moon
gingersnap
Ginkgoales
gentilesse
gunfighter
gingivitis
gangliated
gentlefolk
gangliform
gentlehood
ginglimoid
gunslinger
gentleness
ganglionic
gynandrism
gynandrous
goniometer
goniometry
gonorrheal
gonorrhoea
gonorrheic
generalise
generalist
generality
gangrenous
generosity
generatrix
generation
generative
generously
Genesiacal
geneticist
genethliac
genitively
gunrunning
genevrette
Genevanism
gooney-bird
groceteria
gooseberry
geodesical
geodetical

geomedical
glove-fight
gnoseology
grovelling
goose-flesh
glove-money
geometrise
geometrist
goose-grass
geocentric
glomerular
goose-quill
glomerulus
good-fellow
good-father
grogginess
geophagism
geophagist
geophagous
geophilous
geochemist
good-humour
geothermal
geothermic
geophysics
growing-bag
gnosiology
Grobianism
gloriously
glorifying
goodlihead
goodlyhead
good-liking
growlingly
goodliness
ghoulishly
gloominess
good-morrow
good-mother
groundbait
ground-base
ground-dove
groundedly
ground-hold
groundling
groundless
groundmass
groundplan
groundplot
groundprox
ground-rent
groundsman
geognostic
groundsell
groundsill
good-nature
groundwork
ground-zero
geological
geoponical
gnomonical
gnotobiote
googolplex

geographer
geographic
geotropism
glossology
glossiness
glossarial
goods-train
glossarist
good-sister
Gnosticise
Gnosticism
glottology
gloatingly
ghost-write
geostatics
ghost-story
grotto-work
globularly
geodynamic
goody-goody
gypsophila
gap-toothed
German-band
garlandage
gormandise
gormandism
garbageman
geriatrics
geriatrist
gargantuan
gyrocopter
gyro-carlin
gor-bellied
garnet-rock
garmenture
gorgeously
girlfriend
germinable
garnishing
germicidal
garnierite
gerundival
gorgoneion
gargoylism
garrotting
Gorgonzola
gyrostatic
garishness
gyroscopic
gyrational
gospellise
gasteropod
gashliness
gasometric
Gesundheit
Gasconader
gas-bracket
gastrology
gastralgia
gastralgic
gastronome
gastronomy
Gastropoda

gastrosoph
gastrotomy
gas-turbine
gas-furnace
gut-scraper
Guttiferae
gatling-gun
gate-keeper
gate-legged
get-up-and-go
gutturally
glumaceous
gourdiness
gauge-glass
grudgingly
gauging-rod
glucosuria
glucosuric
grumpiness
gauntleted
gaultheria
gruntingly
gluttonise
gluttonish
gluttonous
gaudy-night
gaudy-green
governance
governable
governante
governessy
government
glycogenic
glycosuria
glycosuric
glyptodont
head-bummer
head-cheese
head-centre
heaven-bred
heaven-born
heaven-sent
heavenward
hoar-headed
head-hugger
headhunter
heathendom
heathenise
heathenish
heathenism
heath-poult
hearing-aid
head-lugged
headmaster
hyalomelan
hyalophane
hyaloplasm
hearse-like
hoarseness
head-stream
heatstroke
headstrong
headsquare

heart's-ease
heart-whole
heart-throb
heart-block
heart-blood
healthless
heartiness
heart-spoon
heartbreak
heart-grief
healthsome
heart-quake
headworker
heavy-laden
heavy-armed
Hebraicism
Hebraistic
hybridiser
Hobbianism
hobble-bush
habiliment
hobblingly
habilatory
habilitate
hebdomadal
hebdomadar
hobjobbing
hobnobbing
hibernacle
habit-maker
habitually
habit-cloth
habitation
hebetation
habitaunce
hobby-horse
hackbuteer
hectically
huckle-bone
hackmatack
hackneyman
hectometre
hectolitre
hectograph
hectorship
hectostere
hocus-pocus
huckstress
hydrazides
hydraulics
hydragogue
hodden-grey
hiddenmost
hiddenness
hodgepodge
hydrically
hidalgoish
hidalgoism
hedonistic
hydromancy
hydropathy
hydromania
hydrotaxis

hydroscope	hygrometry	heliolatry	homeliness	hinge-joint
hydrometer	hygrophobe	helioscope	humbleness	henceforth
hydrometry	hygrochasy	heliometer	homiletics	hen-hearted
hydrotheca	hygrophyte	hollow-eyed	hymeneaeal	hang-glider
hydrophily	hagiologic	heliophyte	hymeneaean	hand-gallop
hydrophane	hagiocracy	Haliotidae	homonymity	hunting-cap
hydrophone	hygrograph	hollowness	homonymous	hunting-cat
hydrochore	high-octane	heliograph	humaneness	hunting-box
hydrophyte	high-placed	heliotrope	humanistic	hunting-cog
hydroplane	high-priced	heliotropy	hemp-nettle	huntiegowk
hydrosomal	high-reared	halloysite	homuncular	hand-in-hand
hydropower	high-raised	hollow-ware	homunculus	handicraft
hydrosomes	high-roller	heliotypic	homeopathy	handicuffs
hydrologic	high-ranker	holophotal	homeomeric	hand-lotion
hydropolyp	high-strung	holophrase	homeomorph	hand-me-down
hydrospace	high-souled	halophytic	homoousian	handmaiden
hydrograph	high-tasted	holophytic	homoplasmy	honorarium
hydrolysis	highwayman	holosteric	hemipteral	handselled
hydrolytic	higry-pigry	holus-bolus	hemipteran	handsomely
hoddy-doddy	hail-fellow	half-sister	hemiplegia	hand-screen
hierarchal	hair-pencil	hylotheism	hemiplegic	handspring
hierarchic	hair-powder	hylotheist	homophonic	henotheism
haematinic	hair-raiser	hylotomous	humgruffin	henotheist
hiera-picra	hairstreak	half-volley	Homorelaps	honourable
haematosis	hair-stroke	half-witted	humoralism	honourably
Haemanthus	hairspring	half-yearly	humoralist	honourless
haematuria	hair-waving	hylozoical	humoristic	honours-man
heedlessly	hoity-toity	Himyaritic	humoresque	Hindustani
hieromancy	Hakenkreuz	hemianopia	humorously	Hanoverian
hierolatry	hokey-pokey	homoblasty	hamesucken	hand-weeded
hieroscopy	heliacally	humpbacked	home-signal	handworked
hyetometer	hullabaloo	home-brewed	hemisphere	handy-dandy
hierophant	Hollandish	hemicyclic	homosexual	honey-eater
hieroglyph	half-a-dozen	homocyclic	homothally	hanky-panky
haemoconia	half-a-crown	home-coming	homotonous	honey-wagon
hierologic	Helianthus	hemichorda	hemitropal	honey-chile
hierocracy	hellbender	homocercal	hemitropic	honey-mouse
hierograph	halobiotic	homochromy	home-thrust	honeymonth
hyetograph	half-cocked	humidifier	homotaxial	honey-crock
haemolysis	helicoidal	humidistat	Homburg-hat	honey-stalk
haemolytic	Heliconian	hammer-beam	Hamburgher	honey-stone
Hieronymic	helicopter	hammer-fish	humbugging	honeybunch
highbinder	hill-digger	hammerhead	humdudgeon	honey-guide
hug-me-tight	half-dollar	hammerlock	humbuggery	honey-sweet
highermost	halberdier	hammerless	humourless	hootananny
high-flying	halfe-horsy	homoeomery	humoursome	Hyoscyamus
high-heeled	halieutics	homoerotic	homozygote	hootenanny
hog-cholera	halleluiah	hammer-pond	homozygous	hookedness
high-handed	hallelujah	homoeopath	hansardise	hoodie-crow
highjacker	holoenzyme	homogamous	hen-harrier	hyoplastra
high-kilted	holography	homogenise	hand-barrow	hootnannie
Highlander	halogenate	homogenate	hand-basket	hoots-toots
hegemonial	halogenous	homogenous	hinderance	heortology
high-minded	holohedral	hamshackle	hendecagon	heptarchic
hegemonism	holohedron	hemihedral	henpeckery	Heptandria
hegemonist	half-hourly	hemihedron	hanselling	Heptateuch
high-necked	helminthic	humming-top	hinderland	heptameter
hogen-mogen	half-kirtle	humiliator	hinderlans	Heptameron
hagiolater	half-length	homologise	hinderlins	heptachord
hagiolatry	helplessly	homologate	hinterland	hopsacking
hagioscope	holing-pick	homologous	hindermost	heptagonal
hygrometer	heliolater	homaloidal	handedness	heptapodic
	heliotaxis	humblingly	hinge-bound	heptatonic

hypnagogic	hypotenuse	horrifying	histrionic	hexametric
Heptagynia	hip-huggers	herald-duck	hesitation	hexandrian
hypabyssal	hippuritic	horologist	hesitatory	hexandrous
hypocritic	hypoxaemia	Horologium	hesitative	hexaplaric
hypocentre	hypoxaemic	horologium	hetmanship	hoydenhood
hypocorism	harman-beck	hare-lipped	hithermost	hey-de-guyes
hypodermal	herbaceous	hurdle-race	hitherside	hey-de-guise
hypodorian	hereabouts	heraldship	hitherward	hazardable
hypodermic	Herbartian	harmlessly	hitch-hiker	inadaptive
hypodermis	hornblende	hurtlessly	hotchpotch	inaccuracy
hyphenated	hard-boiled	Herrnhuter	hot-livered	inaccurate
hypaethral	hard-billed	haranguing	hot-blooded	isabelline
hypaethron	herb-bennet	heriotable	hit-and-miss	inadequacy
hippety-hop	hurl-barrow	harmonical	hot-cockles	inadequate
hypogaeous	hard-bitten	harmoniser	hot-mouthed	ilang-ilang
hypogynous	Heracleian	harmonicon	Hitopadesa	inaugurate
hopping-mad	Heraclidan	harmonious	heterocont	inanimated
hupaithric	Hyracoidea	harpooneer	Heterocera	imaginable
hippiatric	hirudinean	harpoon-gun	heterodont	imaginably
hop-bitters	hirudinoid	harbour-bar	heterodyne	Italianise
hypolydian	hirudinous	harbourage	heterodoxy	Italianism
hypalgesia	hereditary	hard-pushed	heterogamy	Italianist
hypalgesic	horse-faced	herb-robert	heterogeny	Italianate
hopelessly	horse-tamer	hard-riding	heterogony	inapposite
hypanthium	horselaugh	horn-rimmed	hot-brained	inappetent
hippomanes	horrendous	heresiarch	heterokont	inartistic
hippocampi	horse-leech	harassedly	heterology	inaptitude
hypnoidise	hartebeest	heresy-hunt	heteronomy	inactively
hypsometer	horseshoer	haruspical	Heteropoda	inactivate
hypnogenic	horse-thief	haruspices	heterotaxy	inactivity
hypsometry	hermetical	harassment	hateworthy	iracundity
hippophobe	horse-rider	horoscopic	hitty-missy	imbibition
hippophagy	horseflesh	hereticate	heulandite	imbecility
hippophile	horse-cloth	heretofore	hour-circle	inbreeding
hypsophyll	horse-gowan	heritrices	hounds-foot	inbringing
hypnotiser	horse-woman	heritrixes	house-party	imbroccata
hypnogogic	horse-coper	harquebuse	house-agent	imbruement
hippogriff	horsepower	harquebuss	houselling	incrassate
hippodrome	horned-pout	harpy-eagle	housebound	incubation
Hippocrene	horse-bread	hirdy-girdy	housecraft	incubatory
hippogryph	hard-earned	hurryingly	house-proud	incubative
hypophysis	harvestman	hurdy-gurdy	houts-touts	incidental
hyperbaric	harvest-fly	hurly-burly	haustellum	incedingly
hyperbatic	harvest-bug	horizontal	hauntingly	increscent
hyperbaton	Herrenvolk	husbandman	haustorium	inclemency
hyperacute	hornfelses	husbandage	hoveringly	incredible
hyperaemia	horn-footed	hysteresis	hover-mower	incredibly
hyperaemic	hard-fisted	hysteretic	hovercraft	increasing
hop-trefoil	hard-fought	hysterical	hover-train	incogitant
hyperfocal	horography	Hesperides	hawk-beaked	incoherent
hyperbolic	herb-garden	hysteritis	hawk-billed	incohesion
hypergolic	hard-gotten	hystericky	hawser-laid	incohesive
hypersonic	hard-headed	hostelling	Howleglass	inclinable
hypertonic	hard-handed	hospitable	howsomever	inculpable
hyperspace	heroically	hospitably	how-do-you-do	inculpably
hyperdulia	hermit-crab	husking-bee	hawksbeard	inculcator
hypostasis	hartie-hale	histiology	hexactinal	incompared
hypostatic	herbicidal	histogenic	hexaemeron	incumbency
hypotactic	hermitical	historical	hexagynian	incomplete
hypotheses	heroicness	histoblast	hexagynous	incomposed
hypothesis	horridness	histologic	hexahedral	incantator
hypothetic	heroi-comic	histolysis	hexahedron	incunabula
hepatology	herniotomy	histolytic	hexamerous	incandesce

incendiary	indistinct	in-fighting	idiolectic	immorality
incinerate	indisposed	infliction	iridosmine	immurement
inconstant	industrial	inflictive	iridosmium	immeritous
inchoately	indiscreet	infelicity	idiopathic	immiscible
inchoation	indiscrete	infallible	idiot-proof	immaterial
inchoative	inditement	infallibly	iniquitous	immaturely
incapacity	individual	infiltrate	injudicial	immaturity
incipience	individuum	infamonise	injunction	immoveable
incipiency	indexation	infamously	injunctive	ignobility
incurvated	inerasable	infinitude	ink-slinger	innocently
incurrable	inerasably	infinitely	ill-natured	innuendoes
incurrence	Iceland-dog	infinitant	Illecebrum	innominate
incoronate	ice-machine	infinitary	illocution	innumeracy
incorporal	inerasible	infinitate	ill-advised	innumerate
incisiform	inerasibly	infinitive	ill-behaved	innumerous
incasement	inesculent	infernally	ill-defined	ignipotent
incisorial	inelegance	inferrable	ill-feeling	ignorantly
incestuous	inelegancy	informally	illegalise	ignoration
incisively	inefficacy	inferrible	illegality	ionosphere
incitement	ideography	infirmness	idle-headed	ionisation
incitingly	inevitable	inferiorly	Islamicise	innutrient
incitation	inevitably	infarction	Islamicist	innateness
incitative	irenically	infusorial	illuminant	innovation
ischuretic	ineligible	infusorian	illuminism	innovatory
includible	ineligibly	infatuated	illuminist	innovative
incautious	ice-hilling	influenzal	illuminate	Icosandria
incivility	inexistent	ingrateful	illuminati	isogametic
indebtment	ideologist	ingratiate	illuminato	icosahedra
inductance	idealistic	ingle-cheek	ill-looking	idolatress
indictable	inexorable	ingredient	ill-founded	idolatrise
indocility	inexorably	ingression	ill-fortune	idolatrous
indictment	ineloquent	ingressive	idle-pulley	inosculate
inducement	inexpiable	ingeminate	illaqueate	inordinacy
indecently	inexpiably	ingenerate	illustrate	inordinate
indecorous	inexplicit	inglorious	illusively	inoperable
indecision	idempotent	ingestible	illiteracy	inoperably
indecisive	ice-breaker	Ishmaelite	ill-starred	isoleucine
indication	inebritous	inhabitant	illiterate	isogenetic
indicatory	identified	inhibition	illatively	inobedient
indicative	inextended	inhibitory	illaudable	isometrics
indwelling	ideational	inhibitive	illaudably	isoseismal
indefinite	isentropic	ichthyosis	ill-success	isoseismic
indignance	ineptitude	ichthyotic	immeasured	iron-glance
indigo-blue	ineducable	inhalation	immobilise	isocheimal
Indigofera	inequality	inhumanity	immobilism	isocheimic
indigently	irefulness	inhumation	immobility	iron-handed
indigenise	inequation	inherently	immaculacy	isochronal
indigenous	inflamable	inharmonic	immaculate	isothermal
indigested	inflatable	inheritrix	immoderacy	isochasmic
indagation	infeasible	iridaceous	immoderate	ironically
indagatory	infrasonic	itinerancy	immodestly	isoniazide
indagative	infragrant	iridescent	iambically	iron-liquor
indelicacy	infraction	iridectomy	Ismailitic	isoglossal
indelicate	infrahuman	Irishwoman	immolation	isoglottal
indulgence	infibulate	inimically	immemorial	isoglottic
indulgency	infectious	inimitable	immunology	ironmonger
indolently	infidelity	inimitably	immanental	iron-mining
indumentum	inflexible	initialled	imminently	iron-master
iodometric	inflexibly	initialise	immanation	iconolater
Indonesian	inflection	initiation	immortally	iconomachy
indirectly	inflective	initiatory	immortelle	iconomatic
induration	infrequent	initiative	immoralism	iconolatry
indurative	infeftment	idiolectal	immoralist	iconoscope

iconometer	imparadise	instigator	intangibly	intoxicate
iconometry	impartible	instilling	intendment	inurbanely
iconoclasm	impervious	instilment	intoningly	inurbanity
iconoclast	imperilled	inspissate	intentness	inundation
idoloclast	importless	instituter	intenerate	invocation
isomorphic	impartment	institutor	intinction	invocatory
isosporous	impureness	insolvable	intonation	invigilate
isotropism	impersonal	insolvably	iatrogenic	invaginate
isotropous	imperative	insultable	introspect	invigorant
Isoetaceae	importuner	insolidity	introrsely	invigorate
isopterous	impassable	insolvency	introducer	invaluable
inoculable	impassably	inselberge	intercalar	invaluably
inoculator	imposthume	insultment	interramal	involucral
iron-worded	impassible	insolently	interlaced	involucrum
iron-witted	impassibly	insularism	internally	invaliding
isodynamic	impossible	insularity	intermarry	invalidish
ivory-black	imposingly	insolation	interregal	invalidism
isocyanide	impishness	insulation	interceder	invalidate
implacable	imposition	insalutary	interferer	invalidity
implacably	impostumed	insalivate	interreges	involution
impeccancy	impatience	insomnious	intervener	invendible
impeccable	imputation	inseminate	interreign	inventible
impeccably	imputative	insinuator	interregna	invincible
impictured	impoundage	insensible	interferon	invincibly
impudicity	imprudence	insensibly	intervenor	inventress
impediment	impoverish	insentient	interleave	inviolated
impudently	inquirendo	insaneness	interweave	inviolable
impeditive	inquisitor	insanitary	intermezzi	inviolably
impresario	inquietude	insensuous	intermezzo	invariance
impregnant	irradiance	insipidity	interchain	invariable
impregnate	irradiancy	insipience	interphone	invariably
impression	irradicate	insertable	interphase	inveracity
impressure	Israelitic	instructor	intertidal	invertedly
impressive	irregulous	insurgence	intervital	investment
implexuous	irrigation	insurgency	interplead	invitement
impugnable	irrigative	instrument	interclude	invitingly
impugnment	irreligion	insurancer	interplant	inveteracy
imprimatur	irrelation	insistence	internment	inveterate
Implicitly	irrelative	insistency	interunion	invitation
impairment	irrelevant	Insessores	internodal	invitatory
impuissant	irremeable	insatiable	interpolar	inwardness
imprinting	irremeably	insatiably	interposal	ivy-mantled
impalpable	irrenowned	insouciant	interzonal	icy-pearled
impalpably	irresolute	intra-urban	interloper	jabberwock
impalement	irrational	intramural	interposer	jubilantly
impolitely	irritation	intubation	interiorly	jubilation
impendence	irritative	intactness	interwound	jack-a-dandy
impendency	irreverent	intrepidly	intervolve	jackanapes
impenitent	installant	integrable	interspace	Jacobinise
impanation	installing	integrally	interurban	Jacobinism
improbable	instalment	integrator	intergrade	Jacobitism
improbably	inspanning	integument	interbreed	jockeyship
improvable	instantial	intrigante	intertrigo	jackhammer
improvably	insobriety	intriguant	intercross	jocularity
implorator	insociable	intriguing	intergrown	jaculation
improperly	insecurely	intolerant	interested	jaculatory
improvided	insecurity	intimidate	interstice	jocundness
improviser	inspection	intemerate	interstate	jack-priest
imparlance	inspective	intimately	interlunar	jack-rabbit
importance	insufflate	intimation	intertwine	jack-rafter
importancy	insightful	intendancy	intertwist	jocoseness
imperially	inspirable	intendedly	intestinal	judicially
importable	inspirator	intangible	intoxicant	judication

judicatory	journalist	Kantianism	librettist	lucky-piece
judicature	journeyman	kinglihood	lobe-footed	ledger-bait
judicative	journeying	kindliness	lubricator	ledger-line
Judaically	jauntiness	kingliness	lubricious	lady-killer
Judenhetze	jovialness	kinematics	lobulation	lederhosen
jaguarondi	javelin-man	king-of-arms	Lebensraum	lady's-smock
jaguarundi	Juvenalian	kenspeckle	liberalise	leechcraft
jigger-mast	juvenility	king's-chair	liberalism	lieutenant
jaggedness	Jew-baiting	king-salmon	liberalist	laeotropic
juggernaut	jewel-house	kind-spoken	liberality	lherzolite
jiggety-jog	Jew's-mallow	king's-spear	liberation	life-estate
jugglingly	Jew's-myrtle	kinesipath	laboratory	left-footed
Jugendstil	jaw-breaker	kenoticist	liberatory	life-giving
Johnny-cake	jaw-crusher	kookaburra	liberty-man	left-handed
Johnsonian	Jewishness	knobbiness	lobotomise	left-hander
Johnsonese	jaw-twister	Kuomintang	lobster-pot	luffing-jib
Johnsonism	jaywalking	knockabout	laboursome	life-jacket
Jehovistic	joyfulness	knock-kneed	lackadaisy	lifelessly
jeistiecor	joyousness	knobkerrie	lucubrator	life-mortar
jointuress	knat-bottle	knottiness	lactescent	life-rocket
joint-stock	knave-bairn	Karmathian	Lycaenidae	life-renter
joint-stool	klangfarbe	kersantite	locker-room	life-school
jejuneness	knagginess	kirn-dollie	lucifugous	life-saving
jolterhead	knackiness	kerseymere	Luciferian	life-tenant
July-flower	knackwurst	kerygmatic	luciferase	left-winger
jellygraph	kibbutznik	kerchiefed	luciferous	leftwardly
jumblingly	kack-handed	kerb-market	lacrimator	luggage-van
jumble-sale	kidnapping	karyoplasm	locking-nut	leg-warmers
jimson-weed	kidney-bean	kerb-trader	lectionary	lugubrious
Jamesonite	kiddiewink	keratinise	lock-keeper	legibility
juncaceous	klendusity	keratinous	loculament	logicality
junk-bottle	kieselguhr	kerb-vendor	luculently	laggen-gird
junk-dealer	keepership	katabolism	lucklessly	loggerhead
jinrikisha	khediviate	kitten-moth	lack-lustre	logography
jinricksha	knee-length	kite-flying	locomobile	lignifying
jingoistic	knee-timber	kitchen-fee	locomotion	legalistic
Janus-faced	Kafkaesque	kitchendom	locomotory	ligamental
janitorial	kaffir-boom	kettledrum	locomotive	leguminous
janizarian	knife-money	kettle-pins	laciniated	loganberry
jeopardise	knife-board	kittle-pins	licensable	logan-stone
jeopardous	kaisership	Krugerrand	laconicism	lignocaine
japan-earth	kriegspiel	knuckle-bow	licentiate	log-rolling
Japanesery	Krishnaism	lead-arming	licentious	leg-spinner
Japanesque	knighthood	leaf-bridge	Lychnapsia	logorrhoea
jerked-meat	knightless	leaf-cutter	lactoscope	legislator
jerkinhead	knick-knack	leaderette	lactometer	logistical
jardinière	khidmutgar	leadenness	lactogenic	light-faced
jargonelle	khitmutgar	leadership	laccolitic	light-tight
jury-rudder	Kilmarnock	lead-glance	lectorship	light-o'-love
jury-rigged	kilogramme	loan-holder	Lycopodium	legitimacy
juristical	Keltomania	loathingly	lace-pillow	legitimise
jerry-built	kimberlite	leaf-hopper	Lacertilia	legitimist
jasperware	kempery-man	leathering	lachrymary	legitimate
jaspideous	king-at-arms	leaf-insect	lachrymose	lightening
Jesuitical	king-archon	leafleteer	laceration	lighting-up
justiciary	kennel-coal	leaf-mosaic	lacerative	light-tower
justifying	kennelling	loan-office	locust-bean	light-horse
jostlement	kennel-maid	lead-pencil	Locustidae	lighthouse
jet-setting	kingfisher	leaf-sheath	lockstitch	lighterman
journal-box	kinchin-lay	leastaways	lacustrine	light-organ
journalese	Kensington	lean-witted	locust-tree	light-armed
journalise	Kentish-man	libidinist	lacquering	lighterage
journalism	Kentish-rag	libidinous	lacrymator	lightproof

legateship	limburgite	lepidolite	latter-mint	laurustine
leg-pulling	lentamente	lapidarian	lattermost	loud-voiced
leishmania	landammann	lapidarist	lattermath	laurvikite
Leibnizian	longaevous	lapidation	letter-wood	love-affair
leiotrichy	land-breeze	lip-reading	latifundia	love-broker
leisurable	land-bridge	lappet-head	litigation	love-favour
leisurably	lenocinium	leprechaun	Lithistida	levigation
likelihood	linseed-oil	leprechawn	little-ease	livelihead
likeliness	lanceolate	lapper-milk	littleness	lovelihead
lake-lawyer	lanternist	lip-service	litany-desk	livelihood
like-minded	laniferous	lipography	lithomancy	lavallière
lukewarmly	line-fisher	Lippizaner	lithomarge	liveliness
lukewarmth	lanuginose	Lippizzana	litholatry	loveliness
Lollardism	lanuginous	lipomatous	lithophane	love-letter
liliaceous	lanigerous	leproserie	lithophysa	love-making
loll-shraub	long-headed	lap-jointed	lithophyse	love-monger
lumbang-oil	long-haired	leptosomic	lithophyte	lovingness
Limnaeidae	landholder	Leptospira	lithoglyph	living-room
Lammas-tide	land-hunger	Lupercalia	lithoclast	love-potion
lamp-burner	landing-net	laparotomy	lithologic	lever-watch
lime-burner	lentigines	Lipizzaner	lithotomic	lover's-knot
limaciform	lentissimo	loquacious	Lithodomus	liver-fluke
limicolous	lenticular	liquescent	lithoprint	laverbread
lambdacism	land-jobber	liquefying	lithograph	liver-grown
lambdoidal	lanzknecht	liquidator	lithotrite	leviration
lumber-camp	land-lubber	liquidiser	lithotrity	liverwurst
lumber-jack	land-locked	liquidness	Lythraceae	lavishment
lumber-mill	long-legged	lardaceous	liturgical	lavishness
limber-neck	loneliness	lorication	literalise	lavatorial
lumber-room	land-louper	lark-heeled	literalism	lovat-green
lumbersome	land-mining	larvicidal	literalist	levitation
lumpectomy	link-motion	lordliness	laterality	live-weight
lumber-yard	land-owning	laryngitic	literality	loveworthy
limb-girdle	longprimer	laryngitis	literarily	lovey-dovey
lymphocyte	land-pirate	lordolatry	literosity	law-abiding
lymphogram	lansquenet	lust-dieted	literation	lawrencium
lampholder	long-staple	listenable	literature	low-tension
lemniscate	Landsthing	listener-in	lotus-eater	law-officer
lamellated	lonesomely	lysigenous	latescence	low-pitched
lamentable	land-spring	lascivious	lutestring	low-country
lamentably	line-squall	lesbianism	latitation	law-breaker
laminarian	lengthwise	lusciously	Lithuanian	low-profile
laminarise	lengthways	loss-leader	lauraceous	lower-class
lemon-grass	Lingulella	listlessly	launcegaye	loweringly
luminarism	linguiform	last-minute	laurdalite	lawfulness
luminarist	languorous	Lysenkoism	Laundromat	law-burrows
luminosity	languished	lissomness	loundering	lexicology
lamination	languisher	lustreless	laundry-man	loxodromic
lumination	linguister	lustration	louver-door	lexigraphy
luminously	linguistic	lustrously	Laurentian	luxuriance
lampoonery	linguistry	lustreware	laureation	luxuriancy
lampoonist	land-waiter	Lusitanian	loungingly	ley-farming
lumbricoid	long-winded	lethargied	lounge-suit	meandering
Lemuroidea	leopard-cat	lethargise	leuchaemia	meaningful
Lamarckian	leopardess	letter-bomb	loudhailer	measliness
Lamarckism	loose-cover	letter-book	laughingly	meal-monger
lambrequin	lyophilise	latter-born	louping-ill	meat-market
lamb's-tails	lion-hunter	letter-clip	loud-lunged	miasmatous
lumpsucker	looking-for	letter-card	leucopenia	miarolitic
limitrophe	leontiasis	letter-file	leucoplast	meadow-lark
limitarian	Laplandish	letterhead	leucocytic	meagreness
limitation	lipochrome	letterless	louvre-door	meatscreen
limitative	lapidified	litter-lout	Louis-Seize	meal-ticket

myasthenia	maceration	Mohammedan	multiplied	mammy-wagon
myasthenic	mica-schist	Muhammedan	multiplier	mummy-wheat
measurable	mycetology	main-course	multiplane	mummy-cloth
measurably	mycetozoan	maidenhead	millionary	manna-larch
measuredly	mediatress	maidenhair	multipolar	maniacally
mobocratic	medicament	maidenhood	multivocal	mangabeira
Mabinogion	medicaster	maidenlike	multilobed	manzanilla
Maccabaean	medication	maiden-meek	multiloquy	mendacious
mechanical	medicative	maimedness	mulligrubs	Montagnard
Michaelmas	medievally	maidenweed	multi-track	manna-grass
mace-bearer	midden-cock	mainlander	multi-stage	manna-croup
macadamise	madder-lake	mainlining	multistory	mandamuses
mucedinous	madreporic	maisonette	multicycle	mini-budget
muciferous	modifiable	mainpernor	mollifying	montbretia
mock-heroic	midshipman	mainstream	melomaniac	minibuffet
machinator	mud-skipper	mainspring	moliminous	mind-bender
machineman	middle-aged	maintained	malingerer	Manichaean
machine-gun	muddlehead	maintainer	melanaemia	monochasia
mackintosh	middlemost	moisturise	melancholy	monocratic
mycologist	Madelenian	majestical	molendinar	monocyclic
maculation	mud-slinger	make-belief	melanomata	Manicheism
maculature	modalistic	make-weight	Melanesian	monactinal
muck-midden	meddlesome	malvaceous	melanistic	monoclinal
mock-modest	modulation	meliaceous	mylonitise	monoclinic
maconochie	madonnaish	molybdenum	meliorator	monoculous
meconopsis	mud-volcano	molybdosis	mileometer	menacingly
microfarad	mid-morning	malabar-rat	Mallophaga	monocarpic
mucronated	mediocrity	malacology	mellowness	monochroic
mock-orange	mad-brained	melaconite	millocracy	monochrome
microscope	moderniser	melic-grass	malcontent	monochromy
microscopy	modernness	mile-castle	malapropos	manicurist
micrometer	moderatrix	melicotton	malapertly	monocerous
microhenry	moderately	melocotoon	melismatic	monadiform
micrometre	moderation	maledicent	mulishness	monadology
micrometry	moderatism	maladapted	mild-spoken	monkey-boat
microseism	medusiform	maladdress	mill-stream	Mindererus
macrophage	modishness	malodorous	militiaman	monkey-gaff
microphone	meditation	mallee-bird	militantly	monoecious
microphyte	meditative	malleiform	militarily	mindedness
microfiche	medium-term	mallee-fowl	militarise	montero-cap
microlight	mnemonical	millesimal	militarism	monkey-pump
microlitic	meerschaum	millefiori	militarist	monkey-rail
macrobiota	muffin-bell	millennial	mulattress	monkey-rope
macrobiote	mafficking	millennium	molluscoid	monkey-suit
microbiota	magnetical	muliebrity	molluscous	manteltree
microcline	magnetiser	millet-seed	malevolent	monkey-tail
microsomal	magnifical	malfeasant	millwright	manoeuvrer
micrococci	Magnificat	malleation	malaxation	man-servant
micrologic	magnifying	maleficial	membership	munificent
microtomic	Magellanic	maleficent	mimography	munifience
macrospore	megalosaur	malefactor	mumping-day	manifolder
microspore	megalithic	malignance	mummifying	many-folded
microprint	meganewton	malignancy	mamillated	manifoldly
micrograph	mignonette	malaguetta	mumblement	manifestly
macroprism	megaparsec	malignment	mumblingly	monography
micropylar	megascopic	Malthusian	mumble-news	manageable
mycoplasma	magistracy	multifaced	mammogenic	manageably
mock-privet	magistrand	multimedia	mimeograph	management
mycorrhiza	magistrate	melting-pot	mumbo-jumbo	monogamist
mycorhizal	mightiness	Malpighian	membranous	monogamous
muck-raking	Muhammadan	multiphase	memorandum	monogynian
Mucorineae	Mahommedan	mollitious	memorative	monogenism
macaronies		multivious	Mimosaceae	monogenist

monogenous	monarchism	moonstrike	morris-pike	misleading
monogynous	monarchist	map-reading	Morris-tube	misreading
managerial	monorchism	mephitical	mercifully	muster-file
manageress	monorhinal	map-mounter	mortifying	master-hand
many-headed	mineralogy	mopishness	moralistic	masterhood
mind-healer	mineralise	maquillage	myringitis	mesmerical
monohybrid	mineralist	morganatic	Mariolater	Mustelidae
monohydric	mongrelise	myrtaceous	Maryolater	Mustelinae
manchineel	mongrelism	myriadfold	Mariolatry	mesmeriser
mine-hunter	manor-house	margaritic	Maryolatry	mysterious
Manchurian	monorhymed	mordacious	marrow-bone	misbelieve
Manchester	ministeria	marmarosis	myrioscope	miscellany
Munchausen	monastical	mercaptide	marionette	masterless
mendicancy	monistical	mercantile	marrowless	mastermind
Mandingoes	minestrone	marcantant	mirrorwise	misdeeming
Monsignore	ministrant	Myricaceae	marprelate	misseeming
Monsignori	manuscript	miraculous	margravine	misdeemful
Monsignors	ministress	meridional	margravate	mussel-plum
mandibular	minuscular	marketable	maraschino	muster-roll
monticulus	monostylar	market-bell	Morisonian	musket-rest
moniliasis	monstrance	marker-bomb	moroseness	mastership
moniliform	man-stealer	marcescent	markswoman	musket-shot
monologise	minute-bell	marker-flag	meritocrat	mismeasure
monologist	minute-book	market-hall	marathoner	missel-tree
minglement	monotocous	Muraenidae	moratorium	mastectomy
minglingly	minute-drop	merceriser	marguerite	misfeature
mindlessly	monothecal	marvelling	marquisate	misventure
monolithic	minstrelsy	martellato	merrymaker	master-work
monomachia	monotheism	marvellous	merry-night	masterwort
minimalism	monotheist	martensite	mistakable	mystery-man
minimalist	minute-hand	market-town	mustard-gas	mist-flower
monomaniac	minute-jack	Marcgravia	miswandred	mishguggle
monumental	minuteness	morigerate	mustard-oil	misogamist
mint-master	monotonous	morigerous	muscardine	misogynist
minimising	monitorial	marsh-fever	mistakenly	misogynous
manumitted	monetarism	morphogeny	message-boy	mischmetal
manometric	monetarist	marshalled	mismanners	mischanter
man-entered	menstruate	marshaller	maskalonge	misthought
meningitis	menstruous	Marshalsea	maskanonge	masticable
meningioma	manducable	morphology	mystagogic	mosaically
monandrous	mensurable	morphemics	mystagogue	mystically
monzonitic	minauderie	marchantia	mystagogus	masticator
mangosteen	man-queller	merchantry	musk-beetle	mashing-tub
monophasic	manfulness	marshiness	misobserve	muslin-kale
monopodial	mansuetude	morphinism	mossbunker	missionary
monopodium	monovalent	marsh-robin	musicianer	Messianism
monopteral	mine-worker	marshlocks	music-paper	Messianist
monoplegia	monoxylous	march-stone	musicianly	missionise
monopteron	Monaxonida	mirthfully	music-shell	maskinonge
monopteros	money-maker	marginated	musicology	mystifying
monopolise	money-taker	marginalia	musicality	misologist
monopolist	money-bound	marginally	music-folio	moss-litter
manipulate	money-order	morbidezza	music-house	Mesolithic
monophobia	myocardial	martingale	misocapnic	musk-mallow
monophobic	myocardium	marking-ink	music-drama	mesomorphy
monophonic	moon-flower	marking-nut	music-stand	mesomerism
menopausal	myoblastic	martialism	music-stool	misimprove
mini-rocket	myological	martialist	misadvised	mesenteric
mandragora	moon-raised	morbillous	misbehaved	mesenteron
monarchial	myographic	Marcionist	masked-ball	misentreat
Monarchian	moonraking	Marxianism	muster-book	misandrist
menorrhoea	moonshiner	morbidness	missel-bird	Mishnayoth
monarchise	moonstruck	Marcionite	master-card	misconceit

misconduct	mutagenise	motor-lorry	neat-handed	neglection
miswording	mitigation	maturation	near-legged	neglectful
Massoretic	mitigatory	maturative	Neapolitan	neglective
Muscovitic	mitigative	motor-cycle	noblewoman	negligence
miscounsel	matchmaker	metastases	nubiferous	negligible
misjoinder	moth-hunter	metastasis	nubigenous	negligibly
miscompute	match-joint	metastatic	Nibelungen	nigromancy
miscorrect	matchboard	mutessarif	nibblingly	negrophobe
misworship	matchstick	metastable	nebulosity	negrophile
miscontent	metrically	metatheses	nobilitate	niger-seeds
misfortune	mythically	Metatheria	nebulously	night-latch
mass-priest	matricidal	metathesis	Nabathaean	night-watch
misspelled	mythiciser	metathetic	nectareous	night-raven
mysophobia	methinketh	metathorax	nyctalopes	night-taper
mesophytic	matricliny	metatarsal	nyctalopia	negotiable
miscreance	matrifocal	metatarsus	nyctalopic	negotiator
miscreancy	matrilocal	Methuselah	nickelling	night-palsy
miscreated	matriarchy	motiveless	nucleolate	night-heron
misarrange	matricular	motivation	nucleonics	nightshade
miscreator	matellasse	mouldiness	nucleotide	night-shift
misericord	mytiliform	mould-board	nucleation	night-chair
mushroomer	metalepsis	maundering	nuciferous	night-churr
mistrysted	metaleptic	mouse-piece	nyctinasty	nightshirt
mistressly	mettlesome	mouse-sight	nick-nacket	nightpiece
misprision	mutilation	mouthpiece	necromancy	night-rider
misdrawing	metallurgy	mouth-organ	necrolater	night-light
mistrayned	metamerism	moucharaby	necrolatry	night-sight
mesoscaphe	mutinously	moudiewart	nectocalyx	night-glass
mesosphere	methomania	moudiewort	necroscopy	night-cloud
Mosasauros	metromania	maudlinism	necrophile	night-house
mesothorax	mythomania	mourningly	necrophily	night-spell
muscularly	mutton-bird	mournfully	nicrosilal	nightdress
masturbate	mutton-chop	mousseline	necrologic	night-stick
Mussulmans	mutton-fist	mountebank	necropolis	night-steed
masquerade	mutton-head	moustached	nécessaire	night-stool
mosquitoes	matronhood	mountained	Nachschlag	negatively
musquetoon	meteorital	Mousterian	nicotinism	negativism
metabolise	methodical	movability	nickumpoop	negativity
metabolism	meteoritic	movelessly	nucivorous	nihilistic
metabolite	matron-like	mavourneen	nudibranch	nail-biting
mutability	matrocliny	mowdiewart	nidicolous	Naiadaceae
meticulous	motionless	mowdiewort	nidderling	nail-headed
metacentre	mythologer	mixed-media	nidificate	nulla-nulla
metacarpal	metronomic	mixolydian	nidifugous	nullifying
metacarpus	metropolis	maxilliped	nidulation	numberless
mathematic	mythologic	maxillulae	nodulation	nomography
mitten-crab	mythopoeic	myxomycete	nidamental	nympholept
mother-cell	mutton-suet	maximalist	nidamentum	numskulled
mother-city	matronship	myxomatous	noematical	nomologist
mitre-wheel	metrostyle	maxi-single	ne'er-do-weel	nimbleness
mitre-shell	matronymic	mixty-maxty	ne'er-do-well	namelessly
motherhood	metronymic	Mayologist	Noetianism	no-man's-land
mother-land	metaplasia	may-blossom	needle-bath	nominalism
matterless	metaplasis	mayonnaise	needlecord	nominalist
motherless	metaphoric	May-morning	needle-case	nominately
mitre-joint	metaphrase	mozzarella	needle-fish	nomination
methedrine	metaphrast	mizzen-mast	needlessly	nominative
mother-ship	metaphysic	mizzen-sail	needlework	Nemertinea
mother-spot	materially	mezzotinto	niffy-naffy	numerology
mother-to-be	maternally	mezzo-forte	niggardise	numerosity
motherwort	mithridate	mazarinade	nigrescent	numeration
moth-flower	matureness	near-begaun	nigger-head	numerously
metagalaxy	motor-coach	neat-cattle	niggerling	numismatic

nematocyst	nerve-fibre	note-shaver	ombrophobe	overflight
nomothetes	nursehound	notational	ombrophile	overfondly
nomothetic	Norbertine	nutational	orchard-man	overflowed
Nematoidea	nurseryman	natatorial	orcharding	oleiferous
nematology	northwards	natatorium	orchardist	overglance
nummulated	north-bound	native-born	occidental	oleography
nummulitic	northerner	nativeness	once-errand	oreography
nameworthy	narcissism	nativistic	orchestral	overgreedy
namby-pamby	narcissist	noteworthy	orchestics	oleaginous
non-payment	narrow-boat	neurectomy	orchestric	overground
non-natural	narrowcast	nauseating	once-for-all	overgrowth
non-ability	narcolepsy	nauseative	orchideous	open-hearth
non-ferrous	narrowness	nauseously	oscillator	open-handed
nun's-fiddle	nystagmoid	nautically	oncologist	overhanded
nonchalant	nosocomial	nourice-fee	occultness	obeliscoid
non-violent	nosography	neurilemma	osculation	one-sidedly
non-fiction	nesting-box	nourishing	osculatory	overinform
nunciature	nosologist	nautiluses	oecumenism	obediently
non-aligned	nostopathy	neuropathy	occupation	overinsure
nonplussed	nostomania	neurogenic	occupative	overleaven
non-playing	nostologic	neurolemma	occurrence	overlabour
non-smoking	nosophobia	neuroblast	occasional	oreologist
no-nonsense	nasturtium	neuroplasm	occasioner	overlander
non-society	notability	neurotoxin	oscitantly	overlooker
non-joinder	noticeable	Neuroptera	oscitation	ocellation
nincompoop	noticeably	neurolysis	old-maidish	overlaunch
non-content	notodontid	neutralise	old-maidism	overlaying
non-arrival	nathelesse	neutralism	ordainable	open-minded
non-gremial	natterjack	neutralist	ordainment	overmantel
nanosecond	nethermore	neutrality	oedematose	overmaster
nanisation	nethermost	nourriture	oedematous	overmatter
nineteenth	netherward	novicehood	ordonnance	ocean-basin
non-utility	notifiable	novaculite	ordinarily	overnicely
non-starter	notch board	noviceship	ordinately	oceanology
non-current	nothingism	navigation	ordination	ocean-going
Neofascism	net-fishing	novelistic	odd-looking	oceanarium
Neofascist	net-fishery	never-never	old-fogyish	overoffice
Neo-Kantian	nutritious	newfangled	obdurately	overplaced
neogenesis	nit-picking	new-married	obduration	overpraise
neogenetic	nitrifying	newscaster	Ordovician	overpeople
noogenesis	nettle-cell	newsdealer	olde-worlde	overreckon
neoterical	nettle-fish	new-fledged	oleraceous	overriding
neoclassic	nettlerash	newsletter	operations	over-refine
neoplastic	natalitial	newsmonger	opera-cloak	oneirology
neological	nettle-tree	news-reader	opera-glass	overrunner
nuptiality	notonectal	news-vendor	overabound	overrashly
napkin-ring	nationally	news-writer	opera-house	ore-wrought
Napoleonic	notionally	newsworthy	overbidder	overraught
nipplewort	nitrometer	Nazaritism	overbridge	overslaugh
nepenthean	nationhood	opalescent	overboldly	overshadow
nephoscope	nationless	orange-lily	overburden	oversubtle
nephologic	nitro-group	orange-peel	overbought	oversleeve
nephograph	notaphilic	orange-root	overcharge	Odelsthing
nephridium	notarially	orange-tree	operculate	open-stitch
nephrology	Notoryctes	orange-wife	overcolour	overshower
nephralgia	nutcracker	orange-wood	overcanopy	oversupply
nephropexy	nature-cure	ovariotomy	overcaught	overspread
nephrotomy	naturalise	oratorical	overdaring	overstruck
naphthalic	naturalism	Onagraceae	overdosage	overstride
nepotistic	naturalist	ox-antelope	overexcite	overstrain
narratable	nature-myth	oracularly	overexpose	overstrike
nero-antico	naturopath	opaqueness	operettist	overstrong
nurse-child	naturistic	ombrometer	overfreely	overstrung

overstress
overtimely
overturner
overthrust
overthwart
overweight
overwinter
overwisely
officially
officiator
officialty
office-girl
olfactible
off-licence
offendress
obfuscated
off-putting
organicism
organicist
organogram
organogeny
organ-point
organismal
oughtlings
ochraceous
ophicleide
ophthalmia
ophthalmic
ophiolater
ophiolatry
ophiologic
ophiomorph
ochlocracy
othergates
otherwhile
otherwhere
otherworld
otherguess
oligarchal
oligarchic
olivaceous
olive-shell
originally
oxidisable
originator
opinionist
opium-eater
orientated
orientally
orientator
oniromancy
oniroscopy
opisometer
ovipositor
oligoclase
oligopsony
onirodynia
odiousness
obituarist
object-ball
objectless
object-soul
objuration

oak-leather
obligement
obligingly
obligation
obligatory
Owlspiegel
owlishness
oblateness
oblational
obliterate
osmidrosis
osmiridium
ommatidium
osmeterium
obnubilate
omniferous
omnigenous
oenologist
ornamental
ornamenter
omniparity
omniparous
omnipotent
omniscient
ornateness
ornithosis
ornithopod
omnivorous
onomastics
orogenesis
orogenetic
onocentaur
omophagous
omophorion
opotherapy
orological
orographic
odontocete
odontogeny
odontology
odontalgia
odontalgic
odontolite
odontomata
orotundity
orphanhood
orpheoreon
oppression
oppressive
oppugnancy
oppilation
oppilative
oophoritis
opprobrium
opposeless
oppositely
opposition
oppositive
Oireachtas
obsidional
oyster-bank
oyster-farm
oyster-park

obstetrics
oyster-wife
ossiferous
obsoletely
obsoletion
obsoletism
opsomaniac
opsiometer
oesophagus
obsequious
observance
observancy
observable
observably
observator
obstructer
obstructor
ossivorous
outbalance
outlandish
ostraceous
outrageous
outbargain
out-patient
outgassing
outpassion
octodecimo
outgeneral
outperform
out-pension
outmeasure
outjetting
outsetting
out-of-doors
octogenary
octogynous
octahedral
octahedron
octohedron
obtainable
outside-car
ostrich-egg
ostrichism
outfielder
outvillain
obtainment
outfitting
outwitting
ontologist
optologist
outbluster
outclassed
outflowing
optimalise
octamerous
optimistic
oftentimes
ostensible
ostensibly
octandrian
octonarian
octandrous
octonarius

octangular
orthopaedy
osteopathy
optionally
orthocaine
Orthoceras
orthogenic
orthopedia
orthopedic
osteogenic
Osteolepis
outlodging
orthophyre
osteophyte
Ostpolitik
orthoclase
osteoblast
osteoclast
orthopnoea
orthogonal
orthoboric
orthotonic
osteocolla
orthoepist
orthodromy
outpouring
orthograph
orthotropy
orthoprism
orthopraxy
orthoptics
orthoptera
orthoptist
outspeckle
octopodous
octaploidy
octoploidy
outbreathe
otter-shrew
otter-hound
otter-board
otter-trawl
obturation
outwrought
obtuseness
outstretch
optatively
obtruncate
outjutting
outsweeten
out-dweller
outswinger
ouvirandra
oxygenator
onychopagy
onychopora
onyx-marble
oxy-bromide
oryctology
phalangeal
phalangist
play-acting
praecocial

planchette
prancingly
peat-caster
plauditory
peacemaker
plate-layer
planetaria
plane-table
phagedaena
peace-party
prayer-bead
prayer-book
phagedenic
placer-gold
planetical
plate-fleet
plate-glass
prayerless
phanerogam
plate-proof
pease-brose
pease-straw
peacefully
playfellow
plangently
playground
peach-water
peach-bloom
poachiness
peashooter
peacherino
peach-stone
pharisaism
pratincole
planimeter
planimetry
placidness
planigraph
plagiarise
plagiarism
plagiarist
pianissimo
prankingly
planktonic
playleader
phallicism
praeludium
pearl-shell
pearl-white
pearl-diver
phalloidin
phaelonion
pearliness
pearl-stone
pharmacist
plasmodesm
psalmodise
psalmodist
plasmodium
plasmogamy
plasmolyse
pearmonger
praemunire

psammophil
plasmosoma
plasmosome
pragmatise
pragmatism
pragmatist
plain-chant
phaenology
plaintless
phaenotype
planometer
Platonical
peacockery
peacock-ore
peacockish
planoblast
pianoforte
piano-organ
piano-stool
phagocytic
praepostor
peat-reeker
prairie-hen
prairie-dog
pea-trainer
praesidium
playschool
pear-switch
praiseless
praisingly
practician
Plasticine
plasticise
plasticity
plastidule
prattlebox
plastogamy
plastilina
phantomish
plant-house
plant-louse
praetorian
psalterian
plastering
praetorium
psalterium
phantasmal
phantasmic
phantastic
phantasime
practisant
practising
phantastry
plantation
plaguesome
plague-spot
plague-sore
play-writer
playwright
pharyngeal
platypuses
publicness
pebble-ware

puberulent
puberulous
pubescence
pack-animal
peccadillo
piccadillo
piccadilly
piccalilli
piccaninny
pickaninny
pick-cheese
packet-boat
pocket-book
pocket-comb
picket-duty
pocketfuls
pocket-hole
picket-line
pocketless
pickedness
packet-note
packet-ship
pacifiable
pacificism
pacificist
pacificate
pectinated
packing-box
pichiciago
picnicking
peculiarly
poculiform
peculation
pockmantie
pockmarked
pectorally
pycnometer
pictorical
picrotoxin
pycnogonid
pycnospore
pictograph
pycnostyle
pick-pocket
pockpitted
picaresque
pack-saddle
pace-setter
pack-thread
picture-hat
picture-rod
pachymeter
picayunish
podiatrist
pediculate
Pediculati
pediculous
pedicurist
Podocarpus
pedagogics
pedagogism
podagrical
pudding-bag

padding-ken
pudding-pie
paddle-boat
pedologist
podologist
pedal-point
pedal-board
pedal-organ
paddle-wood
pedimental
pedimented
pedantical
peduncular
pedipalpus
Podostemon
pedestrian
paddymelon
paddy-whack
paddy-field
prepayable
preparator
peel-and-eat
prevalence
prevalency
phenacetin
preparedly
pied-à-terre
predaceous
presageful
prelatical
premarital
premaxilla
precarious
predacious
prevailing
prepayment
paedagogic
pteranodon
paedagogue
precaution
poetastery
presbyopia
presbyopic
presbytery
pierceable
prescience
prescriber
preachment
piercingly
pleochroic
pseudo-acid
pseudobulb
pseudocarp
pseudology
pseudimago
pre-Adamite
pleadingly
prevenancy
preferable
preferably
paederasty
pretendant
pretendent

prebendary
precedence
precedency
preference
predevelop
predecease
prerelease
premedical
prevenient
preferment
piece-goods
preferring
prehensile
prepensely
precession
prehension
presension
pretension
prehensory
prehensive
prepensive
preceptial
present-day
presential
paedeutics
precentrix
predestine
predestiny
prelection
prevention
preceptory
prefecture
predentate
preceptive
presentive
preventive
pledgeable
peelgarlic
psephology
poetically
predicable
plebiscite
presidency
pleximeter
pleximetry
prelingual
plenishing
precipiced
precipitin
presidiary
plexiglass
presignify
predispose
preciosity
plesiosaur
paediatric
prediction
prefixture
prehistory
predictive
plenilunar
preciously
previously

pre-glacial
phelloderm
peerlessly
preclusion
psellismus
preclusive
pre-eminent
pleomorphy
pneumatics
pre-emption
pre-emptive
pregnantly
pleonastic
prednisone
Phenogamae
phenogamic
pleromatic
preconceit
preconcert
precordial
precondemn
phenomenal
prepotence
prepotency
piezometer
phenomenon
paedophile
plerophory
premonitor
prepositor
precocious
prepollent
pie-counter
precompose
paedotribe
phenocryst
preconsume
prepossess
Plecoptera
phenotypic
preappoint
puerperium
prearrange
pleurodont
pietra-dura
prefrontal
pleurotomy
pressed-day
press-agent
pleasantly
pleasingly
pressingly
pheasantry
pleasantry
press-money
press-proof
pressurise
prettiness
presternum
plentitude
prestation
presumable
presumably

prefulgent
prejudiced
preludious
pre-qualify
presurmise
presuppose
precursory
precursive
pre-exilian
pterylosis
Pterygotus
pufferfish
puff-pastry
pegmatitic
pugnacious
peg-tankard
pagoda-tree
pigmentary
pugilistic
pogonotomy
pagination
pigeonhole
pigeon-pair
pigeon-post
pigeon-toed
pigeon-wing
pig-sticker
philatelic
primatical
pliability
princified
princehood
princelike
princeling
principial
principled
principate
principium
princessly
prize-fight
prize-money
prize-court
paideutics
pridefully
priggishly
Pliohippus
primiparae
privileged
poikilitic
Philippian
philippina
philippine
Philippise
Philistean
Philistian
philistine
prick-eared
pain-killer
prick-louse
prickly-ash
phialiform
phillumeny
painlessly

prismoidal
poignantly
pliantness
philomathy
poisonable
prison-bars
prison-crop
primordial
prison-door
primordium
primogenit
poison-fang
prisonment
philologer
philosophe
philosophy
philologic
philopoena
philologue
prison-ship
psilocybin
painstaker
priesthood
priest-king
priest-like
priestling
puissantly
puir's-hoose
puir's-house
priestship
poinsettia
puissaunce
psittacine
point-blank
paintiness
paintworks
print-works
paint-brush
pejoration
pejorative
poke-bonnet
pike-keeper
pyknometer
poker-faced
pokerishly
pulsatance
Polyandria
paleaceous
palmaceous
pultaceous
palmatifid
Pulsatilla
palladious
pilgarlick
polyatomic
polyaxonic
Pelmatozoa
pillar-root
pellagrous
Polianthes
polyactine
polyanthus
palm-branch

pall-bearer
phlebolite
palm-butter
phlebotomy
Polychaeta
polychaete
polycyclic
polyclinic
polycrotic
Pelecypoda
polycarpic
polychroic
polychrome
polychromy
polychrest
Pilocarpus
policy-shop
police-trap
polycotton
pulp-cavity
polydactyl
poll-degree
pile-driver
paludament
paludinous
polydipsia
pulverable
Palaeocene
pallescent
palaeogaea
Palaeogene
pulp-engine
pulveriser
palaeolith
pollenosis
palaestral
pollen-tube
palaestric
palaeotype
palmer-worm
Palaeozoic
polt-footed
piliferous
polygraphy
phlegmasia
phlegmatic
palm-grease
polygamist
polygamous
polygynian
polygenism
polygenist
palagonite
polygenous
polygynous
phlegmonic
phlogopite
phlogistic
phlogiston
polyhybrid
polyhedral
polyhedric
polyhydric

polyhedron
polyhalite
Polyhymnia
polyhistor
pulvinated
pollinator
pelvimeter
pulsimeter
pelvimetry
pulvilised
pilliwinks
palliament
pallidness
pillionist
palliation
palliatory
palliative
pellicular
palm-kernel
polemicist
peltmonger
polemonium
polymeride
polymerase
polymerise
polymerism
polymerous
polymastia
polymastic
palimpsest
polymathic
palynology
polynomial
palindrome
Polynesian
Pulmonaria
pillow-bear
pillow-bere
pillowcase
pulsometer
pileorhiza
pillow-lace
pillow-lava
pillowslip
polyonymic
pillorying
polyphagia
polyphasic
Polypodium
Polyphemic
Polyphemus
Polypterus
polyploidy
poll-parrot
pilgrimage
pilgrimise
palfrenier
paltriness
polyrhythm
polishable
palisadoes
pilastered
polishings

polishment
polysemant
palisander
palustrian
palustrine
polystylar
politician
politicise
polytocous
polytheism
polytheist
pilot-whale
pilot-plant
palatalise
politeness
palatinate
pilot-house
pollutedly
pellucidly
polyvalent
palsy-walsy
pome-citron
pummelling
pompelmous
pomiferous
pemphigoid
pemphigous
pump-handle
Pimpinella
pomologist
pumple-nose
Pomeranian
panhandler
Pentandria
panjandrum
Pentateuch
pentameter
Pentameron
pentahedra
pennaceous
pentathlon
pentachord
pentathlum
pinnatiped
pinnatifid
pentaploid
pentagonal
pentapodic
pentapolis
pentatomic
pentatonic
pantaloons
pentagraph
pentaprism
penmanship
pentastich
pentastyle
pennatulae
Pentagynia
pine-beauty
pine-beetle
pine-barren
pine-chafer

Punicaceae
pinacoidal
penicillin
paniculate
pine-carpet
panic-grass
ponderance
ponderancy
ponderable
pince-nezed
pangenesis
pangenetic
penteteric
Pontederia
pony-engine
Pentelican
ponderment
pandermite
Pandemonic
Pontefract
pen-feather
pin-feather
pandectist
pendentive
Pan-African
panegyrise
panegyrist
punch-ladle
pinchpenny
pinchingly
pantherine
punch-drunk
pantheress
pantherish
pencil-case
Pinnipedia
pentimenti
pentimento
Pennisetum
pontifical
pontifices
pencil-lead
pencilling
pennillion
pensionary
pundigrion
panniculus
pinakoidal
pine-kernel
pinakothek
penologist
penelopise
Panglossic
Pan-Slavism
Pan-Slavist
Panamanian
pine-marten
penumbrous
pond-master
penoncelle
pine-needle
penannular
peninsular

pantoscope
pantophagy
pansophism
pansophist
pantomimic
pancosmism
pontonnier
pundonores
pantograph
panton-shoe
panoptical
panopticon
panophobia
panspermic
pancreatic
pancreatin
Pan-Arabism
ponerology
pantrymaid
pancratian
pancratist
panaritium
pancratium
panislamic
punishable
pentstemon
punishment
penetrance
penetrancy
penetralia
penetrable
penetrably
punctually
penetrator
punctuator
pin-striped
punctulate
penitently
punctation
pandurated
pinnulated
Pinguicula
pinguidity
pincushion
penguinery
pin-buttock
pinguitude
panty-waist
pennypiece
penny-pinch
penny-plain
penny-a-line
pennyroyal
pennyworth
pennycress
penny-stane
penny-stone
propaganda
propagable
proratable
propagator
prosaicism
procacious

protanopia
protanopic
propagulum
procaryote
prokaryote
proscriber
proscenium
prosciutto
proud-flesh
ploddingly
Ptolemaean
provenance
promenader
phonematic
Ptolemaist
proverbial
proseuchae
proteaceae
Provençale
proceeding
propendent
pyogenesis
proteiform
promethean
pronephric
pronephros
Prometheum
promethium
phonetical
progenitor
proveditor
propellant
propellent
propelling
proteolyse
propelment
phoneyness
properness
proteinous
propensely
professing
procession
profession
propension
protension
propensity
protensity
propensive
protensive
propertied
protectrix
projectile
projecting
protecting
protestant
projection
protection
provection
projecture
protectory
pro-oestrus
projective
protective

procedural
prosecutor
protervity
proof-sheet
proof-house
proffering
ploughable
ploughgate
plough-iron
ploughland
plough-team
plough-tree
plough-tail
ploughwise
prothallia
prothallic
prothallus
prophesied
prophesier
prophetess
prophetism
provitamin
prodigally
profitable
profitably
providable
proximally
provincial
procidence
prominence
prominency
providence
proairesis
promiseful
prolicidal
prolifical
prohibiter
proficient
prosilient
prohibitor
propitiate
prodigious
prolixious
propitious
profitless
prolixness
propionate
pholidosis
promissory
promissive
profluence
profligacy
profligate
proclaimer
problemist
prowlingly
proglottis
proclivity
phorminges
Phoenician
prognostic
prognathic
phototaxis

proposable
provocable
provokable
provocator
photonasty
phonometer
photometer
phocomelia
photogenic
photometry
prolongate
photophobe
photophily
photophone
photophony
phonophore
photophore
Protophyta
protophyte
pronominal
prosodical
photodiode
phonolitic
photoflood
photoglyph
protoplasm
protoplast
procoelous
pronounced
pronouncer
propounder
profoundly
phonograph
photograph
phototrope
phototropy
protostele
proportion
promontory
Psocoptera
prolocutor
prologuise
prototypal
protoxylem
phonotypic
photolysis
photolytic
phototypic
phosphatic
prompt-book
prospector
prompt-copy
prospectus
promptness
prompt-note
phosphoret
phosphoric
phosphorus
prosperity
prosperous
prompt-side
phosphuret
promptuary

procreator
protracted
proproctor
protractor
protrudent
propraetor
proprietor
poor-relief
programmed
programmer
pyorrhoeal
pyorrhoeic
procrypsis
procryptic
protreptic
protrusile
protrusion
protrusive
poor's-house
prosthesis
prosthetic
proctalgia
prostomial
prostomium
plottingly
proctorial
proctorage
proctorise
prostatism
prostitute
procurable
procurator
procumbent
profundity
profulgent
promulgate
producible
pronuclear
pronucleus
propulsion
propulsory
propulsive
productile
production
productive
propylaeum
pepper-cake
peppercorn
peppermill
peppermint
puppet-play
puppet-show
pepperwort
pupigerous
poplinette
papillated
papillitis
popularise
popularity
pupilarity
papulation
population
populously

pipe-laying
pop-concert
pupiparous
paper-faced
paper-maker
paper-gauge
Piperaceae
piperidine
paper-chase
paper-cigar
paper-birch
papyrology
paper-cloth
paper-knife
paperboard
paper-ruler
piperazine
papistical
papaverine
papaverous
pipe-wrench
popsy-wopsy
Portakabin®
parramatta
permanence
permanency
pyro-acetic
portamento
porraceous
parmacitie
permafrost
Parnassian
parablepsy
paraboloid
parabolise
parabolist
parabemata
parabiosis
parabiotic
pericyclic
periclinal
portcullis
periculous
pyracantha
paradoctor
paradiddle
peridinian
peridinium
peridermal
paradisean
paradisiac
paradisial
paradisian
paradisaic
parodistic
peridotite
pyridoxine
paradoxure
paradoxist
purveyance
parcel-bawd
perdendosi
paraenesis

paraenetic
periegesis
purse-seine
parcel-gilt
Purbeckian
parcelling
Parnellism
Parnellite
purse-pride
perpetrate
purse-proud
pursership
perversely
perversion
perversity
perversive
perceptual
percentage
percentile
pargetting
porpentine
perception
perfection
permeation
porrection
portentous
perceptive
perfective
permeative
persecutor
perpetuate
perpetuity
perceiving
perfervour
parpen-wall
parcelwise
paraffinic
portfolios
poriferous
pyrography
paraglider
pyrogallic
pyrogallol
perigonial
paragonite
perigonium
perigynous
pyrogenous
paragnosis
paraglossa
pyrrhicist
parchmenty
perihelion
pyrrhonian
pyrrhonism
pyrrhonist
perchloric
porphyrite
porphyrous
pyrrhotine
pyrrhotite
persicaria
pertinence

pertinency
parting-cup
parricidal
participle
percipient
perficient
perfidious
pernicious
perjinkety
perjinkity
pernickety
persiflage
partialism
partialist
partiality
persifleur
partialize
parliament
Persianise
portionist
permission
permissive
permitting
persistent
persistive
particular
perviously
parkkeeper
parkleaves
purple-born
Pyrolaceae
paralleled
parallelly
paralogise
paralogism
purple-hued
purblindly
purulently
portliness
paralipsis
pyrolusite
perilously
perplexing
perplexity
paramecium
paramedico
pyrimidine
pyramidion
pyramidist
paramnesia
pyromaniac
pyromantic
portmantle
portmantua
pyromeride
perimysium
parametral
pari-mutuel
parametric
perimetric
pyrometric
peremptory
paramouncy

parentally
paronychia
pyrenocarp
parenteral
parenchyma
parenthood
paranoidal
phrenology
parentless
paronomasy
paronymous
paranormal
phrenesiac
perineural
perforated
personated
personalia
pardonable
pardonably
perforable
personable
personally
percolator
perforator
personator
personalty
perforatus
parrot-beak
parrot-bill
parson-bird
parrot-coal
purposeful
parrot-fish
parsonical
periodical
perfoliate
parvovirus
pardonless
performing
parlour-car
pornocracy
periosteal
periosteum
paraphasia
paraphasic
parapodial
parapodium
peripheral
peripteral
paraplegia
paraplegic
peripheric
paraphilia
parapineal
paraphonia
paraphonic
pyrophoric
pyrophorus
paraphrase
paraphrast
periphrase
perspirate
peripetian

peripeteia
paraphyses
paraphysis
periphyton
parbreaked
pararthria
peroration
porismatic
pyrostatic
perishable
perishably
phrase-book
parascenia
Parisienne
parischane
poristical
puristical
parastichy
paraselene
phraseless
peristomal
periscopic
poroscopic
parasitoid
parasitise
parasitism
peristylar
paratactic
peritectic
pyrotechny
parathesis
perithecia
perstringe
pyretology
peritoneal
puritanise
puritanism
peritoneum
paratroops
perdurance
perdurable
perdurably
permutable
perturbant
perturbate
parturient
percutient
perjurious
pursuantly
pursuingly
porousness
percurrent
percussant
percussion
persuasion
percursory
persuasory
perquisite
percussive
persuasive
parquetted
pirouetter
perruquier

Portuguese
pursuivant
periwigged
periwinkle
peroxidase
peroxidise
pyroxyline
pyroxenite
paroxysmal
paroxytone
postal-card
passageway
passamezzo
post-bellum
push-button
postchaise
post-exilic
pesterment
pasteboard
Pasteurian
paste-grain
pasteurise
pasteurism
possession
possessory
possessive
pasigraphy
posthumous
piscifauna
pestilence
passimeter
pasticheur
pesticidal
pistillode
postillion
passiflora
pistillary
pistillate
postillate
passionary
Passionist
passionate
postliminy
post-letter
post-mortem
postmaster
post-Nicene
pastorally
post-office
pistolling
pastorship
pistol-shot
pistol-whip
post-partum
pastrycook
push-stroke
postscript
positional
positioned
positively
positivism
positivist
positivity

postulancy
pasturable
postulatum
pasquilant
pasquinade
pasty-faced
Puseyistic
pot-wabbler
Petrarchal
Petrarchan
pot-valiant
patibulary
putrescent
putrescine
pathetical
pot-bellied
pettedness
patter-song
putrefying
pathfinder
Patagonian
pitch-wheel
pitch-black
pitchiness
patchcocke
patchboard
pitcherful
pitchstone
pettichaps
patricidal
phthisical
phthisicky
patriciate
pit-village
patricliny
patrialise
patrialism
putridness
patrifocal
patrilocal
patriarchy
petrissage
patristics
patriation
patriotism
petrifying
pottle-deep
petulantly
pitilessly
potamology
patentable
Potentilla
potentiary
potentiate
put-and-take
patination
petiolated
petrolatum
pot-wobbler
pathogenic
pythogenic
petronella
petroleous

patroniser
patrocliny
patrolling
petrolling
pot-boiling
petroglyph
patronless
pathognomy
petromoney
pathologic
patronymic
pityriasis
paternally
Peter-see-me
patereroes
petitioner
potato-trap
pot-hunting
Patavinity
putty-faced
pettychaps
putty-knife
plumassier
plum-colour
pouncet-box
plunderage
plunderous
pluperfect
plume-grass
prudential
pausefully
pruriently
Paulianist
pluckiness
plutolatry
plutocracy
pourparler
pousse-café
Plumularia
pawnbroker
powder-down
powder-horn
pewter-mill
powder-mill
powder-puff
powder-room
power-lathe
power-plant
power-point
power-house
power-drill
power-press
powerfully
pawnticket
pixillated
phylactery
psychiater
psychiatry
psychogram
psychogony
psychology
psychopomp
psychopath

physically
physiocrat
physicking
physiology
Phyllopoda
phyllotaxy
phylloxera
Phytolacca
phytogenic
phytotoxic
phytotoxin
pay-station
puzzle-head
puzzlement
puzzlingly
pozzolanic
pozzuolana
quarantine
Quaker-bird
quaternion
quaternary
quaternate
quaternity
quagginess
qualifying
qualmishly
quaintness
quatorzain
quarriable
quadricone
quadriceps
quatrefoil
quadriform
quadriller
quarrelled
quarreller
quadrumvir
Quadrumana
quadrumane
quadrantal
quadrantes
quarrender
quadrennia
quadrangle
quadruplet
quadruplex
quadrireme
quadrisect
quadratrix
quadrature
quadrivial
quadrivium
quaestuary
quantifier
quartzitic
quartz-mill
quarter-day
quartz-rock
quarterage
quarter-ill
quartering
quarter-boy
quarteroon

quartation	rhapsodise	racket-tail	race-walker	redivision
quantitive	rhapsodist	rickettsia	ride-and-tie	rue-bargain
quenchable	reap-silver	recreation	red-sanders	Riemannian
quenchless	reassemble	recreative	red-lattice	riebeckite
quercitron	reassembly	recogniser	ridability	re-election
queencraft	reassuring	rock-garden	radiciform	re-erection
quernstone	reastiness	rock-hopper	radicalise	re-eligible
queasiness	reactively	race-hatred	radicalism	rheologist
quersprung	reactivate	receivable	radiculose	re-enlister
questingly	reactivity	reclinable	radicality	rheumatoid
questioner	roadworthy	recoilless	ridiculous	rheumatise
queryingly	ready-to-eat	rectifying	redecorate	rheumatism
quinacrine	ready-money	recallable	radication	rheumatize
quinaquina	ready-to-sew	rick-lifter	rededicate	Rheinberry
Quirinalia	rubiaceous	recallment	redeemable	rhetorical
quick-match	Rebeccaism	recolonise	rudder-fish	re-entrance
quick-sandy	Rebeccaite	recklessly	ridge-piece	re-entrancy
quick-water	rub-a-dub-dub	rock-lizard	redeemless	rheotropic
quick-hedge	robber-crab	recommence	rudderless	re-entering
quickthorn	rubber-neck	recumbence	redressive	reed-thrush
quick-firer	riboflavin	recumbency	rodfishing	ruefulness
quickening	rubiginous	recompense	red-figured	refracting
quirkiness	rubrically	Rachmanism	raduliform	refraction
quink-goose	rubricator	recompress	riddle-like	refractory
quick-trick	rabbit-fish	racemation	redolently	refracture
quick-grass	rabbit-hole	raconteuse	riddlingly	refractive
quick-stick	rubbishing	recondense	red-blooded	raft-bridge
quick-lunch	rabbinical	reconciler	redelivery	rifle-range
quiz-master	rebukingly	reconsider	rudimental	rafter-bird
quiescence	rebellious	recontinue	redemption	refreshing
quiescency	rabblement	ricinoleic	redemptory	refreshful
quinsy-wort	rubble-work	recentness	redemptive	reflexible
quint-major	robing-room	reconquest	redundance	rifle-corps
quint-minor	ribbon-fish	raccoon-dog	redundancy	rifle-green
quietening	ribbon-seal	rectorship	riding-boot	reflecting
quintuplet	rib-roaster	receptacle	riding-coat	reflection
quietistic	ribbon-weed	recipience	riding-crop	reflective
quizziness	ribbon-worm	recipiency	riding-hood	refringent
quotatious	roberdsman	rock-pigeon	riding-robe	ruffianish
rear-boiled	robertsman	receptible	riding-suit	ruffianism
road-bridge	ruby-spinel	reciprocal	riding-whip	refulgence
reaccustom	robustious	recuperate	Radiolaria	refulgency
rhabdolith	ruby-silver	recapturer	radioscope	refinement
rear-dorter	robustness	recordable	radioscopy	refundment
readership	rebuttable	rock-ribbed	radiometer	reformable
real-estate	rebatement	rock-rabbit	radiogenic	referrible
reafforest	ruby-throat	rectricial	radiophone	referendum
realisable	rectangled	recurrence	radiophony	refutation
reaming-bit	rockabilly	recurrency	radiosonde	ragmatical
reading-boy	reclaimant	recureless	radiologic	ragged-lady
reallocate	rackabones	rack-renter	radiotoxic	raggedness
road-making	reclassify	rechristen	radiograph	ruggedness
rearmament	rock-badger	rock-salmon	radiolysis	rogue-money
road-mender	rick-burner	recusation	radarscope	regression
Rhamnaceae	rick-barton	rock-temple	rediscover	regressive
reasonable	rock-butter	rock-turbot	redissolve	regretting
reasonably	rock-bottom	recitation	redescribe	regainable
reasonless	recyclable	recitative	redisburse	regainment
readoption	ricocheted	recitativo	redounding	regalement
reappraise	racecourse	recrudesce	redruthite	regularise
reacquaint	recidivism	recoupment	red-murrain	regularity
road-roller	recidivist	recruiting	redcurrant	regelation
road-runner	recreantly	rock-violet	redevelope	regulation

regulatory	rejuvenate	remittance	ripidolite	researcher
regulative	rakishness	remoteness	rope-dancer	rascal-like
ragamuffin	releasable	rumbullion	repression	rascallion
regimental	reluctance	rum-running	repressive	restaurant
regent-bird	reluctancy	rumfustian	repugnance	rose-beetle
regeneracy	rollcollar	rent-an-army	repugnancy	risibility
regenerate	relocation	rent-a-crowd	repairable	rose-chafer
regentship	relievable	rent-charge	ripping-saw	rose-colour
regionally	reliefless	renderable	reptilious	rose-combed
regardable	religioner	runner-bean	repair-shop	rush-candle
regardless	relegation	Ranzellaar	repainting	rest-centre
rigorously	rolling-pin	Ringelmann	repellance	Resedaceae
registered	rollicking	rinderpest	repellancy	residenter
registrant	relentless	rangership	rope-ladder	russel-cord
registrary	relentment	rendezvous	repellence	rose-engine
rightwards	relinquish	ring-finger	repellency	rostellate
right-about	reliquaire	röntgenise	ripple-mark	Russellite
right-of-way	relishable	renegation	ripplingly	respectant
right-lined	Rolls-Royce®	Rh-negative	rope-making	respecting
right-drawn	relational	ranshackle	repentance	respectful
rightfully	relatively	rancidness	roping-down	respective
rehearsing	relativise	ringleader	repinement	rust-fungus
rehandling	relativism	randle-balk	repiningly	rosy-footed
raiyatwari	relativist	randle-tree	ripsnorter	resignedly
reincrease	relativity	ring-master	reprobance	resignment
rain-doctor	relevantly	ring-necked	reprobater	rose-garden
reiterance	relaxation	ranunculus	reproacher	reschedule
reiterated	relaxative	ransomable	rip-roaring	rush-holder
Rhineberry	rallyingly	rondoletto	rapporteur	rest-harrow
Rhinegrave	rampageous	randomiser	reproducer	respirable
rhinestone	rampacious	ransomless	repopulate	rustically
rain forest	rampalllan	rencounter	reportable	respirator
Reichsbank	remediable	randomwise	reportedly	rusticator
Reichsland	remediably	ring-plover	repurchase	reshipment
reichsmark	remedially	ring-porous	repertoire	Russianise
Reichsrath	remediless	rank-riding	reparation	Russianism
raising-bee	romper-suit	renascence	reparatory	Russianist
Rhipiptera	remigation	ring-tailed	reparative	rescission
reim-kennar	ramshackle	ranivorous	rope-stitch	rescissory
reillumine	Ramphastos	renovation	rupestrian	restitutor
rhinolalia	rumple-bane	Rhoeadales	reposition	rustic-ware
rhinoscope	ramblingly	rhomboidal	repository	rustic-work
rhinoscopy	rumblingly	rhomboides	Rh-positive	resolvable
rhizogenic	rum-blossom	rootedness	repatriate	resilience
rhinoceros	rememberer	root-fallen	reputeless	resiliency
rhinotheca	romancical	room-fellow	repetition	resolvedly
rhinophyma	romantical	reorganise	reputation	resultless
Rhizophora	Ruminantia	roof-garden	répétiteur	rustlingly
rhizophore	ruminantly	rhodophane	repetitive	rose-lipped
rhizoplane	remunerate	root-rubber	reputative	restlessly
rhizomorph	Romanistic	room-ridden	repoussage	resolutely
rain-plover	Romanesque	root-sheath	rope-walker	resolution
railroader	rumination	rood-screen	roquelaure	resolutive
reissuable	remonetise	root-system	requirable	rose-laurel
rain-shadow	ruminative	Rhodymenia	requitable	resemblant
reinspirit	remarkable	repealable	requiteful	resembling
roisterous	remarkably	repeatable	requisitor	rose-mallow
rejectable	remorseful	repeatedly	requiescat	resumption
rejectible	remortgage	republican	reredorter	resumptive
rejoindure	remarriage	rupicoline	rarefiable	resentence
rejoiceful	Rome-runner	rupicolous	reregister	rosaniline
rajpramukh	remissible	repudiable	rere-supper	rosin-plant
rejuvenise	remissness	repudiator	Ruritanian	resentment

resonantly	ritornello	river-front	scandalise	shagginess
resinously	rotor-plane	revestiary	scandalous	slanginess
restorable	returnless	ravishment	shard-borne	sparganium
respondent	retardment	revisional	standpoint	staggering
Russophobe	retirement	revisitant	standers-by	swaggering
Russophile	retiringly	revitalise	slanderous	slaughtery
responsory	rôtisserie	revivified	standstill	star-gazing
responsive	rotational	revivalism	shandrydan	stag-headed
resupinate	rat-hunting	revivalist	snake-dance	shag-haired
rose-quartz	**Rottweiler**	revivement	shamefaced	stadholder
reservable	round-eared	revivingly	state-paper	staphyloma
restricted	round-faced	**rowing-boat**	state-cabin	staphyline
resurgence	round-table	rowan-berry	stage-wagon	scatheless
reservedly	roundabout	rewardable	stavesacre	spathulate
restrained	round-nosed	rewardless	sealed-beam	scathingly
restrainer	round-house	rowdy-dowdy	snake-fence	**Scaphopoda**
resorcinol	round-mouth	rhyme-royal	stage-fever	sea-whistle
resorption	route-march	rhythmical	spade-beard	snaphaunce
resorptive	rouseabout	rhythmless	scavenging	snaphaunch
resistance	rough-hewer	**Rhyniaceae**	scavengery	statically
resistible	rough-rider	roysterous	snake's-head	sea-biscuit
resistibly	rough-hound	razzmatazz	scape-wheel	spadiceous
resistless	rough-house	razor-shell	**Swadeshism**	stamineous
resounding	rough-draft	razor-blade	spagerical	sealing-day
rose-window	rough-grind	razor-strop	shale-miner	sealing-wax
rat-catcher	rough-stuff	scarabaeid	state-aided	sea-fishing
retransfer	reunionism	**Scarabaeus**	shade-plant	spagirical
retransmit	reunionist	smaragdine	suaveolent	stabiliser
retractile	roustabout	smaragdite	searedness	spaniolise
retraction	revealable	spatangoid	spacewoman	spaniolate
retractive	revealment	stay-at-home	stagecoach	spatiality
ratability	rove-beetle	sea-bathing	scale-board	stationary
reticulary	revocation	seamanlike	skateboard	stationery
reticulate	revocatory	stalagmite	snake-house	spaciously
rutherford	reviewable	scaramouch	stage-horse	scarifying
ruthenious	revokement	sialagogic	state-house	slack-water
rottenness	revalidate	sialagogue	sea-serpent	stark-naked
rotiferous	revolvency	sea-vampire	sea-leopard	spankingly
retainable	revilement	sea-passage	state-trial	slackening
retailment	revilingly	seamanship	scapegrace	sparkishly
retainment	revalorise	sea-captain	slave-trade	small-wares
retributor	revelation	stalactite	spacecraft	snail-paced
retrieving	revolution	soap-bubble	stagecraft	sea-blubber
retaliator	revelatory	stag-beetle	statecraft	spauld-bone
rattle-head	revelative	soap-boiler	shame-proof	snail-wheel
rattle-pate	raven's-bone	star-bright	shave-grass	snail-shell
ruthlessly	raven's-duck	stabbingly	slave-grown	small-pipes
rattle-trap	revengeful	scabbiness	sea-lettuce	stall-plate
ritt-master	revanchism	shabbiness	sea-feather	stablemate
retinacula	revanchist	slabbiness	scale-stair	stallenger
retinalite	ravenously	searchable	snakestone	stallinger
rationally	river-water	spatchcock	shamefully	stableness
ration-book	river-basin	starchedly	sea-service	small-hours
ration-card	riverscape	spancelled	slave-owner	small-tooth
retrochoir	reversedly	searchless	snaffle-bit	small-craft
retrospect	reversible	stanchless	scaffolder	stable-room
retrograde	revertible	scarcement	scarf-joint	scarlet-hat
retrogress	reverencer	scarceness	· staff-corps	scarlatina
retrorsely	reverently	stanchness	seal-fisher	spallation
ritardando	river-horse	snapdragon	shanghaied	shallowing
returnable	river-mouth	scald-berry	shanghaier	small-sword
ritornelle	river-craft	shandygaff	slang-whang	spasmodist
ritornelli	river-drift	scandalled	slangingly	swan-maiden

starmonger
smalminess
smarminess
swarm-spore
slammerkin
stammering
swan-mussel
seannachie
sea-unicorn
sea-anemone
stagnantly
spawn-brick
Stannaries
stagnation
stannotype
seasonable
seasonably
seasonally
sea-poacher
statoscope
shadowcast
sea-soldier
sea-goddess
Slavophobe
scatophagy
Slavophile
seasonless
shadowless
shadow-mark
sialogogue
shadow-play
slavocracy
sea-monster
stamp-paper
sharp-edged
stamp-hinge
stamp-album
snappingly
sharp-nosed
scampishly
snappishly
scabridity
shagreened
starry-eyed
staurolite
starriness
stair-tower
starr-grass
star-shaped
sparseness
scansorial
seamstress
start-naked
stay-tackle
Spartacist
spasticity
smart-Aleck
smart-Alick
scaithless
skaithless
slantingly
startingly
scantiness

scattiness
smart-money
shaft-horse
slatternly
scattering
smattering
scatter-gun
scapulated
statutable
statutably
sea-burdock
statute-cap
statute-law
sea-surgeon
scaturient
swan-upping
seaquarium
statuesque
starveling
starvation
sea-swallow
stalwartly
subnascent
subtangent
Sabbath-day
sabbatical
submariner
subvariety
subnatural
suboceanic
subacidity
subscribed
subscriber
suboctuple
subdecanal
subtenancy
sabretache
subheading
subgeneric
subterfuge
submediant
subsellium
subdeanery
sabre-tooth
subterrene
subsessile
submersion
subversion
subversive
subcentral
subjectify
subfertile
subletting
subjection
subreption
subsection
subvention
subjective
subreptive
subsequent
sebiferous
subchanter
subshrubby

sublimated
sublimable
subsidence
subsidency
sublingual
subkingdom
subliminal
subdivider
subsidiary
subtilness
submission
submissive
submitting
subsistent
subglobose
subglacial
subtleness
sibilation
sibilatory
subclavian
subintrant
subangular
subcordate
subsoiling
subjoinder
submontane
subroutine
subspecies
subspinous
subaquatic
subaqueous
subtractor
subprefect
seborrhoea
subtrahend
suborbital
subordinal
sobersides
subcranial
subtropics
sybaritish
sybaritism
subarcuate
substratal
substratum
substellar
subatomics
substernal
substation
substitute
subjugator
subfuscous
subsurface
subduement
subduction
subculture
subsultive
Socratical
socialness
societally
secretaire
succeeding
sacredness

secretness
sickerness
sachemship
succession
successful
successive
sick-fallen
saccharide
saccharify
saccharoid
saccharine
saccharase
saccharose
saccharate
succinctly
sucking-pig
sacrificer
sectionise
sickle-bill
sicilienne
sickliness
secularise
secularism
secularist
secularity
sick-listed
sick-making
second-best
second-hand
second-mark
second-rate
sacrosanct
socdolager
sociopathy
sociometry
socdoliger
sacroiliac
socdologer
sociologic
sycophancy
sack-posset
securiform
secernment
securement
secureness
sacerdotal
sacculated
succulence
succulency
secludedly
succursale
succussion
succussive
succubuses
seducement
seducingly
seductress
side-effect
soddenness
suddenness
sad-hearted
side-glance
saddleback

saddle-fast
saddleless
saddle-roof
saddle-room
saddle-sick
saddle-sore
saddle-tree
sedulously
sedan-chair
siderolite
siderostat
sideration
side-saddle
soda-siphon
side-stroke
sedateness
sudatorium
Sadducaean
sidewinder
seecatchie
sherardise
stewardess
shenanigan
steganopod
skew-bridge
sueability
shea-butter
sketchable
sketch-book
stencilled
stenciller
speechless
Spencerian
skew-corbel
stercorary
stercorate
ctcnch-trap
speed-limit
step-dancer
speediness
steadiness
slenderise
speedfully
stereobate
skene-occle
seemelesse
shereefian
stereogram
siege-piece
sieve-plate
shebeening
siege-works
stereopsis
siegecraft
siege-train
stereotomy
stereotype
stereotypy
stepfather
sleigh-bell
sdeignfull
stephanite
see-through

scenically	spermarium	sheathless	sign-manual	schizoidal
sheriffdom	stepmother	sheet-glass	sagination	Schizopoda
specifical	spermatist	sweetening	sogdolager	spinaceous
steriliser	spermatium	sleetiness	sogdoliger	Shivaistic
specialise	stemmatous	sweatiness	sogdologer	spiracular
specialism	sternwards	scent-organ	sugar-candy	spiraculum
specialist	stern-sheet	stentorian	sugar-daddy	shibboleth
speciality	stern-chase	sweetbread	sugar-baker	ship-broker
sterigmata	sternworks	sweet-briar	sugar-maple	shin-barker
speciesism	sternboard	sweet-brier	sage-rabbit	spin-bowler
speciosity	stern-frame	sheltering	sugariness	switchback
speciation	stenograph	sweltering	sugar-house	spitchcock
speciously	seed-oyster	stertorous	sugar-apple	switchgear
specifying	stenotyper	sweetstuff	sugar-wrack	switch-over
shecklaton	sheep-faced	spectatrix	sugar-grass	stitchwork
sneak-thief	stenpoaeic	speculator	Sagittaria	stitchwort
sneakingly	steeple-hat	sleeve-fish	sagittally	spindle-oil
speakingly	sweep-seine	sleeve-hand	sign-writer	skin-diving
sneakiness	sheep's-foot	sleeve-link	sphacelate	slide-valve
steakhouse	sheep's-head	sleeveless	sphaeridia	spider-crab
sneakishly	sleepy-head	swerveless	schlimazel	spinescent
sleekstone	sheepshank	seed-vessel	sphalerite	swine-fever
shellycoat	sheep-biter	stemwinder	scholastic	shire-reeve
shellacked	sheep-plant	sleaziness	schalstein	spider-hole
step-ladder	sweepingly	sneezeweed	schematise	swivel-hook
smell-feast	sleepiness	sneezewood	schematism	Sciaenidae
stellified	steepiness	sneezewort	schematist	spider-like
stelliform	sheep-louse	soft-bodied	schemozzle	snivelling
seemlihead	sheep-track	soft-boiled	sphenogram	spider-line
shellshock	step-parent	soft-billed	sphenoidal	stipellate
stealthily	sheepishly	safe-blower	Sphingidae	shire-horse
steel-plate	sweepstake	sufferance	sphinx-moth	swine-drunk
stellulate	seed-potato	sufferable	Spheniscus	spike-grass
spellingly	shearwater	sufferably	school-bred	stilettoed
stealingly	step-rocket	soft-finned	school-bell	swinestone
swellingly	spear-shaft	soft-footed	school-book	spitefully
seemliness	sperrylite	soft-headed	school-dame	spider-work
shelliness	steersmate	suffigance	schoolgirl	spider-wort
smelliness	sneeringly	suffisance	schoolma'am	sniffingly
steeliness	smeariness	sufficient	schoolmaid	stiffening
shell-money	spear-point	sufflation	school-marm	sniffiness
steelworks	spear-grass	suffragism	school-miss	stiff-rumpt
shellbound	shear-steel	suffragist	school-mate	sail-flying
shell-mound	seersucker	soft-spoken	schoolroom	swingle-bar
spellbound	Spenserian	soft-sawder	school-ship	swing-wheel
shelldrake	stepsister	safety-arch	school-tide	swing-shelf
shellproof	sweet-water	safety-belt	school-time	stingingly
stellately	spectrally	safety-cage	school-term	swingingly
spell-stopt	sheath-bill	safety-plug	schoolward	stinginess
steam-gauge	sweathband	safety-rein	schoolwork	sling-fruit
steam-yacht	spectacled	safety-stop	schipperke	sniggering
steam-navvy	spectacles	signalling	scherzando	swing-stock
spermicide	scent-scale	sage-cheese	sphere-born	slingstone
spermaceti	steatocele	segregable	sphericity	swing-music
spermaduct	scepticise	signet-ring	spheroidal	swing-swang
spermiduct	scepticism	suggestion	sphere-like	stichidium
spermogone	sheet-metal	segmentary	sphereless	ship-holder
sperm-whale	spectre-bat	segmentate	spherulite	stichology
steam-chest	sweetie-pie	suggestive	schorl-rock	slightness
steamtight	sweetheart	sage-grouse	schismatic	smithcraft
steaminess	sheath-fish	seguidilla	schism-shop	sticharion
steam-power	sweat-shirt	signifying	schizocarp	suicidally
steam-crane	scent-gland	Sigillaria	schizogony	spirit-blue

spirit-duck
spiritedly
spirit-leaf
spirit-lamp
spiritless
stibialism
spinigrade
spirituous
skikjöring
sticky-back
skip-kennel
stinkingly
stickiness
smickering
stink-brand
snick-a-snee
slickstone
stinkstone
stifle-bone
stillicide
spiflicate
shield-fern
smifligate
shield-hand
still-birth
spillikins
shillelagh
shieldling
shieldless
shield-maid
Scillonian
stiflingly
still-house
shieldrake
sciolistic
ship-letter
still-stand
stillatory
shieldwall
seismicity
seismogram
seismology
skimmingly
swimmingly
stigmarian
shimmering
ship-master
skirmisher
stigmatise
stigmatism
stigmatist
scientific
skinniness
seignorage
spinnerule
seigneurie
ski-bobbing
spirometer
spirometry
spirophore
sailor-like
sailorless
spirograph

sailor-suit
slit-pocket
skimpingly
skippingly
slippiness
slipperily
ship-rigged
stirringly
stirrup-cup
spinsterly
slipsloppy
slipstream
scissor-leg
slip-string
spinstress
scissor-cut
spissitude
shirtwaist
slit-trench
scintigram
stintingly
shiftiness
stiltiness
shirt-frill
shirt-front
skittishly
stimulancy
stimulable
stimulator
stipulator
ski-running
ski-jumping
shipwright
sojourning
solfataric
saltarello
syllabical
sultanship
self-acting
self-action
salmagundi
salmagundy
self-abuser
syllabuses
self-breath
salubrious
solubilise
salability
solubility
self-binder
salt-butter
self-bounty
Salicaceae
self-cocker
silicified
salt-cellar
siliculose
salicylate
self-colour
solacement
selectness
salicional
salicornia

solecistic
solicitude
solicitant
soliciting
silk-cotton
solicitous
self-deceit
solidified
self-driven
self-denial
self-danger
solidarism
solidarist
solidarity
solid-state
silver-bell
silver-bath
sallenders
silver-foil
salverform
silver-fish
silver-gilt
self-exiled
silver-leaf
silverling
spleenless
sullenness
silverside
silverskin
self-esteem
silver-tree
silverweed
spleen-wort
salifiable
solifidian
self-feeder
self-filler
saliferous
self-glazed
silk-grower
self-giving
sylphidine
sulphonate
sulphurise
sulphurate
sulphurous
self-hatred
salpingian
salvifical
saltigrade
soldiering
self-killed
self-killer
salal-berry
self-loving
solemniser
Solomonian
salamander
solemnness
self-murder
self-mettle
self-motion
shlemozzle

splint-bone
Solanaceae
splint-coal
selenodont
splanchnic
solenoidal
splendidly
silentiary
selenology
silentness
splenative
splintwood
saloon-deck
self-opened
salmonella
silhouette
Salmonidae
syllogiser
salmon-leap
Selbornian
sallowness
seldomness
solipedous
self-poised
self-parody
scleriasis
scleroderm
sultriness
sclerotial
sclerotomy
sclerotium
self-slayer
splash-back
splashdown
self-seeder
self-seeker
sales-clerk
saleswoman
silk-screen
salt-spring
self-severe
self-styled
split-level
splutterer
solutional
solitarian
salutarily
solitarily
solstitial
salutation
salutatory
self-taught
self-unable
Seleucidae
Seleucidan
solivagant
salivation
self-willed
silly-billy
seltzogene
somnambule
sympathise
semi-annual

somebodies
semichorus
semicircle
semicirque
semi-double
semi-divine
semi-drying
Sympetalae
simnel-cake
summerlike
symmetrian
symmetrise
Simmenthal
summertide
summer-tree
summertime
symphilism
symphilous
symphylous
symphonion
symphonist
symphyseal
symphysial
semeiology
summitless
somniloquy
semeiotics
semilucent
simplicity
simulacrum
simplified
simplifier
simpleness
semi-lunate
semi-liquid
similarity
simplistic
similitude
simulation
simulatory
semblative
similative
simulative
simoniacal
seminality
seminarial
seminarian
seminarist
semination
summonable
semi-opaque
somnolence
somnolency
symbolical
symboliser
semiquaver
somersault
samarskite
sombreness
sombrerite
semestrial
sempstress
somatology

semiterete
somatotype
semi-uncial
somewhence
semi-weekly
sunbathing
syntagmata
syncarpous
syndactyly
sandalwood
sandbagged
sandbagger
sand-binder
sand-bunker
sand-cherry
synecology
synecdoche
sinecurism
sinecurist
sand-castle
sand-dollar
sunderance
sense-datum
synaeresis
synderesis
Syngenesia
syngenesis
syngenetic
synteresis
syndetical
synoecious
sanderling
sunderment
syntenosis
sinke-a-pace
sense-organ
Sanhedrist
sentential
sunsetting
sandgroper
sand-grouse
synthectic
Singhalese
synchronal
synchronic
synthronus
sand-hopper
synthesise
synthesist
synthetise
synthetist
syndicator
syneidesis
singing-man
sincipital
sensitised
sensitiser
sun-picture
Sanskritic
single-eyed
synaloepha
single-foot
Sinologist

singleness
sunglasses
synclastic
singletree
sand-launce
sand-lizard
sand-martin
synanthous
synonymist
synonymity
synonymous
synandrium
synandrous
syncopated
syncopator
sun-worship
synoptical
synergetic
syncretise
syncretism
syncretist
sonorously
sand-sucker
senescence
sinisterly
song-school
sinusoidal
synostosis
songstress
sinistrous
sand-saucer
sanctified
sanctifier
sanctimony
sanitarian
senatorial
sanitarily
sanitarist
song-thrush
sanatorium
sanitarium
sanctitude
sanitation
singularly
sensualise
sensualism
sensualist
sensuality
sanguinely
sanguinary
sinfulness
sanguinity
sensuously
songwriter
synaxarion
sporangial
sporangium
stomachful
stomachous
sporadical
stomatitis
saouari-nut
stomatopod

shoebuckle
Scombresox
Scombridae
snow-blower
spot-barred
snobbishly
Scotchness
snow-capped
sword-dance
spondaical
sword-blade
spondylous
shoddiness
swordcraft
scowdering
swordproof
sword-grass
sword-stick
scordatura
sword-guard
stone-canal
shorewards
stone-eater
stone-mason
shower-bath
shore-leave
shovelfuls
shovel-head
score-sheet
stone-throw
spokeshave
Scopelidae
smoketight
smoke-black
slovenlike
shovelling
stone-blind
stove-plant
showerless
stone-snipe
shovelnose
stone-borer
shore-going
score-board
smoke-board
smoke-house
stonehorse
storehouse
shove-groat
stone-break
smoke-dried
stone-fruit
stone-broke
smokeproof
stone-brash
smoke-stack
stone-still
stolenwise
scoffingly
slow-footed
sponge-bath
sponge-cake
sponge-down

spongiform
slow-gaited
spongology
sponginess
stodginess
showground
spongewood
soothsayer
soothingly
smother-fly
smothering
stochastic
slothfully
storiology
stolidness
spoliation
spoliatory
spoliative
Scotifying
showjumper
smock-faced
stork's-bill
shopkeeper
stock-rider
stockinged
stockinger
shockingly
spookiness
stockiness
smock-frock
shock-proof
stockstill
shoal-water
shouldered
shop-lifter
scowlingly
spoil-sport
spotlessly
storm-water
snowmobile
shoemaking
storm-glass
storm-cloud
storminess
stormbound
storm-track
stormproof
slow-motion
stormfully
slow-moving
swooningly
spoondrift
spoonerism
scornfully
spodomancy
stomodaeum
sporophyll
sporophore
sporophyte
scotodinia
sporozoite
snobocracy
scooped-out

sloop-of-war
stoopingly
sloppiness
snow-plough
scorpionic
smrrebrd
shop-soiled
slop-seller
spouseless
Scotswoman
sponsional
sponsorial
spot-stroke
shoestring
short-dated
short-range
smooth-bore
Scotticise
Scotticism
stoutherie
Scottified
short-lived
shoutingly
snortingly
sportingly
shortening
smoothness
snottiness
sportiness
spottiness
short-coats
shortbread
stouthrief
scoutcraft
smooth-shod
sportfully
sportively
sportswear
short-sword
snow-wreath
shop-walker
spot-welder
slow-winged
shop-window
shot-window
Scolytidae
stony-broke
scorzonera
suprarenal
supralunar
sappan-wood
supperless
sapperment
septennial
septennate
septennium
sapiential
suppertime
septemviri
septemvirs
sapphirine
septically
sophically

sapling-cup	separatory	street-door	scrollwise	strip-tease
septicidal	superstore	screech-owl	scrimmager	scrape-good
syphilitic	separatism	screenings	scrummager	seraphical
septillion	separatist	streetlamp	shrimp-girl	strap-hinge
sophistics	super-state	surrealism	scrimshank	strippings
sops-in-wine	separative	surrealist	skrimshank	strophiole
suppliance	superhuman	sergeantcy	scrambling	stripeless
supplicant	superlunar	serjeantcy	scrimpness	scrupulous
supplicate	super-duper	serjeantry	stramonium	stripiness
sepulchral	superexalt	sure-enough	stromatous	scriptoria
supplement	Sapotaceae	screenplay	shrinkable	streperous
supplyment	Septuagint	street-room	string-bean	strepitant
supplanter	sequaclous	serpentine	springbuck	strepitoso
suppleness	sequential	surfeiting	string-band	strepitous
suppletion	serrasalmo	serpent-god	spring-clip	scriptural
suppletory	surfaceman	sarmentose	spring-cart	sororially
suppletive	streamered	serpentise	stringency	sororicide
sepultural	sarracenia	sarmentous	stringendo	surf-riding
saponified	serradella	street-ward	spring-haas	surprising
supineness	sordamente	streetwise	springhead	stressless
supination	stream-gold	sore-falcon	spring-halt	stratocrat
sipunculid	spreaghery	strifeless	stringhalt	stratified
supposable	Serranidae	scrofulous	stronghold	stratiform
supposably	serradilla	surefooted	spring-hare	strategics
saprogenic	streamline	serigraphy	syringitis	strategist
sapropelic	streamling	strigiform	strong-knit	scratch-wig
supposedly	streamless	scrag-whale	spring-lock	scratchily
saprophyte	spread-over	scraggling	springlike	scratching
Sophoclean	surpassing	straggling	sprinkling	scritch-owl
siphonogam	servant-man	struggling	strinkling	shritch-owl
sophomoric	surfactant	stroganoff	springless	struthioid
supporting	scrub-rider '	scrog-apple	stringless	struthious
supporture	strobiloid	sprightful	sereneness	scrutineer
supportive	scribbling	sore-headed	shrinkpack	scrutinise
supercargo	strobiline	surcharged	strong-room	scrutinous
supernally	strobilate	surcharger	springtide	serotinous
superacute	strabismal	survivance	strengthen	Stratiotes
superseder	strabismic	surgically	springtail	strathspey
superdense	strabismus	surmisable	springtime	suretyship
superheavy	surf-bather	serviceman	shrinkwrap	serrulated
supervisal	strabotomy	sortileger	springwood	Sertularia
supergiant	spruce-beer	straitened	springwort	scrounging
supervisor	soricident	strainedly	surrogatum	shroud-line
superaltar	shriche-owl	serving-man	sarcolemma	shroudless
superfluid	stracchino	straighten	sermonette	stravaiger
superalloy	sdrucciola	straightly	Sarcophaga	shrivelled
superclass	strychnine	serpigines	sarcophagi	strivingly
superbness	Saracenism	strait-lace	sarcophagy	scrivening
super-royal	spruceness	sordidness	sardonical	Shrovetide
superposed	strictness	straitness	sermonical	strawberry
superpower	strychnism	servitress	Sorbonical	straw-plait
supersonic	structural	strikingly	surnominal	screw-plate
supertonic	strictured	strokeplay	sermoniser	shrewdness
superiorly	structured	stroke-play	sarcoplasm	strawboard
supersound	stridelegs	striker-out	sorrowless	shrew-mouse
superorder	stridulant	strokesman	surmounted	screw-press
supergrass	stridulate	Struldbrug	surmounter	shrewishly
suppressed	stridulous	serologist	Sorbonnist	spray-dried
suppressor	stridently	shrillness	seriocomic	sustaining
separatrix	Stradivari	surplusage	sarcocolla	sustenance
separately	strideways	strelitzes	servo-motor	systematic
separation	surveyance	strelitzia	Serbo-Croat	sisterhood
superation	shrievalty	scrollwork	scrap-metal	sister-hook

sister-like	saucer-eyed	squirarchy	sky-jumping	translator
sisterless	squeeze-box	square-root	suzerainty	transvalue
systemless	saucerfuls	sauerkraut	tragacanth	transactor
suspensoid	spuleblade	square-sail	thanatosis	transudate
suspension	sauce-alone	squireship	thalassian	transience
suspensory	scutellate	square-toed	tea-tasting	transiency
suspensive	souterrain	square-toes	tear-bottle	transferee
sustention	stupefying	stupration	thatchless	transferor
sustentate	snuff-paper	squarewise	trade-falne	transverse
sestertium	snuff-taker	saussurite	travelator	trans-shape
suspectful	shuffle-cap	Skupshtina	tradesfolk	team-spirit
susceptive	scurfiness	squeteague	tsarevitch	transplant
sustentive	snuffiness	soup-ticket	teaselling	transonics
suscipient	stuffiness	scuttleful	travelling	transposal
suspicious	smut-fungus	stultified	trade-union	transposer
suspirious	snuff-spoon	stultifier	trace-horse	trans-sonic
sisal-grass	snuff-brown	smuttiness	travelogue	transeptal
sash-window	smudginess	soup-tureen	thale-cress	transcribe
satrapical	sluggishly	sauntering	travel-sick	transcript
satyagraha	southwards	shuttering	traversing	transgress
setterwort	southsayer	sputtering	tea-meeting	transistor
satchelled	spur-heeled	stuttering	toad-eating	transition
satellites	south-polar	sluttishly	travertine	transitory
satellitic	south-bound	scurviness	trabeation	transitive
settlement	southerner	spur-winged	trajection	translunar
satin-paper	southernly	savageness	trajectory	transducer
satanology	southering	seven-score	trabeculae	transfuser
satin-stone	Saurischia	sevenpence	trabecular	transmuter
sitophobia	stupidness	sevenpenny	tea-service	translucid
Saturnalia	spuriosity	seventh-day	trafficked	tractility
satyriasis	spuriously	seventieth	trafficker	tractional
satyresque	studiously	savingness	twangingly	tractarian
saturation	skulkingly	seven-a-side	tracheated	traitorism
suturation	squalidity	sovenaunce	Trachearia	traitorous
satisfying	squelching	severeness	tracheitis	traduction
sausage-dog	soullessly	savourless	trachelate	traductive
sousaphone	soup-meagre	sewage-farm	trashiness	tramway-car
stubble-fed	squamiform	sow-thistle	trachytoid	tubicolous
snubbingly	soup-maigre	saw-toothed	tragically	table-water
stubbiness	squamulose	sexpartite	tragi-comic	table-d'hôte
stubbornly	squamosity	saxicoline	thalictrum	table-linen
slubbering	squamation	saxicolous	tear-jerker	table-cloth
slumbering	squandered	saxicavous	track-scout	table-knife
slumberful	squanderer	sexagenary	thankfully	table-cover
slumberous	squint-eyed	Sexagesima	trap-ladder	table-money
squabasher	squint-eyes	six-shooter	thalliform	table-spoon
source-book	stunningly	sex-limited	tea-planter	table-sport
sluice-gate	Sauropsida	sextillion	Thailander	table-music
sculduddry	stumpiness	sexologist	tea-clipper	tobogganer
sound-shift	sculptress	sextonship	trammelled	tub-thumper
'sbuddikins	sculptural	sexlocular	trammeller	tubularian
sourdeline	sculptured	sexivalent	trammel-net	tabularise
soundingly	squirearch	skyjacking	thaumasite	tubularity
sturdiness	square-face	skylarking	traumatise	tabulation
squadronal	square-head	sky-parlour	traumatism	tubulation
squadroned	squirehood	skyscraper	travolator	tabulatory
sound-board	squire-like	scyphiform	tramontana	tabulature
sound-track	squireling	stylistics	tramontane	tibiotarsi
shuddering	scurrility	sky-planted	trampoline	tabernacle
soundproof	squirality	stylopised	trappiness	Tuberaceae
squeezable	scurrilous	stylograph	tranquilly	tuberiform
spumescent	squareness	sky-writing	tea-trolley	tuberosity
stupendous	soubriquet	stypticity	tea-drinker	Tyburn-tree

tubercular	treillaged	triradiate	trick-track	token-money
tuberculin	theologian	trifarious	thick-grown	tillandsia
tuberculum	theologise	tritanopia	trinketing	tiliaceous
tabescence	theologist	tritanopic	triplicate	tale-bearer
toccatella	theologate	Trinacrian	triplicity	tollbridge
tocher-good	trebleness	tripartite	triflingly	telecamera
tocherless	thermogram	twi-natured	tripleness	telecaster
ticker-tape	thermology	thimble-rig	triclinium	tiller-rope
tickety-boo	tree-mallow	thimbleful	thill-horse	tellership
tactically	Thermalite®	thiocyanic	trillionth	telegraphy
ticking-off	theomaniac	triactinal	triglyphic	telegnosis
tactlessly	theomantic	triaconter	triumphant	tilt-hammer
ticklishly	thermionic	third-party	triumphing	telpherman
technician	thermophil	third-class	triumphery	telpherway
technocrat	thermopile	trigeminal	triumviral	telpherage
technicist	thermostat	trioecious	trimmingly	telling-off
technology	thermistor	triternate	triandrian	telemetric
technetium	thermotics	tripewoman	triandrous	talentless
tachometer	'tween-decks	toiletries	triangular	tallow-face
tachometry	theonomous	toilet-roll	trilobated	teleologic
tachograph	tremolando	toilet-soap	tailor-bird	teleonomic
tocopherol	teetotally	trisectrix	teinoscope	teleostean
tectricial	tremolitic	Tridentine	tribometer	tallow-tree
taclturnly	tremorless	trisection	tricoteuse	teleostome
tactuality	theophanic	tridentate	trilobitic	Teleostomi
tachymeter	theopneust	thief-taker	trifoliate	tulip-eared
tachymetry	theophobia	twinflower	tailor-made	telephoner
tachypnoea	theophoric	thingumbob	trimorphic	telephonic
tachygraph	trespasser	thinginess	thixotropy	telepathic
tachylytic	tie-breaker	triggerman	trimonthly	tularaemia
tiddlywink	theurgical	trichiasis	tricostate	tularaemic
tediousome	trekschuit	trichogyne	trilocular	tolerantly
Tudoresque	theistical	triphthong	triapsidal	toleration
tidivation	themselves	trichology	thiopental	talismanic
tide-waiter	treasonous	trip-hammer	trippingly	telesmatic
toddy-ladle	theosopher	trichinous	tripperish	talc-schist
toddy-stick	theosophic	trichromat	tribrachic	telescopic
tsesarevna	theotechny	trichromic	trigrammic	telescreen
trepanning	twentyfold	trithionic	trierarchy	tale-teller
thenabouts	twenty-four	trichroism	tricrotism	Talmudical
trey-antler	twenty-five	teichopsia	tricrotous	televiewer
tree-burial	theatrical	Triphysite	thirstless	televérité
trenchancy	tree-tomato	trichotomy	toilsomely	televisual
theocratic	tweet-tweet	Trichiurus	twin-sister	television
trench-coat	twelvefold	tritically	tristichic	telewriter
treacherer	twelve-note	triniscope	thirteenth	talky-talky
trench-feet	twelve-tone	triliteral	thirtyfold	tilly-fally
theodicean	teeny-weeny	toilinette	twittingly	tilly-vally
tweedledee	tuffaceous	trilineate	twittering	tally-woman
tweedledum	tuftaffeta	triticeous	tripterous	tally-trade
tread-wheel	tuftaffety	trilingual	triturator	tympanites
theodolite	toffee-nose	twilighted	trifurcate	tympanitic
thereabout	tuft-hunter	trivialise	trisulcate	tympanitis
tremendous	toggle-iron	trivialism	tripudiary	Tammanyism
thereafter	tegumental	tuitionary	tripudiate	tamability
thereamong	tiger-shark	tripinnate	tricuspate	timocratic
thereunder	tiger-snake	trinitrate	triquetral	temperance
thereanent	tight-laced	tritiation	triquetrum	temperable
trecentist	tight-lacer	thick-skull	thievishly	temperedly
twelfth-day	tightishly	triskelion	thin-walled	timber-line
theogonist	trilateral	thinkingly	tricycling	timber-mare
thetically	trivalence	thickening	tricyclist	timber-toes
taeniacide	trivalency	trickiness	takingness	timber-tree

tempestive
timber-wolf
timber-yard
tomography
tim-whiskey
time-keeper
time-killer
tumble-cart
tumble-dung
tumbledown
temulently
timeliness
tumblerful
timelessly
tumultuary
tumultuate
tumultuous
tumble-weed
temporally
temporalty
temporiser
tomfoolery
tomfoolish
tambourine
tumorgenic
timbrology
temerously
timorously
tumescence
time-signal
time-switch
time-spirit
time-server
time-saving
temptingly
time-thrust
temptation
tantaliser
tantamount
tennantite
tentacular
tentaculum
tenebrific
tenebrious
tenability
tenderfeet
tenderfoot
tank-engine
tenter-hook
tenderiser
tunbellied
tender-loin
tinder-like
tenderling
tinselling
tunnelling
tenderness
tangential
tendential
tandemwise
tank-farmer
Tanagridae
tennis-ball

tonsilitic
tonsilitis
tension-rod
tennis-shoe
tanglefoot
tanglement
tanglingly
tinklingly
tonelessly
tanglesome
tonalitive
tenemental
tenantable
tuning-fork
tenantless
tenantship
Tintometer®
ten-pointer
ten-pounder
tendrillar
tendrilled
tonishness
tinctorial
tongueless
tonguester
tongue-tied
tongue-work
tropaeolum
troubadour
troubledly
trombonist
trou-de-loup
trowelling
two-year-old
thoughtful
toothpaste
two-wheeled
two-wheeler
tooth-shell
trochoidal
trophology
Trophonian
trochanter
toothbrush
trophesial
trochiscus
trochotron
tropically
tropic-bird
troglodyte
Trollopean
Trollopian
trolloping
trollopish
trolley-car
trolley-man
trolley-bus
trou-madame
thorn-hedge
thorn-devil
thorniness
thorn-apple
tropopause

tromometer
thoroughly
tropophyte
Trogonidae
tropologic
troop-horse
toolpusher
trousseaux
thousandth
trouser-leg
trousering
Trotskyism
Trotskyist
Trotskyite
troctolite
trout-spoon
troutstone
trouvaille
tap-dancing
tophaceous
typhaceous
top-gallant
topicality
typicality
type-cutter
tepidarium
tappet-loom
topography
typography
type-holder
topping-out
topologist
typologist
typhlology
toponymics
top-knotted
top-soiling
tape-record
taperingly
tapestried
tapescript
typescript
typesetter
tapotement
typewriter
topi-wallah
topsyturvy
topazolite
tarmacadam
termagancy
throat-band
threadbare
thread-cell
tersanctus
threatened
threatener
tartareous
throat-full
terra-firma
tirra-lirra
tarpauling
turnaround
terra-rossa

terracotta
thread-worm
throatwort
turnbuckle
turnbroach
tirocinium
taradiddle
targetable
three-parts
turkey-cock
torpescent
turgescent
threescore
threepence
threepenny
three-piece
three-piled
three-sided
three-cleft
terreplein
tortellini
terneplate
torbernite
torpedo-net
three-pound
torpedoist
turret-ship
torrential
tormenting
turpentine
turpentiny
torrent-bow
turkey-trot
torrefying
tortfeasor
thriftiest
thriftless
torch-dance
torchlight
Tyrrhenian
torch-staff
turbinated
Terminalia
terminable
terminably
terminally
terminator
Turritella
turnip-flea
turning-saw
tirling-pin
tirailleur
torpidness
torridness
turbidness
turgidness
Tardigrada
tardigrade
tarsia-work
terrifying
turtleback
turtle-dove
Tyrolienne

tirelessly
turtle-soup
thrombosis
thrombotic
tyrant-bird
threnodial
threnodist
tarantella
Tyrannidae
throneless
throne-room
tiring-room
Turko-Tatar
Turcophobe
Turcophile
terroriser
terrorless
thruppence
thruppenny
tartrazine
tiresomely
teratogeny
teratology
throttling
teratomata
turbulator
turbulence
turbulency
Tartuffian
Tartuffish
Tartuffism
throughway
throughout
through-put
tortuosity
tortuously
thriveless
thrivingly
thrown-silk
throw-stick
testaceous
tassel-gent
tasseiling
tessellate
tusser-silk
tastefully
test-flight
teschenite
tossicated
tosticated
testicular
testifying
test-market
taskmaster
taseometer
testudinal
testudines
tetrabasic
Tetrandria
tetrameral
tetrameter
tetrasemic
tetrathlon

tetrachord	tourmaline	unanimated	upbringing	uncared-for
tetraploid	tournament	unadjusted	unblinking	uncarpeted
tetragonal	trunnioned	unallotted	unblissful	unchristen
tetrapolis	tourniquet	unadmiring	umbellated	ulceration
Tetramorph	truantship	unadmitted	umbilicate	ulcerative
tetraspore	tauromachy	unarmoured	unbelieved	ulcerously
tetrastich	tautomeric	unannealed	unbeliever	uncustomed
tetrastyle	tautophony	unatonable	umbellifer	unclubable
tetractine	tautologic	unavowedly	unbalanced	unctuosity
tetraptote	trumpeting	uranometry	unbonneted	unctuously
tetraethyl	tauntingly	unappeased	unbenignly	undramatic
Tetragynia	trustingly	unapprised	urbanology	undebarred
titubation	trustiness	unappalled	unbundling	undeclared
tête-de-pont	trust-house	unapproved	urbanistic	undeceived
title-sheet	trustfully	unapparent	umbonation	undecimole
Tattersall	truculence	unaspiring	upbuoyance	undoctored
tetchiness	truculency	unabridged	unbloodied	undecisive
tattie-claw	towel-gourd	unarranged	unbrokenly	undreading
tithing-man	towel-horse	unassuaged	unbaptised	undreaming
tattie-shaw	towing-path	unanswered	unbarbered	undressing
titillator	thwartedly	unassigned	unburdened	undefeated
tattlingly	tower-shell	unassailed	unbirthday	undefended
titularity	tawdry-lace	unabsolved	unborrowed	undigested
tattle-tale	tawdriness	unassuming	upbursting	undulately
totemistic	towardness	unassisted	unbespoken	undulating
Titanesque	thwartship	unactuated	unbestowed	undulation
tutworkman	thwartwise	unattached	unbesought	undulatory
totipotent	thwartways	unattained	unbetrayed	undelaying
tutorially	town's-bairn	unattended	unbattered	undomestic
tatpurusha	townswoman	unaltering	unbettered	undeniable
titivation	taxability	unattested	unbuttered	undeniably
thumb-latch	toxicology	unartistic	unbottomed	undrooping
thumbscrew	toxication	unartfully	unbuttoned	undepraved
thumbpiece	taxi-driver	unamusable	unblushing	undeprived
thumbikins	taxi-dancer	unbearable	unbewailed	undeplored
tourbillon	taxidermal	unbearably	unchanging	underjawed
thumb-index	taxidermic	unbeatable	uncharming	underlayer
thumbprint	taxonomist	unblamable	unchastely	undernamed
thumb-stall	toxiphobia	unblamably	unchastity	undertaken
truncately	texturally	unbranched	unclerical	undertaker
truncation	textualism	upbraiding	uncredible	underwater
trundle-bed	textualist	unbeavered	uncleansed	underearth
thundering	twy-natured	umbrageous	uncheerful	underpants
thunder-box	thymectomy	umbratical	uncreating	undervalue
thunder-god	thyrsoidal	unboastful	uncoffined	undirected
thunderous	toyishness	umbraculum	uncritical	underactor
truffle-pig	tryptophan	unbiblical	uncoloured	underscore
truffle-dog	tuzzi-muzzy	unbecoming	uncultured	underscrub
touch-paper	unawakened	unbudgeted	uncumbered	undersexed
truth-value	unacademic	unbedimmed	uncommonly	underbelly
touch-me-not	unavailing	unbedinned	uncommuted	underlease
touch-piece	Ural-Altaic	unbleached	unconfined	undersense
touch-plate	unanalysed	unblenched	uncandidly	underneath
touch-and-go	unanalytic	unbreached	uncanonise	underagent
touchingly	uranalysis	unbreeched	uncensored	undershoot
toughening	unaccented	umbrellaed	unconsoled	undershirt
touchiness	unascended	unbreathed	unconstant	undershrub
touchstone	unanchored	unbeguiled	unconjugal	underlinen
touch-judge	up-and-under	unbegotten	uncensured	underminer
truthfully	unamenable	unbeholden	unconfused	undersized
touring-car	un-American	unbailable	unconsumed	undertimed
trunk-maker	unaffected	unbribable	uncloister	underskirt
truckle-bed	unarguable	upbuilding	uncurbable	undercliff

underslung
underfloor
under-clerk
underclass
underglaze
undervoice
undercover
undernoted
under-power
undertoned
underbough
underworld
underborne
undergoing
underboard
underspend
under-trick
under-craft
undercroft
underdrain
underproof
underbrush
undercrest
underdress
underwrite
underdrive
undergrove
undergrown
underprize
understock
understudy
understeer
underntime
understand
understood
understate
under-tunic
underbuild
underquote
underlying
undismayed
undesigned
undisposed
undescried
undeserved
undeserver
undesiring
undesirous
undisputed
undetected
undeterred
undoubting
undoubtful
undivulged
undiverted
undivorced
undivested
unerasable
unexamined
unexampled
unexacting
unembodied
unexcelled

unenclosed
unescorted
unexciting
unexcluded
unendeared
unendingly
ureteritis
unevenness
uterectomy
uneventful
unexecuted
uneffected
urethritic
urethritis
Uredinales
unedifying
uneclipsed
Ubermensch
uneconomic
uredosorus
uredospore
uredo-stage
unexpiated
unemphatic
unexpected
unexpanded
unemployed
unexplored
unenriched
unerringly
unenslaved
uneasiness
unentailed
unextended
unentitled
uneducated
uneducable
unequalled
usefulness
unenviable
unenviably
unflagging
upflashing
unfeasible
unfeatured
unfocussed
unfadingly
unfrequent
unfrighted
unfaithful
unfriended
unfriendly
unfeigning
unfairness
unfilially
unfillable
unfilleted
unfiltered
unfallible
unfellowed
unfamiliar
unfeminine
unfinished

unforsaken
unfordable
unforcedly
unforgiven
unforcible
unfurrowed
unforeseen
unforested
unforetold
unfortuned
unfastened
unfostered
unfathered
unfettered
unfatherly
unfathomed
unfoughten
unfruitful
ungraceful
ungrateful
ungracious
unguentary
ungainsaid
ungenerous
ungrounded
ungarnered
ungartered
ungathered
ungrudging
ungoverned
unhealable
unheededly
unhygienic
unhelmeted
unholiness
unhallowed
upholstery
uphillward
unhampered
unhomelike
unhumanise
unhindered
unhandsome
unhonoured
unhoped-for
unhardened
unheroical
unheralded
unhurrying
unhistoric
unhouseled
unhouzzled
unhazarded
unicameral
unilateral
univalence
unimagined
univariant
unilabiate
univariate
unipartite
urinalysis
uninclosed

unindeared
uniseriate
unigenitus
unidealism
unitedness
university
unicentral
uninflamed
uninflated
uninfected
uninformed
unitholder
utilisable
uniliteral
unilingual
uniflorous
unimmortal
unisonance
unisonally
univocally
urinoscopy
urinometer
uniformity
univoltine
unicostate
unilobular
unilocular
unimpaired
unimplored
unimproved
unimparted
unimposing
uninspired
unintended
uninuclear
uniqueness
ubiquarian
ubiquitary
ubiquitous
uninvolved
uninvested
uninviting
uniaxially
unjustness
unknighted
unknightly
unkinglike
unkindness
unknowable
unleavened
unlabelled
unlaboured
unlicensed
unladylike
unlifelike
unleisured
unlikeable
unlikeness
unlamented
unliquored
unlistened
unlessoned
unlettered

unliterary
unliveable
unloveable
unlovingly
unlawfully
unmeasured
unmechanic
unmodified
unmeetness
unmailable
unmaidenly
unmellowed
unmolested
unmilitary
unmanacled
unmannered
unmannerly
unmanfully
unmortised
unmerciful
unmorality
unmeriting
unmastered
unmotherly
unmetrical
unmetalled
unmaterial
unmaternal
unmoveable
unmoveably
unmuzzling
uintathere
unnameable
unnumbered
unnurtured
unnoticing
unoccupied
unordained
unordinary
unovercome
urogenital
unobedient
unofficial
unoffended
urochordal
unoriginal
unoxidised
utopianise
utopianism
uxorilocal
uxoriously
uropoiesis
urological
urographic
unossified
unobserved
unobscured
urosthenic
urostegite
unobtained
unorthodox
unplayable
unpeaceful

unplausive	unqualited	unreverted	unstooping	ultroneous
unpickable	unquarried	unreverend	unsmoothed	unthreaded
unpuckered	usquebaugh	unreverent	unsporting	unturnable
unpacified	unquenched	unravished	unsupplied	unthriftly
unprepared	unquotable	unrewarded	unstreamed	untiringly
unpeerable	unreadable	unscalable	unstriated	ulteriorly
unpoetical	unrealised	unshakable	unshrubbed	untortured
unpregnant	uproarious	unshakably	upsurgence	untasteful
unpleasant	unreasoned	unswayable	unscreened	untethered
unpleasing	unreceived	unscabbard	unsurveyed	untruthful
unprizable	unrecalled	unsearched	unstrained	untrueness
unprincely	unreckoned	unstanched	unsurmised	untrussing
unpoisoned	unrecorded	unstarched	unscramble	untrustful
unprisoned	unrecuring	upstanding	unstringed	untowardly
unpriestly	unrideable	unshakenly	unscripted	usucapient
unpillared	unredeemed	unshackled	unscrupled	usucaption
unpolicied	unruffable	unseasoned	unstrapped	unusefully
unpillowed	Ugro-Finnic	unshadowed	unstripped	unutilised
unpolished	unreformed	unsublimed	unstressed	usuriously
unpolitely	unregarded	unsociable	unsistered	unuplifted
unpolluted	upright-man	unsociably	unsisterly	usurpingly
unpampered	unrightful	unsocially	unsatiated	usurpation
unpanelled	unrejoiced	unseconded	unsatiable	usurpatory
unpunished	unreliable	upside-down	unsettling	usurpature
unpunctual	unrelieved	unsteadily	unsizeable	unvaluable
unprofaned	unruliment	ulsterette	ultrabasic	unvendible
unprovable	unruliness	unspecific	ultra-rapid	unviolated
unproperly	unrelished	unspeaking	untearable	unvariable
unploughed	unrelative	unsleeping	unthatched	unveracity
unprofited	unremedied	unswearing	ultrashort	unverified
unpromised	unromantic	unsceptred	ultrafiche	unvirtuous
unprovided	unremarked	unsheathed	unthankful	unvitiated
unprolific	unremitted	unswerving	ultrasonic	unwearable
unproposed	unrendered	unsoftened	ultrasound	unweakened
unprovoked	unransomed	unsafeness	untrampled	unweaponed
unprompted	unrenowned	unschooled	untranquil	unwearying
unproduced	unrepealed	unseizable	Urticaceae	unwieldily
unpeppered	unrepeated	unsuitable	untochered	unwifelike
unpopulous	unrepaired	unsuitably	untuckered	unweighing
unparadise	unrepelled	unsmirched	urticarial	unwrinkled
unpurveyed	unrepented	unsmiled-on	urtication	unwellness
unpurified	unrepining	unshingled	untidiness	unwelcomed
unparallel	unripeness	unspirited	untrenched	unwontedly
upper-class	unreproved	unshielded	untreasure	unwinnowed
unperilous	unreported	unslipping	unthinking	unworkable
unparental	unreposing	unshifting	untainting	unworthily
unparented	unrequired	unstinting	untwisting	unwareness
unpardoned	unrequited	unsaleable	untellable	unwariness
unpurposed	unrespited	unsolvable	untillable	upwardness
upperworks	unresolved	unsolidity	untalked-of	unwiseness
upper-crust	unresented	unsalaried	untalented	unwithered
unperished	unrestored	unsympathy	ustulation	unwithheld
umpireship	unreserved	unsummered	untameable	unwatchful
upper-stock	unresisted	unsymmetry	untameably	unwavering
unperfumed	unratified	ugsomeness	untempered	unyielding
unperjured	unretarded	unsummoned	untimbered	vibraphone
unpassable	unreturned	unsinkable	ultimately	vibraculum
unpossible	unrevealed	unsensible	untuneable	vibrometer
uppishness	unravelled	unsensibly	untendered	vibrograph
unpastoral	unraveller	unsanctify	untenderly	vocabulary
unpastured	unrivalled	unsanitary	untangible	vocabulist
unpathetic	unrevenged	unscorched	untenanted	vice-consul
unpowdered	unreversed	unshowered	untroubled	vice-county

vociferant
vociferate
vociferous
vaccinator
victimiser
vicomtesse
vacuolated
victoriana
victorious
vectograph
viceregent
vocational
victualled
victualler
vacuum-tube
vichyssois
videophone
viewfinder
voetganger
view-halloo
viewlessly
Vietnamese
vignettist
vigilantly
vaginismus
vigorously
vegetarian
vegetating
vegetation
vegetative
vehemently
voice-print
Vulcanalia
voltameter
villanelle
volcanised
villainage
villainess
villainous
Villanovan
Voltairean
Voltairian
Voltairism
volubility
velocipede
validation
vulnerable
volley-ball
velvet-crab
velvet-duck
value-added
velvet-leaf
villeinage
velvet-pile
valleculae
vallecular
voluminous
volumetric
Volapükist
voluptuary
voluptuous
valorously
veldschoen

volatilise
volatility
velutinous
volitional
volitorial
velitation
volitation
volutation
valvulitis
vampire-bat
vomitorium
vine-branch
vanadinite
vindemiate
veneer-moth
Vincentian
vengefully
veneficous
vinegar-eel
vinegar-fly
vinegarish
ventilable
vindicable
ventilator
vindicator
vindictive
vinylidene
vinologist
vine-mildew
venomously
ventricule
ventricose
ventricous
veneration
venus-shell
vanishment
Venetianed
vanity-case
venatorial
vanquisher
violaceous
vapulation
vaporiform
viperiform
vaporosity
vaporously
viperously
vapour-bath
vernacular
varicocele
varicellar
varicosity
varicotomy
veridicous
variegated
verse-maker
verbena-oil
varietally
variegator
verse-smith
verge-board
Vertebrata
vertebrate

vergership
verifiable
viraginian
viraginous
voraginous
vertically
virginally
vortically
virgin-born
vermicelli
vorticella
varnishing
virginhood
vermicidal
vertigines
versionist
vernissage
vermicular
vermifugal
versicular
vorticular
versifying
virologist
Verulamian
virulently
verandahed
variolator
Vertoscope®
variometer
Vireonidae
variolotic
verkrampte
virescence
varitypist
virtualism
virtualist
virtueless
virtuality
virtuosity
virtuously
viscachera
visualiser
visibility
vesiculose
vesiculate
vesication
vesicatory
vesper-bell
vespertine
Visigothic
vespiaries
vestibular
vestibulum
vestmented
visionally
viscometer
visiogenic
viscometry
visionless
viscountcy
vest-pocket
vestry-room
visitorial

visitation
visitative
vascularly
vitrailled
viticolous
Vaticanism
Vaticanist
vaticinate
vitrescent
vitreosity
vitiferous
vitriolise
vitriolate
vitiligate
vitellicle
vitalistic
vitalising
vitalities
vitaminise
vituperate
veterinary
vaudeville
vouchsafed
vauntingly
vivandière
viviparism
viviparity
viviparous
Viverridae
Viverrinae
vivisector
vexingness
voyageable
viziership
vizard-mask
wraparound
whatabouts
weaver-bird
weasel-coot
whale-shark
whale-louse
weasel-word
wharfinger
weak-headed
weak-handed
weak-hinged
wrathiness
weather-gaw
weatherman
weather-map
weathering
weather-bow
weather-box
weatherise
weather-eye
wrathfully
whaling-gun
wearifully
weakliness
weak-minded
weaponless
weapon-shaw
wrap-rascal

whatsoever
wabbliness
wobbliness
wicket-gate
wickedness
wickerwork
Wycliffite
wedding-day
wedding-bed
widershins
widespread
widescreen
wretchedly
wieldiness
whereabout
week-ending
whewellite
whereunder
whereuntil
wheresoe'er
woewearied
weeping-elm
weeping-ash
weedkiller
wheel-chair
wheel-horse
wheel-house
whensoever
wheat-berry
wheatsheaf
wheat-midge
wheat-field
wreathless
woefulness
wheeziness
waffle-iron
wafer-tongs
wafer-irons
wage-freeze
wagon-vault
wagon-train
wage-packet
wag-at-the-wa'
Weimaraner
whidah-bird
wait-a-while
white-faced
white-water
white-hawse
white-beard
white-heart
waiterhood
whitethorn
whitesmith
white-horse
white-brass
writership
whiggamore
Whiggarchy
Whiggishly
wring-staff
weightless
whip-handle

writhingly
weigh-board
weigh-house
writing-ink
whiskified
whisky-jack
whisky-john
whirlybird
whirl-about
whirl-blast
whillywhaw
Whit-Monday
whimpering
whispering
whippeting
whip-socket
whip-stitch
Whitsunday
Whitsun-ale
whimsiness
wainscoted
wrist-watch
whip-tailed
waistcloth
written-off
whitterick
whist-drive
wainwright
whity-brown
whizzingly
Wykehamist
Wallachian
walk-around
well boring
well-beseen
wild-cherry
well-chosen
wildcatter
wildebeest
wilderment
wilderness
welter-race
well-earned
Waldensian
wall-facing
wallflower
well-formed
wild-fowler
well-graced
well-gotten
well-heeled
wellie-boot
wild-indigo
Wolfianism
well-judged
well-liking
wall-lizard
well-minded
well-marked
willow-herb
willow-weed
willow-wren
well-placed

wall-pepper
wall-rocket
wolframite
wolf's-peach
wolf-spider
well-sinker
well-spoken
well-spring
well-thewed
well-to-live
well-turned
wall-to-wall
wilfulness
walnutwood
well-willer
well-wished
well-wisher
walky-talky
willy-nilly
wamblingly
wambliness
woman-hater
woman-child
woman-tired
womenfolks
woman-grown
womanishly
woman-built
womanfully
womenswear
wampum-belt
wampumpeag
wonga-wonga
wine-bibber
wind-broken
wine-cellar
wine-cooler
wind-dropsy
winter-clad
winceyette
wunderkind
wonderland
wanderlust
wonderment
wontedness
winter-tide
wanrestful
wonder-work
wander-year
windfallen
wind-flower
wing-footed
wine-grower
wanthriven
wanchancie
Winchester
windjammer
wentletrap
window-bole
windowless
wantonness
window-pane
window-seat

window-sill
window-sash
wintriness
wondrously
wind-shaken
wind-sucker
wing-sheath
wind-sleeve
windshield
wing-spread
windscreen
wind-tunnel
wine-taster
wine-vaults
wood-boring
wool-comber
wood-carver
wool-carder
wood-cutter
wool-driver
wholesaler
whore's-bird
whole-wheat
wooden-head
whole-plate
woodenness
whorehouse
wrong-timed
wool-grower
wrong-doing
wood-grouse
wrongfully
wrongously
woolly-bear
woolly-hand
woodlander
woolliness
woodpecker
wool-packer
wool-picker
wood-pigeon
wool-staple
whomsoever
wool-shears
wood-spirit
wood-sorrel
woolsorter
woodthrush
wool-winder
wapper-eyed
wappenshaw
wapenschaw
wapinschaw
warrandice
workaholic
warranting
warrantise
wire-bridge
work-basket
worldscale
world-weary
wired-glass
wire-dancer

warmed-over
war-wearied
wardenship
worm-eating
work-fellow
worthwhile
wire-haired
worthiness
worshipped
worshipper
worshipful
Wertherian
Wertherism
warming-pan
working-day
warrioress
warblingly
word-memory
workmaster
war-goddess
werwolfish
werwolfism
wire-puller
work-people
worm-powder
word-square
work-to-rule
wire-walker
wireworker
worryingly
wassailing
wassail-cup
wash-bottle
westernise
westernism
wastefully
washing-day
wishing-cap
wasp-tongue
westwardly
wishy-washy
withdrawal
withdrawer
witness-box
Watteauish
watchmaker
watch-paper
witch-hazel
watch-chain
watch-light
watch-night
watch-clock
witch-alder
withholden
withholder
watch-glass
witchingly
watch-tower
watch-house
witchcraft
watch-strap
watchfully
watch-guard

wattlebark
wattle-bird
wattle-work
wit-snapper
water-gauge
water-table
water-wagon
wit-cracker
water-level
water-meter
water-lemon
water-melon
water-thief
water-wheel
water-shoot
water-chute
water-witch
water-wings
watertight
water-nixie
water-clock
water-elder
water-blink
water-plane
water-plant
water-bloom
water-flood
water-glass
water-plate
watersmeet
water-smoke
water-snake
wateriness
water-power
water-tower
water-borne
water-bound
water-joint
water-motor
water-horse
water-mouse
water-spout
water-break
water-craft
water-brain
water-frame
water-crane
waterfront
waterproof
water-brash
water-brose
watercress
water-ouzel
water-music
waterquake
water-guard
water-twist
water-nymph
wavelength
wave-motion
waveringly
whydah-bird
way-baggage

wry-mouthed
way-traffic
way-freight
way-station
wizen-faced
xylochrome
xylography
xylogenous
xylophagan
xylophonic
xylotomous
xenogenous
xanthopsia
xenophobia
xenarthral
xiphopagic
xiphopagus
xiphosuran
Xyridaceae
xerodermia
xerodermic
xerography
xerophytic
xerostomia
ylang-ylang
yearningly
yeast-plant
yeastiness
yackety-yak
yacht-built
yieldingly
yaffingale
Yggdrasill
Yugoslavic
ythundered
yoke-fellow
yellowback
yellow-bird
yellow-eyed
yellow-girl
yellowness
yellow-root
yellow-soap
yellow-snow
yellow-spot
yellow-weed
yellow-wood
yellow-wort
yellow-wash
yellow-yite
Yankeefied
yerd-hunger
yird-hunger
yerd-hungry
yird-hungry
yard-master
Yarborough
yestereven
yestermorn
yesteryear
ypsiliform
youngberry
youthfully

you-know-who
yourselves
Zoantharia
Zoanthidae
zoanthropy
zebra-finch
zabaglione
zigzagging
zigzaggery
zygobranch
zygodactyl
Zygaenidae
zygomycete
zygomorphy
zygosphene
zwitterion
Zollverein
Zimbabwean
zumbooruck
Zend-Avesta
zinc-blende
zincograph
zincolysis
zone-ticket
zinc-worker
zoolatrous
zoophobous
zoothecial
zoothecium
zoophagous
zoophilism
zoophilist
zoophilous
zoothapsis
zootherapy
zoochorous
zoophytoid
zoogloeoid
zooplastic
zoological
zootomical
zoomorphic
zoosporous
zoographer
zoographic
zootrophic
zootsuiter
zooculture
Zaporogian
zero-valent
zeuglodont

acatalectic
acataleptic
amaranthine
anarchistic
abandonedly
abandonment
academicism
academician
amateurship
anaphylaxis
arachnoidal
anachronism
anachronous
arachnology
anaphorical
apathetical
arabisation
araliaceous
amativeness
anadiplosis
anaplerosis
anaplerotic
acaulescent
anagnorisis
Apatosaurus
araeometric
amatorially
acarologist
analogously
anamorphous
amazon-stone
anacoluthia
anacoluthon
analphabete
anaerobiont
Anacreontic
anaesthesia
anaesthesis
anaesthetic
Acanthaceae
apartmental
anastomoses
anastomosis
anastomotic
abactinally
abbreviator
Albigensian
albugineous
ambiguously
amboina-wood
albuminuria
ambrosially
arboraceous
arborescent
ambuscadoes
asbestiform
arbitrageur
arbitrament
arbitration
arbitrarily
arbitratrix
arbitrement
ambitiously

ambivalence
ambivalency
ambiversion
amboyna-wood
abbey-lubber
acclamation
acclamatory
archaically
archangelic
archaeology
Arcadianism
archduchess
archdukedom
archdiocese
accrescence
Asclepiadic
archegonial
archegonium
ancientness
archenteron
arch-heretic
acclimatise
acclimation
archipelago
Archimedean
acclivitous
architraved
accelerando
accelerator
acculturate
accompanier
accompanist
ascomycetes
accumulator
accommodate
accomptable
ascensional
accentually
alcyonarian
anchor-stock
anchovy-pear
acceptation
arch-prelate
acceptivity
accipitrine
accordantly
accordingly
accustomary
accessorial
ancestorial
accessorily
accusatival
arch-traitor
ascetically
ascititious
accoucheuse
accountable
accountably
accountancy
account-book
arch-villain
audibleness
audaciously

addle-headed
abdominally
audiometric
audio-visual
audiologist
arduousness
audiotyping
audio-typist
androgynous
aldermanity
alder-leaved
aides-de-camp
auditorship
addititious
Amelanchier
alexandrine
alexandrite
Alexandrian
amenability
ametabolism
ametabolous
alembicated
amerciament
anencephaly
anecdotical
anecdotally
abecedarian
awelessness
amethystine
Americanise
Americanism
Americanist
arenicolous
adenomatous
awesomeness
anemometric
axerophthol
amenorrhoea
Areopagitic
averruncate
areosystile
amentaceous
awe-stricken
affranchise
anfractuous
affectation
affectively
affectingly
affectivity
affectioned
affectional
affricative
affrication
affrightful
affiliation
affirmative
affirmation
affirmatory
afforcement
affirmingly
aggravating
aggradation
aggravation

algebraical
aggregately
argie-bargie
argle-bargle
aggregative
aggregation
augmentable
Anglicanism
aiguillette
angelically
algological
angelolatry
angelophany
anglomaniac
agglomerate
anglophobia
anglophobic
anglophilia
anglophilic
anglophonic
Anglo-Indian
Anglo-Norman
Anglo-French
angiography
algorithmic
Augustinian
Argathelian
angst-ridden
agglutinate
agglutinant
achievement
athleticism
achaenocarp
atheistical
ashamedness
Aphaniptera
achromatise
achromatism
aphrodisiac
Aphrodisian
Atharvaveda
athermanous
abhorrently
Atherinidae
animalcular
animalcules
animatingly
amicability
acinaciform
amiableness
abiogenesis
abiogenetic
acidifiable
axiological
alismaceous
axiomatical
amino-acetic
anisocercal
anisomerous
anisotropic
aminobutene
adiaphorism
adiaphorist

adiaphorous
aristocracy
adiathermic
ahistorical
adjectively
adjudicator
adjudgement
adjournment
awkwardness
alkalimeter
alkalimetry
alkalescent
acknowledge
ablactation
allocheiria
auld-farrant
allegorical
allegoriser
all-cheering
all-electric
allelomorph
all-American
allineation
Atlanticism
Atlanticist
aplanospore
all-powerful
alloplastic
allopathist
ailurophile
ailurophobe
ablutionary
allotropism
allotropous
ablatitious
alleviative
alleviation
alleviatory
aimlessness
Arminianism
adminicular
ammophilous
admiralship
atmospheric
armoured-car
armour-plate
annabergite
annihilator
annunciator
Aeneolithic
abnormalism
abnormality
agnosticism
agnatically
anniversary
agoraphobia
agoraphobic
anomalistic
apogamously
apocalyptic
adolescence
aponeurosis
aponeurotic

above-ground
apophyllite
apotheosise
abomination
atomisation
abolishable
abolishment
agonisingly
apoliticism
abolitional
aposiopesis
agonistical
apodictical
apomictical
apollonicon
Apollinaris
apocopation
Azotobacter
apologetics
axonometric
apomorphine
azocompound
aeolotropic
amorousness
acolouthite
amour-propre
avoirdupois
acoustician
adoptianism
adoptianist
apostleship
amontillado
apostolical
about-sledge
apostrophic
apostrophus
Adoptionism
abortionist
adoptionist
apostatical
Apocynaceae
apodyterium
anonymously
appeasement
alphabetise
appeachment
appealingly
appeasingly
appraisable
amphetamine
aspheterise
aspheterism
amplexicaul
appreciable
appreciably
appleringie
appreciator
apple-blight
apple-squire
applicative
application
applicatory
amphisbaena

amphimictic
amphibolite
amphibolous
amphipodous
amphibology
appointment
Amphictyony
appellative
appellation
appallingly
ampullosity
approbative
approbation
approbatory
approximate
approvingly
appropinque
appropriate
aspergation
asportation
appurtenant
appertinent
aspergillum
aspergillus
apparelment
apparelling
aspersorium
apparatchik
apparatuses
asphyxiated
asphyxiator
arquebusade
arquebusier
acquirement
acquisitive
acquisition
acquiescent
acquittance
aerobically
acre-breadth
atrabilious
aerobiology
agrobiology
abracadabra
auricularly
auriculated
agriculture
atrociously
abridgement
aerodynamic
aeroelastic
air-mechanic
air-terminal
arrhenotoky
acriflavine
Aurignacian
arraignment
aerological
agrological
acromegalic
acrimonious
atramentous
air-umbrella

arrangement
abranchiate
acronymania
apron-string
aeronautics
air-corridor
agriproduct
acropetally
agrarianism
aircraftman
aerostation
arrestation
aerostatics
agrostology
aerotropism
arrow-headed
arrow-poison
assuagement
assubjugate
associative
association
assiduously
austereness
assafoetida
assignation
aesthetical
aestivation
abstinently
arse-licking
assimilable
assemblyman
assemblance
assentation
absenteeism
assentingly
abscondence
assortative
abstractive
abstraction
abstriction
assuredness
assertively
absorbingly
Assyriology
adscription
assassinate
assessorial
Aesculapian
auscultator
assay-master
astraphobia
actuarially
attractable
antibilious
Antiburgher
antechamber
autochanger
anticyclone
antecedence
attaché-case
articulable
autecologic
articulated

articulator
astuciously
autocephaly
anticipator
anticathode
autochthons
autochthony
antheridium
autoerotism
antherozoid
artlessness
authentical
Anthesteria
anti-federal
antifouling
autographic
astigmatism
autogravure
autogenesis
antihelices
anti-heroine
astringency
attuitively
attritional
attuitional
attaintment
attributive
attribution
antijacobin
anti-Jacobin
autokinesis
autokinetic
artillerist
antemundane
antimoniate
antimonious
automorphic
attemptable
asthmatical
automatical
attenuation
attentively
antenniform
antinomical
autonomical
Actinomyces
antonomasia
actinometer
antenuptial
astonishing
antineutron
anthomaniac
artiodactyl
anteorbital
authorcraft
anthochlore
anthologise
astronomise
anthologist
anthocyanin
autophagous
autophanous
autoplastic

antependium
antiphonary
antiphrasis
antipyretic
antipathist
antiquarian
antiquation
antiqueness
alternately
altercative
alternative
arterialise
alternating
altercation
alternation
anthracnose
anthracosis
anthracitic
attorneydom
attorneyism
after-effect
autarchical
antirrhinum
after-dinner
alto-relievo
alto-rilievo
anteriority
arteriotomy
anthropical
arthropodal
aftergrowth
arthrospore
afterburner
aftersupper
attestative
attestation
antispastic
anti-Semitic
antistrophe
antithalian
altitudinal
attitudinal
autotrophic
antitypical
antitussive
astoundment
anteversion
anti-vitamin
adumbration
aquaculture
aquiculture
aquafortist
acumination
abusiveness
amusiveness
aquanautics
aquaplaning
aguardiente
aquarellist
acupressure
adulterator
acupuncture
advancement

adventuress
adventurism
adventurist
adventurous
adversative
adverseness
advertently
advertising
adverbially
advisedness
advisership
auxanometer
anxiousness
asynartetic
alycompaine
bramah-press
brabblement
bramble-bush
boat-builder
bear-baiting
branchiopod
branch-pilot
bias-drawing
board-school
brandy-glass
bladder-worm
bladderwort
blamelessly
brazen-faced
blameworthy
branfulness
braggadocio
braggartism
brachiation
beach-master
beach-rescue
beachcomber
Brachiopoda
brachyprism
brachyurous
bearishness
black-market
blackmailer
blackheaded
blackfellow
black-beetle
blackbirder
black-fisher
black-and-tan
black-boding
black-coated
brankursine
blackgrouse
black-browed
black-a-vised
beaumontage
Brahmanical
Brahminical
brain-teaser
brainsickly
brains-trust
blarney-land
blasphemous

bear's-breech
brass-rubber
beautifully
blastogenic
beastliness
bracteolate
beauteously
beauty-sleep
brattishing
bradycardia
bradypeptic
baby-bouncer
bibliogical
bibliolater
bibliolatry
bibliomania
bibliomancy
bibliopegic
bibliophile
bibliophily
bibliopolic
bibliotheca
bubble-shell
baby-sitting
beblubbered
backbreaker
backbencher
back-blocker
back-country
back-draught
bactericide
bacteriosis
bachelordom
bachelorism
bucket-wheel
back-ganging
bacchanalia
buccinatory
bacciferous
backing-down
baccivorous
Bacillaceae
bacillicide
baciliform
Baconianism
bicentenary
buck-passing
bicarbonate
bicorporate
backscatter
bicuspidate
backsliding
backscratch
buck-washing
body-builder
baddeleyite
bed-of-honour
Bodhisattva
body-politic
body-servant
bedevilment
bedevilling
bedizenment

beef-brained
bleach-field
bread-basket
breadthways
breadthwise
breadwinner
Biedermeier
beech-marten
blepharitis
blemishment
beetlebrain
blessedness
breastplate
breast-wheel
breathalyse
breathiness
buffalo-bird
buffalo-robe
buffer-state
buff-leather
baffle-board
bifoliolate
baffle-plate
bifurcation
befittingly
beguilement
begging-bowl
beguilingly
Begoniaceae
bogtrotting
bog-asphodel
Bohemianism
behavioural
blind-felled
blind-storey
bridemaiden
brine-shrimp
bribery-oath
brimfulness
bridgeboard
bridge-drive
bridge-house
blightingly
bricklaying
brickmaking
brickshaped
brilliantly
baillieship
brissel-cock
bristle-tail
bristle-fern
brittleness
bristle-worm
brittle-star
bristliness
Bristol-milk
blizzardous
bull-baiting
bill-chamber
balm-cricket
bulk-carrier
ballet-dance
belle-de-nuit

believingly
balletomane
bullet-proof
billets-doux
bellettrist
bullfighter
balefulness
bullfronted
bell-founder
bell-foundry
bell-heather
belligerent
bulbiferous
bullishness
billionaire
bellicosely
bellicosity
bull-mastiff
balmorality
Baltoslavic
balloon-back
balloon-vine
ballot-paper
biliousness
bellows-fish
bell-ringing
Belorussian
billsticker
belatedness
bull-terrier
bilaterally
belowstairs
belly-dancer
belly-timber
belly-button
Bombacaceae
bombardment
bombilation
bombination
bimillenary
bumble-puppy
bimetallism
bimetallist
bumptiously
bone-breccia
binocularly
Benedictine
benedictive
benediction
benedictory
banteringly
bonnet-laird
bonne-bouche
bonnet-piece
bonnet-rouge
beneficiate
beneficiary
benefaction
beneficence
benefactory
banefulness
benignantly
benightment

bunch-backed
bank-holiday
benchership
benthoscope
bank-manager
bondmanship
bonbonnière
Bonapartean
Bonapartism
Bonapartist
bondservant
bond-service
benevolence
bond-washing
bandy-legged
benzylidine
book-account
buoyantness
bookbinding
blotchiness
broach-spire
boot-catcher
broadcasted
broadcaster
bloody-bones
blood-vessel
bloodletter
bloody-faced
broad-minded
blood-flower
Brobdingnag
blood-bought
bloodsprent
blood-spavin
blood-frozen
bloody-sweat
bloodstream
bloodsucker
blood-guilty
biofeedback
biomedicine
biochemical
brotherlike
brotherhood
booking-hall
bookishness
boorishness
bromidrosis
bookkeeping
blockbuster
block-system
book-learned
bootlicking
bootlegging
biocoenosis
biocoenotic
bookselling
Brotstudien
blotting-pad
boot-topping
biodynamics
Buprestidae
baptismally

bipartition	basket-weave	blunderbuss	change-house	coal-trimmer
biquadratic	bushel-woman	brucellosis	charge-house	chastenment
bureaucracy	bashfulness	bourgeoisie	charge-nurse	charter-hand
bereavement	bastinading	blushlessly	charge-sheet	chantarelle
barrage-fire	bastinadoed	brush-turkey	Cyatheaceae	chanterelle
barbaresque	bashi-bazouk	brutishness	crash-helmet	chastisable
bur-marigold	bushmanship	bauson-faced	coach-office	Chautauquan
bersaglieri	businessman	boutonnière	craniectomy	coadunative
barbarously	bespreading	brusqueness	clavigerous	coagulative
burial-place	bestridable	bourtree-gun	chafing-gear	coadunation
barbastelle	biscuit-root	bountifully	chafing-dish	coagulation
bird-brained	bushwhacker	blunt-witted	craniognomy	coagulatory
bird-batting	beta-blocker	bounteously	coalitional	crapulosity
Burschenism	botheration	bouquetière	coalitioner	coal-whipper
barycentric	bitter-apple	bevel-wheels	charismatic	cabbage-palm
bird-catcher	bitter-cress	bivouacking	craniometer	cabbage-rose
Burseraceae	butter-cloth	bow-windowed	craniometry	cabbage-moth
barge-master	bitter-earth	bewildering	Clavicornia	cabbage-worm
barley-brake	butterflies	bowdleriser	cranioscopy	cabbage-tree
barley-broth	butter-knife	bower-anchor	charity-girl	cabbalistic
barrel-house	between-maid	bewitchment	coadjacency	cubicalness
barrel-organ	betweenness	bowstringed	clanjamfray	cable-length
barge-couple	betweentime	boxing-glove	coadjutress	cable-stitch
barley-sugar	butter-plate	box-junction	crack-halter	cobblestone
barge-stones	butter-print	boysenberry	crackerjack	cybernetics
barley-water	butter-paper	bay-windowed	challenging	cock-and-bull
barefacedly	bittersweet	bryological	chaulmoogra	cockaleekie
bird-fancier	butter-woman	Byzantinism	charlatanic	cock-a-doodle
Bartholomew	butcher-bird	Byzantinist	charlatanry	cocoa-butter
berthon-boat	bathing-suit	claw-and-ball	charmlessly	cock-crowing
burling-iron	bottle-brush	crag-and-tail	chasmogamic	cycadaceous
burnishment	bottle-chart	characinoid	claim-jumper	cachectical
bar-sinister	battledress	chalazogamy	chain-harrow	cacographic
barrier-reef	betel-pepper	clay-brained	chain-letter	cacographer
barbiturate	battlefield	crambo-clink	channelling	cacogastric
bursiculate	bottle-glass	crabbedness	chain-plates	cyclicality
burglarious	batological	chambermaid	chain-smoker	Cochin-China
Barclaycard	bottle-green	chamberlain	chain-bridge	coccidiosis
baron-bailie	bottle-gourd	coarctation	chain-armour	cockleshell
Byronically	bottle-nosed	chance-comer	chain-driven	coconscious
bird-nesting	battleplane	chalcedonic	chain-stitch	coconut-palm
baronetical	battle-piece	chalcedonyx	caaing-whale	coconut-milk
burgomaster	bottle-party	chancellery	cracovienne	cyclopaedia
burrowstown	batsmanship	chancellory	clamorously	cyclopaedic
borborygmic	bathmitsvah	clam-chowder	championess	cuckoo-clock
borborygmus	bathmitzvah	charcuterie	clapperclaw	cyclohexane
bergschrund	botanically	chandlering	crappit-head	cycloserine
barnstormer	biting-louse	clandestine	crappit-heid	cyclothymia
burn-the-wind	botanomancy	crapehanger	clairschach	cyclothymic
burnt-sienna	bottom-glade	Clarencieux	chairperson	cacophonous
barquentine	bottom-grass	coalescence	clairvoyant	cock-sparrow
bird-watcher	bathophobia	crane-necked	chars-à-bancs	cicatricula
bastard-wing	betrothment	Craterellus	classically	code-breaker
bisociative	batholithic	chameleonic	class-leader	codicillary
bisociation	buttock-mail	ceaselessly	class-fellow	cudgel-proof
basket-chair	butyraceous	clavecinist	classifying	caddishness
besiegement	butt-welding	crateriform	chansonnier	cheval-glass
basset-hound	bathyscaphe	chaperonage	chansonette	crémaillère
bastel-house	bathymetric	chapeau-bras	coal-scuttle	crematorial
beseemingly	bathylithic	chaff-engine	coast-waiter	crematorium
besiegingly	bathysphere	chaff-cutter	chanticleer	Caesalpinia
basket-maker	blue-blooded	craggedness	chaotically	crescentade
Baskerville	boulder-clay	changefully	chartaceous	coercionist

crepehanger
cleverality
coenenchyma
crenellated
co-eternally
coefficient
clergy-woman
crepitative
clericalism
crepitation
clericalist
cheliferous
cherishment
credibility
co-existence
check-action
check-string
cream-cheese
clean-shaven
clean-limbed
cleanliness
clean-living
chemotactic
ctenophoran
coenobitism
Chenopodium
chemotropic
creophagous
clear-headed
cheer-leader
cheirognomy
cheiromancy
cheironomic
cheironomer
clearing-nut
Cheiroptera
cherry-stone
cheese-board
cheesecloth
co-essential
cleistogamy
cheese-press
cheese-straw
cheese-wring
creatianism
crestfallen
co-extensive
co-extension
creationism
creationist
creatorship
coeducation
crepuscular
chemurgical
credulously
chequerwise
chequer-work
café-concert
coffee-berry
coffee-house
coffee-stall
coffee-table
cognateness

cognitively
cognitivity
cognitional
cognoscible
cognoscente
cognoscenti
cognominate
cigar-holder
cohortative
climatology
chiragrical
climactical
climacteric
cuir-bouilli
cuir-bouilly
coincidence
coincidency
chip-carving
childminder
chisel-tooth
cliffhanger
chieftaincy
chieftainry
crithomancy
co-inherence
co-inheritor
criminalise
criminative
crimination
criminalist
criminality
criticality
criminatory
criticaster
crinigerous
criminology
chick-a-biddy
click-beetle
chicken-feed
chicken-wire
cliometrics
chimney-nook
chimney-nuik
chiromantic
clinometric
clinochlore
Chilognatha
chiropodial
chirologist
chiropodist
chirography
chinoiserie
chiropteran
Chippendale
crisping-pin
chiaroscuro
chiastolite
co-insurance
chitty-faced
chitterling
chirurgical
culpability
calcariform

call-at-large
collaborate
collapsable
collapsible
calibration
celebration
colubriform
cold-blooded
Calabar-bean
calycanthus
cold-casting
calf-country
collenchyma
colleaguing
culverineer
collegianer
calceolaria
collectable
collectible
collectedly
collectanea
calefacient
calefactive
calefaction
calefactory
cold-forging
californium
cold-hearted
colligative
calcination
colligation
collimation
culmination
cultivation
calciferous
calcigerous
celliferous
culmiferous
calling-crab
Calvinistic
calcicolous
Callitriche
calligramme
calligraphy
Callistemon
colliquable
calcifugous
callipygean
callipygous
columbarium
columnarity
chlamydeous
columniated
calumniator
colonialism
calendarist
colonialist
calendering
colonelship
colonelling
cylindrical
collocation
coleorrhiza

callousness
coleopteral
collocutory
colloquiums
calyptrogen
calorimeter
chlorimeter
chlorometer
colorimeter
calorimetry
chlorimetry
chlorometry
colorimetry
chloroplast
chloroprene
chlorophyll
chloroquine
calisthenic
celestially
calculative
calculating
calculation
colouration
colour-blind
cultureless
collusively
cold-welding
cold-without
comparative
commandment
comradeship
compaginate
companiable
companioned
campaniform
campanology
compass card
compassable
compactedly
compactness
compartment
campanulate
Campbellite
comicalness
commendable
commendably
compendious
commendator
compendiums
competently
competitive
competition
compellable
commemorate
compearance
commensally
compensator
campestrian
commentator
combinative
comminative
combination
commination

compilation
combinatory
comminatory
compilatory
commiserate
complement
commissural
comminution
camel-backed
compliantly
complacence
complacency
complicated
complainant
complaisant
complaining
cameleopard
Camaldolese
Camaldolite
completable
complotting
complexness
camp-meeting
cementation
cementatory
cement-stone
cement-water
compotation
commonality
compotatory
componental
compositive
composition
commotional
commonplace
compossible
commonsense
common-shore
comfortable
comfortably
compost-heap
comfortless
comportment
cymophanous
camaraderie
comprimario
comprisable
compressive
compression
compressure
comstockery
comstockism
comet-finder
Comptometer®
comptroller
communalise
commutative
computative
communalism
commutation
computation
communalist
compunction

computerise
compurgator
communicate
communicant
communistic
comeuppance
come-uppance
compulsitor
combustible
combustious
cinnabarine
connascence
connascency
concatenate
contango-day
consanguine
contaminate
contaminant
Convallaria
containable
containment
confarreate
confabulate
cine-biology
cynicalness
consciously
cony-catcher
conveyancer
canceration
centenarian
congelation
candelabrum
candelabras
candescence
confederate
confederacy
contenement
congenerous
convergence
convergency
congenially
convenience
conveniency
concealable
congealable
concealment
congealment
cancelled
conterminal
condemnable
concernedly
concernment
concernancy
contemplate
contemplant
conferrable
consecrator
concessible
condensable
conversable
conversably
confessedly
conversance

conversancy
concentrate
cinder-track
concert-hall
congestible
connectable
connectible
contestable
convertible
convertibly
conceptacle
conventicle
conceitedly
connectedly
contentedly
conceitless
contentless
consentient
contentment
concentring
concertante
concert-goer
conceptious
contentious
concentered
conjectural
consecutive
consecution
consequence
conceivable
conservable
conceivably
conservancy
conservator
cinchoninic
cantharidic
cantharidal
cantharides
cannibalise
cannibalism
candidature
confiscable
convincible
condisciple
confiscator
considerate
conciseness
confineless
confinement
considering
continental
confidently
continently
cunningness
contingence
contingency
canting-coin
conciliable
cunnilingus
confidingly
consimility
convicinity
convivially

conditioned
consilience
conditional
conditioner
concipiency
candidiasis
conciliator
confirmable
confirmator
consignable
condignness
consignment
centigramme
consistence
consistency
configurate
continuable
continuedly
continually
continuance
continuator
Canellaceae
candle-berry
conflictive
conflicting
confliction
canalicular
canaliculus
confluently
conflagrate
conflagrant
candle-light
candle-power
candle-stick
cinema-organ
CinemaScope®
canonically
connotative
condonation
connotation
consolation
convocation
condolatory
consolatory
consolatrix
consonantal
consonantly
concordance
condolement
consolement
consolidate
concomitant
condominium
consociated
conformable
conformably
cannon-metal
contorniate
concolorate
concolorous
cannon-proof
connoisseur
condottiere

condottieri
convolution
Convolvulus
conspecific
conspicuity
conspicuous
canophilist
conspirator
conurbation
centre-board
centrobaric
contrabasso
contributor
contractile
contractive
contraction
centrically
contracture
contractual
contra-dance
canariensis
centrifugal
canary-grass
congregated
controlment
controlling
congruously
centre-piece
contraption
centripetal
contrariety
contrarious
concrescent
contrastive
congressman
conirostral
contretemps
contra-tenor
cineritious
contrivable
contrivance
controversy
contrayerva
canisterise
cenesthesia
cenesthesis
constrained
constricted
constrictor
constellate
constuprate
constipated
consternate
constituent
cunctatious
construable
constructer
constructor
confutative
conjugative
conjugating
confutation
conjugation

conjuration
conjugality
contumacity
conjunctiva
conjunctive
conjunction
cinquecento
conjuncture
connumerate
conducement
confutement
conjurement
consumerism
consumerist
contubernal
concubinage
concubitant
concubinary
connubially
centuriator
consummator
consumptive
consumption
conquerable
concurrence
concurrency
convulsible
conductible
conductress
conductance
consultancy
condylomata
candy-stripe
clog-almanac
choice-drawn
crotcheteer
cloud-castle
cloudlessly
coordinance
co-ordinance
cloud-topped
Chondrostei
chordophone
crop-dusting
close-banded
close-handed
co-operative
cooperative
co-operation
cooperation
close-hauled
close-barred
closed-chain
closet-drama
close-reefed
choreograph
clover-grass
chokecherry
close-lipped
close-fisted
close-bodied
choregraphy
cholesteric

cholesterol	Cupuliferae	cardinalate	Corrodentia	circumvolve
cholesterin	capillitium	carminative	cardophagus	co-rivalship
cookery-book	copple-stone	cornice-rail	cartophilic	caravansary
cook-general	coping-stone	corrigendum	cormophytic	caravanning
clodhopping	coprolaliac	cornice-ring	cursoriness	caravanette
clothes-line	caprolactam	cornice-pole	corrosively	cordwainery
clothes-pole	coprophagic	cornice-hook	corroborate	curly-headed
clothes-moth	coprophagan	corniferous	corroborant	Carlylesque
clothes-prop	coprophilia	cornigerous	carpogonium	curry-powder
closing-time	cupro-nickel	cardiograph	carpospores	curly-greens
choking-coil	Cypro-Minoan	curling-pond	cartography	cash-account
crocidolite	copiousness	carriageway	curiousness	cost-account
cookie-shine	coprosterol	currishness	Carborundum®	cosmeticise
crookbacked	Capernaitic	certificate	carbonylate	cosmeticism
chock-a-block	cyperaceous	certifiable	carbocyclic	cosmetician
crookedness	coparcenary	certifiably	ceroplastic	castellated
crown-lawyer	coparcenery	curvilineal	cerargyrite	cosmetology
crown-antler	capernoited	curvilinear	coruscation	co-signatory
crocodilite	capernoitie	carnificial	chrismatory	castigation
crocodilian	caper-spurge	cordialness	card-sharper	castigatory
chorologist	caparisoned	cardiomotor	chrysoberyl	cysticercus
chorography	capitularly	carrion-crow	chrysocracy	costiveness
choir-master	carrageenan	carcinomata	chrysocolla	cassiterite
choir-screen	carrageenin	carnivorous	Christendom	casting-vote
choir-stalls	curtal-friar	carcinology	christening	cushion-tire
crossbanded	caryatidean	corbie-steps	christingle	cushion-tyre
cross-garnet	carnationed	corbiculate	caressingly	cassiopeium
crossbarred	curialistic	corniculate	Christiania	cashierment
cross-legged	curtailment	coralliform	Christianly	casuistical
crossbearer	curtail-step	corolliform	chrysalides	castle-guard
cross-leaved	curtain-fire	Carolingian	chrysalises	customarily
cross-tining	currant-cake	coralloidal	Christmassy	custom-built
cloisonnage	currant-wine	carilloneur	chrysoprase	cosmotheism
crossbowman	currant-loaf	carillonist	chrysarobin	cosmothetic
cross-cousin	carnaptious	circle-rider	curatorship	custom-house
cross-stitch	curnaptious	coral-island	circularise	cosmopolite
clostridial	cerebralism	chrominance	circulative	cosmogonist
clostridium	cerebration	ceremonious	circulating	cosmologist
cool-tankard	cerebralist	chromoplast	carburation	cosmopolicy
cephalalgia	curableness	chrome-steel	circulation	cosmosphere
cephalalgic	cerebriform	chromosomal	corrugation	cosmography
Cephalaspis	cerebellous	chromoscope	circularity	cosmocratic
Cappah-brown	carabiniere	chronically	circulatory	cash-payment
captainship	corybantism	chronograph	carbuncular	cash-railway
Cephalopoda	corn-cracker	coronagraph	corpuscular	cesarevitch
cephalotomy	cork-cambium	coronograph	circumciser	cesarewitch
capableness	caricatural	chronologic	carburetion	Cisatlantic
capaciously	correlative	chronologer	carburetted	citharistic
capacitance	correlation	chronometer	carburetter	cathartical
copper-beech	carvel-built	chronometry	carburettor	cataclasmic
copper-faced	curlew-berry	chronoscope	corpulently	cataclastic
cappernoity	carpet-snake	carunculate	circumflect	catechetics
copperplate	corner-stone	carunculous	circumfused	catechising
coppersmith	corbel-table	corporately	carousingly	catechismal
cypress-knee	correctable	carbonalite	circumlunar	catechistic
copper-works	correctible	corporative	cornucopian	catachresis
captivating	corner-teeth	Carbonarism	circumpolar	catacaustic
capriccioso	correctness	corporatism	circumspect	cataclysmic
cypripedium	currentness	carbonation	circumsolar	catadromous
cupriferous	carefulness	corporation	corruptible	catheterism
cupellation	cerographic	corporatist	corruptibly	cathedratic
capillarity	Cirrhipedia	corporality	corruptness	cytogenesis
copple-crown	cornhusking	corporeally		categorical

catch-phrase
catch-the-ten
catallactic
cytological
cataloguise
Cotylophora
catalytical
cotoneaster
cat-and-mouse
Ceteosaurus
cotton-grass
catholicise
catholicism
catholicity
cottonmouth
cotton-plant
cotton-press
cotton-waste
cataplectic
catapultier
cataphonics
cat-cracking
caterpillar
catercorner
cater-cousin
city-slicker
catastrophe
cat's-whisker
citizenship
causatively
church-bench
church-court
church-going
crunchiness
church-mouse
churchwoman
churchwards
causelessly
cauterising
cauligenous
cruciferous
crucigerous
crucifixion
cauliflower
caulicolous
cauliculate
chuckle-head
coupling-box
coulometric
Coulommiers
counselling
caustically
crustaceous
courtierism
courtliness
countrified
countenance
counting-out
courteously
countermand
counterbase
counter-pace
counterpane

countermark
countervail
counter-cast
counterpart
counterseal
counterfeit
cluster-pine
countermine
counter-time
countersink
countersign
counter-view
counterplea
counter-plot
counter-blow
counter-glow
cluster-bomb
counter-bond
counter-move
counter-vote
counter-work
counterfoil
counter-roll
counter-fort
counterdraw
countermure
counter-buff
counter-turn
courtesying
country-seat
countryfied
countryside
countrywide
country-folk
country-rock
cave-dweller
cavillation
cavalierish
cavalierism
civilisable
civil-suited
cavo-rilievo
cavernously
cavernulous
coxcombical
cryobiology
cryophysics
cryosurgery
cryptically
cryotherapy
cryptograph
Cryptogamia
cryptogamic
crystalline
crystallise
crystallite
crystalloid
Cryptomeria
clyster-pipe
deaf-and-dumb
dramaticism
diamagnetic
dramaturgic

dual-control
dead-clothes
diascordium
drap-de-berry
dram-drinker
diadelphous
diametrical
diametrally
diatessaron
dialectical
dialectally
dead-freight
draggle-tail
draughtsman
death-marked
diaphragmal
death-rattle
deathliness
diaphaneity
diachronism
diachronous
diathermacy
diathermous
diaphoresis
diaphoretic
death-stroke
death-duties
drawing-room
diagnostics
diamond-dust
diapophyses
diapophysis
diapositive
dialogistic
dragoon-bird
diabolology
diamorphine
dragon's-head
diacoustics
dual-purpose
diacritical
drastically
diastematic
draft-dodger
diastrophic
diarthrosis
dracunculus
dubiousness
debarcation
debarkation
debasedness
debauchedly
debauchment
debouchment
declarative
declamation
declaration
declamatory
declaratory
doch-an-doris
dictatorial
docibleness
decrescendo

decrepitate
decrepitude
declination
dockisation
declinatory
declinature
ductileness
deceitfully
ducking-pond
declivitous
decollation
décolletage
deckle-edged
decillionth
decelerator
decolourise
Decemberish
decumbently
decemvirate
decumbiture
documentary
decomposite
decameronic
decantation
dichogamous
dichotomise
dichotomist
dichotomous
dicephalous
deceptively
deck-passage
decerebrate
decerebrise
decurrently
decorticate
decursively
dichromatic
doctrinaire
doctrinally
decarbonate
decurionate
decarbonise
dichroscope
decarburise
decussately
decussation
dicotyledon
dock-warrant
dactylology
dactylogram
Dodecagynia
deductively
didacticism
Dodecandria
dodecaphony
dodecastyle
didactylous
dreadnaught
deep-drawing
dreadlessly
dreadnought
dredging-box
dreamlessly

deep-mouthed
dressmaking
deerstalker
dress-length
dress-reform
dress-shield
dress-circle
dyer's-rocket
defeasanced
defraudment
deflagrator
defiantness
defibrinate
defibrinise
deficiently
defectively
differentia
differently
deflexional
diffidently
difficultly
defalcation
defiliation
defoliation
defensative
defenceless
defensively
defloration
deformation
diffractive
diffraction
deforcement
deferential
defeudalise
diffuseness
diffusively
diffusivity
degradation
digladiator
dogmatology
Dogberrydom
Dogberryism
doggishness
dog's-mercury
degustation
degustatory
digestively
digitigrade
deglutinate
deglutitive
deglutition
deglutitory
doggy-paddle
dehydration
dehortative
dehortation
dehortatory
dwindlement
deification
driving-band
driving-gear
drill-barrow
drill-harrow

drill-master
drill-plough
dripping-pan
deictically
deistically
drift-mining
drift-anchor
daisy-cutter
Dukhobortsy
dak-bungalow
Della-Robbia
dull-brained
dolabriform
deliberator
delectation
deliciously
dolefulness
delightedly
delightless
delightsome
Delphinidae
dolphin-fish
dolphinaria
dollishness
doltishness
dulcifluous
delineative
delineation
delinquency
dilapidated
dilapidator
deliriously
dull-sighted
delusionist
dilutionary
deleterious
delitescent
diluvialist
deliverable
delivery-man
deliverance
delivery-van
damnability
demi-bastion
democratise
democratist
domiciliate
domiciliary
dimidiation
dumbfounder
demographic
demographer
demigration
demigoddess
demagnetise
demagogical
demagoguery
demagoguism
damping-down
dampishness
dumpishness
demulsifier
demoniacism

demonianism
demonocracy
domineering
dimensioned
dimensional
demonologic
demonolater
demonolatry
demonomania
diminishing
demonstrate
demarcation
demarkation
damascening
Demosthenic
domesticate
domesticise
domesticity
dame's-violet
damask-steel
demiurgical
demiurgeous
demountable
duniewassal
dinner-dance
dangerously
dinner-table
dinner-wagon
denigration
dentigerous
densimetric
dancing-girl
denticulate
dynamically
dynamograph
dynamometer
dynamometry
denominable
denominator
denumerable
denumerably
denunciator
dining-table
dendrachate
dendroglyph
dendrolatry
dendrometer
dendritical
denitration
Dinotherium
dandy-rigged
denizenship
drop-curtain
Droseraceae
drop-forging
diotheletic
diothelitic
dyotheletic
dyothelitic
Diophantine
deoxidation
dronishness
dioristical

door-knocker
dromophobia
doorstepper
deobstruent
drouthiness
doomwatcher
deoxygenate
deoxygenise
deoxyribose
Dipsacaceae
depravation
depravement
depravingly
deprecative
deprecation
depredation
deprecatory
depredatory
depreciator
dipterocarp
depressible
depth-charge
deprivative
duplicative
deprivation
duplication
duplicature
deprivement
duplicitous
dephlegmate
dependingly
diplomatese
dipsomaniac
diplomatise
deploration
diplomatist
deploringly
diprotodont
depopulator
deportation
diphtheroid
diphthongic
diphthongal
deplumation
depauperate
depauperise
diphycercal
diphysitism
dermatology
durableness
deracialise
directivity
directional
directorate
directorial
directrices
dare-devilry
direfulness
dorsiferous
dereliction
dark-lantern
derangement
daring-hardy

dermography
dorsolumbar
disparately
discalceate
dispatch-box
dispatchful
dastardness
disbandment
discardment
dismayfully
dyspathetic
destabilise
disharmonic
dysharmonic
disfavourer
disgarrison
distantness
dismastment
distasteful
disobedient
disablement
disobliging
desiccative
desecration
desiccation
disaccustom
desideratum
desperately
desperation
desperadoes
dissembling
dismembered
descendable
descendible
disremember
dishevelled
disseminate
dissepiment
disseminule
disbeliever
discernible
discernibly
discernment
discerptive
discerption
distempered
dispensable
distensible
dispensably
dispersedly
dispensator
dissectible
dyspeptical
dissentient
dissentious
disceptator
dissertator
disaffected
disafforest
designative
designation
designatory
desegregate

dissipative
destination
dissipation
distinctive
distinction
distincture
dislikeable
distinguish
duskishness
dissimilate
dispiriting
dissillence
distillable
disciplinal
discipliner
dismissible
dissimulate
destitution
displeasant
displeasing
disyllabism
disyllabify
displeasure
desilverise
disulphuric
disulphuret
desalinator
desultorily
disillusive
disillusion
disembitter
disemployed
disembodied
disimprison
disemburden
disentangle
disinterest
disinfector
disenthrall
disenshroud
disenthrone
desensitise
disinclined
desinential
disunionist
disentrance
disencumber
disannuller
dislocation
dissonantly
despondence
discordance
despondency
discordancy
disbowelled
dishonestly
discomfited
dislodgment
discothèque
discophoran
dissociable
dissociably
disposingly

dispositive
disposition
dyslogistic
despoilment
dishonorary
discoloured
dishonourer
discourtesy
discoursive
discography
disportment
discontinue
dissolutely
dissolutive
dissolution
dissolvable
discomycete
Dasipodidae
disapproval
disarmament
disorganise
describable
distribuend
distributer
distributor
disgraceful
destructive
distractive
distracting
destruction
distraction
disgracious
disordinate
deservingly
deserpidine
disgruntled
descriptive
description
discrepance
discrepancy
disproperty
distressful
distrustful
distressing
disprovable
destroyable
disassemble
disassembly
disputative
despumation
dismutation
disputation
disturbance
disjunctive
disjunction
dysfunction
disjuncture
disquietful
disquietive
disquieting
disquietous
disquietude
discussable

discussible
disguisedly
disgustedly
disaventure
desexualise
dusty-miller
dissymmetry
detrainment
detractress
detectivist
ditheletism
dithelitism
dutifulness
detrimental
doting-piece
dittography
duteousness
determinate
determinant
determinacy
determinism
determinist
deteriorate
deteriorism
deteriority
detestation
dithyrambic
deuteration
deuteranope
deuterogamy
Deuteronomy
doughtiness
druckenness
drunkenness
double-agent
double-blind
double-check
double-cross
double-digit
double-dutch
double-ender
double-edged
double-eagle
double-entry
double-faced
double-form'd
double-fault
double-lived
double-mined
double-quick
double-shade
double-space
double-sharp
double-stout
double-think
douroucouli
Deutschmark
dauntlessly
doubtlessly
dive-bombing
devaluation
divulgation
devolvement

divellicate
devil-dodger
developable
development
diving-board
diving-dress
divining-rod
deviousness
divorceable
divergement
divorcement
divergently
divergingly
divertingly
diversified
devastative
devastating
devastation
divestiture
divisionary
divisionism
devotedness
dovetailing
devotionist
devouringly
down-draught
down-hearted
down-setting
down-sitting
down-the-line
down-to-earth
downtrodden
dexterously
doxographer
dexiotropic
day-labourer
epanalepsis
emanational
emasculator
emancipator
evanescence
evangeliary
evangelical
exaggerator
eradicative
egalitarian
eradication
evagination
examination
exanimation
evasiveness
evanishment
elaborately
elaborative
evaporative
elaboration
evaporation
elaboratory
exasperator
Erastianism
elasticness
elastically
elasticated

exaltedness
exanthemata
elastomeric
Elastoplast®
Eoanthropus
enarthrosis
ejaculative
ejaculation
ejaculatory
embracement
embracingly
ecblastesis
eubacterium
emblematise
emblematist
emboîtement
embellisher
embrocation
embroiderer
embroilment
embarcation
embarkation
embarrassed
embittering
embowelment
embowelling
elbow-grease
embowerment
embryologic
embryonated
exclamative
exclamation
exclamatory
eucharistic
enchainment
eschatology
enchantress
enchantment
excrescence
excrescency
excremental
excrementum
exceedingly
Escherichia
ecclesiarch
escheatable
escheatment
enchiridion
escritorial
eccrinology
encrimsoned
exculpation
exculpatory
excellently
eccaleobion
eucalyptole
encomiastic
encumbrance
excommunion
eccentrical
enchondroma
euchologion
encephaline

encephaloid
encephalous
exceptional
encapsulate
encarnalise
excoriation
excorticate
excursively
encystation
excessively
encouraging
exclusively
exclusivism
exclusivist
encrustment
endearingly
endocardiac
endocardial
endocardium
endochylous
eudaemonism
eudaemonics
eudaemonist
endlessness
endemically
endemiology
endomorphic
endometrial
endometrium
endoplasmic
endophagous
endoplastic
ex-directory
endorsement
elderliness
elder-flower
endospermic
eidetically
endothermic
endotrophic
eremacausis
eye-catching
exercisable
elementally
energetical
elephantine
elephantoid
evening-star
everlasting
exemplarily
exemplarity
esemplastic
exemplified
epeirogenic
eyebrowless
eventualise
eventration
eventuality
eleutherian
electrified
electrician
electricity
ejectamenta

electioneer	Eriodendron	emotionless	expatiation	ectogenesis
electrolier	epipetalous	emotionally	expatiatory	ectogenetic
electronics	episepalous	egotistical	empty-handed	extrication
electrotint	epigenetics	exoskeletal	empty-headed	extrinsical
electrology	epigenesist	exoskeleton	emphyteusis	extemporary
electrocute	epinephrine	erotomaniac	emphyteutic	extemporise
electrolyse	eviternally	erotogenous	enquiration	entomophagy
electrolyte	evidentiary	econometric	exquisitely	entomophily
electrotype	epileptical	emolumental	Eurocentric	ectomorphic
electrotypy	epicheirema	evolutional	eurodollars	extenuative
ejector-seat	epithalamia	explanative	earnestness	extenuating
electorship	epithalamic	explanation	egregiously	extenuation
executively	epithelioma	explanatory	earthliness	extenuatory
executioner	epiphyllous	emplacement	earth-pillar	eating-apple
executorial	epithymetic	explainable	earth-closet	eating-house
executrices	epiphytical	expectative	earthenware	extensively
executrixes	eliminative	expectation	earth-tremor	extensional
everywhence	edification	expectantly	earth-hunger	ectoplasmic
emery-powder	elicitation	expectingly	earthquaked	ectoplastic
enfranchise	elimination	expectorate	ear-piercing	entophytous
efficacious	edificatory	expectorant	erroneously	externalise
efficiently	eliminatory	expediently	europeanise	extirpative
effectively	eligibility	expeditious	Europeanism	externalism
effectually	epidiascope	empiecement	Europeanist	extirpation
exfoliative	epiplastral	euphemistic	Eurypharynx	externalist
exfoliation	epiplastron	espièglerie	Eurypterida	externality
effulgently	enigmatical	expressible	eurypteroid	entertainer
enfeoffment	editorially	expressness	Etruscology	extirpatory
enforceable	epilogistic	expugnation	erratically	enterectomy
enforcement	Eriophorous	explicative	eurythermic	exterminate
enfouldered	epitrochoid	explication	eurythermal	extorsively
engrailment	epigraphist	explicatory	eurhythmics	extortioner
engrammatic	evil-starred	expansively	enslavement	enthralment
Enghalskrug	epistolical	expensively	east-by-north	enthralling
engraftment	epistilbite	expansivity	east-by-south	exteriorise
eagle-winged	existential	expansional	exsiccative	exteriority
eugenically	enjambement	expenditure	exsiccation	enterpriser
engineering	enkephalino	empanelment	easternmost	enterostomy
engrossment	eclecticism	empanelling	exstipulate	enterotoxin
engorgement	eglandulose	exponential	essentially	enterovirus
ergatocracy	ellipticity	explorative	ensanguined	entitlement
ergatomorph	ellipsoidal	exploration	exsanguined	ectothermic
eight-square	enlargement	exploratory	ensepulchre	entrustment
ethological	enlivenment	explosively	elsewhither	equiangular
Ephemeridae	emmenagogic	expromissor	extravagate	educability
ephemerides	emmenagogue	expropriate	extravasate	educational
Echinoderma	Emmenthaler	exploitable	extravagant	equableness
enhancement	enneandrian	eupepticity	estramazone	equibalance
ethnologist	enneandrous	exportation	estranghelo	enunciative
ethnography	enneahedral	expurgation	extradition	enunciation
etherealise	enneahedron	expurgatory	extra-floral	enunciatory
exhortative	ennoblement	empirically	entrainment	edulcorator
exhortation	einsteinium	empiricutic	extrapolate	equidistant
ethereality	egomaniacal	experienced	extractable	enumerative
exhortatory	exorability	Esperantist	extractible	enumeration
etheromania	exorbitance	emperorship	ectoblastic	exuberantly
echo-sounder	exorbitancy	empyreumata	entablature	erubescence
exhaustible	exonerative	expiscation	entablement	erubescency
exhaustless	exoneration	expiscatory	established	ecumenicism
exhaust-pipe	esotericism	exposedness	establisher	elucidative
Elizabethan	exotericism	expositress	estrepement	elucidation
epigastrium	epoch-making	expostulate	entreatable	elucidatory
episcopally	emotionable	expatiative	entreatment	enucleation

equilibrate	flavoursome	faith-healer	finger-glass	forfeitable
equilibrium	flapperhood	faithlessly	finger-grass	forgettable
equilibrist	fratricidal	frightfully	fence-lizard	fire-flaught
equilibrity	franticness	flightiness	fingerplate	fire-fighter
equilateral	frantically	faithworthy	finger-paint	farthingale
equinoctial	fractionate	frigidarium	fingerprint	forthcoming
elusoriness	fractionary	flickertail	fingerstall	furtherance
emulousness	fractionise	feignedness	fender-stool	farthermore
equipollent	fractionlet	frigorifico	finch-backed	furthermore
elutriation	fractiously	frivolously	funambulate	furthersome
emulsionise	featureless	fair-seeming	funambulist	farthermost
Equisetales	flatulently	flirtatious	financially	furthermost
Equisetinae	flag-wagging	fair-weather	Finno-Ugrian	formicarium
equivocally	fabricative	fairy-butter	fund-raising	forcipation
equivocator	fabrication	fallalishly	fenestrated	formication
equivalence	fibrillated	full-acorned	fanatically	fornication
equivalency	fact-finding	full-blooded	functionate	farcicality
envelopment	facsimilist	full-charged	functionary	forbiddance
enviousness	facultative	false-bedded	frowardness	forbiddenly
environment	face-lifting	falteringly	footbreadth	forgiveness
erythematic	facilitator	filter-paper	footballist	furtiveness
erythrocyte	fecundation	fuller's-herb	flocculence	ferriferous
etymologise	facinerious	full-fraught	frondescent	furciferous
etymologist	factory-ship	full-fledged	florescence	forcing-pump
flabbergast	facetiously	full-frontal	flower-clock	furnishment
flamboyance	factualness	full-hearted	floweriness	furnishings
flamboyante	fidgetiness	fulminating	flower-stalk	fortifiable
flamboyancy	faddishness	fulmination	froth-blower	forcibility
flaccidness	fiddle-de-dee	fulminatory	froth-hopper	fernitickle
franc-tireur	fiddlestick	folding-door	florilegium	foreignness
fiançailles	free-and-easy	falsifiable	floriferous	forficulate
francomania	freebootery	fallibility	flowingness	foreknowing
flag-captain	freebooting	folliculose	foolishness	ferulaceous
francophile	Frenchiness	folliculous	flock-master	firelighter
francophobe	fieldworker	fell-lurking	foot-lambert	foraminifer
francophone	field-cornet	filamentary	floorwalker	foraminated
flax-dresser	fremescence	filamentous	flourishing	fire-marshal
fraudulence	fretfulness	full-mouthed	frowstiness	foremastman
fraudulency	freight-shed	feloniously	foot-soldier	farinaceous
frater-house	flesh-market	follow-board	footslogger	fortnightly
flagellated	free-hearted	fulsomeness	footstooled	furunculous
flagellator	fleshliness	fallow-finch	front-ranker	farm-offices
fraternally	flesh-monger	filmography	frontlessly	forfoughten
fraterniser	flesh-colour	felspathoid	frostbitten	ferronickel
fearfulness	flexibility	fell-running	front-runner	ferronnière
feather-pate	freeloading	feldspathic	foppishness	forlornness
feather-palm	freemasonic	filmsetting	fipple-flute	forlorn-hope
feather-edge	freemasonry	Falstaffian	forwardness	ferrography
feather-head	fleurs-de-lis	fulguration	forwandered	furiousness
feather-star	fleurs-de-lys	fell-walking	firmamental	forepayment
flagitation	free-thinker	fume-chamber	farraginous	forereading
fragileness	free-tongued	familiarise	fire-brigade	fore-recited
feasibility	free-thought	familiarity	fire-balloon	fire-raising
franklinite	figure-dance	fomentation	fire-cracker	forestation
frank-pledge	Fehmgericht	Fumariaceae	fire-control	forestaller
frankfurter	fricandeaux	fimbriation	ferociously	foreseeable
flammulated	friableness	Fontarabian	foreclosure	foresignify
fragmentary	flinchingly	fundamental	fardel-bound	foresighted
flap-mouthed	fair-dealing	fanfaronade	far-reaching	foreshorten
flauntingly	fainéantise	fantastical	forgetfully	forespurrer
flannelette	fringilline	finicalness	forget-me-not	ferntickled
flag-officer	frighteners	fingerboard	forbearance	forethinker
flavourless	frightening	fingerguard	fermentable	forethought

first-footer	four-pounder	granophyric	gold-beating	genuineness
foretopmast	fluorimeter	granolithic	gull-catcher	gentilitial
first-fruits	fluorometer	glamorously	gold-digging	gentilitian
fortunately	fluorescein	glass-gazing	goldenberry	gentianella
formularise	fluorescent	glass-blower	galley-foist	gentlemanly
formulation	fluoroscope	Gladstonian	gelseminine	gentlewoman
fortune-tell	fluoroscopy	glassworker	galley-proof	gentlewomen
fortuneless	fluctuating	grasshopper	galley-slave	gonimoblast
fortune-book	fluctuation	glass-cutter	gelders-rose	goniometric
ferruginous	flustration	grass-cutter	gallimaufry	Gongoristic
forevermore	fructuation	geanticline	Gallicanism	generically
forevouched	frustration	ghastliness	gullibility	gonorrhoeic
fire-walking	faultlessly	giant-killer	galliambics	gonorrhoeal
fire-worship	fruitlessly	graptolitic	galliardise	generalship
forewarning	fault-finder	goal-tending	Gallowegian	gangsterism
fire-watcher	fountain-pen	giant-powder	gallowglass	gynostemium
farawayness	flusterment	giant-stride	gallophobia	genetically
fernytickle	four-wheeled	granulative	Gallovidian	genitivally
fish-bellied	four-wheeler	granulation	gallowsness	genouillère
foster-child	fivefingers	gratulation	gallows-bird	geomagnetic
Fastern's-e'en	favouritism	granularity	gallows-ripe	geotactical
foster-nurse	fawningness	gratulatory	gallows-foot	good-brother
fish-farming	fly-dressing	granuliform	gallows-free	grog-blossom
fish-gutting	gradationed	granulocyte	gallows-tree	grouchiness
festinately	gradational	gibberellic	gillravitch	glomeration
fascinating	glauconitic	gibberellin	goldsmithry	good-evening
fissiparism	Graeco-Roman	gable-window	gelatiniser	glove-shield
fascination	glaucescent	gibbousness	gally-bagger	goose-winged
festination	gnatcatcher	gubernation	gally-beggar	geomedicine
fustigation	grandparent	gaberlunzie	gillyflower	globe-flower
fustilarian	grandfather	goddaughter	gully-hunter	goose-flower
fissiparity	grandmaster	godlessness	gymnasiarch	grotesquely
fissiparous	guardedness	goddess-ship	gymnastical	grotesquery
fascia-board	grandeeship	god-forsaken	game-chicken	geometrical
fishing-frog	grandnephew	giddy-headed	gammerstang	Geometridae
fustillrian	grandiosely	Gregarinida	gamogenesis	geotectonic
fastigiated	grandmother	guelder-rose	gemmiparous	glomerulate
fashionable	grandiosity	greenockite	gemmiferous	geochemical
fissionable	gravel-blind	green-keeper	gummiferous	geophysical
fashionably	gracelessly	greenbottle	gambit-piece	globigerina
fushionless	grave-digger	greengrocer	gemological	good-looking
fasciculate	gladfulness	guerrillero	gaming-house	good-morning
fusillation	graphicness	grease-heels	gaming-table	groundburst
fusing-point	graphically	guesstimate	gymnorhinal	ground-elder
fish-packing	graphologic	grease-proof	gemmologist	ground-robin
festschrift	gnathonical	gressorious	gimcrackery	ground-state
fish-torpedo	gravitative	great-nephew	gametangium	groundspeed
fetichistic	gravitation	Grenzgänger	gamotropism	groundsheet
fatidically	graniteware	gaff-topsail	gametophyte	ground-sloth
fothergilla	guaniferous	gegenschein	gemmulation	good-natured
father-in-law	gravimetric	gigantesque	goniatitoid	ground-water
fatefulness	glaringness	giganticide	gendarmerie	geopolitics
fatigue-duty	graving-dock	gigantology	genealogise	gnotobiosis
fatiguingly	goatishness	gain-control	gonfalonier	gnotobiotic
fetch-candle	granitiform	guilelessly	genealogist	gnomonology
fitting-shop	gladioluses	guinea-grass	gonococcoid	glossectomy
fatuousness	gradiometer	gainfulness	geniculated	glossodynia
fetishistic	granivorous	glimmer-gowk	gingerbread	glossolalia
fauxbourdon	glaikitness	gliomatosis	genteelness	goods-engine
four-flusher	Grallatores	geitonogamy	gander-month	gnostically
frugiferous	grammalogue	guiltlessly	gynaecomast	ghostliness
frugivorous	grammatical	gallantness	gynaecology	geostrophic
foul-mouthed	gramophonic	gall-bladder	genuflexion	ghost-writer

groatsworth
globularity
geodynamics
geosyncline
garlandless
gormandiser
germaneness
Germanesque
Germanistic
Germanophil
Gargantuism
Gargantuist
gyrocompass
gyre-carline
garden-glass
garden-house
garnet-paper
garter-snake
garmentless
germinative
germination
gurgitation
girlishness
garnishment
girdlestead
Geraniaceae
gerontophil
gerontology
garbologist
gyrostatics
garrulously
gerrymander
gestational
gestatorial
Gasteropoda
gas-fittings
gesticulate
gaseousness
gastrectomy
gastrologer
gastromancy
gastronomic
gastronomer
gastroscope
gastrostomy
gastrosophy
gas-guzzling
gutta-percha
gatecrasher
gutter-blood
guttersnipe
guttiferous
go-to-meeting
get-together
gutturalise
glutaminase
grumblingly
gouvernante
glumiferous
Glumiflorae
glutinously
gourmandise
gourmandism

grummet-hole
glue-sniffer
glyphograph
glyptotheca
gazing-stock
headborough
heavenwards
haaf-fishing
headhunting
heathenesse
hyacinthine
hyalomelane
head-station
hearse-cloth
heart-easing
heart's-blood
hearth-brush
heartlessly
healthfully
heart-shaped
healthiness
hearth-money
hearth-penny
heart-urchin
hearth-stone
heart-strike
heart-string
heart-struck
heavy-handed
heavy-headed
heavyweight
Hebraically
Hobbistical
hobbledehoy
habilitator
hebdomadary
hobgoblinry
hebephrenia
hebephrenic
haberdasher
hibernation
hibernacula
hibernicise
Hibernicism
habituation
heckelphone
hacking-coat
huckleberry
hectogramme
hucksterage
hucksteress
hide-and-seek
hydra-headed
hydrargyral
hydrargyrum
Hudibrastic
hedge-parson
hedge-school
hedge-priest
hedge-writer
hedge-hyssop
hedging-bill
hiding-place

hydrocarbon
hydropathic
Hydnocarpus
hydromantic
hydrotactic
hydrogenate
hydrometeor
hydrogenous
hydrometric
hydromedusa
hydrophobia
hydrophobic
Hydrophidae
hydrophilic
hydrochoric
Hydrocharis
hydrothorax
hydrophytic
hydrophyton
hydrosomata
hydroponics
hydrologist
hydrosphere
hydrobromic
hydrotropic
hydrography
hideousness
hydrostatic
hydrolysate
hydrocyanic
hierarchism
haematocele
haematology
haematocrit
heedfulness
haemophilia
haemoglobin
hierologist
haemorrhage
haemorrhoid
hierography
hyetography
hierocratic
haemoptysis
haemostasis
haemostatic
Hieronymite
Hieronymian
haemocyanin
hierurgical
huffishness
Haggadistic
high-blooded
highbrowism
high-battled
high-feeding
high-falutin
high-hearted
hog-shoulder
hoggishness
Hegelianism
Highlandman
highly-sexed

hegemonical
high-mettled
hagioscopic
hygroscopic
hygrometric
hygrophytic
hagiologist
Hagiographa
hagiography
hugeousness
high-pitched
high-powered
high-rolling
high-ranking
high-stepper
high-sighted
high-tension
high-voltage
highwrought
hair-brained
hair-breadth
hairdresser
heinousness
hair-raising
hairstylist
hair-trigger
half-and-half
holoblastic
hall-bedroom
half-binding
half-blooded
half-brother
halobiontic
half-baptise
half-checked
helicograph
helichrysum
holocaustic
holocaustal
helve-hammer
halfendeale
Hellenistic
hälleflinta
helleborine
helmet-shell
Heldentenor
helpfulness
holographic
hellgramite
hylogenesis
half-hearted
holohedrism
half-holiday
hellishness
helminthoid
helminthous
half-leather
half-landing
half-measure
hylomorphic
helioscopic
heliometric
heliophobic

heliochrome
heliochromy
heliotropin
heliography
hylophagous
halophilous
halfpennies
hill-pasture
hylopathism
hylopathist
half-pounder
holophytism
hilariously
half-starved
helispheric
holothurian
hallucinate
hylozoistic
home-and-
home
home-and-
away
hemianopsia
hemianoptic
homoblastic
humectation
homocentric
home-crofter
home-defence
hammer-brace
hammercloth
homoeomeric
homoeomorph
homoeotism
homoeopathy
homogeneity
homogeneous
homogeniser
homogenesis
homogenetic
hemihedrism
humming-bird
homoiousian
home-keeping
humiliative
humiliating
humiliation
humiliatory
homological
Hamiltonian
homiletical
hemimorphic
homomorphic
Hymenoptera
homeomerous
hymnologist
homeomorphy
hymnography
homeostatic
homoplastic
hemipterous
homopterous
homophonous

11 i□c□g

humgruffian	heptandrous	hypothecate	harbourless	Heteroptera
hemeralopia	heptamerous	hypothecary	harbour-dues	heteroscian
homesteader	hypoaeolian	hypothesise	hard-pressed	heterospory
hemispheric	heptagynous	hypothetise	harpsichord	heterostyly
hemistichal	hypoblastic	hypothermia	haruspicate	heterotroph
homosporous	hypocycloid	hypothermal	harassingly	heterotopia
home-stretch	hypocorisma	hypothenuse	hart's-tongue	heterotopic
homothallic	hyphenation	hypotensive	hornswoggle	heterotypic
homothermic	haplessness	hypotension	horoscopist	heterotaxis
homothermal	hippeastrum	hypotyposis	heresiology	heterousian
hamstringed	hopefulness	hepatoscopy	heretically	hounds-berry
hemitropous	hypoglossal	hypothyroid	herb-trinity	hound's-tooth
humbuggable	hypogastric	hard-and-fast	hirsuteness	houseparent
homozygosis	hippiatrics	hare-brained	hard-visaged	housefather
hangability	hippiatrist	Heracleidan	hard-wearing	house-factor
hand-breadth	hypallactic	hereditable	hero-worship	housemaster
hunt-counter	hypolimnion	horseradish	hard-working	housekeeper
hinderlands	Hepplewhite	horse-dealer	hardwareman	housewifely
hinderlings	hop-o'-my-	hermeneutic	horny-handed	housewifery
hunter's-moon	thumb	hurley-house	hurly-hacket	householder
hand-feeding	hypnopaedia	horse-riding	hurry-scurry	housemother
handfasting	hippodamist	hermeticity	hurry-skurry	house-arrest
hand-grenade	hippodamous	horse-litter	husbandland	house-broken
hang-gliding	hippocampus	horse-collar	husbandless	haughtiness
hunchbacked	hypnogenous	herpetology	husbandlike	haustellate
handicapped	hypsometric	horse-couper	histaminase	hoverbarrow
handicapper	hypsophobia	horse-doctor	hispanicise	howsomdever
hunting-mass	hypnotistic	horse-drench	hispanicism	hexagonally
hunting-seat	hippopotami	harness-cask	hysteresial	hexametrise
hunting-whip	hippologist	harness-room	Hesperiidae	hexametrist
hunting-tide	hoplologist	harvest-mite	hesperidium	hexaplarian
hunting-song	hypnopompic	harvest-tick	hysteroidal	hexastichal
hunting-horn	hippodromic	harvest-home	hysterogeny	hexateuchal
hunting-crop	haptotropic	harmfulness	hysterotomy	hazardously
hand-knitted	haplography	hurtfulness	hostess-ship	inadaptable
hand-painted	hypsography	horographer	hospitalise	inaugurator
hand-promise	Hippocratic	hard-grained	hospitality	imaginative
hundredfold	hypermarket	hard-hearted	hospitaller	imagination
honorifical	hypergamous	hard-hitting	hostilities	inanimation
hand-running	hyperdactyl	hereinafter	historicise	inalienable
handshaking	hyperactive	hurriedness	historicism	inalienably
handselling	hyperacusis	herring-pond	historicist	isapostolic
honest-to-God	hyperphagia	herring-bone	historicity	itacolumite
hunt-the-gowk	hypercharge	herring-gull	historiated	inappetence
hand-to-mouth	hyperplasia	herring-buss	historiette	inappetency
honour-bound	hyperemesis	horripilate	histologist	inattentive
honour-point	hyperemetic	horripilant	histrionism	inattention
handwriting	hyperinosis	horrisonant	histrionics	inalterable
handwritten	hyperinotic	herbivorous	hasty-witted	inadvertent
handwrought	hyperborean	horrisonous	hetaerismic	inadvisable
honey-waggon	hyperbolise	hurtleberry	hot-tempered	imbrication
honey-badger	hyperbolism	horological	hatlessness	incrassated
honeycombed	hyperdorian	hurdle-racer	hitherwards	incremation
honeymooner	hypersonics	harum-scarum	hatefulness	incoercible
honey-locust	hyperboloid	horn-madness	hatchettite	incremental
honeysuckle	hypertrophy	hard-mouthed	hatti-sherif	inclemently
honey-sucker	hypercritic	hariolation	hetairismic	increasable
hyoscyamine	hypersthene	hercogamous	hotel-keeper	increaseful
hook-climber	hyperlydian	hircocervus	hot-spirited	incredulity
hooliganism	hypostasise	herb-of-grace	heteroclite	incredulous
hyopastral	hypostatise	harrowingly	heterocercy	incognisant
hyoplastron	hypostrophe	harmoniphon	heteroecism	incogitable
heptarchist	hepatectomy	harmonogram	heterograft	incogitancy

incoherence
incoherency
inclination
inclinatory
incriminate
inculcative
inculcation
inculpation
inculcatory
inculpatory
incalescent
incompetent
incumbently
incompliant
Incompletae
incomposite
incommodity
incantation
incantatory
incunabulum
incunabular
inconscient
inconscious
incensement
incense-boat
incontinent
incendivity
inconsonant
incongruent
incongruity
incongruous
incinerator
inconstancy
incapacious
incipiently
incapsulate
incarnadine
incarnation
incurvation
incurvature
incarcerate
incorrectly
incardinate
incertitude
incoronated
incorporate
incorporall
incorporeal
incuriosity
incuriously
incorruptly
incessantly
inclusively
itchy-palmed
india-rubber
indubitable
indubitably
indeciduate
indeciduous
Indo-Chinese
inductively
inductility
inductivity

inductional
indifferent
indefinable
indefinably
indignation
indignantly
indigestive
indigestion
indehiscent
indulgently
indemnified
indomitable
indomitably
indentation
induplicate
independent
indirection
indesignate
industrious
individuate
individable
indivisible
indivisibly
indexterity
index-finger
index-linked
iteratively
inelaborate
inenarrable
ipecacuanha
inescapable
inexcusable
inexcusably
inexcitable
inelegantly
inexecrable
inexecution
inefficient
ineffective
ineffectual
ideographic
inexhausted
inedibility
inexistence
ideological
ineloquence
ideopraxist
inexpectant
inexpedient
inexpensive
idempotency
inebriation
inessential
identically
identifying
inestimable
inestimably
inextension
ineluctable
inequitable
inequitably
infrangible

inflatingly
inflammable
inflammably
infracostal
infecundity
inflexional
infrequence
infrequency
infiltrator
infanticide
infantilism
infantryman
infangthief
infinitival
informative
infirmarian
information
informatics
infernality
informality
informatory
infertility
inferential
inferiority
infestation
infatuation
infeudation
influential
infructuous
ingratitude
ingeniously
ingenuously
ingurgitate
ingathering
inhabitable
inhabitress
inhabitance
inhabitancy
ichthyosaur
ichthyoidal
ichthyolite
Ichthyornis
ichthyology
ichthyopsid
ichnography
ithyphallic
ithyphallus
inheritable
inheritress
inheritance
imitatively
imitability
idioblastic
itinerantly
iridescence
idiographic
idioglossia
iridisation
inimicality
initialling
idiomorphic
idiomatical
idiotically

injudicious
injuriously
inking-table
irksomeness
inkhorn-mate
ill-mannered
ill-favoured
illiberally
illicitness
ill-tempered
ill-affected
illogically
ill-disposed
illuminable
illuminance
illuminator
illuminatus
illimitable
illimitably
ill-informed
illiquation
illaqueable
illiquidity
ill-breeding
ill-wresting
illusionism
illusionist
ill-assorted
illustrious
illustrated
illustrator
ill-humoured
immediately
immediatism
immedicable
immigration
immenseness
immanentism
immanentist
immortalise
immortality
immarginate
immitigable
immitigably
immoveables
ignobleness
innocuously
innominable
ignominious
innumerable
innumerably
innervation
ignoramuses
Ignorantine
ionospheric
innutrition
innavigable
innavigably
ion-exchange
innoxiously
icosandrian
icosandrous
icosahedral

icosahedron
isolability
isomagnetic
inoperative
isolecithal
inobedience
isometrical
isogeotherm
inofficious
inoffensive
iron-founder
iron-foundry
inorganised
iron-hearted
isochronise
isochronism
isochronous
isorhythmic
isoelectric
ironmongery
isotonicity
iconologist
inodorously
isomorphism
isomorphous
iconography
iconostasis
inopportune
inobservant
inobtrusive
inoculative
inoculation
inoculatory
implacental
impeachable
impeachment
implausible
impractical
impecunious
impedimenta
imprecation
imprecatory
implemental
imprecision
impregnable
impregnably
impressible
impressment
impignorate
implicative
implication
impuissance
impulsively
impulsivity
impolitical
impoliticly
impingement
imponderous
impenetrate
impenitence
impenitency
improbative
imploration

improbation	irradiation	insinuating	intromitted	intersperse
imploratory	irreducible	insinuation	intromitter	intertribal
improbatory	irreducibly	insinuatory	intercalate	intercrural
improvement	irreduction	insincerely	intercalary	interpreter
improvisate	irredentism	insincerity	interjacent	intergrowth
improvident	irredentist	insensitive	intertangle	interosseal
imploringly	Israelitish	insentience	internalise	interesting
improvingly	irreflexion	insentiency	interfacing	icteritious
impropriate	irrefutable	insipidness	interfacial	interlunary
impropriety	irrefutably	insipiently	interracial	internuncio
impermanent	irregularly	inseparable	interradial	interludial
imperialise	irreligious	insuperable	interradius	interfusion
imperialism	irrelevance	inseparably	internality	interrupted
Imparkation	irrelevancy	insuperably	intervallic	interrupter
impartation	irremissive	instreaming	intervallum	interruptor
importation	irremission	inscribable	intergatory	intrusively
imperialist	irremovable	instructive	intertarsal	inusitation
imperiality	irremovably	instruction	interactant	inutterable
importantly	irruptively	insertional	interactive	inviability
imperceable	irreparable	inscriptive	interscribe	invectively
impermeable	irreparably	inscription	Interaction	invidiously
impermeably	irresoluble	inscrutable	interocular	invigilator
imperfectly	irresolubly	inscrutably	interbedded	invigorator
imperviable	irretentive	insistently	intermeddle	involucrate
impertinent	irretention	insessorial	intercedent	invalidness
impartially	irrevocable	insatiately	internecine	invalidhood
imperilment	irrevocably	insouciance	internecive	involvement
imperforate	irreverence	insculpture	intermedial	involuntary
impersonate	instatement	inseverable	intermedium	inventively
imperiously	instability	intravenous	interdealer	inventorial
importunate	installment	intrathecal	interregnum	inviolately
importunacy	instaurator	intractable	interneural	investigate
importunely	instantiate	intractably	intercensal	investitive
importuning	insectarium	intrenchant	intercessor	investiture
importunity	insecticide	intrepidity	interdental	jealousness
impastation	Insectivora	integrative	interseptal	jealoushood
imposthumed	insectivore	integration	intersertal	jabberingly
impassively	insectiform	integrality	intercepter	jabberwocky
impassivity	insectifuge	intagliated	interceptor	Jacobinical
impassioned	insectology	intricately	interventor	Jacob's-staff
impostumate	insidiously	intuitively	intersexual	Jacobitical
impetrative	inspectress	intuitivism	interleaves	jactitation
impetration	insufflator	intuitional	interchange	Jack-pudding
impetratory	inspirative	intrinsical	interminate	jocoserious
impatiently	instigative	intriguante	inturbidate	Jacqueminot
impetigines	inspiration	intellected	interlinear	judiciously
impetuosity	instigation	intelligent	interlingua	Judaisation
impetuously	inspiratory	intolerable	intermingle	judgment-day
impoundable	instinctive	intolerably	interlining	Judas-window
impoundment	instinctual	intolerance	interviewee	jagging-iron
imprudently	inspiringly	intemperate	interviewer	John-a-dreams
inquination	inspiriting	intemperant	interfluent	Johnsoniana
inquiration	institorial	intumescent	interallied	joint-tenant
inquiringly	inspissator	intensative	interfluous	jumping-hare
inquisitive	institutive	intenseness	Interglossa	jumping-jack
inquilinism	institution	intendiment	interpolate	jumping-bean
inquisition	institutist	intensively	interrogate	jumping-deer
inquilinity	insalubrity	intensified	interrogant	jimpson-weed
inquilinous	insultingly	intensitive	internodial	jinrickshaw
irreceptive	ipsilateral	intensifier	interiority	jungle-green
irrecusable	inseminator	intentioned	intercourse	janitorship
irrecusably	insensately	intentional	intercostal	juridically
irradiative	insinuative	Istiophorus	interspinal	jury-process

jerrymander
justiceship
justiciable
justifiable
justifiably
journey-work
jaunting-car
juvenescent
joylessness
kwashiorkor
knavishness
kibble-chain
kidney-stone
kidney-vetch
kiddywinkie
knee-capping
keelhauling
keeping-room
knee-tribute
kleptomania
kaisar-i-Hind
knife-switch
kriegsspiel
knick-knacky
killikinick
Kulturkreis
Kulturkampf
Kommersbuch
kymographic
Kimeridgian
Kendal-green
kangaroo-rat
kinderspiel
kind-hearted
kinchin-cove
kinchin-mort
Kentish-fire
kinnikinick
kinematical
king-penguin
kindredness
kindredship
kinesiatric
king's-yellow
kinesiology
kinesipathy
kinetograph
kinetoscope
king-vulture
knowingness
knock-rating
know-nothing
kirk-session
keratophyre
kiss-me-quick
kite-balloon
katabothron
katadromous
kitchen-maid
kitchen-sink
kitchenette
katavothron
knuckle-head

knuckle-bone
load-bearing
leaf-climber
leaf-cushion
leaf-cutting
leave-taking
leader-cable
leaseholder
loathedness
loathliness
loathsomely
leather-back
leather-head
leather-neck
leather-coat
leatherette
leach-trough
leaving-shop
leaping-time
learnedness
loan-society
leaguer-lass
leaguer-lady
librational
labradorite
labefaction
lubricative
lubrication
Lobeliaceae
libellously
labiodental
loblolly-bay
loblolly-boy
libertarian
libertinage
liberticide
libertinism
labyrinthic
labyrinthal
laboriously
liberty-boat
lobby-member
Lochaber-axe
lucratively
lucubration
luckenbooth
lactescence
luckengowan
lickerishly
lichenology
lecherously
lock-forward
lacrimatory
lactiferous
lactifluous
lacrimosely
loculicidal
laciniation
laconically
lycanthrope
lycanthropy
lychnoscope
laccolithic

lactoflavin
lick-platter
Lycopodinae
lacertilian
lachrymator
locorestive
lickspittle
locutionary
lectureship
lacquer-tree
lacrymatory
lacrymosely
ludicrously
lodge-keeper
lady's-mantle
lady's-finger
lady-trifles
leesome-lane
lieutenancy
life-annuity
luffer-board
life-history
lifemanship
life-peerage
life-peeress
life-rentrix
loggan-stone
legibleness
logicalness
logodaedaly
leglessness
leg-of-mutton
logographic
logographer
lignivorous
logomachist
ligamentary
ligamentous
Leguminosae
lagomorphic
Loganiaceae
legionnaire
legerdemain
logarithmic
legislative
legislation
legislature
logistician
light-handed
light-headed
light-legged
lightweight
light-heeled
lightkeeper
light-minded
light-winged
light-footed
legatissimo
leg-business
lignum-swamp
lignum-scrub
lignum-vitae
loiteringly

leishmaniae
laicisation
Leibnitzian
lake-dweller
lukewarmish
Loliginidae
lilliputian
lily-livered
lumbaginous
lamp-chimney
lammergeier
lammergeyer
lymphangial
lumpishness
lamplighter
lamelliform
lamellicorn
lamentation
lemon-yellow
lamentingly
luminescent
limnologist
Lumbricidae
lumbricalis
lamprophyre
limitedness
limitlessly
longanimity
longanimous
landaulette
Lancastrian
long-clothes
linseed-cake
linseed-meal
lingeringly
lanceolated
landfilling
line-fishing
land-grabber
landgravine
landholding
lanthanides
luncheon-bar
lancinating
lancination
landing-beam
landing-gear
landing-ship
lentiginose
lentiginous
longinquity
land-jobbing
lonely-heart
landlordism
land-measure
long-measure
linen-scroll
linen-draper
langoustine
long-playing
line-printer
long-purples
land-spaniel

landscapist
land-steward
long-sighted
landsknecht
line-shooter
lengthiness
long-tongued
languidness
languescent
languishing
linguistics
long-visaged
long-waisted
leopard-wood
loose-limbed
loose-bodied
loose-strife
lion-hearted
lapidifying
Lepidoptera
Lepidosteus
lapidescent
Lepidosiren
Lippizzaner
lapilliform
lipomatosis
leprosarium
leptodactyl
leptocercal
lip-rounding
leptorrhine
lophobranch
lipoprotein
laparoscope
laparoscopy
lapis-lazuli
liquescence
liquescency
liquefiable
Liquidambar
liquidation
large-handed
large-minded
larcenously
larviparous
larrikinism
laryngismus
laryngology
laryngotomy
listeners-in
listening-in
lustfulness
lysigenetic
lastingness
luskishness
lese-majesty
lissomeness
Laserpicium
Laserpitium
lethargical
littérateur
Lutheranism
letter-board

letterpress	luxulyanite	Micawberism	maisterdome	milk-kinship
letter-stamp	luxuriation	mediateness	moisturiser	malakatoone
latifundium	luxuriantly	mediatorial	make-believe	milk-livered
litigiously	luxuriously	mediatrices	Mekhitarist	Melanochroi
latch-string	lixiviation	mediastinal	make-or-break	melanterite
lattice-leaf	leze-liberty	mediastinum	multangular	melancholia
lattice-work	leze-majesty	mediaevally	multanimous	melancholic
lethiferous	meaningless	medico-legal	molybdenite	molendinary
littleworth	meadow-brown	medicinable	Malacca-cane	melanophore
litany-stool	meadow-grass	medicinally	mole-cricket	meliorative
litholapaxy	meadow-sweet	medicine-man	molecularly	melioration
lithogenous	measureless	medievalism	maliciously	malposition
lithochromy	measurement	medievalist	molecatcher	meliphagous
lithophysae	mechanician	maddeningly	maledictive	milk-pudding
lithophytic	mechanistic	madreporite	malediction	malapropism
latrocinium	Machaerodus	middenstead	maledictory	malpractice
lithologist	Machairodus	madefaction	melodiously	malariology
lithotomist	mycodomatia	midshipmate	maladroitly	molestation
lithodomous	mackerel-sky	madrigalian	maladaptive	milk-thistle
lithotomous	machination	madrigalist	maladjusted	malfunction
lithosphere	machine-made	middle-class	millenarism	malevolence
lithography	machine-shop	middle-earth	millenarian	mollycoddle
lithotripsy	machine-work	mud-slinging	millet-grass	mammalogist
lithotritic	machine-tool	middle-sized	millefleurs	mimographer
lithotritor	mocking-bird	middle-world	mulberry-fig	mammiferous
laterigrade	mockingbird	madonnawise	malfeasance	mumpishness
literalness	machicolate	Madonna-lily	mallee-scrub	mamillation
literaliser	mycological	modernistic	malt-extract	mamilliform
literaryism	mock-modesty	medium-dated	malefaction	momentarily
latirostral	macrogamete	mediumistic	malefically	momentously
lateritious	microgamete	muddy-headed	maleficence	mammoth-tree
literatured	macrodactyl	Moeso-gothic	malefactory	mammonistic
lotus-eaters	macroscopic	muffin-fight	malignantly	mammography
latiseptate	microscopic	muffin-worry	multivalent	memorialise
latitudinal	microneedle	Magdalenian	multiracial	memorialist
launderette	microcephal	magnanimity	multiparity	memorabilia
laundry-maid	Micronesian	magnanimous	multiparous	membraneous
louver-board	microsecond	magnetician	multiserial	mimosaceous
laurel-water	micrometric	Maglemosian	Mulciberian	mimetically
laughing-gas	microphonic	magnesstone	melliferous	mansard-roof
laughworthy	microphytic	magnifiable	meltingness	mandarinate
loutishness	microlithic	magnificent	milking-time	manna-lichen
loud-mouthed	macrobiotic	megaloblast	multilineal	Montanistic
leucorrhoea	microampere	megalomania	multilinear	manna-groats
louvre-board	micrococcal	megalopolis	multifidous	miniaturise
loudspeaker	micrococcus	maggotorium	mellifluent	miniaturist
Louis-Treize	micrologist	magisterial	multiplying	monoblepsis
Louis-Quinze	microtomist	magisterium	mellifluous	mind-bending
loup-the-dyke	macrocosmic	magistratic	multiplexer	mind-blowing
laurustinus	microcosmic	Megatherium	milliampere	monochasial
livable-with	microgroove	magazine-gun	millionaire	Manichaeism
love-in-a-mist	micrography	Mahabharata	millionfold	monochasium
level-headed	microtubule	Mohammedis-	multilobate	monoclinous
liver-colour	mycophagist	m	multisonant	monoculture
leviratical	McCarthyite	Mohorovicic	multipotent	mine-captain
levitically	McCarthyism	mail-carrier	multinomial	municipally
law-merchant	mycorrhizal	mail-catcher	multicolour	monocardian
lawlessness	maceranduba	mailing-card	mellivorous	monochromat
low-spirited	macassar-oil	maisonnette	multispiral	monocarpous
low-pressure	mycotrophic	maid-servant	multistorey	Monocotylae
loxodromics	Michurinism	maintenance	multijugate	monocrystal
lexigraphic	micturition	maintopsail	multijugous	Monadelphia
luxulianite	Micawberish	maintopmast	multicuspid	Monodelphia

monodelphic	mineraliser	mirifically	mishallowed	misanthropy
monkey-board	ministering	merogenesis	muscatorium	misoneistic
monkey-bread	ministerial	merogenetic	miscarriage	misinformer
monkey-block	monasterial	marshlander	mismarriage	misinstruct
mendelevium	ministerium	marshmallow	mesoblastic	misdoubtful
monkey-gland	menispermum	mirthlessly	mossbluiter	misconceive
monkey-grass	mine-sweeper	morphologic	music-master	mastoiditis
Monseigneur	monasticism	marshalship	music-seller	misgovernor
minnesinger	Monotremata	marshalling	moss-cheeper	museologist
manneristic	monothelete	merchandise	masochistic	mastodontic
mantelpiece	monothelite	merchantman	musicalness	misconstrue
mantelshelf	monothelism	merchantmen	music-holder	misfortuned
monkey-shine	monothecous	marchioness	mesocephaly	muscovy-duck
monkey-trick	minute-glass	marginalise	misrelation	misspelling
men-servants	many-tongued	morris-dance	master-class	mass-produce
monkey-wheel	munitioneer	martinetism	master-clock	miscreative
munificence	monstrosity	mortice-lock	miscegenate	mistreading
manufactory	monstrously	mortise-lock	misremember	miscreation
manufacture	monitorship	morbiferous	miscegenist	misericorde
mindfulness	mine-thrower	mortiferous	misdemeanor	miserliness
monographic	minute-while	mercilessly	masterfully	mistrustful
monographer	minute-watch	morning-land	misbeliever	misestimate
montgolfier	mensurative	marriage-bed	master-joint	musk-thistle
monogenesis	manducation	morning-tide	miscellanea	moss-trooper
monogenetic	mensuration	morning-gift	muskellunge	musculation
managership	manducatory	morning-room	master-mason	muscularity
mind-healing	mantua-maker	morning-gown	misbecoming	musculature
Munchhausen	monovalence	morsing-horn	misdevotion	masturbator
men-children	monovalency	morning-star	misbegotten	misguidedly
mentholated	money-making	myrmidonian	masterpiece	misguidance
monchiquite	money-market	marlinspike	musket-proof	misjudgment
mancipation	money-lender	marble-edged	mistempered	meshuggenah
mancipatory	money-spider	marble-paper	muster-party	meshuggeneh
manniferous	money-broker	Marantaceae	mispersuade	masculinely
mannishness	money's-worth	Moringaceae	mussel-scalp	masculinise
man-milliner	monozygotic	myringotomy	mussel-scaup	masculinist
mentionable	myocarditis	mirror-image	mise-en-scène	masculinity
monticolour	moor-buzzard	marconigram	mussel-shell	museum-piece
mandibulate	moon-goddess	Mariologist	misfeasance	masquerader
monticulate	mooring-mast	Maryologist	misfeatured	Mussulwoman
monticulous	myoelectric	margraviate	misbestowal	mitrailleur
monological	moonlighter	meritocracy	master-wheel	mutableness
monologuise	moon-madness	Marathonian	mystery-ship	metacentric
monologuist	myographist	meritorious	mystery-play	metachrosis
monolingual	map-measurer	moratoriums	mystery-tour	mathematise
monolatrous	meprobamate	murmuration	missheathed	mutteration
monomyarian	mortar-board	murmuringly	mischievous	mathematics
monomorphic	meroblastic	Marsupialia	Muschelkalk	mothercraft
manumission	moribundity	mercurially	mastication	mutteringly
manumitting	mariculture	murmurously	mussitation	mother-in-law
mononuclear	mercenarism	marquessate	masticatory	mother-naked
meningocele	mercenarily	marquisette	massiveness	mother-right
mentonnière	marcescible	marqueterie	missishness	mother's-mark
monophagous	market-cross	Moravianism	Messiahship	mother-water
manipulable	market-house	Merovingian	miscibility	metagenesis
monopoliser	myrmecology	Marivaudage	mispleading	metagenetic
manipulator	murderously	merrymaking	muscle-bound	matchmaking
monopsonist	market-place	merry-andrew	mésalliance	matchlessly
monophthong	market-price	martyrology	misalliance	metrication
monophysite	morgenstern	mustard-tree	mass-meeting	matrilineal
mind-reading	martensitic	message-girl	mesomorphic	matrilinear
monarchical	market-value	mustachioed	mesenterial	matriclinic
menorrhagia	market-woman	maskallonge	misanthrope	matrimonial

matriarchal	movableness	night-faring	non-provided	nettle-cloth
matriculate	mawkishness	night-waking	none-sparing	nationalise
metalhedyde	moxibustion	nightmarish	non-issuable	nitrosamine
mottle-faced	maxillipede	negotiation	nonetheless	nationalism
metalliding	Myxomycetes	night-walker	nuncupative	nitrosation
metalloidal	maxim-monger	negotiatrix	nuncupation	nationalist
metallogeny	myxomatosis	night-school	nuncupatory	notionalist
metal-worker	Myxophyceae	night-cellar	nun's-veiling	nationality
metallurgic	mixotrophic	night-season	non-existent	Nothofagust
metamorphic	May-meetings	night-shriek	ninny-hammer	nitrogenise
metonymical	neanderthal	night-flying	Nancy-pretty	nitrogenous
mythomaniac	near-sighted	night-flower	neopaganise	nitrocotton
meteoritics	noble-minded	nightingale	neopaganism	notaphilism
methodistic	nubbing-cove	negationist	Neo-Catholic	notaphilist
matroclinic	nectar-guide	nightworker	neovitalism	net-practice
meteorolite	nickel-bloom	night-porter	neovitalist	naturalness
mythologise	neckerchief	night-attire	Neoplatonic	natural-born
mythologian	nucleolated	night-hunter	neologistic	notoriously
metrologist	nickelodeon	noiselessly	Neotropical	naturopathy
mythologist	nickel-ochre	neighbourly	nook-shotten	nature-study
mythopoeist	nickel-steel	noisomeness	nophellnite	Nototherium
meteorology	neck-herring	nail-varnish	napoleonite	nitty-gritty
methodology	noctlvagant	nikethamide	Napoleonism	nautch-girls
meteorogram	nictitation	nulliparity	Napoleonist	naughtiness
mythopoetic	noctivagous	nulliparous	nephologist	nourishable
mythography	nyctinastic	nullifidian	nephrectomy	nourishment
metaplastic	nyctitropic	name-calling	nephritical	naupliiform
metaphorist	noctilucent	nomadically	naphthalene	neuropathic
metaphrasis	noctilucous	name-dropper	naphthalise	neuroleptic
metoposcopy	nick-nackery	nomographer	narratively	neuroticism
metapsychic	necromancer	Nymphalidae	nurse-tender	neurologist
metaphysics	necromantic	nympholepsy	nerve-centre	neurotropic
motor-bandit	necroscopic	nymphomania	nerve-ending	neutraliser
materialise	necrophobia	nomological	nurserymaid	navel-orange
materialism	nyctophobia	nomenclator	northwardly	navel-string
materialist	necrophilia	nominatival	north-easter	novelettish
materiality	necrophilic	numerically	north-wester	novelettlst
motor-launch	necrobiosis	numismatics	northernise	never-fading
Mithradatic	necropoleis	numismatist	northernism	never-ending
Mithridatic	necrologist	nematophore	northermost	Novatianism
Mithraicism	nocuousness	nummulation	narcissuses	Novatianist
motor-driven	necessarian	nonharmonic	narrow-gauge	newscasting
metastasise	necessarily	non-marrying	nervousness	news-theatre
metasilicic	necessitate	non-partisan	nervuration	noxiousness
metasomatic	necessitied	non-metallic	nasofrontal	ob-and-soller
mutationist	necessitous	nondescript	nosographic	opalescence
methylamine	nocturnally	non-resident	nosographer	orange-grass
methylation	nudicaudate	non-delivery	nosological	orange-stick
mould-candle	nudicaulous	nonsensical	nose-nippers	orange-tawny
mould-facing	needfulness	non-feasance	nostradamic	orang-outang
mouse-colour	needlecraft	non-sequitur	Nostradamus	Oxalidaceae
mouth-honour	needle-furze	nonagesimal	nitraniline	onagraceous
mouth-friend	needle-point	nonchalance	notableness	oracularity
moustachial	needle-paper	nunnishness	notice-board	oraculously
mountain-ash	needlewoman	non-violence	notochordal	orbiculares
mountain-cat	Niersteiner	non-elective	netherlings	orbicularis
mountain-dew	Nietzschean	non-election	netherstock	orbicularly
mountaineer	nefariously	non-electric	netherwards	orchestrate
mountainous	nigrescence	nonillionth	nutrimental	orchestrina
mountain-tea	neglectable	nonplussing	nothingness	orchestrion
mountain-top	negligeable	non-unionist	nothing-gift	Orchidaceae
mountenance	negligently	non-specific	nutritively	orchiectomy
moveability	negrophobia	non-priority	nutritional	orchid-house

orchidology	overpayment	objectivate	oyster-patty	orthocentre
oscillative	overreached	objectively	obstetrical	orthophyric
oscillating	oneirodynia	objectivise	oyster-shell	osteophytic
occultation	oneiromancy	objectivism	oyster-tongs	osteoclasis
oscillation	overrunning	objectivist	oyster-woman	osteoplasty
oscillatory	oneiroscopy	objectivity	oyster-wench	orthoborate
oscillogram	overstretch	objurgative	obsignation	Ostrogothic
oecumenical	overstuffed	objurgation	obsignatory	osteologist
occipitally	overtrading	objurgatory	obstinately	orthodontia
old-maidhood	overtedious	oil-painting	obstipation	orthodontic
old-womanish	overthrower	olla-podrida	od's-pitikins	orthoepical
orderliness	overviolent	obliquation	obsolescent	orthodromic
opera-dancer	overweather	obliqueness	od's-bodikins	orthotropic
open-and-shut	overweening	obliquitous	oesophageal	orthography
overachieve	overwrestle	oblationary	observative	osteography
operatively	overwrought	obliterated	observation	orthopraxis
opera-singer	offhandedly	obliviously	observatory	orthostichy
operational	officialdom	Osmundaceae	observantly	orthopteran
over-anxiety	officialese	osmotically	obstructive	orthopteron
over-anxious	officialism	ommatophore	obstriction	orthostatic
overbearing	officiality	obmutescent	obstruction	octuplicate
overblanket	office-block	omniformity	oestrogenic	outbreeding
overbidding	olfactology	omnifarious	observingly	outcrossing
overbrimmed	officiously	oenological	obsessional	obtestation
overbalance	off-scouring	ornamentist	obscuration	octastichon
overburthen	offenceless	omnipresent	obscureness	outstanding
overcoating	offensively	oenophilist	obscurement	obtrusively
operculated	off-coloured	omnipatient	out-paramour	outbuilding
overcorrect	obfuscation	omnipotence	outwardness	outquarters
overcareful	organ-screen	omnipotency	ostracoderm	octave-flute
open-circuit	organically	owner-driver	octachordal	obumbration
overcasting	organisable	omniscience	ostreaceous	ovuliferous
overdraught	ophicalcite	Ornithogaea	ostreophage	obviousness
overdrowsed	ophidiarium	ornithosaur	ostreophagy	oxygenation
opeidoscope	ophthalmist	Ornithopoda	out-of-the-way	onychomancy
overdevelop	ochlophobia	ornithology	out-of-pocket	oxyrhynchus
overearnest	ophiologist	ornithopter	octagonally	oxy-chloride
overfraught	ochlocratic	obnoxiously	ontogenesis	oxy-fluoride
overfreedom	otherwhiles	onomasticon	ontogenetic	oxy-compound
overfreight	Ophiuroidea	ozonisation	octahedrite	oxy-hydrogen
overfulness	oviparousiy	odoriferous	octahedrons	Platanaceae
overflowing	oeil-de-boeuf	ozoniferous	ostrich-farm	placability
overforward	Origenistic	ozonosphere	ostrich-like	phalanstery
oreographic	originative	odorousness	outdistance	play-actress
overgrazing	origination	odontoblast	ontological	plaice-mouth
overgrainer	originality	odontograph	octillionth	praecordial
overgarment	olivine-rock	odontogenic	obtemperate	peat-casting
open-hearted	opinionated	odontologic	optometrist	peacemaking
overhandled	oriel-window	oppignerate	ostentation	planetarium
overhastily	opium-smoker	oppignorate	octonocular	plate-basket
overindulge	orientalise	opprobrious	octingenary	plate-warmer
obediential	Orientalism	opportunely	ostensively	phagedaenic
overleather	orientation	opportunism	octennially	peace-parted
oreological	Orientalist	opportunist	out-and-outer	peace-keeper
overmeasure	orientality	opportunity	orthopaedic	plateresque
open-mouthed	oligomerous	oarsmanship	osteopathic	prayerfully
ocean-stream	Oligochaeta	Ossianesque	orthoscopic	planetoidal
operoseness	oligochaete	obsecration	orthogenics	plate-powder
onerousness	oligochrome	obsidionary	orthopedics	peace-monger
overpicture	oviposition	obsceneness	orthopedist	place-monger
over-precise	onirocritic	oyster-field	osteodermic	planetology
overproduce	ominousness	oyster-knife	osteodermal	player-piano
overpitched	object-glass	oyster-plant	osteogenous	plate-armour

Placentalia	phantasiast	pedal-action	precedently	Pterosauria
place-hunter	piacularity	pedological	preterhuman	pterodactyl
prayer-wheel	planuliform	pad-elephant	premedicate	preconceive
playfulness	pharyngitic	paddle-shaft	premeditate	premovement
platforming	pharyngitis	paddle-wheel	preteritive	phenomenise
peach-brandy	platyrrhine	pedanticise	preterition	phenomenism
pharisaical	publication	pedanticism	prevenience	phenomenist
plagioclase	publishable	pedantocrat	preferrable	pleiomerous
phariseeism	pebble-stone	Podsnappery	Pherecratic	paedophilia
planimetric	pick-and-pick	pedunculate	prehensible	paedophilic
playing-card	peccability	Pedipalpida	presentable	plerophoria
platinotype	peccadillos	Podophyllum	preventable	predominate
planisphere	pococurante	podophyllin	preventible	prenominate
plagiostome	picket-fence	pedestalled	presentably	predominant
Plagiostomi	picket-guard	pedetentous	precentress	premonitive
placket-hole	pocket-glass	preparative	preceptress	prepositive
pearl-barley	pickelhaube	preparation	presentness	premonition
pearl-fisher	pocket-knife	preparatory	presentient	preposition
pearl-millet	pocket-money	Pre-Cambrian	presentment	premonitory
pearl-powder	pocket-piece	presanctify	prefectship	prepollence
pearl-mussel	pocket-sized	presagement	pretentious	prepollency
pearl-button	pacifically	prelateship	prefectural	precognosce
pearl-oyster	pacificator	prevalently	preservable	paedologist
plasmolysis	pectinately	prevaricate	pre-ignition	phenologist
plasmolytic	pectination	premaxillae	plethorical	poenologist
psammophile	pectisation	prevailment	predicament	paedodontic
psammophyte	packing-case	prefatorial	predicative	pre-conquest
plasmatical	peckishness	predatorily	predication	pleiotropic
pragmatical	peculiarise	prefatorily	prelibation	paedotrophy
Phasmatodea	peculiarity	prêt-à-porter	predicatory	pyelography
Phasmatidae	pecuniarily	precautious	preciseness	precontract
pragmatiser	pictorially	prematurely	pleximetric	puerperally
plain-dealer	Pycnogonida	prematurity	prediIected	pleurodynia
phaenogamic	pycnogonoid	plea-bargain	peevishness	pleuritical
Phaenogamae	pictography	presbyteral	Pterichthys	plessimeter
plaintively	pock-pudding	presciently	precipitate	plessimetry
phaenomenon	picture-card	preachiness	precipitant	Pleistocene
plain-spoken	picture-rail	prescindent	preliminary	pleasurable
plainstanes	picture-wire	preschooler	previsional	pleasurably
plainstones	picture-play	pleochroism	precipitous	pleasureful
planogamete	picture-cord	prescission	plenipotent	press-button
piano-school	picture-book	preoccupate	pteridology	pre-stressed
Platonicism	picture-goer	preoccupant	premiership	plentifully
peacock-like	picturesque	preoccupied	predictable	prestigious
peacock-fish	Pickwickian	preacquaint	pietistical	plenteously
peacock-blue	pachydactyl	pseudocubic	paediatrics	Plectoptera
piano-player	pachydermia	pseudograph	paediatrist	peep-through
plano-convex	pachydermic	pre-adamical	prehistoric	prestissimo
phagocytism	pachydermal	pseudomonad	prefigurate	prepunctual
phagocytose	pudibundity	pseudomonas	peelie-wally	prejudgment
prairie-wolf	pedicellate	pseudomorph	pre-election	prejudicate
plantocracy	Pedicularis	pre-adamitic	pre-eminence	prejudicant
practicable	pediculosis	preadmonish	pneumonitis	prelusively
practicably	pediculated	pseudopodia	pleomorphic	presumingly
practically	pedder-coffe	pseudoscope	pre-emptible	prejudicial
plasticiser	pedagogical	plebeianise	pneumatical	preaudience
prattlement	pedagoguery	plebeianism	pneumathode	prelusorily
plantigrade	pedagoguish	paederastic	preambulate	presumptive
phantomatic	pedagoguism	pretendedly	preambulary	presumption
Phaethontic	pudding-pipe	predeceased	plein-airist	pre-existent
praetorship	pudding-time	predecessor	preannounce	pigheadedly
plaster-work	Pedaliaceae	precedented	prerogative	pig-ignorant
phantasmata	paddle-board	preselector	phenogamous	piggishness

pugilistial
pignoration
pigeon-berry
pigeon-flier
pigeon-flyer
pigeon-house
pig-sticking
pig's-whisper
philanderer
privateness
primateship
philatelist
primariness
privatively
primatology
pliableness
pair-bonding
Priscianist
principally
pricelessly
price-fixing
prize-winner
painfulness
philhellene
primiparity
primiparous
primigenial
pairing-time
priming-wire
priming-iron
primitively
primitivism
primitivist
poikilocyte
prickle-back
prickliness
prickly-pear
prickly-heat
phillipsite
prismatical
Psilotaceae
philomathic
psilomelane
poison-gland
Psilophyton
prison-house
philosophic
philosopher
philologian
philologist
poisonously
poison-sumac
philogynist
philogynous
painstaking
priestcraft
psittacosis
pointedness
point-device
point-devise
print-seller
pointlessly
point-of-sale

pointillism
pointillist
point-source
paint-bridge
Primulaceae
poking-stick
polyandrous
palmatisect
palpability
pilgarlicky
pillar-saint
polyactinal
palm-cabbage
police-court
police-force
police-judge
pelican-fish
polycrotism
pilocarpine
polychroism
polychromic
polycarpous
police-state
policewoman
polycrystal
polydactyly
pulveration
pallescence
pollen-grain
poltergeist
pilferingly
Palaearctic
pullet-sperm
palaeotypic
pulverulent
polygraphic
palsgravine
Pelagianism
polygonally
polygenesis
polygenetic
polygonatum
phlegmonoid
phlegmonous
polyglottic
polyglottal
pale-hearted
pulchritude
polyhistory
palpitation
pollination
pillion-seat
pilniewinks
polemically
polymorphic
polymastism
palingenesy
palindromic
pillow-block
pillow-fight
pulmobranch
Pelton-wheel
polyonymous

polyphagous
Polyphemian
polyphonist
polypeptide
pilgrimager
polarimeter
polarimetry
poltroonery
pelargonium
polariscope
Polystichum
Palestinian
polystyrene
pilot-jacket
politicking
politically
polytechnic
pelotherapy
Polytrichum
pull-through
Politbureau
pullulation
pellucidity
pale-visaged
pole-vaulter
palmyra-wood
palmyra-nuts
polyzoarial
polyzoarium
pampas-grass
pomiculture
pumice-stone
Pompeian-red
pampelmoose
pompelmoose
pampelmouse
pompelmouse
pomegranate
pamphleteer
pomological
pompousness
pomfret-cake
Pandanaceae
pentavalent
pentadactyl
pentandrian
pentandrous
panjandarum
pentamerism
pentamerous
pentahedral
pentahedron
pantaletted
pantalettes
pentangular
pentathlete
pinnatisect
pentaploidy
pentazocine
pantalooned
Pentacrinus
pentactinal
pendant-post

pentagynian
pentacyclic
pentagynous
punicaceous
penicillate
Penicillium
paniculated
panic-monger
pinacotheca
panic-struck
ponderation
Pinteresque
ponderingly
panhellenic
Pandemoniac
pandemonium
Pandemonian
ponderosity
ponderously
Pentecostal
penteconter
punt-fishing
panegyrical
panegyricon
pantheistic
pinch-hitter
penthemimer
Punchinello
pantheology
pencil-cedar
pensileness
pensiveness
pinking-iron
pinkishness
pontificate
pontificals
pensionable
pantisocrat
pencil-stone
penological
penultimate
pentlandite
Panglossian
Pan-Slavonic
panomphaean
Pan-American
Pan-Anglican
peninsulate
pennoncelle
pantoscopic
pantophobia
pansophical
pantothenic
pantomimist
pantography
Pantocrator
panspermism
panspermist
penuriously
pancratiast
panislamism
panislamist
panpsychism

panpsychist
penetrative
punctuative
penetrating
penetralian
penetration
punctuation
punctualist
punctuality
Panathenaea
Panathenaic
punctilious
punctulated
penitential
panduriform
pendulosity
pendulously
pennyweight
penny-wisdom
pennywinkle
pinnywinkle
penny-a-liner
propagative
profanation
propagation
profanatory
prosaicness
prosaically
protandrous
profaneness
prolateness
probabilism
probabilist
probability
probational
probationer
protagonist
procaryotic
proud-minded
proterandry
proletarian
proletariat
proteaceous
prosenchyma
procerebral
procerebrum
proper-false
procephalic
phonemicise
phoneticism
phonetician
phonemicist
phoneticist
provenience
progenitrix
progeniture
Procellaria
proteolysis
proteolytic
prolegomena
proterozoic
proterogyny

prose-writer	proclaimant	phosphorism	paper-enamel	perfectible
professedly	problematic	phosphorous	paper-folder	pervertible
proleptical	prognathism	procreative	paper-credit	perceptibly
protectress	prognathous	procreation	paper-muslin	perfectness
projectment	provocateur	protractile	paper-cutter	perpetuable
progestogen	protopathic	protractive	pipe-stapple	persecutive
property-man	provocative	protraction	pipe-stopple	persecution
protectoral	prorogation	protrudable	pipistrelle	perpetually
prosecution	provocation	proprietary	papovavirus	perpetuance
prosecutrix	provocatory	proprietrix	puppy-walker	persecutory
proselytise	photonastic	programming	puppy-headed	perpetuator
proselytism	phototactic	protrusible	permanently	perceivable
proof-reader	protomartyr	Procrustean	permanganic	perceivably
proof-charge	Proboscidea	progressive	pervasively	purificator
proof-spirit	proboscides	progressism	purgatively	paraffinoid
prop-forward	photoactive	progression	parvanimity	paraffin-oil
propforward	proboscises	progressist	portability	paraffin-wax
proof-puller	provokement	prostration	port-admiral	paragraphia
prong-horned	photoperiod	proctodaeal	purgatorial	paragraphic
ploughshare	photo-relief	proctodaeum	purgatorian	paragrapher
plough-staff	photo-resist	prosthetics	parablepsis	pyrogravure
plough-stilt	photometric	prosthetist	parableptic	peregrinate
ptochocracy	prolongable	proctorship	parabolical	paragliding
prothallial	phonophobia	proctoscope	parabolanus	peregrinity
prothallium	photophobia	proctoscopy	pyroballogy	paragenesia
prothalamia	photophobic	prostitutor	parabematic	paragenesis
prothalloid	photophilic	prostatitis	pure-blooded	perigenesis
prophylaxis	photophonic	procuration	parabaptism	paragenetic
prothrombin	photochromy	procuratory	pork-butcher	pyrogenetic
prochronism	Prototheria	protuberate	port-charges	paraglossae
prothoracic	protophytic	protuberant	pericranial	paraglossal
prothoraces	provokingly	profuseness	pericranium	pyrognostic
prophesying	photo-finish	procurement	pyroclastic	Perigordian
prophetical	proposition	producement	periclitate	perigastric
prophetship	photoglyphy	promulgator	parochially	parchedness
prophethood	pronouncing	propylamine	Paracelsian	perchlorate
proximately	protonotary	proxy-wedded	pericentric	perihepatic
prodigalise	protococcal	promycelium	pericentral	porphyritic
proximation	Protococcus	propylitise	paracrostic	purchasable
prodigality	prosopopeia	Procyonidae	pericardiac	pertinacity
promiscuity	protocolise	pop-fastener	pericardial	pervicacity
promiscuous	photocopier	pipe-dreamer	pericardium	pertinently
proliferate	phonologist	peppercorny	pericardian	participate
promiseless	protocolist	pepper-grass	paracetamol	participant
profiterole	protocolled	pepperiness	parachutist	partitively
proliferous	photosphere	papier-mâché	perichylous	participial
prominently	phototropic	pop-festival	peridesmium	partibility
providently	phonography	poppet-valve	paradoxical	percipience
prolificacy	photography	puppet-valve	Paradoxides	partitioner
propitiable	proconsular	peptisation	purse-taking	percipiency
promisingly	provostship	pupillarity	perseverate	porriginous
prohibitive	prolocution	pipe-lighter	perseverant	portionless
prohibition	prolocutrix	papilliform	persevering	parti-coated
prolificity	phonotypist	populariser	purse-seiner	permissible
proficience	protogynous	papillulate	purse-bearer	permissibly
provisional	prospective	paper-hanger	porter-house	permittance
proficiency	prospecting	paper-making	porterhouse	persistence
prosiliency	prospection	paper-sailor	parheliacal	persistency
prohibitory	promptitude	papyraceous	permeameter	particulate
propitiator	phosphorate	piperaceous	perpetrable	parallactic
provisorily	phosphorise	paper-feeder	perpetrator	parallelise
propinquity	phosphorite	paper-weight	parpen-stone	paralleling
poodle-faker	phosphonium	paper-office	perceptible	parallelism

parallelist	paraplectic	persulphate	Pythagorean	plume-pluckt
paraldehyde	paraphiliac	persuasible	Pythagorism	pluriserial
paraleipsis	paripinnate	perquisitor	pot-valorous	plumigerous
Portlandian	pyrophorous	perlustrate	putrescible	pruning-bill
perplexedly	perspirable	periwigging	putrescence	pruning-hook
parsley-pert	paraphraser	part-writing	putrefiable	prudishness
paramedical	periphrases	party-coated	potteringly	pruriginous
pyramidical	periphrasis	party-spirit	pattern-shop	Paulinistic
pyramidally	paraphraxia	passacaglia	pitifulness	pluviometer
paramaecium	paraphraxis	passage-boat	pitchblende	plutologist
paramoecium	peripeteian	piscatorial	patch-pocket	plutonomist
portmanteau	peripatetic	pissasphalt	potting-shed	plutocratic
paramorphic	part-payment	push-bicycle	pettishness	plum-pudding
perimorphic	parapsychic	post-captain	patrilineal	Prussianise
paramastoid	portraitist	pesteringly	patrilinear	Prussianism
perambulate	portraiture	post-exilian	patricianly	plumularian
paramountcy	purpresture	posteriorly	phthiriasis	pavingstone
paramountly	pyrargyrite	pasteuriser	patriclinic	pivot-bridge
perennation	peristalith	pushfulness	pettifogger	powder-flask
paronychial	peristalsis	pasigraphic	patrimonial	powerlessly
paranthelia	peristaltic	post-glacial	petticoated	power-diving
parentheses	peristerite	paschal-lamb	patriarchal	power-driven
parenthesis	parascenium	passiveness	patristical	phylacteric
parenthetic	perispermic	pestiferous	patelliform	psychiatric
perennially	perispermal	pestilently	petalomania	psychically
phrenologic	perishingly	passing-bell	potamogeton	psychodrama
paronomasia	parasuicide	passing-note	potentially	psychedelia
paranephric	parasailing	possibilism	patent-right	psychedelic
perinephric	parishioner	possibilist	patent-rolls	psychodelic
paranephros	paraselenae	possibility	poting-stick	psychograph
partnership	phrasemaker	possibility	pathogenous	psychagogue
phrenetical	part-singing	pessimistic	pathophobia	psychogenic
perineurium	peristomial	postillator	patronising	psychologic
perforative	perissology	Passion-week	patroclinic	psychometer
personalise	phraseology	passionless	patroonship	psychomotor
personative	phraseogram	Passion-tide	pathologist	psychometry
personating	parasitical	Passion-play	petrologist	psychonomic
personalism	parasitosis	Poseidonian	petropounds	psychopathy
percolation	piratically	piscicolous	pathography	physicalism
perforation	pyrotechnic	piscivorous	petrography	physicalist
personation	parotiditis	posological	piteousness	physicality
personalist	perithecial	post-nuptial	patrol-wagon	physiocracy
personality	perithecium	pastoralism	patrolwoman	physiognomy
purposeless	pyritohedra	pastoralist	pataphysics	physitheism
purpose-like	puritanical	pestologist	paternalism	physicianer
park-officer	peritonaeal	pastourelle	paternoster	physiciancy
personified	peritonaeum	postponence	potash-water	physiologic
personifier	peritonitic	postscenium	potass-water	physiologus
periodicity	peritonitis	postulation	potato-apple	physiolater
performable	paratrooper	pustulation	potato-bogle	physiolatry
performance	paratyphoid	postulatory	potato-chips	phylloclade
periodontia	parathyroid	pasture-land	petitionary	ptyalagogic
periodontal	perduration	pastureless	petitioning	ptyalagogue
parlour-maid	permutation	pasquinader	petitionist	phyllomania
pornography	perturbable	post-village	pit-dwelling	phyllotaxis
purportedly	perturbedly	pussywillow	putty-powder	phycophaein
purportless	perturbance	pussyfooter	pluralistic	phytophagic
periostitic	perturbator	Petrarchise	plum-blossom	phytochrome
periostitis	perfunctory	Petrarchism	plumber-work	phycologist
perlocution	persuadable	Petrarchian	pound-master	phytologist
perspective	perfumeless	Petrarchist	pound-weight	phytotomist
perspicuity	parturition	pot-walloner	pound-keeper	phytography
perspicuous	perduellion	pot-walloper	pauselessly	Plymouthite

Plymouthism	quinsy-berry	ribbon-grass	recessively	refractable
Plymouthist	quiescently	rib-roasting	race-suicide	refectioner
phytosterol	quintillion	rebarbative	recessional	refocillate
phycomycete	quilting-bee	Ribesiaceae	recluseness	rifacimenti
phycocyanin	quizzically	rabattement	recountment	rifacimento
quandong-nut	quotability	reclamation	recruitment	refectorian
quaveringly	quoteworthy	rock-and-roll	recoverable	refreshment
quaternion'd	reawakening	rectangular	race-walking	refreshener
qualitative	readability	Rechabitism	reductively	reflexively
qualifiable	rear-admiral	rechallenge	radicalness	reflexology
qualifiedly	reascension	reclaimable	radicellose	reflectance
quacksalver	rhabdomancy	reclaimably	redactorial	refrigerate
quadriennia	rhabdomyoma	rock-breaker	redding-kame	refrigerant
quarrel-pane	Rhabdophora	rice-biscuit	redding-comb	refringency
quarrelling	reamendment	ricocheting	reddishness	raffishness
quadrillion	reach-me-down	ricochetted	riddle-me-ree	ruffian-like
quarrelsome	road-hoggish	rock-climber	redeliverer	refinedness
quarrellous	roadholding	rock-crystal	rodomontade	reformative
quadrennium	realisation	racket-court	rudimentary	reformation
quarrington	reanimation	recremental	redemptible	reformadoes
quadrupedal	reading-lamp	ricketiness	redundantly	reformatory
quadraphony	reading-desk	rocket-motor	riding-cloak	referendary
quadrophony	reading-book	rocket-plane	riding-glove	referential
quadratical	reaping-hook	racket-press	riding-habit	reformulate
quarry-water	reading-room	rocket-range	riding-horse	regretfully
quaestorial	realignment	rickettsiae	rodenticide	regredience
quantometer	reallotment	rickettsial	riding-light	ragged-robin
quarter-back	road-mending	rock-forming	riding-rhyme	regrettable
quarter-jack	readmission	recognitive	riding-skirt	regrettably
quarter-rail	rhamnaceous	recognition	radiocarbon	rigging-loft
quarter-deck	reappraisal	recognitory	radiolarian	rigging-tree
quarter-seal	reappraiser	reclination	radioactive	roguishness
quarter-wind	Rhamphastos	rectipetaly	radio-beacon	regenerable
quarter-road	realpolitik	rectiserial	radiometric	regenerator
quarter-note	reapportion	rocking-tool	radiophonic	regionalise
quarter-tone	rear-roasted	rectifiable	radiologist	regionalism
quarter-bred	rhapsodical	rectilineal	radiography	regionalist
quarter-evil	reassertion	rectilinear	reduplicate	regardfully
queene-apple	reassurance	rock-leather	Rüdesheimer	regurgitate
queen-regent	road-scraper	recollected	rediscovery	regurgitant
queenliness	reactionary	recalescent	redetermine	registrable
queen-mother	reactionist	recalculate	redoubtable	right-handed
queen-stitch	readvertise	recommender	re-enactment	right-hander
queer-basher	ready-witted	race-meeting	reef-builder	right-minded
questionary	ready-to-wear	recumbently	reed-bunting	right-winger
questioning	ready-monied	recombinant	re-encourage	right-angled
questionist	rib-vaulting	recommittal	reed-drawing	righteously
querulously	rubicundity	recantation	re-endowment	rehydration
queez-maddam	rubber-cored	recondition	re-elevation	rhizanthous
quibblingly	rabbet-joint	reconnoitre	re-emergence	rain-chamber
quitch-grass	rubber-stamp	reconstruct	re-existence	reincarnate
quincuncial	rubefacient	receptacula	rheumatical	reiterative
quiveringly	rubefaction	rice-pudding	rheumaticky	reiteration
quick-change	rubrication	receptivity	rheumateese	reinflation
quick-firing	rubbing-post	reciprocate	rhetorician	reification
quick-witted	rubbish-heap	reciprocant	re-emphasise	rhizomatous
quicksilver	rabbit-hutch	recuperable	re-expansion	rhizocarpic
quicken-tree	rabbit-punch	recuperator	reed-sparrow	rhinoscopic
quick-freeze	rebukefully	recordation	re-establish	rhizogenous
quick-frozen	Rabelaisian	recurrently	rheotropism	rhinoplasty
quill-driver	rubble-stone	rack-railway	re-education	rhinologist
quinquereme	ribonucleic	recirculate	reed-warbler	rhizosphere
quinquennia	rebroadcast	rock-sparrow	refrangible	rhinorrhoea

ruinousness	rancorously	rarefaction	reticularly	revoltingly
reinstation	rinforzando	Rastafarian	reticulated	revengeless
reinsertion	ring-stopper	researchful	rate-cutting	revengement
reinsurance	ring-straked	restatement	rother-beast	revendicate
reintegrate	renewedness	rascalliest	rottenstone	revindicate
reintroduce	ring-winding	rush-bearing	rotogravure	revengingly
reinterment	Rhopalocera	rosy-bosomed	retributive	reverberate
reinterpret	rhombohedra	rose-cheeked	retribution	reverberant
rejoicement	root-climber	rosy-cheeked	retributory	reverseless
rejoicingly	rhodium-wood	rose-campion	retrievable	reversional
rejuvenesce	reorientate	Rosicrucian	retrievably	reversioner
rejuvenator	rhododaphne	rose-diamond	retaliative	reverential
releasement	riotousness	residential	retaliation	riverbottom
reliability	root-pruning	respectable	retaliatory	river-dragon
reluctation	rood-steeple	respectably	rattle-brain	river-driver
reluctantly	replaceable	respectless	rattle-pated	river-mussel
relic-monger	replacement	restfulness	rattlesnake	ravishingly
roller-skate	raptatorial	resignation	retinaculum	revisionary
rallentando	republisher	respiration	retinacular	revisionism
roller-towel	rapscallion	rustication	retentively	revisionist
religionary	rapaciously	respiratory	retentivity	rivet-hearth
religionise	repudiative	restiveness	retinispora	revivifying
religionism	repudiation	restitutive	retinospora	revivescent
religionist	reprehender	restitution	retinoscopy	reviviscent
religiosity	repleteness	restitutory	rationalise	rhynchocoel
religiously	representer	resultative	rationalism	rhynchodont
rolling-mill	repleviable	reselection	rationalist	rhyme-scheme
rule-of-thumb	replenished	resplendent	rationality	rhyme-letter
role-playing	replenisher	resemblance	retroactive	rhythmicity
relatedness	repressible	resentfully	retroaction	razzamatazz
relationism	repressibly	resentingly	retrocedent	scarabaeist
relationist	replication	restorative	ratiocinate	scarabaeoid
rallying-cry	repellantly	restoration	retroflexed	sea-lavender
remediation	repellently	respondence	ration-money	svarabhakti
remigration	repulsively	respondency	retro-rocket	scalariform
rumti-iddity	repellingly	Russophobia	retroussage	shamanistic
rompishness	rope-machine	responsible	retrobulbar	stalagmitic
remembrance	repentantly	responsibly	retardative	stalactical
romanticise	repentingly	responsions	Rotarianism	stalactitic
romanticism	ripsnorting	resipiscent	retardation	stalactited
romanticist	reprobative	reservation	retardatory	stalactital
remunerable	reprobation	reservatory	retiredness	scabbedness
remunerator	reprobatory	restrictive	ratatouille	scamblingly
reminiscent	reproachful	restriction	ritournelle	soap-boiling
remonstrate	reprovingly	restructure	rhumb-course	shad-bellied
remonstrant	reprography	resurrector	raunchiness	swag-bellied
remorseless	reportingly	restraining	round-backed	snatch-block
remittently	repartition	restringent	roundedness	starch-grain
rumgumption	reportorial	resuscitate	round-headed	starchiness
ramgunshoch	reposedness	resuscitant	round-leaved	searchingly
rumbustical	reposefully	resistively	round-winged	snatchingly
rumbustious	repetitious	resistingly	round-arched	stanchioned
removedness	raptureless	resistivity	rouge-et-noir	searchlight
ring-carrier	rupturewort	resourceful	rough-legged	star-crossed
rangefinder	rapturously	rescue-grass	rough-coated	starch-paper
renegotiate	requiteless	rosewood-oil	rough-footed	snatch-purse
rinthereout	requirement	rat-catching	rough-spoken	search-party
running-hand	requitement	retraceable	rough-string	sea-scorpion
running-gear	requisition	rat-kangaroo	rouping-wife	snatch-thief
running-knot	requisitory	rateability	raucousness	sea-scouting
renaissance	reradiation	ritualistic	revaccinate	span-counter
randle-perch	ruridecanal	retranslate	rival-hating	stand-patter
Runyonesque	rarefactive	retractable	revaluation	shard-beetle

stand-offish	searing-iron	star-studded	subumbrella	successless
standing-bed	slavishness	spastically	subindicate	Sachertorte
standing-cup	snakishness	scant-o'-grace	subincision	saccharated
standardise	seasickness	swarthiness	Subungulata	succinctory
stage-manage	sea-milkwort	startlingly	subungulate	sacrilegist
spacefaring	spaniel-like	smart-ticket	subrogation	sucking-fish
slave-labour	station-hand	star-thistle	subdominant	sickishness
slate-pencil	staminodium	stactometer	subcontract	sacrificial
shamelessly	stasimorphy	stadtholder	subcontrary	section-mark
space-heater	statistical	smartypants	subcortical	sectionally
stage-effect	slack-handed	shatter-pate	subspecific	Socinianise
sea-hedgehog	shackle-bone	spatterdash	suburbanise	Socinianism
stave-church	shackle-bolt	scatteredly	suburbanite	secondarily
shapeliness	sparklessly	scattershot	suburbanism	second-class
stateliness	sparklingly	scatterling	saburration	second-floor
slaveringly	Stahlianism	scattergood	subarration	second-guess
stage-flower	stall-master	spatter-dock	subornation	sick-nursing
stage-player	small-screen	spatter-work	suburbanity	second-rater
statesmanly	stall-reader	sea-furbelow	subtreasury	seconds-hand
scale-insect	Stahlhelmer	statute-book	subtractive	second-sight
shareholder	small-minded	statutorily	subtraction	sociopathic
slave-holder	snail-flower	sea-purslane	seborrhoeic	sociometric
scaremonger	stalling-ken	sea-cucumber	subordinate	sociologism
state-monger	smallholder	Sabbatarian	subordinary	sociologist
shameworthy	sea-elephant	subpanation	sober-minded	sacrocostal
slave-trader	scarlet-bean	subbasement	subtropical	succourable
stage-fright	swallow-tail	subcategory	subcritical	succourless
scale-armour	shallowness	submarginal	sybaritical	sycophantic
state-prison	swallow-dive	Sabbathless	sober-suited	sycophantry
slate-writer	swallow-hole	subtacksman	substrative	secessional
space-travel	swallow-wort	subscribing	substractor	sick-service
slave-driver	spasmodical	subeconomic	substandard	sacculation
stage-driver	spasmatical	subscapular	substantive	succulently
stage-struck	shawnee-wood	sabre-rattle	substantial	seductively
share-pusher	stainlessly	subdeaconry	subitaneous	side-cutting
spade-guinea	staunchness	submergible	substituent	sedigitated
scaberulous	spawning-bed	submergence	substituted	saddle-cloth
slave-owning	seasonality	subterhuman	subjugation	saddle-girth
stateswoman	sea-rosemary	subdelirium	subluxation	saddle-horse
stagflation	sea-colewort	subaerially	subjunctive	saddle-nosed
snaffle-rein	shadowgraph	subregional	subduedness	sedimentary
scaffoldage	sea-longworm	subterminal	subaudition	sodomitical
scaffolding	shadowiness	submersible	subsumptive	sedentarily
seal-fishing	Slavonicise	subsensible	subsumption	sad-coloured
staff-system	sialorrhoea	subvertical	submultiple	sideropenia
shanghaiing	sialography	subjectship	subcultural	seditionary
shaggedness	sea-dotterel	subsequence	subaxillary	seditiously
spang-cockle	sharp-tailed	subservient	such-and-such	Sadduceeism
swagger-cane	stamp-office	sublimation	sacramental	stewardship
swagger-coat	scalpriform	subdiaconal	sociability	spelaeology
slaughterer	sharp-witted	sublimeness	socialistic	steganogram
spathaceous	sharp-ground	subtileness	sick-benefit	stepbrother
staphylitis	stair-carpet	subdivisive	sick-chamber	speechcraft
swan-hopping	staurolitic	subdivision	sockdolager	speech-crier
suasiveness	seal-rookery	subvitreous	sockdoliger	sketchiness
scapigerous	stair-turret	submissible	sockdologer	speechifier
seaming-lace	sparrow-hawk	submissness	succedaneum	stencilling
staging-base	sea-crawfish	subdistrict	secretarial	speech-maker
sparingness	sparrow-bill	subsistence	societarian	steadfastly
skating-rink	sea-crayfish	sublittoral	secretariat	steady-going
shaving-soap	Shaksperian	subglobular	secretively	spendthrift
staging-post	snapshooter	subclinical	sickeningly	speedometer
staging-area	seamstressy	subimagines	secretional	step-dancing

slenderness	Spermophyta	safe-breaker	school-child	stichometry
siege-basket	spermaphyte	safe-blowing	schoolgoing	smithsonite
stereobatic	spermophyte	safe-cracker	schoolhouse	Smithsonian
stereograph	steam-driven	soft-centred	school-point	smithereens
Stevengraph	spermatical	safe-conduct	schoolwards	spiniferous
stereometer	spermatheca	safe-deposit	spherically	spinigerous
stereometry	spermatozoa	soft-hearted	spheroidise	sliding-keel
skeletonise	Steinberger	sufficience	spherulitic	shiningness
stereoptics	sternsheets	sufficiency	spherometer	smilingness
stereophony	stern-chaser	safe-keeping	schismatise	sailing-ship
stereosonic	sternotribe	suffocative	schism-house	sailing-boat
stereoscope	sternutator	suffocating	schistosity	sliding-rule
stereoscopy	Stegosaurus	suffocation	Schistosoma	swinishness
stereotypic	sceuophylax	suffragette	schistosome	spiritistic
stereotyped	stenochrome	saffron-cake	schottische	spirillosis
stereotyper	stenochromy	soft-shelled	schizogenic	spirit-level
stereotaxia	scenography	safety-catch	Schizanthus	spirituelle
stereotaxic	stenography	safety-match	schizopodal	spiritually
stereotaxis	stenotypist	safety-valve	Schizophyta	spiritualty
sledge-chair	sweep-washer	suffumigate	schizophyte	spirit-world
sdeignfully	sleep-walker	sagaciously	spinach-beet	stickleback
Spergularia	sheep-farmer	segregative	Scitamineae	stickleader
stephanotis	sheep-master	segregation	suitability	stick-insect
shepherdess	steepe-downe	suggestible	spiraculate	slickenside
stethoscope	steeplejack	segmentally	swim-bladder	snickersnee
stethoscopy	steeple-fair	significate	ship-breaker	Skillcentre
sheriffship	sleeplessly	significant	shipbuilder	skilligalee
sheriffalty	steeple-bush	signifiable	stilbestrol	skilligolee
seemingness	sheep-biting	sigillarian	ship-biscuit	stifle-joint
specificate	sheep-silver	sigillation	spin-bowling	spill-stream
specifiable	sleeping-bag	sigmoidally	switchboard	still-hunter
specificity	sleeping-car	sign-painter	switchblade	seismograph
specialiser	sweepstakes	sugar-coated	stitchcraft	seismologic
sleek-headed	steerage-way	Sagittarius	scincoidian	seismometer
speakership	sherris-sack	sight-screen	ship-captain	seismometry
sneck-drawer	spessartite	sight-reader	switch-plant	seismonasty
shell-jacket	spectrality	sightseeing	spindle-legs	skimmington
shell-parrot	stentmaster	sightlessly	spindle-side	shimmy-shake
shellacking	spectacular	sightliness	spindle-tree	skirmishing
steel-headed	sceptically	sight-singer	swivel-block	seismoscope
swell-headed	sceptreless	sagittiform	swivel-chair	stigmatical
stellifying	spectre-crab	sight-player	swine's-cress	scientistic
spellbinder	sleuth-hound	sightworthy	spinescence	seigniorage
steel-plated	sweet-cicely	sign-writing	stipendiate	seigniorial
spelling-bee	sweet-willow	sphragistic	stipendiary	Scientology
stellionate	sheath-knife	schwärmerei	spinelessly	spinnerette
steelworker	sheet-anchor	sphacelated	shiveringly	seigneurial
shell-crater	sweet-potato	scheckaton	stilettoing	spirometric
sperm-candle	spectrology	sphaeridium	slime-fungus	Spirochaeta
steam-jacket	sheet-copper	schrecklich	spider-wheel	spirochaete
steam-packet	spectrogram	Sphagnaceae	stiff-necked	Spinozistic
steam-hammer	scent-bottle	sphagnology	spifflicate	sailor-maker
steam-launch	steatopygia	sphygmology	skilfulness	shin-plaster
spermicidal	shelterless	sphygmogram	stiff-rumped	slipperwort
steam-vessel	sweater-girl	scholiastic	swing-handle	ship-railway
steam-shovel	spectatress	schillerise	sling-backed	stirrup-bone
steam-digger	sheet-rubber	scholarship	swingle-hand	stirrup-dram
steam-plough	speculative	scholar-like	swingletree	stirrup-iron
steam-engine	speculation	schematical	swingeingly	stirrup-pump
steam-boiler	speculatist	sphincteric	swing-plough	spinsterdom
steam-roller	speculatory	sphincteral	swingometer	spinsterish
spermophile	speculatrix	school-board	swing-bridge	spinsterial
Spermaphyta	sleeve-board	schoolcraft	slightingly	spinsterian

scissor-case	self-despair	salmon-berry	sempiternal	synchoresis
scissor-tail	self-devoted	salmon-coble	sempiternum	synthesiser
scissorwise	self-example	salmonellae	somniferous	synthetical
scissor-bill	self-excited	self-offence	summit-level	syndicalism
stilt-walker	self-elected	self-opinion	somnivolent	syndication
Saintpaulia	silver-grain	syllogistic	somniculous	syndicalist
stiltedness	silveriness	saloon-rifle	semi-jubilee	sentimental
stintedness	self-evident	salmon-spear	simpliciter	singing-bird
skittle-ball	self-evolved	seldom-times	simplifying	sinking-ripe
shiftlessly	silver-plate	sallow-thorn	sembling-box	sinking-fund
saintliness	silver-point	salmon-trout	sampler-work	sensitively
swift-winged	silver-paper	self-planted	semi-monthly	sensibility
scintillate	sallee-rover	solipsistic	semanticist	sensitivity
scintillant	silversmith	sclerocauly	somnolently	Sanskritist
shirt-sleeve	silver-stick	scleroderma	sympodially	single-entry
stilt-plover	spleen-stone	sclerometer	symposiarch	Sinological
shift-worker	sylleptical	solarimeter	symbolistic	single-phase
swift-footed	silvestrian	sclerophyll	symbology	singlestick
shinty-stick	sylvestrian	sclerotioid	semipalmate	single-soled
shirt-button	silver-white	sclerotitis	semi-skilled	synanthesis
stimulative	self-feeding	self-sealing	semasiology	synanthetic
stimulating	self-feeling	self-starter	semi-tubular	synonimical
stimulation	self-figured	splash-board	somatically	synonymicon
stipulation	self-fertile	self-subdued	somatogenic	synonymatic
stipulatory	solifluxion	self-sterile	somatologic	syngnathous
sojournment	selaginella	self-seeking	symptomatic	syncopation
syllabarium	self-healing	salesperson	sumptuosity	sinfonietta
sallal-berry	self-harming	splashproof	sumptuously	sindonology
soldatesque	sulphureous	self-support	somatoplasm	sinuousness
self-affairs	sulphur-root	self-service	somatotonia	Sinophilism
saleability	sulphurwort	self-serving	somatotonic	synoptistic
salvability	sulphurator	self-trained	somewhither	sinupallial
solvability	sillimanite	split-screen	Santalaceae	synergistic
syllabicity	solmisation	spluttering	sensational	song-sparrow
saltatorial	saltimbocca	split-second	syntactical	sinisterity
self-assumed	saltimbanco	self-tempted	sansculotte	sand-skipper
self-assured	self-induced	solutionist	synecologic	sinistrally
salableness	salpingitic	self-torment	sansculotte	sinistrorse
self-blinded	salpingitis	self-torture	synecdochic	sanctuarise
self-charity	saltishness	silk-thrower	sang-de-boeuf	sanctifying
self-cocking	selfishness	sclate-stane	synodically	senate-house
salicaceous	self-imposed	salsuginous	Sandemanian	senatorship
self-created	soldiership	self-winding	sincereness	sand-thrower
selectively	saltierwise	silkworm-gut	senselessly	singularise
selectivity	soldierlike	self-worship	sansevieria	singularism
self-culture	soldier-crab	splay-footed	synoeciosis	singularist
self-command	self-invited	somnambulic	syndesmosis	singularity
self-concern	self-knowing	somnambular	syndesmotic	sensualness
self-conceit	self-loading	sympathiser	synoecology	sanguineous
self-concept	self-locking	sympathetic	sinlessness	Sanguinaria
self-content	self-limited	summariness	sunlessness	Sanguisorba
self-centred	soliloquise	summational	sanderswood	sandwich-man
self-control	self-mastery	semi-annular	syntectical	syndyasmian
self-closing	self-misused	semicircled	sententious	sporangiole
selectorial	solanaceous	semi-diurnal	sonofabitch	stomach-ache
salaciously	splenectomy	sympetalous	sin-offering	stomachical
self-covered	splinter-bar	simnel-bread	songfulness	stomachless
self-drawing	selenograph	summer-house	synagogical	stomach-pump
solidifying	self-neglect	simperingly	synchromesh	sloganising
self-defence	splendidous	semi-ellipse	synchronise	Stomatopoda
self-delight	salinometer	symmetrical	synchronism	stomatology
self-denying	splendorous	sempervivum	synchronous	shopbreaker
solid-hoofed	splenetical	symphonious	synchrotron	snow-bunting

scorbutical	snow-leopard	supremeness	supervolute	streetwards
scorchingly	shoe-latchet	saplessness	superpraise	scruffiness
Scotch-Irish	slot-machine	septentrion	suppressant	serigraphic
stoicalness	storm-petrel	septicaemia	suppressive	serigrapher
Scotchwoman	storm-centre	septiferous	suppression	scragginess
sword-bearer	storm-beaten	syphilology	superstruct	sprightless
sword-shaped	storm-window	septifragal	superlunary	serviceable
spondulicks	storm-signal	sophistical	superfusion	serviceably
spondylitis	showmanship	suppliantly	supersubtle	serviceless
swordplayer	storm-tossed	supplicavit	sapotaceous	service-line
sword-dollar	storm-troops	sepulchrous	suppurative	service-pipe
snow-dropper	storm-stayed	Sapindaceae	suppuration	service-wire
stone-falcon	scoundrelly	saponaceous	sequestrate	service-flat
stonewaller	scopolamine	saponifying	sequestrant	service-book
stone-hammer	scotomatous	sipunculoid	sequestered	service-room
store-farmer	spodomantic	sapropelite	surtarbrand	service-tree
store-cattle	Scolopendra	saprolegnia	surface-mail	straight-arm
stone-marten	sporogenous	saprogenous	surbasement	straight-cut
shovel-board	scopophobia	saprophytic	spread-eagle	straightish
smokescreen	scopophilia	suppositive	streakiness	straight-jet
smoke-helmet	scopophilic	supposition	streaminess	straight-out
storekeeper	sporophoric	suppository	screamingly	straightway
smokelessly	sporophytic	saprobiotic	spreadingly	serpiginous
showeriness	sporogonium	siphonogamy	streamingly	strait-laced
scoleciform	snobography	supportable	streamlined	strait-lacer
stone-plover	sporocystic	supportably	surpassable	servitorial
stone-colour	stopping-out	supportless	servant-maid	strike-bound
shower-proof	scorpion-fly	supportress	servant-lass	strike-fault
stone-bruise	Scorpionida	supportment	sarcastical	serological
stoneground	shop-steward	sepiostaire	servantless	scrimshoner
stone's-throw	slow-sighted	supportance	servantship	scrimshandy
stone-curlew	show-stopper	supernatant	servant-girl	scrimpiness
stone-cutter	sponsorship	superjacent	serratulate	stramineous
spokeswoman	short-handed	superlative	scribacious	scrumptious
sponge-cloth	scout-master	superfamily	shrubberied	springboard
snow-goggles	smooth-bored	supertanker	shrubbiness	string-board
smörgåsbord	spottedness	supermarket	strabometer	spring-clean
soothsaying	scouthering	superdainty	stroboscope	strangeness
soothfastly	smooth-faced	superfatted	surf-bathing	stringently
scoriaceous	Scottifying	supernature	scrub-turkey	spring-house
scoring-card	shortchange	superabound	scrub-typhus	springiness
shoeing-horn	short-winded	superoctave	sericulture	stringiness
show-jumping	shooting-box	superscribe	Straduarius	shrinkingly
stock-saddle	spontaneity	superscript	suraddition	serendipity
stocktaking	spontaneous	superfetate	stridulator	strenuosity
stock-market	snotty-nosed	supersedere	screencraft	syringotomy
stock-farmer	shortcoming	supersedeas	sarcenchyme	strenuously
shock-headed	smooth-paced	superheater	surrenderee	string-piece
stock-feeder	short-spoken	supersedure	surrenderer	strongpoint
shopkeeping	short-priced	supercharge	surrenderor	shrink-proof
stockpiling	Scottishman	supercherie	screech-hawk	strengthful
snorkelling	short-staple	superficial	shriekingly	strangulate
stockinette	sportswoman	supervision	surveillant	spring-wheat
stock-jobber	sporulation	superficies	streetlight	spring-water
stock-holder	story-teller	supervisory	surgeonship	stringy-bark
stockbroker	supracostal	superfluity	surgeon-fish	strongyloid
shock-troops	sapucaia-nut	superfluous	sarsen-stone	surrogation
shoe-leather	supremacism	superimpose	serpentlike	sarcomatous
shoulder-bag	suprematism	superintend	serpentinic	sarcoidosis
shouldering	septenarius	superinduce	serpent-star	sorrowfully
smouldering	supremacist	superioress	surrebuttal	sarcophagal
shop-lifting	suprematist	superiority	surrebutter	sarcophagus
stool-pigeon	Septembrist	supernormal	screen-wiper	sartorially

Sorbonnical	suscitation	south-easter	travail-pang	transiently
surmounting	suspiration	south-wester	travail-pain	transsexual
surrounding	sessile-eyed	southernise	thanatology	transceiver
seriousness	sessionally	southernism	thanatopsis	transfixion
sarcocystis	sesame-grass	southermost	thalassemia	transhipper
strap-hanger	susurration	saurischian	thalassemic	transpierce
strap-shaped	sesquialter	studiedness	tharborough	transmitted
scrappiness	sesquioxide	soul-killing	thatch-board	transmittal
Soroptimist	sesquipedal	soup-kitchen	Tragelaphus	transmitter
scriptorial	satiability	spur-leather	trade-fallen	transfigure
scriptorium	situational	squalidness	tracelessly	transilient
scripophile	setter-forth	squandering	tragedienne	transalpine
scripophily	sitting-room	squintingly	trapezoidal	transandine
scrape-penny	sottishness	sauropodous	traversable	translocate
scripturism	settledness	sauropsidan	trabeculate	transponder
scripturist	settling-day	stump-speech	tradeswoman	transposing
surprisedly	satanically	scuppernong	trafficless	transsonics
stratocracy	satin-finish	stump-orator	trafficking	transformed
serotherapy	satanophany	sculpturing	trafficator	transformer
stratifying	satin-stitch	squirearchy	tearfulness	toad-spotted
strategical	sitiophobia	square-built	tear-falling	transported
strategetic	saturnalian	square-dance	twanglingly	transportal
scratch-back	satirically	squarsonage	trachearian	transporter
scratchless	soteriology	squirarchal	Trachinidae	transeptate
stretchless	satisfiable	soul-sleeper	tracheotomy	transcriber
scratch-work	sausage-meat	squashiness	teachership	transuranic
scratch-coat	sausage-roll	saussuritic	traditional	transit-duty
struttingly	sausage-tree	stuntedness	traditioner	transhumant
Struthiones	squeakiness	scuttle-cask	tragi-comedy	translunary
scrutiniser	squeakingly	shuttlewise	thalidomide	translucent
stratopause	squeamishly	shuttlecock	tear-jerking	transfusive
serrulation	shunamitism	scuttle-butt	track-laying	transfusion
sertularian	stubble-rake	stultifying	track-walker	transductor
surturbrand	stumblingly	squattiness	tracklement	toastmaster
scrive-board	slumbrously	stultiloquy	thanklessly	traitorship
shrivelling	slumberland	scurvy-grass	tracklessly	traitorhood
screw-thread	slumberless	savableness	thanksgiver	traducement
scrawlingly	slumbersome	savoir-faire	thankworthy	traducingly
straw-colour	spud-bashing	savoir-vivre	trail-blazer	tobacco-pipe
screw-wrench	scutch-blade	seven-league	Thallophyta	tobacconist
screw-driver	sculduddery	seventeenth	thallophyte	table-napkin
shrew-struck	skulduddery	sovereignly	trammelling	table-tennis
straw-cutter	soundlessly	sovereignty	thaumatrope	table-topped
syssarcosis	sculduggery	severalfold	thaumaturge	tabefaction
sustainable	skulduggery	Sivatherium	traineeship	tubiflorous
sustainedly	sound-shadow	savouriness	train-bearer	tobogganing
sustainment	sounding-rod	sex-reversal	twalpennies	tobogganist
systematise	shuddersome	sexlessness	teaspoonful	tub-thumping
systematism	spumescence	sexagesimal	Trappistine	tibiotarsus
systematics	stupendious	sexennially	tea-equipage	tabernacled
systematist	sauce-crayon	sextodecimo	transpadane	tuberaceous
system-built	studentship	saxophonist	transcalent	tuberculate
sister-in-law	snuff-taking	Styracaceae	transparent	tuberculise
system-maker	soul-fearing	scyphistoma	transmarine	tuberculoma
suspensible	shufflingly	scythe-stone	translation	tuberculose
suspenseful	snuff-dipper	stylisation	tear-stained	tuberculous
susceptible	soulfulness	styliferous	translatory	tacheometer
suspectable	stuffing-box	stylishness	transaction	tacheometry
susceptibly	snuff-colour	stylopodium	transfer-day	ticket-punch
suspectedly	spur-gearing	sky-coloured	transferred	tickettyboo
suspectless	sluggardise	stylography	transferrer	tucking-mill
susceptance	southlander	sky-aspiring	transversal	tectibranch
sustentator	southwardly	tea-canister	transvestic	tickle-brain

technocracy
technically
tichorrhine
tick-tack-toe
taciturnity
tachycardia
tachygraphy
tediousness
trepanation
tsesarevich
therapeutic
Therapeutae
tremblement
tremblingly
theobromine
trenchantly
trencher-cap
trencher-fed
trencher-man
treachetour
treacherous
tree-creeper
thenceforth
trench-fever
Theocritean
treacliness
trendle-tail
trend-setter
teeter-board
therebeside
therewithal
therewithin
theretofore
Twelfth-cake
Twelfth-tide
theogonical
trepidation
trepidatory
theriolatry
theriomorph
treble-dated
theological
theologiser
trellis-work
thermocline
theomachist
thermically
thermoduric
thermograph
thermogenic
thermolysis
thermolytic
thermometer
thermometry
thermonasty
thermionics
thermophile
theomorphic
thermoscope
thermotical
thesmothete
thermotaxic
thermotaxis

theanthropy
teetotalism
teetotaller
treponemata
Theromorpha
theophagous
theopneusty
theophobist
theorematic
theoretical
treasonable
treasonably
theosophise
theosophism
theosophist
tree-surgeon
tree-surgery
theotechnic
trestle-work
theatre-goer
theatricals
theatricise
theatricism
theftuously
tremulously
twelvemonth
twelve-penny
tree-worship
thelytokous
teeny-bopper
tweezer-case
toffee-apple
toffee-nosed
tuft-hunting
toffishness
tufttaffeta
tufttaffeta
tufttaffety
tufttaffety
tagliatelle
toggle-joint
tegumentary
tiger-beetle
tiger-flower
tiger-footed
tight-lacing
tight-lipped
tight-fisted
tightly-knit
tribalistic
tritagonist
trivalvular
thimble-case
twin-brother
thiocyanate
twitch-grass
trindle-tail
third-stream
triceratops
tripetalous
toilet-cloth
toilet-cover
toilet-glass

tripe-visag'd
toilet-paper
trimetrical
tripersonal
toilet-table
trimestrial
tribeswoman
tail-feather
thingliness
thingumajig
triphibious
tritheistic
triphyllous
trichomonad
Trichomonas
trichinella
trichinised
trichinosed
trichinosis
trichinotic
trithionate
trichronous
Trichoptera
thitherward
Trinitarian
trivialness
thick-headed
thick-ribbed
tricksiness
thick-lipped
thick-witted
thick-coming
triumvirate
triennially
triangulate
tridominium
tribologist
tricoloured
trimorphism
trimorphous
thixotropic
thiopentone
trierarchal
thirstiness
thin-skinned
tristichous
thistle-down
taintlessly
twitter-bone
thirty-twomo
tribulation
trituration
tributarily
trifurcated
tribuneship
tribunitial
tribunitian
trisulphine
triquetrous
trisyllabic
trisyllable
teknonymous
telearchics

talkatively
Taliacotian
tale-bearing
telecontrol
tiller-chain
téléférique
telegraphic
telegrapher
telegrammic
telpher-line
telekinesis
telekinetic
telemessage
Teleosaurus
tallow-catch
tallow-faced
teleologism
teleologist
teleprinter
tulipomania
telephonist
telepathise
telepathist
telesthesia
telesthetic
Telescopium
telescopist
tolbutamide
telluretted
Talmudistic
talk-you-down
tally-system
tameability
tympaniform
time-bargain
temperament
temperately
temperative
temperature
timber-hitch
time-expired
tempestuous
tempest-tost
tumefacient
tumefaction
tomographic
time-killing
tumble-drier
tumbling-box
time-machine
Tom-and-Jerry
temporality
temporarily
temporising
time-pleaser
tumorigenic
timbromania
timbrophily
temerarious
time-sharing
time-service
time-serving
temptatious

tummy-button
tentatively
tantalising
tentaculate
tantalus-cup
tentaculite
tenableness
tunableness
tenebrosity
tenaciously
tendencious
tender-dying
tendentious
tunefulness
tank-farming
tennis-court
tonnishness
tangibility
tensibility
tentiginous
tonsillitic
tonsillitis
tennis-match
tensiometry
tonsilotomy
tenementary
tan-coloured
tenuousness
tent-pegging
tendrillous
tonetically
tin-streamer
tonquin-bean
trouble-word
troublesome
trouble-town
troublously
twopenn'orth
trough-fault
trough-shell
thought-wave
thoughtless
thought-sick
trophoblast
tooth-picker
Trochilidae
troth-plight
trochometer
tooth-powder
trophoplasm
tooth-drawer
trophotaxis
trophozoite
Thomistical
troglodytic
troglodytes
troll-my-dame
twofoldness
trommetric
thoroughwax
tropophytic
troposphere
trous-de-loup

trouser-clip	three-bottle	tire-valiant	tough-minded	unaddressed
trouser-suit	torpedo-tube	tardy-gaited	touch-typist	up-and-coming
trout-basket	three-square	tarry-breeks	thuriferous	unamendable
two-storeyed	tormentedly	tessaraglot	truck-farmer	unavertable
trout-stream	terrestrial	testamental	trunksleeve	unaffecting
typicalness	torrentuous	testamentar	tous-les-mois	unaugmented
taphephobia	three-suited	tussac-grass	tautomerism	unashamedly
toplessness	thriftiness	tastelessly	tautometric	unalienable
type-founder	tyroglyphid	tassell-gent	tautochrone	unalienably
type-foundry	Tyroglyphus	tessellated	Teutonicism	unanimously
typographia	torch-bearer	tostication	tautologise	unallowable
topographic	torch-singer	testificate	taurobolium	unannotated
typographic	torch-staves	testimonial	tautologism	unannounced
topographer	terminative	testiculate	tautologist	Uranoscopus
typographer	termitarium	tussock-moth	tautologous	unavoidable
topological	termination	testudinary	tautonymous	unavoidably
typological	terminatory	tissue-paper	trumpet-call	unabolished
tape-measure	terrigenous	tetravalent	trumpet-fish	uranoplasty
tape-machine	turbine-pump	tetradactyl	trumpet-wood	uranography
toponymical	torsiograph	tetrarchate	trumpet-tone	unapostolic
taphophobia	turfing-iron	tetrandrian	trumpet-tree	unappointed
toploftical	tarnishable	tetrandrous	true-seeming	unapproving
tephromancy	terribility	tetramerism	trusteeship	unaspirated
top-priority	torsibility	tetramerous	trustworthy	unagreeable
tap-dressing	territoried	Titianesque	trust-estate	unabrogated
top-dressing	territorial	tetrahedral	trust-buster	unassertive
type-species	Torridonian	tetrahedron	truculently	unassisting
type-setting	torticollis	tetratheism	town-council	unauthentic
typewriting	terricolous	tetraplegia	town-dweller	unattainted
typewritten	terminology	tetraploidy	town-meeting	unattempted
termagantly	turriculate	tetragonous	towing-bitts	unattentive
threatening	thrillingly	tetrapodous	thwartingly	unattending
tarradiddle	turtle-shell	tetrasporic	thwartships	unalterable
threadiness	turtle-stone	tetradrachm	townscaping	unalterably
throatiness	thrummingly	tetractinal	townspeople	unamusingly
throat-latch	thrombocyte	tetrapteran	tax-gatherer	unadvisable
threadmaker	tiring-glass	tetragynian	toxicomania	unadvisably
thread-paper	tiring-house	tetracyclic	taxidermise	unadvisedly
throat-strap	tyrannicide	tetragynous	taxidermist	unblameable
terraqueous	Tironensian	tithe-paying	taxonomical	unblameably
terebration	Tyronensian	totteringly	toxiphagous	umbratilous
terebratula	tyrannosaur	title-holder	toxophilite	unbiassedly
throbbingly	tyrannously	Tattersall's	toxiphobiac	unbeautiful
three-handed	threnetical	tittivation	textureless	umbraculate
three-masted	tiring-woman	tattie-bogle	trypanocide	unblenching
three-parted	turbo-ram-jet	tutti-frutti	Trypanosoma	unblemished
three-master	terroristic	titillation	trypanosome	unbreakable
torpescence	turcopolier	totalisator	thysanurous	umbrella-ant
turgescence	turnpike-man	Titanomachy	thyroiditis	umbrella-fir
turgescency	Tortricidae	thumb-marked	thyrotropin	unbreathing
turret-clock	Terpsichore	tourbillion	Thyrostraca	unbefitting
three-leafed	thrasonical	truncheoned	trysting-day	unbeginning
three-legged	thrust-plane	truncheoner	tryptophane	unblindfold
three-decker	teratogenic	trundle-tail	unawareness	umbriferous
Turneresque	teratologic	thunder-dart	unawakening	unbeknownst
three-leaved	taratantara	thunder-peal	unavailable	umbellately
torpedinous	turbulently	thunderless	unavailably	unballasted
Turbellaria	throughfare	thunder-like	unadaptable	unbelieving
terremotive	through-gaun	thunder-clap	unambiguous	unbeneficed
three-nooked	through-bolt	thunderbolt	unambitious	unbenefited
torpedo-boom	torturingly	true-devoted	unaccusable	unbenignant
three-colour	Targumistic	true-hearted	unaccusably	unbenighted
torpedo-boat	torque-meter	truth-teller	unaccounted	unbendingly

unbrotherly	uncourteous	undesigning	unfurnished	unitisation
unburthened	uncluttered	undistilled	unfortified	utilisation
unbarricade	uncivilised	undisclosed	unforgiving	utilitarian
unburnished	undrainable	undespoiled	unforeknown	uriniparous
unbeseeming	undiagnosed	undistorted	unforgotten	uriniferous
unboundedly	undebauched	undissolved	unfortunate	uninitiated
unceasingly	undecidable	undescribed	unfashioned	unidiomatic
unclassical	undecidedly	undesirable	unfittingly	unillumined
unchastened	undeclining	undesirably	unfeudalise	unipolarity
unchartered	undefinable	undeserving	unfoundedly	uniformness
unchastised	undignified	undestroyed	unfructuous	unicorn-moth
uncuckolded	undyingness	undisturbed	unflustered	unicolorate
uncheckable	undrinkable	undiscussed	unfixedness	unicolorous
uncleanness	undelegated	undisguised	upgradation	unicoloured
unclearness	undelighted	undutifully	unguardedly	unimpeached
unchildlike	undelivered	undoubtable	ungratified	unimpededly
urchin-shows	undemanding	undauntedly	ungrammatic	unimpressed
uncalled-for	undepressed	undoubtedly	ungodliness	unit-pricing
uncollected	undepending	undeviating	unguerdoned	unimportant
uncompanied	underhanded	undividable	unguiculate	uninquiring
uncompacted	undertaking	undividedly	ungallantly	uninspiring
uncommended	undermanned	undeveloped	unguligrade	uninscribed
uncompelled	undermasted	undiverting	ungenteelly	uninucleate
uncommitted	undervaluer	unelaborate	ungentility	uninvidious
uncompliant	under-sawyer	unenchanted	ungenitured	uninventive
uncomplying	underaction	unescapable	ungarmented	unjustified
uncompleted	under-school	unexcitable	ungarnished	unjaundiced
uncomforted	undertenant	unexclusive	ungetatable	unknowingly
uncomatable	underweight	unexcavated	ungazed-upon	unknownness
unconscious	underseller	unendurable	unhealthful	unlearnedly
uncongenial	under-keeper	unendurably	unhealthily	unlaborious
unconcealed	underbearer	unexercised	unhabitable	unlabouring
unconcerned	underletter	uselessness	unhackneyed	unluckiness
uncontemned	undershapen	un-Englished	unhidebound	upliftingly
unconfessed	undercharge	unexhausted	unheedfully	unlightened
unconcerted	undershorts	unevidenced	unheedingly	unlightsome
unconnected	underthirst	urediospore	upholstress	unleisurely
uncontested	underthrust	unemotioned	upholsterer	unlimitedly
unconverted	underbidder	unemotional	unhingement	unlooked-for
unconceived	undermining	unexplained	unhandiness	unliquefied
unconvinced	undersigned	unexpectant	unhandseled	unlistening
uncanniness	underbitten	unexpressed	unhopefully	unloverlike
unconniving	underviewer	unexpensive	unhappiness	unluxuriant
unconfirmed	undersleeve	unexperient	unharnessed	unluxurious
unconvicted	underclothe	unenquiring	unharvested	unmeaningly
uncanonical	undercovert	unessential	unharmfully	unmechanise
uncanonised	underhonest	unequitable	unhurtfully	unmodulated
unconcocted	underlooker	unequivocal	unhurriedly	unmeditated
uncontrived	underworker	unfearfully	unharboured	unmoistened
unconquered	underbreath	unfeathered	unhusbanded	unmalicious
uncurtailed	underpriced	unflavoured	unhazardous	unmelodious
uncurtained	underbridge	unflappable	univalvular	unmalleable
uncertainly	underpraise	unfeelingly	uniserially	unmemorable
uncertainty	underwriter	unflinching	unigeniture	unmindfully
uncorrected	underground	unfailingly	unicellular	unmanliness
uncertified	under-driven	unfeignedly	universally	unmercenary
unchristian	undergrowth	unfaltering	unipersonal	unmortgaged
uncorrupted	under-espial	unfulfilled	unisexually	unmarriable
upcast-shaft	understrata	unfiltrable	uninflected	unmortified
unclubbable	understated	unfinishing	uninforming	unmoralised
uncrushable	undescended	unfermented	uninhabited	unmeritable
uncouthness	undiscerned	unforfeited	uninhibited	unmeritedly
uncountable	undispensed	unforbidden	unification	unmurmuring

unmusically
unmasculine
unmitigable
unmitigably
unmitigated
unmatchable
unmutilated
unmotivated
unnecessary
unneedfully
unnaturally
unnourished
unnavigable
unnavigated
unoperative
unofficious
unofficered
unoffensive
unoffending
unorganised
urochordate
unoriginate
utopianiser
unobnoxious
ulotrichous
unobservant
unobserving
unorthodoxy
unobtrusive
unpeaceable
unplausible
unplausibly
unpractical
unplastered
unpractised
unpublished
unpedigreed
unpreaching
unpreferred
unprevented
unpresuming
unpaintable
unprintable
unpolarised
unpalatable
unpalatably
unpolitical
upping-block
unpensioned
upping-stone
upping-stock
unprocessed
unprofessed
unprojected
unprotected
unprotested
unprophetic
unprovident
unprofiting
unpromising
unprovoking
unpopularly
unpopulated

unperverted
unperfectly
unperceived
unparagoned
unpurchased
unportioned
unperplexed
unpardoning
unperformed
unperishing
unperturbed
unpersuaded
unpossessed
unpassioned
unpatterned
unpitifully
unpityingly
unpatriotic
unpathwayed
unqualified
unqualitied
unquantised
unqueenlike
unquickened
unquietness
unreachable
unreadiness
unrealistic
unreasoning
unreclaimed
unrectified
unreceipted
unrecalling
Utricularia
unreceptive
unrecounted
unrecovered
unreducible
unredressed
unrefracted
unrefreshed
unreflected
unregulated
unregarding
uprightness
unrighteous
unrehearsed
unrejoicing
unreluctant
unreligious
unrelenting
unremaining
unromanised
unremittent
unremitting
unremovable
unrepugnant
unreprieved
unrepentant
unrepenting
unreproving
unreposeful
unrequisite

unrespected
unrescinded
unrestingly
unresentful
unresenting
unrestraint
unresisting
unretentive
unreturning
unretouched
unrevealing
unravelment
unravelling
unrewarding
unstaidness
unshakeable
unshakeably
unsparingly
unswallowed
unstainable
unstaunched
unseaworthy
unsharpened
unsubmerged
unsubjected
unsubduable
unsocialism
unsectarian
unsociality
unsucceeded
unsuccoured
unsteadfast
unspecified
unspeakable
unspeakably
unsweetened
unsheltered
unsoftening
unsighed-for
unsegmented
unscheduled
unscholarly
unskilfully
unsmilingly
unspiritual
unscissored
unsyllabled
unsolicited
unselfishly
unsoldierly
unsandalled
unsentenced
unsensitive
unshockable
unstoppable
unstoppably
unsupported
unseparable
unseparated
unsurpassed
unshrinking
unsprinkled
unsurprised

unscratched
unsustained
unsuspended
unsuspected
unsuspicion
unsatiating
unsettledly
unsatirical
unsaturated
unsatisfied
unslumbrous
unsoundable
unsoundness
unshunnable
unsavourily
ultramarine
untraceable
untravelled
untraversed
unteachable
ultraviolet
ultra-modern
ultrasonics
untractable
urticaceous
untechnical
urticarious
untrembling
untreatable
untremulous
unthinkable
unthickened
untaintedly
untamedness
untempering
untimeously
untunefully
untinctured
unthought-of
untormented
untarnished
unterrified
untouchable
usucaptible
unutterable
unutterably
unusualness
unvocalised
unvulgarise
upvaluation
unvenerable
unveracious
unvarnished
unvisitable
unvitrified
unweathered
unweariable
unweariably
unweariedly
unwedgeable
unweetingly
unwillingly
unwelcomely

unwandering
unwinkingly
unwholesome
unwarranted
unwished-for
unwithering
unwitnessed
unwittingly
unwithstood
unwoundable
vibratility
vibrational
vice-admiral
vociferance
vociferator
vicegerency
vaccination
vaccinatory
victimology
vacillating
vacillation
vacillatory
vice-marshal
vacuolation
vacuousness
viciousness
vectorscope
victoryless
vicar-choral
vicar-forane
vicariously
viceroyship
viceroyalty
vicissitude
vacationist
vacuum-brake
vacuum-clean
vacuum-flask
victuallage
victualless
victualling
vichyssoise
vedette-boat
vagabondage
vagabondise
vagabondish
vagabondism
vigilantism
Vehmgericht
vaivodeship
voivodeship
volcanicity
vulcanicity
valuational
volcanology
vulcanology
villanously
volubleness
velocipeder
valediction
valedictory
vulneration
velvetiness

velvet-paper	verde-antico	weaver-finch	whitethroat	waldgravine
valleculate	verse-monger	whale-fisher	Whitechapel	well-groomed
vellication	vertebrally	wranglesome	white-winged	walking-cane
villication	vertebrated	weak-hearted	white-billed	walking-race
Vallisneria	vermination	weather-gage	white-listed	walking-part
volumometer	verticality	weather-vane	whiteboyism	walking-lady
voluntative	verbigerate	weather-gall	white-collar	walking-leaf
voluntarism	varnish-tree	weather-fend	white-bonnet	walking-beam
voluntarist	vertiginous	weather-helm	white-footed	willingness
voluntarily	vortiginous	weather-ship	white-bottle	walking-fish
Valentinian	vermivorous	weather-side	white-rumped	walking-toad
volitionary	vermiculate	weather-wise	white-eyelid	wellingtons
vomeronasal	vermiculite	weather-sign	whiffletree	walking-twig
vantageless	vermiculous	weathercock	wringing-wet	welwitschia
viniculture	verslibrist	weather-roll	wring-staves	well-judging
vine-dresser	virological	weather-worn	weightiness	well-looking
vine-disease	virilescent	weathermost	whichsoever	well-meaning
Vendémiaire	variolation	whaling-port	whitherward	wall-mustard
veneficious	verboseness	wearisomely	weigh-bridge	well-ordered
vinificator	varsovienne	weapon-schaw	waiting-maid	welcomeness
vine-fretter	variousness	weapon-salve	writing-case	well-rounded
ventilative	verisimilar	weak-sighted	writing-desk	well-stacked
vindicative	verdureless	whatsomever	whiting-time	well-sinking
venditation	verruciform	wealthiness	waiting-list	well-trodden
ventilation	virtue-proof	web-fingered	writing-book	well-thumbed
vindication	visibleness	wobble-board	waiting-room	walnut-juice
vindicatory	vesiculated	wide-chapped	whiting-pout	wolf-whistle
vendibility	vasodilator	wedge-tailed	whitishness	will-worship
vincibility	vespertinal	wedge-heeled	whisky-liver	well-wishing
vinaigrette	vestimental	wedge-shaped	whiskerando	woman-vested
ventricular	viscometric	widdershins	whicket-door	womanliness
ventriculus	viscountess	wedding-cake	whiskeyfied	wing-and-wing
ventriloquy	viscousness	wedding-ring	whitleather	wine-bibbing
venereology	vasopressin	wide-ranging	whitlow-wort	wine-biscuit
vincristine	vasopressor	widow's-bench	whigmaleery	windcheater
venesection	vestry-clerk	widowerhood	Weismannism	want-catcher
vanishingly	visiting-day	wide-watered	waivodeship	winter-apple
venatically	vascularise	whenceforth	whippletree	winter-bloom
venturesome	vascularity	wheedlesome	whipping-boy	winter-berry
venturingly	vasculature	whereabouts	whipping-top	winter-cress
venturously	vasculiform	wherewithal	whimsically	wonderfully
violoncello	vesuvianite	wheresoever	Whitsun-week	wintergreen
voodooistic	vitraillist	weeping-ripe	Whitsuntide	wanderingly
voortrekker	viticulture	weeding-fork	wainscoting	wonderingly
vaporimeter	vaticinator	weeding-hook	wainscotted	Wanderjahre
vaporisable	vitrescible	weeping-rock	whistle-fish	winter's-bark
vapouringly	vitrescence	weeping-tree	whistle-stop	winter-sweet
versatilely	vitrifiable	wheyishness	whistlingly	wind-furnace
variability	vituperable	wreck-master	whist-player	wine-growing
versability	vituperator	wheelbarrow	waist-anchor	winningness
versatility	vouchsafing	wheel-window	wakefulness	winning-post
variational	vivaciously	wheel-plough	weldability	wing-loading
verd-antique	vivacissimo	wheel-animal	well-advised	windlestrae
varicelloid	vivisective	wheelwright	well-behaved	windlestraw
varicellous	vivisection	wheel-cutter	well-beloved	Wensleydale
veraciously	vexillation	wheat-mildew	well-coupled	wine-measure
voraciously	vexillology	Wagneresque	well-dressed	window-blind
veridically	vexatiously	wage-earning	well-defined	window-barne
viridescent	voyeuristic	waggishness	well-derived	winsomeness
Verbenaceae	weasand-pipe	wagon-wright	well-desired	window-frame
verse-making	wearability	white-handed	well-entered	window-glass
variegation	what-d'ye-call	whitewasher	well-founded	window-ledge
verberation	weasel-faced	white-headed	wild-fowling	windsurfing

Windsor-soap	word-perfect	water-skiing	yatteringly
wine-tasting	worsted-work	water-closet	yttriferous
wood-alcohol	werewolfish	watering-can	yttro-cerite
wood-anemone	werewolfism	watering-cap	you-know-what
wool-bearing	wireworking	water-engine	zealousness
wool-combing	wash-and-wear	watering-pot	zoantharian
wood-carving	wassail-bowl	water-souchy	zoanthropic
wool-carding	wassail-bout	waterlogged	zygocardiac
wood-cutting	west-by-north	water-bouget	Zygomycetes
whoremaster	west-by-south	water-monkey	zygomorphic
whole-length	wash-drawing	water-cooled	zygopleural
wholesomely	Wesleyanism	water-cooler	Zygophyllum
whole-hoofed	waste-basket	water-colour	zymological
whole-hogger	wastel-bread	watercourse	zymosimeter
whoremonger	wasterfully	water-bottle	zymotechnic
whole-souled	westernmost	water-doctor	Zanthoxylum
whole-footed	washerwoman	water-splash	zinciferous
whosesoever	wishfulness	water-spider	zinkiferous
whole-stitch	wistfulness	water-sprite	zincography
wood-fretter	wash-gilding	water-spring	Zonotrichia
wrong-headed	wise-hearted	water-spirit	zoomagnetic
wrong-minded	wishing-well	water-tunnel	zoodendrium
wool-growing	washing-line	water-purpie	zootechnics
wrought-iron	washing-blue	water-supply	zootheistic
whorishness	washing-soda	withstander	zoochemical
woollen-mill	wishing-bone	wax-painting	zoophytical
wood-naphtha	wishing-tree	wax-chandler	zeolitiform
wool-stapler	waspishness	waywardness	zooplankton
wood-swallow	wash-leather	X-chromosome	zoogonidium
wood-vinegar	Westminster	xylocarpous	zoomorphism
wood-warbler	wisdom-tooth	xylographic	zoospermium
woody-tongue	Westphalian	xylographer	zoografting
wapper-jawed	wishtonwish	xylophagous	zoographist
wappenschaw	wasp-tongued	xylophilous	zip-fastener
workability	wasp-waisted	xylophonist	Zoroastrian
warrantable	witheringly	xenodochium	zero-grazing
warrantably	witlessness	xenogenesis	zestfulness
warm-blooded	withershins	xenogonctic	
wire-drawing	wither-wrung	xenoglossia	
world-beater	watch-making	Xanthochroi	
worldliness	witch-ridden	xanthophyll	
wire-dancing	witch-finder	Xanthoxylum	
worldly-wise	watch-pocket	xenomorphic	
worm-gearing	witch-doctor	xenoplastic	
warm-hearted	watch-spring	xiphopagous	
worthlessly	witches'-meat	xyridaceous	
worshipable	witenagemot	xeromorphic	
worshipless	without-door	xeranthemum	
worshipping	water-jacket	xerophilous	
warehousing	water-bailie	xerotripsis	
warlikeness	water-hammer	yeard-hunger	
working-face	water-cannon	yeard-hungry	
working-edge	water-barrel	yeast-powder	
working-beam	watered-down	yackety-yack	
working-over	water-meadow	yachtswoman	
wordishness	water-cement	Yugoslavian	
workmanship	water-pepper	Y-chromosome	
workmanlike	water-bearer	yellow-ammer	
wire-netting	water-beetle	yellow-belly	
word-of-mouth	water-thrush	yellow-earth	
word-picture	water-finder	yellow-metal	
word-painter	water-violet	yince-errand	
wire-pulling	water-pistol	yesternight	

anacatharsis
anacathartic
anapaestical
Amarantaceae
anabaptistic
anarchically
academically
amateurishly
amalgamation
amalgamative
anaphylactic
anathematise
avariciously
acaridomatia
availability
agalmatolite
agamogenesis
anagogically
analogically
anatomically
apagogically
acarodomatia
anamorphosis
araeosystyle
analphabetic
anaerobiosis
anaerobiotic
anagrammatic
anaesthetise
anaesthetist
avant-gardism
avant-gardist
acanthaceous
adaptability
anastigmatic
anarthrously
adaptiveness
analytically
ambidextrous
abbreviation
abbreviatory
abbreviature
arborescence
arborisation
ambassadress
ambitionless
abbey-counter
acciaccatura
archdeaconry
accidentally
aecidiospore
Asclepiadean
archegoniate
archetypical
archipelagic
architecture
Archilochian
acceleration
acceleratory
accelerative
accompanyist
accomplished
accomplisher

accumulation
accumulative
accommodable
accommodator
Ascension-day
accentuality
accentuation
anchoretical
anchoritical
accordionist
accurateness
accusatorial
accouchement
accoutrement
addictedness
addle-brained
audiological
androsterone
aldermanlike
aldermanship
alder-liefest
adder's-tongue
additionally
acetaldehyde
amenableness
anencephalia
anencephalic
aye-remaining
aperiodicity
alexipharmic
amelioration
ameliorative
awe-inspiring
anemophilous
anemographic
averruncator
agent-general
amentiferous
adequateness
affectedness
affectionate
arfvedsonite
affrightened
affrightedly
affrightment
apfelstrudel
affrontingly
afforestable
affluentness
aggressively
augmentation
augmentative
anguilliform
argillaceous
angelica-tree
angiocarpous
agglomerated
Anglophabiac
Angiospermae
angiospermal
angiostomous
agglutinable
agglutinogen

achlamydeous
athletically
Alhambresque
atheological
atheromatous
adhesiveness
animalculist
avitaminosis
amicableness
animadverter
alimentation
alimentative
arithmetical
arithmometer
alienability
amitotically
amissibility
aristocratic
Aristolochia
Aristophanic
Aristotelean
Aristotelian
Aristotelism
apiculturist
adjectivally
adjudication
adjunctively
alkalescence
alkalescency
Ankylosauria
Ankylosaurus
all-important
aplanogamete
all-roundness
all-or-nothing
ailurophilia
ailurophobia
allusiveness
alliteration
alliterative
ailourophobe
ailourophile
adminiculate
admonishment
administrant
administrate
atmospherics
armour-bearer
armour-plated
annihilation
annihilative
annunciation
annunciative
announcement
adorableness
avowableness
apodeictical
aforethought
apogeotropic
apothegmatic
apochromatic
anotherguess
aboriginally

apolitically
abolitionary
abolitionism
abolitionist
apoplectical
Apollinarian
apologetical
acoustically
apostolicism
apostolicity
apostrophise
amortisation
abortiveness
apocynaceous
applaudingly
alphabetical
alphamerical
alpha-blocker
appraisement
applausively
alphanumeric
apprehension
apprehensive
appreciation
appreciatory
appreciative
apple-blossom
arpeggiation
appoggiatura
amphigastria
amphisbaenic
amphitheatre
amphibrachic
amphitropous
amphistomous
amphictyonic
ampelography
appendectomy
appendicitis
appendicular
approachable
approach-shot
appropriator
appertaining
appurtenance
apperception
apperceptive
asparaginase
appercipient
apparentness
aspiringness
apparitional
appositeness
appositional
appetisement
appetisingly
asphyxiation
acquaintance
acquiescence
acroamatical
Afro-American
agribusiness
agrobusiness

12 b□e□k

agrochemical	anticipative	attorneyship	black-and-blue
agricultural	autocatalyse	antarthritic	brackishness
aerodynamics	antichthones	afterthought	blackpudding
aeroembolism	autochthones	aethrioscope	black-quarter
agreeability	anticatholic	anthropogeny	blackguardly
arrière-garde	autodidactic	anthropogony	blackcurrant
agroindustry	antediluvial	anthropoidal	beaumontague
air-ambulance	antediluvian	anthropology	brainwashing
acronychally	anthelmintic	anthropotomy	brass-bounder
apron-strings	antherozooid	afterburning	brassfounder
aeronautical	authenticate	antisocially	brass-rubbing
aeroneurosis	authenticity	antasthmatic	blastulation
air-condition	artificially	artistically	blastosphere
air-commodore	antifriction	autistically	blast-furnace
aeroplankton	anti-Gallican	anti-Semitism	boastfulness
acrophonetic	antagonistic	antisepalous	baby-batterer
aircraftsman	antigropelos	antistrophic	Bible-thumper
aerosiderite	antihalation	antistrophon	Bible-pounder
acre's-breadth	autohypnosis	attitudinise	bibliography
assibilation	astringently	altitudinous	bibliologist
assuefaction	auto-immunity	antithetical	bibliomaniac
abstemiously	attributable	antitheistic	bibliopegist
aesthesiogen	artillery-man	antithrombin	bibliopolist
aesthetician	antilegomena	astoundingly	bibliophobia
aestheticise	altaltissimo	ayuntamiento	bibble-babble
aestheticism	automobilism	adulteration	babingtonite
aestheticist	automobilist	adulterously	baby-snatcher
adscititious	antimacassar	advantageous	bobby-dazzler
auspiciously	antimnemonic	adventitious	baccalaurean
absoluteness	antimalarial	adverbialise	buccaneering
assimilation	antemeridian	advisability	buccaneerish
assimilative	automorphism	asynchronism	backbreaking
assentaneous	antimetabole	asynchronous	backboneless
absinthiated	automaticity	amygdaloidal	bactericidal
absent-minded	antoninianus	asymmetrical	bacteriology
abstractedly	astonishment	asymptotical	bacteriostat
abstractness	anti-national	bearableness	bachelor-girl
alstroemeria	antineutrino	blamableness	bachelorhood
assortedness	anthocarpous	bramble-berry	bachelorship
Australasian	astronautics	bramble-finch	bacchanalian
Austronesian	anthoxanthin	blabbermouth	buckle-beggar
abstruseness	Artiodactyla	blanc-de-Chine	becomingness
absorptivity	astrogeology	Branchiopoda	bicameralist
assassinator	anthophilous	brandy-bottle	bicentennial
assessorship	astrophysics	board-measure	backstarting
absquatulate	authorisable	branding-iron	backswordman
auscultation	aetiological	boarding-pike	back-tracking
auscultatory	astrological	brandy-pawnee	backwoodsman
asseverating	astronomical	bladder-wrack	backwardness
asseveration	action-taking	blandishment	backwounding
anti-aircraft	anteprandial	blamefulness	body-building
attractingly	autoptically	brachycephal	bodice-ripper
attractively	antiphonally	brachydactyl	badger-legged
antibacchius	antiphonical	brachygraphy	bed-of-justice
antibarbarus	antiparticle	beachcombing	body-snatcher
anticyclonic	antiparallel	blatherskite	bedazzlement
antecedently	antiperiodic	beatifically	breeches-buoy
anticlerical	antiphrastic	blackballing	breech-loader
articulately	antipathetic	black-hearted	bread-chipper
articulation	antipetalous	black-visaged	bletherskate
articulatory	antipruritic	blackbirding	bletheration
anticipation	alterability	black-fishing	brevipennate
anticipatory	antirachitic	blacklisting	breakfast-set

breakthrough
break-promise
beetle-browed
beetle-headed
blennorrhoea
Byelorussian
breast-girdle
breastplough
breastsummer
breaststroke
breathalyser
breathlessly
breathtaking
buffalo-berry
buffalo-grass
baggage-train
beggarliness
Bignoniaceae
behaviourism
behaviourist
brigade-major
bride-chamber
brimfullness
blithesomely
boiling-point
brinkmanship
brickfielder
brick-nogging
brilliantine
brilliant-cut
blissfulness
Bristol-board
Bristol-brick
blister-steel
boisterously
baking-powder
Balaam-basket
Balaamitical
balladmonger
ballanwrasse
bilharziasis
bilharziosis
ball-bearings
bell-bottomed
ballet-dancer
bullet-headed
balletically
balneologist
ballet-master
balletomania
belletristic
bullfighting
belligerence
belligerency
billingsgate
bolting-hutch
billiard-ball
balance-sheet
balance-wheel
bilingualism
bull-of-the-bog
belittlement
bilateralism

belly-landing
bombacaceous
bomb-disposal
bimillennium
benzaldehyde
benjamin-tree
bantam-weight
banderillero
bonnet-monkey
bandersnatch
beneficially
beneficently
benefactress
benightening
bench-warrant
benumbedness
bunko-steerer
bend-sinister
benevolently
bonny-clabber
biosatellite
bronco-buster
bioscientist
bronchoscope
bronchoscopy
broadcasting
bloodletting
bloodthirsty
bloody-minded
blood-brother
bloodstained
blood-pudding
bloodsucking
broken-backed
biogeography
biomechanics
Bromeliaceae
biometrician
broken-winded
bromhidrosis
biochemistry
brother-in-law
biorhythmics
booking-clerk
boogie-woogie
blockbusting
book-learning
bootlessness
bioflavonoid
blow-moulding
biologically
biographical
book-scorpion
brontosaurus
biosynthesis
biosynthetic
bronze-pigeon
bequeathable
bequeathment
bureaucratic
burial-ground
barratrously
bare-breached

bird-catching
burseraceous
burnet-leaved
barber-monger
birefringent
Berufsverbot
Boraginaceae
birthday-book
birthday-suit
Bertholletia
birding-piece
burying-place
burning-glass
burning-point
burning-house
bertillonage
barrier-cream
barristerial
barometrical
baron-officer
burrowing-owl
bird's-nesting
burnt-almonds
borough-reeve
bird-watching
barmy-brained
bastard-title
basidiospore
beseechingly
basket-making
basket-stitch
bespectacled
Besserwisser
bastinadoing
baselessness
business-like
business-wise
basso-relievo
basso-rilievo
base-spirited
besottedness
bushwhacking
bate-breeding
butter-cooler
butterfly-bow
butterfly-nut
battering-ram
butter-muslin
between-decks
betweentimes
butterscotch
buttery-hatch
bathing-dress
battleground
bottle-holder
battlemented
bottle-opener
bottle-slider
bottle-washer
battological
bottom-sawyer
buttress-root
bathypelagic

butty-collier
bougainvilia
bound-bailiff
blunderingly
boulevardier
bluestocking
blusteringly
bowling-alley
bowling-green
bewilderment
bow-compasses
bewitchingly
buzzard-clock
Characinidae
chalazogamic
Charadriidae
characterise
characterism
crambo-jingle
chalcography
chalcolithic
chance-medley
chalcopyrite
claudication
clare-obscure
chapelmaster
coacervation
clangorously
crash-landing
coachbuilder
clavicembalo
clarinettist
coalitionism
coalitionist
craniologist
clamjamphrie
crackbrained
chaplainship
cradle-scythe
charlatanism
coal-merchant
chain-gearing
charnel-house
channel-stane
channel-stone
clannishness
Cyanophyceae
championship
clapperboard
chairmanship
clair-obscure
clairvoyance
clairaudient
classicality
chassé-croisé
classifiable
Crassulaceae
chaise-longue
crassamentum
claustration
coat-trailing
claptrappery
craftmanship

chartography
craftsmaster
charter-mayor
charterparty
charter-chest
clatteringly
chapter-house
Charterhouse
craft-brother
chastisement
coal-titmouse
chauvinistic
cabbage-white
cable-railway
cable's-length
cable-tramway
cabalistical
cabinetmaker
cockfighting
cucking-stool
coccidiostat
cockieleekie
cachinnation
cachinnatory
cucumber-tree
Cicindelidae
cichoraceous
cuckold-maker
cuckoo-flower
cyclopropane
Cyclostomata
cyclostomous
cacophonical
cacophonious
cock-throwing
code-breaking
cedrelaceous
codification
cremationist
coerciveness
crêpe-de-chine
crenellation
coenesthesia
Coelenterata
coelenterate
Czechoslovak
credibleness
creditworthy
check-weigher
checking-room
checker-berry
checker-board
chemotherapy
coenobitical
chemotropism
creepy-crawly
clear-obscure
cherry-bounce
cheirography
clear-sighted
cheirologist
cherry-laurel
chelromantic

clearing-bank
cheiropteran
cherry-pepper
cheerishness
cheerfulness
cheeseburger
cheese-cutter
cheese-hopper
cheese-monger
cleistogamic
cheese-paring
cheese-rennet
cheese-taster
chesterfield
creatureship
creativeness
crepusculous
cherubically
café-chantant
cigarette-end
cohabitation
cohesibility
cohesiveness
chivalrously
coincidental
coincidently
clincher-work
Cain-coloured
childbearing
childcrowing
childishness
chimerically
cliffhanging
chieftainess
clip-fastener
chief-justice
cliché-ridden
criticalness
chiliahedron
criticisable
chick-a-diddle
clinker-block
clinker-built
chimney-shaft
chimney-piece
chimney-board
chimney-stack
chimney-stalk
chimney-sweep
Chironomidae
chiropractic
chiropractor
chirographer
chiropterous
crimping-iron
crisping-iron
cuisse-madame
cristobalite
chiquichiqui
chirurgeonly
cliquishness
collaterally
culpableness

collaborator
celibatarian
Calyciflorae
calico-flower
calycoideous
calycanthemy
cell-division
collegialism
collegiality
calceamentum
culvertailed
collectorate
collectively
collectivise
collectivism
collectivist
collectivity
Cologne-earth
caliginosity
cultivatable
collision-mat
calligrapher
callisthenic
colliquation
colliquative
calumniation
columniation
calumniatory
calumniously
calamitously
cold-moulding
calendar-line
cylinder-head
cylinder-seal
cylindricity
cylindriform
colonisation
coleopterist
coleopterous
colloquially
coloquintida
chloroformer
chlorimetric
chlorometric
chlorination
calorescence
calisthenics
cold-shoulder
colostration
colossus-wise
cole-titmouse
colluctation
collywobbles
commandingly
companion-way
companionate
compatriotic
compass-plane
compass-plant
Campanularia
come-by-chance
commercially
commencement

commendation
commendatory
cumber-ground
compellation
compellative
commemorable
commemorator
commensalism
commensality
commensurate
compensation
compensatory
commentation
camp-follower
combinations
commiserable
commiserator
commissioned
commissioner
commissarial
commissariat
camiknickers
complacently
cumulo-cirrus
complication
complicative
complaisance
complemental
complimental
complimenter
cumulo-nimbus
complanation
completeness
cumulatively
complexional
complexioned
cement-copper
cementitious
Cominformist
campodeiform
composedness
componential
commodiously
common-riding
commonwealth
camp-preacher
compressible
Combretaceae
cumbrousness
camp-shedding
camp-sheeting
cometography
cymotrichous
compunctious
compurgation
compurgatory
communicable
communicably
communicator
compulsorily
compulsatory
compulsative
compulsively

contabescent
convalescent
contaminable
contagionist
contagiously
cantankerous
canvas-length
containerise
cinnamon-bear
Cantabrigian
connaturally
confabulator
cane-bottomed
conscription
conscionable
conscionably
Cynocephalus
conidiophore
conidiospore
conveyancing
congenerical
cankeredness
concelebrant
concelebrate
conferential
centesimally
congenitally
congeniality
conveniently
cancellarial
cancellarian
cancellation
conterminant
conterminate
conterminous
condemnation
condemnatory
conveyor-belt
contemplable
contemplator
contemptible
contemptibly
contemporary
contemporise
contemptuous
consecration
consecratory
consensually
confessional
confessoress
condensation
conversation
contextually
concentrator
conventicler
consentience
concentrical
consentingly
contesting
convectional
conventional
confectioner
conventioner

concentering
concert-grand
contestation
connectively
consequently
conservatrix
conservation
conservatory
conservatism
conservative
conchiferous
conchologist
cantharidian
cantharidine
convincement
convincingly
confiscation
confiscatory
considerable
considerably
confidential
canting-wheel
contingently
conning-tower
convivialist
conviviality
conditioning
conditionate
conciliation
conciliatory
conciliative
centillionth
cantillation
cantillatory
confirmation
confirmatory
confirmative
consignation
contignation
consignatory
consistently
consistorial
consistorian
continuation
continuative
contiguously
continuously
conglobulate
conglobation
canaliculate
candle-holder
conglomerate
conclamation
canalisation
conclusively
conglutinant
conglutinate
candle-waster
cinemathèque
canonisation
concordantly
console-table
cannon-fodder

concomitance
concomitancy
consolidated
consolidator
consociation
censoriously
conformation
confoundedly
concorporate
contortional
conspectuity
conspiringly
conspiration
contribution
contributory
contributive
contractable
contractedly
centroclinal
contractible
contradictor
congregation
controllable
concremation
confrontment
contranatant
contrapuntal
contrapposto
contrariness
contrariwise
concrescence
centrosphere
congratulant
congratulate
concreteness
contriteness
contriturate
canorousness
contrivement
canister-shot
constabulary
constringent
constriction
constrictive
constipation
constituency
constatation
constitution
constitutive
construction
constructure
constructive
contumacious
conjunctival
contumelious
confusedness
concubitancy
concupiscent
connubiality
Confucianism
Confucianist
centuriation
centuplicate

conduplicate
consummately
consummation
consummatory
consummative
concurrently
conqueringly
conquistador
convulsional
convulsively
consultation
consultatory
consultative
conductivity
centumvirate
cloud-seeding
cloud-chamber
chondriosome
cloud-kissing
coordinately
co-ordinately
coordination
co-ordination
co-ordinative
coordinative
chordophonic
cloddishness
cloven-footed
choreography
cloven-hoofed
cholerically
close-fitting
choreologist
close-tongued
close-mouthed
close-grained
clothes-horse
clothes-brush
clothes-press
choripetalae
cooking-range
cooking-apple
chorizontist
clock-watcher
clownishness
chocolate-box
chorological
chorographic
crossbanding
cross-lateral
crossbencher
cross-bedding
cross-section
cross-lighted
crossing-over
cross-and-pile
cross-country
cross-grained
cross-purpose
cross-current
cross-buttock
crosscutting
cross-examine

Cappagh-brown
cuprammonium
capacitation
copper-bottom
copper-glance
copper-nickel
cypress-swamp
cupping-glass
copying-press
capriciously
captiousness
capillaceous
cupuliferous
co-polymerise
coprophagist
coprophagous
coprophilous
cupboard-love
capercaillie
capercailzie
capitalistic
capitulation
capitulatory
coquettishly
carragheenin
carnal-minded
circassienne
Cordaitaceae
currant-jelly
currant-bread
cerebrotonia
cerebrotonic
corn-chandler
curb-crawling
card-carrying
caricaturist
correlatable
carpetbagger
corn-exchange
curietherapy
Cartesianism
carpet-knight
carte-blanche
carpetmonger
correctional
correctioner
carpenter-bee
carpenter-ant
correctitude
cerographist
cardinal-bird
curvicaudate
cardinalship
cardiography
carriageable
carriage-free
carving-knife
curling-tongs
corning-house
carriage-paid
curling-irons
curling-stone
certificated

carriwitchet
cardiologist
carcinogenic
curvifoliate
curvirostral
curvicostate
curliewurlie
corallaceous
corollaceous
cork-linoleum
carillonneur
circle-riding
carelessness
ceramography
ceremonially
corn-marigold
corn-merchant
curb-merchant
chromosphere
chrome-spinel
chromaticism
chromaticity
chromatogram
chromatopsia
chrematistic
chrome-yellow
chronography
chronologist
chronometric
carbonaceous
corporalship
carbon-dating
corporealise
corporealism
corporealist
corporeality
carpophagous
cartophilist
Carlovingian
corroborable
corroborator
cartological
carton-pierre
cartographer
cartographic
cirro-stratus
cirro-cumulus
carbohydrate
ceroplastics
corpse-candle
christianise
Christianism
Christianity
Christliness
chrisom-cloth
chrestomathy
Christolatry
co-respondent
christophany
chrysophanic
Christ's-thorn
corn-shucking
circumcentre

circumcision
circumfusile
circumfusion
circumfluent
circumfluous
curmudgeonly
circumgyrate
circumjacent
circumlocute
circumnutate
circumstance
circumscribe
circuit-rider
circuitously
caravansarai
caravanserai
cash-and-carry
custard-apple
cashew-apples
cosmetically
costermonger
cushion-plant
coscinomancy
cosmonautics
cosmoplastic
cosmogonical
cosmological
cosmopolitan
cosmopolitic
cosmographer
cosmographic
custom-shrunk
cash-register
catechetical
catachrestic
catacoustics
catadioptric
cathetometer
cytogenetics
categorially
catallactics
cotyledonary
cotyledonous
cattle-lifter
catilinarian
cattle-plague
catamountain
cutinisation
cut-and-thrust
cottonocracy
cathodograph
cataphoresis
cataphractic
cataphysical
cataphyllary
caterwauling
catastrophic
cytotoxicity
courageously
causationism
causationist
churchianity
councilmanic

council-board
council-house
churchpeople
church-parade
church-warden
crush-barrier
cough-mixture
cough-lozenge
cousin-german
cautiousness
chuckie-stane
chuckie-stone
caulking-iron
cruel-hearted
churlishness
coulombmeter
counsellable
court-martial
courtierlike
court-plaster
countenancer
counting-room
countermarch
counter-paled
counter-gauge
counter-tally
counterscarp
counter-weigh
counter-tenor
counter-sense
counter-agent
countercheck
counter-wheel
countershaft
counter-charm
counterlight
counterplead
counter-claim
counter-flory
counter-blast
counter-force
counterpoint
counter-round
counterpoise
counter-brace
counter-drain
counterproof
court-dresser
counter-stand
counter-guard
country-dance
countrywoman
country-house
civilisation
covetousness
covetiveness
cowardliness
cryptography
cryptogamian
cryptogamist
cryptogamous
crystal-gazer
cryptologist

crystallitis
crystal-clear
cryptomnesia
cryptomnesic
cryptanalyst
cryptonymous
dead-and-alive
dramatically
dramatisable
diamagnetism
dramaturgist
deambulatory
dialectician
dialecticism
dialectology
diageotropic
dwarfishness
draughtiness
draught-hooks
draughtboard
draught-horse
draught-house
death-warrant
death-dealing
diaphanously
diathermancy
drawing-paper
drawing-table
doating-piece
drawing-knife
drawing-board
drawing-frame
drawlingness
drainage-tube
diatomaceous
diamond-wheel
diamond-hitch
diamond-field
diamond-drill
diapophysial
diabolically
diatonically
dragon's-blood
dracontiasis
deaspiration
diagrammatic
dearticulate
draft-dodging
diastrophism
deactivation
Dibranchiata
dibranchiate
debilitation
debilitative
debonairness
dubitatively
doch-an-dorach
dictatorship
decrepitness
decreasingly
declensional
decaffeinate
ducking-stool

declinometer
dock-labourer
deceleration
decoloration
decalescence
decomposable
decompressor
deconsecrate
decongestant
decongestion
decongestive
decentralise
decipherable
decipherment
decapitalise
decapitation
dicarpellary
dichromatism
doctrinarian
dichrooscope
dichroscopic
decoratively
decorousness
decasyllabic
decasyllable
decisiveness
decitizenise
decrustation
dactylically
dactyliology
dactyloscopy
deducibility
dodecagynian
dodecagynous
dodecahedral
dodecahedron
didactically
dodecandrous
dodecaphonic
dedicational
dedicatorial
Didelphyidae
diencephalon
dreadfulness
dietetically
diethylamine
deerstalking
dressing-case
dressing-down
dressing-gown
dressing-room
dressing-sack
defraudation
diffareation
deflationary
deflationist
deflagration
defectionist
differentiae
differential
deflectional
defamatorily
definability

definiteness
definitively
deformedness
deforciation
diffrangible
diffusedness
diffusionism
diffusionist
dogmatically
digladiation
digressional
digressively
degenerately
degenerating
degeneration
degenerative
dogtooth-spar
dehumidifier
driving-wheel
driving-shaft
drinking-bout
drinking-horn
Deinotherium
do-it-yourself
dejectedness
dijudication
dollarocracy
Della-Cruscan
deliberately
deliberation
deliberative
dilucidation
dilaceration
delicateness
delicatessen
delightfully
dolphinarium
deltiologist
delamination
delimitation
delimitative
delinquently
dilapidation
deliquescent
doloriferous
dolorousness
delusiveness
dilettantish
dilettantism
dilatability
dilatoriness
delitescence
delivery-pipe
delivery-tube
damnableness
democratical
demi-culverin
demi-distance
demagnetiser
demolishment
demilitarise
demi-mondaine
demoniacally

dementedness
demonologist
diminishable
diminishment
demonstrable
demonstrably
demonstrator
diminutively
demoralising
dimerisation
Domesday-book
domesticated
domesticable
domestically
domesticator
donkey-engine
dunderheaded
dinner-jacket
dentilingual
densitometer
densitometry
dentirostral
denticulated
dunniewassal
dingle-dangle
dynamometric
denomination
denominative
denunciation
denunciatory
Dantophilist
dendrologist
dendrologous
dynastically
do-nothingism
denaturalise
donatistical
denotatively
denouncement
droseraceous
duodecennial
duodenectomy
drongo-cuckoo
drongo-shrike
droughtiness
dyotheletism
dropped-scone
deoppilation
deoppilative
dropping-well
Doomsday-book
deontologist
doomwatching
depravedness
doppel-ganger
depreciation
depreciatory
depreciative
depressingly
depressurise
diprionidian
dephlegmator
depoliticise

diplomatical
diplogenesis
depopulation
departmental
deposition
diphtheritic
diphtheritis
diphthongise
dermatophyte
deracination
directorship
dormer-window
derogatorily
derogatively
dorsiventral
Darlingtonia
dorsiflexion
dormitory-car
duraluminium
derisiveness
dcrivational
derivatively
dispatch-boat
distanceless
diseasedness
dismayedness
dissatisfied
disharmonise
disdainfully
dispauperise
despairingly
disobedience
disaccharide
disaccordant
disadvantage
disadventure
desideration
desiderative
disregardful
dissemblance
disseverance
dysteleology
dishevelling
dishevelment
disseverment
disseminated
disseminator
disrelishing
dysmenorrhea
discerptible
distemperate
disheartened
dispersonate
descensional
dispensation
dispensatory
dispensative
dysaesthesia
dysaesthetic
dissentingly
dessertspoon
dissenterish
dissenterism

disceptation
dissertation
dissertative
disreputable
disreputably
disaffection
disaffiliate
disagreeable
disagreeably
disagreement
dysphemistic
dissipatedly
distinctness
despisedness
despitefully
dispiteously
dissimilarly
dispiritedly
dispiritment
disciplinant
disciplinary
discipleship
distillation
distillatory
dissimulator
displeasedly
displaceable
displacement
desulphurise
desulphurate
disclamation
desalination
disallowance
disallowable
desolateness
disembarrass
disembellish
disembrangle
disinherison
disinterment
disintegrate
disinfectant
disinfection
disincentive
disingenuity
disingenuous
disenchanter
disinflation
disendowment
disintricate
disannulling
disannulment
dislocatedly
despondently
despondingly
discordantly
discoverable
disbowelling
discoverture
Discomedusae
discomedusan
discomfiting
discomfiture

disgorgement
dislodgement
discophorous
despotically
dissocialise
dissociality
despoliation
dissociation
dissociative
discommodity
discommunity
discountable
disconnected
disjointedly
disconnexion
despotocracy
discorporate
discomposure
discourteous
discouraging
discographer
disconsolate
dispossessed
dispossessor
discontented
Discomycetes
disappointed
disoperation
dasyphyllous
desirability
distribution
distributary
distributive
distractedly
destructible
distractible
disgradation
discreetness
disorientate
disgregation
distrainable
distrainment
discriminant
discriminate
disfranchise
dispropriate
distrustless
discreteness
discretional
discretively
desirousness
disprivacied
disprivilege
disestablish
disassociate
disastrously
disputatious
disturbative
disquietness
disauthorise
disqualifier
desquamation
desquamatory

desquamative
disguiseless
disbursement
disguisement
disquisition
disquisitory
disquisitive
discursively
dissuasively
disgustingly
disgustfully
disruptively
disaventrous
dissymmetric
detractingly
detachedness
detectophone
ditheletical
ditheistical
ditriglyphic
detumescence
determinable
determinably
determinedly
dethronement
detruncation
detoxication
dithyrambist
deuteranopia
deuteranopic
deuteroscopy
deuteroplasm
Deuteronomic
daughterling
dough-kneaded
deuch-an-doris
double-acting
double-banked
double-biting
double-bottom
double-charge
double-dealer
double-decked
double-decker
double-dagger
double-figure
double-glazed
double-headed
double-handed
double-locked
double-manned
double-storey
deutoplasmic
doubtfulness
deviationism
deviationist
devil-may-care
devil-in-a-bush
devil-worship
divinatorial
divarication
divertimento
diversionary

diversionist
diverticular
diverticulum
diversifying
divisibility
divisiveness
devotionally
down-and-outer
downwardness
dextrocardia
dextrogyrate
dextrousness
day-blindness
exalbuminous
emasculation
emasculatory
emancipation
exacerbation
evanescently
evangelicism
evangelistic
emargination
exaggeration
exaggeratory
exaggerative
edaciousness
elasmobranch
evaporimeter
evaporograph
epanorthosis
exasperating
exasperation
exasperative
Epacridaceae
exanthematic
enantiopathy
enantiomorph
enantiotropy
enantiostyly
enarthrodial
embranchment
emblazonment
emblematical
embarquement
embitterment
embattlement
embourgeoise
embryologist
embezzlement
exchangeable
eschatologic
enchantingly
encyclopedia
ecclesiology
Ecclesiastes
ecclesiastic
encheiridion
excogitation
excogitative
enclitically
eucalyptuses
encumberment
encumbrancer

eccentricity
encroachment
encephalitic
encephalitis
escapologist
excursionise
excursionist
encirclement
excitability
escutcheoned
exclusionism
exclusionist
excruciating
excruciation
encrustation
endocarditis
endamagement
endometritis
endangerment
endoparasite
endophyllous
endoskeletal
endoskeleton
endosmometer
epencephalic
epencephalon
exercise-book
exercitation
epexegetical
exegetically
eleventh-hour
elementalism
elephant's-ear
etepimeletic
evening-dress
eleemosynary
eternity-ring
exemplifying
execratively
eleutherarch
electrically
electrifying
electroscope
electrometer
electrogenic
electromeric
electrometry
electroshock
electroplate
electropolar
electrosonde
electrotonic
electromotor
electrotonus
electrograph
electron-volt
electrotyper
electrolysis
electrolytic
electrotypic
exenteration
executorship
everydayness

everywhither
effecutation
effectuality
enfeeblement
effiguration
effeminately
efflorescent
effervescent
effusiometer
effusiveness
engraftation
eagle-sighted
Euglenoidina
engagingness
Englishwoman
engine-driver
engine-fitter
egg-and-tongue
egg-apparatus
eighteen-hole
eighteenthly
ephebophilia
exhibitioner
exhilarating
exhilaration
exhilaratory
exhilarative
ephemeridian
ephemerality
euhemeristic
Echinocactus
echinococcus
echinodermal
ethnocentric
ethnological
ethnographer
ethnographic
etheostomine
enhypostasia
enhypostatic
exheredation
etheromaniac
enharmonical
etherisation
echo-sounding
exhaust-value
exhaust-steam
episcopalian
episcopalism
evisceration
epideictical
epidemically
epidemiology
evidentially
evil-favoured
epithalamion
epithalamium
epiphenomena
epididymides
episodically
editorialise
epirrhematic
epigrammatic

emigrational
evil-speaking
epistolarian
epistolatory
evil-tempered
epistemology
Epicureanism
exiguousness
epicycloidal
eclectically
elliptically
ellipsograph
enlargedness
eunuchoidism
exorbitantly
esoterically
exoterically
epoch-marking
exophthalmia
exophthalmic
exophthalmos
exophthalmus
exobiologist
emotionalism
emotionality
emollescence
enormousness
econometrics
econometrist
ecologically
economically
exospherical
egoistically
emolumentary
elocutionary
evolutionary
elocutionist
evolutionism
evolutionist
emphatically
explantation
expediential
expedition
expressional
expressively
expressivity
espagnolette
explicitness
empoisonment
expansionary
expansionism
expansionist
expromission
euphoniously
expropriable
exprobration
exprobratory
exprobrative
exploitation
exploitative
experiential
experimental
experimented

experimenter
empyreumatic
expostulator
expatriation
Euro-American
ebracteolate
Eurocurrency
earnest-penny
earnest-money
earth-created
earthquaking
ear-splitting
eurythermous
enswathement
ecstatically
exsufflicate
exsufflation
East-Indiaman
essentialism
essentialist
essentiality
exsanguinate
exsanguinity
exsanguinous
ex-serviceman
extravagance
extravagancy
extravaganza
extra-marital
entrancement
extraversion
extra-sensory
extra-regular
extraneously
estrangement
extraditable
extra-limital
extrapolator
extra-special
extra-uterine
extra-mundane
extranuclear
entrenchment
entrepreneur
entreatingly
entomologise
entomologist
Entomostraca
extensimeter
extensionist
entanglement
extensometer
extinguisher
extroversion
entoplastral
entoplastron
ectypography
ectoparasite
entertaining
exteroceptor
exterminable
exterminator
extortionary

extortionist
extortionate
Enteromorpha
enthronement
enteropneust
enteroptosis
enterprising
enthusiastic
educationist
edulcoration
exulceration
edulcorative
equidistance
ecumenically
equilibrator
ebullioscope
ebullioscopy
equalisation
equalitarian
equimultiple
equanimously
equipollence
equipollency
equiprobable
equestrienne
Equisetaceae
equisetiform
equatorially
eruptiveness
elucubration
equivocation
equivocatory
equivalently
enviableness
envisagement
eavesdropper
Edwardianism
erythematous
erythroblast
erythromycin
etymological
etymologicon
etymologicum
elytrigerous
Egyptologist
enzymologist
flamboyantly
Franco-German
fraudulently
Frauendienst
flame-thrower
flabelliform
flagelliform
flabellation
flagellation
flagellatory
frame-breaker
frangibility
flash-forward
featheriness
feather-brain
feather-grass
flagitiously

feasibleness
frankalmoign
frankincense
Frankenstein
fearlessness
flammability
flammiferous
flammulation
flannelboard
flannelgraph
fragrantness
fractionally
fractionator
flatteringly
febrifacient
fibrillation
fibrinolysin
fabulousness
Febronianism
factitiously
fictitiously
factionalism
factionalist
fictionalise
factiousness
fecklessness
facilitation
facilitative
fiddle-faddle
fiddlesticks
fiddle-string
French-polish
field-spaniel
fiendishness
frenetically
freight-liner
freight-train
freshmanship
flesh-pottery
flexibleness
freakishness
feeble-minded
feeing-market
free-standing
free-swimming
free-selector
free-thinking
frequentness
free-wheeling
freeze-drying
freezing-down
fugie-warrant
figurability
figure-caster
figuratively
fugitiveness
Fehmgerichte
fricasseeing
Fringillidae
faith-healing
faithfulness
flickeringly
friendliness

fairnitickle
fairnytickle
flippantness
faint-hearted
flint-hearted
flint-knapper
frictionless
flitter-mouse
faintishness
fallaciously
filibusterer
full-bottomed
felicitation
felicitously
false-hearted
filter-passer
fuliginosity
fuliginously
folliculated
folk-medicine
falcon-gentil
falcon-gentle
fellow-member
filtrability
feldspathoid
full-throated
fully-fledged
fume-cupboard
feminineness
fantasticism
fantasticate
finger-and-toe
fence-mending
fennel-flower
fancifulness
fent-merchant
funambulator
financialist
fenestration
functionally
functionless
foot-and-mouth
flocculation
frondiferous
floodlighted
frondescence
flower-delice
flower-deluce
flower-garden
foolish-witty
frolicsomely
floriculture
footplatemen
footslogging
front-bencher
frontiersman
front-of-house
frontispiece
fore-and-after
formaldehyde
forsakenness
fore-admonish
forebodement

forebodingly
forecarriage
faradisation
force-feeding
forbearingly
forset-seller
forgettingly
fermentation
fermentative
fire-fighting
foregoneness
forthrightly
farthingland
farthingless
forth-putting
fornicatress
forbiddingly
forcing-house
forcibleness
foreign-built
ferricyanide
forejudgment
farm-labourer
formlessness
Foraminifera
furunculosis
ferrocyanide
fireproofing
forestalling
forestalment
foreseeingly
foresightful
first-nighter
foretokening
furfuraceous
ferrugineous
fortuitously
forswornness
fire-watching
fast-and-loose
foster-father
foster-mother
foster-parent
fosset-seller
foster-sister
fish-hatchery
fissilingual
fastidiously
fustillirian
fashion-plate
fissirostral
fissicostate
fasciculated
fashiousness
festoon-blind
fish-salesman
father-figure
fatherliness
father-lasher
fathers-in-law
fatigue-party
fatigue-dress
futilitarian

futtock-plate
futurologist
fluidisation
foundationer
frumentation
fourfoldness
Fourieristic
fluorocarbon
fluoridation
fluorimetric
fluorometric
fluorination
fluorescence
fruit-machine
fourteenthly
fructiferous
fault-finding
fountain-head
fountainless
fruitfulness
fructivorous
feverishness
favouredness
fowling-piece
fixed-penalty
guaranteeing
goat-antelope
glaucomatous
glaucescence
guardianship
glandiferous
Grandisonian
grapeseed-oil
grave-clothes
gracefulness
gratefulness
gravel-voiced
graphologist
graminaceous
glaciologist
gladiatorial
gladiatorian
graciousness
gratifyingly
grallatorial
gram-molecule
grammaticise
grammaticism
gram-negative
gramophonist
granodiorite
grapple-plant
graspingness
gram-positive
glassy-headed
grass-widower
glass-blowing
gladsomeness
glass-cutting
geanticlinal
giant's-kettle
giant's-stride
granulocytic

gratuitously
Gibraltarian
gobbledegook
gobbledygook
gibble-gabble
god-forgotten
gregarianism
gregariously
greviousness
greenishness
grease-monkey
great-bellied
great-hearted
guest-chamber
gigantically
gigantomachy
guild-brother
griseofulvin
guilefulness
gainlessness
glimmeringly
glitteringly
galvanoscope
galvanometer
galvanometry
galactagogue
galactometer
gallinaceous
galligaskins
gallows-maker
gall-sickness
gelatination
Gemeinschaft
gambling-hell
gem-engraving
gymnosophist
gemmological
gamopetalous
gamophyllous
gamesmanship
gamesomeness
gamosepalous
genealogical
geniculation
gynodioecism
gonadotropic
gonadotropin
gander-mooner
gynaecomasty
gynaecocracy
genuflection
gingivectomy
gentilitious
Gentianaceae
generatrices
generousness
gangsterland
gang-there-out
genethliacal
genethliacon
genotypicity
Gondwanaland
geomagnetism

good-breeding
gaol-delivery
globe-thistle
geodetically
goose-pimples
grotesquerie
geometrician
globe-trotter
geocentrical
geotectonics
geochemistry
good-humoured
geophysicist
globigerinae
growing-pains
growing-point
Grolieresque
gloriousness
glockenspiel
ghoulishness
ground-beetle
ground-cuckoo
ground-cherry
ground-feeder
groundlessly
ground-pigeon
geognostical
geologically
gnomonically
geopolitical
gnotobiology
gnotobiotics
group-captain
geographical
glossography
glossologist
grossularite
good-tempered
geodynamical
geosynclinal
gormandising
Germanically
Germanophobe
Germanophile
geriatrician
garret-master
garter-stitch
gorgeousness
gyromagnetic
gerontophile
gerontocracy
Gastarbeiter
Gesneriaceae
gasification
gas-discharge
gossip-monger
gesticulator
gossip-writer
Gesellschaft
gasometrical
gas-condenser
gastrocnemii
gastrulation

gastronomist	Hydromedusae	hair-restorer	hemispheroid
gastropodous	hydromedusan	hair-splitter	homothallism
gastrosopher	hydrophobous	hair's-breadth	Humpty-dumpty
gathering-cry	hydrophilite	hallan-shaker	homothermous
get-rich-quick	hydrophilous	Helianthemum	hendecagonal
glucoprotein	hydrophanous	holidaymaker	hunger-bitten
glue-sniffing	hydrochloric	halter-necked	henceforward
gruesomeness	hydrothermal	Hildebrandic	hunger-strike
gluttonously	hydrotherapy	hellgrammite	hindforemost
governmental	hydrophytous	helplessness	hunting-field
governorship	hydrozincite	hylomorphism	hunting-knife
glyphography	hydrobiology	half-mourning	hunting-lodge
glycoprotein	hydrofluoric	heliolatrous	hunting-sword
glyptography	hydroelastic	heliocentric	handkerchief
gazetteerish	hydrological	hollow-ground	Hindoostanee
heat-apoplexy	hydrographer	heliophilous	hindquarters
heaven-fallen	hydrographic	heliochromic	hundred-gated
heaven-gifted	hydrotropism	heliotherapy	huntsmanship
heavenliness	hydrostatics	heliographer	handsomeness
heater-shield	hydroquinone	heliographic	hand's-breadth
heathenishly	hydrodynamic	heliotropism	henotheistic
heather-bleat	hydatidiform	heliogravure	honey-tongued
headmistress	hierarchical	holophrastic	honey-mouthed
headquarters	haematemesis	half-seas-over	honey-buzzard
headshrinker	haematoblast	half-timbered	hooping-cough
heart-failure	haematolysis	hallucinogen	hoodman-blind
heart-warming	haematoxylin	hallucinosis	hood-moulding
heart-rending	haematoxylon	hemp-agrimony	hypocritical
heart-service	haemophiliac	Hemichordata	hypochlorite
heart-to-heart	hierophantic	home-crofting	hypochondria
heartbreaker	hieroglyphic	homochromous	hypocoristic
heartburning	haemorrhagic	hammer-headed	happenstance
heavy-hearted	hierogrammat	homoeomorphy	hypognathism
habeas-corpus	hierographer	homoeomerous	hypognathous
Hobbesianism	hierographic	homoeopathic	hypogastrium
hybridisable	hyetographic	homoeostatic	hypoglycemia
hubble-bubble	heeby-jeebies	humification	hip-hip hurrah
habilitation	high-coloured	homoiomerous	hopelessness
hebdomadarer	hygienically	homologumena	hypnogenesis
hebdomadally	hugger-mugger	homologation	hypnogenetic
Hobson-Jobson	high-fidelity	homelessness	hippocentaur
hobgoblinism	high-faluting	hemimorphism	hippophagist
hebephreniac	higgle-haggle	homomorphism	hippophagous
haberdashery	highly-strung	hemimorphite	hypnotherapy
hibernaculum	hygrophilous	homomorphous	hypnotically
Hibernically	hygrochastic	homonymously	hypnotisable
Hibernianism	hagiological	hymenopteran	hippopotamic
habitability	hagiographer	humanisation	hippopotamus
hebetudinous	hagiographic	humanitarian	hippocrepian
habit-forming	hygrographic	homeopathist	haptotropism
huckle-backed	hog-constable	homeothermal	Hippocratise
hectographic	high-pressure	homeothermic	Hippocratism
hydrargyrism	high-priestly	homeomorphic	hypophrygian
hydraulicked	high-reaching	hymnographer	hypersarcoma
Hudibrastics	high-seasoned	homopolarity	hyperdactyly
hedge-warbler	high-stepping	home-produced	Hypericaceae
hedge-parsley	high-spirited	hemiparasite	hyperacidity
hedge-sparrow	high-sounding	Hemerocallis	hyperidrosis
hedge-creeper	highty-tighty	hamarthritis	hypersensual
hodge-pudding	high-velocity	hamartiology	hypertension
hedge-mustard	heir-apparent	humorousness	hypertensive
hydropathist	heir-by-custom	homesickness	hyperthermal
hydrogeology	hairdressing	homesteading	hyperthermia

hyperalgesia	harmoniously	haussmannise	inconcinnity
hyperalgesic	harmonometer	hexadactylic	inconcinnous
hyperplastic	harmonograph	inadaptation	incendiarism
hyperbolical	harbour-light	irascibility	inconsistent
hypertrophic	horror-struck	inaccurately	incontiguous
hypersthenia	hire-purchase	inaccessible	inconclusion
hypersthenic	heresy-hunter	inaccessibly	inconclusive
hyperpyretic	heritability	inaudibility	inconsonance
hyperpyrexia	horizontally	image-worship	inconsolable
hypostatical	Hispanically	image-breaker	inconsolably
hyposulphate	Hispaniolise	inadequately	incineration
hyposulphite	hysterectomy	inauguration	inconstantly
hypothalamic	hysterically	inauguratory	inconsumable
hypothalamus	hysteromania	inadmissible	inconsumably
hepaticology	hysterogenic	inadmissibly	incoordinate
hypothecator	hospital-ship	inappeasable	incapability
hypothetical	Histiophorus	inapplicable	incapacitate
hephthemimer	histogenesis	inappellable	incurability
hepatologist	histogenetic	inappositely	incorrigible
hypotrochoid	historically	inabstinence	incorrigibly
hepatisation	historiology	inauspicious	incoronation
happy-go-lucky	histological	inarticulacy	incorporator
hereditament	histrionical	inarticulate	incorporeity
hereditarily	hesitatingly	inartificial	incorrodible
horsemanship	hatchet-faced	inartistical	incorrosible
horrendously	hatelessness	inactivation	incorruption
hermeneutics	heteroblasty	iracundulous	incorruptive
hermeneutist	heterocyclic	inadvertence	incestuously
horseshoeing	heteroclitic	inadvertency	incisiveness
hermetically	Heterocontae	incrassation	incatenation
horse-knacker	heterocercal	incrassative	incautiously
herpetofauna	heterochrony	incoagulable	incrustation
herpetologic	heterodactyl	incidentally	incivilities
horse-courser	heteroecious	increasingly	indebtedness
horse-breaker	heterogonous	incognisance	indeclinable
horse-trading	heterokontan	incognisable	indeclinably
horse-trainer	heterologous	incogitative	indoctrinate
harness-maker	heteromorphy	incoherently	indecorously
harvest-feast	heteromerous	inclinometer	indecisively
harvest-field	heteronomous	incalescence	indicatively
harvest-goose	heteroousian	incalculable	Indo-European
harvest-louse	heteroplasia	incalculably	indefeasible
harvest-mouse	heteroplasty	incomparable	indefeasibly
harlequinade	heterophylly	incomparably	indefectible
hard-featured	Heterosomata	incompatible	indifference
hard-favoured	heterosexual	incompatibly	indifferency
heroicalness	heterostyled	incompetence	indefensible
hereinbefore	heterothally	incompetency	indefensibly
horrifically	heterotactic	incompliance	indefinitely
horribleness	heterotrophy	incompletely	indigenously
heroi-comical	heterauxesis	incompletion	Indo-Germanic
herd-instinct	heterozygote	incomunicado	indigestible
horticulture	heterozygous	incommodious	indigestibly
horrifyingly	hound's-tongue	incommutable	indehiscence
heraldically	house-warming	incommutably	indelibility
hurdle-racing	housekeeping	incomputable	indelicately
harmlessness	housey-housey	incunabulist	indemnifying
hurtlessness	house-to-house	incandescent	independence
horometrical	house-breaker	inconvenient	independency
harmonically	house-trained	inconversant	indirectness
harmoniphone	house-steward	inconsequent	indistinctly
harmonichord	house-husband	incontinence	indiscipline
harmoniumist	house-surgeon	incontinency	indissoluble

indissolubly
industrially
indiscreetly
indiscretely
indiscretion
indisputable
indisputably
indetectable
indetectible
indetermined
individually
indivertible
index-linking
ineradicable
ineradicably
inelasticity
inexactitude
inescutcheon
inexecutable
ineffaceable
ineffaceably
inefficiency
inexhaustive
idealisation
inexpectancy
inexpedience
inexpediency
inexpressive
inexpugnable
inexpugnably
inexplicable
inexplicably
inexpansible
inexpungible
inexperience
inexpertness
identifiable
inextricable
inextricably
inextensible
ideationally
inextirpable
inflationary
inflationism
inflationist
inflammation
inflammatory
infraorbital
infibulation
infectiously
inflectional
infrequently
infringement
infelicitous
infiltration
infanticidal
infundibular
infiniteness
infinitively
informidable
infusibility
ingravescent
ingratiating

ingemination
ingloriously
Ishmaelitish
inhabitation
ichneumon-fly
ichthyolatry
ichthyophagy
ichthyolitic
ichthyocolla
ichthyopsida
inhalatorium
ichnographic
inharmonical
inharmonious
inhospitable
inhospitably
iridescently
inimicalness
inimicitious
idiorhythmic
idiosyncrasy
idiothermous
iniquitously
injudicially
injunctively
inking-roller
ill-naturedly
illiberalise
illiberality
ill-beseeming
illegibility
illegitimacy
illegitimate
illumination
illuminative
Islamisation
illimitation
illaqueation
ill-treatment
illustration
illustratory
illustrative
illusiveness
illiterately
immeasurable
immeasurably
immaculately
immoderately
immoderation
immemorially
immunologist
immunisation
immensurable
iambographer
immersionism
immersionist
immutability
immethodical
immaterially
immatureness
immovability
ionophoresis
ignitability

ignitibility
innutritious
isolationism
isolationist
idolatrously
inosculation
inoccupation
inordinately
inordination
inoperculate
isoperimeter
isoperimetry
inobediently
isocheimenal
isochromatic
isochronally
isothermally
isobilateral
ironing-board
isodiametric
isodimorphic
iconomachist
iconophilism
iconophilist
iconoclastic
inobservance
inobservable
isostemonous
implantation
impedimental
impierceable
impregnation
impressively
implicitness
imprisonment
impoliteness
imponderable
impenetrable
impenetrably
impenitently
improvisator
improvidence
impropriator
impermanence
impermanency
imperfection
imperceptive
imperfective
impertinence
impertinency
impartiality
impersistent
imperviously
imperforated
imperforable
impersonally
impersonator
imperishable
imperishably
imperatorial
imperatively
imposthumate
impassionate

imposingness
imputability
impetiginous
imputatively
inquisitress
irrealisable
irrebuttable
irreconciled
irreciprocal
irredeemable
irredeemably
irrefragable
irrefragably
irreflection
irreflective
irreformable
irregularity
irrigational
irrelatively
irrelevantly
irremediable
irremediably
irremissible
irrepealable
irrepealably
irrepairable
irreprovable
irreprovably
irrespective
irrespirable
irresolvable
irresolvably
irresolutely
irresolution
irresponsive
irresistance
irresistlble
irresistibly
irritability
irrationally
irreversible
irreversibly
irreverently
installation
instauration
insubjection
insect-powder
instep-raiser
inspectingly
inspectional
inspectorial
inspectorate
insufferable
insufferably
insufficient
insufflation
instillation
inspissation
insalubrious
insolubilise
insolubility
insalivation
insemination

insomnolence
insanitation
insurability
instructible
instructress
insurrection
instrumental
instrumented
insusceptive
insouciantly
intracardiac
intracranial
intransigent
intransitive
intra-uterine
intramundane
intrenchment
intuitionism
intuitionist
intrinsicate
intriguingly
intellectual
intellection
intellective
intelligence
intelligible
intelligibly
intolerantly
intoleration
intimidation
intimidatory
intemperance
intempestive
intemerately
intumescence
intensifying
inteneration
introversion
introversive
introjection
introvertive
iatrochemist
intromission
intromissive
intromittent
intromitting
introducible
introduction
introductory
introductive
interjacency
interlaminar
internalised
intermaxilla
interoceanic
inter-science
interoceptor
intermeddler
interbedding
interference
intermediacy
intervenient
intermediary

intermediate
interpellant
interpellate
interfemoral
intercession
intercessory
interfertile
interception
interjection
intersection
intervention
intertexture
interceptive
interservice
interchanger
interchapter
interminable
interminably
interlingual
interdigital
intercipient
intertissued
intermission
intermissive
intermittent
interdiction
interdictory
intermixture
interdictive
interpleader
interglacial
interfluence
interclusion
interpleural
interrogatee
intervocalic
interpolable
interrogable
interpolator
interrogator
interfoliate
intercolline
intercommune
interconnect
interlobular
interlocutor
interspinous
interspersal
interspatial
interwreathe
intertraffic
interorbital
interfrontal
intercropped
interfretted
interpretess
interpretate
interpretive
interwrought
interestedly
interosseous
interstellar
interstitial

internuncial
intermundane
intercurrent
interruption
interruptive
intertwining
intussuscept
intrusionist
intoxicating
intoxication
invigilation
invagination
invigoration
inveiglement
invalidation
invulnerable
invulnerably
involutional
involutation
Invertebrata
invertebrate
invisibility
investigable
investigator
invitingness
inveterately
Jack-a-lantern
Jacob's-ladder
Jack-in-office
Jack-in-the-box
Jack-o'-lantern
Jacquard-loom
judgment-debt
judgment-hall
judgment-seat
Jeffersonian
Juglandaceae
jail-delivery
joint-tenancy
jointing-rule
jumping-mouse
jingle-jangle
Jenny-spinner
jeopardously
juristically
jurisdiction
jurisdictive
jurisconsult
jurisprudent
jerry-builder
jesting-stock
Jesuitically
justificator
jet-propelled
journalistic
journey-bated
juvenileness
juvenescence
Krameriaceae
kicking-strap
kickie-wickie
kicksy-wicksy
kidney-potato

kiddiewinkie
knee-breeches
knee-crooking
keeking-glass
Kremlinology
kleptomaniac
knife-and-fork
knife-grinder
knight-errant
knightliness
knick-knacket
klipspringer
kakistocracy
kill-courtesy
kaleidoscope
kaleidophone
kilfud-yoking
kilowatt-hour
Kimmeridgian
kindergarten
kinaesthesia
kinaesthesis
kinaesthetic
kinesipathic
king's-cushion
knowableness
knocking-shop
kerb-crawling
kirschwasser
kurchatovium
kerb-merchant
karyokinesis
keratogenous
keratoplasty
keraunograph
kissing-crust
katzenjammer
kitchen-range
kitchen-wench
kitchen-knave
kitchen-stuff
kettleholder
knuckle-joint
Keynesianism
leap-frogging
leather-cloth
leather-knife
loathfulness
leasing-maker
leaping-house
libidinosity
libidinously
labanotation
loblolly-tree
liberalistic
labyrinthian
labyrinthine
labour-saving
lickety-split
lucifer-match
lock-hospital
lucklessness
localisation

locum-tenency
locomotivity
lycanthropic
licentiously
lactoprotein
Lycopodiales
Lycopodineae
lachrymosely
lachrymation
lachrymatory
lick-trencher
ledger-tackle
lodging-house
lady's-thistle
lady's-fingers
lady's-slipper
lady's-cushion
lieutenantry
life-and-death
left-handedly
life-interest
lifelessness
lugubriously
legacy-hunter
logodaedalic
logodaedalus
loggerheaded
ligniperdous
logging-stone
Liguliflorae
liguliforal
legalisation
lagomorphous
legislatress
light-hearted
lightning-rod
lightning-bug
legitimately
legitimation
laisser-faire
laisser-aller
laissez-faire
laissez-aller
leiotrichous
lake-dwelling
lukewarmness
Lillibullero
Lillibullero
lampadedromy
lampadomancy
lumber-jacket
lymphography
lymphangitis
lomentaceous
luminiferous
Lymantriidae
luminescence
luminousness
limnophilous
limnological
lumbriciform
lamprophyric
lamp-standard

lamb's-lettuce
Lancasterian
long-breathed
long-drawn-out
long-distance
long-division
line-engraver
lanceolately
lantern-jawed
land-grabbing
landgraviate
luncheon-meat
longicaudate
lenticellate
longipennate
landing-field
landing-place
landing-speed
landing-craft
landing-stage
landing-strip
lenticularly
longitudinal
land-lubberly
Lincoln-green
long-standing
lonesomeness
longshoreman
land-surveyor
languageless
linguistical
languishment
land-yachting
leopard's-bane
Laodiceanism
looking-glass
lapidicolous
lepidomelane
lapidescence
lappered-milk
leptosomatic
loquaciously
liquefacient
liquefaction
liqueur-glass
large-hearted
lurking-place
larking-glass
laryngectomy
laryngoscope
laryngoscopy
laryngophony
laryngospasm
liriodendron
lord-superior
lorry-hopping
loss-adjuster
lust-breathed
lese-humanity
lasciviously
lusciousness
listlessness
laticiferous

letter-writer
letter-weight
Little-endian
litholatrous
lithophagous
lithophilous
lithological
lithotomical
lithospheric
Lithospermum
lithographer
lithographic
lithotriptic
lithotriptor
lithotritise
lithotritist
liturgically
liturgiology
literariness
latirostrate
laterisation
lath-splitter
latitudinous
laudableness
launching-pad,
laundry-woman
laureateship
louver-window
lounge-lizard
leucoplastid
leucocytosis
louvre-window
live-feathers
level-pegging
levelling-rod
lovelornness
livery-stable
levorotatory
Liverpudlian
low-watermark
Low-Churchman
Low-Churchism
low-thoughted
low-frequency
lower-bracket
law-stationer
lexicography
lexicologist
loxodromical
luxullianite
laxativeness
lizard-hipped
meat-offering
mean-spirited
meat-salesman
measuring-rod
mealy-mouthed
mobilisation
mechanically
machairodont
macaberesque
mycodomatium
mickey-taking

mock-heroical
machine-ruler
Mechitharist
Macmillanite
machicolated
mucilaginous
microbalance
microcapsule
macrodactyly
microscopist
macrocephaly
microcephaly
microseismic
microphysics
microcircuit
micropipette
microbiology
macrobiotics
microclimate
micrological
microtomical
microcopying
microprinted
microgranite
micrographer
micrographic
macropterous
micropterous
microsurgeon
microsurgery
microtubular
mycoplasmata
mucopurulent
Machtpolitik
mediatorship
mediaevalism
mediaevalist
medicamental
medicine-ball
modification
modificatory
modificative
mid-Victorian
muddleheaded
middle-income
middleweight
mademoiselle
maderisation
moderateness
meditatively
muddy-mettled
meeting-house
mnemotechnic
migrationist
magnetically
magnetisable
magnetometer
magnetograph
magnifically
magnificence
magniloquent
megalomaniac
megalosaurus

Muggletonian
Magnoliaceae
magistrature
mail-carriage
maidenliness
maintainable
moistureless
major-general
majestically
majesticness
make-and-break
milk-and-water
malacologist
molecularity
Malacostraca
melodramatic
malleability
millesimally
miller's-thumb
malversation
mulligatawny
multilateral
multivalence
multivalency
multifaceted
multivariate
multifarious
multivarious
multicauline
multipartite
multiscience
multiseriate
multiversity
multicentral
multidentate
multiseptate
melting-point
milking-stool
multilingual
multicipital
multipliable
multiplicand
multiplicate
multiplicity
mellifluence
multiflorous
multifoliate
multiformity
multivoltine
multicostate
multilobular
multilocular
multiloquent
multiloquous
multipresent
multisulcate
multinuclear
multipurpose
mill-mountain
melanochroic
melancholiac
mallophagous
malformation

malcontented
milk-porridge
malapertness
maltreatment
mill-sixpence
militaristic
molluscicide
Molluscoidea
multungulate
malnutrition
malevolently
mammalogical
mammee-sapota
momentaneous
memorability
memorisation
mendaciously
mind-boggling
man-about-town
Manicheanism
many-coloured
mono-compound
municipalise
municipalism
municipality
monochromasy
monochromist
monochromate
monodramatic
monodelphian
monadelphous
monodelphous
mine-detector
monkey-engine
monkey-flower
monkey-hammer
monkey-jacket
mannerliness
monkey-puzzle
Montessorian
manoeuvrable
monkey-wrench
mangel-wurzel
man-of-war's-man
munificently
minification
manufactural
manufacturer
monofilament
manifoldness
manifestable
manifestible
manifestness
monographist
monogenistic
monticellite
mansion-house
mandibulated
mingle-mangle
monolinguist
mindlessness
manslaughter
monomaniacal

monumentally
monomorphous
minimisation
manometrical
monometallic
minimotorway
monopodially
monopolistic
manipulation
manipulatory
manipulative
monopetalous
monophyodont
monophyletic
monophysitic
monarchistic
mineralogise
mineralogist
monastically
monostichous
monosyllabic
monosyllable
monosepalous
monostrophic
ministration
ministrative
monothalamic
monotheletic
monotheistic
monotonously
munitionette
monitorially
monetisation
menstruation
money-lending
money-changer
money-spinner
money-grubber
moonlighting
myographical
moonstricken
marcatissimo
mordaciously
mercantilism
mercantilist
miraculously
meridionally
marker-beacon
market-garden
Marseillaise
marvellously
Myrmecophaga
myrmecophile
myrmecophily
myrmecologic
market-square
morigeration
marsh-harrier
morphography
morphallaxis
morphologist
merchantable
merchantlike

march-treason
morphotropic
mirthfulness
morris-dancer
Marsileaceae
marlinespike
morning-watch
marriageable
marriage-bone
morning-glory
marriage-ring
morning-dress
morbilliform
Marcionitism
mercifulness
marble-cutter
marbled-white
moralisation
morality-play
myringoscope
Mariolatrous
Maryolatrous
marconigraph
Marcobrunner
marrow-squash
mirror-writer
meristematic
meritocratic
Marattiaceae
meretricious
mercurialise
mercurialism
mercurialist
merry-thought
merry-go-round
massaranduba
miscalculate
mismatchment
mistakenness
message-stick
mystagogical
musicianship
music-teacher
musicologist
mesocephalic
miseducation
misadventure
misadvisedly
master-at-arms
masseranduba
misbehaviour
misleadingly
miscegenator
misdemeanant
misdemeanour
messeigneurs
mysteriously
misbelieving
misreckoning
masterliness
miscellanist
muster-master
misrepresent

master-switch
mastersinger
masterstroke
misfeaturing
missel-thrush
misventurous
moschiferous
mischallenge
mischanceful
mysticalness
misdirection
missionarise
Mastigophora
misplacement
misallotment
mesomorphous
misinterpret
misanthropic
misanthropos
misinformant
misknowledge
misformation
misconstruct
miscontented
mass-produced
misapprehend
mistreatment
mistranslate
mispronounce
mistressless
mistrustless
mistress-ship
mesothelioma
mesothoracic
moss-trooping
misstatement
masturbation
mispunctuate
misjudgement
missummation
misquotation
mitrailleuse
meticulously
mitochondria
metachronism
mathematical
mathematised
mother-church
mother-fucker
mother-figure
motherliness
mother-liquor
motley-minded
matter-of-fact
mothers-in-law
mother-tongue
metagnathous
metagalactic
matriclinous
matriarchate
matriculator
metallically
metalanguage

metallophone
metal-working
metaleptical
metallurgist
metamorphism
metamorphist
metamorphose
mutinousness
mutton-cutlet
mythogenesis
mutton-headed
meteorically
methodically
matroclinous
metropolitan
mythological
metropolises
mythologiser
meteorologic
meteorograph
metrorrhagia
mythographer
metaphorical
metaphrastic
metoposcopic
metapsychics
metaphysical
materialness
motor-scooter
mithridatism
motor-bicycle
motor-tractor
motorisation
maturational
motor-cycling
motor-cyclist
mutessarifat
metasilicate
metasomatism
metathetical
metathoracic
motivational
mound-builder
mouse-buttock
mouth-filling
mouth-to-mouth
mouth-breeder
mourning-band
mourning-dove
mourning-ring
mournfulness
mousquetaire
moustache-cup
mountain-blue
mountain-cork
mountain-flax
mountain-high
mountain-hare
mountain-lion
mountain-meal
mountain-soap
mountain-wood
mountenaunce

moveableness
movelessness
mixobarbaric
mixed-ability
mixter-maxter
mixtie-maxtie
mizzen-course
muzzle-loader
mezzo-rilievo
mezzo-soprano
nubbing-cheat
nebulisation
nobilitation
nebulousness
noctambulism
noctambulist
nickel-silver
nyctitropism
noctilucence
neck-moulding
nectocalyces
necrophagous
necrophiliac
necrophilism
necrophilous
necrophorous
necrological
necropolises
necrographer
nychthemeral
nychthemeron
nicotinamide
nidification
niddle-noddle
noematically
needlessness
neglectingly
neglectfully
negrophilism
negrophilist
negotiatress
night-terrors
night-fishery
night-clothes
nugatoriness
night-brawler
night-crawler
negativeness
nail-head-spar
neighbouring
nail-scissors
name-dropping
nomadisation
Nymphaeaceae
nympholeptic
nymphomaniac
nimble-footed
namelessness
nimble-witted
nominalistic
nomenclature
nomenclative
niminy-piminy

nominatively
numinousness
nimbostratus
numerability
numerousness
nomothetical
nematologist
Nematomorpha
namby-pambies
non-objective
non-scheduled
non-admission
non-residence
non-resistant
non-resisting
non-effective
non-efficient
nonagenarian
non-Christian
nonchalantly
non-fictional
non-alignment
non-flammable
non-alcoholic
non-intrusion
non-combatant
non-conductor
non-communion
non-committal
non-complying
nanoplankton
non-essential
none-so-pretty
nineteenthly
non-attention
non-nucleated
non-Euclidean
non-existence
Neo-Darwinian
Neo-Darwinism
Neo-Darwinist
Neoceratodus
neoterically
Neohellenism
Neo-Christian
neoclassical
Neoplatonism
neoplatonist
neologically
neonomianism
nephelometer
nephelometry
Naples-yellow
nipple-shield
Nepenthaceae
nephological
nephrologist
nephroptosis
Norman-French
noradrenalin
nerve-racking
nurse-tending
nursery-rhyme

north-eastern
north-seeking
north-western
Northumbrian
north-country
northernmost
nursing-chair
narcissistic
narcotherapy
narcotically
narrow-minded
nose-bleeding
nesting-place
nasolacrymal
nasalisation
Nestorianism
nostological
nose-painting
Notodontidae
Netherlander
Netherlandic
notification
nothingarian
nutritionist
nutritiously
Notonectidae
nitromethane
nitrobenzene
nitroaniline
nitroso-group
nitrotoluene
naturalistic
naturopathic
neurasthenia
neurasthenic
nauseousness
neuropathist
neurobiology
neuroanatomy
neurological
neuropterist
neuropterous
neurosurgeon
neurosurgery
neurypnology
navigability
navigational
novelisation
never-failing
nevertheless
neverthemore
newfangledly
new-fashioned
Newfoundland
newspaperman
newspaperdom
newspaperism
orange-flower
ovariotomist
oratorically
oracularness
ombrophobous
ombrophilous

orchard-house
orchard-grass
occidentally
orchestrator
orchidaceous
orchidectomy
orchilla-weed
orchidomania
oscilloscope
oscillograph
oecumenicism
obcompressed
occupational
oncorhynchus
occasionally
old-fashioned
odd-come-short
obdurateness
operatically
opera-glasses
overcanopied
overexertion
overexposure
overestimate
overfullness
overfineness
overfondness
overflourish
one-sidedness
obedientiary
overkindness
overlordship
overmultiply
overniceness
oceanography
oceanologist
one-and-thirty
one-upmanship
overpraising
overpressure
overpopulate
overpersuade
Oreopithecus
overpowering
overreaction
oneirocritic
oneiromancer
overripeness
overrashness
oversubtlety
oversimplify
overstrained
overscutched
overwhelming
overweighted
office-bearer
office-holder
office-hunter
office-seeker
off-reckoning
oughly-headed
organ-gallery
organography

organoleptic
organ-grinder
organisation
organ-builder
ophthalmitis
ophiolatrous
ochroleucous
ophiophagous
ophiophilist
Ophioglossum
ophiological
ophiomorphic
otherworldly
oligarchical
orichalceous
opinionately
opinionative
orienteering
oniroscopist
oligotrophic
oeils-de-boeuf
opisthotonic
opisthodomos
opisthotonos
opisthograph
object-finder
object-lesson
obligingness
obligatorily
oblanceolate
obliteration
obliterative
obliviscence
obmutescence
obnubilation
ornamentally
omnipresence
omnipotently
omnisciently
Ornithischia
ornithomancy
ornithogalum
ornithoscopy
ornithophily
ornithomorph
onomatopoeia
onomatopoeic
otosclerosis
ororotundity
orographical
odontography
odontologist
odontomatous
odontophoral
odontophoran
orphan-asylum
omphalomancy
oppressively
oophorectomy
opposability
oppositeness
oppositional
ourang-outang

obreptitious
obstetrician
ossification
obsolescence
obsoleteness
obsequiously
Observantine
obstreperate
obstreperous
obsessionist
obscurantism
obscurantist
outward-bound
outlandishly
outrageously
outfangthief
outmanoeuvre
oath-breaking
out-pensioner
octogenarian
optimisation
ostentatious
osteomalacia
orthopaedics
orthopaedist
osteopathist
orthogenesis
orthogenetic
osteogenesis
osteogenetic
orthopedical
osteodermous
orthorhombic
orthosilicic
osteoplastic
orthognathic
orthoboracic
orthogonally
orthotonesis
osteological
osteoporosis
orthocousins
orthodontics
orthodontist
orthodromics
orthographer
orthographic
orthotropism
orthotropous
orthopteroid
orthopterist
orthopterous
outspreading
octopetalous
otter-hunting
obtuse-angled
octastichous
octostichous
octosyllabic
octosyllable
octosepalous
octastrophic
oxy-acetylene

platanaceous
placableness
pease-bannock
peace-warrant
praseodymium
planetesimal
peace-keeping
plate-leather
peace-officer
prayerlessly
pease-blossom
prayer-monger
Phanerogamae
Phanerogamia
phanerogamic
phanerophyte
peace-breaker
planet-struck
placentiform
placentation
pease-pudding
peacefulness
peach-yellows
peach-blossom
playing-field
praxinoscope
planispheric
plagiotropic
pearl-tapioca
pearl-sheller
pearl-fishing
pearl-fishery
Pralltriller
pearl-essence
pharmacology
pharmaceutic
psammophytic
plain-dealing
plain-hearted
phaenogamous
plain-clothes
phaeomelanin
Phaeophyceae
platonically
peacock-stone
plano-concave
plano-conical
phagocytical
phagocytosis
plausibility
praiseworthy
practicalism
practicalist
practicality
Platt-Deutsch
plasteriness
plasterboard
plasterstone
phantasmally
phantasmical
practitioner
pharyngology
pharyngotomy

public-school
pebble-powder
peccadilloes
pickerel-weed
pocket-gopher
pocket-pistol
pacification
pacificatory
pectinaceous
packing-paper
packing-sheet
packing-press
picrocarmine
pictorically
pectoriloquy
pictographic
Pecksniffian
Picturephone®
picture-house
picture-frame
pachydacious
pachycarpous
Pachydermata
pachydermous
pedicellaria
pediculation
pudding-faced
pudding-plate
pudding-stone
pedal-clavier
pedal-pushers
pedantically
pedantocracy
pedunculated
paddock-stool
precancerous
preparedness
prelatically
prevaricator
premaxillary
precariously
prevailingly
prefabricate
precautional
poetastering
presbyterial
Presbyterian
presbyterate
pre-eclampsia
preachership
prescription
prescriptive
piercingness
preoccupancy
pseudocyesis
pseudography
pseudo-Gothic
pseudomartyr
pseudonymity
pseudonymous
pseudopodium
pretenceless
pretendingly

predetermine
precedential
preferential
preselection
predesignate
pretermitted
prehensility
precessional
prehensorial
premenstrual
presentially
presentiment
predestinate
preceptorial
prefectorial
presentation
presentative
preventative
preventively
prerequisite
preservation
preservatory
preservative
prechristian
psephologist
plebiscitary
presidential
predigestion
predilection
presidentess
precipitance
precipitancy
precipitable
precipitator
precisianism
precisianist
precisionist
pteridomania
plenipotence
plenipotency
Pteridophyta
pteridophyte
pteridosperm
predisposing
Plesiosaurus
prehistorian
preciousness
previousness
prefloration
preclassical
peerlessness
preclusively
pneumococcus
pre-eminently
pleomorphism
pleomorphous
pneumaticity
pneumatology
pneumothorax
pleonastical
prerogatived
pterosaurian
pterodactyle

paedobaptism
paedobaptist
preponderant
preponderate
precondition
phenomenally
paedogenesis
paedogenetic
paedophiliac
pleiochasium
predominance
predominancy
prefoliation
precociously
preformation
preformative
precognition
precognitive
paedological
phenological
poenological
paedomorphic
paedodontics
pleiotropism
preconstruct
Premonstrant
prepossessed
plecopterous
preposterous
phenotypical
preordinance
Pleuronectes
pleurisy-root
Pre-Dravidian
press-gallery
pre-establish
plessimetric
pleasantness
pleasingness
pleasantries
pheasant's-eye
pleasure-boat
pressure-cook
pleasureless
pressure-suit
pleasure-trip
preassurance
press-cutting
prenticeship
Plectognathi
prestigiator
prestriction
pretty-pretty
pretty-spoken
prejudgement
presumptuous
pregustation
pre-existence
phenylalanin
pugnaciously
pigmentation
pigeon-flying
pigeon's-blood

privat-docent
privat-dozent
philadelphus
privateering
philanthrope
philanthropy
psilanthropy
prince-bishop
princeliness
principality
price-rigging
prize-fighter
pridefulness
price-current
price-cutting
priggishness
philhellenic
philharmonic
primigravida
Philistinise
philistinism
phillumenist
painlessness
primordially
philodendron
primogenital
primogenitor
philosophess
philosophise
philosophism
philosophist
philological
poison-sumach
priestliness
priest-ridden
pointillisme
pointilliste
point-to-point
primulaceous
pyjama-jacket
pejoratively
Polyadelphia
palladianism
palpableness
polyanthuses
phlebotomise
phlebotomist
policy-holder
police-manure
pelican's-foot
police-office
paludicolous
pile-dwelling
paludamentum
pollen-basket
palaeobotany
polyembryony
palaeography
polyethylene
pulverisable
palaeolithic
palaestrical
pulverulence

palification
phlegmagogic
phlegmagogue
Polygalaceae
polygamously
Polygonaceae
polyglottous
polyhistoric
polling-booth
pulvilliform
pillion-rider
polyisoprene
pulp-magazine
polymorphism
polymorphous
palingenesia
palingenesis
palynologist
palindromist
Polonisation
polyneuritis
polypharmacy
polypetalous
polyphyodont
polyphyletic
polyphyllous
polarography
polarimetric
polarisation
polyrhythmic
polysyllabic
polysyllable
polysiloxane
polysyndeton
polysepalous
pilot-balloon
palatability
politicaster
palette-knife
polytheistic
polytonality
polyurethane
pollutedness
pellucidness
pamperedness
pumpernickel
pompholygous
pandanaceous
pentadactyle
pentadactyly
pentateuchal
pandaemonium
pentagonally
pentapolitan
pantaloonery
pentacrinoid
paniculately
pony-carriage
pantechnicon
panhellenion
Panhellenism
Panhellenist
panhellenium

Pan-Germanism
pen-feathered
pin-feathered
panaesthesia
pansexualism
pansexualist
panification
panchromatic
pinchcommons
panpharmacon
Panchatantra
pontifically
pantisocracy
pencil-sketch
pinniewinkle
penalisation
Penang-lawyer
pantophagist
pantophagous
pantomimical
pantographer
pantographic
panspermatic
pancreatitis
panarthritis
Panathenaean
pony-trekking
punctulation
penitentiary
puncturation
penny-wedding
penny-whistle
propagandise
propagandism
propagandist
propaedeutic
procathedral
probationary
pro-marketeer
phonasthenia
protactinium
proscription
proscriptive
proud-hearted
proletariate
proverbially
phonemically
phonetically
progenitress
procellarian
prolegomenon
process-block
propenseness
processional
professional
processioner
professorial
professoress
professorate
protectingly
protestingly
projectional
prosectorial

protectorial
progesterone
property-room
protectorate
protestation
protectively
projectivity
prosecutable
proselytiser
proof-reading
proof-correct
plough-jogger
ploughwright
prophylactic
prothalamion
prothonotary
provincially
profiteering
providential
prolifically
proficiently
provisionary
prolificness
prodigiosity
propitiation
propitiatory
propitiative
prodigiously
propitiously
profitlessly
proditorious
promissorily
protistology
profligately
problematics
proclamation
proclamatory
proglottides
pro-and-conned
phonocamptic
phonotactics
proboscidean
proboscidian
protonematal
photogeology
photosetting
prolongation
photophilous
photochromic
prototherian
phototherapy
pronominally
prosodically
photokinesis
photobiology
photo-fission
proto-history
photoglyphic
protoplasmal
photoelastic
protoplasmic
protoplastic
probouleutic

pronouncedly
profoundness
prosopopeial
phonological
protozoology
protocolling
prosopopoeia
protomorphic
photomontage
photovoltaic
photocopying
photospheric
photo-process
phonographer
photographer
phonographic
photographic
phototropism
photogravure
proconsulate
photo-etching
proportional
proportioned
phonotypical
prototypical
phosphaturia
prospectuses
phosphoresce
prosperously
protractedly
protractible
proprietress
programmatic
programmable
protreptical
protrusively
poor-spirited
proctorially
prostitution
promuscidate
protuberance
promulgation
propugnation
productional
productively
productivity
prosyllogism
progymnasium
pepper-caster
pepper-castor
pupilability
papuliferous
Papilionidae
populousness
paper-marbler
paper-washing
papyrologist
paper-stainer
papistically
Papaveraceae
pergameneous
permanganate
phreatophyte

paraboloidal
paracyanogen
perichaetial
perichaetium
pyrochemical
paroccipital
parochialise
parochialism
parochiality
para-compound
paracentesis
pericynthion
pericarditis
parachronism
peradventure
paradigmatic
parade-ground
paradisiacal
paradise-fish
paradisaical
Paradiseidae
paradoxidian
paradoxology
paradoxurine
porcelainise
porcelainous
permeability
part-exchange
perseverance
perseverator
paraenetical
pyro-electric
paroemiology
porcellanise
porcellanite
porcellanous
porte-cochère
perpetration
perverseness
paraesthesia
purse-strings
perceptional
perfectation
portentously
perfectively
perceptivity
perpetualism
perpetualist
perpetuality
perpetuation
perfervidity
purification
purificatory
purificative
paragnathism
paragraphist
paragnathous
peregrinator
paraglossate
parchmentise
pertinacious
pervicacious
partisanship

parking-place
participable
participator
partitionist
perfidiously
perniciously
parsimonious
Parkinsonism
permissively
persistently
persistingly
permittivity
particularly
perviousness
parallelwise
pyroligneous
purblindness
paralanguage
paralipomena
perilousness
perplexingly
parsley-piert
paramagnetic
paramilitary
pyromaniacal
portmanteaus
portmanteaux
paramorphism
pyromorphite
perimorphous
parametrical
pyrometrical
peremptorily
perambulator
parenterally
paranthelion
parenthesise
perenniality
phrontistery
phrenologise
phrenologist
paronomastic
perinephrium
perineuritis
purpose-built
purposefully
periodically
perfoliation
personifying
performative
periodontics
periodontist
pornographer
pornographic
periostracum
pernoctation
parrot-wrasse
perionychium
perspicacity
perspectival
peripherical
paraphimosis
parapophyses

parapophysis
paraphrastic
periphrastic
perspiration
perspiratory
parapsychism
pyrophyllite
paraquadrate
portrait-bust
porismatical
parascending
peristeronic
parasphenoid
parisyllabic
phrasemonger
parasyntheta
peristomatic
perispomenon
phraseologic
phraseograph
peristrephic
parasiticide
parasitology
paratactical
pyrotechnics
pyrotechnist
pyritiferous
pyritohedral
pyritohedron
pyrithiamine
pyrotartaric
pyrotartrate
percutaneous
perturbation
perturbatory
perturbative
persulphuric
percussional
perquisition
percussively
persuasively
periwig-pated
peroxidation
party-capital
party-verdict
passage-money
postage-stamp
passableness
Pestalozzian
post-doctoral
post-diluvial
post-diluvian
passe-partout
passemeasure
posteriority
possessioned
possessively
post-graduate
posthumously
post-hypnotic
pestiential
passibleness
postillation

passion-fruit
passionately
passion-music
pisciculture
postliminary
postliminous
post-meridian
postmistress
pestological
post-prandial
postponement
postposition
postpositive
Post-Tertiary
positiveness
positivistic
posture-maker
pasque-flower
passy-measure
Puseyistical
pitiableness
pot-walloping
potichomania
putrefacient
putrefaction
putrefactive
patience-dock
pathetically
pattern-maker
pattern-wheel
pitter-patter
pitch-and-toss
pitcher-plant
Patripassian
petrifaction
petrifactive
putting-cleek
putting-green
putting-stone
patrilineage
patriclinous
pettifogging
pettifoggery
patriarchism
patriarchate
patristicism
pottle-bodied
petaliferous
pitilessness
potamologist
potentiality
pathogenesis
pathogenetic
petrogenesis
petrogenetic
patroclinous
petroglyphic
pathological
petrological
petrodollars
pythonomorph
pot-companion
petrographer

petrographic
potato-blight
potato-finger
potato-spirit
plumbiferous
plumbaginous
plumber-block
pound-foolish
prudentially
pluriseriate
pruning-knife
pluriliteral
pluviometric
plurilocular
plummer-block
plum-porridge
Prussianiser
plumulaceous
pavilion-roof
powder-closet
powdering-tub
powder-monkey
power-station
powerfulness
psychiatrist
psychoactive
psychography
psychologism
psychologist
psychometric
psychonomics
psychrometer
psychrometry
psychopathic
psychosocial
psychosexual
psychoticism
psychotropic
physiocratic
physiography
physiognomic
physiologist
phyllotactic
phytonadione
phycoxanthin
phylogenesis
phylogenetic
phytogenesis
phytogenetic
phytobenthos
phytophagous
phycological
phytological
phytographer
phytographic
Phycomycetes
pay-as-you-earn
puzzle-headed
puzzle-monkey
Quaker-colour
quaking-grass
qualificator
quasi-stellar

quacksalving
qualmishness
quadriennial
quadriennium
Quadragesima
quadrumanous
quarrymaster
quadrangular
quadraplegia
quadraplegic
quadriplegia
quadriplegic
quadraphonic
quadrophonic
quadrivalent
quaestionary
quaestorship
quantifiable
quattrocento
quarter-final
quarter-miler
quartern-loaf
quarter-blood
quarter-plate
quarter-bound
quarter-round
quarter-horse
quarter-staff
quarter-guard
quartz-schist
quantisation
quantitative
quantivalent
quaquaversal
quenchlessly
queue-jumping
querimonious
queen-regnant
queen-dowager
queen-consort
queer-bashing
questionable
questionally
questionless
question-mark
quidditative
quick-scented
quick-selling
quick-sighted
quicksilvery
quill-feather
quill-driving
quixotically
quinquenniad
quinquennial
quinquennium
quintessence
quizzicality
quotableness
readableness
readaptation
rhabdosphere
readjustment

reallocation
readmittance
re-annexation
reappearance
rhamphotheca
reassignment
reassemblage
reassumption
road-surveyor
reassuringly
reabsorption
reassessment
reattachment
roasting-jack
re-alteration
reactiveness
reactivation
ready-moneyed
ruby-coloured
rabbeting-saw
rubbing-stone
rabbinically
rabbit-sucker
rabbit-warren
rebelliously
ribble-rabble
rabble-rouser
ribonuclease
robustiously
ruby-throated
ricochetting
rock-climbing
racketeering
racket-ground
Rochelle-salt
racket-tailed
recreational
recognisance
recognisable
recognisably
rocking-chair
rocking-horse
rocking-stone
recriminator
receiving-set
rectirostral
recollection
recollective
recalcitrant
recalcitrate
recalescence
recklessness
recommitment
recommission
recomforture
racemisation
reconveyance
raconteuring
reconsecrate
reconversion
reconcilable
reconcilably
reconsituent

12 r□t□o

reconnoitrer
reconstitute
raccoon-berry
receptacular
receptaculum
receptionist
reciprocally
reciprocator
recuperation
recuperatory
recuperative
recapitalise
recapitulate
recordership
rock-scorpion
reciting-note
recrudescent
reducibility
radicicolous
reductionism
reductionist
ridiculously
radicivorous
radiesthesia
rodomontader
redemptioner
redemptorist
redintegrate
riding-master
riding-school
radiophonics
radiotherapy
radio-thorium
radiobiology
radio-element
radiological
radio-compass
radiographer
radiographic
radio-isotope
radionuclide
redeployment
rediscoverer
redistribute
redoublement
re-embodiment
re-engagement
re-enlistment
rheometrical
rheumatology
rheumatismal
rhetorically
reed-pheasant
roebuck-berry
reflationary
refractorily
refractivity
rifleman-bird
refreshingly
refreshfully
rifle-grenade
reflectingly
reflectively

reflectivity
refrigerator
refoundation
regressively
regressivity
raggle-taggle
regeneration
regeneratory
regenerative
regardlessly
rigorousness
registration
right-and-left
rightfulness
rehabilitate
rainbow-trout
reiteratedly
Rhinegravine
Rhipidoptera
rhizocarpous
rhizogenetic
Rhizocephala
rhinocerical
rhinoceroses
rhinocerotic
rhizophagous
rhizophilous
rhinoplastic
rhinological
rhinorrhagia
rhinorrhoeal
reimposition
reinstalment
reinspection
rail-splitter
reinvigorate
reinvestment
rejuvenation
reliableness
roller-skater
roller-skates
religionless
rolling-stock
relentlessly
relationally
relationless
relationship
relativeness
relativistic
relativitist
remedilessly
ramification
remainder-man
rumble-tumble
rememberable
rememberably
remembrancer
romantically
remuneration
remuneratory
remunerative
reminiscence
Romanisation

remonstrance
remonstrator
ruminatingly
ruminatively
remorsefully
Rembrandtish
Rembrandtism
rumpti-iddity
rambunctious
removability
ring-armature
ring-compound
ring-dropping
ring-dotterel
run-of-the-mill
röntgenogram
röntgenology
renegotiable
running-board
renunciation
renunciatory
renunciative
ranunculuses
ring-streaked
renouncement
rhopaloceral
rhombohedral
rhombohedron
reoccupation
reordination
rooming-house
rhododendron
Rhodophyceae
rhodomontade
root-pressure
root-parasite
root-tubercle
replantation
rope-drilling
reprehension
reprehensive
representant
replevisable
repressively
ripple-marked
reproachable
reproachless
reprographer
reprographic
reproducible
reproduction
reproductive
reparability
repercussion
repercussive
repossession
repatriation
repetitional
repetitively
reputatively
ruralisation
restaurateur
rush-bottomed

rose-coloured
rosy-coloured
rust-coloured
residentiary
residentship
respectfully
respectively
rosy-fingered
resignedness
resting-place
resting-spore
resting-stage
Rosminianism
resolvedness
resplendence
resplendency
restlessness
resoluteness
resolutioner
resumptively
resiniferous
resonance-box
respondentia
Russophobist
Russophilism
Russophilist
responseless
responsorial
responsively
resupination
resipiscence
resipiscency
restrictedly
reservedness
resurrection
resurrective
restrainable
restrainedly
risorgimento
resuscitable
resuscitator
resistlessly
resettlement
resourceless
resoundingly
rushy-fringed
retractility
retractively
reticulately
reticulation
retrenchment
ratification
ratchet-wheel
retainership
retrievement
rattle-headed
ruthlessness
retensionist
retrocession
retrocessive
retrojection
retromingent
retrofitting

retroflected	stapedectomy	sharp-sighted	subminiature
retroflexion	space-heating	stamping-mill	sublibrarian
retropulsion	scavengering	scalping-tuft	submissively
retropulsive	stage-thunder	sharp-tongued	subalternant
retiringness	snake-charmer	sharp-looking	subalternate
rotor-station	stage-whisper	sharp-pointed	soboliferous
rhumb-sailing	shareholding	sharp-toothed	Sabellianism
roundaboutly	slave-holding	scampishness	subumbrellar
round-mouthed	skateboarder	snappishness	subantarctic
route-proving	slave-traffic	scabrousness	subinfeudate
rough-perfect	share-cropper	sparrow-grass	subinspector
rough-grained	slate-writing	star-spangled	subintroduce
rough-wrought	space-station	Shaksperiana	subnormality
reunionistic	shamefulness	snapshooting	subcommittee
revocability	staff-officer	starting-hole	subconscious
revictualled	snaffling-lay	starting-post	subcontinent
revulsionary	staff-college	slantingways	subopercular
revelational	span-farthing	scatteringly	suboperculum
revolutional	staff-surgeon	smatteringly	subapostolic
revolutioner	slang-whanger	scattermouch	subtreasurer
revengefully	staggeringly	scatter-brain	subarachnoid
ravenousness	swaggeringly	shatter-brain	subarrhation
reverberator	swagger-stick	shatter-proof	subordinancy
river-terrace	slaughterman	scapulimancy	sober-blooded
reversionary	slaughterous	sea-buckthorn	subprincipal
revisitation	smash-and-grab	statuesquely	suberisation
revivability	Stakhanovism	sea-butterfly	subarcuation
revivalistic	stakhanovite	stalwartness	substraction
revivescence	staghorn-fern	submaxillary	substantival
revivescency	swashbuckler	Sublapsarian	substantials
reviviscence	seaside-grape	subhastation	substantiate
reviviscency	staying-power	subabdominal	substitution
Rhynchonella	shaving-brush	subacidulous	substitutive
Rhynchophora	shaving-stick	subscribable	substruction
rhythmically	scarificator	suboccipital	substructure
rhythmometer	stabilisator	subscription	subcutaneous
rhythmopoeia	station-wagon	subscriptive	subduplicate
rhytidectomy	station-house	subeditorial	subsultorily
razzle-dazzle	statistician	sabre-rattler	sacramentary
Scarabaeidae	spaciousness	subfeudation	Socratically
shamateurism	sparking-plug	subfeudatory	sectarianise
Spatangoidea	snack-counter	subreference	sectarianism
stalactiform	shawl-pattern	subcelestial	sociableness
star-blasting	Stahlhelmist	submergement	sack-doudling
scabbard-fish	small-clothes	subdelirious	succedaneous
scabbardless	snarling-iron	subterjacent	secretariate
starchedness	snarling-tool	subtemperate	successantly
seal-cylinder	smallholding	subterranean	successional
stand-pattism	scallop-shell	subvertebral	successfully
staddle-stone	stablishment	subfertility	successively
scandalously	stammeringly	subjectively	sick-headache
standing-bowl	stanniferous	subjectivise	saccharoidal
standing-room	scanning-disc	subjectivism	saccharinity
Scandinavian	swainishness	subjectivist	succinctness
standardiser	shadow-boxing	subjectivity	sacrilegious
slanderously	sea-porcupine	subsequently	sectionalism
standard-wing	shadow-figure	subservience	sickle-celled
stage-manager	shadow-flight	subserviency	secularistic
shamefacedly	scatophagous	subthreshold	sickle-shaped
share-capital	seasoning-tub	subdiaconate	second-strike
scapegallows	scatological	sublineation	second-to-none
space-lattice	sharpshooter	subdivisible	sociobiology
scare-heading	sharp-visaged	subsidiarily	sociological

sycophantise
sycophantish
sacerdotally
secessionism
secessionist
seclusionist
succussation
sedge-warbler
sodden-witted
soda-fountain
saddlebacked
saddle-hackle
saddle-pillar
saddle-shaped
saddle-spring
sedulousness
sudoriferous
sudoriparous
side-whiskers
Steganopodes
steganograph
stencil-plate
speechlessly
speech-making
stercoranism
stercoranist
speed-boating
Speedwriting®
stepdaughter
scene-painter
stereochrome
stereochromy
stereography
scene-shifter
stereoisomer
stereometric
stereopticon
stereophonic
stereotactic
stereotropic
stereotyping
sledge-hammer
shepherdling
shepherdless
stethoscopic
sheriff-clerk
sheriff-court
sheriff's-post
specifically
specialistic
speciousness
speckledness
specktioneer
speaking-tube
speakerphone
sneck-drawing
sneakishness
stelliferous
shellshocked
stealthiness
spelling-book
shealing-hill
sheeling-hill

Stellenbosch
swell-mobsman
spermogonium
steam-chamber
steam-whistle
spermaphytic
spermophytic
spermatocele
spermatocyte
spermathecal
stepmotherly
spermatogeny
spermatozoal
spermatozoan
spermatozoic
spermatozoid
spermatozoon
steam-turbine
stern-wheeler
sternutation
sternutatory
sternutative
stegocarpous
stegosaurian
stegophilist
stenographer
scenographic
stenographic
sleep-walking
sheep-scoring
steeplechase
steeple-house
steeple-crown
sheep-shearer
sweepingness
sleeping-pill
sheepishness
sheep-stealer
spear-thrower
spear-thistle
steering-gear
spear-running
speiss-cobalt
sneeshin-mull
sweet-scented
spectre-lemur
sweet-william
steatomatous
sweet-and-sour
spectroscope
spectroscopy
spectrometic
spectrometry
spectrograph
sweet-toothed
steatopygous
stentorphone
stertorously
sweetishness
spectatorial
sheath-winged
sleeve-button
safe-breaking

safe-cracking
safeguarding
sufficiently
softly-softly
suffruticose
segmentation
suggestively
significance
significancy
significator
sugar-refiner
sight-reading
sight-singing
sight-playing
sage-thrasher
sphragistics
sphacelation
Schneiderian
sphygmoscope
sphygmometer
sphygmophone
sphygmograph
schiller-spar
scholastical
sphincterial
schindylesis
schindyletic
schoolboyish
school-doctor
school-divine
school-friend
schoolfellow
school-leaver
schoolmaster
school-taught
schorlaceous
sphericality
schismatical
schizocarpic
Schizaeaceae
schizogenous
schizogonous
schizomycete
schizopodous
schizophrene
schizophytic
schizothymia
schizothymic
scitamineous
suitableness
soixante-neuf
sailboarding
stilboestrol
shipbuilding
ship-chandler
slip-carriage
swindle-sheet
spindle-shell
spindle-whorl
swine-keeping
spine-chiller
seine-fishing
spider-legged

spider-monkey
spider-stitch
spire-steeple
spitefulness
stiff-hearted
spiegeleisen
swinging-boom
swinging-post
sniggeringly
stichometric
stichomythia
stichomythic
spiritedness
spiritlessly
spirit-rapper
spiritualise
spiritualism
spiritualist
spirituality
spirituosity
stickler-like
slickensided
slink-butcher
shield-bearer
spiflication
still-peering
still-piecing
shield-maiden
shieling-hill
spilling-line
shillingless
shilling-mark
shield-shaped
shilly-shally
still-hunting
seismography
seismologist
seismometric
swimming-bell
swimming-bath
swimmingness
swimming-pond
swimming-pool
seismonastic
seismoscopic
scientifical
spinning-mill
seignioralty
seigniorship
skipping-rope
slipperiness
snippetiness
Sciuropterus
stirrup-strap
spinsterhood
spinstership
scissiparity
scissor-blade
scissor-tooth
skirt-dancing
shirtwaister
skittle-alley
spittle-house

scintigraphy	silver-voiced	salutariness	synadelphite
scintillator	self-flattery	solitariness	syngenesious
shift-working	self-focusing	salutational	sonneteering
skittishness	salification	salutatorian	syndetically
stipulaceous	solifluction	salutatorily	sententially
spinulescent	self-gracious	self-violence	synaesthesia
swizzle-stick	self-glorious	splay-mouthed	synaesthetic
self-analysis	sulphonamide	somnambulant	sunshine-roof
self-affected	self-hypnosis	somnambulary	synchronical
self-adhesive	sulphuretted	somnambulism	synchroniser
syllabically	sulphuration	somnambulist	synchroflash
salvationism	self-indeared	somnambulate	syntheticism
salvationist	self-identity	semi-Arianism	singing-hinny
saleableness	selling-price	semi-annually	sensibleness
saltatorious	salvifically	semi-attached	sensitometer
self-anointed	Salviniaceae	semicylinder	single-acting
self-applause	self-interest	semicomatose	single-decker
self-approval	silviculture	semicircular	single-figure
self-absorbed	sylviculture	semi-diameter	single-handed
self-activity	self-involved	semideponent	single-minded
self-begotten	self-judgment	semi-detached	synclinorium
salubriously	self-lighting	Simmenthaler	single-seater
self-balanced	self-luminous	summer-weight	single-wicket
self-betrayal	selflessness	semifinalist	Sinanthropus
silicicolous	salamandrian	semiglobular	synantherous
self-cleaning	salamandroid	sumphishness	synonymously
self-creation	salamandrine	semi-imbecile	sun-and-planet
siliciferous	Solomon's-seal	sempiternity	Syngnathidae
self-critical	self-murderer	somniloquise	sindonophany
self-coloured	splint-armour	somniloquism	synoptically
self-contempt	splinter-bone	somniloquist	sinupalliate
self-consumed	selenography	simultaneity	synarthrosis
solecistical	solenoidally	simultaneous	syncretistic
self-catering	splendidious	simple-minded	sonorousness
solicitation	splendidness	simoniacally	sinisterwise
solicitously	selenologist	seminiferous	sinusoidally
self-deceived	splenomegaly	semantically	sinistrality
self-deceiver	splenisation	somnolescent	sinistrorsal
solidifiable	salsolaceous	semi-official	sinistrously
self-delusion	salmon-colour	symbolically	sanctifiedly
self-depraved	self-occupied	symbololatry	senatorially
self-directed	self-ordained	semi-precious	sanitisation
self-director	salmon-fisher	Semi-Pelagian	sanguiferous
self-disliked	saloon-keeper	semipellucid	sensualistic
self-destruct	sallow-kitten	semiparasite	sanguinolent
self-distrust	salmon-ladder	Simarubaceae	sanguineness
self-devotion	saloon-pistol	Samaritanism	sanguinarily
silver-beater	salmon-tackle	symptomatise	sensuousness
self-exciting	self-pleasing	semitropical	sanguivorous
self-endeared	self-produced	somatopleure	sun-expelling
self-electing	self-portrait	sumpter-horse	sand-yachting
self-election	saltpetreman	Semitisation	sporangiolum
self-exertion	sclerodermia	semiwater-gas	sporadically
self-elective	sclerodermic	santalaceous	stomatodaeum
self-effacing	sclerenchyma	sensationism	shot-blasting
silver-footed	solar-powered	sensationist	shopbreaking
silver-glance	sclerophylly	singableness	snowball-tree
self-evidence	solarisation	syntagmatite	show-business
self-existent	salesmanship	syndactylism	snobbishness
silver-plated	self-schooled	syndactylous	slouch-hatted
self-employed	solitudinous	sand-blasting	stoechiology
salver-shaped	salutiferous	sansculottic	stoichiology
self-educated	self-thinking	synecdochism	slop-clothing

sword-bayonet
snowdrop-tree
sword-breaker
stonewalling
stone-chatter
slovenliness
stone-boiling
spokesperson
stone-breaker
stone-bramble
stone-dresser
stone-cutting
spongicolous
sponge-finger
sponge-fisher
spongologist
sponge-rubber
smotheringly
smotheriness
slothfulness
shoeing-smith
scoring-board
storiologist
snow-in-summer
stock-raising
stockingette
stocking-foot
stock-and-horn
stockingless
stocking-mask
shockingness
stock-in-trade
stocking-sole
slockdolager
stock-jobbing
stock-jobbery
stock-breeder
stockbroking
stockishness
shoulder-belt
shoulder-bone
shoulder-high
shoulder-knot
shoulder-mark
shoulder-note
shoulder-slip
spotlessness
storm-warning
storm-lantern
storm-shutter
stormy-petrel
storm-trooper
stormfulness
scoundreldom
scoundrelism
scornfulness
scolopaceous
Scolopacidae
sporogenesis
scopophiliac
sporophorous
snobographer
stoop-gallant

Scorpaenidae
scorpion-fish
Scorpionidea
scouring-rush
sportability
smooth-browed
smooth-coated
stout-hearted
shortchanger
short-circuit
short-sighted
smooth-leaved
short-clothes
shooting-iron
shooting-star
scoptophilia
Scottishness
smooth-spoken
sportfulness
sportiveness
story-telling
stony-hearted
supraciliary
supra-orbital
supramundane
Septembriser
Septemberish
septennially
septentrions
septemvirate
sapphire-wing
septilateral
sophisticate
supplicating
supplication
supplicatory
supplemental
supplementer
sapindaceous
saponifiable
Sipunculacea
Siphonaptera
saprophagous
saprophytism
suppositious
Siphonophora
siphonophore
siphonostele
supercargoes
supernacular
supernatural
supernaculum
separability
supersedence
supervenient
superrealism
superrealist
supersensual
supersession
supersensory
supervention
soporiferous
supercharger

superhighway
superciliary
supercilious
supercluster
superplastic
supereminent
superimposed
superannuate
superposable
superiorship
superorganic
supererogant
supererogate
superordinal
superfrontal
suppressedly
suppressible
superstratum
separateness
superstition
superhumanly
supermundane
superhumeral
supersubtile
Septuagintal
septuagenary
Septuagesima
sequentially
sequestrator
stream-anchor
sarsaparilla
surface-water
surface-to-air
surface-craft
surpassingly
surf-boarding
scrobiculate
strobiliform
scribblement
scribblingly
strobilation
strabismical
stroboscopic
sprechgesang
strychninism
sprechstimme
structurally
straddle-back
stridelegged
stridulantly
stridulation
stridulatory
Stradivarius
sorbefacient
sir-reverence
street-keeper
surveillance
surrealistic
sergeant-fish
sergeantship
serjeantship
surrejoinder
surveyorship

street-raking
serpent-eater
serpentiform
serpentinely
serpentining
serpentinise
serpentinous
serpent-stone
screen-writer
street-walker
sure-footedly
scraggedness
Strigiformes
stragglingly
strugglingly
sprightfully
service-berry
servicewoman
service-court
surfing-board
straightaway
straightener
straight-edge
straightness
straightways
strait-jacket
strait-lacing
servitorship
survivorship
strikingness
shrill-gorged
shrill-voiced
scrimshander
skrimshanker
serum-therapy
scramblingly
spring-bladed
spring-beauty
spring-beetle
string-course
spring-headed
spring-heeled
strontianite
spring-keeper
spring-loaded
stranglehold
stranglement
strangle-weed
strong-minded
strengthener
strengthless
strangulated
strongylosis
sarcomatosis
sarcophagous
sardonically
sarcoplasmic
surmountable
seriocomical
servo-control
strophanthin
strophanthus
seraphically

strophiolate	stupefactive	traditionist	transmutably
Strepsiptera	stupendously	tragi-comical	translucence
scrupulosity	scutellation	thanksgiving	translucency
scrupulously	shuffle-board	thank-you-ma'am	transfusible
streptoneura	snuff-dipping	thankfulness	transduction
streptococci	spurge-laurel	trail-blazing	tractability
streptomycin	sluggishness	thaumatogeny	toasting-fork
scraper-board	south-eastern	traumatology	toasting-iron
strepitation	south-seeking	thaumaturgic	tractoration
scrophularia	south-western	thaumaturgus	traitorously
scripturally	soughing-tile	training-ship	Traducianism
script-writer	south-country	train-spotter	Traducianist
surprisingly	Southcottian	trampolinist	tobacco-heart
seraskierate	southernmost	tranquillise	tobacco-plant
stratocratic	southernwood	tranquillity	tobacco-pouch
sprat-weather	spuriousness	translatable	table-turning
stratigraphy	studiousness	transparence	Tubuliflorae
scratchingly	skunk-cabbage	transparency	tubulifloral
scratchiness	sculling-boat	transoceanic	tabernacular
scratch-brush	scullery-maid	transudation	tuberiferous
scrutinising	soullessness	transudatory	Tyburn-ticket
scrutinously	Saurognathae	transferable	Tyburn-tippet
stratosphere	slumpflation	transfer-book	tuberculated
stratotanker	stump-oratory	transcendent	tuberculosed
sarrusophone	sculpturally	transference	tuberculosis
shriving-time	squirearchal	transferring	ticket-holder
straw-breadth	squirrel-cage	transversely	ticket-office
shrewishness	squirrel-tail	transversion	ticket-porter
screw-steamer	scurrilously	transleithan	ticket-writer
systematical	square-rigged	transvestism	tactlessness
systematiser	square-rigger	transvestite	ticklishness
sisterliness	soul-stirring	transshipper	technocratic
system-monger	spurtle-blade	transpirable	technicality
suspensorial	squattocracy	transhipping	technicolour
suspensorium	skutterudite	transmigrant	technologist
suspensively	saunteringly	transmigrate	tectonically
sustentation	sputteringly	transmission	tachygrapher
sustentative	stutteringly	transmissive	tachygraphic
susceptivity	sluttishness	transmitting	tsesarevitch
suspiciously	seventy-eight	transpicuous	therapeutics
session-clerk	Sivapithecus	transiliency	therapeutist
session-house	sexcentenary	transplanter	thematically
sesquialtera	sexagenarian	transumption	theocratical
sesquitertia	sexton-beetle	transumptive	trench-mortar
satanophobia	sky-tinctured	transposable	trench-plough
satisfaction	stylographic	transforming	trend-setting
satisfactory	tralaticious	transformism	tremendously
satisfyingly	tralatitious	transformist	thereagainst
stubble-field	thalassaemia	transmogrify	therethrough
stubble-goose	thalassaemic	transmontane	thereinafter
snubbing-post	tragelaphine	transpontine	teeter-totter
slubberingly	traceability	transporting	twelfth-night
slumberingly	tradescantia	trap-shooting	Theriodontia
stubbornness	tradespeople	transportive	Theriomorpha
slumberously	travel-soiled	transuranian	tree-kangaroo
sound-ranging	trabeculated	transuranium	theologaster
sounding-lead	teachability	transgressor	thermo-couple
sounding-line	tracheoscopy	transitional	Thermidorian
studding-sail	tracheostomy	transit-trade	thermography
shuddering-ly	Trachypterus	transitorily	thermolabile
saucepan-fish	tragicalness	transitively	thermometric
stupefacient	tracing-paper	transhumance	thermophilic
stupefaction	traditionary	transmutable	Thesmophoria

12 t◻t◻l

theomorphism	trigonometry	tonelessness	tormentingly
thermostatic	tricorporate	tenant-at-will	tercentenary
thermostable	trigrammatic	tuning-hammer	three-quarter
thermosphere	toilsomeness	tin-streaming	thriftlessly
thermoscopic	thirteenthly	tongue-tacked	torch-thistle
thermotactic	twitteringly	troublemaker	turbinacious
thermotropic	twitterboned	trouble-mirth	Torricellian
teeing-ground	trifurcation	trouble-world	tergiversate
theanthropic	trituberculy	trouble-house	turning-lathe
Theopaschite	tribute-money	trouble-state	turning-point
theopathetic	tripudiation	thoughtfully	terrifically
theophylline	thievishness	trocheameter	turbidimiter
theorematist	telaesthesia	trophobiosis	terribleness
theoretician	telaesthetic	trophobiotic	turriculated
theosophical	talkee-talkee	trophallaxis	tirlie-wirlie
treasure-city	tilley-valley	trochanteric	turtle-necked
trestle-table	telegraphese	tooth-drawing	tirelessness
twenty-four-mo	telegraphist	trophotactic	taramasalata
theatrically	toll-gatherer	trophotropic	tyrannically
theatromania	talking-point	two-sidedness	tyrannicidal
theatrophone	teleosaurian	troglodytism	Turcophilism
twenty-twenty	tallow-candle	trolling-bait	turbocharged
Tagliacotian	teleological	troll-my-dames	turbocharger
toggle-switch	teleostomous	trolley-table	turnpike-road
togetherness	teleprompter	trolley-wheel	throstle-cock
tridactylous	tolerability	thoroughbred	tiresomeness
tripartition	telergically	thorough-bass	teratologist
triadelphous	talismanical	thoroughfare	throttle-pipe
thirdborough	telesmatical	thoroughness	teratomatous
trimethylene	telescopical	tropophilous	through-going
tricephalous	tellurometer	tropological	through-train
tribespeople	teleutospore	tropospheric	through-other
thief-catcher	Telautograph®	troop-carrier	through-stane
trigger-happy	televisional	thousandfold	through-stone
triphthongal	time-bewasted	thousand-legs	tortuousness
trichologist	timocratical	thousand-year	thrivingness
trichiniasis	temperalitie	tootsy-wootsy	testamentary
trichinellae	time-exposure	tapoalteerie	tassel-gentle
trichromatic	time-honoured	type-cylinder	tessellation
trichophyton	timely-parted	tappet-motion	tastefulness
thitherwards	tumbler-drier	typification	testificator
trichotomise	tamelessness	type-founding	testiculated
trichotomous	timelessness	typographist	taskmistress
Trichiuridae	tumultuation	topside-turvy	tussock-grass
triticalness	tumultuously	tapsieteerie	testosterone
thick-sighted	temporaneous	toploftiness	testudineous
thick-skulled	Tamaricaceae	tape-recorder	tissue-typing
thick-skinned	timbrologist	topsyturvily	tetradactyly
thick-and-thin	timbromaniac	terebratulae	tetrarchical
trickishness	timorousness	terebinthine	tetrahedrite
trickstering	temptability	turacoverdin	tetrachordal
triglyceride	temptingness	three-ha'porth	tetrachotomy
triplication	timothy-grass	torrefaction	tetrapolitan
triple-headed	tantalum-lamp	three-centred	tetramorphic
triflingness	tender-hefted	tercel-gentle	tetrasporous
triple-turned	tangentially	Torpedinidae	tetrastichal
Trismegistus	tonsilectomy	tercel-jerkin	tetrastichic
triumphantly	tangibleness	turbellarian	tetrapterous
thigmotropic	tonsillotomy	three-pounder	tetradynamia
triangularly	tintinnabula	Tardenoisian	tetracycline
trinomialism	tenuirostral	three-monthly	tithe-proctor
trinomialist	tennis-player	three-pricker	totalisation
trigonometer	tennis-racket	torrentially	totalitarian

tittle-tattle
titaniferous
tetanisation
Titanosaurus
Thurberesque
thunder-sheet
thunder-plump
thunder-cloud
thunderingly
thunder-drive
thunder-stone
thunder-storm
thunderously
truce-breaker
truth-telling
touchingness
truthfulness
true-love-knot
tautological
trumpet-major
trumpet-shell
trustfulness
tu-whit-tu-whoo
town-planning
towardliness
toxicologist
toxicophobia
toxocariasis
tax-sheltered
taxing-master
tax-collector
toxophilitic
trypaflavine
trypanocidal
Thysanoptera
thyrotrophin
trysting-tree
unanalysable
unanalytical
unaccredited
unascendable
unascendible
unacceptance
unacceptable
unaccustomed
unaffectedly
unachievable
unamiability
unadmonished
unappealable
unappeasable
unapplausive
unapplicable
unapproached
unapparelled
unaspiringly
unappetising
unacquainted
unassuagable
unassociated
unanswerable
unanswerably
unassignable

unassailable
unauspicious
unassumingly
unassistedly
unattractive
unarticulate
unartificial
unattainable
unattainably
unauthorised
unartistlike
unadulterate
unbiasedness
umbrageously
unbecomingly
unbreachable
umbrella-bird
umbrella-tree
unbreathable
unbreathed-on
unbefriended
unblinkingly
unbelievable
unbelievably
Umbelliferae
unbeneficial
urbanologist
urbanisation
unbrokenness
unbetterable
unblushingly
unchaperoned
unchangeable
unchangeably
unchangingly
uncharitable
uncharitably
unchallenged
unclassified
unchasteness
uncreditable
uncheerfully
unchivalrous
uncritically
uncelebrated
uncultivated
uncultivable
uncalculated
uncomeatable
uncommercial
uncomeliness
uncomposable
uncompounded
uncommonness
unconcealing
unconcerning
unconsecrate
unconversant
unconsenting
unconfinable
unconvincing
unconsidered
unconfinedly

uncandidness
unconclusive
uncensorious
unconforming
unconformity
uncontrolled
unconstraint
unconfusedly
uncloistered
uncapsizable
uncoquettish
unchronicled
unchristened
ulcerousness
uncatalogued
uncounselled
unctuousness
uncovenanted
undeceivable
undocumented
undecomposed
undeliberate
undelectable
undelightful
undulatingly
undemocratic
undiminished
undependable
undiplomatic
undertakable
under-hangman
undergarment
underpayment
underpassion
underachieve
undertenancy
underdevelop
underperform
undersealing
underpeopled
underbearing
underletting
under-sheriff
underkingdom
underpinning
underskinker
underblanket
underclothed
underclothes
underpowered
underworkman
under-produce
underdressed
underwriting
underwrought
underdrawing
understratum
understaffed
underutilise
understanded
understander
underfunding
underbuilder

under-turnkey
underrunning
undercurrent
undispatched
undespairing
undismantled
undissembled
undiscerning
undesignedly
undischarged
undiscipline
undiscordant
undiscording
undiscovered
undissolving
undistracted
undisordered
undeservedly
undisturbing
undisputedly
undetermined
undoubtingly
undivestedly
unelaborated
unembittered
unencumbered
unendangered
unendingness
uneventfully
uneconomical
unexpectedly
unexpressive
unexpugnable
unemployable
unemployment
unexpurgated
unerringness
unextenuated
unenthralled
unfranchised
unflaggingly
unflattering
unfadingness
unfrequented
unfrequently
unfrightened
unfaithfully
unfriendship
unfilterable
unfamiliarly
unformalised
unforeboding
unformidable
unfertilised
unforeseeing
unformulated
unforewarned
unfossilised
unfastidious
unfittedness
unfathomable
unfathomably
unfruitfully

unfavourable	unmeasurable	unproclaimed	unrestricted
unfavourably	unmeasurably	unprovokedly	unreservedly
ungracefully	unmechanical	unpronounced	unrestrained
ungratefully	unmechanised	unprosperous	unresistible
ungraciously	unmodifiable	unprocurable	unreturnable
unguentarium	unmodernised	unproductive	unrevealable
ungainliness	unmaintained	unpopularity	unrevengeful
unguiculated	unmanageable	unperfection	unrewardedly
ungentleness	unmanageably	unperceptive	unrhythmical
ungenerously	unmunitioned	unpersecuted	unsearchable
ungroundedly	unmiraculous	unparalleled	unsearchably
ungrudgingly	unmarketable	unperforated	unstanchable
ungovernable	unmercifully	unpardonable	unstableness
ungovernably	unmoralising	unpardonably	unseasonable
unhabituated	unmistakable	unperforming	unseasonably
unhandsomely	unmistakably	upper-bracket	unshadowable
unhyphenated	unmethodical	unperishable	unstatutable
unheroically	unmethodised	unpersuasive	unstatutably
unharmonious	Uintatherium	unpossessing	unsubscribed
unhospitable	unnoticeable	unpassionate	unsublimated
unhistorical	unnaturalise	unpatronised	unsubsidised
unhesitating	unnourishing	unpavilioned	unsubmissive
unilaterally	unoverthrown	unquantified	unsubmitting
unimaginable	unofficially	unquenchable	unsocialised
unimaginably	urolithiasis	unquenchably	unsuccessful
unitarianism	unoriginated	unquestioned	unsuccessive
unincumbered	uxoriousness	uproariously	unsteadiness
uniseriately	unornamental	unreasonable	unsterilised
unidealistic	unornamented	unreasonably	unseemliness
universalise	unoppressive	unrecognised	unspectacled
universalism	Ulotrichales	unrecallable	unswervingly
universalist	unobservance	unreconciled	unsufferable
universality	unobservable	unredeemable	unsufficient
unidentified	unobstructed	unriddleable	unsegregated
unisexuality	unobservedly	unrefreshing	unscientific
uninfluenced	unobtainable	unreflecting	unsailorlike
unionisation	unpeacefully	unreflective	unstimulated
urinogenital	unpreparedly	unreformable	unsalability
unifoliolate	unprelatical	unregimented	unsolicitous
unicorn-shell	unprevailing	unregeneracy	unseminaried
unicorn-whale	unprescribed	unregenerate	unsensitised
unimpressive	unpretending	unregistered	unsanctified
unimpugnable	unpoetically	unrightfully	unsanctioned
unimprisoned	unpleasantly	unrelievable	unsensualise
unimportance	unpleasingly	unrelievedly	unstockinged
unimportuned	unpleasantry	unremembered	unscottified
uninstructed	unprettiness	unromantical	unsepulchred
unintegrated	unprejudiced	unremarkable	unsupposable
unintroduced	unprincipled	unremorseful	unsupervised
uninterested	unprivileged	unremittedly	unsuppressed
ubiquitarian	unpolishable	unrepealable	unstructured
ubiquitously	unpoliteness	unrepeatable	unshrinkable
unkindliness	unpunishable	unrepairable	unscrupulous
unlibidinous	unpunishably	unrepulsable	unscriptural
uglification	unpunctuated	unrepentance	unstratified
unlikelihood	unpropertied	unrepiningly	unsustaining
unlikeliness	unprotesting	unreprovable	unsystematic
unliquidated	unprocedural	unreproached	unsuspecting
unlistened-to	unprofitable	unreportable	unsuspicious
unliveliness	unprofitably	unrequitedly	unsettlement
unloveliness	unprovidedly	unrespective	unsatisfying
unlovingness	unprohibited	unresolvable	unslumbering
unlawfulness	unpropitious	unresponsive	unsculptured

ultrasensual
unthankfully
untrammelled
ultramontane
untranslated
untransmuted
ultramundane
untremendous
unthinkingly
Ustilagineae
ustilaginous
untimeliness
untumultuous
untenability
untenantable
ultroneously
unthoughtful
unthreatened
unterminated
unterrifying
untruthfully
untrustiness
untowardness
unusefulness
usuriousness
usufructuary
unvaccinated
unvulnerable
unventilated
unvanquished
unvariegated
unverifiable
unvirtuously
unvoyageable
unwearyingly
unwieldiness
unwontedness
unworthiness
unworshipped
unworshipful
unwithholden
unwatchfully
unwaveringly
unyieldingly
vibraphonist
vibratiuncle
vocabularian
vocabularied
vice-chairman
vocicultural
vociferosity
vociferation
vociferously
vice-governor
Vacciniaceae
Vaccinoideae
vocalisation
Victorianism
victoriously
vicar-general
vocationally
vacationless
vacuum-packed

vaginicoline
vaginicolous
vigorousness
vegetatively
Vehmgerichte
voicefulness
vainglorious
voiding-lobby
Volga-Baltaic
volcanically
vulcanisable
valuableness
villainously
velocipedean
velocipedian
velocipedist
velvet-guards
velvet-scoter
vilification
voluminosity
voluminously
volumetrical
voluntaryism
voluntaryist
Valenciennes
Velloziaceae
vulvo-uterine
voluptuosity
voluptuously
valorisation
velarisation
valetudinary
volatileness
volitionally
volitionless
volitational
vomiturition
vantage-point
vinicultural
vengefulness
vinification
vinegarrette
vinegar-plant
vindicatress
vendibleness
vindictively
venomousness
venepuncture
venipuncture
ventripotent
vanquishable
vanquishment
violin-string
vaporisation
vaporousness
variationist
variableness
vernacularly
varicoloured
veridicality
viridescence
verbenaceous
vertebration

verification
verificatory
verticalness
versificator
verticillate
vermin-killer
virgin's-bower
vermiculated
virilescence
verisimility
verisimilous
virtuosoship
virtuousness
vesiculation
vasodilatory
viscerotonia
viscerotonic
vestimentary
viscosimeter
viscosimetry
viscoelastic
viscountship
vase-painting
visiting-book
visiting-card
visitational
visitatorial
vaticination
vitreousness
vitrifaction
vitrifacture
vitriolation
vitalisation
vitro-di-trina
vituperation
vituperatory
vituperative
veterinarian
vitativeness
vaudevillian
vaudevillist
vaunt-courier
vivification
viviparously
weal-balanced
whale-fishing
whale-fishery
wranglership
weather-gauge
weather-chart
weather-gleam
weather-glass
weather-cloth
weather-bound
weather-board
weather-house
weather-proof
weather-stain
weather-strip
wrathfulness
weaning-brash
what's-her-name
weak-spirited

what's-his-name
what's-its-name
wicket-keeper
wedding-march
wedding-cards
wedding-dower
wedding-dress
wide-spectrum
wretchedness
whencesoever
whereagainst
wherethrough
weeping-birch
weeding-tongs
weeping-cross
wife-swapping
Wagnerianism
wiggle-waggle
wag-at-the-wall
wag-by-the-wall
whip-and-derry
white-bellied
white-bearded
white-herring
white-livered
white-fronted
white-crested
white-crowned
writer's-cramp
white-pudding
whip-grafting
Whiggishness
weight-lifter
whitherwards
writing-paper
writing-table
waiting-woman
whisky-frisky
whitlow-grass
whigmaleerie
whipping-post
whip-poor-will
whimperingly
whisperingly
whisperously
whimsicality
whip-scorpion
wainscotting
whistle-drunk
waistcoateer
waistcoating
wollastonite
well-becoming
well-breathed
well-balanced
wallcovering
well-dressing
well-directed
well-disposed
welter-stakes
well-educated
welter-weight
well-favoured

well-grounded
well-informed
Wellingtonia
walking-straw
walking-stick
walking-staff
walkie-talkie
williewaught
well-mannered
willow-grouse
will-o'-the-wisp
well-pleasing
well-plighted
wall-painting
well-tempered
well-timbered
wild-williams
wallydraigle
womanishness
woman-queller
wind-changing
wine-coloured
winter-beaten
winter-bourne
winter-cherry
winter-clover
winter-ground
winter-garden
wonder-monger
wonder-struck
winter-weight
wonder-worker
wine-glassful
winding-sheet
winding-stair
wine-merchant
winnowing-fan
window-screen
wondrousness
wing-shooting
Windsor-chair
woodburytype
whole-hearted
wood-engraver
wooden-headed
whole-skinned
wooden-tongue
wrongfulness
wood-hyacinth
woolly-headed
woolly-haired
woodlessness
wood-offering
whooping-swan
whortleberry
workableness
word-building
world-wearied
world-beating
worshipfully
warehouseman
working-class
working-model

working-house
workmistress
warmongering
word-painting
wire-stitched
wire-stringed
wisecracking
wastefulness
washingtonia
washing-board
washing-house
wishing-stone
withdrawment
witheredness
watch-officer
withholdment
watch-crystal
witches'-broom
watchfulness
water-bailiff
water-ballast
water-carrier
watermanship
water-parsnip
water-wagtail
water-parting
water-battery
water-reactor
water-hemlock
water-bellows
water-measure
water-biscuit
water-gilding
water-milfoil
water-diviner
water-blister
water-flowing
water-flowers
watering-call
watering-hole
water-soldier
water-cooling
water-boatman
water-spaniel
water-opossum
water-drinker
waterishness
water-strider
water-turbine
water-buffalo
water-culture
Woulfe-bottle
wave-offering
waveringness
way-passenger
xylobalsamum
xanthochroia
xanthochroic
xanthochroid
xanthomatous
xanthopterin
xiphisternum
xiphophyllus

xerodermatic
xeromorphous
yieldingness
yellow-backed
yellow-billed
yellow-footed
yellow-headed
yellow-hammer
yellow-horned
yellow-legged
yellow-necked
yellow-rumped
yellow-ringed
yellow-rattle
yellow-yowley
yankee-doodle
youthfulness
zygodactylic
zygomycetous
zygomorphism
zygomorphous
zygapophyses
zygapophysis
Zwinglianism
Zwinglianist
Zeitvertreib
zalambdodont
Zantedeschia
zincographer
zincographic
zenith-sector
zoopathology
zoomagnetism
zoogeography
zoochemistry
zoophytology
zoologically
zootomically
zoospermatic
zoographical
Zarathustric
Zeuglodontia

Anacardiaceae
Amaranthaceae
amarantaceous
academicalism
anathematical
anaphrodisiac
anachronistic
arachnologist
anachronously
anaphorically
apathetically
acaridomatium
availableness
araeometrical
acarodomatium
analogousness
anaerobically
anagrammatise
anagrammatism
anagrammatist
avant-gardiste
anastigmatism
ambidexterity
ambidexterous
ambiguousness
arboriculture
ambassadorial
arbitrariness
ambitiousness
archaeologist
archaeopteryx
archbishopric
accidentalism
accidentality
accident-prone
accreditation
Archegoniatae
alcoholometer
alcoholometry
acclimatation
archimandrite
architectonic
architectural
archidiaconal
accelerometer
acculturation
accompaniment
accommodative
accommodating
accommodation
Ascensiontide
acceptability
acceptilation
ascertainable
ascertainment
accessibility
audaciousness
Addressograph®
androdioecism
audio-engineer
audio-location
acetification
adenoidectomy

averruncation
anfractuosity
affreightment
affenpinscher
affirmatively
afforestation
aggravatingly
algebraically
argumentative
argumentation
argentiferous
Anglo-Catholic
Anglo-Saxondom
agglomerative
agglomeration
Anglo-American
angiospermous
agglutinative
agglutination
atheistically
apheliotropic
athematically
aphanipterous
achromatopsia
animalisation
animadversion
animal-worship
adiabatically
arithmetician
acidification
axiomatically
anisophyllous
aristocratism
Aviculariidae
All-hallowmass
All-hallowtide
allegorically
allelomorphic
Atlantosaurus
ailourophobia
ailourophilia
allowableness
admeasurement
armamentarium
almond-blossom
administrable
administrator
admirableness
atmospherical
admissibility
armoured-train
amniocentesis
annexationist
apocatastasis
anomalistical
apocalyptical
apogeotropism
alongshoreman
apophlegmatic
apothegmatise
apothegmatist
apochromatism
aboriginalism

aboriginality
agonistically
apodictically
apomictically
atomistically
abortifacient
apostolically
acotyledonous
alphabetarian
alphabetiform
appealingness
apprehensible
applicability
amphigastrium
amphitheatral
amplification
appellatively
appellational
appendiculate
approximately
approximative
approximation
appropinquate
appropinquity
appropriately
appropriative
appropriation
appertainment
appertainance
aspergillosis
apportionment
acquirability
acquiescently
acquiescingly
agrobiologist
agriculturist
atrociousness
aerodynamical
agreeableness
aerogenerator
acrylonitrile
aerolithology
acrimoniously
air-compressor
airworthiness
agrostologist
associateship
associability
associativity
assiduousness
answerability
aesthetically
assumptionist
assentiveness
arseno-pyrites
absorbability
Austroasiatic
abstractional
assertiveness
Australianism
Assyriologist
assassination
asset-stripper

actualisation
astrapophobia
antiballistic
autobiography
anticoagulant
anticlimactic
anticlinorium
autecological
anticlockwise
autocephalous
antichristian
autocatalysis
autocatalytic
autochthonism
autochthonous
autodigestion
anthelminthic
autoeroticism
asthenosphere
authentically
authenticator
artificialise
artificiality
antigenically
antigropeloes
antihistamine
attainability
attributively
antilogarithm
anti-marketeer
asthmatically
automatically
actinobacilli
attentiveness
antenniferous
antinomianism
actinomycosis
actinomorphic
antinephritic
astonishingly
actinotherapy
antiochianism
anthophyllite
astrophysical
authoritative
authorisation
authoritarian
astrodynamics
anti-personnel
antiquitarian
alternatively
anthropogenic
anthropolatry
anthropomorph
anthropometry
anthropophagi
anthropophagy
anthropopathy
anthroposophy
antispasmodic
antisocialism
antisocialist
antisociality

autoschediaze
autoschediasm
antiscorbutic
antisepticise
antisepticism
attitudiniser
arundinaceous
Aquifoliaceae
aluminiferous
aqua-mirabilis
advantageable
adventuresome
adventurously
advertisement
advisableness
amygdalaceous
anythingarian
branch-officer
boarding-house
bladder-cherry
brachycephaly
brachydactyly
brachiosaurus
brachypterous
beatification
black-and-white
blankety-blank
blanket-stitch
blackguardism
brainsickness
blasphemously
boatswain-bird
brassfounding
brattice-cloth
blastogenesis
beauteousness
baby-battering
bibliographic
bibliographer
bibliolatrist
bibliolatrous
bibliophagist
bibliophilism
bibliophilist
bibliopolical
bibliothecary
bubble-chamber
baby-snatching
baccalaureate
bacteriolysin
bacteriolysis
bacteriolytic
bacteriophage
back-formation
back-pedalling
backscratcher
backwardation
badger-baiting
badger-drawing
bidding-prayer
breechloading
bleeding-heart
breakfast-room

breakableness
breaking-point
beetlebrained
beetle-crusher
breast-feeding
breathing-time
baggage-animal
begging-letter
beginningless
bignoniaceous
blindman's-buff
building-board
building-block
bridge-builder
bridge-of-boats
brilliantness
blister-beetle
Balsaminaceae
Balkanisation
balsamiferous
ballast-heaver
beleaguerment
ball-cartridge
ballet-dancing
belles-lettres
balneotherapy
belligerently
billiard-cloth
billiard-table
Balanoglossus
bullock's-heart
Baltoslavonic
Bildungsroman
bombastically
bamboozlement
bumptiousness
benedictional
bonheur-du-jour
beneficiation
beneficential
bone-turquoise
bioscientific
book-canvasser
bronchoscopic
blood-relation
bloodlessness
Brobdignagian
blood-boltered
broad-spectrum
blood-curdling
biogeographer
broken-hearted
biotechnology
bromeliaceous
biodegradable
brother-german
brotherliness
booking-office
Bloomsburyite
blotting-paper
bureaucratise
bureaucratist
barbarisation

barnacle-goose
bargain-hunter
barbarousness
barrel-chested
Berkeleianism
Berberidaceae
barber-surgeon
barrel-vaulted
barefacedness
birefringence
boraginaceous
Birminghamlse
burying-beetle
burning-mirror
burying-ground
bernicle-goose
barristership
burglariously
burnt-offering
borough-monger
beseemingness
bespottedness
butter-biscuit
butter-fingers
butterfly-weed
butterfly-fish
betweenwhiles
butcher's-broom
bottle-coaster
battle-cruiser
battle-scarred
baton-sinister
button-through
bathymetrical
brutalisation
boundlessness
boundary-layer
boundary-rider
bouillabaisse
bountifulness
boulting-hutch
boustrophedon
bounteousness
bowling-crease
bewilderingly
bowstring-hemp
characterless
chamber-fellow
cranberry-tree
chalcographer
clandestinely
clandestinity
chameleonlike
Chateaubriand
changeability
changefulness
changing-piece
change-ringing
coachwhip-bird
Cyathophyllum
coachbuilding
clarification
craniological

clay-ironstone
cranioscopist
charity-school
coadjutorship
cracker-barrel
challengeable
challengingly
charlatanical
chain-moulding
clamorousness
clapperclawer
clapperboards
clairaudience
classicalness
coarse-grained
craftsmanship
charter-member
coastguardman
coagulability
cabbalistical
cable-moulding
cable-drilling
co-belligerent
cobaltiferous
cabinet-making
cyberneticist
Cyclanthaceae
cacographical
cocainisation
cochleariform
cockle-brained
coconut-butter
cyclospermous
cuckoo-spittle
cock-of-the-rock
Cucurbitaceae
Ciceronianism
cicatrisation
cock-thrappled
cock-throppled
codicological
cheval-de-frise
caesaropapism
coenaesthesis
check-weighman
cream-coloured
clean-timbered
chemoreceptor
cheirographer
clearing-house
cheiropterous
Cheirotherium
clear-starcher
cleistogamous
creosote-plant
chest-register
coeducational
credulousness
cleavableness
coffee-disease
cognomination
cigarette-card
cigarette-butt

climatologist
climatography
climactically
climacterical
cribbage-board
climbing-frame
clincher-built
chieftainship
clishmaclaver
co-inheritance
criminologist
criminousness
crinicultural
chicken-hazard
chinkerinchee
clickety-clack
clickety-click
chimney-corner
chimney-breast
chiromantical
clinopinacoid
clinopinakoid
clinodiagonal
chirographist
criss-cross-row
collaborative
collaboration
caliature-wood
cold-bloodedly
calico-printer
colleagueship
collectedness
collecting-box
collectorship
calcification
Calvinistical
calligraphist
collieshangie
callisthenics
Chlamydomonas
chlamydospore
cylinder-block
cylindrically
cylindraceous
colposcopical
colloquialism
colloquialist
chlorobromide
chlorocruorin
chloroformist
Chloromycetin®
Chlorophyceae
chlorargyrite
calculational
celluliferous
comparatively
comparability
commandership
compagination
combativeness
compatibility
companionable
companionably

companionless
companionship
companionhood
campanologist
compatriotism
compass-timber
compass-window
compass-signal
compassionate
compactedness
Campanulaceae
commercialese
commercialise
commercialism
commercialist
commerciality
campeachy-wood
compendiously
Commelinaceae
commemorative
commemoration
commemoratory
commeasurable
commensurable
commensurably
camphoraceous
combinatorial
commiserative
commiseration
committeeship
complaisantly
complainingly
complementary
complimentary
complexedness
compositeness
compositional
comprehensive
comprehension
compressional
comprovincial
camp-sheathing
commutatively
commutability
computational
communicative
communication
communitarian
communicatory
compulsionist
canvas-climber
concatenation
contabescence
convalescence
convalescency
consanguinity
contaminative
contamination
concavo-convex
cinnamon-stone
confarreation
connaturalise
confabulation

connaturality
confabulatory
conscientious
consciousness
condescending
condescension
confederative
confederation
consenescence
consenescency
cancellariate
concernedness
convexo-convex
contemplative
contemplation
contemplatist
concessionary
confessionary
concessionist
confessorship
conversazione
conversazioni
concentrative
conceptualise
contextualise
conceptualism
concentration
conceptualist
concert-master
conceitedness
contentedness
concentricity
consentaneity
consectaneous
consentaneous
connecting-rod
confectionary
conventionary
confectionery
conceptionist
conventionist
contentiously
convertiplane
conjecturable
conjecturally
consecutively
consequential
conservatoire
conchological
cinchonaceous
candidateship
cannibalistic
considerately
considerative
consideration
consideringly
consimilarity
confidingness
consimilitude
conditionally
configuration
continuedness
canaliculated

candle-dipping
conflagration
candle-lighter
conglomeratic
candle-snuffer
conglutinator
cinematograph
convocational
consolidative
consolidation
concomitantly
confoundingly
contortionate
contortionism
contortionist
conspicuously
cine-projector
conspurcation
conspiratress
contrabandism
contrabandist
contrabassoon
contributable
canary-creeper
contractility
contractional
centricalness
contraceptive
contraception
contradictive
contradiction
contradictory
centrifugally
centrifugence
contrafagotto
centre-forward
confrontation
congruousness
contrapuntist
contrariously
contristation
congressional
Congresswoman
congratulable
congratulator
concretionary
contraterrine
confraternity
Congreve-match
contravention
controversial
controvertist
constrainable
constrainedly
constableship
constablewick
constringency
constellation
constellatory
Constantinian
constupration
consternation
constructable

constructible	carte-de-visite	circumambient	counterfeitly
conjugational	cartelisation	circumambages	counterchange
conjunctively	cornelian-tree	circumduction	countercharge
conjunctional	correspondent	circumductory	counter-signal
connumeration	corresponsive	circumflexion	counter-fleury
concupiscible	corresponding	circumference	counter-motion
concupiscence	carpet-sweeper	circumfluence	counter-poison
consumptively	carpet-slipper	carburisation	counter-spying
consumptivity	cerographical	circumjacency	counter-attack
conquistadors	cardinalatial	circumspectly	counterstroke
convulsionary	cardinalitial	circumscriber	counter-jumper
convulsionist	cartilaginous	corruptionlst	court-cupboard
cinque-spotted	cardiographer	circumvallate	coxcombically
conductorship	carriage-drive	circumventive	cryobiologist
concyclically	certification	circumvention	chymification
condylomatous	cornification	custard-coffin	cayenne-pepper
choreographic	certificatory	costardmonger	cryptographic
choreographer	corrigibility	Casuarinaceae	cryptographer
chorepiscopal	carrion-flower	casualisation	crystal-gazing
cholecystitis	carcinomatous	cost-effective	cryptological
clothes-basket	carcinologist	case-hardening	crystallinity
clothes-screen	carnivorously	casting-weight	cryptanalysis
cook-housemaid	corridor-train	casuistically	diacatholicon
clock-watching	carrier-pigeon	casement-cloth	dramatisation
cloak-and-sword	co-religionist	customariness	dead-colouring
crown-imperial	coralliferous	cosmothetical	diametrically
chopping-board	coralligenous	custodianship	dialectically
chopping-block	Corolliflorae	cosmopolitism	diageotropism
chopping-knife	corollifloral	cosmopolitics	draggle-tailed
cross-hatching	chrome-leather	catechistical	draught-screen
cross-vaulting	ceremonialism	catechumenate	draught-engine
cross-gartered	ceremoniously	catechumenism	draught-animal
cloister-garth	chrome-plating	cytodiagnosis	diaphragmatic
cross-division	chromatically	categorically	deathlessness
cross-springer	chromatograph	categorematic	diaphanometer
crossbreeding	chrome-tanning	cattle-lifting	diachronistic
cross-crosslet	chromatophore	catalytically	diathermanous
cross-quarters	chrematistics	cat-o'-nine-tails	diaphototropy
cross-question	chronobiology	citronella-oil	drawing-master
Capparidaceae	chronographer	cathodography	drawing-pencil
Cephalochorda	corinthianise	cotton-picking	dualistically
cephalothorax	chronological	cotton-spinner	drainage-board
capaciousness	Caryocaraceae	cotton-thistle	drainage-basin
copper-captain	corporateness	catercornered	diagnostician
copper-pyrites	carbonisation	catastrophism	diamond-beetle
copying-pencil	corrosiveness	catastrophist	diamond-powder
caprification	carboniferous	church-officer	dialogistical
copple-crowned	Cercopithecus	church-service	dead-reckoning
capellmeister	corrosibility	causelessness	draftsmanship
cupboard-faith	corroborative	cauterisation	dialypetalous
capercaillzie	corroboration	chuck-farthing	debauchedness
copyrightable	corroboratory	counsel-keeper	declaratively
copartnership	carbonylation	coursing-joint	declamatorily
coriander-seed	cartridge-belt	cruiser-weight	declaratorily
curtain-raiser	Christianness	courts-martial	dictatorially
cerebrospinal	Christianlike	counting-house	deciduousness
card-catalogue	Christmas-tide	courteousness	decrepitation
correlatively	Christmas-time	counter-parole	deceivability
correlativity	Christmas-tree	counter-caster	deceitfulness
cornet-à-piston	chrysanthemum	counteractive	decriminalise
carpet-beating	chrestomathic	counteraction	dichlamydeous
carpet-bedding	Christologist	counter-weight	decelerometer
carpet-bombing	chrysophilite	counterfeiter	documentation

documentalist
decomposition
decompressive
decompression
decontaminate
decontaminant
dichotomously
deceptiveness
deceptibility
deck-passenger
decerebration
decortication
doctrinairism
decarbonation
dichrooscopic
Dicotyledones
dactyliomancy
dactylography
deducibleness
deductibility
dodecaphonist
daddy-long-legs
dreadlessness
dieselisation
dyed-in-the-wool
dwelling-house
dwelling-place
dreamlessness
dress-improver
dressing-table
defeasibility
defibrination
defibrillator
deficientness
defectiveness
defectibility
differentiate
defencelessly
defensibility
deformability
defervescence
defervescency
deferentially
deforestation
diffusiveness
diffusibility
diffusion-tube
dog-periwinkle
daguerreotype
daguerreotypy
dignification
digestibility
dog's-tail-grass
deglutination
driving-mirror
drinkableness
drink-offering
drill-sergeant
drilling-lathe
deipnosophist
delectability
Dolichosauria
Dolichosaurus

dolichocephal
deliciousness
delightedness
dulcification
deliquescence
delirifacient
deliriousness
dilettanteism
deleteriously
domiciliation
damnification
demolitionist
dimensionless
demonological
diminishingly
demonstrative
demonstration
demonstratory
domestication
demythologise
dematerialise
dimethylamine
demiurgically
dunderheadism
dangerousness
dinner-service
dancing-master
densitometric
denticulation
dynamogenesis
Dendrocalamus
dendrological
do-nothingness
denationalise
Dioscoreaceae
diotheletical
diothelitical
dyotheletical
dyothelitical
deoch-an-doruis
deoxidisation
dioristically
deodorisation
deontological
deprecatingly
dipleidoscope
Dipterocarpus
dipping-needle
dephlegmation
deplorability
diplomatology
Diprotodontia
depersonalise
diphthongally
dermatologist
dermatography
darning-needle
dereligionise
derivationist
disparateness
disparagement
discapacitate
disparagingly

dispatch-rider
dastardliness
dishabilitate
disharmonious
dispassionate
distastefully
distant-signal
disnaturalise
disobediently
disobligation
disobligatory
disobligement
désobligeante
disobligingly
disadvantaged
desperateness
dissemblingly
dismemberment
disseveration
disseminative
dissemination
dissepimental
disfellowship
dysmenorrheic
dysmenorrheal
dysmenorrhoea
disrespectful
disheartening
dispersedness
dyspeptically
disceptatious
disreputation
disaffectedly
disaffirmance
desegregation
disagreeables
discharge-tube
despicability
distinctively ·
distinguished
distinguisher
dissimilation
dissimilarity
dispiritingly
dissimilitude
disciplinable
dissimulative
disfiguration
dissimulation
disfigurement
displeasingly
desulphuriser
displantation
desultoriness
disilluminate
disillusioned
disembarkment
disemployment
disembodiment
disengagement
disinterested
disintegrable
disintegrator

disinvestment
disinhibition
disinhibitory
disinvigorate
disconcertion
disconformity
dispositively
dispositioned
dispositional
discommodious
discommission
disconnection
discoloration
dishonourable
dishonourably
disgospelling
dispossession
discontentful
discontenting
discontinuity
discontinuous
dissoluteness
dissolubility
discomycetous
disappearance
disappointing
disequilibria
desirableness
distributable
disgracefully
destructively
distractively
distractingly
destructivist
destructivity
destructional
discreditable
discreditably
disordinately
desertisation
dispraisingly
disarticulate
discriminator
descriptively
descriptivism
disproportion
distressfully
distrustfully
distressingly
discretionary
disestimation
disassimilate
disputatively
disputability
disjunctively
dysfunctional
disquietingly
disguisedness
dispurveyance
detrimentally
determinately
determinative
determination

deterministic
deteriorative
deterioration
detestability
deuterogamist
deuteroscopic
Deuteronomist
daughter-in-law
double-concave
double-crosser
double-dealing
double-founted
double-glazing
double-hearted
double-jointed
double-natured
double-or-quits
double-shotted
double-shuffle
double-tongued
dauntlessness
developmental
devolutionary
devolutionist
divertisement
diversifiable
divertibility
diverticulate
devastatingly
division-lobby
devotionalist
downcast-shaft
downrightness
dexterousness
dextrocardiac
epanadiplosis
evangeliarium
evangeliarion
evangelically
evangelistary
elaborateness
exanthematous
enantiomorphy
enantiodromia
enantiodromic
enantiotropic
embranglement
embracingness
Eubacteriales
embellishment
embarrassment
embryogenesis
embryological
eucharistical
eschatologist
encyclopaedia
encyclopaedic
excrescential
ecclesiolater
ecclesiolatry
encompassment
encomiastical
excommunicate

eccentrically
encroachingly
enchondromata
Encephalartos
encephalocele
encephalotomy
encephalogram
exceptionable
exceptionably
exceptionally
encapsulation
excortication
excursiveness
excusableness
eschscholtzia
excessiveness
excitableness
encouragement
encouragingly
exclusiveness
endearingness
endocrinology
endometriosis
endurableness
endosmometric
emerald-copper
even-Christian
energetically
elephantiasis
elephant's-ears
elephant's-foot
everlastingly
exemplariness
exemplifiable
epeirogenesis
epeirogenetic
electrisation
electrifiable
electrovalent
electromagnet
electroscopic
electrocement
electromerism
electrometric
electioneerer
electrochemic
electrophorus
electrothermy
electromotive
electrography
electrostatic
electrocution
electrotypist
efficaciously
effectiveness
effectualness
efflorescence
effervescible
effervescence
effervescency
eagle-flighted
engine-turning
eighteen-pence

eighteen-penny
ergatomorphic
exhibitionism
exhibitionist
Ephemeroptera
Echinodermata
ethanolamines
ethnocentrism
ethnographica
enhypostatise
epinastically
Eriocaulaceae
epigeneticist
epiphenomenon
enigmatically
epidotisation
epitrachelion
epigrammatise
epigrammatist
emigrationist
enjoyableness
enlightenment
evocativeness
egocentricity
exothermicity
egotistically
economisation
explanatorily
expectorative
expectoration
expeditionary
expeditiously
expressionism
expressionist
expendability
expansiveness
expensiveness
expansibility
exponentially
Euphorbiaceae
explosiveness
expropriation
expurgatorial
experimentist
empyreumatise
expostulative
expostulation
expostulatory
emphysematous
exquisiteness
Eurocommunism
Eurocommunist
egregiousness
earth-movement
earthly-minded
erroneousness
Europocentric
Etruscologist
essentialness
east-north-east
exsanguineous
ensanguinated
eusporangiate

east-south-east
extravasation
extra-galactic
extravagantly
extra-vascular
extra-cellular
extra-metrical
estrangedness
extra-physical
extra-limitary
extrapolative
extrapolation
extrapolatory
extraordinary
extra-tropical
extra-judicial
extra-axillary
establishment
extrinsically
entomological
extemporarily
entomophagous
entomophilous
entomostracan
extenuatingly
extendability
extensiveness
extendibility
extensibility
extensionally
extinguishant
entertainment
exterminative
extermination
exterminatory
exterritorial
Enteropneusta
estate-bottled
educatability
educationally
equidifferent
equidistantly
ecumenicalism
equilibration
ebullioscopic
equinoctially
equiponderate
equiponderant
equipotential
equestrianism
equisetaceous
equitableness
equivocalness
environmental
eavesdropping
erysipelatous
Egyptological
franchisement
Franco-Russian
flagellantism
flame-coloured
feather-weight
feather-bonnet

feather-stitch
feather-duster
frank-tenement
Frankeniaceae
fragmentation
fragmentarily
Flammenwerfer
flannel-flower
fractionalise
fractionalism
fractionation
fractionalist
fractiousness
fibrovascular
fictionalised
facultatively
factorability
factorisation
facetiousness
fiddle-faddler
fiddle-pattern
feeding-bottle
free-selection
frequentative
frequentation
freezing-point
fifth-monarchy
fugaciousness
figure-casting
figure-skating
figure-weaving
fair-and-square
fringilliform
frighteningly
faithlessness
flight-feather
frightfulness
frivolousness
flint-knapping
filibustering
filibusterism
filibusterous
filterability
folk-etymology
full-fashioned
falsification
feloniousness
fellow-citizen
fellow-feeling
fellow-servant
follow-through
filipendulous
fundamentally
finnan-haddock
fantastically
finger-breadth
finger-pointer
fencing-master
funambulation
funambulatory
findon-haddock
functionalism
functionalist

floccillation
floodlighting
flower-service
foolhardiness
floristically
floricultural
foot-land-raker
foot-passenger
flourishingly
floutingstock
formalisation
ferociousness
furaciousness
forgetfulness
fermentitious
forefeelingly
formidability
fertilisation
fortification
fire-insurance
fortississimo
fortitudinous
ferricyanogen
forejudgement
foreknowingly
foreknowledge
foraminiferal
forementioned
ferromagnetic
ferrochromium
ferroelectric
ferroconcrete
ferrosoferric
forgottenness
ferrocyanogen
fire-resistant
fire-resisting
foreshadowing
foresightless
first-begotten
first-offender
fortunateness
formularistic
fortune-teller
fortune-hunter
foster-brother
fissiparously
fishing-tackle
fossilisation
fossiliferous
fatigableness
futurological
future-perfect
feudalisation
founder-member
foundation-net
frumentaceous
frumentarious
fluvioglacial
feuilletonism
feuilletonist
faultlessness
fruitlessness

granddaughter
grandfatherly
grandiloquent
grandiloquous
grandmotherly
gracelessness
graphological
graphemically
gravitational
gravimetrical
granitisation
gratification
graminivorous
glaciological
gladiatorship
graticulation
grammatically
glamorisation
grappling-hook
grappling-iron
glass-painting
glass-grinding
granuliferous
granulomatous
go-as-you-please
gubernatorial
great-grandson
gigantomachia
guilelessness
grief-stricken
Gaidhealtachd
geitonogamous
guiltlessness
galvanisation
galvanoplasty
galactosaemia
galactorrhoea
golden-crested
gillie-wetfoot
Galeopithecus
gymnastically
gumple-foisted
gambling-house
gymnospermous
gametogenesis
Gemütlichkeit
gynodioecious
gonadotrophic
gonadotrophin
gynaecomastia
gynaecologist
gynaecocratic
gentianaceous
gentle-hearted
gentlemanship
gentlemanlike
gentlemanhood
gentlewomanly
gynomonoecism
gynandromorph
goniometrical
generalisable
generalissimo

generationism
genethlialogy
genotypically
genito-urinary
globalisation
geotactically
grotesqueness
geometrically
globe-trotting
geocentricism
geochemically
geochronology
glorification
good-King-Henry
ground-angling
ground-control
groin-centring
ground-officer
good-naturedly
geopolitician
geomorphology
geotropically
grouse-disease
glossographer
glossological
geostationary
globuliferous
Germanisation
Germanophilia
garnetiferous
garnisheement
garlic-mustard
gyromagnetism
gerund-grinder
gerontophilia
gerontologist
gerontocratic
garrulousness
gasteropodous
gas-centrifuge
gesticulation
gesticulatory
gastrocnemius
gastroenteric
gastrological
gathering-peat
gathering-coal
Grumbletonian
gauntlet-guard
glyphographic
glyphographer
glyptographic
heave-offering
heave-shoulder
heaven-kissing
Heath-Robinson
hyalinisation
headquartered
heat-resistant
heartlessness
healthfulness
heart-sickness
heartbreaking

heart-stricken
heart-stirring
hybridisation
hubristically
hibernisation
habitableness
hobby-horsical
hacking-jacket
hide-and-go-seek
hydraulicking
hydraulically
hedge-marriage
hedge-accentor
hydropathical
hydromagnetic
hydrogenation
hydrocephalic
hydrocephalus
hydrometrical
hydromedusoid
hydrochloride
hydrokinetics
hydro-airplane
hydroelectric
hydrosomatous
hydrocracking
hydrostatical
hydrosulphide
hydrosulphite
hydroxylamine
hydrodynamics
haematologist
heebie-jeebies
haemodialysis
hieroglyphist
hierogrammate
haemorrhoidal
High-Churchism
High-Churchman
high-explosive
hygroscopical
hygrometrical
hagiographist
high-stomached
heir-portioner
hair-splitting
hole-and-corner
half-evergreen
Hellenistical
Hildebrandism
helter-skelter
half-heartedly
hole-in-the-wall
helminthiasis
helminthology
holometabolic
helispherical
half-sovereign
Holothuroidea
hallucinative
hallucination
hallucinatory
Hammerklavier

homoeomorphic
homoeroticism
homoeopathist
homoeothermic
homoeothermal
homogenetical
homoiothermic
homoiothermal
homologically
homologoumena
humble-mouthed
homomorphosis
Hymenomycetes
hymenopterous
homeoteleuton
homeothermous
homeomorphism
homeomorphous
hemiparasitic
Hemerobaptist
hemispherical
homosexualist
homosexuality
homeward-bound
hunger-marcher
hunger-striker
Huntingdonian
hunting-ground
hundredweight
honorifically
honeycomb-moth
haphazardness
heptasyllabic
hypocycloidal
hypochondriac
hypochondrium
hyphenisation
hypogylcaemia
hypsophyllary
hypnotisation
hypno-analysis
hippopotamian
hypophosphite
hypercalcemia
hypersarcosis
hyperactivity
hypervelocity
hypermetrical
hypermetropia
hypermetropic
hyperphysical
hyperphrygian
hyperhidrosis
hyperglycemia
hypertrophied
hypertrophous
hypercritical
hypersthenite
hyposulphuric
hypothecation
hare-and-hounds
hermaphrodite
hermeneutical

horse-chestnut
horse-sickness
horse-and-buggy
herpetologist
hard-heartedly
hurricane-lamp
hurricane-deck
horripilation
horticultural
harmonisation
herborisation
harbour-master
haruspication
heresiologist
heresiography
horizontality
hysteranthous
histiophoroid
histrionicism
Hutchinsonian
heteroblastic
heteroclitous
heterochronic
heterocarpous
heterogeneity
heterogeneous
heterogenesis
heterogenetic
heteromorphic
heteroplastic
heteropterous
heterosporous
heterostrophy
heterostylism
heterostylous
heterothallic
heterothermal
heterotrophic
hound-trailing
housewifeship
housewifeskep
housemistress
house-breaking
heuristically
hexactinellid
hexadactylous
hazardousness
inaudibleness
inanimateness
italicisation
inappreciable
inappropriate
inattentively
inadvertently
incredibility
incredulously
incognoscible
inclinational
inclinatorium
incriminatory
incompetently
incommiscible
incompossible

incommunicado
incombustible
incombustibly
inconsciently
incandescence
inconvenience
inconveniency
incondensable
inconversable
incontestable
inconvertible
incontestably
inconvertibly
inconsecutive
inconsequence
incense-burner
inconceivable
inconceivably
inconvincible
inconsiderate
incontinently
inconsistence
inconsistency
inconsonantly
inconspicuous
incongruously
incurableness
incarceration
incorrectness
incorporative
incorporating
incorporation
incorporeally
incuriousness
incorruptible
incorruptibly
incorruptness
indoctrinator
indifferently
indefatigable
indefatigably
indelibleness
induplication
independently
indiscernible
indiscernibly
indispensable
indispensably
indistinctive
indistinction
indissociable
indisposition
indissolvable
industrialise
industrialism
industrialist
indescribable
indescribably
industriously
indissuadable
indissuadably
indeterminate
indeterminacy

indeterminism
indeterminist
individualise
individualism
individuation
individualist
individuality
index-learning
inelaborately
ineffableness
inefficacious
inefficiently
ineffectively
ineffectually
ideographical
inexhaustible
inexhaustibly
inevitability
ineligibility
inexorability
inexpediently
inexpressible
inexpressibly
inexpensively
inexperienced
identicalness
ineducability
infeasibility
infectiveness
inflexibility
inflexionless
infallibilism
infallibilist
infallibility
infundibulate
infinitesimal
inflorescence
informatician
informational
inferentially
influentially
infructuously
ingeniousness
ingenuousness
ingurgitation
Ichthyosauria
Ichthyosaurus
ichthyologist
ichthyography
ichthyopsidan
inhomogeneity
inhomogeneous
inhospitality
imitativeness
inimitability
idiomatically
idiorrhythmic
idiosyncratic
injudiciously
injuriousness
ill-favouredly
Illecebraceae
illocutionary

illegibleness
illogicalness
island-hopping
ill-considered
illustriously
immediateness
immunological
immunotherapy
immarcescible
immarcessible
immiscibility
immutableness
ismaticalness
immaterialise
immaterialism
immaterialist
immateriality
immovableness
innocuousness
ignominiously
iontophoresis
iontophoretic
innovationist
innoxiousness
isobarometric
inoperability
isomerisation
isometrically
isogeothermic
isogeothermal
inofficiously
inoffensively
isoagglutinin
inorganically
isochronously
isodimorphism
isodimorphous
isoelectronic
iconomaticism
inodorousness
inopportunely
inopportunist
inopportunity
inobservation
isostatically
inobtrusively
inoculability
implacability
impracticable
impracticably
impeccability
impecuniosity
impressionism
impressionist
impignoration
implicatively
impalpability
impulsiveness
impolitically
imponderables
impenetration
improbability
improvability

improvisation
improvisatory
improvisatrix
improvidently
impropriation
imperialistic
imperseverant
imperceptible
imperfectible
imperceptibly
imperfectness
impertinently
impartibility
impartialness
impermissible
impermissibly
impersonalise
imperforation
impersonation
impersonality
imperiousness
imparipinnate
importunately
imperturbable
imperturbably
impassability
impassiveness
impossibilism
impossibilist
impassibility
impossibility
impostumation
imputableness
impetuousness
inquisitively
inquisitional
inquisitorial
irreclaimable
irreclaimably
irrecognition
irreciprocity
irrecoverable
irrecoverably
irredeemables
irrefrangible
irrefrangibly
irreligiously
irreplaceable
irreplaceably
irrepressible
irrepressibly
irresponsible
irresponsibly
irritableness
irretrievable
irretrievably
irrationalise
irrationalism
irrationalist
irrationality
irreverential
instantiation
instantaneity

instantaneous
insubordinate
insubstantial
insociability
insectivorous
insectologist
insidiousness
inspectorship
insufficience
insufficiency
insignificant
instigatingly
inspirational
instinctively
instinctivity
instinctually
inspiritingly
institutively
institutional
insolvability
insolubleness
insensateness
insinuatingly
insensitively
insensibility
insensitivity
insupportable
insupportably
insuppressive
instructively
instructional
inscriptively
inscriptional
insusceptible
insusceptibly
insatiateness
insatiability
intravasation
intraparietal
intracapsular
intrapetiolar
intracellular
intra-arterial
intratropical
intransigence
intransigency
intramuscular
integumentary
intricateness
intrinsically
intelligencer
intelligently
intemperately
intensiveness
intangibility
intentionally
iatrogenicity
introversible
iatrochemical
introspective
introspection
introgression
intercalative

intercalation
intergalactic
interlacement
interlaminate
interradially
international
interparietal
intermarriage
interjaculate
interoceptive
interscapular
interrelation
interferingly
interpetiolar
intermediator
intercellular
interpersonal
interdentally
interjectural
interpilaster
intersidereal
interdigitate
intermittence
intermittency
interpolative
interrogative
interlocation
interpolation
interrogation
interrogatory
interposition
intercommunal
intercolonial
interlocution
intercolumnar
interlocutory
interlocutrix
interspecific
interspersion
interbreeding
intertropical
intercropping
interpretable
interpretress
interestingly
interosculate
interosculant
interstratify
interstellary
interlunation
interpunction
intercurrence
interruptedly
intrusiveness
invidiousness
involucellate
involuntarily
inventiveness
invendibility
invincibility
inventorially
inviolateness
inviolability

invariability
invisibleness
investigative
investigation
investigatory
jack-crosstree
judiciousness
judge-advocate
Judaistically
Judas-coloured
juglandaceous
jiggery-pokery
Johnsonianism
jollification
Jamestown-weed
Jenny-long-legs
jargonisation
jurisprudence
jerry-building
justificative
justification
justificatory
jet-propulsion
journey-weight
juxtaposition
Kidderminster
Kletterschuhe
knight-marshal
knights-errant
knight-service
knick-knackery
knickerbocker
kaleidoscopic
kangaroo-apple
kangaroo-grass
kangaroo-thorn
kindergartner
kindly-natured
kinematograph
kinesiologist
kinesipathist
kinesitherapy
knowledgeable
knowledgeably
kapellmeister
kissing-comfit
kiss-in-the-ring
kitchen-garden
kitchen-midden
kittly-benders
kettledrummer
knuckleduster
keyhole-limpet
loathsomeness
leather-jacket
leather-winged
leather-lunged
leasing-making
lead-poisoning
librarianship
labefactation
labyrinthical
labyrinthitis

laboriousness
liberationism
liberationist
lackadaisical
lickerishness
lichenologist
lecherousness
lectisternium
lycanthropist
lactobacillus
Lycopodiaceae
Lecythidaceae
ludicrousness
lady-in-waiting
laevorotation
laevorotatory
life-assurance
left-handiness
lifting-bridge
life-insurance
life-preserver
life-rendering
logographical
lignification
logarithmical
legislatively
legislatorial
light-fingered
lightning-tube
light-infantry
lightsomeness
light-horseman
lighthouseman
light-spirited
leishmaniasis
leishmaniosis
Leibnizianism
laissez-passer
lampadephoria
lymphatically
Lamellicornia
lamellibranch
lemon-coloured
Lamarckianism
limitlessness
long-descended
lance-sergeant
line-engraving
lance-corporal
linsey-woolsey
line-fisherman
landing-ground
land-measuring
land-ownership
long-suffering
land-surveying
languishingly
linguistician
Lepidodendron
lepidopterist
lepidopterous
Lepidostrobus
lipogrammatic

leptocephalic
leptocephalus
leptophyllous
leptospirosis
laryngoscopic
laryngologist
listening-post
Lasiocampidae
lissotrichous
lethargically
letter-carrier
letter-founder
lithesomeness
letter-perfect
letters-patent
litigiousness
lattice-girder
lattice-bridge
luteinisation
Latin-American
lithotriptist
lithontriptic
lithontriptor
launching-ways
launching-site
laughableness
laughing-stock
leucitohedron
leuco-compound
Louis-Quatorze
level-peggings
level-crossing
lavender-water
livery-company
liver-coloured
livery-servant
lawn-sprinkler
lexicographic
lexicographer
lexigraphical
luxuriousness
lozenge-shaped
meadow-saffron
meals-on-wheels
measuring-tape
measuring-worm
mechanisation
mackerel-guide
mackerel-midge
mackerel-shark
machine-gunner
mocking-thrush
machicolation
Machiavellism
Machiavellian
macrodactylic
macroeconomic
microeconomic
microscopical
microdetector
macrocephalic
microcephalic
micrometrical

microfelsitic
microphyllous
macropinakoid
macrodiagonal
microanalysis
microtonality
macromolecule
microcosmical
microcomputer
micro-organism
microprinting
microgranitic
micronutrient
macaronically
mycotoxicosis
mediatisation
mediatorially
medicamentary
medicine-chest
middle-bracket
Middle-Eastern
modernisation
moderatorship
mediterranean
mnemotechnics
mnemotechnist
magnanimously
megacephalous
magnetisation
magnetomotive
magnetosphere
magneto-optics
magnification
magnificently
magniloquence
megalosaurian
Maginot-minded
magnoliaceous
magisterially
megasporangia
magistratical
might-have-been
magazine-rifle
Mohammedanise
Mohammedanism
maiden-tongued
maiden-widowed
maid-of-all-work
Meistersinger
malacological
maliciousness
malacophilous
malacostracan
melodramatist
maladminister
milk-dentition
melodiousness
maladroitness
maladaptation
maladjustment
mallemaroking
malleableness
millefeuilles

millennianism
millenniarism
millennialist
mulberry-faced
Malthusianism
multicamerate
multicapitate
multiramified
multinational
multicellular
Malpighiaceae
multifilament
mellification
mollification
multidigitate
multivibrator
multiplicable
multiplicator
mellifluently
mellifluously
millionairess
multicoloured
multilobulate
multiloculate
multiloquence
multipresence
multitudinary
multitudinous
multinucleate
melanochroous
melancholious
malariologist
Melastomaceae
millstone-grit
molluscicidal
mammaliferous
mummification
momentariness
momentousness
memorableness
membranaceous
manganiferous
Manichaeanism
monochromatic
monochromator
monocotyledon
monodactylous
mine-detection
manufacturing
manifold-paper
manifestative
manifestation
monographical
manageability
monogrammatic
mundificative
mundification
monometallism
monometallist
mononucleosis
meningococcic
meningococcal
meningococcus

mangold-wurzel
manipulatable
monopsonistic
monophthongal
monophysitism
monarchianism
mineralogical
minisubmarine
many-sidedness
ministerially
monosyllabism
monosymmetric
monostrophics
monothalamous
monotrematous
monotheletism
monothelitism
monotelephone
monstrousness
mensurability
mermaid's-glove
mermaid's-purse
mortal-staring
miracle-monger
meridionality
marketability
mercerisation
myrmecologist
marsh-marigold
marsh-samphire
mirthlessness
morphographer
morphogenesis
morphogenetic
morphological
merchandising
morphinomania
morphophoneme
mercilessness
marriage-lines
morning-prayer
mortification
marsipobranch
marble-hearted
mirror-writing
Myristicaceae
Morisonianism
meritoriously
martyrologist
mismanagement
misobservance
music-mistress
musicological
mesocephalism
mesocephalous
musicotherapy
misadvertence
misadventured
misadventurer
master-builder
miscegenation
masterfulness
messenger-wire

mesmerisation
miscellaneous
master-mariner
master-passion
mispersuasion
Messerschmitt
mystery-monger
mischief-maker
mischievously
misshapenness
mystification
mashie-niblick
mastigophoric
mastigophoran
muscle-reading
misemployment
mesencephalic
mesencephalon
misunderstand
misunderstood
misanthropist
misconception
misgovernment
misconjecture
miscomprehend
miscorrection
misappreciate
miserableness
misproportion
mistrustfully
mistrustingly
mesaticephaly
masculineness
mutualisation
mitochondrial
mitochondrion
mathematicise
mathematicism
mathematician
mother-country
mother-of-pearl
metagrabolise
metagrobolise
matchlessness
matchboarding
metrification
matrilineally
matrifocality
matrimonially
matriculation
matriculatory
metallisation
metalliferous
metallography
metallurgical
metempiricism
metempiricist
metamorphoses
metamorphosis
metonymically
mutton-dummies
methodistical
meteorologist

motion-picture
mutton-thumper
metaphosphate
metoposcopist
metapsychical
metaphysician
materfamilias
materialistic
motor-traction
metastability
moulding-board
mouse-coloured
mouthwatering
mouth-breather
mourning-bride
mourning-coach
mourning-cloak
mourning-piece
mourning-stuff
mountebankery
mountebanking
mountebankism
mountain-chain
mountain-sheep
mountains-high
mounting-block
mowing-machine
muzzle-loading
neanderthaler
nyctaginaceae
nectariferous
nickeliferous
nickel-plating
nucleo-protein
noctivagation
nick-nackatory
necromantical
necroscopical
neocssariness
necessitarian
necessitation
necessitously
needle-pointed
nefariousness
niggardliness
neglectedness
negligibility
night-warbling
night-watchman
night-wanderer
negotiability
night-tripping
no-holds-barred
noiselessness
neighbourhood
nullification
noli-me-tangere
nomenclatural
nominatively
numismatology
nemathelminth
namby-pambical
namby-pambyish

namby-pambyism
non-observance
non-acceptance
non-regardance
non-resistance
nonsensically
non-returnable
non-aggression
non-conducting
non-forfeiting
nonconforming
nonconformist
nonconformity
non-collegiate
non-cognisable
non-compliance
non-compounder
non-specialist
non-appearance
non-productive
non-production
non-proficient
non-attendance
non-fulfilment
Neo-Lamarckism
Neo-Lamarckian
Neo-Kantianism
Neo-Melanesian
neoclassicism
neoplasticism
Neo-Plasticism
neoclassicist
neologistical
neogrammarian
nephelometric
nephrological
naphthylamine
normalisation
noradrenaline
nervelessness
nerve-wracking
north-eastward
north-easterly
north-westward
north-westerly
northerliness
nursing-father
narrowcasting
narco-analysis
narcohypnosis
nostalgically
Netherlandish
netting-needle
nitrification
nationalistic
nitrobacteria
nitro-compound
notoriousness
nature-worship
neurastheniac
neurovascular
neuropathical
novocentenary

navigableness
newfangleness
orange-blossom
oraculousness
occidentalise
Occidentalism
Occidentalist
orchesography
orchestration
orchestralist
orchidomaniac
orchidologist
occasionalism
occasionalist
occasionality
old-clothesman
operativeness
overabounding
overabundance
over-anxiously
overbearingly
overcredulity
overcredulous
over-confident
overexcitable
over-exquisite
overflowingly
oreographical
overhastiness
overindulgent
overinsurance
overmultitude
oleomargarine
oceanographic
oceanographer
oceanological
oneiroscopist
overstatement
oversubscribe
overvaluation
offhandedness
olfactologist
officiousness
offensiveness
organogenesis
organotherapy
ophthalmology
ophiomorphous
ochlocratical
otherworldish
oligopolistic
onirocritical
opisthobranch
opisthography
objectivation
objectiveness
objectivistic
objectionable
objectionably
obliviousness
omnicompetent
ornamentation
owner-occupied

owner-occupier
ornithischian
ornithichnite
ornithomantic
ornithologist
obnoxiousness
Orobanchaceae
onomatopoesis
onomatopoetic
odoriferously
ovoviviparous
omoplatoscopy
odontoglossum
odontological
odontophorous
odontornithes
oppignoration
opprobriously
opportuneness
oppositionist
oyster-catcher
oyster-fishery
obstinateness
observational
obstructively
octocentenary
ostodermatous
ostreiculture
ostreophagous
out-settlement
outrecuidance
ontogenically
ontologically
ostensibility
orthopaedical
orthopinakoid
orthodiagonal
orthosilicate
orthognathism
orthognathous
ortho-compound
orthographist
orthostichous
osteomyelitis
outspokenness
otter-trawling
obtuse-angular
outstandingly
obtrusiveness
onychophagist
phalansterism
phalansterian
phalansterist
peaceableness
peacelessness
peace-offering
prayerfulness
prayer-meeting
phanerogamous
planetologist
pease-porridge
phase-contrast
plate-printing

plaigotropous
peach-coloured
pharisaically
planimetrical
platiniferous
plagiostomata
plagiostomous
pianistically
plagiotropism
platitudinise
platitudinous
pearl-shelling
pharmacognosy
pharmacopoeia
pharmaceutics
pharmaceutist
psammophilous
pragmatically
plaintiveness
phaenological
plain-speaking
peacock-throne
peacock-flower
peacock-copper
prairie-turnip
prairie-oyster
plausibleness
practicalness
plantie-cruive
plantain-eater
phantasmalian
phantasmality
platycephalic
pharyngoscope
pharyngoscopy
platyrrhinian
pococurantism
pococurantist
pocket-borough
pocket-picking
packing-needle
pucciniaceous
pycnidiospore
pickle-herring
pycnoconidium
picture-palace
picture-window
picturesquely
Pedicellariae
pedagogically
pudding-headed
pudding-sleeve
paddle-steamer
pedantocratic
podophthalmus
Podostemaceae
pedestrianise
pedestrianism
preparatively
preparatorily
premandibular
Pre-Raphaelite
Pre-Raphaelism

prevarication
predatoriness
prefatorially
prefabricated
prefabricator
precautionary
prematureness
presbytership
prescientific
prescriptible
preoccupation
pseudo-archaic
pseudomonades
pseudomorphic
pre-adamitical
preadmonition
preadaptation
preferability
pretendership
premeditative
premedication
premeditation
preteriteness
predefinition
pretermission
pretermitting
preternatural
preterperfect
Pherecrataean
presentiality
predestinator
pretentiously
precentorship
preserving-pan
psephological
plethorically
predicamental
predicatively
predicability
presidentship
precipitately
precipitative
plebification
precipitation
preliminaries
preliminarily
precipitantly
precipitously
premillennial
pteridologist
plesiosaurian
paediatrician
prehistorical
prefigurative
prefiguration
prefigurement
plenitudinous
phellogenetic
phelloplastic
pneumogastric
pneumonectomy
pneumatically
pneumatolysis

pneumatolytic
pneumatometer
pneumatophore
preambulatory
pre-engagement
prerogatively
piezomagnetic
preconception
preponderance
preponderancy
phenomenalise
phenomenalism
phenomenalist
phenomenality
phenomenology
preconisation
predomination
predominantly
prepositional
premonitorily
piezoelectric
paedomorphism
prepossessing
prepossession
preordainment
preordination
press-fastener
pressure-cabin
pleasure-house
plentifulness
plectognathic
plenteousness
plectopterous
prejudicative
prejudication
prejudicially
presumptively
phenylalanine
pterylography
pigheadedness
pigeon-chested
pigeon-fancier
pigeon-hearted
pigeon-livered
Philadelphian
privateersman
privatisation
primatologist
peirastically
philanthropic
psilanthropic
prince-consort
principalness
principalship
princess-dress
princess-royal
princess-skirt
prices-current
pricelessness
prize-fighting
philhellenism
philhellenist
priming-powder

primitiveness
poikilothermy
primigravidae
prick-me-dainty
prick-the-louse
prismatically
philomathical
prison-breaker
primordialism
primordiality
primogenitary
primogenitive
primogenitrix
primogeniture
prisoners'-base
Psilophytales
philosophical
philosophiser
poisonousness
pointlessness
printing-house
printing-press
pointing-stock
polyadelphous
palpable-gross
pelican-flower
police-officer
polychromatic
polycarbonate
police-station
polycythaemia
polydactylism
polydactylous
polyembryonic
palaeocrystic
pulselessness
palaeographic
palaeographer
palletisation
pelletisation
pulverisation
palaeontology
Palaeotherium
palaeozoology
polygalaceous
polygonaceous
phlogisticate
Phlegethontic
polyhistorian
palmification
pollicitation
polliniferous
Polemoniaceae
palingenesist
palynological
polynomialism
palindromical
poliomyelitis
Polypodiaceae
polyphloisbic
Peloponnesian
polyprotodont
polypropylene

pilgrim-bottle
polysyllabism
polysyllogism
polysynthesis
polysynthetic
polythalamous
palatableness
polytechnical
pompier-ladder
pentadactylic
pentadelphous
panharmonicon
pineapple-weed
Pantagruelism
Pantagruelian
Pantagruelion
Pantagruelist
pentastichous
pentasyllabic
peniciliiform
panic-stricken
ponderability
pandemoniacal
ponderousness
panaesthetism
Pan-Africanism
panegyrically
pantheistical
penthemimeral
panchromatism
pantheologist
pencil-compass
pennilessness
pinking-shears
pontificality
pantisocratic
pandiculation
peninsularity
pontoon-bridge
panspermatism
panspermatist
panophthalmia
pendragonship
pangrammatist
penuriousness
punishability
panpsychistic
penetratively
penetratingly
penetrability
punctiliously
penitentially
pendulousness
penny-farthing
penny-pinching
prosaicalness
probabilities
probabilistic
proparoxytone
phonautograph
proterandrous
proverbialise
proverbialism

proverbialist
probe-scissors
phonendoscope
progenitorial
proteinaceous
prolegomenary
prolegomenous
proterogynous
process-server
processionary
processioning
professoriate
professorship
proleptically
Protestantise
Protestantism
protectionism
projectionist
protectionist
protectorless
prosecutorship
protectorship
profectitious
prosecutrices
prosecutrixes
prophetically
profitability
provincialise
provincialism
provinciality
promiscuously
proliferative
proliferation
proliferously
promise-breach
prolification
prohibitively
provisionally
profit-sharing
problematical
pro-and-conning
prognosticate
protolanguage
provocatively
phonocamptics
protoactinium
photo-receptor
photoperiodic
photochemical
photochromism
photochromics
Protochordata
photophoresis
propositional
proto-historic
photoelectric
photoelectron
photo-emission
pronounceable
pronouncement
protonotarial
protonotariat
Protococcales

prosopopoeial
prosopography
photovoltaics
protospataire
phonographist
photographist
proconsulship
proportionate
proportioning
prospect-glass
prospectively
phosphoretted
phosphorylase
phosphuretted
propraetorial
proprietorial
propraetorian
proprioceptor
procrastinate
progressively
progressivism
progressivist
progressional
plotting-paper
prosthodontia
prostatectomy
procuratorial
pronunciation
protuberation
protuberantly
producibility
pepper-and-salt
popping-crease
papilliferous
Papilionaceae
papillomatous
peptonisation
papaprelatist
paper-hangings
paper-fastener
paper-mulberry
papaveraceous
pervasiveness
phreatophytic
Parnassianism
parabolically
perichondrium
perscrutation
paradoxically
porcelain-clay
porcelaineous
perpendicular
perseveration
perseveringly
pyrheliometer
porcellaneous
purse-snatcher
perfectionate
perfectionism
perfectionist
perfervidness
paraffin-scale
paragraphical

peregrination
perigastritis
parthenocarpy
perihepatitis
parking-ticket
porridge-stick
participative
participating
participation
participantly
participially
partition-wall
perditionable
partitionment
parliamentary
parliamenting
parliament-man
parti-coloured
particularise
particularism
particularist
particularity
parallactical
parallelistic
parallelogram
purple-in-grain
paralelpomena
paralipomenon
perplexedness
pyramidically
paramagnetism
pyrimethamine
perambulation
perambulatory
parencephalon
parenthetical
perennibranch
phrenological
Pyrenomycetes
perinephritis
phrenetically
parrot-disease
purposelessly
parrot-fashion
periodisation
periodicalist
purposiveness
perspicacious
perspectively
perspectivism
perspicuously
paraphernalia
pyrophosphate
parapophysial
peripatetical
parapsychical
parapsychosis
partridge-wood
perishability
pyrosulphuric
parasynthesis
parasynthetic
parasyntheton

perissodactyl
phraseologist
parasitically
pyrotechnical
puritanically
perityphlitis
pyretotherapy
Portulacaceae
perdurability
permutability
perfunctorily
porcupine-wood
percussion-cap
percussionist
perlustration
party-politics
party-coloured
party-spirited
post-communion
passementerie
passenger-mile
Passeriformes
post-existence
possessionate
possessionary
possessorship
pasigraphical
puss-gentleman
paschal-candle
paschal-flower
pestiferously
pessimistical
passion-flower
Passion-Sunday
piscicultural
pusillanimity
pusillanimous
postliminiary
post-operative
postulational
posture-master
phthalocyanin
pitch-farthing
petrification
patrifocality
patrimonially
patriotically
potamological
potentiometer
pathogenicity
petrochemical
petroliferous
patronisingly
pathognomonic
petrocurrency
paterfamilias
potato-disease
putty-coloured
pluralisation
plumbisolvent
plumbosolvent
pauperisation
prudentialism

prudentialist
prudentiality
pruning-shears
pluripresence
powdering-room
powdering-gown
powerlessness
power-politics
power-assisted
phylacterical
psychoanalyse
psychoanalyst
psychiatrical
psychobiology
psychodynamic
psychographic
psychogenesis
psychogenetic
psychohistory
psychokinesis
psychokinetic
psychological
psychometrics
psychometrist
psychrometric
psychrophilic
psychopathist
psychophysics
physharmonica
psychasthenia
psychosomatic
psychosurgery
psychotherapy
physiographic
physiographer
physiognomist
physitheistic
physicianship
physiological
physiotherapy
phyllophagous
phylloquinone
phytoplankton
phytotoxicity
phycoerythrin
quatch-buttock
Quaker-buttons
quaternionist
qualitatively
qualificative
qualification
qualificatory
quadricipital
quadrifoliate
quadrifarious
quatrefeuille
quadrigeminal
quadragesimal
quadrilocular
quadrillionth
quadrilingual
quarrelsomely
quadrilateral

quadriliteral
quadrumvirate
quadringenary
quadrennially
quadrinominal
quadruplicate
quadruplicity
quadraphonics
quadrophonics
quadripartite
quadrisection
quadrivalence
quartz-crystal
quartodeciman
quartz-halogen
quartziferous
quartermaster
quarter-decker
quarter-hourly
quarter-gunner
quantivalence
Queensland-nut
questioningly
questionnaire
querulousness
quincentenary
quincuncially
quingentenary
quick-scenting
quick-tempered
quicksilvered
quick-answered
Quinquagesima
quinquevalent
quintillionth
quilting-frame
quintuplicate
quizzing-glass
quotation-mark
quodlibetical
rhadamanthine
reacclimatise
rhabdomantist
reaffirmation
realistically
road-metalling
reapplication
reappointment
rearrangement
rhapsodically
reactionarism
reactionarist
Rhaeto-Romanic
Rhaeto-Romance
rebecca-eureka
robe-de-chambre
rabble-rousing
rectangularly
Rickettsiales
receivability
rectipetality
recriminative
recrimination

rectification
recriminatory
rectilinearly
receiving-ship
receiving-room
recollectedly
recalcitrance
recommendable
recommendably
recombination
recomposition
recomfortless
recompression
reconcilement
reconsolidate
reconstructor
receptiveness
receptibility
reception-room
reciprocative
reciprocation
reciprocality
recessiveness
recitationist
recrudescence
recrudescency
recrystallise
radialisation
reducibleness
redeemability
redding-straik
redeliverance
rudimentarily
redemptionist
riding-clothes
radio-actinium
radioactivity
radiotelegram
radiolocation
reduplicative
reduplication
redissolution
redevelopment
re-examination
re-embarkation
re-enforcement
reefing-jacket
re-edification
re-eligibility
roe-blackberry
rheumatically
re-exportation
refractometer
refocillation
reflexibility
refrigerative
refrigeration
refrigeratory
Rafflesiaceae
reformability
reference-mark
referentially
refashionment

rogue-elephant
regimentation
rag-and-bone-man
regardfulness
regurgitation
register-plate
registrarship
right-thinking
righteousness
reimbursement
rainbow-chaser
rainbow-tinted
reincarnation
reinforcement
rhinoscleroma
rhizomorphous
reinstatement
reintegration
reinterrogate
railway-stitch
rejuvenescent
roller-bearing
roller-bandage
roller-coaster
roller-skating
religiousness
roll-on-roll-off
rallying-point
remeasurement
rumlegumption
rumelgumption
Romano-British
romanticality
rominiscently
remonstrative
remonstration
remonstratory
remonstrantly
remorselessly
remissibility
remittance-man
rent-collector
ranz-des-vaches
röntgenoscopy
renegotiation
Ranunculaceae
randomisation
rensselaerite
root-and-branch
rhopalocerous
rhombporphyry
reorientation
rhodochrosite
republicanise
republicanism
republication
rapaciousness
reprehensible
reprehensibly
representable
representment
representamen
replenishment

reptiliferous
repulsiveness
reproachfully
rapprochement
repetitionary
repetitiously
requisiteness
restaurant-car
raspberry-bush
Russification
resolvability
resplendently
restoratively
restrictively
rust-resistant
resistance-box
resuscitative
resuscitation
resistibility
rusty-coloured
ritualisation
retranslation
rutherfordium
retributively
rattle-brained
retentiveness
retinoscopist
rationalistic
retroactively
retroactivity
ratiocinative
ratiocination
ratiocinatory
retromingency
retroflection
retrospective
retrospection
retrogressive
retrogression
round-the-clock
round-tripping
rough-and-ready
reunification
revocableness
revaccination
revictualling
revolutionary
revolutionise
revolutionism
revelationist
revolutionist
revenue-cutter
revendication
revindication
reverberative
reverberation
reverberatory
reversibility
reversionally
reverentially
rhyparography
sea-water-green
stalagmometer

stalagmometry
stalagmitical
stalactitical
stalactitious
shabby-genteel
scambling-days
searchingness
starch-reduced
star-catalogue
staccatissimo
search-warrant
swaddling-band
scandal-bearer
scandalmonger
standing-place
standing-stone
shamefastness
state-religion
shamelessness
shapelessness
statelessness
state-of-the-art
seal-engraving
states-general
space-platform
statesmanship
statesmanlike
stagecoaching
stagecoachman
scalenohedron
slate-coloured
skateboarding
Shakespearean
Shakespearian
staff-sergeant
snaffle-bridle
staff-notation
Sparganiaceae
scaphocephaly
scathefulness
Staphyleaceae
Staphylindiae
sea-shouldring
swashbuckling
scaling-ladder
scarification
stabilisation
staminiferous
spadicifloral
station-master
statistically
stalking-horse
small-and-early
scarlet-runner
swallow-tailed
spasmodically
shammy-leather
stainlessness
shadowcasting
sea-gooseberry
seaworthiness
sharpshooting
scalpelliform

scalping-knife
starting-price
starting-point
statute-labour
scapulimantic
sublanceolate
submachine-gun
Sabbath-breach
subeditorship
sabre-battling
subdeaconship
subternatural
sable-coloured
subterraneous
subversionary
subject-matter
subject-object
subventionary
subreptitious
subsequential
subserviently
subtile-witted
subtilisation
subdivisional
subsistential
sublieutenant
subclavicular
subindicative
subindication
subcommission
subcontractor
subcontiguous
subcontinuous
subpopulation
subappearance
subequatorial
subtriangular
subprefecture
subordinately
subordinative
subirrigation
subordination
suburbicarian
subtriplicate
substantively
substantivise
substantivity
substantially
substructural
subjunctively
sacramentally
socialisation
secretaryship
secretary-bird
secretiveness
successlessly
successionist
successorship
sick-feathered
Saccharomyces
saccharimeter
saccharometer
saccharimetry

succinctorium
sucking-bottle
sacrificially
section-cutter
sickle-feather
secondariness
sacrosanctity
sociolinguist
sociologistic
sycophantical
sacerdotalise
sacerdotalism
sacerdotalist
sock-suspender
sick-thoughted
seductiveness
saddle-blanket
saddle-feather
sedimentation
sedimentology
sado-masochism
sado-masochist
sodomitically
sedentariness
side-splitting
seditiousness
scenarisation
spelaeologist
steganopodous
steganography
sketchability
speechfulness
Sterculiaceae
speech-reading
Spencerianism
stercoraceous
stercorarious
steadfastness
Swedenborgian
stereographic
skeletogenous
stereoscopist
stereotropism
sleight-of-hand
stethoscopist
sheriff-depute
seeming-simple
specification
sterilisation
species-monger
speaking-voice
shell-parakeet
swelled-headed
smelling-salts
shell-ornament
steam-carriage
steam-governor
spermatoblast
spermatogenic
spermatophore
Spermatophyta
spermatophyte
spermatotheca

seek-no-further
stern-foremost
Stegocephalia
stenographist
steeplechaser
sleep-learning
sleeplessness
sheep-shearing
sleeping-berth
stepping-stone
sheep-stealing
sherry-cobbler
steering-wheel
sweet-savoured
spectacularly
spectre-shrimp
spectre-insect
sweet-tempered
smelting-house
smelting-works
spectroscopic
spectrography
spectatorship
speculatively
sufficingness
suffocatingly
suffraganship
safety-deposit
suffumigation
signature-tune
sagaciousness
suggestionise
suggestionism
suggestionist
significative
signification
significatory
significantly
sigmoidoscope
sugar-refinery
sugar-refining
sightlessness
schadenfreude
Schwenkfelder
sphagnicolous
sphagnologist
sphygmography
scholarliness
scholasticism
schematically
schoolgirlish
school-leaving
school-marmish
school-teacher
school-trained
sphericalness
spheroidicity
spheristerion
schutzstaffel
schizocarpous
schizogenesis
schizogenetic
schizomycetic

Schizomycetes
schizophrenia
schizophrenic
Schizophyceae
ship-chandlery
ship-carpenter
spindle-legged
spindle-shanks
spindle-shaped
spike-lavender
spinelessness
spine-chilling
seine-shooting
swine's-succory
spifflication
swingebuckler
shingle-roofed
swinging-block
sailing-master
spiritousness
spirit-rapping
spiritualness
spiritualiser
spirit-varnish
stick-in-the-mud
sticking-place
sticking-point
still-piercing
skirl-in-the-pan
still-room-maid
seismographic
seismographer
seismological
stigmatically
spinning-house
spinning-jenny
spinning-wheel
ship-of-the-line
stirpiculture
skittle-ground
shiftlessness
Saint-Simonism
Saint-Simonian
Saint-Simonist
scintillation
skirting-board
snifting-valve
spinuliferous
self-awareness
self-abasement
self-addressed
syllabication
self-admission
self-annealing
self-appointed
self-approving
self-assertive
self-asserting
self-assertion
self-assurance
self-criticism
self-collected
self-communion

self-contained
self-conscious
self-condemned
self-confessed
self-conceited
self-confident
self-confiding
self-convicted
self-conjugate
self-consuming
salaciousness
sale-catalogue
solicitorship
self-deceitful
self-deception
self-defeating
self-denyingly
solidungulate
solidungulous
self-dependent
self-directing
self-direction
self-dispraise
self-executing
soldering-bolt
soldering-iron
self-existence
self-enjoyment
silver-mounted
silver-shafted
sylleptically
silver-tongued
solifidianism
self-financing
self-forgetful
self-fertility
self-governing
sulphadiazine
self-hypnotism
sulphur-yellow
sulphureously
sulphur-bottom
self-induction
self-indulgent
self-infection
self-inflicted
salpingectomy
selling-plater
salviniaceous
self-injection
self-important
soldierliness
self-insurance
self-knowledge
self-levelling
solemnisation
self-murdering
splinter-proof
selenographic
selenographer
splanchnocele
splendiferous
selenological

splenetically
salmon-disease
self-operating
salmonellosis
salmon-fishery
salmon-fishing
syllogisation
self-opinioned
syllogistical
salmon-leister
self-pollution
self-propelled
self-professed
sclerocaulous
sclerodermite
sclerodermous
scleroprotein
self-revealing
self-slaughter
self-sterility
self-sufficing
self-shielding
self-supported
self-surrender
self-surviving
self-sustained
self-satisfied
splutteringly
self-treatment
self-tormentor
silk-throwster
somnambulance
somnambulator
sympathectomy
sympatholytic
sympathetical
semi-automatic
semi-barbarism
semi-barbarian
semiconscious
semiconductor
semicarbazide
symmetrically
summer-seeming
symphyseotomy
symphysiotomy
somniloquence
sympiesometer
symbiotically
simplificator
semilogarithm
simple-hearted
semimenstrual
symbolisation
semioviparous
Semnopithecus
symbolistical
symbolography
semipalmation
semiporcelain
semipermeable
semiperimeter
semiparasitic

semi-sagittate
sempstressing
somatological
symptomatical
sumptuousness
sensationally
syntactically
synecphonesis
synecological
sansculottism
sansculottist
synecdochical
senselessness
sententiously
synchondrosis
synchronicity
synchronistic
synchronology
synchronously
synthetically
syndicalistic
sentimentally
singing-master
sensitisation
sensitiveness
synallagmatic
single-chamber
single-hearted
sun-animalcule
sindonologist
sun-worshipper
synaposematic
synarthrodial
seneschalship
sanctifyingly
sanctimonious
sanitarianism
sanitationist
sandy-laverock
stomatoplasty
shop-assistant
snow-blindness
stoicheiology
scorchingness
stoechiometry
stoichiometry
stop-consonant
swordsmanship
suovetaurilia
smokelessness
scoleciformia
stone-coloured
smoke-consumer
sponge-fishing
sponging-house
soothfastness
scorification
Scotification
shock-absorber
stocking-frame
stock-breeding
shoulder-blade
shoulder-joint

shoulder-strap
swollen-headed
storming-party
scolopendrine
Scolopendrium
stoloniferous
stopping-place
scorpion-grass
scouring-stick
smooth-chinned
smooth-dittied
short-tempered
short-division
sportsmanship
sportsmanlike
shooting-board
shooting-brake
shooting-lodge
spontaneously
shooting-range
shooting-stick
smooth-tongued
supranational
supratemporal
suprasensible
supra-axillary
septentrional
septentriones
syphilisation
syphilophobia
syphilologist
sophistically
sophisticated
sophisticator
supplementary
supplantation
Sipunculoidea
suppositional
supercalender
superlatively
supernational
supersaturate
separableness
superabundant
superaddition
superfetation
supervenience
supersensible
supersensibly
superphysical
superfineness
superficially
superfluidity
superfluously
supereminence
superannuable
superannuated
superdominant
superposition
supercolumnar
superordinate
superordinary
supercritical

separationist
superstitious
superhumanise
superhumanity
supernumerary
sequestration
sequentiality
surface-active
surface-vessel
serialisation
sarcastically
strobilaceous
scribbling-pad
sericiculture
sprocket-wheel
sericulturist
Saracen's-stone
structuralism
structuralist
structureless
screech-martin
screech-thrush
serjeant-at-law
sergeant-major
street-orderly
street-railway
street-sweeper
sarmentaceous
serpent-lizard
surreptitious
street-walking
sprightliness
surchargement
serving-mallet
straightforth
straight-pight
straining-beam
strike-breaker
serologically
shrill-tongued
scrumptiously
strombuliform
spring-balance
spring-cleaner
stringentness
serendipitous
strenuousness
syringomyelia
string-pulling
strengthening
strangulation
surrogateship
sorrowfulness
sarcophaguses
Serbo-Croatian
scrap-merchant
strophiolated
Syrophoenicia
streptococcic
streptococcal
streptococcus
scripophilist
scripturalism

scripturalist
strato-cumulus
stratocruiser
stratigraphic
stratigrapher
strategically
strategetical
stretcher-bond
stratospheric
scrivenership
straw-coloured
systematician
systematology
suspercollate
suspender-belt
systemisation
sustentaculum
sustentacular
suspectedness
suspicionless
sessions-house
sesquiplicate
satanicalness
satin-sheeting
satiricalness
squeamishness
sounding-board
sound-boarding
soundproofing
squeezability
snuff-coloured
spunging-house
south-eastward
south-easterly
south-westward
south-westerly
southerliness
skulking-place
squanderingly
squandermania
squinancy-wort
saurognathous
Sauropterygia
sculpturesque
square-bashing
square-dancing
squirrel-shrew
square-measure
square-pierced
squirarchical
soul-searching
saussuritised
stultiloquent
Sovietologist
savanna-wattle
savanna-forest
seventeenthly
sewing-machine
sowing-machine
Saxifragaceae
sexagesimally
sex-chromosome
sexploitation

sex-intergrade
Scyphomedusae
stylistically
Thalamiflorae
thalamifloral
thanatophobia
thanatography
thalassocracy
thalattocracy
tram-conductor
traceableness
traveller's-joy
tradesmanlike
trade-unionism
trade-unionist
trapezohedron
travel-stained
travel-tainted
traffic-lights
teachableness
traditionally
toad-in-the-hole
thanklessness
tracklessness
thank-offering
thankworthily
tea-plantation
traumatically
thaumatolatry
traumatonasty
thaumaturgism
thaumaturgics
thaumaturgist
train-spotting
tranquilliser
transparently
translational
transnational
transcendence
transcendency
transfer-paper
transferrable
transferrible
transversally
transientness
transshipping
transpiration
transpiratory
transliterate
transmigrator
transmissible
transmittable
transplanting
translocation
transpositive
transposition
transformable
transportable
transportedly
transport-ship
transportance
transcriptive
transcription

transgressive
transgression
transisthmian
transistorise
transatlantic
transit-circle
transitionary
transmutative
transmutation
translucently
transfusively
translucidity
tractableness
toastmistress
tractarianism
tobaccanalian
table-skittles
tablespoonful
tubuliflorous
tuberculation
ticket-of-leave
ticket-writing
tachistoscope
tickly-benders
technicalness
technological
tachometrical
tic-douloureux
tachymetrical
tachygraphist
tiddledywinks
treacherously
thenceforward
thereinbefore
theriomorphic
theologically
thermobalance
thermochemist
thermodynamic
thermographic
thermogenesis
thermogenetic
thermonuclear
thermoplastic
thermophilous
thermosetting
thermotropism
theanthropism
theanthropist
theopaschitic
theorematical
theoretically
treasure-chest
treasure-house
treasurership
treasure-trove
trestle-bridge
theatricalise
theatricalism
theatricality
tremulousness
trisaccharide
tricarpellary

thimble-rigger
twiddling-line
toilet-service
thing-in-itself
tritheistical
trichological
trichromatism
trichopterist
trichopterous
triliteralism
thick-pleached
triple-crowned
thigmotropism
triangulately
triangulation
triangularity
trigonometric
trisoctahedra
triethylamine
tributariness
tritubercular
tribuniticial
tribunitician
triquetrously
trisyllabical
talkativeness
telegraph-wire
telegraph-pole
telegrammatic
telerecording
tolerationist
telescopiform
telautography
televisionary
time-beguiling
time-bettering
time-consuming
temperateness
temperamental
tempest-beaten
tempest-tossed
tempestuously
tumbler-switch
temporariness
temporisation
temporisingly
tumorgenicity
timbrophilist
temerariously
time-signature
temptableness
tantalisation
tantalisingly
Tenebrionidae
tenaciousness
tender-hearted
tenpenny-piece
tangentiality
tendentiously
tonsillectomy
tintinnabulum
tintinnabular
tenant-in-chief

tent-preaching
tongue-doubtie
tongue-in-cheek
tongue-lashing
tongue-twister
Tropaeolaceae
troublesomely
troublousness
twopenceworth
twopennyworth
thought-reader
thoughtlessly
trophoblastic
toothache-tree
trophallactic
troth-plighted
toothsomeness
tooth-ornament
trophotropism
troglodytical
trolling-spoon
thoroughbrace
thorough-going
thorough-paced
thousand-pound
trouser-pocket
trouser-button
trout-coloured
topographical
typographical
topside-turvey
topologically
tippling-house
tape-recording
topsyturvydom
terra-japonica
threateningly
three-farthing
turkey-buzzard
three-per-cents
threepenn'orth
threefoldness
three-cornered
torrentiality
terrestrially
tercentennial
terminatively
terminability
terminational
tergiversator
turnip-lantern
territorially
thrillingness
thremmatology
thrombokinase
tyrannosaurus
turbocharging
terrorisation
turbo-electric
tortoise-plant
tortoise-shell
terpsichorean
thresher-shark

thresher-whale
thrashing-mill
threshing-mill
thrasonically
teratological
throttle-lever
throttle-valve
through-ticket
turquoise-blue
throwing-stick
throwing-table
tarry-fingered
tastelessness
Testicardines
testification
testificatory
tetrachloride
Tetrabranchia
tetrastichous
tetradynamous
tetrasyllabic
tetrasyllable
tithe-gatherer
tattie-lifting
tittle-tattler
Titanotherium
tetartohedral
thunder-darter
thunder-master
thunder-bearer
thunder-shower
thunder-strike
thunder-stroke
thunder-struck
true-disposing
touchableness
truthlessness
thurification
trunk-breeches
tautometrical
tautophonical
tautochronism
tautochronous
Teutonisation
tauromorphous
trumpet-shaped
trumpet-flower
trustlessness
trustworthily
toxicological
toxicophagous
tax-deductible
taxonomically
toxoplasmosis
Thymelaeaceae
trysting-place
trysting-stile
unabbreviated
unambiguously
unambitiously
unaccompanied
unaccentuated
unascertained

unaccountable
unaccountably
un-Americanise
unamiableness
uralitisation
unapostolical
unapprehended
unappreciated
unapprovingly
unappropriate
unassimilable
unassimilated
unarticulated
unanticipated
unadulterated
unadventurous
unadvisedness
unbiassedness
umbraculiform
umbrella-stand
unblessedness
unbridledness
unbelievingly
umbelliferous
unbendingness
unbrotherlike
unbeseemingly
unboundedness
unchastisable
uncleanliness
uncreatedness
urchin-snouted
uncalculating
uncompanioned
uncommendable
uncommendably
uncompetitive
uncompensated
uncomplicated
uncomplaisant
uncomplaining
uncomfortable
uncomfortably
unconsciously
unconcealable
unconcernedly
unconcernment
unconsecrated
unconversable
uncontestable
unconvertible
uncontentious
unconjectured
unconceivable
unconceivably
unconsidering
unconditioned
unconditional
unconformable
unconformably
unconstrained
unconjunctive
unconsummated

unconquerable
unconquerably
uncloudedness
unco-ordinated
uncoordinated
unco-operative
uncooperative
uncertainness
unceremonious
unchristianly
uncircumcised
uncourtliness
undifferenced
undulationist
undomesticate
undepreciated
underhandedly
undercarriage
underachiever
under-shepherd
underniceness
underclassman
underclothing
undergraduate
underprepared
underestimate
understrapper
understanding
underexposure
undescendable
undescendible
undiscernible
undiscernibly
undiscernedly
undistempered
undistinctive
undisciplined
undiscomfited
undishonoured
undiscouraged
undescribable
undistributed
undistracting
undeservingly
undisturbedly
undiscussable
undiscussible
undisguisable
undisguisedly
undutifulness
undeterminate
undauntedness
undeviatingly
undividedness
undiversified
unevangelical
unexaggerated
unembellished
unembarrassed
unexceptional
unexclusively
unexemplified
unelectrified

urediniospore
unenlightened
unemotionally
unexplainable
unexpressible
unexpensively
unexperienced
unearthliness
uneatableness
unestablished
unentertained
unequivocally
unfeelingness
unflinchingly
unfeignedness
unfalteringly
unfamiliarity
unforgettable
unforgettably
unforthcoming
unforgiveable
unforgiveness
unforeseeable
unforeskinned
unfortunately
unfashionable
unfashionably
unguardedness
ungrammatical
ungainsayable
ungenuineness
ungentlemanly
unhealthfully
unhealthiness
unhurtfulness
unicameralism
unilateralism
unicameralist
unilateralist
unilaterality
uninaugurated
unimaginative
uninflammable
uninformative
uninfluential
uninhabitable
unilluminated
unillustrated
unimpeachable
unit-packaging
unimpregnated
unimpressible
unimpassioned
uninquisitive
uninstructive
unintelligent
unintentional
unintermitted
uninteresting
uninterrupted
unjustifiable
unjustifiably
unknowingness

unlearnedness
unlimitedness
unmeaningness
unmacadamised
unmedicinable
unmindfulness
unmentionable
unministerial
unmurmuringly
unmistrustful
unmitigatedly
unnecessarily
unneighboured
unneighbourly
unnaturalness
unnaturalised
unoriginality
unobstructive
unobtrusively
unpracticable
unpractically
unpreoccupied
unprecedented
unpresentable
unpreventable
unpretentious
unpredictable
unpleasurable
unpleasurably
unphilosophic
unpolarisable
unpunctuality
unprophetical
unprovided-for
unpromisingly
unprovisioned
unprovocative
unprogressive
unperpetrated
unperfectness
unperceivable
unperceivably
unperceivedly
unpurchasable
unpersuadable
unpasteurised
unpitifulness
unputdownable
unqualifiedly
unquestioning
unreasoningly
unreclaimable
unreclaimably
unrecognising
unrecollected
unrecommended
unrecompensed
unrecoverable
unrecoverably
unregenerated
unrighteously
uprighteously
unreliability

unrelentingly
unremembering
unremorseless
unremittently
unremittingly
unreplaceable
unrepresented
unreplenished
unreprimanded
unreprievable
unrepentingly
unreproachful
unreproaching
unrestfulness
unrestingness
unresistingly
unreturningly
unscavengered
unsparingness
unstaunchable
unsubstantial
unsociability
unstercorated
unsteadfastly
unspecialised
unspectacular
unspeculative
unsightliness
unscholarlike
unsuitability
unskilfulness
unspiritually
unstigmatised
unsaintliness
unsaleability
unselfishness
unsoldierlike
unsympathetic
unsymmetrical
unsymmetrised
unsensational
unsentimental
unsmotherable
unspottedness
unsupportable
unsupportedly
unsuperfluous
unsurpassable
unsurpassably
unserviceable
unshrinkingly
unscrutinised
unsustainable
unsusceptible
unsuspectedly
unsettledness
unsatisfiable
unsavouriness
untraversable
ultra-virtuous
ultra-tropical
untransparent
untransmitted

untransformed
untremblingly
untheological
untrespassing
untaintedness
Ustilaginales
ustilagineous
untamableness
untenableness
untunableness
untunefulness
utterableness
unterrestrial
unthriftiness
up-to-the-minute
up-to-the-moment
untrustworthy
unvitrifiable
unwillingness
unwelcomeness
unwomanliness
unwholesomely
unwarrantable
unwarrantably
unwarrantedly
unworldliness
unworkmanlike
unwithdrawing
unwithholding
unwittingness
vraisemblance
vibrationless
vibracularium
vice-admiralty
vice-consulate
victimisation
victimologist
vacillatingly
vacuolisation
vice-president
vice-principal
vicariousness
vocationalism
vacuum-cleaner
vegetarianism
voicelessness
villagisation
volcanisation
vulcanisation
vulgarisation
volta-electric
volcanologist
vulcanologist
Voltaireanism
Voltairianism
valedictorian
vulnerability
velvet-fiddler
villeggiatura
volumenometer
velt-mareschal
voluntariness
voluntaristic

Valerianaceae
volatilisable
vantage-ground
viniculturist
vindicability
vindicatorily
Vansittartism
venerableness
ventriloquise
ventriloquial
ventriloquism
ventriloquist
ventriloquous
venereologist
venturesomely
venturousness
viol-de-gamboys
violoncellist
vapourishness
verbalisation
vernalisation
versatileness
variable-sweep
vernacularise
vernacularism
vernacularist
vernacularity
voraciousness
verifiability
verbigeration
varnishing-day
versification
verticillated
vertiginously
versicoloured
vermiculation
verisimilarly
visualisation
visceroptosis
visionariness
viscometrical
viscosimetric
viticulturist
vitrification
vitelligenous
vote-splitting
vouchsafement
vaulting-horse
vaulting-house
vivaciousness
vivisectional
vivisectorium
vivisepulture
vexillologist
vexatiousness
what-d'ye-call-'em
what-d'ye-call-it
weather-headed
weather-beaten
weather-bitten
weatherometer
weather-anchor
weather-driven

weather-symbol
whaling-master
wearisomeness
weaponshawing
wrapping-paper
wide-awakeness
wedding-favour
wedding-finger
wide-stretched
widow's-chamber
whereinsoever
weeding-chisel
weeping-willow
weeping-spring
wheel-carriage
wheeler-dealer
white-favoured
white-breasted
weight-lifting
whithersoever
weight-watcher
waiting-vassal
writing-master
writing-school
whiskerandoed
whirling-table
whipping-cream
whipping-cheer
whimsicalness
whistled-drunk
whistle-blower
wristlet watch
whistling-shop
well-appointed
well-beseeming
well-connected
well-conducted
well-developed
walking-papers
walking-ticket
walking-orders
will-o'-the-wisps
willow-warbler
well-preserved
well-regulated
well-respected
wills-o'-the-wisp
well-thought-of
well-warranted
well-worked-out
wamble-cropped
women-children
woman-suffrage
wing-commander
winter-aconite
wonderfulness
Winter-gardens
wonder-working
wonder-wounded
winding-engine
winkle-pickers
window-curtain
woodcock's-head

whoremasterly
wood-engraving
wholesomeness
whole-coloured
wrong-headedly
wood-germander
wool-gathering
woollen-draper
whooping-cough
wood-sandpiper
wappenshawing
word-blindness
worldly-minded
worthlessness
word-splitting
Wordsworthian
wasterfulness
washhand-basin
washhand-stand
washing-powder
washing-bottle
waspish-headed
witches-butter
water-vascular
water-sapphire
water-carriage
water-chestnut
water-plantain
watering-house
watering-place
water-mocassin
water-softener
water-sprinkle
water-breather
waterproofing
water-dropwort
water-standing
water-hyacinth
wayfaring-tree
xylographical
xanthochroism
xanthochromia
xanthochroous
xanthopterine
xiphiplastral
xiphiplastron
xerodermatous
xerophthalmia
yachtsmanship
yieldableness
yellow-bellied
yellow-bunting
yellow-crowned
yellow-covered
yellow-fronted
yellowishness
yellow-spotted
yellow-yorling
yesterevening
yestermorning
zebra-parakeet
zygodactylism
zygodactylous

zygapophyseal
zygapophysial
Zinjanthropus
Zingiberaceae
zincification
zinkification
zoogeographic
zoogeographer
zoosporangium
zoopsychology
Zarathustrism
Zarathustrian

anacardiaceous
amaranthaceous
amateurishness
anachronically
arachnological
avariciousness
anamnestically
anagrammatical
Acanthocephala
Amaryllidaceae
Albigensianism
arboricultural
ambassadorship
Archaeornithes
archaeological
Asclepiadaceae
archgenethliac
alcoholisation
archiepiscopal
accomplishable
accomplishment
Arctostaphylos
acceptableness
accustomedness
accountability
accountantship
androcephalous
andromedotoxin
audiometrician
androdioecious
andromonoecism
audio-frequency
alder-buckthorn
alexipharmakon
affectionately
aggrandisement
aggressiveness
Anglo-Israelite
angiostomatous
Augustinianism
angustifoliate
apheliotropism
achondroplasia
achromatically
aphoristically
alimentiveness
arithmetically
anisodactylous
aristocratical
acknowledgment
allegorisation
alloiostrophos
allelomorphism
all-overishness
administratrix
administration
administrative
apodeictically
above-mentioned
aforementioned
apothegmatical
apophthegmatic
abominableness

apoplectically
apologetically
alphabetically
alphamerically
alphanumerical
apprehensively
appreciatively
apprenticehood
apprenticement
apprenticeship
amphibological
appendicectomy
Appendicularia
approach-stroke
asparagus-stone
aerobiotically
aerobiological
agrobiological
Africanisation
aerodynamicist
aeroelastician
aerohydroplane
air-vice-marshal
aerenchymatous
arrondissement
air-conditioned
aircraftswoman
agrostological
across-the-board
abstemiousness
aesthesiogenic
auspiciousness
absent-mindedly
abstractedness
abstractionist
absorbefacient
absorptiometer
absorptiveness
asset-stripping
asseveratingly
attractiveness
autobiographer
autocratically
articulateness
anticonvulsant
anticipatorily
anticipatively
antediluvially
antidepressant
authentication
artificialness
anti-federalism
anti-federalist
astigmatically
antagonisation
attainableness
auto-intoxicant
anti-Jacobinism
artillery-plant
antimonarchist
attemptability
antimetathesis
actinobacillus

astrogeologist
astrophysicist
astrologically
astronomically
antiodontalgic
antiphlogistic
antiphonically
antaphrodisiac
antiperspirant
antiperistasis
antiphrastical
antipathetical
antiquarianism
autoradiograph
anthropography
anthropologist
anthropometric
anthropopathic
anthropophuism
auto-suggestion
antiseptically
antiscriptural
altitudinarian
attitudinarian
attitudinising
antithetically
autotypography
altruistically
aquifoliaceous
advantageously
adventitiously
asymmetrically
asymptotically
bear-animalcule
boarding-school
bladder-campion
brachycephalic
brachydiagonal
brachydactylic
brachypinakoid
black-marketeer
blank-cartridge
boa-constrictor
beautification
bibliomaniacal
bacteriologist
bacteriostasis
bacteriostatic
backscratching
bed-sitting-room
bread-and-butter
breeding-ground
bletheranskate
breakfast-table
bremsstrahlung
breathing-while
breathing-space
breathlessness
blithesomeness
Bristol-diamond
blistered-steel
blister-plaster
boisterousness

Baluchitherium
bill-discounter
ballet-mistress
belletristical
bull-headedness
billiard-marker
beneficialness
benzodiazepine
banqueting-hall
biomathematics
bronchiectasis
broncho-dilator
blood-sacrifice
blood-bespotted
brobdingnagian
blood-consuming
blood-poisoning
biodegradation
blockade-runner
bioelectricity
book-mindedness
bioengineering
biographically
biosystematics
barrage-balloon
bargain-counter
Burschenschaft
berberidaceous
burling-machine
barometrically
bird-of-paradise
borough-English
bastardisation
Basidiomycetes
beseechingness
bashi-bazoukery
butter-fingered
butterfly-screw
bathing-machine
bathing-costume
bituminisation
bathygraphical
bougainvillaea
bouleversement
bowdlerisation
characteristic
chamber-counsel
chalcographist
chancellorship
changeableness
chargeableness
claw-hammer-coat
charitableness
clavicytherium
Charley-pitcher
chain-lightning
cyanocobalamin
classification
classificatory
class-conscious
claustrophobia
claustrophobic
Chaetodontidae

chaptalisation
coastguardsman
cabbage-lettuce
cabinet-edition
cabinet-pudding
cock-a-doodle-doo
cyclanthaceous
coconut-matting
cucurbitaceous
cadaverousness
coelanaglyphic
chevaux-de-frise
creditableness
chemoreception
chemoreceptive
Chenopodiaceae
chemosynthesis
cheirographist
cheiromantical
clear-starching
co-essentiality
chest-protector
cigarette-paper
climatological
chivalrousness
coincidentally
chincherinchee
child-resistant
crinkum-crankum
chicken-hearted
chicken-livered
cairngorm-stone
chimney-sweeper
chimney-swallow
chittagong-wood
clitter-clatter
collapsability
collapsibility
Calycanthaceae
calligraphical
colliquescence
calamitousness
colonel-in-chief
calorification
chlorpromazine
chlorite-schist
chloritisation
colour-sergeant
comparableness
commandantship
compatibleness
companion-hatch
campanological
compassionable
campanulaceous
commensurately
commensuration
compensational
commentatorial
commissionaire
commissaryship
Camelopardalis
complexionless

composing-stick
commodiousness
common-or-garden
compossibility
commonsensical
comprehensible
comprehensibly
compunctiously
compurgatorial
combustibility
campylotropous
consanguineous
contagiousness
cantankerously
concavo-concave
connaturalness
conscriptional
centenarianism
condescendence
concelebration
convexo-concave
contemporanean
contemperation
contemperature
contemptuously
condensability
concessionaire
contesseration
conversational
conversaziones
convertibility
concentrically
conventionally
conceivability
conservational
conservatorium
cinchonisation
centimetre-gram
confidentially
continentalism
continentalist
conditionality
contiguousness
continuousness
conglobulation
conglomeration
conclusiveness
conglutination
conglutinative
cinematography
convocationist
cannonball-tree
consociational
censoriousness
conformability
Convolvulaceae
conspiratorial
contracyclical
contractedness
contractionary
contradictable
contradictious
centrifugalise

centrifugation
congregational
contraindicant
contraindicate
controllership
centralisation
contraposition
contrapositive
centripetalism
contrarotating
congratulation
congratulatory
congratulative
controvertible
controvertibly
constitutional
construability
constructional
constructively
constructivism
contumaciously
censurableness
conjunctivitis
contumeliously
centuplication
conquistadores
consubstantial
convulsiveness
conductibility
consuetudinary
consulting-room
Crouched-friars
coordinateness
co-ordinateness
chondrogenesis
chondrocranium
cholelithiasis
cholecystotomy
cloak-and-dagger
chorographical
cross-reference
cross-sectional
cross-infection
Crossopterygii
capparidaceous
captain-general
copper-bottomed
copper-fastened
capriciousness
Caprifoliaceae
capitalisation
coquettishness
cornet-à-pistons
correspondence
correspondency
current-bedding
cardinal-bishop
cardinal-deacon
cardinal-flower
cardinal-priest
curvilinearity
cardiomyopathy
carcinomatosis

carcinogenesis
carcinological
corticosteroid
cardiovascular
corolliflorous
caramelisation
chromatography
chromatosphere
chronometrical
cartographical
cartridge-paper
Christ-cross-row
Christological
circumambience
circumambiency
circumambulate
circumbendibus
corpuscularian
circumforanean
circumferentor
circumgyration
circumgyratory
circumlocution
circumlocutory
circumlittoral
circumnutation
circumnutatory
circumnavigate
circumposition
circumstantial
circumspection
circumspective
circumscissile
corruptibility
circuit-breaker
circuitousness
circumvolution
cost-accountant
cost-accounting
Castanospermum
castle-building
casement-window
cosmopolitical
cosmographical
castrametation
catechetically
catachrestical
catechumenical
catechumenship
catadioptrical
Catherine-wheel
cathodographer
courageousness
Crutched-friars
council-chamber
counsel-keeping
counsellorship
counterbalance
counter-salient
counter-passant
counter-battery
counter-measure
counter-changed

counter-skipper
counter-opening
counter-trading
counter-wrought
counter-subject
counter-current
country-dancing
coxcombicality
cryobiological
cryptaesthesia
cryptaesthetic
cryptographist
crystallisable
crystallomancy
diamantiferous
diaheliotropic
dialectologist
diaphanousness
diachronically
diathermaneity
death-practised
diaphototropic
diamond-wedding
diamondiferous
dragon-standard
deceivableness
decolonisation
decolorisation
decimalisation
decompoundable
decontaminator
deconsecration
dechristianise
decorativeness
dicotyledonous
dactyliography
dodecasyllabic
dodecasyllable
diesel-electric
dress-rehearsal
dressing-jacket
dyer's-greenweed
defeasibleness
daffadowndilly
deflagrability
differentially
differentiator
defenestration
definitiveness
diffractometer
daguerreotyper
degenerateness
dogtooth-violet
dog's-tooth-grass
drill-husbandry
deliberateness
deliberatively
delectableness
dolichocephaly
delightfulness
dolomitisation
deliverability
demobilisation

democratically
diminutiveness
demoralisation
demi-semiquaver
dinoflagellate
dynamo-electric
dynamometrical
denominational
denominatively
denitrificator
dinitrobenzene
dioscoreaceous
dipterocarpous
depolarisation
diplomatically
deplorableness
diplostemonous
departmentally
deposit-receipt
dermatological
derogatoriness
durchkomponirt
Durchmusterung
disdainfulness
disacknowledge
disaccommodate
disadventurous
disregardfully
dysteleologist
dysmenorrhoeal
dysmenorrhoeic
discerpibility
disrespectable
distemperature
dispensability
distensibility
dispensational
dispensatorily
dispensatively
dessert-service
dissertational
disceptatorial
disserviceable
disaffiliation
disaffirmation
despicableness
despitefulness
dispiteousness
distinguishing
dispiritedness
disciplinarian
disciplinarium
displeasedness
desulphuration
displenishment
disillusionary
disillusionise
disembarkation
disimpassioned
disembowelment
disemboguement
disincarcerate
disengagedness

disinheritance
disintegration
disintegrative
disinfestation
disinvestiture
disingenuously
disenthralment
disenchantment
disenchantress
disinclination
disinformation
disincorporate
disentrainment
disenfranchise
disencumbrance
discombobulate
discomboberate
disconcertment
discomfortable
disconformable
despoticalness
dissociability
discommendable
discount-broker
disconnectedly
discountenance
disjointedness
discolouration
discourteously
discouragement
discouragingly
disconsolately
disconsolation
discontinuance
discontentedly
discontentment
dissolutionism
dissolutionist
dissolubleness
dissolvability
disapplication
disappointment
disapprobation
disapprobatory
disapprobative
disappropriate
disapprovingly
disequilibrium
disarrangement
distributional
distributively
distractedness
destructionist
disorderliness
disorientation
discriminately
discriminating
discrimination
discriminatory
discriminative
discretionally
disassociation
disputatiously

disputableness
disqualifiable
disfurnishment
disquisitional
discursiveness
disgustingness
disgustfulness
dissymmetrical
detestableness
detoxification
Deuteronomical
daughterliness
daughters-in-law
double-breasted
double-declutch
double-flowered
double-stopping
dividing-engine
devil-on-the-neck
devalorisation
davenport-trick
divertissement
diverticulated
diverticulitis
diverticulosis
devitalisation
dextrorotation
dextrorotatory
daylight-saving
dazzle-painting
exacerbescence
evangelicalism
evangelisation
egalitarianism
examine-in-chief
Elasmobranchii
enantiomorphic
enantiostylous
emblematically
embellishingly
eschatological
exclaustration
encyclopaedian
encyclopaedism
encyclopaedist
excrementitial
ecclesiologist
ecclesiastical
Ecclesiasticus
excommunicable
encephalograph
excruciatingly
endoradiosonde
endosmotically
epexegetically
electrovalency
electrogenesis
electioneering
electrochemist
electrothermal
electrothermic
electrotherapy
electronically

electrogilding
electrobiology
electrowinning
electroplating
electrostatics
electroculture
effeminateness
effervescingly
engagement-ring
eigen-frequency
exhilaratingly
ethnologically
etherification
enharmonically
Elizabethanism
epidemiologist
enigmatography
epigrammatical
epistolography
epistemologist
existentialism
existentialist
eulogistically
econometrician
emphaticalness
expressionless
expressiveness
euphorbiaceous
empire-building
experienceless
experimentally
empyreumatical
euphuistically
edriophthalmic
early-Victorian
extra-parochial
extracanonical
extravehicular
extraneousness
extraforaneous
extra-condensed
extracorporeal
extractability
extrinsicality
extemporaneity
extemporaneous
entomostracous
extensionalism
extensionality
extinguishable
extinguishment
eutrophication
entertainingly
enterocentesis
esterification
extortionately
enthronisation
enterprisingly
enthusiastical
enthymematical
equiangularity
educationalist
eburnification

equiponderance
emulsification
erythropoiesis
etymologically
flamboyant-tree
flagelliferous
fraternisation
flat-footedness
flagitiousness
flag-lieutenant
fibrocartilage
factitiousness
facinorousness
fiddle-faddling
federalisation
French-Canadian
French-polisher
feeble-mindedly
free-spokenness
figurativeness
fringillaceous
flight-recorder
friendlessness
faint-heartedly
fairy-godmother
fallaciousness
folding-machine
falsifiability
fellow-creature
fellow-commoner
filiopietistic
follow-my-leader
fellow-townsman
Finlandisation
fundamentalism
fundamentalist
fundamentality
fantasticality
finger-alphabet
finger-painting
finger-pointing
fingerprinting
finger's-breadth
food-controller
flowery-kirtled
frolicsomeness
floriculturist
forward-looking
fermentability
fermentescible
forthrightness
farthingsworth
formidableness
forbiddingness
foraminiferous
ferro-manganese
ferromagnesian
foreordination
ferroprussiate
forisfamiliate
foreshortening
forethoughtful
furfuraldehyde

fortune-telling
fortuitousness
fire-worshipper
foster-daughter
fastidiousness
fashionmonging
fatherlessness
fatiguableness
futtock-shrouds
foundation-stop
fructification
fivepenny-piece
favourableness
glanduliferous
grandiloquence
grace-and-favour
gram-equivalent
grangerisation
Gnathobdellida
graphitisation
grammaticaster
gregariousness
greisenisation
greywacke-slate
galvanoplastic
galactophorous
galactopoietic
galeopithecoid
galeopithecine
gold-of-pleasure
gelatinisation
genealogically
gynaecological
gentleman-cadet
gynomonoecious
gynandromorphy
gentrification
generalisation
general-purpose
genethliacally
genethlialogic
gooseberry-bush
gooseberry-fool
gooseberry-moth
gooseberry-wine
glove-stretcher
geocentrically
good-fellowship
good-for-nothing
good-humouredly
geothermometer
groundlessness
geognostically
ground-squirrel
geomorphologic
geographically
geosynchronous
gerontological
gyrostabiliser
Gasteromycetes
gutter-merchant
heaven-directed
heavenly-minded

heathenishness
heather-mixture
heather-bleater
heather-bluiter
heather-blutter
heavier-than-air
heart-searching
heart-heaviness
healthlessness
hebraistically
hobbledehoydom
hobbledehoyish
hobbledehoyism
hebetudinosity
hickery-pickery
huckleberrying
hydromagnetics
hydrocephalous
hydromechanics
hydronephrosis
hydronephrotic
hydrogeologist
hydrocellulose
hydro-aeroplane
hydrobiologist
hydropneumatic
hydrocoralline
hydrocortisone
hydrographical
Hydropterideae
hydrosulphuric
hydroextractor
hydrodynamical
hierarchically
haematogenesis
hieroglyphical
Hierosolymitan
hierogrammatic
hierographical
hyetographical
high-handedness
highly-seasoned
high-mindedness
hygroscopicity
hagiographical
hygrographical
high-principled
high-priesthood
half-a-sovereign
holier-than-thou
helminthologic
holometabolism
heliosciophyte
half-pennyworth
Haloragidaceae
hallucinogenic
humidification
homoeomorphism
homoeomorphous
homoeothermous
homoeoteleuton
homogenisation
homoiothermous

Hamamelidaceae
hemispheroidal
humoursomeness
hunting-leopard
handicraftsman
handkerchieves
hen-and-chickens
hundred-per-cent
hunt-the-slipper
honourableness
hypocritically
hypochondriasm
hypochondriast
hypocoristical
hypodermically
hippety-hoppety
hypomixolydian
hippopotamuses
haplostemonous
hypercatalexis
hypercalcaemia
hyperbatically
hypernatraemia
hyperacuteness
hypersensitise
hypersensitive
hyperaesthesia
hyperaesthesic
hyperaesthetic
hyperglycaemia
hyperinflation
hyperbolically
hyperconscious
hypertrophical
hypercriticise
hypercriticism
hypostatically
hyposulphurous
hepaticologist
hypothetically
hephthemimeral
hypothyroidism
hermaphroditic
hereditability
hereditariness
horse-godmother
herpetological
herring-fishery
horticulturist
harmoniousness
horror-stricken
heresiographer
hysterectomise
hospitableness
histopathology
histogenically
histochemistry
historiography
histrionically
heterochromous
heterochronism
heterochronous
heteromorphism

heteromorphous
heterophyllous
heterosomatous
heterostrophic
heterothallism
house-physician
Hexactinellida
inadequateness
imaginableness
inalienability
Italianisation
inapprehension
inapprehensive
inappreciation
inappreciative
inapproachable
inapproachably
inappositeness
inauspiciously
inarticulately
inarticulation
inartificially
inalterability
inartistically
inadvisability
incidentalness
incredibleness
incogitability
inclinableness
incommensurate
incompleteness
incommodiously
incompressible
incommunicable
incommunicably
inconscionable
inconveniently
inconsequently
inconsiderable
inconsiderably
inconsistently
incontiguously
inconclusively
incontrollable
incontrollably
incoordination
incapacitation
incorporealism
incorporeality
incestuousness
incautiousness
indubitability
indecomposable
indecipherable
indoctrination
indecorousness
indecisiveness
indifferentism
indifferentist
indefiniteness
indigenisation
indemonstrable
indiscerptible

indistinctness
indiscoverable
indisposedness
indescribables
indestructible
indestructibly
indiscreetness
indiscriminate
indiscreteness
indeterminable
indeterminably
indivisibility
inexcusability
ineffectuality
inevitableness
idealistically
inexorableness
inexpiableness
inexpressibles
identification
inframaxillary
infralapsarian
infrangibility
inflation-proof
inflammability
infrastructure
infectiousness
inflexibleness
inflectionless
ingloriousness
inhabitiveness
ichthyosaurian
ichthyolatrous
ichthyophagist
ichthyophagous
ichthyological
ichnographical
inharmoniously
inimitableness
idiopathically
iniquitousness
ill-naturedness
illegitimately
illegitimation
ill-conditioned
illustrational
illustratively
illiterateness
immobilisation
immaculateness
immoderateness
immunosuppress
immethodically
innumerability
inordinateness
inoperableness
inorganisation
isodiametrical
ivory-porcelain
implacableness
implausibility
impracticality
implementation

impregnability
impressibility
impressionable
impressiveness
imponderabilia
improvableness
impermeability
imperfectively
imperviability
imperviousness
imparisyllabic
imperturbation
impassableness
imposthumation
impassibleness
impoverishment
inquisiturient
irrecognisable
irreconcilable
irreconcilably
irreducibility
irrefutability
irrelativeness
irremovability
irreproachable
irreproachably
irreproducible
irreparability
irrespectively
irresolubility
irresoluteness
irresponsively
irrestrainable
irresuscitable
irresuscitably
irrevocability
insufficiently
insignificance
insignificancy
inspirationism
inspirationist
institutionary
insalubriously
insensibleness
insanitariness
inseparability
insuperability
insuppressible
insuppressibly
insurrectional
instrumentally
insurmountable
insurmountably
inscrutability
insusceptively
insatiableness
intra-abdominal
intramercurial
intramolecular
intransitively
intransmutable
intractability
integrationist

intuitionalism	jingoistically	levelling-staff	malfunctioning
intuitionalist	jurisdictional	lavender-cotton	Monochlamydeae
intrinsicality	joukery-pawkery	loving-kindness	monocarpellary
intellectually	knapping-hammer	lexicographist	monochromatism
intelligential	kneading-trough	measurableness	manifold-writer
intelligentsia	Kremlinologist	moccasin-flower	manageableness
intelligentzia	knight-bachelor	macadamisation	monolingualism
intolerability	knight-banneret	mackerel-breeze	Monoplacophora
intempestivity	knight-errantry	mock-heroically	monoprionidian
intangibleness	knitting-needle	macrodactylous	monophthongian
intentionality	kindergartener	macroeconomics	mineralisation
iatrochemistry	kinetheodolite	microeconomics	monosaccharide
introductorily	know-nothingism	micro-meteorite	ministerialist
intermaxillary	Kupferschiefer	microdetection	Menispermaceae
Internationale	keratinisation	macrocephalous	monotheletical
interactionism	kissing-strings	microcephalous	monotheistical
interactionist	leaden-stepping	micropegmatite	monotonousness
interdependent	leather-mouthed	microseismical	munition-worker
interpenetrant	leading-strings	microchemistry	money-scrivener
interpenetrate	libidinousness	microminiature	myocardiopathy
interferential	libertarianism	microbiologist	Mephistopheles
intermediately	liberalisation	micrologically	Mephistophelic
intermediation	labyrinthodont	microcomponent	Mephistophilis
intermediatory	licentiousness	macrosporangia	Mephostophilus
interpellation	lecythidaceous	microsporangia	morganatically
interferometer	lieutenantship	microprocessor	miraculousness
interferometry	left-handedness	microstructure	marketableness
intercessional	luggage-carrier	mucoviscidosis	market-gardener
intercessorial	legalistically	medicamentally	murdering-piece
interjectional	legislatorship	medicine-bottle	marvellousness
intersectional	light-heartedly	Middle-American	myrmecophagous
intersexuality	legitimateness	middle-distance	myrmecophilous
interlineation	lighter-than-air	muddleheadedly	myrmecological
interlingually	Leibnitzianism	meddlesomeness	Marcgraviaceae
intermigration	lumbersomeness	meditativeness	Marchantiaceae
intermittently	lamellirostral	magniloquently	morphinomaniac
intermittingly	long-headedness	megasporangium	morphophonemic
interplanetary	luncheon-basket	megasporophyll	marriage-broker
interambulacra	longitudinally	Mohorovicician	marriage-favour
Intermolecular	longs-and-shorts	maidenhair-tree	marble-breasted
intercommunion	linguistically	maintenance-man	marble-constant
intercommunity	long-windedness	major-generalcy	meretriciously
interconnexion	lyophilisation	majesticalness	martyrological
interior-sprung	lepidodendroid	multarticulate	miscalculation
interlocutrice	lapidification	Malacopterygii	mustard-plaster
interlocutress	lipogrammatism	malacostracous	misacceptation
interspatially	lipogrammatist	malodorousness	misadventurous
intergradation	leptodactylous	millenarianism	misadvisedness
interpretation	loquaciousness	multiracialism	mysteriousness
interpretative	laryngoscopist	multifariously	miscellanarian
interestedness	laryngological	milking-parlour	mesdemoiselles
interpunctuate	lasciviousness	multiple-choice	mismeasurement
interruptively	lithochromatic	multiplication	misogynistical
intertwinement	lithographical	multiplicative	mischief-making
intertwiningly	lithontriptist	multifoliolate	mastigophorous
intussuscepted	lithonthryptic	multinucleated	misimprovement
invincibleness	liturgiologist	multicuspidate	misinterpreter
inviolableness	latitudinarian	multi-ownership	misanthropical
invariableness	louping-on-stane	mylonitisation	misinformation
inveterateness	leucocythaemia	malcontentedly	misinstruction
Jack-by-the-hedge	leucocytopenia	malappropriate	miscomputation
Jack-in-the-green	leucocytolysis	melastomaceous	miscontentment
Johannisberger	love-in-idleness	militarisation	misapplication

mass-production
misappropriate
misarrangement
mistranslation
mushroom-anchor
mesaticephalic
mispunctuation
mosquito-weight
meticulousness
mathematically
mathematicised
matriarchalism
metalinguistic
metallographer
metallographic
mettlesomeness
metempsychoses
metempsychosis
methodicalness
mythologically
metropolitical
meteorological
metaphorically
metaphosphoric
metoposcopical
metapsychology
metaphysically
motivelessness
mourning-border
mountain-beaver
mountaineering
mountain-laurel
mountain-marrow
mountain-tallow
muzzle-velocity
neanderthaloid
nebuchadnezzar
noctambulation
nectareousness
nyctaginaceous
nuclear-powered
necessarianism
neck-sweetbread
Nudibranchiata
nudibranchiate
Nietzscheanism
neglectfulness
night-wandering
night-blindness
night-flowering
night-foundered
night-fossicker
nimble-fingered
nomenclatorial
namby-pambiness
non-performance
nonsensicality
non-restrictive
non-electrolyte
non-involvement
non-concurrence
non-communicant
non-compearance

non-cooperation
non-contentious
non-operational
neocolonialism
Neopythagorean
north-eastwards
north-westwards
north-north-east
north-north-west
narcocatharsis
narcosynthesis
norepinephrine
nutritiousness
nitrocellulose
nitroglycerine
naturalisation
nature-printing
noteworthiness
neuropathology
neuroradiology
neuroanatomist
Neuropteroidea
neurohypnology
neutralisation
never-never-land
newfangledness
newspaper-woman
newsworthiness
orange-coloured
orange-squeezer
oecumenicalism
onchocerciasis
old-gentlemanly
odd-come-shortly
old-established
overburdensome
overcompensate
over-confidence
overcapitalise
overcorrection
over-determined
overestimation
oleaginousness
open-handedness
overindulgence
open-mindedness
ocean-greyhound
overprotective
overproduction
overpopulation
overpoweringly
oneirocritical
over-refinement
overspecialise
overscrupulous
over-the-counter
overwhelmingly
organ-harmonium
organometallic
organisability
organisational
ophthalmoscope
ophthalmoscopy

ophthalmometer
ophthalmometry
opinionatively
onirocriticism
oligopsonistic
oligocythaemia
opisthoglossal
opisthocoelian
opisthocoelous
opisthographic
obligatoriness
omnibenevolent
omnicompetence
Ornithodelphia
ornithodelphic
ornithophilous
ornithological
ornithomorphic
omnium-gatherum
orobanchaceous
onomatopoiesis
otolaryngology
oppressiveness
obsequiousness
observableness
obstructionist
obstreperously
outward-sainted
outlandishness
outrageousness
optoelectronic
ottrelite-slate
ostrich-feather
optimalisation
optimistically
ostentatiously
octingentenary
orthochromatic
orthophosphate
osteoglossidae
osteo-arthritis
osteoarthrosis
orthographical
orthopterology
oxy-haemoglobin
prayerlessness
plane-polarised
planet-stricken
planing-machine
pharmacologist
pharmacopoeial
pharmacopoeian
pharmacopolist
pharmaceutical
plasmapheresis
pragmaticality
piano-accordion
prairie-chicken
Praeraphaelite
praiseworthily
practicability
Plantaginaceae
plant-formation

phantasmagoria
phantasmagoric
plague-stricken
platycephalous
public-spirited
pococuranteism
picture-gallery
picture-writing
pachydermatous
precariousness
predaciousness
prefabrication
plea-bargaining
presbyterially
preaching-house
preaching-friar
preaching-cross
prescriptively
pseudo-archaism
pseudaesthesia
pseudomembrane
pseudomorphism
pseudomorphous
pseudonymously
pseudepigrapha
pseudepigraphy
pseudosolution
pseudosymmetry
predeterminism
predeterminate
predevelopment
preferentially
premeditatedly
predesignation
predesignatory
pre-Reformation
presentability
preventability
presentimental
predestinarian
predestination
predestinative
presentational
presentiveness
preventiveness
preservability
psephoanalysis
plethysmograph
premillenarian
plenipotential
pteridophilist
predisposition
predictability
phelloplastics
pneumoconiosis
pneumoconiotic
pneumodynamics
pneumokoniosis
pneumatologist
pleonastically
phenobarbitone
piezomagnetism
preconcertedly

preponderantly
pyelonephritic
pyelonephritis
piezochemistry
precociousness
paedomorphosis
preposterously
prearrangement
Pleuronectidae
pleurapophyses
pleurapophysis
pleasure-ground
pleasure-giving
pressure-helmet
pleasure-seeker
prettification
plectognathous
presupposition
presumptuously
phenylbutazone
pterylographic
pugnaciousness
pugilistically
pigeon-breasted
pigeon-fancying
philanthropist
psilanthropism
psilanthropist
pribble-prabble
prince-imperial
princesse-skirt
princesse-dress
poikilothermal
poikilothermic
prick-the-garter
prison-breaking
philosopheress
philosophaster
philosophistic
philologically
prittle-prattle
printing-office
painter-stainer
pyjama-trousers
palmatipartite
palaeobotanist
polyembryonate
palaeogeography
palaeographist
palaeanthropic
Palaeanthropus
palaeopedology
palaeethnology
phlegmatically
palagonite-tuff
polemoniaceous
polymerisation
palingenetical
pillow-fighting
Polyplacophora
polysaccharide
polishing-paste
polishing-slate

polysyllabical
polysynthetism
palato-alveolar
politicisation
polytheistical
pamphleteering
pentadactylism
pentadactylous
pinnatipartite
pennatulaceous
Pontederiaceae
pincer-movement
Pentecostalist
Pontefract-cake
Pan-Americanism
pantomimically
pantopragmatic
pantographical
penetrableness
penny-a-linerism
penny-in-the-slot
pennystone-cast
propaedeutical
probabiliorism
probabiliorist
proscriptively
proud-stomached
Protevangelium
phonematically
proletarianise
proletarianism
prosencephalic
prosencephalon
proceleusmatic
progenitorship
propeller-shaft
professionally
professorially
proventriculus
property-master
protectiveness
prothonotarial
prothonotariat
profitableness
provincial-rose
promise-keeping
promise-breaker
promise-crammed
providentially
prohibitionary
prohibitionism
prohibitionist
propitiatorily
prodigiousness
propitiousness
protistologist
prognosticator
phototelegraph
photoperiodism
photosensitise
photosensitive
photochemistry
photobiologist

protoplasmatic
photo-engraving
protozoologist
Protospathaire
Prototracheata
photogrammetry
photographical
provost-marshal
proportionable
proportionably
proportionally
proportionless
proportionment
prolocutorship
photosynthesis
photosynthetic
phosphor-bronze
phosphorescent
phosphoprotein
prosperousness
proprietorship
proprioceptive
procryptically
procrastinator
progressionary
progressionism
progressionist
protrusiveness
prostaglandins
prosthodontics
prosthodontist
procuratorship
pronunciamento
productibility
productiveness
peppermint-drop
papilionaceous
popularisation
paradigmatical
paroemiography
pyrheliometric
purse-snatching
perfectibilian
perfectibilism
perfectibilist
perceptibility
perfectibility
portentousness
perceptiveness
paragrammatist
parthenocarpic
Porphyrogenite
pertinaciously
perfidiousness
perniciousness
pernicketiness
parliament-cake
parliament-heel
parsimoniously
permissibility
permissiveness
particularness
purple-coloured

parallelepiped
parallelopiped
parallel-veined
paraleipomenon
paralinguistic
peremptoriness
parenchymatous
pyrenomycetous
paronomastical
pardonableness
personableness
purposefulness
periophthalmus
periodontology
parlour-boarder
person-to-person
perlocutionary
pyrophotograph
pyrophosphoric
paraphrastical
periphrastical
peripateticism
parapsychology
partridge-berry
pararosaniline
perishableness
Perissodactyla
phraseological
parasitologist
paratactically
percutaneously
perturbational
porcupine-grass
persuasibility
percussion-fuse
percussion-lock
persuasiveness
pasteurisation
possessiveness
pestilentially
Passifloraceae
passionateness
pisciculturist
post-millennial
postmastership
postpositional
postpositively
Petrarchianism
Petrarchianist
Pythagoreanism
phthalocyanine
patresfamilias
patrialisation
petticoat-tails
patriarchalism
potentiometric
pathologically
petrologically
petrographical
potassium-argon
Plumbaginaceae
pluviometrical
plutodemocracy

Prussification
powder-magazine
psychoanalysis
psychoanalytic
psychochemical
psychodramatic
psychodynamics
psycholinguist
psychometrical
psychoneurosis
psychoneurotic
psychophysical
psychosomatics
physiognomical
phyllotactical
Phytolaccaceae
phytopathology
phytogenetical
phytogeography
quadriennially
quadrigeminate
quadrigeminous
quadragenarian
quadrangularly
quadrisyllabic
quadrisyllable
quantification
quattrocentism
quattrocentist
quartz-porphyry
quarter-gallery
quantitatively
quaquaversally
querimoniously
question-master
quicksilvering
quicksilverish
quinquagesimal
quinquevalence
quinquefarious
quinquennially
quinquefoliate
quinquecostate
quilting-cotton
quintessential
quizzification
reaping-machine
reasonableness
reappraisement
reacquaintance
rear-view-mirror
road-worthiness
rabbeting-plane
rubber-solution
rabbit-squirrel
Rabelaisianism
rebelliousness
ribbon-building
robustiousness
rectangularity
Rochelle-powder
Rickettsiaceae
receivableness

rectilinearity
receiving-house
receiving-order
recalcitration
recolonisation
recommencement
recommendation
recommendatory
reconnaissance
reconsecration
recondensation
reconciliation
reconciliatory
reconstitution
reconstruction
reconstructive
reception-order
rice-polishings
recapitulation
recapitulatory
recapitulative
recurvirostral
recitation-room
recoverability
radicalisation
ridiculousness
riding-breeches
redintegration
riding-interest
radiotelemeter
radiotelephone
radiotelephony
radiotelegraph
radiosensitise
radiosensitive
radiochemistry
radioastronomy
radio-strontium
radioautograph
redistillation
redistribution
reed-instrument
rheumatologist
refrangibility
refractoriness
reflexological
reflectionless
reflectiveness
reformationist
regressiveness
regularisation
regeneratively
regardlessness
rehabilitation
rehabilitative
rhinencephalic
rhinencephalon
rhinoceros-bird
Rhinocerotidae
Rhizophoraceae
reintroduction
reinvigoration
rejuvenescence

relentlessness
relinquishment
rampageousness
remedilessness
rummelgumption
rumblegumption
rummlegumption
reminiscential
remonetisation
remarkableness
remorsefulness
Rembrandtesque
rambunctiously
röntgenography
running-banquet
ranunculaceous
rhombenporphyr
reorganisation
repudiationist
reprehensively
representation
representative
reproductively
reproductivity
repetitiveness
requisitionary
requisitionist
Rosicrucianism
respectability
respectfulness
Russianisation
restitutionism
restitutionist
resultlessness
resinification
restorationism
restorationist
restorableness
responsibility
responsiveness
Russo-Byzantine
restrictionist
rostrocarinate
resurrectional
restrainedness
resistance-coil
resistlessness
retransmission
retaliationist
retrocognition
retro-operative
retrogradation
roundaboutedly
roundaboutness
rough-and-tumble
revalorisation
revengefulness
revivification
rewardableness
rhyparographer
rhyparographic
rhynchophorous
stalactitiform

starch-hyacinth
swaddling-cloth
scandalmonging
scandalisation
scandalousness
standing-ground
standard-bearer
slanderousness
shamefacedness
stage-direction
scaremongering
Shakespeariana
space-traveller
scale-staircase
spade-husbandry
slaughter-house
slaughterously
scaphocephalic
scaphocephalus
staphylococcal
Staphylococcus
swathing-clouts
sea-gilliflower
sea-gillyflower
station-manager
stationariness
spatiotemporal
shawl-waistcoat
spawning-ground
seasonableness
star-of-the-earth
star-of-the-night
stamping-ground
snapping-turtle
stamp-collector
sparrow-blasted
slantendicular
slantindicular
slatternliness
scatter-brained
shatter-brained
statuesqueness
Sabbatarianism
Sabbath-breaker
subgenerically
submergibility
subterposition
subterrestrial
submersibility
subtersensuous
subject-heading
subjectiveness
subjectivistic
subminiaturise
submicroscopic
submissiveness
subalternation
subinfeudation
subinfeudatory
subinsinuation
subconsciously
subcontrariety
subcontinental

subarborescent	sufferableness	self-controlled	symmetrisation
substantivally	segregationist	self-correcting	simultaneously
substantialise	suggestibility	solecistically	simplification
substantialism	suggestiveness	solicitousness	simplificative
substantialist	Sigillariaceae	solidification	simplistically
substantiality	Schwenkfeldian	self-dependence	semi-occasional
substantiation	sphaerocrystal	self-discipline	semi-officially
substitutional	sphygmographic	self-displeased	symbolicalness
substitutively	schematisation	self-destroying	semaphorically
subcutaneously	school-divinity	self-determined	sempstress-ship
sacramentalism	schooner-rigged	self-effacement	symptomatology
sacramentalist	schoolmasterly	self-explaining	sensationalism
sacrament-house	schoolmistress	self-expression	sensationalist
sacramentarian	school-teaching	self-employment	sansculotterie
successionally	schismatically	self-enrichment	sansculottides
successionless	schizognathous	silver-shedding	sonnet-sequence
successfulness	schizomycetous	silversmithing	synchronically
successiveness	schizophyceous	self-flattering	sentimentalise
sacchariferous	skimble-skamble	self-fulfilling	sentimentalism
sacrilegiously	spindle-shanked	self-fulfilment	sentimentalist
secularisation	swindge-buckler	self-generating	sentimentality
sociobiologist	stiletto-heeled	self-government	singing-gallery
sycophantishly	swingling-stock	sulphanilamide	single-breasted
succulent-house	stichometrical	sulphapyridine	synonymousness
spelaeological	spiritlessness	sulphathiazole	synaposematism
steganographer	spirit-stirring	self-heterodyne	sinistrorsally
steganographic	spiritualistic	self-inductance	sanctification
speechlessness	spirituousness	self-indulgence	sanguification
speech-training	sticky-fingered	self-immolation	sensualisation
stereoisomeric	shillingsworth	self-importance	sanguinariness
stereometrical	shilly-shallier	self-interested	sanguinivorous
skeleton-shrimp	seismometrical	self-justifying	sandwich-boards
siege-artillery	stigmatiferous	salamander-like	sporangiophore
stereospecific	stigmatisation	self-management	sporangiospore
stereoscopical	scientifically	self-neglecting	stomachfulness
stereotactical	spirochaetosis	salmon-coloured	stomatogastric
shelf-catalogue	snipper-snapper	saloon-carriage	Scombresocidae
stethoscopical	stirrup-leather	self-punishment	stolchelometry
sheriff-officer	ship's-carpenter	self-protecting	stoechiometric
specialisation	snip-snap-snorum	self-protective	stoichiometric
shell-limestone	spinthariscope	self-proclaimed	sword-swallower
smelling-bottle	scintilloscope	self-propulsion	shove-halfpenny
steel-engraving	scintillometer	saltpetre-paper	smoking-concert
spermatogenous	shifting-boards	sclerophyllous	stocking-filler
spermatogonium	self-accusation	self-revelation	stocking-stitch
spermatophytic	self-accusatory	self-sufficient	shoulder-girdle
spermatorrhoea	self-affrighted	self-suggestion	shoulder-height
stegocephalian	self-admiration	self-supporting	stoope-gallaunt
stegocephalous	self-abnegation	self-sustaining	stomping-ground
sceuophylacium	self-assumption	self-sustenance	scorpion-spider
stenographical	self-absorption	self-satisfying	swoopstake-like
steeplechasing	self-advertiser	solitudinarian	snow-spectacles
steeple-crowned	salubriousness	solitaire-board	stout-heartedly
sheep-whistling	solubilisation	self-tormenting	Scottification
sleepy-sickness	silicification	self-torturable	short-sightedly
spectacularity	self-comparison	somnambulistic	shooting-jacket
sheet-lightning	self-commitment	somnambulation	Supralapsarian
sweet-and-twenty	self-complacent	semi-centennial	suprasegmental
spectroscopist	self-condemning	semiconducting	sapphire-quartz
spectrological	self-consequent	semicarbazones	sophistication
spectrographic	self-confidence	semicircularly	supplicatingly
stentorophonic	self-consistent	semi-elliptical	supplementally
stertorousness	self-conviction	symmetrophobia	saponification

supposititious	spring-mattress	transcendently	trinitrophenol
suppositionary	strand-scouring	transversality	trinitrotoluol
supercargoship	servo-mechanism	transfer-ticket	trinkum-trankum
supernaturally	strepsipterous	transvestitism	triconsonantal
superabundance	scrupulousness	transsexualism	triconsonantic
superscription	Syrophoenician	transliterator	trisoctahedron
supercelestial	surprisingness	transmigration	trituberculism
superterranean	stratification	transmigratory	trituberculate
supersensitive	stratigraphist	transmigrative	telegraph-cable
soporiferously	stretching-bond	transmissional	telegraph-plant
superphosphate	stretching-iron	transmissivity	telegraph-board
superficialise	scrutinisingly	transplantable	talking-machine
superficiality	strawberry-leaf	transformistic	telangiectasis
superciliously	strawberry-mark	transformation	telangiectatic
supervisorship	strawberry-tree	transformative	tallow-chandler
superelevation	screw-propeller	transmogrified	teleologically
supereminently	systematically	transport-rider	teleprocessing
superintendent	suspensibility	transportingly	telephonically
superincumbent	susceptibility	transportation	telephotograph
superannuation	suspiciousness	transitionally	telepathically
superinduction	sesquipedalian	transitoriness	telesmatically
superconductor	sesquipedality	transitiveness	telescopically
supercontinent	sesquisulphide	transfusionist	teletypewriter
superfoetation	soteriological	traction-engine	telautographic
supererogation	satisfactorily	traitorousness	temperamentful
supererogatory	sausage-bassoon	tobacco-stopper	tumbling-barrel
supererogative	stumbling-block	tabularisation	tumultuousness
superessential	stumbling-stone	tabernacle-work	tumorigenicity
superstruction	soul-confirming	tacheometrical	tintinnabulant
superstructure	squadron-leader	tachistoscopic	tintinnabulary
superstructive	soul-destroying	tachygraphical	tintinnabulate
superovulation	stupendousness	tide-waitership	tintinnabulous
superexcellent	slug-foot-second	theocratically	troubleshooter
septuagenarian	south-eastwards	trencher-friend	thought-reading
sequaciousness	south-westwards	trencher-knight	thought-process
spread-eagleism	south-south-east	treacle-mustard	thoughtfulness
Sarraceniaceae	south-south-west	tremendousness	Trochelminthes
serratirostral	skunk-blackbird	theriomorphism	trophoneurosis
surpassingness	Sturmabteilung	theriomorphous	two-dimensional
scrubbing-board	sauropterygian	therianthropic	two-for-his-heels
scrubbing-brush	squirearchical	thermochemical	tropologically
scribbling-book	squirrel-monkey	thermodynamics	topsyturviness
strobilisation	scurrilousness	thermo-electric	threadbareness
strabismometer	stultification	thermometrical	turf-accountant
sericitisation	stultiloquence	Theopaschitism	three-halfpence
straddle-legged	Sovietological	theosophically	three-halfpenny
sergeant-at-arms	savanna-sparrow	theatricalness	three-farthings
serjeant-at-arms	saxifragaceous	tree-worshipper	turpentine-tree
street-railroad	thalassography	thimble-rigging	thriftlessness
serpentiningly	traveller's-tree	third-programme	tariff-reformer
serpentine-rock	traffic-manager	trimethylamine	terminableness
serpent-goddess	traffic-returns	tripersonalism	tergiversation
serpent-worship	traffic-signals	tripersonalist	turbine-steamer
sure-footedness	Trachypteridae	tripersonality	torsion-balance
sprightfulness	traditionalism	trichobacteria	territorialise
serviceability	traditionalist	trichomoniasis	territorialism
straining-piece	traditionality	triphenylamine	territorialist
strike-breaking	traditionarily	trichinisation	territoriality
striking-circle	tragi-comically	trichophytosis	terminological
shrill-shriking	thaumatography	trichotomously	thromboplastin
spring-cleaning	thaumaturgical	Trinitarianism	tyrannicalness
spring-carriage	transvaluation	tridimensional	turbo-generator
spring-ligament	transcendental	trivialisation	terror-stricken

thrashing-floor	uncertificated	unintoxicating	unsplinterable
threshing-floor	uncorroborated	unknightliness	unsympathising
terotechnology	unchristianise	unknowableness	unsophisticate
through-ganging	uncircumcision	unmalleability	unstrengthened
through-traffic	uncrystallised	unmannerliness	unsurmountable
turquoise-green	undecomposable	unmanufactured	unscrupulously
testamentarily	undecipherable	unmentionables	unscripturally
testimonialise	undiminishable	unmerchantable	unsystematical
tetradactylous	undemonstrable	unmarriageable	unsystematised
tetrachotomous	undomesticated	unmercifulness	unsisterliness
tetrasporangia	undeniableness	unmathematical	unsuspectingly
tetragrammaton	undervaluation	unmatriculated	unsuspiciously
tatterdemalion	underdeveloped	unmetaphorical	unsatisfaction
tittle-tattling	under-secretary	unmetaphysical	unsatisfactory
true-lover's-knot	undermentioned	unmaterialised	ultra-Neptunian
tautologically	under-clerkship	unostentatious	ultramicrotome
trumpet-tongued	undernourished	unpraiseworthy	ultramicrotomy
town-councillor	under-constable	unpracticality	unthankfulness
thysanopterous	under-populated	unpreparedness	ultramontanism
thymelaeaceous	undergraduette	unpretendingly	ultramontanist
thyrotoxicosis	understrapping	unpremeditated	ultracrepidate
unaccomplished	understandable	unpremeditable	untranslatable
unaccommodated	understatement	unpoeticalness	untranslatably
unaccounted-for	undespairingly	unprepossessed	untransferable
unaffectedness	undesignedness	unpleasantness	untransmutable
unacknowledged	undiscoverable	unpresumptuous	ultrastructure
unavoidability	undiscoverably	unprofessional	unthinkability
unapprehensive	undesirability	unpropitiously	unthinkingness
unappreciative	undistractedly	unproportioned	Ustilaginaceae
unapproachable	undeservedness	unprosperously	untameableness
unapproachably	undeterminable	unproductively	ultimogeniture
unappropriated	uterogestation	unproductivity	ultroneousness
unaspiringness	unexpectedness	unpurchaseable	unthoughtfully
unacquaintance	unextinguished	unpassableness	untruthfulness
unassumingness	unentertaining	unquestionable	untowardliness
unattractively	unenterprising	unquestionably	unvanquishable
unauthenticity	unenthusiastic	unreadableness	unwatchfulness
unartificially	unflappability	uproariousness	unyieldingness
unbearableness	unflatteringly	unrecognisable	vibroflotation
unblamableness	unfaithfulness	unrecognisably	vice-chancellor
umbrageousness	unfriendedness	unreconcilable	vice-consulship
unbecomingness	unfriendliness	unreconcilably	vociferousness
unbusinesslike	unforeknowable	unreciprocated	victoriousness
uncheerfulness	unfruitfulness	unrecapturable	vice-presidency
uncomprehended	ungracefulness	unreflectingly	vicar-apostalic
uncompromising	ungratefulness	unrightfulness	vicesimo-quarto
uncommunicated	ungraciousness	unreliableness	videotelephone
uncommunicable	ungroundedness	unromantically	vigesimo-quarto
uncontaminated	unhandsomeness	unremunerative	vegetativeness
unconscionable	unhesitatingly	unremorsefully	vaingloriously
unconscionably	unincorporated	unreproducible	volcanological
unconfederated	universalistic	unresolvedness	vulcanological
uncongeniality	universitarian	unresponsively	vulnerableness
uncontemplated	unidentifiable	unrestrictedly	voluminousness
unconventional	utilitarianise	unreservedness	volumetrically
unconceiveable	utilitarianism	unrestrainable	Valentinianism
unconciliatory	unidirectional	unrestrainedly	voluptuousness
unconsolidated	unilluminating	unrhythmically	valerianaceous
uncontradicted	uniformitarian	unsectarianism	valetudinarian
uncontrollable	unintellectual	unsociableness	volatilisation
uncontrollably	unintelligible	unsuccessfully	vindictiveness
uncontrolledly	unintelligibly	unsuitableness	verse-mongering
uncontroverted	unintermitting	unspiritualise	verticillaster

verisimilitude
vasodilatation
vasodilatatory
vitrescibility
vitriolisation
vitalistically
vitilitigation
vituperatively
viviparousness
vivisectionist
what-d'you-call-'em
what-d'you-call-it
weather-prophet
weather-station
wearing-apparel
weak-mindedness
weapon-schawing
wedding-garment
widow-bewitched
weeding-forceps
wheeler-dealing
wreath-filament
weightlessness
whispering-dome
whippersnapper
whittie-whattie
whistle-blowing
well-acquainted
Wilhelmstrasse
willing-hearted
well-thought-out
wonder-stricken
wind-instrument
window-dressing
window-shopping
whole-heartedly
woollen-drapery
wood-nightshade
wappenschawing
warrant-officer
worcester-sauce
worcesterberry
worshipfulness
working-drawing
westernisation
washing-machine
withering-floor
watch-committee
witches'-thimble
water-barometer
water-repellent
water-resistant
watertightness
watering-trough
water-colourist
water-breathing
water-privilege
xylopyrography
xylotypography
xanthomelanous
xiphihumeralis
yellow-breasted
yellow-centaury

yellow-yoldring
yttro-tantalite
yttro-columbite
zebra-parrakeet
Zygobranchiata
zygobranchiate
zingiberaceous
zinziberaceous
zinckification
zincographical
zenith-distance
zoophytologist
Zoroastrianism

anacreontically
anaesthesiology
anaesthetically
amaryllidaceous
ambulance-chaser
arboriculturist
asclepiadaceous
acclimatisation
architectonical
Archichlamydeae
archiepiscopate
archiepiscopacy
ancestor-worship
accountableness
andromonoecious
affranchisement
argumentatively
angustirostrate
achondroplastic
atherosclerosis
abiogenetically
Aristotelianism
adjutant-general
ankylostomiasis
acknowledgeable
acknowledgeably
acknowledgement
all-changing-word
allotriomorphic
atmospherically
armoured-cruiser
annihilationism
Annunciation-day
anomalistically
apocalyptically
apophthegmatise
apophthegmatist
Apollinarianism
amphitheatrical
approachability
appropinquation
appropriateness
acquisitiveness
agriculturalist
air-chief-marshal
air-conditioning
aircraft-carrier
anticlericalism
anticholinergic
antichristianly
autographically
anti-Gallicanism
antimonarchical
automorphically
astronavigation
authoritatively
astrodynamicist
antepenultimate
antiperistaltic
arterialisation
autoradiography
attorney-general
anthropobiology

anthropocentric
anthropogenesis
anthropological
anthropomorphic
anthropophagite
anthropophagous
anthropopathism
anthropopsychic
anthroposophist
autoschediastic
antitrinitarian
antivivisection
adventurousness
brachycephalous
brachydactylous
brachistochrone
blast-furnaceman
bibliographical
bubble-and-squeak
bacteriological
bacchanalianism
bed-and-breakfast
before-mentioned
bomb-calorimeter
boning-telescope
banqueting-house
bronchoscopical
blood-and-thunder
blood-guiltiness
biogeochemistry
biogeographical
biodestructible
bioastronautics
bioluminescence
bargain-basement
Bartholomew-tide
basidiomycetous
butterfly-flower
butterfly-orchis
chamber-hangings
chamberlainship
clandestineness
chargé-d'affaires
coconsciousness
cockneyfication
Caesalpiniaceae
Czechoslovakian
chenopodiaceous
chemopsychiatry
clearing-station
crease-resistant
crease-resisting
cigarette-holder
criminalisation
crimping-machine
co-instantaneity
co-instantaneous
cold-bloodedness
collenchymatous
Callitrichaceae
colposcopically
chloramphenicol
companion-ladder

compassionately
compartmentally
commendableness
compendiousness
competitiveness
commission-agent
complementarily
complementarity
compotationship
comfortlessness
comprehensively
comprehensivise
compressibility
communalisation
computerisation
communicatively
communicability
combustibleness
canvas-stretcher
conscience-proof
conscientiously
conscriptionist
condescendingly
Cinderella-dance
congealableness
contemplatively
contemptibility
contemporaneity
contemporaneous
consecratedness
confessionalism
confessionalist
conversationism
conversationist
conceptualistic
consentaneously
conventionalise
conventionalism
conventionalist
conventionality
contentiousness
consecutiveness
consequentially
conceivableness
conservationist
conservatorship
considerateness
consideratively
confidentiality
configurational
continuation-day
cinemicrography
cinematographic
cinematographer
consolation-race
connoisseurship
conspicuousness
contractability
contractibility
contradictively
contradictorily
controllability
confrontational

contrapropeller
contravallation
controversially
canisterisation
constitutionist
constructionism
conjunctiveness
conjunctionally
consumptiveness
conquerableness
consubstantiate
cholangiography
chondrification
cloud-compelling
chondropterygii
cloud-cuckoo-land
cloud-cuckoo-town
cholecystectomy
cholecystostomy
crook-shouldered
cross-laterality
crossing-sweeper
crossopterygian
caprifoliaceous
Capernaitically
cerebrovascular
correlativeness
correspondently
correspondingly
carriage-forward
carnivorousness
ceremoniousness
chromatographic
chromoxylograph
chronologically
carpometacarpus
Caryophyllaceae
corporification
Christadelphian
chrestomathical
Christy-minstrel
circumambagious
circumferential
circumforaneous
circumincession
circuminsession
circumnavigable
circumnavigator
circumstantiate
circumstantials
circumspectness
circumscribable
circumscriptive
circumscription
corruptibleness
circumvallation
co-significative
casement-curtain
cosmopolitanism
cataclysmically
categoricalness
catch-as-catch-can
catallactically

cytomegalovirus	dishabilitation	evangelistarion	extemporisation
citronella-grass	disharmoniously	enantiomorphism	externalisation
countermandable	dispassionately	enantiomorphous	exteriorisation
countervailable	distastefulness	exchangeability	ebullioscopical
counteractively	disobligingness	encyclopaedical	equalitarianism
counterfeisance	disadvantageous	excrementitious	equiprobability
counter-security	dysteleological	ecclesiological	Erziehungsroman
counter-flowered	dysmenorrhealic	encomiastically	flamboyante-tree
counter-movement	disrespectfully	excommunication	feather-boarding
counter-approach	dishearteningly	excommunicatory	franking-machine
counter-irritant	dispensableness	encephalography	fragmentariness
counter-proposal	dessertspoonful	evening-primrose	fractionisation
counter-pressure	disreputability	everlastingness	Frenchification
counter-evidence	disaffectedness	exemplification	French-polishing
crypto-communist	disaffectionate	eleutherodactyl	field-sequential
crypto-Christian	disafforestment	electrification	free-heartedness
crystallisation	disagreeability	electromagnetic	freezing-mixture
crystallography	distinctiveness	electronegative	fifth-monarchism
diamagnetically	distinguishable	electrotechnics	fifth-monarchist
diaheliotropism	distinguishably	electrometrical	flibbertigibbet
diaphragmatitis	distinguishment	electrochemical	faithworthiness
diaphototropism	displeasingness	electrothermics	fellow-traveller
drawn-threadwork	desilverisation	electrophoresis	fantasticalness
decalcification	disillusionment	electrophoretic	ferro-molybdenum
decolourisation	disimprisonment	electrokinetics	formularisation
decomposability	disentanglement	electroanalysis	fashionableness
decontaminative	disinterestedly	electropositive	foundation-stone
decontamination	disinflationary	electrodynamics	foul-mouthedness
decipherability	disentrancement	electromyograph	flutter-tonguing
doctrinarianism	dissociableness	enfranchisement	grandiloquently
decarbonisation	dyslogistically	efficaciousness	gravitationally
decarburisation	discommodiously	ergatandromorph	granitification
dieselhydraulic	discommendation	exhibitionistic	gramophonically
dyer's-yellowweed	discontinuation	echinodermatous	granulitisation
dressing-station	discontinuously	ethnomusicology	Gleichschaltung
differentiation	dissolvableness	etherealisation	greenery-yallery
defencelessness	disorganisation	episcopalianism	great-grandchild
diffrangibility	disgracefulness	Eriocaulonaceae	gillie-whitefoot
daguerreotypist	destructiveness	epidemiological	gentlemanliness
degenerationist	destructibility	epitheliomatous	gentleman-at-arms
deindustrialise	distractibility	epistemological	gynandromorphic
drilling-machine	desertification	éclaircissement	goniometrically
dolichocephalic	disarticulation	expeditiousness	good-conditioned
deleteriousness	descriptiveness	euphemistically	gooseberry-stone
democratisation	disproportional	expressionistic	geochronologist
democratifiable	distressfulness	experientialism	good-naturedness
demagnetisation	distrustfulness	experientialist	gnotobiological
demulsification	discretionarily	experimentalise	gnotobiotically
demonstratively	disassimilative	experimentative	geomorphologist
demonstrability	disputativeness	experimentalism	glossographical
dimethylaniline	disquisitionary	experimentation	gastroenteritis
denitrification	desexualisation	experimentalist	Götterdämmerung
dephlogisticate	determinability	edriophthalmian	gathering-ground
departmentalise	dithyrambically	edriophthalmous	governor-general
departmentalism	double-barrelled	extra-illustrate	hobbledehoyhood
dermatoglyphics	double-facedness	extraordinaries	hackney-carriage
direction-finder	dividend-warrant	extraordinarily	hackney-coachman
director-general	devil-worshipper	extra-provincial	hydropathically
durchkomponiert	developmentally	extra-judicially	hydrometallurgy
dorsiventrality	diversification	extra-curricular	hydrobiological
dorsibranchiate	devitrification	entrepreneurial	Hydrocorallinae
dissatisfaction	emancipationist	entomologically	hydrostatically
dissatisfactory	evangelicalness	extemporariness	hydrodynamicist

15 m□c□o

hyetometrograph
hierogrammatist
high-gravel-blind
heir-presumptive
holocrystalline
hellenistically
half-heartedness
helminthologist
heliotropically
half-wellingtons
homochlamydeous
hemicrystalline
homogeneousness
humanitarianism
homeopathically
hendecasyllabic
hendecasyllable
hypochondriacal
hypochondriasis
hypnotisability
hypophosphorous
hypercatalectic
hyperadrenalism
hyperthyroidism
hypercritically
hepaticological
hard-and-fastness
hermaphroditism
herb-Christopher
hermeneutically
harvest-festival
hard-heartedness
hospitalisation
historiographic
historiographer
heterocercality
heterodactylous
heterogeneously
heterosexuallty
hexachlorophane
hexachlorophene
inaccessibility
imaginativeness
inadmissibility
inapprehensible
inapplicability
inappropriately
inattentiveness
inadvisableness
incredulousness
incalculability
incomparability
incompatibility
incommensurable
incommensurably
incomprehensive
incomprehension
incommutability
incommunicative
inconsequential
inconsiderately
inconsideration
inconspicuously

incongruousness
incapaciousness
incorrigibility
indubitableness
indefeasibility
indefensibility
indigestibility
indemnification
indistinctively
indisciplinable
indissolubility
indistributable
indeterminately
indetermination
individualistic
indivisibleness
inexcusableness
inefficaciously
ineffectiveness
ineffectualness
ideographically
inexplicability
inexpensiveness
inextensibility
infrangibleness
inflammableness
infundibuliform
infinitesimally
ichthyodorulite
ichthyodorylite
ichthyopterygia
idiosyncratical
injudiciousness
ill-favouredness
illimitableness
illustriousness
immunochemistry
immensurability
immortalisation
innumerableness
inoperativeness
isoperimetrical
inofficiousness
inoffensiveness
icositetrahedra
inopportuneness
inobtrusiveness
impracticalness
imprescriptible
impressionistic
imponderability
impenetrability
improvisatorial
impermeableness
imperviableness
imperishability
importunateness
inquisitiveness
inquisitorially
irreconcilement
irreducibleness
irreductibility
irredeemability

irrefragability
irrefutableness
irreligiousness
irremissibility
irremovableness
irrepealability
irreprehensible
irreprehensibly
irreparableness
irresolvability
irresistibility
irretentiveness
Irrationalistic
irrevocableness
irreversibility
instantaneously
insubordinately
insubordination
insubstantially
insignificative
insignificantly
inspirationally
institutionally
insensitiveness
inseperableness
insuperableness
instructiveness
insurrectionary
insurrectionism
insurrectionist
instrumentalism
instrumentation
instrumentalist
instrumentality
inscrutableness
intransigentism
intransigentist
intransmissible
intractableness
intrinsicalness
intellectualise
intellectualism
intellectualist
intellectuality
intelligibility
intolerableness
intemperateness
intensification
introsusception
interfascicular
intertanglement
interlamination
internationally
interjaculatory
interscholastic
interdependence
interpenetrable
interferometric
interpersonally
intertentacular
interjectionary
interventionism
interventionist

interchangeable
interchangeably
interchangement
interdigitation
interclavicular
interambulacral
interambulacrum
interrogatively
intercollegiate
interconnection
intercolonially
interpretership
interprovincial
interestingness
interosculation
interstratified
intersubjective
intertwistingly
intussusceptive
intussusception
invulnerability
involuntariness
Jack-in-the-pulpit
Jack-of-all-trades
Johnny-head-in-air
Jungermanniales
jurisprudential
jerry-come-tumble
justifiableness
juxtapositional
knick-knackatory
knitting-machine
kilogram-calorie
kind-heartedness
kitchen-gardener
katathermometer
lob-lie-by-the-fire
logographically
logarithmically
light-headedness
light-mindedness
landing-carriage
landscape-marble
long-sightedness
lepidopterology
lophobranchiate
lissencephalous
lithochromatics
laughing-jackass
low-spiritedness
lexicographical
meadow-saxifrage
mechanistically
Michaelmas-daisy
machine-readable
macroscopically
microscopically
microtechnology
micropegmatitic
Microchiroptera
microphotograph
micromillimetre
micromicrocurie

micromicrofarad
microdissection
microelectronic
microanalytical
macrocosmically
macrosporangium
microsporangium
microsporophyll
medicine-dropper
Middle-Easterner
middle-of-the-road
middle-stitching
Megacheiroptera
magneto-electric
magisterialness
malacopterygian
mole-electronics
multiarticulate
maldistribution
multitudinously
multinucleolate
malconformation
malpractitioner
malpresentation
malassimilation
miniaturisation
manic-depressive
monochlamydeous
Monocotyledones
monocrystalline
manneristically
manoeuvrability
montmorillonite
monarchianistic
mineralogically
menispermaceous
monosymmetrical
Mephistophelean
Mephistophelian
margaritiferous
meroblastically
market-gardening
marsh-cinquefoil
morphophonemics
mortiferousness
morning-sickness
marriage-licence
marriage-portion
Marsipobranchii
myristicivorous
meritoriousness
messenger-at-arms
miscellaneously
misbecomingness
mischievousness
misintelligence
misconstruction
misappreciative
misappreciation
misapprehensive
misapprehension
misproportioned
mistrustfulness

mesaticephalous
metalinguistics
metamathematics
methodistically
metropolitanate
materialisation
materialistical
mountain-bramble
mountain-leather
mountain-railway
near-sightedness
noble-mindedness
necromantically
necessitousness
neighbourliness
numismatologist
nemathelminthic
Nemathelminthes
nonsensicalness
non-intervention
non-intrusionist
non-commissioned
non-contributory
non-professional
non-profit-making
Neo-Christianity
nepheline-basalt
north-eastwardly
north-westwardly
north-countryman
nothingarianism
notwithstanding
nationalisation
nitro-derivative
nature-knowledge
neurophysiology
neuropsychiatry
new-Common-
wealth
overbearingness
overdevelopment
overforwardness
open-heartedness
oceanographical
oneirocriticism
ophthalmoscopic
ophthalmoplegia
ophthalmologist
Ophioglossaceae
ochlocratically
opisthognathous
Opisthobranchia
objectification
omnibenevolence
omnidirectional
owner-occupation
ornithodelphian
ornithodelphous
ornithorhynchus
odoriferousness
odontostomatous
opprobriousness
observationally

ostreiculturist
optoelectronics
ontogenetically
orthophosphoric
orthopsychiatry
onychocryptosis
phase-difference
peasecod-bellied
peasecod-cuirass
pharisaicalness
plagiostomatous
platitudinarian
pharmacognosist
pharmacognostic
pragmaticalness
peacock-pheasant
prairie-schooner
practicableness
plantaginaceous
phantasmagorial
Platyhelminthes
packet-switching
picture-restorer
picture-moulding
picturesqueness
pedagoguishness
Pre-Raphaelitish
Pre-Raphaelitism
Pre-Raphaelistic
phenakistoscope
Presbyterianise
Presbyterianism
preacquaintance
pseudohexagonal
pseudepigraphic
presence-chamber
predeterminable
preferentialism
preferentialist
preternaturally
presentableness
pretentiousness
presentationism
presentationist
preservationist
precipitability
precipitousness
plenipotentiary
predictableness
prehistorically
pneumatological
phenomenalistic
phenomenologist
prepositionally
preformationism
preformationist
phenolphthalein
preconstruction
prepossessingly
pleuro-pneumonia
pleasurableness
pleasure-seeking
prestidigitator

phenylketonuria
phenylketonuric
philanthropical
philosophically
printing-machine
police-constable
police-inspector
polychloroprene
polycrystalline
palaeobotanical
palaeographical
palaeogeography
palaeolimnology
palaeomagnetism
palaeontologist
palaeontography
palaeophytology
palaeozoologist
pulchritudinous
pulmobranchiate
pillow-structure
polyphloesboean
Polyprotodontia
polishing-powder
polysyllabicism
polysynthetical
polyunsaturated
pantechnicon-van
pencil-sharpener
pantopragmatics
panophthalmitis
Pan-Presbyterian
penetrativeness
punctiliousness
probationership
phonautographic
prosenchymatous
phonemicisation
properispomenon
professionalise
professionalism
processionalist
proof-correcting
proof-correction
prohibitiveness
problematically
prognosticative
prognostication
provocativeness
phototelegraphy
photomechanical
photosensitiser
photozincograph
photolithograph
photomicrograph
photoelasticity
photoconductive
photoconducting
protozoological
protospatharius
photogrammetric
provost-sergeant
proportionately

proportionality
photoxylography
prospectiveness
phosphorescence
phosphorylation
procreativeness
proprietorially
programmability
procrastinative
procrastinating
procrastination
procrastinatory
progressiveness
propylitisation
pergamentaceous
paradoxicalness
porcelain-cement
perpendicularly
pyro-electricity
paroemiographer
paragraphically
paraheliotropic
parthenogenesis
parthenogenetic
parliamentarism
parliamentarian
parliamentarily
parliament-hinge
parliament-house
particularistic
paralinguistics
portmanteau-word
parenthetically
phrenologically
personalisation
purposelessness
personification
perspicaciously
perspicuousness
pyrophotography
portrait-gallery
portrait-painter
peristaltically
parasympathetic
perissodactylic
perissosyllabic
parasiticalness
pyrotechnically
perfunctoriness
party-government
passenger-pigeon
pessimistically
pusillanimously
post-millenarian
postulationally
Pithecanthropus
Patripassianism
plumbaginaceous
paulo-post-future
poverty-stricken
powdering-closet
psychobiologist
psychobiography

psychochemistry
psychographical
psychogenetical
psychogeriatric
psychohistorian
psychometrician
psychrometrical
psychopathology
psychophysicist
psychosomimetic
psychotherapist
psychotomimetic
physiographical
physiologically
physicochemical
physiotherapist
phytogeographic
phytogeographer
quatercentenary
quasihistorical
quarrelsomeness
quadruplication
quadripartition
quarter-sessions
quartermistress
questionability
question-begging
quick-wittedness
quick-conceiving
quinquagenarian
quintuplication
reafforestation
Rhamphorhynchus
reapportionment
readvertisement
recrementitious
receiver-general
receiving-office
recollectedness
reconvalescence
reconcilability
reconsideration
reconsolidation
recoverableness
rudimentariness
riding-committee
radiotelegraphy
radiogoniometer
radiogramophone
redetermination
rheumatological
re-establishment
refrangibleness
refreshment-room
refortification
regionalisation
right-handedness
right-mindedness
rainbow-coloured
reinterrogation
railway-carriage
railway-crossing
romanticisation

remonstratingly
remorselessness
röntgenotherapy
rent-restriction
rhombencephalon
rhombenporphyry
reproachfulness
repetitiousness
respectableness
resurrectionary
resurrectionise
resurrectionism
resurrectionist
resurrection-man
resurrection-pie
resourcefulness
ritualistically
retrievableness
rationalisation
retrospectively
retrogressively
retrogressional
roundaboutation
roundaboutility
round-shouldered
Rhynchobdellida
Rhynchocephalia
stalagmitically
stalactitically
shabby-gentility
stand-offishness
standing-rigging
standardisation
slave-trafficker
space-travelling
scaphocephalous
staphylorrhaphy
swathing-clothes
seaplane-carrier
stapling-machine
star-of-Bethlehem
shadow-pantomime
stamping-machine
slantingdicular
Sabbath-breaking
sublapsarianism
subterraneously
subject-superior
subintellection
subintelligence
subintelligitur
subcommissioner
subspecifically
suburbanisation
subordinateness
sober-mindedness
substratosphere
substantiveness
substantialness
substitutionary
socialistically
successlessness
Second-adventist

second-in-
command
secundogeniture
seconds-pendulum
sociolinguistic
sociobiological
sycophantically
saddler-sergeant
saddler-corporal
sedimentologist
sado-masochistic
steganographist
speechification
stereochemistry
stereographical
stereoisomerism
seeming-virtuous
speaking-trumpet
steam-navigation
spermatoblastic
spermatogenesis
spermatogenetic
sleeping-draught
sleeping-partner
smelting-furnace
spectroscopical
speculativeness
softly-sprighted
significatively
Schrecklichkeit
sphaerosiderite
schillerisation
Spheniciformes
school-inspector
schoolmastering
schoolmasterish
spheroidisation
schistosomiasis
schizophrenetic
stiff-neckedness
sticking-plaster
seismographical
stilpnosiderite
self-abandonment
self-affirmation
syllabification
self-approbation
self-advancement
self-complacence
self-consequence
self-considering
self-confidently
self-consistency
self-constituted
self-capacitance
self-degradation
self-destructive
self-destruction
self-determining
self-examination
self-explanatory
self-explication
self-forgetfully

Selaginellaceae
sulphaguanidine
self-humiliation
sulphur-bacteria
sulphureousness
self-improvement
self-liquidating
selenographical
self-opinionated
syllogistically
saloon-passenger
self-observation
self-pollination
self-portraiture
sclerodermatous
self-slaughtered
self-substantial
self-sufficiency
self-sustainment
self-sovereignty
self-vindication
sympathomimetic
sympathetically
semi-documentary
symmetricalness
semi-independent
semimanufacture
Semi-Pelagianism
semitransparent
symptomatically
sensation-monger
synecologically
synecdochically
sense-perception
sententiousness
synchronisation
synchronistical
synchronousness
single-heartedly
synarthrodially
sanctimoniously
singularisation
sandwort-spurrey
stoicheiometric
stoechiological
stoichiological
sword-and-buckler
shoulder-clapper
shoulder-slipped
shoulder-shotten
scolopendriform
shooting-gallery
slotting-machine
spontaneousness
septentrionally
supplementation
supplementarily
suppositionally
supportableness
supercalendered
superlativeness
supernaturalise
supernaturalism

supersaturation
supernaturalist
superabundantly
superheterodyne
superficialness
superfluousness
superplasticity
superimposition
superintendence
superintendency
superincumbence
superinducement
superconductive
superconducting
superordination
superstitiously
superstructural
superexcellence
superexaltation
spread-eaglewise
scribaciousness
scribbling-paper
sericiculturist
sarcenchymatous
sergeant-drummer
surreptitiously
serviceableness
straightforward
strait-waistcoat
strombuliferous
shrink-resistant
scripture-reader
stratigraphical
stretching-frame
stretcher-bearer
strawberry-shrub
systematisation
susceptibleness
sesquicentenary
south-eastwardly
south-westwardly
slumpflationary
seventeen-hunder
thanatognomonic
thalassographic
thalassographer
thankworthiness
traumatological
training-college
transparentness
transferribilty
transliteration
transfiguration
transfigurement
transplantation
transilluminate
transpositional
transmogrifying
transportedness
transcriptively
transcriptional
transgressively
transgressional

transmutability
tuberculisation
ticket-collector
Tectibranchiata
tectibranchiate
technologically
therapeutically
treacherousness
theriomorphosis
therianthropism
thermochemistry
theorematically
treasonableness
theosophistical
trinitrobenzene
trinitrotoluene
trigonometrical
thin-skinnedness
trisyllabically
telegraphically
telephotography
temperamentally
tempestuousness
tentaculiferous
tender-heartedly
tendentiousness
two-pair-of-stairs
troubleshooting
troublesomeness
thoughtlessness
topographically
typographically
threepenceworth
threepennyworth
thrombo-embolism
tarsometatarsal
tarsometatarsus
torque-converter
testament-dative
tetrasporangium
Tetrabranchiata
tetrabranchiate
Tetractinellida
tetrasyllabical
totalitarianism
true-heartedness
trustworthiness
trypanosomiasis
unavailableness
unaccommodating
unascertainable
unavoidableness
unapostolically
unapprehensible
unauthenticated
unauthoritative
unalterableness
unadvisableness
unblameableness
unchangeability
unchallengeable
unchallengeably
uncompanionable

uncompassionate
uncomplaisantly
uncomplainingly
uncomplimentary
uncomprehensive
uncomprehending
uncommunicative
unconscientious
unconsciousness
unconcernedness
unconsentaneous
unconditionally
uncanonicalness
uncontroversial
unconstrainable
unconstrainedly
uncooperatively
unco-operatively
unceremoniously
unchristianlike
uncircumscribed
undemonstrative
underhandedness
under-the-counter
under-employment
under-production
under-privileged
underestimation
understandingly
undistinguished
undisciplinable
undesirableness
undetermination
unexceptionable
unexceptionably
unexceptionally
unforgivingness
unfortunateness
unfossiliferous
ungrammatically
ungentlemanlike
unhealthfulness
unimaginatively
unidiomatically
unintentionally
unintermittedly
uninterpretable
uninterestingly
uninterruptedly
unnecessariness
unobjectionable
unobjectionably
unobtrusiveness
unpeaceableness
unpractisedness
unprecedentedly
unpremeditation
unprepossessing
unphilosophical
unprotectedness
unprotestantise
unpronounceable
unproportionate

unprogressively
unparliamentary
unpatriotically
unqualifiedness
unrecommendable
unreconciliable
unreconstructed
unrighteousness
unrelentingness
unremittingness
unstatesmanlike
unseaworthiness
unsubstantiated
unsteadfastness
unselfconscious
unsymmetrically
unsportsmanlike
unsophisticated
unsuspectedness
unsatisfiedness
ultracentrifuge
unteachableness
ultramicroscope
ultramicroscopy
ultrasonography
ultra-Protestant
untransmigrated
untransmissible
untractableness
untrustworthily
unverifiability
unwholesomeness
vice-chamberlain
vicissitudinous
victualling-yard
victualling-ship
victualling-bill
vehicle-actuated
vindicativeness
ventriloquially
ventriloquistic
venturesomeness
vertiginousness
vasoconstrictor
viscosimetrical
vascularisation
weather-notation
weather-boarding
wheel-animalcule
wringing-machine
weighing-machine
whirling-dervish
whirling-machine
well-accomplisht
well-conditioned
wall-gillyflower
well-intentioned
well-upholstered
wonder-mongering
window-gardening
wrong-headedness
woody-nightshade
warrantableness

world-without-end
warm-heartedness
withdrawing-room
water-equivalent
xylotypographic
xeroradiography
zoogeographical
zoophytological

Words arranged according to
EVEN LETTERS

baba	laic	cage	mace	wane	nach	gawk	harl	kain
caba	marc	cake	made	ware	oath	hack	haul	kaon
Cama	saic	came	mage	wase	pash	haik	jail	lain
capa	talc	cane	make	wate	path	hank	jarl	larn
casa	Waac	cape	male	wave	rach	hark	kail	lawn
Dada	**bald**	care	mane	wawe	rash	hask	mail	main
data	band	case	mare	yale	rath	hawk	mall	maun
a-la	bard	cate	mase	yare	sash	jack	marl	naan
gaga	baud	cave	mate	yate	tach	jark	maul	nain
jala	bawd	dace	maté	**baff**	tanh	lack	nail	pain
na-ha	card	dale	maze	caff	tash	laik	pail	pawn
naka	Dard	dame	name	calf	tath	lank	pall	rain
lava	daud	Dane	nape	daff	wash	lark	paul	raun
caka	dawd	dare	nare	faff	**Babi**	lawk	pawl	rawn
Kama	eard	date	nave	gaff	cadi	mack	rail	sain
ana	fand	daze	naze	haaf	dali	maik	sail	sawn
cava	fard	eale	pace	haff	dari	mark	saul	ta'en
a-la	gaed	ease	page	half	gadi	mask	taal	tarn
ama	gaid	face	pale	kaif	haji	mawk	tael	vain
ana	gaud	fade	pane	naïf	kadi	nabk	tail	wain
ava	gawd	fake	papo	raff	kaki	nalk	tall	warn
nama	hand	fame	pare	Waaf	kali	nark	vail	yarn
nana	hard	fane	pâté	waff	kami	pack	wail	yawn
nara	haud	fare	pate	waif	kati	paik	wall	**capo**
naya	kaid	fate	pave	yaff	Magi	park	waul	dado
naga	laid	faze	race	zarf	mali	pawk	wawl	dago
Naia	land	gade	rade	**bang**	maxi	rack	yawl	fado
Naja	lard	gage	rage	cang	Nazi	raik	**balm**	faro
nala	laud	gale	rake	dang	Paki	rank	barm	gajo
nana	maid	game	rale	darg	Pali	sack	calm	gapó
baca	mand	gane	rape	fang	qadi	sank	caum	halo
papa	mard	gape	rare	gang	rabi	sark	tarm	haro
Pará	maud	gare	rase	hagg	ragi	tack	gaum	jato
bara	nard	gate	rate	hang	raki	talk	haem	kago
baua	paid	gave	rave	kang	rami	tank	halm	kayo
bawa	pand	gaze	raze	lang	rani	task	harm	mako
aca	pard	hade	safe	magg	saki	walk	hawm	Nato
aga	rag'd	hake	**sage**	marg	sari	wank	kaim	paco
aja	raid	hale	sake	pang	sati	wark	ma'am	Pavo
Rama	rand	hame	sale	ragg	taxi	wauk	maim	sago
ana	said	hare	same	rang	vagi	yack	malm	taco
ata	sand	hate	sane	sang	vali	yank	marm	taro
Saba	sard	have	sate	T'ang	wadi	zack	naam	**barp**
saga	wadd	haze	save	tang	wali	**Baal**	palm	calp
aha	Wafd	jade	Saxe	vang	zati	bael	saim	camp
aka	waid	jake	tace	wang	**hadj**	bail	warm	carp
ala	wald	jane	take	yang	hajj	ball	**barn**	caup
ana	wand	jape	tale	**bach**	**back**	bawl	bawn	damp
apa	ward	kade	tame	bash	balk	call	cain	gamp
ara	yald	kaie	tane	bath	bank	carl	cann	gasp
a-ta	yard	kale	tape	cash	bark	caul	caul	gaup
axa	yaud	kame	tare	dash	bask	dahl	damn	gawp
ara	babe	lace	tate	each	bauk	Dáil	darn	harp
asa	bade	lade	vade	eath	calk	earl	dawn	hasp
ama	bake	lake	vale	fash	cark	fail	earn	jasp
arb	bale	lamé	vare	gash	cask	fall	fain	jaup
aub	bane	lame	vase	hash	cauk	farl	faun	lamp
amb	bare	lane	wade	hath	cawk	Gael	fawn	Lapp
arb	base	lare	wage	lakh	dank	gall	gain	palp
amb	bate	lase	wake	lash	dark	gaol	gaun	ramp
amb	baye	late	wale	lath	dawk	Gaul	hain	rasp
amb	cade	lave	wame	mash	faik	hail	harn	salp
anc	café	laze		math	fank	hall	jann	samp

4 □a□s

tamp	cast	tatu	abut	odso	mead	névé	beck	pell
vamp	daft	**calx**	obit	**Adar**	meed	peke	berk	real
warp	dalt	faix	ybet	odor	meld	Pele	deck	reel
wasp	dant	falx	**ibex**	**Ades**	mend	pene	desk	seal
yapp	dart	lanx	**ably**	Ides	need	père	feck	seel
yaup	dawt	Manx	obey	odds	pend	rede	geck	seil
yawp	east	**baby**	**acta**	**adit**	read	reke	heck	sell
baur	fact	cagy	**scab**	edit	redd	rete	jerk	teal
bawr	fart	caky	**acid**	**adaw**	reed	sele	keck	teel
carr	fast	cany	ecad	**adry**	rend	semé	keek	teil
fair	gait	cavy	iced	D-day	seed	sere	leak	tell
gair	gant	Davy	scad	eddy	seld	sese	leek	veal
gaur	gart	easy	scud	edgy	send	teme	meek	veil
haar	gast	fady	**ache**	idly	tead	tene	merk	vell
hair	haet	gaby	acme	V-day	teed	tête	neck	weal
laer	haft	gamy	acne	**bema**	teld	vele	neuk	weel
lair	ha'it	gazy	acre	beta	tend	were	peak	weil
maar	halt	hazy	ecce	deva	veld	we're	peck	well
mawr	hart	jasy	eche	gena	vend	we've	peek	we'll
Nair	hast	jazy	scye	geta	weed	wexe	penk	yell
pair	haut	lacy	**scog**	keta	weid	yede	perk	zeal
parr	kant	lady	scug	leva	weld	yeve	reak	**beam**
sair	kart	laky	**scul**	mesa	wend	**beef**	reck	berm
tahr	lant	lazy	**scam**	peba	yead	deaf	reek	deem
vair	last	many	scum	pela	yeed	delf	reik	derm
waur	malt	maty	**icon**	sera	yeld	jeff	seek	fehm
yarr	mart	mazy	scan	seta	yerd	kerf	serk	ferm
baas	mast	nary	**ecco**	tela	Zend	leaf	teak	germ
bass	matt	navy	echo	Veda	**bede**	neif	weak	geum
bats	oast	oaky	**scup**	vega	bene	pelf	week	helm
caps	pact	oary	**Acer**	vela	bere	reef	welk	herm
dais	pant	pacy	icer	vena	bete	reif	yelk	leam
kans	part	paly	scar	Vera	bête	seif	yerk	neem
lass	past	racy	scur	weka	cede	self	yesk	neum
mags	raft	taky	**echt**	Xema	cere	serf	yeuk	perm
Mars	rait	vary	scat	zeta	dele	teff	**bell**	ream
mass	rant	wady	scot	**Beeb**	deme	terf	ceil	seam
nabs	rapt	waly	scut	herb	dene	**berg**	cell	seem
naos	rast	wany	**ecru**	kemb	dere	leng	deal	team
oats	salt	wary	**scaw**	kerb	feme	meng	deil	teem
pais	saut	wavy	scow	Serb	fere	peag	dell	term
pass	tact	waxy	**achy**	verb	fête	tegg	feal	vehm
pays	tait	yawy	icky	wemb	gene	yegg	feel	weem
rams	taut	zany	scry	**aesc**	hebe	**beth**	fell	**aeon**
rats	tatt	**jazz**	**Edda**	merc	he-he	eech	geal	bean
sans	taut	razz	idea	**bead**	hele	hech	heal	been
sass	tawt	**abba**	odea	bend	heme	mesh	heel	bein
says	vant	obia	**odic**	dead	here	nesh	heil	dean
tass	vast	**Abib**	**adze**	deed	hete	pech	hell	deen
taws	vaut	**abac**	edge	deid	jeté	pegh	he'll	dern
wats	waft	**abed**	idée	feed	leke	sech	herl	eevn
yaws	wait	abid	idle	fend	leme	yeah	jeel	fern
baft	want	ibid	**idol**	feod	lere	**beni**	jell	gean
baht	wart	'zbud	idyl	feud	leve	cedi	keel	hern
bait	wast	**abbé**	odal	geld	Mede	deli	kell	hewn
Balt	watt	able	odyl	head	mene	kepi	leal	jean
bant	**babu**	abye	udal	heed	mere	meri	meal	keen
bast	balu	oboe	**Adam**	held	mese	peni	mell	kern
batt	bapu	**obol**	Edam	hend	mete	peri	merl	lean
bayt	masu	**ebon**	idem	herd	meve	semi	mewl	**mean**
can't	Rahu	T-bar	**Eden**	lead	meze	yeti	neal	mein
cant	tabu	**ibis**	Odin	lend	nene	**benj**	peal	nemn
cart	tapu	**abet**	eddo	lewd	nete	**beak**	peel	**neon**

pean	lehr	gest	Jesu	chid	cher	lima	bike	pisé
peen	leir	heat	menu	khud	khor	lira	bile	pize
pein	meer	heft	Peru	shad	shir	mica	bine	rice
peon	near	hent	zebu	shed	thar	mina	bise	ride
pern	ne'er	hept	**deev**	she'd	thir	Mira	bite	rife
rean	pear	hest	derv	shod	Thor	Nipa	cide	rile
reen	peer	jeat	perv	thud	whe'r	pica	ciré	rime
rein	rear	jest	**deaw**	whid	whir	pika	cite	rine
sean	sear	kelt	meow	**ghee**	**rhus**	pila	cive	ripe
seen	seer	kent	**aery**	shoe	she's	piña	dice	rise
sewn	serr	kept	bevy	thae	this	pipa	dike	rite
Tean	tear	kest	defy	thee	thus	pita	dime	rive
teen	teer	lcat	demy	whee	**chat**	rlma	dine	sice
tern	tehr	leet	deny	**chef**	chit	riva	dire	side
vein	veer	left	dewy	**chug**	chut	sida	dite	sike
wean	wear	lent	eery	shag	ghat	sika	dive	sile
ween	weir	lest	hery	shog	khat	sima	eine	sine
yean	year	Lett	levy	thig	phot	Siva	fife	sipe
zein	**ceas**	meat	rely	thug	phut	tika	fike	sire
bego	cess	meet	reny	whig	shat	vina	file	site
demo	deus	melt	sexy	shat	shot	visa	fine	size
hero	fegs	ment	tedy	shet	shut	vita	fire	tice
leno	feis	neat	very	shit	that	viva	five	tide
memo	fess	nest	**Geëz**	shah	what	zila	gibe	tige
pepo	gens	nett	lezz	**chai**	whet	**dieb**	gite	tike
peso	hers	newt	**afro**	Shri	whit	limb	give	tile
re-do	jess	next	**afar**	Thai	whot	sibb	hide	time
sego	Keys	peat	**affy**	**chik**	**chou**	zimb	hike	tine
veto	lees	pelt	**agha**	dhak	thou	**disc**	hire	tire
zero	lens	pent	egma	**bhel**	thru	fisc	hive	tite
deep	less	pert	**aged**	chal	**chiv**	zinc	jibe	vibe
heap	mess	pest	egad	dhal	shiv	**bind**	jive	vice
help	mews	reft	igad	shul	**chaw**	bird	kibe	vide
hemp	ness	rent	**agee**	**ahem**	chew	died	kike	vile
hesp	news	rest	ague	cham	chow	eild	kine	vine
jeep	reis	seat	ogee	chum	dhow	find	kipe	visé
keep	reps	sect	ogle	sham	phew	gied	kite	vise
kelp	sens	sent	ogre	shim	shaw	gild	lice	vite
kemp	seps	sept	ygoe	them	shew	gird	life	vive
leap	sess	sett	**agog**	wham	show	hied	like	wide
neap	tems	sext	**ugli**	whim	thaw	hild	lime	wife
neep	vers	teat	**egal**	whom	thew	hind	line	wile
peep	Zeus	telt	**ogam**	**chin**	whew	kild	lire	wine
reap	**beat**	tent	**agen**	khan	whow	kind	lite	wipe
repp	beet	test	agin	phon	**ahoy**	lied	live	wire
seep	belt	text	agon	shan	chay	lind	mice	wise
temp	bent	vent	**agio**	shin	shay	mild	mike	wite
weep	best	vert	Igbo	shun	they	mind	mile	wive
yelp	celt	vest	**agar**	than	whey	pied	mime	yite
bear	cent	weet	eger	then	**chez**	rind	mine	**biff**
beer	cert	weft	**egis**	thin	phiz	sild	mire	fief
dear	debt	welt	**Ogpu**	thon	whiz	sind	mise	jiff
deer	deft	went	**eggy**	when	biga	tied	mite	lief
fear	dent	wept	ugly	whin	Bixa	tind	nice	miff
feer	feat	wert	**rhea**	shoo	dika	vied	nide	nief
gear	feet	west	shea	thro	dita	vild	nife	niff
hear	felt	yelt	shwa	**chap**	diva	wild	Nike	riff
heir	fent	yest	**Thea**	chip	gila	wind	nine	tiff
Herr	fett	yett	**whoa**	chop	hila	yird	pice	**bigg**
jeer	geat	zest	**chub**	ship	hiya	**aide**	pike	bing
keir	geit	**beau**	**chic**	shop	kina	aîné	pile	biog
lear	gelt	genu	choc	whop		bice	pine	ding
leer	gent	Jehu	**chad**	char		bide	pipe	ging

hing	kick	riem	wisp	riot	Skye	alme	clip	flay
king	kink	Sium	**bier**	ript	**skeg**	aloe	clop	fley
ling	kirk	**airn**	birr	ritt	skug	blae	flap	gley
ming	lick	bien	girr	sift	**skim**	blee	flip	illy
ping	link	cion	kier	silt	**akin**	blue	flop	oldy
rigg	lirk	Dian	liar	sist	ikon	clue	plap	play
ring	mick	Finn	lier	tift	skin	else	plop	ploy
sing	milk	firn	pier	tilt	**skeo**	flee	slap	slay
ting	mink	gien	tiar	tint	skio	floe	slip	sley
wing	mirk	ginn	tier	tipt	**skep**	flue	slop	**amla**
zing	nick	girn	tirr	vint	skip	glee	**alar**	emma
bish	pick	hisn	**bias**	wilt	**sker**	glue	blur	**amid**
dich	pink	jinn	cits	win't	skyr	olpe	slur	**amie**
dish	rick	kiln	dies	wist	**skis**	plié	**alas**	smee
fish	rink	kirn	digs	**Ainu**	**skat**	slae	alms	ympe
high	risk	lien	diss	aitu	skit	slee	plus	**smog**
hish	sick	limn	fils	**Dieu**	**skaw**	sloe	**alit**	smug
kish	silk	linn	hiss	lieu	skew	slue	blat	**amah**
kith	sink	lion	kiss	rimu	**okay**	ylke	blet	umph
lich	tick	mien	Lias	**Mirv**	skry	**clef**	blot	**impi**
lith	tink	pion	miss	**view**	**alfa**	**clag**	Blut	**amok**
nigh	wick	pirn	piss	**jinx**	alga	cleg	clat	**amyl**
pish	wink	sien	Riss	minx	alma	clog	clot	**imam**
pith	yirk	sign	siss	**airy**	flea	flag	flat	**amen**
rich	**bill**	winn	vibs	city	glia	fleg	flit	G-man
sich	birl	cill	**ain't**	dixy	ilea	flog	glit	omen
sigh	cirl	Zion	airt	fiky	ilia	gleg	glut	**ambo**
Sikh	cirl	**Biro®**	bint	lily	ilka	glug	plat	ammo
sinh	dial	bito	bitt	limy	Olea	plug	plot	umbo
sith	dill	ciao	cist	miny	olla	slag	slat	**amir**
tich	dirl	cito	dict	miry	plea	slog	slit	emir
wish	fill	dido	diet	mity	ulna	slug	slot	omer
with	gill	fico	dint	mixy	**blab**	**blah**	slut	smir
divi	girl	Fido	dirt	nixy	bleb	**glei**	**clou**	smur
dixi	hill	figo	ditt	oily	blob	vlei	**Slav**	**amis**
hi-fi	jill	fino	fiat	piny	blub	**flak**	alew	emys
kiri	kill	giro	fist	pioy	club	elul	alow	Xmas
kiwi	lill	kilo	fitt	pipy	flab	**alum**	blew	**emit**
midi	mill	kino	gift	pity	flub	clam	blow	omit
mini	nill	lido	gilt	pixy	glib	clem	claw	smit
nidi	nirl	lilo	girt	ricy	glob	flam	clew	smut
nisi	pill	lino	gist	rimy	pleb	glam	clow	ympt
pili	pirl	mico	hilt	sizy	slab	glim	flaw	**emeu**
pipi	rial	milo	hint	tidy	slob	glum	flew	ombu
siri	riel	mino	hipt	tiny	slub	plim	flow	**smew**
tiki	rill	miso	hist	viny	**bloc**	plum	glow	**Emmy**
tipi	sial	rivo	jilt	vizy	**alod**	slam	plow	**anna**
titi	sill	silo	kilt	wily	blad	slim	slaw	anoa
wili	till	tiro	kist	winy	bled	slum	slew	anta
bilk	tirl	vino	lift	wiry	clad	ylem	slow	**Inca**
bink	vial	vivo	lilt	**fizz**	clod	**blin**	**flax**	inia
birk	vill	wino	lint	gizz	fled	clan	flex	**knob**
bisk	viol	**gimp**	list	hizz	glad	élan	flix	knub
dick	virl	jimp	milt	tizz	gled	flan	flux	snab
dink	wiel	kilp	mint	**ajee**	glid	glen	ilex	sneb
dirk	will	limp	mist	**ajar**	olid	plan	ulex	snib
disk	yill	lisp	mitt	**Ajax**	pled	**also**	**alay**	snob
fink	**Bimm**	pimp	mixt	**ekka**	plod	alto	ally	snub
firk	film	ripp	oint	okra	sled	Clio	blay	**sned**
fisk	firm	risp	Pict	skua	slid	oleo	bley	**snod**
gink	gism	simp	piet	**ski'd**	alae	olio	clay	**ance**
hick	jism	simp	pint	skid	albe	**blip**	cloy	ante
jink	pium	wimp	rift	**akee**	alee	clap	elmy	**knee**

once	bona	fond	gole	rore	mong	hook	noll	loun
unbe	bora	food	gone	rose	nong	howk	noul	lown
unce	coca	ford	gore	rosé	pong	jock	nowl	moan
unde	coda	foud	hole	rote	rong	jook	poll	moon
knag	cola	goad	home	roué	song	jouk	pool	morn
snag	coma	gold	hone	rove	tong	konk	roil	mown
snig	coxa	good	hope	soke	**booh**	kook	roll	noon
snog	dona	gowd	hore	sole	bosh	lock	rotl	Norn
snug	Doña	hoed	hose	some	both	look	roul	noun
ankh	dopa	hold	hote	sone	coch	mock	soil	nown
inch	Dora	hond	hove	sore	cosh	monk	soul	poon
anti	EOKA	hood	howe	to-be	coth	nock	sowl	porn
unci	fora	kond	jobe	toge	doth	nook	toil	pown
anal	Hova	load	joke	toke	gosh	pock	toll	roan
anil	iota	loid	jole	tole	Goth	polk	tool	roin
anan	jota	lord	Jove	tome	hogh	pook	wool	roon
anon	kola	loud	lobe	tone	josh	pork	yowl	soon
anno	kora	mold	lode	tope	loch	pouk	**boom**	sorn
info	loma	mood	loge	tore	losh	rock	coom	sown
inro	lota	pond	lome	tose	loth	rook	corm	toon
into	mona	pood	lone	tote	moth	soak	doom	torn
onto	mora	road	lope	toze	nosh	sock	dorm	toun
unco	mowa	roed	lore	vole	pooh	sook	foam	town
undo	moxa	rood	lose	vote	posh	souk	form	woon
Unio	noma	sold	lote	woke	roch	took	gorm	worn
unto	nova	sord	love	wore	soph	touk	holm	zoon
knap	roma	toad	lowe	wove	tosh	wock	loam	**boko**
knop	Rosa	toed	mode	yode	yogh	work	loom	coco
snap	rota	told	moke	yoke	**foci**	york	norm	coho
snip	soda	void	mole	yore	Holi	youk	poem	dodo
gnar	sofa	woad	mome	yowe	lobi	**boil**	roam	gobo
knar	soja	wold	mope	zone	loci	boll	room	gogo
knur	sola	wood	more	**coff**	Loki	bowl	roum	hobo
oner	soma	word	mose	coif	modi	coal	soom	homo
snar	sora	yold	mote	coof	mooi	coil	soum	joco
anas	soya	yond	moue	corf	nodi	coll	sowm	jomo
anus	toga	you'd	move	doff	not-I	cool	toom	kolo
onus	tola	**bode**	moze	dowf	Sofi	cowl	worm	koto
gnat	vola	bole	node	goaf	soli	doll	zoom	loco
knit	Xosa	bone	nole	goff	sori	dool	**boon**	logo
knot	yoga	bore	nome	golf	topi	dowl	born	loto
knut	zoea	code	none	goof	tori	eorl	bos'n	Moho
onst	zona	coke	nope	gowf	yogi	foal	boun	moko
snot	**bomb**	cole	nose	hoof	yoni	foil	coin	mono
unit	boob	come	note	houf	**bock**	fool	conn	Moro
unau	comb	cone	oose	howf	book	foul	coon	no-no
anew	doab	cope	ooze	koff	bosk	fowl	corn	poco
anow	doob	core	poke	loaf	bouk	goal	doen	polo
enew	sorb	cose	pole	loof	cock	goel	down	so-ho
enow	tomb	cote	pome	poof	conk	gool	eoan	solo
gnaw	womb	cove	pone	pouf	cook	gowl	foen	so-so
knew	**douc**	coze	pope	roof	cork	howl	föhn	toco
know	torc	doge	pore	sowf	dock	joll	foin	to-do
snow	zoic	dole	pose	toff	dook	jowl	goon	toho
onyx	**bold**	dome	posé	wolf	folk	kohl	gown	toko
Pnyx	bond	done	pote	woof	fork	loll	horn	yo-ho
envy	bord	dope	robe	wowf	gonk	moil	john	yo-yo
inby	coed	dose	rode	**boyg**	gook	moll	join	zobo
inky	cold	dote	roke	dong	gouk	mool	koan	**comp**
inly	cond	dove	role	gong	gowk	moyl	loan	co-op
only	cord	doze	Rome	hogg	hock	Noël	loin	coop
boba	dowd	fone	rone	hong	hoik	noil	loon	coup
boma	fold	fore	rope	long	honk		lorn	cowp

dorp	hors	nout	joky	spry	brig	drop	dray	stap
doup	hoss	nowt	lory	upby	brog	frap	drey	step
dowp	joss	oont	moly	upsy	crag	grip	fray	stop
golp	koss	poet	mony	**aqua**	drag	prep	gray	**star**
goop	loos	polt	mopy	**arba**	drug	prop	grey	stir
holp	loss	poot	movy	area	frig	trap	orby	**utas**
hoop	löss	port	nosy	aria	frog	trip	orgy	utis
loop	mods	post	nowy	Orca	grig	wrap	pray	**état**
loup	moss	pott	oosy	orra	grog	**arar**	prey	stet
moop	noes	pout	oozy	proa	prig	brer	troy	stot
moup	nous	ront	poky	urea	prog	**bras**	urdy	**staw**
noop	oons	root	poly	Ursa	trig	Eros	X-ray	stew
noup	oops	rort	pony	urva	trog	fris	**Druz**	stow
pomp	pons	rout	pory	**Arab**	trug	gris	friz	**Styx**
poop	poss	rowt	posy	crab	**arch**	iris	friz	**stay**
romp	sols	soft	roky	crib	pruh	kris	trez	stey
roop	soss	soot	ropy	drab	arak	pros	**used**	**aula**
roup	sous	sort	rory	drib	trek	prys	**esne**	aura
soap	toss	sout	rosy	drub	**aril**	urus	esse	buba
soop	wots	toft	toby	frab	aryl	**aret**	isle	buna
soup	**boat**	tolt	tody	grab	oral	brat	**Esth**	duma
sowp	bolt	toot	tony	grub	Ural	brit	**asci**	dura
yoop	boot	tort	Tory	**croc**	vril	brut	Asti	gula
boar	bort	tost	towy	eric	**arum**	crit	Tshi	huia
Boer	bott	tout	**pozz**	uric	brim	drat	**asar**	hula
boor	bout	towt	**epha**	**ared**	Brum	erst	ksar	huma
bowr	coat	volt	**epic**	arid	cram	fret	tsar	juba
coir	coft	won't	spec	brad	dram	frit	user	juga
cour	colt	wont	spic	bred	drum	grat	**Isis**	jura
doer	coot	woot	**apod**	brod	from	grit	**ashy**	Musa
door	Copt	wort	sped	crud	gram	grot	**Esky®**	puja
dorr	cost	wost	spud	drad	grim	prat	espy	puma
dour	cott	yont	**apse**	grid	grum	tret	ismy	puna
four	doat	**non-U**	épée	irid	pram	trot	I-spy	pupa
goer	doit	tolu	spae	prad	prim	writ	**frau**	rusa
goor	dolt	zobu	spie	prod	prom	prau	stoa	Ruta
hoar	don't	**coax**	spue	trad	tram	prau	**stab**	sura
hoer	dort	hoax	**opah**	trod	trim	Urdu	stob	tuba
hour	dost	roux	**spik**	arse	Urim	**arew**	stub	tufa
jour	dout	**body**	opal	brae	Aran	arow	**atoc**	tuna
loor	font	bogy	**Spam®**	bree	bran	braw	otic	yuca
lour	foot	bony	**J-pen**	Brie	bren	brew	**sted**	yuga
mohr	fort	cony	open	cree	cran	brow	stud	zupa
moor	goat	copy	span	crue	gran	craw	**ethe**	**bulb**
poor	gout	cosy	spin	dree	grin	crew	stie	curb
pour	holt	coxy	spun	erne	iron	crow	stye	dumb
roar	hoot	cozy	upon	Erse	trin	draw	**stag**	numb
soar	host	dogy	**upgo**	frae	tron	drew	**etch**	**fusc**
sour	hout	domy	**spar**	free	wren	drow	itch	**auld**
torr	jolt	dopy	spur	gree	**arco**	frow	**etui**	bund
tour	loft	dory	**epos**	grue	Argo	grew	**atok**	burd
voar	loot	doty	opus	orfe	arvo	grow	**atom**	curd
your	lost	doxy	upas	orle	brio	prow	item	duad
boss	lout	dozy	**spat**	pree	broo	trew	stem	fund
coms	lowt	fogy	spet	tree	ergo	trow	stum	guid
coss	moat	foxy	spit	trie	Kroo	**Crax**	**eten**	hued
does	moit	fozy	spot	true	proo	crux	Eton	Kurd
doss	molt	goby	**spiv**	urdé	trio	oryx	sten	muid
dows	moot	go-by	urge	urge	urao	prex	stun	quad
foes	mort	gory	**spaw**	Graf	**crap**	**army**	**otto**	quid
foss	most	holy	spew	prof	crop	'Arry	**atap**	quod
Goss	mott	homy	**apex**	tref	drap	arty	**atop**	rudd
hols	nott	joey	spay	**brag**	drip	bray	atop	rued

rund	cuif	husk	vuln	curt	uvea	oxen	wyte
sudd	duff	junk	yuan	duct	avid	expo	zyme
sued	fuff	luck	auto	duet	ivy'd	oxer	ayah
surd	guff	lurk	bubo	dunt	evoe	axes	myth
tund	gulf	lusk	bufo	dust	aval	axis	gyal
turd	huff	muck	duro	fust	evil	exes	myal
buke	humf	murk	euro	gust	oval	exit	ryal
cube	luff	musk	huso	hunt	ovum	cyma	lyam
cure	muff	oulk	judo	hurt	even	eyra	cyan
curé	puff	puck	Juno	just	oven	Lyra	hymn
cute	ruff	pulk	ludo	luit	aver	myna	Lyon
duce	surf	punk	ouzo	lunt	ever	sync	syen
dude	tuff	ruck	sumo	lust	over	dyad	hypo
duke	turf	rusk	bump	must	Aves	dyed	pyro
dule	zurf	suck	burp	mutt	evet	eyed	sybo
dune	bung	sulk	cusp	oust	avow	fyrd	typo
dupe	burg	sunk	dump	punt	swab	kynd	tyro
dure	dung	tuck	gulp	putt	swob	rynd	gymp
euge	fung	Turk	gump	quat	awed	synd	tymp
fume	hung	tusk	hump	quit	owed	tynd	dyer
fuse	lung	yuck	jump	runt	swad	wynd	oyer
fuze	quag	buhl	lump	rust	owre	byke	eyas
gude	rung	bull	mump	suet	swee	byre	eyes
gule	sung	burl	pulp	suit	twae	byte	nyas
huge	bush	cull	pump	tuft	twee	cyme	oyes
hule	cush	curl	quep	yuft	swag	cyte	cyst
jube	dush	dual	quip	yurt	swig	dyke	eyot
juke	eugh	duel	quop	guru	twig	dyne	kyat
June	gush	dull	rump	juju	hwyl	eyne	pyat
jure	hush	fuel	sump	kudu	twal	eyre	pyet
jute	lush	full	tump	kuku	dwam	fyke	pyot
luce	much	furl	burr	lulu	swam	fyle	ryot
luge	mush	gull	curr	pulu	swim	gybe	xyst
luke	ouch	gurl	duar	tutu	swum	gyre	iynx
lune	ouph	hull	furr	Zulu	swan	gyte	jynx
lure	pugh	hurl	guar	yunx	twin	gyvé	lynx
lute	push	lull	huer	buoy	swap	hyke	eyry
mule	rukh	muil	muir	bury	swop	hylo	gyny
mure	rush	mull	nurr	busy	ewer	hype	oyez
muse	ruth	murl	puer	duly	ower	kyle	azym
mute	such	null	puir	duty	iwis	kyne	azan
nude	sukh	nurl	purr	fumy	'twas	kyte	czar
nuke	tush	pull	buss	fury	ywis	lyme	tzar
puce	euoi	purl	cuss	guly	swat	lyne	
puke	Sufi	wull	fuss	hugy	swot	lyre	
pule	Tupi	culm	huss	judy	twat	lyse	
pure	Zuñi	mumm	lues	July	twit	lyte	
rube	buck	quim	muss	jury	away	pyne	
rude	buik	turm	nuts	puly	awny	pyre	
rule	bulk	Würm	ours	pumy	awry	ryfe	
rume	bunk	burn	puss	puny	M-way	ryke	
rune	burk	curn	Russ	quay	owly	rype	
rusé	busk	duan	suds	quey	sway	ryve	
ruse	cusk	durn	suss	ruby	tway	syce	
sure	duck	guan	tuts	ruly	swiz	syke	
tube	dunk	gurn	aunt	tuny	ixia	syne	
tule	dusk	muon	buat	yuky	axle	sype	
tune	fuck	ourn	bunt	buzz	axel	tyde	
yuke	funk	quin	bust	fuzz	axil	tyke	
yule	gunk	ruin	butt	Günz	exul	tyne	
buff	huck	sunn	cuit	lutz	exam	type	
bumf	hulk	tuan	cult	quiz	axon	tyre	
cuff	hunk	turn	cunt	tuzz	exon	tyte	

5 □a□a

Bahai	palay	dance	mardy	gazer	palea	vales	panga	gamin
bajan	panax	fancy	nandu	Hades	palet	valet	parge	habit
balas	papal	farce	paddy	haler	paned	vaned	raggy	hakim
banal	papaw	farci	panda	harem	panel	varec	range	harim
Banat	pavan	farcy	pandy	hater	paper	wader	rangy	Hasid
basal	pawaw	fasci	pardi	haven	parer	wafer	saiga	jagir
basan	qanat	ganch	pardy	haver	paseo	wager	sarge	Kafir
bazar	rabat	gaucy	ragde	haves	pated	wages	sargo	kalif
cabal	radar	gawcy	randy	hazel	paten	waked	saugh	kamis
cabas	rajah	haick	sandy	hazer	pater	waken	taiga	labia
cacao	ramal	hance	tardy	jaded	paved	waker	tanga	labis
caman	ratan	hanch	vardy	jäger	paven	waler	tango	Ladin
camas	rayah	hatch	waddy	jakes	paver	wamed	tangy	lakin
canal	Sabal	lance	waide	james	payed	waned	targe	lamia
carat	Sakai	lanch	Babee	jasey	payee	waney	waugh	lapis
daman	salad	larch	Babel	javel	payer	water	bathe	Latin
damar	salal	latch	bagel	jawed	racer	waved	cache	madid
daraf	sapan	lauch	baked	kaneh	raged	waver	dacha	Mafia
datal	Satan	march	baken	Karen	rager	wavey	eathe	magic
fanal	Tacan	match	baker	label	rakee	waxen	hashy	malic
farad	talar	nance	baler	laced	raker	waxer	kacha	mania
fatal	tamal	nancy	based	lacet	ramee	yager	lathe	manic
galah	tasar	natch	bases	lacey	ranee	yamen	lathi	Manis
gayal	Tatar	pance	caber	laded	raper	yawey	lathy	maria
gazal	vagal	Parca	cadet	laden	rased	baffy	macho	marid
hakam	varan	parch	caged	lager	rated	daffy	mashy	matin
halal	vasal	Pasch	cagey	laker	ratel	gaffe	maths	mavis
hamal	barbe	patch	camel	lapel	rater	halfa	nache	maxim
hanap	cabby	rance	cameo	laser	ravel	Jaffa	pacha	nadir
haram	daube	ranch	caneh	lated	raven	Naafi	pasha	Nasik
jalap	dauby	ratch	caper	laten	raver	samfu	pashm	nazir
japan	gabby	saice	caret	later	rayed	taffy	rache	oasis
Javan	gamba	saick	carex	latex	razed	waefu'	raphe	panic
jawan	garbe	sauce	cater	laver	razee	waift	rathe	panim
kabab	Garbo	sauch	cates	layer	Saber	wauff	sadhu	Paris
kaiak	iambi	saucy	cavel	macer	saker	yarfa	tache	patin
karat	jambe	watch	daker	maker	salep	badge	washy	patio
kayak	jambo	yacca	Dalek	maned	salet	baggy	yacht	pavid
lagan	jambu	baddy	dared	maneh	samel	barge	bania	pavin
lahar	Kaaba	Bände	dares	manes	samen	cadge	baric	pavis
lavas	kasba	bandh	dated	manet	samey	cadgy	basic	rabic
lazar	lay-by	bandy	dater	maser	saree	cargo	basil	rabid
macaw	mamba	bardy	dazed	mater	sated	dagga	basin	radii
madam	mambo	bawdy	eager	matey	saved	darga	basis	radio
makar	maybe	caddy	eared	mazer	saver	fadge	batik	radix
malar	rabbi	candy	easel	naked	savey	fango	bavin	ramie
malax	samba	cardi	eaten	naker	sawed	faugh	cabin	rapid
Malay	sambo	cardy	eater	named	sawer	gadge	calid	ratio
marah	sauba	daddy	eaves	namer	sayer	gauge	calif	ravin
Masai	tabby	dandy	faced	nares	tabes	haugh	calix	sabin
Mayan	taube	faddy	facer	nates	tacet	jaggy	camis	sahib
nahal	warby	garda	facet	navel	taken	kanga	canid	sakia
naiad	yabby	gaudy	faker	navew	taker	kaugh	Canis	salic
Naias	zambo	handy	fakes	oaken	tales	laigh	Carib	salix
naras	bacca	hards	famed	oaker	tamer	large	cavie	sapid
nasal	bacco	hardy	fated	oared	tapen	largo	cavil	sarin
natal	baccy	iaido	galea	oases	taper	laugh	danio	sasin
naval	banco	kandy	gaper	oaten	tapet	madge	daric	satin
nawab	barca	labda	gases	oaves	tater	maggs	davit	savin
Nayar	batch	laldy	gated	paced	taver	mange	facia	sayid
paean	caeca	lande	gavel	pacer	tawer	mango	Fagin	tabid
pagan	casco	lardy	gayer	pacey	taxed	mangy	fakir	tacit
palas	catch	Mahdi	gazel	pager	taxer	naggy	gamic	tafia

takin	dally	waulk	sauna	pagod	cabré	Hanse	gaitt	favus
Tamil	dault	yauld	saunt	parol	cadre	harsh	garth	Gadus
tamin	eagle	balmy	Sawny	racon	caird	Hausa	haith	galut
tamis	early	barmy	sayne	radon	cairn	hause	hasta	gamut
tapir	easle	calmy	Taino	rayon	carry	hawse	haste	Janus
tapis	fable	damme	taint	razor	dairy	karst	hasty	jarul
tatie	farle	gamma	tanna	sabot	darre	lapse	haute	kaput
tawie	fatly	gammy	taunt	sajou	eagre	lasso	janty	larum
taxis	fault	gaumy	tawny	salon	fa'ard	lassu	jarta	Larus
vakil	gable	halma	varna	salop	faery	maise	katti	lay-up
valid	gaily	hammy	vaunt	sapor	fairy	manse	laith	magus
vapid	gally	haoma	yawny	saros	faurd	marsh	laity	mahua
varix	gault	jammy	baboo	savor	garre	massa	Malta	manul
vatic	hable	kaama	bacon	savoy	hairy	massé	malty	manus
wazir	haily	kamme	baloo	Saxon	harry	massy	manta	maqui
zamia	hallo	karma	baron	sayon	karri	mayst	manto	mazut
banjo	haply	lammy	bason	taboo	kauri	paisa	manty	oakum
gadje	hauld	magma	baton	tabor	labra	paise	masty	ramus
ganja	haulm	mamma	bayou	talon	laird	palsy	matte	sagum
gauje	hault	mammy	cabob	taroc	lairy	pansy	Nantz	salue
hadji	hayle	padma	caboc	tarok	laura	parse	nasty	sarus
hajji	kayle	palmy	cagot	tarot	lavra	Parsi	natty	tabun
lapje	ladle	rammy	canoe	tatou	maire	passé	panto	taluk
zanja	laxly	salmi	canon	tatow	Maori	patsy	pants	talus
balk'd	macle	Salmo	cañon	taxon	marry	pause	parti	Taxus
balky	madly	Sammy	capon	taxor	nacre	paysd	party	vacua
barky	maile	talma	capot	vapor	naira	raise	pasta	vague
darky	manly	tammy	carob	wagon	narre	rasse	paste	vagus
gawky	maple	ba'ing	carol	wahoo	padre	saist	pasty	value
Haikh	marle	banns	carom	yahoo	pagri	salse	patte	varus
haiku	marls	canna	caxon	yapok	paire	sansa	patté	wamus
hanky	marly	canny	dados	yapon	parry	sarsa	patty	Yakul
laika	matlo	carny	Dagon	calpa	raird	sasse	Rasta	calve
lanky	nalla	daine	fagot	campy	sabra	sassy	ratty	carve
larky	padle	daint	fanon	dampy	sabre	say-so	saith	carvy
lawks	pagle	daunt	favor	gappy	sacra	sayst	Sakta	Fauve
manky	palla	daynt	galop	gaspy	saury	taish	Sakti	halva
narky	pally	faine	gazon	happy	taira	tansy	salty	halve
pakka	paoli	faint	gazoo	harpy	tarre	tarsi	sauté	larva
palki	paolo	fanny	halo'd	jaspé	tarry	tasse	tanti	malva
parka	parle	fauna	halos	kalpa	tayra	tawse	tarty	mauve
parki	parly	fayne	havoc	kappa	vairé	valse	taste	naeve
parky	patly	garni	jabot	nappe	vairy	waist	tasty	naevi
pawky	raile	gaunt	Jacob	nappy	warre	warst	tatts	naive
ranke	rally	harns	kabob	palpi	zabra	Bantu	tatty	navvy
sanko	rawly	haunt	kapok	pampa	balsa	basta	vasty	Saiva
sarky	rayle	Jaina	Karoo	pappy	basse	baste	vaute	salve
tacky	sable	jaunt	kayoe	paspy	basso	basto	vawte	salvo
tanka	sadly	laund	kazoo	Ralph	caese	batta	walty	savvy
wacke	saily	lawny	labor	raspy	canst	batts	waltz	valve
wacky	salle	mains	Maçon	Salpa	carse	batty	wanty	varve
yakka	sally	manna	Magog	sampi	cause	cacti	warty	waive
badly	sault	maund	magot	sappy	daisy	canto	waste	Yahve
bally	tabla	nanna	mahoe	talpa	earst	canty	yarta	mahwa
baulk	table	nanny	major	tappa	false	carta	yarto	Yahwe
bayle	tally	naunt	manor	taupe	farse	carte	zante	barye
cable	tauld	paint	maror	waspy	fatso	caste	babul	calyx
calla	vails	panne	mason	zappy	gadso	catty	cajun	satyr
caple	vault	raine	mayor	bairn	gassy	earth	camus	baize
cauld	walla	rainy	nabob	bajra	gauss	faith	capul	darzi
caulk	wally	rayne	nagor	bajri	gawsy	Fanti	caput	gauze
daily	wanle	saine	napoo	barré	hadst	fasti	datum	gauzy
dalle	wanly	saint	paeon	barre	halse	fatty	Fagus	hamza

jazzy	abysm	sculk	scrum	adown	relax	recce	genet	vexer
kanzu	abyss	scull	schwa	adays	relay	reech	heben	weber
maize	obese	sculp	scowl	sdayn	reman	Reich	here's	xebec
matza	abate	scamp	scowp	bedad	renal	retch	hevea	Xeres
matzo	about	schmo	addax	begad	renay	secco	hewed	yeven
sarza	Abrus	acini	ad-man	began	repay	teach	hewer	yewen
tazza	above	icing	adrad	begar	resay	tench	jebel	zebec
tazze	abaya	scand	idea'd	begat	Sebat	terce	jewel	beefs
wanze	abuzz	scant	ideal	bekah	sedan	teuch	kevel	beefy
zanze	éclat	scena	ydrad	belah	segar	vetch	keyed	deify
abeam	ictal	scend	adobe	belay	selah	welch	leger	delft
abear	ocean	scene	edict	bemad	sepad	wench	lenes	feoff
abram	octad	scent	educe	bepat	sepal	beady	leper	leafy
abray	octal	scone	educt	beray	sérac	bendy	levee	neafe
E-boat	sceat	ycond	adder	cedar	serai	deedy	level	reify
I-beam	scrab	accoy	adeem	de-bag	seral	fendy	lever	terfe
obeah	scrae	acton	adieu	debar	setae	geode	mêlée	beige
Q-boat	scrag	actor	adred	decad	Teian	heady	merel	belga
U-boat	scram	ichor	advew	decal	telae	heedy	mesel	cerge
abaca	scran	scion	edged	decay	terai	kendo	meted	deign
abaci	scrap	scoog	idler	dedal	teras	leady	meter	feign
aback	scrat	scoop	udder	delay	Texan	neddy	nebek	hedge
abide	scraw	scoot	ydred	denay	texas	needs	nebel	hedgy
abode	scray	scrog	edify	deray	vegan	needy	neper	heigh
a'body	yclad	scrow	adage	dewan	velar	perdu	nevel	henge
X-body	scuba	scapa	addio	fecal	venae	perdy	never	heugh
abbey	acock	scape	ad-lib	femal	venal	ready	newel	hewgh
abcee	scudi	scapi	admin	feral	debby	reddy	penes	kedge
abies	scudo	scopa	admit	fetal	derby	reede	peter	kedgy
ablet	ackee	scope	admix	feuar	gerbe	reedy	rebec	ledge
absey	acred	Scops	Eddic	genal	herby	seedy	rebel	ledgy
objet	F-clef	acari	sdein	gerah	kembo	teade	refel	legge
abaft	G-clef	acerb	addle	geyan	o'erby	teddy	refer	leggy
aboil	icker	acorn	adult	Hecat	webby	Vedda	relet	leugh
abrim	ocher	ochre	edile	hemal	yerba	veldt	remex	menge
abrin	ocker	ochry	Idola	he-man	beach	weedy	renew	merge
absit	ocrea	scare	idyll	hepar	beech	Yezdi	reney	neigh
Eblis	octet	scarf	oddly	hexad	belch	zerda	repel	peggy
Iblis	scree	scarp	odyle	jehad	bench	bedel	reset	reign
obiit	screw	scart	edema	jelab	Decca®	bedew	revel	renga
abele	ycled	scary	Adeni	kebab	de-ice	begem	revet	sedge
obeli	scaff	score	adunc	kenaf	deuce	beget	Seder	sedgy
oboli	sci-fi	scorn	idant	kesar	fence	belee	sedes	serge
U-bolt	scoff	scurf	adios	leear	fetch	benet	semée	teugh
A-bomb	scuff	T-cart	idiom	legal	hence	beret	semen	venge
H-bomb	scuft	scuse	idiot	leman	heuch	besee	sesey	verge
V-bomb	acrid	acute	odeon	medal	keech	beset	seven	wedge
aband	ictic	scath	adapt	Medau	ketch	betel	sever	weigh
abuna	scail	scatt	adept	mesal	leach	bevel	sewed	fecht
abune	sclim	Scots	adopt	metal	leech	bever	sewel	hecht
ebony	scrim	scuta	L-dopa	pecan	letch	bewet	sewen	Lethe
obang	scrip	scute	adore	pedal	leuch	bezel	sewer	meshy
T-bone	acold	ictus	adorn	pekan	Mecca	Ceres	sexed	meths
abbot	icily	occur	adust	penal	mercy	debel	seyen	Pecht
abhor	P-Celt	scaud	Idist	perai	peace	defer	tehee	Peght
ablow	Q-Celt	scaup	odism	Pesah	peach	Deneb	telex	tea-ho
abord	scala	scaur	odist	petal	peece	deter	tenet	techy
abort	scald	schul	add-to	petar	pence	devel	tepee	wecht
ybore	scale	scoug	adyta	recal	Perca	eeven	terek	aecia
abase	scall	scoup	adsum	recap	perce	feces	tewel	aegis
abash	scalp	scour	odeum	redan	perch	fever	Texel	aerie
abask	scaly	scout	odium	regal	reach	fezes	veney	aesir
abuse	scold	scrub	odour	regar	react	gemel	vexed	bedim

befit	resit	repla	penny	xenon	reird	temse	weete	selva
begin	retie	reply	peony	Xerox®	repro	tense	wefte	senvy
belie	revie	seeld	reins	delph	retro	terse	yesty	serve
besit	semie	seely	renne	dempt	retry	verse	zesty	servo
betid	semis	selle	segno	heaps	seare	verso	beaut	verve
bewig	sepia	tell'd	seine	heapy	serra	verst	beaux	weave
cedis	seric	telly	senna	hempy	serre	weise	begum	deawy
ceria	serif	tesla	teend	kelpy	serry	welsh	begun	fetwa
debit	serin	veale	teene	kempt	teary	wersh	bemud	bedye
demic	sewin	vealy	teeny	leapt	terra	yeast	bevue	beryl
demit	telic	veily	teind	nempt	terry	beath	Cebus	cetyl
denim	tenia	weald	tenné	peepe	tetra	benty	cecum	Debye
devil	tepid	welly	terne	peppy	veery	berth	debug	herye
eerie	tewit	beamy	veena	seepy	verry	betty	début	ceaze
fecit	Vedic	derma	veiny	Tempe	weary	cento	degum	feeze
Felis	venin	fehme	weeny	tempi	weird	certy	demur	heeze
fetid	vezir	femme	wenny	tempo	yeard	death	femur	leaze
gelid	xeric	fermi	bebop	tempt	yearn	deity	fetus	leeze
genic	becke	gemma	befog	vespa	zebra	delta	gebur	lezzy
genie	decko	gemmy	begot	weepy	beast	depth	genus	mezzo
genii	dekko	heame	below	beard	beard	derth	get-up	neeze
genip	fenks	herma	berob	cease	cease	festa	jésus	peaze
geoid	gecko	jemmy	besom	beare	cense	gents	Jesus	peize
helix	jerky	lemma	besot	beery	deism	genty	ledum	seaze
jerid	kecks	neume	béton	berry	deist	gesto	lemur	seize
kefir	leaky	pelma	celom	ceorl	dense	heath	let-up	senza
legit	nerka	reame	décor	deare	desse	hefte	negus	teaze
lenis	Neski	reamy	decoy	dearn	feast	hefty	nexus	weize
lepid	peaky	regma	demob	deary	fesse	hertz	rebus	afear
levin	pecke	seame	demon	decry	geese	jetty	rebut	offal
levis	perky	seamy	demos	deere	geist	kelty	recur	oflag
lewis	pesky	vehme	depot	feare	gesse	lefte	regur	after
media	reeky	weamb	felon	ferry	gesso	lefty	rerun	offer
medic	weeke	beano	fetor	geare	heast	lento	revue	often
Melia	welke	being	gemot	genre	heist	lepta	sebum	affix
melic	welkt	benne	genoa	Genro	herse	meaty	sedum	Afric
meril	be-all	benni	genom	Gerry	Jesse	meith	segue	afrit
merit	belle	cerne	helot	heard	lease	mesto	serum	afald
mesic	belly	feint	heroe	heare	leash	neath	set-up	afoot
metic	ceili	fenny	heron	heart	least	netty	tenue	'sfoot
metif	cella	ferny	jeton	hejra	leese	peaty	velum	afire
métis	cello	gerne	kebob	henry	mease	pelta	venue	afore
nelis	dealt	henna	lemon	herry	Mensa	petty	venus	yfere
nepit	fella	henny	mebos	jerry	mense	reata	zebub	afoul
Pekin	felly	jenny	Médoc	Jewry	messy	reate	bevvy	eggar
penie	ferly	jeune	melon	leare	meuse	recta	deave	ogham
penis	gelly	ken-no	meson	learn	neese	recti	deeve	agger
peril	gerle	kerne	metol	leary	neist	recto	delve	aglee
petit	heald	leant	peeoy	leery	newsy	rente	heave	aglet
pewit	hello	leany	pekoe	lepra	pease	resty	heavy	agley
rebid	jeely	Lemna	redox	mear'd	peise	rewth	helve	agree
redia	jello	Lerna	repot	meare	perse	seity	keeve	agued
re-did	jelly	Lerne	segol	merry	perst	septa	kerve	egger
redip	meal'd	meane	sekos	metre	peyse	set-to	leave	egret
refit	mealy	means	Señor	metro	reast	teeth	leavy	ngwee
régie	medle	meant	sepoy	Negro	reest	tenth	neive	ogee'd
re-jig	merle	meany	seron	peare	reist	tenty	nerve	ogler
rejig	neeld	meint	serow	pearl	reuse	terts	nervy	agoge
relic	neele	meiny	seton	peart	sease	testa	peavy	again
remit	nelly	mesne	telos	pedro	seise	teste	peeve	agrin
renig	newly	meynt	tenon	peery	seism	testy	reave	ngaio
renin	realm	penna	tenor	perry	sense	vertu	reeve	ogmic
resin	redly	penne	venom	petre	sessa	vesta	reive	Ugric

agila	thack	their	rhomb	theow	whore	shewn	Bibby	aided
agile	theca	thrid	rhumb	thiol	whorl	shown	bilbo	aider
Agama	thick	thrip	rhyme	throb	whort	showy	kimbo	aînée
agami	whack	khoja	shama	throe	chase	thawy	limbo	airer
agene	which	shoji	shame	throw	chasm	thews	nimbi	bided
agent	chide	thuja	Shema	whoop	chess	thewy	Niobe	bidet
aging	chode	cheka	thema	whoot	chest	thowl	ribby	biped
agone	khadi	choke	theme	chape	chose	chaya	timbó	biter
agony	kheda	choky	thumb	chaps	chuse	khaya	zimbi	cider
aglow	shade	khaki	thyme	chips	ghast	shaya	aitch	cimex
agood	shady	shake	thymy	shape	ghest	they'd	Binca®	civet
igloo	cheek	shako	zhomo	shaps	ghost	Thuya	birch	dicer
agape	cheep	shakt	ahind	shope	phase	ghazi	bitch	dicey
Egypt	cheer	shaky	ahint	whipt	phese	whizz	cinch	diker
igapo	chief	ahold	bhang	chara	shash	bigae	circa	dikey
aggri	chiel	ahull	chank	chard	shush	cigar	circs	dimer
aggro	Khmer	chalk	chant	chare	these	cimar	cisco	diner
aggry	pheer	chela	china	chark	those	cital	diact	diver
agora	sheel	child	chine	charm	whish	dinar	disco	Dives
agast	sheen	chile	chink	charr	whisk	dital	ditch	dizen
agist	sheep	chili	chino	chart	whiss	divan	filch	eider
egest	sheer	chill	chunk	chary	whist	diwan	finch	eisel
agate	sheet	choli	chynd	chère	whose	filar	fitch	fiber
aguti	shied	chyle	ohone	chert	whoso	final	hilch	fifer
agave	shiel	dhole	phang	chirk	Xhosa	hilar	hitch	filed
ogive	shier	dholl	phene	chirl	chute	jihad	linch	filer
agaze	shoed	f-hole	phone	chirm	dhoti	kisan	milch	filet
ahead	shoer	ghyll	phony	chirp	photo	ligan	mince	finer
aheap	shoes	phyla	rhine	chirr	rhyta	lilac	niece	fired
cheap	shred	phyle	rhino	chirt	shite	limax	piece	firer
cheat	shrew	shale	rhone	chord	shote	linac	pilch	fiver
Chian	shyer	shall	shand	chore	shott	liras	pinch	fives
chiao	theek	shalm	shank	churl	theta	Midas	pitch	fixed
ihram	thief	shalt	shan't	churn	thete	minar	since	fixer
phial	three	shaly	shend	churr	Thoth	nidal	ticca	gibel
sheaf	threw	shelf	shent	mhorr	white	Nisan	tinct	giber
sheal	wheel	shell	shine	phare	whity	nival	titch	gilet
shear	wheen	she'll	shiny	shard	chout	nizam	Vinca	given
Shiah	chafe	shill	Shona	share	choux	pi-jaw	wince	giver
shoal	chaff	shily	shone	shark	ghaut	pilau	winch	hiker
shoat	chaft	shola	shunt	sharn	ghoul	pilaw	witch	hired
thrae	chufa	shyly	thana	sharp	rheum	pipal	yince	hirer
thraw	chuff	thelf	thane	sherd	shout	pirai	zilch	hiver
uhlan	shaft	thilk	thank	shere	shrub	rimae	zinco	hives
wheal	shift	thill	thine	shire	shrug	rival	zincy	jiber
whear	theft	thole	thing	shirk	thou'd	riyal	biddy	kidel
wheat	thoft	tholi	think	shirr	thous	Sican	dildo	kiley
Chubb	wheft	Thule	thong	shirt	thrum	simar	diode	libel
dhobi	whiff	whale	whang	shore	uh-huh	sisal	giddy	liber
Sheba	whift	whelk	whine	shorn	whaup	sitar	Hindi	lifer
chace	ahigh	whelm	whiny	short	whaur	Sivan	Hindu	liger
chack	phage	whelp	chaos	there	chave	sizar	kiddy	liken
chaco	thagi	while	chook	therm	chevy	tical	middy	liker
check	thegn	whilk	choom	third	chive	tidal	misdo	limen
chica	thigh	whole	pheon	thirl	chivy	titan	rindy	limes
chich	shchi	champ	phlox	thorn	shave	vicar	tiddy	limey
chick	chain	chimb	she'ol	thorp	sheva	vinal	tilde	lined
chock	chair	chime	shook	uhuru	Shiva	viral	vifda	linen
chuck	choir	chimp	shool	whare	shive	vital	vilde	liner
Phoca	ohmic	chomp	shoon	wharf	shove	vivat	vivda	liter
shack	sheik	chump	shoot	where	chewy	wigan	widdy	lived
shock	thaim	chyme	shrow	whirl	shawl	witan	winds	liven
shuck	theic	rhime		whirr	shawm	zigan	windy	liver

lives	tired	dishy	sigil	title	minor	piert	titty	skoal
miler	titer	eight	Sinic	villa	nicol	tiara	virtu	skran
mimer	vibes	fiche	sirih	villi	nidor	Tisri	vista	skeer
miner	vibex	fichu	sit-in	viola	Nilot	titre	visto	skeet
miser	video	fight	tibia	viold	ninon	birse	vitta	skied
miter	viner	fishy	tie-in	wield	niton	birsy	width	skier
mixed	vinew	hight	Tilia	willy	picot	cissy	witty	skiey
mixen	viper	hithe	timid	yield	pi-dog	didst	fit-up	skyer
mixer	vireo	kight	vigia	biome	pilot	dipso	gibus	skyey
mizen	vitex	kithe	vigil	disme	pilow	first	gigue	skiff
Niger	viver	lichi	virid	filmy	piñon	gipsy	hilum	skoff
nisei	vives	licht	visie	gimme	piton	giust	hilus	skail
oiler	vlxen	light	visit	gismo	pivot	kiosk	miaul	skein
Plcea	widen	lithe	Vitis	gizmo	rigol	miasm	Mimus	sklim
oiked	winey	litho	vivid	hiems	rigor	midst	minus	P-Kelt
oiker	wiper	miche	vizir	jimmy	silo'd	missy	mix-up	Q-Kelt
oilea	wired	might	Rioja	limma	siroc	nisse	nidus	skald
oilei	wirer	niche	dicky	pigmy	tigon	rinse	nisus	skelf
oiler	wives	night	dinky	sigma	timon	sissy	picul	skelm
oiney	wizen	pight	dirke	biont	Timon	tipsy	Picus	skelp
oiped	zibet	pithy	finks	Diana	tiros	biota	pikul	skill
oiper	zizel	richt	kinky	eigne	vigor	birth	pilum	skulk
oixel	jiffy	right	micky	fiend	vison	bitte	pilus	skull
Ribes	miffy	rishi	milky	finny	visor	bitty	pin-up	skimp
ricer	niffy	sight	mirky	giant	vizor	dicta	pious	akene
ricey	biggy	sithe	picky	hiant	widow	diota	pipul	skene
rider	bilge	tichy	pinko	hinny	cippi	dirty	pique	skink
Rigel	bilgy	tight	pinky	jinni	dippy	ditto	risus	skint
Riley	binge	tithe	pisky	jinns	gilpy	ditty	sinus	skunk
rimed	bingo	Vichy	risky	kiang	gippo	fifth	Sioux	okapi
rimer	ciggy	wight	silky	liana	gippy	fifty	sirup	skart
ripen	dinge	withe	sinky	liane	hippo	filth	tle-up	skirl
riper	dingo	withy	wicky	liang	hippy	firth	tip-up	skirr
risen	dingy	bifid	zinke	ligne	jimpy	fisty	titup	skirt
riser	dirge	ci-gît	zinky	linny	lippy	fitte	virus	skyre
rived	fidge	cilia	aisle	ninny	nippy	gilts	bivvy	ukase
rivel	hinge	civic	aizle	piano	pippy	girth	civvy	skate
riven	jingo	civil	bible	piend	timpз	killy	divvy	skite
river	kidge	dlglt	bield	pinna	tippy	kitty	kieve	skyte
rivet	liege	dinic	billy	pinny	Wimpy®	linty	lieve	skive
Sicel	ligge	dixie	birle	piony	wispy	mifty	mieve	skivy
sided	linga	finis	dilli	riant	yippy	miltz	nieve	Alban
sider	lingo	kinin	dilly	sient	zippy	minty	rieve	algae
Sikel	lingy	licit	dimly	tinny	aiery	mirth	sieve	algal
silen	midge	lie-in	field	'tisn't	cirri	misty	silva	alias
siler	mingy	likin	fille	viand	diary	Mitty	viewy	Allah
silex	misgo	limit	filly	visne	fiars	nifty	pioye	allay
sinew	piggy	linin	fitly	winna	fibre	ninth	sibyl	almah
siren	ridge	lipid	gilly	aidos	fiere	nitty	vinyl	altar
siver	ridgy	livid	girly	bigot	fiery	pietà	diazo	alway
sixer	siege	mimic	hillo	bijou	fiord	piety	dizzy	bleak
sized	singe	Minié	hilly	bipod	firry	pinta	fizzy	blear
sizel	tinge	minim	lisle	bison	hijra	pinto	Mirza	bleat
sizer	virga	mix-in	mille	cibol	liard	piste	piezo	bloat
ribet	virge	nihil	mirly	divot	liart	pitta	pizza	clean
iger	Virgo	nitid	nirly	eikon	libra	riata	ritzy	clear
iled	winge	nixie	piel'd	gigot	litre	sieth	tizzy	cleat
iler	wingy	oidia	qibla	giron	livre	silty	winze	cloak
imed	zingy	pipit	rifle	jigot	micro	Sitta	ajwan	cloam
imer	bigha	pixie	rille	livor	mitre	sixth	eject	eliad
imes	bight	ricin	sidle	miaow	nitre	sixty	djinn	Elian
inea	dicht	rigid	sigla	mid-on	nitry	tilth	fjord	elvan
ined	dight	Rigil	silly	milor	picra	tinty	skean	fleam

float	allel	all-in	plumy	blood	blush	flout	emeer	smirk
gleam	alley	allis	slime	bloom	clash	glaum	emmer	smirr
glean	almeh	blain	slimy	cloop	clasp	glaur	emmet	smore
glial	aloed	bluid	slump	cloot	class	Glaux	emmew	umbra
gloat	alter	claim	ulema	elbow	close	glout	emmew	umbre
ileac	blaes	eldin	aland	flood	flash	ileum	imbed	amass
iliac	bleed	elfin	alang	floor	flask	ileus	immew	amiss
Iliad	bleep	eloin	aline	Fluon®	flesh	ilium	impel	amuse
Ilian	bluey	elsin	alone	fluor	flisk	oleum	smeek	omasa
ollav	claes	flail	bland	gloom	flosh	Ulmus	umbel	smash
plead	cleek	flair	blank	gluon	floss	alive	umber	amate
pleat	cleep	fluid	blend	kloof	flush	blive	amigo	Amati
sloan	elder	glaik	blent	pleon	glass	clave	image	amity
ulnae	elmen	glair	blind	sloom	glisk	cleve	imago	emote
ulnar	elpee	oldie	blini	sloop	gloss	clove	omega	empty
alibi	elver	oleic	blink	sloot	plash	glove	imshi	smite
all-be	elves	olein	blond	aleph	plasm	olive	imshy	smith
clubs	fleer	plaid	blunk	clepe	plast	slave	amain	smote
fly-by	fleet	plain	blunt	clipe	plesh	slive	ambit	umpty
glebe	flier	plait	clang	clipt	plush	slove	amnia	Y-moth
gleby	flies	slaid	clank	clype	slash	alowe	amrit	amour
globe	fluey	slain	cline	Elaps	slish	blown	immit	ampul
globy	flyer	sloid	cling	elope	slosh	blowy	immix	embus
plebs	gleed	sluit	clink	elops	sluse	clown	smaik	imaum
slubb	gleek	ulmin	clone	flype	slush	flawn	smoke	imbue
alack	gleet	ulyie	clonk	glyph	alate	flawy	smoko	smous
Alice	glued	ulzie	clung	slept	all-to	flown	smoky	smout
black	gluer	alike	clunk	slipe	blate	flaxy	amble	amove
block	gluey	bloke	eland	slipt	blite	aleye	ample	emove
clack	olden	cloke	flank	slope	blitz	alkyd	amply	smowt
cleck	plied	flake	fling	slops	clote	alkyl	emule	amaze
click	plier	flaky	flint	slopy	cloth	allyl	imply	anear
clock	plies	fluke	flong	slype	elate	cloye	small	annal
cluck	sleek	fluky	flung	alarm	élite	playa	smalm	annat
elect	sleep	glike	flunk	alary	elute	sloyd	smalt	antae
fleck	sleet	slake	gland	alert	flite	blaze	smell	antar
flick	slued	ylike	glans	alure	flitt	cloze	smelt	Anzac
flock	slyer	alula	glent	blare	flota	glaze	smile	eniac
glacé	ulcer	slily	glint	blore	flote	glazy	smolt	in-car
place	aleft	slyly	klang	blurb	flute	gloze	ymolt	ingan
plack	aloft	blame	llano	blurt	fluty	plaza	amend	in-law
plica	bluff	blimp	olent	Clare	flyte	amban	amene	inlay
pluck	cleft	blimy	plane	clary	glitz	amman	ament	Invar®
slack	cliff	clame	plank	clerk	illth	embar	amine	knead
slice	clift	clamp	plant	flare	plate	embay	among	snead
slick	cloff	climb	plink	flary	platy	imbar	emend	sneak
Vlach	flaff	clime	plong	flirt	Pluto	omlah	emong	sneap
blade	fluff	clomb	plonk	flora	slate	omrah	ambos	unbag
blude	gliff	clump	plunk	flory	slaty	smear	ammon	unbar
elide	glift	e-la-mi	slane	flurr	sloth	umiak	embog	uncap
elude	pluff	elemi	slang	glare	zloty	amice	embow	undam
glade	'slife	flame	slant	glary	album	amici	embox	unhat
glady	align	flamm	sling	glory	algum	amuck	impot	Uniat
glede	elegy	flamy	slink	slurb	all-up	smack	smoor	unlaw
glide	éloge	fleme	slung	slurp	almug	smock	smoot	unlay
glode	elogy	flimp	slunk	ultra	Alnus	amide	ambry	unman
slade	glogg	flume	Algol	blasé	aloud	imide	amort	unpay
slide	plage	flump	allod	blash	blaud	amber	D-mark	unsay
albee	aloha	glume	allot	blast	claut	ameer	emery	untax
aldea	alpha	llama	allow	bless	cloud	Ampex®	imari	enact
alder	elchi	plumb	alloy	blest	clour	embed	ombre	knack
alien	algid	plume	aloof	bliss	clout	ember	smarm	knock
allée	algin	plump	altos	blist	flour	emcee	smart	snack

sneck	Indic	incog	unity	koban	zoeae	touch	cooey	losen
snick	infix	indol	ankus	Kodak®	zoeal	voice	coper	loser
snuck	intil	ingot	annul	Koran	zonae	vouch	cored	lover
V-neck	Inuit	inion	Anzus	lobar	zonal	yoick	corer	lovey
anode	inwit	onion	endue	local	bobby	zocco	cosec	lower
cnida	on-dit	snood	ennui	logan	bombe	boody	coved	lozen
snide	snail	snook	ensue	loral	bombé	borde	coven	model
angel	unbid	snool	incur	loran	booby	coudé	cover	modem
anger	undid	snoop	incus	lotah	cobby	doddy	covet	mohel
anker	unfit	snoot	incut	lovat	combe	dowdy	covey	moner
annex	unfix	ungod	indue	loyal	combo	fonda	cowed	money
ended	unkid	ungot	Injun	modal	combs	fonds	cower	moped
endew	unlid	union	input	molal	comby	fordo	cozen	morel
enmew	unlit	unsod	knout	molar	corbe	goldy	domed	mores
ensew	unpin	unwon	oncus	monad	dobby	good-o	donee	mosey
enter	unrid	inapt	onkus	monal	Dolby®	goody	Donet	moted
Enzed	unrig	inept	snout	monas	doubt	Gouda	doper	motel
indew	unrip	snipe	uncus	moral	forby	horde	dopey	moten
index	untie	snips	uncut	morat	gombo	howdy	doree	motet
infer	until	snipy	undue	moray	hobby	lordy	doseh	motey
inker	untin	unapt	undug	nodal	howbe	moody	doter	moved
inlet	unwit	angry	ungum	nomad	lobby	noddy	dover	mover
inner	unzip	antre	knave	no-man	looby	poddy	dowed	mowed
inset	ensky	Anura	knive	nopal	mobby	ronde	dowel	mower
inter	snake	enarm	gnawn	notal	nobby	rondo	dower	nomen
kneed	snaky	enorm	knowe	novae	pombe	rowdy	doyen	Nones
kneel	snoke	entry	known	noway	sorbo	soddy	dozed	nonet
oncer	ancle	enure	snowk	noxal	womby	solde	dozen	nosed
one-er	anele	gnarl	snowy	noyau	yobbo	soldi	dozer	noser
onset	angle	gnarr	inbye	podal	zombi	soldo	fogey	nosey
sneer	Anglo	inarm	bobac	pokal	bocca	sonde	fomes	noted
snoek	anile	Indra	bobak	polar	bonce	sorda	forel	noter
unbed	ankle	indri	bolas	Pomak	botch	sordo	fouet	novel
undée	ingle	inerm	borax	poral	coach	toady	fovea	nowed
under	inkle	inert	bowat	powan	coact	todde	foxed	Nowel
unfed	inula	infra	boyar	Qoran	cocci	toddy	foyer	noyes
unget	knell	inorb	boyau	romal	cocco	tondo	godet	podex
unkcd	knelt	intra	comal	roman	conch	woody	goter	poked
unket	knoll	intro	copal	roral	couch	wordy	golem	poker
unled	onely	inure	coral	rotal	dolce	zonda	goner	poley
unlet	snell	inurn	cowan	rowan	douce	bogey	gooey	poney
unmew	uncle	knarl	coxal	royal	force	bohea	hogen	porer
unpeg	anima	knurl	domal	sofar	hoick	boned	holey	poser
unpen	anime	knurr	donah	solah	hooch	boner	homer	power
unred	anomy	snare	Donat	solan	hotch	boree	homey	rodeo
unset	enema	snark	dorad	solar	loach	borel	honey	Roger
unsew	enemy	snarl	Doras	sonar	mooch	borer	hooey	roker
unsex	gnome	snary	dotal	soral	mouch	botel	hosed	Romeo
unwed	mneme	snirt	douar	sowar	nonce	bowed	hosen	roneo
unwet	anana	snore	Douay	today	notch	bowel	hotel	roped
in-off	an-end	snort	dowar	toga'd	poach	bower	hoten	roper
knife	anent	unarm	focal	Tokay	ponce	bowes	hovel	rosed
on-off	Anona	angst	foray	toman	pooch	bowet	hoven	roset
snafu	inane	anise	fouat	tonal	porch	boxen	hover	rover
sniff	ancon	gnash	gonad	topaz	potch	boxer	jodel	rowel
snift	anion	inust	gopak	Torah	pouch	codex	joker	rowen
snuff	annoy	knosp	goral	toran	roach	cokes	jokey	rower
unify	end-on	snash	gowan	total	rotch	coley	joyed	rozet
anigh	endow	snush	hogan	vocal	sonce	comer	lobed	sober
antic	enjoy	enate	horal	volae	souce	comet	loden	soger
anvil	enrol	snath	Jonah	volar	souct	coney	loner	soken
enfix	envoi	uneth	joram	woman	sowce	cooed	lorel	solen
entia	envoy	unite	jowar	yojan	torch	cooee	losel	soler

soree	forge	folio	hooky	moult	doing	jokol	hoard	horsy
sorel	forgo	gonia	jocko	moyle	Donna	kotow	hoary	house
sorex	gorge	goyim	kooky	noble	donné	Logos	hoord	howso
sowed	gouge	iodic	nooky	nobly	donne	lolog	houri	joist
sower	Hodge	ionic	poaka	noils	downa	lotos	howre	joust
toged	hough	logia	poake	nould	downy	moron	kokra	loast
token	jougs	logic	pocky	noule	found	motor	loord	loess
toned	lodge	logie	polka	poilu	fount	nohow	loure	loose
toney	longa	loric	porky	polly	foyne	nomos	loury	lossy
topee	longe	loris	pouke	poule	going	robot	Moira	louse
topek	lough	louis	rocky	poulp	gonna	rotor	moiré	lousy
toper	moggy	modii	rooky	poult	horny	Sodom	moire	lowse
totem	podge	moria	socks	roble	hound	Solon	moory	moist
towel	podgy	motif	vodka	roily	joint	sopor	morra	moose
tower	pogge	movie	wonky	roule	Koine	topos	morro	mopsy
toyer	pongo	nomic	works	socle	loony	Wolof	mourn	morse
voces	porgy	noria	yolky	soily	lound	**coapt**	mowra	mossy
volet	rouge	oobit	yonks	soole	lownd	compo	poort	mouse
vomer	rough	oorie	Yorks	sowle	lowne	compt	powre	moust
voter	soggy	podia	zooks	soyle	moony	co-opt	roary	mousy
vowed	sorgo	polio	**bodle**	voilà	morné	corps	soare	noise
vowel	sough	posit	bogle	voile	morne	coupe	sopra	noisy
Woden	tonga	potin	boule	voulu	mound	coupé	sorra	noose
woken	tongs	powin	boult	woold	mount	coypu	sorry	Norse
women	tough	robin	coaly	world	noint	golpe	worry	poesy
wooed	vouge	Romic	coble	would	nonny	goopy	you're	poise
wooer	wodge	roric	colly	yodle	no-one	hoppy	yourn	popsy
woven	wonga	rorid	cooly	you'll	Norna	koppa	yours	posse
woxen	**boche**	rorie	could	**comma**	nouns	loopy	yourt	poyse
yodel	bothy	rosin	coyly	commo	poind	loupe	zorro	roast
yokel	docht	rosit	do-all	coomb	point	moppy	**boast**	roist
zoned	foehn	rozit	doilt	coomy	porno	morph	boose	roosa
zooea	hoo-ha	sodic	doily	dogma	pound	oomph	boost	roose
comfy	Mocha	solid	dolly	dooms	pownd	poppa	bossy	roost
go-off	mothy	sonic	doole	doomy	powny	poppy	bouse	rouse
goofy	sopha	Tobit	dowle	dormy	poynt	poupe	bousy	roust
houff	Sophi	tonic	fogle	douma	ronne	poupt	bowse	royst
howff	Sophy	topic	folly	foamy	round	roopy	coast	sonse
loofa	Sotho	toric	fonly	forme	rownd	roupy	coost	sonsy
roofy	tophi	torii	foulé	gormy	royne	soapy	copse	souse
sol-fa	toshy	toxic	foyle	homme	sonne	soppy	copsy	sowse
sowff	**bogie**	toxin	godly	horme	sonny	soupy	corse	toast
toffy	bolix	tozie	golly	loamy	sound	zoppo	corso	toise
woofy	bonie	vogie	goold	momma	sownd	**board**	doest	torse
bodge	cobia	vomit	gooly	mommy	sowne	boart	dorse	torsk
boggy	cogie	yogic	holla	Norma	tonne	boord	douse	torso
bongo	colic	yogin	hollo	pommy	towny	bourd	dowse	tossy
borgo	colin	zooid	holly	roomy	wound	bourg	foist	touse
bouge	comic	zoril	hooly	rowme	young	bourn	fossa	tousy
bough	conia	zowie	hotly	tommy	**boron**	coarb	fosse	towse
coign	conic	**hodja**	jolly	wormy	bosom	cobra	godso	towsy
conga	covin	kopje	joule	**bonne**	boson	copra	goose	woosh
congé	dogie	pooja	koala	bonny	Cobol	courb	goosy	worse
congo	dolia	**booky**	lolly	boong	cocoa	courd	gorse	worst
corgi	Doric	bosky	lowly	borne	codon	coure	gorsy	zoism
cough	Doris	cocky	moble	borné	cohoe	court	gosse	zoist
dodge	dovie	conky	molla	bound	cohog	cowry	hoast	**aorta**
dodgy	dowie	cooky	molly	bowne	colon	doorn	hoise	booth
doggo	Eolic	corky	moola	conne	color	doura	hoist	boots
doggy	eosin	forky	mools	corno	dodos	dowry	hoose	booty
donga	folia	hokku	mooly	cornu	donor	goary	hoosh	botte
dough	folic	honky	mould	corny	honor	Goura	horse	coate
foggy	folie	hooka	mouls	count	hoo-oo	gourd	horst	coati

conte	wootz	boozy	upsey	sprog	arras	cruck	brief	brogh
conto	worth	colza	spiff	up-bow	array	Draco	brier	dregs
costa	youth	motza	apage	epopt	artal	erect	creed	grège
coste	bogus	pozzy	spahi	apart	arval	erica	creek	grego
cotta	bolus	toaze	apaid	apert	Aryan	erick	creel	tragi
couth	bonus	touze	aphid	apery	bread	Eruca	creep	ortho
doeth	bosun	towze	aphis	aport	break	eruct	cried	prahu
dorts	cogue	woozy	April	appro	bream	frack	crier	argil
dorty	comus	apeak	apsis	opera	briar	fract	cries	armil
dotty	donut	apian	épris	spard	broad	frock	cruel	aroid
foots	focus	appal	optic	spare	creak	grace	cruet	arris
footy	forum	appay	spain	spark	cream	grece	dried	arsis
forte	hocus	ephah	speir	spart	croak	grice	drier	artic
forth	ho-hum	speak	split	sperm	Croat	orach	dryer	braid
forty	hokum	spean	spoil	spire	dread	oracy	erred	brail
fouth	jorum	spear	sprig	spirt	dream	price	erven	brain
fowth	jotun	speat	sprit	spiry	drear	prick	freed	broil
goaty	kokum	spial	uptie	spore	dryad	pricy	freer	Bruin
goety	lobus	splat	spake	sport	freak	pruce	freet	bruit
gotta	locum	splay	spike	spurn	friar	trace	fried	craig
gouty	locus	sprad	spiky	spurt	graal	track	frier	drail
hosta	lotus	sprag	spoke	spyre	great	tract	fries	drain
how-to	modus	sprat	apple	apish	groan	treck	fryer	droil
jolty	mogul	spray	apply	apism	groat	trice	greed	droit
jonty	mohur	spyal	aptly	spasm	kraal	trick	Greek	Druid
loath	Momus	uplay	spald	sposh	oread	trock	green	erbia
lofty	mop-up	uptak	spale	spate	organ	truce	grees	Ernie
los'te	mopus	apace	spall	spite	orval	truck	greet	frail
lotto	Morus	epact	spalt	spitz	praam	wrack	grief	fraim
molto	nodus	epoch	speld	sputa	prial	wreck	gruel	freit
monte	notum	space	spelk	appui	pro-am	wrick	orbed	fruit
month	Notus	spacy	spell	appuy	tread	aredd	order	grail
motte	novum	speck	spelt	opium	treat	arede	oriel	grain
motto	pop-up	specs	spile	spaul	triad	brede	ormer	graip
motty	rogue	spica	spill	spout	trial	bride	preen	grein
mouth	roguy	spice	spilt	sprue	Trias	credo	pried	groin
north	roque	spick	spule	sprug	troad	crude	prief	krait
ponty	solum	spicy	spume	uprun	troat	crudy	priep	orbit
porta	solus	apode	spumy	spawl	urban	erode	prier	orcin
Porte	sorus	epode	opine	spawn	ureal	grade	pries	orgia
porty	togue	spade	spane	spewy	urial	gride	proem	orgic
potto	ton-up	spado	spang	epoxy	urman	gryde	pryer	ornis
potty	tonus	spide	spank	apayd	urnal	irade	treen	orpin
roate	top-up	spode	spend	spayd	wreak	predy	tried	orris
ronte	toque	apeek	spent	upbye	araba	pride	trier	preif
rooty	torus	apnea	spina	equal	Araby	prude	tries	traik
rorty	vogue	après	spine	squab	aroba	trade	tryer	T-rail
route	woful	mpret	spink	squad	bribe	tride	urdee	trail
routh	yokul	spaer	spiny	squat	grebe	trode	urger	train
rowth	hoove	speed	spunk	squaw	oribi	uredo	urned	trait
softa	loave	speel	up-end	equip	probe	Ardea	arefy	Troic
softy	moove	speer	apoop	squib	tribe	ardeb	craft	vraic
soote	poove	spied	apron	squid	urubu	ariel	croft	brake
sooth	poovy	spiel	ephod	squit	brace	Aries	draff	braky
sooty	solve	spies	ephor	brace	aread	arles	draft	broke
south	volva	spred	speos	brach	areal	armed	drift	crake
sowth	volve	spree	spoof	brack	arear	armet	graff	drake
tooth	wolve	upjet	spook	bract	argal	arrêt	graft	grike
toots	you've	upled	spool	brick	argan	arses	griff	gryke
torte	Kotys	upped	spoom	broch	Arian	ártel	grift	proke
totty	polyp	upper	spoon	brock	A-road	breed	gruff	trike
volta	bonze	upsee	spoor	crack	arrah	breem	kraft	troke
volte	booze	upset	sprod	crick	crock	breer	trefa	wroke

b**r**i**l**l
brûlé
drill
drily
drôle
droll
dryly
frill
grill
krill
prole
proll
trild
trill
troll
trull
truly
urali
wryly
a**r**o**m**a
brame
breme
brume
crame
cramp
crême
crime
crimp
cromb
crome
crumb
crump
drama
drome
frame
fremd
frump
grama
grame
grime
grimy
groma
grume
prima
prime
primo
primp
primy
tramp
trema
tromp
trump
a**r**e**n**a
brand
brank
brent
brine
bring
brink
briny
brond
brunt
crane
crank
crena
crine
crone
cronk
crony
drank
drant
drent
drink
drone
drony
drunk
franc
frank
frena
frond
front
grand
grant
grind
grone
grunt
irony
krang
krans
kranz
kreng
krona
krone
orang
orant
prang
prank
prent
prink
print
prone
prong
prune
prunt
trant
trend
trine
trona
tronc
trone
trunk
urena
urent
urine
wring
wrong
wrung
yrent
a**r**b**o**r
argol
argon
argot
ariot
armor
arrow
arson
brood
brook
brool
broom
crook
croon
cruor
drook
drool
droop
ergon
ergot
error
Freon®
groof
groom
M-roof
Orion
orlop
prior
proof
trior
troop
try-on
urson
vroom
wroot
c**r**a**p**e
craps
crapy
crêpe
crept
crypt
drape
drupe
erupt
grape
graph
grapy
gripe
grope
grype
grypt
props
trape
tripe
trope
wrapt
yrapt
I**r**a**q**i
a**r**d**r**i
ard-ri
arere
brere
crare
crore
drere
frore
frorn
frory
prore
urari
a**r**i**s**e
arish
arose
brash
brass
brast
brisk
brose
brush
brust
crash
crass
cress
crest
crise
crisp
cross
crost
cruse
crush
crust
crusy
dress
drest
dross
druse
drusy
erase
erose
frass
fresh
frisk
frist
frost
frush
frust
grasp
grass
grese
grise
grist
grisy
gross
Irish
prase
presa
prese
press
prest
prise
prism
prose
prosy
pryse
trash
trass
tress
trist
truss
trust
tryst
wrast
wrest
wrist
a**r**ê**t**e
arett
broth
brute
crate
crith
crwth
Erato
frate
frati
frith
froth
grate
grith
grits
irate
orate
prate
praty
trite
troth
truth
urate
urite
wrate
wrath
write
wrote
wroth
a**r**c**u**s
argue
argus
arnut
croup
crout
drouk
fraud
fry-up
grouf
group
grout
kraut
orgue
proud
proul
trout
Ursus
vrouw
b**r**a**v**a
brave
bravi
bravo
breve
crave
cruve
drave
drive
drove
grave
gravy
greve
grove
preve
privy
prove
Provo
yrivd
b**r**a**w**l
brawn
braws
brown
crawl
crewe
crowd
crown
drawl
drawn
drown
frown
frowy
growl
grown
prawn
prowl
trawl
trews
wrawl
b**r**a**x**y
druxy
prexy
proxy
O**r**i**y**a
proyn
X-rays
b**r**a**z**e
brize
craze
crazy
croze
Druze
frize
frizz
froze
graze
grize
Oryza
prize
A**s**i**a**n
assai
assay
asway
eskar
essay
Isiac
Islam
Oscan
Oscar
oshac
pshaw
psoas
usual
d**s**o**b**o
p**s**y**c**h
a**s**i**d**e
a**s**h**e**n
asker
askew
aspen
asper
asses
asset
aster
esker
ester
islet
issei
osier
usher
usnea
O**s**a**g**e
Tsuga
usage
V-sign
A**s**d**i**c
aspic
astir
aswim
g-suit
osmic
ossia
ostia
e**s**i**l**e
istle
psalm
d**s**o**m**o
ysame
a**s**a**n**a
usen't
a**s**s**o**t
escot
estoc
estop
psyop
e**s**t**r**o
psora
usure
usurp
usury
a**s**c**u**s
astun
issue
pseud
a**t**l**a**s
atman
attap
attar
ethal
ottar
stead
steak
steal
steam
stean
stear
stoae
stoai
stoat
strad
strae
strag
strak
strap
straw
stray
U-trap
U-**t**u**b**e
s**t**a**c**k
stich
stick
stock
é**t**u**d**e
stade
stedd
stede
study
e**t**h**e**r
etwee
other
otter
steed
steek
steel
steem
steen
steep
steer
stied
sties
stoep
strep
strew
styed
styes
utter
s**t**a**f**f
stiff
stuff
é**t**a**g**e
stage
stagy
stogy
i**t**c**h**y
a**t**r**i**a
atrip
attic
ethic
ettin
staid
staig
stain
stair
steil
stein
stoic
stoit
stria
strid
strig
strip
a**t**o**k**e
stake
stoke
a**t**i**l**t
atoll
ettle
Itala
stal'd
stale
stalk
stall
stela
stele
stell
stilb
stile
still
stilt
stola
stole
stull
stulm
style
styli
stylo
utile
a**t**i**m**y
atomy
etyma
stamp
steme
stime
stimy
stoma
stomp
stump
styme
a**t**o**n**e
atony
ctene
stand
stane
stang
stank
stend
stent
sting
stink
stint
stond
stone
stong
stonk
stonn
stony
stung
stunk
stunt
e**t**h**o**s
stood
stook
stool
stoop
stoor
strop
strow

stroy	judas	juice	luxes	gurge	humid	husky	mummy	humpy
atopy	jugal	juicy	muley	judge	hutia	junky	pulmo	jumpy
étape	jumar	junco	murex	lunge	Kufic	lucky	queme	lumpy
staph	jural	kutch	mused	lungi	lucid	mucky	rummy	mumps
stept	jurat	lunch	muser	Lurgi	lupin	murky	rusma	pulpy
stipa	kulak	lurch	muset	muggy	lurid	musky	summa	puppy
stipe	kulan	mulch	muted	mulga	mucic	pucka	Suomi	purpy
stope	lunar	mulct	numen	mungo	mucid	pukka	tummy	quipo
stupa	mural	munch	ousel	nudge	mucin	pulka	turme	quipu
stupe	Musak	Musca	outed	outgo	mudir	punka	yummy	sumph
otary	Muzak®	Musci	outer	pudge	mujik	quake	bunny	tumpy
stare	nugae	mutch	ouzel	pudgy	music	quaky	burnt	turps
stark	pupae	ounce	pubes	puggy	musit	sulky	curny	burqa
starn	pupal	punce	puker	purge	nubia	Turki	dunno	burro
starr	quean	punch	puler	ruggy	oubit	tusky	dunny	burry
start	quoad	quack	Pulex	surge	ourie	yucky	funny	curry
stere	Qurân	quich	purée	surgy	pubic	yukky	guana	durra
stern	rudas	quick	puzel	vuggy	pubis	bugle	guano	fuero
stire	rumal	runch	queen	vulgo	pudic	build	gunny	furry
stirk	Ruman	succi	queer	aught	pugil	built	quant	guard
stirp	rural	sulci	quiet	buchu	pumie	bulla	quina	gurry
store	subah	Turco	ruler	bushy	Punic	bully	quine	hurra
stork	Sudan	yucca	rumen	cushy	pupil	burly	quint	hurry
storm	sugar	buddy	Rumex	duchy	purim	cully	quonk	kukri
story	sumac	cuddy	runed	gushy	purin	curly	ruing	kurre
sture	surah	curdy	rupee	hushy	putid	dully	runny	lubra
sturt	sural	fundi	suber	lushy	put-in	duple	suing	lucre
styre	surat	guide	super	musha	quail	duply	suint	lurry
uteri	tubae	gundy	tubed	mushy	quair	fugle	Sunna	mucro
U-turn	tubal	hurds	tuber	nucha	quoif	fully	Sunni	Munro
stash	tubar	muddy	tuned	oucht	quoin	Guelf	sunny	murra
ytost	yulan	Munda	tuner	ought	quoit	guild	tunny	murre
state	zupan	oundy	tupek	ouphe	Rubia	guile	buxom	murry
stoun	bubby	outdo	tutee	pushy	rubin	guilt	duroy	outré
stoup	bumbo	puddy	buffa	qui-hi	runic	gully	eusol	quark
stour	busby	ruddy	buffe	ruche	run-in	gurly	furol	quart
stout	cubby	suede	buffi	rushy	rupia	gusla	furor	quern
strum	fubby	auger	buffo	sushi	rutin	gusle	tuton	query
strut	gumbo	aurei	cuffo	audio	Sufic	gusli	guyot	quire
stave	hubby	buses	fuffy	audit	Sufis	guyle	humor	quirk
stive	jumbo	Butea	gulfy	aulic	tulip	hullo	jupon	quirt
stivy	jumby	buyer	huffy	aumil	tumid	hully	juror	sucre
stove	nubby	cubeb	luffa	auric	tunic	hurly	kudos	Sudra
stewy	outby	culet	puffy	auxin	tupik	murly	mucor	surra
stown	rugby	culex	quaff	bunia	bunje	nulla	muton	sutra
ataxy	rumba	cumec	quiff	burin	bunjy	pusle	pudor	tuart
ethyl	rumbo	cupel	ruffe	buy-in	ouija	qualm	put-on	buist
aurae	tubby	curer	surfy	cubic	bucko	quell	rumor	bulse
aural	turbo	cusec	tuffe	cubit	bucku	quill	run-on	bursa
bubal	bunce	cutey	turfy	Cufic	bulky	quilt	sudor	burse
buran	bunch	cuvée	budge	cumin	bunko	quoll	sutor	burst
Cuban	bunco	duper	buggy	cupid	burka	ruble	Tudor	bussu
curat	butch	duvet	bulge	curia	burke	rumly	tumor	cuish
ducal	culch	fumet	bulgy	curie	busky	sully	tutor	curse
ducat	curch	fusee	bungy	curio	ducks	surly	yupon	curst
dural	cutch	fuzee	burgh	cutie	ducky	tulle	bumph	dulse
eupad	dunce	gules	dungy	cut-in	dumka	dummy	bumpy	dunsh
fugal	dunch	julep	durgy	cutin	dumky	duomo	cuppa	durst
fural	dutch	luces	fudge	cutis	dusky	guimp	dumpy	fubsy
furan	guaco	Luger	fuggy	dulia	funky	gumma	duppy	fussy
gulag	gulch	lumen	fungi	fugie	hulky	gummy	gulph	guess
gular	hunch	Lurex	gunge	fusil	hunks	lumme	guppy	guest
human	hutch	luter	gungy	humic	hunky	lummy	humph	guise

gutsy	tutti	avert	swoln	awful	hymen	gyron
guyse	tutty	evert	'twill	dwaum	hyper	hyson
hurst	augur	every	twill	swoun	kyley	kyloe
hussy	durum	ivory	twilt	two-up	lycée	lysol
muist	Eurus	ovary	swami	awave	Pyrex®	nylon
mulsh	fucus	overt	swamp	'twixt	ryper	pylon
musse	fugue	avast	a-wing	aways	sycee	syboe
mussy	Fusus	avise	bwana	swayl	syker	sybow
nurse	Gueux	aviso	dwine	bwazi	syren	synod
pudsy	humus	kvass	owing	axial	syver	xylol
pulse	jugum	ovist	swang	exeat	tyler	zygon
purse	lupus	evite	swank	exact	tyned	gyppo
pursy	mucus	ovate	swine	exode	tyred	gyppy
pussy	put-up	avoué	swing	exude	xylem	lymph
quash	queue	avize	swink	oxide	nyaff	myope
quasi	Rubus	avyze	swone	excel	hypha	myops
quest	run-up	sweal	swung	exeem	hythe	nymph
quist	sun-up	swear	twang	exies	kythe	sylph
sudsy	tuque	sweat	twank	expel	lythe	aygre
tuism	curve	tweak	twine	oxter	sythe	Cymry
wurst	curvy	swack	twink	axoid	Tyche	hydra
aunty	guava	twice	twiny	oxlip	Typha	hydro
bunty	murva	swede	ewhow	axile	ayrie	lyart
busty	suave	a-week	swoon	exalt	cylix	myrrh
butte	vulva	aweel	swoop	exile	cynic	gypsy
butty	bunya	awned	swapt	exult	eyrie	kydst
cutto	butyl	awner	swept	ixtle	Eytie	Eyeti
cutty	Kuo-yü	owler	swipe	exeme	hylic	fytte
duett	quayd	owlet	swopt	exine	hyoid	lytta
dusty	queyn	owner	award	axiom	kylie	typto
furth	Surya	owsen	aware	extol	kylin	gyrus
fusty	buaze	sweel	awarn	ox-bot	kylix	Pyrus
gusto	buzzy	sweep	awmry	ox-bow	Kyrie	syrup
gutta	furze	sweer	awork	exert	lyric	sylva
gutty	furzy	sweet	dwarf	extra	lysin	xylyl
junta	fuzzy	tweed	sward	exist	lysis	Czech
junto	huzza	tweel	sware	ox-eye	myoid	Aztec
jutty	huzzy	'tween	swarf	bylaw	pyoid	izzet
kurta	kudzu	tweer	swarm	byway	pyxis	Uzbeg
lusty	muzzy	tweet	swart	cycad	sybil	Uzbek
mufti	avian	twier	swerf	cymar	typic	azygy
musth	uveal	twoer	swire	gynae	xylic	azoic
musty	evict	twyer	swirl	gyral	Xyris	ozeki
nutty	evade	swift	sword	hyrax	ayelp	azyme
punto	ivied	swage	swore	lyyar	cycle	ozone
punty	avail	owche	sworn	mynah	cyclo	azure
purty	avoid	await	'twere	pygal	gyeld	azurn
putti	ovoid	owrie	twerp	pyral	myall	azury
putto	evoke	swain	twire	rybat	myoma	izard
putty	avale	sweir	twirl	symar	pygmy	azote
quite	mvule	twain	twirp	typal	rymme	azoth
quits	ovolo	awake	awash	tyran	ayont	pzazz
quota	ovule	awoke	ewest	zygal	by-end	
quote	uvula	dwale	swash	sybbe	dying	
quoth	avant	dwalm	swish	lynch	eying	
quyte	Avena	dwell	Swiss	synch	gynny	
runty	avens	dwelt	twist	Hyads	hyena	
rusty	avine	kwela	aweto	hynde	hying	
rutty	evens	swale	swath	kynde	kyang	
suety	event	swaly	swats	tynde	lying	
suite	ovine	swell	swith	cyder	tying	
tuath	avion	swelt	swits	dykey	vying	
tufty	evhoe	swill	twite	hyleg	cyton	

bahada	pavane	datary	gambir	gaucho	pardie	raider	careen
bajada	rafale	galaxy	harbor	rancho	raddle	sadder	casein
balata	ramate	malady	jabber	sancho	randie	sander	casern
banana	ravage	panary	jamber	ear-cap	saddle	sawder	cave-in
batata	salade	papacy	nabber	madcap	waddie	wander	cavern
cabala	salame	salary	sambar	calcar	waddle	warder	fade-in
cabana	savage	vagary	sambur	cancer	wandle	zander	have-on
cañada	savate	bazazz	tamber	dancer	bandog	caddis	lateen
Carapa	takahe	pazazz	yabber	lancer	lapdog	bandit	ramean
Havana	tamale	balboa	iambus	lascar	wardog	pandit	Sabean
jacana	vacate	lambda	lay-bys	rancor	gardai	saidst	sateen
jataka	zarape	baobab	barbet	saucer	sandhi	landau	take-in
kabala	lalang	earbob	gag-bit	calces	haiduk	saddhu	tavern
kabaya	padang	iambic	gambet	caucus	caudal	may-dew	gazebo
kamala	parang	barbed	gambit	faeces	daedal	caudex	make-do
kanaka	calash	dabbed	hagbut	falces	fardel	baldly	sapego
karaka	camash	day-bed	rabbet	fasces	pardal	bawdry	fade-up
Malaga	gamash	nabbed	rabbit	fauces	sandal	hardly	make-up
mañana	paraph	tabbed	sabbat	lances	sardel	laidly	race-up
maraca	calami	tan-bed	talbot	mancus	vandal	law-day	rave-up
nagana	jawari	babble	hatbox	saccos	fandom	lay-day	take-up
palama	manati	bauble	haybox	catcht	mandom	man-day	career
panada	nagari	bawbee	jawbox	fat-cat	randem	mayday	fadeur
panama	safari	bawble	pay-box	faucet	random	pay-day	laveer
papaya	salami	cabbie	tar-box	lancet	tandem	Tagday	pasear
Paraná	tamari	dabble	babbly	mascot	Dardan	tawdry	cameos
samara	tatami	faible	carboy	ramcat	farden	camera	caress
satara	Wahabi	gabble	dawbry	waucht	garden	catena	jabers
tamara	carack	gamble	day-boy	Manchu	hadden	galena	kamees
Bayard	damask	garble	marbly	catchy	hagden	Ganesa	cadent
cafard	padauk	hamble	wambly	patchy	hagdon	kamela	caveat
canard	saxaul	jabble	fascia	talcky	hand-in	lagena	gayest
farand	Balaam	jambee	calcic	war-cry	harden	pakeha	jacent
hazard	napalm	lambie	calced	bardic	lardon	patera	lament
maraud	salaam	lay-bye	rancid	Dardic	madden	tapeta	latent
mazard	papain	marble	raucid	banded	maidan	valeta	latest
nasard	wabain	rabble	eatche	barded	maiden	zabeta	manent
navaid	catalo	ramble	gauche	candid	pardon	zareba	mayest
tabard	Galago	wabble	gaucie	gadded	randan	maleic	parent
tarand	kakapo	wamble	manche	handed	randon	fag-end	patent
vaward	lavabo	warble	mascle	landed	sadden	hareld	sayest
Banate	macaco	yabbie	Parcae	padded	warden	lag-end	talent
canapé	paramo	gas-bag	raucle	parded	nandoo	salewd	tavert
carafe	rabato	may-bug	caecal	sanded	nardoo	tag-end	bateau
damage	bazaar	rag-bag	cancel	wadded	vaudoo	wax-end	cadeau
eatage	camass	ratbag	faecal	warded	hard-up	barege	gâteau
façade	cavass	sag-bag	faucal	baddie	paid-up	camese	bakery
galage	harass	casbah	laical	caddie	bandar	carème	barely
garage	kavass	kasbah	marcel	candie	candor	facete	basely
gavage	naiads	jambok	parcel	candle	carder	galère	calefy
hamate	vakass	barbel	pascal	caudle	dander	gamete	eatery
karate	basalt	gambol	rancel	daddle	gadder	kabele	gaiety
lanate	caract	jambul	rascal	daidle	gander	manège	gamely
lavage	galant	carbon	tarcel	dandle	hander	paleae	gamesy
madame	karait	rabbin	caecum	dawdle	ladder	raceme	jadery
malate	naiant	bamboo	talcum	faddle	lander	sagene	lamely
manage	natant	gabbro	cancan	haddie	larder	sapele	lately
oarage	savant	yah-boo	falcon	handle	lauder	varech	madefy
palace	talant	barber	farcin	lac-dye	madder	tapeti	namely
palate	vacant	camber	garçon	laddie	mandir	rameal	napery
parade	tamanu	dabber	gascon	laldie	padder	vakeel	palely
parage	caranx	dauber	mascon	paddle	pandar	hareem	papery
pavage	canary	gabber	fascio	paidle	pander	baleen	rakery

rarefy	sagged	ranger	jaghir	habile	paging	labial	facies
rarely	tagged	saggar	Jashar	halide	paling	narial	ladies
safely	tanged	sagger	Jasher	halite	paring	parial	matins
safety	wagged	sangar	lasher	hamite	paving	racial	rabies
sagely	war-god	sauger	lather	karite	paying	radial	radius
samely	bangle	tagger	masher	labile	racing	samiel	sanies
sanely	bargee	yagger	rasher	larine	raging	Babism	Babist
tabefy	cangue	haggis	rather	malice	raking	barium	galiot
tamely	daggle	sargus	washer	marine	raping	favism	lariat
tawery	dangle	valgus	bathos	maxixe	raring	kalium	laxist
wafery	dargle	baggit	hachis	narine	rating	labium	malist
watery	fangle	catgut	laches	native	raving	laxism	Maoist
wavery	gadgie	caught	pathos	patine	rawing	Magism	Marist
yarely	gaggle	faggot	rachis	pavise	saving	Maoism	papist
Maffia	gangue	gadget	raphis	ranine	sawing	nanism	racist
raffia	gargle	garget	cachet	rapine	saying	Nazism	Ramist
baffle	haggle	haught	sachet	ratine	taking	papism	rapist
Caffre	jangle	maggot	cachou	ratite	taming	racism	sadist
gaufre	langue	naught	Pakhtu	ravine	tawing	radium	Samiot
raffle	maigre	parget	Pashtu	Sabine	taxing	Ramism	tanist
waffle	malgre	raught	bashaw	saline	wading	sadism	Taoist
yaffle	mangle	target	cashaw	samite	waking	Sapium	tapist
zaffre	maugre	taught	cashew	sasine	waning	Taoism	jabiru
bagful	paigle	waught	haw-haw	satire	waving	Valium®	cagily
barful	raggee	pangfu'	eathly	sative	waxing	banian	cavity
canful	raggle	gangly	gashly	savine	banish	camion	easily
earful	taigle	jangly	rashly	tamine	barish	cation	family
hatful	tangie	laughy	sashay	tamise	caliph	Fabian	gasify
jarful	tangle	mangey	cafila	vagile	Danish	fanion	hazily
lapful	waggle	margay	capita	valine	dawish	gabion	ladify
lawful	wangle	tangly	Carica	valise	eadish	Janian	laxity
manful	mangal	waggly	carina	wahine	famish	kalian	lazily
panful	mangel	Raphia	Dalila	walise	garish	kation	mazily
sapful	Targum	pathic	farina	tariff	harish	Latian	Nazify
vatful	jargon	washed	kafila	baaing	jadish	Magian	pacify
waeful	laggen	daphne	kamila	baking	lakish	malign	parity
halfen	laggin	lathee	la-di-da	basing	lamish	Marian	racily
samfoo	largen	mashie	lamina	bating	Lapith	nasion	ramify
gaffer	margin	pachak	manila	caking	latish	nation	rarity
gaufer	pangen	Gadhel	marina	caning	lavish	Parian	ratify
Kaffer	tangun	fathom	maxima	caring	marish	radian	salify
Kaffir	waggon	mayhem	patina	casing	oafish	ration	sanify
zaffer	wangan	pashim	sahiba	caving	palish	Sabian	sanity
haffet	wangun	sachem	salina	cawing	papish	Salian	satiny
haffit	bang-up	fat-hen	saliva	daring	pariah	Samian	vanity
carfax	hang-up	lathen	tahina	earing	parish	talion	warily
carfox	badger	machan	vagina	eating	radish	wanion	masjid
barfly	banger	Pathan	zariba	facing	rakish	Zabian	sanjak
day-fly	cadger	Sathan	maniac	fading	ravish	calico	garjan
gadfly	dagger	sazhen	manioc	gaming	rawish	caligo	gas-jar
mayfly	danger	washen	panisc	gaping	sakieh	casino	hanjar
saw-fly	gagger	wash-in	taxied	gating	vanish	Ladino	jamjar
bagged	ganger	Pakhto	varied	having	Cabiri	manito	fan-jet
banged	gauger	Pashto	barite	haying	tahini	matico	gas-jet
fagged	hangar	lash-up	camise	hazing	wakiki	magilp	ram-jet
fanged	hanger	mayhap	canine	jawing	wapiti	cahier	banjax
gagged	jaeger	wash-up	caribe	lacing	panick	caviar	tankia
hagged	jagger	basher	dacite	lading	panisk	cavier	backed
hanged	laager	bather	Danite	lawing	Daniel	pavior	hawked
jagged	lagger	Cathar	dative	laying	facial	rapier	marked
lagged	langur	dasher	facile	making	garial	varier	masked
nagged	manger	father	famine	maying	gavial	capias	narked
ragged	nagger	gather	gamine	naming		caries	racked

ranked	talker	saulge	ballet	mammae	maunna	pawner	barock
tacked	tanker	saulie	ballot	mammee	taenia	tanner	padouk
tanked	tasker	tailye	batlet	Palmae	tannic	vanner	paiock
vacked	walker	bablah	callet	malmag	zarnec	warner	pajock
cackle	wanker	nallah	camlet	warmth	canned	faints	yapock
darkie	yacker	pallah	carlot	haemal	damned	magnes	cagoul
darkle	yakker	wallah	eaglet	hammal	darned	Bannat	jarool
fankle	yanker	bailli	gablet	harmel	fanned	basnet	kagool
hackee	faikes	fallal	gallet	mahmal	hained	cannot	kagoul
hackle	sakkos	hallal	gas-lit	mammal	maenad	carnet	waboom
hankie	backet	sallal	haglet	wadmal	manned	gannet	baboon
hawkie	banket	vallum	hamlet	wadmol	pained	garnet	batoon
mackle	basket	caplin	harlot	hammam	tanned	magnet	cacoon
palkee	casket	fallen	haslet	badman	vanned	oak-nut	ganoin
parkee	gasket	fall-in	haulst	bagman	wanned	walnut	gazoon
rankle	hawkit	gallon	mallet	barman	faunae	larnax	lagoon
tackle	jacket	hallan	pallet	batman	jaunce	magnox	Mahoun
talkie	lasket	kaolin	raylet	cabman	jaunse	barney	maroon
wankle	market	lallan	sallet	caiman	launce	carney	racoon
Yankee	nacket	marlin	samlet	carman	paunce	dainty	ratoon
yankie	packet	maslin	tablet	cayman	pawnce	fainly	sagoin
haikai	racket	raglan	tallat	daemon	pawnee	fainty	saloon
kaikai	tacket	ratlin	tallet	daimen	raunge	gainly	manoao
Naskhi	darkey	Gallio	tallot	gammon	sarnie	jaunty	palolo
jackal	darkly	halloo	taslet	gasman	vaunce	mainly	saloop
barkan	hackly	call-up	varlet	haemin	pad-nag	maundy	favour
barken	hawkey	cat-lap	wallet	harman	gaunch	painty	labour
calkin	lackey	dallop	ballow	harmin	hainch	sarney	savour
catkin	lankly	earlap	callow	lawman	haunch	sawney	tabour
darken	parkly	gallop	fallow	layman	launch	Tannoy®	valour
gaskin	rankly	oar-lap	gallow	madman	paunch	vainly	vapour
harken	dahlia	gallop	hallow	mammon	raunch	dagoba	dadoes
malkin	halloa	oar-lap	mallow	ragman	tannah	macoya	dagoes
mawkin	paella	tail-up	matlow	salmon	cannel	Masora	famous
nankin	pallia	wallop	sallow	warman	carnal	pagoda	favous
napkin	lablab	bailer	tallow	daimio	darnel	payola	haloes
parkin	Gaelic	batler	wallow	warm-up	fannel	sapota	hamous
walk-in	Gallic	bawler	hallux	dammar	faunal	haboob	kaross
walk-on	garlic	caller	bailey	dammer	tarnal	day-old	patois
back-up	ballad	fabler	barley	farmer	wannel	gadoid	ramous
mark-up	balled	gaoler	bawley	gammer	magnum	ganoid	cahoot
backer	callid	hauler	faulty	hammer	painim	haloed	cavort
balker	fabled	jailer	galley	lammer	paynim	haloid	dacoit
banker	failed	jailor	parlay	mammer	cannon	laroid	dakoit
barker	gabled	mailer	parley	palmar	tannin	Samoed	far-out
calker	macled	nailer	railly	palmer	bagnio	cajole	galoot
canker	mailed	pallor	valley	rammer	catnap	capote	lavolt
cauker	marled	railer	vaulty	warmer	catnep	favose	lay-out
cawker	nailed	sailer	waylay	yammer	catnip	galore	mahout
dacker	palled	sailor	Y-alloy	lacmus	sannup	hamose	mazout
daiker	pallid	tailor	kalmia	Lammas	banner	lanose	pay-out
hanker	sailed	tatler	caimac	magmas	canner	parole	ragout
hawker	sallad	vallar	karmic	salmis	darner	pavone	way-out
janker	tabled	wailer	tarmac	wammus	dauner	radome	barony
lacker	tailed	waller	calmed	dammit	dawner	ramose	canopy
larker	walled	callus	dammed	mammet	earner	vamose	jalopy
marker	bailee	caules	jammed	marmot	fanner	far-off	paeony
masker	bailie	caulis	maimed	maumet	fawner	lay-off	parody
packer	faille	gallus	palmed	mawmet	gainer	pay-off	savory
parker	mallee	Majlis	rammed	haymow	garner	kalong	saxony
racker	pallae	Pallas	Talmud	calmly	lanner	sarong	yarpha
ranker	rallye	Rallus	warmed	warmly	mainor	galosh	calpac
tacker	sallee	ballat	lammie	Tammuz	manner	satori	capped

happed	yapper	tagrag	warray	passer	hantle	tattoo	mantis
lampad	yawper	jarrah	warrey	pauser	jantee	gas-tap	pastis
lapped	campus	barrel	cassia	raiser	mantle	baiter	saltus
mapped	carpus	carrel	nausea	cassis	pattée	banter	rat-tat
napped	gaupus	laurel	tarsia	lapsus	pattle	barter	tautit
rapped	gawpus	parral	Vaisya	lassos	rattle	baster	daftly
sapped	jaspis	parrel	parsec	passus	saithe	batter	earthy
tapped	kalpis	patrol	capsid	tarsus	tattie	baxter	fastly
warped	lampas	sacral	gassed	basset	tattle	cantar	gantry
cample	mawpus	saurel	halsed	saw-set	tawtie	canter	lastly
dapple	palpus	Bairam	Hassid	tasset	wattle	cantor	paltry
lappie	pampas	labrum	lapsed	wadset	rag-tag	captor	pantry
magpie	pappus	marram	passed	samshu	tautog	carter	partly
rappee	wampus	marrum	dassie	pad-saw	nautch	caster	pastry
sample	carpet	sacrum	falsie	causey	canthi	castor	saltly
taupie	jampot	vagrom	hassle	marshy	baetyl	cauter	tartly
tawpie	lappet	barren	laesie	nay-say	battel	darter	vastly
wampee	Rajput	garran	laisse	maltha	cartel	easter	wastry
hatpeg	rat-pit	garron	lassie	mantra	cautel	factor	datura
kalpak	sawpit	hadron	Parsee	mantua	dactyl	faitor	facula
carpal	tan-pit	latron	passée	Raetia	hartal	falter	garuda
carpel	tappet	macron	tassie	Tantra	mantel	faster	lacuna
lappel	tappit	matron	warsle	Cantab	martel	fatter	Laputa
palpal	pawpaw	napron	massif	Baltic	pastel	fautor	macula
rappel	damply	natron	taisch	haptic	pastil	gaiter	manuka
wampum	barque	patron	causal	lastic	santal	garter	masula
dampen	basque	warran	damsel	lactic	wastel	gas-tar	mazuma
happen	caique	warren	eassel	mantic	bantam	halter	natura
hatpin	calque	barrio	eassil	mastic	factum	hatter	papula
jampan	casque	hair-do	hansel	nastic	fantom	kantar	radula
parpen	haique	Karroo	haysel	nautic	pactum	laster	ranula
sampan	Jacque	larrup	pausal	tactic	partim	latter	tabula
sanpan	manqué	satrap	ransel	batted	tam-tam	martyr	valuta
sappan	marque	Labrus	tahsil	casted	barton	master	Varuna
taipan	masque	labrys	tarsal	fantad	batten	matter	caduac
tampon	sacque	Laurus	tarsel	fantod	caftan	natter	salued
tarpan	saique	madras	tassel	fatted	canton	palter	valued
tarpon	garrya	narras	varsal	gaited	captan	panter	cayuse
yaupon	latria	tarras	vassal	hatted	carton	parter	lagune
Sappho	Sauria	Taurus	balsam	malted	Caxton	paster	macule
camper	capric	walrus	hansom	mantid	danton	pastor	manure
capper	fabric	barrat	passim	masted	fan-tan	patter	mature
carper	iatric	barret	ransom	matted	fasten	rafter	nasute
damper	matric	cabrit	causen	parted	fatten	ranter	nature
dapper	tanrec	carrat	damson	patted	harten	raptor	papule
gasper	tauric	carrot	kamsin	raited	hasten	raster	parure
hamper	barred	garret	parson	ratted	kaftan	ratter	rasure
harper	darred	garrot	raisin	salted	kanten	saeter	razure
jasper	garred	hairst	ramson	tasted	latten	salter	salute
lapper	haired	labret	Samson	wafted	marten	santir	Baluch
mapper	hatred	parrot	sarsen	wanted	martin	santur	galuth
napper	jarred	sap-rot	camsho	warted	panton	sartor	kabuki
pamper	manred	tabret	catsup	battle	pantun	tartar	ramuli
pauper	marred	waurst	caesar	battue	partan	taster	saluki
ramper	paired	barrow	causer	cantle	parton	tatter	canuck
rapper	ramrod	farrow	falser	castle	patten	wafter	Kanuck
rasper	sacred	harrow	halser	cattle	rattan	waiter	casual
sapper	tarred	marrow	hassar	daftie	ratten	wanter	manual
tamper	warred	narrow	hawser	dartle	ratton	waster	vacuum
tapper	wax-red	tarrow	kaiser	dartre	santon	yatter	Paduan
vamper	bajree	yarrow	mahsir	dautie	tartan	cactus	Papuan
wapper	cabrie	matrix	Mauser	dawtie	tauten	cantos	saguin
warper	faerie	fairly	parser	Fantee	wanton	cantus	Saturn

taguan	lawyer	'sblood	schema	scummy	scurvy	eddied	weyard
baguio	magyar	oblong	sclera	iconic	Scotia	admire	wezand
Basuto	sawyer	abloom	accend	scenic	acetic	advice	aerate
lanugo	raiyat	abvolt	screed	sconce	Scotic	advise	became
gazump	gay-you	ubique	accede	acanth	scathe	sdaine	bedaze
faquir	larynx	sbirri	achene	acinus	scythe	edging	behave
jaguar	ladyfy	aboral	ocreae	econut	scatch	eddish	bejade
valuer	razzia	Oberon	scheme	acknow	scotch	oddish	belace
maquis	dazzle	sbirro	sclere	scanty	scutch	addict	belate
kaputt	razzle	Iberis	screak	echoic	schtik	adrift	bename
yaourt	hamzah	aburst	schelm	accord	acetal	Idoist	berate
Basutu	matzah	uberty	scream	echoed	acetyl	oddity	betake
maguey	matzoh	abased	screen	ecbole	scutal	odd-job	beware
raguly	banzai	abuser	access	eclose	scutum	addled	cerate
salvia	ranzel	abated	accent	ochone	acater	Idolum	cetane
carved	Tarzan	obital	accept	scrobe	scoter	Idolon	debase
salve'd	mahzor	abator	octett	T-cloth	acates	Adamic	debate
valved	panzer	obiter	scient	octopi	scatty	odd-man	decade
varved	aboard	abatis	yclept	o'clock	Scotty	Adonia	decane
garvie	abraid	abattu	ochery	accoil	accuse	Adonic	decare
larvae	ablate	abound	screwy	school	acture	Edenic	deface
halvah	ablaze	absurd	scuffy	schorl	scouse	Adonai	defame
Jahveh	abrade	obtund	Scogan	scroll	scruze	Adonis	dégagé
Yahveh	oblate	ybound	scried	scrowl	scruff	adsorb	delate
carvel	obtain	abduce	accite	scroop	scouth	addoom	derate
larval	abdabs	abjure	acmite	echoer	actual	adjoin	female
marvel	ablaut	obdure	active	across	scruto	adoors	Hecate
valval	oblast	objure	scribe	echoes	scrump	eddoes	hexane
varvel	abbacy	obtuse	scrike	T-cross	octuor	odious	legate
carven	obeche	ablush	scrine	accost	schuss	adroit	let-a-be
mauvin	abacus	abouts	scrive	schout	acquit	idiocy	menace
calver	ibices	abduct	aching	ectopy	occult	adipic	ménage
carver	abided	abrupt	acting	scopae	schuit	adorer	metage
halver	ibidem	ibexes	scaith	scyphi	schuyt	odds-on	negate
salver	obtend	obeyer	tchick	ice-pan	scrunt	adytum	pedate
salvor	abrégé	achage	schism	scapus	occupy	editor	pelage
taiver	abseil	ice-axe	action	ochrea	scaury	adduce	pesade
valvar	abbess	octane	schizo	scoria	scowth	adjure	rebate
waiver	obsess	octave	scrimp	scarab	ectype	adduct	reface
calves	abject	sclate	schist	sciroc	scryde	adjust	regale
canvas	absent	sclave	script	acarid	scryne	befana	relate
halves	object	scrape	acuity	accrue	scryer	gelada	remade
naevus	obtect	scraye	acajou	écarté	scazon	Gemara	remake
parvis	obtest	sclaff	achkan	écurie	Eddaic	petara	rename
tan-vat	obvert	ack-ack	scilla	scarce	adward	retama	resale
jarvey	yblent	acrawl	Scylla	scarre	ideaed	terata	retake
savvey	ybrent	scrawl	scaled	scerne	adnate	zenana	sea-ape
bagwig	ubiety	scrawm	scalae	scorse	ideate	bedaub	sebate
earwig	oblige	octavo	sculle	scarth	'sdeath	decarb	sedate
talweg	abeigh	éclair	ocelli	scorch	admass	aefald	senate
Yahweh	obeism	Octans	schlep	octroi	edible	belaud	serape
earwax	obiism	octant	ocular	ice-run	adverb	demand	sesame
paxwax	obsign	sceatt	scalar	scarer	addend	herald	sewage
calxes	ablins	occamy	scaler	scorer	adread	petard	tenace
baryta	oboist	ice-bag	ocelot	acarus	adhere	regard	velate
satyra	abolla	icebox	sculpt	Acorus	advene	relaid	behalf
sayyid	abulia	scabby	scolex	Scarus	addeem	remand	serang
haüyne	obelus	acacia	accloy	accrew	Idaean	repaid	bedash
Kabyle	obolus	icicle	schmoe	ochrey	adieus	repand	detach
papyri	obi-man	ice-cap	scampi	scarey	advent	resaid	Pesach
banyan	Abroma	acedia	scamel	scarry	advert	retard	rehash
baryon	absorb	acidic	acumen	scurfy	adieux	reward	seraph
canyon	abroad	eczema	iceman	scurry	adagio	wesand	teraph

decani	belamy	tercio	herden	Aeneid	serein	tepefy	weight
Dewali	denary	Velcro®	leaden	behead	Verein	venery	gewgaw
dewani	fegary	red-cap	lead-in	beheld	wedeln	deific	peshwa
debark	legacy	sea-cap	ledden	defend	Herero	leafed	method
demark	petary	teacup	redden	depend	hereto	sexfid	lethee
reback	senary	de-icer	reeden	jereed	teredo	neaffe	rechie
remark	telary	fencer	tendon	legend	beweep	sea-fog	teehee
repack	tetany	mercer	send-up	nereid	meneer	keffel	sea-hog
becall	bezazz	cercus	bedder	remead	meteor	netful	bethel
befall	cembra	hep-cat	bender	remeid	rehear	penful	lethal
bemaul	jerboa	mercat	deader	reread	rêveur	pepful	methyl
bewail	terbic	sea-cat	deodar	tele-ad	sea-ear	deafen	seghol
derail	nebbed	tercet	feeder	bemete	veneer	sea-fan	derham
detail	red-bud	sea-cow	fender	delete	Cereus	heifer	pelham
devall	seabed	beachy	gelder	hexene	Jewess	reefer	pea-hen
jezail	tebbad	descry	gender	kebele	recess	sea-fir	sephen
mesail	webbed	leachy	header	recede	revers	perfet	reship
mezail	feeble	peachy	leader	redeye	sevens	Ceefax®	aether
recall	kebbie	reechy	lender	remede	behest	sea-fox	hether
rerail	leg-bye	tetchy	melder	renege	bepelt	belfry	kephir
retail	pebble	vetchy	mender	retene	bereft	deafly	lecher
serail	remble	serdab	needer	revere	bewept	deffly	menhir
tenail	Seabee	geodic	pedder	secede	cement	perfay	nether
becalm	semble	herdic	reader	Selene	deceit	wet-fly	pether
cedarn	bedbug	Wendic	redder	sememe	decent	zeugma	Senhor
demain	tea-bag	beaded	reeder	serene	defeat	Belgic	tether
detain	lebbek	bedded	render	severe	defect	begged	wether
regain	nebbuk	bended	seeder	terete	deject	legged	zephyr
remain	reebok	gelded	sender	vegete	dement	menged	Tethys
retain	gerbil	headed	tedder	venewe	desert	pegged	red-hat
legato	herbal	leaded	tender	hereof	detect	sea-god	red-hot
melano	jerbil	reeded	Veadar	sea-egg	detent	sedged	tewhit
pedalo	verbal	seeded	vender	secesh	detest	wedged	heehaw
rebato	sea-bun	sended	vendor	Tebeth	devest	beagle	nephew
decamp	Berber	tedded	weeder	seseli	gerent	dengue	hegira
revamp	Herbar	tended	welder	bedeck	hereat	feague	hejira
repair	member	wedded	weldor	nebeck	recent	gee-gee	jemima
sea-air	hen-bit	weeded	vendis	rebeck	recept	league	medina
dedans	sea-bat	wended	re-edit	zebeck	refect	meagre	Nerita
lemans	dew-bow	beadle	verdet	bedell	regent	reggae	Peziza
megass	Bembex	cendré	verdit	befell	regest	teagle	regina
repass	peg-box	heddle	meadow	cereal	reheat	Teague	retina
bejant	red-box	meddle	deadly	merell	reject	wedgie	vesica
bezant	feebly	need-be	heyday	newell	relent	beegah	zeriba
decant	pebbly	needle	lewdly	reheel	repeat	length	celiac
defast	sea-boy	peddle	needly	repeal	repent	beigel	heliac
depart	sea-cob	perdie	verdoy	resell	reseat	tergal	begild
desalt	deuced	perdue	genera	retell	resect	red-gum	begird
hexact	fenced	reddle	geneva	reveal	resent	tergum	behind
levant	peacod	tendre	Hedera	sea-eel	revert	pen-gun	belied
nefast	fescue	vendee	oedema	beseem	revest	beggar	defied
pedant	rescue	vendue	pereia	beteem	sedent	hedger	denied
pesant	seiche	red-dog	peseta	redeem	select	kedger	levied
pezant	cercal	sea-dog	pesewa	telesm	détenu	ledger	period
recant	mescal	keddah	Reseda	bemean	réseau	legger	rebind
recast	pencel	zendik	semeia	Berean	teledu	leiger	relied
redact	pencil	feodal	Seneca	beseen	celery	lenger	remind
repast	tercel	feudal	senega	decern	hereby	merger	renied
secant	beacon	sendal	telega	demean	heresy	seggar	rewind
sejant	deacon	beldam	terefa	herein	merely	venger	aedile
tenant	leucin	seldom	veleta	hereon	remedy	verger	bedide
tewart	percen	deaden	zereba	Nemean	revery	height	belike
zelant	re-echo	head-on	reverb	secern	severy	keight	belive

bemire	sewing	relier	reckan	heeler	leg-man	kernel	retold
beside	teeing	senior	reckon	heller	merman	pennal	reword
betide	vexing	verier	weaken	keeler	met-man	regnal	second
betime	besigh	bekiss	welkin	mealer	penman	ternal	aerobe
bêtise	ceriph	cecils	beaker	medlar	red-man	vennel	become
cerise	fetich	demiss	decker	pedlar	seaman	vernal	before
cerite	fetish	genius	jerker	peeler	sermon	weanel	begone
debile	Jewish	medius	keeker	reeler	tegmen	Memnon	behote
decide	nebish	nelies	leaker	sealer	vermin	pennon	behove
décime	newish	regius	pecker	seller	yeoman	rennin	Belone
defile	perish	remiss	seeker	tellar	yeomen	lean-to	belove
define	relish	series	becket	teller	yes-man	deaner	decode
delice	seriph	begift	reskew	Mejlis	beamer	henner	decoke
demise	zenith	begirt	bed-key	peplos	reamer	keener	démodé
deride	gemini	delict	feckly	peplus	seamer	kenner	demote
derive	Yezidi	demist	kecksy	Tellus	seemer	penner	denote
desine	medick	depict	meekly	leglet	teamer	seiner	depone
desire	aerial	desist	weakly	pellet	termer	tenner	depose
device	Belial	dewitt	weekly	reflet	termor	feints	devote
devise	denial	heriot	realia	reglet	dermis	tennis	genome
feline	fecial	legist	Aeolic	vellet	Geomys	bennet	hexose
ferine	ferial	Nesiot	celled	zealot	Hermes	ben-nut	ketone
levite	fetial	oecist	gelled	bellow	Jeames	dennet	merome
Medise	genial	relict	heeled	fellow	kermes	gennet	metope
nerine	medial	resist	keeled	mellow	kermis	jennet	perone
nerite	menial	sexist	peeled	reflow	Termes	kennet	peyote
pelite	mesial	Vedist	sealed	sea-law	vermes	Nernst	rebore
penile	penial	verist	veiled	yellow	vermis	peanut	re-done
petite	refill	review	cellae	deflex	besmut	peinct	remote
rebite	retial	meninx	felloe	reflex	cermet	rennet	remove
recipe	serial	bepity	jeelie	reflux	fewmet	sennet	repone
recite	venial	cecity	keelie	deploy	holmet	sennit	repose
redlae	xenial	dewily	mealie	fealty	hermit	begnaw	resole
refine	aecium	eerily	wellie	lealty	pelmet	dernly	revoke
régime	cerium	ferity	peg-leg	medley	permit	keenly	setose
regive	cesium	geminy	redleg	mellay	sea-mat	leanly	veloce
relide	helium	lenify	Beulah	o'erlay	semmit	meanly	venose
reline	Medism	lenity	fellah	ro ally	sea-maw	melney	behoof
relive	medium	levity	health	really	sea-mew	teensy	let-off
remise	merism	verify	keblah	realty	seemly	teenty	set-off
repine	Nerium	verily	sealch	replay	termly	fedora	belong
reside	sepium	verity	sealgh	dermic	hernia	femora	debosh
resile	sexism	Seljuk	wealth	fehmic	neb-neb	hebona	zeroth
re-site	tedium	deejay	bedlam	vehmic	pen-nib	Pecora	neroli
retire	Vedism	beaked	beflum	deemed	fennec	pelota	bemock
revile	verism	decked	peplum	desmid	neanic	redowa	betook
revise	xenium	necked	replum	gemmed	genned	remora	retook
revive	benign	peaked	vellum	helmed	kenned	Sencdora	rework
rewire	Delian	recked	berlin	hemmed	leaned	serosa	befool
sea-ice	design	deckle	Ceylon	red-mad	Leonid	xeroma	befoul
sedile	Fenian	heckle	leglan	teamed	penned	desorb	behowl
Semite	legion	keckle	leglen	gemmae	Pernod®	resorb	bemoil
senile	lesion	reekie	leglin	hermae	Seanad	heroic	ben-oil
teniae	median	reskue	merlin	dermal	veined	behold	betoil
Venice	mesian	selkie	merlon	vermil	beanie	beyond	defoul
venire	region	Neskhi	replan	desman	meanie	devoid	reboil
venite	resign	seckel	vellon	fenman	meinie	keloid	recoil
belief	medico	teckel	dewlap	gemman	peenge	new-old	retool
relief	merino	beckon	cellar	gemmen	pennae	peloid	sea-owl
besing	megilp	jerkin	dealer	german	séance	record	befoam
hewing	defier	meeken	feeler	germen	beenah	reload	deform
hexing	denier	merkin	feller	germin	fennel	remoud	megohm
seeing	métier	perkin	healer	hetman	kennel	resold	reform

bemoan	semple	Leerie	bewray	lessor	fettle	beat-up	vertex
besoin	sempre	pearce	dearly	Mensur	feutre	peg-top	centry
ceroon	teepee	peerie	defray	sensor	gentle	pent-up	deathy
dehorn	temple	retree	hearsy	teaser	jestee	redtop	deftly
heroin	weepie	reurge	hearty	tensor	keltie	beater	featly
heroon	sea-pig	searce	near-by	verser	kettle	bestar	gently
reborn	peepul	serrae	nearly	census	leetle	bestir	gentry
rejoin	pen-pal	terrae	pearly	lenses	leftie	better	heathy
renown	bedpan	lea-rig	rearly	menses	lettre	bettor	meetly
seroon	deepen	dearth	verrey	Messrs	meathe	center	neatly
zeloso	hempen	hearth	yearly	mewses	mestee	debtor	nextly
recoup	hen-pen	search	geisha	sepsis	mettle	dexter	peltry
bezoar	key-pin	bedral	Persic	versus	nestle	felter	pertly
detour	reopen	ferrel	hersed	bed-sit	nettle	fester	sentry
devoir	sea-pen	neural	jessed	eel-set	pestle	fetter	vestry
devour	weapon	petrel	new-sad	tea-set	pettle	fewter	beluga
memoir	helper	petrol	seised	verset	seethe	getter	Betula
retour	Hesper	retral	sensed	leasow	settee	heater	cedula
tenour	keeper	tetryl	versed	seesaw	settle	hector	cesura
velour	kemper	verrel	heaste	feisty	tee-tee	jester	fecula
betoss	Keuper	betrim	jessie	jersey	teethe	kelter	ferula
heroes	leaper	megrim	keksye	kersey	tentie	lector	medusa
Merops	peeper	retrim	lessee	measly	testee	lentor	mezuza
serous	pepper	hen-run	measle	reasty	ventre	letter	nebula
venous	reaper	Herren	pensée	reesty	vertue	mentor	regula
vetoes	semper	neuron	persue	yeasty	cestui	nectar	remuda
besort	temper	perron	deasil	bertha	cental	Nestor	tegula
decoct	vesper	serran	mensal	Dectra	dental	neuter	benumb
dégoût	weeper	Terran	pensel	tertia	dentel	pelter	fecund
dehort	yelper	weirdo	pensil	Celtic	dentil	pester	gerund
deport	delphs	bedrop	teasel	gestic	festal	petter	refund
detort	herpes	rewrap	versal	hectic	lentil	pewter	retund
devout	bespat	bearer	vessel	Keltic	meatal	rector	secund
get-out	bespit	hearer	weasel	lentic	mental	reiter	aemule
let-out	bespot	jeerer	jetsam	Lettic	rectal	renter	Beaune
refoot	despot	nearer	jetsom	pectic	rental	rester	bemuse
report	keppit	rearer	pensum	peptic	septal	sector	ceruse
repost	sexpot	tearer	semsem	septic	ventil	setter	cesure
resort	tea-pot	terror	sensum	belted	vestal	teeter	deduce
retort	deeply	wearer	geason	bestad	centum	tenter	defuse
revolt	sea-pay	cerris	jetson	bestud	mentum	tester	defuze
set-out	teapoy	debris	kelson	betted	rectum	tetter	deluce
betony	jerque	degras	lessen	debted	restem	vector	delude
felony	ferric	derris	lesson	heated	septum	venter	deluge
gelosy	metric	nebris	messan	heptad	beaten	welter	demure
gemony	tenrec	serras	nelson	letted	dentin	wester	denude
lemony	betrod	Sèvres	peason	melted	deuton	yester	depute
melody	feared	terras	pepsin	netted	jetton	centos	ferule
memory	geared	berret	person	pentad	lenten	certes	heaume
pelory	Hebrid	ferret	reason	petted	lepton	cestus	jejune
leipoa	meered	learnt	season	retted	melton	gentes	legume
besped	metred	pearst	seisin	seated	nekton	meatus	nebulé
helped	retrod	regret	telson	teated	newton	rectus	nebule
leaped	seared	searat	tenson	tented	pecten	set-tos	peruke
lepped	tetrad	secret	ven'son	vented	pectin	testes	peruse
neaped	beurré	terret	versin	vested	seston	testis	rebuke
pea-pod	dearie	territ	mess-up	vetted	sextan	vestas	recule
repped	decree	wet-rot	censer	wetted	sexton	septet	recure
deepie	degree	decrew	censor	beetle	teston	sestet	recuse
kelpie	féerie	Hebrew	geyser	berthe	Teuton	sextet	reduce
kemple	George	redraw	keasar	centre	weeten	bestow	refuge
people	hearie	redrew	leaser	certie	gentoo	dentex	refuse
sea-pie	hearse	betray	lesser	debtee		tettix	refute

relume	serval	aflame	ignite	Ghebre	sheers	chikor	shimmy
repure	vervel	efface	ageing	thible	shiest	choker	thumby
repute	weevil	affair	agoing	chibol	shyest	chukar	whimmy
resume	heaven	offcut	ogling	Theban	threat	chukor	whimsy
résumé	Hesvan	off-day	aguish	Gheber	cheeky	shaker	khanga
retuse	kelvin	afield	ogrish	Thebes	cheery	shikar	thanna
secure	leaven	offend	ageism	Shebat	cheesy	chokey	phenic
seduce	verven	effere	egoism	thibet	sheeny	Shelta	phonic
tenure	beaver	effete	Ugrian	chubby	sheepy	Thalia	shined
velure	delver	afresh	ageist	shabby	sheety	thulia	chance
venule	heaver	affeer	egoist	cha-cha	wheely	cholic	change
bepuff	nerver	effeir	egoity	chacma	wheezy	childe	Chinee
rebuff	peever	afters	uglify	chicha	chafer	chylde	shinne
returf	reaver	affect	uglily	Thecla	shofar	shelve	thence
bebung	reiver	afreet	eggler	chicle	chaffy	khalif	whence
bedung	server	effect	egally	phocae	chuffy	chilli	whinge
besung	weaver	eftest	agamic	thecae	shifty	phalli	chinch
beduck	weever	afghan	ogamic	chichi	whiffy	shalli	thanah
begunk	beeves	affied	agamid	shtchi	chigoe	thalli	phenol
debunk	delves	affine	agenda	thecal	chigre	tholoi	phenyl
becurl	leaves	office	agonic	chicon	chagan	phylum	phonal
refuel	pelves	effing	egence	whacko	shogun	whilom	rhinal
sequel	pelvis	offing	eggnog	shucks	shaggy	chalan	khanum
sexual	selves	offish	agency	checky	Shaiva	choler	phonon
beduin	velvet	affirm	egency	chicly	sheila	thaler	thin'un
beguin	vervet	effigy	ogdoad	thicky	chaise	whaler	Shinto
repugn	cervix	off-key	ignore	whacky	choice	pholas	chenar
return	lenvoy	afflux	ugsome	khodja	Shiite	tholos	chinar
sequin	peavey	efflux	ignomy	rhodic	shrike	tholus	shiner
tea-urn	renvoy	afford	agapae	chided	shrine	whiles	thenar
tenuto	redwud	afloat	Egeria	shaded	shrive	chalet	whiner
repulp	deawie	afront	agaric	shaduf	theine	khalat	chinks
tenues	peewee	effort	agorot	chadar	thrice	khilat	whenas
tenuis	wee-wee	offput	egesta	chador	thrive	shalot	chenet
bedust	meawes	affrap	kgotla	chider	thyine	whilst	why-not
deduct	peewit	affret	agouta	shoder	sheikh	chalky	chenix
degust	key-way	affray	agouti	Rhodes	shyish	chilly	chancy
Jesuit	leeway	offset	ogival	shadow	shriek	shelly	chanty
penult	seaway	effuoc	agryze	shoddy	shrink	shelly	chinky
redult	deixis	Q-fever	agazed	chaeta	shtick	shelty	chunky
reluct	bedyed	afawld	phrase	phaeic	shrill	shelvy	phoney
requit	bedyde	affyde	sheave	chield	thrill	whally	shandy
result	desyne	Aglaia	theave	shield	chrism	whelky	shanny
Telugu	re-type	iguana	thrave	shrewd	Shiism	whilly	shanty
beauty	Aegypt	agname	wheare	thread	thairm	wholly	shindy
decury	fezzed	agnate	thrang	cheese	shairn	ahimsa	shinny
deputy	bezzle	agnail	sheath	pheere	shrimp	rhumba	shinty
nebuly	heezie	ignaro	thrash	pheese	theirs	chemic	thingy
penury	teazle	aghast	shrank	pheeze	thrips	rhymed	thinly
rebury	benzal	egg-box	thwack	phoebe	Christ	shamed	whinny
pelvic	benzil	eggcup	thrall	thieve	shrift	rhombi	chintz
fervid	benzol	Agadah	chiasm	threne	theist	thymol	chroma
heaved	benzyl	agreed	thrawn	wheeze	thrift	shaman	shroud
leaved	meazel	agrégé	chiaus	thresh	thrist	chimer	shrowd
nerved	teazel	egress	shears	shreek	chukka	rhymer	choose
peeved	seizin	ogress	she-ass	shreik	Shakta	shamer	chrome
reeved	tenzon	eggery	'sheart	shtetl	shiksa	shamus	shrove
revved	weazen	agogic	thwart	phlegm	choked	Themis	throne
weaved	geezer	agnise	phrasy	Phleum	shaked	thymus	throve
oeuvre	seizer	agrise	sheafy	cheero	Shakti	chemmy	throwe
renvoi	fezzes	agrize	shoaly	threap	shekel	chummy	shroff
devvel	afeard	aguise	phobia	threep	shaken	shammy	throng
nerval	afraid	aguize	phobic	cheers		shamoy	whoosh

dhooti	chorus	whiten	vimana	vicary	fitché	riddle	lineal
she-oak	pharos	ghetto	bicarb	vivary	miscue	tiddle	pineal
phloem	Bharat	whatso	ligand	bizazz	litchi	windle	pileum
thrown	charet	rhetor	lizard	pizazz	fiscal	pie-dog	live-in
chromo	thirst	whites	ribald	limbec	tincal	dik-dik	pigeon
throat	thorax	chatty	riband	niobic	nincom	Mindel	side-on
choosy	charry	chitty	ribaud	air-bed	nincum	tindal	wigeon
dhooly	cherry	whitey	rizard	big-bud	sitcom	diadem	wivern
phooey	cherty	should	visaed	dibbed	viscum	dirdum	cicero
theory	chirpy	chaufe	vizard	disbud	niacin	wisdom	line-up
chapka	gharry	chouse	wisard	fibbed	oilcan	bidden	pile-up
shaped	sharny	chauff	wizard	jibbed	piecen	Diodon	diseur
chypre	sherry	chough	binate	limbed	siccan	gilden	fineer
rhaphe	shirty	sheuch	dilate	nibbed	tin-can	hidden	linear
chapel	shorty	sheugh	finale	nimbed	viscin	linden	biceps
chopin	thirty	shough	fixate	pig-bed	zircon	midden	citess
shapen	thorny	though	hidage	ribbed	gilcup	milden	cizers
shippo	wherry	thrush	kinase	dibble	hiccup	ridden	divers
shaper	whirry	wheugh	libate	dimble	air-car	sindon	pileus
chappy	Phasma	shrunk	ligate	fimble	circar	Hindoo	vivers
chippy	phasic	chaunt	linage	jirble	kit-car	wind-up	bident
choppy	physic	thrust	lipase	kibble	mincer	bidder	bisect
shoppy	Chasid	rheumy	micate	liable	piecer	binder	digest
whippy	phased	shaved	mid-age	nibble	pincer	cinder	direct
cheque	chassé	shavie	milage	nimble	siccar	didder	divert
chequy	chasse	shovel	mirage	timbre	sircar	finder	divest
charta	chaste	thivel	pipage	viable	wincer	gilder	eident
chorea	ghesse	cheven	pirate	wimble	circus	girder	piment
choria	bhisti	chevin	rivage	kit-bag	discus	hidder	rident
dharma	chesil	shaven	silage	Liebig	Pisces	hinder	silent
dharna	chisel	shivoo	silane	jibbah	viscus	kidder	Tibert
dhurra	chosen	shaver	tirade	kirbeh	gib-cat	lieder	virent
khurta	Xhosan	shiver	tisane	gimbal	Kitcat	minder	wisent
sharia	physio	shover	vidame	timbal	tib-cat	pinder	cicely
sheria	chaser	chivvy	visage	gibbon	tip-cat	sirdar	cidery
sherpa	phases	showed	vivace	Lisbon	bitchy	tinder	fikery
shirra	phasis	thewed	pilaff	ribbon	fitchy	wilder	finely
cherub	rhesus	chowri	siwash	bibber	hitchy	winder	finery
choric	theses	shewel	Divali	dibber	pitchy	windas	likely
chared	thesis	thowel	Diwali	disbar	wincey	mildew	lively
ahorse	whisht	shower	miladi	fibber	zincky	window	livery
charge	chasmy	thawer	eirack	gibber	windac	fiddly	misery
choree	chesty	thewes	hijack	jibber	gilded	kindly	nicely
thorpe	ghosty	chewet	air-arm	libber	girded	midday	nicety
thyrse	whisky	chowry	disarm	limber	kidded	mildly	ninety
wharve	chatta	rhexis	misaim	mimbar	lidded	six-day	nitery
kharif	whatna	they're	dizain	minbar	minded	tiddly	oilery
sherif	phatic	they've	gitano	timber	misdid	vildly	pinery
church	photic	they'll	mikado	air-bus	ridded	cinema	rifely
Thorah	rhotic	wheyey	virago	Limbus	rinded	kinema	ripely
gharri	thetic	rhizic	mid-air	nimbus	tinded	pineta	rivery
thyrsi	thatch	phizog	vitals	gibbet	winded	Vipera	sinewy
bharal	thetch	ghazal	aidant	tidbit	birdie	viséed	tigery
choral	chital	ghazel	dicast	titbit	diddle	bireme	tilery
Charon	rhythm	Bimana	dikast	nimbly	dièdre	misère	timely
shoran	chaton	cicada	libant	Riccia	dildoe	Nicene	titely
thoron	chitin	cicala	bigamy	kincob	dindle	picene	vilely
chi-rho	chiton	gitana	binary	diacid	fiddle	silene	vinery
cherup	photon	pirancda	digamy	minced	girdle	sirene	vively
sharer	phyton	piraya	Hilary	viscid	kiddle	kilerg	widely
shorer	rhyton	Pitaka	litany	zinced	kindle	ripeck	wifely
charas	shut-in	pitara	milady	circle	middle	cineol	winery
Charis	whaten	vihara	piracy	fiacre	piddle	eisell	wisely

piaffe	zingel	mishmi	tibiae	aikido	silken	riglin	airman
piffle	lingam	Tishri	virile	libido	simkin	tiglon	disman
riffle	air-gun	withal	visile	cimier	siskin	villan	firman
siffle	biggin	dirham	visite	pitier	ticken	violin	gigman
aidful	biogen	dirhem	visive	tinier	wicken	billy-o	hit-man
dinful	fingan	lichen	aiding	visier	ginkgo	niello	oil-man
fitful	liggen	richen	ailing	vizier	kick-up	Rialto	pieman
sinful	pidgin	siphon	airing	wizier	link-up	fillip	pig-man
tinful	piggin	sithen	biding	civics	pick-up	birler	pin-man
wilful	six-gun	within	biting	Sirius	bicker	filler	pitman
biffin	virgin	righto	dicing	oikist	bilker	killer	'simmon
tiffin	gingko	bishop	diving	timist	dicker	miller	tinman
differ	air-gap	high-up	filing	vibist	kicker	pillar	bismar
liefer	bigger	mishap	fining	milieu	licker	rifler	dimmer
niffer	digger	cipher	firing	airily	milker	siller	gimmer
pilfer	dinger	cither	fixing	dimity	nickar	tiller	gimmor
titfer	finger	dither	giving	fixity	nicker	titler	kimmer
filfot	ginger	either	hiding	jiminy	picker	villar	limmer
misfit	jigger	fisher	hieing	minify	ricker	violer	nimmer
kid-fox	lidger	higher	hiring	nidify	risker	willer	simmer
lingua	lieger	hither	liking	oilily	sicker	killas	zimmer
digged	ligger	lither	liming	tidily	sinker	villus	litmus
dinged	linger	micher	lining	vilify	sirkar	aiglet	kismet
figged	nigger	mither	living	vivify	ticker	billet	dismay
hinged	pinger	nicher	mining	willy	tinker	diglot	firmly
jigged	rigger	sigher	niding	wirily	wicker	fillet	sienna
minged	ringer	tither	pieing	kibitz	winker	firlot	zinnia
pigged	sieger	wisher	piping	gidjee	picket	giblet	bionic
ridged	singer	wither	riding	jigjig	ticket	giglet	finnac
rigged	virger	zither	rising	jig-jog	wicket	giglot	Finnic
ringed	winger	fishes	siding	jimjam	wisket	gillet	picnic
singed	air-gas	lights	sizing	finjan	dickey	gimlet	dinned
wigged	biogas	nights	tiling	picked	mickey	jillet	finned
winged	dinges	pithos	timing	pinked	rickly	killut	ginned
biggie	dingus	riches	tiring	ticked	sickly	millet	nid-nod
bingle	oil-gas	sithes	viking	wicked	tickey	nirlit	pinned
ciggie	fidget	tights	wiping	zinked	tickly	oillet	pioned
dingle	Giggit	mishit	wiring	birkio	tinkly	piglet	sinned
gidgee	lingot	Vishnu	Fifish	fickle	sialic	piolet	tinned
giggle	midget	eighty	fikish	kie-kie	aisled	rillet	dinnle
gilgie	mid-gut	highly	finish	kinkle	billed	violet	fiancé
gingle	nidget	linhay	minish	mickle	hilled	willet	girnie
higgle	widget	mighty	bikini	pickle	milled	Kisleu	jinnee
jiggle	nilgau	nighly	miriti	pinkie	misled	pillau	minnie
jingle	dingey	nighty	tisick	rickle	nilled	Kislev	nix-nie
kingle	dinghy	richly	filial	sickie	nirled	billow	pinnae
lingle	giggly	minima	finial	sickle	titled	pillow	pinnie
mingle	jingly	silica	simial	silkie	willed	willow	pirnie
niggle	kingly	lilied	tibial	tickle	billie	diplex	tinnie
piggie	niggly	pitied	bivium	tinkle	diploe	bieldy	winnle
pingle	singly	tidied	cilium	winkle	gillie	mislay	nig-nog
single	tingly	cilice	civism	nickel	girlie	wieldy	Dipnoi
tingle	wiggly	dirige	Lilium	dinkum	nirlie	willey	dirndl
wiggle	lithia	divide	minium	nickum	vielle	mia-mia	ginnel
fisgig	Mishna	divine	oidium	birken	dialog	filmic	girnel
fizgig	Mithra	finite	bilian	firkin	mid-leg	Micmac	lienal
gilgai	lithic	fixive	minion	girkin	pin-leg	dimmed	lionel
nilgai	dished	liaise	pinion	kirkin'	kiblah	nimmed	signal
gingal	niched	lipide	simian	libken	zillah	rimmed	simnel
jingal	tithed	picine	Sirian	milken	nielli	diamyl	lignum
lingel	lichee	pinite	titian	misken	billon	dismal	finnan
ridgel	eighth	ribibe	virion	pipkin	diplon	gimmal	lignin
ridgil	highth	simile	vision	sicken	Hielan'	hiemal	mignon

kidnap
dinner
finner
ginner
limner
pinner
pioner
signer
signor
sinner
tinner
winner
dip-net
linnet
lionet
oilnut
pig-nut
pinnet
pirnit
signet
sinnet
minnow
winnow
jitney
kidney
lionly
pioney
riancy
aikona
eidola
kia-ora
lipoma
mimosa
bifold
lipoid
milord
siloed
bizone
citole
dipole
ditone
filose
kinone
Nilote
Nivôse
picoté
pilose
pinole
ribose
rimose
virose
mid-off
rip-off
tip-off
simorg
kibosh
titoki
nim-oil
rigoll
til-oil
biform
simoom
Aizoon

disown
Minoan
simoon
gigolo
kimono
giaour
rigour
vigour
limous
pilous
rimous
timous
tiroes
vinous
virous
dim-out
fit-out
rig-out
bijoux
dipody
simony
biopic
hippic
dipped
hipped
hispid
limpid
lipped
nipped
pipped
ripped
sipped
tipped
dimple
disple
fipple
hirple
lippie
nipple
pimple
ripple
simple
sipple
tipple
wimple
yippee
simpai
dispel
lippen
Nippon
pigpen
pippin
Rippon
tie-pin
diaper
diapir
dipper
kipper
lisper
nipper
ripper
simper
sipper

tipper
zipper
cippus
hippus
limpet
pit-pat
sippet
tinpot
tippet
biopsy
dimply
gilpey
jimply
pimply
ripply
simply
bisque
cinque
cirque
risque
risqué
sierra
midrib
mihrab
citric
nitric
picric
ric-rac
vitric
fibred
Nimrod
pierid
tiara'd
tie-rod
cierge
fierce
kierie
lierne
pierce
sirree
tierce
ti-tree
oil-rig
diarch
hijrah
sirrah
fibril
mitral
nitryl
Vibram®
citrin
citron
fibrin
fiorin
micron
mikron
vibrio
riprap
sitrep
mirror
cirrus
citrus
miurus

Pieris
vivres
pierst
pig-rat
tirrit
fin-ray
air-sea
fiesta
miasma
mid-sea
siesta
vizsla
air-sac
biased
pissed
birsle
fissle
hirsle
kiss-me
missee
tissue
kirsch
kitsch
diesel
hirsel
missal
missel
tinsel
lissom
bisson
gipsen
Nissen
fiasco
finsko
giusto
sissoo
kisser
rinser
dieses
diesis
dipsas
lisses
miasms
miosis
misses
missis
missus
misset
jigsaw
pit-saw
rip-saw
linsey
mid-sky
milsey
missay
pigsny
pigsty
tinsey
winsey
sistra
biotic
cistic
fistic

tic-tac
tietac
bitted
cisted
ditted
fitted
gifted
kilted
listed
pioted
pitted
tilted
vista'd
witted
bistre
bittie
filtre
histie
kiltie
kirtle
kittle
lintie
little
mistle
pintle
tiptoe
tittle
virtue
vittae
vittle
wintle
distal
distil
kittul
lintel
listel
pistil
pistol
rictal
vistal
wittol
diatom
dictum
victim
biotin
bitten
kitten
listen
litten
mitten
piston
pitten
Wilton
bistro
tiptop
bister
bitter
bittor
bittur
dieter
fictor
filter

fitter
hitter
jitter
kilter
lictor
lifter
linter
lister
litter
milter
minter
mister
nipter
pitter
qintar
rioter
ritter
sifter
sinter
sister
sittar
sitter
tilter
titter
tinter
viator
victor
winter
witter
cistus
dittos
hiatus
rictus
diktat
dittit
dittay
filthy
kittly
riotry
vintry
wintry
wistly
cicuta
fibula
ligula
pilula
situla
tipula
vicuña
liquid
dilute
disuse
figure
fixure
ligule
ligure
minute
misuse
pilule
titule
simurg
kiaugh
pituri

lifull
ritual
vidual
visual
Siouan
liquor
lituus
fiaunt
minuet
misust
piquet
kikuyu
titupy
silvae
silvan
liever
riever
silver
Milvus
bigwig
tie-wig
wigwag
wigwam
viewer
nitwit
airway
midway
viewly
jinxed
biaxal
diaxon
dioxan
dioxin
pinxit
Libyan
Minyan
Pinyin
piazza
fizzed
fizzle
mizzle
pizzle
sizzle
vizzie
zigzag
fizzen
gizzen
mizzen
fizzer
rizzar
rizzer
rizzor
mizzly
djebel
ejecta
djinni
ajowan
sklate
skeary
ski-bob
skreen
sklent
skeely

skeery
skiing
skaith
skeigh
skyish
skrimp
skolia
skelly
skilly
skyman
akimbo
skimpy
skinny
skarth
ski-run
skerry
skurry
sketch
skater
skrump
skivie
skiver
skivvy
skewed
skewer
skyway
ukiyo-e
skryer
albata
alpaca
cloaca
Alcaic
Altaic
algate
alkane
alnage
cleave
eluate
fluate
oleate
please
sleave
ullage
ulnare
bleach
ollamh
pleach
Alhagi
alkali
almain
Altair
always
eluant
olfact
pliant
Albany
Almany
bleaky
bleary
floaty
gleamy
sleazy
globed

global	pliers	elding	blunge	floppy	glutei	flavin	immane
globin	albeit	flying	elance	slippy	flotel	sliven	impale
labby	albert	plying	flange	sloppy	gluten	sloven	impave
glibly	client	ulling	flense	claque	platan	claver	smeath
plebby	eldest	bluish	glance	clique	platen	clever	embank
slabby	fluent	elfish	plonge	cloqué	pluton	clover	embark
slobby	oldest	elvish	plunge	plaque	blotto	glover	imbark
slubby	slyest	gluish	blanch	cliquy	Clotho	oliver	immask
placed	almery	oldish	blench	gloria	elater	plover	impark
placid	fleecy	sleigh	clench	cleric	elutor	slaver	embail
cleché	gleety	slyish	clinch	all-red	fluter	sliver	emball
cliché	sleeky	Alpini	clunch	florid	plater	claves	imparl
cloche	sleepy	Allium	elench	alerce	slater	clavis	embalm
flèche	sleely	Albion	flanch	florae	ulster	clevis	impawn
plicae	sleezy	eloign	flench	floral	cloths	olivet	impair
eltchi	olefin	ultion	planch	plural	flatus	slavey	impact
flocci	cliffy	albino	plinth	alarum	Plutus	blowed	impart
glycol	clifty	Alpino	clonal	aldrin	ulitis	clawed	umlaut
flacon	fluffy	ultimo	plenum	florin	zlotys	flawed	smeary
glycin	pluffy	allies	blanco	Glires	blotty	flewed	smudge
ulicon	alogia	plaint	planar	claret	clotty	flowed	emydes
Alecto	alegge	bluidy	planer	floret	flatly	slewed	amidst
placer	blague	glairy	blinks	clarty	glitzy	blowse	amadou
slicer	plague	sluicy	clonus	clergy	plotty	blowze	smiddy
glacis	flugel	sloken	llanos	flurry	pleura	flow-on	smudgy
ilices	plagal	ulikon	Olenus	slurry	allude	blow-up	amoeba
elicit	flagon	flukey	elanet	alisma	allure	blower	impend
placet	plug-in	alalia	planet	clusia	blouse	flower	ampere
placit	slogan	slalom	blanky	glossa	clause	glower	impede
plucky	alegar	alumna	blenny	plasma	flaune	blowsy	emmesh
Elodea	alight	blamed	clingy	closed	flouse	blowzy	immesh
alidad	blight	flamed	flinty	plaste	illude	slowly	smeech
bladed	flight	plumed	plenty	plissé	illume	alexia	smeeth
sleded	ill-got	clambe	slangy	Flysch	ill-use	alexic	ambery
slided	plight	flambé	slinky	closer	cleuch	alexin	empery
bludge	slight	alumni	blintz	flaser	cleugh	flaxen	umbery
bludie	bluggy	flamen	glioma	ulosis	clough	klaxon	smegma
fledge	claggy	fly-man	algoid	closet	floush	ellxir	émigré
gledge	cloggy	clamor	almond	blashy	pleuch	flexor	imagos
pledge	flaggy	glamor	alcove	classy	pleugh	plexor	smight
sledge	plaguy	clumps	aldose	flashy	plough	ilexes	smoggy
sludge	slaggy	glumps	ill-off	fleshy	sleuth	plexus	smugly
aludel	all-hid	flemit	alsoon	flisky	slouch	cloyed	amrita
glider	elchee	climax	allons	flossy	slough	flayed	empire
slider	Elohim	blimey	almous	flushy	illupi	gleyed	imbibe
all-day	elshin	clammy	Cloots	glassy	albugo	E-layer	smoile
cloddy	ultima	clumpy	ellops	glossy	flaunt	flayer	umpire
clodly	allied	clumsy	all-out	plashy	cloudy	player	impish
fledgy	illiad	flimsy	almost	plushy	fleury	slayer	omnium
gladly	Pleiad	glumly	bloody	sloshy	floury	clayey	amnion
sludgy	albite	glumpy	bloomy	slushy	glaury	blazon	omnify
allege	Aldine	plummy	floosy	elytra	Slavic	glazen	smoked
allele	allice	plumpy	floozy	alated	gloved	blazer	smoker
fleece	alpine	slimly	gloomy	plated	slived	glazer	amelia
sleeve	alsike	slimsy	sloomy	slated	clavie	blazes	emblic
fleech	alvine	slummy	Clupea	blithe	Slovak	impala	emulge
sleech	blaise	slumpy	aliped	clothe	A-level	ambage	amylum
aldern	blaize	planta	elapse	blotch	O-level	embace	emblem
alpeen	glaive	clinic	slip-on	clatch	Y-level	embale	smalto
altern	illipe	clonic	slap-up	clutch	alevin	embase	ambler
albedo	plaice	plongd	slip-up	fletch	cloven	empale	smiler
alleys	sluice	blende	eloper	flitch	eleven	empare	umbles
Elaeis	bluing	blonde	klepht	glitch	elevon	imbase	amulet

omelet	empusa	unease	snubby	unsewn	anyhow	unlink	enamel
smilet	ampule	Uniate	onycha	endear	unthaw	unpick	gnomon
implex	émeute	unlace	ink-cap	ensear	angina	infill	mnemon
smilax	empuse	unlade	Cnicus	unbear	intima	uncial	one-man
employ	immune	unmade	knicks	undear	engild	unwill	enamor
smalmy	immure	unmake	anicut	ungear	engird	indium	animus
smelly	impure	unrake	ant-cow	unless	enwind	infirm	ynambu
amomum	impute	unsafe	knacky	inbent	invis'd	unfirm	ananke
amtman	smouse	untame	anodic	incept	inwind	ensign	anonym
amenta	ambush	unware	cnidae	incest	unbind	enzian	ananas
omenta	smouch	in-calf	snudge	indent	ungild	Indian	unknit
omened	impugn	unhang	unedge	infect	ungird	indign	unknot
amende	amount	aneath	anodal	infeft	unkind	angico	Ancona
emunge	embusy	encash	enodal	infelt	untied	indigo	ancora
amends	smoyle	sneath	anadem	infest	unwind	antiar	Angola
amoove	amazon	uneath	entera	ingest	ancile	envier	angora
emmove	indaba	unlash	ennead	inject	Andine	inlier	Annona
impone	inyala	enrank	indeed	insect	endite	gneiss	entomb
impose	enjamb	unbark	intend	insert	endive	'snails	enwomb
smooch	enlard	unmask	on-lend	intent	enfire	unbias	intomb
smooth	inlaid	unpack	unbend	invent	engine	undies	untomb
imbosk	inland	untack	unfeed	invert	ensile	unkiss	enfold
emboil	inward	end-all	unhead	invest	entice	anoint	infold
emboss	onward	engaol	unlead	unbelt	entire	engirt	inroad
imboss	unhand	entail	unread	unbent	incise	enlist	intoed
embost	unlaid	enwall	annexe	unfelt	incite	indict	in-word
import	unmard	infall	enlevé	unkent	indite	insist	uncord
impost	unpaid	inwall	entêté	unkept	ingine	unbitt	unfold
embody	unsaid	onfall	incede	unmeet	inside	ungilt	ungord
emboly	anlace	unnail	indene	unnest	intime	ungirt	unhood
imbody	anlage	unvail	infere	unpent	intine	unwist	unload
amerce	ansate	encalm	inhere	unrent	intire	enmity	unlord
amorce	encage	ungain	sneeze	unrest	invite	entity	unsold
embrue	encase	enhalo	unhele	unseat	Kneipe	snaily	untold
emerge	encave	incavo	undeaf	unsent	ondine	unmiry	ancome
imbrue	enface	encamp	unself	untent	on-line	untidy	Ankole
smirch	engagé	unhasp	enmesh	unwept	onside	antlia	anyone
amoral	engage	unfair	sneesh	ingénu	undine	angled	encode
umbral	enlace	unhair	undeck	sneery	unfine	ankled	encore
umbrel	enrace	in-laws	unmeek	sneezy	unhive	unclad	engore
umbril	enrage	endart	anneal	unific	unlike	unglad	enmove
embryo	enragé	enfant	enseal	sniffy	unlime	unglue	enrobe
amoret	ensate	enrapt	unheal	snifty	unline	analog	enzone
imbrex	entame	indart	unleal	snuffy	unlive	unclog	income
smarmy	incage	infant	unreal	enigma	unripe	unplug	indole
smarty	incase	intact	unreel	Onagra	untile	inulin	in-joke
smirky	incave	uncart	unseal	onager	unwire	inclip	insole
smirry	infame	unfact	unseel	anight	unwise	angler	intone
smurry	infare	angary	unveil	knight	unwive	antler	invoke
amused	ingate	infamy	unweal	knaggy	anting	anklet	inwove
omasal	inhale	sneaky	unwell	snaggy	ending	englut	oncome
omasum	inlace	uneasy	enseam	snugly	enring	inflow	snooze
amuser	inmate	unwary	inseam	inched	inning	unclew	unbone
emesis	innate	enable	inseem	unshed	onding	influx	uncope
tmesis	insane	snebbe	unhelm	unshod	unking	snelly	undone
emetic	intake	snubbe	unseam	unshoe	enrich	anemia	unlove
smatch	invade	unable	unteam	anthem	inwith	anemic	unpope
smutch	unbare	ink-bag	Andean	inship	unlich	anomic	unrobe
amatol	uncage	anabas	intern	unship	unwish	gnomic	unrope
emetin	uncape	Anubis	undern	anchor	uncini	mnemic	unyoke
smiter	uncase	knobby	unhewn	anther	antick	anomie	one-off
smithy	uncate	knubby	unrein	unshot	enlink	gnomae	unroof
smutty	undate	snobby	unseen	unshut	inwick	animal	enlock

inlock	snippy	instep	unbusy	morale	tooart	booboo	doucet
inwork	unique	unstep	unduly	nocake	volant	gombro	forçat
uncock	anuria	unstop	unruly	nomade	vorant	bomber	tom-cat
uncork	oniric	instar	snivel	nonage	boyaux	cobber	roucou
undock	inbred	uniter	uneven	nonane	botany	comber	coccyx
unhook	unbred	unstow	knives	notate	covary	dobber	botchy
unlock	untrod	knotty	gnawed	noyade	donary	goober	coachy
unwork	enerve	snotty	unawed	pomace	goramy	jobber	conchy
enroll	enfree	Anoura	unowed	pomade	gowany	robber	poachy
ensoul	entrée	induna	knawel	potage	horary	towbar	pouchy
entoil	unfree	infula	answer	pot-ale	nonary	morbus	touchy
in-foal	untrue	insula	gnawer	romage	notary	combat	bonduc
insoul	anarch	pneuma	knower	rosace	oogamy	fox-bat	Nordic
uncoil	enarch	ungula	anyway	rotate	Romany	gobbet	aoudad
uncool	inarch	ensued	one-way	socage	rosary	nobbut	bonded
uncowl	anarak	endure	anoxia	solace	rotary	sorbet	codded
unfool	anorak	ennuyé	anoxic	sorage	volary	wombat	corded
unroll	antrum	ensure	undyed	togate	votary	woobut	dodded
unsoul	engram	incuse	uneyed	to-name	zonary	woubit	doodad
enform	ingram	induce	enzyme	towage	tombac	fog-bow	fordid
inform	ingrum	infuse	oneyre	volage	tombic	bombax	godded
unform	untrim	inhume	ungyve	voyage	tomboc	Bombyx	hooded
enjoin	entrap	injure	oneyer	zonate	bobbed	bow-boy	loaded
inborn	enwrap	insure	encyst	Zouave	box-bed	cowboy	nodded
intown	inwrap	intuse	snazzy	gobang	combed	doubly	podded
inworn	unprop	unrude	posada	kobang	forbad	lowboy	sordid
unborn	unwrap	unrule	sonata	bodach	forbid	pot-boy	volded
ungown	snarer	unsure	torana	fogash	hotbed	tomboy	woaded
unmown	snorer	untune	yojana	potash	jobbed	wobbly	wooded
unsown	indris	engulf	comarb	jowari	lobbed	concha	worded
untorn	Andrew	ingulf	mosaic	souari	mobbed	lorcha	boddle
unworn	undraw	unturf	Romaic	mohawk	morbid	coccid	boodle
inhoop	anerly	unhung	sodaic	Polack	robbed	forced	boodle
unhoop	energy	unsung	coward	monaul	sobbed	roscid	coddle
indoor	gnarly	anough	dotard	morall	bobble	voiced	doodle
undoer	in-tray	enough	Poland	no-ball	cobble	bosche	fondle
unmoor	knurly	inrush	Roland	to-fall	comble	bouche	fondue
endoss	snarly	onrush	soland	you-all	corbie	bouclé	hoddle
ingoes	snorty	annuli	togaed	domain	doable	couché	howdie
snooks	unpray	incubi	toward	sodain	dobbie	douche	noddle
enroot	entrez	unhusk	woman'd	dorado	dog-bee	louche	noodle
inmost	ink-sac	untuck	bocage	pomato	double	potche	poodle
oncost	unused	annual	borage	potato	foible	rotche	poudre
unbolt	enisle	uncurl	borane	robalo	forbye	touché	roadie
unboot	inisle	unfurl	borate	solaño	gobble	coccal	toddle
uncolt	snaste	ungual	bovate	tomato	hobble	coucal	voidee
unlost	unison	unturn	comate	vorago	hombre	non-com	woodie
unroot	enosis	Anguis	cowage	hot-air	mobbie	non-con	fog-dog
unsoft	gnosis	ungues	dog-ape	mohair	mobble	toucan	hopdog
unwont	unisex	unguis	dogate	morass	nobble	poncho	doodah
incony	anatta	incult	donate	noways	rouble	mob-cap	good-oh
oniony	anetic	induct	dosage	potass	sombre	toecap	houdah
snooty	united	indult	dotage	sowans	wobble	box-car	howdah
unholy	snathe	Innuit	douane	Volans	zombie	concur	bordel
uniped	knitch	insult	forage	cobalt	dor-bug	forcer	goidel
unipod	snatch	intuit	forane	comart	sow-bug	soccer	ooidal
unsped	snitch	unhurt	homage	dopant	bosbok	voicer	rondel
inspan	instal	unjust	iodate	dotant	tombak	coccus	condom
unspun	instil	unsuit	lobate	go-cart	corbel	Dorcas	goddam
sniper	unital	anbury	locale	go-kart	bobbin	hoicks	bolden
unspar	Gnetum	injury	locate	monact	bonbon	yoicks	cordon
inkpot	anatto	snouty	lorate	sonant	corban	bobcat	god-den
snappy	one-two	unbury	lovage	tonant	dobbin	doocot	golden

6 □o□d□o

hodden	pop-eye	ponent	botfly	bought	top-hat	homing	porism
hoiden	toneme	potent	dor-fly	bowget	Tophet	lobing	sodium
holden	zooeae	rodent	hop-fly	dought	moshav	loring	Sofism
houdan	cosech	sobeit	loggia	forgat	forhow	losing	tomium
hoyden	joseph	to-rent	cogged	forget	pochay	loving	yogism
Jordan	Molech	coteau	dogged	forgot	poshly	lowing	Aonian
loaden	moneth	pole-ax	fogged	fought	coaita	moving	Dorian
louden	soneri	bowery	gorged	gorget	conima	mowing	Eolian
sodden	copeck	comedy	hogged	hogget	copita	nosing	gonion
soldan	kopeck	comely	jogged	loggat	lorica	poking	Ionian
Soudan	boreal	foreby	logged	'mongst	vomica	poling	Jovian
wooden	foveal	homely	pongid	mought	oomiac	posing	logion
hoodoo	lozell	lonely	sogged	nougat	zodiac	robing	lotion
koodoo	Nowell	lovely	bodgie	nought	bodied	roding	morion
voodoo	roseal	lowery	boggle	rotgut	copied	roping	motion
hold-up	sorell	moiety	boogie	rought	honied	roving	notion
bonder	zooeal	oogeny	bougie	sought	monied	sowing	Popian
bordar	boreen	popery	coggie	congou	bodice	toling	potion
border	come-on	ropery	coggle	coggly	bolide	towing	bonito
conder	govern	rosery	coigne	doughy	boride	toying	domino
condor	modern	rosety	congee	goggly	bovine	woning	dosi-do
dodder	moreen	solely	goggle	googly	conine	wooing	Loligo
fodder	nosean	sorely	google	longly	cosine	yoking	solito
folder	poleyn	towery	joggle	morgay	cotise	zoning	vomito
holder	poteen	volery	loggie	roughy	docile	boyish	zorino
loader	solein	gowf-ba'	morgue	boshta	dorise	cowish	copier
moider	solemn	confab	pongee	lochia	iodide	coyish	cosier
nodder	voteen	hoofed	porgie	sophia	iodine	dotish	cozier
polder	bolero	poufed	soigné	Gothic	iodise	dovish	foliar
ponder	comedo	roofed	toggle	sophic	iolite	eolith	hosier
pouder	forego	sol-fa'd	tongue	Sothic	ionlse	goyish	rosier
powder	non-ego	woofed	woggle	mothed	mobile	modish	bodies
solder	pomelo	coffee	googol	bothie	moline	mopish	bogies
sordor	Toledo	coffle	mongol	towhee	motile	morish	conics
voider	torero	poffle	dodgem	kowhai	motive	polish	golias
wonder	bo-peep	pouffe	gorgon	nochel	norite	popish	modius
yonder	co-heir	toffee	hoggin	bothan	no-side	Romish	monies
rondos	dog-ear	loofah	longan	Cochin	notice	tonish	movies
sordes	howe'er	boxful	long-on	eothen	novice	toyish	sonics
voudou	poseur	joyful	moggan	Goshen	nowise	solidi	aorist
row-dow	to-tear	potful	morgen	lochan	oolite	Morisk	bonist
boldly	voyeur	woeful	noggin	boo-hoo	podite	oomiak	codist
box-day	bogeys	boffin	pop-gun	forhoo	police	jovial	forint
coldly	Boreas	bowfin	pot-gun	yoo-hoo	polite	monial	holist
fondly	coleus	coffin	gorgio	dog-hep	solive	Novial	Ionist
goodly	soleus	confer	sorgho	dog-hip	somite	oorial	loriot
hobday	sowens	doffer	bodger	nosh-up	sopite	podial	modist
lordly	vowess	goffer	codger	bother	tonite	social	monist
loudly	cogent	golfer	cogger	cosher	votive	tomial	soviet
Monday	covent	gowfer	conger	fother	boding	bonism	bodily
woodsy	covert	loafer	cougar	gopher	boning	corium	codify
bodega	dolent	roofer	dodger	josher	boring	dolium	comity
modena	domett	wolfer	dogger	kosher	boxing	Dorism	cosily
monera	foment	woofer	fogger	mother	coming	eonism	gorily
novena	forest	comfit	forger	pother	cooing	folium	holily
womera	honest	confit	hogger	rother	coping	holism	homily
dog-end	loment	konfyt	jogger	tocher	coving	iodism	hominy
token'd	lowest	soffit	lodger	tosher	doping	Ionism	modify
to-rend	modest	confix	logger	tother	doting	ionium	moyity
cohere	molest	dogfox	longer	tophus	dozing	Lolium	nosily
Docete	moment	forfex	monger	log-hut	foxing	monism	notify
Eocene	motett	bob-fly	sodger	pot-hat	goring	nomism	novity
foveae	nocent		bouget	rochet	holing	podium	oozily

policy	yorker	norlan'	holmic	horned	kobold	nobody	forpit
polity	bosket	pollan	doomed	mooned	locoed	oology	hotpot
ropily	cocket	pollen	formed	morned	toroid	polony	loupit
rosily	docket	poplin	roomed	bonnie	toxoid	sodomy	moppet
rosiny	dooket	roll-on	wormed	bounce	zonoid	cow-pea	poppet
Torify	locket	collop	commie	donnée	bog-ore	hoop-la	roopit
hobjob	nocket	dollop	dormie	Downie®	botone	copped	roupit
conjee	pocket	foul-up	formal	Hornie	comose	couped	toupet
poojah	pookit	gollop	formol	jounce	coyote	hopped	cowpox
moujik	poukit	lollop	normal	loonie	ionone	looped	comply
log-jam	rocket	roll-up	pommel	lounge	jocose	lopped	pompey
donjon	socket	boiler	bow-man	Moonie	lobose	mopped	popply
popjoy	booksy	bowler	common	pointe	mopoke	pooped	mosque
cocked	cocksy	collar	con-man	pounce	morose	popped	torque
corked	donkey	cooler	cowman	pownie	nodose	sopped	moorva
forked	folksy	dollar	dodman	rounce	porose	topped	cobric
hooked	hockey	fowler	dolman	townee	sobole	torpid	forrad
pocked	hookey	gollar	dolmen	townie	tofore	copple	horrid
soaked	horkey	holler	foeman	tonnag	hop-off	corpse	torrid
worked	jockey	howler	foemen	cornel	bogong	coupee	boorde
yolked	low-key	jowler	fogman	nounal	oolong	couple	bo-tree
zonked	monkey	loller	hodman	zoonal	so-long	doppie	bourne
bookie	holloa	moiler	log-man	xoanon	golosh	hoopoe	bourse
cockle	boiled	poller	Mormon	coiner	moloch	hopple	coarse
cookie	bolled	poplar	norman	conner	colobi	koppie	coerce
honkie	cowled	roller	pot-man	corner	bogoak	popple	corrie
kookie	doiled	sollar	rodman	downer	mocock	souple	course
nookie	foiled	soller	Rouman	horner	Mohock	topple	cowrie
rookie	howled	toiler	socman	joiner	cocoon	toupee	gourde
hookah	jowled	toller	topman	moaner	cohorn	oompah	hoarse
bodkin	mobled	yodler	towmon	mooner	cojoin	compel	Lowrie
docken	polled	boules	toyman	sorner	Eozoon	gospel	pourie
dodkin	pot-lid	dowlas	boomer	Cornus	go-down	vorpal	roarie
joskin	rolled	oodles	Colmar	Somnus	godown	pompom	soirée
look-in	soiled	collet	commer	zounds	corozo	coppin	source
morkin	souled	goblet	dormer	bonnet	rococo	coupon	sourse
soaken	toiled	goglet	former	cobnut	rotolo	gowpen	toorie
work-in	boulle	goslet	roamer	cornet	yo-ho-ho	hog-pen	bodrag
cock-up	collie	howlet	roemer	donnat	bow-oar	holpen	toe-rag
hook-up	coolie	job-lot	roomer	donnot	colour	loupen	fourth
lock-up	coulée	toilet	wormer	hornet	dolour	pompon	Moirai
mock-up	doolie	follow	commis	posnet	honour	tompon	borrel
bosker	goalie	go-slow	cormus	sonnet	notour	morpho	corral
cocker	mollie	hollow	cosmos	tow-net	comous	bopper	sorrel
conker	noulde	mob-law	kosmos	fornix	dodoes	cooper	worral
cooker	poulpe	bollix	commit	bouncy	hoboes	copper	worrel
corker	voulge	pollex	commot	bounty	iodous	couper	fogram
corkir	bow-leg	Pollux	format	coonty	joyous	dopper	pogrom
docker	dog-leg	coolly	mommet	county	nodous	hooper	forren
forker	loglog	doyley	motmot	gooney	noyous	hopper	sovran
hocker	coolth	foully	commix	johnny	porous	looper	gooroo
hooker	koolah	gooley	cornea	mornay	cohort	lopper	horror
howker	mollah	hooley	cornua	mounty	cop-out	mopper	pourer
korkir	moolah	motley	goanna	powney	not-out	popper	roarer
locker	tol-lol	mouldy	hobnob	rouncy	volost	romper	tourer
looker	coelom	podley	Cognac	townly	gomoku	souper	gourds
mocker	Moslem	volley	poonac	woundy	bosomy	topper	morris
porker	bollen	woolly	zoonic	corona	colony	torpor	forrit
rocker	codlin	yowley	conned	jojoba	corody	corpus	hog-rat
soaker	goblin	cosmea	corned	korora	gobony	bowpot	torret
socker	gollan	holmia	donned	Pomona	monody	compot	worrit
worker	koulan	cosmic	downed	Eozoic	monosy	cowpat	borrow
yonker	moulin	formic	gowned	conoid	motory	forpet	morrow

sorrow	gossip	rotted	co-star	forthy	louver	upland	upkeep
forray	toss-up	sotted	coster	hostry	soever	upward	upleap
gourdy	bowser	wonted	cottar	loathy	solver	opiate	appear
hourly	cooser	wotted	cotter	mostly	wolver	T-plate	sphear
Norroy	dorser	bootee	couter	mouthy	corves	update	upbear
pomroy	dosser	bottle	doater	poetry	corvus	upgaze	upbear
poorly	douser	coatee	doctor	portly	hooves	upmake	uprear
sourly	dowser	dottle	dorter	softly	loaves	uprate	uptear
foussa	fossor	footle	douter	toothy	looves	uptake	splent
gossib	josser	foutre	foetor	tootsy	wolves	sprang	sprent
bossed	motser	goatee	footer	worthy	corvet	upgang	upbeat
fossed	mouser	goitre	foster	youthy	convex	uphang	uprest
hoised	poiser	goutte	fouter	copula	Volvox	splash	speedy
poised	rosser	hogtie	goiter	gopura	convey	sprack	sphery
soused	rouser	hottie	hooter	koruna	convoy	sprawl	spiffy
tossed	tonsor	jostle	hotter	morula	cobweb	sprain	spoffy
cossie	tosser	loathe	jolter	motuca	bobwig	appair	apogee
donsie	touser	montre	jotter	Podura	cotwal	sphaer	epigon
fo'c'sle	towser	mottle	lofter	rosula	kotwal	optant	spight
mossie	worser	pontie	loiter	rotula	godwit	upcast	spigot
mousie	wowser	postie	looter	Torula	wou-wou	upwaft	ypight
mousle	gooses	pottle	low-tar	Yoruba	bowwow	yplast	spahee
mousmé	louses	rootle	mooter	zonula	powwaw	apiary	upshot
mousse	noesis	softie	mortar	toluic	powwow	speary	epeira
nousle	souses	soothe	mouter	jocund	wow-wow	epocha	optima
possie	comsat	sortie	Pooter	rotund	forwhy	ipecac	upbind
pousse	corset	tootle	porter	cohune	Norway	spaced	uphild
sonsie	cosset	tottie	poster	colure	bonxie	spiced	upwind
sowsse	dowset	toutie	potter	lobule	coaxer	apache	éprise
tousle	lowsit	wortle	pouter	locule	hoaxer	specie	épuisé
borsch	posset	sontag	powter	module	coryza	apical	ophite
bonsai	bow-saw	hootch	rooter	nodule	corymb	epical	optime
consul	log-saw	aortal	rorter	solute	cotyle	spacer	splice
dorsal	bolshy	boatel	roster	vocule	covyne	spicer	spline
dorsel	forsay	coital	rotter	volume	oocyte	apices	sprite
dossal	goosey	costal	router	volute	polype	specks	up-line
dossel	gousty	coutil	sorter	zonule	polypi	spacey	uprise
dossil	mousey	foetal	soutar	coburg	ronyon	speccy	upside
fossil	tolsey	fontal	souter	gomuti	bowyer	specky	spring
housel	contra	hostel	sowter	lobuli	polyps	epodic	spying
morsal	footra	mortal	tolter	loculi	Toryfy	apodal	upping
morsel	foutra	pontal	tooter	moduli	boozed	apedom	uppish
podsol	noctua	pontil	totter	bohunk	foozle	spider	upfill
tolsel	rostra	portal	touter	mocuck	mozzie	spadix	uphill
tonsil	aortic	postal	zoster	Podunk	nozzle	spuddy	up-till
torsel	Coptic	postil	Boötes	toluol	sozzle	append	Ophism
woosel	noetic	bottom	coitus	column	touzle	spread	option
dorsum	nostoc	montem	Cortes	jötunn	borzoi	spredd	aphids
possum	poetic	tom-tom	costus	colugo	donzel	upheld	optics
coosen	pontic	boston	Cottus	gomuto	podzol	uplead	speiss
coosin	zoetic	bouton	foetus	modulo	gozzan	upsend	splint
cousin	booted	cotton	fortis	coquet	zoozoo	apiece	spoilt
foison	cotted	gotten	nostos	locust	bonzer	ephebe	sprint
godson	doited	looten	pontes	loquat	boozer	sphene	uplift
gossan	dotted	moutan	portas	robust	rozzer	sphere	uprist
horson	foetid	ponton	sortes	roquet	boozey	speech	uptilt
loosen	footed	rottan	doitit	voguey	sozzly	ephebi	sphinx
poison	jotted	rotten	tomtit	corvid	tolzey	appeal	uppity
poyson	lotted	soften	kowtow	corvée	appaid	upwell	spiked
tocsin	moated	too-too	cortex	louvre	appayd	spleen	spoken
toison	motto'd	boater	vortex	coeval	spraid	uplean	opaled
tossen	potted	bolter	costly	hooven	uphand	speedo	spalle
worsen	rooted	colter	couthy	hoover	uphaud	upheap	spulye
							spilth

apollo	sperse	squall	errant	dredge	orrery	archon	'Arriet
epulis	spurge	squeak	triact	drudge	troely	arghan	artist
opulus	spurne	squeal	truant	fridge	prefab	arshin	brainy
upblow	uphroe	Aquila	Arcady	grudge	trifid	brehon	freity
upflow	updrag	equine	creaky	trudge	griffe	orphan	fruity
apeman	eparch	équipe	creamy	bridal	trifle	urchin	grainy
epimer	sparth	squire	creasy	credal	armful	archer	orbity
spined	spiral	squiff	croaky	iridal	artful	orchis	frijol
spence	sparer	squish	dreamy	gradin	ireful	orchat	Trojan
sponge	sports	squill	dreary	trader	urnful	archly	grakle
spunge	sperst	squirm	freaky	gradus	Gräfin	arnica	broken
spinal	spirit	squier	friary	irides	gryfon	orbita	kraken
spinel	aperçu	squirr	greasy	credit	prefer	pruina	wroken
eponym	éperdu	squint	treaty	aridly	drafts	troika	broker
opener	updraw	squirt	ersatz	cruddy	profit	urtica	proker
spinar	upgrew	equity	Arabic	Friday	orifex	braird	trek-ox
spinet	upgrow	squiny	arable	fraena	prefix	araise	crikey
upknit	sparry	arcana	criblé	friend	crafty	Argive	aralia
openly	sporty	argala	treble	breese	draffy	arkite	arolla
spinny	spurry	armada	tribal	breeze	drifty	arride	brolga
spongy	upbray	errata	arabin	creese	dry-fly	arrive	frolic
spunky	sposhy	argand	graben	freeze	bregma	arsine	Uralic
apnoea	aphtha	Briard	briber	frieze	tragic	braide	grille
aplomb	spathe	errand	Arabis	greece	frigid	braise	grilse
uphold	spetch	friand	Erebus	greese	brigue	braize	proleg
appose	spital	Ormazd	crabby	greete	brogue	bruise	arilli
aptote	sputum	arcade	drabby	griece	dragée	cruise	prelim
oppose	spot-on	arcane	drably	grieve	drogue	cruive	trillo
splore	apathy	breare	grubby	kreese	Progne	ermine	proler
upcome	spotty	crease	trebly	preeve	gri-gri	fraise	armlet
uprose	upstay	create	graced	priefe	frugal	froise	prolix
sprong	spauld	ergate	priced	prieve	brogan	graile	brolly
splosh	epaule	grease	broché	breech	dragon	graine	drolly
uplock	spouse	greave	crèche	creesh	origan	greige	frilly
uplook	spruce	ornate	croche	ordeal	origin	orcine	orally
upboil	sprung	preace	orache	orcein	trigon	oreide	trilby
upcoil	sprush	prease	oracle	arrear	trogon	oroide	trolly
uproll	upgush	triage	troche	breeks	Trygon	orpine	premia
uptown	uprush	troade	uracil	cruels	droger	praise	uremia
uptorn	upcurl	urbane	drachm	uraeus	fragor	preife	bromic
uproar	upfurl	wreake	bracer	ardent	tragus	proine	dromic
apport	uphurl	areach	grocer	argent	troggs	pruine	eremic
sprout	oppugn	breach	tracer	arpent	aright	ursine	uremic
upmost	upturn	breath	tricar	arrect	bright	arcing	premed
uproot	spruit	broach	trocar	arrest	fright	crying	gramme
aphony	spouty	creach	crocus	driest	frigot	drying	trémie
spooky	up-over	creagh	cruces	freest	wright	erring	trompe
spoony	spivvy	eriach	fracas	orgeat	gru-gru	frying	grumph
epopee	spewer	preach	grices	orient	bragly	prying	dromoi
apepsy	upsway	wreath	précis	priest	craggy	trying	brumal
opaque	apexes	wroath	fricht	urgent	dreggy	urging	primal
aporia	spayad	argali	tricot	artery	froggy	urning	crumen
Sparta	spryer	arrack	bricky	breezy	groggy	arrish	dromon
spirea	spryly	orgasm	cricky	briery	trigly	dreich	crambo
spiric	epizoa	ordain	pricey	creeky	Brahma	droich	cremor
sparid	apozem	Greats	tricky	creepy	Orphic	dryish	framer
spired	squama	groats	iridic	freely	arched	graith	primer
a-per-se	equate	Arnaut	eroded	freety	orchid	wraith	tremor
sparge	squame	arrant	traded	greedy	Archie	erbium	trimer
sparke	square	breast	bridge	greeny	Brahmi	truism	crumbs
sparre	squash	creant	bridie	griesy	archil	proign	dromos
sparse	squawk	criant	bridle	gryesy	orchel	orgies	primus
sperre	squail	dreamt	cradle	ornery	orchil	aroint	fremit

gromet	kroner	frappé	priser	grotto	driven	brazil	isohel
prompt	kronor	graple	proser	crater	graven	drazel	eschar
brumby	pruner	griple	crases	cratur	proven	frazil	eschew
crampy	branks	grippe	crasis	frater	craver	brazen	espied
crimpy	crants	triple	crises	grater	driver	frozen	ashine
crumby	Erinys	trophi	crisis	orator	drover	grazer	aspine
crummy	Kronos	drupel	irises	prater	graver	prizer	aspire
crumpy	Uranus	propel	krises	ureter	prover	frizzy	assize
drumly	brunet	propyl	preses	writer	trover	espada	essive
frumpy	cronet	crepon	uresis	Brutus	bravos	Tswana	oscine
Grammy	erenow	fripon	urosis	gratis	graves	Asgard	aswing
grimly	brandy	trapan	cruset	iritis	travis	island	aspick
grumly	branky	trepan	groset	trevis	trevis	usward	Ostiak
grumpy	branny	crypto	prosit	frutex	brevet	ashake	aswirl
primly	bronzy	troppo	brashy	pre-tax	cravat	ashame	espial
trimly	cranky	draper	brassy	fratry	grivet	aslake	ostial
Aranea	cranny	griper	brisky	fretty	privet	astare	osmium
crania	franzy	groper	brushy	frothy	trivet	escape	ostium
Urania	frenzy	proper	cressy	gritty	crowed	estate	ascian
Iranic	fringy	cripes	crispy	grotty	browse	osmate	assign
irenic	granny	trapes	crusty	pretty	drawee	askari	Ossian
ironic	pranky	tripos	drosky	truthy	drowse	assail	ustion
uranic	tranny	armpit	drossy	wrathy	frowie	aswarm	Eskimo
branle	trendy	drapet	frisky	trauma	prawle	escarp	assist
brenne	krantz	croppy	frosty	around	growth	askant	T-shirt
bronze	areola	drappy	grassy	ground	crewel	aslant	aseity
cringe	arroba	drippy	grisly	Ormuzd	trowel	assart	ossify
frenne	areole	dropsy	prismy	arbute	prewyn	astart	ash-key
fringe	arkose	grippy	prissy	argute	brewer	usable	asylum
Fronde	broose	prepay	trashy	armure	drawer	isabel	ashlar
grande	creole	preppy	tressy	arouse	grower	ash-bin	ashler
grange	droome	trappy	trusty	brouze	brewis	isobar	ostler
orange	groove	triply	wristy	croupe	browst	psyche	tsamba
prance	orgone	trophy	protea	crouse	frowst	ash-can	Ostmen
prince	oriole	Griqua	arctic	croûte	brawly	psycho	isomer
trance	triode	frorne	cretic	grouse	brawny	Isodia	usance
transe	brooch	crural	critic	ordure	browny	used-up	ashore
branch	arioso	froren	erotic	triune	crawly	ascend	aslope
brunch	arroyo	dry-rot	iritic	troule	drowsy	yshend	astone
cranch	arbour	arista	uretic	troupe	frowsy	Essene	osmose
crunch	ardour	crista	grated	trouse	frowzy	osteal	assoil
drench	armour	crusta	pratie	brough	growly	esteem	aswoon
french	proofs	friska	wrethe	crouch	wraxle	astern	esloin
Granth	try-out	frusta	writhe	drouth	cruxes	ossein	essoin
trench	ormolu	erased	cratch	grouch	orexis	asleep	astoop
wrench	argosy	irised	crotch	trough	praxis	asmear	osmous
pranck	armory	crosse	crutch	arguer	prayed	assess	asport
crenel	arrowy	crusie	fratch	draunt	arayse	assets	aspout
crinal	briony	graste	grutch	irrupt	argyle	ascent	assort
trinal	broody	grysie	wretch	argufy	grayle	aspect	assott
uranyl	broomy	triste	brutal	croupy	groyne	assent	escort
urinal	bryony	wrasse	crotal	groupy	proyne	assert	astony
frenum	droopy	cresol	protyl	grouty	trayne	astert	isopod
kronen	grooly	trisul	trotyl	trouty	Argyll	ostent	ash-pan
uranin	groovy	arisen	breton	trivia	crayon	ashery	ash-pit
bronco	priory	grison	Briton	graved	Troyan	astely	Ostrea
drongo	grappa	orison	craton	gravid	brayer	esnecy	escroc
eringo	tropic	prison	Cretan	proved	crayer	osiery	psoric
eryngo	draped	aristo	cretin	drivel	prayer	useful	astral
franco	trepid	fresco	croton	frivol	aroynt	isogon	escrol
gringo	tripod	presto	erg-ten	gravel	greyly	usager	asarum
pronto	uropod	eraser	proton	grovel	crazed	asthma	ashram
ironer	craple	groser	triton	travel	prized	ischia	estrum

usurer	sticky	étrier	attone	statue	sudate	tumble	succus
Osiris	stocky	Atkins	otiose	stitch	tubage	humbug	sulcus
astrut	stadda	ethics	stooge	statal	tubate	gubbah	dulcet
esprit	stadia	atwixt	stoope	stater	musang	jubbah	mud-cat
escrow	stedde	strict	strobe	stator	queach	bulbil	muscat
astrex	stodge	strift	strode	otitis	sumach	bulbul	dun-cow
astray	studio	stripy	stroke	status	curari	jumbal	bunchy
estray	steddy	atokal	strove	stithy	gurami	dubbin	outcry
osprey	stodgy	stoker	strong	struma	jupati	tulban	punchy
tsetse	Athena	stokes	strook	stound	kumari	turban	Buddha
tsotsi	attend	italic	stroll	attune	ourali	pueblo	sundra
isatin	steeld	stoled	stroam	strung	ourari	bulbar	tundra
Isatis	Athene	stolid	attorn	stouth	out-ask	bus-bar	mundic
osmund	ethene	stelae	strown	struck	aumail	cumber	budded
assume	steeve	stalag	stroup	strunt	eucain	durbar	funded
assure	stieve	etalon	strout	stoury	fusain	Gueber	buddle
astute	strene	stolen	utmost	staved	supawn	lubber	bundle
oscule	itself	stolon	utopia	stived	fugato	lumbar	burdie
escudo	streak	stalko	atopic	steven	fumado	lumber	cuddie
pseudo	streek	stelar	etypic	stiver	rubato	number	cuddle
issuer	atweel	stylar	stupid	stover	turaco	outbar	Culdee
asquat	streel	stylus	staple	staves	durant	rubber	curdle
psywar	stream	stilet	steppe	stawed	jumart	tubber	duddie
Ostyak	atween	stylet	stipel	stewed	jurant	burbot	fuddle
ottava	Etnean	otalgy	step-in	stownd	mutant	numbat	guddle
strata	strewn	stalky	stop-go	stowre	nutant	rubbet	huddle
steard	stress	stilly	step-up	stewer	outact	rubbit	hurdle
strand	attent	stilty	stupor	stower	subact	surbet	muddle
Utgard	attest	stemma	stapes	ataxia	curacy	turbit	puddle
ethane	street	atomic	stipes	ataxic	eutaxy	turbot	ruddle
steale	steedy	etymic	pteria	ptyxis	lunacy	sunbow	rundle
steane	steely	stemme	yttria	stayed	lunary	outbox	subdue
steare	steepy	stimie	athrob	ethyne	queasy	aumbry	Suidae
strafe	steery	stymie	steric	stayne	queazy	bubbly	sundae
strake	stifle	ataman	yttric	stayre	sudary	busboy	pug-dog
straff	stuffy	etymon	eterne	stay-in	sugary	dumbly	sun-dog
attach	stigma	stamen	starve	stayer	hubbub	humbly	numdah
strath	staged	stumer	sterve	curara	bulbod	jumbly	purdah
attack	stigme	stumpy	stirre	kumara	cubbed	nubbly	sundri
atlask	stogie	stanza	storge	Purana	dubbed	rubbly	dumdum
strack	stager	atonic	starch	Tupaia	numbed	cutcha	durdum
straik	stagey	ethnic	sterol	bumalc	outbid	kutcha	quidam
Y-track	stogey	stoned	pterin	Judaic	rubbed	puncta	burden
attain	stuggy	stance	stereo	aubade	rum-bud	muscid	guidon
atwain	etcher	stanze	attrap	aurate	subbed	muscae	gulden
strain	striga	stonne	starer	butane	sunbed	muscle	hudden
strawn	attire	stanch	storer	cubage	surbed	nuncle	hurden
stramp	étoile	stench	Pteris	curare	turbid	quiche	lurdan
strass	striae	stanck	stirps	curate	bubble	tusche	lurden
stealt	stride	atonal	uterus	fumage	bum-bee	buccal	pudden
strait	strife	stonen	storax	furane	bumble	furcal	sudden
steady	strike	stanzo	styrax	humane	burble	sulcal	tundun
steamy	Strine	stingo	starry	jubate	fumble	Tuscan	huddup
strawy	stripe	atoner	storey	jugate	Guebre	vulcan	dudder
stable	strive	stoner	stormy	lunate	humble	nuncio	dunder
atabeg	a'thing	stingy	sturdy	luxate	jumbie	puncto	furder
atabek	string	stinty	ptisan	mucate	jumble	hub-cap	guider
atabal	k'thibh	Atropa	ptosis	murage	mumble	juicer	judder
stably	staith	stroma	stasis	mutate	nubble	succor	murder
stubby	strich	stromb	statua	nutate	outbye	cuscus	pudder
atocia·	atrial	strond	static	outage	rubble	juncus	rudder
stacte	atrium	stroud	stated	pupate	rumble	ruscus	sudder
stucco	Ethiop	at-home		rugate	suable	succès	sunder

fundus	turfed	kurgan	lum-hat	rupiah	busked	Sukkot	buglet
Turdus	cuffle	outgun	outhit	buriti	fucked	sunket	bullet
pundit	duffle	burgoo	sunhat	burial	husked	tucket	cullet
subdew	muffle	gung-ho	Pushtu	autism	musked	musk-ox	cutlet
sun-dew	purfle	budger	lushly	cubism	sucked	duskly	duplet
cuddly	ruffle	bugger	muchly	curium	tusked	turkey	gullet
puddly	cupful	Bulgar	oughly	dudism	buckie	quelea	gurlet
Sunday	dueful	bulger	Auriga	Humism	buckle	mucluc	mullet
sundry	duffel	burger	cubica	mutism	huckle	public	nutlet
eureka	fulfil	fulgor	Judica	nudism	junkie	curled	outlet
murena	jugful	hunger	kufiya	purism	luckie	guiled	pullet
superb	mugful	lugger	Lucina	Sufism	muckle	mulled	runlet
but-end	rueful	mugger	lumina	bunion	muskle	humlie	sublet
butene	tubful	nuggar	numina	dupion	ruckle	ouglie	sunlit
mug-ewe	cuffin	purger	Punica	durian	runkle	outlie	curlew
quaere	muffin	rugger	rumina	durion	suckle	ruelle	outlaw
Sûreté	puffin	sungar	Tulipa	fusion	sunkie	tuille	duplex
tuyère	ruffin	tugger	buried	Humian	muskeg	putlog	dually
humeri	turfen	turgor	busied	Julian	punkah	Guelph	guilty
ourebi	buffer	vulgar	dutied	Tupian	bunkum	Gullah	gulley
puteli	duffer	fungus	rubied	turion	bumkin	mullah	hurley
cuneal	furfur	outgas	audile	Zuñian	buskin	nullah	mulley
luteal	puffer	Tungus	augite	subito	dusken	quelch	outlay
puteal	suffer	vulgus	dunite	junior	lucken	nuclei	pulley
museum	sulfur	budget	fusile	punier	murken	mukluk	qualmy
Augean	surfer	nugget	futile	curios	rumkin	suslik	wurley
dudeen	buffet	quight	gunite	kumiss	sucken	fullam	mummia
Humean	outfit	hungry	humite	aurist	suck-in	Muslim	Suomic
Judean	tuffet	jungly	lumine	cubist	tuck-in	dualin	bummed
lucern	subfeu	quaggy	lupine	cueist	cuckoo	dunlin	gummed
lutein	curfew	bushed	munite	curiet	duikep	fullan	hummed
luzern	guffaw	hushed	murine	Humist	bucker	muflon	mummed
tureen	outfox	pushed	musive	jurist	bulker	murlan	summed
pumelo	suffix	euchre	mutine	lutist	bunker	murlin	bummle
tupelo	outfly	qui-hye	nubile	nudist	busker	muslin	guimpe
tuxedo	purfly	nurhag	pumice	purist	ducker	pull-in	nutmeg
auteur	quagga	quahog	purine	quaint	Dunker	pull-on	hummel
fureur	bugged	muzhik	rubine	queint	duyker	purlin	kümmel
aureus	fulgid	burhel	rusine	quoist	fucker	sullen	mulmul
duress	hugged	bushel	rutile	aurify	hunker	duello	pummel
funest	jugged	muchel	supine	bulimy	husker	burlap	hummum
humect	lugged	nuchal	sutile	busily	junker	Dunlop	Burman
lucent	lunged	Durham	busing	humify	kunkar	pull-up	busman
outeat	rugged	fulham	buying	munify	kunkur	bugler	culmen
ouvert	sungod	humhum	during	mutiny	lurker	buller	cummin
pudent	tugged	eughen	luging	nudity	mucker	burler	cupman
queest	turgid	euphon	luting	punily	pucker	butler	gunman
bureau	budgie	Kuchen	musing	purify	Quaker	culler	musmon
dukery	bungee	rushen	outing	purity	sucker	curler	outman
dupery	bungie	tuchun	puling	rubify	tucker	cutler	subman
hugely	bungle	Pushto	rueing	bunjee	Tunker	fuller	summon
humefy	burgee	tu-whoo	ruling	bunjie	tuskar	guiler	tutman
mutely	burgle	author	tubing	jug-jug	tusker	guller	bummer
nudely	guggle	gusher	tuning	gurjun	yucker	guslar	cummer
purely	gurgle	husher	dudish	outjet	ruckus	guyler	fulmar
rubefy	juggle	lusher	kufiah	outjut	turkis	hurler	hummer
rudely	jungle	musher	mulish	buckra	bucket	muller	mummer
rudery	luggie	Nuphar	Munich	burkha	busket	outler	murmur
surely	lungie	outher	punish	funkia	junket	puller	rummer
surety	jungli	pusher	quaich	Gurkha	musket	purler	summar
tumefy	cudgel	rusher	quaigh	pulkha	junket	sutler	summer
puffed	fungal	wuther	rudish	quokka	musket	cullis	hummus
ruffed	durgan	cushat		Turkic	sucket	auklet	submit

summat	rugose	furphy	muesli	cup-tie	muster	curvet	avatar	
summit	cut-off	humpty	munshi	cuttle	mutter	survew	ovator	
muu-muu	put-off	murphy	Russki	cuttoe	nutter	kurvey	avoure	
lummox	run-off	purply	bursal	guttae	ouster	purvey	avouch	
bunnia	bugong	supply	cursal	guttle	punter	survey	avaunt	
duenna	dugong	tumphy	gunsel	hurtle	putter	suivez	evovae	
guinea	oulong	pulque	mussel	hustle	quoter	outwin	avowed	
quanta	judogi	murrha	pussel	justle	rutter	pulwar	avowal	
quinoa	nut-oil	cupric	russel	lustre	suitor	tulwar	avowry	
quinta	suborn	lubric	tussal	mustee	tufter	outwit	avoyer	
Hunnic	zufolo	rubric	outsum	puntee	cultus	runway	sweard	
muonic	humour	furred	Bunsen	puttee	custos	subway	awhape	
quinic	huzoor	outred	tutsan	puttie	quotes	lunyie	ywrake	
burned	rumour	putrid	bursar	quethe	fustet	gunyah	awrack	
dunned	tumour	currie	curser	rustle	tut-tut	yum-yum	aweary	
punned	aurous	cursor	cursor	rustre	surtax	bunyip	sweaty	
ruined	dumous	durrie	cusser	subtle	curtly	huzza'd	two-bit	
sunned	fumous	quarte	fusser	suttee	curtsy	fuzzle	kwacha	
turned	humous	runrig	guiser	suttle	justly	guzzle	owl-car	
vulned	mucous	Tuareg	hussar	turtle	subtly	muzzle	twicer	
nuance	putois	gurrah	nurser	cultch	suetty	nuzzle	swaddy	
quince	rufous	hurrah	pulsar	quatch	sultry	puzzle	a'where	
quinie	rugous	burrel	purser	quetch	aucuba	wuzzle	twyere	
quinte	bug-out	musrol	quasar	quitch	lucuma	puzzel	awheel	
quinze	buy-out	murram	tusser	curtal	lunula	buzzer	sweert	
numnah	cut-out	quorum	tussis	subtil	Luzula	nuzzer	sweeny	
quench	dugout	murren	gusset	custom	mutuca	aviate	owlery	/
funnel	eulogy	murrin	outset	multum	suburb	aviary	sweeny	
gunnel	sulpha	outrun	outsit	quotum	queued	ovibos	sweepy	
quinol	cupped	quarto	russet	tum-tum	cupule	avocet	sweety	
runnel	cusped	Führer	subset	Austin	curule	avidly	tweeny	
tunnel	cuspid	hubris	sunset	burton	cuouae	avalle	twight	
guanin	humped	turret	pursew	button	future	evejar	twiggy	
guenon	jumped	burrow	gun-shy	luiten	jujube	avulse	ewghen	
quango	pumped	furrow	pudsey	lutten	lunule	évolué	awhile	
burn-up	pupped	tutrix	puisny	muntin	mutule	evolve	twaite	
turnip	supped	hurray	Russky	mutton	nucule	evulse	awning	
turn-up	dumple	murray	lustra	pultan	puture	svelte	a-weigh	
burner	mud-pie	murrey	quotha	pulton	suture	uvulae	owlish	
cunner	purpie	quarry	cultic	pultun	tubule	ovular	sweirt	
gunner	purple	quirky	fustic	putten	eunuch	uvular	awaked	
punner	rumple	sunray	fustoc	sultan	cumuli	evilly	awaken	
ruiner	supple	surrey	luetic	suntan	tumuli	ovally	awoken	
runner	curpel	quartz	rustic	duetto	mutual	avenge	twelve	
turner	lumpen	cuesta	bunted	bust-up	mutuum	avenue	twilit	
wunner	luppen	russia	busted	dust-up	auburn	evince	owelty	
burnet	bumper	sub-sea	butted	outtop	autumn	avanti	twilly	
gurnet	cupper	cursed	gutted	aunter	lucumo	avenir	swampy	
punnet	dumper	cussed	hutted	Auster	august	evenly	swimmy	
runnet	jumper	pulsed	jutted	bunter	tumult	evzone	twined	
curney	lumper	Aussie	nutted	buster	augury	Evipan®	swinge	
quinsy	mumper	bursae	putted	butter	luxury	Svarga	twinge	
aurora	pulper	cuisse	quited	cuiter	curved	averse	twiner	
cupola	pumper	nursle	runted	culter	fulvid	overdo	swanky	
judoka	Rumper	puisne	rusted	cutter	outvie	overgo	swanny	
mucosa	supper	pursue	rutted	duster	pulvil	overby	twangy	
cuboid	rumpus	tussle	suited	guitar	vulval	overly	twenty	
fucoid	Vulpes	hussif	tufted	gunter	culver	Avesta	awsome	
mucoid	output	Bursch	auntie	gutter	pulver	ovisac	ywroke	
dumose	pulpit	putsch	bustee	hunter	quaver	avoset	awrong	
furole	puppet	tussah	bustle	hurter	quiver	ivy-tod	swoosh	
furore	put-put	tusseh	buttle	Kultur	vulvar	kvetch	awmous	
quooke	sumpit	bukshi	buttle	luster	turves	avital	swiper	
							swipes	

swipey
two-ply
Swarga
Swerga
awmrie
swarve
swerve
swarth
swaraj
owerby'
swardy
swarty
swirly
twirly
swashy
swishy
twisty
swathe
awatch
swatch
switch
twitch
ewftes
swathy
swound
swoune
swivel
sweven
swownd
swowne
two-way
swayed
swayer
awayes
excamb
expand
oxland
exhale
oxgate
oxgang
oxtail
extant
extasy
exedra
exodic
exodus
exceed
expend
extend
oxhead
extern
excess
except
expect
expert
exsect
exsert
extent
exogen
oxygen
ox-bird
excide
excise

excite
expire
extine
extirp
expiry
axilla
exilic
oxalic
oxslip
oxalis
oxymel
examen
exomis
exempt
exonym
extold
Oxford
exposé
expose
exhort
export
extort
exopod
exequy
exarch
exotic
exited
excuse
exhume
expugn
exeunt
ox-eyed
aye-aye
by-lane
by-name
cytase
gyrate
hypate
lynage
lyrate
mygale
zymase
pygarg
bypath
dynamo
bypass
by-past
byzant
dynast
gyrant
tyrant
bye-bye
dyable
dybbuk
cymbal
symbol
tymbal
dyadic
syndic
pye-dog
gylden
Hyades
syndet

hyaena
Cybele
pyrene
xylene
myself
rypeck
lyceum
wyvern
eyeful
fylfot
myogen
Pythia
mythic
Pythic
hyphae
lychee
rythme
hyphal
hyphen
python
syphon
Typhon
cypher
mythos
mythus
typhus
Myrica
Syriac
eyliad
myriad
byline
bylive
by-time
lysine
pyrite
zymite
dyeing
eyeing
pyeing
typing
tyring
cytisi
hylism
lyrism
Syrism
Lydian
Syrian
Tyrian
Cynips
hylist
lyrist
typist
syrinx
typify
cyclic
eyelid
syrlye
myelin
myelon
cycler
cyclus
by-plot
eyalet

eyelet
by-blow
bye-law
byrlaw
by-play
pyemia
gymmal
nyanza
cyanic
gymnic
hymnic
hypnic
pycnic
pyknic
hymned
byrnie
hymnal
hypnum
cyanin
pycnon
pyoner
Hypnos
cygnet
gynney
Lycosa
myxoma
Pyrola
xyloma
zygoma
ayword
byroad
byword
cymoid
cytoid
hypoid
jymold
xyloid
zymoid
bygone
cymose
cytode
dynode
gyrose
pyrope
tylote
xylose
zygose
zygote
zymome
kybosh
bywork
by-form
byroom
tycoon
dyvour
cymous
gyrous
pylons
tyroes
myopia
myopic
gypped
gyppie

tympan
nympho
eye-pit
hydria
pyuria
Cymric
hydric
cyprid
hybrid
cypris
cyprus
hybris
byssal
gypsum
myosin
hyssop
byssus
cyesis
Hyksos
myosis
cystic
myotic
mystic
cystid
Eyetie
myrtle
tystie
hyetal
system
syntan
oyster
xyster
Myrtus
syrtes
syrtis
xystos
xystus
syntax
lyfull
Tyburn
dysury
syrupy
sylvia
sylvan
lynxes
hydyne
syzygy
izzard
Azrael
azodye
ozaena
azalea
Ozalid®
azonic
azonal
azione
czapka
dzeren
azotic

aracan	Saracen	papable	catasta	cabbala	**barchan**	balcony
aracal	tabaret	papally	Karaite	falbala	car-coat	calcine
aravan	takahea	parable	Maranta	hagbolt	day-coal	dancing
araway	tanager	parafle	rabatte	Kabbala	fascial	farcing
·ataian	Wahabee	payable	Sabaoth	lamb-ale	faucial	fascine
·atalan	**Falange**	ratable	**Bahadur**	patball	gas-coal	larceny
atapan	galanga	ratably	Balanus	pay-bill	panchax	Marconi
·atayan	sarangi	salable	calamus	ragbolt	paschal	nascent
araday	**earache**	salably	Calanus	saw-bill	**bawcock**	vaccine
¶alakah	Halacha	savable	Carabus	tap-bolt	dawcock	**halcyon**
alavah	Maratha	sayable	caracul	wax-bill	haycock	manchoo
acamar	Marathi	takable	karakul	way-bill	**cascade**	man-cook
amadar	navarho	tamable	labarum	**bambino**	falcade	raccoon
ajawah	panache	taxable	ladanum	carbine	sarcode	salchow
ayaway	paratha	taxably	macaque	dabbing	**catched**	**baccara**
nacadam	sagathy	**mahatma**	Tabanus	daubing	catchen	baccare
¶alayan	tamasha	paracme	vacatur	ear-bone	catcher	cascara
acarat	**baladin**	**caranna**	Varanus	hatband	fancied	mascara
ajamas	canakin	carauna	**cambial**	hayband	fancier	tax-cart
alamae	cap-à-pie	lasagna	catboat	jambone	farcied	**cap-case**
alatal	dataria	lasagne	jambeau	jawbone	hatchel	carcase
an-Arab	fanatic	rabanna	pap-boat	lambent	hatcher	carcass
atamar	faradic	savanna	**rag-baby**	nabbing	hatchet	fascism
amadan	galabia	talaunt	**hawbuck**	rabboni	larchen	fascist
at-a-tat	jalapic	**caracol**	layback	rawbone	latchet	laicise
abaean	jalapin	catalog	sambuca	salband	manchet	sarcasm
agaman	Latakia	gasahol	saw-buck	saw-buck	Märchen	talcose
aharan	malacia	laxator	**carbide**	day-book	marcher	**baccate**
arafan	malaria	marabou	gambado	gas-buoy	marches	calcite
atanas	manakin	matador	man-body	jambool	mascled	falcate
anadar	Nasalis	Panadol®	naebody	law-book	matched	marcato
·aratah	navarin	parados	**babbler**	rag-book	matcher	paucity
atagan	paladin	paradox	basbleu	**Barbary**	parched	saccate
aramba	Panagia	paragon	cambrel	catbird	patched	**Bacchus**
atawba	patagia	parasol	dabbler	daubery	patcher	calcium
alance	Patarin	parazoa	darbies	gabbard	rancher	catchup
amaica	ramakin	sabaton	gabbler	gabbart	ratchet	farceur
avarch	ratafia	salamon	gambier	halberd	satchel	jacchus
abasco®	Sarapic	sapajou	gambler	halbert	saucier	patch-up
acance	Sarapis	Tagalog	gambrel	Hamburg	watcher	rancour
acancy	satanic	talayot	garbler	hauberk	watchet	raucous
alance	savarin	**catalpa**	has-been	lambert	**calcify**	sanctum
alando	tabanid	**bagarre**	jambier	may-bird	farcify	Sanctus
abaret	talaria	catarrh	mad-bred	tan-bark	**Bacchic**	sarcous
adaver	tamarin	cavalry	marbled	**cambism**	bacchii	talcous
amaieu	Tataric	macabre	marbler	cambist	macchie	**bandeau**
aramel	vanadic	palabra	rabbler	earbash	sarcoid	band-saw
aravel	**malarky**	tanagra	rambler	gambist	**carcake**	cardiac
alafel	**banally**	zamarra	tabbied	iambist	gas-coke	handbag
alabea	batable	zamarro	wabbler	lambast	oatcake	handcar
alatea	capable	**babassu**	warbler	rag-bush	pancake	handjar
anaper	cavalla	bagasse	**cabbage**	tarbush	**bascule**	handsaw
zaret	cavally	Bahaism	cabbagy	**babbitt**	bauchle	hard-pan
¶anager	datable	Bahaist	camboge	barbate	calculi	land-law
¶anatee	eatable	Dadaism	gamboge	hay-bote	catcall	landman
aiades	fadable	Dadaist	garbage	rabbity	falcula	land-rat
alaver	fatally	fadaise	**cambric**	Sabbath	law-calf	Landtag
anacea	hatable	Lamaism	garboil	**cambium**	masculy	land-tax
apaver	makable	Lamaist	lambkin	harbour	saccule	Mazdean
arapet	manacle	malaise	parboil	jambeux	sacculi	Pandean
ara-red	namable	Sabaism	**bar-bell**	tambour	saucily	sandbag
avager	nasally	**Bahaite**	barbola	**jambiya**	vascula	sand-bar
	pacable	canasta	barbule	lamboys	**sarcoma**	sandman

Wardian	banding	saidest	lakelet	cayenne	earflap	gangrel
yardman	candent	sawdust	lameter	ha'penny	half-cap	haggler
habdabs	farding	bandits	layered	Karenni	half-day	jangler
caddice	gadding	caudate	racemed	pageant	half-pay	langrel
candock	gardant	mandate	sad-eyed	taverna	halfway	langued
cardecu	jamdani	candour	sage-tea	camelot	saffian	languet
daddock	landing	carduus	sakeret	catelog	fat-face	laugher
haddock	madding	eardrum	tagetes	have-not	maffick	mangler
paddock	nandine	handful	tapered	mamelon	baffler	mangoes
pandect	padding	hand-gun	taperer	matelot	maffled	tangled
candida	pardine	handout	wagerer	name-son	palfrey	tangler
bandied	sanding	hard-run	wakened	page-boy	raffler	tangoed
candied	sardine	pandour	wakener	paletot	rat-flea	wangler
candies	wadding	sardius	watered	saveloy	tax-free	baggage
dawdler	warding	taedium	waterer	waveson	hafflin	langaha
handled	yardang	vaudoux	wavelet	lace-ups	halflin	bargain
handler	band-box	war-drum	waverer	Cabeiri	half-wit	ganglia
handsel	bandook	tardive	rake-off	camelry	mafflin	languid
handset	bandrol	hagdown	face-off	madeira	Mayfair	sangria
hard-set	caldron	man-days	take-off	pareira	parfait	tanghin
ländler	cardoon	baseman	Fabergé	vanessa	rag-fair	baggily
mandrel	caudron	cameral	parerga	vareuse	bagfuls	largely
paddler	eardrop	case-law	saw-edge	cavetto	caffila	mangold
pardner	hard-got	caseman	catechu	G-agents	canfuls	nargile
raddled	hard-won	catenae	capelin	galeate	hatfuls	nargily
saddler	lardoon	cateran	Galenic	gaseity	jarfuls	oak-gall
sand-bed	mandioc	caveman	gametic	gazette	jawfall	tangelo
sand-eel	Pandion	danelaw	hare-lip	jadeite	panfuls	May-game
dandify	pandoor	faceman	javelin	Janeite	daffing	pangamy
hand-off	sand-box	game-bag	malefic	Lacerta	gaffing	war-game
bandage	sand-boy	gamelan	paresis	layette	half-one	bagging
faldage	sand-hog	gametal	paretic	magenta	pakfong	banging
fardage	wardrop	gateman	racemic	majesty	ratfink	fagging
yardage	bandore	gateway	ramekin	maleate	damfool	gagging
baldric	caldera	kamerad	rape-oil	navette	jaw-foot	ganging
Baldwin	gaudery	lace-man	rarebit	palette	saffron	gauging
baudric	laddery	lateral	ravelin	paneity	half-ape	hanging
bawdkin	mandira	Lateran	tabetic	ramenta	fanfare	jagging
gaudgie	mandora	name-day	basenji	V-agents	gas-fire	lagging
hard-hit	pandora	paterae	canella	baleful	hayfork	margent
mandril	pandore	raceway	Capella	baneful	oak-fern	pangene
maudlin	pandura	tapetal	dazedly	bateaux	salfern	panging
sand-pit	pay-dirt	wakeman	eagerly	cage-cup	warfare	pargana
Vaudois	sanders	zareeba	fadedly	cajeput	wayfare	ragging
hardoke	yard-arm	cadence	gabelle	careful	catfish	sagging
may-duke	baddish	cadency	gazelle	caseous	gabfest	tagging
Vandyke	baldish	faience	hazelly	dareful	garfish	tangent
bawdily	caddish	fayence	jadedly	easeful	hagfish	wagging
candela	caddyss	ha'pence	labella	fade-out	oar-fish	waygone
daedale	faddish	latence	lamella	fateful	raffish	hangdog
dandily	faddism	latency	mace-ale	gaseous	saw-fish	jargoon
gaudily	faddist	patency	nacelle	gazeful	taffeta	languor
handily	hardish	valence	nakedly	hateful	taffety	day-girl
hardily	Kaddish	valency	padella	haveour	gangway	faggery
mandala	maddest	calends	parella	mazeful	hangman	haggard
mandola	Mahdism	kalends	parelle	rageful	pangram	jaggery
pardale	Mahdist	caperer	patella	rameous	tangram	laggard
rag-doll	maidish	caterer	sabella	take-out	Haggada	raggery
sand-fly	maidism	cat-eyed	sacella	taleful	raggedy	saggard
tardily	pay-desk	faceted	save-all	tapetum	bangled	taggers
wax-doll	Qaddish	gateleg	zanella	wakeful	cargoes	waggery
balding	rag-dust	havened	maremma	wameful	dangler	bargest
bandana	saddish	haverel	caserne	cadenza	fangled	haggish

largess
largish
margosa
waggish
haughty
maggoty
naughty
paughty
saw-gate
hangout
gang-bye
bathyal
cathead
each-way
fat-head
lashkar
mashlam
mash-vat
nashgab
Paphian
pathway
rachial
rawhead
saphead
warhead
wash-day
yakhdan
yashmak
cathode
kathode
raphide
rawhide
cashier
machree
tar-heel
yachter
kachcha
naphtha
bathmic
Kashmir
machair
mashlim
mashlin
cat-hole
ear-hole
jawhole
manhole
rat-hole
nathemo
bashing
dashing
lashing
lathing
machine
manhunt
mashing
washing
cathood
dash-pot
fashion
machzor
manhood
tachyon

wash-pot
wanhope
fashery
hachure
jaghire
kacheri
lathery
saxhorn
hashish
pachisi
rathest
tachism
tachist
machete
bashful
bathtub
Bauhaus
gashful
man-hour
mashlum
mash-tub
mash-tun
wash-out
wash-tub
cachexy
bashlyk
basilar
Caliban
Canidae
capital
capitan
caritas
Dalilah
datival
Gadidae
habitat
Harijan
janizar
laminae
laminar
Laridae
latitat
magical
marital
matinal
maximal
paginal
radical
Ranidae
Ratitae
sahibah
salival
talipat
taxicab
taximan
vaginae
vaginal
vaginas
Vatican
wanigan
marimba
paxiuba
carioca

tapioca
Matilda
basinet
cabinet
caliber
calipee
caliver
carices
galilee
lamiger
lamiter
latices
Latiner
Malines
mariner
matinée
matinee
patined
radicel
radices
ravined
sakiyeh
salices
salicet
samisen
satinet
tabinet
taliped
talipes
varices
satisfy
caliche
kamichi
malicho
basidia
Cabiric
canikin
Fatimid
Hamitic
Hasidic
lacinia
manikin
pacific
Palilia
papilio
Ramilie
salicin
satiric
Tamilic
panicky
bacilli
barilla
cariole
dariole
lapilli
mamilla
manilla
manille
maniple
maxilla
panicle
papilla
patible

rabidly
radiale
radicle
rapidly
ravioli
sanicle
tacitly
validly
vanilla
vapidly
variola
variole
cariama
patient
radiant
salient
sapient
valiant
variant
bar-iron
Capitol
caribou
galipot
halidom
halimot
haricot
janitor
malison
manihoc
Manihot
manitou
parison
paritor
sad-iron
saligot
talipot
warison
calibre
cariere
caviare
laniard
laniary
Babiism
mafioso
Naziism
balista
batiste
jacinth
labiate
Radiata
radiate
sagitta
Samiote
satiate
satiety
variate
variety
badious
cacique
carious
cazique
fatigue
habitué

halibut
halitus
haviour
maximum
Panicum
paviour
Salique
sanious
saviour
various
Panjabi
manjack
Mas-John
mah-jong
zanjero
backpay
backsaw
barkhan
Gaekwar
Gaikwar
hack-saw
jackdaw
jackman
jarkman
markman
packman
pack-rat
packway
parkway
tank-car
walkway
pack ice
backset
backsey
bark-bed
cackler
hackler
hacklet
hackney
nankeen
tackled
tackler
Zadkiel
package
sackage
tankage
banksia
hawkbit
lack-all
pawkily
back-end
backing
balking
banking
carking
gaskins
hacking
hawking
lacking
mankind
marking
packing
parking

racking
Rankine
ranking
sacking
sarking
tacking
talking
tanking
tasking
vacking
walking
yanking
backhoe
backlog
hack-log
jackpot
markhor
backare
cankery
hackery
jankers
saw-kerf
tankard
dankish
darkish
hawkish
jackass
larkish
mawkish
parkish
rackett
rackety
tackety
hackbut
sackbut
sackful
sarkful
tankful
walk-out
Sankhya
fabliau
hallian
hallway
kail-pat
mail-bag
mail-car
mailman
mail-van
pallial
Paulian
pay-load
rail-car
railman
railway
tableau
wallaba
wallaby
carlock
daglock
earlock
fallacy
Gallice
laylock

oar-lock
padlock
raploch
warlock
ballade
May-lady
caulker
dallied
dallier
earlier
gaulter
haulier
nail-bed
rallied
rallier
sallied
tallied
tallies
vaulted
vaulter
bailiff
hayloft
haulage
tallage
tally-ho
baillie
haploid
mail-gig
marl-pit
racloir
tabloid
taillie
tailzie
tall-oil
cat-like
lac-lake
manlike
warllke
day-lily
gall-fly
hallali
may-lily
tail-fly
caulome
gas-lamp
gas-lime
Kallima
oak-lump
ballant
balling
bawling
bay-line
cabling
callant
calling
Calluna
carline
catling
cauline
darling
daylong
eanling
fabling

failing	tailard	palmiet	Barnaby	tannery	taloned	gavotte
falling	vallary	barmaid	bannock	badness	valonea	hap'orth
fatling	warlord	barmkin	cannach	carnose	wagoner	lavolta
gadling	Baalism	gas-main	jannock	earnest	basoche	baroque
gallant	ballast	palm-oil	pannick	farness	caroche	Canopus
galling	carlish	harmala	zarnich	fatness	galoche	Carolus
garland	Carlism	saw-mill	Kannada	faunist	panocha	jacobus
halling	Carlist	wadmoll	cain-hen	gabnash	Aaronic	madoqua
harling	earless	calmant	daunder	garnish	caloric	cacodyl
kaoline	gallise	carmine	fainted	gayness	calorie	kakodyl
Karling	Gaulish	catmint	haunted	harness	canonic	paronym
Lallans	hapless	caymans	haunter	Jainism	Canopic	tan-ooze
lalling	hatless	damming	jauntee	laxness	carotid	pampean
lawland	lawless	farming	launder	madness	carotin	salpian
madling	law-list	garment	maunder	mannish	galopin	calpack
mailing	napless	haemony	nainsel'	mannose	Jacobin	earpick
marline	oarless	harmine	painted	pannose	Japonic	rampick
marling	pay-list	harmony	painter	patness	laconic	Tampico
nailing	rayless	jamming	pannier	rawness	lanolin	tappice
oakling	sacless	jasmine	sainted	sadness	mahonia	ba'spiel
palling	sapless	lamming	saunter	tarnish	masonic	camp-bed
pallone	taplash	maiming	tainted	varnish	paeonic	dappled
Pauline	wayless	payment	taunter	waeness	parodic	day-peep
railing	Baalite	ragment	vaunted	wanness	parotic	lamprey
ralline	fat-lute	raiment	vaunter	wannish	parotid	sampler
ratline	gallate	ramming	damnify	Cainite	parotis	sapples
ratling	tallith	sarment	magnify	gahnite	sagouin	rampage
sailing	ballium	Tammany	sawn-off	kainite	saponin	dauphin
sapling	balls-up	varment	carnage	magnate	saronic	nauplii
tabling	callous	varmint	pannage	magneto	Saxonic	Sapphic
tail-end	fall-guy	warming	tannage	mannite	taborin	garpike
tailing	fall-out	wayment	wainage	Samnite	valonia	rampike
tallent	gallium	daymark	paunchy	tannate	bazooka	happily
tanling	gall-nut	earmark	raunchy	gainful	gazooka	lamp-fly
wailing	malleus	farmery	jauntie	hafnium	paiocke	maypole
walling	pailful	mammary	cannily	mainour	pajocke	tadpole
warling	pallium	May-morn	cannula	painful	palooka	wax-palm
wauling	parlour	palmary	faintly	caporal	cagoule	campana
wawling	parlous	palmyra	fannell	majorat	kagoule	capping
balloon	railbus	saimiri	gauntly	man-o'-war	panoply	carping
call-box	wailful	waymark	paenula	Masorah	façonné	gasping
call-boy	wall-rue	badmash	saintly	mayoral	Madonna	happing
earldom	baclava	farmost	canning	samovar	Mahound	jampani
galleon	Pahlavi	gas-mask	damning	j'adoube	gasohol	kampong
galliot	pavlova	harmost	darning	barocco	cacoepy	lamping
galloon	gallows	marmose	dawning	patonce	jaloppy	lapping
hallion	sallowy	oak-mast	earning	baloney	Camorra	mapping
hallyon	tallowy	palmist	fanning	baronet	canonry	napping
kail-pot	wall-eye	rammish	fawning	bayonet	masonry	parpane
mail-box	Cadmean	magmata	haining	cacolet	savoury	parpend
maillot	nagmaal	mammate	manning	cajoler	vapoury	parpent
nail-rod	oatmeal	mammoth	panning	calomel	baboosh	rampant
paillon	palm-cat	marmite	tanning	caloyer	caboose	rapping
tallboy	pap-meat	palmate	vanning	caromel	carouse	rasping
Walloon	wadmaal	wax-moth	warning	damosel	jalouse	salpinx
fahlerz	Calmuck	cadmium	yawning	damozel	papoose	sapping
fahlore	gammock	harmful	daunton	halogen	vamoose	T'ai-p'ing
failure	hammock	palmful	maintop	jaconet	zamouse	tamping
gallery	Kalmuck	balneal	rainbow	Rasores	calotte	tapping
mallard	mammock	dawn-man	wannion	Samoyed	dacoity	vamping
maulgre	man-made	gainsay	cannery	tabooed	dakoiti	wappend
May-lord	larmier	harn-pan	gauntry	taborer	fagotto	warping
nailery	malmsey	taeniae	laundry	taboret	garotte	camphor

campion	carract	manrent	car-sick	tassell	Laotian	wattled
harpoon	carrect	Marrano	cassock	balsamy	maltman	wax-tree
lampion	farruca	marring	hassock	gaysome	manteau	zabtieh
lampoon	hatrack	padrone	lassock	Lakshmi	mantram	zaptieh
marplot	hayrick	padroni	ransack	satsuma	mantrap	caitiff
Rajpoot	matrice	pairing	passade	waesome	Mantuan	cast-off
rampion	patrick	sacring	passado	bausond	martial	laithfu'
tampion	patrico	tarring	wayside	cassino	Martian	mastiff
bagpipe	tarrock	taurine	banshee	cassone	partial	Tartufe
gas-pipe	hag-ride	vagrant	dabster	dapsone	Raetian	cartage
Campari	tan-ride	warrand	daisied	gassing	raftman	lastage
carpark	barrier	warrant	Dansker	paisano	rat-trap	vantage
carport	carried	warring	falsies	parsing	salt-cat	waftage
jaspery	carrier	bar-room	gagster	passant	salt-fat	wantage
lampern	farrier	carrion	hag-seed	passing	salt-pan	wastage
mappery	hair-eel	carry-on	hamster	pausing	tactual	wattage
pampero	hair-net	gadroon	harshen	raising	Watteau	cantrip
rampart	harried	patriot	harslet	tar-sand	zaptiah	captain
rampire	harrier	patroon	hayseed	war-song	cattabu	eastlin
rapport	married	taproom	kamseen	bassoon	mastaba	fantail
sampire	marrier	taproot	lassoed	caisson	cantico	gastric
vampire	parried	warrior	lassoes	ear-shot	castock	mastoid
dampish	tarried	satrapy	mahseer	mansion	haptics	mattoid
gampish	tarrier	Macrura	maister	passion	hattock	nartjie
harpist	vaurien	padrero	mawseed	samshoo	Lactuca	rat-tail
Lappish	caprify	patrero	mayster	tap-shoe	lattice	rattlin
mappist	sacrify	fairish	paisley	tar-spot	mastich	salt-pit
pappose	barrage	labrose	palsied	caesura	mattock	sautoir
Rappist	farrago	madrasa	pansied	Hansard	nautics	tag-tail
vampish	lairage	matrass	parsley	maestro	tactics	Tantric
wampish	caproic	matross	parsnep	mansard	bastide	wagtail
waspish	darrain	Maurist	passkey	Massora	battler	want-wit
way-post	hair-oil	sacrist	sarsden	tapstry	canteen	xanthic
palpate	hairpin	caprate	sarsnet	falsish	cantlet	xanthin
Rappite	labroid	carroty	tapster	falsism	cantred	partake
warpath	sauroid	nacrite	tarsier	Parsism	cantref	battels
earplug	naartje	narrate	wabster	falsity	castled	battill
pappous	paprika	parroty	waisted	varsity	earthen	cattalo
hanquet	bairnly	haircut	waister	wadsett	fanteeg	earthly
basqued	caerule	nacrous	yapster	caesium	farthel	hartely
lacquer	carrell	natrium	falsify	caestus	farther	hastily
lacquey	fairily	marrowy	salsafy	danseur	gantlet	Kartell
marquee	marrels	darrayn	salsify	masseur	manteel	nastily
masquer	pay-roll	bass-bar	massage	passout	mantlet	nattily
parquet	safrole	batsman	passage	saksaul	martlet	nautili
racquet	hadrome	Capsian	paysage	Tarsius	mast-fed	pantile
marquis	macramé	capstan	sapsago	cassava	mauther	saltily
Pasquil	macrami	cat's-ear	sausage	massive	mawther	tactile
Pasquin	barring	cat's-paw	catskin	passive	narthex	tastily
fair-day	cab-rank	darshan	catsuit	cat's-eye	oak-tree	tattily
fairway	cadrans	daysman	caustic	Vaishya	pad-tree	daytime
pairial	Cairene	daystar	lawsuit	capsize	panther	laytime
pair-oar	caprine	gadsman	parsnip	man-size	panties	May-time
patrial	earring	magsman	pay-slip	caltrap	pantler	pastime
saurian	fairing	marshal	vassail	cartway	partlet	ragtime
taurean	farrand	oarsman	warship	castral	partner	wartime
Zairean	farrant	Pan-Slav	wassail	Dantean	ratteen	baiting
saprobe	gas-ring	passman	capsule	dart-sac	rattler	banteng
barrace	jarring	rakshas	falsely	factual	saltier	banting
barrack	ladrone	ramstam	harshly	fast-day	tartlet	basting
barrico	latrine	tapsman	jap-silk	gas-trap	tattler	batting
caprice	madroña	tar-seal	Marsala	Kantian	waltzer	bay-tine
carrack	madroño	sassaby	Salsola	lacteal	wastrel	cantina

canting	laetare	tantrum	faculty	cam-wood	papyrus	abjoint
casting	lantern	caitive	fatuity	dagwood	jazzman	obloquy
darting	martyry	captive	Nahuatl	oak-wood	dazzler	absolve
easting	mastery	factive	vacuate	rag-wool	jazzily	Iberian
Fastens	mattery	tantivy	vacuity	sap-wood	canzona	obtrude
fasting	nattery	mar-text	valuate	day-work	canzone	uberous
fatting	parture	fabular	cajuput	hayward	canzoni	abysmal
gas-tank	pastern	faculae	famulus	haywire	fanzine	abyssal
halting	pasture	facular	fatuous	lapwork	madzoon	abashed
hatting	pattern	hamular	hamulus	madwort	matzoon	abusage
karting	rapture	hanuman	pabulum	maw-worm	mazzard	abusion
Lagting	rattery	lacunae	ramulus	nayward	matzoth	obesity
lantana	saltern	lacunal	vacuous	nayword	bazzazz	abusive
lasting	saltire	lacunar	Jacuzzi®	ragwork	pazzazz	abuttal
malting	tantara	Laputan	Latvian	ragworm	abraxas	obitual
martini	tartare	maculae	garvock	ragwort	Abbasid	ebb-tide
matting	Tartary	macular	vaivode	saw-wort	ablator	abetted
mattins	tattery	natural	waivode	vanward	abscind	abetter
paktong	wafture	pabular	navvied	war-worn	abscond	abutted
pantine	wastery	paludal	salvoes	waxwork	obscene	abutter
panting	baptise	papulae	salvage	wayward	abactor	abattis
parting	baptism	papular	mauvais	wayworn	obscure	abstain
patting	baptist	radulae	naevoid	bagwash	abscess	abettor
raiting	cattish	radular	naïvely	car-wash	absciss	abature
ratting	Dantist	ramular	valvula	mapwise	abidden	abjurer
saltant	fantasm	samurai	valvule	Yahwist	abiding	abought
salting	fantast	tabulae	carving	Manxman	Abaddon	ébauche
tantony	fantasy	tabular	parvenu	Marxian	abreact	aboulia
tartana	fastish	calumba	salving	Marxism	absence	obovoid
tartane	fattest	cacumen	Calvary	Marxist	abreast	obovate
tartine	fattish	caducei	halvers	bauxite	obverse	abaxial
tasting	Kantism	calumet	taivert	man-year	obsequy	Achaean
tatting	Kantist	manurer	canvass	satyral	observe	Achaian
wafting	lactase	natured	Fauvism	barytes	abigail	octaval
waiting	lactose	papules	Fauvist	calyces	abthane	scraich
wanting	maltase	raguled	harvest	calyxes	obligee	scranch
wasting	Maltese	saluter	parvise	lazy-bed	abridge	scratch
bastion	maltose	babuche	Saivism	baby-sit	obligor	scrauch
caltrop	rattish	Baluchi	Yahvist	barytic	ebriose	Achates
cantdog	Saktism	capuche	larvate	katydid	absinth	scraper
cantion	saltish	manumit	naïveté	ladykin	ebriate	scraggy
caption	tactism	paludic	naïvety	satyric	ebriety	scraigh
cartoon	tartish	parulis	Saivite	satyrid	obviate	scraugh
caution	battuta	patulin	valvate	calycle	oblique	ectasis
faction	cantata	Tamulic	carve-up	ladyfly	obvious	oceanic
Gasthof	cantate	mazurka	narwhal	taxying	abalone	oceanid
hautboy	hastate	yamulka	hag-weed	varying	obelion	octadic
paction	lactate	zakuska	man-week	baryton	obolary	sciarid
partook	partita	zakuski	matweed	dasypod	abolish	sciatic
salt-box	partite	casuals	mayweed	ladycow	ebbless	scrapie
taction	saltate	vacuole	oarweed	dasyure	obelise	accablé
wart-hog	saltato	vaguely	ragweed	halyard	obelisk	octapla
Zantiot	vastity	calumny	tarweed	lanyard	ability	scrawly
bastard	cab-tout	babudom	cat-walk	tanyard	abandon	acharné
battery	canthus	galumph	gadwall	babyish	ebonise	Sciaena
capture	faitour	January	gas-well	calypso	ebonist	scranny
castory	hauteur	saburra	jaywalk	easy-osy	ebonite	scrawny
cattery	mastful	saguaro	maxwell	ladyish	abroach	Actaeon
cautery	pantoum	saouari	warwolf	ladyism	abdomen	ichabod
dastard	paste-up	vaquero	lapwing	zanyism	abiosis	octagon
eastern	rastrum	babuism	lauwine	Dasypus	abiotic	échappé
factory	santour	casuist	waxwing	ladybug	obconic	schappe
facture	tactful	vacuist	barwood	marybud	abrooke	scrappy

ice-boat	scribal	scandal	scepsis	Scottie	edacity	oddsman
scabbed	scriech	scanned	sceptic	acutely	educate	odyssey
scabies	scritch	scanner	scapple	scatole	adrenal	edition
scabrid	scriber	scented	scapula	scuttle	addenda	adjunct
ice-belt	accinge	scunner	scopula	scytale	adherer	adducer
scabble	accidie	acantha	sceptre	scotoma	odd-even	odoured
scybala	aclinic	Scandic	sceptry	scotomy	uddered	adjudge
iceberg	acridin	Scandix	scopate	acetone	adverse	adaxial
ice-bird	actinia	scantle	scyphus	ecotype	idlesse	eddying
ice-blue	actinic	scantly	acarian	acetose	edifice	decadal
ice-cube	schisma	schnell	accrual	ecstasy	edified	decanal
ecocide	echidna	economy	Icarian	Scotish	edifier	getaway
acyclic	scriene	schnook	scoriac	Scotism	adagios	jemadar
scuchin	actinon	schnaps	scoriae	Scotist	admiral	megabar
ice-cold	scrimpy	scenary	Acarida	acetate	admirer	megarad
Acadian	eclipse	scenery	acorned	scutate	advised	tetanal
scudded	echinus	schnorr	scarfed	acatour	adviser	welaway
scudder	occiput	iciness	scarlet	acetous	adhibit	debauch
scudler	achieve	iconise	scarped	ichthys	sdeigne	hexarch
acidify	scrieve	aconite	scarper	acaudal	advisor	mesarch
scedule	ocellar	ichnite	scarred	accusal	idalian	penance
scuddle	schlich	acrobat	scarves	scrubby	odaller	rematch
academe	schlock	scholar	scorner	scrunch	udaller	tenancy
academy	occlude	scrotal	scorper	accused	od's-life	xerarch
acidity	scalade	accoied	scorser	accuser	idyllic	veranda
scleral	scalado	accoyed	scarify	ictuses	odd-like	bedazed
science	scalder	acrogen	scorify	scauper	idolise	behaved
screech	scalled	acroter	écorché	scourer	idolism	belated
screich	scalpel	October	acaroid	scouter	idolist	bemazed
acceder	scalper	scooped	acerbic	scruffy	odalisk	benamed
schemer	scolder	scooper	ochroid	scourge	odylism	betaken
screwed	sculler	scooter	scorpio	acouchy	adulate	cedarod
screwer	ecology	scroggy	scurril	scourie	adamant	ceramet
ycleped	acclaim	scrooge	Acarina	octuple	oddment	Cetacea
acreage	oceloid	scrouge	acarine	scruple	Adamite	debased
screigh	P-Celtic	ecbolic	eccrine	scrummy	edental	debaser
icteric	Q-Celtic	ectopia	ice-rink	scrumpy	adenoid	debater
écuelle	scaldic	ectopic	ocarina	acquire	identic	decayed
ack-emma	sculpin	octofid	scoring	actuary	odontic	defacer
Acheron	Iceland	scholia	acerose	accurse	adenoma	delayed
echelon	scalene	accoyld	actress	accurst	adenine	delayer
ycleap'd	scaling	schoole	accrete	acquest	adonise	fedayee
ycleepe	scallop	scrowle	acerous	scourse	oddness	felafel
ocreate	scollop	scroyle	ochrous	acquite	Odonata	legatee
octette	acaleph	account	Scirpus	actuate	idiotcy	medalet
icterus	schlepp	echoing	ice-spar	scrunty	od-force	metamer
screeve	oculist	ectozoa	scissel	Sciurus	idiotic	métayer
scherzo	schloss	octopod	scissil	scavage	odzooks	penates
ice-free	acolyte	accompt	acushla	scowder	adjoint	rebater
scoffer	acolyth	accourt	ice-show	scowrer	adjourn	related
scaffie	oculate	accoast	scissor	scowrie	adapted	relater
ice-fall	ocellus	echoise	Scotian	ice-worm	adapter	relayed
scuffle	schmock	echoism	schtick	ectypal	adopted	remanet
ice-floe	schmuck	echoist	Scotice	acrylic	edaphic	renayed
ice-foot	scamper	sciolto	scatter	ecdysis	adaptor	repaper
aciform	schmoes	eclogue	scutter	scrying	adipose	retaken
ice-fern	Scomber	octopus	scythed	advance	adermin	retaker
ice-fish	scumber	scrotum	scyther	ideally	odorant	velamen
scaglia	scummed	acronym	acetify	adharma	address	velated
Scoggin	scummer	icepack	Scotify	od's-bobs	addrest	deraign
ice-hill	scamble	ice-pick	scutage	oddball	adpress	derange
ecthyma	schmelz	scupper	Scotchy	edictal	odorate	mélange
actinal	scumble	acapnia	ichthic	eductor	odorous	relâche

seraphs	levator	herbist	rescind	bending	bemedal	deleble
bedawin	megafog	herbose	hen-coop	dead-end	federal	vexedly
ceramic	megaron	nebbish	reactor	deodand	general	beteeme
cerasin	megaton	sea-bass	sea-cook	feeding	Genevan	meseems
fedarie	metazoa	verbose	sea-crow	feuding	hederal	dejeune
gelatin	peraeon	herbous	percept	gelding	Peneian	demeane
heparin	relator	sea-blue	mercery	heading	peregal	demesne
hepatic	senator	terbium	mercury	leading	renewal	Gehenna
hexadic	telamon	berceau	net-cord	lending	Senecan	sejeant
keramic	venator	dew-claw	peccary	mending	several	develop
keratin	genappe	pea-coat	rescore	pendant	terefah	hebenon
megabit	hetaera	pea-crab	sea-card	pendent	vegetal	pereion
melanic	hetaira	redcoat	metcast	pending	veteran	reredos
melanin	Megaera	sea-coal	pen-case	reading	beseech	semeion
nematic	remarry	teuchat	percase	redding	decency	temenos
pelagic	bécasse	meacock	percuss	reeding	defence	benempt
regalia	because	peacock	tea-cosy	seeding	Rebecca	receipt
relaxin	degauss	percoct	leucite	sending	recency	bebeeru
remanié	delapse	petcock	ketchup	tedding	regence	bepearl
sebacic	megasse	sea-cock	red-cowl	tendenz	regency	jewelry
sematic	relapse	deicide	beadman	verdant	remercy	pereira
Serapic	defaste	beached	dead-pan	wedding	tedesca	revelry
Serapis	penalty	beechen	dead-pay	weeding	tedesco	terebra
tetanic	pesante	belcher	headman	welding	delenda	decease
vedalia	regatta	bencher	headway	yeading	bejewel	defense
veganic	Vedanta	leechee	herdman	dendron	fevered	demerse
velaria	devalue	leuchen	seed-lac	dew-drop	geneses	recense
velaric	pegasus	merchet	Vendean	feedlot	Jezebel	release
venatic	petasus	peacher	lewdsby	herdboy	leveret	reverse
xerafin	renague	perched	heyduck	seedbox	meseled	reversi
xerasia	revalue	percher	sea-dace	tendron	referee	reverso
aefauld	tetanus	reached	sea-duck	readapt	reneger	rêveuse
cenacle	lesbian	reacher	vendace	readopt	renewer	teleost
débâcle	membral	rescued	verdict	feodary	reverer	beneath
default	remblai	rescuer	wet-dock	feudary	seceder	celesta
hexapla	sea-bean	teacher	bendlet	Jeddart	venerer	celeste
legally	sea-bear	welcher	dead-men	perdure	demerge	dejecta
mesally	sea-beat	wencher	dead-set	verdure	deterge	démenti
metally	sea-boat	mercify	headset	weedery	remerge	détente
penally	Serbian	deictic	leidger	feudist	revenge	genette
regally	kebbock	helcoid	meddler	geodesy	reweigh	memento
retable	kebbuck	percoid	needler	herdess	telergy	seventh
seeable	nebbich	teachie	peddler	key-desk	dépêche	seventy
tenable	setback	teach-in	readier	reddest	bedevil	vedette
venally	wetback	tea-cake	reed-bed	reddish	benefic	Benelux
bepaint	herblet	key-cold	seedbed	sea-dust	benefit	cereous
besaint	herb-tea	percale	re-edify	tea-dish	ceresin	détenue
delaine	pebbled	rescale	send-off	vendiss	demerit	renegue
demaine	sea-beet	sea-calf	vendage	Wendish	generic	réseaux
demayne	herbage	sex-cell	headrig	deodate	genesis	revenue
depaint	cembalo	wet-cell	readmit	feu-duty	genetic	bereave
dewanny	netball	leucoma	seedlip	deedful	heretic	deceive
pesaunt	geebung	newcome	seed-oil	heedful	nemesia	deserve
remains	henbane	o'ercome	tendril	lead-out	nemesis	receive
repaint	sea-bank	welcome	Veddoid	needful	pedesis	reserve
aerator	verbena	descant	deedily	read-out	pedetic	reseize
celadon	webbing	descend	headily	sea-dove	reverie	beef-ham
decagon	red-book	descent	needily	let-down	selenic	sea-foam
decapod	gerbera	fencing	readily	meadowy	senecio	A-effect
delator	herbary	leucine	seedily	set-down	telesis	perfect
hexagon	newborn	Meccano®	beldame	dead-eye	venefic	perfidy
hexapod	sea-bird	peccant	beading	bedeman	zetetic	beeftea
legator	sea-born	percine	bedding	bederal	beseeke	deified

deifier	lengthy	bewhore	desirer	reticle	retinue	jellied
feoffee	penguin	Jethart	devilet	vehicle	serious	re-alter
feoffer	weigh-in	lechery	devisee	vesicle	tedious	replied
leaflet	Bengali	leghorn	deviser	vexilla	believe	replier
sea-fret	bergylt	sea-hare	femiter	melisma	relieve	Wealden
self-fed	pergola	Senhora	helices	seriema	relievo	well-fed
leafage	seagull	Peshito	helixes	verismo	Mes-John	well-set
serfage	wergild	rechate	pedicel	beginne	perjink	jellify
deaf-aid	bergama	Cepheus	perigee	defiant	perjure	sell-off
jeofail	begging	beehive	reciter	deviant	perjury	well-off
jetfoil	geogeny	sea-hawk	refined	hemione	weekday	geology
sexfoil	geogony	Cebidae	refiner	lenient	peekabo	keelage
beefalo	hedging	decimal	regimen	mediant	deckled	négligé
dew-fall	logging	Delilah	reliver	reliant	heckler	neology
dewfull	Neogene	devisal	remiges	resiant	necklet	realign
menfolk	o'ergang	Felidae	repiner	benison	leakage	sea-legs
merfolk	pegging	Felinae	resider	debitor	necktie	healthy
penfold	reagent	feminal	resiner	demigod	perkily	wealthy
sea-folk	wedging	fenitar	retired	devisor	peskily	declaim
tenfold	beggary	genipap	retiree	genitor	sea-kale	new-laid
perfume	belgard	genital	reviler	heritor	serkali	reallie
perfumy	sea-girt	genizah	reviser	leg-iron	decking	realtie
beffana	leggism	geoidal	reviver	lexicon	Jenkins	reclaim
leafing	lengest	helical	semiped	melilot	jerking	sea-like
reefing	Newgate	heliman	veliger	merinos	necking	cellule
self-end	sea-gate	helipad	vetiver	pea-iron	peaking	heal-all
feoffor	tergite	jemidar	Yezidee	peridot	pecking	sea-lily
sea-food	weighty	lexical	Zezidee	perigon	reeking	deplume
serfdom	bee-glue	medical	besiege	retinol	sea-king	réclame
ten-foot	sea-gown	Mexican	seringa	revisor	weekend	reclimb
web-foot	tea-gown	Oedipal	bedight	revivor	peckish	Bellona
deiform	Heshvan	pedicab	behight	semilog	bee-kite	berline
eelfare	lethean	pelican	benight	sericon	aeolian	ceiling
fee-farm	recheat	pemican	betight	venison	bell-jar	dealing
fen-fire	red-head	recital	delight	periapt	bellman	decline
perform	red-heat	reginal	fetiche	deciare	heel-tap	devling
sea-fire	sea-haar	retinae	Jericho	devilry	hell-cat	feeling
welfare	recheck	retinal	relight	Félibre	keelman	fonland
bedfast	Methody	retiral	aecidla	retiary	meal-man	gelling
jewfish	beshrew	revisal	deficit	hérissé	realgar	healing
net-fish	lethied	revival	delimit	métisse	seal-wax	heeling
perfuse	meshuga	seminal	deliria	pelisse	tea-lead	Hellene
redfish	cepheid	seminar	Geminid	periost	tea-leaf	hem-line
sea-fish	Mechlin	semitar	legitim	sepiost	jellaba	herling
selfish	nephric	vesicae	levitic	veriest	deflect	keeling
selfism	technic	vesical	neritic	deviate	fetlock	lee-lane
selfist	keyhole	bewitch	pelitic	genista	hemlock	merling
serfish	beshame	dehisce	periwig	mediate	neglect	peeling
leafbud	bethumb	mediacy	revisit	rebirth	pellach	recline
pea-fowl	bethump	menisci	sebific	seriate	pellack	reeling
sea-fowl	beshine	bedizen	sedilia	teniate	pellock	replant
Belgian	beshone	bemired	Semitic	bezique	re-elect	sea-lane
verglas	bethink	besides	sericin	decidua	reflect	sealant
yeggman	meshing	betided	tenioid	dedimus	replace	sea-line
beagler	methane	betimes	betitle	detinue	replica	sealing
feigned	methink	decibel	cedilla	devious	sea-loch	seeling
leaguer	red-hand	decided	delible	helibus	wedlock	set-line
leughen	rethink	decider	gelidly	Oedipus	Wenlock	telling
Neogaea	nephron	defiler	hemiola	perique	yelloch	veiling
weighed	perhaps	deliver	legible	relique	ceilidh	welling
weigher	reshape	demirep	legibly	repique	seclude	wetland
lee-gage	becharm	denizen	pedicle	residua	bellied	yelling
heigh-ho	beghard	derider	petiole	residue	hellier	zealant

begloom	new-made	reinter	serosae	reboant	bespake	retrial
bell-boy	Heimweh	vernier	Veronal®	rebound	bespoke	sea-road
bellhop	seam-set	reunify	redoubt	recount	sea-pike	tear-bag
hell-box	desmoid	peonage	debouch	redound	seppuku	tear-gas
hellion	germain	teenage	deforce	refound	leg-pull	bedrock
keelson	mermaid	deontic	devoice	remount	reapply	defrock
reallot	sea-maid	pennill	rejoice	repoint	redpoll	derrick
Realtor®	vermeil	Reynold	retouch	resound	respell	detract
rebloom	beamily	pen-name	seconde	aerosol	serpula	metrics
sea-lion	gemmule	eevning	secondo	decolor	despond	rebrace
well-won	sea-mile	kenning	begored	Mesozoa	dew-pond	re-erect
wet-look	vermell	leaning	beloved	metopon	heaping	refract
yealdon	vermily	leonine	betoken	begorra	helping	retrace
dewlapt	beaming	meaning	decoder	demonry	keeping	retract
declare	desmine	pennant	demoded	felonry	kemping	secrecy
deplore	ferment	pennine	deposer	helotry	leaping	terrace
meal-ark	gemming	penning	devoted	heronry	perpend	tetract
pedlary	germane	regnant	devotee	recoure	perpent	verruca
sea-lark	hemming	remnant	Helodea	rejourn	respond	bedridd
sealery	hetmans	seining	kerogen	velours	sea-pink	degrade
sea-lord	lemming	veining	oenomel	zedoary	serpent	detrude
cellist	reamend	vernant	recover	delouse	tenpins	regrade
declass	reaming	re-endow	recower	Genoese	terpene	regrede
hellish	seeming	reunion	remodel	heroise	vespine	tetrode
keyless	segment	ternion	removed	heroism	weeping	bearded
legless	teaming	deanery	remover	rehouse	yelping	berried
realise	teeming	fernery	reposed	remorse	peep-toe	berries
realism	tegmina	hennery	tenoner	bemouth	besport	debrief
realist	termini	re-entry	venomed	velouté	deep-fry	decreed
reclose	verminy	rein-arm	xerotes	aerobus	jeepers	decreet
recluse	fermion	reynard	regorge	decorum	jeopard	decried
rellish	gemmery	ternary	aerobic	pelorus	leopard	decrier
sexless	seamark	fennish	bedouin	Xenopus	peppery	deerlet
deflate	beamish	fewness	begonia	behoove	respire	ferried
deplete	kermess	kernish	celomic	devolve	seaport	hearken
fellate	sea-moss	newness	demonic	resolve	tempera	hearted
mellite	bee-moth	peonism	demotic	revolve	tempore	hearten
neolith	fermata	redness	deposit	metonym	tempura	learned
Peelite	gemmate	setness	hedonic	bespeak	bedpost	learner
perlite	lemmata	teentsy	henotic	leap-day	despise	Negroes
reality	permute	wennish	kenosis	net-play	hey-pass	pearled
reflate	regmata	wetness	kenotic	respeak	sea-pass	pearler
replete	termite	kernite	ketosis	respray	tempest	perrier
zeolite	fermium	keynote	meconic	templar	despite	regreet
becloud	teemful	neonate	meconin	bespice	respite	reorder
jealous	new-mown	pennate	meiosis	henpeck	sea-path	retried
kellaut	aeonian	reunite	meiotic	respect	bespout	sea-reed
perlous	Aetnean	ternate	melodic	bespeed	eelpout	serried
sell-out	bean-bag	dernful	mesonic	deep-fet	helpful	terreen
zealful	hernial	heinous	metonic	deep-sea	jerquer	terrier
zealous	Lemnian	veinous	metopic	keepnet	mesquin	wearied
beslave	lernean	beknave	nepotic	perplex	mesquit	petrify
hellova	Kennick	beknown	Neronic	telpher	re-equip	redraft
helluva	redneck	fern-owl	Pelopid	templed	bear-cat	terrify
Pehlevi	re-enact	neo-Nazi	peloria	templet	betread	ferrugo
replevy	beinked	deposal	peloric	tempter	cerrial	peerage
bellows	dernier	femoral	reposit	seepage	decrial	verruga
mellowy	hennaed	Jehovah	xerosis	serpigo	hearsay	detrain
yellowy	meander	menorah	xerotic	Delphic	meercat	geordie
besmear	pennied	nemoral	recoyle	delphin	meerkat	georgic
Permian	pennies	removal	remould	despair	ne'erday	Hebraic
term-day	reannex	reposal	demount	despoil	retread	negroid
vermian	re-enter	Seconal®	heroine	vespoid	retreat	pearlin

pedrail
recruit
refrain
retrain
retrait
tear-pit
terrain
weirdie
zebroid
heureka
bed-roll
Cedrela
dearnly
febrile
ferrule
heartly
merrily
peartly
wearily
weirdly
zebrula
zebrule
begrime
neuroma
reframe
reprime
bearing
cedrine
gearing
hearing
herring
jeering
key-ring
leering
neurine
neurone
pébrine
Petrine
pow-rent
regrant
regrind
reprint
searing
tearing
terrene
terrine
veering
wearing
zebrine
bedroom
gearbox
heirdom
legroom
rear-dos
red-root
reproof
sea-room
tea-room
bedropt
decrypt
pedrero
petrary
bearish

beprose
defrost
depress
heiress
heurism
leg-rest
leprose
leprosy
metrist
nearest
necrose
Negress
peeress
rearise
recross
redress
refresh
regress
repress
reprise
sea-risk
tea-rose
wearish
zebrass
bedrite
betroth
cedrate
Debrett
ferrate
ferrety
ferrite
Negrito
regrate
retrate
rewrite
rewrote
secreta
secrete
serrate
defraud
fearful
ferrous
leprous
petrous
regroup
tearful
deprave
deprive
redrive
reprive
reprove
repryve
decrown
reprize
beeswax
censual
deiseal
felspar
hessian
Jersian
Jew's-ear
key-seat
mensual

Messiah
Messias
newsman
Persian
redsear
sea-star
seismal
sensual
Telstar
persico
seasick
bedside
seaside
bee-skep
feaster
heister
hepster
leister
measled
measles
Meissen
oersted
Perspex®
red-seed
webster
welsher
versify
message
beastie
cesspit
deasoil
deistic
hership
leg-slip
leg-spin
mess-tin
Perseid
redskin
seismic
vessail
netsuke
beastly
densely
hersall
herself
messily
pensile
sea-salt
sensile
sessile
tensely
tensile
tersely
beesome
jessamy
ceasing
jessant
leasing
peasant
pepsine
persant
persona
retsina

sea-sand
sensing
teasing
versant
versine
versing
weasand
cession
gemsbok
leg-show
mersion
neuston
newsboy
peascod
pension
session
tea-shop
tension
tersion
version
wet-shod
bedsore
berserk
censure
dessert
leisure
measure
pessary
seasure
sensory
seysure
tessera
Persism
persist
sensism
sensist
density
felsite
tensity
versute
Celsius
deasiul
pea-soup
Perseus
reissue
sea-slug
pensive
tensive
zemstvo
leasowe
peishwa
bestead
bestial
central
dextral
dextran
gentian
meat-man
neutral
oestral
peat-hag
peatman
rent-day

rest-day
tea-tray
tertial
tertian
text-man
textual
ventral
vestral
bedtick
bestick
bestuck
lettuce
pontact
pentice
peptics
restock
testacy
cestode
pentode
peptide
testudo
bestrew
centner
centred
feather
feller
genteel
heathen
heather
hen-toed
kestrel
leather
meat-tea
mettled
neither
peat-bed
rentier
reutter
seethed
seether
seltzer
settled
settler
tea-tree
tent-bed
tent-peg
test-bed
vent-peg
weather
web-toed
yew-tree
beatify
certify
left-off
rectify
restaff
restiff
testify
centage
lentigo
nest-egg
restage
tentage

tentigo
ventage
ventige
vertigo
vestige
weftage
beatnik
benthic
bestain
bestrid
centric
certain
cestoid
deltaic
deltoid
dentoid
Deutzia
dextrin
lentoid
meat-pie
penthia
pertain
rectrix
tectrix
tent-pin
testril
westlin
pertake
beet-fly
bestill
deathly
fertile
gentile
gestalt
meat-fly
pettily
reptile
restyle
sectile
sextile
tenthly
test-fly
testily
textile
bedtime
centime
leptome
septime
tea-time
beating
Beltane
belting
betting
bez-tine
dentine
destine
destiny
felting
gestant
getting
heating
heptane
jesting

letting
meeting
melting
neoteny
Neptune
netting
pelting
pentane
pentene
peptone
petting
reptant
resting
retting
sea-tang
seating
sestina
sestine
setting
sextans
sextant
tenting
testing
ventana
venting
vesting
vetting
weeting
westing
wetting
benthos
destroy
festoon
keitloa
lection
menthol
mention
neutron
peat-bog
rection
section
septuor
settlor
sextuor
testoon
Gestapo
red-tape
bestorm
century
dentary
denture
feature
gesture
hectare
lectern
lecture
lecturn
leotard
lettern
nectary
peatary
peatery
perturb

rectory	medusae	jejunum	network	sferics	cheater	chicory
restart	medusan	Réaumur	o'erword	affront	phraser	shicksa
restore	mezuzah	regulus	seaward	offside	sheared	thecate
rettery	nebulae	seculum	sea-ware	offscum	shearer	check-up
sea-term	nebular	tenuous	sea-worm	offtake	sheaved	thick'un
sea-turn	perusal	Xenurus	sea-worn	effulge	sheaves	chaddar
sectary	refusal	recurve	webworm	off-ward	theater	Cheddar
testern	refutal	seruewe	weyward	affying	wheaten	chuddah
texture	regulae	Servian	sea-wave	agnamed	sheathe	chuddar
venture	regular	service	betwixt	agraffe	sheathy	khaddar
venturi	secular	pervade	Zeuxian	agrapha	thiamin	Rhodian
vesture	tegulae	bevvied	re-exist	agnatic	cheaply	chidden
vettura	tegular	heavier	zeuxite	agravic	chiasma	shedder
western	nelumbo	oeuvres	recycle	oghamic	phratry	shidder
yestern	defunct	sea-view	kerygma	agraste	theatre	shudder
dentist	felucca	selvage	belying	egg-bird	Chianti	whidder
Kentish	sebundy	vervain	defying	egg-cell	thwaite	shadily
leftism	beaufet	heavily	denying	agaçant	shea-nut	chiding
leftist	cerumen	nervule	levying	egg-case	thiasus	shading
lentisk	deluded	servile	relying	egg-cosy	chlamys	shadoof
Lettish	deluder	weevily	renying	ague-fit	chobdar	rhodora
pectise	lemures	cervine	revying	ogreish	she-bear	rhodium
pectose	peruser	fervent	benzoic	igneous	chubbed	rhodous
peltast	rebuker	heaving	benzoin	egg-flip	shebeen	khediva
pentise	rebuses	leaving	Neozoic	Ogygian	Chablis	khedive
pentose	reduced	nervine	benzole	agogics	Thebaic	shadowy
peptise	reducer	revving	benzene	egghead	Thebaid	chaetae
pertuse	refugee	servant	benzine	agrised	shabble	cheetah
pettish	refuser	serving	seizing	igniter	shebang	shreddy
sea-tost	refuter	weaving	weazand	against	rhabdom	thready
ventose	reputed	beavery	seizure	agilely	rhubarb	cheeper
Ventôse	requiem	nervure	benzoyl	agelong	phobism	cheerer
wettish	securer	pervert	bezzazz	ageless	phobist	cheesed
dentate	seducer	servery	affable	agility	chabouk	chiefer
gestate	rejudge	dervish	affably	egality	chibouk	sheeted
meltith	resurge	peevish	effable	agamoid	rhabdus	shoe-peg
peltate	beaufin	nervate	affaire	eggmass	choc-bar	thieves
restate	decuria	Servite	offbeat	agamous	choctaw	wheeled
septate	legumin	velvety	off-come	agonise	choc-ice	wheeler
septett	Lemuria	fervour	X-factor	agonist	shy-cock	whoever
sestett	petunia	nervous	off-duty	agnomen	checker	whyever
sextett	refugia	servewe	offence	ignorer	chicken	wheenge
tektite	sequoia	between	effendi	ignoble	chocker	wheesht
testate	beguile	seaweed	offered	ignobly	shicker	cheerio
centaur	decuple	hen-wife	offerer	aground	shocked	choenix
centrum	medulla	sea-wife	affear'd	egg-plum	shocker	Phoenix
featous	rebuild	reawake	offense	aggrace	shucker	phrenic
jestful	recuile	sea-wall	offhand	aggrade	thicken	Rhaetia
lentous	sequela	sea-wolf	African	igarapé	thicket	Rhaetic
meat-tub	setuale	setwall	affined	aggress	whacked	shoe-tie
oestrum	tequila	werwolf	officer	aggrate	whacker	wheelie
oestrus	beguine	redwing	affiche	agister	whicker	cheerly
pestful	genuine	sea-wind	offload	agistor	Chicago	chiefly
restful	sequent	sea-wing	afflict	ego-trip	chéchia	sheerly
tentful	requere	redwood	ufology	egotise	chuckie	wheedle
tertius	require	bedward	off-line	egotism	phacoid	wheeple
zestful	beauish	bedwarf	aftmost	egotist	rhachis	wheezle
centavo	bequest	bedwork	sfumato	agitate	chuckle	phlegmy
festive	repulse	dew-worm	pfennig	agitato	shackle	shoeing
restive	request	eelworm	afforce	Iguvine	thickly	phaeton
mestiza	Senussi	felwort	efforce	pheazar	chicane	threnos
mestizo	requite	leeward	affoord	phrasal	chicano	wheeson
decuman	tenuity	legwork	offpeak	cheapen	phocine	chiefry

phaeism
phrensy
bheesty
thretty
Phoebus
threave
chaffer
chuffed
shafted
shafter
shifted
shifter
whiffer
whiffet
shuffle
whiffle
chiffon
chigger
shagged
shogged
thigger
thuggee
chagrin
thiggit
chignon
Ahriman
shaitan
shrinal
shriech
shritch
chained
shrived
shrivel·
shriven
shriver
thrived
thriven
thriver
aheight
shright
Shiitic
shrilly
thrilly
whaisle
whaizle
chrisom
Christy
thrifty
thristy
shrieve
chukker
shakily
shaking
chikhor
chikara
shikari
chekist
shake-up
challan
Chilean
chiliad
Chilian
ghilgai

shellac
thalian
chalice
Shylock
Chaldee
chalder
Chelsea
childed
childer
chilled
phellem
philter
shelled
sheller
shelter
shelves
thalweg
thiller
whelked
khalifa
challis
cheloid
ghillie
phallic
phallin
sheltie
shilpit
thallic
childly
thalami
chalone
choline
phalanx
whaling
shallon
shallop
shallot
shallow
cholera
choltry
philtre
whalery
thylose
wholism
chelate
thulite
chillum
phallus
thallus
thulium
chalaza
champac
champak
chamade
chamber
chamfer
chamlet
chimley
chimney
chumley
shammed
shammer
shimmer

thumbed
thumper
whimper
whimsey
chymify
chamois
khamsin
rhombic
Thummim
shamble
thimble
whample
whemmle
whimple
whomble
whommle
whummle
thymine
rhomboi
rhombos
shampoo
chambré
chimera
chimere
chamise
chamiso
chemise
chemism
chemist
Rhemish
Rhemist
rhymist
Thomism
Thomist
Shemite
themata
chymous
Rhamnus
rhombus
thammuz
chinwag
thannah
whangam
phonics
chancel
chancer
changer
channel
chanter
chantey
chunder
chunnel
chunner
chunter
shanked
shunned
shunter
thankee
thanker
thinker
thinned
thinner
thonder

thonged
thunder
whangee
whene'er
whinger
thanage
rhonchi
chantie
chindit
Chinkie
phone-in
shindig
shingle
shingly
phoneme
shining
whining
chanson
chantor
chinook
phantom
ahungry
chancre
chantry
chondre
chondri
shandry
Chinese
Rhenish
shiness
shyness
khanate
phenate
phonate
rhenium
chanoyu
chintzy
chloral
theorbo
thrombi
shroudy
chooser
choosey
shooter
theorem
throned
thrower
whoopee
whooper
through
whoop
chaotic
chloric
chookie
chromic
chronic
theoric
throw-in
shoogle
chronon
shmoose
throaty
whoobub
chapeau

chapman
chip-hat
shiplap
shipman
ship-way
shophar
shopman
whipcat
whip-saw
chaplet
chapped
chapter
chipped
chipper
chopper
chopped
shopper
whipped
whipper
whippet
whopper
chappie
rhaphis
shapely
chopine
shaping
ship-boy
shippon
shop-boy
whip-top
chapati
chupati
shipful
shopful
chequer
chordal
gharial
shariat
sheriat
thereat
theriac
thermae
thermal
whereas
whereat
cherubs
thereby
whereby
charact
charade
charger
charley
charmed
charmer
charnel
charred
charter
chirper
sharded

sharker
sharpen
sharper
sherbet
shereef
shirker
shirred
shorten
thorned
wharves
where'er
wherret
whirler
whirred
whirret
whorled
sheriff
thurify
churchy
charlie
charpie
chervil
choroid
dhurrie
gherkin
sherris
shortie
therein
thermic
Thermit®
theroid
thyroid
wherein
charily
chorale
chortle
sharply
shortly
thirdly
whirtle
charing
chorine
pharynx
sharing
shoring
chariot
charpoy
cheroot
chorion
Pharaoh
thereof
thereon
thermos
whereof
whereon
therapy
charism
cherish
chorist
whereso
whorish
Bharati
charity

thereto
thirsty
thorite
whereto
charqui
chirrup
choreus
churrus
thorium
thyrsus
Chesvan
physics
bhistee
chasmed
chasten
chessel
chested
Chislev
ghessed
shaster
shyster
whisker
whisket
whiskey
whisper
chasmic
Chassid
chassis
phasmid
ghastly
ghostly
thistle
thistly
thyself
whistle
chasing
shastra
chesnut
château
khotbah
khutbah
shittah
whittaw
photics
chatted
chattel
chatter
chitter
chutney
khotbeh
shatter
shotted
shotten
shutter
thether
thither
thother
whate'er
whatten
whether
whetted
whetter
whither

whitret	Sinaean	bizarre	gibbous	discard	birding	wire-man
thatcht	aidance	rivalry	limbous	discern	eilding	wiretap
shittim	finance	simarre	niobium	discerp	finding	wire-way
whatsis	viranda	filasse	Circean	discord	gilding	licence
whatsit	virando	Sivaism	pit-coal	discure	girding	silence
shottle	citadel	tirasse	bibcock	pilcorn	hilding	vivency
shuttle	didakei	vinasse	biocide	piscary	kidding	videnda
whitely	dilated	ailanto	discide	rip-cord	lindane	bigener
whittle	dilater	Sivaite	zincode	sincere	misdone	cinerea
rhatany	filabeg	piragua	air-crew	tip-cart	ridding	dimeter
rhytina	filacer	bivalve	birchen	viscera	wilding	fire-new
whiting	filazer	kit-boat	Circaea	circusy	winding	hive-bee
whatnot	hicatee	Niobean	circled	die-cast	air-drop	livered
whitlow	lie-abed	pigboat	circler	diocese	bird-dog	minever
photism	limacel	tie-beam	circlet	discase	diadrom	pie-eyed
whitish	limaces	dieback	ditcher	discuss	jib-door	pig-eyed
shotgun	minaret	finback	filcher	giocoso	wild-dog	pikelet
shot-put	vilayet	limbeck	finched	miscast	windrow	pin-eyed
shut-out	visaged	bilboes	fitchée	pincase	Windsor	pipe-key
Whitsun	giraffe	dibbler	fitchet	viscose	bindery	ridered
shut-eye	hidalga	kimboed	fitchew	siccity	cindery	rivered
thruway	hidalgo	nibbler	hitcher	zincite	pindari	riveret
shrubby	piranha	timbrel	kitchen	linctus	tindery	riveted
chaunce	cidaris	wimbrel	linchet	viscous	windore	riveter
thrutch	dibasic	yibbles	pilcher	zincous	middest	sinewed
rheumed	dika-oil	fimbria	pinched	diedral	piedish	tile-red
shouter	Filaria	air-bell	pincher	findram	pin-dust	vinewed
chaunge	jigajig	diabolo	pitched	misdeal	wild-ass	widener
theurgy	piratic	hip-belt	pitcher	misdraw	wildish	wizened
thought	Titania	oil-belt	tinchel	wild-cat	Yiddish	disedge
chauvin	titanic	piebald	witchen	wildoat	biodata	diverge
thrummy	Vinalia	pinball	zincked	wind-bag	misdate	lineage
Shavian	vis-à-vis	timbale	zincify	piddock	hind-gut	mileage
shaving	vitamin	dibbing	discage	viaduct	mindful	cimelia
Cheviot	vivaria	disband	ribcage	windock	wind-gun	dimeric
chevron	Zizania	fibbing	biscuit	diddler	lie-down	Dioecia
shivery	ziganka	hip-bone	circuit	fiddler	mildewy	eidetic
showman	citable	jibbing	discoid	fiddley	sitdown	eirenic
chowder	disable	mirbane	kinchin	girdled	bipedal	fivepin
Shawnee	disally	ribband	tie-clip	girdler	fire-bar	kinesis
show-off	finable	ribbing	zincoid	hindleg	fireman	kinetic
showghe	finagle	rib-bone	oil-cake	kiddier	firepan	mimesis
showbiz	finally	ribbony	air-cell	kiddies	five-bar	mimetic
showily	fixable	jib-boom	miscall	kindler	liberal	nine-pin
chewink	hirable	pit-brow	piccolo	kindred	lineman	niterie
showing	likable	disbark	vincula	lip-deep	literal	piperic
thawing	livable	fibbery	Zincala	misdeed	live-oak	silesia
show-box	mirable	fig-bird	Zincali	misdeem	mineral	Sirenia
showery	miracle	filbert	Zincalo	misdiet	pikeman	sirenic
wheyish	ridable	gilbert	discant	misdoer	sidecar	tide-rip
whey-tub	sizable	libbard	fir-cone	piddler	sideral	cineole
whizzed	vitally	misborn	hircine	pig-deer	sideway	firefly
whizzer	digamma	oil-bird	mincing	riddler	Tibetan	fixedly
rhizoid	gisarme	tilbury	Miocene	tiddled	tide-way	micella
rhizome	sixaine	air-base	piscina	tiddler	tile-hat	micelle
rhizine	dilator	diabase	piscine	tiddley	time-lag	mineola
bimanal	disavow	gibbose	wincing	windage	vinegar	miserly
didakai	girasol	air-bath	zincing	wind-egg	virelay	mixedly
die-away	jigajog	hip-bath	jim-crow	disdain	wide-gab	nigella
Nicaean	limaçon	kibbutz	pilcrow	giddily	wine-bag	tigerly
picamar	mirador	limbate	discept	windily	wine-fat	vitelli
pitapat	picador	niobite	hiccupy	bidding	wine-sap	vixenly
pitarah	tinamou	oil-bath	miscopy	binding	wine-vat	dilemma

aileron	misfell	digging	Xiphias	pig-herd	licitly	sick-man
bibelot	misfile	figging	fighter	withers	ribible	silk-hat
dice-box	pinfold	hinging	fish-net	zithern	rigidly	silk-man
filemot	pitfall	jigging	high-fed	highest	risible	dinky-di
firebox	sixfold	misgone	highmen	highish	silicle	milk-leg
firedog	tinfuls	pigging	high-set	mightst	timidly	pickeer
firepot	disfame	ridging	lighted	Sikhism	visible	pickled
live-box	tiffany	rigging	lighten	lithate	visibly	pickler
pi-meson	tiffing	ringent	lighter	lithite	vividly	sick-bed
side-box	six-foot	ringing	mishmee	dishful	ripieno	sickled
viceroy	difform	singing	nighted	fishful	didicoi	tickler
vine-rod	disform	sirgang	righten	lithium	didicoy	tinkler
viretot	misfare	tinging	righter	mid-hour	divisor	kick-off
wide-boy	misfire	wigging	sighted	pithful	kirimon	zinkify
dirempt	misform	Zingana	sighter	sighful	liaison	linkage
fire-arm	piffero	Zingane	tighten	wishful	pig-iron	sinkage
Viverra	pilfery	Zingani	fishify	without	silicon	ricksha
cineast	pin-fire	Zingano	cichlid	Ziphius	similor	milkily
disease	diffuse	kingdom	fishgig	eightvo	Vidicon®	riskily
diseuse	liefest	king-rod	fish-oil	lich-owl	visitor	silkily
diverse	pig-fish	pidgeon	lithoid	fisheye	biliary	dickens
fideism	pinfish	widgeon	Mishnic	bifilar	ciliary	kirking
fineish	sitfast	figgery	nightie	digital	miliary	licking
finesse	ziffius	gingery	xiphoid	finical	mimicry	milking
license	gin-fizz	Midgard	airhole	liminal	riviera	picking
misease	diagram	niggard	dishelm	militar	rivière	pinking
niceish	dingbat	niggcry	lichtly	mimical	tiniest	sinking
ailette	gingham	piggery	lightly	minicab	Ciliata	ticking
biretta	lingual	wiggery	lithely	minicar	ciliate	winking
dinette	ringman	Zingara	nightly	minimal	filiate	zinking
liberty	ring-taw	Zingare	pightle	similar	miniate	hip-knob
lineate	ringway	Zingari	pinholc	simitar	nimiety	kirkton
minette	dingoes	Zingaro	pithily	sinical	viciate	linkboy
pileate	giggler	biggest	rightly	vicinal	vitiate	milk-cow
pimento	higgler	biggish	sightly	bilimbi	bilious	milk-sop
pipette	jingler	disgest	Sinhala	viliaco	bivious	misknow
vidette	jinglet	disgust	tightly	cimices	fidibus	hickory
direful	kinglet	jiggish	wightly	citizen	milieux	pickery
firebug	mingler	piggish	dishome	divider	minibus	pinkish
hideous	niggler	riggish	diphone	diviner	minimum	sickish
hideout	piggies	fidgety	dishing	filibeg	minimus	rickets
lifeful	pingler	virgate	fishing	Filices	mini-sub	rickety
line-out	ringlet	hip-gout	miching	limited	nimious	milk-run
mixed-up	singlet	kingcup	nithing	limiter	pili-nut	riskful
niveous	tingler	vingt-un	sighing	limites	pitiful	pickaxe
piceous	wiggler	misgave	sithens	miniver	Ricinus	pink-eye
pinetum	wing-led	misgive	tithing	minivet	siliqua	billman
pipeful	winglet	disgown	wishing	vibices	silique	disleaf
piteous	diagrid	bighead	fish-god	visitee	simious	disleal
silenus	king-hit	dish-rag	highboy	visiter	vicious	disload
time-gun	king-pin	fish-day	high-low	tidings	vidimus	fig-leaf
timeous	pilgrim	fish-fag	high-top	viliago	rilievo	milldam
time-out	pinguid	fish-way	right-oh	divisim	disject	mislead
wileful	pinguin	high-hat	mishapt	finikin	disjoin	pig-lead
Minerva	ringbit	highman	bighorn	militia	misjoin	air-lock
piaffer	ringgit	highway	cithara	minikin	jinjili	dialect
piffler	gingall	lichway	cithern	mirific	pig-jump	hillock
pigfeed	gingili	mishear	dichord	silicic	disjune	hip-lock
riffler	lingula	Mishnah	die-hard	vivific	linkman	killick
milfoil	riggald	Mithras	dishorn	finicky	milk-bar	killock
tinfoil	singult	pinhead	fishery	hijinks	milkman	misluck
kinfolk	virgule	pithead	Highers	kibitka	pickmaw	niblick
misfall	biogeny	pith-hat	kithara	civilly	sick-bay	sillock

billies	violent	ailment	ginning	ciboria	biophor	hip-roof
dialled	violone	diamond	limning	cipolin	pit-prop	pierrot
dialler	willing	dimming	pianino	kilobit	dip-pipe	vitriol
fielded	witling	dinmont	pinning	limosis	airport	digraph
fielder	billion	figment	pioning	mitosis	bit-part	disrupt
fitlier	billy-oh	fitment	sinning	mitotic	dioptre	library
hillmen	gillion	pigment	tinning	Nilotic	dispark	cirrose
killdee	hilltop	rimming	winning	nimonic	dispart	diarise
vialled	killcow	siamang	midnoon	sinopia	disport	diarist
wielder	killjoy	siemens	Signior	sinopis	diapase	digress
willies	million	filmdom	diandry	virosis	dispose	diorism
yielder	pill-box	pismire	giantry	binocle	dispost	fibrose
airlift	pillion	pit-mirk	ginnery	pinocle	hippish	Midrash
biology	witloof	air-miss	kiln-dry	eidolon	dispute	piarist
pillage	zillion	biomass	signary	girosol	picquet	tigress
tillage	diglyph	dimmish	Signora	kiloton	diarial	tigrish
village	pillory	dismask	Signore	dimorph	diarian	cirrate
diploid	Sillery	dismast	signory	bigotry	diurnal	citrate
mislaid	titlark	dismiss	bigness	Titoism	lip-read	diorite
sialoid	aidless	filmish	dimness	Titoist	misread	disrate
sirloin	aimless	kirmess	disnest	ricotta	Nitrian	librate
villain	airless	midmost	Finnish	ridotto	Pierian	migrate
villein	biblist	siamese	fitness	riposte	sierran	misrate
dislike	dialist	titmose	lioness	risotto	disrobe	nitrate
mislike	dialyse	bismuth	lionise	vicomte	microbe	nitrite
riblike	finless	mismate	lionism	linocut	pibroch	picrate
siclike	girlish	sigmate	pianism	pirogue	vitrics	picrite
pig-lily	kinless	mim-mou'd	pianist	display	nitride	titrate
sillily	lidless	dismayd	Sienese	misplay	pierced	vibrate
diploma	lipless	dismayl	witness	dispace	piercer	vibrato
dislimb	pipless	mizmaze	Zionism	nit-pick	tiaraed	cirrous
dislimn	ribless	siameze	Zionist	six-pack	tiercel	citrous
millime	rimless	dipnoan	dignity	dimpled	midriff	fibrous
aiblins	sinless	Linnean	lignite	diopter	nigrify	Librium®
air-lane	tieless	bionics	pinnate	pimpled	nitrify	nitrous
billing	villose	finnack	lion-cub	rippier	vitrify	vitraux
biplane	violist	finnock	signeur	rippler	pierage	vitreum
birling	wigless	minnick	bifocal	ripplet	vitrage	disseat
birlinn	willest	minnock	bilobar	simpler	diarchy	kinsman
cieling	witless	pinnace	bipolar	simplex	microhm	miasmal
dilling	giblets	pinnock	bitonal	tippler	air-raid	miasmas
diplont	tillite	winnock	bivouac	kippage	air-rail	Rigsdag
dislink	violate	Dionaea	bizonal	silphia	fibroid	Riksdag
filling	pill-bug	fiancée	digonal	simpkin	fibroin	Rissian
girlond	vialful	Limnaea	dipolar	oil-palm	ligroin	airsick
hidling	villous	lioncel	kilobar	air-pump	milreis	dissect
hidlins	mislive	pinnoed	pivotal	dipping	tigroid	biassed
Hieland	billowy	pioneer	divorce	dispend	vitrail	fibster
Hielant	pillowy	pionies	Minorca	dispone	vitrain	hipster
hirling	willowy	dignify	sirocco	hipping	fierily	linseed
kidling	mill-eye	lignify	zimocca	limping	misrule	minster
killing	dialyze	signify	bigoted	lipping	nitrile	misseem
kitling	pigmean	lignage	bilobed	lisping	diorama	misstep
midland	pigmeat	biontic	disobey	lispund	fibroma	oil-seed
mid-Lent	gimmick	finnsko	litotes	nipping	citrine	pigsney
milling	mimmick	giantly	picotee	pimping	disrank	Pilsner
pigling	titmice	Pianola®	pivoted	pipping	firring	til-seed
rifling	mismade	pinnula	pivoter	pit-pony	migrant	tipster
rigling	air-mail	pinnule	Siporex	ripping	tigrine	tipsify
sibling	riempie	misname	visored	sipping	vibrant	kitschy
tilling	sigmoid	sirname	vizored	timpani	Vitrina	airship
titling	mismake	visnomy	widower	timpano	vitrine	cissoid
villany	oil-mill	dinning	timothy	tipping	disroot	hirstie

kid-skin	tin-tack	rioting	diethyl	airward	skulker	cleaved
kinship	pintado	sifting	riotize	die-work	ski-lift	cleaver
kip-skin	riptide	Sistine	fibular	figwort	P-Keltic	floatel
Liassic	bistred	sittine	figural	misword	Q-Keltic	floater
miasmic	dirt-bed	sitting	ligular	ribwork	skaldic	gleaner
midship	dirtied	tilting	pilular	ribwort	skulpin	pleaded
missaid	fifteen	tinting	simular	tinware	ukelele	pleader
missuit	fifties	witting	situlae	Midwest	ukulele	pleased
niks-nie	fig-tree	diction	titular	pigwash	skyline	pleaser
oilskin	fin-toed	fiction	vitular	airwave	skolion	sleaved
pigskin	fir-tree	miction	bitumed	midwive	skylark	alfalfa
pigsnie	kirtled	mistook	bitumen	biaxial	skellum	alkalis
pissoir	mista'en	mixtion	dilutee	dioxide	skilful	Alsatia
sibship	oil-tree	pint-pot	diluter	Pinxter	skimmed	Eleatic
firstly	sixteen	tintype	figured	dioxane	skimmer	ellagic
fissile	sixties	tittupy	misuser	mid-year	skummer	flea-pit
himself	tiptoed	bistort	rivulet	pixy-led	skimmia	gliadin
missile	vintner	bittern	liquefy	Digynia	skinker	ulnaria
oil-silk	vistaed	bitters	divulge	disyoke	skinned	bleakly
rissole	distaff	cistern	liturgy	misyoke	skinner	cleanly
tipsily	lift-off	cittern	simurgh	bicycle	skinful	clearly
lissome	mintage	dietary	viduage	biryani	skipped	flyable
winsome	vintage	Diptera	hirudin	pitying	skipper	pliable
biasing	dirt-pie	distort	minutia	tidying	skippet	pliably
Diasone	distain	disturb	piously	mitzvah	skepsis	Almaine
dissent	histoid	fixture	vihuela	sizzler	skeptic	cleanse
ginseng	histrio	gittern	diluent	fizzgig	skepful	illapse
hissing	littlin	history	minuend	dizzily	skirret	alfaquí
linsang	pigtail	jitters	piquant	fizzing	skirted	clean-up
missend	pintail	jittery	dilutor	dizzard	skirter	club-law
missent	victrix	littery	kikumon	gizzard	sky-sign	clubman
missing	mistake	mid-term	sit-upon	rizzart	ekistic	flyboat
rinsing	dirtily	misterm	sinuose	bizzazz	skysail	blabbed
sinsyne	distill	mistery	liquate	pizzazz	skitter	blabber
airstop	distyle	mixture	pituita	djibbah	sketchy	blubber
fission	fictile	picture	pituite	ejector	skatole	clabber
ginshop	fifthly	sintery	sinuate	Mjölnir	skittle	clobber
hip-shot	fistula	victory	situate	sjambok	skullle	clubbed
kip-shop	mistell	wintery	viduity	ajutage	skating	ill-bred
mission	mistily	dietist	limulus	akvavit	skiving	slabbed
pie-shop	mistold	Pictish	liqueur	skiable	skyward	slabber
piss-pot	ninthly	pietism	mimulus	ski-bobs	skew-put	slobber
pit-stop	pistole	pietist	Silurus	sky-bred	alcázar	slubbed
ribston	sixthly	Pittism	sinuous	ikebana	almanac	slubber
fissure	wittily	riotise	viduous	skyborn	cloacae	plebify
piastre	airtime	biotite	dibutyl	sky-blue	cloacal	globoid
missish	big-time	dictate	Rigveda	skyclad	flea-bag	elf-bolt
hirsute	mistime	Hittite	civvies	skidpan	flyaway	flybelt
fissive	biltong	listeth	milvine	skudler	ilkaday	globule
missive	dietine	nictate	nirvana	skid-lid	pliancy	flybane
air-trap	distant	pittite	silvern	skeeter	alcaide	flyblow
dip-trap	distend	vittate	silvery	skreigh	alcalde	flybook
fist-law	distent	wistiti	lievest	skreaky	alcayde	ale-bush
mint-man	distune	bittour	mid-week	skiffle	algates	globose
mistral	dittany	fistful	misween	skegger	aliases	globate
victual	fitting	giltcup	pigweed	sky-high	alkanet	glebous
virtual	histone	listful	midwife	skriech	allayer	globous
bittock	hitting	mistful	oil-well	skriegh	alnager	clachan
diptych	kitteny	riotous	witwall	skyjack	bleared	glacial
distich	listing	sistrum	miswend	skelder	bloated	placcat
mistico	misting	wistful	miswent	skelter	bloater	placebo
pin-tuck	mistune	fictive	viewing	skilled	cleaner	blacken
tietack	pitting	Miltown	fir-wood	skillet	clearer	blocked

blocker	slidder	altezza	illicit	climate	slyness	alarmed
blucher	gliding	fly-flap	plainly	plumate	alength	blarney
clacker	sladang	bluffer	albinos	alumium	alunite	blurred
clichéd	sliding	cliffed	cloison	alumnus	planxty	gloried
clicker	gladdon	clifted	ellipse	clamour	flâneur	slurred
clicket	pledgor	flaffer	slàinte	glamour	blintze	clarify
clocked	alodium	bluffly	fly-kick	Olympus	Alcoran	glorify
clocker	gladful	ill-fame	olykoek	plumbum	Alkoran	clarkia
flacker	gladius	olefine	flyleaf	plumous	also-ran	floruit
flacket	bluecap	plafond	ill-luck	alannah	all-over	alertly
flecked	gleeman	elegiac	elfland	Cluniac	allowed	clerkly
flecker	illegal	flag-day	ululant	plantar	almoner	pleroma
flicker	fluence	plug-hat	ululate	blanket	blooded	plerome
glacier	fluency	clogged	alumnae	blended	bloomer	flaring
placket	already	clogger	alameda	blender	flooded	glaring
plucked	alférez	flagged	alamode	blinded	floored	alerion
plucker	aliened	flogged	clamber	blinder	floorer	clarion
slacken	alienee	plaguey	clammed	blinked	flyover	clerisy
slacker	alleged	plugged	clamper	blinker	allonge	florist
slicken	alleyed	plugger	climbed	blunder	Clootie	oloroso
slicker	altered	slogger	climber	blunger	floosie	clarity
slocken	bleeder	slugger	clumber	blunker	floozie	flare-up
flaccid	bleeper	elegant	flamfew	clanger	fluoric	all-star
placoid	cleeked	all-good	glimmer	clinker	alforja	alms-man
slackly	fleeced	elegise	plumber	flanged	aloofly	Elysian
slickly	fleecer	elegist	plummet	flanker	bloosme	glossal
alicant	fleerer	elogist	plumpen	flannel	alsoone	allseed
glucina	sleeken	oligist	plumper	flannen	alcohol	all-seer
glycine	sleeker	blighty	slammed	flinder	pleopod	alms-fee
slicing	sleeper	flighty	slammer	flunkey	almonry	blasted
elector	sleeved	elogium	slimmed	klinker	alcorza	blaster
olycook	ulcered	plagium	slimmer	planned	clypeal	blessed
ulichon	albergo	allheal	slumber	planner	klipdas	blister
electro	alledge	althaea	slummer	planter	slipway	blusher
placard	allergy	all-hail	plumage	plonker	clapnet	blushet
plectra	sleechy	fly-half	alembic	plunder	clapped	bluster
plectre	algesia	alchemy	Olympia	plunger	clapper	clasper
alecost	algesis	alchymy	Olympic	plunker	clipped	classed
glucose	aloetic	Althing	plumbic	slander	clipper	cluster
glycose	cleekit	ale-hoof	plumpie	slanted	flapped	clyster
elocute	Elzevir	elfhood	plumply	slender	flapper	flasher
placate	sleekit	alphorn	plumula	slinger	flipper	flasket
placita	sloe-gin	althorn	plumule	slinker	plopped	fleshed
plicate	alveole	Elohist	slimily	elenchi	slapped	flesher
floccus	alveoli	almirah	aliment	glenoid	slapper	flushed
alodial	elderly	fluidal	alimony	alonely	slipped	flusher
alidade	fleetly	Pleiade	alumina	blandly	slipper	fluster
cladode	sleekly	Pleiads	clamant	blankly	slopped	glassen
bladder	alterne	Alcides	clement	blindly	clippie	glisten
bludger	blueing	claimer	element	bluntly	clupeid	glister
clodded	fleeing	glaiket	flaming	planula	glyphic	glosser
fledged	alienor	glaived	Fleming	slantly	glyptic	oldster
gladded	blue-rot	plaided	flummox	clangor	ale-pole	plashet
gladden	glue-pot	plaited	plumcot	plenipo	alepine	plaster
glidder	algebra	plaiter	alamort	llanero	sloping	slashed
pledgee	allegro	sleided	plumery	planury	flip-dog	slasher
pledger	alveary	alright	slumbry	plenary	clypeus	sloshed
pledget	sleepry	sleight	alumish	alongst	cliquey	plusage
plodded	altesse	alginic	blemish	illness	aliquot	classic
plodder	bluette	fluidic	Flemish	oldness	Floréal	classis
sledded	clued-up	glaikit	glimpse	planish	floreat	clastic
sledger	gleeful	glairin	plumist	plenish	glareal	elastic
slidden	blue-eye	ileitis	plumose	plenist	cleruch	elastin

Glossic	slatted	flaunty	cloying	immerse	emanant	impresa
plasmic	slatter	Glaucus	flaying	amnesty	eminent	imprese
plasmid	slither	eluvial	ally-tor	omneity	amongst	impress
plasmin	slitter	Flavian	play-box	impetus	emongst	imprest
plastic	slotter	fluvial	playboy	amygdal	amanita	umbrose
plastid	flotage	pluvial	clayish	smuggle	amenity	embrute
pliskie	blotchy	clavier	playful	imagine	emanate	emeriti
closely	glottic	flivver	glazier	imagery	amentum	emirate
fleshly	glottis	klavier	glazing	imagism	omentum	imbrute
closing	plottie	Slavify	glozing	imagist	ominous	amorous
blesbok	all-time	elevens	alizare	umwhile	ammonal	umbrous
blossom	old-time	flavine	ambatch	amphora	immoral	embrave
elf-shot	blatant	flavone	ambages	imbiber	umbonal	improve
elision	flotant	olivine	embased	impinge	ambones	embrewe
elusion	flutina	Slovene	empanel	empight	embowed	embrown
fly-slow	fluting	Slavdom	impanel	empiric	embowel	imbrown
plessor	flyting	clivers	ommatea	omnific	embower	Ameslan
plosion	platane	clovery	embargo	ambient	empower	ambs-ace
closure	platina	olivary	embathe	omniana	imbower	ames-ace
elusory	plating	plovery	empathy	ambitty	imposer	smasher
Flustra	slating	slavery	imbathe	impiety	umbones	amusing
alyssum	elation	slavish	Amharic	omniety	smoothe	smash-up
close-up	elution	Slavism	impavid	impious	ammonia	amusive
Elysium	elytron	clavate	amiable	omnibus	embolic	emitted
elusive	fletton	elevate	amiably	smoke-ho	emporia	emptied
plosive	glutton	eluvium	embayld	smokily	ampoule	emptier
elytral	platoon	flavour	impaint	smoking	embound	empties
flat-cap	cloture	blowsed	empaire	amalgam	impound	omitted
flotsam	ill-turn	blowzed	empayre	amildar	embosom	omitter
fly-trap	olitory	plowter	ambassy	implead	imbosom	smatter
glottal	elitism	alewife	ampassy	emplace	embogue	smother
gluteal	elitist	flowage	embassy	implode	embolus	smutted
plateau	flutist	blowfly	impasse	implied	embread	umpteen
pluteal	clotbur	ill-will	embaste	smeller	Umbrian	smytrie
blather	elytrum	ellwand	impaste	smelter	amtrack	smittle
blatter	gluteus	flowing	impasto	smolder	embrace	emetine
blether	plotful	glowing	smacker	ymolten	emerods	imitant
hletted	pluteus	slowing	smicker	amplify	emersed	emotion
blither	elative	plywood	smicket	amyloid	smarten	emption
blotted	clausal	all-work	smectic	emulsin	impregn	amatory
blotter	pleurae	blawort	smickly	emblema	smarago	imitate
clatter	pleural	blewart	emicant	emplume	umbrage	amateur
clitter	flounce	blow-dry	omicron	ambling	ambroid	amative
clothed	aliunde	flowery	emicate	amylene	embraid	emotive
clothes	albumen	slowish	smidgen	emplane	embroil	amputee
clotted	clouded	blewits	smudger	implant	smartie	imputer
clotter	clouted	blowgun	smidgin	smiling	emerald	smouser
clutter	fleuret	blow-out	smeddum	embloom	smartly	ampulla
flatlet	ill-used	flexile	amoebae	emulsor	amarant	imburse
flatted	plouter	flexion	empeach	implore	Amerind	impulse
flatten	claucht	fluxion	emperce	amylase	amorini	empyema
flatter	claught	flexure	impeach	amylate	amorino	amazing
flitted	flaught	plexure	ambered	emulate	imprint	endarch
flitter	slouchy	fluxive	ammeter	implate	embryon	enhance
flutter	sloughy	ally-taw	umbered	implete	embryos	infancy
glitter	albumin	play-day	immerge	emulous	umbrere	infarct
glutaei	alluvia	play-way	amnesia	emblaze	amorism	unlatch
glutted	plaudit	play-act	amnesic	imamate	amorist	innards
platted	blaubok	playlet	amoebic	amental	amorosa	inwards
platter	bloubok	play-pen	imperil	omental	amoroso	onwards
plotted	blouson	play-off	emperor	amender	empress	unhandy
plotter	fleuron	clay-pit	impearl	emonges	emprise	unhardy
slather	pleuron	allying	immense	amenage	imbrast	annates

ansated
Antares
engaged
Engager
enraged
inhaler
inlayer
invader
kneader
sneaker
unbaked
unbated
undated
uneared
uneaten
unfaded
unfamed
unfazed
ungazed
unjaded
unladen
unmated
unnamed
unpaged
unpanel
unpaper
unpared
unpaved
unraced
unraked
unravel
unsated
unsaved
untaken
untamed
untaxed
unwaked
unwares
unwater
unwayed
enlarge
enrange
antacid
entasis
inhabit
insanie
invalid
unwarie
entayle
envault
unhable
unmanly
unvaile
uncanny
unpaint
unsaint
unhappy
ondatra
unmarry
infaust
inhaust
andante
annatta

annatto
inearth
infanta
infante
unearth
unfaith
unhasty
unlaste
sneak-up
ant-bear
anybody
knobbed
knobber
snubbed
snubber
knobble
knobbly
knubble
knubbly
snabble
ant-bird
knacker
knicker
knocker
snicker
unacted
unscrew
V-necked
gnocchi
onychia
insculp
knuckle
unscale
enactor
knock-on
inscape
unicorn
unicity
knock-up
snick-up
unidea'd
unideal
snodded
snoddit
snidely
anodyne
anodise
enteral
knee-cap
knee-pan
inherce
unperch
unteach
underdo
unheedy
unready
unweldy
enterer
entêtée
indexer
indexes
ingener
integer

invexed
kneeled
kneeler
one-eyed
sneerer
sneezer
unbeget
unfeued
unmeted
unsewed
unsexed
unvexed
enfeoff
undeify
ant-eggs
inveigh
undergo
anaemia
anaemic
angelic
Angevin
annelid
anoesis
anoetic
antefix
endemic
enteric
inherit
interim
invenit
angerly
injelly
antenna
inbeing
inferno
interne
unbeing
unmeant
angekok
enderon
enfelon
enteron
envelop
envenom
unbegot
unkempt
unheard
unheart
unlearn
unweary
incense
intense
inverse
unherst
unleash
unsense
entente
in-depth
ingesta
Insecta
insecty
unneath
untenty

angelus
ingénue
knees-up
unbegun
innerve
inweave
unnerve
unreave
unreeve
unweave
ink-feed
sniffer
snifter
snuffer
unified
unifier
unoften
onefold
snaffle
sniffle
snuffle
uniform
anagram
snagged
snigger
snugged
anagoge
anagogy
sniggle
snuggle
endgame
anthrax
enthral
inthral
uncheck
encheer
enwheel
enchafe
anthoid
enchain
inchpin
unchain
ant-hill
enshell
inshell
unchild
unshale
unshell
Anthony
enchant
in-thing
unshent
unthink
unshoot
unshape
unwhipt
encharm
inkhorn
inshore
onshore
uncharm
unchary
unshorn

enchase
enthuse
inchase
inphase
unshout
anchovy
unshewn
unshown
anginal
indican
inqilab
intimae
unvital
unhitch
unwitch
unfilde
antigen
enfiled
enginer
enliven
enriven
enticer
incised
inciter
indices
inditer
infidel
insider
insinew
inviter
unaided
unaimed
unaired
unfiled
unfired
unfixed
unhired
unlimed
unlined
unmixed
unoiled
unrimed
unrisen
unriven
unrivet
unsinew
unsized
untiled
untired
unwiped
unwived
innings
unhinge
enlight
insight
undight
unright
unsight
indicia
inhibit
insipid
oneiric
uncivil

anticke
unpinkt
entitle
infield
unfitly
angioma
ancient
antient
insigne
andiron
antilog
endiron
environ
incisor
unvisor
anxiety
ungirth
unwitty
annicut
antique
anxious
envious
invious
uncinus
snakily
unaking
snakish
Anglian
antliae
unclean
unclear
uncloak
englobe
inglobe
anelace
anglice
inflect
inflict
unblock
unplace
include
anglify
analogy
unplait
unslain
unalike
inflame
unplumb
unplume
angling
aniline
endlang
endlong
England
incline
inkling
unblent
unblind
unsling
unslung
ant-lion
engloom

unclipt
analyse
analyst
anglist
enclasp
enclose
endless
enflesh
English
inclasp
inclose
inulase
unalist
unbless
unblest
unclasp
unclose
unflesh
unflush
anility
inflate
encloud
uncloud
enclave
enslave
unalive
unglove
unblown
analyze
f-number
anomaly
anemone
unsmart
animism
animist
endmost
gnomish
animate
enemata
enomoty
unsmote
enamour
onymous
Ananias
in-kneed
in-and-in
anonyma
ensnare
ensnarl
insnare
unsnarl
onanism
onanist
oneness
inanity
unknown
insofar
unmoral
unroyal
unvocal
unwoman
enforce
inforce

invoice
unvoice
ancones
annoyed
endogen
endowed
endower
enjoyer
ingowes
intoner
inwoven
snooded
snooker
snooper
snoozer
unbowed
uncover
ungored
unhoped
unloved
unmoved
unnoted
unposed
untoned
unwooed
unwoven
unyoked
unzoned
engorge
enrough
unrough
unionic
encomia
entomic
entopic
intotic
inconie
unsolid
ennoble
snoozle
ungodly
unmould
unnoble
enround
inconnu
ingoing
injoint
ungoing
unbound
undoing
unfound
unjoint
unmount
unround
unsound
unwound
undozoa
intozoa
unbosom
unboard
undoors
unhoard
undorse

indorse
in-house
unhorse
unhouse
unloose
unroost
unsonsy
insooth
uncouth
unsoote
unworth
involve
antonym
unspeak
inspect
unspide
knapped
knapper
snapped
snapper
snipped
snipper
snippet
unspied
unspoke
inaptly
Ineptly
knapple
unaptly
unspell
unspilt
sniping
unspent
inspire
inspyre
anapest
unequal
anyroad
entreat
inbreak
intreat
untread
engrace
infract
unbrace
unfrock
untrace
intrude
untride
enarmed
gnarled
gnarred
inbreed
knarred
knurled
snarled
snarler
snorkel
snorter
unarmed
undried
unorder
untried

unurged
engraff
engraft
indraft
ingraft
anarchy
android
aneroid
energic
energid
engrail
engrain
entrail
entrain
inertia
ingrain
introit
unbroke
angrily
entrold
inertly
introld
snirtle
untruly
enframe
enprint
entrant
inbring
intrant
snaring
snoring
undrunk
unwrung
entropy
ancress
encrust
engrasp
engross
entrism
entrist
entrust
incrust
ingress
intrust
uncross
undress
untruss
untrust
encraty
ingrate
untruth
unwrite
anurous
ingroup
onerous
snarl-up
engrave
on-drive
indrawn
ingrown
uncrown
ungrown
anorexy

unusual
aniseed
Knesset
onestep
unasked
anosmia
end-ship
gnostic
oneself
one-shot
Oniscus
gnathal
initial
instead
onstead
unstrap
D-notice
unstack
unstick
unstock
unstuck
another
ensteep
knitted
knitter
knotted
knotter
snotter
unsteel
snatchy
gnathic
unstaid
unstrip
enstyle
install
instill
knittle
anatomy
anytime
enstamp
one-time
instant
uniting
enation
unction
unition
unitary
anatase
unitise
instate
unstate
unitive
angular
annular
infulae
inhuman
insular
ungulae
unhuman
enounce
injunct
annulet
endurer

end-user
incudes
inducer
infuser
injurer
inquiet
insurer
snouted
uncured
unfumed
unguled
unqueen
unquiet
unruled
unsured
untuned
unruffe
indulge
aneurin
indusia
insulin
unlucky
in-built
unbuild
unbuilt
anguine
ensuing
unburnt
unfunny
unguent
unsunny
engulph
ingulph
enguard
enquire
enquiry
inquere
inquire
inquiry
unguard
anguish
inburst
inquest
insulse
uncurse
unpurse
annuity
unquote
annulus
incubus
incurve
andvile
knevell
knavery
knavish
snowcap
snowman
unswear
snow-ice
anywhen
ensweep
snow-fed
unowned

unsweet
indwell
indwelt
inkwell
know-all
snow-fly
snowily
entwine
inswing
intwine
knowing
untwine
know-how
snow-box
unswept
unaware
unsworn
anywise
endwise
entwist
intwist
snowish
untwist
anyways
endways
inexact
ungyved
enzymic
envying
inlying
undying
untying
innyard
snuzzle
Mozarab
oolakan
tokamak
copalba
joyance
monarch
nomarch
noyance
polacca
romance
sonance
sonancy
tobacco
toparch
monarda
notanda
towards
dowager
forager
foramen
forayer
gowaned
homager
nodated
nonaged
po-faced
Romanes
rosacea
rosaker

royalet
sofa-bed
togated
voyager
zonated
botargo
gouache
Bobadil
boracic
botanic
cohabit
conaria
domatia
gonadic
Koranic
Logania
monacid
monadic
nomadic
novalia
podalic
Polaris
potamic
Romanic
rosalia
somatic
Sotadic
vocalic
volatic
romaika
coracle
coralla
dowable
locally
losable
lovable
loyally
modally
morally
movable
movably
notable
notably
potable
ropable
rowable
royally
totally
vocable
vocally
volable
womanly
Cocagne
cocaine
hosanna
moraine
posaune
romaunt
sodaine
borazon
donator
dos-à-dos
hob-a-nob

monaxon	combine	potcher	wood-wax	sordine	someway	foveola
nonagon	cowbane	pouched	córdoba	sordini	cogence	foveole
rotator	dogbane	torcher	conduce	sordino	cogency	loverly
conacre	fog-bank	touched	conduct	tondino	Moresco	morello
podagra	hopbind	toucher	hordock	voiding	potence	Moselle
polacre	hopbine	vouchee	howdy-do	wood-ant	potencé	notedly
sowarry	jobbing	voucher	soldado	wording	potency	novella
Molasse	mobbing	wotcher	doodler	good-now	morendo	novelle
morassy	pot-bank	boscage	fondler	good-son	bone-bed	rosella
Mosaism	robbing	soccage	good-den	road-hog	boneset	roselle
potassa	sobbing	coccoid	good-e'en	bordure	coherer	roseola
Romansh	sorbent	conceit	hog-deer	doddard	covelet	rozelle
Zolaism	boobook	conchie	road-bed	doddery	covered	soberly
coranto	log-book	log-chip	roe-deer	moidore	coveted	vowelly
loyalty	low-brow	Noachic	soldier	powdery	cozener	codeine
royalty	top-boot	rotchie	toadied	rondure	doe-eyed	doyenne
volante	bobbery	toeclip	toddler	coldish	dovelet	fore-end
bonasus	bombard	hoe-cake	wondred	goddess	foreleg	someone
conatus	cowbird	box-calf	bondage	goldish	foremen	boredom
notaeum	forbore	cow-calf	condign	goodish	foresee	Comecon
pomatum	Homburg	doucely	cordage	loudish	forever	copepod
popadum	jobbery	zoccolo	pondage	wood-ash	honeyed	dovecot
solanum	lombard	coxcomb	sondage	wordish	hose-net	foretop
Totanus	low-born	non-come	wordage	cordate	however	holesom
Volapük	mowburn	concent	boudoir	cordite	lobelet	moneron
copaiva	poe-bird	doucine	conduit	fold-out	lovered	pomeroy
bonanza	poy-bird	porcine	foudrie	foodful	moneyed	popedom
bogbean	robbery	voicing	hordein	gold-bug	moneyer	somehow
corbeau	wosbird	volcano	lordkin	Gordius	nose-led	sorehon
forbear	bobbish	gorcrow	non-drip	hoodlum	notelet	toheroa
Hobbian	bombast	ponchos	wood-oil	Hordeum	pop-eyed	bone-dry
rowboat	combust	torchon	wood-tin	woodcut	powered	forearm
Sorbian	hobbish	concept	condole	hoedown	rose-red	tone-arm
hogback	Hobbism	concupy	condyle	low-down	towered	bone-ash
roebuck	Hobbist	forceps	dowdily	wood-owl	come-off	Couéism
forbade	mobbish	concern	gondola	dogdays	foreign	Couéist
forbode	Sorbish	concert	hold-all	goldeye	lozenge	doveish
cobbler	soubise	concord	moodily	good-bye	lozengy	moreish
doubler	Corbett	dogcart	rowdily	Docetae	somewhy	nor'-east
doublet	Moabite	popcorn	sondeli	forecar	bone-oil	poseuse
double-u	sorbate	sorcery	wordily	foreday	cole-tit	dogeate
doubted	comb-out	concise	condemn	forelay	cometic	dozenth
doubter	box-coat	concuss	goddamn	foreman	coterie	fouetté
gobbler	conceal	corcass	bonding	forepaw	Docetic	foveate
gombeen	dog-crab	low-cost	codding	foreran	dovekie	honesty
hobbler	Joycean	boycott	condone	foresaw	forelie	lomenta
low-bred	morceau	toccata	cording	foresay	fox-evil	lorette
nobbler	ponceau	douceur	cow-dung	gomeral	Gobelin	modesty
wobbler	Roscian	Roscius	folding	hoseman	godetia	mofette
corbell	top-coat	concave	fondant	love-day	gomeril	momenta
howbeit	concoct	bondman	fordone	Mohegan	Homeric	mozetta
nombril	gorcock	cordial	holding	molerat	Homerid	nonette
cowbell	concede	good-day	loading	nosebag	lobelia	nonetto
dog-belt	botcher	goodman	Londony	nosegay	polemic	novelty
dogbolt	coachee	Gordian	lording	nose-rag	poperin	podesta
fog-bell	coacher	hoodman	mordant	notepad	roper-in	polenta
loobily	concrew	mondial	mordent	polecat	rose-hip	poverty
low-bell	couchee	roadman	nodding	rodeway	soredia	roseate
nobbily	moocher	road-map	podding	rokelay	tonemic	rosette
tombola	moucher	roadway	road-end	ropeway	tonetic	rosetty
tombolo	notched	rondeau	roading	rose-bay	totemic	bodeful
bobbing	notchel	woodman	rondino	sokeman	zooecia	Boletus
bowbent	poacher	wood-tar	sodding	someday	corella	coteaux

cover-up
doleful
foregut
forerun
hopeful
pokeful
rose-bud
rose-bug
rose-cut
pole-axe
homelyn
golf-bag
oooftah
pouftah
Wolfian
wolfram
confect
confide
coffret
comfrey
hop-flea
oomfret
poofter
ooufter
sol-faed
forfair
forfeit
wolfkin
boxfuls
cot-folk
goofily
Norfolk
potfuls
souffle
soufflé
topfull
confine
forfend
golfing
oafing
roofing
wolfing
hoof-rot
hotfoot
mouflon
roof-top
tomfool
wolf-dog
oonfire
comfort
confirm
conform
zoeform
codfish
confess
confest
confuse
cowfish
dogfish
hog-fish
toffish
wolfish
confute

conflux
loofful
congeal
couguar
low-gear
Morglay
songman
Vosgean
Vosgian
torgoch
fougade
boggler
congree
cougher
doggrel
goggled
goggler
joggled
long-leg
mongrel
roughen
rougher
soignée
tongued
toughen
long-off
foggage
long-ago
long-oil
long-pig
roughie
song-hit
toughie
foggily
roughly
soggily
toughly
Dodgems
zoogamy
co-agent
cogging
dogging
doggone
forging
forgone
hogging
jogging
lodging
logging
longing
nogging
sogging
zoogeny
zoogony
longbow
lorgnon
boggard
boggart
congery
cowgirl
dodgery
doggery
forgery

hoggery
mongery
toggery
congest
doggess
doggish
hoggish
longest
longish
doughty
foughty
zorgite
congrue
songful
sorghum
forgave
forgive
bowhead
dog-head
go-ahead
godhead
hop-head
hothead
lochial
log-head
moth-eat
Pooh-Bah
pot-head
tow-head
Gothick
toshach
cowhide
boshter
cochlea
cowheel
potheen
cowhage
pochoir
bothole
doghole
foxhole
mochell
pothole
toe-hold
top-hole
bow-hand
cowhand
forhent
fox-hunt
nothing
boyhood
godhood
hoghood
pothook
coehorn
coshery
cothurn
cowherd
foghorn
mothery
non-hero
nowhere
pochard

pot-herb
pothery
yoghurt
dobhash
sophism
sophist
göthite
oophyte
box-haul
dorhawk
goshawk
bolivar
comical
comital
conical
co-rival
co-tidal
domical
holiday
logical
loricae
Mohican
nodical
nominal
somital
topical
toxical
cowitch
goyisch
Morisco
oomiack
to-pinch
codices
conifer
fomites
lobiped
lorimer
loriner
molimen
moniker
no-fines
nominee
porifer
posited
rooinek
rosined
rotifer
soliped
sorites
vomited
cotinga
foliage
Moringa
moriche
potiche
tonight
bodikin
codicil
cohibit
colitis
comitia
conidia
domicil

dominie
gonidia
gonidic
hominid
monilia
motivic
notitia
oolitic
politic
robinia
solicit
somitic
soritic
colicky
bouilli
codilla
codille
docible
foliole
gorilla
Modiola
mouillé
solidly
zorille
zorillo
coniine
totient
bog-iron
box-iron
copilot
Honiton
horizon
monitor
norimon
positon
tow-iron
colibri
goliard
hosiery
poniard
rosiere
topiary
foliose
Corinth
foliate
Goliath
modiste
sociate
society
comique
copious
corious
holibut
modicum
noxious
solidum
solidus
conject
conjoin
conjure
conjury
bonjour
bookman

cork-mat
cork-oak
folkway
Hock-day
Lockian
lock-jaw
lockman
lockram
mooktar
rocklay
rock-tar
work-bag
work-day
workman
yolk-sac
cockade
mockado
booklet
cockled
cockney
cork-leg
look-see
rockier
corkage
dockage
lockage
mockage
soakage
cockshy
work-shy
booksie
cockpit
hook-pin
pockpit
pork-pie
rock-oil
cockily
rock-elm
rockily
book-end
booking
corking
docking
Dorking
looking
mocking
rocking
soaking
working
kolkhoz
rock-cod
top-knot
work-box
worktop
bonkers
conkers
cookery
folk-art
jookery
joukery
mockery
monkery
pockard

rockery
rookery
bookish
dockise
Lockist
monkish
rookish
Yorkish
Yorkist
box-kite
bookful
cookout
lockful
lock-nut
lockout
lookout
workful
work-out
cockeye
donkeys
sockeye
coal-gas
coalman
coal-tar
cobloaf
coeliac
pollman
poll-tax
roll-bar
rouleau
souldan
toll-bar
tollman
toolbag
woolfat
woolman
Zoilean
would-be
collect
cowlick
dorlach
hoolock
pollack
pollicy
pollock
pot-luck
rollick
rollock
rowlock
collide
collude
roulade
boulder
boulter
bowlder
coal-bed
colleen
collied
collier
coulter
dollied
dollier
dowlney

foulder	morling	Wormian	cornice	zoonomy	romneya	torpedo
goolies	norland	dormice	dornick	coining	coronae	compeer
moulder	oodlins	Formica	downa-do	conning	coronal	complex
moulten	pollent	hommock	poinado	donning	coronas	compter
poulder	polling	commode	tornade	fornent	locoman	coupler
poulter	rolling	formula	tornado	horning	soroban	couplet
woolded'	soiling	pommele	bouncer	joining	sororal	morphew
woolder	toiling	roomily	bounded	loaning	morocco	pompier
woolled	tolling	booming	bounden	looning	boloney	poppied
woollen	tooling	command	bounder	morning	bosomed	torpefy
woolsey	top-line	commend	corn-fed	nooning	colonel	compage
worlded	towline	comment	counsel	poynant	coroner	Solpuga
jollify	yowling	commons	counted	sorning	coronet	complin
low-life	coal-box	commune	counter	town-end	ionomer	dolphin
mollify	dolldom	dooming	données	coin-box	monomer	low-paid
collage	moellon	dormant	down-bed	corn-cob	no-hoper	morphia
college	rollmop	foaming	founder	downbow	popover	morphic
noology	roll-top	formant	hornlet	gownboy	soboles	cowpoke
tollage	toolbox	forming	joannes	moon-bow	borough	compile
zoology	toylsom	gormand	joinder	moon-god	soroche	hop-pole
hollaho	boilery	hog-mane	jointed	country	boronia	pompelo
coal-oil	bollard	hormone	jointer	donnard	colonic	soapily
coal-pit	collard	noumena	lounder	donnart	coronis	soppily
coal-tit	foolery	Rommany	lounger	donnerd	monodic	company
colloid	forlore	rouming	Moonies	donnert	monofil	compend
couloir	forlorn	souming	moonset	foundry	monosis	componé
douleia	foulard	torment	mounted	joinery	moronic	compony
toolkit	lollard	tormina	mounter	cognise	oogonia	dopping
wool-oil	pollard	towmond	poinder	Cornish	Polonia	forpine
godlike	poulard	towmont	pointed	cornist	polonie	hopping
rodlike	pouldre	mormaor	pointel	coyness	porosis	looping
godlily	poultry	Mormops	pointer	donnish	robotic	lopping
jollily	soilure	commère	pounced	donnism	rosolio	mopping
lowlily	coalise	foumart	pouncet	hog-nose	sorosis	pompano
worldly	coolish	Kommers	pounder	hornish	mono-ski	popping
coelome	dollish	woomera	rounded	hornist	corolla	sooping
coulomb	fogless	wormery	roundel	hotness	monocle	sopping
fog-lamp	foolish	bog-moss	rounder	lowness	Bologna	topping
bogland	forlese	cosmism	sounder	moonish	to-torne	volpino
boiling	godless	cosmist	wounder	roinish	to-worne	complot
bowline	goulash	koumiss	younker	roynish	hobodom	pompion
bowling	jobless	topmast	coinage	so-and-so	homolog	pompoon
codling	joyless	topmost	cornage	tonnish	monocot	soapbox
colling	mollusc	commute	tonnage	townish	Monodon	soupcon
Collins	mollusk	formate	coontie	bornite	potoroo	tompion
coolant	rodless	doomful	corn-bin	cognate	Solomon	cob-pipe
cotland	sonless	holmium	corn-pit	connate	coloury	compare
cowling	topless	roomful	corn-rig	connote	sojourn	compart
foiling	Zoilism	commove	council	cornett	hoboism	compere
fooling	Zoilist	coon-can	hobnail	cornute	hop-oast	comport
fopling	Coalite®	corneal	johnnie	cornuto	molossi	coopery
forlana	collate	corn-law	moonlit	hornito	poloist	coppery
forlend	hoplite	cornual	mountie	Sonnite	soloist	corpora
forlent	jollity	corn-van	poon-oil	youngth	cocotte	coupure
fowling	pollute	gownman	toe-nail	zoonite	coconut	foppery
godling	zoolite	horn-mad	bonnily	hornbug	colobus	oospore
golland	zoolith	Johnian	cornfly	hornful	homonym	row-port
gosling	roll-out	moineau	jointly	horn-nut	toponym	zoopery
gowland	soulful	noonday	roundle	moanful	compear	compass
holland	toilful	poundal	roundly	round-up	Gosplan	compast
howling	poll-axe	somnial	soundly	worn-out	compact	compose
logline	gooleys	tonneau	tonnell	connive	coppice	compost
lowland	holm-oak	connect	youngly	moon-eye	hospice	foppish

hoop-ash	courage	cob-swan	sonship	consist	röntgen	doating
lompish	moorage	dog's-ear	souslik	possess	rootlet	dotting
porpess	porrigo	Dogstar	sow-skin	zoisite	sonties	footing
rompish	bourkha	mobsman	topsail	Hotspur	soother	fortune
compete	Goorkha	moss-hag	top-soil	corsive	souther	hosting
compote	to-brake	rodsman	topspin	torsive	toothed	jotting
compute	borrell	topsman	toustie	boatman	fortify	lotting
towpath	courtly	Cossack	worship	Comtian	mortify	montane
hog-plum	four-ale	dogsick	forsake	costean	pontiff	montant
nonplus	hoarily	fossick	mousaka	footbar	pontify	mooting
pompous	log-roll	hopsack	console	foot-jaw	bottega	portend
coequal	lorrell	nonsuch	consols	footman	cortège	portent
rorqual	moor-ill	pot-sick	consult	footpad	cottage	posting
bouquet	noursle	toisech	fossula	tootway	footage	potting
conquer	sorrily	gorsedd	loosely	Fortran	hostage	pouting
docquet	woorali	topside	lousily	fox-trap	montage	rooting
rocquet	wourali	torsade	moistly	koftgar	pontage	rotting
torqued	gourami	boaster	noisily	mootman	portage	routine
jonquil	no-trump	bobsled	nousell	Noetian	postage	routing
bourlaw	courant	bolster	tossily	portman	pottage	sorting
courlan	dourine	booster	woosell	portray	rootage	sotting
door-man	horrent	coaster	consume	post-bag	voltage	soutane
doormat	louring	conster	noisome	post-day	bobtail	tontine
doorway	mooring	corslet	noysome	postman	contain	totting
four-oar	pouring	corsned	toysome	post-war	cottoid	wotting
journal	roaring	cowshed	woesome	root-cap	couthie	coction
Locrian	soaring	dossier	bousing	rostral	doitkin	coition
moorman	soprani	foister	consent	bortsch	fox-tail	control
moor-pan	soprano	holster	godsend	contact	goat-fig	dogtrot
poor-law	souring	lobster	horsing	conteck	hoatzin	footboy
to-break	torrent	mobster	housing	dog-tick	noctuid	footrot
correct	touring	moisten	mousing	mortice	nostril	foot-ton
morrice	bourbon	monster	pop-song	portico	postflx	fox-trot
nourice	bourdon	mousmee	rousant	boutade	routhie	goat-god
porrect	boxroom	roaster	rousing	bootleg	tootsie	hot-trod
sourock	fourgon	rodster	sossing	bottled	tortrix	jog-trot
touraco	godroon	roister	sousing	bottler	voltaic	pontoon
comrade	moorlog	rooster	tossing	box-tree	boat-fly	porthos
corrade	morrion	rouster	tousing	costrel	coctile	portion
corrode	poor-box	royster	bowshot	cottier	cortile	post-box
corrody	sour-sop	toasted	cop-shop	cow-tree	goutfly	tom-trot
joy-ride	corrupt	toaster	forsloe	dottled	hostile	zootype
boarder	towrope	worsted	forslow	dottrel	loathly	contort
bourder	Moorery	consign	forsook	fontlet	loftily	costard .
bourrée	woorara	corsage	gorsoon	footmen	monthly	couture
coarsen	boarish	borscht	gossoon	forties	noctule	lottery
courier	boorish	bolshie	hoosgow	fortlet	pontile	montero
courser	dog-rose	bonsoir	hotshot	goateed	soothly	monture
fourses	low-rise	conseil	monsoon	goitred	sootily	nocturn
gourmet	Mooress	corsair	non-stop	hop-tree	tortile	non-term
hoarder	moorish	cowslip	poisson	hostler	youthly	postern
hoarsen	nourish	doe-skin	pop-shop	loathed	contemn	posture
journey	poorish	dogship	pot-shop	loather	costume	pottery
log-reel	sourish	dogskin	pot-shot	moither	zootomy	torture
moorhen	to-brusd	donship	torsion	mottled	boating	tottery
mourner	tourism	foxship	tosspot	mottoed	bolting	voiture
poursew	tourist	godship	toyshop	mottoes	bottine	Zostera
sorrier	morrhua	hog-skin	gossipy	mouthed	bottony	coltish
tourney	poursue	log-ship	consort	mouther	coating	Comtism
worried	zoarium	non-skid	goosery	norther	contend	Comtist
worrier	borstal	non-slip	morsure	poitrel	content	contest
horrify	box-seat	nonsuit	mousery	posteen	contund	contuse
torrefy	coastal	poussin	tonsure	pouther	cottony	cottise

doltish
goatish
hostess
hottish
loutish
mortise
ooftish
poetess
poetise
portess
softish
sottish
wottest
costate
portate
wotteth
contour
dortour
nostrum
portous
post-bus
rostrum
routous
costive
tortive
cottown
dogtown
context
zootaxy
bostryx
copular
gopuram
jocular
lobular
locular
modular
morular
nodular
popular
vocular
Yoruban
zonular
Columba
rotunda
coluber
columel
focused
focuses
hocused
ioduret
noduled
non-user
volumed
voluted
zonulet
torulin
volubil
volutin
soluble
voluble
volubly
wofully
roguing

toluene
voluspa
goburra
roguery
roguish
voguish
coquito
locusta
lobulus
loculus
modulus
nocuous
torulus
Zonurus
nouveau
convict
couvade
voivode
louvred
convoke
convene
convent
corvine
dogvane
hop-vine
solvent
wolving
convert
couvert
poovery
wolvish
solvate
volvate
convive
woiwode
cow-weed
hog-weed
pop-weed
cob-wall
forwent
morwong
boxwood
dogwood
logwood
forward
forwarn
forworn
godward
hogward
lobworm
norward
woeworn
hogwash
nor'-west
coaxial
co-exist
bogy-man
copy-cat
cotylae
holydam
polygam
polyact
cotyles

loxygen
polymer
polypes
Corypha
coryphe
polynia
holy-ale
bodying
copying
Corydon
fogydom
polygon
polypod
Polyzoa
hop-yard
bogyism
copyism
copyist
fogyish
fogyism
Toryism
Kotytto
Corylus
polypus
toby-jug
polynya
foozler
sozzled
boozily
woozily
boozing
forzato
booze-up
apparat
splatch
upcatch
upwards
apparel
opiated
speaker
speared
sprayed
sprayer
upmaker
splashy
aphagia
aphasia
aphasic
aplasia
apraxia
sprawly
spraint
spray-on
sphaere
upraise
Appalto
upvalue
Apician
epochal
spacial
special
epicede

épicier
species
specter
specify
epacrid
epacris
speckle
specula
spicily
spicula
spicule
epicene
spacing
apocope
epicarp
epicure
spectra
spectre
spicery
epicism
epicist
opacity
spicate
opacous
spadger
spadoes
spidery
epidote
apodous
spodium
apteral
spaeman
spheral
appeach
spredde
speeded
speeder
speeler
sphered
spieler
spreagh
aphelia
aphelic
aphesis
aphetic
apperil
apteria
ephebic
sphenic
spheric
splenic
spleeny
ephebos
up-tempo
ephedra
spheare
appease
aplenty
ephebus
speed-up
upheave
apteryx
spreaze

spreeze
apogeal
apogean
epigeal
epigean
epigram
spignel
apagoge
epagoge
apogamy
epigene
epigone
epigoni
epigons
epigyny
upcheer
spy-hole
apehood
upshoot
upthrow
upwhirl
apsidal
oppidan
optical
optimal
uprisal
aphides
apsides
épuisée
spoiled
spoiler
uppiled
uprisen
upriver
upsides
spairge
spriggy
springe
springy
spright
upright
uptight
yplight
epeirid
Ophidia
ophitic
apricot
epsilon
upsilon
ypsilon
Ophiura
optimum
spikily
spelean
applied
spelder
spelled
speller
spelter
spilled
spiller
apology
speldin

spulyie
spulzie
upclimb
opaline
opulent
spiling
up-along
upflung
upclose
epilate
spilite
applaud
upblown
ipomoea
spumous
sponsal
spinach
spinode
spancel
spaniel
spanker
spanned
spanner
span-new
spencer
spender
spinner
spinnet
spinney
spondee
sponger
spin-off
apanage
spinage
open-air
opuntia
spongin
spunkie
spangle
spangly
spindle
spindly
spinule
open-end
opening
opinion
sponson
sponsor
spin-dry
aptness
Spanish
spinose
spinate
spinous
spinout
spun-out
spondyl
splotch
apposer
opposer
spoofer
spooler
spooney

spoorer
splodge
splodgy
aphonia
aphonic
aphotic
aptotic
opsonic
opsonin
appoint
upbound
upgoing
upwound
apropos
uphoard
uphoord
upcoast
uphoist
uprouse
upspeak
upspear
apoplex
apepsia
upspake
upspoke
Spartan
sporran
spuriae
spur-way
upbreak
oporice
upgrade
sparger
sparred
sparrer
spersed
spiraea
sporter
spurner
spurred
spurrer
spurrey
eparchy
sparthe
sperthe
sparoid
spermic
spiroid
upbraid
uptrain
up-train
sparely
sparkle
spirtle
sporule
spurtle
spireme
epergne
operand
operant
sparing
spirant
upbring

uptrend — upsurge — breaded — Grobian — bricken — tractor — uredine
approof — upbuild — breaker — cry-baby — brocked — precept — bridoon
sparrow — appulse — briared — tribade — brocket — triceps — predoom
appress — upburst — broaden — tribady — cracked — brocard — prudery
apprise — spawner — creamer — crabbed — cracker — dry-cure — tridarn
operose — upsweep — croaker — cribbed — cricket — grocery — iridise
oppress — spa-well — dreader — crubeen — crickey — procure — prudish
upbrast — upswell — dreamed — drabber — crochet — tracery — aridity
epurate — upswing — dreamer — drabbet — crocket — tricorn — crudity
operate — upswept — dryades — drabler — drucken — Grecise — erudite
spirity — upswarm — ergates — dribber — erected — Grecism — gradate
éperdue — epaxial — greaser — driblet — erecter — precast — predate
approve — epoxide — greaten — drubbed — fracted — precess — erodium
updrawn — aphylly — greater — grabbed — frocked — precise — iridium
upgrown — uplying — greaves — grabber — fructed — process — triduum
episode — spryest — oreades — grubbed — pricker — tricksy — uredium
apostil — epizoan — treader — grubber — pricket — uricase — bradawl
spasmic — epizoic — treater — problem — proceed — brucite — arsenal
spastic — epizoon — wreaked — triblet — trachea — grecque — creedal
apishly — squamae — wreaker — crab-oil — tracked — tractus — freeman
apostle — squabby — arraign — frabbit — tracker — trochus — freeway
epistle — squacco — arrange — brabble — tricker — urachus — trueman
opuscle — squaddy — breathe — cribble — trochee — cracowe — ardency
opossum — aquafer — breathy — drabble — trucker — graddan — oriency
aphthae — squared — preachy — dribble — wrecker — gradual — urgence
spatial — squarer — wreathe — dribbly — crucify — Irideae — urgency
epithem — squashy — wreaths — fribble — brocage — irideal — arreede
epithet — aquaria — wreathy — grabble — trucage — iridial — breeder
spathed — aquatic — break-in — gribble — arachis — iridian — briered
spattee — aquavit — creatic — grubble — braccia — predial — creeper
spatter — squalid — erratic — prabble — braccio — pridian — dry-eyed
spitted — squawky — organic — pribble — breccia — triduan — freemen
spilten — equable — priapic — proball — brockit — dry-dock — freezer
spitter — equably — triacid — tribble — cricoid — predict — friezed
spotted — equally — triadic — wrybill — ericoid — produce — greeted
spotter — squally — triatic — armband — orectic — product — grieced
sputter — equator — broadly — prebend — practic — traduce — griever
upstage — squalor — dreadly — proband — brickle — bridled — orderer
spathic — squatty — errable — probang — bricole — bridler — praeses
sputnik — squelch — friable — tribune — bruckle — dredger — creeshy
upstair — squeaky — friarly — bribery — crackle — drudger — arsenic
apetaly — equerry — greatly — arabise — crackly — prodded — creepie
spatula — aqueous — treacle — Arabism — dry-cell — trodden — ermelin
spatule — squeeze — treacly — Arabist — erectly — trudgen — freebie
spittle — squeezy — treadle — probate — freckle — trudger — freesia
epitome — Equidae — triable — probity — freckly — prodigy — Friesic
épatant — equinal — creator — tribute — gracile — sraddha — griesie
upstand — squinch — organon — crab-nut — grackle — brodkin — troelie
spit-box — squitch — treason — araceae — grockle — trade-in — uraemia
upstood — aquifer — triaxon — Arician — prickle — cruddle — uraemic
epitaph — squiffy — preasse — brecham — prickly — crudely — briefly
upstare — squishy — breadth — brochan — trickle — gradely — cruells
upstart — equinia — arcanum — crucial — trickly — griddle — cruelly
apatite — squirmy — Arnaout — crucian — truckle — treddle — greenly
upstate — squinny — erratum — Grecian — drachma — Urodela — griesly
epitaxy — Aquilon — organum — proctal — bracing — urodele — grysely
spousal — equinox — Priapus — trochal — brucine — credent — orderly
appuied — creance — treague — trucial — iracund — erodent — freeing
appuyed — triarch — organza — brocade — tracing — gradine — orleans
epaulet — truancy — Arabian — precede — erector — gradino — freedom
spouter — friande — drybeat — brachet — precook — prudent — praetor
splurge — arcaded — grab-bag — bracken — proctor — trading — treetop
splurgy — arrased — — bracket — Procyon — trident — pre-empt

free-arm
arietta
ariette
cruelty
greenth
Croesus
fraenum
orifice
preface
prefect
proface
prefade
crofter
draftee
drafter
drifter
grafter
grifter
proffer
trifler
griffin
traffic
trefoil
triffid
gruffly
profile
trifoly
truffle
urnfuls
profane
draft-ox
dry-foot
griffon
prefard
preform
triform
dry-fist
profess
profuse
drag-bar
drag-man
frogman
grogram
program
trigram
brigade
tragedy
bragged
cragged
dragged
drag-net
drogher
droguet
drugged
drugger
drugget
frigger
frogged
froglet
prigger
trigger
frogbit
draggle

fragile
gregale
tragule
wriggle
origami
trigamy
brigand
oregano
origane
orogeny
progeny
dragoon
E-region
triglot
gregory
frigate
archway
Brahman
Orphean
orthian
preheat
archlet
arsheen
orphrey
bruhaha
archaic
Brahmin
armhole
trehala
arshine
errhine
prehend
arch-foe
orthros
archery
orchard
Orphism
archeus
Orpheus
archive
arrival
artisan
orbital
ordinal
ordinar
arbiter
armiger
braided
brained
broider
broiler
bruiser
cruiser
drainer
ermined
fruited
fruiter
grained
grainer
greisen
groined
orbiter
ordinee

praiser
trailer
trained
trainee
trainer
arriage
droichy
freight
cruisie
druidic
prairie
traikit
armilla
article
Braille
frailly
greisly
treille
orcinol
traitor
arriéré
arriero
orgiast
traipse
artiste
frailty
Orvieto
project
traject
frijole
prejink
trekked
trekker
brokage
Prakrit
arcking
erl-king
brokery
Fraktur
Grallae
Trullan
Uralian
trilobe
prelacy
prelect
prelude
cruller
grilled
Grolier
proller
trilled
troller
trolley
orology
trilogy
urology
brulyie
brulzie
trellis
arc-lamp
prelims
erelong
praline

prolong
Trilene®
trollop
arblast
armless
artless
braless
prelate
prelaty
prolate
trilith
uralite
urolith
arillus
Krilium®
frampal
grammar
gremial
tram-car
tramway
trumeau
cromack
grimace
primacy
bromide
brimmed
brimmer
brommer
brummer
crammed
crammer
cramped
crampet
crimmer
crimper
crumpet
drummed
drummer
grommet
grummet
krimmer
premier
primmed
prommer
trammel
tramper
trimmed
trimmer
trommel
trumpet
primage
Aramaic
Brummie
crampit
drumlin
gremlin
kremlin
primsie
bramble
brambly
crimple
crumble
crumbly

crumple
drumble
frumple
grimily
grumble
grumbly
primely
primula
trample
tremble
tremolo
briming
bromine
cremona
crimine
crimini
dromond
framing
primine
priming
crampon
crimson
gramary
primary
primero
uromere
Arimasp
cramesy
gramash
grumose
premise
premiss
promise
bromate
cremate
eremite
primate
promote
brimful
brumous
frame-up
grampus
grumous
premium
primeur
premove
Araneae
brinjal
cranial
frontal
grandad
grandam
grannam
Iranian
iron-pan
trangam
trental
truncal
Uranian
tranect
wryneck
grenade

uranide
branded
brander
bran-new
brinded
bringer
bronzed
bronzen
cringer
drinker
drunken
Erinyes
fringed
fronded
fronted
grandee
granfer
granger
grantee
granter
grinder
grinned
grunter
prancer
printer
pronged
prunted
tranced
tranter
trinket
trunked
wringed
wringer
wronger
cranage
branchy
bronchi
broncho
crunchy
Frenchy
tranche
araneid
bran-pie
crinoid
frantic
grannie
prenzie
trannie
transit
trenail
wren-tit
prancke
brangle
bransle
brantle
brindle
crankle
cringle
crinkle
crinkly
crunkle
frankly
grandly

granule
gruntle
prankle
pronely
trangle
trindle
tringle
trundle
wrangle
wrinkle
wrinkly
wrongly
grandma
erg-nine
ironing
pruning
urinant
crannog
franion
fronton
grantor
grunion
princox
pronaoi
pronaos
transom
grandpa
granary
iron-ore
trinary
urinary
brinish
crinose
dronish
dryness
ironise
ironist
trenise
uranism
wryness
crenate
crinate
crinite
erinite
granite
pronate
pronota
trinity
uranite
urinate
bran-tub
cranium
proneur
pronoun
trankum
trinkum
uranium
uranous
urinous
areolae
areolar
kroo-man
ortolan

preoral	tripsis	brasset	trisula	protein	grouchy	crowder
arboret	trophic	brisken	wrestle	write-in	wrought	crowned
brooder	trypsin	brisket	irksome	britska	droukit	crowner
crooked	tryptic	brushed	presume	britzka	groupie	crownet
crooner	aripple	brusher	triseme	brattle	proudly	drawler
cryogen	cripple	cresset	urosome	brittle	trouble	draw-net
triolet	dropfly	crested	art-song	crottle	croupon	drowned
triones	dropple	crisper	Krishna	fritfly	croûton	drowner
trooper	grapple	crosier	present	irately	triumph	growler
brioche	gripple	crossed	prosing	prattle	arcuate	oreweed
Armoric	propale	crushed	Bristol	protyle	arbutus	prowler
drookit	propyla	crusher	dry-shod	tritely	arduous	trawler
ergodic	tripoli	Dresden	erasion	erotema	trivial	brewage
prootic	tripple	dressed	erosion	eroteme	crevice	brownie
troolie	griping	dresser	frisson	Tritoma	privacy	crowdie
criollo	propane	freshen	grysbok	grating	bravado	prawlin
croodle	propend	fresher	brasero	orotund	privado	crewels
Bryozoa	propene	freshet	brisure	prating	provide	brewing
kroo-boy	propine	Frisbee	drosera	pretend	bravoes	drawing
armoire	propone	frisker	erasure	protend	brevier	growing
armoury	trepang	frisket	frisure	tritone	preview	crow-toe
arnotto	crypton	frosted	grosert	writing	drive-in	draw-boy
trionym	gryphon	grasper	Irishry	Brython	prevail	Erewhon
crop-ear	krypton	grasser	irisate	oration	travail	artwork
cryptal	drapery	grisled	brush-up	fratery	travois	brewery
prepack	drip-dry	Irisher	brusque	friture	provoke	froward
prepuce	grapery	presser	friseur	oratory	bravely	dry-wash
tripody	prepare	Prestel®	frustum	preterm	drevill	prowess
cropped	tripery	prosper	grassum	urethra	gravely	prowest
cropper	oropesa	tressed	press-up	British	privily	frowsty
crupper	propose	tressel	trismus	brutish	craving	grown-up
drapier	tropism	trussed	erosive	cretism	crivens	proximo
dripped	tropist	trusser	fretsaw	erotism	driving	bruxism
droplet	croptul	trustee	Grotian	protest	graving	drayman
drop-net	drop-out	truster	protean	protist	prevene	grey-lag
dropped	trap-cut	tryster	urethan	crittur	prevent	greyhen
dropper	trapeze	wrester	erotica	fretful	provand	drayage
frappée	briquet	presage	protect	proteus	provant	argyrla
fripper	croquet	prisage	brothel	protium	provend	traybit
grapnel	prequel	brassie	brother	tritium	provine	treybit
gripped	orarian	crispin	critter	write-up	proving	grayfly
gripper	araroba	drastic	dratted	pretext	bravery	fraying
prophet	ard-righ	eristic	fretted	prothyl	bravura	praying
prop-jet	prurigo	griskin	fritted	arousal	gravure	Gruyère
propped	trireme	prosaic	fritter	braunch	proverb	'Arryish
trapped	orarion	prussic	gritter	craunch	previse	greyish
trapper	prerupt	trysail	grutten	frounce	proviso	preyful
triplet	prorate	droshky	pretzel	praunce	provost	trayful
triplex	orarium	briskly	prithee	trounce	treviss	brazier
tripped	artsman	bristle	prythee	arouser	breveté	crozier
tripper	crusian	bristly	trotted	crouper	brevity	frizzed
trippet	crustae	crassly	trotter	graupel	gravity	grazier
wrapped	crustal	crisply	withen	grouper	pravity	wrizled
wrapper	crystal	crossly	written	grouser	private	prezzie
propage	Drusian	dry-salt	wrythen	prouler	privity	crazily
cryptic	trishaw	freshly	brutify	trouper	trivium	drizzle
drappie	trisect	grisely	frutify	trouter	crow-bar	drizzly
drip-tip	crusade	gristle	gratify	brought	draw-bar	frazzle
erepsin	crusado	gristly	protégé	draught	grow-bag	frizzle
graphic	preside	grossly	fratchy	drought	brawler	frizzly
Graphis	prosody	grysely	arctoid	drouthy	brawned	grizzle
krypsis	brasier	prosily	oratrix	fraught	crawler	grizzly
prepaid		trestle	proteid	froughy	crowded	grazing

trizone
assagai
Isiacal
askance
ashamed
assayer
escapee
escaper
essayed
essayer
T-shaped
U-shaped
V-shaped
yslaked
ascarid
ascaris
Asianic
Asiatic
Aspasia
astatic
Islamic
ismatic
astatki
assault
astable
Ismaili
Israeli
Osmanli
usually
ascaunt
escalop
Astarte
esparto
Tsabian
isobare
isobase
isobath
asocial
psychic
isochor
usucapt
asudden
isodoma
isodont
assegai
isleman
essence
assever
isoetes
osiered
osselet
osseter
asperge
ascesis
ascetic
askesis
astelic
asteria
asterid
osteoid
osteoma
asperse
asteism

osseous
isogram
isagoge
lsegrim
isogamy
isogeny
tsigane
ash-heap
escheat
ischial
oscheal
isohyet
ash-hole
asphalt
asthore
ischium
isthmus
asphyxy
estival
ascites
ashiver
assizer
Oscines
assiege
ascidia
aspidia
aspirin
ossific
ossicle
ostiole
ostiary
osmiate
ostiate
osmious
isokont
Psalter
asylums
asklent
isoline
useless
isolate
Ishmael
isomere
asinico
asunder
isonomy
tsunami
asinine
Asmoday
escolar
asconce
estover
osmosis
osmotic
psionic
estoile
astound
esloyne
essoyne
espouse
Isopoda
asepsis
aseptic

aspread
csárdás
estreat
Osirian
ascribe
escribe
astrict
estrich
ostraca
ostrich
astride
estrade
usurped
usurper
astroid
ostraka
escroll
ashrama
astrand
c-spring
G-string
tsarina
usuring
tsardom
estrepe
tsarism
tsarist
usuress
asprout
usurous
asprawl
ash-tray
isatine
isotone
isotron
isotope
isotopy
isotype
esotery
oscular
osmunda
assumed
assured
assurer
assuage
escuage
asquint
issuant
esquire
estuary
ossuary
T-square
osculum
asswage
asexual
astylar
espying
atlases
steaded
stealed
stealer
steamed
steamer

strawed
strawen
strayed
strayer
strange
attaché
ptyalin
steamie
stearic
stearin
attaint
straint
athanor
attaboy
ethanol
strappy
stealth
stratum
stratus
stibial
stabbed
stabber
stabler
stubbed
atabrin
atebrin
stabile
stibble
stubble
stubbly
stibine
stibium
stacked
stacket
sticked
sticker
atactic
stichic
stickit
stickle
stichoi
stichos
stucco'd
stuccos
etacism
itacism
otocyst
stickup
stuck-up
stodger
studded
studden
studied
studier
stiddie
staddle
studdle
student
stadium
stretch
steeled
steepen
steeper

steerer
strewed
strewer
utterer
atresia
etaerio
etheric
steekit
sthenic
streaky
steeple
steeply
utterly
streamy
étrenne
attempt
atheise
atheism
atheist
steep-to
streety
stretta
stretto
'strewth
atheous
steep-up
staffer
stiffen
stifled
stifler
stuffed
stuffer
stiffly
ataghan
Stygian
stagger
stagily
staging
étagère
stagery
etchant
etching
ethical
stoical
strigae
stained
stainer
staired
stoiter
Striges
striker
striped
stripes
stripey
strived
striven
striver
stringy
staithe
strigil
staidly
utricle
stridor

ethiops
athirst
striate
atokous
Italian
stellar
atelier
stalked
stalker
stalled
stelled
stiller
stilted
stilter
étalage
otology
otalgia
styloid
stalely
stelene
Italiot
Stilton
stylise
stylish
stylist
utilise
athleta
athlete
otolith
stylate
stylite
utility
atalaya
stomach
stammel
stammer
stamper
stemmed
stempel
stummed
stummel
stumper
ethmoid
stemple
stimuli
stumble
stumbly
atamans
stamina
stamnos
stembok
stemson
atomise
atomism
atomist
itemise
stomata
Etonian
stengah
stand-by
standen
stander
staniel

stannel
stanyel
stinged
stinger
stinker
stinted
stinter
stonied
stonker
stunned
stunner
stunted
stenchy
ctenoid
stand-in
stannic
stencil
utensil
atingle
stonily
stentor
stonern
stand-to
stand-up
Ottoman
stooden
stooker
stooped
stooper
stroken
stroker
strowed
strower
atrophy
strophe
atropia
atropin
etiolin
stoolie
strobic
strooke
strodle
Atropos
stroppy
stop-gap
utopian
stapler
stepney
stepped
stepper
stopped
stopper
stop-off
stupefy
stypsis
styptic
stapple
stipple
stipule
stopple
stipend
stoping
stupent

stepson	statant	aurally	quiblin	dulcify	subduer	quieter
utopism	station	buyable	tumbril	muscoid	mundify	auberge
utopist	Stetson	curable	cue-ball	quickie	guidage	outedge
eternal	stature	ducally	quibble	furcula	mueddin	queechy
star-man	statism	dupable	bugbane	quackle	quadric	aurelia
star-map	statist	durable	cubbing	quickly	quiddit	auxesis
sternal	statute	durably	cumbent	sun-cult	quodlin	auxetic
stirrah	stative	fugally	dubbing	curcuma	muddily	Eugenia
attract	strumae	humanly	gubbins	outcome	quiddle	eugenic
otaries	staunch	jurally	husband	succumb	ruddily	eutexia
starken	étourdi	mutable	lumbang	buccina	rundale	numeric
star-led	stouten	mutably	numbing	mud-cone	ducdame	subedit
starlet	strudel	rulable	rubbing	outcrop	budding	suberic
starred	Etruria	rurally	subbing	puccoon	duodena	suberin
starter	stoutly	sueable	tubbing	succory	funding	aureola
starved	attuent	tunable	turband	dulcose	guiding	aureole
sterlet	attuite	tunably	turbant	muscose	lurdane	cure-all
sterned	stovies	eucaine	turbine	nutcase	mundane	jumelle
stirpes	stoving	lucarne	turbond	outcast	nundine	pucelle
stirred	atavism	muraena	gumboot	success	pudding	queenly
stirrer	stew-can	bugaboo	nun-buoy	succose	turdine	queerly
storied	stewpan	curaçoa	dun-bird	succuss	bundook	quietly
storage	stowage	curator	fubbery	dulcite	gumdrop	rubella
starchy	stewing	Euratom	lubbard	furcate	outdoor	rubeola
ptarmic	stowing	fusarol	outburn	juncate	puldron	lucerne
starlit	stewpot	subatom	rubbery	Succoth	duddery	lugeing
starnie	athwart	sumatra	sun-bird	sulcate	outdare	dukedom
steroid	steward	dumaist	sunburn	fulcrum	outdure	eugenol
athrill	staying	Judaise	turbary	fuscous	sundari	gude-son
pteryla	curaçao	Judaism	cubbish	punch-up	burdash	juke-box
starkly	cutaway	Judaist	furbish	punctum	Kurdish	mu-meson
startle	Judaean	mulatta	kurbash	putchuk	Luddism	Euterpe
startly	nunatak	mulatto	rubbish	quechua	sun-disk	funèbre
sterile	oulakan	Bubalus	surbase	Quichua	tun-dish	duresse
sternly	runaway	punalua	tubbish	succour	Luddite	eupepsy
iterant	subadar	rub-a-dub	mud-bath	succous	outdate	rulesse
otarine	durance	subaqua	sun-bath	Muscovy	surdity	aureate
staring	surance	bugbear	surbate	quadrat	humdrum	aureity
styrene	mutanda	bum-boat	turbith	subdean	put-down	burette
uterine	aurated	cudbear	bulbous	subdual	rubdown	buvette
pterion	duramen	gunboat	bumbaze	suidian	run-down	cuneate
stardom	lunated	mud-boat	humbuzz	subdual...	sun-dawn	cunette
stir-fry	Musales	outbrag	Dunciad	sundial	sundown	curette
attrist	mutagen	sun-beam	sun-clad	burdock	funeral	cuvette
attrite	putamen	sun-bear	surcoat	puddock	gude-man	fumette
iterate	sudamen	sun-beat	tulchan	ruddock	humeral	lunette
starets	sugared	tug-boat	succuba	subduce	juvenal	musette
staretz	nuraghe	cutback	succubi	subduct	lumenal	puberty
start-up	nuraghi	jumbuck	succade	sun-deck	numeral	bureaus
sternum	queachy	outback	suicide	fuddled	puberal	bureaux
stirrup	bubalis	Purbeck	bunched	fuddler	ruderal	dureful
Sturnus	cumarin	fumbler	butcher	huddled	subedar	duteous
yttrium	Fumaria	humbles	futchel	hundred	tutelar	hugeous
ataraxy	lunatic	jumbler	guichet	hurdies	tutenag	humerus
etesian	puparia	mumbler	gutcher	hurdler	rudesby	luteous
stasima	Puranic	numbles	luncher	muddied	lucency	museful
statice	subacid	outbred	lurcher	muddler	pudency	quietus
statics	subarid	rumbler	mulcted	puddler	quiesce	tubeful
statued	sudanic	tumbler	muncher	ruddied	tumesce	tuneful
stetted	turacin	tumbrel	muscled	ruddier	pudenda	huff-cap
stotter	tutania	lumbago	puncher	rundled	bug-eyed	mud-flap
stutter	autarky	gumboil	quicken	rundlet	murexes	mud-flat
stately	rusalka	ouabain	succeed	subdued	quieten	ruffian

runflat	dung-fly	push-pin	cubicle	sucking	murlain	bullate
surfman	nut-gall	muchell	cuticle	bucksom	nuclein	duality
turfman	bugging	mud-hole	funicle	musk-cod	purloin	nullity
outface	bulging	mushily	fusible	musk-pod	ruellia	quality
suffice	fulgent	out-half	humidly	tuck-box	surloin	sublate
surface	hugging	euphony	lucidly	Dunkirk	tuilyie	build-up
muffled	jugging	gushing	luridly	hunkers	tuilzie	built-up
muffler	juggins	pushing	tumidly	puckery	sunlike	bull-pup
purfled	lugging	ruching	tunicle	buckish	surlily	full-out
quaffer	lunging	Ruthene	audient	duskish	mud-lump	nucleus
ruffled	mugging	cubhood	auditor	luskish	mug-lamb	pull-out
ruffler	muggins	cushion	humidor	murkish	sublime	mud-lava
funfair	outgone	euphroe	musimon	puckish	sun-lamp	outlive
furfair	pugging	fushion	rubicon	Turkess	culling	gulleys
surfeit	pungent	mud-hook	curiosa	Turkish	curling	nut-meal
buffalo	purging	nunhood	furioso	Sukkoth	cutling	Würmian
cupfuls	rugging	nut-hook	ju-jitsu	tuck-out	Euglena	bummock
huffily	surgent	Pushtoo	puniest	buck-eye	furlana	hummock
jugfuls	surging	futhark	Sufiism	bullbat	furlong	mummock
mugfuls	tugging	futhorc	dubiety	hurl-bat	hurling	outmode
outfall	turgent	futhork	muriate	nucleal	Juglans	mummied
puffily	burgeon	Kuh-horn	bulimus	nuclear	nulling	mummify
tubfuls	dudgeon	outhire	cubitus	outleap	outland	rummage
zuffolo	dungeon	outhyre	curious	Pullman	outline	duumvir
puffing	gudgeon	tushery	dubious	quillai	purline	turmoil
surfing	Guignol	duchess	dutiful	Tullian	purling	bummalo
turfing	murgeon	Cushite	euripus	lullaby	bulldog	mulmull
buffoon	outgrow	Kurhaus	furious	bullace	bullion	pug-mill
outflow	sunglow	outhaul	rubious	bullock	cullion	rummily
outfoot	surgeon	pushful	Punjabi	gun-lock	full-hot	augment
puff-box	budgero	quahaug	subject	mullock	mullion	butment
bus-fare	buggery	ruthful	subjoin	putlock	nucleon	fulmine
gunfire	busgirl	cubical	outjump	rullock	outlook	gumming
puffery	Hungary	cubital	outjest	nuclide	quillon	humming
dun-fish	puggery	kufiyah	buckram	builded	rullion	hutment
huffish	surgery	luminal	buck-saw	builder	bullary	mumming
lubfish	burgess	Muridae	junkman	bullied	butlery	summand
mud-fish	muggish	musical	musk-bag	bull-pen	cutlery	summing
pupfish	outgush	puritan	musk-cat	cullied	dullard	summons
subfusc	puggish	Surinam	musk-rat	duelled	guildry	cup-mark
subfusk	suggest	Lusiads	musk-sac	dueller	gullery	mummery
suffuse	nuggety	culices	Turkman	fuelled	mudlark	nummary
sunfast	outgate	jubilee	buckeen	fueller	sutlery	summary
sun-fish	vulgate	juniper	buckler	full-fed	Auslese	summery
tubfast	fulgour	Jupiter	suckler	guilder	budless	budmash
tubfish	fungous	lucifer	turkies	gullied	bugloss	Burmese
suffete	outgive	lucigen	bulkily	gullies	bullish	cup-moss
sulfate	rug-gown	mucigen	cuckold	outlier	cubless	durmast
turfite	bush-cat	murices	duskily	purlieu	cutlass	outmost
burghal	bushman	pubises	huskily	queller	dualism	quamash
burglar	cuphead	quoiter	luckily	quilled	dualist	rummish
Jungian	lum-head	bubinga	murkily	quillet	dullish	submiss
aufgabe	mukhtar	augitic	muskily	quilted	euclase	summist
bungler	sub-head	bulimia	sulkily	quilter	fullest	Suomish
burgher	hushaby	culicid	bucking	sullied	fullish	surmise
juggler	bushido	cutikin	busking	wurlies	gullish	furmety
outgoer	Fuehrer	juridic	duck-ant	nullify	gutless	furmity
puggree	luthier	mudiria	ducking	qualify	hueless	gummata
burgage	push-off	tunicin	fucking	fullage	outlash	gummite
luggage	Buphaga	audible	hulking	sullage	outlast	pug-moth
fungoid	kuchcha	audibly	husking	built-in	publish	sun-myth
tung-oil	bush-tit	auricle	lurking	Guelfic	sumless	gummous
cupgall	fuchsia		quaking	mullein	sunless	hummaum

7 □u□v□r

outmove	quantum	guipure	murrine	quassia	burthen	suction
quantal	ruinous	gunport	outrank	subsoil	bustler	tuition
quinnat	turndun	outpart	purring	sunsuit	curtsey	subtype
quintal	turn-out	outport	guerdon	fussily	custrel	austere
quintan	auroral	purport	gunroom	ourself	further	bustard
quondam	autocar	Purpura	murrion	outsell	hustler	buttery
dunnock	automat	purpure	outroop	outsole	lustres	culture
furnace	autovac	support	outroot	fulsome	murther	custard
guanaco	cupola'd	suspire	sun-roof	subsume	nut-tree	multure
huanaco	cupolar	dumpish	eutropy	bussing	puttied	mustard
funnies	humoral	lumpish	guy-rope	cuisine	puttier	nurture
quannet	sudoral	mumpish	outrope	cursing	quitted	outturn
quintet	Euronet	outpost	bulrush	bus-stop	quitter	pulture
turnkey	humogen	purpose	cuirass	fuss-pot	rustler	rupture
turn-off	out-over	suppose	currish	gumshoe	rustred	tuatara
turnoff	aurochs	surpass	guarish	gunshot	turtler	tuatara
dunnage	bubonic	cuspate	outrush	mudscow	justify	vulture
gunnage	bucolic	turpeth	querist	mugshot	Austric	vulturn
tunnage	dulosis	outpour	sucrase	outshot	curtail	cultism
quinche	dulotic	pulpous	sucrose	questor	curtain	cultist
quantic	eulogia	sulphur	sunrise	rum-shop	dust-bin	eustasy
quintic	out-owre	surplus	tutress	suasion	huitain	runtish
funnily	autopsy	suppawn	cuprite	sunspot	sustain	ruttish
sunnily	judoist	cumquat	eucrite	bursary	outtake	curtate
outname	culotte	kumquat	cuprous	Bursera	cuittle	guttate
surname	autobus	outroar	Quercus	cursory	ductile	oustiti
burning	autocue	quartan	furrowy	guisard	dustily	gustful
cunning	autonym	surreal	guereza	nursery	eustyle	hunt's-up
dunning	gunplay	currach	quartzy	suasory	lustily	hurtful
funning	outplay	outrace	cumshaw	tussore	Mustela	lustful
guanine	outpray	outride	fur-seal	subsist	outtalk	lustrum
gunning	auspice	bur-reed	Hulsean	Hussite	outtell	punt-gun
ounning	mudpack	burrhel	kursaal	pulsate	pustule	surtout
quinine	outpace	curried	outsoar	russety	rustily	furtive
quinone	suspect	currier	outspan	burst-up	subtile	curtaxe
ruining	jump-jet	furrier	outstay	cursive	rut-time	subtext
running	outpeep	guarded	pursual	jussive	bunting	augural
sunning	outpeer	hurried	Russian	suasive	butt-end	cupular
tunning	rump-fed	ouvrier	Tuesday	tussive	buttons	jugular
turning	sumpter	quarrel	tussock	outsize	buttony	lunular
munnion	jump-off	quarter	outside	austral	curtana	sutural
runnion	pulpify	quartet	subside	dustman	duotone	tubular
gunnera	bumpkin	queried	subsidy	dust-pan	gutting	tumular
gunnery	culprit	sucrier	bukshee	fustian	hunting	augurer
gurnard	lumpkin	putrefy	bursted	lustral	hutting	fucused
nunnery	pumpkin	curragh	bursten	muntjac	jutting	fucuses
quinary	dum-palm	outrage	burster	muntjak	munting	sutured
turnery	duopoly	ouvrage	cuisser	nuptial	mustang	pupunha
burnish	jumpily	duarchy	guesser	out-tray	muttony	lupulin
dulness	lumpily	murrain	guesten	quetzal	nutting	subunit
dunnish	pulpily	quartic	outstep	quittal	putting	bubukle
fulness	cupping	bunraku	punster	suntrap	quiting	queuing
furnish	jumping	buirdly	pursuer	buttock	rusting	fuguist
Hunnish	lumping	burrell	Quashee	custock	rutting	auguste
nunnish	nut-pine	puerile	quester	eustacy	subtend	cumulus
outness	pupping	supreme	Russify	futtock	suiting	tumulus
pug-nose	rump-end	supremo	gunship	justice	sultana	purview
quinate	supping	currant	ludship	lustick	tufting	surview
ruinate	suspend	current	lugsail	puttock	yu-stone	suavely
Sunnite	suspens	furring	nunship	quetsch	auction	curving
burnous	vulpine	guaraná	outsail	subtack	pultoon	pulvini
burn-out	pumpion	Guaraní	pursuit	custode	quittor	culvert
muonium	subplot	guarani	Quashie	custody	ruction	quavery

subvert	fuzzily	overall	swigger	swipple	excheat	exuvial
curvate	muzzily	overfly	twiggen	two-part	extinct	lyra-way
curvity	buzzing	overply	twigger	dwarfed	excited	pyjama'd
outvote	subzone	overtly	swaggie	swarded	exciter	pyjamas
suavity	buzzard	overjoy	Swahili	swarmer	expired	bycatch
vulvate	subzero	oversow	two-hand	swerver	exhibit	hyraces
fulvous	aviator	overtop	two-inch	sworder	exciton	lyrated
survive	ivy-bush	overarm	awaking	twirler	excitor	dynamic
survewe	avocado	Everest	dwelled	swarthy	expiate	hydatid
outwear	ovicide	ivorist	dweller	twiscar	axillae	myiasis
outwick	evacuee	overuse	swallet	swasher	axillar	pyralid
burweed	Avicula	evirate	swelled	swisher	exclude	Pyralis
cudweed	evictor	Avernus	sweller	twisted	explode	pyramid
outweed	evocate	overbuy	swelted	twister	exalted	pyramis
outweep	Ovidian	overdue	swelter	two-step	exclaim	synaxis
huswife	oviduct	overrun	swiller	awesome	explain	dyeable
gunwale	evident	overawe	swollen	twasome	exploit	gyrally
outwalk	avidity	overdye	twilled	twosome	explant	rybauld
out-wall	ivresse	overeye	ewe-lamb	swatter	oxblood	Lycaena
outwell	aviette	Avestan	swaling	swither	explore	tyranne
mugwump	aviform	Avestic	two-line	Switzer	axolotl	tyranny
outwent	oviform	evasion	swallow	swotter	exility	Zygaena
outwind	ovoidal	evasive	sweltry	twitted	oxalate	synapse
outwing	uveitis	ovation	aweless	twitten	exclave	dynasty
bug-word	evolute	evitate	awnless	twitter	example	synapte
bugwort	ovulate	avoutry	twelfth	switchy	exempla	eye-beam
bulwark	avenger	uva-ursi	swamper	twitchy	exemple	cymbalo
cutworm	evangel	swearer	swimmer	twattle	examine	eyeball
lugworm	eventer	sweated	ewe-milk	two-time	exomion	eyebolt
mudwort	oven-tit	sweater	owl-moth	two-tone	Oxonian	pyeball
mugwort	evening	swabbed	gwiniad	awfully	axinite	symbole
outward	aventre	swabber	gwyniad	awkward	oxonium	myrbane
outwork	evanish	swobbed	Owenian	swaying	exposal	eyebrow
outworn	dvandva	swobber	twankay	swizzle	exposed	symbion
sunward	avionic	twibill	swing-by	extatic	exposer	eye-bath
tutwork	ovarian	awlbird	ewe-neck	oxy-acid	expound	lyncean
Pugwash	overeat	swaddle	swanker	axially	extreat	lynchet
sunwise	overfar	twaddle	swankey	exhaust	exurban	hyacine
outwith	overlap	twaddly	swinger	expanse	uxorial	syncope
juryman	overlay	twiddle	swinked	exacter	extract	rye-corn
jurymen	overman	twiddly	twinned	exactly	extrude	syncarp
ruby-red	overpay	Swedish	twin-set	exscind	exarchy	hylding
buoyage	overran	owl-eyed	twinter	exactor	exordia	eye-drop
quayage	overtax	sweeper	swindge	exocarp	extrait	lyddite
butyric	avarice	sweered	dwindle	execute	exurbia	byreman
queynie	overact	sweeten	swindle	exedrae	extreme	Hygeian
guayule	averred	tweeter	swingle	oxidant	express	hymenal
buoyant	averted	two-eyed	twangle	exoderm	exarate	type-bar
burying	ivoried	sweetie	twinkle	exodist	excreta	mycetes
busying	overfed	awheels	twining	oxidase	excrete	synergy
rubying	overget	sweetly	swinery	oxidise	exergue	mycelia
jury-box	overnet	tweedle	Owenism	exudate	oxy-salt	pyaemia
buzz-saw	overred	swifter	Owenist	oxidate	exotica	pyaemic
Günzian	oversea	swiftly	swinish	ox-fence	oxytone	pyretic
guzzler	oversee	twafald	twoness	externe	excusal	pyrexia
huzzaed	overset	twifold	Owenite	axle-box	expunct	pyrexic
muzzler	oversew	twofold	swooned	excerpt	exhumer	synesis
puzzler	average	twyfold	ywroken	exhedra	expunge	lyceums
quizzed	over-age	two-foot	swapped	expense	expurge	hyperon
quizzer	dvornik	two-four	swapper	extense	excudit	xylenol
quizzes	overbid	swagman	swopped	exogamy	excurse	bynempt
buzz-wig	overhit	swagged	swopper	exigent	expulse	Cyperus
muezzin	overlie	swagger	two-pair	exegete	exuviae	eye-flap

myogram
nylghau
syzgial
syngamy
Pythian
mynheer
Lychnic
lychnis
typhoid
eye-hole
wych-elm
by-thing
eyehook
typhoon
mythise
mythism
mythist
tychism
Lythrum
pythium
typhous
cynical
lyrical
symitar
typical
cylices
lymiter
pyrites
pyxides
myringa
syringa
syringe
pyritic
pyxidia
hygiene
Syriasm
cytisus
Dyticus
Mytilus
eyeliad
syllabi
byplace
byrlady
dyslogy
myology
cycloid
hyaloid
myalgia
myalgic
myeloid
myeloma
cyclone
dyeline
hyaline
cyclops
cyclist
eyelash
eyeless
myalism
hyalite
pygmean
pygmoid
Lyomeri

by-and-by
cyanide
hymnody
Lymnaea
hypnoid
lying-in
dyingly
lyingly
vyingly
cyanine
hymning
hypnone
hymnary
cyanise
gymnast
hymnist
kyanise
cyanate
cyanite
kyanite
pycnite
syenite
gyrocar
synodal
bycoket
bygones
bywoner
hypogea
pyrogen
tyloses
tyrones
xylogen
zymogen
Byronic
dysodil
hypoxia
hypoxic
mycosis
mycotic
pyloric
pyrosis
sybotic
sycosis
synodic
synovia
tylosis
xylonic
Xylopia
zygosis
zygotic
zymosis
zymotic
bygoing
gyronny
lycopod
mylodon
tylopod
dyvoury
hyloist
pylorus
pyropus
synonym
lymphad

nymphae
nymphal
rye-peck
dyspnea
nymphet
lyophil
nymphic
sylphid
syrphid
nymphly
tympana
tympano
tympany
symptom
Syrphus
cyprian
hydride
dyarchy
hydroid
myrrhic
pyrrhic
rye-roll
cyprine
hydrant
Cypriot
myrrhol
cypress
gytrash
hydrate
hydrous
hydroxy
dyester
byssoid
byssine
eye-shot
eye-spot
eyesore
myosote
myotube
Cyathea
mystify
cystoid
systole
systyle
syntony
mystery
cyathus
hypural
dysuria
dysuric
Sylvian
sylvine
sylvite
rye-wolf
Tynwald
eye-wink
dye-wood
dye-work
eye-wash
Czechic
tzigany
azygous
Szekler

Azilian
azulejo
tzimmes
azimuth
azymite
azymous
ozonise
azurean
czardas
azurine
czarina
czardom
czarism
czarist
azurite
azotise
azotous

caracara
jararaca
jararaka
katakana
lava-lava
maharaja
matamata
Ramayana
sasarara
takamaka
saraband
carapace
catalase
database
malaxage
malaxate
palamate
paravane
vanadate
parasang
calabash
Malagash
maharani
databank
tamarack
paravail
galapago
cataract
paravant
calamary
Malagasy
balanced
valanced
Jamaican
balancer
navarchy
tamandua
kalamdan
qalamdan
malander
marauder
hazardry
habanera
Kamadeva
Mahadeva
parabema
Samaveda
tapadera
bayadère
Canarese
Fagaceae
Gadarene
Japanese
Javanese
Kanarese
Nazarene
paramese
paranete
Taxaceae
galabeah
maravedi
kaka-beak
Nazarean

panacean
tara-fern
tapadero
law-agent
malapert
parakeet
parament
Japanesy
lamasery
savagely
savagery
paraffle
paraffin
canaigre
harangue
galangal
radar-gun
barathea
Halachic
Halachah
marathon
matachin
Ramadhan
yataghan
rajaship
tabashir
cavatina
galabiya
salaried
tamarind
baladine
basanite
calamine
calamite
canalise
carabine
catamite
faradise
fayalite
laxative
macarise
macarize
magazine
mazarine
nasalise
Nazarite
paganise
palatine
papalise
paradise
parasite
Patarine
sanative
saxatile
taxative
Wahabite
zaratite
garaging
managing
maraging
salading
dahabieh
galabiah

galabieh
paganish
vagarish
hara-kiri
tamarisk
kaka-bill
malarial
palatial
patagial
cabalism
Caladium
faradism
fatalism
macarism
navalism
paganism
papalism
paradigm
patagium
ranarium
samarium
satanism
vanadium
Wahabism
Batavian
Canadian
halation
Hawaiian
lavation
malarian
natation
pacation
ranarian
Tatarian
taxation
vacation
palamino
cavalier
gasalier
vagaries
cabalist
calamint
Fanariot
fatalist
Lazarist
papalist
salariat
satanist
banality
calamity
capacity
fatality
nasality
natality
rapacity
sagacity
salacity
satanity
damaskin
malarkey
caballed
canaille
parallel

rataplan
caballer
parallax
marasmic
marasmus
japanned
savannah
japanner
carap-nut
Casanova
parabola
paranoea
paranoia
Saratoga
catacomb
paranoic
Garamond
paranoid
vagabond
caracole
matadore
parabole
paragoge
sagamore
zabaione
macaroni
carap-oil
parafoil
lavaform
macaroon
parazoan
parazoon
talapoin
cacafogo
tapacolo
paramour
tamanoir
vavasour
vanadous
gadabout
layabout
marabout
racahout
tacahout
catatony
lavatory
natatory
paradoxy
paralogy
sanatory
vavasory
mad-apple
may-apple
oak-apple
paragram
paradrop
banausic
harassed
tanaiste
damassin
harasser
hamartia
Marattia

basaltic
galactic
tac-au-tac
cadastre
lamantin
canaster
varactor
tarantas
vacantly
macahuba
malamute
tapaculo
catapult
paraquat
Paraguay
catalyse
kamacyte
paralyse
catalyst
kala-azar
damboard
garboard
lap-board
larboard
pax-board
way-board
saw-blade
vambrace
madbrain
sauba-ant
jambeaux
barbecue
barbicel
barbican
tabby-cat
Barbados
waybread
pax-brede
daybreak
parbreak
has-beens
gambogic
Darbyite
lamblike
babbling
baubling
dabbling
gabbling
garbling
lambling
marbling
rabbling
rambling
saibling
tabbying
wabbling
wambling
warbling
Cambrian
lambskin
carbolic
Kabbalah
jambolan

tan-balls
zambomba
carbonic
rabbinic
rawboned
carbonyl
galbanum
saw-bones
tabbinet
lambency
gabbroic
gabbroid
lambdoid
tarboosh
may-bloom
gambroon
barbaric
jamboree
Hamburgh
carbaryl
jabberer
carburet
barberry
bayberry
hagberry
waxberry
lambaste
gambeson
iambuses
sabbatic
barbated
rabbeted
barbette
barbital
rambutan
rabbiter
Babbitry
rabbitry
tamboura
mawbound
faubourg
hatbrush
tarboush
tar-brush
carboxyl
jambiyah
barchane
calceate
fasciate
catch-all
bacchant
bar-chart
farcy-bud
cascabel
matchbox
patch-box
sauce-box
watch-box
nancy-boy
fascicle
farcical
sarcodic
watch-dog

Sarcodes
marchesa
marchese
pasch-egg
pancheon
ranchero
pancreas
sauciest
hatchery
hatchety
patchery
calcific
fanciful
watchful
catchfly
lancegay
bacchiac
man-child
cancrine
batching
catching
fancying
Fasching
hatching
matching
patching
ranching
dabchick
bacchian
falchion
panchion
sanction
bacchius
patchily
sanctify
sanctity
carcajou
latchkey
watch-key
Caecilia
marcella
cancelli
saeculum
vasculum
calcular
saccular
vascular
calculus
saccules
sacculus
lancelet
rascally
marchman
ranchman
sauceman
watchman
Garcinia
vaccinia
nascence
vaccinal
mancando
falconer
larcener

parcener
Maecenas
balconet
carcanet
falconet
sarcenet
falconry
nascency
fasciola
cancroid
fasciole
parclose
bad-cloth
wax-cloth
tau-cross
watch-out
manciple
saucepan
calcspar
catch-pit
caschrom
mascaron
baccarat
Fascista
saucisse
Fascisti
narcissi
Fascismo
Fascists
narcoses
narcosis
narcotic
alcated
anceted
dancette
dancetté
dancetty
farceuse
calc-tuff
aw-court
natchway
nandmaid
andward
yardland
yardwand
baldpate
card-case
card-game
nandmade
aardbake
nardface
nardware
andrace
naid-pale
nandrake
sand-bath
aardvark
aardback
nardhack
aardtack
aid-back
andmark
sand-bank

sand-lark
handball
hand-ball
handrail
landfall
landrail
sand-wasp
landmass
hand-cart
handfast
sand-cast
sand-dart
bandeaux
landlady
laudable
mandible
laudably
cardecue
caudicle
Sadducee
handicap
caudices
lah-di-dah
candidly
gaudy-day
bald-head
hand-held
hardhead
land-herd
handbell
daydream
hardbeam
hand-sewn
hard-fern
Mandaean
sand-heap
sand-peep
Landwehr
baldness
handless
hardness
landless
maidless
wardress
saddlery
cardigan
hay-de-guy
sand-shoe
dandy-hen
bardship
hardship
land-ship
wardship
landwind
hand-line
hardline
land-line
land-mine
sand-pipe
dandriff
bandying
bardling
daidling

handling
paddling
sandling
waddling
band-fish
dandyish
land-fish
sandwich
sandyish
baldrick
baudrick
hand-pick
handbill
hand-mill
landfill
landgirl
mandrill
sand-hill
dandyism
Mahdiism
Mazdaism
Mazdeism
Paddyism
hand-list
Mahdiist
tawdrily
vandyked
baudekin
landskip
sand-flea
daedalic
Vandalic
hard-a-lee
sardelle
sand-flag
Magdalen
mandolin
caudillo
gardyloo
handclap
landslip
pardalis
bandelet
handplay
pandemia
pandemic
Landsmål
cardamom
bandsman
bandyman
cardamon
handyman
landsman
mandamus
randomly
bandanna
gardenia
sardonic
hardened
tap-dance
war-dance
cardinal
labdanum

laudanum
fandango
Mandingo
gardener
hardener
pardoner
Pandanus
sardonyx
maidenly
wardenry
mandioca
cardioid
handhold
hardwood
landlord
maidhood
card-vote
handsome
hardcore
sand-hole
sand-mole
ward-mote
wardrobe
aardwolf
tandoori
handbook
handwork
land-roll
hand-loom
sand-worm
ward-room
bawd-born
hand-horn
waldhorn
ward-corn
land-poor
Baudrons
bald-coot
hand-post
sandwort
mandorla
land-crab
sandarac
laddered
wandered
banderol
falderal
mandarin
wanderoo
handgrip
sand-trap
larderer
wanderer
landdros
land-army
panderly
sawdusty
faldetta
caudated
banditti
bandster
mandator
sand-star

carditis
banditry
sand-dune
dandruff
handcuff
sand-pump
handfuls
handover
sandiver
pandowdy
caudexes
Kalevala
baselard
face-card
race-card
savegard
waveband
casemate
catenate
lacerate
latewake
macerate
makebate
name-tape
pale-face
racemate
rape-cake
waterage
danelagh
race-path
bareback
cakewalk
lacebark
baseball
race-ball
date-palm
lacerant
name-part
catenary
water-boa
water-bed
hateable
makeable
nameable
rateable
saleable
takeable
tameable
water-bag
water-bug
water-bus
water-box
paper-boy
rateably
saleably
cadenced
face-ache
water-cow
water-dog
babeldom
calendar
calender

kalendar
lavender
taberdar
calendry
paper-day
danegeld
gapeseed
pale-dead
rape-seed
lace-leaf
farewell
harebell
rakehell
cameleon
gate-vein
male-fern
Pareoean
paderero
paterero
bateleur
cameleer
cave-bear
hare's-ear
bareness
baseless
baseness
bateless
careless
cateress
dateless
faceless
fadeless
fameless
gameness
gateless
haleness
hateless
lameness
lateness
makeless
maneless
mateless
nameless
paleness
rareness
safeness
sageness
sameness
saneness
sateless
tameless
tameness
tapeless
vaneless
wakeless
wareless
waveless
bakemeat
basement
batement
casement
danegelt
easement

fakement
gazement
haterent
lavement
mazement
pavement
water-fly
saw-edged
water-god
parergon
water-gap
oak-egger
water-gas
catechol
water-hen
mageship
canephor
case-shot
cagebird
game-bird
rarefied
tape-tied
Bakelite®
bale-fire
baregine
base-line
cameline
capeline
date-line
facetiae
galenite
gate-fine
laterite
maderise
malefice
palewise
racemise
racemize
sagenite
tapeline
wakerife
water-ice
wavelike
cageling
catering
lace-wing
layering
papering
ravening
tapering
valeting
wakening
watering
wavering
babelish
camelish
hamewith
waterish
maverick
cane-mill
material
matériel
Babeeism

babelism	wage-work	saw-frame	langrage	manganin	Gadhelic	marinade
Galenism	garefowl	half-calf	language	waggoner	pachalic	marinate
racemism	case-worm	half-back	margrave	garganey	parhelic	maritage
Jamesian	gapeworm	gaff-sail	langlauf	tangency	pashalik	navigate
Naperian	sale-room	taffrail	gang-bang	bargoose	bachelor	paginate
Sahelian	tapeworm	half-mast	bar-graph	cargoose	cachalot	palisade
Salesian	waveform	fat-faced	bang-tail	gas-globe	cacholot	radicate
valerian	base-born	sad-faced	hangnail	mangrove	Baphomet	saginate
gaselier	careworn	daffodil	Sangraal	waygoose	raphania	salivate
face-lift	fade-down	gas-field	Sangrail	langspel	Raphanus	sanitate
Galenist	take-down	half-dead	malgrado	margaric	Sathanas	vaginate
maledict	kakemono	hayfield	Sangrado	sangaree	sash-cord	validate
water-jet	racegoer	half-beak	matgrass	hanger-on	bathrobe	calipash
kabeljou	have-nots	half-term	oat-grass	margarin	mashloch	hari-kari
camellia	ravenous	half-year	hangable	kangaroo	cash-book	camisado
labelled	waverous	calfless	tangible	badgerly	sash-tool	capitano
lapelled	barefoot	half-text	mangabey	largesse	wash-bowl	palisado
panelled	gate-post	caffeine	tangibly	sargasso	bathroom	habitans
ravelled	hanepoot	calf-time	Haggadic	pargeted	washroom	harigals
lamellae	hare-foot	half-life	Haggadah	targeted	sash-door	habitant
patellae	lace-boot	half-pike	jaggedly	bangster	fashious	latitant
waterlog	category	half-tide	raggedly	daughter	cache-pot	radicant
date-plum	water-pot	half-time	cargeese	gangster	bathorse	vaginant
labellum	water-pox	baffling	gangrene	laughter	saw-horse	janizary
sacellum	date-tree	halfling	Sangreal	pargeter	war-horse	laminary
Waterloo	water-ram	maffling	sap-green	gadgetry	Mathurin	lapidary
gabeller	name-drop	calf-lick	vargueño	pang-full	gatherer	salivary
lamellar	water-rat	caffeism	fangless	hangover	lathyrus	sanitary
patellar	water-ski	half-pint	pangless	law-giver	fatherly	Caribbee
satelles	cavesson	half-tint	barghest	gargoyle	cathisma	satiable
capellet	caper-tea	calfskin	hangnest	wash-ball	tachisme	variable
water-lot	palestra	half-blue	laughful	oathable	tachiste	cabin-boy
dalesman	maieutic	matfelon	Langshan	warhable	machismo	panic-buy
gavelman	majestic	lawfully	hangbird	washable	Lachesis	variably
salesman	galeated	manfully	hangfire	cachucha	mathesis	mariachi
talesman	gazetted	hawfinch	narghile	cathedra	bathetic	maniacal
waterman	lamented	calf-love	sanguine	cathodic	Japhetic	cariacou
caverned	talented	half-done	dangling	cathodal	pathetic	havildar
cayenned	patentee	half-note	gaggling	washed-up	rachitic	zamindar
maternal	parental	half-tone	gangling	rachides	catheter	Sapindus
paternal	ramentum	half-loaf	jangling	raphides	cathetus	samizdat
taverner	water-tap	half-cock	laughing	cashmere	rachitis	variedly
hazelnut	gamester	half-moon	tangling	hasheesh	bathcube	saliceta
cameloid	man-eater	half-door	wangling	bashless	cathouse	Balinese
case-load	patentor	half-hour	way-going	nathless	madhouse	Galilean
galenoid	sales-tax	half-boot	languish	pathless	tap-house	caginess
gatefold	latently	saffrony	ganglion	rashness	man-hours	calipers
pagehood	tapestry	gas-fired	gangliar	Panhagia	wash-away	easiness
barebone	wage-fund	half-bred	sanglier	pathogen	cachexia	haziness
dane-hole	malemute	far-forth	bargaist	kachahri	cathexis	laziness
gamesome	Mameluke	tafferel	tangoist	naphthol	Cathayan	maziness
matelote	palebuck	fanfaron	sanguify	pashmina	calisaya	raciness
racemose	ramequin	warfarin	nargileh	rathripe	Saxicava	wariness
bale-dock	mameluco	warfarer	pangolin	yachting	camisard	waviness
cagework	take-over	wayfarer	bargello	bathmism	badinage	waxiness
casebook	fade-away	half-step	pangamic	taghairm	camisade	manifest
case-work	take-away	taffetas	Targumic	Cathaian	capitate	navicert
game-cock	waterway	far-flung	bargeman	wash-dirt	carinate	wariment
gavelock	pale-eyed	kaffiyeh	gangsman	parhelia	fatigate	facilely
havelock	water-yam	gangland	manganic	rachilla	kamikaze	natively
laverock	panegyry	hatguard	margined	Valhalla	laminate	basinful
sage-cock	half-face	rat-guard	mangonel	Walhalla	lapidate	Faringee
salework	halfpace	vanguard	marginal	catholic	Latinate	daring-do

malinger	nativist	farinose	mah-jongg	mackinaw	malleate	wax-light
daringly	pacifist	halicore	marjoram	back-comb	palliate	faulchin
gapingly	satirist	halimote	backband	backbond	tail-gate	ballyhoo
ragingly	basicity	palinode	backhand	backword	tail-race	hailshot
ravingly	calidity	varicose	backward	pack-load	talliate	call-bird
savingly	caninity	gasiform	backyard	backbone	vaultage	gaol-bird
takingly	facility	janiform	lackland	back-rope	wall-game	jail-bird
Manichee	Ladinity	maniform	parkland	bank-note	way-leave	fail-dike
padishah	lapidify	napiform	parkward	darksome	kaoliang	nail-file
parishen	Latinity	natiform	back-date	lack-love	caillach	tail-pipe
papisher	nativity	paliform	bank-rate	packfong	fall-back	caulking
ravisher	rabidity	raniform	sack-race	hawk-moth	hallmark	dallying
vanisher	rapidity	variform	backlash	backwork	tailback	rallying
garishly	salinity	vasiform	backwash	bank-book	bail-ball	sallying
lavishly	sapidity	cavicorn	backpack	hack-work	pall-mall	tallying
rakishly	vagility	naricorn	hark-back	rackwork	gall-wasp	vaulting
basilica	validity	makimono	talk-back	taskwork	galleass	sail-fish
cavitied	vapidity	calicoes	backfall	bankroll	galliass	wallfish
ladified	panicked	halitous	rack-rail	jack-fool	mail-cart	call-girl
ramified	radialia	maxi-coat	sark-tail	backroom	fabliaux	Gaulism
ratified	cavilled	palimony	back-hair	dark-room	tableaux	Harleian
salified	panicled	palinody	darkmans	backdown	gallabea	Gaullist
Catiline	mamillae	vanitory	bankable	mark-down	gallabia	faultily
kalinite	maxillae	Calippic	talkable	back-door	bailable	haploidy
laciniae	papillae	calibred	walkable	backmost	fallible	tailskid
Latinise	Ramillie	taxiarch	backache	hackbolt	mailable	mail-clad
maritime	panislam	marigram	tacked-on	jackboot	sailable	hallaloo
maximise	carillon	variorum	lackaday	sack-coat	fallibly	gallumph
Nazirite	papillon	janitrix	markedly	backspin	caulicle	bailsman
salicine	vanillin	papistic	backveld	larkspur	Gallican	Paul's-man
sanidine	bacillar	sadistic	hawkweed	cankered	mallecho	sally-man
sanitise	caviller	Taoistic	hawkbell	jack-tree	cable-car	tallyman
satirise	mamillar	radiated	barkless	sack-tree	ballocks	table-mat
vaticide	papillar	Labiatae	dankness	Valkyrie	halluces	vallonia
basilisk	variolar	parietal	darkness	Walkyrie	table-cut	parlance
basidial	bacillus	sagittal	lankness	mackerel	garlicky	parlando
familial	facially	varietal	rankness	walker-on	palladic	badlands
basidium	labially	Calixtin	cackless	jackaroo	Rallidae	ballonet
fakirism	radially	sapi-utan	saikless	jackeroo	balled-up	wall-knot
familism	talisman	banister	rack-rent	backdrop	balladry	nail-bomb
Hasidism	hacienda	canister	talkfest	tank-trap	pallidly	bail-bond
Latinism	Panionic	ganister	packaged	jacketed	gable-end	railroad
Marinism	gabioned	magister	backchat	marketed	nail-head	Calliope
nativism	patience	radiator	talk-show	racketed	railhead	call-note
pacifism	radiance	varistor	backbite	backstop	wallsend	nail-hole
Basilian	salience	haliotis	backfire	marketer	carl-hemp	tail-rope
Cabirian	sapience	papistry	backside	racketer	gall-less	badly-off
magician	valiance	tanistry	balkline	basketry	railless	taglioni
Parisian	variance	Canicula	jack-pine	pack-mule	sailless	bail-dock
pavilion	national	capitula	parklike	sackfuls	tailless	ballcock
Tamilian	rational	kaliyuga	waukrife	bankrupt	tallness	eagle-owl
familiar	maligner	navicula	darkling	walk-over	wall-less	ball-room
gasifier	malignly	vaginula	tackling	walk-away	bailment	sail-room
pacifier	radiancy	fatigued	bank-high	hawk-eyed	earliest	tail-boom
ratifier	saliency	habitude	jack-high	fahlband	wall-newt	call-loan
canities	valiancy	latitude	backfill	gaillard	raillery	hall-door
Ramilies	mariposa	manicure	back-lill	galliard	faultful	wall-moss
Familist	Saxicola	radicule	bank-bill	halliard	ladleful	hall-moot
had-I-wist	manifold	vaginule	walk-mill	kailyard	tableful	mail-boat
Hasidist	marigold	habitual	wauk-mill	railcard	lallygag	sail-boat
Latinist	tapiroid	taciturn	banksman	sail-yard	daylight	sail-loft
Marinist	baritone	carjacou	marksman	ball-game	fanlight	tail-coat
maximist	camisole	banjoist	tacksman	fail-safe	gaslight	wall-wort

wallwort	daemonic	saintdom	magnesia	camomile	vaporous	dauphine
tail-spin	harmonic	manna-dew	vainesse	canonise	batology	samphire
calliper	salmonid	main-deck	magnetic	caponise	cacodoxy	sapphire
galloper	gammoner	nainsell	mannitol	Caroline	cacology	sampling
walloper	salmonet	fainness	magneton	datolite	Mayology	sapphism
gallipot	rag-money	gainless	samnitis	gasoline	taxonomy	campaign
wall-tree	farm-toun	painless	gannetry	Jacobite	magot-pie	Tarpeian
ballyrag	palmiped	rainless	mainstay	jarosite	favoured	nauplius
mail-drag	palm-tree	saintess	carnauba	lanoline	laboured	parpoint
cauldron	balmoral	vainness	painture	Maronite	savoured	sapphist
pauldron	Palmerin	vauntery	tainture	pavonine	vapoured	gas-poker
wallaroo	Parmesan	magnific	carnival	saponite	barogram	paspalum
fall-trap	marmoset	vauntful	panorama	Saxonise	nanogram	pamphlet
eagle-ray	harmosty	carnifex	sayonara	saxonite	tabourin	rampsman
sailorly	Sarmatia	pawnshop	Savoyard	Taborite	favourer	jampanee
ballista	dalmatic	launcher	baronage	valorise	labourer	harpings
galluses	haematic	rain-bird	cabotage	vaporise	vapourer	rampancy
balletic	magmatic	jaundice	sabotage	canoeing	tabouret	earphone
balloted	palmitic	mainline	wagonage	fagoting	savourly	lamphole
palleted	Sarmatic	fainting	sago-palm	tabooing	parousia	pappoose
ballotee	palmated	haunting	marocain	baronial	jalousie	pay-phone
tarlatan	palmette	jaunting	makomako	cacomixl	carousal	ratproof
varletto	haematin	painting	mahogany	manorial	carousel	war-proof
table-top	palmitin	taunting	wagon-bed	rasorial	carouser	lamp-hour
harlotry	palmetto	vauncing	wagon-box	laconism	galowses	lamppost
varletry	gas-meter	vaunting	babouche	Saxonism	famously	bagpiper
gall-duct	gas-motor	faintish	barouche	Taxodium	panoptic	cap-paper
kail-runt	mammetry	saintish	farouche	Baconian	garotted	rag-paper
day-level	maumetry	saintism	pabouche	Bajocian	garotter	tar-paper
gallivat	mawmetry	daintily	caboodle	Catonian	barostat	wax-paper
wallowed	razmataz	jauntily	canoodle	Favonian	maroquin	bagpipes
wallower	badmouth	pannikel	Ganoidei	Jacobian	paroquet	Pan-pipes
cableway	panmixia	cannikin	Saxondom	Laconian	man-of-war	vampiric
Galloway	panmixis	mannikin	carotene	Maeonian	calotype	rapparee
wall-eyed	barnyard	pannikin	gasogene	Maronian	kalotype	pamperer
waylayer	gainsaid	larnakes	gasolene	pavonian	paroxysm	tamperer
farm-hand	mainland	magnolia	gazogene	Racovian	paronymy	Capparis
farmyard	mainyard	cannulae	Masorete	salopian	camphane	dapperly
caimacam	rain-band	gauntlet	Samoyede	palomino	vamplate	lampasse
naumachy	taeniate	carnally	Masoreth	caponier	warplane	carpeted
Talmudic	vauntage	paynimry	Carolean	gasolier	gas-plant	lappeted
warmed-up	manna-ash	earnings	Jacobean	sabotier	hat-plant	hampster
calmness	rain-wash	gainings	napoleon	calorist	palpable	rampauge
gaumless	sannyasi	cannonry	caboceer	canoeist	palpably	manpower
harmless	mainsail	taenioid	saboteur	canonist	salpicon	tax-payer
warmness	rainfall	nainsook	baroness	parodist	gazpacho	jacquard
mammifer	maintain	mainboom	canoness	Saxonist	Campodea	may-queen
earmuffs	fainéant	sainfoin	mayoress	majority	Talpidae	marquess
lammiger	mainmast	barndoor	cajolery	saponify	pappadom	basquine
dalmahoy	balneary	main-door	barometz	havocked	camphene	marquise
palm-wine	cannabic	carneous	wagonful	carolled	earpiece	vanquish
wagmoire	damnable	raincoat	taboggan	masoolah	say-piece	daiquiri
kaimakam	gainable	rainbowy	·caboched	caroller	harp-seal	hair-band
haymaker	tannable	bannered	caboshed	wagon-lit	dampness	caproate
law-maker	cannibal	mannered	cabochon	paroemia	lampreys	carriage
way-maker	cannabin	gauntree	parochin	marooner	samplery	hair-wave
Mammalia	cannabis	rain-tree	Zalophus	ratooner	campagna	laureate
mammilla	paint-box	Ragnarök	Carolina	naloxone	zampogna	marriage
yarmulka	damnably	bannerol	japonica	malodour	camp-shot	patriate
yarmulke	barnacle	raindrop	maiolica	canorous	camp-fire	carry-all
harmalin	pannicle	banneret	majolica	saporous	camphine	hair-ball
palm-play	wainscot	lanneret	canopied	savorous	camphire	hair-tail
sarmenta	maenadic	mannerly	parodied	valorous	campsite	hauriant

capricci	sapropel	ear-shell	pansophy	fastness	paltrily	partwork
iatrical	satrapal	gas-shell	causerie	fattrels	partaken	salt-work
barracan	sacraria	mass-bell	sanserif	hartbees	lantskip	maltworm
matrices	Saururae	passless	Massorah	mastless	partaker	hawthorn
carrycot	macrural	cat's-meat	caesural	mattress	kantikoy	lanthorn
sabre-cut	hair-grip	far-spent	Passeres	saltless	battalia	tattooer
Labridae	Laurasia	passment	Sanscrit	saltness	mantilla	watt-hour
fairydom	lacrosse	pay-sheet	Sanskrit	tactless	dactylic	captious
harridan	madrasah	pauseful	hausfrau	tartness	tantalic	cautious
Labrador	garrison	marsh-gas	passer-by	tautness	pantiled	dartrous
sacredly	sarrasin	day-sight	cassette	vastness	bastille	factious
fair-lead	warrison	batswing	falsetto	waitress	pastille	fastuous
hairbell	sacristy	lassoing	masseter	wartless	nastalik	hautbois
hair-seal	Mahratta	canstick	danseuse	farthest	Santalum	lacteous
fairness	garreted	cat-stick	masseuse	maltreat	tantalum	xanthous
hairless	parroted	malstick	Passover	battle-ax	pantalon	eastmost
haurient	barrette	mapstick	causeway	Bartlemy	santalin	faltboat
farriery	garrotte	Parsiism	causeyed	lactific	martello	raft-port
caprifig	carritch	faustian	man-sized	earth-fed	batteler	salt-foot
madrigal	parritch	gaussian	capsizal	pantofle	dactylar	salt-wort
warragal	barrator	day-shift	gastraea	Tartuffe	Dactylis	wartwort
warrigal	narrator	manshift	eastland	faithful	nautilus	earth-pea
kauri-gum	parroter	baasskap	eastward	tasteful	naythles	Xantippe
larrigan	barratry	Marsilea	castrate	wasteful	tantalus	Zantippe
tarragon	parrotry	Marsilia	salt-cake	fantigue	mantelet	hag-taper
darraine	carraway	mamselle	salt-lake	martagon	party-man	bacteria
hairline	narrowly	sassolin	tartrate	gas-tight	raftsman	Hatteria
pairwise	matrixes	capsular	xanthate	earth-hog	Rastaman	bacteric
carrying	rat-rhyme	causally	canthari	Banthine®	ragtimer	tartaric
dairying	sarrazin	tasselly	castrati	gantline	tautomer	nattered
harrying	rakshasa	vassalry	pastrami	ianthine	caatinga	raftered
marrying	cab-stand	balsamic	fastback	part-time	Castanea	raptured
parrying	hatstand	marshman	cant-rail	rattline	cantoned	tattered
tarrying	camstane	ransomer	way-train	salt-mine	pattened	parterre
fairyism	nauseate	parsonic	castrato	xanthine	tartaned	Sauterne
darraign	palstave	Sassanid	Gasthaus	bantling	pastance	Tartarie
larrikin	ratsbane	raisonné	manteaux	eastling	cantonal	pastoral
caprylic	tasswage	bassinet	taste-bud	farthing	tautonym	pastural
harrumph	palstaff	sarsenet	vartabed	Lagthing	santonin	cast-iron
lacrimal	tau-staff	massoola	pantable	mantling	saltando	hapteron
lacrymal	haystack	basswood	partible	naething	fastener	calthrop
dairyman	saw-shark	password	tastable	rattling	fattener	banterer
barranca	cat's-tail	tarsioid	earth-bag	tattling	hastener	barterer
hadronic	lay-stall	camstone	wait-a-bit	waltzing	hastings	palterer
matronal	rat's-tail	capstone	canticle	wattling	saw-tones	patterer
patronal	camshaft	gas-stove	particle	baitfish	earth-nut	cantoris
safranin	lay-shaft	lapstone	pastiche	paitrick	martenot	halteres
barranco	naissant	ragstone	pasticci	salt-lick	martinet	Raptores
warrener	nauseant	camshoch	nautical	malt-mill	wantonly	Tartarus
matronly	lapsable	mass-book	tactical	wanthill	xanthoma	bastardy
vagrancy	passable	pass-book	canticum	Baathism	cartload	dastardy
warranty	passible	lasslorn	masticot	partyism	cart-road	easterly
pair-bond	raisable	mansworn	canticoy	Tantrism	tattooed	latterly
cabriole	passably	mass-john	mastodon	xanthium	gantlope	masterly
capriole	passibly	pap-spoon	tarted-up	Bactrian	raft-rope	pastorly
carriole	massacre	ram's-horn	day-to-day	malt-kiln	salt-cote	tartarly
hair-work	capsicum	maestoso	masthead	Parthian	Zantiote	fantasia
gairfowl	capsicin	caesious	wartweed	Sartrian	part-song	mantissa
hair-worm	waesucks	nauseous	xanthene	xanthian	dart-moth	bartisan
nacreous	massicot	cat's-foot	paste-eel	eastlins	gag-tooth	partisan
carry-out	hassocky	mar-sport	Pantheon	Baathist	jaw-tooth	cactuses
satrapic	Hassidic	passport	xanthein	Tantrist	saw-tooth	hastated
sauropod	mansuete	Tarsipes	daftness	wait-list	canthook	factotum

maltster	casually	tar-water	abidance	abetment	scudding	actinian
partitur	casualty	banxring	abnegate	abutment	academia	activist
mastitis	manually	bauxitic	Abderite	abetting	academic	acridity
gastrula	Saturnia	capybara	Ibsenite	abutting	acidosis	activity
sastruga	saturnic	navy-yard	Ibsenism	abstrict	schemata	schiller
Xanthura	laburnum	easy-care	Abderian	abutilon	acierage	schimmel
zastruga	lacunose	baby-talk	obtemper	abattoir	acierate	actinoid
cartouch	maculose	lazy-jack	obtected	absterge	scienced	echinoid
salt-bush	paludose	Davy-lamp	absentee	abstruse	screw-cap	schizoid
salt-junk	papulose	Caryocar	objector	obstruct	screechy	ochidore
fauteuil	ramulose	Ganymede	abjectly	obdurate	screeder	Echinops
malt-dust	sabulose	lady-fern	absently	obturate	sclerema	schizont
earthwax	Januform	lady-help	observer	obduracy	sclereid	acrimony
castaway	caducous	cagyness	abdicate	ybounden	acoemeti	scrimped
bartizan	fabulous	satyress	obligate	absurdly	icterine	scrimply
partizan	pabulous	laryngal	abdicant	abducent	sclerite	scoinson
sapucaia	paludous	larynges	obeisant	obtusely	scheming	ecliptic
carucage	papulous	ladyship	obligant	ablution	screwing	scrimure
carucate	patulous	ladybird	aboideau	obtusity	achenial	aculeate
hamulate	ramulous	ladyfied	aboiteau	abductor	achenium	ocellate
jaculate	sabulous	calycine	abridger	abruptly	schellum	scalable
lacunate	kalumpit	ladylike	obliging	obi-woman	screamer	scolecid
maculate	haruspex	satyrisk	oblivion	abeyance	Achernar	scoleces
maturate	manubria	navy-list	obsidian	abeyancy	screener	scilicet
radulate	saburral	calycled	abricock	oceanaut	scleroma	ice-ledge
saturate	paduasoy	navy-blue	ebriated	scrabble	scleroid	scullery
tabulate	baguette	babyfood	absinthe	scramble	sclerose	ecologic
vapulate	maquette	babyhood	obliquid	scratchy	ocherous	schläger
lacunars	haqueton	calycoid	abampere	scrag-end	sclerous	scalding
saturant	baluster	ladyhood	abomasum	écraseur	eclestic	scolding
lacunary	valuator	barytone	abomasus	scragged	screwtop	sculling
salutary	salvable	lady-love	T-bandage	scraggly	accentor	scaldini
valuable	Calvados	many-root	abundant	sciatica	accepter	scallion
valuably	salvific	Dasyurus	ébéniste	scraping	acceptor	scullion
caruncle	aasvogel	lawyerly	ebenezer	Occamism	scienter	scaldino
faburden	mauveine	calyptra	abrogate	Accadian	schedule	scaly-leg
talukdar	navvying	kalyptra	absonant	occasion	screever	ice-lolly
Saturday	valvular	caryatic	absorbed	Oceanian	ice-field	acalepha
caducean	valvelet	caryatid	absorber	Occamist	ecofreak	acalephe
caduceus	Salvinia	calycule	obsolete	scrawler	scoffing	Scolopax
maturely	galvanic	larynxes	ebionise	scrap-man	scuffler	schleppy
babushka	tadvance	many-eyed	Ebionite	sciaenid	scaffold	Scalaria
capuchin	calvered	zarzuela	ebionism	scrannel	ice-front	scalprum
baculine	malvasia	dazzling	abnormal	octaroon	ice-house	scelerat
baculite	malvesie	canzonet	abhorred	octapody	Schizaea	ocularly
daturine	larvated	gadzooks	abhorrer	scrapped	activate	ecclesia
fabulise	fauvette	marzipan	absolute	eclampsy	echinate	occlusal
lazulite	war-weary	mahzorim	obvolute	ice-apron	scribble	occlusor
lazurite	cam-wheel	abradant	absolver	schapska	scribbly	sculpsit
matutine	ragwheel	Abbaside	ubiquity	scrattle	schiedam	oculated
paludine	earwiggy	ablative	aberrate	octantal	accident	sculptor
manuring	tarwhine	abrasive	aberrant	sceattas	occident	Scolytus
naturing	batwoman	abbatial	obtruder	scabbard	actively	scalawag
manurial	day-woman	abeahism	Aberdeen	iceblink	scriggle	scamping
masurium	madwoman	ablation	eburnean	scybalum	scriggly	scumming
naturism	ragwoman	abrasion	aborigen	Scabiosa	acridine	scampish
paludism	war-whoop	oblation	aborigin	scabious	actinide	scomfish
Laputian	wanworth	abram-man	abortive	scabrous	actiniae	scumfish
fabulist	gas-works	obtainer	abortion	ice-bound	actinide	scambler
naturist	wanwordy	obscurer	abstract	ice-craft	scribing	schmaltz
caducity	waywiser	abscissa	obituary	ice-cream	actinism	ecumenic
maturity	gas-water	abscisse	abatable	acicular	actinium	schmooze
vacuolar	tap-water	obedient	obstacle	acid-head	activism	scammony

scimitar	scrofula	scathing	educible	ideogram	seraphic	denarius
scent-bag	scuppaug	Scottish	eduction	addorsed	detached	senarius
scent-box	ice-plant	Scythian	adscript	advowson	seraphim	ceramist
scenical	Scopolia	Scottify	edacious	odiously	teraphim	legalist
scandent	scapular	scutella	educator	adroitly	xeraphim	regalist
scentful	Scopelus	scuttler	edgeways	advoutry	seraphin	femality
acanthin	scaphoid	Scotsman	addendum	adaptive	metaphor	feracity
acanthus	sceptred	scotopia	edgeless	adoptive	regather	legality
scanning	sceptral	scotopic	idleness	adaption	Hepatica	regality
scenting	acerbate	scot-free	adherent	adoption	velamina	tenacity
scandium	acervate	ecstasis	udderful	adequate	déraciné	venality
Scandian	ochreate	ecstatic	adhesive	adequacy	gelatine	veracity
scansion	scordato	acaudate	edgewise	adorable	hematite	remarked
scontion	scarabee	accurate	adhesion	adorably	hepatise	bedarken
scantily	scirocco	ecaudate	idlehood	Odyssean	hepatite	remarker
scantity	acorn-cup	occupate	edgebone	adespota	legalise	medallic
economic	Scaridae	occupant	edifying	editress	legatine	metallic
scene-man	acaridan	accuracy	odograph	adjutage	melamine	bewailed
scincoid	accredit	scrubbed	ad-libber	adjutant	melanite	detailed
schnapps	scarless	scrubber	edginess	adjuvant	negative	Heraclid
scenario	scarcely	scrunchy	additive	adducent	penalise	medalled
aconitic	scornful	scourger	advising	adjuring	petaline	metalled
aconitum	scorched	scouther	addition	adductor	relative	pedalled
acknowne	scorcher	occupied	advisory	adjuster	sedative	petalled
ectosarc	scirrhus	sciurine	addicted	adjustor	sepaline	tenaille
accolade	scurrile	scouring	admitted	mesaraic	serafile	befallen
octonary	scarfing	scouting	adultery	métayage	tetanise	seraglio
scrowdge	scarping	occupier	bdellium	separate	velarise	derailer
accorder	scarring	acquaint	idyllian	seladang	debasing	hexaplar
ectoderm	scorning	scrutiny	idyllist	megawatt	defaming	pedaller
acrolein	scarfish	scrupler	odalique	relaxant	delaying	retailer
echoless	scorpion	octuplet	adularia	legatary	derating	hexaglot
ectogeny	scurrier	scout-law	idoliser	bedabble	menacing	becalmed
scoopful	Scorpius	actually	adulator	menarche	relaxing	detainee
scroggie	acerbity	sciuroid	idolater	revanche	renaying	detainer
scrouger	scarcity	acquired	idolatry	heraldic	repaying	regainer
eclogite	scurvily	occurred	Adamical	retarded	retaking	retainer
scooping	scarmoge	acquiral	Adamitic	veranda'd	megalith	cedar-nut
acrolith	acarpous	accursed	odometer	rehandle	geraniol	pecan-nut
acromial	ochreous	acoustic	udometer	verandah	betacism	Decapoda
acrotism	scarious	occulted	odometry	demander	geranium	Hexapoda
scholium	scorious	accustom	Edentata	regarder	legalism	lecanora
sciolism	ectropic	actuator	aduncate	retarder	melanism	melanoma
acromion	scarf-pin	occultly	edentate	rewarder	petalism	metabola
eclosion	eccrisis	scavager	adenoids	sea-adder	regalism	metanoia
scholion	eccritic	scavenge	odontist	heraldry	teratism	Nematoda
sciolist	ecostate	scowther	aduncity	metamere	veganism	teratoma
schooled	ice-skate	scowling	identify	Serapeum	velarium	hecatomb
scrolled	acescent	ice-water	identity	Cesarean	aeration	metazoic
scrounge	ice-sheet	ice-yacht	adynamia	cetacean	dedalian	ceratoid
schooner	scissile	advanced	adynamic	fedayeen	delation	keratoid
scoop-net	acosmism	idealess	odontoma	Pegasean	deration	nematoid
Ochotona	scission	adjacent	odontoid	secateur	gelation	petaloid
Octopoda	acosmist	idealise	aduncous	bejabers	legation	sepaloid
ectozoic	ice-stone	ideative	adenitis	decadent	negation	sesamoid
ectozoan	scissors	idealism	advocate	remanent	Pelagian	teratoid
ectozoon	scissure	adnation	advocaat	Pelagian	regalian	tetanoid
octoroon	Scotland	ideation	advocacy	sedately	relation	keratose
ichorous	Scotican	idealist	idiolect	Pelasgic	sedation	let-alone
sciolous	scattery	ideality	admonish	deranged	venation	megapode
echogram	scutiger	Adiantum	idiotish	bedaggle	vexation	nematode
acrostic	scutcher	idocrase	idiotism	redargue	Zelanian	metazoan
accoutre	Scottice	educable	ideology	resalgar	pedalier	metazoon

sea-acorn	sea-beach	tea-chest	headmark	meddling	geodesic	legendry
belabour	jet-black	merciful	dead-fall	peddling	vendetta	seven-day
melanous	sea-beast	peaceful	dead-wall	reedling	geodetic	repetend
petalous	semblant	heich-how	headrail	seedling	seedy-toe	reverend
sepalous	bee-bread	descried	headlamp	yeldring	reed-stop	Genevese
megavolt	tea-bread	merchild	dead-cart	seed-fish	lewdster	teleseme
demagogy	leg-break	describe	headfast	herdwick	verditer	terebene
hexapody	tea-break	perceive	beddable	dead-lift	vendeuse	venereal
negatory	sea-bream	reactive	readable	dead-pull	dead-pull	mezereum
pedagogy	herb-beer	zecchine	vendible	Seidlitz	feed-pump	mezereon
petalody	herbless	kerchief	weldable	pendulum	headhunt	venerean
sepalody	verbless	sea-cliff	readably	pendular	readjust	pederero
vexatory	herbaged	fetching	vendibly	seed-plot	sea-devil	hereness
behappen	keybugle	leaching	headache	feudally	demerara	redeless
pétanque	kerb-side	perching	pendicle	hebdomad	serenata	sereness
remarqué	sea-blite	reaching	headachy	beadsman	metewand	cerement
gematria	sea-brief	rescuing	dead-head	headsman	meteyard	decedent
hetaeria	pebbling	teaching	feed-head	herdsman	rereward	deferent
hetairia	feeblish	pea-chick	seed-leaf	leadsman	beverage	referent
debarred	redbrick	reaction	dead-deal	seedsman	defecate	reselect
métairie	gerbille	Teucrian	seldseen	mesdames	delegate	reverent
hetairai	herbelet	zecchino	headgear	ready-mix	federate	teletext
decagram	red-belly	rescript	deadness	reddenda	generale	tenement
hexagram	verbally	tetchily	deedless	tendance	generate	vehement
veratrum	reabsorb	Leucojum	headless	tendence	hebetate	cemetery
betatron	pembroke	teocalli	heedless	perdendo	leverage	serenely
bevatron	new-blown	aesculin	leadless	reddendo	regelate	severely
negatron	sea-boots	mescalin	lewdness	deadener	relegate	bedeafen
veratrin	herbaria	percolin	needless	leadenly	renegade	feverfew
repairer	membered	Aesculus	seedless	pendency	renegate	telergic
relapsed	seaborne	tercelet	seedness	tendency	selenate	sea-eagle
relapser	berberis	henchman	weedless	verdancy	serenade	revenger
xeransis	Cerberus	henchmen	weldless	dead-wood	sewerage	sewer-gas
semantra	dew-berry	newcomer	dead-beat	dendroid	vegetate	petechia
gelastic	fen-berry	welcomer	dead-heat	headword	venerate	telethon
pedantic	peaberry	seicento	dead-meat	reed-rond	ceterach	secesher
semantic	seaberry	deaconry	headrest	dead-rope	telepath	celeriac
Vedantic	teaberry	peccancy	needment	headnote	telemark	Genesiac
xerantic	nebbishe	seacunny	readiest	headrope	femerall	jeremiad
repartee	verbatim	tea-cloth	weldment	seadrome	renegado	remedied
decanter	deuce-ace	beech-oil	hey-de-guy	seed-lobe	benefact	weregild
departer	leachate	cercaria	headship	headlong	generant	benefice
Levanter	bescrawl	mercuric	seed-shop	deadlock	hebetant	ceresine
recanter	pew-chair	geocarpy	feldsher	dead-work	relevant	deletive
recaptor	merchant	leach-tub	dead-shot	herd-book	revenant	pelerine
redactor	penchant	leucitic	dead-wind	yeldrock	telecast	reremice
cerastes	pencraft	seecatch	reed-bird	bead-roll	vegetant	rerevise
pedantry	reactant	Mercator	bendwise	head-boom	delegacy	selenide
tenantry	sea-chart	teuchter	dead-fire	headroom	federacy	selenite
velatura	sea-coast	berceuse	deadline	dead-born	federary	telecine
denature	seacraft	selcouth	dendrite	seed-corn	femetary	televise
peracute	petchary	hen-court	feed-pipe	dead-bolt	resemble	vegetive
resalute	fencible	reoccupy	headline	headmost	December	legering
megabyte	peccable	bedcover	head-tire	seed-coat	remember	receding
megadyne	peacocky	dead-hand	lead-line	feldspar	defenced	renewing
bedazzle	Percidae	headband	need-fire	verdured	Seleucid	sewering
keyboard	deicidal	headland	readvise	gendarme	tedesche	feverish
lee-board	leechdom	reed-band	reed-pipe	reed-wren	tedeschi	herewith
pegboard	deucedly	reed-rand	seed-like	renderer	defended	Jeremiah
seaboard	tea-caddy	headrace	seed-time	tenderer	beheadal	fedelini
tea-board	bescreen	reed-mace	der-doing	verderer	rebeldom	Benedick
membrane	nescient	seedcake	headring	feldgrau	tenendum	remedial
verbiage	sea-chest	feed-back		tenderly	defender	selenium

telefilm	deletory	reheater	reaffirm	hedgepig	levirate	peripety
deletion	feretory	rejecter	self-pity	kedgeree	levitate	refinery
Hegelian	hegemony	rejector	menfolks	hedgerow	medicare	periagua
Menevian	telegony	repeater	perfumed	beggarly	medicate	bewigged
redesign	repeople	repenter	perfumer	heighten	meditate	meringue
Venetian	hereupon	resenter	reef-knot	lee-gauge	Merimake	Feringhi
peperino	bepepper	resetter	beef-wood	rephrase	remigate	besieger
genetics	cerebric	selector	selfhood	sea-heath	resinate	rejigger
Benedict	meteoric	semester	serfhood	bethwack	seminate	meninges
derelict	deferred	decently	self-love	bethrall	vesicate	vexingly
remediat	deterred	recently	sea-froth	methodic	mericarp	perished
reverist	referred	revestry	leaf-roll	menhaden	pedipalp	zenithal
teleview	rehearse	revenued	self-born	methadon	pericarp	lecithin
celerity	tenebrae	verecund	self-sown	beshadow	semitaur	decipher
heredity	rere-arch	hebetude	sea-floor	neshness	genitals	perisher
legerity	research	reperuse	sea-front	meshugga	dedicant	Jewishly
reaedify	cerebral	henequen	self-lost	meshugge	hesitant	Neritina
serenity	deferral	henequin	perforce	nephrite	vesicant	verified
severity	referral	bedeguar	renforce	tephrite	celibacy	aegirine
temerity	cerebrum	reneguer	seafarer	technics	delicacy	aegirite
bevelled	here-from	bejesuit	new-found	cephalic	rotiracy	decisive
debelled	telegram	sederunt	deaf-mute	kephalic	seminary	definite
jewelled	teletron	bereaved	leaf-curl	methylic	deniable	derisive
levelled	tenebrio	deserved	key-fruit	sea-holly	leviable	feminine
newelled	deferrer	received	keffiyeh	béchamel	reliable	feminise
rebelled	veneerer	reserved	leg-guard	mechanic	deniably	feticide
refelled	sewer-rat	receival	sea-grape	bechance	roliably	genitive
repelled	genetrix	bereaven	weighage	methanol	mediocre	Leninite
revelled	deceased	deceiver	bergfall	Nethinim	heliacal	lenitive
reveille	demersed	decemvir	berghaan	methinks	meniscus	lewisite
sewellel	recessed	receiver	eelgrass	nephroid	periodic	medicine
beveller	reversed	never-was	sea-grass	dethrone	begirded	melilite
jeweller	releasee	hereaway	sergeant	mesh-work	rekindle	melinite
leveller	demersal	Teletype®	bergmehl	recharge	devildom	redivide
rebeller	reversal	reef-band	Neogaean	sea-horse	bewilder	regicide
repealer	releaser	beefcake	pea-green	lethargy	heliodor	resinise
repeller	releasor	leaf-base	sea-green	Bethesda	reminder	retinite
reteller	reverser	self-hate	sengreen	Mephisto	zemindar	Semitiac
revealer	reversis	self-made	seigneur	methysis	beniseed	sericite
reveller	dementia	leaf-fall	meagrely	hen-hussy	Pekinese	Tebilise
rebellow	fenestra	red-faced	vengeful	Peshitta	beriberi	deviling
redeploy	Nemertea	perfecti	hedgehog	mephitic	perigeal	refining
meseemed	telestic	deifical	lengthen	Peshitto	perineal	repining
bedesman	bewetted	perfecto	hedge-hop	mephitis	periderm	retiring
meresman	dejected	leaf-scar	re-ignite	sea-hound	perineum	reviling
peter-man	demented	reoffend	fee-grief	bee-house	Medicean	reviving
redeemer	repeated	hen-flesh	beagling	hen-house	Oedipean	semi-ring
tenesmus	reverted	self-heal	feigning	tea-house	perigean	devilish
beseemly	revetted	self-help	weighing	resinata	deviless	peridial
hereunto	selected	deafness	seignior	perisarc	dewiness	remigial
demeanor	nepenthe	leafless	hey-go-mad	medicaid	eeriness	aecidium
betel-nut	recentre	selfless	bergamot	celibate	sexiness	delirium
Denebola	resettle	selfness	geogonic	decimate	desinent	devilism
Hereford	pedestal	self-left	mergence	dedicate	pediment	feminism
dene-hole	sebesten	sea-fight	reagency	defilade	penitent	Leninism
werewolf	bee-eater	tea-fight	vergency	delibate	redirect	peridium
behemoth	begetter	serfship	Wedgwood	delicate	regiment	Semitism
feverous	bepester	belfried	peignoir	depilate	renitent	decision
generous	besetter	leaf-like	geognost	derivate	resident	derision
Hereroes	defector	self-life	weigh-out	geminate	reticent	lenition
selenous	deserter	self-like	geognosy	heritage	sediment	Lewisian
temerous	detector	deifying	seignory	hesitate	sepiment	meridian
ceremony	receptor	self-will		levigate	delivery	petition

recision	Seminole	demi-lune	hell-gate	sealskin	beslaver	pelmatic
religion	semitone	geniture	oeillade	cellular	newly-wed	helmeted
revision	tedisome	pedicure	telltale	beplumed	beflower	besmutch
sedition	demi-wolf	perilune	tell-tale	sea-lemon	bellower	deemster
bénitier	aeriform	refigure	well-made	wealsman	deflower	geometer
verifier	reniform	reticule	sea-loach	Hellenic	fellowly	seamster
Semitics	retiform	semilune	heel-ball	reclined	mellowly	teamster
verities	demijohn	semi-mute	keelhaul	declinal	wellaway	geometry
feminist	desirous	semi-nude	fellable	bed-linen	deflexed	sea-mouse
Leninist	geminous	decidual	healable	jetliner	reflexed	vermouth
Semitist	perilous	residual	sellable	recliner	reflexly	sea-mount
debility	resinous	semibull	tellable	sea-lungs	Wesleyan	rein-hand
felicity	demi-volt	residuum	mealy-bug	well-knit	Vellozia	re-engage
felinity	heliport	medieval	pellucid	bellcote	permeate	vernicle
feminity	semi-soft	believer	pellicle	bell-rope	team-mate	penny-dog
gelidity	decisory	desilver	replacer	healsome	re-embark	fern-seed
resinify	derisory	reliever	hellicat	hell-hole	neomycin	meunière
revivify	petitory	reviewal	Helladic	meal-poke	pemmican	penneech
senility	revisory	reviewer	secluded	well-hole	gemma-cup	penneeck
tepidity	hemiopia	semi-axis	welladay	meal-worm	new-model	lernaean
devilkin	hemiopic	perigyny	well-head	well-room	Bermudas	reindeer
hemiolia	semi-opal	Heliozoa	well-read	hell-born	germ-cell	beinness
hemiolic	demiurge	serjeant	well-deck	well-born	beamless	keenness
devilled	pedigree	Medjidie	pell-mell	well-worn	helmless	leanness
pedicled	decigram	verjuice	well-seen	well-to-do	seamless	meanness
perilled	lexigram	vee-joint	fellness	well-doer	seemless	reinless
petioled	genitrix	sea-jelly	realness	bellwort	teemless	reinsert
periblem	heritrix	benjamin	veilless	keelboat	termless	reinvest
vexillum	herisson	perjured	zealless	well-boat	seam-rent	penny-fee
petiolar	lewisson	perjurer	bell-tent	jelly-pan	germaine	teen-aged
periplus	geniuses	deck-hand	defluent	telluric	teamwise	teenager
aerially	heliosis	neck-band	hell-bent	declared	term-time	sennight
genially	teniasis	deck-game	refluent	hell-bred	seemlier	deanship
medially	demissly	necklace	bellyful	well-bred	bedmaker	fernshaw
mesially	remissly	peekaboo	pellagra	meal-tree	helmsman	hernshaw
serially	meristic	neckweed	geologic	tellural	Germanic	meantime
venially	periotic	neck-beef	neologic	cellarer	sermonic	bean-king
bedimmed	semiotic	neck-gear	belly-god	declarer	vermined	weanling
nepionic	veristic	neckwear	aeglogue	cellaret	helminth	yeanling
legioned	befitted	feckless	negligee	déclassé	germinal	deontics
resigned	remitted	meekness	verligte	realiser	terminal	re-enlist
defiance	belittle	reckless	geologer	mellitic	sermoner	fern-ally
deviance	remittee	weakness	penlight	perlitic	terminer	kernelly
lenience	redistil	neckline	red-light	zeolitic	beam-ends	vernally
reliance	remittal	penknife	sealyham	reclothe	terminus	sea-nymph
resiance	meristem	keckling	fellahin	declutch	sermonet	reinsman
perianth	seriatim	reckling	bellbind	neo-Latin	geomancy	pennoned
regional	helistop	weakling	bell-bird	fellatio	seamanly	seine-net
beginner	demister	weakfish	hell-fire	belleter	yeomanly	pernancy
designer	depicter	reckoner	hell-kite	deflater	yeomanry	beanpole
resigner	depictor	weakener	meal-tide	deflator	geomyoid	mean-tone
hemionus	deviator	Geckones	meal-time	geolatry	reimpose	reinform
benignly	mediator	deck-load	realtime	zealotry	team-work	mean-born
deviancy	register	peak-load	seal-pipe	well-curb	gemmeous	cernuous
leniency	remitter	neck-bone	bellying	jealouse	reimport	penny-pig
semicoma	remittor	desk-work	replying	reillume	re-embody	gesneria
helicoid	resistor	beak-iron	seal-ring	well-hung	vehmique	wet-nurse
pezizoid	selictar	beck-iron	dealfish	bellpush	mesmeric	penn'orth
lepidote	deviltry	neckatee	well-nigh	bellpull	re-emerge	reinette
pericope	geriatry	weak-eyed	well-wish	bell-buoy	sea-marge	neonatal
peridote	registry	hellward	Wellsian	jealousy	besmirch	reinfund
perigone	retinula	well-far'd	velleity	sea-level	dermatic	reinfuse
semi-dome	vesicula	dealbate	oerlikon	replevin	hermetic	reinsure

reanswer	demonise	bemoaner	reconvey	sea-perch	degraded	heartlet
decorate	genocide	dehorner	aerodyne	temporal	begrudge	retrally
denotate	kerosine	renowner	genotype	vesperal	perradii	ferryman
derogate	leporine	aerobomb	serotype	pepperer	befriend	merryman
desolate	meionite	Cenozoic	metonymy	temperer	defreeze	serranid
detonate	melodise	Mesozoic	deep-laid	Hesperis	pearl-eye	befringe
helotage	memorise	menopome	bed-plate	Hesperus	refreeze	refringe
lemonade	mesolite	merosome	helpmate	hen-party	repriefe	bedrench
meconate	peroxide	aerofoil	jetplane	jeopardy	reprieve	retrench
pejorate	serotine	jeroboam	keepsake	tea-party	retrieve	neuronal
perorate	tenorite	rehoboam	key-plate	despisal	deer-neck	petronel
relocate	xenotime	tenoroon	seaplane	despiser	bear's-ear	tetronal
renovate	becoming	decolour	template	despotic	near-beer	Serranus
resonate	beloving	decorous	hemp-palm	herpetic	dearness	zebrinny
segolate	aerolith	nemorous	neoplasm	despatch	fearless	fearsome
cenotaph	demolish	venomous	pea-plant	dempster	heirless	yearlong
sea-orach	regolith	secodont	tea-plant	sempster	nearness	year-book
mesocarp	xenolith	aerology	geophagy	despotat	peerless	heirloom
debonair	memorial	aeronomy	keepsaky	ten-pound	searness	deer-horn
aerodart	demonism	cetology	vespiary	hempbush	tearless	ferreous
aeronaut	hedonism	demology	hen-padle	sea-power	rearrest	hen-roost
resonant	helotism	gemology	Vespidae	deep-dyed	reorient	rearmost
xenogamy	meconium	menology	bespread	geophyte	febrific	Cecropia
demobbed	metopism	merogony	deep-read	neophyte	petrific	heartpea
redouble	pelorism	oenology	hemp-seed	seaquake	terrific	tetrapla
débouché	bezonian	pedology	resplend	verquere	pea-rifle	tetrapod
heroical	Demonian	pelology	neoprene	mesquite	dearnful	terrapin
penoncel	demotion	penology	sea-piece	verquire	weariful	decrepit
resorcin	Devonian	serology	leap-year	jerquing	retrofit	necropsy
rejoicer	devotion	sexology	reappear	bearward	tetragon	perruque
heroicly	melodion	tenotomy	deepness	near-hand	verrugas	terraria
lemon-dab	Neronian	recourse	helpless	rearward	bedright	pear-tree
keloidal	remotion	resource	besprent	decrease	heirship	retrorse
beholden	sea-onion	begorrah	deep-felt	degrease	searcher	rear-arch
beholder	Senonian	metopryl	helpmeet	ferriage	bearbine	tetrarch
bepowder	aerobics	aerogram	neopagan	gear-case	bepraise	wear-iron
recorder	hedonics	mesotron	peep-show	recreate	Hebraise	pear-drop
seconder	melodics	devourer	Memphite	pearl-ash	nearside	tear-drop
secondly	demonist	democrat	neaptide	reproach	pearlite	heart-rot
Genovese	demotist	repoussé	semplice	deer-park	rearmice	petrosal
kerosene	hedonist	Senoussi	tempting	rear-rank	berrying	reprisal
peroneal	Jehovist	heronsew	Delphian	near-gaun	dearling	new-risen
mesoderm	melodist	tenon-saw	Memphian	pearmain	decrying	necrosis
melodeon	nepotist	gerontic	dewpoint	reordain	ferrying	neuroses
demoness	tenorist	besotted	bespoken	rear-lamp	learning	neurosis
peroneus	detoxify	retorted	serpulae	deer-hair	pearling	ferritic
deforest	ferocity	revolted	zeppelin	recreant	retrying	heuretic
deponent	remodify	deportee	Responsa	retroact	yearling	Nearctic
redolent	serosity	begotten	geoponic	segreant	yearning	necrotic
behovely	velocity	dehorter	weaponed	February	deer-lick	neuritic
recovery	venosity	reporter	response	bearable	near-silk	neurotic
remotely	besouled	resorter	tenpence	terrible	Hebraism	ferreted
besought	récollet	retorter	reopener	wearable	negroism	serrated
xenophya	deformed	revolter	tenpenny	sea-robin	Georgian	decretal
oenophil	reformed	sea-otter	weaponry	bearably	pearlies	detrital
heroship	bepommel	aerostat	geophone	terribly	Hebraist	secretin
geropiga	deformer	devoutly	peep-hole	terraced	retraitt	ferreter
semolina	reformer	reposure	weephole	tetracid	heartily	regrater
Señorita	recommit	resolute	deepmost	verrucae	bearskin	regrator
veronica	renowned	revolute	hesperid	metrical	deerskin	detritus
demoniac	denounce	resolved	tempered	jerrican	terrella	metritis
aerolite	renounce	resolver	sea-purse	jerrycan	petrolic	Negritos
cenobite	besognio	revolver	leap-frog	tetradic	Negrillo	neuritis

serratus
aegrotat
secretly
pear-push
beer-pump
tear-duct
depraved
deprived
deprival
reproval
reprover
sea-rover
regrowth
tearaway
tetraxon
defrayed
betrayal
defrayal
betrayer
defrayer
terrazzo
messmate
messuage
persuade
redshare
seascape
sea-snake
bed-staff
newshawk
red-shank
sea-snail
Jew's-harp
newscast
red-start
feasible
leasable
reusable
sensible
tensible
feasibly
sensibly
pease-cod
versicle
bedsocks
persicot
Messidor
feast-day
bedstead
reascend
kenspeck
newspeak
deisheal
newsreel
seashell
peesweep
eel-spear
herseems
reassess
reascent
reassert
feastful
menseful
senseful

mem-sahib
perspire
redshire
sea-snipe
sea-swine
beeswing
feasting
sea-stick
newsgirl
seismism
sensuism
reassign
red-shirt
sensuist
tee-shirt
perseity
sensilla
tessella
teaseled
mersalyl
teaseler
weaseler
verselet
weaselly
verse-man
Welshman
Bessemer
reasoned
seasoned
personal
seasonal
reasoner
seasoner
keeshond
felstone
gemstone
keystone
pea-stone
seashore
ten-score
penstock
sea-stock
cesspool
sesspool
mess-room
newsroom
sea-storm
mess-john
teaspoon
velskoen
sensuous
redshort
sea-scout
seas-tost
menstrua
sea-shrub
lease-rod
leisured
measured
tesserae
mensural
tesseral
mensuren

measurer
bedstraw
pea-straw
set-screw
felsitic
reassume
reassure
pea-soupy
peishwah
feast-won
left-hand
leftward
Lettland
text-hand
westward
centiare
meat-safe
test-case
peat-hagg
reattach
left-bank
peat-bank
meat-ball
reattain
restrain
bestiary
tertiary
textuary
vestiary
vertebra
death-bed
beatable
bed-table
rentable
tea-table
testable
denticle
lenticle
pentacle
tentacle
testicle
hectical
lenticel
vertical
verticil
death-cap
death-cup
vertices
pentadic
pettedly
septleva
neat-herd
aesthete
bestreak
peat-reek
bestsell
bestrewn
leathern
yestreen
deftness
lectress
meatless
meetness

neatness
nextness
pertness
rectress
restless
seatless
weetless
peetweet
seat-belt
seat-rent
sentient
vestment
feathery
heathery
leathery
beatific
pettifog
deathful
vestigia
heptagon
pentagon
heath-hen
peatship
bestride
dextrine
gentrice
perthite
tentwise
ventaile
vent-pipe
beetling
centring
fettling
left-wing
nestling
restring
seething
settling
teething
testrill
centrism
Hertzian
neutrino
destrier
fewtrils
centoist
centrist
restrict
gentrify
lent-lily
dentalia
Reptilia
gentilic
Pentelic
dentelle
vent-plug
sextolet
festally
mentally
rectally
rent-a-mob
septimal
testamur

neotenic
Newtonic
tectonic
Teutonic
sentence
pectinal
sentinel
lentando
pectines
bentwood
centroid
bestrode
centrode
dextrose
peat-hole
rest-home
tent-pole
tent-rope
vent-hole
pentroof
jestbook
tent-work
text-book
textbook
benthoal
rent-roll
sept-foil
rest-room
bestrown
meltdown
next-door
peat-moor
dextrous
feateous
featuous
oestrous
peat-moss
vertuous
beetroot
sea-trout
westmost
centuple
septuple
sextuple
Zentippe
heatspot
dentaria
septaria
neoteric
bettered
centered
featured
lettered
nectared
textured
vestured
rent-free
sesterce
heptarch
pentarch
gestural
pectoral
rectoral

sectoral
textural
vestural
deuteron
setter-on
setter-up
hectorer
lecturer
letterer
pesterer
pewterer
restorer
venturer
vesturer
death-ray
hectorly
westerly
pertused
jettison
pentosan
centesis
meatuses
rectitic
septette
sestette
sextette
teetotal
teetotum
testatum
sestetto
sectator
testator
rectitis
rest-cure
test-tube
destruct
centaury
aestival
festival
left-over
bestowal
bestower
geotaxis
ventayle
sentry-go
mestizas
mestizos
denudate
depurate
peculate
regulate
bequeath
mezuzahs
débutant
depurant
petulant
recusant
penumbra
benumbed
renumber
zerumbet
semuncia

peduncle
befuddle
bemuddle
refunder
beau-pere
cerulean
cerulein
teru-tero
feculent
relucent
tegument
temulent
demurely
jejunely
securely
bemuffle
gefuffle
kefuffle
nenuphar
beauxite
cerusite
delusive
deputise
Jebusite
lemurine
nebulise
reguline
regulise
relumine
resupine
xenurine
reducing
reputing
seducing
reburial
tenurial
nebulium
peculium
refugium
decurion
delusion
lemurian
Peruvian
refusion
Venusian
Venutian
Vesuvian
peculiar
Merulius
beautify
jejunity
repurify
security
sedulity
tequilla
republic
medullae
sequelae
beguiler
medullar
sexually
remurmur
resubmit

sequence	penwoman	offshore	egg-tooth	chick-pea	shred-pie	choirman
refusnik	sea-woman	eftsoons	agitprop	thickset	sheep-pen	shrimper
lemuroid	pen-wiper	offshoot	agitated	shuddery	threapit	thrissel
medusoid	bedwards	off-sorts	agitator	shedding	threepit	thlipsis
levulose	seawards	oft-times	egg-whisk	shoddily	sheep-pox	thripses
jelutong	red-water	effulged	thraward	rhodanic	three-ply	chainsaw
mezuzoth	sea-water	effusive	pheasant	who-dun-it	shoe-tree	theistic
nebulous	re-expand	affusion	thrawart	shaddock	sheep-run	Christie
sedulous	re-export	effusion	thearchy	Rhodesia	shrew-run	thristle
tenuious	cetywall	off-white	shraddha	Rhodites	sheep-rot	christom
Beaufort	hexylene	offwards	thraldom	shadbush	phreatic	christen
delusory	Terylene®	aguacate	Theaceae	khedival	bheestie	Christly
demurred	demyship	eglatere	wheat-eel	she-devil	sheet-tin	shrieved
recurred	lecythis	agraphia	wheat-ear	shadower	threaten	shrieval
required	Lecythus	agraphic	wheatear	shoe-lace	three-way	shakable
demurral	lekythos	agraphon	cheatery	shoe-nail	chaffery	shake-bag
delubrum	merycism	agnation	wheat-fly	wheel-cut	Shafiite	chokidar
demurrer	Pepysian	agrarian	sheathed	shredded	chaffing	Shaktism
requirer	beryllia	Ignatian	shear-hog	sheepdog	shafting	Shekinah
Jesuitic	desyatin	yglaunst	thrasher	chiefdom	shifting	shake-out
rebutted	dewy-eyed	egg-apple	Theatine	threaden	whiffling	shikaree
requited	benzoate	egg-bound	thiamine	sheep-dip	shiftily	shake-rag
petuntse	seizable	agedness	phrasing	shielder	shift-key	choliamb
petuntze	weazened	egg-dance	sheading	shredder	shuffler	Chaldaic
rebuttal	terzetta	ague-cake	shealing	threader	whiffler	chiliasm
requital	terzetto	agrémens	shearing	shrewdly	shofroth	chiliast
rebutton	off-and-on	agrément	shoaling	Phoebean	chaffron	phyllary
rebutter	off-board	agrestic	thwacker	chiefess	shag-bark	childbed
requiter	off-break	agrestal	phialled	shoeless	shagreen	philabeg
seductor	off-drive	egg-fruit	shear-leg	chiefest	thuggery	philibeg
Jesuitry	offender	egg-glass	shearman	chiefery	Whiggery	chaliced
recurved	aftereye	ugliness	chiasmus	thievery	chugging	pholades
resurvey	afferent	aguishly	shrapnel	cheerful	shogging	while-ere
teguexin	efferent	ignition	whoa-ho-ho	chee-chee	thigging	shell-egg
perviate	effetely	aglimmer	thrapple	threshel	Whiggish	Chaldean
cervical	offering	agrimony	theatric	Phaethon	thuggism	Chellean
selvedge	affeered	ignitron	shea-tree	shoe-shop	Whiggism	sheltery
fervidly	affected	egoistic	theatral	thresher	shaggily	khalifah
nerve-end	affecter	aglitter	chiastic	sheeling	shigella	shelf-ful
heaviest	effecter	agalloch	thwarted	sheeting	shogunal	shellful
servient	effector	Agamidae	Rh-factor	shieling	shagroon	Chelifer
weeviled	efficacy	egomania	thwarter	thieving	phthalic	khalifat
nervular	official	agential	thwartly	wheeling	phthalin	khilafat
cervelat	effigies	Aganippe	thwartly	wheezing	chthonic	whole-hog
nervelet	affinity	agonised	thebaine	sheepish	phthisic	phyllite
weevilly	affirmer	agiotage	shabbily	shrewish	phthisis	shell-ice
leavings	affiance	ignorant	rhabdoid	thievish	thridace	thalline
fervency	effierce	ignominy	rhubarby	cheewink	chair-bed	childing
heavenly	affluent	agrology	chechako	shlemiel	choirboy	chilling
pervious	effluent	agronomy	Phocidae	shoe-bill	sheikdom	shelling
beavered	afflated	agnostic	shock-dog	Rhaetian	choicely	shelving
perverse	afflatus	egg-plant	Phocaena	cheekily	Shaivite	shilling
renverse	effluvia	Egyptian	thickety	cheerily	sheiling	childish
renverst	pfenning	egg-purse	shocking	wheezily	shriving	phallism
velveret	afforest	aggrieve	shucking	sheep-ked	thriving	thallium
Helvetic	offprint	agar-agar	whacking	wheedler	Shaivism	chilily
velveted	sforzato	Ygdrasil	thickish	phlegmon	shrieker	shell-lac
servitor	affright	eggshell	chuckies	three-man	shrinker	thalamic
eelwrack	affronté	egestive	check-key	wheelman	thriller	Philomel
sea-wrack	affrayed	egg-slice	chaconne	shoe-rose	chainlet	whale-man
webwheel	off-shake	egestion	chicaner	threnode	chrismal	thalamus
reawaken	off-stage	egg-spoon	check-off	shoehorn	chairman	philamot
dey-woman	offsider	egg-timer	chiccory	threnody		philomot

Chelonia	thanedom	rhyolite	chaperon	phorminx	chestnut	shauchle
chalonic	Rhinodon	theorise	chapatti	chirpily	phisnomy	shouther
phalange	thanadar	shooting	chupatti	Cherokee	physique	shauding
phalloid	Shandean	throwing	chapiter	shiralee	physeter	shauchly
phelloid	chinless	whooping	whipster	short-leg	Cheshvan	shouting
phylloid	shunless	chromium	chipmuck	chorally	whosever	ghoulish
thalloid	thinness	theorist	chipmunk	shareman	shetland	shrunken
phyllode	thinnest	theodicy	chop-suey	shireman	white-ale	thrummed
phyllome	Chancery	rheocord	Chordata	shoreman	white-arm	thrummer
shale-oil	thundery	rheotome	theriaca	churinga	white-ant	chausses
whale-oil	thankful	theosoph	choriamb	chorioid	châteaux	chaunter
shalloon	phenogam	chlorous	chordate	thyreoid	Whiteboy	thruster
thallous	shanghai	shoot-out	shortage	thyrsoid	thetical	chauntry
phyllody	rhonchal	throw-out	thirlage	charlock	whitecap	choultry
cheliped	chin-chin	rheology	wharfage	charcoal	white-eye	Shivaite
thole-pin	rhonchus	theogony	charlady	churn-owl	Whitweek	Shivaism
chalkpit	whinchat	theology	pharmacy	shark-oil	thatness	cheville
chyluria	whinnied	theonomy	cherubic	short-oil	whatness	chevalet
choleric	phengite	thropple	thurible	share-out	shattery	chivalry
phylarch	shunning	theocrat	cherubim	thereout	photo-fit	chevrony
chaldron	shunting	chloasma	cherubin	whereout	white-fly	shivaree
children	thanking	throated	whirl-bat	theropod	photogen	cheverel
thyloses	thinking	throstle	whorl-bat	shirt-pin	thatched	cheveril
thylosis	thinning	throttle	thoracic	short-rib	thatcher	cheveron
phyletic	thinnish	rheostat	thoraces	wharf-rat	chitchat	show-card
chelator	Ghanaian	shipyard	sharp-cut	charisma	white-hot	show-yard
shelduck	phenolic	whip-hand	shortcut	chorused	chat-show	showcase
shamiana	phenylic	shipmate	shore-due	Pharisee	what-like	chow-mein
chummage	shingled	whiplash	whoredom	whoreson	chatting	thawless
champart	chenille	whipjack	Thursday	chorisis	shotting	thewless
chemical	chandler	whip-tail	thirteen	sharp-set	shutting	thowless
chymical	shingler	chaplain	charneco	thornset	whetting	chow-chow
chimaera	shingles	shapable	charmful	Sheraton	whitling	shawling
champers	chinampa	shepherd	therefor	thirster	shot-clog	show-bill
shimmery	phonemic	shop-bell	thurifer	Charites	white-leg	showgirl
shameful	Chinaman	chapless	wherefor	thorough	rhythmic	showroom
whim-wham	shin-bone	shipless	chiragra	chirrupy	rhythmed	show-down
shamming	phinnock	shipment	choragic	wherever	rhythmal	show-boat
thumping	thin-sown	chop-chop	choregic	thyroxin	rhythmus	chawdron
champion	phantomy	chip-shot	choragus	chasuble	whitener	whey-face
whimsily	thin-spun	whipbird	choregus	physical	shot-hole	Phrygian
shamanic	chondral	rhaphide	churchly	physicky	shut-down	chay-root
rhomboid	chondrin	ship-tire	thermite	Chasidic	white-out	choy-root
shampoo'd	phoner-in	chipping	charming	phosgene	photopia	rhizobia
shamrock	chondrus	chopping	charring	chasseur	photopic	whizzing
thumbpot	phonetic	shipping	chirping	thisness	chutzpah	whizz-kid
chimeric	rhinitis	shopping	churning	thusness	white-pot	rhizopod
whimbrel	shantung	whipping	sharking	chastely	photopsy	rhizopus
chemurgy	whenever	whopping	sharping	whiskery	rhetoric	Himalaya
chamisal	chlorate	shop-girl	shirring	whispery	shot-free	divagate
shamisen	chromate	shop-sign	shirting	chestful	whittret	titanate
phimosis	thio-salt	rhopalic	thirding	ghastful	Rhytisma	vicarage
rhematic	throbbed	chapelry	wharfing	phosphor	phytosis	vicarate
thematic	thrombin	ship-load	whirling	khuskhus	whatever	dilatant
ohmmeter	thrombus	whipcord	whirring	chastise	white-wax	gigawatt
whomever	thio-acid	rhapsode	churlish	thuswise	thataway	divan-bed
chinkara	shrouded	chapbook	sharpish	whisking	thousand	dinarchy
whiniard	thronged	ship-worm	shortish	thespian	thrum-cap	vizarded
whinyard	choo-choo	whipworm	chartism	chastity	shoulder	bilander
chantage	chloride	shopworn	phormium	physalia	shouldst	filander
phantasm	chlorine	shop-door	thermion	whistler	chauffer	risaldar
phantasy	chlorite	rhapsody	wherries	physalis	theurgic	misandry
thingamy	chromite	chaptrel	chartist	chessman	shrugged	ribaldry
						ribaudry

wizardly	vivacity	air-built	winchman	mindless	likewake	wire-heel
wizardry	hijacker	diabolic	zirconia	piedness	literate	nineteen
Bixaceae	disabled	disbench	zirconic	rindless	liveware	vice-dean
Limaceae	rivalled	air-bends	piscinae	vildness	pipe-case	ciseleur
Vitaceae	misallot	jibbings	diaconal	wildness	side-face	life-peer
pikadell	disallow	ribbonry	piecener	windless	tide-gate	rice-beer
pita-hemp	pita-flax	wig-block	discinct	misdight	tide-race	fineless
rivaless	disannul	timbered	discandy	birdshot	tide-wave	fineness
Titaness	disannex	airborne	pince-nez	bird-lice	limewash	fireless
vicaress	lima-wood	disburse	Cinchona	bird-lime	side-path	hiveless
bivalent	pinacoid	misbirth	disclose	Hinduise	literati	lifeless
divalent	pinakoid	airburst	oilcloth	wildfire	fire-back	likeness
filament	girasole	bilberry	discrown	wildlife	fire-mark	niceness
ligament	pinafore	nisberry	disclost	windpipe	fire-walk	pipeless
hidalgas	disadorn	diabasic	hiccuped	wind-side	kite-mark	rifeness
hidalgos	picaroon	nimbused	disciple	fiddling	likewalk	ripeness
kinakina	rigadoon	bimbashi	mince-pie	hind-wing	pipe-rack	riteless
dilative	bigamous	disbosom	linchpin	kindling	sidewalk	tideless
finalise	bimanous	nimbuses	sinciput	middling	tidemark	timeless
fixative	biparous	diabetic	visceral	misdoing	wine-cask	tireless
limacine	digamous	diabetes	miscarry	piddling	tire-ball	vileness
liparite	titanous	air-brush	diocesan	riddling	live-rail	wideness
Picariae	citatory	disbowel	circussy	windmill	time-ball	wifeless
rivalise	dilatory	pilchard	hiccatee	Hinduism	vine-gall	wireless
titanite	filatory	jib-crane	circiter	kindlily	wine-palm	witeless
vitalise	libatory	gimcrack	piscator	vindaloo	riverain	hive-nest
vitative	minatory	jimcrack	cincture	diademed	Sicelain	lifebelt
bifacial	didapper	disclaim	lincture	riddance	literato	life-rent
bilabial	disapply	aircraft	tincture	sindings	firedamp	virement
filarial	misapply	miscible	hiccough	hiddenly	wire-hair	river-god
riparial	disagree	vincible	discount	wild-wood	sideways	river-hog
vicarial	filagree	biscacha	miscount	airdrome	live-bait	dimethyl
finalism	binaural	bizcacha	piecrust	wind-cone	cinerary	fireship
sinapism	cicatrix	viscacha	viscount	wind-rode	literacy	side-show
Titanism	disarray	vizcacha	air-cover	windrose	literary	fire-bird
titanium	misarray	milch-cow	discover	wind-sock	siserary	liveried
vitalism	dicastic	ditch-dog	Biscayan	wild-fowl	vicenary	rice-bird
vivarium	didactic	biocidal	hindward	lindworm	vinegary	side-wind
bibation	gigantic	miscreed	wild-land	wild-born	river-bed	wire-bird
cibation	Sinaitic	discrete	windward	wild-boar	hireable	dimerise
citation	didactyl	witch-elm	birdcage	fiddious	likeable	fireside
dilation	disaster	Circaean	birdbath	bird-bolt	liveable	hivelike
fixation	pilaster	discreet	birdcall	hind-foot	rideable	lifelike
himation	pinaster	bitchery	windfall	hindmost	sizeable	life-line
libation	simaruba	witchery	wind-gall	Piedmont	silenced	life-size
ligation	disabuse	miscegen	wind-sail	Pindaric	wiseacre	lifetime
limation	filature	pinchgut	air-drain	wildered	libeccio	likewise
nidation	fixature	pinch-hit	air-drawn	pindaree	cider-cup	live-wire
picarian	ligature	diactine	windlass	hinderer	ricercar	mimetite
riparian	picayune	mischief	misdealt	mind-cure	silencer	nine-mile
Sicanian	pirarucu	circling	biddable	windburn	tiger-cat	pipelike
Titanian	air-brake	filching	diadochi	misdoubt	fire-edge	pipeline
bigamist	rim-brake	pinching	diddicoi	windowed	Tineidae	piperine
digamist	mid-brain	pitching	diddycoy	bird-eyed	videndum	pipe-wine
finalist	bioblast	witching	bindweed	Cinerama®	disendow	riverine
timariot	tie-break	zincking	birdseed	cider-and	fireweed	side-line
vitalist	limbmeal	dipchick	hindhead	hiveward	pike-head	siderite
dicacity	limbless	circuity	misdread	side-band	Miserere	sidewise
finality	diablery	hitchily	bindi-eye	sideward	tiger-eye	viperine
hilarity	misbegot	zinckify	bird's-eye	time-card	vine-leaf	wife-like
minacity	gibbsite	vinculum	kindless	vineyard	cinereal	wire-line
rivality	nibbling	circular	kindness	Airedale	live-well	wise-like
vitality	air-brick	piacular	mildness	liberate	sidereal	

zibeline	tides-man	mirepoix	live-axle	ringside	ringster	righting
hireling	nine-inch	wide-body	fire-eyed	ring-time	oil-gauge	lightish
nidering	hibernal	fire-opal	wide-eyed	ringwise	disgavel	tightish
riveting	Zigeuner	fine-spun	nine-eyes	giggling	gingival	ditheism
sideling	tiger-nut	lifespan	airframe	higgling	misgiven	eighties
tireling	time-unit	wide-open	giff-gaff	jingling	ridgeway	ditheist
vice-king	pigeonry	dimetric	niffnaff	kingling	ring-dyke	rightist
wiseling	dive-bomb	lime-tree	riff-raff	mingling	diaglyph	mightily
file-fish	fire-bomb	pine-tree	hip-flask	niggling	ginglymi	nightjar
line-fish	side-comb	pipe-tree	diffract	pingling	Mithraea	fishskin
liverish	time-bomb	dihedral	Jiffybag	ridgling	Mishnaic	fish-glue
pipe-fish	firewood	disenrol	pig-faced	singeing	Mithraic	night-man
side-dish	fivefold	mire-drum	airfield	singling	highland	siphonic
tigerish	lifehold	side-drum	midfield	wingding	nigh-hand	lichened
tilefish	lime-wood	dihedron	oil-field	jingoish	fishcake	sithence
viperish	ninefold	vine-prop	disflesh	kingfish	lichgate	diphenyl
vixenish	pine-wood	sidearms	piffling	tinglish	lichwake	siphonal
fire-risk	side-road	firebrat	misfaith	ring-dial	night-ape	lichenin
limerick	wifehood	liver-rot	misfeign	jingoism	mishmash	dishonor
rice-milk	wivehood	river-rat	fitfully	jingoist	wish-wash	lichanos
side-kick	cicerone	fine-draw	wilfully	linguist	fish-hawk	siphonet
biserial	fire-bote	wire-draw	sinfonia	cingulum	highjack	dichroic
tidemill	fire-hose	linearly	disfrock	lingular	fishball	cichloid
time-bill	lifesome	diseased	oil-fired	singular	fish-tail	fishpond
dimerism	literose	licensed	pilferer	gingelly	highball	highroad
dioecism	nine-hole	cineaste	diffused	kings-man	hightail	withhold
tigerism	pine-cone	licensee	diffuser	liegeman	pithball	fish-bone
limekiln	side-note	finesser	disfavor	Virginia	fish-farm	high-lone
Milesian	time-zone	licenser	oil-gland	biogenic	fishable	wishbone
Sikelian	tiresome	licensor	disgrace	Diogenic	tithable	fish-hook
sirenian	wire-rope	diversly	disgrade	diagonal	dishabit	night-owl
fivepins	wirewove	dicentra	wing-case	virginal	dithecal	high-born
kinesics	lifelong	lineated	misgraff	diggings	nightcap	eight-oar
kinetics	livelong	pileated	jingbang	virginly	night-dog	highmost
ninepins	sidelong	rivetted	airgraph	kinghood	eight-day	tithe-pig
nineties	ciceroni	bidental	biograph	kingwood	withheld	high-bred
Siceliot	fire-hook	pipe-stem	diagraph	ring-road	fish-meal	withered
Sikeliot	fire-lock	fire-step	ring-bark	diagnose	eighteen	dishorse
wine-list	firework	side-step	ring-walk	kid-glove	fish-weir	litharge
side-view	life-work	bisector	ring-tail	ringbone	high-gear	pilhorse
fidelity	pilework	digester	ring-wall	ring-dove	highness	pith-tree
livelily	pipework	director	nit-grass	ding-dong	nighness	pichurim
ciderkin	sidelock	mimester	rib-grass	ping-pong	pithless	hitherto
wine-skin	tide-lock	sin-eater	ringhals	singsong	richness	higher-up
bi-weekly	time-work	videotex	misgraft	ringwork	high-test	ditherer
libelled	wirework	directly	diggable	ringworm	mightest	disherit
rivelled	dice-coal	misentry	singable	lipgloss	rich-left	highbrow
vine-clad	niger-oil	silently	zingiber	king-bolt	night-foe	withdraw
rice-glue	pine-wool	ciselure	liegedom	kingpost	lightful	withdrew
fire-flag	fireworm	fine-tune	wingedly	ring-bolt	mightful	litherly
fire-plug	pile-worm	fire-tube	kingless	wingspan	rightful	dichasia
vitellin	wire-worn	sinecure	ringless	king-crab	night-fly	richesse
side-slip	live-born	time-fuse	wingless	fingered	pishogue	sightsee
libeller	time-worn	Nibelung	wingbeat	jiggered	night-hag	fish-stew
micellar	rice-soup	tile-hung	pinguefy	disgorge	eighthly	air-house
vitellus	side-door	bisexual	siege-gun	lingerie	withwind	dishouse
dice-play	dimerous	ritenuto	kingship	lingerer	fish-dive	ginhouse
fire-clay	viperous	bile-duct	wing-shot	ziggurat	fishwife	fish-guts
lineally	lifeboat	life-buoy	king-bird	king-crow	high-rise	dishevel
pipeclay	nine-foot	lime-twig	disguise	gingerly	pithlike	tightwad
linesman	pilewort	giveaway	kinglike	diegesis	Vichyite	digitate
riverman	pipewort	hideaway	king-size	fidgeted	fighting	litigate
sidesman	side-post	riverway	misguide	lingster	lighting	militate

nitigate
ibilate
ilicane
ilicate
idivate
itivate
icinage
izirate
iriyani
itigant
nilitant
nitigant
ibilant
igilant
isitant
imitary
nilitary
ivipary
itiable
itiable
icisbei
icisbeo
igisbeo
itiably
libiscus
lividend
ilipend
iriness
miness
niriness
iliness
itiless
iziness
idiness
niness
viliness
viriness
liligent
irigent
iriment
niment
niniment
ivisect
ivinely
initely
ibingly
bingly
inished
inisher
ilipina
iticica
ilified
iminite
ivilise
igitise
ivinise
ivisive
ilicide
ripipe
ninimise
igidise
ilicide
imilise

sinicise
viricide
viridite
viticide
dividing
limiting
visiting
diminish
dividivi
lixivial
minipill
vizirial
dirigism
lixivium
minimism
nihilism
silicium
Sinicism
virilism
civilian
division
Sicilian
viridian
Filipino
vitiligo
vilifier
vivifier
civilist
minimist
nihilist
civility
divinify
divinity
lividity
nihility
rigidify
rigidity
silicify
timidity
vicinity
viridity
virility
vividity
mimicked
mimicker
miniskis
filially
visioned
visional
pimiento
visioner
cicinnus
silicone
Visigoth
filiform
piliform
pisiform
liripoop
sibilous
filioque
filigree
siriasis
ciliated

disinter
minister
sinister
vitiator
ministry
silicula
disinure
finitude
ridicule
silicule
dividual
kibitzer
misjudge
disjoint
hip-joint
disjunct
jiu-jitsu
kirkward
kirkyard
milkmaid
rickyard
nickname
kickback
milk-walk
pickback
rick-rack
tick-tack
hickwall
silktail
milk-warm
rinkhals
kickable
dinky-die
wickedly
milk-weed
pick-me-up
milkless
pinkness
sickness
tick-shop
kickshaw
rickshaw
sicklied
milklike
tickling
tinkling
milkfish
ticklish
tick-tick
sick-list
sicklily
jickajog
kinkajou
nickelic
sick-flag
sickener
jirkinet
milkwood
mirksome
sink-hole
milk-loaf
linkwork
picklock

tick-tock
silkworm
kickdown
kirktown
kink-host
milkwort
pinkroot
wickered
milk-tree
pickerel
bick-iron
licker-in
zikkurat
sickerly
picketed
diskette
nicky-tam
linkster
picketer
Pinkster
ricketty
pink-eyed
billiard
mill-hand
milliard
willyard
diallage
disleave
milliare
millrace
rillmark
mill-tail
vIlliago
willyart
milliary
sillabub
tillable
violable
dilly-bag
fillibeg
millibar
billyboy
violably
pirlicue
biblical
billy-can
hillocky
dislodge
villadom
killadar
silladar
field-dew
billhead
millième
Niflheim
killdeer
fitliest
dialogic
dialogue
killogie
diplogen
villagio
pillager

villager
mislight
silly-how
hillside
dialling
fielding
yielding
mill-girl
disloign
niellist
diploidy
villainy
misliker
hielaman
rifleman
gig-lamps
diplomat
violence
airliner
cislunar
milliner
hidlings
billfold
girlhood
millpond
nielloed
billbook
billhook
hillfolk
mill-work
pill-worm
hill-fort
pillwort
diplopia
filliped
milleped
milliped
I illiput
rifle-pit
gillaroo
jillaroo
killcrop
dialyser
dialyses
dialysis
dielytra
dialytic
villatic
billeted
filleted
ciclaton
mirliton
violator
gillyvor
billowed
pillowed
willowed
williwaw
disloyal
filmland
firmware
filmable
gimmicky

dismoded
firmless
firmness
pin-maker
wig-maker
dismally
diamanté
pin-money
filmgoer
biomorph
mismarry
sigmatic
mismated
mismetre
mismatch
diameter
viameter
biometry
titmouse
dismount
Zionward
kirn-baby
winnable
cinnabar
binnacle
pinnacle
picnicky
dianodal
limnaeid
Siennese
Viennese
Linnaean
signieur
giantess
signless
lientery
midnight
dianthus
lion-like
fiendish
kirn-milk
biennial
giantism
signally
bionomic
cinnamic
visnomie
cinnamon
misnomer
Bignonia
minneola
kiln-hole
dipnoous
ligneous
signpost
pinniped
Diandria
Signoria
vigneron
Dionysia
pianiste
finnesko
lignitic

limnetic
pinnated
signeted
bien-être
pianette
vignette
tinnitus
biannual
winnowed
winnower
lipomata
bilobate
pilotage
dinosaur
Minotaur
bifocals
kilowatt
misogamy
disorbed
divorcee
divorcer
Girondin
disorder
misorder
virogene
linoleum
mid-ocean
timoneer
minoress
vinolent
pinochle
piroshki
pirozhki
Sinophil
finochio
ricochet
simoniac
cimolite
licorice
limonite
minorite
nicotine
picotite
pisolite
sinopite
Timonise
pivoting
binomial
ciborium
rigorism
Timonism
nicotian
Tironian
rigorist
simonist
Timonist
minority
pilosity
vinosity
pivot-man
widow-man
ritornel
Dinornis

liposome	rispings	dieresis	tinselry	mistreat	bitterly	pit-viper
ribosome	sixpenny	diuresis	Pilsener	ointment	sisterly	silverly
ditokous	misproud	fibrosis	rinsings	mirthful	winterly	silvatic
nidorous	biophore	hidrosis	diaspora	histogen	distaste	disvouch
rigorous	diaphone	dicrotic	misshood	vintager	hiatuses	viewdata
timorous	displode	dioritic	bioscope	airtight	dietetic	fin-whale
vigorous	disprove	diuretic	diaspore	gift-shop	mistitle	viewable
kilovolt	disproof	fibrotic	diastole	diatribe	dictator	pin-wheel
kidology	diapiric	hidrotic	dip-slope	girtline	lift-pump	viewless
misology	dioptric	hieratic	oilstone	uintaite	distrust	midwifed
Sinology	hippuric	aigrette	ribstone	dirtying	mistrust	miswrite
sitology	disperse	libretti	sixscore	littling	bistoury	airwoman
vinology	dispurse	libretto	tinstone	fiftyish	mistryst	pig-woman
virology	hipparch	migrator	die-stock	misthink	disusage	bijwoner
kilogram	kipperer	vibrator	kinsfolk	mistrial	figurate	airwards
lipogram	simperer	pirrauru	linstock	histrion	ligulate	midwived
Limousin	Hippuris	tirrivee	miasmous	district	misusage	midwives
timously	dispirit	tirrivie	fissiped	filthily	simulate	mixy-maxy
risoluto	disposed	nitroxyl	fissured	mistaken	titubate	tityre-tu
biconvex	disposal	miasmata	disserve	fistulae	figurant	Zizyphus
Linotype®	diapason	piassaba	minstrel	biathlon	simulant	pixy-ring
misogyny	disposer	piassava	airstrip	fistular	titubant	didymium
airplane	dispatch	first-aid	diestrus	pistolet	liquable	digynian
dioptase	rispetto	airspace	airscrew	distally	liquidly	dicyclic
dispeace	disputer	diastase	Dioscuri	wittolly	virulent	pityroid
displace	lispound	dissuade	kiss-curl	diatomic	minutely	hidy-hole
misplace	diapause	misshape	dissever	mistimed	liturgic	didymous
tin-plate	displume	misstate	diastyle	mittimus	disunite	digynous
bioplasm	air-power	oil-shale	fistiana	miltonia	figuline	dihydric
air-plant	cinquain	tipstaff	tilt-yard	diatonic	figurine	dihybrid
bioplast	disquiet	pig's-wash	filtrate	Miltonic	minutiae	sitz-bath
displant	misquote	airshaft	misteach	mittened	vituline	zigzaggy
pie-plant	rib-roast	piss-a-bed	mint-mark	distance	diluvial	dizzying
limpidly	microbic	rinsable	gilt-tail	pittance	fiducial	mizzling
dispread	microbar	rinsible	cistvaen	listener	diluvium	sizzling
misplead	didrachm	Dipsacus	distrain	distinct	dilution	piazzian
jimpness	wirricow	dipsades	kistvaen	virtuosa	diluvian	mitzvoth
oil-press	Pieridae	first-day	air-to-air	dirt-road	diluvion	diazepam
diopside	Pierides	diastema	distract	giltwood	disunion	pizzeria
disprize	microdot	misspend	distrait	histioid	Siculian	ejective
misprise	pier-head	misspeak	bistable	virtuose	Silurian	ejection
misprize	hirrient	misspell	liftable	virtuosi	figurist	djellaba
rippling	fiercely	himseems	pintable	gift-book	silurist	Mjöllnir
simpling	nitrogen	hipsters	ditty-bag	tint-tool	piou-piou	skean-dhu
pin-prick	diarrhea	misspelt	ditty-box	virtuoso	disunity	Akkadian
silphium	diarchic	misspent	bittacle	virtuous	aiguille	skiagram
simplism	diarchal	dissight	fistical	tilt-boat	ritually	skiatron
mispoint	migraine	kitschly	viaticum	pitty-pat	visually	skua-gull
misprint	piercing	disseise	distichs	victoria	viburnum	sky-diver
oil-paint	fibrilla	disseize	birthdom	wistaria	piquancy	skull-cap
pinpoint	microlux	biassing	pintados	wisteria	liguloid	skilless
simplist	dioramic	gin-sling	birthday	historic	siluroid	skylight
simplify	vibronic	Riesling	giftedly	littered	sinusoid	skelping
Hispanic	citrange	tinsmith	gilt-head	wintered	bibulous	skilling
diapente	vibrancy	dip-stick	lintseed	tin-terne	bicuspid	skulking
dispence	citreous	lipstick	disthene	dipteral	liquored	skillion
dispense	vitreous	pigswill	fiftieth	littoral	liquesce	skelloch
disponee	mirrored	midships	sixtieth	pictural	sinuated	skeletal
disponge	hierarch	tipsy-key	distress	dipteran	situated	skeleton
dispunge	hierurgy	dissolve	listless	sitter-in	sinuitis	skimming
fippence	micrurgy	lipsalve	mistress	gift-wrap	nieveful	skimping
sixpence	vibrissa	missilry	tintless	titterer	disvalue	skim-milk
disponer	diereses	tinselly	victress	dipteros	sirvente	skimpily

skin-game	Alsatian	black-cat	clodpole	aldehyde	fluidise	clammily
skene-dhu	illation	placidly	gladiole	olefiant	plaiding	clumsily
skinhead	alkalies	all-clear	gladsome	ill-faced	plaining	flimsily
skin-deep	alkalify	black-fox	gladioli	gliffing	plaiting	fly-maker
skinless	sleazily	glucagon	clodpoll	cly-faker	plainish	glumella
skinking	algaroba	glycogen	alienage	all-fired	albinism	plumulae
skinning	alkaloid	elf-child	alienate	ill-fated	alpinism	flim-flam
skin-wool	albacore	elective	ulcerate	ill-faurd	illinium	plumular
akinesia	fleasome	blacking	blueback	all-fours	illision	flamelet
akinesis	aleatory	blocking	alterant	all-fives	fluidics	plumelet
eklogite	alcatras	clecking	blueweed	sluggard	alpinist	clemence
skipjack	elf-arrow	clicking	bluebell	elegiast	algidity	aluminum
skipping	cleanser	slicking	blueness	flagrant	fluidify	flamenco
sky-pilot	oleaster	blackish	clueless	plagiary	fluidity	flamingo
skirling	pliantly	blockish	sleepery	slug-a-bed	plaidman	clamancy
skirting	pleasure	election	alder-fly	eligible	alliance	clemency
skirmish	clearway	alacrity	allergic	eligibly	albicore	plimsole
skyscape	slobland	pluckily	allergen	alogical	ellipses	slummock
ski-stick	club-face	slack-jaw	elder-gun	slugfest	ellipsis	plimsoll
ekistics	glabrate	blackleg	blue-chip	plug-ugly	elliptic	plumbous
ski-slope	club-haul	placeman	bluebird	flagship	cloister	alum-root
sketcher	clubable	placenta	algerine	flagging	plaister	plumiped
skittish	club-head	black-neb	elsewise	flogging	slaister	slime-pit
skittles	glibness	glyconic	ilmenite	plugging	illiquid	plum-tree
skewbald	glibbery	glucinum	bleeding	sluggish	altitude	climatic
skew-back	slabbery	floccose	bluewing	plaguily	elflocks	climatal
skywards	slobbery	blackout	fleering	flagella	clambake	clematis
altarage	club-line	electric	fleeting	elegance	plumbate	flammule
clearage	blabbing	glyceric	sleeking	elegancy	plum-cake	plum-duff
cleavage	clubbing	glycerol	sleeping	flagpole	plumbago	Plymouth
lea-bane	ill-being	glyceryl	bluefish	slag-wool	plumb-bob	blinkard
floatage	slubbing	electrum	alienism	flag-worm	blamable	blindage
floatant	clubbish	plectrum	Algerian	slughorn	blamably	elongate
pleasant	clubbism	electron	allerion	slogorne	flambéed	plantage
Alhambra	plebeian	glycerin	ulterior	oligarch	glumness	plantain
cloak-bag	clubbist	plectron	alienist	alighted	slimness	Plantago
clean-cut	glabella	electret	alterity	blighted	slimmest	plank-bed
clear-cut	globulin	glacises	sleepily	flighted	flambeau	clinical
oleander	globular	plicated	fluellin	plighted	flummery	Blenheim
Oleaceae	globulet	placitum	alveolar	blighter	glimmery	glanders
Ulmaceae	globally	block-tin	alveolus	plighter	plumbery	planless
cleavers	alebench	blacktop	alderman	slightly	slumbery	plangent
alcahest	olibanum	elicitor	alternat	all-giver	blameful	blankety
alkahest	ill-blood	flichter	Alderney	alphabet	plumaged	all-night
Almagest	clubroom	floccule	bluenose	blah-blah	Olympiad	blind-gut
bleacher	fly-blown	flocculi	gleesome	alchemic	Alemaine	flanched
alkaline	club-moss	clodpate	fluework	elkhound	plumbite	planched
alkalise	glabrous	gladiate	bluegown	ale-house	slimline	clanship
elvanite	slyboots	eludible	ulcerous	although	blimbing	clincher
lea-bite	club-foot	bludgeon	bluecoat	ultimata	clamming	flincher
allaying	clubroot	pledgeor	allegory	alginate	climbing	elenchus
oleating	ale-berry	gladness	sloetree	alligate	clumping	planchet
bloating	globated	bladdery	blue-grey	ultimate	plumbing	klondike
cleaning	club-rush	gliddery	alveated	plein-air	slamming	blending
clearing	blockade	ill-deedy	cliental	claimant	slimming	blinding
cleaving	blockage	sliddery	alley-tor	plainant	slumming	blinking
floating	glaciate	cladding	alley-taw	ultimacy	blimpish	clanging
gleaming	flock-bed	clodding	fluently	Pleiades	glumpish	clanking
gleaning	placable	gladding	alleluia	albiness	plumpish	clinking
gloaming	clack-box	plodding	sloebush	plainful	slimmish	flinging
bleading	blackboy	sledding	blue-buck	almighty	plumbism	glancing
bleasing	placably	sledging	alleyway	albitise	Olympian	planking
Albanian	blackcap	cloddish	sloe-eyed	algicide	olympics	planning

planting	blood-tax	floridly	flashing	flatting	illusion	flix-weed
plonking	blood-wit	clerkess	flushing	flitting	flautist	Flextime®
plunging	floodway	florigen	plashing	fly-tying	cloudily	flax-mill
slanging	clypeate	clerihew	slashing	glutting	pleurisy	flax-lily
slanting	slip-case	flurried	alms-dish	platting	cloudlet	gloxinia
blandish	slippage	alarming	plastics	plotting	alburnum	flax-comb
bluntish	slipware	blurring	classify	slitting	glaucoma	flexuose
clannish	slap-bang	blurting	flashily	flatfish	aleurone	flexuous
slangish	slap-dash	flirting	glassify	flattish	glaucous	flexural
Blennius	flapjack	glorying	glassily	sluttish	illusory	plexuses
flintify	slapjack	slurring	glossily	clothier	claustra	flax-bush
flintily	sliprail	clerkish	classman	clitella	flaunter	play-mare
slangily	slop-pail	flirtish	glassman	flotilla	clausula	playmate
bloncket	elephant	altruism	blastoid	glutelin	alguazil	clay-bank
planulae	flippant	ultraism	blast-off	platelet	slave-ant	playback
planular	oliphant	alarmist	alms-folk	ill-timed	clavicle	clay-marl
plantlet	alopecia	altruist	elf-shoot	plateman	clavecin	playable
clansman	slippery	ultraist	blossomy	old-timer	claviger	cloyless
clinamen	slipshod	florally	flesh-pot	platanna	cleveite	cloyment
Klansman	slip-shoe	plurally	plastral	platinic	Slavonia	play-debt
clangour	slop-shop	clarence	alastrim	platonic	Slavonic	clay-pipe
plant-pot	elaphine	florence	klystron	plutonic	eleventh	playtime
clinique	flip-side	clarinet	plastron	platinum	slovenly	clay-mill
planuria	clapping	gloriosa	fly-spray	Platanus	slovenry	play-bill
flânerie	clipping	gloriole	closeted	plethora	pluviose	playgirl
plenarty	flapping	glareous	blastula	flatlong	olive-oil	Illyrian
elenctic	flipping	glorious	floscule	clotpoll	pluvious	clay-cold
planetic	plopping	glory-pea	oldsquaw	flat-worm	clovered	claymore
plankton	slapping	ultrared	class-war	platform	slaverer	cloysome
glandule	slipping	plurisie	platband	flatuous	cleverly	playsome
plantule	slopping	alfresco	flatmate	flatboat	clavated	playbook
klondyke	clapdish	all-risks	flat-race	flat-foot	elevated	playroom
gliomata	clap-sill	eldritch	flatware	gluttony	Olivetan	play-goer
allocate	glyptics	all-round	slate-axe	platypus	elevator	playsuit
allopath	floppily	ale-stake	plateasm	ulstered	slivovic	blizzard
pleonasm	sloppily	glissade	flatways	clithral	clawback	blazoner
Eldorado	clip-clop	plussage	plateaux	clitoral	slowback	blazonry
allosaur	clop-clop	glossary	clotebur	elaterin	blowball	alizarin
pleonast	flip-flap	flush-box	cloth-cap	flatiron	blowlamp	impanate
allogamy	flip-flop	blastema	elatedly	clitoris	glowlamp	emmarble
Pliocene	slipslop	alms-deed	flathead	Ulothrix	flywheel	smear-dab
bloomers	slip-knot	glosseme	glutaeal	platysma	clawless	ommateum
bloomery	clupeoid	fly-sheet	flittern	cloudage	flawless	immanent
gloomful	clip-hook	ill-spent	slattern	ill-usage	slowness	immanely
blood-hot	slip-dock	blistery	flatness	alguacil	clowney	empathic
fluoride	slopwork	blustery	glutaeus	flounder	blowpipe	immanity
fluorine	slop-bowl	clustery	plotless	fly-under	clowning	imparity
fluorite	slipform	flustery	ill-treat	sloughed	clownish	smearily
blooming	flypaper	plastery	blithely	plougher	blowhole	embarked
flooding	claptrap	blissful	flattery	sloucher	slowpoke	embanker
flooring	klephtic	blushful	glittery	allusive	glow-worm	empacket
glooming	slip-over	glassful	slattery	illumine	slow-worm	embalmer
allodial	aliquant	flesh-fly	sluttery	illusive	blowdown	impannel
algorism	claqueur	flash-gun	plateful	plaudite	slow-down	embarred
allodium	eloquent	glossina	slothful	plausive	slow-foot	empatron
Ultonian	cliquish	allspice	blotched	alluring	flowered	impasted
bloodily	cliquism	glassine	fletcher	clouding	old-world	impasto'd
gloomily	clarsach	Glassite	flatwise	flourish	flowerer	embattle
Algonkin	glorybox	blasting	blotting	alluvial	floweret	immantle
floodlit	clerical	blessing	clothing	alluvium	alewives	imparter
algology	altrices	blushing	clotting	allusion	flexible	amiantus
blood-red	cleruchy	clashing	flatling	alluvion	flexibly	immature
allotted	clerkdom	clasping		Claudian	flax-seed	Emmanuel

Immanuel	amniotic	embodied	imitable	endanger	encaenia	inscribe
emaciate	immitted	ammonite	emetical	enlarger	undamned	onychite
amicable	embitter	immobile	umptieth	uncaught	unearned	unactive
amicably	imbitter	impolite	smithers	untaught	unfanned	enacting
smacking	smokable	imposing	smithery	unbathed	unmanned	knocking
smocking	smoke-box	ammonium	smothery	uncashed	unpained	unaching
emiction	smoke-dry	embolism	emitting	undashed	unsained	knackish
emictory	smallage	emporium	emptying	unpathed	untanned	onychium
omadhaun	small-ale	impolicy	omitting	unsashed	unwarned	enaction
smidgeon	impleach	impocket	smuttily	unwashed	enraunge	inaction
smudgily	small-arm	embossed	imitancy	uneathes	unpannel	unscaled
amidmost	implicit	empoison	amitosis	unvaried	ungainly	inoculum
amadavat	impledge	embosser	emptysis	annalise	Ansafone®	unicolor
amperage	emulgent	immortal	amitotic	Infamise	infamous	insculpt
amnesiac	smeltery	importer	imitator	innative	undamped	anaconda
amberite	smileful	imposter	amethyst	invasive	unsapped	aniconic
emperise	emulsive	impostor	ambulate	unnative	untapped	ensconce
imbecile	smaltite	omoplate	amputate	engaging	unwarped	insconce
emperish	implying	omophagy	ambulant	inlaying	ensample	anechoic
imperial	smelling	smorzato	smoulder	sneaking	encarpus	anecdote
imperium	smelting	emery-bag	smouldry	sneaping	unbarred	inscroll
impetigo	smallish	embraced	impudent	uncaring	unhaired	knockout
impelled	emulsion	American	impurely	unfading	unmarred	enacture
impeller	emulsify	embracer	immunise	unlading	unpaired	inedible
amberoid	smalmily	amaracus	umquhile	unmaking	untarred	cnidaria
amoeboid	implunge	imbrices	immunity	unsating	unfairly	unadored
amberous	emulsoid	umbriere	impunity	enravish	intarsia	inedited
empeople	amelcorn	emergent	impurity	sneakish	uncaused	unedited
immersed	umble-pie	amortise	ampullae	uniaxial	unhalsed	unrepaid
Emmental	smallpox	emerging	impugner	invasion	unraised	antedate
embezzle	implorer	emersion	empurple	annalist	envassal	enterate
amygdala	amuletic	smarmily	impurple	insanity	intarsio	under-age
amygdale	omelette	ombrella	embusqué	sneakily	sneaksby	antenati
emigrate	emulator	umbrella	embussed	uneasily	unbaited	underarm
emigrant	impluvia	umbrello	empyreal	unwarily	unhatted	unrepair
smugness	employed	imprimis	empyrean	unbacked	unsalted	antepast
smuggled	employee	amaranth	empyesis	unbanked	untasted	interact
smuggler	employer	embryons	amazedly	unbarked	unwanted	underact
imaginal	emblazon	improper	endamage	unhacked	unwasted	untenant
imaginer	emendate	smirbrd	indagate	unmarked	unmantle	underbid
imagines	emendals	ambrosia	inhalant	unmasked	unfasten	unwebbed
amygdule	amenable	impresse	unbarbed	unpacked	infantry	enfeeble
Amphibia	amenably	imprison	sneak-cup	unracked	unvalued	ensemble
omphalic	emongest	embrasor	unbanded	untackle	undazzle	under-boy
omphalos	amandine	umbratic	uncandid	unmasker	anableps	underbuy
omohyoid	eminence	umbrated	unwarded	unpacker	snobbery	unfenced
amphipod	eminency	umbrette	unsaddle	uncalled	snobling	intercom
amphoric	immolate	amoretti	inlander	unfabled	snubbing	intercut
amphorae	umbonate	amoretto	inwardly	ungalled	snobbish	undercut
emphases	embolden	emeritus	onwardly	unhailed	snubbish	enneadic
emphasis	emborder	improver	innately	unmailed	snobbism	intended
emphatic	empolder	emissary	insanely	unsailed	anabolic	unbedded
umpirage	imborder	amusable	unsafely	unwalled	anabasis	unbended
ambivert	impolder	amusedly	unsafety	unfallen	anabatic	undeeded
imminent	immodest	smash-hit	unwarely	intaglio	unabated	underdid
immingle	immoment	emissile	unwatery	entailer	unobeyed	unheeded
impishly	imponent	emissive	unlawful	enwallow	snack-bar	unneeded
ambition	impotent	omissive	enlarged	unhallow	unicycle	unseeded
ambiance	smoothie	amissing	ungauged	unfaulty	knickers	untended
ambience	smoothen	smashing	unhanged	undammed	inscient	unwedded
omnivore	smoother	emission	unpanged	unharmed	knackery	unweeded
omniform	smoothly	omission	entangle	unmaimed	enactive	underdog
empierce	ammoniac	amusette	untangle	unwarmed	inactive	unfeudal

unseldom	unveiled	unsecret	unsexual	unchaste	unrigged	anticous
engender	underlie	interrex	unnerved	unchosen	unringed	environs
entender	unhealth	undersea	interval	anthesis	untinged	antibody
Enzedder	underlap	unleased	once-over	enthetic	unwigged	antilogy
intender	underlip	unsensed	interwar	unthatch	unwinged	antimony
untender	annealer	unversed	underwit	unshaved	unkingly	antinomy
antecede	unveiler	Anderson	endeixis	unshaven	unfished	undipped
knee-jerk	entellus	unperson	unseized	unchewed	antiphon	unripped
unbeseem	underlet	unreason	unafraid	unthawed	unbishop	enfierce
knee-deep	interlay	unseason	knife-box	Anthozoa	encipher	gneissic
interess	underlay	incenser	snuffbox	unvizard	uncipher	unbiased
antevert	unreally	incensor	knife-boy	enfilade	antithet	unkissed
indecent	endermic	Intelsat	snuffers	ensilage	unpitied	unmissed
inherent	unhelmed	underset	sniffing	envisage	anticize	unbitted
interest	unseamed	intersex	snuffing	indicate	incisive	undinted
unbereft	underman	undersay	unifying	intimate	infinite	unfitted
undecent	intermit	undersky	snifily	uncinate	undivine	ungifted
undesert	intermix	enfested	sniffler	antimask	enticing	unlisted
underfed	unseemly	indebted	snuffler	incitant	inviting	unsifted
underfur	unkenned	indented	unifilar	indicant	ungiving	indictee
unhedged	unpenned	infefted	snugness	intimacy	unliving	unvirtue
enveigle	unreined	inserted	snuggery	unribbed	untiring	infilter
inveagle	unweaned	invected	anagogic	enviable	unfilial	antistat
inveigle	unweened	inverted	snugging	inviable	incivism	incisure
enneagon	unyeaned	unbelted	sniggler	unviable	intimism	intitule
sneeshan	antennae	unheated	knightly	unlimber	oncidium	unviewed
sneeshin	enceinte	unmelted	anaglyph	enviably	envision	antitype
untether	internee	unnetted	inchoate	encircle	incision	snake-eel
unnethes	antennal	unseated	inch-tape	ungilded	intimist	snake-fly
angelica	enkernel	untented	ensheath	ungirded	infinity	snake-oil
Annelida	infernal	untested	enthrall	unlidded	intimity	snake-pit
antefixa	internal	unvented	unshaded	unminded	unfixity	antliate
undefied	unkennel	unwetted	unshadow	engirdle	untidily	enallage
andesine	antennas	incentre	enshield	enkindle	unlicked	unpliant
andesite	unheroic	intertie	unthread	unriddle	unlinked	unilobed
ankerite	anaerobe	ungentle	inchmeal	unwisdom	unmilked	unilobar
anserine	antelope	unsettle	enshrine	unbidden	unpicked	analecta
unbelief	envelope	invertin	inshrine	unhidden	unpinked	unplaced
entering	kneehole	unbeaten	unthrift	unridden	unsicker	Anglican
indexing	anteroom	knee-stop	unshaked	unkindly	unfilled	analects
sneering	ante-post	ancestor	unshaken	antisera	unmilled	included
sneezing	undevout	ant-eater	anthelia	indigene	unrifled	influent
unseeing	unhelped	enfetter	anthelix	inficete	untilled	analogic
knee-high	unreaped	inceptor	enthalpy	unlineal	untitled	analogue
endemial	unpeople	indenter	anthemia	anti-hero	unwilled	analogon
ungenial	Interpol	infector	unrhymed	engineer	unwieldy	in-flight
endemism	underpin	injector	unshamed	inkiness	undimmed	unallied
ingenium	unheppen	inserter	unchancy	incident	unfilmed	analcime
annexion	unweapon	inventor	enshroud	indigent	Indiaman	analcite
inhesion	untemper	inverter	unshroud	indigest	infirmly	unsluice
unbenign	underpay	invertor	enthrone	indirect	insignia	unslaked
anterior	endeared	investor	unthrone	enginery	unpinned	inflamed
inferior	inferred	onsetter	inch-worm	entirely	unsigned	unblamed
interior	interred	unfetter	unshaped	entirety	untinned	inflamer
under-jaw	unfeared	undertow	unshapen	snailery	ensigncy	inclined
invecked	ungeared	ancestry	enchoric	unlikely	antidote	unclench
undecked	unpeered	intently	unshared	unlively	Antilope	one-liner
unrecked	enhearse	ungently	encharge	untimely	antinode	unbloody
angekkok	inhearse	unmeetly	one-horse	unwifely	antipode	antlered
unfelled	unhearse	infecund	uncharge	unwisely	antipole	unclosed
unhealed	integral	annexure	unchurch	unwilful	antipope	analyser
unpeeled	underrun	insecure	anchoret	enridged	ensiform	encloser
unsealed	unlearnt	underuse	enchased	unhinged	unciform	incloser

analyses	inholder	undoomed	ensphere	anorthic	unusably	insulate
analysis	unfolder	unformed	insphere	enarched	one-sided	intubate
enclisis	unloader	unwormed	one-piece	anarchal	unuseful	undulate
analytic	unsolder	informal	unsphere	energise	ants'-eggs	ungulate
enclitic	unlordly	unformal	anapaest	unpraise	unespied	injurant
inflated	endoderm	uncommon	snippety	knurling	inessive	insulant
unelated	entoderm	informer	snapshot	snarling	inustion	insurant
enclothe	unsolemn	insomnia	knapping	snorting	unisonal	undulant
unclothe	enforest	uncoined	snapping	unerring	inkstone	uncurbed
unclutch	indolent	uncoyned	snipping	inertial	anasarca	undubbed
inflator	innocent	ungowned	snappish	untruism	angstrom	unrubbed
inflatus	insolent	unmoaned	snap-link	entrails	anisette	unturbid
uncloudy	unhonest	announce	unspoilt	enormity	inositol	encumber
enslaved	endogeny	inconnue	snappily	unbroken	inasmuch	unbudded
ungloved	ontogeny	enjoiner	unspoken	engramma	initiate	unfunded
uncloven	uncomely	unbonnet	unipolar	unframed	one-track	unguided
enslaver	unhomely	endozoic	unopened	entremes	unsteady	unbundle
unblowed	unlovely	entozoic	snip-snap	intromit	instable	unburden
unflawed	unroofed	entozoal	anaphora	encrinic	unstable	unsued-to
enflower	snootful	endozoon	end-paper	unironed	unitedly	unmuffle
inflexed	unjoyful	entozoon	inspired	unpruned	anathema	unruffle
unglazed	engorged	encolour	unspared	entrance	knotweed	unpurged
inimical	unforged	unjoyous	snap-brim	infringe	on-stream	enhunger
animally	ungorged	oncology	inspirer	intrince	knitwear	indulger
gnomonic	unrouged	ontology	inspirit	entrench	instress	unvulgar
mnemonic	unbought	unlopped	Anoplura	indrench	knotless	unburied
unsmooth	unforgot	unsoaped	unsprung	intrench	snottery	enlumine
unamused	unfought	incorpse	uniquely	encrinal	unstuffy	induciae
animated	unsought	uncouple	inequity	engroove	snatcher	induline
animator	unbodied	unholpen	iniquity	ingroove	snitcher	induviae
unimbued	indocile	unsoured	enervate	enormous	gnathite	infusive
inundate	unionise	endorsed	increase	intrepid	anything	enduring
inundant	unpolite	enmossed	increate	undraped	gnatling	indusial
unknight	incoming	unhoused	inornate	unproper	knitting	induvial
unanchor	intoning	unpoised	inurbane	entrepot	knotting	aneurism
unenvied	oncoming	endorsee	uncreate	infra-red	unstring	indusium
unending	unboding	unloosen	encroach	antrorse	snottily	infusion
unaneled	unloving	unpoison	unpreach	introrse	Gnetales	unsucked
in and-out	unmoving	endorser	inerrant	entresol	anatomic	untucked
uninured	unmodish	entoptic	undreamt	enfrosen	unatoned	unbuckle
endosarc	unpolish	enzootic	entreaty	unarisen	instance	insucken
un-mosaic	unsocial	unpoetic	inarable	unprison	instinct	Anguilla
untoward	encomium	intorted	unbraced	enuresis	instancy	annulled
annotate	unionism	unbolted	ungraced	undrossy	knot-hole	unculled
innovate	encomion	unfooted	unpriced	untrusty	one-to-one	uncurled
insolate	unionist	unposted	untraced	anoretic	knotwork	undulled
intonate	unholily	unrooted	entr'acte	enuretic	unctuous	unpulled
invocate	unbooked	unrotted	ungraded	unpretty	anatropy	annually
endocarp	uncooked	unsorted	untraded	unargued	unstarch	unguilty
endogamy	undocked	unwonted	encradle	unground	unstated	ungummed
uncombed	unlocked	ungotten	unbridle	engraved	unstitch	unsummed
unforbid	unlooked	unrotten	intruder	unproved	unstrung	unburned
untombed	unworked	uncostly	intrados	engraven	unstruck	unsunned
undouble	onlooker	unworthy	unfriend	undriven	instruct	unturned
unforced	unsocket	encolure	enfreeze	unproven	unstayed	inguinal
unvoiced	engouled	involute	engrieve	engraver	Annulata	innuendo
unfolded	enrolled	insomuch	unfreeze	ingrowth	Ungulata	annulose
unhooded	uncowled	unsolved	unbreech	anorexia	annulate	undulose
unloaded	unpolled	endodyne	unpriest	anorexic	inaurate	anourous
unlorded	unsoiled	anaphase	unartful	unprized	incubate	incubous
unwooded	unsouled	knapsack	intrigue	unfrozen	indurate	undulous
unworded	enroller	knapscal	androgen	inkstand	inhumane	infusory
unsodden	informed	knapweed	anarchic	unusable	inhumate	anguiped

incurred
unfurred
enquirer
inquirer
unburrow
intuited
unhunted
unsuited
unsubtle
unbutton
enaunter
inductor
insulter
industry
unjustly
incurved
aneurysm
unmuzzle
univocal
univalve
snivelly
unevenly
universe
unavowed
snowball
snowfall
snow-capt
knowable
anywhere
snowless
snow-shoe
snow-bird
snowlike
snowline
snow-flea
snow-cold
snow-boot
snowdrop
answerer
unawares
enswathe
inswathe
unswathe
unswayed
snow-eyes
inexpert
encyclic
ankylose
enhydros
encysted
soda-lake
coranach
tomahawk
nowadays
donatary
Monarcho
romancer
monarchy
nomarchy
toparchy
mokaddam
notandum
colander

Polander
pomander
solander
cowardly
cowardry
monandry
towardly
Moraceae
Rosaceae
Sotadean
voyageur
votaress
covalent
god-awful
pot-au-feu
coxalgia
Cocaigne
coraggio
Podargus
do-naught
monachal
Jonathan
borachio
Monachus
potashes
foramina
sonatina
boracite
botanise
conative
coramine
donative
dopamine
focalise
localise
locative
monazite
moralise
nodalise
nomadise
notarise
polarise
Romanise
rotative
royalise
soda-lime
sodalite
sodamide
solanine
solarise
tonalite
topazine
totalise
vocalise
vocative
volatile
womanise
Romanish
tovarish
womanish
conarial
domanial
gonadial

monaxial
notarial
conarium
domatium
donatism
iotacism
localism
modalism
monadism
moralism
nomadism
Romanism
rosarium
royalism
solarism
solarium
solatium
somatism
vocalism
colation
conation
donation
dotation
Horatian
jobation
Kolarian
lobation
location
Moravian
nodation
notation
Novatian
novation
Polabian
potation
rogation
Romanian
rosarian
Rotarian
rotation
solation
vocalion
vocation
zonation
botanist
Donatist
loyalist
modalist
moralist
Romanist
royalist
solarist
somatist
vocalist
votarist
locality
modality
molality
molarity
morality
nodality
polarity
sodality

tonality
totality
vocality
voracity
so-called
totalled
rocaille
corallum
moraller
movables
tomalley
toxaemia
toxaemic
morainic
domainal
morainal
johannes
bona-roba
Coca-Cola®
coracoid
homaloid
Polaroid
comatose
oogamous
potatoes
tomatoes
donatory
moratory
potatory
rogatory
rotatory
zoiatria
podagric
sowarree
monaural
podagral
Moharram
potassic
Romansch
mocassin
bonassus
molasses
cobaltic
monastic
romantic
colature
logboard
mopboard
hot-brain
zooblast
bombycid
morbidly
sow-bread
sombrero
combless
tombless
cobblery
sombrely
morbific
doubtful
bomb-site
comb-wise
cobbling

doubling
doubting
hobbling
lobbying
not-being
wobbling
boobyish
boobyism
hobbyism
zombiism
hobbyist
lobbyist
gorblimy
morbilli
gor-belly
pot-belly
combined
Sorbonne
combings
bobbinet
tolbooth
doubloon
sombrous
bobby-pin
forborne
row-barge
zomboruk
dobber-in
mowburnt
cowberry
dogberry
foxberry
combated
sorbitol
fogbound
pot-bound
boob-tube
fox-brush
conchate
conclave
non-claim
couchant
morceaux
ponceaux
forcible
boschbok
log-cabin
coach-box
touch-box
voice-box
forcibly
coccidia
Coccidae
coachdog
conceder
roncador
forcedly
concrete
torchère
dog-cheap
botchery
louchely
forceful

pouchful
voiceful
coccyges
godchild
coactive
conceive
botching
coaching
couching
notching
poaching
touching
dobchick
coaction
Noachian
conceity
Roccella
concolor
torcular
Cocculus
coachman
Golconda
volcanic
log-canoe
toucanet
conchoid
zoochore
souchong
box-cloth
poaceous
zoochory
forcipes
hotchpot
concerto
sorcerer
moccasin
zoocytia
concetti
concetto
concause
conclude
coach-way
hoactzin
bondmaid
food-card
woodland
woodward
gold-lace
good-dame
wood-sage
woodwale
good-lack
holdback
wood-lark
cordwain
gold-wasp
moldwarp
wood-wasp
hold-fast
Bordeaux
rondeaux
fordable

voidable
wood-ibis
wood-acid
rondache
toddy-cat
rowdedow
rowdydow
sordidly
pondweed
gold-leaf
wood-meal
rood-beam
how-d'ye-do
toodle-oo
goodyear
boldness
coldness
cordless
fondness
foodless
goldless
goodness
hoodless
lordless
loudness
top-dress
voidness
woodless
wordless
soldiery
bondager
woodshed
lordship
wood-chat
roadshow
woodbind
woodwind
gold-mine
gold-size
gold-wire
goodsire
goodtime
goodwife
load-line
pond-life
roadside
woodbine
woodlice
woodmice
wood-mite
wood-pile
fondling
fordoing
lordling
toadying
toddling
yoldring
dowdyish
goldfish
rowdyish
toad-fish
toadyish
hoodwink

wood-tick	wonderer	forepart	noteless	coveting	foreslow	rose-tree
goodwill	corduroy	honey-ant	roseless	foreking	foreplay	love-drug
dowdyism	lordosis	molecast	soleness	forewing	role-play	fox-earth
rowdyism	lordotic	tolerant	soreness	honeying	bogey-man	rose-drop
toadyism	goadster	cometary	toneless	lowering	lodesman	home-brew
goodlier	loadstar	monetary	voteless	nose-ring	governor	forensic
dog-daisy	roadster	novenary	zoneless	popeling	cokernut	homeosis
pond-lily	woodruff	rosemary	bodement	sobering	love-knot	somerset
wood-skin	gold-rush	hover-bed	coherent	towering	rose-knot	Rodentia
Goidelic	toad-rush	honey-bee	co-regent	novelish	foreknow	domestic
bordello	wood-rush	loveable	forefeet	pokerish	modernly	toreutic
jordeloo	sow-drunk	moveable	forefelt	rosefish	solemnly	forested
condylar	wood-pulp	ropeable	forehent	yokelish	Copepoda	rosetted
toadflax	doldrums	money-bag	forelent	homesick	rose-comb	forestal
moody-mad	gold-dust	honeybun	forewent	lovesick	foretold	lomentum
bondsman	rondavel	November	home-felt	rose-pink	foreword	momentum
goadsman	wood-evil	hover-bus	love-feat	bone-mill	popehood	tomentum
roadsman	cordovan	money-box	love-nest	mole-hill	rosewood	fomenter
woodsman	good-even	moveably	love-seat	mote-hill	solenoid	forester
condense	hobdayed	bone-ache	movement	soredial	yoke-toed	go-getter
toe-dance	boneyard	novercal	non-elect	soterial	borecole	lodestar
voidance	forehand	hover-car	non-event	bogeyism	borehole	molester
cordiner	foreland	Rome-scot	powerful	Docetism	dolesome	cogently
Londoner	foresaid	bone-idle	hover-fly	nobelium	dovecote	Coventry
gold-ends	foreward	co-meddle	lozenged	novelism	forebode	covertly
goldenly	homeland	fore-edge	somewhen	solecism	foregone	forestay
mordancy	homeward	noveldom	dogeship	soredium	jokesome	forestry
woodenly	nose-band	Poseidon	foreship	tokenism	lonesome	honestly
cord-wood	Romeward	loreador	popeship	totemism	lovesome	modestly
wood-hole	bone-cave	honey-dew	comether	Wodenism	nose-cone	momently
wood-note	bone-lace	nose-herb	together	zooecium	rotenone	nocently
woodwose	code-name	bonehead	somewhat	Bohemian	wobegone	non-entry
word-lore	coverage	cole-seed	foreshew	cohesion	love-song	potently
wood-roof	cozenage	forehead	foreshow	comedian	forelock	rose-hued
cold-work	foredate	forelend	forelimb	hotelier	homework	molecule
road-book	forename	foreread	forewind	motelier	lovelock	nonesuch
woodcock	home-made	pokeweed	lovebird	Gobelins	more-pork	rose-bush
woodwork	love-game	rope's-end	cohesive	polemics	notebook	bone-dust
wordbook	Lovelace	sorehead	coteline	Docetist	ropework	love-suit
gold-foil	moderate	somedele	covetise	forebitt	rose-bowl	moreover
wood-coal	note-case	nose-leaf	dolerite	forelift	foredoom	rove-over
wood-wool	somegate	rose-leaf	dovelike	novelist	comedown	dove-eyed
wood-worm	tolerate	tone-deaf	foreside	noverint	forenoon	mole-eyed
wood-born	yoke-mate	foredeck	foretime	polemist	home-born	conflate
wondrous	rose-rash	forepeak	home-fire	solecist	home-town	hog-frame
foldboat	come-back	bone-meal	home-life	totemist	lovelorn	loaf-cake
rood-loft	fore-rank	forefeel	homelike	homelily	foregoer	hoof-mark
wood-opal	mopehawk	foretell	hosepipe	lovelily	covetous	roof-rack
toad-spit	rope-walk	hose-reel	lobeline	foreskin	cole-wort	wolf-pack
bordered	sore-hawk	somedeal	monetise	moleskin	forefoot	golf-ball
doddered	coverall	foremean	nose-dive	bowelled	foremost	goofball
powdered	dovetail	foreseen	noselite	coverlid	lobe-foot	korfball
wondered	foresail	forebear	novelise	modelled	rose-root	bouffant
foedarie	home-farm	boneless	polemise	rowelled	fore-body	dog-faced
rood-tree	forewarn	coreless	rope-ripe	towelled	somebody	confider
folderol	rope-yarn	doneness	roselike	vowelled	dowel-pin	confrère
ponderal	moderato	goneness	soberise	novellae	homespun	coiffeur
wood-wren	someways	homeless	solecise	foreplan	honeypot	dowfness
borderer	cosecant	hopeless	sometime	hoveller	Moresque	hoofless
dodderer	co-tenant	loneness	somewise	modeller	dog-eared	roofless
fodderer	covenant	loveless	vomerine	yodeller	dowel-rod	solfeggi
ponderer	forecast	moveless	vowelise	coverlet	home-bred	dog-fight
solderer	foremast	noseless	covering	cole-slaw	lop-eared	roof-like

sol-faing
wolfling
wolf-fish
sol-faism
forfairn
Wolffian
conflict
sol-faist
wolf-skin
golf-club
gonfalon
moufflon
joyfully
woefully
confined
gonfanon
confiner
wolf-note
soffioni
confront
conferva
coffered
conferee
roof-tree
confused
confetti
confound
coiffure
longhand
bongrace
fox-grape
long-wave
roughage
long-haul
long-tail
longwall
long-hair
cowgrass
dog-grass
log-glass
longways
lopgrass
rotgrass
poignant
zoograft
congiary
doggy-bag
dough-boy
doggedly
rough-dry
long-head
Congoese
Congreve
long-term
jongleur
longueur
congress
long-legs
longness
songless
congreet
lodgment
longship

rough-hew
yongthly
songbird
long-life
long-nine
longwise
song-like
coughing
forgoing
goggling
joggling
tonguing
roughish
toughish
long-firm
Mongolic
coagulum
long-slip
forgeman
Gorgonia
zoogenic
doggoned
congener
doughnut
co-agency
zoogloea
conglobe
foxglove
longsome
mongoose
songbook
longhorn
mongcorn
pop-group
gorgeous
long-togs
longboat
long-spun
boughpot
doggerel
hoggerel
gorgerin
longeron
fougasse
Golgotha
boughten
foughten
long-stop
gongster
songster
long-stay
longeval
forgiven
God-given
moth-ball
top-heavy
sophical
poshteen
cochlear
poshness
dochmiac
forhaile
po'chaise

dochmius
Rochelle
bonhomie
bothyman
nowhence
forhooie
pooh-pooh
sopheric
cothurni
sopherim
oophoron
Lothario
cosherer
motherly
pochette
foxhound
cot-house
cowhouse
dog-house
hothouse
log-house
pothouse
yoghourt
moshavim
boniface
cogitate
dominate
loricate
motivate
nominate
rosinate
solidare
solidate
volitate
komitaji
dominant
toxicant
volitant
docimasy
poticary
solidary
solitary
sociable
sociably
zodiacal
Gobiidae
louis-d'or
Porifera
Rotifera
bonibell
coliseum
domineer
bodiless
boniness
cosiness
coxiness
doziness
foxiness
foziness
holiness
nosiness
ooziness
poriness

ropiness
rosiness
lorikeet
politely
foliaged
jowing-in
cooingly
hopingly
jokingly
losingly
lovingly
mopingly
movingly
posingly
rovingly
eolithic
polished
polisher
dolichos
boyishly
coyishly
modishly
mopishly
popishly
tonishly
toyishly
codified
modified
notified
domicile
eolipile
homicide
Ionicise
logicise
mobilise
monitive
positive
soricine
totitive
volitive
vomitive
positing
vomiting
solidish
politick
conidial
gonidial
conidium
Doricism
gonidium
Molinism
solidism
dominion
logician
monition
nolition
position
Socinian
volition
politico
codifier
modifier
notifier

politics
homilist
Molinist
solidist
docility
mobility
motility
motivity
nobility
solicity
solidify
solidity
tonicity
toxicity
popinjay
monicker
bouillon
cotillon
modiolar
modiolus
son-in-law
jovially
socially
éolienne
motional
notional
doridoid
hominoid
soricoid
zopilote
rosin-oil
coliform
coniform
covinous
dominoes
modiwort
monitory
vomitory
Eohippus
positron
goliardy
forinsec
komissar
kolinsky
holistic
logistic
monistic
nomistic
poristic
sovietic
foliated
societal
podiatry
lodicula
moribund
lodicule
solitude
howitzer
forjudge
goujeers
conjugal
log-juice
conjoint

conjunct
conjurer
conjuror
nonjuror
bookland
cookmaid
dockland
dockyard
folkland
bookcase
book-mate
folk-tale
lock-gate
rock-cake
work-mate
book-oath
bookmark
pockmark
rock-lark
cocktail
fork-tail
rock-fall
hock-cart
lockfast
rock-salt
mockable
workable
booked-up
polka-dot
forkedly
workaday
worky-day
forkhead
rockweed
cork-heel
monk-seal
rock-hewn
workwear
bookless
workless
book-debt
bookrest
bookshop
cookshop
pork-chop
workshop
cockshot
cockshut
cockbird
rock-bird
booklice
hock-tide
corkwing
porkling
rockling
monk-fish
rock-fish
work-girl
rock-alum
locksman
mon-khmer
corkwood
monkhood

rock-wood
workload
booklore
cork-sole
folklore
rock-dove
rock-rose
worksome
folk-song
bookwork
cook-book
folkrock
rock-cook
rock-cork
rock-work
workbook
workfolk
bookworm
cookroom
hook-worm
workroom
book-post
cockboat
cockloft
folkmoot
workboat
cockspur
cork-tree
folk-free
cockerel
looker-in
looker-on
cock-crow
docketed
pocketed
socketed
jockette
cockatoo
lockstep
rocketer
rocketry
cocksure
folk-tune
dock-dues
work-over
rockaway
soakaway
cockeyed
Cockayne
wool-card
woolward
coal-face
tollgate
kohlrabi
wool-pack
woolsack
coalball
roll-call
toll-call
wool-ball
foulmart
toll-bait
rouleaux

rollable	hollands	wool-dyed	pommetty	downwind	cornered	colophon
tollable	moslings	formiate	zoometry	coincide	down-trod	colonise
coolabah	moulinet	room-mate	dormouse	cornpipe	bountree	dolomite
box-lobby	toilinet	doom-palm	worm-tube	down-line	cognosce	monoxide
follicle	wool-comb	doum-palm	cornland	downpipe	goings-on	motorise
pollical	dollhood	worm-cast	downland	downtime	zoonoses	polonise
hoolican	world-old	tommy-bar	downward	hornpipe	zoonosis	sodomise
foolscap	coal-hole	cosmical	join-hand	moonrise	zoonitic	Sodomite
bollocks	toilsome	doomsday	townland	noontide	bonneted	sororise
pollices	holly-oak	worm-seed	corn-cake	bouncing	cornuted	monolith
soul-scat	woolwork	worm-gear	moon-face	bounding	top-notch	nohowish
soul-scot	boll-worm	foamless	poundage	founding	cornetto	bobolink
hollidam	toolroom	formless	mooncalf	lounging	round-top	colonial
colluder	fool-born	gormless	town-talk	mounting	cornetcy	monomial
cow-leech	toil-worn	dormient	corn-ball	poinding	sonnetry	motorial
dog-leech	Coalport	tommy-gun	downfall	pointing	corn-cure	oogonial
roll-neck	foalfoot	topmaker	down-haul	rounding	jointure	sororial
soul-bell	goalpost	formulae	horntail	sounding	roundure	coronium
woolfell	collapse	formalin	moonsail	townling	downrush	motorium
coolness	lollipop	formular	round-arm	wounding	cornhusk	oogonium
foulness	colloque	formally	fountain	moon-fish	downturn	polonism
soilless	colloquy	normalcy	mountain	roundish	conniver	polonium
soulless	collared	normally	downcast	youngish	cognovit	Boeotian
toilless	dollared	doomsman	mountant	corn-mill	moon-eyed	Dodonian
fowl-pest	toll-free	hormonic	boundary	downhill	coenzyme	Polonian
colliery	pouldron	hog-maned	corn-baby	hornbill	moon-type	robotics
toplofty	solleret	commence	coenobia	horn-rims	Notogaea	colonist
collogue	Lollardy	communal	loanable	corn-kist	toxocara	monodist
lollygag	Mollusca	hormonal	sound-bar	bouncily	coronate	monotint
collagen	coalesce	noumenal	sound-bow	woundily	sororate	motorist
hooligan	coulisse	terminal	sound-box	townskip	coronach	oologist
colleger	noblesse	noumenon	hobnobby	corn-flag	monomark	jocosity
holla hoa	dolly-tub	commando	corniced	roundlet	monorail	morosity
tool-shed	poplitic	commoner	cornacre	downflow	motorail	nodosity
soul-shot	zoolitic	coamings	corniche	zoonomia	coco-palm	porosity
coal-mine	polluted	commoney	cornicle	zoonomic	monocarp	sonority
goal-line	toileted	commonly	tornadic	cognomen	colorant	sorority
poulaine	roulette	dormancy	pound-day	gownsman	roborant	motor-jet
poultice	lollette	Hogmanay	tom-noddy	townsman	sonorant	co-worker
soil-pipe	potlatch	zoomancy	horngeld	mornings	coronary	cocoplum
boulting	bog-Latin	wormwood	moonseed	fornenst	homogamy	rosoglio
moulding	dog-Latin	roomsome	co-inhere	pound-net	honorary	monoglot
moulting	collator	worm-hole	corn-beef	corn-snow	monogamy	motorman
wooling	pollster	formwork	hornbeak	loan-word	porogamy	notornis
coalfish	polluter	coumaric	rowndell	poon-wood	motor-bus	cocoanut
foul-fish	zoolater	commerce	hornbeam	corn-pone	Monoecia	Podogona
tolldish	toiletry	commerge	moonbeam	down-come	monoacid	holozoic
goal-kick	zoolatry	zoomorph	mounseer	coon-song	motor-car	coco-wood
soul-sick	dog-louse	non-moral	countess	corn-moth	conoidic	coronoid
wool-mill	coal-dust	boom-iron	hornfels	hornbook	conoidal	corocore
woollies	low-lived	coumarin	hornless	hornwork	toroidal	horologe
coal-flap	top-level	tommy-rot	moonless	joint-oil	do-gooder	locomote
wool-clip	golliwog	formerly	corn-rent	cornworm	loco-weed	monopode
foul-play	gollywog	pop-music	downbeat	hornworm	Holocene	monotone
loblolly	polliwig	cosmesis	cornific	down-town	homogeny	soporose
coelomic	polliwog	cosmetic	somnific	torn-down	jocosely	iodoform
Moslemin	pollywig	dogmatic	fountful	downpour	monogeny	corocoro
nobleman	pollywog	poematic	joint-fir	corneous	morosely	doloroso
noblemen	follow-on	non-metal	roentgen	cornloft	nomogeny	locofoco
dolly-mop	follow-up	pot-metal	moonshee	count-out	cocoa-fat	dolorous
pollinia	follower	commuter	township	downmost	toboggan	jocorous
pollinic	hollowly	doomster	Zoanthus	hornwort	toboggin	sonorous
top-liner	volleyed	noometry	moonshot	moonwort	do-nought	soporous

homodont	gospodar	zoophyte	poorwill	forspend	poisoner	postdate
monodont	hospodar	porphyry	coercion	godspeed	Volsungs	postface
colotomy	torpidly	torquate	courtier	hogshead	cousinly	rostrate
dosology	cod-piece	cotquean	to-broken	potsherd	cousinry	rout-cake
doxology	complete	conquest	courtlet	goose-egg	Cotswold	software
homology	morpheme	mosquito	door's-man	forspeak	dog's-nose	foot-bath
homotony	oosphere	non-quota	no-trumps	top-shell	fog-smoke	footpath
horology	toe-piece	door-yard	doorknob	zoosperm	forswore	koftgari
lobotomy	morphean	gourmand	courante	dog-sleep	hog-score	post-nati
monogony	compress	hour-hand	Sobranje	forswear	moss-rose	boot-jack
monology	hot-press	moor-band	Sobranye	monsieur	potstone	coatrack
monopoly	Morpheus	moorland	sovranty	mouse-ear	roestone	footmark
monotony	soapless	door-case	botryoid	dog's-meat	rot-stone	postmark
nomology	box-pleat	poor-rate	fourfold	forspent	top-stone	softback
nosology	compleat	kourbash	sour-cold	boastful	zoospore	boattail
podology	complect	doornail	botryose	houseful	forsooth	contrail
pomology	soap-test	four-ball	foursome	noiseful	non-stock	football
posology	compages	four-part	hourlong	horsefly	forsworn	footfall
tocology	complied	pot-roast	moorcock	house-fly	voussoir	moot-hall
tokology	complice	horrible	moorfowl	goosegob	couscous	softball
topology	compline	poor's-box	poor-john	goosegog	kouskous	mortmain
coloured	comprise	horribly	doorpost	hoosegow	hot-short	root-hair
honoured	co-optive	worricow	four-foot	kok-sagyz	dog's-body	bootlast
coco-tree	loop-line	worrycow	moor-pout	conspire	sob-story	contract
hologram	morphine	porridge	bourtree	solstice	zooscopy	contrast
logogram	porpoise	corridor	touristy	boasting	gossypol	portlast
monogram	zoophile	forrader	Socratic	coasting	gossipry	portrait
nomogram	coupling	joy-rider	doorstep	hoisting	tonsured	root-fast
tomogram	soap-dish	court-day	tournure	housling	conserve	contrary
honourer	co-option	horridly	sourpuss	roasting	construe	costmary
mobocrat	Pompeian	hoarhead	borrowed	roisting	coistrel	mortuary
monocrat	sorption	hog-reeve	sorrowed	roysting	coistril	noctuary
tomorrow	complier	four-leaf	borrower	toasting	coystrel	loo-table
colossal	comprint	yourself	sorrower	god-smith	coystril	mootable
colossus	compiler	doorbell	sour-eyed	forswink	moss-crop	portable
molossus	cow-pilot	bourgeon	four-eyes	joy-stick	bowsprit	sortable
joyously	top-proud	fourteen	moussaka	mopstick	souse-tub	bontebok
holoptic	loophole	dourness	mossland	pot-stick	corseted	cottabus
Holostei	soap-work	poorness	constate	bonspiel	cosseted	kottabos
monohull	poppy-oil	sourness	dog'sbane	pot-still	fossette	post-obit
sonobuoy	soap-root	sorriest	log-slate	Volscian	noisette	monticle
motorway	soapwort	coarsely	moss-hagg	moistify	housetop	postiche
gonocyte	soap-tree	courtesy	toiseach	forsaken	moisture	soutache
holotype	corporal	hoarsely	forslack	mousekin	sob-stuff	cortical
homodyne	zooperal	sobriety	fox-shark	consoler	low-slung	poetical
homotype	copperas	horrific	hog's-back	consular	forswunk	vortical
logotype	corporas	mournful	moss-back	tonsilar	Fosseway	cortices
monotype	non-party	non-rigid	borstall	corselet	hoistway	vortices
homonymy	composed	lorry-hop	coxswain	moss-flow	horseway	hotted-up
homotypy	compesce	fourthly	bobstays	dorsally	powsowdy	rootedly
monogyny	porpesse	coercive	constant	consommé	boss-eyed	bolt-head
toponymy	composer	sourdine	forswatt	Comsomol	coat-card	goatherd
Zoophaga	hospitia	to-bruise	possible	Komsomol	portland	goatweed
tow-plane	not-pated	boarding	loose-box	hoastman	postcard	goutweed
volplane	compital	coursing	horse-boy	hoistman	post-paid	jolthead
soap-bark	hospital	courting	houseboy	horseman	boatrace	mort-head
soap-ball	computer	mourning	possibly	houseman	bootlace	nowt-herd
complain	zoopathy	worrying	goose-cap	Norseman	contrate	softhead
cow-plant	compound	boarfish	horsecar	consumer	footpace	portière
pot-plant	jodphurs	coarsish	lop-sided	gossamer	footpage	fortieth
poppadum	soap-suds	poortith	house-dog	consumpt	foot-race	boat-deck
hopped-up	Porphyra	sorryish	mouse-dun	nonsense	mortgage	mortbell
souped-up	Zoophyta	door-sill	consider	loosener	mort-safe	soft-sell

northern	moot-hill	zootrope	vortexes	solvency	cony-wool	apically
southern	post-mill	boat-song	copulate	louvered	polyzoan	epically
footgear	voltaism	dogtooth	lobulate	converge	polyzoon	spaceman
footwear	worthies	goat-moth	loculate	converse	polypous	specimen
root-beer	contrist	boat-hook	modulate	pop-visit	hoky-poky	spicknel
bootless	fortuity	boot-hook	populace	corvette	polygony	Apocynum
coatless	port-winy	footwork	populate	convexed	polypody	spacious
doctress	worthily	koftwork	rosulate	convexly	polysomy	specious
fortress	bootikin	soft-boil	conurbia	conveyal	roly-poly	spectral
fostress	cootikin	footworn	Columbic	conveyer	polyuria	spectrum
portress	goatskin	poltroon	Columban	conveyor	polyarch	spicated
rootless	tortilla	post-horn	conurban	dog-weary	rosy-drop	epicotyl
softness	coutille	post-town	homuncle	forweary	polyaxon	spadices
sootless	footslog	soft-soap	corundum	cobwebby	polygyny	spadeful
wontless	portolan	goitrous	mocuddum	dog-whelk	foozling	upadaisy
footrest	Noctilio	porteous	jocundly	bobwheel	forzando	spadille
rout-seat	hosteler	porthors	rotundly	cog-wheel	colza-oil	spadillo
sortment	cost-plus	tortious	document	joy-wheel	douzeper	epidemic
mortific	soft-slow	tortuous	monument	cow-wheat	mozzetta	spademan
pontific	hostelry	footpost	co-author	dog-wheat	bozzetto	spadones
oathful	mortally	goutwort	roburite	box-wagon	bouzouki	spadroon
mouthful	zootomic	hoot-toot	solutive	bob-white	appanage	epidural
soothful	bottomed	hout-tout	focusing	non-white	uplander	apodosis
toothful	costumed	poltfoot	hocusing	toywoman	upwardly	epidotic
worthful	Northman	zootypic	botulism	forwards	apparent	speed-cop
youthful	costumer	southpaw	populism	godwards	spragged	splendid
pontifex	contempt	boutique	locution	forwaste	sprangle	splendor
cottaged	continua	montaria	non-union	dog-watch	spray-gun	spreader
portague	fortuned	dog-tired	solution	pomwater	upcaught	appendix
portigue	boutonné	tottered	volution	Norweyan	splasher	ephemera
Portugee	continue	boottree	roturier	co-extend	upgather	appetent
cottager	fontange	cost-free	populist	polygala	aphasiac	speedful
soft-shoe	portance	goat's-rue	volumist	holydame	aphanite	aphetise
poetship	sortance	nocturne	coquilla	polymath	optative	appetise
nostwhat	bostangi	post-free	nonuplet	pony-tail	speaking	appetite
contline	fontanel	doctoral	columned	corybant	upmaking	spaewife
contrite	contango	dotterel	columnal	polygamy	apiarian	speeding
contrive	continuo	postural	columnar	polypary	apiarist	splenial
doctrine	softener	southron	volutoid	polyacid	sprackle	apterium
port-fire	tontiner	contorno	nodulose	molybdic	up-market	splenium
portoise	root-knot	root-crop	torulose	polygene	appalled	aphelian
port-wine	don't-know	fosterer	nodulous	polyseme	sprawler	aphelion
post-time	moltenly	loiterer	populous	polygeny	spearman	Ephesian
ortoise	rottenly	mouterer	locutory	polymery	Sphagnum	spherics
ootling	boat-load	posturer	hocussed	polysemy	upraised	splenius
goatling	coltwood	potterer	mofussil	coryphee	aplastic	speedily
ostling	foothold	torturer	coquette	polyphon	sprattle	sphenoid
oathing	post-road	totterer	locustae	iodyrite	splatter	spheroid
mortling	roothold	doctorly	moquette	polypide	epiblast	apterous
mottling	softwood	porterly	roquette	polypine	speciate	upreared
non-thing	bolthole	souterly	loquitur	polypite	spectate	appearer
northing	bolt-rope	portesse	coquetry	pony-skin	spiccato	après-ski
softling	boothose	cortisol	robustly	polyglot	space-bar	spreathe
soothing	footnote	soothsay	solvable	Polymnia	spice-box	spreethe
southing	foot-rope	southsay	Corvidae	polyonym	epicycle	upsetter
ortyish	footsore	costated	convolve	polyzoic	epicedia	appestat
goat-fish	porthole	footstep	convulse	copyhold	specific	spherule
monteith	Postcode	aortitis	volvulus	cotyloid	speckled	upheaval
bootlick	post-hole	footrule	convince	holy-rood	speculum	speedway
dog-trick	postpone	posttool	Corvinae	polypoid	spiculum	epifocal
orthink	soft-core	footmuff	convener	polysome	specular	opificer
boatbill	zoetrope	foot-pump	convenor	bodywork	spicular	spiffing
oothill	zoothome	zootoxin	souvenir	copybook	epicalyx	spoffish

apograph	spalpeen	open-door	spur-gear	epistyle	squamose	preacher
epigraph	spelaean	spandrel	spurless	epithema	squamous	treacher
spyglass	spellful	spandril	aperient	spot-weld	squab-pie	wreather
apogaeic	apologia	epinosic	sparsely	apothegm	squadron	Arianise
epigaeal	epilogic	Upanisad	sportful	upstream	squarson	Aryanise
epigaean	apologue	epinasty	Spirifer	spotless	squatted	creatine
apagogic	epilogue	spinette	spark-gap	sputtery	squattle	creative
epagogic	apolline	spinster	opera-hat	spiteful	squatter	kreatine
Spigelia	applying	spansule	appraise	spitcher	squamula	organise
epigamic	spelding	open-eyed	sportive	epitrite	squamule	treatise
epigones	spelling	up-to-date	sparling	spit-fire	aqualung	urbanise
epigeous	spilling	splotchy	sparring	spitting	squelchy	urbanite
spageric	epyllion	upholder	sperling	spotting	squeegee	arcading
spagiric	spelikin	opponent	sporting	upstairs	squeaker	breaking
spagyric	spilikin	spoofery	spurling	spottily	squealer	croaking
upthrust	opulence	spookery	spurning	spatular	aqueduct	dreaming
apricate	apple-pie	spoon-fed	spurring	epitomic	squeezer	drearing
oppilate	epilepsy	spoonful	sparkish	epitonic	equipage	groaning
optimate	appliqué	aphorise	spur-rial	spathose	squirage	treading
speisade	speldrin	apposite	spurrier	upstroke	equitant	treating
spoilage	opalised	epsomite	sparsity	spittoon	squireen	broadish
opsimath	epulotic	opposite	sportily	aphthous	squiress	freakish
spritely	spilitic	opposing	spirilla	epitasis	squirely	triaxial
spoilful	epilator	spooming	sparkler	apatetic	squiffer	Arianism
sphingid	applause	spookish	sporular	spit-curl	squiggle	ordalium
sprigged	spillway	aphorism	sparklet	spousage	squilgee	organism
springle	Apollyon	opsonium	spirally	sprucely	squiggly	priapism
springal	spy-money	aphorist	sperm-oil	appuying	aquiline	trialism
springer	epimeric	spookily	spermous	upturned	equinity	Arcadian
sphinges	apomixis	spoonily	spurious	oppugner	equivoke	creation
uppishly	spondaic	uplocked	operetta	aplustre	equipped	Croatian
aphicide	Spaniard	sprocket	apyretic	splutter	squirrel	Graafian
optimise	spendall	upfollow	operatic	upcurved	squinter	Orcadian
uprising	spun-yarn	apron-man	spirated	spivvery	squirter	ordalian
Aprilish	open-cast	Epyornis	spirited	spavined	breakage	arbalist
Ophitism	openable	aphonous	aperitif	spawning	preamble	arcanist
optimism	opinable	optology	operator	spryness	cream-bun	organist
aphidian	opinicus	sprouted	spiritus	sphygmic	triarchy	triadist
Aprilian	epanodos	uprootal	opercula	sphygmus	organdie	trialist
ophidian	openness	uprooter	Spergula	Squamata	trial-day	creakily
optician	spanless	upsprang	aperture	aquacade	arrasene	croakily
optimist	spinneys	Epiphany	approval	squamate	Briarean	dreamily
sprinkle	spintext	epopoeia	approver	squabash	Priapean	drearily
optional	spinnery	apoplexy	upgrowth	aquanaut	arbalest	greasily
split-new	spinifex	upspring	apyrexia	squabble	armament	organity
ypsiloid	apanaged	epipolic	spur-ryal	squander	ornament	triality
apricock	up-anchor	opopanax	Sporozoa	squarely	arcanely	urbanity
ophiurid	spanking	epiploic	apprizer	squasher	creamery	break-jaw
ophiuran	spanning	epiploon	apostate	equalise	dreamery	breaskit
splitted	spending	upsprung	apostasy	squaring	ornately	treadler
uplifted	spinning	apophyge	episodic	squarish	urbanely	orgasmic
uptilted	sponsing	epiphyte	episodal	aquarium	dreadful	Armagnac
splinter	sponsion	opaquely	episperm	aquarian	dreamful	ordainer
splitter	spinnies	approach	epistler	equation	freakful	breadnut
sprinter	spongily	spar-hawk	episemon	Aquarius	gronful	cream-nut
uplifter	spangled	spur-gall	episcope	aquarist	wreakful	ergatoid
aptitude	open-plan	spermary	epispore	aquatint	triangle	creasote
spuilzie	spangler	operable	apospory	equality	arraught	kreasote
spikelet	spanglet	sparable	episcopy	squawker	breathed	break-out
spike-oil	spongoid	spiracle	upas-tree	equalled	wreathed	freak-out
spekboom	span-roof	sporidia	apositia	squailer	wreathen	creatrix
spillage	span-long	sporadic	opuscula	squaller	breather	Triassic
spoliate	spontoon	Sparidae	opuscule	squawman	broacher	triapsal

orgastic	tracheae	precinct	brideman	Graecism	pro-forma	triglyph
breasted	bracteal	procinct	credenda	Armenian	triforia	prohibit
errantly	tracheal	trachoma	credenza	Artesian	profuser	orthicon
errantry	dry-clean	trichoid	credence	Friesian	profiter	orthodox
truantry	crackers	trichord	prudence	pre-exist	profound	Archaean
armature	crockery	trochoid	uredines	prie-dieu	drift-way	archaeus
creature	trickery	urochord	prodrome	breezily	bregmata	archness
treasure	graceful	fructose	trade-off	free-city	trigraph	orthoepy
treasury	wrackful	trichome	prodromi	greedily	braggart	archaise
break-vow	wreckful	broccoli	gridlock	tree-lily	cragfast	archwise
broadway	crucifer	gracioso	gridiron	orsellic	fragrant	prehnite
cribbage	crucifix	araceous	gradatim	orielled	pregnant	archaism
cribrate	trichina	croceous	creditor	orseille	tragical	archaist
trabeate	crocoite	gracious	predator	urceolus	frigidly	orchella
tribrach	erectile	precious	proditor	greenlet	preggers	orchilla
crab-yaws	erective	crackpot	traditor	freedman	progress	prehuman
dry-bible	practice	precepit	free-hand	Armenoid	trigness	arch-poet
probable	practise	tric-trac	arsenate	freehold	fragment	orthopod
probably	practive	brick-red	tree-calf	freeload	froggery	orchitic
drabness	procaine	precurse	free-fall	argemone	groggery	orthotic
crablike	proclive	tricorne	treenail	arsehole	priggery	orchitis
crabwise	tractile	brockram	artefact	gruesome	grog-shop	archduke
cribbing	tractive	procurer	brief-bag	true-love	drag-shot	archlute
drubbing	trichite	tractrix	green-bag	free-soil	dragline	try-house
grabbing	trochite	dricksie	friended	freeborn	bragging	archival
grubbing	bricking	brick-tea	Greekdom	true-born	briguing	ordinand
drabbish	cracking	price-tag	friendly	grievous	dragging	drainage
grub-kick	frocking	brocatel	free-reed	tree-moss	drugging	fruitage
cribella	pricking	Cricetus	tree-fern	free-cost	frigging	grainage
cribbled	tracking	brochure	freeze-up	free-port	frogling	irrigate
drabbler	tricking	fracture	freeness	true-bred	prigging	irritate
dribbler	trucking	preclude	treeless	greegree	frogfish	ordinate
fribbler	wrecking	trackway	trueness	tree-frog	priggish	urticate
dribblet	brackish	trachyte	praefect	oriented	priggism	arm-in-arm
tribally	trickish	graduand	pre-elect	arrestee	proggins	artifact
tribunal	trochisk	bride-ale	greenery	oriental	druggist	irritant
crab-wood	brachial	eradiate	griefful	arrester	Erdgeist	ordinant
cribrose	erection	graduate	greenfly	arrestor	wrigglor	urticant
cribwork	fraction	bride-bed	arpeggio	Argestes	frugally	ordinary
frabjous	friction	credible	breeched	ardently	cragsman	fruit-bud
crab-tree	traction	gradable	triethyl	priestly	dragoman	fruit-bat
tribasic	fructify	credibly	treeship	urgently	dragsman	Druidess
drabette	trickily	tridacna	breeches	driftage	Trigynia	orpiment
tributer	crackjaw	producer	free-shot	draft-bar	erogenic	broidery
orichalc	trochlea	traducer	arsenide	trifocal	orogenic	fruitery
trochaic	freckled	aridness	arsenite	urnfield	trigonic	fruitful
braccate	oracular	gradient	Graecise	drift-ice	dragonné	fruit-fly
croceate	tricolor	drudgery	tree-line	crofting	original	erringly
cruciate	bracelet	prideful	breeding	grafting	trigonal	pryingly
eructate	bractlet	tradeful	briefing	trifling	origanum	tryingly
trackage	tricklet	prodigal	creeping	draffish	dragonet	ornithic
tractate	drachmae	Bradshaw	freezing	gruffish	dry-goods	graithly
truckage	drachmai	bridging	greening	graffiti	oragious	prairied
wreckage	trackman	cradling	greesing	graffito	tragopan	arginine
proclaim	truchman	grudging	greeting	greffier	frog-spit	artifice
armchair	truckman	prodding	ordering	craftily	Fragaria	fruitive
crucible	drachmas	trudging	Friesish	truffled	progeria	troilite
brickbat	draconic	drudgism	Greekish	profiler	erigeron	braiding
tricycle	arachnid	brodekin	greenish	artfully	brighten	bruising
brocaded	brick-nog	predella	arterial	irefully	frighten	fruiting
Dracaena	cracknel	tredille	free-will	profaner	dragster	graining
tracheid	trecento	gridelin	praedial	drift-net	brightly	groining
preceese	areca-nut	urodelan	proemial	driftpin	drag-hunt	praising

training	uralitic	krameria	princely	iron-clay	Triodion	drop-kick
brainish	prolixly	trimeric	frank-fee	brinkman	cryonics	graphium
frailish	drammach	cremorne	prankful	frontman	arborist	eruption
prairial	crummack	cromorne	trunkful	transmit	armorist	graphics
Braidism	trumeaux	gramarye	wrongful	transmew	arsonist	dry-point
druidism	dromical	premorse	transfer	ordnance	errorist	pre-print
troilism	bromidic	Trimurti	transfix	brand-new	droopily	Trappist
Arminian	premedic	trimaran	crane-fly	ironwood	priority	propylic
fruition	drumhead	gramercy	branchia	frondose	brooklet	propylon
irrision	première	premised	bronchia	iron-mole	creosote	trippler
Orbilius	cromlech	promisee	branched	ironwork	kreosote	propolis
vraicker	gromwell	promiser	prong-hoe	princock	arborous	drupelet
articled	Aramaean	promisor	tranship	frontoon	creodont	tripeman
trail-net	brimless	premises	brancher	araneous	bryology	araponga
Arvicola	grimness	frame-saw	drencher	wrongous	oreology	arapunga
pruinose	grumness	kromesky	trencher	print-out	arboured	crepance
train-oil	primness	aromatic	bronchus	brine-pan	armoured	prepense
irrisory	trimness	dramatic	Araneida	brine-pit	ergogram	propense
brainpan	drumbeat	eremitic	brandied	Arenaria	cryotron	triploid
arbitral	trumpery	primatic	crannied	dry-nurse	groo-groo	triphone
artistic	crimeful	trematic	frenzied	print-run	armourer	triptote
truistic	grumphie	prompted	brandise	iron-gray	cryostat	trap-rock
frailtee	dram-shop	eremital	bronzite	iron-grey	dry-plate	trip-hook
Orvietan	Brumaire	primatal	iron-mine	prenasal	prophase	drop-goal
artistry	drumfire	prometal	Ironside	grandson	triplane	trap-door
bruilzie	Frimaire	gram-atom	prentice	frenetic	triptane	drop-wort
prejudge	grimoire	tram-stop	transire	granitic	wrappage	prop-root
frijoles	tram-line	cremator	bringing	uranitic	kreplach	troparia
trekking	brimming	promoter	bronzing	crenated	gripsack	prepared
brokenly	cramming	promotor	cringing	crinated	trap-ball	preparer
brake-van	drumming	prompter	drinking	brunette	trap-fall	properly
arillate	primming	trimeter	grinding	prenatal	trippant	property
grillade	trimming	fremitus	grinning	pronotal	tropical	proposal
grillage	drumfish	Primates	grunting	pronotum	tripedal	proposer
arillary	frumpish	promptly	prancing	pronator	tripodal	crepitus
trilobed	Aramaism	brim-full	pranking	urinator	drip-feed	propound
preludio	cramoisy	cram-full	printing	transude	grapheme	cropfuls
drollery	grumpily	primeval	trunking	transume	trappean	wrapover
prolific	bromelia	Craniata	wringing	tranquil	frippery	triptych
urologic	Tremella	brancard	brandish	areolate	prophecy	prophyll
prologue	crumpled	drunkard	Frankish	arrogate	prophesy	trapezia
arc-light	promulge	iron-sand	prankish	priorate	trophesy	truquage
Araldite®	frampler	frondage	iron-sick	argonaut	drop-shot	truqueur
drilling	grumbler	frontage	prandial	arrogant	arapaima	frequent
drolling	premolar	ironware	eryngium	preorder	dropsied	prurient
frilling	trampler	truncate	francium	arboreta	trophied	prorogue
grilling	trembler	bran-mash	Orangism	arboreal	drop-ripe	pruritic
trilling	primally	ironbark	trunnion	armozeen	dropwise	pruritus
trolling	criminal	iron-mail	frontier	prioress	eruptive	brassard
drollish	crumenal	transact	bronzify	cryogeny	graphite	aristate
trillium	fromenty	irenical	crankily	armozine	trephine	crispate
orillion	frumenty	ironical	Brunella	arsonite	trip-wire	cristate
trillion	frampold	irenicon	prunella	brookite	cropping	crustate
frillies	tram-road	granddad	brindled	cryolite	dripping	dressage
trilemma	primrose	Aranidae	gruntled	ergotise	dropping	dry-stane
prolamin	trombone	frondeur	iron-clad	trioxide	gripping	frescade
prolonge	crummock	grandeur	wrinkled	crooning	propping	ore-stare
arillode	drammock	princess	prunelle	drooking	trapping	prostate
gralloch	drummock	frondent	franklin	proofing	tripling	trespass
trollopy	crumhorn	transect	prunello	armorial	tripping	brassart
prolapse	krumhorn	transept	granular	troopial	wrapping	grossart
breloque	primrosy	grindery	wrangler	ergotism	cropsick	press-bed
prelatic	cromorna	orangery	frontlet	creolian		erasable

cross-bun	trashily	erythema	protasis	provoker	prizable	asperges
crossbar	trustily	frotteur	erotetic	trivalve	cruzeiro	ushering
crossbow	Griselda	oratress	protatic	gravelly	grizzled	asterisk
grass-box	bristled	frothery	protrude	trevally	grizzler	especial
press-box	wrestler	grateful	prothyle	gravamen	prize-man	asterism
trash-can	crosslet	trothful	protozoa	province	Brezonek	Essenism
crosscut	wristlet	truthful	brouhaha	cravenly	trizonal	Asterias
presidia	trisemic	wrathful	traumata	previous	brazenly	asperity
prosodic	trisomic	froth-fly	croupade	traverse	brazenry	esterify
presidio	Erysimum	protégée	groupage	crevasse	escalade	esteemed
crusader	freshman	crotched	arguable	provisor	escalate	islesman
triskele	Irishman	crutched	arquebus	travesty	escapade	asteroid
urostege	pressman	wretched	arguably	breveted	estacade	asperous
grosbeak	proseman	britches	trouncer	graviton	escalado	assessor
ark-shell	presumer	cratches	grounded	gravitas	escapado	asbestic
Brussels	presence	bratchet	grounden	grave-wax	estancia	assenter
trossers	prisoner	crotchet	grounder	driveway	islander	assentor
crescent	fresh-new	brattice	trouvère	drawback	escargot	asserter
prospect	frescoed	brettice	fräulein	drawable	astatine	assertor
trashery	prismoid	trotline	trouveur	crown-cap	Islamise	asbestos
friskful	dry-stone	bratling	trousers	draw-well	Islamite	osteitis
pressful	dry-stove	fretting	argument	draw-gear	ashaming	usefully
tristful	iriscope	fritting	argutely	browless	assaying	usufruct
trustful	brush-off	trotting	crousely	browbeat	essaying	isagogic
pressfat	grass-oil	writhing	fraudful	growlery	essayish	isogamic
presager	frescoer	brattish	troutful	brow-tine	escapism	isogonic
groschen	bristols	erethism	trauchle	erewhile	Islamism	isogonal
crush-hat	frescoes	frothily	brougham	brawling	ossarium	isogloss
brassica	griseous	gratuity	draughty	browning	espalier	asphodel
prescind	uroscopy	prettify	droughty	browsing	escapist	isthmian
crescive	crashpad	prettily	Ursuline	crawling	essayist	eschalot
prestige	wrest-pin	wrathily	drouking	crowning	escallop	ischemia
pristine	wrist-pin	writhled	grouping	drowning	escalope	ischemic
brisling	cross-ply	crotalum	grouting	frowning	escarole	asthenia
brushing	cross-rib	prattler	trouting	growling	assassin	asthenic
crashing	preserve	Crotalus	proudish	prowling	osnaburg	ischuria
crossing	fresh-run	brutally	troupial	trawling	isabella	esthetic
crushing	grisgris	prytanea	Freudian	brownish	ash-blond	asphyxia
dressing	cross-row	tritonia	croupier	crawfish	isobront	aspirate
frisking	irisated	protonic	groupist	crow-bill	isobaric	estimate
frosting	cross-tie	cretonne	triunity	Brownism	isochasm	oscitate
grasping	dress-tie	pretence	troubled	Brownian	isocracy	ostinato
grassing	grisette	protense	troubler	Brownist	isocheim	Ustilago
gressing	frustule	write-off	troutlet	crownlet	isochime	aspirant
pressing	pressure	fretwork	croupous	trewsman	isocline	oscitant
trussing	tressure	grattoir	ordurous	trawl-net	psychism	espiègle
trusting	crossway	trottoir	orgulous	crowfoot	C-section	ossified
briskish	presbyte	trot-cozy	trout-rod	frowards	psychics	oscinine
crossish	prostyle	critique	frou-frou	crown-saw	psychist	aspiring
freshish	urostyle	pratique	triumvir	brewster	psychoid	ascidium
tristich	frottage	criteria	creutzer	frowster	isochore	aspidium
Irishism	protease	ureteric	kreutzer	draw-tube	isocryme	ascidian
prosaism	tritiate	urethrae	breviate	wraxling	isodicon	astigmia
Erastian	urethane	ureteral	proviant	proximal	isodomum	Ossianic
pression	pratfall	urethral	breviary	Fraxinus	isodomon	assignee
Prussian	protract	brethren	provable	greyness	asperate	assiento
trustier	writable	oratorio	provably	argyrite	osier-bed	assignor
prosaist	critical	Arcturus	provided	trey-tine	assemblé	assignat
brassily	erotical	preterit	provedor	grayling	assemble	assisted
crustily	protocol	britzska	provider	crayfish	assembly	ash-leach
friskily	tritical	Protista	providor	grey-fish	ascender	isolable
frostily	Triticum	bretesse	bravados	grey-coat	usheress	psaltery
Prussify	frutices	erotesis	crivvens	grey-eyed	asperger	isologue

psellism	issuable	Atlantis	etherise	striving	stem-form	attorney
psalmist	issuably	stealthy	atheling	Atticism	atomiser	atropous
psalmody	esculent	straitly	steeling	ethicism	stomatic	atmology
psilosis	astutely	stub-nail	steening	stoicism	stomatal	ethology
psilotic	pseudery	stibnite	steering	ethicist	stembuck	stropped
Psilotum	assuming	stabbing	steeving	strickle	stanzaic	strontia
isolator	astucity	stabling	strewing	strinkle	standard	atmolyse
psammite	Esquimau	stubbing	uttering	stricken	stinkard	stepdame
isomeric	issuance	stablish	steepish	strigose	stunkard	stephane
isomorph	Assyrian	stubbled	etherial	Strigops	stannate	stoppage
isometry	ashy-grey	stibbler	etherism	Ethiopic	stunsail	stuprate
isonomic	stearate	stubborn	Athenian	stripped	stannary	stop-bath
Isengrim	stravaig	stoccata	etherion	stripper	stone-bow	utopiast
assonate	stramash	stockade	etherist	stair-rod	ethnical	atypical
assonant	athanasy	staccato	strelitz	striated	stone-fly	etypical
ascorbic	steam-car	sticcado	streaked	striatum	stanchel	stupidly
Asmodeus	straicht	sticcato	streaker	strictly	stancher	stopless
essonite	straucht	stoccado	steepled	attitude	stanchly	stepwise
astonish	stranded	stickful	streamer	utriculi	stannite	stepping
Estonian	straddle	stacking	atheroma	stairway	standing	stopping
essoiner	atrament	sticking	athetoid	stake-net	stinging	stapelia
astomous	strategy	stocking	steel-pen	stallage	stinking	stippled
estopped	straggle	stockish	attemper	stellate	stinting	stipuled
estoppel	strangle	stockist	stressed	stillage	stunning	stippler
espousal	stranger	stickily	attested	stalwart	standish	stipular
espouser	straight	stockily	streeted	stolidly	Stundism	stop-cock
assorted	straught	stickjaw	streltzi	stilbene	Stundist	step-down
assotted	straggly	stick-lac	attester	stall-fed	stingily	stipites
assorter	attached	stickler	attestor	stalagma	stuntman	stop-over
aseptate	straw-hat	stockman	Strepyan	stilbite	stanhope	staphyle
ash-plant	steadied	stuccoed	staffage	stalking	stand-off	star-pav'd
isopodan	Ottamite	stuccoer	stiff-bit	stalling	stenlock	star-gaze
Isoptera	ptyalise	stock-pot	stifling	stilling	stone-oil	sternage
isoprene	stearine	stud-farm	stuffing	stilting	stentour	storable
isopleth	steatite	studding	stiffish	stiltish	stannous	star-read
psephite	steading	studying	stuffily	stallion	stink-pot	sturgeon
psephism	stealing	stodgily	stigmata	stellion	stone-pit	starkers
ostracod	steaming	stud-book	staggard	stillion	stone-rag	starless
ostracon	steaning	studwork	stagnate	stellify	ethnarch	stirless
estridge	straying	studious	stagnant	stultify	stone-raw	startful
esurient	ptyalism	stud-bolt	stage-box	stallman	sting-ray	stormful
astragal	strabism	steerage	stegodon	Atalanta	stenosed	pterygia
ostreger	ottavino	strewage	stag-head	Italiote	stenosis	sterigma
usurping	steadier	ytterbia	staghorn	utiliser	stenotic	staragen
ostrakon	stradiot	atremble	stag-hunt	ptilosis	stromata	starched
astringe	steadily	steenbok	itchweed	athletic	etiolate	starcher
estrange	steamily	steelbow	itch-mite	stiletto	strombus	sturdied
usurious	stratify	attercop	Stahlism	stemmata	stroddle	eternise
espresso	attacker	ethercap	Stahlian	stumpage	stronger	starlike
tsaritsa	strammel	ettercap	strigate	atomical	strongly	sternite
tsarevna	strained	stretchy	striddle	stomachy	strophic	sturnine
ash-stand	straunge	attender	stridden	stampede	strobila	starling
isostasy	strainer	ethereal	strident	stampedo	atropine	starring
asystole	steatoma	steepe-up	stringed	stemless	Ottomite	starting
isospory	stratose	strepent	stringer	ptomaine	strobile	starving
isothere	strap-oil	utterest	Atticise	stamping	stooping	sterling
isotherm	stratous	steevely	ethicise	stemming	stroking	stirring
isotonic	strapped	stievely	strigine	stumming	strowing	storming
isotropy	strapper	strength	attiring	stumpily	strobili	Storting
isotopic	Atlantic	Strephon	staining	stumbler	atropism	storying
esoteric	steam-tug	Atherina	steining	stimulus	atrocity	starfish
osculate	straiten	atherine	striking	stamened	otiosity	startish
osculant	Atlantes	athetise	striping	staminal	stroller	eternity

8 ⊔u⊔e⊔t

starrily	rutabaga	fusarole	rumbelow	mutchkin	quiddity	tuneless
stormily	pupa-case	ducatoon	tunbelly	curculio	quiddler	suberect
sturdily	runagate	hula-hoop	turbaned	furcular	guidance	dukeship
startled	Gujarati	runabout	turbined	muscular	outdance	superhet
pterylae	Judaical	curatory	turbinal	surculus	duodenal	tumefied
startler	autarchy	fumatory	turbines	buncombe	nundinal	euxenite
iterance	muqaddam	juratory	curb-roof	Dutchman	duodenum	gudesire
sturnoid	mutandum	mutatory	nut-brown	Dutchmen	pundonor	juvenile
star-nose	subahdar	nugatory	cumbrous	Turcoman	puddingy	Puseyite
stereome	Musaceae	sudatory	cumbered	dulcimer	suddenly	queenite
yttrious	Rutaceae	eupatrid	cumberer	Dulcinea	suddenty	quietive
starwort	Sudanese	subacrid	lumberer	Puccinia	quadroon	suberise
pteropod	subagent	Muharram	numberer	succinic	outdoors	sure-fire
starspot	humanely	Muharrem	outburst	vulcanic	sun-drops	yuletide
star-trap	sugar-gum	curatrix	sunburnt	Buccinum	subduple	dukeling
starosta	eulachon	Jurassic	sunburst	succinum	sundered	queening
sternson	oulachon	Rumansch	Burberry	succinct	murderer	quieting
starosty	putamina	Judaiser	lubberly	bum-clock	sunderer	queerish
uteritis	sudamina	curassow	lumberly	putchock	cul-de-sac	eugenism
star-turn	bubaline	cunabula	mulberry	luscious	outdated	eumerism
star-dust	curarine	hula-hula	surbased	outcross	suedette	lutecium
sternway	curarise	cubature	subbasal	sun-cured	punditry	lutetium
ataraxia	curative	subacute	rubbishy	cup-coral	quidnunc	Puseyism
ataraxic	eutaxite	punaluan	surbated	subcosta	dun-diver	quietism
storeyed	humanise	eucaryon	sunbathe	outcaste	superadd	aurelian
stasimon	mutative	eukaryon	outbound	quickset	fuselage	Eusebian
otoscope	putative	eucalypt	dulciana	furcated	gude-dame	Lutetian
statuary	ruralise	eucaryot	Furcraea	sulcated	numerate	Sumerian
statable	sugaring	eukaryot	fulcrate	dulcitol	pucelage	superior
statical	tuna-fish	rubaiyat	punctate	muscatel	suberate	eugenics
statedly	puparial	cupboard	purchase	juncture	superate	eugenist
stitched	humanism	outboard	surcease	punctule	tutelage	lutcnist
stitcher	puparium	dumb-cane	sun-crack	puncture	Gujerati	quietist
stetting	ruralism	hub-brake	pub-crawl	punctual	lukewarm	queerity
stotious	sudarium	outbrave	guacharo	Quechuan	suzerain	super-jet
statured	aularian	sunbeamy	lug-chair	Quichuan	funerary	aureoled
étatisme	duration	curbable	outclass	Guicowar	numeracy	cupelled
Etruscan	Eurasian	hubbuboo	subclass	gurdwara	numerary	luteolin
struggle	lunarian	Quebecer	runcible	quadrate	tutelary	rubellan
Struthio	lunation	turbocar	succubae	cub-drawn	queen-bee	nucellar
stoutish	luxation	turbidly	Mulciber	quadrans	tuneable	bucellas
Etrurian	mutation	outbreed	succubas	quadrant	auger-bit	nucellus
strummed	nudation	subbreed	succubus	quiddany	superbly	queenlet
strummel	nutarian	outbreak	Muscidae	fundable	tubercle	superman
strumose	nutation	dumb-bell	muscadel	guidable	Lupercal	supernal
strumous	pupation	curbless	suicidal	buddleia	pudendal	suberose
strumpet	Rumanian	dumbness	duncedom	outdwell	pudendum	tuberose
strutted	sudation	turbofan	muscadin	fundless	queendom	fusel-oil
strutter	Turanian	dumb-show	mud-clerk	sun-dress	queerdom	tube-worm
stived-up	humanist	purblind	hurcheon	ruddiest	funereal	numerous
stovaine	lunarist	sun-blind	luncheon	quadriga	tube-well	suberous
stowlins	lutanist	curbside	nuncheon	sun-dried	super-ego	tuberous
stewpond	ruralist	jumboise	puncheon	outdrive	mule-deer	tube-foot
stowdown	audacity	burbling	butcher's	bundling	muleteer	eudemony
stowaway	fugacity	humbling	butchery	fuddling	cureless	pure-bred
ethylate	furacity	mumbling	cutchery	hurdling	hugeness	dule-tree
stay-lace	humanity	rumbling	quackery	muddying	muteness	funebral
stay-tape	queasily	tumbling	bunching	puddling	nudeness	eupepsia
staysail	rurality	sun-blink	butching	ruddying	pureness	suversed
ethylene	autarkic	turbo-jet	muscling	outdrink	rudeness	cuneatic
stayless	autacoid	sun-baked	zucchini	Buddhism	ruleless	eupeptic
stay-down	humanoid	quibbler	function	sundries	sureness	eutectic
stay-bolt	fumarole	furbelow	junction	Buddhist	tubeless	pubertal

quaestor	lungeing	bush-rope	pulingly	auricula	quillaja	bully-off
supertax	outgoing	mushroom	punisher	furibund	full-face	nucleoli
nubecula	lung-fish	hush-boat	mulishly	pudibund	full-page	full-cock
quietude	dung-hill	cushiony	mutinied	rubicund	nuclease	bull-horn
subequal	hungrily	euphoria	purified	Punjabee	nucleate	hull-down
sufflate	quagmiry	Eutheria	auditive	cunjevoi	sublease	quill-pen
suffrage	bungalow	euphoric	culicine	junk-yard	bull-calf	bullfrog
outflash	pungence	out-Herod	cutinise	muck-rake	pull-back	bullyrag
outflank	subgenus	Lutheran	fugitive	buck-wash	full-sail	cullysim
puffball	burganet	duchesse	punitive	duck-hawk	outlearn	burletta
pug-faced	burgonet	fughetta	quailing	rucksack	nucleary	bulletin
surfaced	burgundy	zuchetta	mudirieh	duck-tail	gullable	furlough
surfacer	fulgency	Cushitic	judicial	musk-ball	gullible	turlough
gulfweed	pungency	Kushitic	musk-ball	buckcart	bully-boy	buplever
outfield	bung-hole	nuthatch	pugilism	musk-cavy	curlicue	pullover
bun-fight	mungoose	zuchetto	rubidium	lucky-bag	purlicue	outlawry
gunflint	dung-fork	bughouse	audition	lucky-dip	publican	dull-eyed
outfight	lung-book	mug-house	munition	bulkhead	publicly	full-eyed
puff-bird	mungcorn	nut-house	musician	duckweed	bullhead	gunlayer
surf-bird	subgroup	outhouse	punition	buckbean	bull's-eye	guimbard
outfling	lungwort	hush-hush	auxiliar	muck-heap	bull-beef	hummocky
purfling	Bulgaric	bush-buck	fusilier	musk-deer	fuel-cell	outmoded
ruffling	budgeree	push-pull	purifier	musk-pear	dullness	rummager
surf-fish	dungaree	push-over	nudities	duskness	fullness	nutmeggy
gunflint	puggaree	Tunicata	burinist	luckless	nullness	mummying
turf-clad	tung-tree	dubitate	luminist	sucklers	full-pelt	duumviri
ruefully	fulgural	fumigate	pugilist	tuskless	guileful	duumvirs
outfrown	budgerow	jubilate	cupidity	buckshee	full-aged	Gurmukhi
subfloor	hungerly	mucilage	futility	tuckahoe	duologue	gunmaker
buff-coat	vulgarly	muricate	humidify	junk-shop	sunlight	nummular
surf-boat	Tungusic	musicale	humidity	tuck-shop	bullshit	pulmonic
buffered	funguses	mutilate	humility	buckshot	full-time	summoner
furfural	Tunguses	pumicate	lucidity	duck-shot	nucleide	pulmones
furfurol	tungstic	pupilage	nubility	buckling	suilline	furmenty
furfuran	budgeted	pupilate	pudicity	duckling	building	turmeric
sufferer	tungsten	ruminate	tumidity	junk-ring	bull-ring	bummaree
dumfound	hung-over	supinate	tunicked	suckling	bullying	submerge
puff-puff	gurgoyle	suricate	musicker	duckbill	cullying	submerse
outflush	push-ball	tunicate	auricled	tuck-mill	duelling	outmarch
surf-duck	push-cart	sukiyaki	audience	puckfist	fuelling	dummerer
suffixal	bush-baby	nudicaul	julienne	buckskin	gull-wing	murmurer
kuffiyeh	euphrasy	subimago	tubicole	musk-plum	outlying	summerly
mud-guard	Dukhobor	fumigant	auriform	cuckoldy	qualming	surmisal
outguard	bushveld	jubilant	cubiform	Turkoman	quilling	surmiser
burgrave	lushness	luminant	fusiform	buskined	quilting	gummosis
outglare	muchness	ruminant	muriform	suckener	sullying	outmatch
nut-grass	ruthless	rutilant	nubiform	duck-pond	qualmish	gunmetal
dung-cart	suchness	tulipant	tubiform	duckmole	bullyism	luxmeter
burglary	Cuthbert	culinary	luminous	funkhole	duellist	summitry
huggable	euphuise	luminary	muticous	murksome	full-tilt	surmount
surgical	fuchsine	pupilary	mutinous	musk-rose	guiltily	quandang
ruggedly	fuchsite	dutiable	nubilous	muck-worm	sublimed	turnback
turgidly	push-bike	music-box	numinous	buckhorn	fugleman	quintain
dungmere	rush-like	guaiacum	auditory	bunkered	quillman	quandary
hung-beef	suchlike	fusileer	fumitory	suckered	quill-nib	ruinable
dung-heap	suchwise	mutineer	punitory	buckaroo	muslined	runnable
bung-vent	rush-ring	business	music-pen	quakerly	sublunar	sunn-hemp
judgment	euphuism	puniness	autistic	junketed	muslinet	burnt-ear
jugglery	euphuist	muniment	juristic	huckster	sullenly	quintett
surgeful	subhuman	rudiment	muriatic	musketry	bulldoze	outnight
quagmire	euphonia	futilely	puristic	muckluck	duelsome	bunny-hug
bungling	euphonic	supinely	Sufistic	musk-duck	nucleole	quencher
juggling	ruthenic	musingly	muriated	quillaia	bull-hoof	burnside
			quaintly			

Burnsite	dumosity	quippish	currying	nursling	ductless	guttural
huon-pine	fumosity	sumphish	hurrying	outswing	dustless	nurtural
quantise	gulosity	pulpmill	querying	pursuing	huntress	putter-on
quintile	mucosity	supplial	quirkish	questing	hurtless	multurer
turnpike	rugosity	puppyism	guardian	quisling	justness	mutterer
Burnsian	Jugoslav	gumphion	outreign	gunsmith	lustless	nurturer
quantify	Yugoslav	gumption	quarrier	ouistiti	rustless	kurtosis
quantity	suborner	subprior	quartier	gunstick	suitress	eustatic
dunnakin	Eurobond	supplier	guerilla	Russniak	furthest	guttated
turnskin	autosome	murphies	murrelet	question	quit-rent	subtitle
quenelle	humorous	outpoint	outremer	huissier	quotient	subtotal
euonymin	rumorous	sun-print	outrance	outskirt	subtlety	rum-ti-tum
euonymus	sudorous	lumpy-jaw	Quirinal	sunshiny	multifid	subtrude
turnsole	tumorous	suspense	Quirinus	pulsejet	multifil	cultivar
quandong	bunodont	tuppence	curranty	pulsojet	cultigen	cumulate
quantong	autology	rum-punch	currency	vulsella	dust-shot	cupulate
turncock	autonomy	lumpenly	guaranty	subsolar	buntline	jugulate
turn-down	autotomy	tuppenny	cupreous	subsonic	lustrine	lunulate
turncoat	ourology	pulpwood	muir-poot	nuisance	subtribe	subulate
turnspit	humoured	pump-hood	muir-pout	purse-net	wurtzite	tubulate
runner-up	rumourer	rump-bone	eutropic	cuss-word	hustling	tumulary
pug-nosed	autocrat	sulphone	outroper	outscold	lustring	suburbia
burnouse	autopsia	sunproof	quart-pot	gunstone	puttying	suburban
quincunx	Rumonsch	pump-room	eutrophy	mudstone	quitting	cucumber
turnover	autoptic	rump-post	bulrushy	rubstone	rustling	cucurbit
automata	culottes	mud-puppy	guernsey	sunstone	turtling	furuncle
cupolaed	tucotuco	purpuric	eucritic	puss-moth	outthink	luculent
autocade	tug-of-war	cutpurse	turreted	gunstock	Austrian	muculent
auto-da-fé	autodyne	purpurin	Quirites	outscorn	duettino	purulent
automate	autolyse	purposed	surround	outshoot	duettist	autunite
subovate	autotype	supposed	outrival	outsport	subtlist	Eugubine
tutorage	autogyro	supposal	surroyal	rum-shrub	subtrist	lupuline
Autobahn	sulphate	supposer	outstand	subshrub	multeity	queueing
autocarp	humpback	supposes	bud-scale	subserve	sultrily	futurism
autoharp	suppeago	pulpited	outstare	humstrum	cuitikin	futurist
Euromart	supplant	pulpitum	purslane	outstrip	outtaken	luxurist
autogamy	culpable	sumpitan	substage	cursores	pustular	futurity
cuboidal	culpably	pulpiter	sun-shade	cursitor	curtal-ax	Lucullic
fucoidal	puppy-dog	quipster	fuss-ball	pulsator	subtilly	Lucullan
suborder	cuspidal	pulpitry	purslain	bursitis	subtilty	mutually
humoresk	puppodum	puppetry	outsmart	numskull	Funtumia	Musulman
aurorean	puppydom	sulphury	puissant	cum-savvy	customed	autumnal
European	jumped-up	outpower	pursuant	substyle	huntsman	Huguenot
tutoress	cuspidor	musquash	questant	outsized	puntsman	cumulose
autogeny	subpoena	surquedy	suasible	subsizar	customer	rugulose
rugosely	pump-head	guardase	pussy-cat	cultrate	subtonic	tubulous
Kuroshio	pump-well	outreach	tussocky	lustrate	sultanic	susurrus
eulogise	rumpless	guardant	pulsidge	suit-case	subtense	Augustan
suboxide	suppress	surrebut	outsider	dust-bath	hustings	augustly
tutorise	jump-seat	curricle	cursedly	dust-ball	dust-hole	subucula
tutoring	puppy-fat	lubrical	outspeak	quatrain	punt-pole	durukuli
sutorial	supplied	rubrical	nutshell	dust-cart	dust-bowl	tucutuco
tutorial	cut-price	guéridon	outswell	subtract	lustrous	sucurujú
eulogium	outprize	outrider	mug-sheep	gustable	dust-coat	surucucu
europium	sulphide	putridly	outsleep	quotable	subtopia	outvoice
tutorism	sulphite	quartern	outswear	suitable	multiped	outvalue
Ausonian	surplice	nutrient	pulsific	quotably	multiple	pulville
Huronian	surprise	quartett	purseful	suitably	multiply	pulvilli
Junonian	tump-line	furriery	outsight	mustache	lustique	pulvilio
sutorian	dumpling	outright	burschen	rustical	Suctoria	outvenom
autogiro	lumpfish	quarried	outshine	justicer	cultured	pulvinar
eulogist	puppyish	murrhine	sunshine	buttress	quatorze	pulvinus
humorist	purplish	quartile	guessing	curtness	cultural	quivered

subverse	evolvent	overseen	overload	swabbing	twinkler	exhedrae
culverin	avulsion	overween	overlord	swobbing	swan-song	extensor
quaverer	evulsion	overkeep	oversold	twichild	twin-born	expected
sun-visor	evil-doer	overleap	overword	two-digit	swine-pox	exserted
curvated	uvularly	overbear	evermore	swaddler	swine-sty	exceptor
curveted	uvulitis	overhear	everyone	twaddler	twin-axis	expecter
curvital	ovenware	overpeer	ovariole	twiddler	swooning	expertly
outvoter	aventail	overseer	overcome	Swadeshi	two-piece	exigible
vulvitis	evenfall	overwear	overdone	Zwieback	swap-shop	exiguity
survival	evenness	overyear	overdose	sweet-bay	swapping	exogamic
survivor	evangely	overseas	overtone	tweezers	swopping	exigence
surveyal	eventful	averment	overwore	two-edged	twopence	exigency
kurveyor	oven-bird	overbeat	overlong	sweeping	twopenny	exiguous
purveyor	eventide	overheat	overbook	sweeting	sword-arm	exegesis
surveyor	evincive	overhent	overlook	sweetish	sword-cut	exegetic
outweary	avenging	overneat	overwork	sweep-net	swarming	exchange
outwrest	eventing	overwent	overboil	owreword	swerving	excitant
outweigh	ovenwood	aversely	over-cool	owrecome	dwarfish	expirant
outworth	evensong	overshoe	oversoul	sweet-oil	sword-law	expiable
outwards	even-down	overshot	overtoil	sweetpea	swordman	exciting
sunwards	evanesce	overkind	overworn	sweet-sop	owerloup	expiring
outwatch	eventual	overwind	overdoer	sweep-saw	two-sided	excision
cut-water	avionics	aversive	ovarious	two-faced	swastika	ex-libris
quixotic	oviposit	overbite	overcoat	Swiftian	swashing	expiator
quixotry	overhand	overfine	overpost	swiftlet	swishing	exultant
duty-paid	overlaid	overfire	overspin	owl-glass	swissing	axillary
butyrate	overland	overgive	overfree	Ewigkeit	twisting	explicit
ruby-tail	overlard	overlive	overarch	swagshop	two-score	excluded
jurymast	overhale	overnice	overcrop	swagsman	owl-train	exploded
butylene	overlade	override	overtrip	twigsome	twittery	exploder
busyness	overname	overripe	overbrow	two-horse	switchel	explorer
eurythmy	overpage	overside	overcrow	swaining	twitcher	exemplum
quayside	overrake	oversize	overdraw	swainish	swotting	examplar
eucyclic	overrate	overtime	overgrow	swelldom	twitting	exemplar
buoyance	overtake	overtire	overstep	twelvemo	twattler	examinee
buoyancy	overgang	overwise	ovaritis	owl-light	two-timer	examiner
busybody	overhang	averring	overstay	twilight	sway-back	eximious
duty-free	overrash	overking	overrule	swelchie	swayling	oxymoron
zugzwang	overwash	overwing	overture	dwelling	excavate	oximeter
fuzz-ball	overrack	overfish	overruff	swelling	exhalant	exanthem
quizzery	overrank	overfill	overhung	swilling	ox-warble	exponent
huzzaing	overtalk	overkill	overmuch	swellish	expander	ox-tongue
puzzling	overtask	aversion	overbulk	swell-mob	expandor	extolled
quizzing	overcall	eversion	overfull	swill-tub	execrate	axiology
quizzify	overfall	overlier	overburn	swimwear	exocrine	exhorter
subzonal	overgall	overview	overturn	swimming	exacting	exporter
pulza-oil	overhaul	overskip	overjump	swimsuit	exaction	exposure
aviation	oversail	over-club	overdust	swan-mark	executer	exoplasm
aviarist	overlain	overclad	overbusy	swanherd	executor	exophagy
aviatrix	overhair	overslip	overswim	swan-neck	executry	exequial
evacuate	overpass	overplus	everyway	swannery	oxidiser	exequies
evacuant	overcast	overblow	oversway	twinship	extended	exorable
evection	overmast	overflow	evasible	swan-shot	expender	Oxbridge
eviction	overpart	overcloy	svastika	swanlike	extender	extruder
evadable	overpast	overplay	evitable	awanting	expedite	extrados
oviducal	everyday	Everyman	kvetcher	swanking	exterior	exercise
evidence	overfeed	oversman	avowable	swinging	ox-pecker	exertive
avadavat	overhead	overknee	avowedly	twanging	excelled	exorcise
avifauna	overread	ivory-nut	a-weather	twinling	expelled	exordial
availing	overleaf	overbold	awearied	twinning	expellee	exorcism
evaluate	oversell	overfold	swealing	swingism	external	exordium
evulgate	overveil	overfond	swearing	swan-skin	externat	exertion
evilness	overteem	overhold	sweating	swindler	axle-tree	exorcist

extremer	syndesis	pyxidium	hypogene	tympanum	dye-works
uxorious	syndetic	typifier	pyroxene	dyspnoea	eye-water
extrorse	Cyrenaic	hylicist	Tyrolese	lymphoma	lynx-eyed
exergual	lykewake	Cyrillic	hypogeal	lyophobe	syzygial
existent	type-face	kyrielle	hypoderm	symploce	syzygies
axe-stone	typecast	hygienic	hypogeum	symphony	dyhydric
exosmose	myxedema	mytiloid	hypogean	dyspepsy	ozoniser
exospore	hymeneal	lyriform	Tyrolean	symposia	czaritza
oxytocin	hymenean	pyriform	hypothec	dyspathy	czarevna
exitance	Pyrenean	pyritous	by-motive	sympathy	
exoteric	tyreless	myriapod	cytosine	Symphyla	
exhumate	synergic	myriopod	dysodile	cyprides	
excubant	synergid	Syriarch	mylonite	Tyrrhene	
excuse-me	synechia	myristic	tyrosine	hydrogen	
expunger	lyre-bird	syrinxes	Xylonite®	myrrhine	
excusive	type-high	gymkhana	zylonite	hydremia	
excursus	hymenial	syllabub	synovial	hydromel	
exuviate	mycelial	syllabic	Byronism	Hydromys	
pyjamaed	pyrexial	syllable	sybotism	hydranth	
cynanche	hymenium	syllabus	syconium	Cyprinus	
synarchy	mycelium	cyclical	hypocist	Cypriote	
bylander	Hyperion	cycle-car	by-corner	pyrrhous	
gynandry	syrenian	Hyblaean	Pyrosoma	hydropic	
hypalgia	mycetoma	byrlakin	Tylopoda	hydropsy	
synaphea	pyrenoid	cyclamen	hypobole	hydroski	
dynamite	type-body	cyclonic	pyrosome	hydroxyl	
lyra-wise	synedria	eyeliner	sycomore	eye-rhyme	
sybarite	synectic	cyclopic	mylodont	Hydrozoa	
sycamine	rye-flour	cyclopes	zygodont	eyeshade	
lyra-viol	myograph	cyclosis	cytology	eyestalk	
cymatium	syngraph	kyllosis	mycology	gypsydom	
dynamism	eyeglass	pyelitic	typology	eyesight	
gyration	rye-grass	myclitis	xylology	Ayrshire	
dynamics	syngamic	pyelitis	synopses	hyoscine	
dynamist	dysgenic	wye-level	synopsis	gypsyism	
tyrannic	myogenic	cycleway	synoptic	eye-salve	
zygaenid	pyogenic	dyslexia	gyrostat	gypseous	
tyrannis	lychgate	dyslexic	pyrostat	rye-straw	
hydatoid	mythical	myrmidon	cynosure	syssitia	
hyracoid	Typhoean	pygmaean	dysodyle	myositic	
sycamore	Typhoeus	dysmelia	gyrodyne	myositis	
gyratory	syphilis	dysmelic	lysozyme	myosotis	
dynatron	hyphenic	myomancy	pyrolyse	dyestuff	
synapsis	pythonic	symmetry	pyroxyle	ryotwari	
dynastic	Tychonic	pyengadu	hypogyny	mystical	
synaptic	typhonic	cyanogen	synonymy	Tyrtaean	
synanthy	kyphosis	ayenbite	Nymphaea	by-street	
synastry	kyphotic	pyonings	dysphagy	syntagma	
myoblast	dye-house	cyanuret	sympodia	cyathium	
cymbidia	dytiscid	gymnasia	dyspneic	systolic	
rye-bread	Dytiscus	gymnasic	eye-piece	systemic	
symbolic	myriadth	cyanosed	by-speech	systemed	
symbiont	cylinder	cyanosis	dyspneal	syntonic	
syncline	syringes	hypnosis	nymphean	syntonin	
lynch-law	typified	cyanotic	lyophile	eye-tooth	
hyacinth	cytisine	hypnotic	sylphide	dystopia	
syncopic	pyridine	syenitic	sylphine	mystique	
syncopal	pyritise	hypogaea	symphile	hysteria	
dyschroa	pygidial	myxomata	nymphish	hysteric	
syncarpy	cynicism	hylobate	sylphish	cystitis	
syndical	hylicism	xylocarp	symphily	syntexis	
syndings	lyricism	gyroidal	tympanic	sylviine	
syndrome	pygidium	xyloidin	tympanal	sylvatic	

catamaran	catalepsy	paraclete	tarantara	gas-bottle	canceleer
maharajah	lazaretto	Balaclava	galactose	barbitone	cancelier
Malayalam	fabaceous	cataplexy	tarantass	rabbeting	marcelled
Nabataean	fagaceous	rabatment	tarantism	sabbatine	parcelled
tacamahac	sagapenum	balaam-box	cacafuego	jawbation	sarcology
calamanco	paraffine	Balaamite	paracusis	talbotype	hatchling
calavance	paraffiny	Marasmius	malagueña	Babbitism	masculine
caravance	Varangian	japanning	paraquito	sabbatise	rascaldom
catafalco	harangued	carap-nuts	carap-wood	sabbatism	calculary
jacaranda	haranguer	Jagannath	sapan-wood	lambitive	calculose
caravaned	carangoid	parabolas	catalyser	harbourer	fanciless
caravaner	salangane	paradoxal	paralyser	tambourin	matchless
maharanee	falangism	paranoiac	catalysis	lamb's-wool	rascalism
camanachd	falangist	cataloger	catalytic	bacchanal	calculate
katabasis	Walachian	paradoxer	paralysis	panchayat	falculate
katabatic	tabasheer	baragouin	paralytic	wanchancy	laccolite
Pan-Arabic	cataphyll	catatonia	paranymph	calceated	laccolith
parabasis	catarhine	catatonic	vambraced	fasciated	rascality
paralalia	Malathion®	katabolic	parbuckle	pancratic	calculous
parataxis	malachite	macaronic	sarbacane	saccharic	catchment
balalaika	parachute	macaronis	Barbadian	saccharin	hatchment
palatable	barathrum	madarosis	Barbadoes	catchable	parchment
palatably	Carabidae	parabolic	may-beetle	matchable	sarcomata
man-at-arms	dahabiyah	paragogic	warble-fly	patchable	calcaneal
paravaunt	fanatical	paralogia	cambiform	bacchante	calcanean
malaxator	galabiyah	paranoeic	gambogian	Saccharum	Mancunian
paramatta	paradisal	parapodia	tarboggin	Maccabean	vaccinial
Taraxacum	Samaritan	paratonic	tabbyhood	sauce-boat	Gasconade
paparazzo	satanical	catamount	Cambridge	hatchback	balconied
canal-boat	Tabanidae	paramount	gambolled	watch-bill	tap-cinder
carambola	Varanidae	paramorph	jambolana	dance-band	carcinoma
carambole	dahabiyeh	calaboose	cabbalism	fascicled	falconine
cavalcade	karabiner	babacoote	cabbalist	calcicole	parcenary
canal-cell	maharishi	catalogue	carbamide	ear-cockle	Gasconism
damascene	balanitis	paragogue	carbamate	fascicule	larcenist
parasceve	Nazaritic	macaw-palm	carbonade	fasciculi	sauciness
bavardage	paradisic	palampore	carbonado	catch-crop	fascinate
calandria	parasitic	damasquin	harbinger	match-cord	lancinate
farandole	camarilla	palanquin	carbuncle	sarcocarp	vaccinate
farandine	sabadilla	catarrhal	lambently	watch-case	calcaneum
gabardine	capacitor	hamadryad	jawboning	march-dike	larcenous
cat-and-dog	caparison	maladroit	Carbonari	march-dyke	vaccinium
hazardous	cavaliero	parabrake	carbonise	calcedony	lanceolar
hazardize	lavaliere	tanagrine	rabbinism	Sarcodina	gas-cooker
dahabeeah	Wahabiism	paragraph	rabbinist	rancidity	gas-cooled
lamaserai	palafitte	calabrese	carbonate	gauchesco	patchocke
palace-car	Wahabiite	gala-dress	rabbinate	gaucherie	patchouli
zapateado	capacious	gama-grass	rabbinite	rancheria	patchouly
Japaneses	malarious	canal-rays	sanbenito	parchedly	match-play
palaverer	rapacious	banausian	zamboorak	haecceity	Sarcoptes
parameter	sagacious	camass-rat	bamboozle	fancy-free	sarcoptic
parapeted	salacious	Malaysian	barbarian	calcifuge	catchpole
cadaveric	vagarious	Dadaistic	gas-burner	bacciform	catchpoll
catalexis	damaskeen	lamaistic	hamburger	falciform	marchpane
catamenia	palankeen	rajahship	jabbering	lanciform	mancipate
Hamamelis	kalamkari	harassing	barbarise	sacciform	barcarole
paralexia	lazar-like	palaestra	barbarism	watch-fire	calcarine
paramecia	caballine	cadastral	carburise	dance-hall	gas-carbon
paramedic	caballing	bay-antler	barbarity	raccahout	calcarate
Saracenic	caballero	macaw-tree	carburate	rascaille	cancerate
bagatelle	cataclasm	tarantula	barbarous	lance-jack	cancerous
panatella	cataclysm	galantine	barbastel	caecilian	rancorous
savagedom	cataplasm	rabatting	cambistry	matchlock	saucerful

saucer-eye	dandy-cart	Landsmaal	panderism	raven-bone	gas-engine
Caucasian	labdacism	pandemian	sand-grass	wagenboom	malengine
fancy-sick	Sadducism	cardamine	pandurate	Camembert	habergeon
fascistic	manducate	hardiment	caldarium	water-bird	paper-girl
pancosmic	candidacy	randomise	panderous	caper-bush	salesgirl
sarcastic	candidate	Dardanian	landgrave	water-bath	Watergate
saucisson	caddie-car	Sardinian	waldgrave	water-butt	water-gate
marcasite	Candlemas	sardonian	hard-drawn	mareschal	water-head
narcissus	handlebar	card-index	caddis-fly	paper-coal	mane-sheet
dancettee	hard-metal	tap-dancer	yardstick	water-cock	makeshift
dance-tune	raddleman	Valdenses	candytuft	paper-clip	cane-chair
narcotine	saddle-bag	Waldenses	handstaff	layer-cake	date-shell
falcation	saddle-bar	sand-snake	bandstand	wafer-cake	name-child
narcotise	saddle-lap	fandangle	band-stone	water-cell	water-hole
narcotism	saddle-pin	maddingly	handstand	canescent	rakeshame
narcotist	sand-devil	gardening	Landsting	latescent	waveshape
Manchuria	candle-end	maddening	sandstone	tabescent	canephora
raucously	paddle-box	pardoning	faldstool	water-cool	canephore
sanctuary	saddle-bow	bawdiness	laudation	gas-escape	catechise
catchweed	candle-nut	faddiness	pandation	taxed-cart	catechism
lance-wood	land-reeve	gaudiness	handsturn	water-cart	catechist
matchwood	dandified	handiness	Landsturm	water-core	Galenical
catchword	dandyfunk	hardiness	laudatory	water-cure	haverings
fancywork	land-agent	maidenish	mandatary	paper-case	sagenitic
patchwork	hardihead	sandiness	mandatory	water-cask	facetious
watchword	band-wheel	tardiness	sand-storm	patercove	parecious
cardiacal	handshake	land-force	laudative	raven-duck	water-jump
dandiacal	hardshell	mandiocca	card-punch	water-deck	kabeljouw
sand-dance	maid-child	baldmoney	hand-punch	calendrer	gavelkind
landwards	hardihood	handtowel	hard-cured	water-deer	Sabellian
bald-faced	card-sharp	hardnosed	hard-ruled	eavesdrip	water-leaf
baldpated	land-shark	landloper	landaulet	calendula	saleslady
hand-paper	hardliner	Land-rover®	paedeutic	gaberdine	labelloid
sandpaper	sandpiper	wardrober	paideutic	haberdine	lamelloid
cardialgy	land-pilot	cardboard	landowner	eavesdrop	waterlily
land-yacht	Daedalian	hardboard	handiwork	water-drop	capelline
sand-yacht	fardel-bag	dandiprat	handywork	cavendish	labelling
bald-eagle	landslide	dandyprat	cameraman	make-peace	panelling
card-table	bandelier	handspike	barefaced	make-ready	ravelling
sand-table	bandoleer	sand-spout	camerated	wavemeter	water-lens
landdamne	bandolier	baldaquin	caretaker	cafeteria	water-line
bandwagon	sandalled	ealdorman	casemaker	dare-devil	tabellion
galdragon	paedology	hand-organ	casemated	papeterie	lamellose
sand-mason	bandoline	sand-break	face-saver	parenesis	panellist
paediatry	land-plane	garderobe	lace-paper	rakehelly	waterless
hard-paste	magdalene	sandarach	lacerated	madeleine	baseplate
gaudeamus	mandoline	sand-crack	pacemaker	pademelon	face-cloth
land-value	sand-blind	sand-pride	ratepayer	baneberry	face-plate
bandy-ball	dandelion	bard-craft	camera-shy	naseberry	faveolate
paddy-bird	land-flood	handcraft	lake-basin	vade-mecum	lamellate
bandobast	mandilion	sand-grain	lacerable	take-leave	name-plate
Laodicean	mandylion	band-brake	laterally	water-flag	patellate
Sadducean	bandalore	hand-brake	talegalla	water-flea	satellite
dandy-cock	bandolero	banderole	macerator	paper-file	wavellite
hand-screw	hand-clasp	dandy-roll	matelassé	waterfall	water-main
sand-screw	hand-glass	mandarine	cave-earth	wages-fund	paper-mill
baldachin	sand-blast	wandering	rare-earth	hare's-foot	water-mill
land-scrip	sand-glass	ganderism	saleratus	water-flow	water-mole
lardy-cake	vandalise	hand-press	wager-boat	water-fern	ravelment
baldi-coot	vandalism	hardgrass	camelback	water-fowl	watermark
bandicoot	lardalite	landdrost	paperback	water-gage	Falernian
mad-doctor	waldflute	paederast	water-buck	galengale	case-knife
landscape	landamman	panderess	water-bull	water-gall	careenage

pageantry	watershed	halfpenny	narghilly	rachidian	Catharism
eagerness	cadetship	carfuffle	ganglions	Sanhedrim	Catharist
fadedness	caressing	calf's-foot	gangliate	Sanhedrin	lathyrism
mare's-nest	haversine	lay-figure	gangplank	pachyderm	ratherest
nakedness	raree-show	half-cheek	Targumist	washed-out	ratherish
satedness	water-shot	half-shift	bargander	cashierer	yachtsman
taperness	cadential	half-shell	jargoneer	machmeter	cache-sexe
maternity	lacertian	half-hitch	laggingly	cachaemia	Manhattan
paternity	maieutics	half-miler	jargonise	cachaemic	wash-stand
cavernous	case-study	half-timer	jargonist	tachogram	bashfully
gate-money	gazetteer	half-light	largeness	pathogeny	bashawism
gate-tower	parentage	half-title	manganese	dash-wheel	lachrymal
late-comer	have-at-him	gas-filled	manginess	dachshund	haphazard
Malebolge	mare's-tail	jaw-fallen	ranginess	bakhshish	latitancy
paregoric	wapentake	half-blood	manganate	kathakali	garibaldi
wake-robin	sales-talk	half-close	manganite	mashallah	harigalds
case-bound	vasectomy	half-plate	marginate	gas-helmet	laminated
gaze-hound	bakestone	raffinose	manganous	gas-holder	patinated
macedoine	gazetting	raffinate	baignoire	waghalter	radicated
race-going	hare-stane	ray-fungus	gangboard	pathology	vaginated
bakeboard	lacertine	half-royal	wang-tooth	cacholong	Laminaria
baseboard	lamenting	calfdozer	langspiel	parhelion	sanitaria
basecourt	parenting	half-dozen	bargepole	natheless	basically
bakehouse	valentine	mayflower	Pan-German	batholite	capitally
gate-house	balection	oar-footed	sangfroid	batholith	fatigable
panegoism	caseation	safflower	haggardly	bathylite	habilable
racehorse	calenture	saffroned	bangsring	bathylith	habitable
warehouse	cane-sugar	wax-flower	margarine	tachylite	habitably
wase-goose	date-sugar	calf-bound	tangerine	tachylyte	laminable
water-poet	waveguide	half-bound	badger-dog	wash-cloth	magically
bakeapple	balefully	half-pound	gargarise	nachtmaal	manically
paper-pulp	banefully	half-round	gargarism	cat-hammed	maritally
sage-apple	carefully	half-board	margarite	sachemdom	maximally
water-polo	fatefully	half-price	dangerous	nathemore	navigable
water-pump	hatefully	half-track	mangostan	Bathonian	radically
water-pipe	wakefully	fanfarade	haggishly	ham-handed	laminator
cameo-part	face-guard	half-breed	waggishly	dashingly	navigator
davenport	safeguard	malformed	laughsome	manhandle	Caribbean
palempore	water-vole	fanfarona	pargasite	panhandle	panic-bolt
water-pore	water-vine	warfaring	gadgeteer	machinery	satin-bird
racetrack	water-weed	wayfaring	targeteer	machinist	marischal
sale-price	laserwort	Sanforise	maggot-pie	washiness	parischan
paper-reed	navelwort	half-truth	haughtily	machinate	cabin-crew
sage-green	water-work	half-crown	naughtily	washing-up	fatiscent
canefruit	water-worn	ham-fisted	faggoting	fashioner	variscite
water-rail	taperwise	raffishly	pargeting	machzorim	zamindari
cane-brake	caterwaul	gas-fitter	largition	dashboard	basipetal
cameo-rôle	water-wave	hamfatter	mangetout	wash-board	taoiseach
lace-frame	yakety-yak	half-sword	langouste	bathhouse	calibered
wavefront	safety-net	languaged	mangouste	wash-house	salimeter
page-proof	panegyric	pay-gravel	law-giving	parhypate	tasimeter
cane-trash	safety-pin	gaugeable	parge-work	jaghirdar	taximeter
careerism	rarefying	laughable	fat-headed	washerman	gaminerie
careerist	half-hardy	laughably	gas-heater	bacharach	capitella
gatecrash	half-baked	Langobard	sapheaded	bath-brick	varicella
sagebrush	half-faced	Largactil®	wash-basin	catharsis	taxidermy
tape-grass	half-caste	Haggadist	bath-salts	cathartic	manifesto
water-rate	mafficker	languette	bathybius	katharsis	satinetta
oakenshaw	halfpence	larghetto	cachectic	sash-frame	satinette
wapenshaw	palfreyed	bargainer	cathectic	gathering	lapideous
water-seal	parfleche	langridge	yacht-club	Mathurine	salicetum
haversack	Rafflesia	tanghinin	cathedral	ratheripe	satisfied
waterside	ramfeezle	languidly	rachidial	catharise	satisfier

basinfuls	variolite	sapi-outan	jack-plane	dalliance	fallalery
rapid-fire	papillous	vaginulae	back-cloth	wallpaper	Carlylese
racing-car	variolous	halieutic	backplate	Gaeltacht	Carlylism
radiogram	laticlave	variously	pack-cloth	malleable	faultless
taking-off	radionics	fatiguing	sackcloth	talliable	sail-cloth
racing-bit	gabionade	marihuana	Jack-slave	kailyaird	wall-plate
galingale	galiongee	marijuana	hackamore	paillasse	mallemuck
lamington	gabionage	babirussa	jacksmith	palliasse	table-maid
malingery	Salientia	habituate	jack-knife	gallabeah	waulk-mill
variegate	patiently	capitulum	balkingly	gallabiah	Paulinian
Manichean	radiantly	basin-wide	jack-snipe	gallabieh	Laplander
ravishing	rationale	satinwood	Balkanise	table-beer	mallander
vanishing	saliently	vanity-bag	gawkiness	table-book	mallender
caliphate	sapiently	yakity-yak	lankiness	day-labour	tail-ender
basilical	valiantly	Varityper®	larkiness	gallabiya	gallonage
basilican	malignant	salicylic	pawkiness	Paulician	gallantly
fatidical	Fabianism	ramifying	tackiness	vallecula	gallingly
pacifical	Fabianist	ratifying	wackiness	galli-crow	gallinule
satirical	Magianism	salifying	talking-to	gally-crow	railingly
vaticinal	rabidness	vanity-box	task-force	warlockry	wailingly
basifixed	rapidness	banjulele	backwoods	gaelicise	caulinary
laminitis	Sabianism	jack-sauce	hawk-nosed	gaelicism	gallantry
lapidific	tacitness	backwards	bark-bound	gallicise	garlandry
vaginitis	validness	parklands	dark-house	gallicism	earliness
basilicon	vapidness	parkwards	pack-horse	Palladian	kaolinise
laciniate	malignity	backwater	backspeer	wallydrag	manliness
malicious	latifondi	bank-paper	backspeir	balladeer	Paulinism
panicking	halitosis	lack-Latin	backspaul	called-for	Paulinist
maxi-skirt	Napierian	tank-wagon	backtrack	balladist	kaolinite
maniplies	Saxifraga	tanka-boat	back-green	callidity	gallinazo
Ramillies	saxifrage	hawksbill	jack-fruit	pallidity	malleolar
caliology	hagiarchy	walkabout	lack-brain	palladium	mall-coach
hagiology	marigraph	back-pedal	pack-train	palladous	call-money
Mariology	janitross	back-bench	pack-drill	sallee-man	gallooned
palillogy	maxi-dress	barkeeper	hankering	cailleach	ball-point
radiology	calibrate	hackneyed	backcross	rail-fence	rail-borne
varioloid	satin-spar	Yankeedom	cankerous	eagle-eyed	sail-borne
maxillula	wapinshaw	hackberry	task-group	gaol-fever	rail-motor
papillule	wax-insect	lack-beard	Valkyrlur	jail-fever	sailboard
radial-ply	janissary	Yankeeism	back-crawl	mallee-hen	tail-board
papilloma	magistral	bank-agent	hawkishly	paillette	wall-board
cavilling	varieties	packaging	mawkishly	ballsed-up	jailhouse
vacillant	radiately	lark's-heel	jack-straw	ladlefuls	malleolus
bacillary	Calixtine	packsheet	market-day	cauliform	Fallopian
capillary	Pakistani	back-chain	market-man	cablegram	wall-space
mamillary	raciation	gawkihood	bank-stock	calligram	gallopade
maxillary	radiation	backshish	marketeer	panlogism	Callippic
papillary	satiation	mark-white	racketeer	faulchion	gallophil
labialise	variation	backfisch	jack-staff	eagle-hawk	galloping
labialism	magistery	backpiece	packstaff	cailliach	walloping
papillose	radiatory	pack-cinch	backstage	tailpiece	callipers
racialism	sagittary	backbiter	backstall	gauleiter	sallyport
racialist	macintosh	lack-linen	cask-stand	gall-midge	harlequin
radialise	sagittate	rank-rider	marketing	tail-light	gas-liquor
sapidless	caliatour	darklings	racketing	Carlylean	tan-liquor
hariolate	radiative	backsight	saskatoon	table-leaf	gaol-break
mamillate	variative	back-block	basketful	haplology	jail-break
marialite	basifugal	jack-block	talkative	cable-laid	sail-broad
papillate	canicular	backslide	backstays	sail-fluke	sailor-hat
papillote	capitular	jackalled	jack-stays	mail-plane	sailor-man
radiality	manipular	Raskolnik	rack-punch	sailplane	galleried
vacillate	navicular	back-slang	pack-twine	tableland	mail-order
variolate	radicular	Jack-a-Lent	backsword	tailplane	cauld-rife

mail-train	mammalian	palmation	faintness	Kainozoic	caponiere
wall-fruit	farm-place	haematite	gauntness	jaborandi	laborious
ballerina	marmalade	palmitate	raininess	Haloragis	havocking
ballerine	mammalogy	calmative	tawniness	panoramic	Damoclean
sailoring	harmaline	palm-sugar	lawn-mower	Saponaria	wagon-load
tailoring	barm-cloth	harmfully	rainbowed	razorable	wagon-lock
ball-proof	Carmelite	barmizvah	rain-bound	vaporable	panoplied
ball-dress	Tasmanian	basmizvah	haanepoot	capotaine	carolling
jaileress	harmonica	batmizvah	mannequin	capotasto	paroemiac
nail-brush	harmonics	fainéance	Wagnerian	mayoralty	paroemial
tailoress	garmented	fainéancy	mainbrace	razor-back	saloon-bar
wall-cress	lawmonger	gainsayer	mainframe	razor-bill	saloon-car
ballasted	man-minded	rain-maker	rain-print	razor-clam	marooning
ballistic	warmonger	rain-water	rainproof	man-orchis	baboonery
haplessly	salmonoid	rain-gauge	laundress	baroscope	baboonish
lawlessly	gas-mantle	bain-marie	mainprise	paroicous	saloonist
tallyshop	salmon-fly	sannyasin	mannerism	major-domo	taxonomer
Gallisise	gammoning	taeniasis	mannerist	Mahometan	cacotopia
callosity	badminton	paintable	paintress	baronetcy	Salomonic
mahlstick	salmon-fry	lagniappe	Wagnerism	barometer	taxonomic
maulstick	balminess	lawn-party	Wagnerist	bayoneted	vasomotor
table-talk	barminess	dannebrog	Wagnerite	can-opener	lagomorph
balloting	harmonise	Barnabite	magnesian	gasometer	masonried
gall-stone	harmonist	barnacled	gannister	manometer	savourily
hailstone	mammonish	launderer	garnishee	razor-edge	vapouring
hallstand	mammonism	maunderer	garnisher	Masoretic	wagon-roof
marlstone	mammonist	panniered	tarnished	Samoyedic	barograph
ballot-box	Harmonite	saunterer	tarnisher	cacodemon	Camorrism
lallation	mammonite	painterly	varnisher	barometry	Camorrist
maelstrom	harmonium	magnifico	faunistic	gasometry	labourism
kallitype	sarmentum	magnified	saintship	nanometre	labourist
hail-storm	palm-honey	magnifier	earnestly	majorette	vapourish
tablature	harm-doing	saintfoin	garnishry	salopette	favourite
palletise	farmhouse	nanny-goat	carnosity	vaporetto	Labourite
varletess	palmhouse	carnahuba	magnesite	wagonette	manor-seat
Hallstatt	palmipede	raincheck	magnesium	pay-office	jalousied
callously	hammerman	mainsheet	Parnassus	camouflet	majorship
Pavlovian	marmoreal	sainthood	magnetics	razor-fish	mayorship
gallivant	palmarian	jaundiced	magnitude	parochial	panoistic
Hallowmas	barmbrack	mainliner	dae-nettle	halophile	wagons-lit
bailiwick	hammering	raintight	day-nettle	halophily	cacoethes
gallowses	yammering	pannikell	caen-stone	cacophony	dacoitage
Hallowe'en	hammerkop	carnelian	rain-stone	halothane	catoptric
paulownia	hammer-toe	saintlike	carnation	parochine	garotting
tallow-dip	farmeress	saintling	damnation	saxophone	fagottist
wallowing	marmarise	cannelure	magnetron	masochism	raconteur
eaglewood	haemostat	vainglory	tarnation	masochist	manoeuvre
table-ware	paymaster	carnalise	barnstorm	halophyte	canopying
table-work	say-master	carnalism	damnatory	Aaronical	parodying
galliwasp	palmistry	carnalist	garniture	canonical	campeador
sallowish	Dalmatian	dauntless	rainstorm	laconical	palpebral
tablewise	farmstead	taintless	magnetise	parodical	jam-packed
tallowish	harmattan	cannulate	magnetism	Zapodidae	pay-packet
parleyvoo	Sarmatian	carnality	magnetist	Maeonides	rag-picker
Barmecide	haematoid	magnalium	carnotite	vaporiser	rampicked
naumachia	palmately	rain-cloud	magnetite	calorific	tan-pickle
haemocyte	haematoma	cannonade	gainfully	Jacobinic	jaspidean
gammadion	harmotome	cannoneer	painfully	Jacobitic	lampadary
Talmudist	calmstane	cannonier	Carnivora	parotitis	lampadist
mammiform	calmstone	fawningly	carnivore	vaporific	dapple-bay
bar-magnet	caumstane	warningly	taint-worm	sapodilla	camp-fever
palm-civet	caumstone	yawningly	Caenozoic	zapotilla	raspberry
haymaking	gammation	canniness	Cainozoic	halobiont	salpiform

Malpighia
lampshade
camp-chair
harp-shell
lamp-shell
sapphired
lamplight
nauplioid
rat-poison
lamp-black
lamp-glass
mappemond
tamponade
carpenter
tamponage
campanile
campanili
Campanula
carpingly
gaspingly
rampantly
raspingly
happening
campanero
campanist
gaspiness
happiness
nappiness
sappiness
harpooner
lampooner
camphoric
rasp-house
bagpiping
gaspereau
wapper-jaw
tampering
barperson
damp-proof
layperson
jasperise
pauperess
pauperise
pauperism
vampirise
vampirism
jasperous
waspishly
campesino
carpet-bag
carpet-bed
tappit-hen
carpeting
palpitant
wasp-stung
camp-stool
carpet-rod
palpation
raspatory
palpitate
tarpaulin
sasquatch
banqueted

banqueter
lacquerer
parqueted
Jacquerie
hacqueton
marquetry
parquetry
banquette
harquebus
pasquiler
matriarch
patriarch
tarriance
fair-faced
hair-waver
macroaxis
macrobian
Lauraceae
patrician
barracuda
barricade
barricado
matricide
parricide
patricide
barracker
batrachia
capriccio
matricula
fabricant
latrociny
barracoon
macrocopy
Capricorn
macrocosm
fabricate
macrocyte
Dalradian
hag-ridden
macrodome
parrhesia
sapraemia
sapraemic
sacrifice
caprifole
capriform
dairy-farm
tauriform
carrageen
cat-rigged
iatrogeny
Tarragona
cairngorm
fairyhood
hair-shirt
hair-piece
darraigne
parrakeet
caerulean
patrolman
hair-slide
barrelled
bas-relief

lap-roller
laurelled
patrolled
patroller
barrelage
macrology
patrology
sacrilege
bairnlike
fairylike
fairyland
matriliny
caprylate
garrulity
haircloth
natrolite
saprolite
barrelful
garrulous
dairymaid
matrimony
patrimony
sacrament
lacrimary
lacrymary
lacrimose
lacrymose
lagrimoso
carronade
cab-runner
warranted
warrantee
warrantor
matronage
patronage
jarringly
safranine
warrantor
hairiness
matronise
patroness
patronise
tarriness
pair-royal
cabriolet
gadrooned
garryowen
patriotic
pair-horse
hair-spray
hair-space
Sauropoda
kauri-pine
madrepore
parroquet
hair-drier
hair-dryer
fairy-ring
hair-brush
hair-grass
macrurous
sacrarium
Laurasian

madrassah
sacristan
barrister
lairdship
patristic
hadrosaur
bairn-team
barret-cap
parrot-jaw
garreteer
garrotted
garrotter
hairst-rig
carrytale
fairy-tale
hairstyle
bairn-time
latration
narration
day-return
gas-retort
narratory
parrot-cry
Mauritius
narrative
Harrovian
galravage
marrowfat
marrow-men
marrowsky
harrowing
narrowing
sabre-wing
barrow-boy
marrowish
saprozoic
marshalcy
fan-shaped
man-slayer
Hanseatic
Pan-Slavic
raiseable
ranshakle
camstairy
waistboat
waistbelt
hause-bane
waistband
waistcoat
cassocked
ransacker
sapsucker
false-card
waist-deep
pad-saddle
Hassidism
camsheugh
haustella
panspermy
far-seeing
camsteary
baksheesh
Parseeism

sassafras
falsified
falsifier
massagist
paysagist
pass-check
waist-high
hawsehole
day-school
falsehood
wassailer
capsaicin
wassailry
mausolean
tahsildar
hause-lock
cat-silver
hanselled
tasselled
vassalage
tarsalgia
marshland
waistline
capsulary
capsulise
causeless
pauseless
vassaless
capsulate
causality
sassolite
mausoleum
hansom-cab
baisemain
facsimile
Balsamina
parsimony
passament
passement
cassimere
massymore
Sassanian
Sassenach
cassonade
passenger
parsonage
pausingly
Cassandra
falseness
harshness
Jansenism
Jansenist
massiness
parsonish
Vaishnava
oarswoman
passional
passioned
haustoria
mansionry
marsupial
passepied
sans-appel

pansophic
hawsepipe
marsupium
Caesarean
Caesarian
lapstreak
wasserman
passers-by
cassareep
casserole
dayspring
hamstring
hamstrung
maistring
passerine
kaiserdom
cassaripe
sassarara
Caesarism
Caesarist
kaiserism
Massorete
palsgrave
lassitude
wadsetter
cassation
causation
causative
cassoulet
far-sought
massively
passivism
passivist
passivity
cassowary
falsework
marshwort
pansexual
balthasar
balthazar
eastwards
castrated
salt-water
cantharid
cantharis
martially
partially
tactually
salt-marsh
cantharus
gastraeum
lanthanum
earth-bred
cantabile
taste-bulb
cantabank
waste-book
earthborn
earth-bath
Cactaceae
tactician
faith-cube

pasticcio
party-call
manticora
manticore
masticate
tacticity
vastidity
cattleman
rattlebag
Bartlemew
wattmeter
panthenol
Parthenon
battle-cry
saltpetre
pantheism
pantheist
battle-axe
earthflax
Tartufian
earthfall
pantoffle
cactiform
Rastafari
earthfast
Tartufish
Tartufism
cartogram
pantagamy
castigate
waste-gate
fastigium
cartwheel
hartshorn
pantihose
salt-rheum
mastoidal
captaincy
last-ditch
fantailed
fat-tailed
part-timer
cartridge
eastlings
partridge
gastritis
Xanthippe
captainry
party-jury
partaking
Castalian
castellan
Castilian
Tantalean
Tantalian
martelled
battology
cartilage
cartology
tautology
cantilena
earthling
maltalent

pantiling
party-line
santolina
wasteland
battalion
malt-floor
pantaleon
Pantaloon
cartulary
cartelise
dactylist
faithless
tactilist
tantalise
tantalism
tasteless
pantalets
tactility
tantalate
tantalite
cantaloup
castellum
cautelous
salt-glaze
pantomime
Baltimore
caste-mark
mattamore
Daltonian
Martinmas
Waltonian
santonica
bastinade
bastinado
bartender
Eastender
fasten-e'en
cartonage
dartingly
haltingly
lastingly
pantingly
rantingly
waitingly
battening
fastening
fattening
rattening
cantiness
Cantonese
Daltonism
fattiness
hastiness
nastiness
nattiness
pastiness
saltiness
tattiness
wantonise
wasteness
castanets
factional
pactional

bastioned
cautioner
salt-money
salt-works
gastropod
cant-board
cautionry
dart-board
Xanthoura
cart-horse
cart-house
malt-horse
malt-house
masthouse
oast-house
salt-horse
tattooist
rantipole
salt-spoon
waste-pipe
bacterial
bacterian
cantorial
factorial
latter-day
raptorial
sartorial
sartorian
Tartarean
Tartarian
cart-track
vantbrace
easterner
master-key
Sauternes
wasterife
factorage
pasturage
waiterage
bacteroid
castor-oil
latter-wit
bastardly
dastardly
pastorale
bantering
cauterant
factoring
faltering
mastering
raftering
waitering
yattering
lanterloo
martyrdom
masterdom
tantarara
bacterise
cauterise
cauterism
factorise
martyrise
ranterism

rapturise
rapturist
tartarise
vant-brass
wart-cress
masterate
pastorate
bacterium
castoreum
masterful
matterful
rapturous
sartorius
wasterful
Baltoslav
Bantustan
baptismal
Cartesian
earth-star
fantasied
fantastic
saltishly
baptistry
fantastry
fantasise
fantasist
Dantesque
fantasque
vastitude
cast-steel
cart's-tail
factotums
jactation
lactation
mactation
partition
saltation
partitura
saltatory
factitive
partitive
cartouche
pantoufle
tactfully
captivate
captivity
part-owner
earthwolf
party-wall
zante-wood
earthward
earthwork
earthworm
pantryman
manurance
saturated
lacunaria
maturable
naturally
saturable
tabularly
jaculator
saturator

tabulator
larum-bell
majuscule
ranunculi
facundity
nature-god
cacuminal
matutinal
paludinal
Baculites
datum-line
casualise
casualism
valueless
vacuolate
Saturnian
saturnine
saturnism
saturnist
vagueness
haruspicy
manubrial
bahuvrihi
Casuarina
Paludrine
salubrity
manubrium
casuistic
casuistry
maquisard
palustral
vacuation
valuation
fatuitous
vacuously
Yajurveda
Malvaceae
larvicide
carvacrol
larviform
malvoisie
larvikite
marvelled
varvelled
laevulose
valveless
Calvinism
Calvinist
galvanise
galvanism
galvanist
salvarsan
canvasser
harvester
valvassor
calvities
salvation
salvatory
Galwegian
law-writer
jaywalker
Rauwolfia
Darwinian

Darwinism
waxworker
way-warden
waywardly
war-wasted
cat-witted
fat-witted
Manxwoman
padymelon
laryngeal
easy-chair
calycinal
satyrical
Satyridae
Satyrinae
many-sided
labyrinth
manyplies
Maryology
lady-smock
lady's-maid
lazy-bones
lazy-tongs
easy-going
caryopsis
Magyarise
Magyarism
caryatids
Zanzibari
ranzelman
gauziness
jazziness
manzanita
wayzgoose
balzarine
lazzarone
lazzaroni
gauze-tree
ablatival
abactinal
absconder
obscenely
obscenity
obscurely
obscurant
obscurity
abscissae
abscissas
abscisses
obedience
'sbodikins
abodement
abidingly
abnegator
abseiling
obsecrate
obversely
obsession
obversion
obsessive
objectify
abjection
objection

obreption	abstinent	sclereide	scallawag	scantling	sceptical
obtention	obstinate	icterical	aculeated	scentless	scapulary
obvention	obstetric	Icteridae	ocellated	ichnolite	scapeless
objective	obstruent	scleritis	scale-beam	economics	scapolite
obsequial	obturator	Acheulean	scaly-bark	economise	scopulate
obsequies	obfuscate	Acheulian	ochlocrat	economist	scapement
obsequent	abounding	scheelite	scolecoid	scantness	ecophobia
observant	obtundent	screaming	scald-crow	Scansores	scaphopod
observing	absurdity	octennial	scolecite	schnapper	Scyphozoa
obeisance	about-face	screw-nail	occludent	schnorkel	acariasis
abdicable	objurgate	screening	schlieren	schnorrer	Scorpaena
oblivious	about-ship	sclerotal	scale-fern	scenarise	scaraboid
ebrillade	abduction	sclerosed	scald-fish	scenarist	Aceraceae
obsignate	abruption	sclerosis	scale-fish	iconostas	acaricide
ebriosity	about-turn	sclerotia	ecologist	aconitine	scarecrow
obviation	obovately	sclerotic	scald-head	schnauzer	score-card
obliquely	sciamachy	screw-pile	scaldings	ichneumon	acaridean
obviously	scrabbler	screw-pine	scale-leaf	schnozzle	acaridian
obliquity	scrambler	accension	scalp-lock	scholarch	score-draw
obbligato	scrap-book	accession	scalelike	acrobatic	scorodite
ebullient	scratcher	accessary	scaleless	echolalia	scarpetti
obeliscal	ice-anchor	accessory	scalpless	octonarii	scarpetto
abolition	Octandria	accentual	schlemiel	scholarly	scarified
abominate	octameter	sciential	schlemihl	scrog-bush	scarifier
obumbrate	octahedra	eclectics	scale-moss	scrog-buss	scart-free
abondance	scrape-gut	eccentric	acclimate	scroddled	scorifier
abundance	scraggily	acceptant	Icelander	accordant	scare-head
abundancy	scrap-heap	scientism	Icelandic	according	scirrhoid
Ebenaceae	octachord	scientist	scaliness	accordion	scorching
abandoned	Sciaridae	acceptive	scalloped	acropetal	scirrhous
abandonee	sciatical	scheduled	scoliosis	acroteria	Ecardines
abrogator	oceanides	screeving	scoliotic	ectogenic	scarpines
absorbent	scrap-iron	screw-worm	acalephan	acrophony	scorpioid
absorbing	octaploid	screw-wise	scelerate	ectotherm	scurriour
obcordate	scrawling	scaff-raff	ecclesial	ectophyte	acarology
obsolesce	sciaenoid	scagliola	occlusion	schollast	scare-line
abdominal	achaenium	ice-hockey	occlusive	schoolbag	ectropion
obconical	octagonal	Ockhamism	aooluthic	school-day	ectropium
ebionitic	octapodic	Ockhamist	scolytoid	schoolman	scarf-ring
obnoxious	eclampsia	echinated	sculpture	scroll-saw	scarfskin
abnormity	eclamptic	scribable	acellular	school-age	accretion
abnormous	scrappily	activator	acclivity	octoploid	accretive
abhorrent	scrapping	scribbler	acclivous	schooling	scorbutic
abhorring	octastich	accidence	scale-work	schoolboy	scarfwise
abbotship	octastyle	scrivener	scallywag	schoolery	écossaise
obvoluted	ice-action	occipital	scummings	scrollery	acescence
obvolvent	scrap-yard	Achillean	scambling	ectoblast	acescency
aberrance	ice-bucket	schilling	scumbling	ectoplasm	ecosphere
aberrancy	scybalous	octillion	schmaltzy	scrounger	scissorer
obtruding	acock-bill	scrimmage	ecumenics	octopodes	ecosystem
eburneous	aciculate	echidnine	ecumenism	sciosophy	acetabula
aborigine	scuddaler	actionist	acuminate	acropolis	scytheman
obtrusion	acidified	Actinozoa	scombroid	ectomorph	scattered
obtrusive	acidulate	schizopod	scamp-work	accompany	scatterer
abysmally	acidulous	écritoire	aciniform	acrospire	scatheful
abashless	academist	scrippage	acanthoid	ectocrine	Scotified
abasement	schematic	scrimpily	acanthine	Octobrist	scutiform
abashment	screwball	scrimshaw	sconcheon	accoutred	Scotchman
obeseness	screw-bolt	scriptory	scuncheon	octostyle	scutching
abusively	screecher	scripture	acanthous	octopuses	scutcheon
abstainer	screeding	schistose	scintilla	acronymic	scutellar
abatement	screw-down	schistous	ichnology	Octogynia	scatology
obstinacy	accedence	schiavone	iconology	scapegoat	acetylene

scutellum
acetamide
scotomata
acuteness
ecstasied
Scotistic
ecstasise
ichthyoid
occupance
occupancy
accusable
scrutable
scrutator
scrubbing
scrub-bird
scaup-duck
scoundrel
acquiesce
scrub-fowl
scrum-half
scouthery
Sciuridae
scrubland
actualise
actualist
actuality
scrummage
scrutoire
actuarial
occurrent
occurring
acquittal
acoustics
acquitted
occulting
actuation
occultism
occultist
occupying
scavenger
ecdysiast
scazontic
adiabatic
adnascent
Edwardian
adjacency
adiaphora
idealiser
idealless
idealogue
advantage
edibility
edictally
educement
education
educatory
educative
Adrenalin®
adverbial
adherence
idle-wheel
udderless
idle-worms

adversely
admeasure
adversary
adversity
advertent
advection
adventure
Adventist
advertise
adjective
adventive
adderwort
edificial
oddfellow
admirable
admirably
advisable
advisably
Admiralty
ad-libbing
advisedly
adviceful
adminicle
admission
admissive
admitting
addiction
admixture
addictive
odd-jobman
odd-jobber
adulterer
edelweiss
adulthood
addlement
odalisque
Odelsting
adulation
adulatory
odd-man-out
adumbrate
udometric
ademption
Adamitism
edematose
edematous
aduncated
odontalgy
adenoidal
identical
identikit
adenomata
Adansonia
idiopathy
idiomatic
advocator
adsorbent
adsorbate
idiophone
idiotical
admonitor
idioticon
idioblast

idioplasm
adjoining
ideologic
ideologue
ideograph
idiograph
advoutrer
adaptable
adipocere
adoptious
adiposity
adornment
adoringly
addressed
addressee
addresser
adpressed
addressor
adoration
odorously
editorial
adjutancy
adjuvancy
adjunctly
adducible
odourless
adduction
adductive
megafarad
metabasis
metabatic
debatable
get-at-able
reparable
reparably
repayable
separable
separably
separator
megagauss
separatum
pedal-bone
cedar-bird
bepatched
debauched
debauchee
debaucher
decalcify
renascent
sea-anchor
megascope
defaecate
defalcate
demarcate
Decandria
Hexandria
celandine
demandant
demanding
pen-and-ink
regardant
regarding
retardant

rewarding
decaudate
retardate
nefandous
regardful
rewardful
decadence
decadency
Hexateuch
recalesce
remanence
remanency
hexameter
menagerie
metameric
cesarevna
Decameron
decametre
secateurs
megadeath
megahertz
revalenta
ceraceous
cetaceous
sebaceous
setaceous
Pelasgian
de-bagging
selachian
seraphims
megaphone
seraphine
seraphins
decathlon
refashion
decachord
hexachord
melaphyre
semaphore
metaphase
Hepaticae
hepatical
relatival
venatical
feralised
velarised
ceratitis
hepatitis
keratitis
pedatifid
cebadilla
cevadilla
menadione
decalitre
reradiate
retaliate
behaviour
feracious
nefarious
tenacious
veracious
vexatious
seraskier

Heraclean
defaulter
hexaploid
metalloid
befalling
bewailing
medalling
metalline
metalling
pedalling
medallion
tenaillon
medallist
metallise
metallist
metaplasm
debarment
recalment
repayment
besainted
remainder
retaining
degarnish
decagonal
decapodal
decapodan
hexagonal
Telamones
teratogen
demagogic
keratosis
melanosis
melanotic
metabolic
pedagogic
megajoule
peraeopod
belamoure
ceratodus
decalogue
demagogue
pedagogue
sex-appeal
melampode
megaspore
remarqued
repairman
relay-race
debarring
mepacrine
petaurine
veratrine
debarrass
Dekabrist
hetaerism
hetaerist
hetairism
hetairist
petaurist
repassage
relapsing
delapsion
decastich

hexastich
semantics
bez-antler
pecan-tree
oenanthic
decastyle
hexastyle
Melastoma
semanteme
departing
desalting
Levantine
recaption
redaction
semantron
decastere
departure
depasture
recapture
repasture
Xenarthra
pedantise
pedantism
rebaptise
rebaptism
se-baptist
decantate
devastate
Cerastium
megacurie
melanuria
melanuric
devaluate
tenaculum
cedarwood
medaewart
metal-work
Decagynia
Hexagynia
megacycle
bedazzled
semblance
sea-beaten
herb-Paris
semblable
semblably
herbicide
verbicide
sea-breach
herb-Peter
redbreast
sea-breeze
cembalist
herbalist
verbalise
verbalism
verbalist
verbality
Serbonian
cerberian
herbarian
verbarian
herb-grace

berberine	mercenary	headshake	weed-grown	depending	rebellion
herborist	rencontre	headphone	geodesist	legendary	jewellery
verberate	sea-canary	needy-hood	feedstock	legendist	cerealist
herbarium	deaconess	seldshown	geodetics	deference	cere-cloth
eel-basket	hercynite	headpiece	headstick	reference	beseeming
nebbisher	bed-closet	headliner	headstock	reverence	besetment
verbosely	mercaptan	hen-driver	feedstuff	vehemence	bevelment
verbosity	peach-palm	jet-driven	headstall	vehemency	deferment
Verbascum	peace-pipe	pen-driver	seed-stalk	referenda	determent
sea-bather	teacupful	headlight	headstone	telemeter	determine
sea-bottle	cercarian	dendritic	perdition	tête-bêche	redeeming
kerbstone	mercurial	seed-field	rendition	telegenic	revetment
sea-bottom	red-carpet	veldskoen	vendition	redevelop	nevermore
herbivora	geocarpic	Mendelian	teudatory	telemetry	decennial
herbivore	mercerise	penduline	heedfully	venereous	perennial
perchance	mercurous	seed-plant	needfully	hereafter	sexennial
reactance	mercy-seat	feudalise	meadow-rue	sevenfold	hereunder
sea-change	Reichsrat	feudalism	relevance	jewelfish	teleonomy
sex-change	Reichstag	feudalist	relevancy	bevel-gear	secernent
merciable	Leicester	Mendelism	severance	beleaguer	decennary
peaceable	percussed	feudality	hederated	detergent	vexedness
peaceably	percussor	headcloth	screnader	revenging	belemnite
reachable	Leuciscus	pendulate	vegetated	revengive	perennate
rescuable	bescatter	pendulous	telepathy	fever-heat	perennity
teachable	peach-tree	dead-alive	federarie	petechiae	decennium
beach-ball	leucotome	ready-made	generalia	petechial	demeanour
peach-blow	leucotomy	neodymium	deferable	repechage	developed
leuco-base	peacetime	reed-knife	delegable	telepheme	developer
beccaccia	reacquire	bendingly	generable	telephone	hegemonic
leucocyte	reactuate	pendently	generally	telephony	heterosis
nescience	beech-wood	verdantly	referable	telephoto	semeiotic
leucaemia	peach-wood	deadening	relegable	generical	heterodox
percheron	descrying	headiness	renewable	genetical	heteropod
new-create	dead-march	heediness	reverable	heretical	pereiopod
beccafico	readvance	neediness	severable	venefical	reredorse
beech-fern	dead-water	readiness	severally	beneficed	reredosse
perciform	feed-water	reediness	vegetable	benefited	reremouse
hercogamy	head-water	seediness	vegetably	redeliver	heteronym
beachhead	lead-paint	weediness	venerable	teredines	reserpine
bench-hole	pendragon	reddendum	venerably	benedight	rehearsal
describer	sea-dragon	redding-up	defecator	Genesitic	rerebrace
perceiver	hendiadys	tendinous	generator	selenitic	rehearser
Herculean	teddy-bear	seed-coral	revelator	televisor	redecraft
pencilled	weedicide	dead-point	venerator	remediate	meteoroid
penciller	pendicler	headboard	severalty	terebinth	bebeerine
percaline	mendicant	bead-house	peter-boat	selenious	celebrant
vetchling	mendacity	dead-house	resembler	genealogy	deferring
pencil-ore	mendicity	feldspath	hereabout	teleology	deterrent
fenceless	re-educate	reed-organ	seneschal	peneplain	deterring
merciless	reddleman	seed-drill	beseeched	rebel-like	gemel-ring
mescalism	headreach	headframe	beseecher	bevelling	penetrant
peaceless	dead-level	dead-drunk	remercied	debelling	peregrine
reachless	needle-tin	deodorant	level-coil	jewelling	referring
teachless	beadledom	rendering	redescend	leger-line	rehearing
percolate	seed-pearl	tendering	senescent	levelling	terebrant
Neocomian	lend-lease	bead-proof	telescope	peneplane	veneering
bench-mark	needleful	herd-groom	telescopy	rebelling	telegraph
beech-mast	needle-gun	deodorise	jewel-case	refelling	meteorism
Hercynian	heddle-eye	head-dress	repercuss	repellant	meteorist
percental	re-edifier	readdress	beheading	repellent	tenebrism
descended	verdigris	reed-grass	defendant	repelling	tenebrist
descender	deid-thraw	tenderise	dependant	revealing	tenebrose
peccantly	headchair	verdurous	dependent	revelling	celebrate

celebrity	debenture	self-borne	sea-girdle	perinaeal	penitency
cerebrate	deceptory	leaf-trace	beggardom	perinatal	renitency
desecrate	defeature	leaf-green	vee-gutter	semi-bajan	residence
meteorite	dejectory	performer	Neo-Gothic	demi-lance	residency
penetrate	mesentery	perfervid	weightily	hesitance	reticence
tenebrity	refectory	perforans	weighting	hesitancy	reticency
terebrate	repertory	perforant	sedge-wren	dedicated	bedizened
meteorous	retexture	seafaring	wedgewise	dedicatee	deliverer
revel-rout	sedentary	self-wrong	nephralgy	medicated	perimeter
tenebrous	defeatism	perfervor	nephratic	meditated	demi-deify
petersham	defeatist	self-trust	Rechabite	cevitamic	demi-devil
Teleostei	cementite	welfarism	methadone	genitalia	peripetia
bedelship	dementate	welfarist	pethidine	decidable	decidedly
reversely	tête-à-tête	beef-broth	methodise	decimally	deliverly
reversing	deceitful	perforate	methodism	definable	refinedly
decession	resentful	self-drive	methodist	definably	retiredly
demersion	deceptive	sea-fisher	red-heeled	demisable	decimetre
detersion	defective	selfishly	reshuffle	derivable	hemihedry
recension	detective	perfusion	nephogram	derivably	perimetry
recession	receptive	perfusive	tephigram	desirable	delineate
reversion	resentive	beefsteak	metheglin	desirably	femineity
secession	retentive	self-study	technical	devisable	serinette
necessary	revertive	leaf-stalk	red-haired	helically	deviceful
remeasure	selective	Delftware	nephritic	heritable	sericeous
necessity	reperusal	self-aware	nephritis	heritably	devil-fish
teleosaur	reservoir	fee-faw-fum	tephritic	levigable	meningeal
defensive	deserving	sergeancy	technique	lexically	Feringhee
detersive	decemviri	vengeance	penholder	medicable	besieging
recessive	decemvirs	geography	pew-holder	medically	Pekingese
celestial	reservist	zeugmatic	nephology	revisable	redingote
fenestral	jewel-weed	vengeable	methylene	revivable	benighted
nemertean	remedying	vengeably	nepheline	revivably	benighten
nemertian	beefeater	weighable	nephalism	seminally	benighter
select-man	self-faced	hedgebill	nephalist	veritable	delighted
semestral	self-abuse	weigh-bank	netheless	veritably	perishing
Terentian	perfecter	hedge-born	cephalate	decimator	periphery
metestick	perfectly	sedge-bird	lethality	dedicator	fetichism
telestich	perfector	hedge-bote	methylate	depilator	fetichist
nepenthes	leaf-metal	neighbour	nephelite	hesitator	fetishism
seventeen	self-begot	berg-adder	segholate	Semi-Saxon	fetishist
seventies	renfierst	berg-cedar	cephalous	Pedipalpi	feticidal
seventhly	kerfuffle	feignedly	bethumbed	demitasse	genitival
begetting	pen-friend	lengthily	mechanics	perinaeum	Heliicidae
besetting	self-pious	lengthful	redhanded	peripatus	levitical
Celestine	new-fallen	penguinry	bethankit	semilatus	medicinal
merestone	self-slain	seigniory	mechanise	devil-crab	Neritidae
nemertine	bedfellow	Vergilian	mechanism	Meliaceae	regicidal
relenting	gerfalcon	bengaline	mechanist	periscian	regiminal
repeating	jerfalcon	sedgeland	dethroner	meniscoid	semifinal
repentant	pew-fellow	vengement	nephrosis	dehiscent	veridical
revetting	self-image	bergamask	tephrosis	desiccant	reminisce
deception	feoffment	bergomask	recherché	heliscoop	mediciner
defection	perfumery	pergunnah	lethargic	periscope	felicific
dejection	newfangle	bergander	Sephardic	desiccate	peridinia
desertion	deafening	merganser	Sephardim	zemindari	retinitis
detection	leafiness	sea-ginger	Senhorita	zemindary	semi-rigid
detention	self-doubt	beggingly	lecherous	periodate	sericitic
reception	bee-flower	legginess	methystic	remindful	derisible
refection	leaf-nosed	seignoral	Zechstein	mediaeval	deficient
rejection	self-moved	geognosis	mephitism	semi-metal	deliriant
resection	web-footed	Zeuglodon	réchauffé	venireman	desipient
retention	leaf-mould	beggar-man	bethought	desinence	recipient
selection	reef-point	tea-garden	methought	penitence	resilient

helipilot	demi-gorge	resistant	leakiness	realmless	realising
decilitre	peridotic	resistent	perkiness	cellulite	reblossom
religiose	resinosis	depiction	deck-house	well-smack	reclusion
delicious	semitonic	deviation	sex-kitten	bedlamism	seclusion
delirious	peribolos	mediation	tea-kettle	bedlamite	reclusory
demipique	semicolon	seriation	hellwards	wellanear	reclusive
Leviticus	perimorph	heliotype	hell-hated	ceilinged	seclusive
redivivus	peribolus	decistere	well-famed	sex-linked	red-letter
religious	Menippean	depicture	bellyache	sea-lentil	sea-letter
seditious	hemiopsia	deviatory	weel-faird	feelingly	pelletify
periaktos	perisperm	Hemiptera	weel-faur'd	healingly	Bellatrix
Periclean	semi-Arian	mediatory	well-faurt	reelingly	Neolithic
aetiology	periproct	mediatise	jellybean	tellingly	deflation
heliology	pedigreed	depictive	beslobber	declinant	depletion
semiology	denitrify	mediative	beslubber	reclining	fellation
semifluid	devitrify	resistive	bellibone	Ceylonese	reflation
petiolule	Félibrige	pedicular	belly-band	hellenise	repletion
semiplume	demiurgic	reliquiae	welly-boot	Hellenism	Sellotape®
devilling	helidrome	reticular	hellebore	Hellenist	depletory
pericline	peridrome	retinulae	deflected	mealiness	pellitory
perilling	pericrany	retinular	fetlocked	replenish	pelletise
pétillant	semigrand	semi-lunar	neglecter	ceylanite	zealotism
sea-island	hemitrope	vehicular	reflected	ceylonite	depletive
decillion	serigraph	vesicular	reflecter	declinate	bell-punch
vexillary	heritress	deviously	deflector	reclinate	jealously
aerialist	meliorism	seriously	reflector	well-known	well-built
genialise	meliorist	tediously	bellicose	bell-tower	zealously
periclase	denigrate	reliquary	replicate	peel-tower	keelivine
periplast	denitrate	residuary	vellicate	red-looked	keelyvine
serialise	meliorate	deciduate	bell-metal	well-borer	declivity
serialism	meliority	deciduous	refluence	hellhound	re-elevate
serialist	remigrate	deliquium	well-being	seal-point	declivous
aeriality	seniority	Pediculus	well-meant	well-doing	fellow-man
geniality	demiurgus	residuous	veilleuse	well-found	sea-lawyer
legislate	retiarius	reticulum	Beelzebub	peel-house	reflowing
petiolate	semibreve	believing	well-set-up	well-house	yellow-boy
sepiolite	heliostat	relieving	belly-flop	dewlapped	yellow-dog
seriality	devil's-bit	pericycle	jelliform	aeolipilc	yellowish
veniality	devilship	verifying	jellyfish	aeolipyle	deflexion
bedimming	peninsula	perilymph	neologian	well-spent	defluxion
devilment	demission	heliozoan	red-legged	cellarman	reflexion
refitment	remission	heliozoic	Pellagrin	Keplerian	deflexure
remitment	remissory	serjeancy	negligent	tellurian	reflexive
melismata	tediosity	serjeanty	geologise	telluride	permeance
defiantly	demissive	bed-jacket	geologist	beglerbeg	germ-layer
leniently	remissive	pea-jacket	neologise	cellarage	permeable
semi-angle	leviathan	verjuiced	neologism	well-drain	permeably
beginning	registrar	Seljukian	neologist	declarant	germicide
benignant	revictual	perjurous	healthily	tellurion	vermicide
designing	hemistich	deck-cargo	wealthily	cellarist	vermicule
legionary	semiotics	beekeeper	healthful	tellurise	desmodium
regionary	geriatric	leukaemia	heel-piece	deflorate	vermifuge
Fenianism	mediatrix	neckverse	declaimer	hell-broth	vermiform
fetidness	mediately	herkogamy	reclaimer	tellurate	termagant
gelidness	peristyle	deck-chair	well-aimed	tellurite	Geomyidae
tepidness	seriately	neck-piece	well-given	cellarous	mermaiden
benignity	peristome	weeknight	well-lined	tellurium	seemlihed
designate	befitting	neck-cloth	well-oiled	tellurous	vermeille
gelignite	besitting	berkelium	well-timed	beplaster	seemliest
designful	penistone	weak-kneed	hell-black	déclassée	gemmology
Meliboean	refitting	week-ender	celluloid	realistic	permalloy
demi-monde	remittent	reckoning	bell-glass	hellishly	vermilion
semivowel	remitting	jerkiness	cellulose	reclusely	germ-plasm

hermandad
segmental
tegmental
fermented
geomancer
germander
segmented
sermoneer
geomantic
beamingly
germanely
seemingly
germinant
permanent
beaminess
Germanise
Germanish
Germanism
Germanist
jemminess
pelmanism
seaminess
sermonise
sermonish
terminism
terminist
germinate
hetmanate
terminate
verminate
germanium
tegmentum
verminous
newmarket
sea-margin
mesmerise
mesmerism
mesmerist
seamy-side
beemaster
kermesite
hermetics
besmutted
permitted
permitter
hermitage
dermatoid
geometric
geometrid
gemmation
termitary
hermitess
pegmatite
permutate
gemmative
reimburse
herniated
lean-faced
seannachy
reinhabit
seine-boat
Zernebock
penny-bank

Lemnaceae
sennachie
Bernadine
meandered
beanfeast
jeannette
penniform
meanwhile
fernticle
kennel-man
kennelled
pennyland
beingless
pennalism
penniless
vernalise
vernality
neonomian
reanimate
Memnonian
pennoncel
meaningly
teknonymy
beingness
Mennonite
penninite
re-enforce
reinforce
reinvolve
reinspect
reinspire
penny-post
meandrian
Wernerian
Deinornis
penny-rent
re-entrant
wernerite
meandrous
Keynesian
Wednesday
benne-seed
benni-seed
deinosaur
rennet-bag
veinstuff
beanstalk
pennatula
reinstall
sea-nettle
ternately
jenneting
veinstone
resnatron
vernation
means-test
reinstate
Ceanothus
Pernettya
reinsurer
heinously
jenny-wren
pennywort

penny-wise
neo-Nazism
aeromancy
belomancy
ceromancy
oenomancy
resonance
memoranda
decorated
desolater
zero-rated
sea-orange
sea-orache
aerotaxis
celomatic
melomania
melomanic
oenomania
xenomania
denotable
deposable
memorable
memorably
removable
removably
revocable
revocably
decorator
desolator
detonator
renovator
resonator
menopause
redoubted
demobbing
recombine
resorbent
retoucher
tenor-clef
bee-orchis
reconcile
rejoicing
second-day
decoy-duck
beholding
recording
secondary
recondite
redolence
redolency
aerometer
decoherer
mekometer
oenometer
pedometer
pew-opener
recoveree
recoverer
hecogenin
xenomenia
devotedly
reposedly
xeroderma

recoveror
aerometry
behoveful
reposeful
recomfort
reconfirm
decongest
besom-head
xenophobe
xenophoby
xerophagy
aeroshell
mesophyll
nemophila
oenophile
oenophily
xenophile
xerophily
aerophone
Oenothera
telophase
xerochasy
aerophyte
mesophyte
xerophyte
Belonidae
genocidal
Meropidae
meropidan
memoriter
menominee
pelorised
aerolitic
aerobiont
defoliant
négociant
depositor
repositor
defoliate
negotiate
felonious
ferocious
melodious
véronique
recollect
remoulade
mesogloea
aeroplane
mesoblast
decollate
décolleté
reformade
reformado
recommend
reformism
reformist
deformity
reconnect
denouncer
refounder
rejoinder
renouncer
recoinage

bemoaning
recognise
serotonin
aeromotor
melocoton
mesomorph
xeromorph
merozoite
aerospace
recompact
decomplex
decoupage
devonport
decompose
recompose
reconquer
democracy
menorrhea
xenograft
aerotrain
bezoardic
aerodrome
melodrama
melodrame
velodrome
devouring
aerograph
cerograph
memoirism
memoirist
xenocryst
heronshaw
bemonster
meroistic
lemon-sole
rehousing
detorsion
retorsion
repossess
refortify
reportage
befortune
besotting
remontant
reporting
repotting
revolting
veloutine
decoction
decontrol
detortion
reboation
retortion
decocture
Mecoptera
decoctive
retortive
resoluble
reconvene
resolvent
revolving
reconvert
lemon-weed

genotypic
metonymic
zelotypia
net-player
reapparel
temptable
red-plague
respecter
bespeckle
hen-paddle
hey-presto
despoiler
peep-sight
delphinia
geophilic
Memphitic
hen-paidle
Delphinus
pemphigus
leg-puller
red-polled
Neopilina
serpulite
Melpomene
despumate
geoponics
responder
responser
bespangle
weepingly
responsor
terpineol
serpentry
responsum
deep-toned
neophobia
merpeople
reappoint
Hesperian
desperado
jeoparder
peppering
tempering
pepper-box
pepper-pot
sea-parrot
temporary
temporise
temptress
desperate
temperate
deiparous
deep-drawn
Herpestes
pen-pusher
heapstead
perpetual
bespatter
bespotted
herpetoid
sempitern
cespitose
despotism

despotate	learnedly	decrement	leprosity	neesberry	pensioner
geophytic	decreeing	detriment	betrothal	sea-sleeve	versioner
neophytic	bear-berry	herriment	heir-at-law	versified	newshound
recreance	deerberry	herryment	gear-stick	versifier	bedspread
recreancy	georgette	merriment	negritude	cease-fire	censorial
retreaded	heart-free	recrement	betrothed	versiform	censorian
rearrange	metrifier	reprimand	regretted	newsagent	jetstream
heartache	petrified	terramara	rewritten	news-sheet	menstrual
Wehrmacht	retroflex	terramare	secretage	leasehold	redstreak
gear-ratio	terrified	derring-do	red-rattle	beasthood	sensorial
learnable	febrifuge	derringer	necrotomy	geosphere	berserker
béarnaise	serrefile	herringer	neurotomy	deistical	keystroke
ferry-boat	bear's-foot	sea-ranger	ferreting	seismical	berserkly
heart-beat	deprogram	serranoid	regrating	hem-stitch	leisurely
reprobacy	ferrogram	jeeringly	detrition	Jew's-pitch	Jew's-trump
sea-robber	neurogram	leeringly	neuration	sea-spider	cee-spring
heart-bond	pearl-gray	terrenely	secretion	beastings	gee-string
heartburn	tetragram	veeringly	serration	beestings	jesserant
reprobate	pearl-grey	metronome	ferrotype	ressaldar	measuring
retribute	neuroglia	beeriness	decretory	tessellae	newsprint
metrician	bedraggle	merriness	secretary	tessellar	sea-strand
retrocede	segregate	Petrinism	secretory	weasel-cat	sea-sorrow
refracted	hearth-tax	weariness	serrature	teaselled	feast-rite
retracted	negrohead	weirdness	territory	teaseller	geyserite
sea-rocket	gear-wheel	beer-money	decretist	weaseller	menstruum
febricula	tear-sheet	deer-hound	necrotise	beastlike	sensorium
febricule	gear-shift	year-round	regretful	lease-lend	pease-soup
terricole	tear-shell	beer-house	decretive	teaseling	celsitude
terracing	deprehend	deer-mouse	secretive	sea-salmon	bed-sitter
detractor	reprehend	rear-dorse	rearousal	ceaseless	jet-setter
refractor	searching	rearhorse	defrauder	menseless	versatile
retractor	near-white	rearmouse	fearfully	news-flash	Jew's-stone
negro-corn	hearth-rug	tetrapody	tearfully	senseless	news-stand
serricorn	Hebraical	bedropped	rear-guard	pensility	cessation
metricise	negroidal	negrophil	retroussé	tensility	sensation
metricist	recruital	neuropath	reproving	sensillum	sea-satyre
reprocess	debruised	détraquée	sea-roving	pease-meal	tessitura
verrucose	Hebraiser	tetrarchy	retrovert	gelsemine	sensitise
deprecate	recruiter	terrorise	depravity	jessamine	sensitive
febricity	rear light	terrorism	heartwood	persimmon	pea-souper
metricate	heartikin	terrorist	zebra-wood	pessimism	reassurer
verrucous	pearlitic	terrarium	pearl-wort	pessimist	sea-squill
heart-dear	retroject	pearl-spar	Hebrewess	Gelsemium	sea-squirt
Hebridean	petrolled	heart-sick	Hebrewism	messenger	tee-square
Hebridian	necrology	defroster	tetroxide	personnel	pensively
perradial	neurology	depressed	defraying	personify	persevere
reproduce	petrolage	heartseed	newspaper	personage	peaseweep
bedridden	petrology	medresseh	persuader	teasingly	fesse-wise
betrodden	tetralogy	redresser	Teeswater	lessoning	leastwise
retrodden	neuralgia	refreshen	geostatic	reasoning	leastways
degrading	neuralgic	refresher	Messianic	seasoning	test-match
depredate	heartland	pearl-sago	sensually	peasantry	leftwards
tetradite	heartling	heuristic	feiseanna	denseness	westwards
perradius	tear-gland	peirastic	news-value	messiness	besteaded
degree-day	Negrillos	heartsome	leaseback	newsiness	meat-eater
reprieval	beardless	wearisome	lease-band	personise	melt-water
retrieval	heartless	represent	fen-sucked	tenseness	tent-maker
deer-fence	weariless	depressor	Persicise	terseness	test-paper
gear-lever	febrility	detrusion	persecute	hessonite	centrally
hearkener	neurility	jerry-shop	Menshevik	personate	dextrally
pearl-eyed	serrulate	repressor	persienne	newswoman	neutrally
retriever	petroleum	heart-sore	penstemon	sessional	textually
pearl-edge	merrymake	leprosery	messieurs	versional	ventrally

restraint	heath-fowl	tectonics	rectorial	pettishly	tegularly
meat-paste	centigram	centenier	sectarial	leptosome	depurator
vertebrae	hectogram	sentencer	sectarian	death-song	peculator
vertebral	pentagram	septennia	sectorial	pentosane	regulator
death-bell	vestigial	jestingly	septarian	pertusion	debutante
vestibule	heptaglot	meltingly	tectorial	dentistry	penumbral
depth-bomb	vestigium	peltingly	tentorial	pertusate	betumbled
death-blow	centrical	pentangle	textorial	ventosity	decumbent
heath-bird	rectrices	rectangle	vectorial	death-trap	recumbent
west-about	tectrices	sea-tangle	yesterday	peat-stack	refurbish
petticoat	restringe	weetingly	peat-creel	seat-stick	nelumbium
heathcock	tea-things	pertinent	perturbed	beatitude	semuncial
menticide	neoteinia	centenary	perturber	certitude	requicken
pesticide	neoteinic	septenary	restarter	rectitude	sea-urchin
tentacled	perthitic	centonist	westerner	pettitoes	demulcent
geotactic	certainly	jettiness	setter-off	testatrix	sepulchre
death-cell	ventricle	meatiness	heptarchy	neat-stall	sequacity
tentacula	certainty	Neptunist	pentarchy	dentation	beau-ideal
fettucine	reptilian	peptonise	sestertia	dentition	gerundial
fettucini	rentaller	pettiness	death-roll	gestation	delundung
Celticism	festilogy	sextoness	featurely	mentation	redundant
Kelticism	festology	testiness	sea-turtle	reptation	secundine
Pentecost	pestology	Teutonise	bettering	septation	fecundate
pepticity	pentalpha	Teutonism	centering	tentation	fecundity
septicity	reptiloid	Teutonist	gettering	testation	gerundive
verticity	deathlike	bentonite	lettering	gestatory	feculence
ventiduct	fertilely	centonate	nectarine	jettatura	feculency
death-damp	pentylene	destinate	reiterant	vestiture	temulence
death-duty	pestilent	festinate	venturing	destitute	temulency
gentleman	deathless	pectinate	vetturini	restitute	oecumenic
sentience	depthless	neotenous	vetturino	gestative	refusenik
sentiency	fertilise	neptunium	weltering	tentative	reputedly
bestrewed	gentilise	sectional	westering	kent-bugle	beauteous
feathered	gentilish	destroyed	centurion	restfully	ceruleous
gentlemen	gentilism	destroyer	letter-box	zestfully	rebukeful
settle-bed	mentalism	oestrogen	bent-grass	Centaurus	refulgent
weathered	mentalist	benthonic	hectorism	festively	resurgent
kentledge	fertility	geotropic	neoterise	restively	securitan
aesthesia	gentility	leitmotif	neoterism	aestivate	nebuliser
aesthesis	meat-plate	leitmotiv	neoterist	festivity	Jebusitic
aesthetic	mentality	westbound	rectoress	festivous	deducible
centre-bit	pectolite	dextrorse	texturise	delta-wing	reducible
genteelly	sectility	neat-house	death-rate	deathward	pecuniary
weatherly	tent-cloth	penthouse	deuterate	pentoxide	repudiate
centreing	ventilate	pesthouse	dexterity	vestryman	beautiful
heathenry	dentalium	rest-house	lectorate	sentry-box	decubitus
Weltgeist	destemper	centipede	rectorate	petulance	pecunious
zeitgeist	September	heptapody	reiterate	petulancy	penurious
neutretto	centumvir	peat-spade	deuterium	recusance	genuflect
kettleful	septemfid	pentapody	dexterous	securance	medullary
ventifact	septemvir	septuplet	nectarous	Jerusalem	republish
certified	peat-smoke	sextuplet	pesterous	tegulated	sexualise
certifier	septimole	vertiport	septarium	deludable	sexualism
rectified	sentiment	red-tapism	setter-out	rebukable	sexualist
rectifier	testament	red-tapist	tentorium	refusable	medullate
testified	testimony	centurial	tetterous	refutable	sexuality
testifier	vestiment	hesternal	venturous	refutably	beguinage
death-fire	pentamery	letter-gae	test-drive	regularly	genuinely
dentiform	death-mask	mentorial	yestereve	reputable	repugnant
lentiform	Neptunian	nectareal	deathsman	reputably	refurnish
restiform	Newtonian	nectarean	pertussal	resumable	desulphur
septiform	pectineal	nectarial	tea-taster	secularly	resurrect
tectiform	sextantal	Nestorian	pertussis	securable	fenugreek

demurrage	leavenous	offhanded	agonistes	thickener	threefold
decurrent	beaver-rat	Africaner	agonistic	thicketed	three-foot
demurring	perverter	Afrikaner	agonising	thick-eyed	three-four
recurrent	renversed	affidavit	ignorance	whichever	cheechako
recurring	fervorous	Afrikaans	ignorable	chock-full	sheer-hulk
requiring	peevishly	office-boy	ignoramus	chuck-full	threshold
reguerdon	pervasion	officinal	agrologic	shock-head	shoeshine
jequirity	pervasive	efficient	agronomic	thickhead	threshing
requester	Helvetian	officiant	Agapemone	phacoidal	sheep-hook
sequester	servitude	affiliate	egg-powder	Shechinah	phlebitis
demulsify	velveteen	officiate	aggrieved	rhachides	phrenitic
decursion	velveting	officious	aggregate	rhachitis	phrenitis
recursion	nervation	affirmant	aggressor	thick-knee	sheet-iron
repulsion	nervature	affianced	aggravate	phycology	sheet-lead
revulsion	helvetium	afflicted	agistment	chickling	sheep-lice
cerussite	nervously	affluence	egotheism	chuckling	shoeblack
decussate	sea-walled	effluence	egotistic	thick-lips	wheel-lock
requisite	net-winged	ufologist	agitation	checklist	thief-like
decursive	seaworthy	afflation	agitative	chocolate	chiefling
recursive	seawardly	effluvial	wheat-bird	phacolite	wheedling
repulsive	hen-witted	effluvium	thearchic	phacolith	cheerless
revulsive	deoxidise	affluxion	wheat-crop	checkmate	chiefless
desuetude	deoxidate	effluxion	wheat-corn	chicaning	shredless
penultima	re-examine	Afro-Asian	theandric	chicanery	sheepmeat
rebutting	hedyphane	off-putter	phraseman	thickness	shrew-mice
reductant	Hesychasm	sforzando	cheapener	check-rein	threeness
reluctant	Hesychast	affricate	theaceous	checkroom	phaenogam
resultant	beryllium	aforehand	sheat-fish	thickskin	threnodic
resulting	denyingly	affronted	wheat-germ	thick-sown	chaetodon
deduction	Aepyornis	affrontée	shear-hulk	check-till	chaetopod
reduction	dehydrate	aforesaid	sheathing	chickweed	three-pair
seduction	benzidine	aforetime	thrashing	shadberry	three-pile
desultory	benzoline	offseason	cheap-jack	shadeless	three-part
sepulture	mezzanine	offsaddle	thwacking	rhodolite	wheel-race
Jesuitism	terza-rima	off-stream	phialling	rhodamine	shoe-brush
reductase	mezzotint	off-street	shearling	whodunnit	sheep-scab
degustate	off-chance	offspring	thralldom	rhodanise	chiefship
reluctate	off-colour	off-the-peg	wheat-meal	shadiness	sheep's-bit
resultful	off-centre	effulgent	shoal-mark	rhodanate	sheepskin
deductive	offerable	effulging	wheat-moth	rhodonite	wheel-spin
reductive	after-clap	sgian-dubh	cheapness	rhodopsin	threesome
seductive	after-crop	sgraffiti	shoalness	Rhodesian	sheep's-eye
tenuously	aftercare	sgraffito	thrasonic	shade-tree	Thyestean
pervicacy	after-damp	agnatical	whoa-ho-hoa	khedivial	sheep-tick
nerve-cell	efference	Iguanidae	theatrics	khedivate	chieftain
belvedere	aftergame	Iguanodon	thwarting	shadowing	threatful
fervidity	afterglow	eglantine	wheat-worm	shoemaker	sheepwalk
serviette	afterings	egg-beater	shoalwise	cheek-bone	wheelwork
pelviform	after-life	Yggdrasil	chlamydes	sheet-bend	sheep-wash
net-veined	aftermost	agreeable	chub-faced	wheelbase	theftboot
vervelled	aftermath	agreeably	shebeener	three-card	theftbote
weevilled	afternoon	ignescent	chubb-lock	sheep-cote	chafferer
servilely	oftenness	egregious	Ghibeline	shield-may	chaffinch
sexvalent	offensive	agreement	chibouque	shielduck	shuffling
tervalent	effectual	ague-proof	chabazite	three-deck	whiffling
nerveless	aftertime	egression	chickadee	rhoeadine	whifflery
servilism	affecting	agrestial	chickaree	shredding	chaffless
servility	affection	ignitable	cha-cha-cha	shield-bug	shaftless
fervently	offertory	ignitible	chechacho	cheese-vat	theftuous
leavening	affective	agriology	chechaquo	phrenesis	shift-work
servantry	effective	agalactia	phycocyan	phrenetic	shageared
heaviness	afterward	Agamemnon	checkered	threnetic	thigh-bone
nerviness	afterword	egomaniac	shickered	sheepfold	

phagocyte	shillelah	wholistic	thinkable	thanatoid	Theobroma
chagrined	sheltered	wholesale	phantasma	think-tank	rheotrope
shogunate	shelterer	wholesome	phantasms	whinstone	theocrasy
thegither	challenge	shell-sand	shank-bone	whunstane	throwster
chihuahua	cholaemia	thelytoky	thenabout	phonation	throttler
phthalein	cholaemic	philately	Phenician	phenotype	throatily
phthalate	wholefood	chelation	shanachie	phonotype	ship-canal
chthonian	shellfire	child-wife	phenacite	phonotypy	shapeable
shlimazel	shellfish	shellwork	ahungered	phonatory	chaprassi
chain-bolt	khalifate	Phillyrea	phonmeter	phonetism	chuprassy
chair-days	philogyny	whillywha	thunderer	phonetist	rhipidion
choiceful	phylogeny	shamianah	whencever	thanatism	rhipidate
chain-gear	shell-heap	champaign	thin-belly	thanatist	rhipidium
chain-gang	whale-head	champagne	whingeing	Chinatown	chapleted
choir-girl	shell-hole	chemicked	chanteuse	thingummy	ship-fever
sheikhdom	childhood	thymocyte	chanceful	chinovnik	whipper-in
shrinkage	cheloidal	thymidine	changeful	Rhinewine	shipshape
shrieking	phillibeg	chambered	phonogram	China-ware	rhaphides
shriek-owl	shelf-life	chamberer	rhonchial	shantyman	shop-floor
chairlift	philology	chamfered	shanghai'd	whinnying	chapeless
shrilling	chilblain	whimperer	thanehood	throw-away	rhopalism
thrillant	childlike	champerty	thinghood	theomancy	shapeless
thrilling	shell-like	shamefast	Rhynchota	theomachy	chipolata
chainless	shell-lime	rhamphoid	phengites	theopathy	rhapontic
chain-mail	whale-line	thumb-hole	Chantilly	chromatic	whip-snake
chain-pier	childless	whimsical	phenakism	chromatin	shopwoman
shrimp-net	shell-less	thumbkins	phenakite	rheotaxis	whipcordy
chain-pump	cholelith	thumb-knot	phenology	theomania	ship-money
shrimping	chalumeau	rhumb-line	phonology	shootable	chop-logic
chain-rule	whole-meal	shambling	rhinology	chloracne	rhapsodic
chain-shot	Philomela	thumbling	shingling	throbbing	ship-pound
Christian	Philomene	chameleon	chandlery	theorbist	whip-round
Christmas	shale-mine	rhymeless	shineless	thrombose	chipboard
thriftier	shelf-mark	shameless	thankless	shrouding	shipboard
thriftily	shell-marl	thumbless	phenolate	throw-down	shopboard
chainwork	philomath	champlevé	phonolite	rheometer	chop-house
shakeable	Thelemite	chamomile	rhinolith	theoretic	chaparral
chokebore	chelonian	thumb-mark	phonemics	Chlorella	shipwreck
chokedamp	phalangal	thumbnail	phenomena	shroffage	whip-graft
shake-down	phalanger	shamanism	shiningly	cheong-sam	chaperone
choke-full	phalanges	shamanist	whiningly	throughly	shop-front
shakiness	phalanxes	shampooed	phoniness	throngful	shophroth
choke-pear	philander	shampooer	thingness	theophagy	whip-stock
shakerism	phalangid	shambolic	whininess	theophany	whipstaff
Chaldaean	phelonion	chamfrain	chincough	rheochord	whipstall
chiliarch	childness	chemurgic	Rhineodon	chronical	ship-owner
phillabeg	chillness	thumb-ring	Shintoism	theoriser	chequered
chiliagon	wholeness	chemostat	Shintoist	chloritic	charlatan
chaldaism	phellogen	rhymester	phonopore	chromidia	thereaway
Chalybean	shallowly	Thomistic	chondrify	rhyolitic	theriacal
whale-boat	phyllopod	chemistry	chancroid	chronicle	thermally
shellback	philhorse	chymistry	chondroid	theorique	shore-boat
whale-back	Chilopoda	thumb-tack	chondrule	throbless	thornback
whalebone	philippic	chemitype	Shangri-la	theologer	Charybdis
shellbark	philopena	chemitypy	chinaroot	theosophy	cherubims
chalybite	phylarchy	shamateur	Phanariot	chlorosis	charabanc
tholobate	choleraic	rhyme-word	chantress	chlorotic	char-à-banc
whale-calf	sheldrake	shemozzle	chondrite	rheologic	shirt-band
thylacine	shelfroom	shimozzle	chancrous	theogonic	whirl-bone
chelicera	phalarope	thin-faced	thundrous	theologic	thorn-bush
cholecyst	Philister	chincapin	thaneship	theotokos	Characeae
shellduck	chelaship	chinkapin	chinstrap	theologue	shore-crab
shellduck	thalassic	phantasim	phonetics	theocracy	short-coat

character	charwoman	chastener	photopsia	Himalayan	disanoint
shortcake	chernozem	whiskered	white-rent	dilatancy	viragoish
share-crop	pharaonic	whisperer	shot-proof	jigamaree	disappear
charge-man	thermotic	whosoever	rhetorise	dilatable	Cisalpine
chartered	charlotte	Chassepot	white-seam	dilatator	dika-bread
charterer	chiropody	phosphide	white-salt	financial	cicatrice
sharpener	therapsid	phosphene	phytotomy	financier	cicatrise
sharp-eyed	whirlpool	phosphine	whetstone	disanchor	misassign
shortener	therapist	phosphate	phytotron	vitascope	rivalship
Thargelia	chartroom	phosphite	phototype	disaccord	Sivaistic
charmeuse	third-rate	Phasmidae	phototypy	Ricardian	sizarship
chargeful	Chartreux	Chassidic	whitewing	ribaudred	vicarship
sherifian	sharesman	chiselled	whitewood	vivandier	Dinantian
shortfall	shoresman	ghost-like	whiteware	girandola	gigantean
therefrom	thirdsman	whistling	whitewash	girandole	didactics
wherefrom	shore-side	phaseless	chatoyant	hit-and-run	cigar-tree
therefore	cherished	ghost-moth	rheumatic	tip-and-run	digastric
wherefore	chorister	Thysanura	rheumatiz	tie-and-dye	disattune
chiragric	whore's-egg	ghastness	shrubbery	bicameral	dicastery
shortgown	pharisaic	chest-note	shouldest	bilateral	disattire
churchman	sharkskin	chase-port	thrum-eyed	bivalence	gigantism
churchway	short-slip	chest-tone	chauffeur	bivalency	bipartite
church-ale	dharmsala	thesaurus	theurgist	mirabelle	ribattuta
churching	whorishly	ghost-word	thoughted	cigarette	ailanthus
shorthand	chorusing	phossy-jaw	thoughten	gigahertz	misadvise
third-hand	sharp-shod	whittawer	shrubless	vivamente	disbranch
short-horn	short-stop	whitebeam	thrumming	filaceous	air-bubble
churchism	thyristor	white-bear	chaussure	limaceous	misbecome
thermical	shirt-stud	whitebait	thrusting	micaceous	disbodied
Thersitic	thorntree	whitebass	thrust-hoe	vinaceous	diablerie
whirligig	shirt-tail	photocall	chevrette	disaffect	oil-beetle
Thermidor	thirstily	photocell	shovel-hat	giraffine	kirbigrip
thereinto	short-time	photocopy	chevalier	disaffirm	kirby-grip
thirtieth	thyratron	rhotacise	shovelled	sisal-hemp	misbehave
whereinto	short-term	rhotacism	shoveller	piratical	air-bridge
short-life	thirstful	chatterer	chivalric	misavised	fimbriate
chirology	thereupon	shattered	shaveling	vitaliser	disbelief
chorology	whereupon	shuttered	chevelure	mirabilia	misbelief
therology	thereunto	white-face	shovelful	mirabilis	diabology
Charolais	whereunto	whitefish	chavender	cigarillo	diabolise
shoreline	charivari	photogram	chevroned	bivariant	diabolism
charmless	thorow-wax	photogene	shivering	bilabiate	liability
chartless	shore-weed	photogeny	showmanly	bivariate	viability
shirtless	whirlwind	phytogeny	chaw-bacon	vicariate	ribbon-man
shoreless	churr-worm	White-head	chowkidar	visagiste	Ribbonism
short-list	shoreward	Whitehall	showpiece	bibacious	disbursal
thornless	therewith	thatching	show-place	bifarious	timber-man
cheralite	wherewith	white-hass	shawlless	dicacious	disburden
theralite	short-wave	shotfirer	showiness	hilarious	limburger
churn-milk	thyroxine	white-lady	shewbread	minacious	oil-burner
pheromone	wherryman	phytology	showbread	vicarious	timbering
shire-moot	cherry-pie	châtelain	showering	vivacious	gibberish
cherimoya	cherry-pit	white-lime	showerful	misallied	misbeseem
chirimoya	cherry-bob	whet-slate	whey-faced	misallege	misbestow
pharyngal	thirtyish	rhythmics	chrysalid	rivalling	gibbosity
pharynges	chorizont	rhythmise	chrysalis	rivalless	kibbutzim
pharynxes	physician	rhythmist	chrysanth	mica-slate	gibbously
chironomy	physicked	whitening	whizz-bang	piña-cloth	mischance
chariness	physicism	whiteness	rhizobium	disarming	mischancy
sharpness	physicist	chitinous	rhizocarp	misaunter	discharge
shortness	physic-nut	shot-tower	rhizocaul	disavowal	mischarge
thereness	Chasidism	whatsoe'er	rhizoidal	disavouch	pinchbeck
whereness	chastened	photophil	Rhizopoda	pinafored	aitchbone

pinchcock	hircosity	kilderkin	ricercata	libellant	fire-drill
circadian	viscosity	hinder-end	eider-duck	libelling	firebrand
piccadill	pitch-tree	niddering	eiderdown	niderling	fire-irons
diacodion	piscatrix	wildering	vice-regal	vitelline	viverrine
pitch-dark	piscatory	tinder-box	fivepence	zibelline	fire-arrow
viscidity	siccative	wild-grape	line-fence	life-blood	fireproof
diacodium	dischurch	Pindarise	ninepence	fire-alarm	firecrest
kitchener	cinctured	Pindarism	pike-perch	vitellary	rice-grass
discredit	linctuses	Pindarist	diaereses	fire-blast	wine-press
miscredit	discourse	wildgrave	wire-sewed	riderless	wire-grass
miscreant	viscounty	Yiddisher	bigeneric	riverless	biserrate
nip-cheese	piacevole	misdesert	diaeresis	sinewless	fire-grate
tip-cheese	discovert	mind-curer	fivepenny	wine-glass	linearity
miscreate	discovery	mindfully	ninepenny	lineality	line-grove
witchetty	air-cavity	window-bar	vicereine	lineolate	fine-drawn
pisciform	witch-wife	window-tax	life-weary	libellous	wiredrawn
pitchfork	piece-work	wind-swift	wine-berry	rice-flour	five-a-side
pinchfist	diachylon	kiddywink	cinereous	lineament	riverside
miscegene	diachylum	window-box	vitecetum	tiger-moth	diversify
miscegine	hindrance	windswept	river-flat	Hibernian	diversely
hitch-hike	windwards	hivewards	linen-fold	vicennial	finessing
zinc-white	wild-water	sidewards	disengage	pigeon-pea	river-sand
diactinal	wind-gauge	fire-eater	air-engine	wide-angle	dimension
discoidal	bird-table	fire-water	divergent	mire-snipe	diversion
diacritic	find-fault	life-saver	diverging	fixedness	licensure
diactinic	vindicate	limewater	oil-engine	givenness	diversity
circuitry	middleman	mine-layer	river-head	hibernise	hideosity
witch-knot	misdeemed	pipe-layer	rivet-head	mixedness	side-issue
discalced	middle-age	rice-paper	bioethics	tiredness	tiger's-eye
zinc-bloom	tie-dyeing	rice-water	side-wheel	Gibeonite	fire-stick
zircalloy	fiddle-bow	tide-water	time-sheet	hibernate	livestock
pieceless	hindberry	cinematic	side-chain	Simeonite	vine-stock
circulate	wild-geese	cineramic	hidey-hole	piperonal	river-tide
niccolite	bird's-foot	cineraria	rivet-hole	tire-woman	disesteem
discolour	hind-wheel	kinematic	wire-photo	life-force	misesteem
miscolour	wind-shak'd	literatim	kinetical	fire-power	pikestaff
oil-colour	wind-chart	disenable	mimetical	fire-robed	directrix
mincemeat	wind-chest	liberally	vicesimal	hive-honey	disentail
piecemeal	disdained	life-table	vigesimal	nine-holes	tiger-tail
witch-meal	riddlings	literally	Viperidae	side-bones	disentomb
discumber	hindsight	miserable	pine-finch	Ciceronic	lipectomy
discomfit	wind-tight	miserably	timepiece	siderosis	diverting
discommon	Mindelian	side-table	life-sized	hide-bound	eigentone
discandie	rix-dollar	tide-table	videlicet	lime-hound	firestone
mincingly	bird-alane	timetable	firelight	sideboard	libertine
circinate	bird-alone	wine-vault	limelight	firehouse	limestone
diaconate	wild-olive	cinerator	pipe-light	pine-house	milestone
cincinnus	misdemean	fife-major	sidelight	timenoguy	pipestone
zirconium	vindemial	liberator	sideritic	Didelphia	rivetting
air-cooled	windingly	literator	time-limit	didelphic	sin-eating
cinchonic	bird's-nest	time-lapse	mine-field	pineapple	tile-stone
zinc-colic	giddiness	wine-party	rice-field	disemploy	wine-stone
hiccuping	windiness	literatus	eirenicon	misemploy	bisection
pitchpine	hiddenite	wire-gauze	live-birth	Didelphys	digestion
pitchpipe	wild-honey	river-boat	ninetieth	fire-break	direction
wincopipe	wind-hover	disembody	dioecious	pipe-dream	lineation
discerner	wind-bound	river-bank	river-jack	pipe-organ	videotape
dip-circle	bird-louse	disembark	firefloat	firebrick	directory
sincerely	wild-goose	libecchio	fireplace	pipe-track	fire-storm
piece-rate	yird-house	timescale	time-clock	side-track	line-storm
sincerity	wind-break	virescent	riverlike	wisecrack	bidentate
viscerate	misdirect	nine-score	tiger-lily	rice-grain	dioestrus
discursus	hind-brain	ricercare	divellent	fire-drake	digestive

directive	singleton	fidgeting	xiphoidal	dichroite	biohazard
divertive	vingt-et-un	ringstand	Ziphiidae	fish-spear	militancy
ime-juice	misguggle	ring-ousel	high-viced	high-speed	sibilance
vice-queen	ring-shake	ring-ouzel	highlight	mishappen	sibilancy
direfully	wing-shell	misgiving	eightieth	bishopric	vigilance
hideously	king's-hood	misgovern	tight-knit	lithopone	digitated
piteously	disguised	ginglymus	fish-slice	bishopdom	Filicales
imeously	disguiser	fish-sauce	high-place	bishopess	pixilated
side-burns	king-sized	highlands	tight-lace	fisherman	digitalin
ireguard	misguided	big-headed	high-flier	sight-read	Digitalis
feguard	misguider	dish-faced	high-flyer	night-robe	militaria
vire-guard	pilgrimer	dish-water	lithology	high-grade	civically
pile-ducts	ringsider	high-taper	night-line	cipher-key	dividable
pinervate	bilge-keel	mid-heaven	nightlong	fish-creel	finically
nine-owner	Virgilian	plgheaded	sight-line	high-dried	limitable
iverweed	sing-along	lithiasis	dishallow	bilharzia	litigable
vide-awake	ting-a-ling	rightable	dithelism	night-rail	mitigable
iver-wall	liege-lord	withhault	high-blest	Richardia	similarly
iger-wolf	Cingalese	Mithraism	high-class	night-rule	visitable
iver-wing	liegeless	Mithraist	lightless	dithyramb	divinator
iger-wood	lingulate	fish-garth	nightless	ciphering	mitigator
sideswipe	virgulate	Mithraeum	rightless	withering	visitator
iverwort	ring-small	fightback	sightless	high-proof	vigilante
iveryman	jiggumbob	fight-back	Sinhalese	tight-rope	bilimbing
ife-cycle	Virginian	fishyback	dish-cloth	citharist	Liliaceae
niff-naffy	wing-snail	light-ball	dithelete	night-rest	Tiliaceae
nisfeasor	ring-snake	night-bell	fish-plate	witherite	Cicindela
difficult	ringingly	right-bank	dish-clout	Cichorium	biliteral
diffident	singingly	night-bird	high-blown	high-grown	diligence
disfigure	dinginess	tithe-barn	high-flown	withdrawn	dividedly
nisfallen	minginess	fish-scrap	light-mill	dichasial	limitedly
niffiness	virginity	pithecoid	nightmare	eightsman	citizenry
in-footed	biogenous	night-crow	nightmary	nlght-side	midinette
six-footer	virginium	night-cart	dishumour	sightseer	siliceous
pilferage	diagnoses	lithocyst	mishanter	lightship	vimineous
different	kingdomed	dithecous	siphonage	lithistid	disinfect
nisfaring	ring-money	night-club	lichenoid	night-soil	misinform
pilfering	diagnosis	light-dues	mishandle	eightsome	disinfest
differari	king-cobra	Nithsdale	sighingly	lightsome	bilingual
differaro	misgrowth	right down	siphuncle	lithesome	dining-car
disforest	singspiel	high-level	lightning	sight-sing	fining-pot
diffusely	king-apple	tightener	dishonest	nightspot	riding-rod
diffusion	ridge-pole	righteous	fishiness	Xiphosura	vikingism
diffusive	bilge-pump	tithe-free	lichenism	diphysite	disinhume
diffluent	gingerade	eight-foil	lichenist	dichasium	finishing
disfavour	kingcraft	eightfold	lichenose	night-tide	Tisiphone
ing-canal	fingertip	nightfall	lightness	dichotomy	pixie-hood
ing-dance	hip-girdle	eight-foot	litheness	lithotome	bicipital
disgracer	niggardly	light-foot	pithiness	lithotomy	Cimicidae
sing-maker	finger-end	nightfire	rightness	night-time	libidinal
ing-gauge	fingering	night-fowl	tightness	withstand	mirifical
biography	jingo-ring	night-gear	siphonate	withstood	civilised
ingually	lingering	dichogamy	dishonour	withouten	civiliser
inguaite	niggerdom	nightgown	lichenous	wishfully	digitiser
piggyback	ridge-rope	high-chair	dichromat	fish-guano	dirigible
idgeback	niggerish	sight-hole	fish-woman	nightwear	divisible
iggy-bank	niggerism	diphthong	dish-cover	night-walk	divisibly
idge-bone	ring-cross	right-hand	dish-towel	right-wing	dirigisme
disgodded	gingerous	eight-hour	high-toned	withywind	siciliana
ing-fence	disgusted	night-hawk	dichromic	nightward	siciliano
ingleted	piggishly	Cichlidae	fish-joint	night-work	dimidiate
ing's-evil	misgotten	lithoidal	dichroism	rightward	dirigiste
single-end	ridge-tile	Xiphiidae	fish-louse	light-year	lixiviate

cilicious	kirkyaird	misleared	billionth	Cimmerian	kidney-ore
litigious	pickaback	niellated	millionth	rigmarole	pivotally
lixivious	dicky-bird	diallagic	mill-tooth	dismissal	pilot-boat
silicious	sickleman	wieldable	millepede	diametral	widow-bird
finicking	milk-vetch	yieldable	millipede	biometric	Aizoaceae
mimicking	Nickie-ben	billabong	fillipeen	diametric	finocchio
midi-skirt	pickeerer	rifle-bird	mislippen	sigmation	biconcave
mini-skirt	lickpenny	dialectal	title-poem	sigmatron	divorcive
miniskirt	sick-berth	millocrat	title-page	sigmatism	Girondism
disillude	sick-leave	Violaceae	filliping	dismayful	Girondist
sitiology	milk-shake	billycock	millepore	lion-tamer	Dinoceras
Dixieland	pick-thank	pillicock	Millerian	picnicked	milometer
sigillary	milk-white	dialectic	pilloried	picnicker	Nilometer
limitless	kickshaws	biblicism	title-role	pinnacled	tin-opener
ciliolate	sick-tired	biblicist	pillar-box	finnochio	filoselle
sigillate	milk-float	dislocate	Hitlerism	dianoetic	kilometre
titillate	nickelled	title-deed	Hitlerist	lienteric	misoneism
disimmure	milk-gland	birlieman	pillarist	lioncelle	misoneist
visioning	silk-gland	fieldfare	pillorise	lion-heart	kilohertz
visionary	nickelise	villiform	Hitlerite	significs	pirouette
lividness	nickelous	billy-goat	millerite	dignified	pilot-flag
rigidness	milken-way	sialogram	fieldsman	lignified	pilot-fish
ripienist	winkingly	mirligoes	fillister	signified	Sinophile
timidness	sickening	villagery	Willesden	signifier	Sinophily
visionist	milkiness	biologist	aimlessly	gianthood	widowhood
vividness	pinkiness	dialogise	girlishly	signalman	binominal
bipinnate	riskiness	dialogist	sinlessly	lignaloes	limonitic
vivianite	silkiness	dialogite	witlessly	signalled	nicotinic
silicosis	zinkenite	mill-wheel	rifle-shot	signaller	pisolitic
silicotic	milk-molar	hill-billy	dislustre	limnology	disorient
vizierial	risk-money	misliking	villosity	fiend-like	nicotiana
Minitrack®	kink-cough	title-leaf	billeting	signal-box	kilolitre
citigrade	Dicksonia	gillflirt	filleting	signalise	bifoliate
filigreed	kink-hoast	jillflirt	millstone	pinnulate	simonious
filigrain	milk-house	titleless	violation	bionomics	pilot-jack
filigrane	sick-house	wieldless	ciclatoun	Sinningia	sinoekete
mini-dress	milk-tooth	dial-plate	violative	winningly	disoblige
minidress	pick-tooth	sialolith	mill-owner	signboard	filoplume
visitress	pickapack	diplomacy	billowing	pinnipede	cipollino
vizierate	sink-a-pace	diplomate	fieldward	kidnapped	misoclere
vizirship	wink-a-peep	willemite	fieldwork	kidnapper	pilotless
dimissory	tinkering	Finlander	willowish	signorial	hit-or-miss
viciosity	Pinkerton	uitlander	pillow-cup	giant-rude	visor-mask
vitiosity	lickerish	villanage	Diplozoon	dinner-set	ritornell
sinistral	silk-grass	villenage	gimmickry	kiln-dried	liposomal
misintend	sickishly	millennia	diamagnet	Signorina	Sinologue
filiation	ticket-day	violently	sigmoidal	pignerate	dimorphic
miniation	nickstick	willingly	pin-making	pignorate	nicompoop
vitiation	rickstick	violin-bow	bismillah	diandrous	simon-pure
miniature	ricketily	millenary	gimmalled	Dionysiac	timocracy
Ricinulei	minkstone	millinery	dismality	Dionysian	eidograph
ridiculer	picketing	diclinism	dismember	witnesser	minorship
bilirubin	rickstand	hilliness	firmament	giantship	timorsome
biliously	kick-start	silliness	pigmental	pianistic	limousine
pitifully	milk-sugar	violinist	Simmental	dianetics®	bimonthly
viciously	milk-punch	diclinous	air-minded	vignetter	bilobular
siliquose	pick-purse	villanous	diamonded	pinnately	bilocular
dividuous	sick-nurse	nielloing	pigmented	dignitary	binocular
disinvest	billiards	billboard	wit-monger	signatory	widow-wail
vilifying	dill-water	mill-board	mismanage	signature	Dicotylae
air-jacket	misleader	fill-horse	dismantle	signeurie	kilocycle
disjaskit		gill-house	filminess	winnowing	displayed
nick-nacky		mill-horse	gigmanity	piano-wire	displayer

hippiatry	piepowder	vitriolic	dissident	tittlebat	dictyogen
dispraise	diaphysis	cirrhopod	himseemed	fifteener	diatropic
mispraise	Lippizana	cirripede	diosgenin	sixteener	virtuosic
hippocras	lip-reader	disrupter	first-foot	kintledge	dietarian
air-pocket	diurnally	disrepair	first-hand	diathesis	diet-bread
fig-pecker	gier-eagle	micropsia	biosphere	diathetic	diuturnal
hip-pocket	pier-table	micropyle	dip-switch	diathermy	historian
mispickel	microbial	disruptor	biestings	sixteenmo	Listerian
hippodame	microbian	misreport	disseisin	littleane	pictorial
Cispadane	hierocrat	disrepute	disseizin	tiptoeing	viatorial
hispidity	ditrochee	librarian	disseisor	mistletoe	Victorian
limpidity	microchip	hierarchy	disseizor	fifteenth	dirt-track
diapyesis	vibracula	mirroring	tinselled	sixteenth	distorted
diapyetic	didrachma	vibrissae	air-splint	diatretum	disturbed
sImpleton	nigricant	dioristic	firstling	histogram	disturber
displease	misreckon	Midrashim	missilery	pictogram	filter-bed
misplease	microcopy	nitro-silk	dieselise	mistigris	pistareen
misprised	microcard	microsome	dissolute	histogeny	historify
simplices	microcosm	nigrosine	fissility	vintaging	bitter-pit
disprison	fibrocyte	Nigritian	midsummer	dirt-cheap	filter-tip
simpliste	microcyte	hieratica	dissemble	lintwhite	litter-bin
gin-palace	Hieracium	nigritude	dissembly	uintahite	pictarnie
dispelled	hierodule	vibratile	dissimile	pintailed	binturong
hippology	nitriding	microtome	winsomely	pint-sized	diet-drink
dispensed	pieridine	microtomy	die-sinker	mistaking	disthrone
dispenser	tiercelet	microtone	dissenter	tint-block	sistering
dispondee	tierceron	nitratine	dissunder	distilled	tittering
limpingly	Pierrette	libration	hissingly	distiller	victorine
lispingly	nitrified	migration	missingly	lintelled	bitterish
nippingly	vitrified	nitration	dissonant	pistoleer	dipterist
rippingly	microfilm	titration	tipsiness	pistolled	historism
lippening	cirriform	vibration	kinswoman	tip-tilted	Listerise
Nipponese	fibriform	fioritura	pigsconce	dittology	Listerism
timpanist	mlcroform	fioriture	dib-stones	histology	victoress
disproval	mitriform	libratory	Dioscorea	girthline	winterise
disproved	vitriform	migratory	missioner	fistulose	birth-rate
disproven	hierogram	vibratory	diastolic	mirthless	micturate
rib-plough	microgram	dicrotism	kinsfolks	vistaless	dipterous
disprofit	disregard	dicrotous	tissipede	fistulous	jitterbug
dispcople	misregard	vibrative	dissipate	distemper	litter-bug
dispersal	diarrheal	Vitruvian	midstream	mistemper	winter-bud
dioptrics	diarrhoea	gilravage	air-strike	histamine	pietistic
hit-parade	diarrheic	microwire	pin-stripe	birthmark	dietitian
disperser	vibraharp	mitre-wort	sisserary	victimise	dietetics
dispurvey	mitraille	microwatt	first-rate	diatomite	lintstock
pimpernel	livraison	microwave	kieserite	Miltonian	dictatrix
diaphragm	fibrillae	dissuader	first-time	dittander	siltstone
disparage	fibrillar	misshaped	pipsqueak	oil-tanker	dictation
nipperkin	hierology	misshapen	pit-sawyer	distantly	nictation
bioparent	micrology	tipstaves	missaying	fittingly	siltation
diapering	fibroline	tipstaffs	mint-sauce	hintingly	dictatory
simpering	tirra-lyra	diastasic	filtrable	siftingly	dictature
Hipparion	disrelish	diastasis	virtually	wittingly	nictitate
dioptrate	fibreless	diastatic	distraint	piston-rod	pint-stoup
disparate	pier-glass	miasmatic	Cistaceae	dirtiness	mint-julep
disparity	fibrolite	biostable	dietician	kittenish	mistaught
hippurite	microlite	mid-season	distichal	Miltonism	riotously
disposing	microlith	first-born	fisticuff	mistiness	wistfully
disposure	misrelate	dissocial	pistachio	niftiness	tittivate
simpatico	fibromata	dissected	viaticals	tintiness	kittiwake
lippitude	fieriness	tipsy-cake	witticism	wittiness	birthwort
disputant	fibrinous	dip-sector	gilt-edged	distingué	titubancy
dispauper	cirrhosis	dissector	histidine	fictional	simulated

figurable	witwanton	cleavable	slack-bake	clockwise	bluffness
titularly	viewiness	floatable	blackball	ale-draper	fly-fisher
simulator	rigwoodie	pleadable	blackband	clodpated	all-father
simulacra	viewpoint	clearcole	block-book	gladiator	elegiacal
simulacre	airworthy	almandine	blackbird	blade-bone	clogdance
figurante	nitwitted	pleaseman	block-coal	bladdered	flagrance
minuscule	midwiving	blear-eyed	blackcock	fledgling	flagrancy
simulcast	bipyramid	clear-eyed	alicyclic	glidingly	flag-waver
bifurcate	Didynamia	albarello	glycocoll	slidingly	sluggabed
bisulcate	airy-fairy	oleaceous	placoderm	gladiolus	Oligocene
hirundine	cityscape	ulmaceous	clackdish	slide-rule	plague-pit
liquidise	Sisyphean	alpargata	elucidate	slide-rest	flugelman
liquidate	lily-white	bleaching	placidity	Aldebaran	flagellum
liquidity	Sibylline	bleachers	Blackfeet	allemande	alignment
minuteman	bicyclist	bleachery	Blackfoot	alienable	elegantly
virulence	Sibyllist	cloacinal	blackfish	allenarly	sloganise
virulency	pityingly	allayment	clock-golf	alterable	uliginous
minute-gun	dizygotic	bleakness	blackgame	illegally	flageolet
liquefied	dimyarian	cleanness	blackhead	alienator	sloggorne
liquefier	Himyarite	clearness	blockhead	albescent	sloghorne
liquified	pixy-stool	aleatoric	flaccidly	altercate	slughorne
liturgics	pizzicato	alkalosis	blackjack	all-ending	oligopoly
liturgist	zigzagged	algarroba	place-kick	allegedly	oligarchy
divulgate	dizziness	algarrobo	blacklead	sleeve-dog	flagstick
Siluridae	mizzonite	cloakroom	blacklist	blaeberry	ill-gotten
Tipulidae	sitzkrieg	albatross	fleckless	blueberry	flagstaff
Hirudinea	diazeuxis	clear-skin	placeless	sleeve-nut	flightily
sinusitis	ejaculate	cleansing	plackless	fleet-foot	blighting
fiduciary	ejectment	allantoic	blackmail	Elaeagnus	flagstone
minutiose	djellabah	allantoid	placement	fleeching	slightish
ritualise	T-junction	allantois	placentae	alpenhorn	flagitate
ritualism	skiamachy	altar-tomb	placental	elsewhere	plightful
ritualist	skiascopy	olfaction	ale-conner	sloethorn	ill-headed
visualise	Ukrainian	olfactory	blackness	illegible	ill-haired
visualist	skiagraph	clianthus	slackness	illegibly	alchemist
visuality	sky-colour	olfactive	slickness	allegiant	ill-humour
piquantly	skedaddle	pleasurer	glucinium	alleviate	Elohistic
Liguorian	sky-diving	clearwing	electoral	blue-black	claimable
Ripuarian	skeesicks	altarwise	electrode	sleepless	alligator
liquorice	skrimmage	clubbable	glyceride	alveolate	ultimatum
liquorish	skyjacker	ill-boding	electrify	elaeolite	Pleiocene
divulsion	skijoring	blubbered	glycerine	alternant	plain-cook
sinuosity	ski-kiting	slabberer	slack-rope	fleetness	plain-darn
divulsive	skill-less	globe-fish	electress	glueyness	illiberal
pituitrin	akoluthos	slab-sided	electrise	sleekness	altimeter
sinuately	skilfully	glabellae	glucoside	alternate	glaireous
liquation	skunk-bird	glabellar	block-ship	allegoric	cleithral
sinuation	skin-diver	globalise	plicately	albespine	allicholy
situation	skin-tight	globulite	elocution	albespyne	sleighing
pituitary	skinflick	flabellum	placation	blue-green	illimited
sinuously	skinflint	globulous	plication	algebraic	illicitly
silver-fir	sky-rocket	alabamine	elocutory	blueprint	eloinment
silvering	skirtless	clubwoman	placatory	bluegrass	pleiomery
silver-fox	ski-school	clubhouse	placitory	eldership	fluidness
silverise	sketchily	elaborate	plicature	clientage	plainness
sieve-tube	skatology	alabaster	floccular	clientèle	plaid-neuk
mid-wicket	sky-troops	globosity	fluctuant	bluestone	albinotic
rigwiddie	skew-table	fly-bitten	electuary	albertite	cloisonné
midwifing	skew-whiff	slabstone	fluctuate	alleluiah	albinoism
midwifery	okey-dokey	alack-a-day	flocculus	aloeswood	plainsman
viewphone	clearance	olecranal	blackwood	cliff-face	ellipsoid
tim-whisky	pleasance	olecranon	clockwork	cliffhang	altissimo
mid-winter	cloacalin	blackbuck	black-wash	cly-faking	plainsong

cloistral	clamourer	slantwise	clip-joint	class-book	slate-grey
plaintiff	elongated	slantways	Glyptodon	glass-crab	cloth-hall
slaistery	clinoaxis	allowance	clapboard	flashcube	blotching
plaintful	plantable	allopathy	clip-board	close-down	glottides
plaintive	glengarry	allocable	slip-board	clustered	flatlings
plainwork	sling-back	allowable	flophouse	plastered	ulotrichy
ill-judged	blind-coal	allowably	clapbread	plasterer	elutriate
slakeless	clinician	allocarpy	slapstick	blessedly	clitellar
flakiness	plangency	pleonaste	klephtism	all-seeing	plutology
flukeworm	blunderer	blood-bird	slop-built	glass-gall	flatulent
ululation	glandered	blood-bath	slopewise	blast-hole	clitellum
plumdamas	plunderer	almond-oil	clepsydra	blaspheme	ill-temper
slammakin	slanderer	blood-dust	eloquence	blasphemy	glutamine
climbable	slant-eyed	fluoresce	plaquette	flesh-hood	plate-mark
flammable	flannelly	ill-omened	floreated	flesh-hook	glutamate
plume-bird	slenderly	oleo-resin	floriated	classical	Plutonian
climactic	plenteous	allowedly	alarm-bell	fleshings	platinoid
clampdown	blindfold	blood-feud	altricial	classific	blatantly
climb-down	blindfish	floodgate	cleruchia	glossitis	plutonomy
slumberer	flanching	bloodheat	clerecole	classible	platinise
flambeaux	glenoidal	floorhead	clericals	close-knit	Platonise
plumbeous	Glenlivet	allophone	clericate	glasslike	Platonism
alum-shale	plentiful	illogical	clericity	fleshling	Platonist
clam-shell	blond-lace	algorithm	Florideae	blissless	Plutonism
flame-leaf	flintlock	Algonkian	floridean	blushless	Plutonist
plumb-line	plant-lice	alloplasm	floridity	classless	slatiness
blameless	planuloid	bloodless	alarmedly	fleshless	glutenous
flameless	plant-like	bloodlust	clarified	flesh-meat	glutinous
plumbless	plantling	bloomless	clarifier	blastment	platinous
plumeless	plenilune	allotment	glorified	fleshment	plutonium
plumulose	plant-lore	floodmark	floriform	classmate	plethoric
alum-slate	blindless	aloofness	flirt-gill	closeness	plate-rack
plumulate	clankless	alcoholic	ultra-high	flushness	plate-rail
plume-moth	plantless	fluorosis	glory-hole	alms-woman	plate-room
alimental	Olenellus	allomorph	clerk-like	elastomer	plot-proof
elemental	alinement	Algonquin	all-ruling	plasmodia	clathrate
ill-manned	aloneness	blood-rain	clerkling	plus-fours	elaterite
Alemannic	blandness	bloodroot	clerkless	alms-house	elaterium
clemently	blankness	elbow-room	pluralise	blast-pipe	plate-ship
flamingly	blindness	allograph	pluralism	alms-drink	platitude
eliminant	bluntness	allotrope	pluralist	classroom	flotation
flamingos	planarian	allotropy	plurality	glass-rope	blutwurst
aluminise	Planorbis	oleograph	flaringly	blush-rose	cloth-yard
plumpness	plenarily	fluorspar	glaringly	flustrate	flouncing
sliminess	klinostat	bioodshed	clarendon	glass-soap	clouterly
aluminate	alongside	bloodshot	alertness	closeting	fleurette
eliminate	blind-side	floodtide	clarionet	flesh-tint	ploughman
aluminium	planisher	allotting	cluripara	blastular	slouch-hat
aluminous	slinkskin	bloodwood	flare-path	floscular	flaughter
glomerule	sling-shot	blood-worm	clerkship	elusively	ploughmen
glomeruli	slung-shot	blood-wite	floristic	fleshworm	slaughter
plumb-rule	plenitude	flippancy	floristry	glassware	ploughing
glamorise	plane-tree	flap-eared	claret-cup	glasswork	slouching
alembroth	planetoid	aliphatic	claret-jug	glasswort	ploughboy
glomerate	planation	slop-basin	clergyman	flûte-à-bec	eleutheri
clamorous	ill-nature	slap-happy	flurrying	sloth-bear	illuminer
glamorous	planetary	slippered	elastance	flute-bird	flourishy
slumbrous	glandular	Clupeidae	glissando	plutocrat	Aleuritis
flame-tree	slangular	olephilic	plasmatic	slate-club	pleuritic
alum-stone	klendusic	elopement	classable	clatterer	pleuritis
plum-stone	clinquant	slopingly	glossator	flatterer	plausible
climature	slinkweed	slip-coach	flash-back	slot-meter	plausibly
climatise	blindworm	slop-pouch	flash-bulb	slate-gray	album-leaf

cloudland	ill-wisher	impeccant	immitting	emanation	ambrosial
cloudless	clownship	impendent	omnibuses	emanatory	ambrosian
clout-nail	flax-wench	impending	ambiguity	emunctory	embrasure
alburnous	plexiform	Ember-days	ambiguous	emanatist	impresari
clout-shoe	fluxional	imperfect	smoke-ball	emanative	amorosity
claustral	flexitime	amber-fish	smoke-bomb	ominously	umbratile
plaustral	clay-eater	ambergris	smoke-bush	immorally	ambrotype
flaunting	play-actor	immediacy	smoke-jack	immovable	amorously
claustrum	played-out	impeticos	smokeless	immovably	improving
clausulae	plaything	immediate	smokiness	imposable	improvise
clausular	flay-flint	imperious	smoke-room	immolator	smart-weed
fluviatic	clay-slate	umbellule	smoke-sail	emboscata	embrazure
slave-born	Alcyonium	impellent	smoke-tree	impotence	amassable
slavocrat	play-world	impelling	impleader	impotency	smasheroo
clavicula	play-going	embellish	small-arms	immodesty	amissible
clavicorn	clay-court	umbellate	small-bore	smoothing	omissible
claviform	playhouse	embedment	small-coal	smoothish	amassment
slave-fork	play-spell	empennage	emplecton	impolitic	amusement
slave-hunt	playgroup	emmetrope	implicate	impounder	amusingly
clove-hook	playfully	impetrate	emplectum	impostume	omittance
Slovakian	alizarine	immensely	small-debt	important	Ametabola
Slovakish	imbalance	ampersand	implodent	importune	smatterer
clavulate	immanacle	immersion	emulgence	imposture	smothered
Slavonian	impacable	immensity	impliedly	embodying	smotherer
Slovenian	immanence	Emmenthal	amplified	omophagia	umpteenth
elevenses	immanency	impetuses	amplifier	omophagic	emptiness
Slavonise	embargoed	impetuous	small-hand	smorzando	emotional
olivenite	embargoes	Ember-week	amyloidal	smart-alec	emptional
Slavophil	empathise	embezzler	emollient	embreathe	amatorial
clove-pink	ommatidia	amperzand	emolliate	improbity	amatorian
Oliverian	impavidly	smug-faced	smell-less	Americana	imitation
ill-versed	impatiens	amygdalin	smileless	embracing	imitative
slavering	impatient	imageable	emolument	embraceor	ambulance
cleverish	ambagious	Amygdalus	implement	embracery	immutable
flavorous	embarking	smuggling	emblemise	imprecise	immutably
slave-ship	emballing	imageless	emblemata	embrocate	imputable
slavishly	embalming	imagining	smilingly	imbricate	imputably
clove-tree	embayment	imaginary	ampleness	imprecate	ambulator
clavation	empanoply	imaginist	smallness	americium	amputator
elevation	embarring	imagistic	gmelinite	embracive	ambulacra
elevatory	embarrass	amphibian	amblyopia	imprudent	ambuscade
slivovica	embassade	amphibole	emplaster	emergence	ambuscado
slivovitz	ambassage	amphiboly	emplastic	emergency	impudence
slivowitz	embassage	omphacite	amplosome	embroglio	amourette
olive-yard	empaestic	amphigory	emblossom	imbroglio	amaurosis
slow-march	impassion	omphaloid	implosion	amorphism	amaurotic
slow-match	impassive	ampholyte	implosive	amorphous	ombudsman
slow-paced	impartial	amphioxus	smell-trap	embroider	embussing
blowvalve	embattled	Amphipoda	amplitude	amornings	impulsion
flowmeter	impastoed	emphysema	small-talk	amaryllid	impulsory
clew-lines	impaction	emphasise	small-time	amaryllis	impulsive
flyweight	impactite	emphlysis	emulation	amoralism	empyreuma
flowingly	amianthus	imminence	impletion	amoralist	amazement
glowingly	immatured	imminency	emulative	impromptu	amazonian
blowtorch	emaciated	impingent	emulously	embrangle	amazingly
slowcoach	smock-race	impinging	impluvium	imbrangle	amazon-ant
slow-hound	emication	empirical	implexion	smartness	amazonite
flower-bed	amidships	umbilical	amino-acid	Amarantus	unbalance
flowerage	amoebaean	ambitious	amendable	embryonal	undamaged
flowering	impedance	umbilicus	emendable	embryo-sac	unmanaged
flowerpot	imperator	immigrant	emendator	embryonic	incapable
flower-bud	umber-bird	immigrate	amendment	embryotic	incapably
alewashed	impeacher	immission	eminently	ombrophil	uncapable

uneatable	entamoeba	anecdotal	underdone	intenible	interplay
unfadable	unrazored	unscarred	unheeding	inheritor	unbespeak
unmakable	uncanonic	unscathed	engendure	ingenious	underplay
unmanacle	unsavoury	unscythed	interdash	unserious	interpret
unnamable	unhappily	anacruses	unheedful	unbelieve	underpeep
unpayable	unmarried	unaccused	unneedful	interject	unpeopled
unsalable	sneak-raid	unscoured	indecency	interjoin	unperplex
unsatable	unpalsied	anacrusis	inference	underkeep	untempted
unsayable	encaustic	unadmired	inherence	interknit	interpage
untamable	unpartial	unadvised	inherency	underking	underpaid
untamably	unearthed	snideness	unrenewed	interleaf	interpone
indagator	encanthis	unadapted	unsevered	intellect	underplot
inhalator	infantile	unadopted	entelechy	interlace	underprop
ungarbled	unearthly	unadorned	sneeze-box	interlock	interpose
unharbour	andantino	inodorous	undeceive	interlude	underpass
unhatched	infantine	antenatal	undeserve	unhealthy	unhelpful
unmatched	unhasting	ink-eraser	unreserve	underlaid	enhearten
unwatched	unhatting	undebased	interface	underlain	unbearded
Antarctic	unwasting	undecayed	unperfect	annealing	unhearsed
enranckle	incaution	undefaced	underfeed	index-link	unlearned
enhancive	enrapture	undelayed	interfold	interline	unwearied
unhandled	unbaptise	unrebated	underfelt	interlink	knee-drill
unsaddled	unnatural	unrelated	underfong	underline	endearing
unhandily	unmanured	unrelaxed	angel-food	underling	inferring
uncandour	unmatured	enterable	interflow	underfling	integrand
unpapered	unsaluted	inferable	underflow	unfeeling	integrant
unwakened	infatuate	intenable	underfoot	unveiling	interring
unwatered	unvarying	unseeable	interfere	interlope	unbearing
unbasedly	undazzled	untenable	underfire	interlard	unfearing
uncareful	anabranch	endecagon	angel-fish	angerless	under-roof
unbaffled	inebriant	inter-arts	interfuse	indexless	unheard-of
untangled	inebriate	underbear	unselfish	unrealise	interrupt
unbashful	inebriety	interbred	undergrad	unrealism	under-ripe
invalidly	unobvious	underbred	inveigler	unreality	unredrest
in-patient	anabolism	interbank	unfeigned	unjealous	integrate
invariant	inability	inselberg	unweighed	unzealous	integrity
inhabitor	snub-nosed	underbush	intergrow	envermeil	underrate
insatiate	anabiosis	underbite	undergird	annexment	unfearful
insatiety	anabiotic	underclad	undergown	interment	underseal
unsatiate	unabashed	underclay	antechoir	undermine	intersect
unmasking	knob-stick	undercoat	sneeshing	unseeming	underside
unpacking	ink-bottle	intercede	underhand	intermure	intensify
unmanlike	anacharis	unreached	underhung	innermost	undersign
unwarlike	unactable	endeictic	angelhood	undermost	undersoil
engarland	sneck-draw	angel-cake	angelical	internode	intensely
unfailing	knock-down	unwelcome	antefixal	unpennied	inversely
ungallant	inscience	intercrop	endemical	indemnify	underself
inharmony	knackered	undercook	indexical	antennule	undersell
inpayment	knickered	undercool	undecimal	unmeaning	incessant
unharming	anucleate	intercept	antefixes	antennary	unceasing
unharmful	enucleate	undercast	endenizen	internist	uncessant
undaunted	knocker-up	intercity	undecided	Inverness	undersong
unhaunted	inscriber	underclub	undefiled	indemnity	intension
unpainted	onychitis	interdeal	undefined	undernote	inversion
untainted	knock-knee	underdraw	undesired	unbeknown	undershot
uncannily	Anschluss	interdict	unmerited	knee-cords	incensory
unsaintly	inoculate	underdeck	unrefined	enveloped	intersert
undawning	unicolour	underdoer	unrevised	unbeloved	insensate
unharness	enactment	unheedily	undelight	unremoved	intensate
incarnate	unscanned	unreadily	andesitic	unrevoked	intensity
ungainful	unscented	intendant	enteritis	anaerobic	intensive
unpainful	aniconism	interdine	indelible	knee-holly	inversive
endamoeba	aniconist	unbending	indelibly	knee-joint	indecorum	ancestral

intestacy	in-between	anchorman	ancipital	unsisting	analogous
insect-net	knee-swell	enchorial	antiviral	unwitting	unclaimed
ungenteel	interwind	anchor-ice	undivided	indiction	unplained
unsettled	underwing	uncharged	unlimited	insisture	unplaited
entertain	underwood	uncharmed	unvisited	undiluted	ankle-jack
uncertain	interwork	uncharnel	anticivic	unfigured	unplumbed
entertake	underwork	uncharted	insipidly	indirubin	inclement
undertake	interzone	anchorage	invisible	antiquely	Englander
infertile	uneffaced	anchoress	invisibly	anxiously	unblended
insectile	ineffable	anchorite	uncivilly	enviously	unblinded
undertime	ineffably	uncharity	incipient	antiquark	unblunted
intestine	unifiable	anthurium	insipient	antiquary	unplanked
onsetting	snuff-dish	unghostly	inhibitor	antiquate	unplanned
undertint	unoffered	on-the-spot	insidious	antiquity	unplanted
undertone	knife-edge	unshutter	invidious	insinuate	inclining
unresting	snuffling	antipapal	unpitiful	antitypal	ingle-nook
unweeting	knifeless	uncinated	unsickled	antitypic	unalloyed
inception	snuff-mill	antipathy	unwinking	unpitying	unblooded
indention	snuff-mull	inaidable	infielder	snakebird	unfloored
infection	uniformed	unaidable	snail-like	snakebite	unclipped
ingestion	uniformly	unlikable	anticline	snake-cult	analeptic
injection	knife-rest	unlivable	infilling	innkeeper	anglophil
insection	enigmatic	unridable	unwilling	unskilled	unslept-in
insertion	sniggerer	unsizable	ancillary	snakelike	ingle-side
intention	sniggling	untirable	inviolate	unskilful	Englisher
invention	knightage	indicator	infirmary	unskimmed	unblessed
undertook	anaglypta	antipasto	angiomata	unskinned	unclassed
indenture	ensheathe	antiscian	infirmity	snakiness	unfleshed
insectary	insheathe	engiscope	antiknock	snakeroot	unglossed
inventory	unsheathe	insincere	indignify	snakeweed	inelastic
invertase	anthracic	enkindled	undignify	snakewood	uncleship
intestate	encheason	unkindled	anciently	snakewise	endlessly
unrestful	anthocyan	unriddler	indignant	unallayed	unfleshly
incentive	unchecked	unbinding	ancientry	uncleaned	inclusion
inceptive	unshocked	unwinding	Indianise	uncleared	enclosure
infective	unshackle	unmindful	Indianist	unpleased	Englishry
ingestive	anthocarp	engine-man	unfitness	unpleated	inclosure
intentive	uncheered	inside-car	indignity	uncleanly	anglesite
invective	unchained	incidence	antidotal	unclearly	inclusive
inventive	unshrived	indigence	antinodal	unpliable	unblotted
antelucan	unshriven	indigency	antipodal	unpliably	unclothed
unsecular	unchrisom	on-licence	anti-novel	ankle-boot	inflation
undeluded	unthrifty	enlivener	antipodes	unelected	inflative
unrebuked	inshallah	unripened	unpiloted	unplucked	unclouded
unreduced	enchilada	unsinewed	antimonic	analectic	unillumed
unrefuted	enshelter	antigenic	antinomic	anglicise	onslaught
unsecured	inkholder	antihelix	antitoxic	anglicism	ingluvial
unseduced	innholder	unlived-in	antitoxin	anglicist	ingluvies
unbeguile	inshelter	unmixedly	indigotin	unfledged	inflowing
ungenuine	anthology	antiserum	unripping	unpledged	angle-worm
ingenuity	anthelion	untimeous	antispast	influence	anglewise
ingenuous	anchylose	snail-fish	indispose	unaltered	inflexion
in-service	enthymeme	angiogram	antitrade	analgesia	influxion
interview	anthemion	unmingled	unpierced	analgesic	inflexure
intervein	enchanted	enlighten	anti-trust	influenza	unamiable
intervale	enchanter	unlighted	unbiassed	Englified	unimpeded
intervene	one-handed	unsighted	gneissoid	one-legged	anamnesis
unnerving	unchanged	unsightly	snail-slow	unclogged	anemogram
unpervert	unshunned	antiphony	gneissose	unplagued	enamelled
undervest	unthanked	unsighing	ungirthed	unplugged	enameller
innervate	anthropic	unwishing	unwittily	inelegant	anemology
endeavour	unwhipped	antichlor	insistent	analogise	unsmiling
underwear	unshapely	unwishful	unfitting	analogist	animalise

9 □n□t□m

animalism	unroyally	incommode	insolvent	ungrudged	untrusser
animalist	unwomanly	endowment	endolymph	untrodden	intrusion
animality	annotator	engoûment	uniplanar	inerudite	intrusive
anomalous	innovator	enjoyment	snaphance	snare-drum	unfretted
gnomonics	intonator	enrolment	unapparel	unfreeman	unwritten
unamended	undoubted	informant	anaplasty	unordered	unwriting
mnemonist	uncombine	endosmose	knapscull	energetic	Encratism
unimposed	untouched	insomniac	inspector	unorderly	un-British
enamorado	ensorcell	announcer	anopheles	enfreedom	Encratite
unamerced	unvoicing	encounter	inspheare	intriguer	energumen
enumerate	endoscope	unbounded	snapper-up	androgyny	inbrought
inamorata	endoscopy	uncounted	snipe-fish	intrigant	indraught
inamorato	unconcern	unfounded	unspoiled	anarchial	inwrought
inumbrate	uncordial	unjointed	knapskull	anarchise	unfraught
animistic	unfolding	unmounted	unapplied	anarchism	unwrought
onomastic	unloading	unpointed	unspilled	anarchist	onerously
Mnemosyne	incondite	unrounded	inspanned	anorthite	unprovoke
unamusing	indolence	unsounded	inaptness	engrained	ungravely
animosity	indolency	unwounded	ineptness	engrainer	engraving
unemptied	innocence	unsoundly	unaptness	ingrained	engravery
unsmitten	innocency	incognita	inopinate	unbraided	introvert
animating	insolence	incognito	unopposed	unbruised	uncrowded
animation	oncometer	unbosomer	anaphoric	undrained	uncrowned
animatism	onion-eyed	ontologic	Kniphofia	unpraised	undrowned
enamoured	uncovered	endomorph	unsparing	untrained	ingrowing
unengaged	unmoneyed	uncoupled	uniparous	introitus	unbrizzed
Anonaceae	endogenic	endorphin	unspotted	introject	unashamed
unentered	oncogenic	encolpion	anaptyxis	undrilled	unassayed
unindexed	ontogenic	endosperm	unsquared	andrology	unessayed
unsnuffed	unmovedly	endospore	inequable	onirology	anastasis
ananthous	unhopeful	encompass	unequable	andromeda	anastatic
unincited	unconfine	encolpium	unequally	entrammel	unusually
uninvited	unconform	incorrect	inerrancy	untrimmed	unessence
enunciate	uncongeal	unmourned	end-reader	increment	unshered
unanxious	endophagy	unworried	increaser	inurement	gnostical
unenvious	endophyte	encourage	uncreated	encrimson	unisonant
unknelled	entophyte	entourage	undreaded	snort-mast	unisonous
un-English	Unionidae	uncourtly	undreamed	entremets	uniserial
anonymity	unlogical	endocrine	untreated	incremate	inusitate
inanimate	unionised	inpouring	unwreaked	unfranked	unassumed
unanimity	unmotived	incorrupt	enwreathe	unprinted	unassured
anonymous	unnoticed	uncorrupt	inbreathe	engrenage	unisexual
unanimous	unpoliced	envoyship	inwreathe	intrinsic	initially
unendowed	unrosined	onion-skin	unwreathe	unwrinkle	initiator
anandrous	endomixis	intorsion	inorganic	angriness	Gnetaceae
onanistic	unpolitic	endosteal	inerrable	inertness	unstocked
inanition	indocible	En-Tout-Cas®	inerrably	encrinite	unstudied
inunction	unsolidly	entoptics	entrechat	ungroomed	anathemas
uninjured	encomiast	uncouthly	intricacy	encrypted	unuttered
uninsured	innoxious	infortune	Antrycide	entrapper	unstifled
unknowing	inworking	unfortune	infracted	uncropped	unstuffed
unenvying	onlooking	intortion	unfrocked	unpropped	instigate
annoyance	unworking	Angostura	untracked	entropion	snatchily
unlocated	unbookish	endosteum	anorectic	unprepare	unethical
unsolaced	unmoulded	unpopular	infractor	entropium	unattired
endogamic	ungodlike	involucel	unprecise	engrossed	unstained
enjoyable	ungodlily	involuted	entrecôte	engrosser	unstriped
enjoyably	unworldly	unfocused	intricate	unbrushed	Anatolian
unlosable	enrolling	insoluble	introduce	uncrossed	installed
unlovable	untoiling	insolubly	unpredict	undressed	instilled
unmovable	endoblast	involucre	unbridged	unpressed	unstilled
unmovably	endoplasm	innocuity	unbridled	untressed	inutility
unpotable	entoblast	innocuous	uncrudded	untrussed	unstamped

anatomise	inaudibly	incubuses	woman-born	Johannean	bombinate
anatomist	inducible	incurvate	monarchal	Johannine	combinate
instanter	infusible	incurvity	Holarctic	cocainise	torbanite
unstinted	indusiate	unmuzzled	monarchic	cocainism	top-booted
instantly	induviate	unavoided	monarchic	cocainist	zoobiotic
gnathonic	infuriate	snivelled	romancing	vocalness	sorb-apple
inotropic	incurious	sniveller	soda-scone	monatomic	pot-barley
unstopped	indubious	univalent	somascope	monaxonic	Roxburghe
unstopper	injurious	unavenged	mosaicism	moratoria	Lombardic
Unitarian	uncurious	universal	mosaicist	potato-pit	robber-fly
unsterile	undutiful	knaveship	non-access	rosa-solis	bombardon
ant-thrush	unsubject	knavishly	cowardice	potato-rot	bombproof
knotgrass	unluckily	snow-water	Monandria	woman-post	Hobbesian
enstatite	unfuelled	snowscape	hob-and-nob	coral-rock	bobbysock
institute	unquelled	unswaddle	hot-and-hot	zoiatrics	bombastic
unitively	unsullied	knowledge	forage-cap	coral-reef	bombasine
unstaying	unqualify	snow-berry	covalency	copatriot	booby-trap
endurance	annulling	snow-white	God-a-mercy	coral-root	bog-butter
insulance	inquiline	snow-finch	copacetic	podagrous	combatant
insurance	uncurling	snowfield	logaoedic	potassium	combating
undulancy	unbuilt-on	snowfleck	pomace-fly	Monastral	tombstone
angulated	annualise	snowflick	dogaressa	Mozartian	combative
annulated	annulment	indweller	moraceous	copartner	bombazine
undulated	inburning	snowflake	pomaceous	coral-tree	moschatel
pneumatic	unturning	snow-blind	rosaceous	rowan-tree	touchable
endurable	innuendos	snow-blink	volageous	monactine	notchback
endurably	unfurnish	snow-plant	coral-fish	monastery	touch-back
incunable	inquinate	inswinger	cotangent	cobaltite	concubine
incurable	untutored	knowingly	notaphily	vocabular	concocter
incurably	infusoria	snowiness	toxaphene	vol-au-vent	concyclic
inhumanly	pneumonia	snow-bound	womanhood	coral-wort	concoctor
insularly	pneumonic	snow-goose	monachism	doubtable	coccidium
insurable	unsuspect	snow-break	monachist	porbeagle	touch-down
uncurable	anguipede	snowdrift	Fomalhaut	bomb-happy	concierge
untunable	unrumpled	snow-broth	botanical	bow-backed	bob-cherry
untunably	inculpate	untwisted	foraminal	corbicula	concreate
incubator	unguarded	snowstorm	monadical	forbiddal	couchette
insulator	unhurried	snow-guard	Totaninae	forbidden	force-feed
unhumbled	incurrent	inexactly	cohabitee	morbidity	pouchfuls
untumbled	incurring	unextinct	localiser	double-bar	coccygeal
incumbent	inquiring	unexcited	moraliser	bomb-ketch	coccygian
unsuccess	uncurrent	unexpired	polarised	dor-beetle	touch-hole
inculcate	anguished	unexalted	polariser	doubleton	coach-hire
infuscate	unguessed	unexposed	romaniser	double-you	coach-horn
uncurdled	unpursued	enzymatic	totaliser	soubrette	conceited
unsubdued	incursion	engyscope	vocaliser	combretum	conchitis
unsued-for	insulsity	untypical	womaniser	double-axe	colchicum
intumesce	incursive	undyingly	logarithm	wobbegong	conciliar
unqueened	injustice	ankylosed	notabilia	woebegone	dog-collar
inquietly	unburthen	ankylosis	covariant	bombshell	porcelain
unqueenly	encurtain	anhydride	rotavirus	gorblimey	torch-lily
unquietly	uncurtain	anhydrite	solacious	pot-boiler	force-land
unduteous	inductile	enhydrite	souari-nut	corbeille	touch-line
untuneful	annuitant	anhydrous	voracious	corbelled	forceless
unruffled	insultant	enhydrous	womankind	doubtless	touchless
anguiform	insulting	soda-water	Corallian	hobbyless	voiceless
unguiform	unsuiting	Mozarabic	coralloid	bombilate	coccolite
indulgent	induction	rotatable	woman-like	bobbin-net	coccolith
insurgent	intuition	sofa-table	coralline	Hobbinoll	forcemeat
endungeon	unhurtful	copataine	rotaplane	sobbingly	coxcombic
inrushing	inductive	rotavator	totalling	combining	box-camera
unmusical	intuitive	woman-body	corallite	nobbiness	coxcombry
inaudible	inaugural	rocambole	soya-flour	Sorbonist	touch-mark

volcanian	toodle-pip	woodiness	coadjutor	bone-weary	Powellism
concenter	soldierly	wordiness	low-downer	pokeberry	powerless
volcanoes	noodledom	coadunate	row-dow-dow	love-feast	towerless
colcannon	poodle-dog	Cobdenite	moudiwart	côtelette	vowelless
concentre	goodyears	golden-eye	moudiwort	foreteeth	covellite
jobcentre	road-sense	bond-woman	mowdiwart	novelette	forecloth
douceness	cowdie-gum	rood-tower	mowdiwort	solenette	locellate
volcanise	doodlebug	wood-borer	wood-nymph	poker-face	nose-flute
volcanism	wood-reeve	wood-honey	Mondayish	womenfolk	powellite
volcanist	cordiform	hood-mould	co-tenancy	dove's-foot	sole-plate
voice-over	condignly	road-borne	love-match	foreigner	Dobermann
no-account	road-agent	wordbound	polemarch	monergism	honeymoon
Corchorus	good-cheap	coldhouse	rope-dance	rowel-head	homeomery
forcepses	woodchuck	roadhouse	sovenance	foreshock	lowermost
force-pump	wood-shock	voodooism	tolerance	fore-wheel	copes-mate
porcupine	cold-short	voodooist	fore-caddy	nose-wheel	jokesmith
doucepere	goldfinch	wood-horse	homewards	love-shaft	novennial
coach-road	Cordaites	woodhouse	Romewards	love-child	solemnify
concordat	goldminer	woodlouse	code-named	somewhile	come-and-go
torch-race	good-sized	woodmouse	forenamed	forethink	governall
concerned	good-night	loudmouth	homemaker	something	foreanent
concerted	goldfield	hordeolum	love-maker	foreshore	governing
concurred	goldfinny	good-speed	notepaper	love-charm	no-meaning
zoechrome	goldsinny	doddipoll	pome-water	somewhere	governess
concertos	wood-fibre	doddypoll	robe-maker	hope-chest	modernise
sorceress	goodliest	toddy-palm	rope-maker	foreshewn	modernism
sorcerous	roadblock	goldspink	rose-water	foreshown	modernist
worcester	woodblock	gowdspink	forecabin	Homeridae	notedness
vouchsafe	Cordelier	wood-spite	covetable	polemical	soberness
concisely	gondolier	holderbat	pole-vault	nose-piece	solemness
torch-song	condyloid	gold-brick	sore-eagle	fore-cited	solemnise
concision	condyloma	road-craft	tolerable	noveliser	modernity
colcothar	condolent	woodcraft	tolerably	sometimes	solemnity
toccatina	cordyline	road-train	dodecagon	forenight	foreknown
touch-tone	word-blind	cold-frame	moderator	foresight	jobernowl
touch-type	gold-cloth	doddering	tolerator	lovelight	forewoman
zoocytium	gold-plate	foddering	sokemanry	doleritic	rose-topaz
concluded	wood-flour	soldering	bone-earth	cohesible	foreboder
concourse	bond-slave	wondering	cole-garth	dope-fiend	foretoken
boschveld	condemned	powder-box	foretaste	coheritor	forewomen
concavely	goddamned	cord-grass	honey-bear	sorediate	home-comer
concavity	condiment	goldcrest	powerboat	monecious	love-token
coachwhip	goldsmith	toad-grass	moveables	womenkind	rope-soled
touchwood	wordsmith	foederati	money-bill	foreskirt	ropeworks
coachwork	Jordanian	ponderate	honey-blob	foregleam	rose-noble
nonce-word	Londonian	ponderous	bower-bird	bone-black	foregoing
bold-faced	condenser	wonderful	honey-bird	foreslack	forepoint
gold-laced	Domdaniel	wonderous	honeycomb	someplace	homebound
good-faced	pond-snail	cold-drawn	honey-cart	nose-bleed	horehound
road-maker	mordantly	soi-disant	lower-case	rose-elder	forecourt
toad-eater	golden-rod	roadstead	lower-deck	bowelling	cole-mouse
top-drawer	Cobdenism	goldstick	power-dive	modelling	dove-house
wood-paper	dowdiness	food-stuff	coherence	rowelling	fore-horse
wood-waxen	goodiness	cordotomy	coherency	towelling	rope-house
cordially	hoydenish	wood-stamp	forereach	gore-blood	foretooth
wood-screw	hoydenism	bondstone	foreteach	power-loom	Coregonus
conductor	Londonese	goldstone	dose-meter	pole-clipt	forespeak
mordacity	Londonise	loadstone	foreweigh	dowerless	mole-spade
conducive	Londonish	toad-stone	sovereign	foreclose	love-apple
condiddle	Londonism	wood-stone	oogenesis	honeyless	rose-apple
boodie-rat	moodiness	condition	oogenetic	loverless	forespend
road-metal	rowdiness	toadstool	yoke-devil	moneyless	hoverport
gold-fever	Soudanese	wood-sugar	Rome-penny	powellise	hovel-post

homeopath	moneywort	loaf-sugar	zoogloeic	Tocharish	noviciate
fore-brace	poker-work	confluent	long-house	Tokharish	novitiate
rope-trick	money-wise	roof-guard	long-coats	cothurnus	politique
towel-rack	wolfsbane	poignancy	lodgepole	mother-lye	gorillian
homecraft	Confucian	long-dated	doggerman	sophister	moniplies
home-croft	wolf's-claw	long-eared	box-girder	sophistic	dosiology
fore-brain	Forficula	long-faced	conger-eel	sophistry	koniology
towel-rail	forficate	long-range	congeries	nowhither	sociology
forefront	confidant	zoography	hop-garden	dominance	gorilline
love-arrow	confident	forgeable	songcraft	dominancy	cotillion
coheiress	confiding	tonga-bean	mongering	comitadji	modillion
rose-cross	cowfeeder	hobgoblin	Gongorism	cogitable	nonillion
voyeurism	confrérie	dough-ball	Gongorist	comically	foliolose
home-truth	coffee-pot	Longobard	long-drawn	conically	socialise
home-grown	coiffeuse	longicorn	congested	logically	socialism
coseismal	coffee-bug	roughcast	moygashel	nominable	socialist
forensics	coffee-cup	rough-draw	doggishly	nominally	foliolate
nor'-easter	wolf's-foot	cough-drop	hoggishly	topically	joviality
coseismic	solfeggio	longaeval	rough-shod	toxically	socialite
coverslip	configure	tonguelet	gong-stick	dominator	sociality
rowel-spur	forfeiter	toughener	longitude	nominator	motion-man
foresteal	top-flight	mongrelly	forgather	co-rivalry	coriander
forest-oak	golf-links	goggle-box	forgetter	solitaire	motionist
homestead	boyfriend	borghetto	forgotten	Rosinante	notionist
potential	vow-fellow	lorgnette	doughtily	Rozinante	solidness
toreutics	roof-plate	god-gifted	forgetful	comitatus	polianite
novelties	confining	lodge-gate	forgetive	yohimbine	soliloquy
forestage	goofiness	long-chain	songfully	Politburo	sociopath
forestair	coffinite	longshore	congruent	koniscope	hodiernal
forestall	hoof-bound	rough-hewn	congruity	Coniferae	topiarian
forest-fly	wolf-hound	long-lived	congruous	policeman	goliardic
homestall	roof-board	long-sixes	forgiving	poriferal	monitress
yoke-stalk	corf-house	long-field	longevity	poriferan	topiarist
lobectomy	confronté	Mongolian	longevous	rotiferal	solipsism
topectomy	wolf-tooth	sow-gelder	song-cycle	dosimeter	solipsist
cope-stone	coffer-dam	mongoloid	hotheaded	focimeter	logistics
forestine	confervae	coagulant	mop-headed	konimeter	covin-tree
go-getting	conformal	Congolese	moth-eaten	homiletic	foliation
hone-stone	loaf-bread	Mongolise	not-headed	police-dog	Comintern
lodestone	comforter	mongolism	tow-headed	dosimetry	foliature
momentany	conferred	coagulate	pothecary	Cominform	Komintern
bolection	conferrer	long-cloth	gothicise	Kominform	societary
dog-eat-dog	confirmed	lodgement	Gothicism	coping-saw	sovietise
coverture	confirmee	songsmith	lophodont	sociogram	sovietism
love-story	confirmer	zoogamete	cochleate	towing-net	goniatite
momentary	conformer	zoogamous	potholing	comings-in	sociative
motettist	goffering	congenial	top-hamper	boning-rod	coticular
tomentose	hoofprint	gorgonian	bonhommie	loving-cup	lodiculae
nonentity	solferino	rough-neck	sophomore	holing-axe	Solifugae
potentate	confirmor	gorgoneia	Gothamist	dominical	copiously
molestful	loaferish	longingly	Gothamite	Dominican	noxiously
momentous	cod-fisher	bogginess	bonhomous	Dorididae	rosin-weed
tomentous	confessed	dogginess	cochineal	homicidal	codifying
molecular	rodfisher	fogginess	fox-hunter	Hominidae	modifying
love-juice	confestly	gorgonise	mob-handed	political	notifying
home-ruler	wolfishly	podginess	pot-hanger	Soricidae	hobjobber
forejudge	confessor	roughness	pot-hunter	soritical	Poujadism
dolefully	confusion	sogginess	Tocharian	domiciled	Poujadist
hopefully	godfather	toughness	Tokharian	politicly	conjugate
home-guard	confiteor	morganite	mother-wit	boliviano	conjoined
yo-heave-ho	comfiture	zoogenous	coshering	volitient	conjuring
go-between	confiture	zoogonous	mothering	solicitor	non-juring
come-o'-will	solfatara	mongooses	moth-proof	nobiliary	forjaskit

forjeskit	workfolks	poult-foot	coelostat	commendam	dormitive
cockmatch	cockyolly	holly-fern	molluscan	commensal	formative
folk-dance	look-round	collegial	foolishly	Rosminian	normative
bookmaker	rock-bound	collegian	godlessly	Roumanian	corn-salad
rockwater	Doukhobor	bow-legged	joylessly	Roumansch	roundarch
rock-basin	booklouse	dog-legged	collision	commander	downwards
pockmanky	cockhorse	zoologist	collusion	commenter	horn-maker
book-tally	cookhouse	colligate	dolly-shop	low-minded	moon-faced
cock-padle	lockhouse	collegium	popliteal	tormented	moonraker
workmanly	workhorse	jollyhead	dog-letter	commonage	countable
work-table	workhouse	lowlihead	mollities	tormentil	woundable
cocklaird	volksraad	hollyhock	toilet-set	zoomantic	connubial
tonka-bean	folk-craft	loll-shrob	cowl-staff	commingle	sound-body
cork-screw	rock-brake	colloidal	bolletrie	foamingly	bonnibell
cockscomb	rock-drill	coal-fired	zoolatria	communing	mound-bird
booked-out	rock-'n'-roll	coal-miner	zoolithic	commentor	coenobite
cockle-hat	rock-tripe	coalfield	pollutant	communion	coenobium
rock-perch	dock-cress	coal-black	coalition	hodmandod	Cornaceae
boxkeeper	rockcress	mould-loft	collation	tormentor	connected
jockteleg	cock-broth	hoplology	pollution	communard	connecter
cockneyfy	mocker-nut	coal-plant	collotype	communise	low-necked
cockle-bur	monk's-seam	worldling	collative	communism	pound-cake
folk-weave	jockstrap	tol-lolish	pollutive	communist	connector
cocksfoot	cockateel	coal-plate	soul-curer	loaminess	moonscape
fork-chuck	cockatiel	jolliment	soulfully	Mormonism	townscape
rock-shaft	rocketeer	Moslemism	colluvies	roominess	fornicate
lock-chain	forky-tail	Coelomata	boulevard	comminate	tornadoes
bookshelf	bookstall	coelomate	worldwide	comminute	point-duty
cock-a-hoop	bookstand	collimate	coal-owner	community	count-down
cockshoot	docketing	mollymawk	Tod-lowrie	Mormonite	lounge-bar
monkshood	Folketing	collinear	following	cosmonaut	pounce-bag
Yorkshire	honky-tonk	non-linear	Hollywood	tormentum	rounceval
workpiece	pocketing	pollen-sac	holloware	torminous	roundelay
cockfight	socketing	Hollander	mouldwarp	worm-holed	round-eyed
folk-right	bookstore	lowlander	doomwatch	zoomorphy	young-eyed
rock-pipit	pocketful	lollingly	worm-eaten	cosmorama	pointedly
Cockaigne	folk-music	dolliness	cosmocrat	boomerang	pounce-box
workplace	rock-guano	godliness	formicant	commorant	bounteous
Volkslied	cockswain	jolliness	formicary	cormorant	sound-film
look-alike	donkey-man	lowliness	formicate	rosmarine	townsfolk
rock-plant	monkey-bag	nobleness	commodore	woomerang	corniform
bookplate	monkey-jar	soiliness	commodity	worm-grass	hound-fish
rock-flour	monkey-pot	pollinate	worm-fence	commissar	round-fish
locksmith	jockeyism	pollinium	worm-fever	job-master	hornyhead
dog-kennel	monkeyish	poll-money	cosmogeny	tommy-shop	Roundhead
rock-snake	monkeyism	soil-bound	cosmogony	committal	corn-shuck
mockingly	monkey-run	coal-house	worm-wheel	commutual	joint-heir
soakingly	foolhardy	coal-mouse	topmaking	dogmatics	sound-hole
boskiness	low-loader	cool-house	pommelled	committed	moonshine
cockiness	toolmaker	toll-house	sommelier	committee	moonshiny
corkiness	mouldable	toolhouse	cosmology	godmother	roundhand
forkiness	fool-happy	goalmouth	boom-slang	zoometric	down-throw
rockiness	colleague	tollbooth	Commelina	coemption	loan-shark
work-woman	jollyboat	colloquia	formulary	commotion	hobnailed
cockroach	roll-about	pot-liquor	formalise	cosmotron	downright
workforce	hoolachan	bowler-hat	formalism	dormition	moonlight
book-token	collected	forlornly	formalist	formation	cornfield
cork-borer	collector	foolproof	formulise	dogmatory	pointillé
hook-nosed	collocate	foul-brood	normalise	dormitory	poinciana
rock-borer	collodion	Lollardry	formality	dogmatise	councilor
cock-robin	poulterer	coal-brass	formulate	dogmatism	bountiful
folkloric	mollified	goslarite	normality	dogmatist	cornelian
rock-solid	mollifier	collyrium	non-member	commutate	point-lace

moon-glade	hornstone	colonelcy	horologic	homonymic	soapworks
poenology	moonstone	bolometer	monologic	homotypic	zoophorus
foundling	sonneting	coco-de-mer	monotonic	Monogynia	pompholyx
moon-blind	cognation	coroneted	Solomonic	monotypic	soupspoon
somnolent	cognition	hodometer	topologic	toponymic	corporeal
youngling	connation	monometer	locomotor	golomynka	Popperian
boundless	connature	potometer	homomorph	monoxylon	corporify
countless	sonnetary	tonometer	Notodonta	colocynth	cooperage
jointless	cornetist	monomeric	homologue	zoophagan	nonpareil
pointless	sonnetise	poromeric	monocoque	comptable	comptroll
soundless	sonnetist	monoceros	monologue	complaint	co-operant
woundless	connotate	bolometry	colourman	comprador	cooperant
loin-cloth	cognitive	hodometry	mobocracy	zooplasty	coopering
corn-flour	connotive	horometry	monocracy	poppycock	coppering
cornemuse	moonquake	Notonecta	monotroch	compacted	godparent
zoonomist	down-quilt	box-office	nomocracy	hop-picker	poppering
moon-knife	moanfully	Lotophagi	gonorrhea	hop-pocket	non-person
foiningly	connivent	monophagy	logorrhea	compactly	copperish
bonniness	downswing	homophile	sojourner	compactor	zooperist
downiness	joint-worm	iodophile	homograft	torpedoer	co-operate
horniness	round-worm	toxophily	loxodrome	torpedoes	cooperate
jointness	woundwort	monorhyme	loxodromy	dog-paddle	corporate
roundness	sound-wave	colophony	monodrama	hooped-pot	porporate
soundness	connexion	do-nothing	monotreme	torpidity	nonparous
youngness	connexive	homophone	Nototrema	pompadour	poppy-seed
corn-borer	Johnny-raw	homophony	colourant	completed	corpuscle
going-over	down-gyved	monophony	colouring	completer	foppishly
moon-loved	down-lying	monorhine	holocrine	co-sphered	rompishly
boondocks	Dodonaean	gonophore	hodograph	morphemic	corposant
down-going	Notogaean	monochord	holograph	morphetic	composure
townhouse	coronated	notochord	homograph	complexly	composite
cornopean	monolater	molochise	logograph	soapberry	pomposity
John-apple	logomachy	monophase	logogriph	complexus	torpitude
sound-post	monomachy	holophote	monograph	poppy-head	compotier
Cointreau®	Colocasia	holophyte	Monotropa	comprisal	hospitage
corn-bread	homogamic	logothete	nomograph	dolphinet	soopstake
corner-man	homotaxic	nomothete	rotograph	loop-light	hospitale
hornwrack	homotaxis	monodical	tomograph	zoophilia	competent
downgrade	monobasic	colorific	colourist	comptible	computant
Boanerges	monogamic	dolomitic	motocross	compliant	soapstone
town-crier	monomania	dolorific	colourful	compelled	computist
down-train	Notogaeic	honorific	pomoerium	gospeller	hospitium
corn-brake	porogamic	sodomitic	homousian	corpulent	pompously
corncrake	motorable	soporific	Molossian	gospelise	pot-pourri
corner-boy	Novocaine®	notoriety	motor-ship	soup-plate	porphyria
cornbrash	rotovator	notorious	rotor-ship	compander	porphyrio
foundress	monolatry	mono-skier	monopsony	companied	zoophytic
jointress	holocaust	corolline	colosseum	compendia	complying
pointsman	ionopause	loco-plant	monostich	hoop-snake	torquated
roundsman	polonaise	monocline	pogo-stick	rompingly	coequally
youngster	novodamus	monoplane	colostric	toppingly	conqueror
countship	motor-boat	corollary	monostyle	component	courbaril
tonnishly	motor-bike	homoplasy	colostomy	compandor	soar-eagle
cognisant	motorcade	monoamine	co-portion	companion	doorn-boom
coenosarc	monorchid	cocoa-nibs	Homoptera	soapiness	correctly
goings-out	hodoscope	colonnade	monoptote	soppiness	corrector
sonneteer	horoscope	cocoonery	colostrum	gowpenful	court-card
downstage	horoscopy	Bolognese	monocular	topping-up	fourscore
downstair	poroscope	homopolar	cocoa-wood	gomphosis	pop-record
round-trip	poroscopy	gonococci	homotypal	morphosis	comradely
cornstalk	monoecism	horologer	toponymal	morphotic	Notre-Dame
youngthly	do-goodery	homoeosis	co-polymer	zoophobia	corrodent
cornstone	do-goodism	homotonic	holotypic	zoophoric	joy-riding

torridity	poorhouse	horse-foot	looseness	pousowdie	hostlesse
courtesan	boar-spear	goose-fish	lousiness	goose-wing	north-east
courtezan	corrupter	fog-signal	moistness	copsewood	poetresse
fourpence	corruptly	consigned	mossiness	coastward	south-east
journeyed	sobriquet	consignee	noisiness	housework	zootheism
journeyer	court-roll	consigner	worseness	lousewort	bottleful
tourneyer	poor's-roll	consignor	consensus	coastwise	portreeve
bourgeois	boardroom	Monsignor	consonous	mooseyard	pontifice
fourpenny	hoar-frost	goose-girl	poison-nut	pontianac	volte-face
lowrie-tod	sour-crout	moss-agate	poisonous	pontianak	fortified
tournedos	Fourcroya	horsehide	poison-ivy	portrayal	fortifier
Monroeism	nourisher	horsehair	monsoonal	post-nasal	mortified
courgette	courtship	household	torsional	post-natal	mortifier
courteous	touristic	mouse-hole	hop-scotch	boot-faced	mouthfuls
horrified	boorishly	mouse-hunt	dogshores	bootmaker	coltsfoot
torrefied	sourishly	goose-herd	non-smoker	mortgagee	soothfast
board-foot	worrisome	noosphere	zooscopic	mortgager	forty-five
court-fool	co-present	conspirer	zoosporic	portrayer	Portuguee
cobriform	corrasion	conscient	doss-house	root-eater	contagion
toe-ragger	corrosion	conscious	joss-house	rostrated	contagium
board-game	bourasque	forsaking	lobscouse	toothache	voltigeur
corrigent	corrosive	loose-leaf	dog's-tooth	footfault	youthhead
corrugate	door-stead	tonsillar	horseplay	mouthable	goat's-hair
door-cheek	door-stone	joss-block	gossiping	hootnanny	soft-shell
four-wheel	hoar-stone	consultee	gossypine	mortgagor	youthhood
court-hand	nouriture	consulter	horse-pond	root-cause	mouth-harp
mournival	Socratise	house-leek	Gossypium	contralti	doctrinal
coercible	coarctate	houselled	fossorial	contralto	Noctuidae
coercibly	boardwalk	consulage	tonsorial	post-haste	bobtailed
court-leet	borrowing	coastline	conscribe	soft-paste	container
log-roller	sorrowing	house-line	constrict	mortician	contriver
coprology	gourd-worm	moss-plant	construct	foeticide	tortrices
courtlike	sorrowful	consultor	toast-rack	porticoed	footlight
courtling	courtyard	dog-salmon	conserver	porticoes	fortnight
four-flush	four-by-two	boastless	consorted	corticoid	tortricid
hour-glass	constancy	fossilise	consorter	monticule	rostellar
coprolite	moustache	horseless	construer	poeticule	bootblack
correlate	bog-spavin	houseless	consortia	forthcome	fortalice
door-plate	constable	noiseless	constrain	toothcomb	noctiluca
hourplate	house-boat	consolate	bowstring	conticent	portulaca
no-trumper	horseback	consulate	bowstrung	zootechny	soothlich
worriment	roast-beef	fossulate	house-room	contactor	hosteller
fogramite	house-bote	horsemeat	conscript	poeticise	postiller
fogramity	house-coat	roast-meat	goustrous	poeticism	fortilage
hog-ringer	fossicker	housemaid	monstrous	vorticism	nostology
porrenger	house-carl	noisomely	moss-grown	vorticist	sortilege
porringer	goose-club	consuming	goose-step	vorticose	sortilegy
hour-angle	mouse-deer	horsemint	possessed	corticate	nostalgia
louringly	house-duty	rousement	sob-sister	posticous	nostalgic
roaringly	bolstered	gossamery	horseshoe	contadina	sootflake
soaringly	corsleted	house-mate	possessor	contadine	hostilely
sopranino	holstered	poison-gas	mouse-trap	contadini	monthling
hoariness	howsoever	poison-oak	joss-stick	contadino	northland
sopranist	roisterer	sons-in-law	corsetier	Southdown	portolano
sorriness	roysterer	goose-neck	forsythia	bottle-gas	postulant
sour-dough	bobsleigh	goosander	horsetail	soft-pedal	southland
boarhound	Bolshevik	pop-singer	mouse-tail	voltmeter	postilion
hoarhound	poussette	cousinage	corseting	pontlevis	mortalise
pourpoint	roussette	voisinage	cosseting	zoothecia	mouthless
four-hours	house-flag	rousingly	top-sawyer	northerly	toothless
pourboire	dorsiflex	consonant	housewife	southerly	worthless
sour-gourd	housefuls	bossiness	sousewife	bottle-imp	footcloth
four-horse	goosefoot	horsiness	horsewhip	pottle-pot	footplate

hostility	foot-pound	footstalk	colubrine	polyvinyl	spectacle
mortality	root-bound	foot-stall	volucrine	monyplies	spectator
mortcloth	footboard	portatile	rogueship	polyploid	specialty
postulate	moot-court	coatstand	roguishly	polyglott	space-band
tortility	boathouse	font-stone	hocussing	polyamide	spice-bush
rostellum	foot-loose	mort-stone	coquetted	polyonymy	epicyclic
contumacy	moothouse	footstool	volunteer	Houyhnhnm	spice-cake
mouth-made	porthouse	hortation	voluntary	polyandry	epicedial
contemned	post-horse	sortation	nocuously	polygonal	epicedian
contemner	posthouse	sortition	cocus-wood	polytonal	epicedium
contemper	root-house	hortatory	convector	polyzonal	epiclesis
costumier	toothpick	hortative	convocate	polyposis	specified
contumely	dottipoll	portative	convolute	polyzooid	epicritic
contemnor	coeternal	contoured	pot-valour	polymorph	spicilege
northmost	doctorial	routously	dog-violet	polyzoary	spaceless
southmost	nocturnal	costively	converter	polygonum	speckless
zootomist	coat-frock	boatswain	polverine	Polyporus .	apiculate
continual	contorted	howtowdie	wolverene	holy-cruel	speculate
pottingar	couturier	northward	wolverine	polyarchy	spiculate
cottonade	voiturier	southward	convertor	polygraph	epicentre
boutonnée	fosterage	toothwort	wolvishly	polyester	spiciness
contender	porterage	mouthwash	non-voting	polyptych	apocopate
contented	boat-train	north-west	solvation	polystyle	Epicurean
continued	cotter-pin	south-west	convivial	holystone	epicurise
continuer	sooterkin	toothwash	convexity	body-curer	epicurism
pontoneer	doctorand	forthwith	Norwegian	bodyguard	spaceship
pontonier	footprint	lobulated	porwiggle	polyaxial	space-suit
pottinger	fostering	nodulated	boxwallah	Polygynia	space-time
routineer	loitering	non-usager	pot-waller	polytypic	apocrypha
cotton-gin	pottering	jocularly	forwander	pozzolana	spade-bone
joltingly	root-prune	popularly	bow-window	wooziness	apodictic
poutingly	rostering	joculator	forwarder	monzonite	spade-foot
continent	torturing	modulator	forwardly	douzepers	spadillio
softening	tottering	Columbian	nor'-wester	appanaged	opodeldoc
contangos	foster-son	columbine	sou'-wester	aplanatic	spodumene
hottentot	posterior	columbary	coaxially	speakable	epedaphic
Hottentot	coat-dress	columbate	coaxingly	ups-a-daisy	epidermal
post-entry	doctoress	columbite	cony-catch	apparatus	spider-man
dottiness	Pooterism	columbium	polywater	speal-bone	spider-leg
goutiness	porteress	homuncule	polymathy	spraickle	spider-web
loftiness	posturist	homunculi	Corydalis	sprauchle	epidermic
Montanism	soft-grass	coruscant	polybasic	uplandish	epidermis
Montanist	doctorate	coruscate	Polygamia	apparency	spadesman
routinism	posterity	loquacity	polygamic	speak-easy	spadassin
routinist	Southroun	toluidine	corybants	sphacelus	epidosite
sootiness	torturous	jocundity	polymasty	splay-foot	spadework
voltinism	contested	rotundate	corymbose	spearfish	speed-boat
fortunate	poetaster	rotundity	molybdate	spragging	speed-ball
sostenuto	route-step	conundrum	molybdous	spearhead	spleuchan
continuum	sottisier	volumeter	polygenic	splashily	up-perched
souteneur	doltishly	columella	polymeric	splashing	upper-case
totting-up	loutishly	toruffled	cotyledon	apparitor	appendage
fortunize	sottishly	Roquefort	polyhedra	appalling	appendant
post-woman	loathsome	voluminal	coryphaei	sprawling	sphendone
soft-goods	toothsome	Zonuridae	polyphagy	spearmint	splendent
pontooner	youthsome	Lotus-land	bodyshell	sphagnous	spreading
portioned	cortisone	locuplete	coryphene	Appaloosa	splendour
portioner	contusion	columnist	polyphone	sphaerite	ephemerae
postponer	poetastry	wofulness	polyphony	spear-side	ephemeral
soft-nosed	contusive	torulosis	polythene	spear-wood	appetence
zootrophy	rootstock	colubriad	polyphase	spearwort	appetency
portfolio	fortitude	Solutrean	copyright	opobalsam	apheresis
zoetropic	coat-style	Solutrian	polypidom	specially	epaenetic

ephemerid	upaithric	spymaster	upholster	apartness	epitomise
ephemeris	sprightly	spinnaker	opportune	apertness	epitomist
splenetic	uprightly	sponsalia	sprouting	spareness	Spatangus
ephemeron	aphidical	spendable	uprooting	spur-royal	epitapher
speechify	Epeiridae	epinician	apportion	spur-rowel	epitaphic
sprechery	speirings	epinicion	spoonwise	aperiodic	upstaring
speechful	apsidiole	up-and-down	spoonways	spark-plug	epitaxial
spherical	sprinkler	sponge-bag	apophatic	sportsman	spauld-ill
appetiser	ephialtes	spinneret	epiphanic	spiraster	spruce-fir
speerings	ophiology	spanaemia	epipolism	operosely	epaulette
splenitis	upfilling	spanaemic	epiphragm	oppressor	spout-hole
appetible	Ophiurida	spongeous	epiphytal	operosity	upgushing
spreckled	ophiuroid	spiniform	apophyses	spiritual	spoutless
appealing	apriorism	open-chain	epiphyses	spirituel	oppugnant
appellant	apriorist	open-field	apophysis	spare-time	upburning
upwelling	apriority	sponsible	epiphysis	operating	upturning
speedless	spoilsman	spongiose	epiphytic	spiriting	up-current
appellate	spritsail	spongious	sportance	epuration	up-putting
uppermost	splitting	epinikian	spermaria	operation	spluttery
spleenish	sprinting	epinikion	spermatia	spiration	apivorous
spleenful	uplifting	spangling	spermatic	spiritism	spawn-cake
sphenodon	upsitting	spindling	spermatid	spiritist	spewiness
upheaping	splintery	spineless	spartanly	spiritoso	upsy-daisy
ephedrine	spike-fish	spinulose	sportable	spiritful	aphyllous
speedster	spike-nail	spinulate	approbate	spirit-gum	sphygmoid
appertain	spikenard	spinulous	up-pricked	spiritous	epizootic
upsetting	spikiness	eponymous	spark-coil	aperitive	epizeuxis
spherular	spike-rush	open-ended	sperm-cell	operative	aquabatic
speedwell	spokesman	spininess	spiracula	opercular	squabbler
apoenzyme	spokewise	opinioned	sporocarp	upbrought	squabbish
epigraphy	appliance	up-and-over	spore-case	up-draught	square-leg
spaghetti	appliable	open-armed	sporocyst	upwrought	aqua-regia
epigaeous	spellable	spin-drier	sporidial	operculum	aquarelle
Spigelian	spoliator	spin-dryer	sporidesm	upgrowing	squamella
apogamous	spellbind	spindrift	sporidium	spirewise	squashily
epigynous	spulebane	Upanishad	sparterie	apprizing	aqua-vitae
spagerist	spulebone	epinastic	sparsedly	apostatic	equaliser
spagirist	epilobium	spinosity	sparteine	epistasis	squalidly
spagyrist	applicant	open-steek	sporogeny	epistatic	aquariums
upcheered	apple-cart	spondulix	Spirogyra	epistaxis	aquariist
up-Channel	applicate	Spinozism	spur-wheel	spasmatic	aquatinta
upthunder	spelldown	Spinozist	apartheid	episodial	squawking
optimates	apologise	opsomania	epirrhema	epistemic	aquaplane
opsimathy	apologist	opposable	apprehend	apostille	equalling
optically	epilogise	epeolatry	spur-whang	apishness	squailing
spoil-bark	spellican	ephoralty	eparchate	episcopal	squalling
sphincter	spellikin	spoon-bait	appraisal	epistoler	equalness
Ophiuchus	spillikin	spoonbill	appraiser	epistolet	squatness
epainetic	apple-jack	upholding	upbraider	apostolic	squamosal
spriteful	apple-john	opponency	X-particle	epistolic	aquaboard
April-fish	opal-glass	optometer	spirillar	spasmodic	aquadrome
spoil-five	opulently	optometry	uptrilled	opusculum	squadrone
spring-bed	spillover	spoon-feed	sparkling	spatially	squarrose
springlet	epileptic	spoon-food	spareless	sputterer	squatting
springald	speldring	optophone	sparkless	apathetic	squelcher
springily	spilosite	spoon-hook	spireless	apothecia	squeakily
sprigging	apple-tree	aphoriser	sportless	epithesis	squeaking
springing	epilation	spoonmeat	spirality	epithetic	squeakery
springbok	epulation	appointed	sporulate	epitheton	squealing
spring-box	apple-tart	appointee	spirillum	spot-check	squeamish
spring-gun	applauder	upbounden	apartment	spotlight	squeezing
spoil-heap	apple-wife	appointor	sporangia	spatulate	squinancy
uplighted	apomictic	up-country	sparingly	apetalous	squirarch

equitable	irradiate	crab-louse	practicum	precision	tradesman
equitably	ortanique	crab-apple	Trachinus	processor	predesign
squiralty	broad-leaf	tribesman	trochilus	truck-shop	prudishly
equivalve	cream-laid	proboscis	brick-kiln	prick-spur	eruditely
squibbing	breadline	arabesque	trochlear	precisive	iridotomy
squireage	dreamland	crabstick	truck-load	Brechtian	erudition
aquilegia	treadling	grub-stake	crackling	precatory	gradation
equisetic	broadloom	probation	freckling	fricative	predation
squiredom	dreadless	probatory	prickling	precative	tradition
equisetum	dreamless	tributary	trickling	fructuary	predatory
equipment	wreakless	probative	truckling	fructuate	proditory
equivocal	treadmill	traceable	truculent	fructuous	predative
equipoise	arrayment	traceably	bractless	Cracovian	traditive
equivoque	treatment	tractable	frockless	brickwall	predevote
equipping	area-sneak	tractator	graceless	prickwood	bridewell
squinting	breakneck	bric-à-brac	priceless	brickwork	free-lance
squirting	broadness	track-boat	price-list	trachytic	grievance
squint-eye	greatness	brick-clay	traceless	Brachyura	trierarch
breakaway	triatomic	Ericaceae	trackless	brickyard	irrelated
ergataner	trialogue	frock-coat	truceless	graduated	free-range
arracacha	organ-pipe	precocial	gracility	gradually	freezable
pre-adamic	breadroom	tricycler	oraculous	graduator	freemason
breakable	breadroot	tricyclic	tricolour	Iridaceae	greenback
creatable	creatress	precocity	draconian	Traducian	green-bone
treatable	broadside	procacity	Uriconian	bridecake	order-book
great-aunt	bread-tree	crocodile	Arachnida	predicant	breed-bate
broad-bean	breastpin	precedent	pre-cancel	traducing	proembryo
dreamboat	broadtail	preceding	arachnoid	predictor	arc-en-ciel
breakback	triactine	procident	dracontic	eradicate	friedcake
broad-brim	creatural	procedure	precentor	predacity	brief-case
broadband	treasurer	brick-dust	draconism	predicate	friending
friarbird	break-wind	crackdown	erectness	tridactyl	free-bench
greatcoat	broadwise	tracheide	preconise	dredge-box	creepered
cream-cake	cream-wove	cricketer	priciness	grudgeful	green-eyed
bread-corn	broadways	crocheted	proconsul	predefine	trieteric
broadcast	organzine	proceeder	Urochorda	predigest	arle-penny
Triandria	crab-eater	bracteole	trichosis	tredrille	truepenny
errand-boy	crab-faced	procreant	tricrotic	predikant	freeze-dry
Dryasdust	trabeated	tracheary	precipice	predilect	greengage
breakdown	grub-screw	précieuse	preceptor	prideless	pre-engage
break-even	trebuchet	bracteate	trackroad	tradeless	freesheet
organelle	trabecula	procreate	procuracy	credulity	free-wheel
ervalenta	tribadism	Tracheata	precurrer	credulous	tree-shrew
grease-gun	crab's-eyes	tracheate	traceried	urodelous	creep-hole
trial-fire	crabbedly	crucified	trichroic	bridemaid	breeching
breakfast	crab-sidle	crucifier	trichrome	trademark	greenhand
arraigner	cribellar	cruciform	urochrome	tridymite	greenhorn
triangled	tribology	eruciform	precursor	tridental	arsenical
preachify	drabbling	truck-farm	procaryon	Uredineae	free-diver
breathily	fribbling	crack-hemp	procaryot	uredinial	free-liver
dreamhole	aryballos	practical	tricerion	tridented	free-rider
preachily	fribblish	trichinae	crack-rope	prudently	tree-lined
breathing	tribalism	Trochidae	procuress	tradename	artemisia
preaching	tribalist	practised	procerity	crudeness	arteritis
treachery	tribeless	practiser	cracksman	credendum	praesidia
breathful	cribellum	proclitis	precisian	uredinium	pre-exilic
treachour	prebendal	proctitis	fricassee	uredinous	arteriole
erratical	Orobanche	trachitis	processed	prodromal	arseniate
organical	arabinose	trichitic	trickster	prodromic	arsenious
organised	Trubenise®	triclinic	tricuspid	prudhomme	triecious
organiser	tribunate	trochilic	precisely	prodromus	Orwellian
armadillo	tribunite	Fructidor	tricksome	Gradgrind	Greekling
irradiant	prebiotic	fractious	prick-song	bridesman	gruelling

briefless
Greekless
griefless
orderless
irreality
urceolate
triennial
tree-snake
tree-onion
cruelness
greenness
Orleanism
Orleanist
freewoman
freewomen
praecoces
praenomen
free-board
freebooty
free-space
pre-employ
pre-emptor
free-trade
arrearage
tree-trunk
brier-root
greenroom
greensand
grief-shot
priest-rid
free-style
argentine
Argentino
freestone
priestess
argentite
orientate
arrestive
irregular
Greenwich
greenweed
brier-wood
greenwood
proenzyme
oriflamme
drift-bolt
orificial
prefacial
trifacial
trifocals
proffered
profferer
prefigure
trefoiled
drift-land
craftless
driftless
profilist
trifolium
profanely
gruffness
profanity
preferred

preferrer
triformed
triforium
craftsman
draftsman
dry-fisted
professed
drift-sail
profusely
professor
profusion
profiteer
profiting
prefatory
profluent
drift-weed
drift-wood
prefixion
fragrance
fragrancy
frogmarch
pregnance
pregnancy
frog-eater
orography
urography
bregmatic
pragmatic
pregnable
programme
tragedian
brigadier
frigidity
drag-chain
drug-fiend
fragilely
traguline
wriggling
tragelaph
frugalist
fragility
frugality
dragomans
trigamist
trigamous
trigynian
dragonfly
brigandry
dragoness
dragonise
dragonish
dragonism
Origenism
Origenist
aragonite
originate
erogenous
trigonous
trigynous
prognoses
prognosis
drag-hound
frogmouth

gregarian
Gregorian
Gregarina
gregarine
progestin
frigatoon
drug-store
frightful
tregetour
Brahmanic
orthoaxis
trihybrid
Archibald
Orchideae
trihedral
trihydric
trihedron
orchidist
orthodoxy
orthoepic
arch-felon
archaiser
Brahminee
arthritic
arthritis
Brahminic
arch-fiend
archology
prehallux
archilowe
archimage
archangel
orphanage
archontic
arch-enemy
prehensor
orphanism
arthrosis
arthropod
orthopedy
orthoptic
Arthurian
arch-druid
orpharion
archeress
orchestic
orchestra
architect
orthotics
arch-stone
orthotone
archetype
orthotist
archducal
archduchy
archivolt
archivist
arrivance
arrivancy
irritancy
ordinance
urticaria
drainable

irrigable
irritable
irritably
trainable
irrigator
irritator
train-band
fruit-cake
braincase
brain-dead
armigeral
cruiseway
broiderer
fruiterer
praiseful
frying-pan
Orpington
Irvingism
Irvingite
freighter
ornithoid
artichoke
druidical
artificer
arrivisme ·
arriviste
vraicking
treillage
armillary
artillary
brainless
fruitless
argillite
orgillous
frailness
traitorly
drain-pipe
arbitrage
orris-root
arbitrary
arbitress
traitress
arbitrate
brainsick
orgiastic
croissant
traipsing
drain-trap
armistice
fruit-tree
drain-tile
articular
orbicular
irriguous
fruitwood
brainwash
brainwave
projector
prejudice
Prakritic
brakeless
brokerage
prokaryon

prokaryot
brakes-man
brake-shoe
krakowiak
arillated
trilobate
Trilobita
trilobite
prolicide
frolicked
prolactin
prelector
preludial
urolagnia
orologist
prologise
urologist
trellised
brilliant
prolamine
trilinear
prolonger
drollness
trollopee
prolepses
prolepsis
proleptic
prolapsus
grill-room
arblaster
artlessly
prelusion
prolusion
prelusory
prolusory
prelusive
prelatial
trilithic
prolately
prelation
prolation
trilithon
prelature
proletary
prelatess
prelatise
prelatish
prelatism
prelatist
uralitise
prolative
prolixity
Brummagem
grammatic
crammable
drum-major
cramp-bone
cramp-bark
promachos
cremocarp
trump-card
dromedare
dromedary

primaeval
trumpeted
trumpeter
trumped-up
bromoform
cramp-fish
Cro-Magnon
krummhorn
cramp-iron
bromeliad
grimalkin
brambling
crumpling
grumbling
primuline
trampling
tremblant
trembling
tremolant
tremulant
crimeless
primality
tremolite
tremulate
tremulous
Gramineae
promenade
prominent
griminess
premonish
primeness
criminate
criminous
primrosed
trampolin
primipara
primarily
cramp-ring
trimerous
cremaster
trimester
premosaic
promuscis
promising
promissor
crumb-tray
primatial
primitiae
primitial
primitias
dramatics
drumstick
Trematoda
trematode
trematoid
brimstone
brimstony
prompting
cremation
premotion
promotion
crematory
dramaturg

premature
prompture
aromatise
dramatise
dramatist
eremitism
primitive
promotive
trimethyl
framework
grandaddy
frontager
iron-cased
truncated
drinkable
grantable
printable
grand-aunt
brinjarry
prongbuck
prenubile
wring-bolt
pronuclei
wry-necked
trunk-call
transcend
crankcase
irenicism
grenadier
wrong-doer
grenadine
Orangeman
cranreuch
orangeade
brandered
princelet
trinketer
Frankenia
orange-tip
princekin
drunkenly
trancedly
transenna
princedom
cranberry
trinketry
Orangeism
princesse
wrong-foot
transform
transfuse
trunkfish
branchiae
branchial
bronchial
branchlet
Frenchify
drink-hail
transhume
branching
trenchand
trenchant
wrenching

truncheon
branchery
pronghorn
trenchard
franchise
trunk-hose
crinoidal
frenzical
principal
Crinoidea
iron-miner
iron-sided
Ironsides
principia
frangible
principle
transient
brand-iron
grandiose
crenelled
irenology
uranology
urinology
Franglais
granuloma
brandling
brangling
crinoline
front-line
trunk-line
wrangling
prunellos
granulary
frontless
granulose
printless
crenulate
granulate
granulite
translate
granulous
trinomial
trunk-mail
ironsmith
transmute
transmove
Brunonian
droningly
brand-name
crankness
frankness
grandness
proneness
wrongness
uraninite
francolin
transonic
iron-mould
iron-bound
front-page
drone-pipe
grandpapa
transpire

transport
transpose
trunk-road
front-rank
brandreth
prankster
transship
dronishly
pranksome
print-shop
grandsire
uraniscus
granitoid
ironstone
arenation
crenation
prenotion
pronation
urination
crenature
granitise
granitite
urinative
orang-utan
pronounce
transumpt
transvest
frontward
trunk-work
frontwise
frontways
Grundyism
arrogance
arrogancy
areolated
preorally
Areopagus
crookback
cryoscope
cryoscopy
preoccupy
broom-corn
preordain
areometer
cryometer
ergometer
eriometer
kryometer
cryogenic
crookedly
arboreous
arboretum
erroneous
arrow-head
Bryophyta
bryophyte
Armorican
Oriolidae
creolised
brooklime
proofless
prooemion
proof-mark

prooemium
ergonomic
proof-read
arrowroot
broomrape
ergograph
groomsman
priorship
troop-ship
arrow-shot
areostyle
preoption
proof-text
brookweed
trionymal
crop-eared
cryptadia
crop-marks
prepacked
drop-scene
drop-scone
trepidant
propodeon
propodeum
tripudium
fripperer
graphemic
prophetic
gruppetto
uropygial
propagule
propagate
uropygium
cryptical
dropsical
graphical
trappings
graphitic
propriety
prepollex
propelled
propeller
propylaea
tropology
crapulent
crepoline
crippling
propylene
grapeless
propylite
crapulous
trepanned
trepanner
gripingly
gropingly
treponema
proponent
drepanium
cryptogam
triploidy
proptosis
cropbound
wrapround

cryptonym
draperied
draperies
properdin
drop-drill
troparion
drop-press
grapeseed
tropistic
trapesing
grapeshot
tripe-shop
preputial
trap-stick
grapetree
trap-stair
Tripitaka
crepitant
drip-stone
drop-stone
prepotent
crepitate
grapevine
tripewife
triptyque
trapezial
trapezoid
trapezium
trapezius
frequence
frequency
triquetra
briquette
croquette
Iroquoian
prorector
triradial
prurience
pruriency
prorogate
ore-rested
prerosion
ororotund
proration
ore-raught
Aristarch
crispated
Crustacea
crustated
urn-shaped
prismatic
prostatic
crushable
graspable
crossbeam
truss-beam
crossbred
crossbill
crossband
wristband
press-book
crossbite
frostbite

dress-coat
prosector
trisector
prosecute
presidial
prosodial
prosodian
trust-deed
president
wrist-drop
prosodist
presidium
crash-dive
crescendo
crosiered
cross-eyed
freshener
brasserie
triskelia
crossette
cross-fade
crossfall
brush-fire
crossfire
dress-form
crossfish
press-gang
trisagion
cross-head
grasshook
preschool
eristical
prosaical
Aristides
grisaille
irascible
irascibly
prescient
brassière
trustiest
prussiate
prescious
crossjack
preselect
drysalter
bristling
crash-land
grassland
wrestling
crestless
crustless
frostless
graspless
trustless
proselyte
prosimian
gris-amber
grist-mill
irksomely
erasement
presuming
press-mark
grass-moth

prison-van	protected	bruteness	troubling	breveting	estate-car
presentee	britschka	cretinism	troutling	privation	ashamedly
presenter	graticule	triteness	troutless	privatise	essayette
frost-nail	triticale	cretinous	troublous	gravitate	estafette
presently	protector	prytaneum	proudness	privative	Ascaridae
briskness	Briticise	prothorax	triumphal	graveyard	ismatical
crassness	Briticism	trot-cosey	proud-pied	crow's-bill	ascarides
crispness	criticise	Brythonic	triumpher	crown-bark	estaminet
crossness	criticism	trattoria	trousseau	tri-weekly	Islamitic
freshness	eroticism	fraternal	fraudster	crow-berry	Ismailian
grossness	eroticist	oratorial	Proustian	crow's-foot	assaulter
prosiness	fruticose	oratorian	croustade	trawl-fish	assailant
prisonous	triticism	oratories	arcuation	crown-gall	establish
crossover	write-down	pretermit	irruption	crown-head	Ismailism
frescoing	erythemal	erythrina	proustite	draw-sheet	Israelite
frescoist	fritterer	troth-ring	irruptive	dry-waller	usualness
prose-poem	prothesis	criterion	arduously	trowelled	Kshatriya
grass-plot	prothetic	erythrism	triumviri	troweller	ash-bucket
crossroad	brotherly	preterist	triumviry	crown-land	ash-blonde
prescribe	tritheism	writeress	proveably	trawl-line	isobathic
proscribe	tritheist	erythrite	trivially	crewelist	isocratic
preserver	Crataegus	preterite	gravy-boat	crownless	isocyclic
cross-ruff	brutified	triturate	provocant	draw-plate	isochimal
grosgrain	gratified	craterous	Dravidian	brownness	isoclinal
pre-shrink	gratifier	Britisher	bravadoes	crow's-nest	psychical
crush-room	froth-fomy	protester	provident	brow-bound	isoclinic
press-room	Arctogaea	bretasche	provedore	grewhound	psychogas
prescript	frithgild	protistic	gravidity	brew-house	psychoses
proscript	protogine	brutishly	travailed	crowfoots	isochoric
erostrate	protogyny	protestor	provoking	crown-post	psychosis
frustrate	dratchell	grotesque	drivelled	frowardly	psychotic
prostrate	erstwhile	gratitude	driveller	prowessed	usucapion
dress-suit	fratching	gritstone	gravelled	crow-steps	isochrone
cross-sill	crotchety	prototype	grovelled	crow-quill	isocrymal
wrist-shot	fratchety	writative	groveller	crownwork	isodomous
press-stud	Arctiidae	fretfully	travelled	drawn-work	isodontal
crosstree	erethitic	bratwurst	traveller	proximate	Isidorian
grass-tree	proteinic	protoxide	trivalved	proximity	espérance
trashtrie	truthlike	prettyish	privilege	argy-bargy	Esperanto
cross-talk	brattling	prettyism	gravel-pit	graywacke	assembler
irisation	crotaline	protozoan	prevalent	greywacke	ascendant
grossular	gratulant	protozoic	trivalent	greybeard	ascendent
tressured	brutalise	protozoon	graveless	arsy-versy	ascending
proseucha	crotalism	araucaria	frivolity	arhythmia	osteoderm
proseuche	frothless	traumatic	frivolous	arhythmic	osmeteria
brusquely	trothless	arquebuse	Provençal	tray-cloth	usherette
prescutum	truthless	trouncing	preventer	prayingly	ashen-grey
crosswalk	wrathless	groundman	provender	greyhound	aspergill
crosswind	brutality	ground-oak	graveness	dray-horse	osteogeny
brushwood	gratulate	groundsel	drove-road	grey-goose	ascetical
brushwork	protamine	groundage	preverbal	prayerful	osteology
crossword	Aretinian	grounding	pre-vernal	prayer-rug	aspen-like
crosswort	pretended	ground-hog	traversed	prize-crew	osteopath
frostwork	pretender	ground-ash	traverser	Brazilian	aspersoir
press-work	arytenoid	ground-nut	travertin	brazeless	ushership
crosswise	Britannia	ground-ivy	yravished	prize-list	ascension
presbyter	Britannic	argus-eyed	prevision	prozymite	aspersion
presbyope	cretinoid	trousered	provision	craziness	aspersory
presbyopy	gratingly	trout-farm	provisory	prize-ring	ostensory
Bretwalda	pratingly	draughter	provostry	assayable	ascensive
prothalli	protonema	grouchily	brevetted	escapable	aspersive
write-back	protandry	draught-ox	privateer	escalator	ostensive
frithborh	Britoness	wrought-up	privately	asparagus	aspectual

essential	isolation	isosteric	Utraquism	athetosis	string-tie
ascertain	isolative	Psittacus	Utraquist	attempter	stringily
osteotome	asymmetry	isotactic	strap-work	steersman	strigging
osteotomy	psammitic	isotheral	strapwort	atheistic	stringent
asbestine	esemplasy	isotropic	straw-worm	stressful	stringing
assertion	isomerise	esoterism	steadying	steel-trap	Stringops
assertory	isomerism	Ashtaroth	straw-yard	street-car	stairhead
asbestous	isomerous	Ashtoreth	stable-man	streetway	strip-leaf
assentive	isometric	assurance	stable-boy	streetage	stridling
assertive	asymptote	pseudaxis	stabilise	attention	stripling
asafetida	isoniazid	assumable	stability	street-boy	stainless
isagogics	asyndetic	assumably	stock-dove	streetful	strip-mine
isogamete	asyndeton	assurable	sticheron	attentive	staidness
isogamous	isinglass	assumedly	stockfish	attenuant	Ethiopian
isogenous	isonomous	assuredly	stockinet	attenuate	stripping
asthmatic	asininity	assuaging	stichidia	strenuity	striation
ischiadic	asynergia	assurgent	stock-lock	strenuous	striature
ischiatic	isenergic	astucious	stockless	steel-wool	stricture
escheator	assonance	issueless	stock-list	steel-ware	strictish
isohyetal	ascorbate	Esquimaux	atacamite	steelwork	utricular
ischaemia	osmometer	pseudopod	stockpile	otherwise	utriculus
ischaemic	escopette	pseudonym	stack-room	steelyard	stair-well
asphaltic	associate	assumpsit	stock-room	staff-duty	stair-work
asphaltum	asmoulder	estuarial	stock-whip	stiffener	stairwise
Esthonian	assoilzie	estuarian	stockwork	stuff-gown	stokehold
oscitancy	astounded	estuarine	stackyard	stiff-neck	stoke-hole
estimable	estoppage	assuasive	stockyard	stiffness	stellated
estimably	estopping	assuetude	stadia-rod	staffroom	Stellaria
aspirator	ascospore	asexually	studiedly	staff-tree	style-book
estimator	escortage	stratagem	studentry	stag-dance	still-born
astichous	iso-octane	stramaçon	stud-horse	stagnancy	stilt-bird
ascitical	esophagus	stramazon	stud-groom	Stigmaria	stylobate
aspidioid	isopodous	steamboat	utterance	stigmatic	stalactic
oscillate	isopolity	steam-coal	athematic	stag-party	italicise
ostiolate	asepalous	steam-dome	utterable	stegodont	italicism
espionage	isopropyl	strategic	Athenaeum	stage-door	stolidity
ossifraga	psoriasis	steadfast	steel-blue	staggered	stalk-eyed
ossifrage	psoriatic	straggler	ytterbium	staggerer	stiltedly
assistant	escribano	strangler	steel-clad	stage-hand	stall-feed
ossicular	Ostracoda	strangles	stretched	stegomyia	styliform
assiduity	Ostracion	strangely	stretcher	stage-name	otologist
assiduous	ostracise	strap-game	attendant	staginess	still-head
ossifying	ostracism	strangury	steep-down	stegnosis	still-hunt
Isokontae	astraddle	strap-hang	athetesis	stegnotic	still-life
isokontan	astrodome	steam-haul	ethereous	staghound	stalkless
psalm-book	esurience	steatitic	steel-gray	stage-play	styleless
psalteria	esuriency	steadiest	steel-grey	Stagirite	Ptolemaic
isologous	usurpedly	strayling	etherical	Stagyrite	stalemate
esplanade	astrofell	strapless	streakily	stegosaur	staleness
esclandre	Ostrogoth	strawless	streaking	Stahlhelm	Stalinism
Asplenium	astrakhan	attainder	steenkirk	itchiness	stillness
isallobar	astrolabe	straining	atheology	ethically	stalworth
psalmodic	astrology	steatosis	steerling	stoically	still-room
asclepiad	estranged	stratonic	utterless	steinbock	stylistic
asclepias	estranger	strappado	stream-ice	staircase	stylishly
Asclepios	Astrantia	strapping	streamlet	strike-pay	athletics
Asclepius	astronomy	steam-pipe	stream-tin	stridence	stellular
ashlaring	astronaut	steam-port	streaming	stridency	stomachal
ashlering	estrapade	straw-rope	strewment	strifeful	stomached
ostleress	astrophel	straw-stem	uttermost	strikeout	stomacher
psaltress	tsarevich	steamship	otherness	stairfoot	stomachic
uselessly	isostatic	Atlantean	steepness	string-bag	atomicity
psalm-tune	isosceles	steam-trap	utterness	string-pea	stamp-duty

stammerer	stink-trap	athrocyte	état-major	butadiene	lumbricus
ethmoidal	stenotype	steradian	statocyst	audacious	numbskull
etymology	stenotypy	Pteridium	stutterer	fugacious	dumb-cluck
stimulant	stonewall	storm-drum	statuette	furacious	quibbling
stimulate	stink-wood	star-jelly	stitching	humankind	turbulent
stamp-mill	stoneware	stornelli	statehood	autarkist	suability
stamineal	stonework	stornello	stitchery	Judas-kiss	sun-bonnet
staminode	stonewort	sternebra	statelily	sugar-loaf	husbandly
staminody	stromatic	storiette	stateless	humanlike	husbandry
staminoid	stoolball	storyette	statolith	sugar-lump	tubbiness
staminate	strouding	store-farm	statement	sugarless	turbinate
stamp-note	stroke-oar	stern-fast	stational	sugar-mill	dumbfound
atomistic	atmometer	pteryglal	stationer	eudaemony	zumbooruk
stump-work	strongman	pterygoid	stateroom	sugar-mite	turboprop
stingaree	strongyle	pterygium	statesman	humanness	lumberman
stannator	strong-box	otorrhoea	stateside	ruralness	sunburned
sting-bull	strongarm	star-wheel	statistic	fumatoria	lumber-pie
stink-ball	strongest	starchily	statutory	subatomic	lumbering
stink-bomb	strongish	star-shell	statewide	sugar-palm	rubberise
stink-bird	atrophied	attrahent	strumatic	subalpine	furbisher
stonechat	strobilae	starshine	staunchly	sugar-pine	rubbishly
stone-coal	atrocious	Storthing	struggler	sugar-plum	nut-butter
ethnocide	strobilus	ptarmigan	stouthrie	subaerial	rum-butter
stone-cell	attollent	Sturnidae	strumitis	Judaistic	sunbather
stone-cold	strolling	starlight	strumming	subahship	curbstone
stonecrop	ethologic	sternitic	stoutness	subastral	outbounds
ethnicism	stropping	startling	strutting	Judas-tree	bum-baylie
stone-cast	strossers	startlish	attuition	subaction	mumchance
atonicity	strontium	sterilise	structure	subaltern	punctated
ethnicity	atmolysis	stormless	attuitive	duralumin	purchaser
stone-dead	step-dance	ottrelite	stevedore	Euraquilo	surcharge
stone-deaf	stop-watch	sterility	stove-pipe	eucalypti	cunctator
stander-by	step-fault	sternmost	atavistic	eucaryote	punctator
stintedly	stepbairn	staringly	stownlins	eukaryote	subclause
cteniform	stapedial	star-anise	stewardry	cumbrance	outcrafty
sting-fish	stupidity	starkness	stewartry	subbranch	quickbeam
stonefish	stapedius	sternness	stay-maker	cupbearer	hunchback
standgale	stupefied	stercoral	strychnia	sunbeamed	punch-ball
stanchlng	stupefier	star-nosed	strychnic	sun-beaten	succubine
stanchion	stepchild	starboard	itsy-bitsy	quebracho	quick-born
stinkhorn	styptical	Pteropoda	nunataker	gutbucket	succubous
stone-hard	stippling	star-apple	Gujarathi	outbacker	punch-bowl
stone-hawk	stipulary	sternport	sugar-ally	Quebecker	Juncaceae
ethnology	stipulate	stern-post	sugar-bean	Québecois	punch-card
stone-lily	stop-press	star-drift	sugar-beet	rudbeckia	muscadine
atonalism	stuporous	star-proof	sugar-cube	mum-budget	muscle-man
stingless	step-stone	storeroom	autarchic	turbidity	quickener
stintless	stipitate	star-crost	subarctic	bubble-car	quick-eyed
stoneless	Staphylea	star-grass	sugar-cane	tumble-car	succeeder
atonality	etiquette	storm-stay	subahdary	bumble-bee	butcherly
stone-mill	star-gazer	store-ship	out-and-out	humble-bee	cutcherry
atonement	storiated	storm-sail	subagency	humble-pie	zucchetto
atoningly	eternally	pterosaur	mutagenic	numble-pie	dulcified
stoniness	storm-beat	uterotomy	tularemia	Bumbledom	quick-fire
stenopaic	storm-belt	star-stone	tularemic	humblesse	lunch-hour
stone-pine	story-book	attrition	cutaneous	bubble-gum	punctilio
stand-pipe	storm-bird	iteration	musaceous	tumble-bug	muscology
itineracy	attribute	iterative	rutaceous	humbugged	quicklime
ethnarchy	stirabout	sterculia	tufaceous	humbugger	succulent
itinerant	storm-cock	storm-wind	Judas-hole	cubby-hole	juiceless
itinerary	ataractic	sternward	sudaminal	lumbrical	sulcalise
itinerate	storm-cone	stasidion	Tupaiidae	sun-bright	surculose
stoneshot	attractor	Ctesiphon	eutaxitic	dumb-piano	musculous

guacamole	quadrigae	superheat	suffragan	Bulgarian	authorish
curcumine	quadrifid	auger-hole	ruffianly	Hungarian	authorism
dulcamara	quadrille	queenhood	surf-canoe	vulgarian	Eucharist
vulcanian	burd-alane	superhive	puff-paste	fulgurant	Lutherism
buccaneer	guideline	numerical	surficial	vulgarise	Lutherist
buccanier	guideless	Eumenides	sufficing	vulgarism	authority
surcingle	subdolous	juvenilia	surfacing	fulgurate	rush-grown
subcantor	fundament	subeditor	suffocate	fulgurite	eurhythmy
succentor	humdinger	quaeritur	puff-adder	vulgarity	push-start
juiciness	mundanely	quaesitum	ruff-a-duff	fulgorous	outhauler
quickness	puddening	tube-skirt	curfuffle	fulgurous	pushfully
vulcanise	duodenary	museology	buff-wheel	hungerful	ruthfully
vulcanism	curdiness	queen-like	surfeited	lung-grown	push-cycle
vulcanist	muddiness	cupelling	surfeiter	Tungusian	dubitancy
runcinate	ruddiness	pure-blood	buffaloes	suggester	jubilance
succinate	mundanity	queenless	fulfilled	judgeship	jubilancy
succinite	burdenous	rubellite	fulfiller	fungosity	luminance
vulcanite	mundungus	luteolous	subfamily	budgeting	muricated
Turcophil	purdonium	supermart	muffin-cap	purgation	mutilated
turcopole	outdoorsy	outermost	muffin-man	budgetary	rutilated
punch-prop	guide-post	tunesmith	muffineer	purgatory	tunicated
susceptor	guide-rail	luteinise	puffingly	tungstate	puritanic
nuncupate	sundering	queerness	huffiness	purgative	Ruritania
succursal	guide-rope	quietness	puffiness	outgiving	cubically
hut-circle	murderess	supernova	turfiness	rug-headed	dubitable
muscarine	murderous	eudemonia	wulfenite	bush-metal	dubitably
subcostal	guideship	eudemonic	sunflower	bushwhack	judicable
quickstep	quadruman	juke-joint	surf-board	push-chair	musically
quicksand	quadruped	Euterpean	turf-spade	rushlight	fumigator
successor	quadruple	queen-post	turf-drain	bushel-man	judicator
dulcitude	subdivide	superpose	furfurole	busheller	mutilator
lunch-time	sun-downer	superplus	suffering	sun-helmet	ruminator
Dulcitone	Oudenarde	funebrial	dufferdom	euchology	supinator
furcation	Gujerathi	rune-craft	dufferism	euphemise	luminaire
guncotton	eumelanin	mugearite	furfurous	euphemism	Rubiaceae
sulcation	numerable	superstar	huffishly	Ruthenian	quail-call
succotash	numerably	supersede	suffusion	euthenics	auriscope
suscitate	numerally	queenship	buff-stick	bug-hunter	music-case
subcaudal	superable	rulership	muffettee	mug-hunter	subincise
punctured	superably	supersalt	outfitter	authentic	music-demy
succourer	numerator	quietsome	buffeting	gushingly	luminesce
punctuate	numeraire	queen's-arm	fungibles	pushingly	luciferin
Muscovian	superbity	queen-size	fungicide	bushiness	rubicelle
muscovado	ouzel-cock	curettage	turgidity	euphonise	Juniperus
Muscovite	tubercled	eutectoid	Ausgleich	euthanasy	pumiceous
muscovite	queen-cake	tubectomy	fungiform	euthenist	rubineous
quadratic	supercold	humectant	fungoidal	mushiness	audiogram
auld-warld	tubercule	subentire	cudgelled	oughtness	tuning-key
subduable	lutescent	humectate	cudgeller	rushiness	tuning-peg
subdeacon	pubescent	Bucentaur	bungaloid	euphonium	tuning-pin
quadratus	quiescent	humective	surgeless	ruthenium	music-hall
guide-book	rubescent	rune-stave	judge-made	cushioned	audiphone
bundobust	rufescent	nubeculae	judgement	cushionet	punishing
duodecimo	tumescent	dune-buggy	fulgently	euchloric	Munichism
fuddle-cap	supercool	duteously	pungently	lush-house	Culicidae
ruddleman	pudendous	hugeously	tuggingly	authorial	juridical
hundreder	Juneberry	musefully	turgently	bushcraft	municipal
cuddeehih	superfine	tunefully	subgenera	bush-fruit	Pulicidae
subduedly	cuneiform	supervene	bulginess	euphorbia	humiliant
hundredor	superfuse	supervise	pudginess	authoring	auxiliary
Dundreary	superflux	auger-worm	surgeoncy	wuthering	judiciary
hundredth	aubergine	outerware	dungeoner	authoress	humiliate
cul-de-four	pug-engine	tumefying	outgrowth	authorise	judicious

musicking	buck's-horn	guillemot	sublessor	gummatous	out-of-date
fusillade	buckthorn	oubliette	outlustre	summative	dupondius
audiology	buckshish	tuillette	burlesque	guinea-hen	auxometer
pupillage	cuckoldly	nullified	sublethal	guinea-pig	autotelic
pupillary	musk-gland	nullifier	bully-tree	turntable	suboffice
curialism	musk-plant	qualified	qualitied	turnabout	autophoby
curialist	cuckoldom	qualifier	subletter	turn-screw	autophagy
eudialyte	cuckoldry	bullwhack	bulletrie	burnt-cork	autophony
pupillate	duck's-meat	guildhall	sublation	pugnacity	bucolical
fusionism	muckender	gully-hole	outlaunch	quinidine	autotimer
fusionist	quakingly	bugle-horn	sun-lounge	turn-penny	sudorific
humidness	bulkiness	bullfinch	quillwort	quintette	autopilot
lucidness	duskiness	full-timer	hummocked	quintetto	autopista
luridness	funkiness	purloiner	submicron	tunny-fish	autoflare
tumidness	huskiness	bullfight	mummy-case	turnagain	autoclave
lunisolar	luckiness	full-blood	mummified	bunny-girl	tug-of-love
tubicolar	muckiness	full-blast	mummiform	quenching	buxomness
auditoria	murkiness	guileless	nutmegged	quantical	autosomal
audiophil	muskiness	guiltless	turmagant	funnelled	autonomic
quail-pipe	punkiness	qualmless	duumviral	funnel-net	autotoxin
music-rack	quakiness	pullulate	hummeller	tunnelled	autopoint
music-roll	sulkiness	full-blown	pummelled	tunneller	autoroute
music-room	musk-pouch	qualamdan	surmullet	tunnel-net	autocracy
tulip-root	cuckoo-fly	sublimely	nummuline	quinoline	dulocracy
auditress	buckhound	subliming	nummulary	outnumber	Eurocracy
tutiorism	buckboard	Muslimism	bummaloti	cunningly	autograft
tutiorist	duck-board	sublimise	nummulite	runningly	autograph
juniority	bucktooth	sublimate	submental	funniness	autotroph
ludicrous	cuckoo-bud	sublimity	augmented	sunniness	autocross
Sufiistic	Euskarian	outlinear	augmenter	turnround	tutorship
curiosity	junkerdom	sublinear	outmantle	turnip-fly	Junoesque
dubiosity	Quakerdom	Ausländer	culminant	turnip-top	suboctave
furiosity	junkerism	cullender	fulminant	subnormal	subocular
tulip-tree	Quakeress	outlander	augmentor	Turnerian	out-of-work
auricular	Quakerish	sublunary	mud-minnow	quintroon	autolysis
cuticular	Quakerism	burliness	pulmonary	vulnerary	autolytic
funicular	duskishly	curliness	dumminess	vulnerate	autocycle
curiously	musketeer	surliness	gumminess	burnisher	Autolycus
dubiously	bucketing	sublunate	rumminess	furnished	pump-water
dutifully	junketing	nucleolar	culminate	furnisher	sulphatic
furiously	musketoon	bulldozer	fulminate	turnstile	vulpicide
funiculus	huckstery	bull-nosed	Pulmonata	turnstone	nutpecker
tulip-wood	bucketful	mullioned	pulmonate	nunnation	suspected
mutinying	muck-sweat	guilloche	fulminous	ruination	suspicion
purifying	turkey-hen	cullionly	submentum	furniture	auspicate
nutjobber	bull-dance	full-bound	summing-up	subneural	cuspidore
subjected	curl-paper	bull-board	submerged	quintuple	cuspidate
subjacent	cut-leaved	nucleolus	submersed	ruinously	subpoena'd
subjugate	full-faced	full-speed	summerset	quinquina	puppyhood
Punjaubee	nucleated	full-split	summarily	subniveal	supplicat
muck-raker	rue-leaved	nullipara	murmuring	subnivean	surprisal
buck-wagon	bully-beef	full-cream	submarine	guanazolo	surpliced
Puck-hairy	bugle-band	full-orbed	summering	cupolated	surprised
huckaback	cup-lichen	butlerage	summarise	Mucorales	surpriser
hunky-dory	bugle-call	full-front	summarist	autogamic	suppliant
luckie-dad	full-scale	bully-rook	murmurous	automatic	bumptious
luck-penny	duplicand	full-dress	surmaster	aurorally	gumptious
musk-melon	publicise	bull-trout	submissly	automaton	mumpsimus
duck's-foot	publicist	full-grown	surmising	autolatry	sumpsimus
buckwheat	duplicate	publisher	gummosity	autoscopy	bumpology
musk-sheep	duplicity	sublessee	submitted	mutoscope	suspended
musk-shrew	publicity	dualistic	submitter	ouroscopy	suspender
tusk-shell	Euclidean	bullishly	summation	autos-da-fé	suspensor

bumpiness	outrigger	substance	mussitate	dustiness	furtively
dumpiness	subregion	Dunstable	pulsative	fustiness	cultivate
jumpiness	subrogate	guessable	sun-spurge	gustiness	multi-wall
lumpiness	surrogate	pursuable	cursively	lustiness	tuptowing
pulpiness	murrained	puissaunt	suasively	nuttiness	cumulated
vulpinism	surreined	subsacral	guesswork	rustiness	lunulated
vulpinite	guerrilla	subsecive	guestwise	sultaness	tubulated
sulphonic	surrejoin	subsidise	pulse-wave	austenite	Tubularia
pulpboard	currajong	pussyfoot	substylar	sultanate	suturally
purpureal	kurrajong	bursiform	quittance	outtongue	purulence
out-porter	curry-leaf	subsoiler	cultrated	tuitional	purulency
supporter	outrelief	gumshield	outtravel	dust-cover	subungual
sun-parlor	guardless	Mussulman	rusty-back	subtropic	eunuchoid
outparish	puerilism	vulsellae	justiciar	subtopian	eunuchism
suppurate	puerility	Kunstlied	rusticial	multipede	lupulinic
dumpishly	querulous	musselled	mustachio	multiplet	luxuriant
lumpishly	supremacy	Mussulmen	rusticise	multiplex	luxuriate
mumpishly	supremely	ourselves	rusticate	multipara	luxurious
purposely	nutriment	subsellia	rusticity	juxtapose	queue-jump
supposing	querimony	nurselike	custodial	auctorial	Lucullean
purposive	supremity	nurseling	custodian	butter-fat	Lucullian
turpitude	guaranies	nun's-flesh	quotidian	butter-pat	mutualise
pulpiteer	guarantee	pulseless	custodier	cut-throat	mutualism
puppeteer	gunrunner	subsultus	furtherer	gutter-man	cucullate
pulpstone	outrunner	vulsellum	murtherer	Hunterian	mutuality
bump-start	quarenden	Quasimodo	dust-devil	suctorial	susurrant
culpatory	quarender	nursemaid	sutteeism	austerely	lucubrate
jump-start	rum-runner	fulsomely	justified	butterfly	augurship
lump-sugar	surrender	cuisinier	justifier	butterine	subursine
outpourer	currently	nuisancer	multifoil	dust-brand	Augustine
sulphuret	purringly	out-sentry	dusty-foot	muttering	curviform
sulphuric	guarantor	curstness	multiform	nurturant	vulviform
sumptuary	surrendry	fussiness	butty-gang	vulturine	surveille
sumptuous	mucronate	gutsiness	fustigate	butter-box	pulvillar
gunpowder	outrooper	mussiness	lustihead	dustproof	pulvilled
supplying	eutrophic	outspoken	dust-sheet	rust-proof	pulvillio
subphylum	eutrapely	Russophil	butt-shaft	cultorist	pulvillus
surquedry	eutropous	bursarial	multihull	culturist	pulvinule
turquoise	guard-rail	cursorial	lustihood	dust-brush	pulvinate
guardable	guard-ring	outspread	sustained	guitarist	subversal
guard-book	guard-room	subscribe	sustainer	vulturish	culver-key
rubrician	guardsman	substract	curtilage	vulturism	subverter
curricula	quirister	substruct	fustilugs	austerity	pulverine
guard-cell	Buprestis	sunstruck	quit-claim	butterbur	quavering
curry-comb	guard-ship	subseries	subtilely	buttercup	pulverise
hurricane	hubristic	outstrain	musteline	butternut	quiverish
hurricano	currishly	outstrike	pustulant	putter-out	pulverous
lubricant	sunrising	sunstroke	subtilise	vulturous	quiverful
lubricate	Cupressus	cursorily	subtilist	cutty-sark	subvassal
rubricate	buhrstone	outspring	ductility	multitude	curvesome
lubricous	burrstone	guest-room	pustulate	curtation	curvetted
outredden	nutrition	guest-rope	subtilety	gustation	curveting
putridity	turret-gun	subscript	subtility	guttation	curvation
puerperal	lucrative	sussarara	pustulous	luctation	curvature
quartered	nutritive	questrist	customary	quotation	curvative
aubrietia	currawong	pulse-rate	custumary	quotition	surviving
guardedly	quarryman	substrata	customise	ructation	surveying
hurriedly	quarry-sap	substrate	Huttonian	dust-storm	nut-wrench
quarterly	quarrying	pulsatile	mutton-ham	gustatory	nut-weevil
quartette	quartzose	nurse-tend	suntanned	gustative	jut-window
quartetto	quartzite	russeting	juttingly	quotative	outworker
quercetum	puissance	pulsation	subtenant	hurtfully	subwarden
putrefied	pursuance	pulsatory	sustinent	lustfully	tutworker

outwardly	overcarry	overtrade	twiddling	swindling	expansion
outwitted	overhaste	evergreen	sweepback	swingling	expansive
quixotism	overhasty	overgreen	sweet-corn	twangling	exuberant
Eumycetes	overvalue	overdraft	'tween-deck	twinkling	exuberate
Eutychian	everybody	overgrain	sweetener	twin-plane	execrable
eurytherm	overscore	overtrain	sweet-flag	twiningly	execrably
urywoman	overperch	overtrump	sweetfish	swan-goose	exactment
urywomen	overreach	overprint	sweet-gale	swinishly	exactness
duty-bound	overreact	overproof	owle-glass	swingtree	exactress
muzzle-bag	oversexed	overdress	ownerless	swing-wing	executrix
puzzle-peg	overweigh	overgrass	sweetmeal	twentyish	executant
puzzledom	avertedly	overpress	sweetmeat	twenty-two	execution
quizzical	overmerry	overtrust	sweetness	swept-back	executory
puzzolana	overweary	overwrest	ownership	two-parted	executive
buzzingly	ivory-gate	overwrite	sweet-talk	owl-parrot	exodermal
fuzziness	overcheck	overproud	sweetwood	sword-bean	exodermis
muzziness	overshade	overdrive	sweetwort	swart-back	exudation
ovibovine	overwhelm	overcrowd	swift-foot	sword-belt	oxidation
evacuator	overshine	overgrown	swiftness	sword-bill	exudative
avocation	overshoot	overgraze	two-footed	sword-cane	exceeding
evocation	overthrow	overprize	twiforked	swordfish	extendant
evocatory	overshirt	overissue	twiformed	sword-hand	expedient
evocative	overpitch	overstock	two-forked	swarajism	excellent
oviductal	overrider	overstudy	twyforked	swarajist	excelling
evidently	overripen	ivory-tree	twyformed	sword-knot	expellant
oviferous	oversized	oversteer	two-fisted	swordlike	expellent
evaginate	overtimer	overstrew	swaggerer	swordless	expelling
ovigerous	overdight	overstaff	swag-belly	awareness	extermine
evagation	overnight	overstuff	two-headed	swartness	excerptor
avoidance	oversight	overstain	two-handed	two-roomed	extempore
available	avertible	overstand	two-hander	swordplay	extensile
availably	eversible	overstink	sweirness	sword-rack	excelsior
avoidable	overskirt	overstunk	awakening	swordsman	extension
ivy-leaved	everglade	overstare	two-leafed	sword-tail	extensity
evolvable	overalled	overstate	two-leaved	twoseater	excessive
avalanche	oversleep	overruler	sweltered	twistable	expensive
evolution	overgloom	overbuild	twalpenny	awesomely	extensive
ovulation	overflush	overlusty	twa-lofted	two-storey	oxcentric
evolutive	overcloud	uvarovite	two-legged	awe-struck	exsertile
ovalbumin	overblown	overswear	swallower	awestrike	exceptant
aventaile	overflown	everywhen	twalhours	twostroke	excepting
oven-ready	overglaze	overswell	two-lipped	swashwork	expectant
evangelic	overinked	over-exact	twelfthly	twitterer	expecting
avengeful	overcover	overexert	swimmable	switchman	exception
evincible	overpower	overlying	swimmeret	switching	exsection
evincibly	overtower	avisement	swampland	twitching	exsertion
événement	overgorge	avisandum	two-masted	twattling	expertise
evanition	overbound	evasively	two-master	two-timing	exceptive
avuncular	overcount	eviternal	swingboat	awfulness	axle-guard
eventuate	overgoing	ovotestis	swing-back	swivel-gun	extenuate
evaporate	overmount	evitation	ewe-necked	swivel-eye	ex-service
oviparity	overwound	avouterer	twin-screw	awkwardly	exogamous
oviparous	overboard	avizefull	swing-door	tway-blade	oxygenise
overcatch	Averroism	avizandum	swans-down	exhalable	oxygenate
overmatch	Averroist	swear-word	swansdown	excavator	exogenous
overwatch	overpoise	two-by-four	swingeing	excambion	oxygenous
overdated	overroast	two-bottle	swine-fish	excambium	exegetics
overladen	ivory-palm	twice-born	swinehood	excaudate	exegetist
overtaken	overspill	ewe-cheese	swineherd	expatiate	oxy-halide
avertable	overspend	twice-laid	Zwanziger	Excalibur	exchanger
overhaile	overspent	twice-told	twentieth	exhausted	exchequer
overpaint	overgreat	two-decker	twin-birth	exhauster	excitancy
overhappy	overtrick	twaddling	Zwinglian	expansile	excisable

excitable	extremely	synaptase	myoglobin	cyclopean	pyrometer
expirable	excrement	zygantrum	Ayahuasco	cyclopian	xylometer
exsiccant	extremism	cymbidium	wych-hazel	cyclopses	hypoxemia
expiscate	extremist	cymbiform	Typhaceae	syllepses	hypoxemic
exsiccate	extremity	eyebright	mythicise	syllepsis	pyrogenic
oxy-iodide	extrinsic	symbolics	mythicism	sylleptic	pyroxenic
exciseman	expressly	symbolled	mythicist	cyclorama	zymogenic
exhibiter	extrusion	symbology	typhoidal	cyclotron	hypoderma
excipient	extrusory	cymbalist	typhlitic	byrlaw-man	pyrometry
exhibitor	extrusive	symbolise	typhlitis	myrmecoid	hypogeous
extirpate	exaration	symbolism	mythology	myomantic	mycophagy
ex-librism	excretion	symbolist	syphiloid	lyam-hound	Xylophaga
ex-librist	exoration	symbiosis	syphiloma	lyomerous	xylophage
Axminster	excretory	symbiotic	syphilise	symmetral	cymophane
expiation	excretive	dyscrasia	Typhonian	symmetric	pyrophone
expiatory	extravert	syncretic	hyphenise	cyaniding	sycophant
exultance	extrovert	rye-coffee	hyphenism	hymnodist	xylophone
exultancy	existence	synclinal	pythoness	pycnidium	gynophore
explicate	exosphere	syncoptic	hyphenate	hypnogeny	hylophyte
explainer	exosporal	syncopate	mythopoet	hypnoidal	zygophyte
exploiter	exosmosis	dyschroia	Cytherean	hymnology	mycorhiza
exilement	exosmotic	synchrony	Xyridales	hypnology	Lycosidae
exploring	exostosis	syncytial	cynically	cyanamide	synodical
exclusion	exoticism	syncytium	lyrically	dyingness	cytokinin
explosion	excusable	synchysis	typically	wyandotte	mylonitic
exclosure	excusably	syndicate	wylie-coat	gymnasial	synovitis
exclusory	exsuccous	syndactyl	Syriacism	gymnasien	zymolitic
exclusive	expurgate	syndromic	cylindric	gymnastic	myxovirus
explosive	exculpate	Mycenaean	lysimeter	gymnosoph	gyroplane
expletory	excurrent	Pyrenaean	lysigenic	gymnasium	cytoplasm
expletive	excursion	hyperbola	synizesis	hypnotoid	hypoblast
exemplify	expulsion	hyperbole	syringeal	cyanotype	tycoonery
exemplary	exquisite	Aylesbury	Cynipidae	hypnotise	bytownite
examinant	excursive	hypercube	Mytilidae	hypnotism	tycoonate
examining	expulsive	type-metal	pyritical	hypnotist	cytotoxic
examinate	pyracanth	cynegetic	hygienics	hypogaeal	cytotoxin
exemption	gynaecoid	syneresis	hygienist	hypogaean	hypotonic
exanthema	gynaeceum	pyreneite	Syrianism	myrobalan	mycologic
exanimate	rybaudrye	type-genus	hypinosis	gyromancy	mycotoxin
exonerate	synangium	lysergide	pyridoxin	pyromancy	zymologic
axiomatic	hydathode	hypergamy	Myriapoda	Hylobates	hylozoism
Oxfordian	synapheia	synergism	myriorama	pyrolater	hylozoist
exponible	dynamical	synergist	Myristica	hypomania	hypocotyl
expositor	Pyralidae	pyrethrin	typifying	hypomanic	zygosperm
excoriate	pyramidal	pyrethrum	syllabics	hypotaxis	zygospore
exfoliate	dynamiter	Hyaenidae	syllabled	pyromania	cymograph
extolling	pyramides	Hypericum	syllabify	typomania	kymograph
extolment	pyramidic	byrewoman	syllabary	zygomatic	xylograph
expounder	sybaritic	hyperopia	syllabise	pyrolatry	hypocrisy
extorsive	pyramidon	lyme-hound	syllabism	hypocaust	hypocrite
extortion	hypallage	Mycetozoa	dyslectic	hyponasty	synodsman
exposture	zygaenoid	synedrial	cyclicism	gyrovague	hyson-skin
extortive	zygaenine	synedrion	cyclicity	hypogaeum	hypostyle
exopodite	tyranness	lyme-grass	Wyclifite	gyroscope	pygostyle
exequatur	tyrannise	typewrite	pyelogram	pyroscope	Cynosurus
uxoricide	tyrannous	synedrium	myologist	synoecise	cytolysis
extractor	synagogal	synectics	syllogise	synoecism	mylohyoid
extricate	dynamotor	dysentery	syllogism	synoecete	pyrolysis
extradite	synagogue	gyrfalcon	cycloidal	gynoecium	pyrolytic
exarchist	cymagraph	eye-glance	cyclolith	synoicous	pyroxylic
exarchate	by-passage	myography	cyclamate	myxoedema	pyroxylin
exerciser	synanthic	syngamous	hyalonema	xyloidine	synonymic
exorciser	Byzantine	dysgenics	hyalinise	eye-opener	zymolysis

dysphagia
dysphagic
dysphasia
lymphatic
nymphalid
nymphaeum
sympodial
sympodium
nymphical
Syrphidae
lyophilic
nymph-like
sylph-like
tympanist
dyspnoeal
dysphonia
dysphonic
dysphoria
dysphoric
dyspnoeic
lyophobic
symphonic
symptosis
symptotic
dyspepsia
dyspeptic
symposiac
symposial
symposium
symphysis
symphytic
Symphytum
mydriasis
mydriatic
hydrocele
by-product
hygrodeik
hybridise
hybridism
hybridity
hybridous
hydraemia
hydrofoil
pyorrhoea
by-ordinar
hydrology
hygrology
hydrolyse
hydrolyte
hydrangea
cyprinoid
hydronaut
hydriodic
Pyrrhonic
hydroptic
hygrophil
hydropult
hydrostat
hygrostat
hydrosoma
hydrosome
hygristor
hydration

hydraulic
hydrovane
dyer's-weed
dyer's-weld
hydroxide
hydrozoan
hydrazine
hydrozoon
eye-shadow
eye-splice
eyestrain
eye-string
gypsywort
Myrtaceae
dystectic
syntactic
cystocele
cystocarp
mysticism
cystidean
myrtle-wax
syntheses
dysthesia
dysthetic
synthesis
synthetic
mystified
mystifier
cystiform
mystagogy
nystagmic
nystagmus
Cystoidea
ayatollah
hyetology
systaltic
nyctalops
cystolith
systemise
bystander
syntonous
dystrophy
dystopian
hysterics
mysteries
oyster-bed
hysteroid
cystotomy
dysthymia
dysthymic
Sylviidae
Sylviinae
sylvanite
sylvinite
rye-whisky
ozocerite
dziggetai
ozokerite
azimuthal
ozonation
azeotrope
czarevich

calamander	paraphasic	palaeolith	parbreaked	catch-basin
salamander	paraphyses	lavatorial	jaw-breaker	watch-chain
Naiadaceae	paraphysis	natatorial	law-breaker	patchcocke
caravaneer	parathesis	parapodial	lambrequin	talc-schist
macadamise	paradisaic	catabolism	way-baggage	sarcocolla
palatalise	capacitate	katabolism	cabbage-fly	fascicular
caravaning	mazarinade	natatorium	garbageman	fasciculus
carapacial	palatinate	paralogism	wabbliness	farcically
Pan-Arabism	paradiddle	parapodium	wambliness	watch-clock
datamation	taradiddle	sanatorium	Balbriggan	catch-drain
malaxation	parapineal	Patagonian	dabblingly	rancidness
Panamanian	paradisean	macaronies	ramblingly	satchelled
caravanned	carabineer	parabolist	wamblingly	pancreatic
caravanner	paradisiac	paradoxist	warblingly	pancreatin
catafalque	fanaticise	paranormal	barbellate	Manchester
malabar-rat	parasitise	paramouncy	gambolling	fancifully
paratactic	vanadinite	Palaeozoic	carbonnade	watchfully
maladapted	law-abiding	paraboloid	rabbinical	calciferol
salal-berry	natalitial	laparotomy	carbuncled	watch-guard
damasceene	paradisial	malacology	carbon-copy	watch-glass
Lamarckism	fanaticism	satanology	lambdoidal	watch-house
Lamarckian	Nazaritism	paradoctor	may-blossom	cancrizans
maraschino	panaritium	paradoxure	gabbroitic	manchineel
parascenia	parasitism	cataloguer	namby-pamby	sanctified
hazardable	paradisian	palaeotype	Camberwell	sanctifier
maladdress	carabinier	Pan-African	barber-shop	fan-cricket
parabemata	capability	Tanagridae	Hamburgher	calceiform
damageable	Patavinity	catarrhine	halberdier	cancriform
manageable	ratability	cavalryman	cat-burglar	sanctimony
manageably	salability	catarrhous	jabberwock	calc-sinter
paraselene	tamability	paratroops	law-burrows	sanctitude
manageress	taxability	malapropos	Yarborough	match-joint
savageness	parasitoid	harassedly	ear-bussing	parcel-bawd
management	calamitous	harassment	gambit-pawn	cancellate
Japanesery	cavalierly	samarskite	sabbatical	calculable
caramelise	parabiosis	Eatanswill	Sabbath-day	calculably
papaverine	paralipsis	radarscope	balbutient	watch-light
catamenial	cabalistic	palaestric	rabbit-fish	parcelwise
managerial	fatalistic	palaestral	lamb's-tails	rascal-like
paramecium	parabiotic	bagassosis	rabbit-hole	cancelling
Saracenism	canaliculi	parastichy	barbituric	parcelling
paramedico	paraglider	wag-at-the-wa'	harbourage	rascallion
cadaverous	lavallière	tarantella	harbour-bar	parcel-gilt
papaverous	paraplegia	pararthria	tambourine	sarcolemma
Japanesque	paraplegic	catastasis	saccharase	cancellous
parametric	paralleled	catacumbal	saccharate	narcolepsy
japan-earth	parallelly	ragamuffin	bacchanals	vascularly
parametral	zabaglione	malaguetta	wanchancie	calculuses
catalectic	parablepsy	catapultic	saccharide	laccolitic
cataleptic	paraglossa	canary-seed	saccharine	calculated
malaperty	paramnesia	canary-bird	pancratium	sacculated
paraffinic	paraenesis	canary-wood	fasciation	calculator
haranguing	paragnosis	day-boarder	pancratian	matchmaker
paraphrase	paraenetic	babblative	pancratist	watchmaker
cataphract	palaeogaea	lambdacism	saccharify	parchmenty
paraphrast	paranoidal	gas-bracket	cat-cracker	dance-music
Nabathaean	Palaeocene	fat-brained	saccharoid	marcantant
paraphilia	Palaeogene	mad-brained	saccharose	calcinable
paraphonia	catalogize	iambically	sauce-alone	Gasconader
cataphonic	palagonite	barbed-wire	marchantia	malcontent
paraphonic	parabolise	babblement	matchboard	carcinogen
marathoner	paragonite	gabblement	patchboard	watch-night
paraphasia	paralogise	rabblement	Maccabaean	carcinosis

balconette	candidness	maidenhair	paedeutics	wavelength
fascinator	handedness	pardonable	paideutics	make-weight
vaccinator	handy-dandy	pardonably	sand-bunker	make-belief
falcon-eyed	randle-balk	sardonical	sand-sucker	Madelenian
calceolate	saddleback	maidenhead	vaudeville	game-dealer
lanceolate	saddle-fast	maidenweed	paddy-whack	tale-teller
raccoon-dog	bald-headed	jardinière	land-owning	tape-record
cancionero	hand-weeded	maiden-meek	tawdry-lace	patereroes
Marcionite	hard-headed	pardonless	sage-rabbit	gamekeeper
Marcionist	saddleless	gaudy-night	case-harden	gate-keeper
Sarcophaga	candle-fish	wardenship	gametangia	mace-bearer
sarcophagi	candlewick	maidenlike	lacerative	tale-bearer
sarcoplasm	saddle-sick	tap-dancing	face-saving	carelessly
sarcophagy	handselled	Waldensian	cameration	fadelessly
catchpenny	daydreamer	padding-ken	catenarian	namelessly
watch-paper	candle-bomb	cardinally	catenation	casemented
cascarilla	candle-wood	landing-net	laceration	pace-setter
barcarolle	paddle-wood	maidenhood	maceration	water-frame
calcareous	saddle-sore	Mandingoes	racemation	paper-faced
cancer-root	saddle-roof	land-jobber	laterality	water-flood
saucerfuls	candle-coal	card-holder	barebacked	waterfront
Marcgravia	saddle-room	landholder	race walker	water-guard
saucer-eyed	hand-me-down	handsomely	wage-packet	water-glass
narcescent	candle-doup	hard-fought	baseballer	paper-gauge
matchstick	paddle-boat	hand-lotion	race-hatred	water-gauge
narcissism	candle-tree	handworked	calefactor	sage-cheese
pancosmism	randle-tree	land-locked	malefactor	catechumen
narcissist	saddle-tree	hard-boiled	lake-lawyer	water-horse
march-stone	paddy-field	sand-dollar	paperboard	canephorus
watch-strap	candy-floss	cardiology	water-brash	catechiser
cat-catcher	dandy-fever	land-louper	water-brain	catechesis
watch-tower	Tardigrada	sand-hopper	laverbread	catechotic
jaw-crusher	tardigrade	cardiogram	water break	rarefiable
Manchurian	gaudy-green	hard-gotten	water-blink	base-minded
lascivious	paedagogic	paedophile	water-brose	wateriness
band-saucer	paedagogue	handspring	water-bloom	maledicent
hard-handed	dandy-horse	land-spring	water-borne	maleficent
handmaiden	sand-cherry	madder-lake	paper-birch	taperingly
cardialgia	bawdy-house	balderdash	water-bound	waveringly
sandbagged	sand-lizard	land-bridge	paper-chase	maleficial
sandbagger	land-pirate	land-breeze	water-crane	lace-pillow
sand-basket	sand-binder	wander-year	water-craft	materially
hand-gallop	tawdriness	pandermite	sales-clerk	javelin-man
hard-earned	dawdlingly	sanderling	watercress	wafer-irons
sand-launce	hard-riding	banderilla	paper-cigar	hare-lipped
mandragora	land-mining	badderlock	tapescript	water-joint
paediatric	maudlinism	gander-moon	calescence	sauerkraut
hand-barrow	hard-billed	sandgroper	canescence	Hakenkreuz
card-castle	hard-fisted	paederasty	latescence	paper-knife
sand-castle	hard-bitten	pandurated	tabescence	water-lemon
hand-martin	candelabra	sand-grouse	paper-cloth	Magellanic
handmaster	candelilla	wanderlust	water-clock	camerlengo
hand-waiter	sandalwood	caddis-case	dame-school	camerlingo
hard-master	band-clutch	candescent	paleaceous	matellasse
mandibular	bardolatry	faldistory	camel-corps	satellitic
dandy-brush	landammann	paedotribe	water-chute	lamellated
handicraft	randomwise	band-string	parenchyma	satellites
manducable	tandemwise	Landsthing	calendarer	water-level
hand-screen	paddymelon	land-lubber	sacerdotal	safe-blower
Sadducaean	Pandemonic	eard-hunger	bareheaded	paper-maker
handicuffs	randomiser	land-hunger	water-elder	water-melon
handectist	mandamuses	eard-hungry	barelegged	water-music
cardaceous	hand-in-hand	hard-pushed	gate-legged	taseometer

water-meter	Lacertilia	gangrenous	mathematic	sanitation
water-motor	parentally	tanglefoot	bathometer	validation
water-mouse	wafer-tongs	gauge-glass	bathymeter	galimatias
tabernacle	parenthood	baggage-car	fathometer	capitalist
Capernaite	man-entered	sanguinary	pachymeter	lapidarist
capernoity	parenteral	sanguinely	tachometer	maximalist
maternally	water-tower	laughingly	tachymeter	sanitarist
paternally	hamesucken	tanglingly	bathymetry	Vaticanist
water-nymph	baserunner	languished	tachometry	radicality
water-nixie	water-wheel	languisher	tachymetry	sanitarily
camelopard	water-wagon	sanguinity	cachinnate	habitaunce
face-to-face	saleswoman	ganglionic	bathing-box	palisadoes
face-powder	water-wings	gangliform	washing-day	saxicavous
malevolent	water-witch	gangliated	machine-gun	habilatory
categorise	safety-cage	hang-glider	bathing-hut	caricatura
Jamesonite	safety-rein	laggen-gird	rat-hunting	caricature
date-coding	safety-belt	tangential	panhandler	parischane
categorial	panegyrise	marginalia	machineman	hagiocracy
Caledonian	panegyrist	jargonelle	mashing-tub	maniacally
Cameronian	safety-plug	marginally	machinator	fatiscence
wave-motion	safety-arch	gauging-rod	fashionist	habit-cloth
categories	safety-stop	pangenesis	wash-bottle	palindrome
categorist	malfeasant	pangenetic	tachypnoea	facileness
case-worker	mafficking	marginated	fatherland	nativeness
faceworker	half-a-crown	gargantuan	cash-credit	capitellum
racecourse	daffodilly	languorous	fatherless	varicellar
ravenously	half-a-dozen	Panglossic	fathership	taxidermic
barefooted	half-length	rangership	fatherhood	taxidermal
case-bottle	way-freight	margaritic	bathyscape	native-born
hateworthy	palfrenier	mangosteen	bathyscaph	laniferous
nameworthy	waffle-iron	targetable	pathetical	lanigerous
water-ouzel	half-yearly	pargetting	bashawship	saliferous
water-plane	halfe-horsy	daughterly	cashew-nuts	manifestly
water-plate	gaff-rigged	gargoylism	lachrymary	satisfying
water-plant	bafflingly	Rachmanism	lachrymose	faying-face
waterproof	caffeinism	sad-hearted	taxi-dancer	radiograph
water-power	half-witted	yacht-built	palisander	panic-grass
waterquake	half-kirtle	Nachschlag	Caricaceae	savingness
wage-freeze	half-sister	Sanhedrist	Salicaceae	takingness
paper-ruler	lawfulness	cathode-ray	capitalise	cariogenic
sage-grouse	manfulness	cashiering	laminarise	radiogenic
care-crazed	yaffingale	cash-keeper	radicalise	baking-soda
water-snake	half-cocked	tachograph	capitalism	malingerer
cameo-shell	half-dollar	tachygraph	radicalism	variegated
watersmeet	half-volley	pathogenic	sanitarium	variegator
wapenschaw	half-hourly	pathognomy	Vaticanism	Manichaean
raven's-bone	gas-furnace	naphthalic	capitation	garishness
water-smoke	kaffir-boom	pathfinder	cavitation	lavishness
water-shoot	calf-ground	sash-window	habitation	rakishness
water-spout	far-fetched	gashliness	janizarian	banishment
caper-sauce	batfowling	bathmizvah	laminarian	famishment
raven's-duck	margravate	catholicon	lapidarian	lavishment
lamentable	margravine	catholicos	lapidation	ravishment
patentable	barge-board	pathologic	latitation	vanishment
water-table	mangabeira	nathelesse	nanisation	Manicheism
lamentably	ragged-lady	batholitic	navigation	facilitate
majestical	jaggedness	bathylitic	pagination	· habilitate
parentless	raggedness	tachylytic	patination	pacificate
talentless	war-goddess	fathomable	radication	vaticinate
watertight	daggle-tail	fathomless	sagination	pacifiable
tapestried	tanglement	sachemship	salifiable	salifiable
water-thief	marguerite	fathom-line	salivation	habiliment
water-twist	tanglesome	baphometic	sanitarian	maxi-single

lapidified	calico-bush	lackadaisy	yackety-yak	balloonist
pacificism	palimpsest	jack-a-dandy	back-number	wall-rocket
facilities	radiophone	backvelder	hackbuteer	Mallophaga
pacificist	radiophony	Yankeefied	lack-lustre	gallophile
vaginismus	satin-paper	hawk-beaked	bankruptcy	gallophobe
Parisienne	bacitracin	lark-heeled	markswoman	tailor-made
salicional	pasigraphy	hackneyman	galliambic	sailorless
radiciform	calibrator	parkkeeper	palliament	tailor-bird
caliginous	taxi-driver	Kafkaesque	parliament	galleryite
familiarly	wapinschaw	bark-beetle	oak-leather	sailor-like
familistic	radiosonde	rack-renter	palliative	ballerinas
nativistic	hagioscope	parkleaves	wall-facing	sailor-suit
laciniated	radioscope	pack-thread	malleation	caulescent
hagiologic	satin-stone	backsheesh	palliation	pallescent
radiologic	radioscopy	bank-cheque	Paulianist	ballistite
capillaire	magistrand	backbiting	palliatory	ballistics
maxillulae	magistrate	rank-riding	calliature	eagle-stone
panislamic	magistracy	hawk-billed	gallabiyah	table-spoon
maxilliped	papistical	back-blocks	Wallachian	table-sport
Radiolaria	Haliotidae	backslider	valleculae	tally-trade
radiolysis	sagittally	maskalonge	vallecular	ballet-girl
variolotic	varietally	packing-box	cauliculus	parlour-car
mamillated	Sagittaria	barkentine	table-cloth	tallow-face
papillated	radiotoxic	tank-engine	fallacious	fallowness
hagiolater	capitulate	napkin-ring	table-cover	sallowness
Mariolater	manipulate	marking-ink	pallidness	fallow-chat
variolator	paniculate	pack-animal	table-d'hôte	gallows-lee
papillitis	capitulant	maskanonge	palladious	tally-woman
hagiolatry	capitulary	maskinonge	nail-headed	tallow-tree
Mariolatry	patibulary	marking-nut	bailieship	table-water
habit-maker	fatiguable	mackintosh	mallee-bird	galley-west
talismanic	latifundia	jackanapes	earlierise	halloysite
radiometer	halieutics	backworker	hail-fellow	galley-worm
variometer	manicurist	sack-posset	mallee-fowl	barleycorn
ration-card	habitually	hanky-panky	wall-pepper	barley-bree
nationless	taciturnly	backspauld	pall-bearer	barley-broo
malignment	radiculose	banker-mark	cauliflory	Barmecidal
sapiential	balibuntal	cankeredly	galloglass	tarmacadam
nationally	pari-mutuel	back-friend	gaultheria	haemoconia
rationally	salicylate	jack-priest	wall-lizard	palmaceous
malignance	vanity-case	marker-flag	faultiness	parmacitie
malignancy	varitypist	marker-bomb	rallyingly	Talmudical
nationhood	lap-jointed	canker-worm	nail-biting	maimedness
ration-book	panjandrum	background	malleiform	warmed-over
marionette	hackmatack	walk-around	table-knife	palm-kernel
manifolder	jack-rabbit	ear-kissing	sail-flying	harmlessly
manifoldly	backhanded	basketball	halleluiah	mammogenic
varicocele	cack-handed	market-hall	hallelujah	salmagundi
capitoline	kack-handed	racket-tail	table-linen	salmagundy
saxicoline	pack-saddle	marketable	ball-flower	carmagnole
anitorial	back-garden	market-bell	wallflower	haemolysis
capitolian	backhander	packet-ship	gallomania	haemolytic
Mabinogion	backwardly	backstairs	table-money	harmonical
varicosity	backmarker	basket-hilt	table-music	harmonicon
Cavicornia	backpacker	talky-talky	garlandage	Salmonidae
salicornia	backgammon	walky-talky	sapling-cup	harman-beck
calico-wood	jackhammer	backstroke	sailenders	salmon-leap
acinorous	tank-farmer	packet-note	gatling-gun	Haemanthus
anivorous	jack-rafter	basketwork	Laplandish	Tammanyism
saxicolous	taskmaster	market-town	falling-off	salmonella
varicotomy	hawksbeard	packet-boat	wall-to-wall	sarmentose
calico-tree	rackabones	backstitch	railroader	harmonious
babiroussa	masked-ball	basketfuls	ballooning	sarmentous

10 □a□m□n

warming-pan
harmoniser
garmenture
palm-grease
hammerhead
hammer-beam
hammerless
May-morning
hammer-fish
palm-branch
hammer-pond
hammerlock
palmer-worm
marmarosis
Lammas-tide
ragmatical
palmatifid
Karmathian
haematinic
haematuria
haematosis
barmitsvah
barmitzvah
basmitsvah
basmitzvah
batmitsvah
batmitzvah
map-mounter
palm-butter
mammy-wagon
mainlander
taeniacide
gainsaying
balneation
maintained
maintainer
cannibally
cannabinol
paint-brush
panniculus
manna-croup
wainscoted
launcegaye
garnierite
maundering
sauntering
mainpernor
painlessly
magnifical
Magnificat
magnifying
manna-grass
faint-heart
rain-shadow
daintiness
jauntiness
paintiness
hauntingly
tauntingly
vauntingly
gaingiving
mainlining
pawnticket

pain-killer
carnallite
Parnellite
Parnellism
cannelloni
cannel-coal
manna-larch
gauntleted
rain-plover
capnomancy
cannon-game
cannonball
cannon-shot
rain-forest
balneology
main-course
rain-doctor
mainspring
wainwright
pawnbroker
laundry-man
Laundromat
garnishing
varnishing
carnassial
Parnassian
magnetical
mainstream
gainstrive
painstaker
walnutwood
garnet-rock
magnetiser
ca'ing-whale
paintworks
Sapotaceae
cacodaemom
laboratory
pagoda-tree
capodastro
razor-blade
baronetage
halogenate
baronetess
cajolement
tapotement
Hanoverian
cacogenics
Napoleonic
carotenoid
nanosecond
halogenous
barometric
gasometric
manometric
camouflage
law-officer
canophobia
panophobia
canophilia
cacophonic
halophytic
manor-house

canonicals
saponified
gadolinite
Jacobinise
gadolinium
Jacobinism
Jacobitism
laconicism
Carolinian
calorifier
canonicity
carotinoid
vaporiform
canonistic
halobiotic
parodistic
cacomistle
Mahommedan
saloon-deck
mayonnaise
madonnaish
paronomasy
maconochie
cacotopian
Zaporogian
batologist
Mayologist
taxonomist
vaporosity
malodorous
canorously
valorously
vaporously
vapour-bath
favourable
favourably
mavourneen
favourless
savourless
laboursome
gamotropic
laeotropic
cacography
cacotrophy
Camorrista
razor-shell
famousness
razor-strop
wagon-train
panoptical
panopticon
catoptrics
raconteuse
manoeuvrer
wagon-vault
paronychia
calotypist
paroxysmal
paroxytone
paronymous
Ramphastos
rajpramukh
cappuccino

rampacious
jaspideous
marprelate
harpy-eagle
dapple-grey
Malpighian
rampageous
dauphiness
sapphirine
campaigner
carpellary
rampallian
wampumpeag
wampum-belt
parpen-wall
wappenshaw
salpingian
campanular
sappan-wood
damping-off
camphorate
lampholder
harpooneer
lampoonery
wasp-tongue
harpoon-gun
Camptonite
lampoonist
carphology
damp-course
carpophore
jasperware
vampire-bat
rapporteur
dapperness
sapperment
dapperling
lapper-milk
bar-parlour
tatpurusha
wapper-eyed
campestral
lappet-head
carpet-moth
tappet-loom
tarpauling
lamp-burner
masquerade
banqueteer
banqueting
lacquering
man-queller
parquetted
harquebuse
harquebuss
marquisate
pasquinade
pasquilant
vanquisher
matriarchy
patriarchy
laurdalite
patrialise

hair-waving
map-reading
patrialism
laureation
patriation
fair-haired
hair-raiser
fairy-beads
macrobiota
macrobiote
patriciate
fairy-cycle
matricidal
parricidal
patricidal
barracking
batrachian
matricliny
matrocliny
patricliny
patrocliny
matricular
sarracenia
barracoota
capricious
lauraceous
fabricator
barracouta
sacredness
hair-pencil
fair-headed
fair-leader
matrifocal
patrifocal
sacrificer
carragheen
iatrogenic
saprogenic
fair-minded
carrying-on
sacroiliac
laurvikite
day-release
matrilocal
patrilocal
patrolling
barrel-bulk
barrelfuls
tauromachy
barramunda
barramundi
fairy-money
parramatta
lacrimator
lacrymator
barrenness
patronless
Fahrenheit
matronship
farrandine
matron-like
warrandice
warrantise

warranting	tarsia-work	lansquenet	tastefully	salt-spring
lawrencium	Marshalsea	daisy-wheel	wastefully	cartophily
Laurentian	daisy-chain	palsy-walsy	fastigiate	tautophony
matronymic	waistcloth	causewayed	saltigrade	earthquake
patronymic	falsidical	capsizable	pantograph	master-card
matronhood	haustellum	fast-handed	paste-grain	master-hand
barrenwort	man-stealer	way-traffic	lactogenic	masturbate
barring-out	panspermic	gastralgia	castigator	lattermath
patroniser	camsteerie	gastralgic	earth-house	natterjack
capreolate	mansuetude	carthamine	earthiness	Tattersall
hair-powder	false-faced	partialize	paltriness	factorable
warrioress	falsifying	tartrazine	tattlingly	pasturable
fair-boding	pausefully	Watteauish	day-tripper	bastard-bar
gadrooning	passiflora	Kantianism	jaw-twister	raft-bridge
patriotism	marsh-fever	martialism	last-minute	masterless
macrophage	Cassegrain	partialism	cantillate	matterless
satrapical	sausage-dog	Cantuarian	martellato	parturient
Sauropsida	far-sighted	castration	tautologic	cartwright
hairspring	passageway	martialist	earth-light	factorship
macroprism	day-scholar	partialist	pantaloons	mastership
fair-spoken	wassail-cup	factuality	manteltree	pastorship
sapropelic	bass-fiddle	partiality	tantaliser	mastermind
madreporic	marshiness	tactuality	nautiluses	rafter-bird
saprophyte	tasseiling	earth-board	cantaloupe	bastardise
fair-ground	wassailing	pasteboard	cantilever	Eastertide
bairn's-part	causticity	hartebeest	pantomimic	Eastertime
wanrestful	caespitose	earthbound	cartomancy	gas-turbine
Saurischia	easselward	masticable	tautomeric	easterling
laurustine	easselgate	pasticheur	lactometer	bastardism
patristics	marshlocks	fantoccini	tantamount	nasturtium
sacrosanct	tassel-gent	particular	cartonnage	lanternist
fairy-stone	hanselling	nautically	martingale	latter-mint
macrospore	cassolette	tactically	parting-cup	saltarello
narratable	ransomable	cactaceous	bastinaded	pastorally
sabretache	ransomless	mastectomy	Fastens-eve	bacterioid
hairstreak	cassumunar	participle	Battenberg	masterhood
parrot-beak	passimeter	masticator	wantonness	waiterhood
garrotting	passamezzo	fastidious	cantonment	patter-song
parrot-fish	raising-bee	hartie-hale	panton-shoe	master-work
parrot-bill	parsonical	rattle-pate	martensite	latter-born
hair-stroke	parson-bird	tattle-tale	bantingism	tartareous
sabre-tooth	maisonette	wattlebark	casting-net	eastermost
parrot-coal	passionate	rattle-head	cautionary	lattermost
barratrous	passionary	pantheress	factionary	masterwort
galravitch	Cassiopeia	battlement	gag-toothed	gasteropod
narrowcast	haustorium	battleship	gap-toothed	canterbury
marrowless	bassoonist	tattie-shaw	saw-toothed	wanthriven
narrowness	Passionist	wattle-bird	cartoonist	lactescent
marrow-bone	nauseously	pantherine	factionist	baptistery
narrow-boat	pansophism	pantherish	Bartholomew	earth-shine
barrow-tram	pansophist	salt-cellar	Gastropoda	fantastico
cassia-bark	hawser-laid	tattie-claw	gastronome	bartisaned
nauseative	man-servant	battledore	gastrosoph	earth-smoke
nauseating	marsh-robin	wattle-work	gastrology	lactoscope
Pan-Slavism	cat's-cradle	battledoor	gastronomy	pantoscope
pay-station	mass-priest	cattle-grid	gastrotomy	earth-table
way-station	Caesarship	rattle-trap	xanthopsia	cantatrice
Pan-Slavist	kaisership	tactlessly	captiously	factitious
hamshackle	hansardise	pasty-faced	cautiously	pasteurise
ramshackle	Massoretic	Tartuffish	factiously	pasteurism
ranshackle	Sanskritic	Tartuffism	earth-plate	Carthusian
marshalled	basset-horn	Tartuffian	pantophagy	Malthusian
marshaller	saussurite	faithfully	cartophile	Pasteurian

ear-trumpet	palustrian	obtainable	eburnation	oceanology
salt-butter	balustered	obtainment	aberdevine	schalstein
wait-a-while	larvicidal	ebracteate	Ubermensch	scrag-whale
panty-waist	malvaceous	abscission	aboriginal	ice-breaker
pantrymaid	salvifical	obediently	aborigines	scabbiness
pastrycook	marvelling	'sbuddikins	abortively	scabridity
value-added	marvellous	abnegation	aborticide	acidifying
paludament	valvulitis	abreaction	obtruncate	academical
maturative	galvaniser	abbey-laird	Aberdonian	acidimeter
naturalise	salverform	able-bodied	abbreviate	acidimetry
tabularise	canvas-back	abbey-piece	Abyssinian	schematise
naturalism	harvest-bug	object-ball	obituarist	schematism
jaculation	harvest-fly	abjectness	abstracted	schematist
maculation	harvestman	objectless	abstracter	eczematous
maturation	canvas-work	object-soul	abstractor	screech-owl
papulation	calves'-foot	obsequious	abstractly	accelerate
salutation	parvovirus	observable	abstemious	accelerant
saturation	day-wearied	observably	abstention	scleriasis
tabulation	war-wearied	observance	abstinence	screenplay
vapulation	jaywalking	observancy	abstinency	screenings
naturalist	ear-witness	observator	abiturient	scleroderm
salutarily	Marxianism	abdication	abstergent	sclerotial
jaculatory	baby-walker	obligation	abstersive	sclerotium
salutatory	baby-farmer	obligatory	abstersion	sclerotomy
tabulatory	many-headed	obliterate	obstetrics	Acherontic
maculature	satyresque	obligement	abstrusely	schemozzle
manuscript	satyagraha	abridgment	obstructer	screw-plate
caruncular	laryngitic	obligingly	obstructor	screw-press
ranunculus	laryngitis	obsidional	obdurately	accessible
caoutchouc	baby-ribbon	ebullition	abjuration	accessibly
matureness	baby-minder	ebullience	obduration	accentuate
nature-cure	lady-killer	ebulliency	objuration	acceptable
nature-myth	calyciform	obeliscoid	obturation	acceptably
Janus-faced	satyriasis	abominable	abjunction	scientific
lanuginose	baby-sitter	abominably	obfuscated	acceptance
raduliform	Maryolater	abominator	absurdness	acceptancy
cacuminous	Maryolatry	abundantly	obtuseness	scherzando
lanuginous	many-folded	abrogative	éboulement	scoffingly
paludinous	Babylonish	abrogation	obnubilate	scaffolder
naturistic	Babylonian	absorbable	abruptness	ecphractic
manumitted	palynology	absorbedly	above-board	ecthlipsis
maquillage	papyrology	absorbency	above-named	ice-hilling
casualness	karyoplasm	obsoletely	oceanarium	ecchymosed
vacuolated	barysphere	obsoletism	scrambling	ecchymosis
datum-level	Dasyuridae	obsoletion	ocean-basin	ecchymotic
vacuum-tube	lady's-smock	abiogenist	scratching	ecphonesis
calumniate	calyptrate	ebionitism	scratchily	activation
Saturnalia	raiyatwari	abdominous	scratch-wig	scribbling
calumnious	caryatidic	abnormally	octandrian	scritch-owl
naturopath	caryatidal	absorptive	octandrous	activeness
fabulosity	caryatides	absorption	scrape-good	scrivening
fabulously	baby-jumper	abhorrence	octamerous	accidented
datum-plane	razzmatazz	abhorrency	octahedral	accidental
haruspical	dazzlement	absolutely	octahedron	occidental
haruspices	dazzlingly	absolutism	ocean-going	scaithless
daguerrean	Ranzellaar	absolution	scraggling	acriflavin
jaguarondi	lanzknecht	absolutist	octangular	scrimmager
jaguarundi	manzanilla	absolutory	actability	schism-shop
saouari-nut	canzonetta	absolvitor	occasional	schismatic
salubrious	canzonette	ubiquarian	occasioner	actionable
balustrade	Abraham-man	ubiquitary	octaploidy	schizocarp
lacustrine	oblateness	ubiquitous	scrap-metal	Echinoidea
palustrine	oblational	aberration	Sciaenidae	schizoidal

echinoderm	accoucheur	scepticism	accusative	Adullamite
Achitophel	accordable	scyphiform	occupative	idoloclast
actinolite	accordance	Scopelidae	accubation	adulterate
Schizopoda	accordancy	scapulated	accusation	adulterant
schizogony	acromegaly	Scaphopoda	occupation	adulteress
scrimpness	octogenary	scape-wheel	scoutcraft	adulterine
schipperke	acroterial	scarlatina	accusement	adulterise
scrimshank	acroterium	acervation	scrutineer	adulterous
scriptoria	acroterion	scordatura	scrutinise	adelantado
scriptural	octodecimo	score-board	scrutinous	edulcorate
achievable	ectodermic	scarabaeid	acquainted	edulcorant
ocellation	ectodermal	Scarabaeus	actualités	odd-looking
scale-board	acrogenous	aceraceous	scrummager	addle-pated
scald-berry	ectogenous	ochraceous	acquirable	adolescent
ochlocracy	scooped-out	accredited	scrub-rider	idolatress
ecological	octohedron	scarceness	occurrence	idolatrise
schlimazel	acrophobia	scarcement	acoustical	Odelsthing
Iceland-dog	acrophonic	scarlet-hat	occultness	idolatrous
Scillonian	ectophytic	scarifying	acquitment	adamantean
scale-stair	sciolistic	scornfully	acquitting	adamantine
ecclesiast	schoolmaid	ecardinate	accustomed	idempotent
Scolytidae	schoolward	scurfiness	accultural	Adamitical
sculptress	school-dame	scurviness	accumulate	odontalgia
sculptured	school-mate	scurrility	scrupulous	odontalgic
sculptural	schoolma'am	scorpionic	scavengery	adenectomy
sculduddry	school-marm	scurrilous	scavenging	identified
acolouthic	school-bell	scarf-joint	scowdering	odontomata
acolouthos	school-term	achromatic	scowlingly	odontocete
ice-machine	school-ship	achromatin	adjacently	odontogeny
scampishly	school-tide	scaramouch	adiaphoron	odontolite
ecumenical	school-time	scorzonera	ideational	odontology
acuminated	scrollwise	acarophily	idealistic	edentulous
Scombridae	schoolgirl	acorn-shell	edibleness	idiopathic
Scombresox	school-miss	accrescent	edaciously	advocation
scandalise	octoploidy	score-sheet	idle-headed	advocatory
scandalled	school-book	ecospecies	adhesively	idiolectic
scandalous	schoolwork	icosahedra	adderstone	idiolectal
iconoclasm	schorl-rock	Icosandria	adder's-wort	admonitive
iconoclast	scrollwork	scissor-cut	adversaria	admonition
scenically	schoolroom	scissor-leg	advertence	admonitory
acanaceous	school-bred	acetabulum	advertency	ideologist
acinaceous	acroamatic	acetabular	adventurer	adsorption
scent-gland	accountant	scotodinia	advertiser	idiot-proof
scantiness	accounting	scatheless	adjectival	ideography
scintigram	scrounging	scatter-gun	idle-pulley	odiousness
iconolater	octopodous	scattering	edifyingly	adroitness
iconolatry	ectomorphy	Scotifying	additament	adaptative
economical	accomptant	Scotchness	admirative	adaptation
iconomachy	accomplice	scattiness	admiration	adaptively
economiser	accomplish	scathingly	advisatory	edaphology
iconomatic	eccoprotic	Scottified	advisement	adequately
iconometer	echopraxia	Scotticise	advice-boat	adequative
iconometry	echopraxis	Scotticism	additively	editorship
scent-organ	accostable	scutellate	admiringly	adjuration
scansorial	accoutring	acotyledon	adhibition	adjuratory
scent-scale	scrofulous	scuttleful	additional	adjunctive
iconoscope	acronychal	acatalepsy	administer	adjunction
acrobatism	acronymous	scatophagy	sdeignfull	sdrucciola
octonarian	octogynous	scaturient	advisorate	adjudgment
acrobatics	icy-pearled	Scotswoman	admissible	adjudicate
octonarius	acephalous	ichthyosis	admittable	adjustable
scrog-apple	scapegrace	ichthyotic	admittedly	adjustment
scholastic	scepticise	accurately	admittance	devanagari

metagalaxy	hexahedral	hexaplaric	semblative	descendent
separately	decahedron	metallurgy	lesbianism	deaconship
relaxative	hexahedron	metaplasia	kerb-market	Fescennine
reparative	metalepsis	metaplasis	membranous	mercantile
separative	metaleptic	hexaemeron	herbicidal	percentile
separatism	metacentre	regainable	herbaceous	descending
defamation	meganewton	retainable	Serbo-Croat	descension
relaxation	decadently	detainment	pebble-ware	deaconhood
reparation	Dewar-flask	regainment	kerb-vendor	geocentric
separation	metaphrase	retainment	feebleness	bedclothes
separatist	metaphrast	repainting	herb-bennet	teichopsia
melanaemia	detachable	penannular	Jew-baiting	sea-captain
defamatory	seraphical	melanomata	Leibnizian	leucoplast
reparatory	detachedly	teratomata	verbena-oil	percipient
separatory	decathlete	megalosaur	red-blooded	mercaptide
metacarpal	detachment	Nematoidea	herb-robert	perceptive
metacarpus	Metatheria	teratogeny	kerb-trader	perception
separatrix	metaphoric	pedal-organ	membership	leucopenia
megaparsec	metathorax	devalorise	Herbartian	peace-party
metatarsal	metaphysic	melaconite	Selbornian	perceptual
metatarsus	metatheses	metabolise	sea-burdock	redcurrant
pedal-board	metathesis	metabolite	sea-biscuit	percurrent
sedan-chair	metathetic	revalorise	sea-bathing	percursory
debauchery	decapitate	senatorial	sea-blubber	merceriser
revanchism	delaminate	venatorial	bedchamber	Reichsland
revanchist	deracinate	demagogism	leuchaemia	Reichsrath
renascence	desalinate	metabolism	neoclassic	Reichsbank
melancholy	gelatinate	pedagogism	merchantry	reichsmark
megascopic	revalidate	pedagogics	peach-bloom	percussant
defalcator	negatively	decalogist	leechcraft	percussive
bel-accoyle	relatively	decapodous	peacockery	percussion
demandable	debasingly	hepatology	peacockish	rescission
regardable	debatingly	nematology	peacock-ore	peach-stone
rewardable	defacingly	teratology	leucocytic	rescissory
regardless	delayingly	nematocyst	peccadillo	percutient
rewardless	menacingly	decampment	beech-drops	seecatchie
retardment	megalithic	pedal-point	teschenite	gem-cutting
verandahed	gelatinise	remarriage	peacherino	reacquaint
heraldship	keratinise	repatriate	geochemist	reaccustom
rehandling	relativise	repairable	reschedule	rencounter
decandrian	negativism	repair-shop	beccaficos	peach-water
hexandrian	relativism	decagramme	mercifully	headmaster
decandrous	ceramicist	metastable	peacefully	hendecagon
hexandrous	relativist	tenantable	henceforth	mendicancy
herald-duck	negativity	pedantical	deactivate	veldschoen
sewage-farm	relativity	tenantless	reactivate	mendacious
sexagenary	tenability	department	bescribble	needle-case
debateable	relational	tenantship	tetchiness	needle-bath
femaleness	gelatinoid	hexactinal	reactively	lead-pencil
sedateness	gelatinous	xenarthral	kerchiefed	dead-weight
debasement	keratinous	recapturer	perceiving	beadleship
defacement	legalistic	metastases	reactivity	needle-fish
rebatement	melanistic	metastasis	fen-cricket	beadlehood
regalement	retaliator	metastatic	tea-clipper	needlecord
legateship	remarkable	devastator	pencil-case	meddlesome
Sexagesima	remarkably	devastivit	pencil-lead	needlework
metamerism	recallable	denaturant	pencilling	seed-vessel
Melanesian	Heraclidan	denaturise	beach-la-mar	heedlessly
sea-anemone	dérailleur	decagynian	perchloric	needlessly
decamerous	derailment	hexagynian	percolator	dead-nettle
hexamerous	recallment	decagynous	peacemaker	head-centre
hexametric	retailment	hexagynous	percentage	dead-letter
decahedral	Heracleian	herb-garden	descendant	feed-heater

hey-de-guise	head-bummer	dependency	repellance	meteoritic
hey-de-guyes	headhunter	decelerate	repellence	celebrated
head-cheese	Zend-Avesta	degenerate	repellancy	genevrette
reed-thrush	meadow-lark	regenerate	repellency	meteorital
deadliness	beadswoman	degeneracy	rebellious	celebrator
dead-lights	seed-oyster	regeneracy	redeemable	desecrater
dead-finish	rendezvous	reverencer	redeemless	desecrator
tea-drinker	telecamera	referendum	determiner	penetrator
tendrilled	Resedaceae	sereneness	telesmatic	telewriter
tendrillar	telepathic	severeness	secernment	cerebritis
weedkiller	federalise	televérité	teleonomic	Lebensraum
dendriform	federative	cerebellum	telegnosis	defeasible
fer-de-lance	generalise	cerebellar	decennoval	defensible
lead-glance	generative	redevelope	never-never	releasable
hebdomadal	revelative	tête-de-pont	redecorate	reversible
hebdomadar	seven-a-side	telemetric	heterogamy	defensibly
seldomness	vegetative	tenemental	heterotaxy	reversedly
ready-money	vegetating	reverently	Heterocera	Peter-see-me
wedding-bed	federalism	vehemently	benevolent	teleostean
reading-boy	Genevanism	revengeful	heterogeny	nécessaire
wedding-day	defecation	detergence	penelopise	defeasance
leadenness	delegation	detergency	developing	seven-score
pendentive	donegation	Betelgeuse	ceremonial	teleostome
tendential	federation	Betelgeuze	hegemonial	Teleostomi
geodynamic	generation	genethliac	hegemonism	fenestrate
perdendosi	hebetation	telephonic	semeiotics	revestiary
seed-potato	regelation	telephoner	hegemonist	deceptible
dendroidal	relegation	lederhosen	generosity	defectible
Dendrophis	ronegation	jewel-house	Heteropoda	delectable
dendrobium	revelation	hereticate	heretofore	detectable
headworker	vegetarian	rededicate	heterocont	detectible
dendrology	vegetation	hereditary	heterodont	detestable
dendrogram	veneration	veterinary	heterokont	receptible
readoption	federalist	remediable	selenodont	rejectable
headsquare	generalist	remediably	heterodoxy	rejectible
perdurable	generality	Genesiacal	heterogony	repeatable
renderable	oedematose	répétiteur	heterology	revertible
perdurably	oedematous	remediless	heteronomy	delectably
tenderness	revelatory	beneficent	selenology	detestably
tenderfeet	generatrix	redelivery	semeiology	receptacle
leadership	benefactor	feverishly	generously	dejectedly
readership	telecaster	benedicite	temerously	dementedly
lead-arming	relevantly	repetitive	reredorter	repeatedly
tenderling	resemblant	benefiting	heterodyne	seventh-day
perdurance	resembling	beneficial	redemptive	seventieth
gelder-rose	Decembrist	repetition	redemption	nepenthean
tender-loin	rememberer	television	sevenpence	desertless
tenderfoot	Decemberly	geneticist	sevenpenny	recentness
deodoriser	hereabouts	bedevilled	peremptory	relentless
tenderiser	Seleucidae	remedially	redemptory	selectness
leaderette	Seleucidan	Venetianed	deferrable	relentment
dead-ground	telescreen	veneficous	penetrable	resentment
geodesical	Rebeccaite	heresiarch	referrible	regentship
geodetical	redescribe	reregister	penetrably	regent-bird
head-stream	beseeching	Benedictus	tenebrific	repertoire
ready-to-eat	Rebeccaism	televisual	researcher	semestrial
dead-stroke	senescence	televiewer	rehearsing	pedestrian
headstrong	telescopic	repealable	penetralia	fenestella
ready-to-sew	aerenchyma	revealable	penetrance	Nemertinea
head-lugged	defendable	revealment	penetrancy	repentance
head-hugger	dependable	genealogic	veneer-moth	resentence
yerd-hunger	dependably	teleologic	tenebrious	deceptious
yerd-hungry	dependence	bedellship	telegraphy	mesenteric

beweltered	perforable	methomania	seminality	meningioma
debentured	leaf-bridge	mechanical	demi-cannon	periegesis
mesenteron	ley-farming	methinketh	dedicatory	meningitis
rere-supper	performing	nephropexy	depilatory	periphrase
deceivable	perfervour	dethroning	hesitatory	perishable
receivable	perforated	Aethiopian	vesicatory	relishable
reservable	perforator	nephrology	pedipalpus	perishably
deceivably	perforatus	nephrotomy	medicaster	perithecia
deservedly	self-driven	technology	retinacula	Jewishness
reservedly	beef-brewis	technocrat	beribboned	delightful
decemviral	self-esteem	reshipment	redisburse	benighting
lever-watch	net-fishery	netherward	bewitchery	hemichorda
Pelecypoda	net-fishing	lethargied	bewitching	peripheric
heresy-hunt	sea-fishing	lethargise	mediocrity	peripheral
self-danger	Neofascism	hen-harrier	heliacally	decipherer
self-taught	Neofascist	nethermore	seriocomic	semichorus
pen-feather	self-styled	nethermost	dehiscence	periphyton
sea-feather	self-murder	Methuselah	meliaceous	debilitate
self-parody	beefburger	nephoscope	periscopic	delimitate
self-hatred	deaf-mutism	mephitical	desiccator	felicitate
self-abuser	leaf-cutter	medicament	rediscover	legitimate
perficient	self-exiled	sexivalent	behind-hand	revisitant
perfective	geographic	delicately	periodical	legitimacy
self-acting	geographer	decimalise	behind-door	verifiable
perfection	Belgravian	dedicative	bewildered	semicircle
self-action	sergeantcy	derivative	desiderata	decisively
perfidious	verge-board	devitalise	deliberate	definitely
self-feeder	weigh-board	hesitative	desiderate	derisively
self-seeder	sea-goddess	medicative	delineable	femininely
self-severe	meagreness	meditative	demirepdom	genitively
leafleteer	seigneurie	recitative	peripeteia	periwigged
self-deceit	vengefully	retinalite	semiterete	deridingly
new-fledged	lengthways	revitalise	desireless	repiningly
self-denial	lengthwise	seminarial	defilement	retiringly
self-seeker	weigh-house	decimalism	definement	revilingly
self-mettle	penguinery	revivalism	refinement	revivingly
fee-fi-fo-fum	neogenesis	tepidarium	repinement	devilishly
red-figured	neogenetic	decimation	retirement	revivified
leaf-sheath	seignorage	dedication	revilement	decivilise
self-binder	Bergsonism	delibation	revivement	definitive
self-giving	Bergsonian	deligation	aedileship	legitimise
self-killed	zeuglodont	deliration	desiderium	semi-divine
self-willed	geognostic	denization	perihelion	femininism
self-filler	ledger-bait	depilation	peripetian	peridinium
self-killer	vergership	derivation	semi-weekly	recidivism
beef-witted	ledger-line	gemination	peridermal	definition
perfoliate	weightless	hesitation	sebiferous	peridinian
self-slayer	nephralgia	levigation	perimetric	redivision
self-glazed	hen-hearted	leviration	hemihedral	legitimist
self-unable	déshabillé	levitation	perineural	recidivist
leaf-insect	methodical	medication	hemihedron	feminility
newfangled	methedrine	meditation	peritectic	femininity
leaf-mosaic	bêche-de-mer	recitation	pedimented	legibility
reafforest	technetium	remigation	pedimental	periwinkle
self-loving	nephograph	seminarian	regimental	penicillin
self-motion	nephridium	semination	delineator	deficience
self-cocker	technician	velitation	residenter	desipience
self-bounty	technicist	vesication	penitently	recipience
self-colour	rechristen	recitativo	beliefless	resilience
leaf-hopper	cephalagra	decimalist	reliefless	meridional
self-poised	nephologic	revivalist	heliograph	revisional
self-opened	cephalopod	seminarist	melic-grass	petitioner
self-breath	cephalitis	feminality	vexingness	religioner

deficiency	hemitropal	perigynous	well-chosen	well-judged
recipiency	lexigraphy	serjeantcy	well-thewed	reillumine
resiliency	serigraphy	serjeantry	declaimant	well-turned
demi-ditone	denigrator	perjinkety	reclaimant	fell-runner
felicitous	meliorator	perjinkity	well-minded	bell-turret
veridicous	heritrixes	perjurious	bell-ringer	yellow-wash
semicirque	remissible	weak-handed	well-wished	yellowback
feministic	periosteal	verkrampte	seal-fisher	yellow-weed
semi-liquid	periosteum	jerked-meat	well-wisher	fellow-heir
definitude	remissness	weak-headed	declaiming	mellowness
genialness	redissolve	deckle-edge	well-liking	yellowness
hemiplegia	peninsular	beekeeping	well-sinker	fellowship
hemiplegic	aeciospore	deck-tennis	meal-ticket	yellow-bird
periclinal	helioscope	fecklessly	bell-siller	yellow-yite
petiolated	registrant	recklessly	well-willer	yellow-girl
feuilleton	registrary	weak-minded	well-placed	yellow-snow
heliolater	heriotable	weakliness	cellulosic	yellow-wood
legislator	resistible	weak-hinged	cellulated	yellow-soap
heliolatry	resistibly	Berkeleian	cellulitis	yellow-root
medium-term	mediatress	jerkinhead	belly-laugh	yellow-wort
melismatic	resistless	week-ending	bell-flower	yellow-spot
heliometer	belittling	Neo-Kantian	sex-limited	deflowerer
designable	Cerinthian	deck-bridge	bellamoure	yellow-eyed
designedly	geriatrics	deck-quoits	declinable	reflexible
resignedly	geriatrist	bellhanger	reclinable	deployment
designless	peristylar	dealbation	sealing-day	permeative
designment	peristomal	well-marked	peel-and-eat	permeation
resignment	desistance	fell-walker	heulandite	germicidal
Helianthus	desistence	peelgarlic	declension	vermicidal
semi-uncial	remittance	well-earned	telling-off	vermicelli
regionally	resistance	pellucidly	Bedlington	vermicular
benignancy	heliotrope	neglectful	declinator	gemmaceous
hemianopia	heliotropy	deflective	sealing-wax	geomedical
designator	heliotypic	neglective	sea-leopard	tea-meeting
semi-annual	registered	reflective	reallocate	reim-kennar
semi-double	hemipteral	reflecting	fellmonger	vermifugal
helicoidal	peripteral	deflection	meal-monger	permafrost
peritoneal	hemipteran	neglection	well-to-live	termagancy
peritoneum	heliotaxis	re-election	well-boring	seemlihead
lepidolite	geniculate	reflection	well-formed	seemliness
peridotite	pediculate	pellicular	well-gotten	seemelesse
perigonial	reticulate	sexlocular	cellophane®	German-band
perigonium	semi-lunate	secludedly	well-spring	segmentate
Heliconian	vesiculate	sealed-beam	well-spoken	segmentary
decinormal	Pediculati	belladonna	declarable	germinable
lexicology	reticulary	belly-dance	deplorable	terminable
meritocrat	semilucent	hellbender	deplorably	reaming-bit
desirously	reliquaire	well-beseen	well-graced	terminably
perilously	pedicurist	bell-wether	declaredly	sermonical
resinously	tediousome	well-heeled	dealership	helminthic
melicotton	vesiculose	wellie-boot	tellership	hetmanship
helicopter	meticulous	deflagrate	bellarmine	penmanship
Cecidomyia	pediculous	jellygraph	cellar-flap	seamanship
hemisphere	periculous	negligible	cellar-book	beam-engine
semi-opaque	deliquesce	re-eligible	declarator	fermentive
heliophyte	semiquaver	negligibly	real-estate	seamanlike
delinquent	believable	geological	realisable	Terminalia
relinquish	relievable	neological	declassify	terminally
reciprocal	medievally	negligence	reclassify	permanence
heritrices	reviewable	pellagrous	red-lattice	permanency
semi-drying	perimysium	healthless	belletrist	sermoniser
decigramme	hemicyclic	healthsome	aeolotropy	sermonette
hemitropic	pericyclic	bell-shaped	sea-lettuce	sea-monster

terminator	penny-stone	xerodermia	decolonise	revolvency
Dermaptera	teinoscope	xerodermic	decolorise	sea-poacher
Dermoptera	Pennisetum	xenogenous	recolonise	geophagism
team-spirit	pennatulae	aerometric	aerologist	temptation
red-murrain	teeny-weeny	redolently	aeronomist	vespiaries
mesmerical	pennyworth	lemon-grass	gemologist	geophagist
new-married	memorandum	belongings	oenologist	geophagous
Weimaraner	zero-valent	aerophobia	pedologist	neoplastic
mesmeriser	derogately	xenophobia	penologist	tea-planter
permissive	desolately	aerophobic	serologist	respectant
permission	melomaniac	oesophagus	sexologist	despicable
permutable	decorative	henotheism	melocotoon	despicably
hermetical	demoralise	henotheist	demonology	henpeckery
hermitical	denotative	mesothorax	mesomorphy	respectful
seamstress	depolarise	mesophytic	meconopsis	respective
dermatogen	derogative	xerophytic	decorously	respecting
geometrise	devocalise	denominate	venomously	telpherage
permitting	memorative	detoxicate	mesosphere	perplexing
geometrist	pejorative	peroxidase	decompress	perplexity
hermit-crab	decoration	detoxicant	recompress	telpherman
dermatosis	denotation	depositary	recoupment	bedpresser
pegmatitic	derogation	negotiable	resorptive	helplessly
dermatitis	desolation	demoniacal	desorption	deep-seated
Pelmatozoa	detonation	velocipede	resorption	hemp-nettle
seannachie	pejoration	becomingly	recompense	telpherway
penny-a-line	peroration	Mesolithic	decomposer	serpigines
pennycress	relocation	demolisher	decompound	deoppilate
pernickety	renovation	demobilise	reconquest	despairful
vernacular	revocation	depositive	leiotrichy	temptingly
pennaceous	aerobatics	peroxidise	besom-rider	despairing
pernicious	derogatory	lenocinium	devourment	delphinium
Deinoceras	desolatory	demolition	aerogramme	besprinkle
meandering	revocatory	deposition	menorrhoea	deep-sinker
re-entering	debonairly	reposition	seborrhoea	delphinoid
ferntickle	menopausal	demoticist	aerotropic	pemphigoid
fernticled	aeronautic	kenoticist	aerography	geophilous
leontiasis	aerotactic	devotional	cerography	pemphigous
lean-witted	resonantly	serotinous	demography	ten-pointer
re-enlister	deforciant	depository	xerography	reap-silver
kennel-maid	heroicness	repository	democratic	leg-pulling
kennelling	rejoiceful	aerobiosis	repoussage	Neapolitan
pennillion	penoncelle	aerobiotic	reconsider	weeping-ash
kennel-coal	reconciler	hedonistic	remorseful	geoponical
meaningful	heroically	Jehovistic	demoiselle	weeping-elm
tennantite	heroi-comic	nepotistic	remortgage	weaponless
reunionism	resorcinol	defoliator	decoctible	despondent
reunionist	mesoscaphe	negotiator	reportable	respondent
deontology	debouchure	recoilless	besottedly	serpent-god
herniotomy	second-hand	decollated	reportedly	weapon-shaw
terneplate	second-rate	deformable	devoutness	responsive
penny-plain	second-mark	reformable	deportment	serpentine
pennypiece	recordable	deformedly	xerostomia	serpentise
penny-pinch	second-best	recommence	recontinue	desponding
reinspirit	recondense	aeroengine	aerostatic	responsory
reincrease	beforehand	debonnaire	depopulate	deep-rooted
re-entrance	remoteness	redounding	repopulate	pepper-cake
re-entrancy	denotement	resounding	resolutely	respirable
pennyroyal	dénouement	nero-antico	resolutive	temperable
lemniscate	revokement	recogniser	devolution	leopard-cat
penny-stane	beforetime	rejoindure	resolution	desperados
vernissage	demonetise	decolorate	revolution	Hesperides
tennis-ball	remonetise	decolorant	resolvable	temperedly
tennis-shoe	mesomerism	Demogorgon	resolvedly	deep-freeze

vesper-bell	detracting	petroleous	heart's-ease	newscaster
leopardess	refracting	neurolysis	petrissage	belshazzar
keepership	detraction	serrulated	depressant	pease-brose
jeopardise	re-erection	petrolatum	pearl-shell	versicular
reappraise	refraction	necrolater	decrescent	persicaria
sexpartite	retraction	necrolatry	retrospect	persecutor
vespertine	metrically	merrymaker	refreshful	sense-datum
peppermill	tetrachord	metromania	degressive	reassemble
peppermint	retrochoir	necromancy	depressive	reassembly
temporally	detractory	petromoney	redressive	news-reader
temporalty	neurectomy	Tetramorph	regressive	news-vendor
kempery-man	refractory	tetrameral	repressive	fesseewise
temperance	terracotta	tetrameter	depressing	kenspeckle
peppercorn	deprecator	hearing-aid	refreshing	newsdealer
jeopardous	refracture	detruncate	tetrastich	newsletter
pepperwort	degradable	Serranidae	degression	bed-swerver
temporiser	reproducer	ferronière	depression	persiflage
respirator	searedness	refringent	regression	persifleur
deep-browed	serradella	retransfer	repression	versifying
sea-passage	serradilla	merry-night	decrassify	message-boy
despisable	recrudesce	beer-engine	serrasalmo	deaspirate
tempestive	depredator	ferrandine	tetrasemic	perspirate
perpetrate	pearl-diver	petronella	pearl-stone	jeistiecor
perpetuate	near-begaun	metronomic	tetraspore	measliness
despotical	decreeable	metronymic	heart-spoon	reastiness
sempstress	bear-leader	retransmit	necroscopy	yeastiness
despiteful	near-legged	Herrenvolk	leproserie	beeswinged
perpetuity	tetraethyl	Tetrandria	metrostyle	seismicity
despiteous	hearse-like	ne'er-do-weel	tetrastyle	leg-spinner
ten-pounder	retrieving	ne'er-do-well	secretness	tessellate
geophysics	tear-jerker	deer-forest	redruthite	teaselling
desquamate	fearlessly	fearsomely	secretaire	sea-soldier
seaquarium	peerlessly	pearmonger	dew-retting	weasel-word
perquisite	febrifugal	dearbought	regretting	weasel-coot
degreasant	petrifying	fearnought	tetrathlon	verse-maker
beer-garden	terrifying	rear-boiled	heart-throb	leishmania
rearmament	wearifully	heortology	neurotoxin	densimeter
reproacher	zebra-finch	beer-bottle	seersucker	densimetry
recreative	terra-firma	tear-bottle	deprivable	personable
reorganise	retrograde	roar-dorter	depravedly	reasonable
recreation	beard-grass	neuroplasm	pearl-white	seasonable
ferro-alloy	segregable	Neuroptera	heart-whole	reasonably
beer-barrel	retrogress	terreplein	pear-switch	seasonably
recreantly	heart-grief	necrophile	defrayable	reasonless
neuroblast	bedraggled	negrophile	defrayment	red-sanders
heartbreak	Tetragynia	decryption	leastaways	seasonless
jerry-built	neurogenic	ferroprint	felspathic	kersantite
reprobance	tetragonal	necrophily	dessiatine	personalia
heart-blood	petroglyph	metropolis	dessyatine	personally
heart-block	searchable	necropolis	Persianise	personalty
tetrabasic	searchless	tetrapolis	persuasive	seasonally
reprobater	Herrnhuter	tetraploid	sensualise	personated
retributor	ferry-house	negrophobe	Messianism	Kensington
depreciate	heartiness	tetraptote	sensualism	personator
meerschaum	pearliness	neuropathy	persuasion	tersanctus
leprechaun	yearningly	heart-quake	geostatics	cessionary
leprechawn	recruiting	perruquier	Messianist	pensionary
deprecable	Hebraicism	terrorless	sensualist	sense-organ
detractive	Hebraistic	retrorsely	sensuality	newsmonger
refractive	necrologic	Petrarchal	Jew's-mallow	versionist
retractile	petrolling	Petrarchan	sea-swallow	seismology
retractive	neurilemma	terra-rossa	gensdarmes	tension-rod
tetractine	neurolemma	terroriser	persuasory	seismogram

sensuously
peashooter
newsworthy
yeast-plant
fesse-point
menstruate
censurable
leisurable
measurable
mensurable
censurably
leisurably
measurably
measuredly
sea-surgeon
sea-serpent
censorship
sea-service
tea-service
perstringe
censorious
menstruous
news-writer
persistent
persistive
verse-smith
pease-straw
jet-setting
sensitised
sensitiser
reissuable
reassuring
kerseymere
Jew's-myrtle
left-handed
neat-handed
bestraddle
death-adder
left-hander
leftwardly
westwardly
bestraught
Benthamite
bestialise
centralise
neutralise
Benthamism
bestialism
centralism
neutralism
textualism
Cestracion
centralist
neutralist
Septuagint
textualist
bestiality
centrality
dextrality
neutrality
meat-market
test-market
restrained

pea-trainer
restrainer
death-agony
rest-harrow
neat-cattle
peat-caster
Vertebrata
vertebrate
vestibulum
vestibular
pettichaps
pettychaps
pesticidal
septicidal
meatscreen
fettuccine
tentaculum
lenticular
tentacular
testicular
nectocalyx
hectically
septically
vertically
heptachord
pentachord
rent-a-crowd
testaceous
pettedness
testudinal
testudines
centre-half
nettlerash
centre-back
centre-rail
feather-bed
weather-bow
weather-box
heathendom
beetlehead
weather-eye
nettle-cell
gentleness
settlement
weather-gaw
heathenise
weatherise
feathering
leathering
weathering
genteelish
heathenish
nettle-fish
genteelism
heathenism
Wertherism
Wertherian
aesthetics
kettle-pins
peat-reeker
bestseller
geothermic
geothermal

weatherman
weather-map
centrefold
gentlehood
mettlesome
gentlefolk
nettle-tree
kettledrum
wentletrap
restlessly
vestmented
rest-centre
beetle-eyed
beatifical
dentifrice
certifying
rectifying
testifying
centigrade
hectograph
pentagraph
vectograph
Heptagynia
Pentagynia
heptagonal
pentagonal
lentigines
vertigines
pentahedra
rent-charge
bestridden
cestoidean
left-winger
rectricial
tectricial
centricity
ventricose
ventricous
restricted
beetmister
centrifuge
ventricule
death-knell
ventilable
Pentelican
test-flight
centillion
septillion
sextillion
pestilence
reptilious
Sertularia
gentilesse
fertiliser
centilitre
hectolitre
ventilator
centumviri
septemviri
septemvirs
Celtomania
Keltomania
lentamente

pentimenti
pentimento
Heptameron
Pentameron
centimetre
hectometre
centimeter
heptameter
pentameter
peg-tankard
septennate
nesting-box
sextonship
centennial
sentential
septennial
septennium
rectangled
pertinence
pertinency
melting-pot
Heptandria
Pentandria
rent-an-army
pectinated
certiorari
lectionary
seltzogene
festoonery
peltmonger
sectionise
destroying
geotropism
vest-pocket
tea-trolley
centrosome
deltiology
dextrously
feateously
left-footed
dextrogyre
deutoplasm
heptapodic
pentapodic
pentaprism
pentapolis
pentaploid
heath-poult
letter-card
perturbate
welter-race
perturbant
restorable
neoterical
letterhead
yesteryear
betterness
fetterless
letterless
betterment
pesterment
heptarchic
hectorship

lectorship
rectorship
dexterwise
letter-file
westernise
pewter-mill
sestertium
westernism
letter-clip
pectorally
texturally
reiterance
letter-bomb
letter-wood
fetterlock
letter-book
tenter-hook
yestermorn
nectareous
bettermost
setterwort
reiterated
see-through
yestereven
death's-head
hectostere
Leptospira
tea-tasting
pentastich
lentissimo
leptosomic
centesimal
Kentish-man
Vertoscope®
Kentish-rag
pentastyle
death-token
pentathlum
pentathlon
teetotally
pentatomic
pentstemon
heptatonic
pentatonic
heatstroke
penteteric
death-throe
restitutor
Heptateuch
Pentateuch
restaurant
centaurian
destructor
bestowment
death-watch
death-wound
vestry-room
get-up-and-go
Betulaceae
bequeathal
dehumanise
depurative
regularise

regulative
reputative
secularise
secularism
denudation
depuration
deputation
peculation
recusation
refutation
regulation
reputation
Verulamian
secularist
regularity
secularity
depuratory
regulatory
petulantly
benumbment
decumbence
recumbence
decumbency
recumbency
penumbrous
denunciate
repurchase
defunctive
defunction
peduncular
sequacious
sepulchral
Gesundheit
refundment
seguidilla
redundance
redundancy
gerundival
recuperate
rejuvenate
remunerate
requiescat
demureness
jejuneness
recureless
reputeless
secureness
deducement
securement
seducement
rejuvenise
oecumenism
tegumental
temulently
refulgence
resurgence
refulgency
resupinate
repudiable
delusively
rebukingly
seducingly
beautician

beautifier
dehumidify
delusional
cecutiency
medusiform
securiform
sea-unicorn
aeruginous
ceruminous
leguminous
velutinous
peculiarly
repudiator
republican
returnable
returnless
sequential
repugnance
repugnancy
Beaujolais
Lemuroidea
nebulosity
nebulously
sedulously
resumptive
resumption
demurrable
requirable
recurrence
decurrency
recurrency
venus-shell
decussated
requisitor
deductible
rebuttable
requitable
Jesuitical
resultless
seductress
requiteful
reluctance
reluctancy
sepultural
beauty-spot
heavy-armed
serviceman
fervidness
nerve-fibre
heavy-laden
sea-vampire
pelvimeter
servo-motor
pelvimetry
heavenward
heaven-sent
servant-man
serving-man
heaven-born
heaven-bred
perviously
perversely
weaver-bird

perversive
perversion
perversity
beaver-wood
beaver-tree
fervescent
velvet-leaf
servitress
velvet-pile
velvet-crab
velvet-duck
betweenity
sea-whistle
werwolfish
werwolfism
leg-warmers
bed-wetting
deoxidiser
recyclable
kerygmatic
dehydrater
dehydrator
benzocaine
Benzedrine
mezzo-forte
mezzotinto
benzpyrene
effaceable
effacement
affability
aficionado
afterbirth
offendress
effeteness
after-guard
aftergrass
after-image
effeminate
effeminacy
effeminise
after-light
afterpiece
afterpains
affeerment
aftershave
aftershaft
effectuate
effectible
affectedly
effectless
oftentimes
affettuoso
aftertaste
effervesce
afterworld
afterwards
Africander
Afrikander
Africanise
Africanism
Africanist
efficacity
Africanoid

office-girl
affiliable
affinitive
officially
officialty
efficience
efficiency
officiator
affirmable
affirmance
effigurate
afflictive
afflicting
affliction
off-licence
affluently
effloresce
effleurage
afrormosia
effortless
off-putting
affricated
affrighted
affrighten
effrontery
affrontive
affronting
effulgence
effusively
egg-and-dart
eglandular
age-bracket
egg-binding
egocentric
egg-capsule
Yggdrasil
ignipotent
agglutinin
agonisedly
agonistics
ignoration
ignorantly
ugsomeness
ignobility
Ugro-Finnic
agronomial
agrologist
agronomist
agapanthus
Egyptology
egurgitate
aggrandise
aggressive
aggression
agitatedly
pheasantry
wheat-berry
phraseless
phrase-book
wheat-field
sheathless
sheath-fish
sheath-bill

phialiform
wheat-midge
theatrical
cheapskate
wheatsheaf
shear-steel
thwartways
thwartedly
thwartship
thwartwise
shea-butter
shearwater
shoal-water
chlamydate
shebeening
chubbiness
shabbiness
Ghibelline
shibboleth
rhabdolith
check-clerk
thickening
chucker-out
chickenpox
chicken-run
thick-grown
shockingly
checklaton
shecklaton
phocomelia
shock-proof
chockstone
thick-skull
chock-tight
check-taker
chuck-wagon
shuddering
whidah-bird
whydah-bird
shoddiness
Rhodymenia
rhodophane
shade-plant
khidmutgar
khediviate
shadow-mark
shadowcast
shadowless
shadow-play
Rh-negative
shoemaking
chrematist
chief-baron
sheep-biter
wheel-chair
three-cleft
shield-hand
shield-maid
shieldrake
threadbare
shieldwall
thread-cell
shield-fern

shieldless	chiffonier	Childermas	shimmering	shanghaied
shrewdness	Whiggarchy	chalcedony	whimpering	shanghaier
shielding	whiggamore	cholagogic	Chamber-lye	chinchilla
Rhoeadales	shag-haired	cholagogue	Chamaerops	thinginess
thread-worm	phagocytic	thill-horse	chamberpot	thinkingly
cheesecake	phagedaena	chalkiness	chimney-pot	rhinolalia
phrenesiac	phagedenic	chilliness	Chambertin	chandlerly
cheese-mite	shagreened	shelliness	chimney-top	phonolitic
sheep-faced	shagginess	childishly	themselves	phenomenal
cheerfully	Whiggishly	phallicism	shamefaced	phenomenon
sheet-glass	phthisical	Chalcidian	shamefully	phonematic
cheechalko	phthisicky	thalliform	thumb-index	phonometer
wheel-horse	Thailander	philologic	whimsiness	shenanigan
wheel-house	Rheinberry	philologue	thumbikins	phantomish
cheeriness	chain-cable	philologer	champignon	whensoever
cheesiness	shritch-owl	whale-louse	thimbleful	phonophore
wheeziness	chain-drive	chalumeaux	thimble-rig	rhinophyma
sheepishly	chaise-cart	shale-miner	thumb-latch	shandrydan
shrewishly	chaiseless	shell-money	chemonasty	phanerogam
thievishly	choiceness	philomathy	rhomboidal	chondritic
Phoenician	thriveless	shell-mound	rhomboides	chank-shell
sheep-louse	shrivelled	phalangeal	whomsoever	rhinestone
phlegmonic	shriche-owl	whaling-gun	thumbpiece	rhinoscope
phlegmasia	thrivingly	phalangist	thumbprint	rhinoscopy
phlegmatic	shrinkpack	phyllotaxy	shame-proof	phonetical
sheet-metal	shrinkable	phalloidin	chimerical	rhinotheca
shrew-mouse	shrinkwrap	phylloxera	rhyme-royal	phenotypic
phlebolite	shrillness	phelloderm	thumb-stall	phonotypic
threnodial	chair-organ	shallowing	thumbscrew	thanatosis
phaelonion	choir-organ	Phyllopoda	chemisette	thingumbob
threnodist	cheirology	whole-plate	chemotaxis	chinquapin
Chaetopoda	cheironomy	philopoena	Rhyniaceae	shandygaff
phaenology	shrimp-girl	philippina	phantasime	phoneyness
phlebotomy	chain-smoke	philippine	shin-barker	theomaniac
phrenology	chain-store	Philippise	thin-walled	chloralism
phaenotype	Christiana	Philippian	phantasmic	chromatics
shlemozzle	Christmasy	child-proof	phantasmal	theomantic
sheep-plant	theistical	shellproof	phantastic	chromatype
three-piece	Christless	whale-shark	phantastry	thrombosis
three-piled	thriftless	Philistean	Rhineberry	thrombotic
threepence	thriftiest	philistine	thenabouts	shroudless
threepenny	Christlike	Philistian	chinachina	shroud-line
three-parts	Christhood	thalassian	rhinoceros	throneless
three-pound	shrievalty	wholesaler	phenacetin	theotechny
cheek-pouch	chairwoman	chalkstone	phenocryst	Shrovetide
sheepshank	chokeberry	shellshock	changeable	chrome-alum
three-sided	choliambic	philosophe	thunder-box	throne-room
sheep's-head	chiliarchy	philosophy	changeably	thiopental
threescore	shellacked	child-study	chanceless	throughout
sheep's-foot	chiliastic	philatelic	changeless	through-put
sheep-track	chalkboard	phillumeny	thunder-god	throughway
shoestring	chalybeate	whole-wheat	changeling	theophobia
thief-taker	childbirth	whillywhaw	thundering	theophanic
threatened	shellbound	shellycoat	chandelier	theophoric
threatener	thale-cress	Rhamnaceae	channelled	chloridate
cheek-tooth	phylactery	chemiatric	chancellor	chlorinate
shoebuckle	chelicerae	chimpanzee	thunderous	theodicean
chiff-chaff	thalictrum	chemicking	change-over	chloridise
shaft-horse	shelldrake	chemically	thankfully	chlorinise
chuffiness	pholidosis	thymectomy	Rhinegrave	Rh-positive
shiftiness	shillelagh	chimney-can	phonograph	chromidium
chaffingly	challenger	chamaeleon	phenogamic	chronicity
shuffle-cap	sheltering	chambering	Phenogamae	chronicler

phlogistic	choriambic	pharyngeal	chiselling	khitmutgar
phlogiston	thereanent	chironomic	chasmogamy	white-water
hrown-silk	Thermalite®	chironomid	physiology	chatoyance
heopneust	pharmacist	chironomer	physiocrat	thousandth
heologate	thereamong	Chironomus	ghost-story	rheumatise
heosophic	thereabout	sharp-nosed	chest-voice	rheumatize
chlorophyl	whereabout	thyrsoidal	ghost-write	thaumasite
heosopher	whirl-about	chersonese	whisky-jack	rheumatism
phlogopite	thorn-apple	charioteer	chessylite	rheumatoid
heodolite	thereafter	thermophil	whisky-john	Chautauqua
heologise	whirl-blast	lherzolite	chittagong	shouldered
heologian	cherubical	thermopile	white-beard	Chaucerism
heologist	shortbread	thermotics	white-brass	Chaucerian
heogonist	cherubimic	choreology	whity-brown	chaudfroid
heologist	charabancs	thermology	whatabouts	chauffeuse
chionodoxa	shard-borne	thermogram	thetically	theurgical
chromosome	short-coats	thermostat	photodiode	thoughtful
chloroform	third-class	Chiroptera	chatterbox	shoutingly
heonomous	charactery	third-party	chattering	ghoulishly
chronology	churn-drill	shire-reeve	chittering	chauvinism
chromogram	Charadrius	chirurgeon	shuttering	chauvinist
chronogram	short-dated	chirurgery	whitterick	chaulmugra
chronotron	thorn-devil	sherardise	white-faced	chaud-mellé
chloroquin	charge-hand	short-range	photoflood	thruppence
chlorodyne	ahorseback	Chartreuse	photograph	thruppenny
chromotype	chargeable	dharmshala	photogenic	chauntress
heotropic	chargeably	churn-staff	phytogenic	shave-grass
heocratic	chargeless	wheresoe'er	photoglyph	shove-groat
hrow-stick	sharp-edged	whore's-bird	white-heart	Shivaistic
hroat-band	shortening	chorus-girl	thatchless	shovel-head
hrottling	shereefian	pharisaism	white-horse	shovelling
hroatwort	thirteenth	short-sword	white-hawse	shovelnose
hroat-full	Charleston	charitable	chota hazri	chivalrous
hiocyanic	sheriffdom	charitably	shot-window	shovelfuls
vhip-handle	shirt-frill	charity-boy	Phytolacca	chevrotain
chaptalise	shirt-front	thirstless	châtelaine	chevesaile
shop-walker	chirograph	chartulary	photolysis	chevisance
chip-basket	shore-going	thereunder	photolytic	whewellite
vhip-tailed	chirognomy	whereunder	rhythmical	chewing-gum
chapfallen	churchward	thoroughly	rhythmless	shower-bath
chopfallen	churchyard	whereuntil	photometer	showerless
chaplaincy	church-rate	shirtwaist	photometry	showground
chaplainry	thorn-hedge	shorewards	photonasty	showjumper
ship-master	churchless	cherry-bean	Whit-Monday	thixotropy
vhippeting	church-text	whirlybird	Ahithophel	chrysalids
shopkeeper	church-goer	cherry-plum	whatsoever	chrysophan
ship-letter	shire-horse	thirtyfold	photophily	chrysolite
shop-window	charthouse	cherry-coal	photophobe	chrysotile
ship-rigged	whorehouse	chessboard	photophone	rhizogenic
shop-lifter	chirpiness	physicking	photophore	whizzingly
ship-holder	thorniness	physically	photophony	rhizomorph
hapsodise	wharfinger	whist-drive	rhetorical	rhizoplane
hapsodist	phorminges	chasse-café	chitarrone	Rhizophora
vhip-socket	charmingly	chasteness	whitesmith	rhizophore
shop-soiled	churlishly	whispering	phototrope	dilatation
Rhipiptera	thermionic	ghastfully	whitethorn	divagation
shipwright	thermistor	phosphoric	phototropy	disavaunce
chaparajos	shore-leave	phosphorus	phototypic	mica-schist
chaparejos	Charollais	phosphoret	phytotoxic	didascalic
ship-broker	short-lived	phosphuret	phytotoxin	vizard-mask
chopsticks	chiromancy	phosphatic	phototaxis	vivandière
vhip-stitch	cherimoyer	whiskified	Whitsun-ale	hit-and-miss
cheque-book	Ahuramazda	Chassidism	Whitsunday	misandrist

ritardando
dinanderie
minauderie
dilacerate
picaresque
Titanesque
ligamental
nidamental
nidamentum
sisal-grass
hidalgoish
hidalgoism
dilapidate
disanimate
divaricate
vitaminise
vitalising
viraginian
vitalities
disability
ridability
limaciform
viraginous
filariasis
vitalistic
tirailleur
pinacoidal
pinakoidal
pinakothek
dilatorily
bigamously
disappoint
disapprove
disapparel
cicatrices
binaurally
disarrange
misarrange
bizarrerie
cicatrixes
didactical
disastrous
pilastered
bipartisan
picayunish
miraculous
dika-butter
bivalvular
disadvance
misadvised
litany-desk
air-bladder
Zimbabwean
riebeckite
nimbleness
tie-breaker
misbehaved
limb-girdle
nibblingly
fimbriated
diabolical
disbelieve
misbelieve

big-bellied
ribbon-weed
ribbon-seal
ribbon-fish
ribbon-worm
timbrology
timber-yard
timber-mare
limber-neck
disbarment
disburthen
Gilbertine
kimberlite
limburgite
timber-line
Gilbertian
Gibberella
timber-wolf
timber-toes
timber-tree
diabetical
kibbutznik
pin-buttock
witch-alder
discharger
wit-cracker
disclaimer
disc-harrow
mischanter
pitch-black
discobolus
witchcraft
viscachera
piccadillo
piccadilly
discrepant
kitchendom
discretely
kitchen-fee
pitcherful
discretive
discretion
biochemist
miscreance
miscreancy
miscreated
miscreator
Winchester
discreetly
piscifauna
zincograph
piece-goods
hitch-hiker
witch-hazel
circuiteer
bitchiness
pitchiness
filchingly
pinchingly
witchingly
kinchin-lay
circuitous
disculpate

miscellany
circulable
piccalilli
zinc-blende
disc-floret
circularly
zincolysis
circulator
disc-plough
disc-flower
discommend
circumvent
circumcise
circumflex
circumpose
discommode
discompose
nincompoop
discomfort
mischmetal
viscometer
viscometry
circumduce
circumfuse
circummure
miscompute
circumduct
cincinnate
diaconicon
disconcert
disconnect
disconsent
discontent
misconceit
miscontent
circensian
Vincentian
piccaninny
misconduct
pince-nezed
cinchonine
cinchonise
air-cooling
tinctorial
cinchonism
zinc-worker
disc-jockey
disclosure
discipline
discophile
pinchpenny
Discophora
sincipital
discordant
miscorrect
discordful
discursive
discerning
discursion
discursist
diachronic
discursory
discussive ·

die-casting
air-cushion
Circassian
discission
discussion
pincushion
pitchstone
discutient
discourage
discounsel
miscounsel
discourser
diacaustic
diacoustic
discounter
pie-counter
viscountcy
discoverer
pitch-wheel
ditch-water
winceyette
misdrawing
windfallen
windjammer
wildcatter
wildebeest
vindicable
windscreen
vindictive
vindicator
mindedness
fiddle-back
mind-bender
fiddlehead
misdeemful
middle-aged
riddle-like
misdeeming
kiddiewink
mind-healer
fiddlewood
middlemost
bird-pepper
middlebrow
mindlessly
dildo-glass
hirdy-girdy
windshield
wind-shaken
bird-cherry
wild-cherry
kindliness
disdainful
riddlingly
bird-hipped
bird-witted
bird-skiing
wind-sleeve
Diadelphia
wind-flower
vindemiate
hiddenness
wild-indigo

biodynamic
midden-cock
hiddenmost
wild-fowler
giddy-paced
bird-spider
kind-spoken
mild-spoken
hinderland
cinder-path
hinderlans
wilderness
rinderpest
wilderment
tinder-like
nidderling
hinderlins
wind-broken
Cinderella
hinderance
cinder-cone
hindermost
wind-dropsy
Mindererus
Hindustani
bird-strike
pied-à-terre
yird-hunger
yird-hungry
wind-sucker
wind-tunnel
window-pane
window-sash
windowless
window-seat
window-sill
window-bole
tiddlywink
wire-dancer
side-saddle
fire-warden
cine-camera
Piperaceae
vinegar-eel
vinegar-fly
liberalise
literalise
mineralise
piperazine
life-saving
pipe-laying
time-saving
vinegarish
bipedalism
cinerarium
liberalism
literalism
cineration
liberation
literation
sideration
kinematics
liberalist

iteralist
mineralist
liberality
literality
literarily
fire-walker
wire-walker
fire-basket
life-jacket
bimetallic
wine-vaults
bipetalous
dipetalous
disepalous
liberatory
mineralogy
dive-dapper
pine-carpet
wire-haired
pine-barren
fire-raiser
five-parted
mile-castle
pine-marten
fire-master
tide-waiter
wine-taster
literature
disembogue
disembroil
disembosom
river-basin
disembowel
disenchain
disenchant
river-craft
fire-screen
widescreen
virescence
disenclose
life-school
Oireachtas
river-drift
disendowed
aide-de-camp
life-tenant
pine-needle
file-leader
viceregent
live-weight
wine-cellar
nineteenth
pine-kernel
pike-keeper
time-keeper
lifelessly
timelessly
tirelessly
pine-beetle
life-renter
pine-beauty
time-server
wizen-faced

side-effect
fire-office
river-front
liver-fluke
mimeograph
wired-glass
disengaged
divergence
divergency
liver-grown
pine-chafer
river-horse
time-thrust
fire-shovel
kinesipath
wine-bibber
like-minded
sidewinder
vine-mildew
livelihead
likeliness
liveliness
timeliness
five-finger
line-fisher
piperidine
life-giving
time-killer
time-signal
likelihood
livelihood
misericord
viperiform
vitellicle
fire-blight
kite-flying
side-glance
fire-plough
dice-player
mixed-media
dilemmatic
mileometer
river-mouth
pigeon-pair
disennoble
hibernacle
Vireonidae
fire-engine
pigeon-wing
pigeon-toed
pigeonhole
pigeon-post
ride-and-tie
dive-bomber
tiresomely
siderolite
Ciceronian
fire-policy
literosity
mine-worker
wireworker
life-rocket
wine-cooler

vice-county
bioecology
diseconomy
vice-consul
viperously
life-mortar
siderostat
widespread
cider-press
didelphine
didelphian
diremption
fine-spoken
videophone
didelphous
time-spirit
disespouse
five-square
line-squall
Viverridae
wire-bridge
plleorhiza
Viverrinae
pipe-wrench
vine-branch
pile-driver
wine-grower
disenslave
fire-escape
life-estate
riverscape
tiger-snake
tiger-shark
licensable
niger-seeds
diseaseful
widershins
licentiate
disentrain
silentiary
digestible
divertible
divestible
digestedly
directness
directress
silentness
divestment
misentreat
Directoire
disentwine
bimestrial
liberty-man
dilettante
dilettanti
minestrone
side-stroke
licentious
disenthral
bidentated
disentitle
Nibelungen
fine-tuning

sinecurism
sinecurist
fire-bucket
wire-puller
lime-burner
file-cutter
mine-hunter
eigenvalue
disenvelop
disenviron
liverwurst
time-switch
river-water
pin-feather
disfeature
misfeature
difficulty
diffidence
fitfulness
sinfulness
wilfulness
niffy-naffy
disfurnish
difformity
difference
differency
misfortune
diffusible
diffusedly
Singhalese
biographic
diagraphic
biographer
air-grating
ring-tailed
king-salmon
ring-master
hinge-bound
king's-chair
siegecraft
ringleader
singleness
minglement
ring-necked
gigglesome
single-foot
singletree
single-eyed
king-of-arms
wing-sheath
pilgrimage
kingliness
ring-finger
minglingly
kingfisher
pilgrimise
disguising
pinguidity
ginglimoid
kinglihood
linguiform
jingoistic
linguistic

linguister
linguistry
Pinguicula
pinguitude
hinge-joint
Ringelmann
Lingulella
singularly
ring-plover
diagometer
diagonally
virginally
singing-man
virginhood
virgin-born
biogenesis
diagenesis
biogenetic
diagenetic
disglorify
ring-porous
diagnostic
wing-footed
wing-spread
ridge-piece
siege-piece
fingermark
fingernail
digger-wasp
jigger-mast
didgeridoo
finger's-end
nigger-head
fingerless
king-archon
niggardise
fingerling
niggerling
disgarnish
pilgarlick
gingersnap
fingerhold
fingerhole
fingerbowl
fingerpost
king's-spear
disgustful
disgusting
siege-train
jiggety-jog
king-at-arms
disgruntle
gingivitis
siege-works
bilge-water
high-handed
fish-ladder
Highlander
dish-washer
Lithuanian
highjacker
high-ranker
light-armed

highwayman	wishing-cap	high-strung	dining-room	ridiculous
fish-farmer	siphonogam	light-tower	living-room	filibuster
Mishnayoth	tithing-man	mishguggle	tiring-room	disinvolve
right-about	fishing-rod	silhouette	riding-boot	Lipizzaner
high-raised	dishonesty	fish-gutter	riding-coat	disjection
high-tasted	bichromate	rightwards	riding-crop	misjoinder
dishearten	dichromate	wishy-washy	firing-step	disjointed
fish-manure	dithionate	night-watch	diving-suit	disjunctor
fish-carver	withholden	digitately	riding-suit	sinke-a-pace
dishabille	withholder	disimagine	disinhibit	sick-making
high-octane	light-organ	limitative	disinherit	nick-nacket
pichiciago	fishmonger	militarise	nidificate	sick-fallen
night-chair	dichromism	mitigative	vitiligate	rick-barton
lithoclast	high-souled	similative	Filicineae	silk-screen
night-cloud	high-roller	visitative	filicinean	pickedness
night-churr	light-o'-love	militarism	diminished	wickedness
right-drawn	diphyodont	minimalism	silicified	fickleness
nightdress	dichroitic	viviparism	minimising	sickle-bill
Lithodomus	right-of-way	digitation	libidinist	pick-cheese
lighterage	lithophane	divination	risibility	sickliness
lightening	nightpiece	limitarian	visibility	tinklingly
high-necked	xiphopagic	limitation	militiaman	ticklishly
high-heeled	xiphopagus	litigation	sicilienne	dickcissel
lighterman	bishop-bird	mitigation	divisional	sick-listed
Michaelmas	lithoprint	sibilation	digitiform	rick-lifter
eighteenth	night-palsy	tidivation	libidinous	nickelling
eighteenmo	eightpence	titivation	nihilistic	nickumpoop
high-reared	eightpenny	visitation	similitude	Dickensian
fish-kettle	lightproof	militarist	Sigillaria	pickaninny
light-faced	lithophysa	minimalist	pixillated	ticking-off
rightfully	lithophyse	finicality	titillator	link-motion
lithograph	lithophyte	militarily	visionless	pick-pocket
night-glass	hitherward	similarity	visionally	Ginkgoales
hip-huggers	high-priced	viviparity	bipinnaria	silk-cotton
lithoglyph	night-rider	viviparous	ricinoleic	ticker-tape
diphtheria	hitherside	divinatory	Visigothic	sickerness
diphtheric	highermost	mitigatory	ripidolite	wickerwork
light-horse	hithermost	sibilatory	visitorial	silk-grower
night-heron	disharmony	militantly	digitorium	wicket-gate
lighthouse	disherison	vigilantly	mini-rocket	tickety-boo
night-house	disheritor	cicisbeism	fimicolous	picket-line
mithridate	night-raven	disincline	limicolous	rickettsia
high-minded	fish-trowel	disinclose	nidicolous	picket-duty
highbinder	withdrawal	liliaceous	viticolous	rick-burner
mightiness	withdrawer	tiliaceous	ciliophora	gillravage
lighting-up	nightshade	biliverdin	disimprove	misleading
fish-finger	night-steed	citizeness	misimprove	diallagoid
tightishly	night-spell	divineness	viziership	silly-billy
ditheistic	air-hostess	divineress	limitrophe	fieldboots
high-kilted	night-sight	finiteness	ministrant	millocracy
high-placed	Lithistida	citizenise	ministress	dialectics
tight-laced	night-stick	piliferous	sinistrous	biblically
tight-lacer	night-shift	vitiferous	ministeria	violaceous
lithologic	nightshirt	pitilessly	tibiotarsi	dielectric
night-light	eightscore	vivisector	disinthral	rifle-corps
high-flying	night-stool	diligently	sinisterly	digladiate
right-lined	vichyssois	dining-hall	minibuffet	Diplodocus
diphyletic	xiphosuran	diving-bell	mini-budget	dilly-dally
ditheletic	light-tight	riding-whip	diminutive	tilly-fally
night-latch	lithotrite	bilinguist	diminution	millefiori
litholatry	lithotrity	visiogenic	diminuendo	biological
lithomancy	lithotomic	riding-hood	siliculose	rifle-green
lithomarge	night-taper	riding-robe	nidifugous	sialagogic

sialagogue	dismalness	Pilocarpus	simplicity	nitrifying
sialogogue	cismontane	Dinosauria	biopoiesis	microfarad
villainage	pigmentary	disordered	simplistic	cirrigrade
villeinage	mismanners	disorderly	dispelling	hierograph
villainess	Simmenthal	digoneutic	hippomanes	micrograph
wieldiness	airmanship	pirouetter	dispondaic	vibrograph
hill-digger	diamantine	air-officer	dispensary	fibreglass
yieldingly	Riemannian	disorganic	cispontine	nitro-group
Cisleithan	biomorphic	sitophobia	Pimpinella	ditriglyph
villainous	air-marshal	lipochrome	ripping-saw	hieroglyph
dislikable	mid-morning	ricocheted	disprofess	diarrhoeic
dislikeful	Kilmarnock	pilot-house	disprovide	diarrhoeal
diplomatic	dismissive	simoniacal	displosion	microhenry
fieldmouse	dismission	nicotinism	hippophagy	diorthosis
millennial	dismissory	tirocinium	hippophile	diorthotic
millennium	biometrics	riboflavin	hippophobe	cirrhipede
villanelle	big-mouthed	disownment	dispersant	piercingly
willy-nilly	sign-manual	ritornelle	dioptrical	vitrailled
tirling-pin	cinnabaric	ritornelli	disparager	mitre-joint
tillandsia	lignocaine	ritornello	dispersive	jinrikisha
Villanovan	picnicking	misologist	dispersion	fibrillate
bibliomane	Limnaeidae	Sinologist	dispersold	fibrillary
millionary	dignifying	vinologist	dispermous	hierologic
bibliopegy	lignifying	virologist	hippuritic	micrologic
bibliophil	signifying	rigorously	dispirited	microlight
pillionist	pianoforte	timorously	disparates	fibrillose
bibliopole	fianchetto	vigorously	disposable	fibrillous
bibliology	biennially	pilot-plant	disposedly	tirra-lirra
bibliopoly	simnel-cake	dimorphism	dispossess	miarolitic
billposter	signalling	dimorphous	dispassion	microlitic
fieldpiece	pinnulated	kilogramme	dispositor	hierolatry
girlfriend	cinnamonic	lipography	disputable	hieromancy
millwright	mignonette	mimography	disputably	nigromancy
pillorying	piano-organ	timocratic	hippety-hop	micrometre
bill-broker	kirn-dollie	misobserve	dispatcher	micrometer
rifle-range	Pinnipedia	birostrate	dispiteous	nitrometer
tiller-rope	kidnapping	bijouterie	diophysite	vibrometer
pillar-root	dinner-pail	vicomtesse	biophysics	micrometry
dialysable	dinnerless	pilot-whale	Lippizzana	fibrinogen
title-sheet	dinner-time	mixolydian	Lippizaner	Dibranchia
millesimal	dinner-gown	misogynist	disqualify	citronella
fieldstone	dinner-hour	misogynous	cinque-pace	Hieronymic
billet-head	sign-writer	diaphanous	cinque-foil	vitriolate
millet-seed	witness-box	hippiatric	disquieten	vitriolise
mill-stream	pianissimo	dispraiser	disquietly	vitreosity
billet-doux	piano-stool	Hippocrene	lip-reading	Cirrhopoda
gimlet-eyed	pinnatifid	nit-picking	misreading	hierophant
tilly-vally	signet-ring	hippocampi	rip-roaring	hiera-picra
pillow-lava	vignettist	hippodrome	diurnalist	Cirripedia
pillowcase	pinnatiped	diapedesis	rib-roaster	higry-pigry
pillow-lace	disnatured	diapedetic	fibreboard	disruptive
willow-herb	Finno-Ugric	ripple-mark	fibroblast	disruption
willow-weed	lion-hunter	simpleness	microbiota	microprint
pillow-bere	kidney-bean	dimplement	hierocracy	micropylar
pillow-bear	Hitopadesa	displenish	micrococci	microphone
pillowslip	Mimosaceae	nipplewort	ditrochean	vibraphone
pilliwinks	bilocation	displeased	microcline	microphyte
willow-wren	misogamist	hippogriff	vibraculum	hierarchic
fieldwards	bipolarity	hippogryph	jinricksha	hierarchal
disloyally	bitonality	ripplingly	pierceable	mirrorwise
disloyalty	bivouacked	simplified	fierceness	mitre-shell
mismeasure	misocapnic	misprision	bierkeller	disrespect
biomedical	lipomatous	simplifier	microfiche	nigrescent

vitrescent
digressive
microseism
digression
nicrosilal
microsomal
microscope
microspore
hieroscopy
microscopy
fibrositis
librettist
microtomic
picrotoxin
gilravager
mitre-wheel
biorhythms
first-aider
dissuasive
dissuasion
miasmatous
dissuasory
wit-snapper
diastaltic
dissociate
first-class
dissective
dissecting
dissection
dissidence
diastemata
diaskeuast
misseeming
misspelled
linseed-oil
dissheathe
first-floor
first-fruit
pig-sticker
midshipman
bioscience
dissoluble
dissilient
dissolvent
missel-bird
dissolving
tinselling
missel-tree
kieselguhr
lissomness
dissembler
dissimilar
dipsomania
jimson-weed
first-night
die-sinking
dissenting
dissension
dissonance
dissonancy
missionary
missionise
ripsnorter

six-shooter
dissipable
dissipated
dissertate
disservice
lip-service
minstrelsy
pin-striped
first-thing
dissatisfy
dissevered
bissextile
Vietnamese
air-traffic
distraught
dirt-eating
virtualism
filtration
virtualist
virtuality
victualled
victualler
tilt-hammer
mistrayned
distrainee
distrainer
distrainor
distracted
mint-master
ritt-master
pietra-dura
histoblast
distichous
giftedness
eisteddfod
little-ease
diothelete
littleness
virtueless
diothelite
diothelism
kittle-pins
diathermic
diathermal
distressed
listlessly
mistressly
fifty-fifty
mirthfully
Dictograph
pictograph
histogenic
filthiness
wintriness
distringas
diatribist
histrionic
distribute
mistakable
mistakenly
distilland
distillate
pistillate

pistillary
distillery
histologic
pistol-whip
pistol-shot
distilling
pistolling
pistillode
histolysis
histolytic
mist-flower
victimiser
hitty-missy
Tintometer®
mixty-maxty
listenable
birthnight
distensile
distensive
distension
distention
kitten-moth
fitting-out
mitten-crab
listener-in
distinctly
distinguée
dictionary
distrouble
misthought
diatropism
fictionist
virtuosity
histiology
virtuously
dirt-rotten
birthplace
fifty-pence
dictaphone
victoriana
hinterland
disturbant
filterable
historical
pictorical
bitterness
sisterless
birthright
picture-hat
distortive
sister-like
winter-tide
bitter-king
bitterling
Cistercian
distortion
diuturnity
winter-clad
bitterwood
sisterhood
sister-hook
victorious
bitter-root

litter-lout
bitter-spar
picture-rod
dietetical
uintathere
dictatress
fictitious
mistrysted
figurative
simulative
figuration
nidulation
simulation
titubation
titularity
simulatory
simulacrum
sipunculid
minuscular
Didunculus
bifurcated
liquidness
liquidiser
liquidator
minute-hand
vituperate
minute-jack
lieutenant
figurehead
minute-bell
diluteness
minuteness
minute-book
minute-drop
virulently
liquefying
liturgical
bituminate
dijudicate
dilucidate
hirudinean
bituminise
disutility
fiducially
hirudinoid
bituminous
hirudinous
visualiser
biquintile
sinusoidal
bisulphate
disulphate
bisulphide
disulphide
liquescent
pit-village
misventure
sieve-plate
silver-bath
silverweed
silver-leaf
silver-bell
silverside

silverling
silver-fish
silver-gilt
silverskin
silver-foil
silver-tree
view-halloo
viewlessly
viewfinder
tim-whiskey
miswandred
disworship
misworship
miswording
didynamian
didynamous
vinylidene
pityriasis
disyllabic
disyllable
dicynodont
Himyaritic
zigzaggery
zigzagging
piezometer
mizzen-sail
mizzen-mast
fizzenless
diazeuctic
ski-bobbing
skaithless
skrimshank
skyjacking
ski-jumping
sky-jumping
skikjöring
skulkingly
skylarking
akolouthos
skimmingly
skimpingly
skinniness
skin-diving
skene-occle
sky-planted
skip-kennel
Skupshtina
skippingly
sky-parlour
skirmisher
ski-running
ekistician
skyscraper
skateboard
sketchable
sketch-book
skittishly
sky-writing
skew-corbel
skew-bridge
cloacaline
floatation
almacantar

pleasantly	electively	fleece-wool	oligarchic	climatical
pleasantry	electivity	Illecebrum	oligarchal	alang-alang
float-board	flaccidity	bluey-green	flight-deck	alineation
altar-cloth	flick-knife	allergenic	flightless	elongation
illaudable	elecampane	blue-cheese	slightness	plantation
illaudably	clockmaker	fleechment	flagitious	blind-alley
flea-beetle	electorate	bluethroat	alphabetic	planoblast
flea-circus	electoress	sleepiness	All-Hallows	clinically
bleariness	electorial	sleetiness	alchemical	blind-drunk
sleaziness	glaciology	fleeringly	alphameric	blonde-lace
illatively	Plecoptera	fleetingly	alphametic	plunderage
floatingly	flock-paper	allegiance	Alphonsine	flunkeydom
gloatingly	electrical	ulteriorly	ultimately	slenderise
pleadingly	clock-radio	alleviator	alligation	blanketing
pleasingly	electrogen	aldermanic	plain-chant	blundering
alkalinity	electromer	aldermanly	claircolle	flunkeyish
pliability	electronic	aldermanry	alliaceous	flunkeyism
oleaginous	placer-gold	alternance	alliterate	flannelled
flea-bitten	blacksmith	alternatim	illiterate	glance-coal
altazimuth	Blackshirt	alternator	sluice-gate	glanderous
altarpiece	slickstone	blue-tongue	illiteracy	plunderous
altar-rails	glucosuria	allegorise	oleiferous	slanderous
cleansable	glycosuria	allegorist	Albigenses	flindersia
altar-stone	glucosuric	olde-worlde	sleigh-bell	plangently
float-stone	glycosuric	blue-collar	eloignment	klangfarbe
clear-story	fly-catcher	blue-bonnet	altisonant	sling-fruit
olfactible	blackthorn	ulcerously	altitonant	planigraph
pliantness	flocculate	bluebottle	elliptical	flint-glass
illaqueate	flocculent	bluebreast	cloistress	flint-heart
ill-advised	clack-valve	algebraist	plaintless	planchette
bleary-eyed	blackwater	allegretto	cloistered	plant-house
clubmaster	slack-water	sleekstone	cloisterer	ilang-ilang
club-headed	glad-hander	alpenstock	flake-white	clinginess
slubbering	gladiatory	fluentness	ill-looking	flintiness
glebe-house	pledgeable	clientship	glumaceous	slanginess
ill-behaved	all-dreaded	sleepy-head	slumberful	glancingly
flabbiness	fledgeling	fly-flapper	glimmering	slangingly
slabbiness	bladder-nut	ill-feeling	slumbering	clantingly
flabellate	ill defined	old-fogyish	slammerkin	clannishly
globularly	ploddingly	fluffiness	slumberous	glandiform
fly-by-night	gladsomely	all-firedly	blamefully	plentitude
alabandine	clodhopper	ill-fortune	plume-grass	plenilunar
alabandite	Clydesdale	fly-fishing	clamminess	plant-louse
club-footed	slide-valve	ill-founded	clumpiness	blancmange
elaborator	gleemaiden	plagiarise	clumsiness	clinometer
plebiscite	alterative	flag-waving	flimsiness	planimeter
glaciation	illegalise	plagiarism	old-maidish	planometer
glacialist	ulcerative	plagiarist	old-maidism	clinometry
blackamoor	alienation	flag-basket	Plumularia	planimetry
blackboard	allegation	flagrantly	Flamingant	flanconade
black-bully	alteration	oligoclase	alimentary	glendoveer
blackberry	ulceration	plaguesome	elementary	clangorous
click-clack	illegality	plague-sore	eliminable	plenishing
block-chain	bluejacket	plague-spot	flaminical	alongshore
placidness	elderberry	clogginess	clementine	clingstone
elucidator	albescence	flagginess	flamingoes	clinkstone
slackening	sleeve-hand	sluggishly	eliminator	slingstone
blackfaced	blue-pencil	Flagellata	flamboyant	plane-table
blackguard	fleeceless	flagellate	plum-colour	planetical
glycogenic	sleeveless	flagellant	clomiphene	planktonic
blackheart	sleeve-fish	flugelhorn	glomerular	planetaria
blockhouse	sleeve-link	Glagolitic	glomerulus	ill-natured
pluckiness	allegeance	oligopsony	plumassier	klendusity

glandulous	floppiness	blister-fly	blithering	flourished
blanquette	slippiness	blistering	flattering	albuminise
slang-whang	sloppiness	blustering	glittering	illuminism
clanswoman	clypeiform	clustering	slatternly	Eleusinian
ylang-ylang	slipsloppy	glistering	blithesome	illuminist
allopathic	flapdoodle	plastering	clothes-peg	albuminoid
allocation	glyptodont	Glaswegian	clothes-pin	albuminous
algolagnia	pluperfect	blusterous	blottesque	plauditory
allogamous	flap-dragon	flesh-eater	cloth-eared	glauconite
gliomatous	all-purpose	glass-faced	plate-fleet	pleurodont
Allosaurus	flyposting	glassfulls	slothfully	pleurotomy
pleonastic	slipstream	blissfully	plate-glass	illustrate
floorboard	slip-string	blasphemer	clottiness	fluviatile
elbow-chair	eloquently	flash-house	plottingly	fluvialist
floorcloth	cliquiness	glasshouse	sluttishly	slavocracy
almond-tree	flirtation	elasticate	elytriform	clavicular
almond-eyed	clarabella	flashiness	elutriator	clavichord
altogether	floribunda	fleshiness	blitzkrieg	olivaceous
all-overish	ultrabasic	glassiness	flatulence	glove-fight
blood-guilt	clarichord	glossiness	flatulency	slave-grown
blood-group	alarm-clock	blushingly	plutolatry	clove-hitch
algophobia	oleraceous	plastilina	plate-layer	glove-money
allophonic	floridness	classified	flute-mouth	eleventhly
pleochroic	florideous	elasticise	Platonical	slovenlike
allochiria	ultrafiche	Plasticine	gluttonise	slave-owner
blood-horse	clarifying	plasticise	gluttonish	Slavophile
bloodhound	glorifying	classicism	slit-pocket	Slavophobe
fluoridate	clergiable	classifier	gluttonous	cloverleaf
fluorinate	alarmingly	classicist	glottology	cleverness
gloominess	flirtingly	elasticity	flat-footed	olive-shell
fluoridise	altruistic	plasticity	plate-proof	flavescent
Pliohippus	florilegia	plastidule	platypuses	slave-trade
floodlight	cleromancy	clasp-knife	slit-trench	flavouring
blood-money	pleromatic	flashlight	ulsterette	claw-hammer
alcoholise	Clarenceux	plesiosaur	almucantar	clew-garnet
alcoholism	florentine	clistogamy	cloud-built	slow-gaited
algologist	ultroneous	plasmogamy	cloudburst	slow-winged
pleomorphy	gloriously	plastogamy	cloudberry	clownishly
sloop-of-war	plerophory	Blastoidea	flaunching	slow-moving
fluorotype	alarm-radio	blastomere	fleur-de-lis	slow-motion
blood-plate	ultra-rapid	blastoderm	fleur-de-lys	slow-footed
Algonquian	florescent	plasmodesm	allurement	flower-head
allotropic	floristics	blossoming	albumenise	flower-bell
oleography	ultrasonic	plasmodium	glauberite	flowerless
blood-royal	ultrashort	plasmosoma	ploughland	flower-show
bloodstain	clerestory	blastopore	ploughgate	flower-girl
bloodstone	ultrasound	plasmosome	plough-tail	blow-by-blow
bloodstock	all-rounder	glossology	ploughable	plexiglass
Bloomsbury	clergyable	plasmolyse	plough-team	flexihours
blood-sized	Alismaceae	blastocyst	slaughtery	pleximeter
allocution	Clusiaceae	flash-point	ploughwise	pleximetry
illocution	glossarial	glass-paper	plough-tree	alexanders
blood-wagon	glossarist	clostridia	plough-iron	fluxionary
floodwater	ill-starred	glass-snake	albuminate	fluxionist
bloody-eyed	flash-board	close-stool	illuminate	play-acting
blepharism	flesh-broth	closet-play	illuminati	playschool
flippantly	flesh-brush	flosculous	illuminato	playleader
clapperboy	clish-clash	flesh-wound	illuminant	playfellow
clappering	glass-coach	plutocracy	cloudiness	allycholly
flapperish	ill-success	elatedness	allusively	clay-pigeon
slipperily	glass-cloth	glitterand	illusively	Alcyonaria
slop-seller	closed-door	blitheness	alluringly	playwright
clapped-out	cluster-cup	blethering	floutingly	play-writer

clay-ground	emmenology	implicitly	ammoniated	improvably
playground	ampelopsis	smell-feast	impoundage	improvided
blizzardly	emmetropia	amplifying	embonpoint	improviser
emparadise	emmetropic	small-hours	impossible	emery-wheel
imparadise	impersonal	smalminess	embossment	embrowning
immanation	immeasured	smelliness	empoisoned	emissivity
impanation	Emmentaler	emollition	importable	emasculate
embasement	impervious	emulsifier	importless	ametabolic
impalement	smifligate	emblements	immortelle	smithcraft
immaterial	emigration	emblematic	immortally	emetically
empanelled	amygdaloid	ameliorate	impostumed	smother-fly
immanental	emigratory	Amblyopsis	importance	smattering
embargoing	imaginable	small-pipes	importuner	smothering
empathetic	imaginably	implorator	importancy	smuttiness
smeariness	emphractic	Amblystoma	imposthume	amatorious
ommatidium	amphibrach	small-sword	omophagous	smut-fungus
amiability	amphibolic	emplastrum	omophorion	amateurish
impatience	amphibious	emplastron	smart-Aleck	amateurism
ambagitory	Amphictyon	emulatress	smart-Alick	imputative
embankment	amphimacer	small-tooth	emery-board	ambulation
embarkment	amphimixis	small-wares	improbable	amputation
imparlance	Amphineura	implexuous	improbably	imputation
embalmment	amphiscian	employable	imbroccata	ambulatory
impalpable	emphatical	employment	umbraculum	ambulacral
impalpably	amphoteric	emblazoner	emery-cloth	ambulacrum
impairment	Amphitryon	emblazonry	imprudence	ambuscados
impassable	ambivalent	emendation	amercement	impureness
impassible	omniparity	amendatory	imbruement	immurement
impassably	omniparous	emendatory	smrrebrd	impudently
impassibly	amritattva	amanuenses	emergently	ambushment
ambassador	immiscible	amanuensis	impregnate	ammunition
embassador	omniscient	amino-group	impregnant	impudicity
impartible	umpireship	emancipate	smaragdine	impugnable
impartment	omniferous	emancipist	smaragdite	impugnment
immaculate	omnigenous	eminential	umbrageous	immunology
immaculacy	ambidexter	immoralism	emarginate	ampussy-and
immaturely	imminently	immolation	amerciable	impuissant
immaturity	impishness	umbonation	smarminess	amazedness
Ambarvalia	umbilicate	immoralist	embroidery	Amazon-like
emaciation	empiricism	immorality	umbrellaed	Angaraland
smickering	imbibition	embouchure	emerald-cut	unbalanced
smock-faced	empiricist	emboldener	smart-money	unhazarded
smock-frock	Ampicillin®	immoderate	imprimatur	unsalaried
amido-group	omnipotent	immoderacy	ombrometer	indagative
smudginess	ambisonics	immoveable	Amaranthus	unparadise
imperative	omnivorous	empoverish	amarantine	indagation
impeccable	embittered	impoverish	imprinting	inhalation
impeccably	impictured	embowelled	Amerindian	incapacity
impeccancy	embitterer	immodestly	embryonate	unmanacled
impendence	smoke-board	smoothness	embryogeny	unparallel
impendency	smoke-black	smooth-shod	embryology	indagatory
ember-goose	smoke-dried	smooth-bore	embryotomy	enjambment
impediment	smoke-house	ammoniacal	ombrophile	unbarbered
impenitent	smokeproof	ammoniacum	ombrophobe	unwatchful
impeditive	smoke-stack	embodiment	emery-paper	infarction
imbecility	smoketight	impolitely	improperly	unsanctify
imperilled	amalgamate	imposingly	impressive	uncandidly
imperially	ampliative	immobilise	impression	inwardness
amoebiform	ampliation	immobilism	impresario	unhardened
immeritous	small-craft	imposition	impressure	unpardoned
umbellifer	implacable	immobility	umbratical	unmaidenly
umbellated	implacably	embolismic	embryulcia	unhandsome
immemorial	amylaceous	embolismal	improvable	incandesce

unnameable	invalidish	unobtained	ineducable	underdress
unsaleable	invalidism	snobocracy	uneducable	intendment
untameable	unfamiliar	unobscured	uneducated	underdrive
untameably	invalidity	inobedient	unedifying	intendancy
innateness	uniaxially	unobedient	unadmiring	unrendered
insaneness	invariance	knobkerrie	unadmitted	untendered
unsafeness	annalistic	unobserved	anadyomene	untenderly
unwareness	unsatiated	knobbiness	anadromous	engendrure
encasement	untalked-of	unabridged	inadaptive	ingenerate
enfacement	infallible	snubbingly	inadequate	intemerate
engagement	unbailable	snobbishly	inadequacy	intenerate
enlacement	unfallible	inebritous	unadjusted	inveterate
enragement	unmailable	unabsolved	unheralded	inveteracy
incasement	infallibly	anabaptise	unregarded	undefended
uncared-for	entailment	anabaptism	unretarded	sneezeweed
unwavering	unhallowed	anabaptist	unrewarded	unreverend
unmaterial	anharmonic	unscramble	underagent	antecedent
unlabelled	enharmonic	snick-a-snee	unrelative	enlevement
unpanelled	inharmonic	knockabout	undelaying	unreverent
unravelled	ungainsaid	anaclastic	anhelation	unrevenged
unraveller	untainting	Anschauung	annexation	knee-length
unmaternal	ungarnered	unscabbard	indexation	unremedied
unlamented	unmannered	unacademic	inveracity	unrepealed
unparented	unmannerly	unscreened	unveracity	unrepelled
untalented	endamoebae	anucleated	unremarked	unrevealed
unparental	entamoebae	unaccented	unbewailed	ante-bellum
unlawfully	antagonise	enschedule	unmetalled	unredeemed
unmanfully	infamonise	inactivate	unrecalled	sneezewood
intangible	uncanonise	knackiness	undebarred	ungenerous
untangible	antagonism	inactively	unrepaired	sneezewort
intangibly	antagonist	inactivity	untenanted	undeterred
enlargedly	unlaboured	uneclipsed	underactor	underearth
ensanguine	infamously	unscripted	underboard	unreversed
endangerer	encampment	knick-knack	interbreed	antecessor
encashment	unhampered	knock-kneed	underbuild	interested
unfathomed	unpampered	inoculable	underbelly	undefeated
unfathered	uncarpeted	unscalable	inselberge	undetected
ungathered	unfairness	knuckle-bow	underborne	unrepeated
unfatherly	engarrison	anacolutha	underbough	unrepented
unpathetic	unpassable	inoculator	underbrush	unresented
insalivate	unransomed	unicameral	interchain	unreverted
invaginate	intactness	onocentaur	underclass	indecently
invalidate	unfaithful	uneconomic	under-craft	inherently
inhabitant	untasteful	unicentral	interceder	antepenult
insanitary	sneak-thief	anecdotage	under-clerk	undeceived
unsanitary	unfastened	onychopagy	undercrest	undeserved
insatiable	incautious	anecdotist	unmerciful	unreceived
invariable	enraptured	unschooled	unpeaceful	unreserved
unsatiable	unbattered	onychopora	undescried	undeserver
unvariable	ungartered	unsceptred	undercliff	unperfumed
insatiably	unmastered	unscorched	intercalar	underfloor
invariably	unpastured	anacardium	unwelcomed	interferon
sneakiness	unpastoral	anachronic	intercross	interferer
uneasiness	unbaptised	unicostate	undercroft	intergrade
unwariness	incantator	inaccurate	interclude	underglaze
engagingly	insalutary	inaccuracy	undercover	undergoing
sneakingly	invaluable	unoccupied	underdrain	unfeigning
unfadingly	unvaluable	unscrupled	incendiary	unweighing
unravished	invaluably	anacrustic	invendible	enneagonal
sneakishly	andalusite	unactuated	unreadable	undergrove
unpacified	Andalusian	knackwurst	unvendible	intergrown
unratified	infatuated	unidealism	intendedly	undergrown
invaliding	unladylike	cnidoblast	unheededly	encephalic

encephalin	undeplored	unbearable	intentness	snaffle-bit
encephalon	unrealised	unpeerable	inventress	knife-money
enkephalin	unfellowed	untearable	unmeetness	uniflorous
unmechanic	unmellowed	unwearable	indebtment	snuff-paper
antechapel	underlayer	unbearably	infeftment	uniformity
untethered	endermical	unmetrical	insentient	snuff-spoon
indelicate	underminer	endearment	investment	snuff-taker
ingeminate	intermarry	interregna	intertwine	Onagraceae
inseminate	endermatic	interregal	unsettling	enigmatise
indelicacy	unhelmeted	interreges	under-trick	enigmatist
undeniable	intermezzi	unsearched	intertrigo	sniggering
unreliable	intermezzo	unwearying	intertwist	anagogical
knee-timber	underneath	interreign	undertaken	knagginess
undeniably	internodal	integrally	undertaker	unigenitus
ante-Nicene	internment	interramal	undertimed	knightless
enregiment	underntime	integrator	under-tunic	knighthood
incedingly	infernally	undepraved	undertoned	anaglyphic
sneeringly	internally	undeprived	intestinal	anaglyptic
unperished	undernamed	unreproved	incestuous	enthraldom
unrelished	Enneandria	unbetrayed	infectious	anthracene
unverified	undernoted	understand	enfestered	inchoately
indecisive	once-for-all	interspace	unbettered	unsheathed
indefinite	unrejoiced	interstate	unfeatured	anthracite
undecisive	unheroical	understate	unfettered	inchoative
unfeminine	unrecorded	infeasible	unlettered	inchoation
undesiring	unseconded	insensible	unrestored	enthralled
unmeriting	unbeholden	unfeasible	unbestowed	anthracoid
unrepining	enterocele	unsensible	interurban	unshackled
indecision	unbesought	insensibly	integument	unshadowed
endemicity	unbecoming	unsensibly	insecurely	unshielded
infelicity	unreposing	underspend	unrecuring	unthreaded
unbedimmed	enterolith	understeer	interunion	uncheerful
unbedinned	unreformed	interstice	insecurity	unshifting
undesigned	unrenowned	undershirt	unbeguiled	unchristen
unbenignly	indecorous	underskirt	unreturned	unthriftly
undecimole	angelology	unlessoned	unrequired	unshakable
undesirous	enterotomy	unreasoned	unrequited	unshakably
unperilous	unreported	unseasoned	undervoice	unshakenly
inheritrix	unbegotten	undersense	intervolve	anthelices
anteriorly	unresolved	understood	undervalue	anchylosed
inferiorly	interphase	underscore	unleavened	anchylosis
interiorly	interplant	understock	intervener	anthemwise
unremitted	interplead	insensuous	intervenor	anthomania
unresisted	enterprise	undershoot	unbeavered	unthankful
enregister	underprize	underscrub	intervital	enchanting
unbelieved	unbespoken	undershrub	interweave	unchanging
unrelieved	interpolar	uncensored	underwrite	unthinking
unbeliever	unweaponed	uncensured	underworld	unshingled
unperjured	underpants	unleisured	angel-water	Anthonomus
underjawed	interphone	unmeasured	underwater	enthronise
unreckoned	underproof	Insessores	interwound	anthropoid
unweakened	unpeppered	underslung	unseizable	anthophore
interleave	untempered	understudy	interzonal	antheridia
underlease	interposal	undersexed	knife-board	anchorless
unhealable	interposer	enneastyle	snuff-brown	anchor-ring
untellable	unrespited	undersized	unoffended	uncharming
interlaced	under-power	ingestible	unaffected	anchor-hold
unwellness	underquote	insertable	uneffected	anchoretic
underlying	ance-errand	invertible	inefficacy	anchoritic
underlinen	once-errand	unbeatable	sniffiness	enthusiasm
interlunar	inferrable	intertidal	snuffiness	enthusiast
interloper	inferrible	invertedly	sniffingly	unchastely
undeclared	integrable	ancestress	unofficial	unchastity

unthatched
unshrubbed
unshowered
intimately
antipathic
incitative
indicative
incitation
indication
intimation
invitation
unrivalled
indicatory
invitatory
antimasque
anti-matter
untimbered
invincible
invincibly
Antiochene
indiscrete
indiscreet
encircling
Antiochian
intinction
encincture
unkindness
unhindered
antiaditis
incinerate
unliterary
enticeable
unlikeable
unliveable
unrideable
unsizeable
entireness
unlikeness
unripeness
unwiseness
enticement
incitement
inditement
invitement
anti-Semite
indigenise
unlifelike
unwifelike
infidelity
anti-heroic
engine-room
indigenous
unlicensed
antisepsis
antiseptic
indigested
undigested
undirected
undiverted
undivested
incidental
indigently
indirectly

unkinglike
unwithheld
enrichment
insightful
unrightful
Antichthon
in-fighting
antitheism
Antichrist
antitheist
antiphonic
antiphonal
antiphoner
unwithered
antitheses
antithesis
antithetic
annihilate
anticipate
infinitate
intimidate
invigilate
anticipant
infinitant
infinitary
unmilitary
untidiness
incisively
infinitely
enticingly
incitingly
invitingly
untiringly
unfinished
infinitive
inhibitive
anticivism
inhibition
incivility
insipidity
unfilially
incipience
insipience
incipiency
incisiform
ancipitous
inhibitory
antibiosis
antibiotic
unvitiated
infinitude
individual
individuum
unpickable
unsinkable
inviolable
unfillable
untillable
inviolably
unbiblical
unyielding
unwieldily
anticlimax

anticlinal
unpillared
anxiolytic
inviolated
unfilleted
unviolated
unpillowed
infirmness
undismayed
ensignship
indignance
unwinnowed
antimonate
invigorate
invigorant
undivorced
Indigofera
antipodean
antilopine
antimonide
antimonite
antimonial
antisocial
incisorial
antinomian
environics
indigo-blue
antilogous
oneirology
snail-paced
indisposed
undisposed
undisputed
antifreeze
antitragus
antidromic
antiproton
snail-shell
angiosperm
gneissitic
infiltrate
indictable
unbirthday
enlistment
indictment
unlistened
insistence
indistinct
insistency
unvirtuous
unhistoric
unfiltered
unsistered
unsisterly
antistatic
infibulate
undivulged
unliquored
antiquated
insinuator
snail-wheel
snake-dance
snake-fence

snake-house
snake's-head
snakestone
unpleasant
unbleached
unpleasing
uncleansed
unilabiate
unclubable
unilobular
ingle-cheek
inflective
inflictive
inflection
infliction
unilocular
includible
unaltering
unsleeping
influenzal
ineligible
ineligibly
analogical
unflagging
inelegance
inelegancy
analphabet
Anglo-Irish
encloister
uncloister
inflamable
unblamable
unblamably
anglomania
inclemency
inclinable
unblenched
unblinking
unilingual
unbloodied
unallotted
unslipping
anglophobe
anglophone
ineloquent
unclerical
antler-moth
inglorious
analysable
unblissful
unblushing
Englishism
Englishman
Anglo-Saxon
inflatable
analytical
unilateral
uniliteral
unploughed
unplayable
inflexible
inflexibly
unplayable

unimpaired
unimparted
inimically
animadvert
anamnestic
anemograph
unimagined
unemphatic
unsmiled-on
enamelling
enamellist
unimplored
animalcula
animalcule
unemployed
anemometer
anemometry
unamenable
gnomonical
mnemonical
unsmoothed
unembodied
unimposing
unimmortal
anemophily
un-American
anamorphic
unsmirched
enumerator
unimproved
unamusable
onomastics
inimitable
inimitably
animatedly
enamouring
inundation
unentailed
uninuclear
anonaceous
unintended
unannealed
unendeared
unindeared
uninfected
uninvested
unknighted
unknightly
unanchored
enunciable
unenviable
unenviably
unendingly
unenriched
uninviting
unentitled
enantiosis
enunciator
uninflamed
unanalysed
unenclosed
uninclosed
unanalytic

uninflated
unenslaved
inanimated
unanimated
uninformed
uninvolved
uninspired
unknowable
unanswered
untowardly
innovative
annotation
innovation
insolation
intonation
invocation
unmorality
endogamous
innovatory
invocatory
unromantic
entombment
undoubtful
undoubting
insouciant
unforcible
enforcedly
unforcedly
endoscopic
unfordable
enfoldment
unpowdered
intolerant
unloveable
unmoveable
unmoveably
unforeseen
engouement
incoherent
unhoped-for
incohesive
unhomelike
incohesion
Indonesian
endodermic
endodermal
endodermis
ungoverned
unforetold
endogenous
undomestic
unforested
unmolested
indolently
innocently
insolently
uncoffined
unconfined
unconfused
unfoughten
encoignure
unforgiven
untochered

unmotherly
endophytic
entophytic
entophytal
endorhizal
innominate
intoxicate
incogitant
intoxicant
insociable
unsociable
unsociably
unholiness
unpolitely
annoyingly
intoningly
unlovingly
unpolished
unmodified
unpolicied
unnoticing
indocility
insolidity
unsolidity
unsocially
unconjugal
unworkable
entoilment
unpolluted
endopleura
informally
uncommonly
endosmosis
endosmotic
uncommuted
enjoinment
insomnious
unbonneted
incoronate
endopodite
oncologist
ontologist
entomology
endomorphy
uncoloured
unhonoured
incomplete
incompared
incorporal
incomposed
insobriety
encourager
endocrinic
endocrinal
endocritic
unborrowed
inconstant
unconstant
endorsable
unpossible
unboastful
unforsaken
unconsoled

unhouseled
unconsumed
unpoisoned
unpoetical
unwontedly
unworthily
unbottomed
unfortuned
unsoftened
undoctored
unfostered
untortured
unmortised
involution
unpopulous
involucral
involucrum
unfocussed
insolvable
unsolvable
insolvably
insolvency
unhouzzled
unapparent
unspeaking
Gnaphalium
unappalled
snaphaunce
snaphaunch
anaplastic
unspecific
inspective
inspection
inappetent
anopheline
unappeased
anapaestic
snappingly
snappishly
unuplifted
inaptitude
ineptitude
inspanning
inapposite
end-product
inoperable
inspirable
inoperably
snapdragon
unipartite
unsporting
unapprised
unspirited
inspirator
unapproved
inspissate
anaphylaxy
anaptyctic
inequation
inequality
unequalled
uniqueness
iniquitous

inurbanely
unarranged
unbreached
unbreathed
encroacher
enervative
entreative
enervating
entreating
increasing
uncreating
undreading
undreaming
enarration
enervation
inurbanity
unordained
entreasure
untreasure
unbribable
ungraceful
infraction
ungracious
incredible
uncredible
incredibly
unproduced
introducer
ingredient
ungrudging
onirodynia
unfriended
unfriendly
untrueness
unbreeched
inbreeding
androecium
energetics
unpriestly
unartfully
unprofaned
unprofited
infragrant
intriguant
unpregnant
intriguing
androgenic
intrigante
unoriginal
unfrighted
anarchical
unorthodox
infrahuman
anarthrous
inordinate
inordinacy
unordinary
unfruitful
snortingly
unerringly
inartistic
unartistic
unbrokenly

unprolific
untrampled
oniromancy
intramural
unpromised
entremesse
undramatic
unprompted
unprincely
unbranched
untrenched
entrancing
inbringing
unwrinkled
encrinitic
encrinital
untranquil
undrooping
unarmoured
enormously
intrepidly
entrapment
enwrapment
enwrapping
encryption
androphore
Entryphone®
unprepared
unproperly
unproposed
infrequent
unfrequent
introrsely
incrassate
inerasable
inerasible
unerasable
inerasably
inerasibly
increscent
introspect
untrustful
ingressive
engrossing
undressing
untrussing
ingression
infrasonic
unprisoned
oniroscopy
ingratiate
uncritical
ingrateful
ungrateful
untruthful
unarguable
intra-urban
ungrounded
untroubled
unprovable
unprovided
unprovoked
unprizable

unassailed	anatropous	aneurismal	snow-capped	voyageable
one-sidedly	unctuously	unpuckered	anywhither	solacement
unascended	knat-bottle	untuckered	unawakened	Romanesque
unusefully	unstarched	unsublimed	indwelling	womanfully
ink-slinger	instituter	unqualited	snow-plough	lovat-green
gnashingly	institutor	Anguillula	snow-blower	woman-grown
unossified	instrument	unsummoned	angwantibo	notaphilic
Gnosticise	instructor	unsummered	snowmobile	woman-hater
unaspiring	insurancer	unsurmised	snow-wreath	coradicate
Gnosticism	undulately	unguentary	answerable	cohabitant
anastigmat	incubative	unturnable	answerably	soda-siphon
unassigned	indurative	unquenched	answerless	womanishly
unassisted	unhumanise	innuendoes	unswerving	rosaniline
unisonally	undulating	infusorial	untwisting	tonalitive
unisonance	insularism	infusorian	unswayable	volatilise
anastomose	annulation	inculpable	onyx-marble	movability
gnoseology	incubation	inculpably	unexpanded	non-ability
gnosiology	induration	unsupplied	unexacting	notability
end-stopped	inhumation	unpurposed	unexecuted	volatility
unescorted	insulation	incurrable	unoxidised	notarially
uniseriate	intubation	innutrient	inextended	non-aligned
anastrophe	undulation	unquarried	unextended	covariance
anisotropy	pneumatics	unhurrying	unexcelled	notational
inosculate	angularity	incurrence	unexpected	rotational
inesculent	annularity	inquirendo	inexpiable	vocational
unassuaged	inhumanity	unfurrowed	inexpiably	monadiform
unassuming	insularity	inquisitor	unexciting	foraminous
unattached	incubatory	annuntiate	unexpiated	voraginous
initialise	undulatory	insultable	inexplicit	donatistic
initiative	incunabula	unquotable	unexcluded	modalistic
initiation	uncurbable	unsuitable	unexplored	moralistic
unsteadily	incumbency	unsuitably	unexampled	Romanistic
initialled	uncumbered	unjustness	unexamined	colatitude
unattained	unnumbered	insultment	inexorable	Mohammedan
unstrained	annunciate	industrial	inexorably	homaloidal
initiatory	injunctive	uncustomed	inexistent	Monaxonida
unstrapped	injunction	unbuttoned	unhygienic	topazolite
gnotobiote	inculcator	inductance	encyclical	moratorium
unitedness	unpunctual	unbuttered	unsymmetry	monadology
unattended	unbundling	uncultured	ankylosaur	potamology
unstreamed	unburdened	unnurtured	enzymology	somatology
unstressed	innumerate	inaugurate	unsympathy	potato-trap
unattested	innumeracy	incurvated	enhydritic	somatotype
instigator	untuneable	unpurveyed	encystment	podagrical
knottiness	inducement	unsurveyed	Solanaceae	conacreism
snottiness	innumerous	aneurysmal	Mosasauros	non-arrival
unstringed	indumentum	unmuzzling	woman-built	no-man's-land
unstripped	inquietude	knave-bairn	coral-berry	coral-snake
unstriated	insufflate	univocally	loganberry	logan-stone
installant	unruffable	unavailing	rowan-berry	monastical
instalment	engulfment	univoltine	romancical	romantical
instilment	anguifauna	snivelling	comanchero	copartnery
installing	indulgence	univalence	woman-child	cobalt-blue
instilling	insurgence	unevenness	monarchise	monactinal
unutilised	indulgency	uneventful	monarchial	woman-tired
anatomical	insurgency	univariate	monarchism	vocabulary
unatonable	unbudgeted	univariant	Monarchian	novaculite
unstanched	unruliness	university	monarchist	vocabulist
unstinting	unruliment	unovercome	mosaically	Volapükist
instantial	enduringly	inevitable	coparcener	forbearant
unitholder	unpunished	inevitably	towardness	forbearing
unstooping	unpurified	unavowedly	cowardship	Hobbianism
unctuosity	injudicial	unswearing	monandrous	hot-brained

Bombycidae	concretive	touchstone	cordillera	rope-dancer
corbiculae	concretism	cowcatcher	socdolager	forehanded
morbidness	concretion	concettism	socdoliger	cote-hardie
forbidding	concretist	concettist	socdologer	rose-garden
morbidezza	cow-chervil	toccatella	sogdolager	rope-ladder
double-take	forcefully	conclusive	sogdoliger	moderately
double-park	couch-grass	concluding	sogdoliger	foretaught
double-talk	coach-horse	conclusion	sogdoliger	forefather
double-bass	coach-house	conclusory	condolence	foregather
doubleness	poachiness	low-country	rondoletto	co-relative
sombreness	touchiness	coach-wheel	lordolatry	love-making
double-chin	conceitful	woodlander	sordamente	rope-making
double-gild	touchingly	coadjacent	condensate	moderatism
sombrerite	colchicine	gold-washer	wooden-head	monetarism
double-flat	coactivity	good-father	golden-seal	co-relation
gombeen-man	conchiform	cordialise	soddenness	moderation
doubletree	touch-judge	bordraging	woodenness	Pomeranian
bomb-vessel	conciliate	road-making	condensery	toleration
double-hung	conciliary	toad-eating	gold-end-man	monetarist
hobble-bush	torchlight	cordiality	hoydenhood	rope-walker
double-dyed	zooculture	loudhailer	hodden-grey	rose-mallow
double-eyed	coxcomical	cordwainer	foudroyant	fore-hammer
doubtfully	dolcemente	pond-master	loud-voiced	fore-damned
hobby-horse	touch-me-not	good-nature	bond-holder	sovenaunce
wobbliness	non-content	wood-carver	good-mother	love-favour
doubtingly	pop-concert	conducible	wood-boring	rose-laurel
hobblingly	concinnity	rood-screen	road-roller	moderatrix
pot-boiling	coccineous	conductive	wood-sorrel	covenanted
soubriquet	concinnous	conduction	good-morrow	forecasted
gor-bellied	forcing-pit	mordacious	wondrously	covenantee
pot-bellied	concentric	hoddy-doddy	roadworthy	forecastle
corbelling	concentred	sordidness	wood-spirit	covenanter
morbillous	volcanised	rowdy dowdy	word-square	covenantor
bobbin-lace	conchoidal	moudiewart	borderland	forecaster
Sorbonical	hog-cholera	mowdiewart	wonderland	tolerantly
Sorbonnist	zoochorous	road-mender	ponderable	honeybunch
hot-blooded	conchology	bowdlerise	road-bridge	money-bound
booby-prize	touch-plate	cordierite	borderless	lower-class
comburgess	touch-piece	cowdie-pine	ponderment	hovercraft
Homburg-hat	concipient	soldiering	wonderment	honey-chile
Colbertine	conceptive	bowdlerism	borderline	honey-crock
Norbertine	conception	woodpecker	powder-mill	fore-advise
torbernite	voice-print	good-fellow	ponderance	power-drill
bombardier	touch-paper	moudiewort	ponderancy	robersdman
robber-crab	forcipated	mowdiewort	wonder-work	molendinar
combustive	hotchpotch	word-memory	powder-room	lovey-dovey
combustion	conceptual	hoodie-crow	powder-down	sore-headed
dog-biscuit	coacervate	gold-beetle	powder-horn	foreseeing
bobbysoxer	concordant	gold-beater	foederatus	foreteller
combatable	concurrent	goody-goody	wood-grouse	yoke-fellow
hop-bitters	non-current	gold-thread	powder-puff	hopelessly
nonchalant	concertina	cold-chisel	condescend	movelessly
moucharaby	concerning	woodthrush	toddy-stick	tonelessly
touch-and-go	concurring	bond-timber	goods-train	copesettic
conclavist	concordial	goodlihead	coadjutant	rose-beetle
notch-board	concertino	wood-pigeon	loud-lunged	rove-beetle
coach-built	coach-stand	goodliness	road-runner	bonesetter
concoctive	torch-staff	lordliness	good-humour	honey-eater
concoction	vouchsafed	gold-digger	coadjutrix	love-letter
hot-cockles	concessive	good-liking	wood-cutter	coherently
forcedness	concussive	good-sister	bondswoman	love-affair
torch-dance	concession	goldilocks	goodlyhead	poker-faced
concretely	concussion	toddy-ladle	how-do-you-do	womenfolks
			sore-falcon	

powerfully	rose-combed	fore-quoted	rough-draft	fox-hunting
honey-guide	solenoidal	honey-wagon	doggedness	pot-hunting
towel-gourd	money-order	bowerwoman	congregate	nothingism
foreshadow	dolesomely	bowerwomen	congregant	mother-land
rose-chafer	lonesomely	roof-garden	long-headed	mother-cell
boneshaker	love-monger	wolframite	tongueless	motherless
somewhence	coregonine	God-fearing	long-legged	tocherless
towel-horse	fore-notice	Wolfianism	tongue-tied	mother-ship
forechosen	foreboding	conflation	mongrelise	mother-city
dower-house	home-coming	confabular	toughening	motherhood
power-house	polemonium	confection	non-gremial	tocher-good
home-thrust	love-potion	non-fiction	mongrelism	bothersome
note-shaver	somebodies	confidante	tongue-work	mother-to-be
foreshewed	poke-bonnet	confidence	longaevous	motherwort
foreshowed	dove-colour	confidency	toggle-iron	mother-spot
rose-window	rose-colour	confederal	tonguester	oophoritis
lovelihead	cometology	coffee-bean	goggle-eyed	sophistics
comeliness	ponerology	coffee-mill	doughfaced	moth-hunter
homeliness	forecourse	toffee-nose	rough-grind	solivagant
loneliness	covetously	coffee-room	rough-hound	nominately
loveliness	lobe-footed	coffee-tree	rough-house	cogitative
cohesively	loveworthy	forfeiture	song-thrush	comitative
forefinger	noteworthy	joyfulness	rough-hewer	dominative
covetingly	power-plant	woefulness	long-winded	nominative
coweringly	Coleoptera	coffin-nail	doughiness	nominalism
hoveringly	power-press	confinable	top-gallant	solidarism
loweringly	power-point	coffin-ship	coagulable	cogitation
come-hither	hokey-pokey	dog-fancier	googolplex	domination
pokerishly	comeupance	coffin-bone	coagulator	ionisation
polemicist	come-upance	tomfoolery	gorgoneion	lorication
zone-ticket	homeopathy	tomfoolish	Gorgonzola	motivation
comédienne	bone-spavin	golf-course	congeneric	nomination
home-signal	foreordain	bow-fronted	noogenesis	solitarian
rose-lipped	coleorhiza	wolf's-peach	congenetic	toxication
pome-citron	love-broker	wolf-spider	morganatic	volitation
comedietta	foreground	confirmand	congenital	nominalist
Docetistic	home-brewed	conferment	conglobate	solidarist
novelistic	honey-stalk	conferring	zoogloeoid	comicality
solecistic	sobersides	confirming	gorgeously	logicality
totemistic	tower-shell	coffer-fish	hodgepodge	solidarity
dowel-joint	womenswear	conformist	rough-rider	solitarily
power-lathe	honey-sweet	conformity	loggerhead	topicality
hogen-mogen	lover's-knot	conference	longprimer	topi-wallah
money-maker	honey-stone	confervoid	songwriter	docimastic
honeymonth	somersault	non-ferrous	congestive	dominantly
token-money	potentiate	confiscate	congestion	coriaceous
homeomeric	hover-train	confusedly	rough-stuff	foliaceous
homeomorph	potentiary	cod-fishery	songstress	morigerate
honey-mouse	come-at-able	cod-fishing	forgettery	vociferate
hover-mower	comestible	rodfishing	forgetting	vociferant
fore-and-aft	domestical	confession	long-staple	noticeable
governable	co-sentient	confutable	congruence	noticeably
Copernican	money-taker	solfataric	congruency	motiveless
modernness	Potentilla	confounded	forgivable	politeness
solemnness	robertsman	forfeuchen	wonga-wonga	noviceship
government	forest-born	forfoughen	Sophoclean	homiletics
rose-engine	forest-bred	confluence	sophically	novicehood
governance	forest-tree	zoographic	tophaceous	coniferous
governante	rope-stitch	zoographer	Cochlearia	morigerous
cone-in-cone	code-number	long-haired	cochleated	pomiferous
moderniser	forerunner	poignantly	dochmiacal	poriferous
solemniser	Rome-runner	dough-baked	moth-flower	rotiferous
governessy	rose-quartz	song-school	sophomoric	solipedous

vociferous
police-trap
towing-path
Cotingidae
lovingness
holing-pick
robing-room
roping-down
rowing-boat
toxiphobia
polishable
boyishness
coyishness
modishness
mopishness
tonishness
toyishness
polishment
oolishings
dolichurus
Dolichotis
nobilitate
solicitant
moditiable
notifiable
soricident
positively
solidified
cohibitive
politicise
soliciting
positivism
cohibition
politician
solifidian
positivist
docibility
positivity
positioned
positional
volitional
moniliform
moliminous
solicitous
moniliasis
solicitude
jovialness
socialness
sociologic
bouillotte
borismatic
goniometer
goniometry
sociometry
motionless
Polianthes
notionally
totipotent
eosinophil
monitorial
volitorial
vomitorium
Morisonian

codicology
docimology
toxicology
horizontal
rosin-plant
sociopathy
goliardery
solid-state
forinsecal
Louis-Seize
rôtisserie
logistical
monistical
poristical
goliathise
Corinthian
podiatrist
societally
policy-shop
hobjobbing
conjecture
conjugally
conjugated
Conjugatae
non-joinder
conjointly
conjunctly
conjurator
rock-rabbit
cock-paddle
cock-paidle
rock-garden
rock-badger
bookmaking
pockmarked
bookmarker
cork-jacket
work-basket
cocktailed
fork-tailed
rock-salmon
cork-carpet
pockmantie
dock-master
workmaster
rockabilly
cock-a-bondy
kookaburra
forkedness
hookedness
cockneydom
cockneyish
cockneyism
cork-heeled
bookseller
work-fellow
mock-heroic
folk-memory
rock-temple
work-people
bookkeeper
lock-keeper
cockteaser

cockchafer
workaholic
rock-lizard
rock-ribbed
bookbinder
rock-pigeon
cocksiness
folksiness
rock-violet
pockpitted
cockyleeky
cockalorum
poikilitic
working-day
looking-for
locking-nut
corking-pin
book-holder
mock-modest
folklorist
rock-hopper
top-knotted
rock-bottom
work-to-rule
you-know-who
folk-speech
mock-orange
locker-room
cockernony
mock-privet
forkit-tail
pocketless
cockatrice
pocket-comb
pocket-hole
pocket-book
lockstitch
pocketfuls
rock-turbot
book-muslin
book-hunter
cork-cutter
rock-butter
monkey-gaff
monkey-rail
monkey-tail
jockeyship
monkey-rope
donkey-work
monkey-boat
donkey-pump
monkey-pump
monkey-suit
wool-carder
wool-packer
poll-parrot
coalmaster
colleagued
mould-board
doulocracy
collective
collecting
rollicking

collection
follicular
coelacanth
collocutor
cool-headed
goal-tender
Zollverein
fool-begged
coal-cellar
goal-keeper
poll-degree
soullessly
boll-weevil
coal-heaver
mollifying
collegiate
Howleglass
zoological
loll-shrub
wool-shears
doll's-house
wool-winder
mouldiness
woolliness
wool-picker
fowl-plague
Collembola
coelomatic
collimator
coulometer
coulometry
Hollandish
Bollandist
fowling-net
cooling-off
codlin-moth
rolling-pin
pollenosis
poplinette
toilinette
pollinator
pollen-tube
wool-comber
toilsomely
rollcollar
coal-porter
woolsorter
foul-spoken
colliquate
colliquant
colloquise
colloquial
colloquium
colloquist
tollbridge
collar-beam
dollarless
dollarship
Lollardism
collar-bone
collar-work
collar-stud
collarette

wool-driver
wool-grower
Rolls-Royce®
worldscale
coalescent
molluscoid
molluscous
collatable
pollutedly
toiletries
toilet-roll
toilet-soap
mollitious
zoolatrous
wool-staple
collateral
toolpusher
coal-bunker
coal-cutter
hot-livered
hollow-ware
world-weary
hollowness
noblewoman
hollow-eyed
woolly-hand
volley-ball
woolly-bear
worm-eating
commeasure
cosmically
formicaria
formidable
formidably
cosmodrome
commodious
coomceiled
room-follow
formlessly
cosmogonic
room-ridden
cosmolatry
commentate
commandant
commentary
commonable
commonweal
commandeer
commonness
commandery
gormandise
commanding
tormenting
gormandism
commingled
commonalty
communally
communique
worm-powder
cosmopolis
Commiphora
cormophyte
zoomorphic

commercial
coumarilic
cosmoramic
commissary
commission
commissure
commutable
cosmetical
noematical
commitment
committing
dogmatiser
commutator
hot-mouthed
commixtion
commixture
corn-maiden
downwardly
moonraking
foundation
down-market
downfallen
mountained
roundabout
moon-raised
corn-factor
down-easter
sound-board
point-blank
hobnobbing
town's-bairn
Donnybrook
youngberry
coenobitic
pornocracy
connective
connection
corniculum
cornucopia
fornicator
horned-pout
mountebank
counteract
pouncet-box
loundering
counselled
corn-dealer
counsellor
founderous
round-eared
hornfelses
counter-spy
poinsettia
lounge-suit
corn-weevil
round-faced
loan-office
Zoanthidae
corn-thrips
moonshiner
zoanthropy
Zoantharia
corn-whisky

round-house
bounciness
coincident
loungingly
soundingly
corn-miller
councillor
horn-rimmed
councilman
bountihood
corn-kister
cornflakes
hornblende
somnolence
somnolency
somniloquy
cornel-tree
cornflower
moon-flower
cognominal
somnambule
round-mouth
down-and-out
round-nosed
loan-holder
Johnsonese
boondoggle
corn-dodger
Johnsonism
Johnsonian
corncockle
corn-dollie
corn-popper
horn-footed
conniption
soundproof
corn-spirit
country-box
cornerwise
countryman
corn-brandy
cognisable
cognisably
connascent
sound-shift
cognisance
joint-stock
joint-stool
hounds-foot
sound-track
round-table
down-at-heel
downstream
moonstrike
downstairs
downstroke
cornstarch
connatural
non-natural
moonstruck
jointuress
cornhusker
corn-cutter

connivance
connivence
connivancy
connivency
count-wheel
townswoman
Johnny-cake
gooney-bird
coromandel
monovalent
monomachia
monomaniac
homotaxial
honorarium
coloration
coronation
monogamist
homogamous
monogamous
monocarpic
Podocarpus
coloratura
cocoa-beans
motor-coach
motor-cycle
monorchism
monoecious
horoscopic
poroscopic
conoidical
homogenate
Homorelaps
homocercal
jocoseness
moroseness
homogenise
monogenism
monogenist
homogenous
monocerous
monogenous
bolometric
iodometric
holohedral
holohedron
notonectal
homosexual
tobogganer
holophrase
monophobia
nosophobia
monophobic
monothecal
monotheism
monotheist
homothally
monorhymed
homophonic
monophonic
monorhinal
monochroic
monochrome
homochromy

monochromy
tocopherol
monochasia
monophasic
holophytic
nomothetic
holophotal
nomothetes
monolithic
dolomitise
sororicide
colonially
sororially
monoplegia
monoclinic
monoclinal
motor-lorry
homoblasty
homoplasmy
colonnaded
holoenzyme
homologate
homoeopath
gonococcic
gonococcal
gonococcus
homoeomery
homologise
lobotomise
locomobile
locomotive
monologise
monopolise
monopodial
nosocomial
Horologium
horologium
monopodium
locomotion
Solomonian
horologist
monologist
monopolist
nomologist
nosologist
podologist
pomologist
topologist
homologous
homotonous
monotocous
monotonous
locomotory
pogonotomy
dolorously
sonorously
notodontid
rotor-plane
ionosphere
colour-wash
colour-ways
colour-fast
colourable

honourable
colourably
honourably
gonorrheic
gonorrheal
colourless
honourless
sojourning
loxodromic
honours-man
gonorrhoea
logorrhoea
doxography
holography
horography
logography
monography
nomography
nosography
tomography
topography
homoerotic
mobocratic
monocratic
joyousness
porousness
no-nonsense
goloe-shoes
monostylar
Podostemon
colostrous
goloptious
holosteric
monopteral
monopteron
monopteros
homoousian
coconut-oil
monoculous
coconut-shy
monogynian
toponymics
homonymity
homocyclic
monocyclic
homozygote
homonymous
homozygous
monogynous
monoxylous
monohydric
monohybrid
Notoryctes
complanate
compearant
complacent
soup-maigre
co-optative
non-playing
coaptation
co-optation
complainer
compradore

zoophagous	comparable	four-parted	tourniquet	Mousterian
zooplastic	comparably	corroboree	log-rolling	bolshevist
compaction	copperhead	court-baron	coprolalia	dog's-fennel
compacture	colporteur	courtcraft	coprolitic	boisterous
torpidness	corporeity	nourice-fee	four-in-hand	roisterous
torpedoist	copperskin	corrective	torrent-bow	roysterous
torpedo-net	corporally	correction	touring-car	lobster-pot
corpse-gate	cow-parsley	porrection	four-inched	conspectus
comprehend	dog-parsley	four-o-clock	torrential	consuetude
complement	cow-parsnip	porraceous	horrendous	horse-faced
couplement	copper-nose	correctory	botryoidal	goose-flesh
completely	copper-work	fourscorth	Bourbonism	horseflesh
soup-meagre	copper-worm	corrodible	Bourbonist	boastfully
completive	comparison	court-dress	door-to-door	dorsifixed
dopplerite	comparator	horridness	four-footed	coastguard
completion	cooperator	torridness	four-poster	dorsigrade
complexion	co-operator	hoar-headed	coprophagy	goose-grass
morphemics	corporator	coarseness	corruptive	consignify
complexity	romper-suit	hoarseness	correption	Monsignore
completory	composedly	four-leafed	corruption	Monsignori
compressed	torpescent	four-legged	foursquare	Monsignors
compressor	compassing	courtesied	corrosible	horse-gowan
complected	compassion	cowrie-pine	morris-pike	constipate
complicate	colposcope	sourdeline	nourishing	conspirant
complicant	colposcopy	poor-relief	co-presence	conspiracy
complicacy	compass-saw	journeying	correspond	worshipful
compliable	Compositae	Fourierism	court-sword	top-soiling
compliment	compositor	journeyman	Morris-tube	solstitial
dolphin-fly	corpuscule	fourteenth	Socratical	conscience
morphinism	compatible	fourteener	four-stroke	worshipped
zoophilism	computable	source-book	sorrowless	worshipper
zoophilist	hospitable	door-keeper	board-wages	moss-litter
complicity	compatibly	tour-letter	house-agent	constitute
soup-ticket	hospitably	four-seater	moustached	forsakenly
compliance	low-pitched	four-leaved	constative	consultant
compliancy	compatriot	yourselves	codswallop	consolable
zoophilous	competence	horrifying	rouseabout	horse-leech
compulsive	competency	torrefying	roustabout	consilient
gospellise	competitor	mournfully	Constantia	consulship
compelling	compotator	corrigible	constantan	consultive
compulsion	computator	corregidor	non-starter	consulting
corpulence	soap-bubble	courageful	constantly	houselling
corpulency	compounder	court-guide	horse-bread	consultory
pompelmous	soup-tureen	Bourignian	consubsist	tonsilitic
compulsory	compluvium	corrigenda	gooseberry	corselette
compilator	nonplussed	courageous	housebound	tonsilitis
compensate	non-payment	corrugated	consecrate	horselaugh
cowpuncher	porphyrite	corrugator	consociate	consummate
porpentine	zoophytoid	fourth-rate	housecraft	consumable
companying	porphyrous	fourchette	consectary	consumedly
louping-ill	coequality	court-house	non-society	consimilar
compendium	conqueress	poor's-house	fossicking	howsomever
hopping-mad	conquering	coordinate	hopsacking	poison-fang
componency	mosquitoes	co-ordinate	horse-cloth	poisonable
topping-out	journal-box	hour-circle	horse-coper	foisonless
morphogeny	four-handed	gourdiness	tossicated	cousinship
compromise	journalese	coercively	loose-cover	sops-in-wine
low-profile	tournament	mourningly	pousse-café	bousingken
soap-boiler	journalise	worryingly	loss-leader	consonance
zoophobous	tourmaline	tourbillon	bolshevise	consonancy
morphology	journalism	courtierly	mousseline	cousinhood
complotted	journalist	four-figure	bolstering	consensual
colportage	pourparler	nourriture	bolshevism	dog's-tongue

non-smoking
comstocker
zoosporous
couscousou
mouse-piece
house-proud
sousaphone
house-party
horsepower
consequent
goose-quill
conservant
horse-rider
consortism
consortium
constraint
constringe
monstrance
consistent
mouse-sight
possessive
possession
horseshoer
consistory
possessory
corsetière
horse-thief
horse-tamer
topsyturvy
moisturise
mossbunker
horse-woman
popsy-wopsy
coastwards
contraband
contrabass
foot-candle
soft-sawder
contravene
contrahent
coat-hanger
voetganger
boat-racing
bootmaking
costeaning
foot-racing
Noetianism
contradict
contrarily
root-fallen
footballer
goat-sallow
contraplex
foot-warmer
hootnannie
costean-pit
contraprop
zoothapsis
portmantua
contracted
portmantle
post-partum
contractor

postmaster
contraltos
goat's-beard
north-bound
south-bound
toothbrush
foeticidal
postscript
vorticella
vorticular
fonticulus
monticulus
poetically
vortically
corticated
tosticated
contactual
rootedness
wontedness
contadinas
Cortaderia
Pontederia
zootherapy
soft-headed
bottle-feed
bottle-head
bottle-neck
pottle-deep
jostlement
bootlegger
röntgenise
southering
bottle-fish
zoothecial
cottierism
zoothecium
post-bellum
Rottweiler
northerner
southerner
southernly
bottle-nose
hop-trefoil
contrecoup
bottle-tree
tortfeasor
bootlessly
post-letter
Pontefract
pontifical
pontifices
post-office
fortifying
mortifying
youthfully
coat-of-arms
Montagnard
Portuguese
forthgoing
contiguity
contagious
contiguous
root-sheath

postchaise
post-Nicene
Voltairean
costliness
portliness
worthiness
contritely
loathingly
soothingly
fortuitism
Voltairism
contrition
Voltairian
fortuitist
postliminy
bootlicker
foot-licker
soft-billed
goat-willow
soft-finned
fortuitous
sow-thistle
contribute
Portakabin®
postal-card
postillate
rostellate
nostologic
sortileger
hostelling
tortellini
postillion
postulancy
boot-closer
postulatum
bottom-land
zootomical
bottomless
contemning
bottom-fish
nostomania
coati-mondi
coati-mundi
portamento
route-march
voltameter
continuate
cottontail
continuant
cottonseed
cotton-weed
rottenness
contendent
contingent
contending
cotton-mill
contention
low-tension
pontonnier
continuity
fontanelle
fontinalis
continence

forty-niner
continency
hootananny
hootananny
cotton-wood
cotton-boll
cotton-wool
cotton-worm
coetaneous
continuous
portentous
cotton-tree
controvert
mouth-organ
zootrophic
soft-bodied
portfolios
portionist
tortuosity
controlled
soft-boiled
controller
tortuously
polt-footed
soft-footed
post-mortem
bogtrotter
fortepiano
mouthpiece
soft-spoken
south-polar
toothpaste
nostopathy
souterrain
montero-cap
footbridge
jolterhead
couturière
forthright
doctorship
contortive
fosterling
doctor-fish
contortion
fox-terrier
co-eternity
foster-home
coat-armour
montbretia
contestant
tooth-shell
poetastery
contesting
fortissimo
costus-root
soothsayer
southsayer
hoity-toity
goat's-thorn
hoots-toots
houts-touts
root-rubber
goatsucker

portcullis
posthumous
foot-guards
zootsuiter
worthwhile
northwards
southwards
post-exilic
contexture
contextual
root-system
loculament
copulative
popularise
copulation
lobulation
modulation
nodulation
population
volutation
jocularity
popularity
copulatory
holus-bolus
homuncular
homunculus
loquacious
jocundness
volumetric
documental
monumental
lotus-eater
solubilise
non-utility
solubility
volubility
solutional
poculiform
voluminous
coquelicot
roquelaure
coquimbite
rogue-money
columnated
populously
hocus-pocus
Colubridae
voluptuary
Locustidae
locust-bean
robustness
coquetting
coquettish
goluptious
robustious
voluptuous
locust-tree
convective
convictive
convictism
convection
conviction
louvre-door

convulsant
pot-valiant
convulsive
convulsion
convalesce
convoluted
convenable
convenient
convincing
convention
convenance
conventual
non-violent
conversant
convertend
convergent
conversely
convertite
converging
conversion
louver-door
convexedly
convexness
conveyable
conveyance
woewearied
cobwebbery
pot-wabbler
pot-wobbler
Boswellise
Boswellism
Boswellian
forwarding
co-existent
polyvalent
polymathic
corydaline
polyhalite
polygamist
polygamous
polycarpic
polymastia
corybantic
polymastic
polydactyl
corybantes
polyactine
molybdenum
molybdosis
polymerase
polysemant
polymeride
polymerise
polygenism
polymerism
Polynesian
polygenist
polygenous
polymerous
polyhedric
polyhedral
polyhedron
Polychaeta

polychaete
coryphaeus
polychrest
polyphagia
polytheism
polytheist
Polyphemic
Polyphemus
polychroic
polychrome
polychromy
polyphasic
polyrhythm
cotyliform
polydipsia
polyhistor
polyploidy
polyclinic
polyanthus
pony-engine
copying-ink
polyonymic
Polyandria
copyholder
polynomial
Polypodium
polytocous
rosy-footed
polycotton
polygraphy
polycrotic
copywriter
polystylar
polyatomic
Polypterus
cony-burrow
polyaxonic
copy-typing
polygynian
copy-typist
polycyclic
Polyhymnia
polygynous
polyhydric
polyhybrid
pozzolanic
monzonitic
pozzuolana
mozzarella
aplanatism
splanchnic
upwardness
spray-dried
sphacelate
sphalerite
apparelled
aplacental
apparently
spear-grass
splash-back
splashdown
optatively
speakingly

apparition
spear-point
sphaeridia
aphaeresis
spear-shaft
epiblastic
specialise
specialism
speciation
specialist
speciality
spectacled
spectacles
spectatrix
spacecraft
epicycloid
speciesism
specifical
specifying
apocalypse
speculator
apiculture
epicanthic
epicanthus
epicentral
speciosity
spaciously
speciously
spectre-bat
spectrally
apochromat
apocarpous
spacewoman
apocryphal
apocryphon
spade-beard
spadiceous
epididymis
apodeictic
epideictic
epidemical
spodomancy
epidiorite
spider-like
spider-line
epidermoid
spider-hole
spider-work
spider-wort
spider-crab
epidotised
splenative
upper-class
apperceive
upper-crust
appendices
splendidly
spread-over
appendixes
sphereless
sphere-like
ephemerist
sphere-born

ephemerous
speedfully
spreaghery
speechless
Spheniscus
speediness
appetitive
appetising
appetition
sphericity
appealable
speed-limit
spleenless
spleen-wort
sphenoidal
spheroidal
sphenogram
appearance
appeasable
upper-stock
spherulite
upperworks
apterygial
Apterygota
spiflicate
epigraphic
epigrapher
apagogical
epagomenal
epigenesis
epigenetic
epiglottic
epiglottis
spagerical
spagirical
epigastric
oppilative
optimalise
aprication
oppilation
upside-down
spring-hare
springtail
spring-haas
spring-cart
spring-halt
Sphingidae
springhead
springless
springlike
springtide
springtime
spring-clip
springwood
spring-lock
springwort
springbuck
uppishness
sprightful
upright-man
aphidicide
ypsiliform
optimistic

sprinkling
uphillward
ophiologic
ophicleide
ophiolater
ophiolatry
split-level
ophiomorph
opsiometer
optionally
epeirogeny
spoil-sport
splintwood
splint-bone
splint-coal
sphinx-moth
spike-grass
spokeshave
spoliative
spallation
spoliation
spoliatory
spuleblade
spellbound
applicable
applicably
applicator
epiloguise
apologetic
spellingly
spillikins
epilimnion
Apollonian
opalescent
upflashing
spell-stopt
apolitical
applausive
applauding
apolaustic
apple-woman
epimeletic
apomorphia
spumescent
spondaical
open-handed
eponychium
spinaceous
sponge-cake
sponge-bath
Spencerian
Spenserian
spancelled
spongewood
sponge-down
open-hearth
spinnerule
spinigrade
epenthesis
epenthetic
open-minded
sponginess
spankingly

sponsional	spur-winged	ophthalmic	squalidity	greasiness
spongiform	sportingly	spot-barred	squamiform	dreariment
spindle-oil	sparkishly	epithemata	equanimous	creatively
spaniolate	spermicide	apothecary	aquaplaner	dreamingly
spaniolise	upbraiding	opotherapy	equatorial	freakishly
sponsorial	spermiduct	spot-welder	squamosity	creatinine
opinionist	spirometer	sputtering	aquafortis	organicism
spin-bowler	spirometry	apothecial	squadroned	organicist
spongology	apprentice	epithelial	squadronal	creativity
epanaphora	upbringing	apothecium	squamulose	friability
spinescent	sporangial	epithelium	squelching	organismal
spinstress	sporangium	epithermal	squeteague	irradiance
spinsterly	spuriosity	apotheoses	equestrian	creational
open-stitch	spermogone	apotheosis	squeezable	irrational
up-and-under	spuriously	spotlessly	squeeze-box	irradiancy
spondylous	spirophore	spitefully	squirarchy	drearihood
opsomaniac	sporophore	spatchcock	equivalent	drearisome
spoondrift	sporophyte	spitchcock	equitation	urbanistic
opposeless	sporophyll	spottiness	squirality	arbalister
spoonerism	sportswear	epitomical	squireship	dreadlocks
spookiness	oppressive	epitomiser	squire-like	ordainable
appositely	oppression	upstanding	squireling	great-niece
oppositely	spirit-lamp	spatangoid	squirehood	ordainment
appositive	spiritedly	apotropaic	squirearch	organogeny
oppositive	spirit-leaf	apotropous	equivocate	arragonite
apposition	spiritless	epitaphian	equipotent	treasonous
opposition	operettist	epitaphist	squint-eyed	urbanology
aphoristic	spirit-blue	spot-stroke	squint-eyes	organogram
appointive	operations	spathulate	pre-Adamite	triaconter
optologist	spirituous	spauld-bone	broad-arrow	ergatogyne
uproarious	spirit-duck	spruce-beer	bread-board	broadpiece
apron-stage	operculate	spouseless	breadberry	organ-point
upholstery	approvable	spruceness	broad-based	preappoint
éprouvette	approvance	epaulement	broadcloth	prearrange
epiplastra	sperm-whale	opium-eater	bread-crumb	proairesis
apoplectic	approximal	upsurgence	errand-girl	triapsidal
apopemptic	sperrylite	upbuilding	triandrian	broadsheet
epiphonema	sporozoite	oppugnancy	triandrous	cream-slice
apophthegm	apostatise	upbursting	Armageddon	bread-stick
epiphytism	epispastic	splutterer	arcaneness	broadsword
opaqueness	episodical	upbuoyance	ornateness	breadstuff
spermaceti	epistemics	spawn-brick	greasewood	breastrail
sparganium	episternal	epexegesis	ornamental	breast-feed
spermarium	episternum	epexegetic	arbalester	breast-deep
spermatium	spasticity	epizootics	ornamenter	truantship
Spartacist	spissitude	aquamanale	cream-faced	breast-high
spermatist	aposematic	squabasher	dreadfully	triactinal
spermaduct	episematic	aquamanile	break-front	breast-knot
opprobrium	opisometer	aquamarine	breadfruit	breastbone
appreciate	apostolate	squamation	arraigning	breastwork
spiraculum	episcopate	aquabatics	triangular	great-uncle
spiracular	episcopant	squandered	broad-gauge	creaturely
opera-cloak	episcopacy	squanderer	breathless	tread-wheel
sporadical	epistolary	square-face	wreathless	dreamwhile
aphrodisia	episcopise	square-sail	breath-test	dream-world
sparseness	epistolise	square-head	preachment	breakwater
spur-heeled	epistolist	squareness	treacherer	tribrachic
sportfully	spasmodist	squarewise	irradicate	Grobianism
spirograph	aposporous	square-toed	drearihead	cribration
opera-glass	apostrophe	square-toes	creaminess	trabeation
opera-house	epistrophe	square-root	dreaminess	trabeculae
sportiness	spatiality	equability	dreariness	trabecular
sportively	ophthalmia	equanimity	freakiness	trebleness

problemist
drabbiness
crib-biting
Brobdignag
cribriform
aryballoid
tribometer
prebendary
frabjously
erubescent
erubescite
arabesqued
crab-stones
crackajack
proctalgia
eructation
tractarian
proclaimer
trochanter
crackbrain
tricycling
tricyclist
ericaceous
precocious
procacious
Crocodilia
Crocodilus
precedence
procidence
precedency
procedural
trachelate
cricketing
crocheting
proceeding
procoelous
Trachearia
prick-eared
brick-earth
tracheated
procreator
tracheitis
brickfield
crucifying
gracefully
Cruciferae
trace-horse
practisant
trochiscus
trickiness
crocoisite
practising
triclinium
practician
erectility
proclivity
tractility
fractional
tractional
trichinous
brachiopod
Trichiurus
trichiasis

brecciated
prickly-ash
truckle-bed
truculence
truculency
oracularly
prick-louse
bricklayer
procumbent
brickmaker
precompose
arachnidan
precondemn
preconceit
preconcert
fricandeau
Dracontium
trecentist
iracundity
precentrix
draconites
preconsume
proctorage
trochoidal
urochordal
proctorise
troctolite
proctorial
tricrotism
graciosity
preciosity
tricrotous
oryctology
trichology
trichotomy
trochotron
graciously
preciously
trichogyne
precipiced
preceptive
dry-cupping
preceptial
preceptory
precipitin
procurable
precursive
precordial
trichroism
trichromic
Greco-Roman
trichromat
procaryote
precarious
precursory
procurator
tricostate
tricuspate
fricasseed
precession
procession
track-scout
trick-track

brocatelle
groceteria
tricoteuse
crack-tryst
preclusive
precaution
preclusion
trachytoid
brachydome
brachylogy
brachyural
procrypsis
procryptic
brachyaxis
gradualism
eradiation
graduation
gradualist
graduality
predecease
eradicable
predicable
producible
predictive
productile
productive
traductive
prediction
production
traduction
iridaceous
predaceous
predacious
iridectomy
eradicated
eradicator
Bridgerama
bridle-hand
bridle-path
cradlewalk
bridgehead
bridle-rein
bridgeless
bridle-road
gradienter
trade-falne
pridefully
prodigally
bridegroom
prodigious
drudgingly
grudgingly
prednisone
predentate
tridentate
Tridentine
credential
prudential
Uredinales
bridesmaid
bride's-cake
uredo-stage
iridescent

iridosmine
predestine
bradyseism
iridosmium
predestiny
predispose
uredospore
tradesfolk
uredosorus
creditable
creditably
trade-union
predevelop
freelancer
trierarchy
free-handed
irrelative
irrelation
tree-mallow
free-labour
freemartin
greencloth
free-school
green-drake
friendless
friendship
friendlily
irrelevant
irremeable
irremeably
breezeless
free-select
Irreverent
Froebelism
Froebelian
free-verser
greenfinch
arpeggiate
arpeggione
greenheart
breechless
greenhouse
free-minded
breeziness
greediness
pre-eminent
creepingly
grievingly
free-fisher
free-diving
praesidium
irreligion
pre-exilian
arse-licker
araeometer
araeometry
creepmouse
free-for-all
tree-tomato
free-fooder
freeholder
freeloader
praecocial

praetorium
praetorian
free-soiler
irrenowned
grievously
free-footed
freebooter
praepostor
irresolute
pre-emptive
pre-emption
free-spoken
arles-penny
free-trader
cruet-stand
greensward
greenshank
kriegspiel
greenstone
greenstuff
araeostyle
arrestable
arrestment
priestship
priest-like
priest-king
priestling
orientally
priesthood
orientated
orientator
praemunire
tree-burial
praeludium
irregulous
freedwoman
freedwomen
proficient
arefaction
prefecture
proffering
craft-guild
draft-horse
profligate
profligacy
craftiness
triflingly
griffinish
griffinism
trafficked
trafficker
trifoliate
truffle-dog
artfulness
irefulness
prefulgent
profulgent
truffle-pig
profundity
prefrontal
trifurcate
preferable
preferably

preferment	frigorific	arrhythmia	Araliaceae	prominence
preferring	gregarious	arrhythmic	trilobitic	prominency
preference	brightness	orthotonic	trilobated	gramineous
trifarious	frightened	orthotropy	prolicidal	tremendous
professing	brightsome	archetypal	frolicking	promontory
profession	frightsome	Urticaceae	prelection	premonitor
profitable	triglyphic	ordinately	trilocular	trampoline
profitably	arthralgia	irrigative	frolicsome	trombonist
profitless	arthralgic	irritative	prolocutor	grimlooked
profoundly	Brahmanism	urticarial	preludious	framboesia
profluence	orthoboric	fruitarian	trolley-bus	gramophone
prefixture	prohibiter	irrigation	trolley-car	gramophony
orographic	prohibitor	irritation	trolley-man	primiparae
prognathic	orthoclase	ordination	prolifical	tremorless
urographic	orthocaine	urtication	orological	trimorphic
pragmatise	Orthoceras	ordinarily	urological	primordial
drag-racing	orchideous	dreikanter	prologuise	primordium
pre-glacial	orthodromy	brainchild	brilliance	premarital
pragmatism	archdeacon	fruiteress	trillionth	fremescent
pragmatist	orthoepist	praiseless	brilliancy	promiseful
trigrammic	orthograph	greisenise	Ural-Altaic	promissive
programmed	archegonia	broidering	prolongate	Arimaspian
programmer	orthogenic	armigerous	trilineate	promissory
fragrantly	orthogonal	fruitfully	prelingual	promptuary
pregnantly	arch-chimic	craigfluke	trilingual	dramatical
tragically	arch-pirate	freightage	Trollopean	eremitical
tragi-comic	archbishop	freight-car	trolloping	primatical
tragacanth	archaicism	ornithopod	trollopish	Prometheum
frigidness	Brahminism	ornithosis	Trollopian	promethean
drug-addict	archaistic	prairie-dog	drill-press	promptness
bragadisme	arch-flamen	braininess	prelatical	prompt-side
triggerman	archontate	praisingly	trilateral	promethium
fragmented	archonship	prairie-hen	triliteral	prompt-note
fragmental	prehensile	artificial	prolixness	prompt-book
cragginess	prehensive	fruit-knife	prolixious	prompt-copy
dregginess	prehension	treillaged	tramway-car	dramaturge
grogginess	orphanhood	armipotent	grammarian	dramaturgy
braggingly	prehensory	arvicoline	grammatist	wry-mouthed
priggishly	arthromere	traitorism	gramicidin	premaxilla
trigeminal	orpheoreon	traitorous	crumb-brush	iron-handed
frog's-march	Arthropoda	arbitrable	crumb-cloth	truncately
frog's-mouth	archeology	arrière-ban	premedical	truncation
brigandage	orthopraxy	arbitrator	trumpeting	iron-master
dragonnade	orthopedia	brainstorm	trammelled	transactor
Trogonidae	orthopedic	artistical	trammeller	front-bench
dragonhead	orthoptera	Articulata	trammel-net	pronuclear
brigandine	orthopaedy	articulate	brome-grass	pronucleus
brigantine	orthoprism	projectile	primogenit	grandchild
dragonlike	orthoptics	projective	Bramah-lock	transcribe
dragon-fish	orthoptist	projecting	frame-house	Trinacrian
originally	orthopnoea	projection	grumpiness	transcript
dragon-root	orthophyre	trajection	trimmingly	irenically
dragon-tree	Arthuriana	trajectory	promulgate	ironically
orogenesis	arch-priest	projecture	drumbledor	arenaceous
orogenetic	orcharding	prejudiced	tremolando	grand-ducal
urogenital	archer-fish	brake-block	tremolitic	transducer
originator	orchardist	crake-berry	frame-maker	granddaddy
progenitor	orchard-man	trekschuit	tromometer	wrong-doing
frog-hopper	orchestics	brokenness	tramontana	granadilla
prognostic	prehistory	broken-down	tramontane	grenadilla
proglottis	orchestric	prokaryote	promenader	orange-peel
troglodyte	orchestral	drakestone	trimonthly	fringeless
Krugerrand	architrave	brake-wheel	criminally	grangerise

orange-wife	iron-glance	arrogantly	trappiness	gripe-water
princelike	translunar	trioecious	trippingly	prepayable
brandering	granularly	cryoscopic	graphitise	prepayment
bronze-wing	uranalysis	cryogenics	triplicity	Triphysite
cringeling	urinalysis	cryometric	eruptional	pre-qualify
princeling	granulitic	arrow-grass	graphitoid	triquetral
trinketing	crenulated	ergophobia	uropoiesis	triquetrum
Grangerism	crinolette	troop-horse	proprietor	frequenter
orange-lily	granulater	eriophorum	propellant	frequently
orange-wood	granulator	cryophorus	crippledom	craquelure
princehood	translator	proof-house	propylaeum	triradiate
orange-root	trunk-maker	broodiness	prepollent	pruriently
orange-tree	grandmamma	droopiness	propellent	prerelease
princessly	pronominal	broodingly	propelment	proratable
transeptal	drink-money	droopingly	tropologic	crustacean
wrongfully	transmuter	Ordovician	propulsive	press-agent
transferee	urinometer	ergodicity	propelling	prostatism
transferor	uranometry	crook-kneed	propulsion	crispation
transfuser	grand-niece	ordonnance	crapulence	crustation
transgress	brontosaur	cryoconite	propulsory	prestation
brant-goose	iron-worded	ergonomics	grape-louse	cross-armed
brent-goose	ironmonger	bryologist	tripinnate	trespasser
branchiate	francophil	ergonomist	propendent	crispature
branchless	transonics	oreologist	prepensely	crispbread
trench-feet	craniology	crio-sphinx	propensely	crossbreed
trenchancy	craniotomy	brood-pouch	prepensive	crossbench
bronchiole	wrongously	armourless	propensive	crossbones
branch-work	transplant	armour-clad	trepanning	fresh-blown
trench-coat	pronephric	areography	propension	cross-birth
franchiser	pronephros	oreography	propensity	frostbound
bronchitic	transposal	broomstaff	propionate	crossbower
bronchitis	transposer	proof-sheet	cryptogamy	cross-claim
grant-in-aid	granophyre	broomstick	tryptophan	cross-check
frangipane	grandstand	pro-oestrus	graptolite	trisection
principle	trans-shape	ergosterol	Trophonian	criss-cross
frangipani	wring-staff	wrap-rascal	cryptology	trisectrix
Franciscan	crankshaft	trap-ladder	graphology	prosecutor
crinoidean	crank-sided	drop-hammer	trophology	presidiary
crankiness	cranesbill	trip-hammer	cryptogram	prosodical
cringingly	trans-sonic	propraetor	proproctor	presidency
gruntingly	grindstone	tropic-bird	tropopause	fresherdom
prancingly	triniscope	tropically	tropophyte	pressed-day
prankingly	urinoscopy	drupaceous	preparedly	urostegite
princified	trinitrate	tripudiate	properness	proscenium
transitive	frenetical	tripudiary	propertied	triskelion
iron-mining	wrong-timed	prophetess	tripartite	prosperity
principial	transudate	tripleness	proportion	presternum
principium	pronounced	graplement	preparator	prosperous
transition	grand-uncle	prophesied	wraparound	crescentic
fringillid	pronouncer	tripperish	proposable	crescented
principled	tranquilly	trophesial	prepossess	prospector
frantic-mad	transvalue	prophetism	crêpe-soled	prospectus
trunnioned	transverse	prophesier	grapestone	trustfully
transience	frontwards	graphemics	prepositor	dressguard
transiency	print-works	tropaeolum	crepuscule	grass-green
transitory	brandy-ball	tripterous	propitiate	presageful
iron-witted	brandy-snap	drop-letter	prepotence	presignify
transistor	Areopagite	grapefruit	prepotency	grass-grown
iron-liquor	areolation	propagable	triphthong	dress-goods
crenellate	arrogation	propagulum	propitious	urosthenic
trundle-bed	Eriocaulon	propaganda	propounder	prosthesis
translucid	artocarpus	propagator	crop-duster	prosthetic
crinolined	argonautic	triplicate	tripewoman	trust-house

brassiness	grass-snake	Trotskyist	groundedly	Provençale
crustiness	cross-staff	fritillary	groundsell	driving-box
drossiness	dress-shirt	prattlebox	ground-zero	cravenness
friskiness	cross-stone	Crotalidae	groundless	prevenient
frostiness	frost-smoke	gratility	ground-rent	preventive
grassiness	proseuchae	crotalaria	groundling	provincial
grisliness	pressurise	erotomania	groundsill	prevention
trashiness	bressummer	arithmetic	groundplan	provenance
trustiness	brusquerie	pretendant	groundplot	prevenancy
crushingly	grasswrack	pretendent	groundsman	graveolent
friskingly	grass-widow	protensive	ground-hold	previously
graspingly	brushwheel	writing-ink	ground-dove	travertine
pressingly	Irishwoman	pretension	groundwork	traversing
trustingly	wrist-watch	protension	groundprox	proverbial
tristichic	freshwater	orotundity	arguteness	gravestone
prosaicism	presbytery	protensity	trousering	brevetting
prescience	presbyopia	pratincole	trouser-leg	Gravettian
cristiform	presbyopic	protanopia	trou-de-loup	provitamin
Aristippus	proteaceae	tritanopia	argumentum	crown-agent
prosciutto	tritiation	protanopic	proud-flesh	Drawcansir
crassitude	prothallia	tritanopic	fraudfully	crew-necked
prostitute	prothallic	cretinised	crouch-ware	crowkeeper
trisulcate	prothallus	grotto-work	fraughtage	crown-glass
prosilient	protracted	proteolyse	draught-bar	crown-graft
drysaltery	protractor	protoplasm	draughtman	crown-green
crosslight	protective	protoplast	draught-net	crow-shrike
presumable	protecting	arctophile	croupiness	brawniness
presumably	protection	Protophyta	troubledly	drowsiness
dressmaker	critically	protophyte	triumphant	drawlingly
press-money	tritically	triternate	triumphery	frowningly
cross-match	cretaceous	oratorical	triumphing	growlingly
drosometer	triticeous	writership	trousseaux	prowlingly
prison-bars	protectory	fraternise	troutstone	crown-jewel
present-day	protectrix	fraternity	trout-spoon	crewellery
prisonment	brother-man	protervity	fraudulent	arc-welding
prison-ship	arytaenoid	erythritic	triumviral	trowelling
presentive	written-off	urethritic	trivialise	crewelwork
presential	protreptic	triturator	trivialism	crow-flower
Krishnaism	brutifying	ureteritis	provocable	growing-bag
presension	gratifying	urethritis	provection	brow-antler
prison-door	gratefully	Fratercula	provocator	drawing-pen
prison-crop	truthfully	protestant	providable	drawing-pin
prismoidal	wrathfully	protostele	providence	ore-wrought
gressorial	Arctogaeic	Britishism	proveditor	Erewhonian
prostomial	Arctogaean	frithsoken	prevailing	crown-piece
prostomium	erotogenic	frithstool	provokable	drawbridge
aristology	wretchedly	grith-stool	gravel-walk	Brownshirt
aristocrat	crotcheted	prototypal	privileged	brownstone
crosspiece	frothiness	protrudent	travelogue	draw-string
drosophila	grittiness	protrusile	drivelling	crown-wheel
erysipelas	prettiness	protrusive	gravelling	proximally
presuppose	wrathiness	protrusion	grovelling	Fraxinella
crash-proof	writhingly	truth-value	travelling	grey-haired
press-proof	fratricide	protoxylem	travel-sick	grey-headed
crosspatch	bratticing	trou-madame	prevalence	grey-wether
crossroads	erethismic	traumatise	trivalence	dray-plough
prescriber	trithionic	traumatism	prevalency	trey-antler
proscriber	proteiform	arcubalist	trivalency	argyrodite
cross-refer	gratuitous	trouvaille	travelator	grey-coated
presurmise	proteinous	troubadour	travolator	prayer-bead
grass-roots	erethistic	ground-base	grave-maker	prayerless
frustrated	Trotskyite	groundmass	gravimeter	arty-crafty
cross-ratio	Trotskyism	groundbait	gravimetry	prayer-book

prize-court
prize-fight
brazil-wood
prize-money
brazen-face
brazenness
asparagine
escalation
escalatory
astarboard
estanciero
escapeless
escapement
assafetida
estatesman
Islamicise
Asiaticism
Islamicist
ascariasis
essayistic
assailable
assailment
escallonia
escalloped
Ismailitic
Israelitic
escapology
assay-piece
escarpment
escadrille
espadrille
isabelline
isocyanide
isochasmic
isocheimic
isocheimal
psychiater
psychiatry
psychopath
psychopomp
psychogony
psychology
psychogram
Psocoptera
usucapient
usucaption
isochronal
isodynamic
Isoetaceae
assemblage
osteoblast
osteoclast
osteocolla
ascendable
ascendible
ascendance
ascendence
ascendancy
ascendency
asseverate
osmeterium
aspergilla
osteogenic

asceticism
asterisked
especially
asteriated
Osteolepis
Asteroidea
asteroidal
osteopathy
osteophyte
assessable
ostensible
ostensibly
assessment
aspectable
assertable
assentient
asbestosis
assentator
asafoetida
usefulness
isogametic
isogenetic
Isoglossal
isoglottic
isoglottal
escheatage
escharotic
ischuretic
asphyxiate
asphyxiant
estimative
aspiration
estimation
oscitation
aspiratory
oscitantly
ossiferous
assibilate
assimilate
aspiringly
osmiridium
aspidistra
oscillator
astigmatic
assignable
assignment
ossivorous
osmidrosis
assistance
estipulate
Ashkenazim
psilocybin
psalterium
psalterian
psellismus
psalmodise
psalmodist
ashlar-work
isoleucine
Ishmaelite
asymmetric
psammophil
isomorphic

isometrics
asymptotic
isoniazide
asyntactic
asynchrony
asynartete
isentropic
astomatous
assonantal
associable
astonished
assoilment
astounding
assortment
ascomycete
isopterous
isopticise
asepticism
Ostpolitik
psephology
usurpation
usurpatory
usurpature
ascribable
asarabacca
ostrich-egg
astrictive
ostrichism
astriction
ostraceous
astragalus
usurpingly
astrologic
astrologer
astrolatry
estrangelo
astringent
astronomic
astronomer
usuriously
ascription
escritoire
tsarevitch
isoseismic
isoseismal
asystolism
isosporous
tsesarevna
psittacine
isothermal
isotropism
isotropous
osculation
ustulation
osculatory
usquebaugh
escutcheon
astuteness
assurgency
pseudimago
assumingly
pseudocarp
pseudo-acid

pseudology
pseudobulb
assumptive
assumption
asexuality
assythment
stravaiger
Athanasian
strawboard
strawberry
ethambutol
steam-crane
steam-chest
stracchino
strategics
strategist
atramental
straggling
straighten
straightly
steam-gauge
attachable
attachment
strap-hinge
strathspey
steakhouse
Stradivari
steadiness
steaminess
stealingly
stratified
strabismic
strabismal
strabismus
stratiform
Stratiotes
attackable
attainable
strainedly
attainment
attainture
steam-navvy
steatocele
stramonium
strabotomy
stratocrat
straw-plait
steam-power
strait-lace
straitness
steamtight
stealthily
straitened
steam-yacht
stibialism
stablemate
stableness
stable-room
stubbiness
stabbingly
stubble-fed
stabiliser
stubbornly

sticharion
stochastic
stickiness
stockiness
stockinged
stockinger
stichidium
stichology
stock-rider
stockstill
sticky-back
stodginess
stadholder
studiously
otter-board
attendment
attendance
attendancy
ethereally
streperous
otherguess
strengthen
othergates
otter-hound
strepitant
steeliness
steepiness
strepitoso
strepitous
strelitzia
strelitzes
steeple-hat
streamless
streamline
streamling
athermancy
stream-gold
streamered
steel-plate
attempered
steersmate
stressless
Etheostoma
otter-shrew
street-ward
otter-trawl
streetlamp
attestable
streetwise
street-room
street-door
attenuated
attenuator
otherwhere
otherwhile
otherworld
steelworks
staff-corps
stiffening
stifle-bone
stuffiness
stiflingly
stiff-rumpt

stigmatise	Ptolemaean	stenotyper	sturdiness	strychnine
stigmatism	Ptolemaist	stone-throw	startingly	strychnism
stagnation	stolenwise	etiolation	stirringly	stay-at-home
stigmarian	stall-plate	stroganoff	steriliser	tularaemia
stigmatist	stylopised	stromatous	pterylosis	tularaemic
stagnantly	still-stand	strokeplay	pteranodon	sugar-apple
stagecoach	utilisable	stroke-play	stark-naked	sugar-baker
stagecraft	stylistics	strokesman	start-naked	subarcuate
stag-headed	stilettoed	strong-knit	stercorate	autarchist
staggering	stellulate	stronghold	stereobate	Judaically
stag-beetle	stamp-album	strong-room	stercorary	sugar-candy
stage-fever	stemmatous	strophiole	starmonger	put-and-take
stage-horse	stomachful	strobilate	stertorous	cup-and-ball
steganopod	stomachous	stoopingly	stereotomy	sugar-daddy
stage-wagon	stomodaeum	strobiline	storiology	cup-and-ring
strideways	stammering	strobiloid	stereogram	humaneness
stridelegs	stamp-hinge	attornment	stereopsis	curateship
strifeless	stemwinder	atmologist	stereotype	mutagenise
stripeless	stumpiness	ethologist	stereotypy	sugar-grass
attirement	stimulable	atmosphere	stormproof	subangular
striker-out	stimulancy	step-dancer	star-bright	sugar-house
stridently	stimulator	step-ladder	stern-sheet	queasiness
string-band	stamineous	step-parent	stork's-bill	sugariness
stringhalt	stamp-paper	stepfather	storm-track	curability
string-bean	stomatopod	stephanite	stirrup-cup	dupability
stringless	stomatitis	utopianise	sternwards	durability
stringendo	Stannaries	utopianism	sternworks	mutability
stringency	stink-brand	stupration	storm-water	subacidity
stripiness	stone-brash	stupidness	starry-eyed	sueability
strikingly	stone-break	stupefying	state-aided	durational
strivingly	stone-blind	stypticity	statecraft	nutational
strigiform	stone-broke	stepsister	state-cabin	humanistic
strinkling	stony-broke	stipellate	statically	autarkical
strippings	stone-borer	stipulator	stuttering	Muhammadan
strip-tease	ethnically	stupendous	statuesque	Muhammedan
strictness	stone-canal	stepmother	stitchwork	eudaemonia
strictured	standers-by	step-rocket	stitchwort	eudaemonic
stair-tower	stone-eater	staphyline	state-house	euharmonic
stridulate	stone-fruit	staphyloma	stationary	sugar-maple
stridulant	stenograph	eternalise	stationery	Muraenidae
stridulous	stanchless	star-gazing	state-paper	fumatorium
Italianate	stanchness	starvation	statoscope	sudatorium
stellately	stonehorse	eternalist	statutable	subatomics
Italianise	stench-trap	sternboard	statutably	Eurafrican
Italianism	stinginess	stormbound	statute-cap	mulattress
Italianist	stingingly	stern-chase	state-trial	eubacteria
stillatory	stinkingly	attractant	statute-law	hupaithric
stalwartly	stintingly	attractive	ythundered	rub-a-dub-dub
still-birth	stunningly	attraction	Struldbrug	subaqueous
stalactite	stencilled	storm-cloud	attunement	subaquatic
stolidness	stenciller	uterectomy	struggling	sugar-wrack
stallenger	stone-mason	starveling	stouthrief	eucaryotic
stylograph	stenpoaeic	stern-frame	struthioid	eukaryotic
stalagmite	stentorian	stormfully	struthious	eucalyptol
still-house	stannotype	sterigmata	stoutherie	eucalyptus
stiltiness	standpoint	starr-grass	staurolite	curb-market
stallinger	Ctenophora	storm-glass	structured	dumb-waiter
stellified	ctenophore	Pterygotus	structural	Purbeckian
stultified	itinerancy	starchedly	stove-plant	turbidness
stillicide	stone-snipe	star-shaped	stavesacre	jumble-sale
stultifier	standstill	storehouse	stewardess	tumble-cart
stelliform	stone-still	starriness	ethylamine	curb-vendor
ateleiosis	stinkstone	storminess	stay-tackle	tumble-weed

humbleness	Munchausen	humdudgeon	super-duper	surfaceman
mumble-news	subchanter	hurdle-race	Jugendstil	tuffaceous
mumblement	nunciature	muddlehead	superexalt	outfielder
tumblerful	succubuses	subduement	euhemerise	bufflehead
dumbledore	juncaceous	out-dweller	quietening	buff-jerkin
rubble-work	suicidally	quadrennia	euhemerism	bumfreezer
tumbledown	punch-drunk	cuddlesome	euhemerist	suffigance
bumble-foot	butchering	pundigrion	superfluid	gunfighter
outbreathe	quickening	hurdy-gurdy	supergrass	surfeiting
tumble-dung	succeeding	quadrireme	supergiant	surf-riding
humbuggery	quick-firer	quadriceps	aubergiste	ruefulness
humbugging	bunch-grass	quadrisect	superheavy	fulfilment
purblindly	quick-grass	quadrivial	Bucephalus	fulfilling
fumblingly	quick-hedge	quadrivium	superhuman	buffalo-nut
humblingly	bunchiness	quadriller	Judenhetze	muffin-bell
jumblingly	functional	quadricone	juvenility	luffing-jib
mumblingly	auscultate	quadriform	tuberiform	buffoonery
rumblingly	punch-ladle	Buddhistic	mucedinous	outflowing
bumbailiff	succulence	cul-de-lampe	superiorly	sufferable
lumbricoid	quick-lunch	pudding-bag	Puseyistic	sufferably
mumbo-jumbo	succulency	suddenness	quietistic	subfertile
tunbellied	dulciloquy	burdensome	superlunar	pufferfish
rumbullion	muscularly	pudding-pie	aureomycin	sufferance
outbalance	subculture	pundonores	supernally	rumfustian
turbulence	quick-match	duodenitis	gubernator	suffisance
turbulency	Vulcanalia	fund-holder	sure-enough	subfuscous
turbulator	subcentral	dunderpate	superorder	outfitting
husbandage	buccinator	dunderhead	eudemonics	dumfounder
husbandman	succinctly	rudderless	numerosity	curfew-bell
lumbang-oil	lusciously	sunderment	tuberosity	burglarise
turbinated	suscipient	wunderkind	autecology	subglacial
rum-blossom	susceptive	rudder-fish	numerology	sunglasses
cumbrously	Turcophile	sunderance	numerously	fungicidal
zumbooruck	Turcophobe	dunderfunk	surefooted	surgically
lumber-yard	subcordate	Quadrumana	superposed	ruggedness
lumber-jack	succursale	quadrumane	superpower	turgidness
outbargain	muscardine	quadruplet	super-royal	dung-beetle
rue-bargain	successful	quadruplex	super-state	luggage-van
lumber-camp	successive	quadrumvir	superseder	quagginess
curb trader	succussive	subdivider	auger-shell	bunglingly
rubber-neck	quick-stick	Tuberaceae	supersonic	jugglingly
cumberless	succession	Juvenalian	superstore	cudgelling
numberless	succussion	numeration	mutessarif	cudgel-play
cumberment	quick-sandy	superation	supersound	subgeneric
lumber-mill	quick-trick	superalloy	quaestuary	outgeneral
cumbersome	quickthorn	lukewarmth	lutestring	subglobose
lumbersome	punctulate	lukewarmly	rupestrian	juggernaut
lumber-room	punctually	suzerainty	supertonic	budgerigar
rubbishing	punctuator	superaltar	puberulent	turgescent
sunbathing	Muscovitic	superacute	puberulous	suggestive
dumbstruck	Dutchwoman	superbness	bureaucrat	outgassing
outbluster	Dutchwomen	superclass	supervisal	suggestion
bubbly-jock	quick-water	queencraft	supervisor	humgruffin
surcharged	subdeanery	Lupercalia	suretyship	dung-hunter
surcharger	quadrangle	tuberculum	surf-bather	rush-candle
cunctative	quadratrix	tuberculin	ruffianish	bushranger
subcranial	quadrantal	tubercular	ruffianism	Buchmanite
cunctation	quadrantes	pubescence	suffragism	subheading
punctation	quadrature	quiescence	sufflation	Buchmanism
subclavian	subduction	tumescence	suffragist	bush-harrow
nutcracker	duodecimal	quiescency	puff-pastry	bushmaster
cunctatory	subdecanal	supercargo	surfactant	ruthlessly
outclassed	fuddy-duddy	superdense	sufficient	bush-shrike

euphuistic	pupigerous	duck-legged	guillotine	turnbroach
bushelling	tulip-eared	junk-dealer	nucleotide	vulnerable
oughtlings	rudimental	huckle-bone	nucleonics	runner-bean
euphonical	music-folio	lucklessly	bullionist	turnaround
cub-hunting	audiograph	musk-beetle	full-cocked	subnascent
euphonious	tuning-fork	muck-midden	bull-roarer	burnishing
ruthenious	punishable	duck-billed	full-bottom	burnettise
euthanasia	mulishness	cuckoldise	butlership	burnet-moth
Euthyneura	punishment	husking-bee	dull-browed	subnatural
rush-holder	music-house	subkingdom	bullet-head	turnbuckle
euchlorine	munificent	sucking-pig	subletting	quintuplet
mushroomer	fugitively	cuckoo-pint	bullet-tree	quinsy-wort
Euphrosyne	humidifier	cuckoo-spit	full-summed	automatism
euphoriant	audibility	junk-bottle	guilty-like	humoralism
authorless	fusibility	lucky-piece	outmeasure	automation
authorship	judicially	Quaker-bird	mummy-cloth	automatist
euphorbium	munifience	dukkeripen	submediant	humoralist
rutherford	musicianer	huckstress	curmudgeon	Euromarket
eurhythmic	musicianly	musket-rest	mummifying	autogamous
push-stroke	culiciform	musket-shot	duumvirate	automatons
push-button	cupidinous	Turko-Tatar	pummelling	suborbital
ouvirandra	fuliginous	bucketfuls	nummulitic	autoscopic
Punicaceae	rubiginous	bulk-buying	nummulated	subordinal
dubitative	pugilistic	buck-jumper	submontane	out-of-doors
judicative	humiliator	turkey-cock	Kuomintang	suboceanic
puritanise	humidistat	turkey-trot	summonable	autogenous
ruminative	numismatic	full-handed	fulmineous	humoresque
luminarism	audiometer	nucleation	Pulmonaria	Tudoresque
puritanism	fusionless	full-sailed	humming-top	tumorgenic
dubitation	rupicoline	hurl-barrow	summerlike	autochthon
fugitation	auditorium	hullabaloo	summertide	autotheism
fumigation	luminosity	hurly-burly	summertime	autotheist
jubilation	nucivorous	publicness	curmurring	autodidact
judication	rupicolous	duplicator	submersion	Mucorineae
lumination	tubicolous	curled-pate	submariner	Eurovision
Lusitanian	musicology	outlodging	summer-tree	tutorially
mutilation	luminously	bull-headed	cummerbund	eulogistic
rumination	mutinously	full-length	surmisable	humoristic
Ruritanian	audiophile	bull-beggar	submissive	Euroclydon
supination	music-paper	bull-necked	submission	autoplasty
luminarist	nudibranch	bull-beeves	summitless	Yugoslavic
musicality	music-stand	nullifying	hug-me-tight	auto-immune
pupilarity	music-shell	qualifying	submitting	bubonocele
pupiparous	music-stool	guilefully	surmounted	automobile
fumigatory	subintrant	mulligrubs	surmounter	automotive
judicatory	juristical	full-circle	mummy-wheat	autonomics
duniwassal	puristical	guiltiness	guinea-fowl	autonomist
Ruminantia	quaintness	full-rigged	guinea-worm	autonomous
jubilantly	auriculate	full-winged	guinea-corn	humorously
ruminantly	funiculate	qualmishly	quinacrine	humourless
judicature	lucifugous	dull-witted	pugnacious	humoursome
muliebrity	subjective	sublimable	quink-goose	autography
rubiaceous	subjection	subliminal	quenchable	autocratic
music-drama	subjectify	sublimated	quenchless	autoerotic
luciferase	subjugator	muslin-kale	quantitive	Eurocratic
supineness	subjoinder	sullenness	quantifier	autostrada
Luciferian	outjetting	outlandish	tunnelling	autoptical
auriferous	outjutting	nulla-nulla	quint-major	suboctuple
luciferous	buck-rabbit	Euglenales	surnominal	pump-handle
muciferous	muck-raking	sublingual	quint-minor	pulp-cavity
nubiferous	buck-basket	nucleolate	turning-saw	humpbacked
nubigenous	musk-mallow	full-voiced	turnip-flea	supplanter
nuciferous	Aufklärung	full-bodied	quinaquina	suspectful

auspicious	rubrically	outside-car	Australian	mutton-fist
suspicious	lubricious	cursedness	lustration	fustanella
lumpectomy	lubricator	cussedness	fustianist	sustenance
sun-picture	rubricator	subsidence	nuptiality	subtenancy
cuspidated	putridness	subsidency	dust-jacket	button-hold
rumple-bane	quarterage	subspecies	Australorp	button-wood
suppleness	quarter-boy	outspeckle	subtractor	button-hole
subprefect	quarrender	substellar	rustic-ware	button-hook
supplement	quarter-day	substernal	justiciary	austenitic
suppletive	quartering	outsweeten	multicycle	button-bush
suppletion	quarter-ill	nursehound	Eustachian	mutton-suet
pumple-nose	puerperium	guest-house	rustically	auctionary
purple-born	quarrelled	pursuivant	rustic-work	tuitionary
suppletory	quarreller	nun's-fiddle	pultaceous	auctioneer
suppressed	quarteroon	gunslinger	rusticator	subtropics
suppressor	putrefying	mud-slinger	lustreware	lustrously
purple-hued	outrageous	outswinger	turtleback	multiphase
supplicate	surrogatum	guessingly	lustreless	multiplane
supplicant	puir's-hoose	pursuingly	subtleness	multiplied
surprising	guard-house	questingly	cuttlefish	multiplier
bumpkinish	puir's-house	subsoiling	cuttle-bone	multipolar
suppliance	quarriable	questioner	turtle-dove	butter-bake
dumpy-level	quirkiness	subspinous	huntiegowk	quaternate
mumping-day	hurryingly	mud-skipper	quatrefoil	quatorzain
pulp-engine	queryingly	substitute	turtle-soup	quaternary
suspensive	quercitron	Mussulmans	hurtlessly	culturable
turpentine	supralunar	Russellite	multifaced	buttery-bar
out-pension	burramundi	subsultive	putty-faced	subterrene
suspension	currant-bun	subsellium	tuftaffeta	butter-bean
turpentiny	guaranteed	mussel-plum	tuftaffety	mustard-gas
suspensoid	quarantine	russel-cord	justifying	butter-bird
suspensory	gunrunning	pulsimeter	Guttiferae	butter-wife
sulphonate	rum-running	pulsometer	sultriness	muster-file
supperless	Quirinalia	guest-night	austringer	butter-dish
suppertime	mucronated	purse-pride	rustlingly	butter-fish
supportive	subreptive	Russophile	sustaining	butter-milk
supporting	subreption	purse-proud	cultriform	quaternion
outperform	eutrapelia	Russophobe	lust-dieted	quaternity
suspirious	quersprung	subsequent	bur-thistle	culturally
supporture	suprarenal	subsurface	putty-knife	gutturally
supposable	putrescent	subscribed	multilobed	butterdock
supposably	putrescine	subscriber	Mustelidae	muster-book
supposedly	cuirassier	subshrubby	subtilness	mustard-oil
purposeful	quernstone	bursarship	Mustelinae	muster-roll
surpassing	turret-ship	pursership	multiloquy	butter-boat
outpassion	Turritella	tusser-silk	custom-made	butterwort
out-patient	nutritious	nurseryman	customable	custard-pie
puppet-show	subroutine	gut-scraper	multimedia	butter-tree
puppet-play	furrow-weed	outstretch	customised	subterfuge
sulphurate	burrow-duck	substratal	sustentate	butter-bump
surplusage	quartz-mill	substratum	button-ball	multi-stage
sulphurise	quartz-rock	subsistent	hunting-box	cutty-stool
outpouring	quartzitic	purse-seine	hunting-cog	multistory
lumpsucker	Russianise	subsessile	hunting-cap	multi-track
sulphurous	Russianism	outsetting	hunting-cat	quotatious
supplyment	substation	sunsetting	buttoned-up	rust-fungus
musquetoon	Russianist	Pulsatilla	mutton-head	tub-thumper
surrealism	puissaunce	pulsatance	subtangent	tuft-hunter
quartation	puissantly	fuss-budget	mutton-chop	cultivable
surrealist	pursuantly	numskulled	sultanship	multivocal
burr-walnut	nurse-child	subtrahend	mutton-bird	multivious
curriculum	subsection	australite	sustentive	cultivator
curricular	subsidiary	fustianise	sustention	cumulative

cumulation
suturation
tubularian
tubulation
tubularity
tubulature
cucurbital
furuncular
futureless
luculently
purulently
futurition
luxuriance
luxuriancy
cucumiform
cumuliform
futuristic
cucullated
autumnally
futurology
lugubrious
lucubrator
tumultuate
tumultuary
augustness
tumultuous
curvaceous
curvacious
outvillain
mud-volcano
pulvilised
subvention
pulvinated
suaveolent
culvertage
pulverable
subvariety
subversive
subversion
pulveriser
curvetting
survivance
purveyance
surveyance
outwrought
sun-worship
tutworkman
outwitting
ruby-throat
jury-rigged
ruby-silver
July-flower
ruby-spinel
eurypterid
Eurypterus
jury-rudder
quiz-master
puzzle-head
puzzlement
quizziness
puzzlingly
tuzzi-muzzy
evacuative

evacuation
Aviculidae
Avicularia
aviculture
evidential
availingly
evaluative
evaluation
evolvement
evil-minded
evil-worker
ivy-mantled
even-handed
avenaceous
avengeress
avengement
evincement
evangelise
evangelism
evangeliar
evangelist
avant-garde
even-minded
evanescent
avanturine
aventurine
eventually
evaporable
evaporator
ovipositor
overhanded
overlander
overcaught
overraught
overrashly
overdaring
overlaying
overlaunch
overlabour
overcanopy
overmantel
overmaster
overmatter
ivory-black
overabound
avaricious
averseness
overweight
over-refine
overreckon
overpeople
overleaven
overoffice
overthwart
overshadow
Averrhoism
Averrhoist
overcharge
overthrust
overshower
overbidder
overnicely
overtimely

overwisely
ever-living
overriding
overwinter
overplaced
Everglades
oversleeve
overflight
overglance
overslaugh
overflowed
overinform
overinsure
overdosage
overboldly
overfondly
overbought
overlooker
overcolour
ovariotomy
everyplace
overspread
overbridge
overfreely
overgreedy
overpraise
overground
overgrowth
overstrain
overstress
overstride
overstrike
everything
overstrong
overstrung
overstruck
overburden
overrunner
overturner
oversupply
oversubtle
everywhere
overexcite
overexpose
eviscerate
eviternity
avouchable
avouchment
sweathband
sweatiness
sweat-shirt
Swadeshism
sweetbread
sweet-briar
sweet-brier
'tween-decks
sweetening
sweetheart
sweepingly
sweetie-pie
tweedledee
tweedledum
sweepstake

sweep-seine
sweetstuff
tweet-tweet
sweet-water
swaggering
owlishness
sweltering
twelvefold
twelve-note
twelve-tone
twilighted
swellingly
twelfth-day
swimmingly
swan-maiden
swine-drunk
swine-fever
swingingly
twangingly
twin-sister
swingle-bar
twinflower
swing-music
swan-upping
swing-swang
swing-shelf
swinestone
swing-stock
twi-natured
twy-natured
swan-mussel
swing-wheel
twenty-five
twentyfold
twenty-four
swooningly
sword-blade
swordcraft
sword-dance
swerveless
sword-guard
sword-grass
dwarfishly
swordproof
sword-stick
swarm-spore
Owlspiegel
twittering
zwitterion
switchback
switchgear
switch-over
twittingly
swivel-hook
two-wheeled
two-wheeler
awkwardish
two-year-old
excavation
exhalation
exsanguine
expatiator
expatriate

expansible
expansibly
exhaust-gas
exhaustive
exhaustion
oxy-bromide
exobiology
exuberance
exuberancy
execrative
execration
execratory
exactitude
exacerbate
executable
executress
executancy
oxidisable
expendable
extendable
extendible
extendedly
exheredate
expeditate
experiment
expeditive
expedition
expedience
experience
expediency
exteriorly
excellence
excellency
externally
excerpting
excerption
extemporal
extensible
expectedly
expertness
expectance
expectancy
exceptious
extenuator
exaggerate
exogenetic
oxygenator
exegetical
exhilarate
exhilarant
excitative
excitation
expiration
excitatory
expiratory
extinctive
extinction
exsiccator
extincture
excitement
extinguish
exhibitive
exhibition

exhibitory	excursuses	synecdoche	eye-legible	cytochrome
extirpable	exuviation	hyperdulia	myological	xylochrome
extirpator	synaxarion	syneidesis	syllogiser	pyrophoric
exaltation	pyracantha	hymeneaeal	cycloidian	pyrophorus
exultation	gynandrism	hymeneaean	hyalomelan	hypophysis
exultantly	synandrium	typesetter	cyclometer	hypotheses
explicable	gynandrous	hyperfocal	hyalophane	hypothesis
explicator	synandrous	hypergolic	hyaloplasm	hypothetic
explicitly	hypalgesia	synergetic	cyclopedia	mycorhizal
exulcerate	hypalgesic	Lysenkoism	cyclopedic	mylonitise
exploitage	dynamitard	cybernetic	cycloramic	Tyrolienne
exultingly	sybaritish	pyrenocarp	cyclostome	mycoplasma
exploitive	sybaritism	type-holder	cyclostyle	hylozoical
examinable	pyramidion	mycetozoan	eyelet-hole	hypocorism
examinator	dynamicist	mycetology	cyclothyme	Lycopodium
exenterate	pyramidist	pyretology	symmetrise	hypodorian
ox-antelope	gyrational	synecology	symmetrian	cytologist
axinomancy	dynamistic	typewriter	hypnagogic	mycologist
axiomatics	Lycaenidae	hyperspace	hypnogogic	typologist
excogitate	Tyrannidae	hypersonic	hypnogenic	hylotomous
expositive	Zygaenidae	hypertonic	pycnogonid	xylotomous
exposition	Hyracoidea	dysenteric	hypnoidise	zygomorphy
expository	dynamogeny	type-cutter	cyanometer	gyrocopter
axiologist	synaloepha	dysgraphia	pycnometer	zygosphene
exportable	synaeresis	dysgraphic	pyknometer	cymotrichy
exophagous	dynastical	myographic	gymnasiast	mycorrhiza
exopoditic	tyrant-bird	Syngenesia	gymnosperm	zygobranch
exurbanite	hypanthium	pyogenesis	pycnospore	pyrography
exprobrate	synanthous	syngenesis	gymnosophy	typography
excruciate	hypaethral	syngenetic	pycnostyle	xylography
extractant	hypaethron	Lythraceae	hypnotiser	hypocritic
extricable	hypabyssal	Lychnapsia	Pyrolaceae	synoptical
extractive	myoblastic	mythically	pyromaniac	hypostasis
extraction	symbolical	typhaceous	pyrogallic	synostosis
exorbitate	symboliser	mythiciser	pyrogallol	gyrostatic
exorbitant	dyscrasite	pythogenic	hypoxaemia	hypostatic
uxorilocal	synclastic	mythologic	hypoxaemic	pyrostatic
excrementa	syncretise	mythologer	hypogaeous	pyrolusite
extra-mural	syncretism	syphilitic	myxomatous	myxomycete
extraneity	syncretist	mythomania	hypotactic	zygomycete
extraneous	syncopated	hyphenated	pyromantic	pyroxyline
uxoriously	syncopator	typhlology	zygodactyl	hypolydian
expressage	myocardial	mythopoeic	synoecious	synonymist
excrescent	myocardium	Myricaceae	gyroscopic	synonymity
expressive	synchronic	Xyridaceae	pyro-acetic	hypogynous
expression	synchronal	typicality	pyrotechny	synonymous
extra-solar	syncarpous	cylindrite	pyromeride	hyoplastra
expressman	eye-catcher	cylindroid	pyroxenite	dysphemism
expressure	syndicator	myriadfold	hypodermic	lyophilise
expressway	syndactyly	lysigenous	hypodermal	sylphidine
exasperate	synderesis	myringitis	hypodermis	symphilism
exospheric	syndetical	syringitis	pyrogenous	symphilous
exosporous	Cyperaceae	pyrimidine	xylogenous	tympanitic
exothermic	Wykehamist	mytiliform	pyrometric	tympanites
exothermal	gyre-carlin	pyridoxine	hypocentre	tympanitis
exoterical	hyperaemia	myrioscope	hypotenuse	nympholept
exhumation	hyperaemic	syllabical	cynophobia	dysprosium
excusatory	hyperacute	syllabuses	mysophobia	symphonion
expunction	hyperbolic	by-election	xylophagan	symphonist
exsufflate	hyperbaric	cyclically	hylotheism	lymphogram
expurgator	hyperbatic	cyclo-cross	hylotheist	lymphocyte
expugnable	hyperbaton	Wycliffite	xylophonic	sympathise
exculpable	typescript	cyclograph	sycophancy	Sympetalae

symphyseal
dyophysite
symphysial
symphylous
dyer's-broom
hygrochasy
hydrically
hydrochore
hybridiser
Tyrrhenian
hydrograph
hygrograph
hydragogue
pyorrhoeic
pyorrhoeal
pyrrhicist
hydrologic
hydrolysis
hydrolytic
hydromania
hydromancy
hydrometer
hygrometer
hydrometry
hygrometry
Cyprinidae
by-drinking
pyrrhotine
pyrrhotite
pyrrhonism
pyrrhonian
pyrrhonist
hydrophane
hydroplane
cypripedia
hydrophily
hydropolyp
hydrophone
hygrophobe
hydropathy
hydropower
hydrophyte
hygrophyte
hydrospace
hydrosomal
hydrosomes
hydroscope
hygroscope
hydrotheca
hydrotaxis
hydraulics
hydrazides
byssaceous
myasthenia
myasthenic
hypsometer
hypsometry
byssinosis
eye-spotted
gypsophila
hypsophyll
eye-servant
eye-service

eyas-musket
Hyoscyamus
mystically
myrtaceous
dyothelete
dyothelite
synthesise
synthetise
dyothelism
synthesist
synthetist
synthectic
mystifying
syntagmata
hyetograph
mystagogic
mystagogue
mystagogus
nystagmoid
cyathiform
nyctalopia
nyctalopic
nyctalopes
systemless
systematic
hyetometer
syntenosis
nyctinasty
dystrophia
dystrophic
oyster-bank
oyster-park
oyster-farm
hysterical
hystericky
oyster-wife
mystery-man
synthronus
mysterious
hysteresis
synteresis
hysteretic
hysteritis
cystoscope
cystoscopy
dysthymiac
Tyburn-tree
eye-witness
azobenzene
azeotropic
czarevitch

553

11 □a□d□n

Calabar-bean
Palaearctic
paramaecium
camaraderie
caravanette
parasailing
caravanning
farawayness
malakatoone
catacaustic
caravansary
paramastoid
taratantara
parabaptism
maladaptive
Malacca-cane
damascening
parascenium
paraldehyde
Camaldolese
Camaldolite
cat-and-mouse
hazardously
parabematic
paracetamol
paraselenae
paragenesia
paragenesis
paragenetic
paranephric
paranephros
Pan-American
paramedical
paraleipsis
Paracelsian
managership
paraffin-wax
paraffinoid
paraffin-oil
Pan-Anglican
paraphraser
paraphraxia
paraphraxis
catachresis
paraphiliac
Marathonian
cataphonics
Panathenaea
Panathenaic
parathyroid
Mahabharata
pataphysics
parachutist
capacitance
fanatically
satanically
magazine-gun
parasitical
carabiniere
malariology
canariensis
vacationist
caparisoned

parasitosis
cavalierish
cavalierism
canalicular
capaciously
rapaciously
sagaciously
salaciously
canaliculus
maladjusted
damask-steel
catallactic
cataplectic
parallactic
paraplectic
paragliding
paralleling
parallelise
parallelism
parallelist
capableness
salableness
savableness
parablepsis
parableptic
paraglossae
paraglossal
cataclasmic
cataclastic
cataclysmic
parabolanus
laparoscope
laparoscopy
paramoecium
vagabondage
vagabondise
vagabondish
vagabondism
satanophany
katabothron
katavothron
parabolical
paradoxical
Paradoxides
ratatouille
paramountcy
paramountly
paramorphic
cataloguise
palaeotypic
maladroitly
catadromous
katadromous
paratrooper
paragrapher
paragraphia
paragraphic
malapropism
paracrostic
parapsychic
harassingly
macassar-oil
Marantaceae

paranthelia
rabattement
catastrophe
parasuicide
catapultier
paratyphoid
catalytical
canary-grass
carbocyclic
marble-paper
marble-edged
cabbage-moth
cabbage-palm
cabbage-rose
cabbage-tree
cabbage-worm
garbologist
cabbalistic
dak-bungalow
carbonalite
carbonylate
Carbonarism
carbonation
carbuncular
jabberingly
Carborundum®
jabberwocky
barbaresque
carburetted
carburetter
carburation
carburetion
carburettor
barbarously
barbastelle
gambit-piece
Sabbathless
rabbet-joint
Sabbatarian
barbiturate
rabbit-hutch
rabbit-punch
harbour-dues
harbourless
saccharated
bacchanalia
Barclaycard
wax-chandler
pancratiast
cat-cracking
paschal-lamb
fascia-board
sauce-crayon
farcicality
fasciculate
calcicolous
sarcocystis
parchedness
hatchettite
calcifugous
bacciferous
calciferous
calcigerous

marchioness
sarcoidosis
sanctifying
cancellated
vasculiform
rascalliest
masculinely
masculinise
masculinist
masculinity
vascularise
vascularity
matchlessly
laccolithic
calculating
calculation
sacculation
vasculature
calculative
sad-coloured
tan-coloured
matchmaking
watch-making
sarcomatous
marconigram
dancing-girl
sarcenchyme
carcinology
carcinomata
fascinating
lancinating
calcination
fascination
lancination
vaccination
vaccinatory
larcenously
lanceolated
calceolaria
sancho-pedro
sarcophagal
sarcophagus
patch-pocket
watch-pocket
Nancy-pretty
catch-phrase
mancipation
mancipatory
calcariform
canceration
rancorously
sarcastical
marcescible
Lancastrian
latch-string
watch-spring
laicisation
narcissuses
catch-the-ten
rat-catching
raucousness
sanctuarise
baccivorous

hardwareman
hand-painted
paediatrics
paediatrist
handfasting
mandibulate
Sadduceeism
handicapped
handicapper
landscapist
manducation
manducatory
candidiasis
paedodontic
candidature
hand-feeding
randle-perch
candle-berry
paddle-wheel
paddle-shaft
candle-light
saddle-girth
handselling
saddle-cloth
candle-power
saddle-nosed
paddle-board
saddle-horse
hard-hearted
hard-wearing
tap-dressing
land-measure
candle-stick
maid-servant
tardy-gaited
handshaking
sand-thrower
card-sharper
hard-visaged
sandwich-man
landfilling
hard-hitting
landsknecht
sand-skipper
candelabras
candelabrum
bandy-legged
paedologist
Magdalenian
fardel-bound
baddeleyite
Pandemoniac
Pandemonian
Sandemanian
pandemonium
landing-beam
Pandanaceae
hard-and-fast
landing-gear
garden-glass
cardinalate
maddeningly
garden-house

landing-ship	water-bailie	facetiously	patent-rolls	Sanguisorba
hand-knitted	rateability	water-jacket	water-thrush	hang-gliding
land-jobbing	saleability	Canellaceae	lamentation	large-minded
landholding	tameability	lamellicorn	race-suicide	barge-master
landlordism	water-barrel	lamelliform	balefulness	Targumistic
hard-working	water-bottle	patelliform	banefulness	ramgunshoch
cardiomotor	water-bouget	waterlogged	carefulness	jagging-iron
hand-to-mouth	paper-credit	gaberlunzie	fatefulness	marginalise
cardiograph	water-colour	safe-blowing	gaseousness	Gargantuism
hard-mouthed	water-cement	water-meadow	hatefulness	Gargantuist
cardophagus	water-cannon	paper-making	wakefulness	Panglossian
paedophilia	water-closet	water-monkey	rate-cutting	kangaroo-rat
paedophilic	water-cooled	paper-muslin	dame's-violet	dangerously
land-spaniel	water-cooler	tabernacled	water-violet	waggishness
Wanderjahre	catercorner	capernoited	paper-weight	barge-stones
hand-breadth	paper-cutter	Capernaitic	cave-dweller	tax-gatherer
land-grabber	cater-cousin	capernoitie	lake-dweller	haughtiness
panduriform	watercourse	paternalism	safety-catch	naughtiness
dandy-rigged	water-doctor	cavernulous	safety-match	gangsterism
hard-grained	calendering	paternoster	safety-valve	maggotorium
hand-promise	calendarist	cavernously	panegyrical	langoustine
hand-grenade	haberdasher	navel-orange	panegyricon	laughworthy
wanderingly	paper-enamel	café-concert	malfeasance	gas-guzzling
mandarinate	watered-down	safe-conduct	half-landing	cash-railway
gander-month	water-engine	malevolence	half-baptise	cash-payment
hard-pressed	pad-elephant	paper-office	baffle-plate	bashi-bazouk
paederastic	dare-devilry	gametophyte	halfpennies	cachectical
handwritten	make-believe	categorical	baffle-board	machicolate
handwriting	safe-deposit	warehousing	half-hearted	cash-account
handwrought	safe-keeping	Laserpicium	half-measure	tachycardia
landgravine	cameleopard	caterpillar	half-leather	cathedratic
waldgravine	pale-hearted	water-pepper	half-checked	pachydactyl
sanderswood	tale-bearing	water-purpie	half-binding	pachydermal
candescence	tape-measure	salesperson	haaf-fishing	pachydermia
caddishness	race-meeting	water-pistol	half-blooded	pachydermic
faddishness	paper-feeder	Laserpitium	halfendeale	cashierment
candy-stripe	paper-folder	safe-breaker	half-and-half	Machaerodus
paedotrophy	water-finder	safe-cracker	malfunction	wash-leather
land-steward	game-chicken	hare-brained	saffron-cake	pathography
landaulette	water-hammer	name-dropper	half-holiday	tachygraphy
hand-running	paper-hanger	make-or-break	half-pounder	pathogenous
maceranduba	catechismal	gatecrasher	calf-country	naphthalene
barefacedly	catechistic	water-spider	gaff-topsail	naphthalise
gametangium	catechising	water-spirit	fanfaronade	wash-gilding
tape-machine	catechetics	water-skiing	half-brother	Machairodus
calefacient	pale-visaged	paper-sailor	raffishness	bathmitsvah
race-walking	malefically	water-splash	gas-fittings	bathmitzvah
name-calling	maleficence	caressingly	half-starved	parheliacal
wage-earning	watering-can	water-supply	margraviate	catholicise
Rabelaisian	watering-cap	navel-string	hangability	catholicism
calefaction	watering-pot	water-spring	tangibility	catholicity
labefaction	lateritious	water-sprite	barge-couple	panhellenic
madefaction	materialise	caper-spurge	ragged-robin	pathologist
malefaction	materialism	water-souchy	Haggadistic	bachelordom
rarefaction	materialist	parentheses	languescent	bachelorism
tabefaction	materiality	parenthesis	sang-de-boeuf	batholithic
calefactory	laterigrade	parenthetic	rangefinder	bathylithic
malefactory	face-lifting	patent-right	large-handed	mathematics
calefactive	malediction	lacertilian	Sanguinaria	bathymetric
rarefactive	valediction	Palestinian	sanguineous	mathematise
water-bearer	maledictory	Valentinian	laughing-gas	washing-blue
camel-backed	valedictory	water-tunnel	languishing	washing-line
water-beetle	maledictive	lamentingly	languidness	machine-made

washing-soda	variegation	papier-mâché	basket-weave	gallophobia
bathing-suit	Manichaeism	pasigraphic	basket-chair	sailor-maker
machine-shop	ravishingly	calibration	market-place	pallescence
machination	vanishingly	satin-stitch	market-woman	Vallisneria
machine-tool	parishioner	hagioscopic	racket-court	Callistemon
wash-and-wear	fatidically	panic-struck	market-house	cable-stitch
machine-work	pacifically	magistratic	market-price	haplessness
fashionable	satirically	calisthenic	market-cross	hatlessness
fashionably	facilitator	sagittiform	racket-press	lawlessness
tacheometer	habilitator	Hamiltonian	talkatively	saplessness
tacheometry	pacificator	variational	yackety-yack	tally-system
bathophobia	vaticinator	magisterial	Jack-pudding	ballet-dance
pathophobia	paripinnate	canisterise	galliambics	ballot-paper
taphephobia	famillarise	magisterium	mail-catcher	call-at-large
taphophobia	familiarity	Sagittarius	galliardise	Callitriche
cathartical	laciniation	paniculated	tagliatelle	balletomane
father-in-law	maliciously	capitularly	nail-varnish	table-tennis
washerwoman	lapidifying	manipulable	mail-carrier	table-topped
Sachertorte	Bacillaceae	manipulator	gally-beggar	parlour-maid
wash-drawing	bacillicide	fatigue-duty	gally-bagger	callousness
bathyscaphe	bacilliform	latifundium	fallibility	wall-mustard
bathysphere	lapilliform	latitudinal	day-labourer	Gallovidian
yachtswoman	mamilliform	fatiguingly	cauliculate	tallow-catch
catheterism	papilliform	variousness	valleculate	tallow-faced
bashfulness	hagiologist	taciturnity	caulicolous	gallows-bird
lachrymator	Mariologist	habituation	Gallicanism	gallows-free
Marivaudage	radiologist	mariculture	hallucinate	gallows-foot
farinaceous	papillulate	panjandarum	mallee-scrub	Gallowegian
salicaceous	panislamism	bank-manager	sallee-rover	sallow-thorn
radicalness	panislamist	back-ganging	hall-bedroom	fallow-finch
radioactive	carillonist	rack-railway	tail-feather	gallowglass
caricatural	carilloneur	tank-farming	hälleflinta	eagle winged
radio-beacon	maxillipede	dark-lantern	fault-finder	gable-window
satlability	radiolarian	backscratch	cauliflower	gallowsness
variability	capillarity	backscatter	calligraphy	gallows-ripe
ratiocinate	vacillating	backbencher	haplography	gallows-tree
radiocarbon	cavillation	park-officer	calligramme	barley-water
Taliacotian	hariolation	back-blocker	cauligenous	galley-slave
Sapindaceae	mamillation	backsliding	rallying-cry	galley-foist
labiodental	vacillation	maskallonge	baillieship	barley-brake
palindromic	variolation	rat-kangaroo	warlikeness	galley-proof
lapidescent	vacillatory	walking-beam	gall-bladder	barley-broth
facinerious	capillitium	hacking-coat	sallal-berry	barley-sugar
varicelloid	lapis-lazuli	walking-cane	cable-length	palm-cabbage
radicellose	maxim-monger	packing-case	fallalishly	map-measurer
varicellous	panic-monger	backing-down	faultlessly	haemocyanin
taxidermise	radiometric	walking-fish	Carlylesque	Talmudistic
taxidermist	nationalise	walking-leaf	Maglemosian	May-meetings
latiseptate	nationalism	walking-lady	gallimaufry	warm-hearted
satisfiable	nationalist	walking-part	rallentando	farm-offices
satin-finish	rationalise	walking-race	sailing-boat	mammiferous
daring-hardy	rationalism	walking-toad	calling-crab	mammography
Hagiographa	rationalist	walking-twig	mailing-card	haemoglobin
hagiography	nationality	talk-you-down	garlandless	mammalogist
radiography	rationality	bank-holiday	gallantness	man-milliner
gaming-table	malignantly	back-country	table-napkin	warm-blooded
caaing-whale	ration-money	backbreaker	marlinspike	salmon-berry
palingenesy	salinometer	Baskerville	Paulinistic	harmonogram
eating-house	Dasipodidae	mackerel-sky	sailing-ship	salmonellae
gaming-house	californium	back-draught	balloon-back	garmentless
eating-apple	janitorship	mawkishness	balloon-vine	salmon-coble
gazing-stock	latirostral	basket-maker	callipygean	salmon-spear
pavingstone	radiophonic	market-value	callipygous	harmoniphon

salmon-trout	mannishness	favouritism	patricianly	hair-brained
mammonistic	harness-room	carousingly	matriclinic	hairdresser
carminative	varnish-tree	Jacob's-staff	matroclinic	sabre-rattle
haemophilia	magnesstone	wagon-wright	patriclinic	saurischian
haemoptysis	garnet-paper	paronychial	patroclinic	patristical
balm-cricket	magnetician	wasp-waisted	capriccioso	laurustinus
lammergeier	painstaking	malpractice	matriculate	macroscopic
lammergeyer	carnationed	palpability	latrocinium	hairstylist
haemorrhage	barnstormer	ear-piercing	sacrocostal	narratively
haemorrhoid	walnut-juice	Campbellite	macrocosmic	narrow-gauge
law-merchant	gainfulness	camp-meeting	fabrication	harrowingly
balmorality	painfulness	sampler-work	fabricative	waist-anchor
hammercloth	carnivorous	carpogonium	macrodactyl	Falstaffian
palmyra-nuts	saponaceous	lamp-chimney	tarradiddle	marshalling
hammer-brace	sapotaceous	Cappah-brown	labradorite	rapscallion
gammerstang	papovavirus	naupliiform	fair-dealing	Pan-Slavonic
palmyra-wood	cacogastric	lamplighter	fair-seeming	batsmanship
haemostasis	baron-bailie	harpsichord	barrier-reef	marshalship
haemostatic	gamogenesis	wax-painting	fair-weather	oarsmanship
haematocrit	baronetical	pampelmoose	sacrificial	false-bedded
haematocele	Napoleonism	pampelmouse	carrageenan	passibility
haematology	Napoleonist	pamphleteer	carragenin	passacaglia
palmatisect	napoleonite	wappenschaw	barrage-fire	daisy-cutter
mammoth-tree	parochially	damping-down	madrigalian	maisterdome
harmfulness	canophilist	campaniform	madrigalist	haustellate
fainéantise	halophilous	salpingitic	macrogamete	panspermism
paint-bridge	saxophonist	salpingitis	farraginous	panspermist
cannibalise	cacophonous	campanology	saprogenous	parsley-pert
cannibalism	masochistic	campanulate	larrikinism	mass-meeting
damnability	canonically	parpen-stone	laurel-water	falsifiable
wainscotted	laconically	wasp-tongued	patrol-wagon	passage-boat
wainscoting	vaporisable	lamprophyre	caprolactam	sausage-meat
maintenance	vasodilator	wapper-jawed	saprolegnia	salsuginous
launderette	calorimeter	cappernoity	sacrilegist	sausage-roll
magnifiable	vaporimeter	dampishness	matrilineal	sausage-tree
carnificial	calorimetry	waspishness	matrilinear	cat's-whisker
magnificent	Carolingian	carpospores	patrilineal	caustically
manniferous	Jacobinical	campestrian	patrilinear	wassail-bout
manna-groats	Jacobitical	pampas-grass	patrolwoman	wassail-bowl
rain-chamber	parotiditis	malposition	barrel-house	tassell-gent
raunchiness	cavo-rilievo	carpet-snake	barrel-organ	Caesalpinia
jaunting-car	halobiontic	palpitation	garrulously	marshlander
manna-lichen	Baconianism	panpsychism	matrimonial	causelessly
saintliness	laboriously	panpsychist	patrimonial	pauselessly
dauntlessly	saponifying	masquerader	sacramental	marshmallow
taintlessly	saloon-rifle	marqueterie	lacrimosely	facsimilist
cannon-metal	Madonna-lily	Jacqueminot	lacrymosely	bauson-faced
magnanimity	madonnawise	marquessate	lacrimatory	passing-bell
magnanimous	paronomasia	lacquer-tree	lacrymatory	maisonnette
fawningness	batological	barquentine	warrantable	passing-note
cannon-proof	taxonomical	pasquinader	warrantably	bar-sinister
maintopmast	lagomorphic	marquisette	patronising	sarsen-stone
maintopsail	panomphaean	matriarchal	pairing-time	cassiopeium
gain-control	savoir-faire	patriarchal	carrion-crow	passionless
carnaptious	savoir-vivre	carriageway	pair-bonding	Passion-play
Saintpaulia	nasofrontal	marriage-bed	patroonship	Passion-tide
laundry-maid	vapouringly	far-reaching	sauropodous	Passion-week
manneristic	savouriness	hair-raising	sauropsidan	Marsupialia
Wagneresque	cacographer	tarry-breeks	sapropelite	pansophical
tarnishable	cacographic	taurobolium	madreporite	mass-produce
harness-cask	gamotropism	macrobiotic	saprophytic	kaisar-i-Hind
garnishment	vasopressin	saprobiotic	hair-breadth	hamstringed
earnestness	vasopressor	fairy-butter	hair-trigger	mansard-roof

Sanskritist	nautch-girls	bactericide	nature-study	obtemperate
palsgravine	earth-hunger	master-wheel	manumission	obsecration
basset-hound	fact-finding	masterpiece	manumitting	obsessional
cassiterite	farthingale	master-clock	vacuolation	absenteeism
causatively	part-singing	martyrology	vacuum-clean	object-glass
saussuritic	mastoiditis	pasture-land	vacuum-flask	obtestation
sansculotte	captainship	master-class	vacuum-brake	objectively
sansevieria	castellated	pastoralism	calumniator	objectivise
varsovienne	Santalaceae	pastoralist	saturnalian	objectivism
massiveness	dactylogram	pastureless	naturopathy	objectivist
passiveness	tautologise	raptureless	haruspicate	objectivate
mantua-maker	tautologism	easternmost	saburration	objectivity
want-catcher	tautologist	garter-snake	harum-scarum	observantly
cantharidal	tautologous	banteringly	casuistical	observingly
cantharides	mantelshelf	falteringly	valuational	observation
lanthanides	mantelpiece	yatteringly	facultative	observatory
cantharidic	dactylology	dastardness	fatuousness	observative
part-payment	earthliness	bacteriosis	vacuousness	obliterated
factualness	pantalooned	master-joint	salvability	abridgement
partibility	bastel-house	Gasteropoda	vaivodeship	obsidionary
waste-basket	wastel-bread	Fastern's-e'en	waivodeship	obliviously
parti-coated	faithlessly	factory ship	carvel-built	obsignation
party-coated	tastelessly	cauterising	parvanimity	obsignatory
Pantocrator	tantalising	pattern-shop	Calvinistic	obliqueness
lattice-leaf	tantalus-cup	part-writing	larviparous	obviousness
particulate	pantaletted	parturition	harvest-home	obliquation
earth-closet	pantalettes	masterfully	harvest-mite	obliquitous
participial	saltimbanco	rapturously	harvest-tick	abolishable
participant	pantomimist	wasterfully	bay-windowed	abolishment
participate	saltimbocca	bastard-wing	waywardness	abolitional
tautochrone	tautomerism	Baltoslavic	fauxbourdon	abomination
mastication	tautometric	baptismally	papyraceous	obumbration
masticatory	canting-coin	pantisocrat	calycanthus	abandonedly
lattice-work	bastinadoed	lactescence	barycentric	abandonment
mastodontic	bastinading	hatti-sherif	lady's-finger	ob-and-soller
rattle-pated	martensitic	fantastical	laryngology	absorbingly
battle-piece	waiting-list	party-spirit	laryngismus	obsolescent
battlefield	waiting-maid	saltishness	laryngotomy	abiogenesis
pantheology	tautonymous	pantoscopic	labyrinthal	abiogenetic
battleplane	lastingness	pantothenic	labyrinthic	abdominally
farthermore	waiting-room	earth-tremor	baby-sitting	obnoxiously
farthermost	martinetism	hart's-tongue	Maryologist	abnormalism
rattlesnake	casting-vote	partitioner	lady's-mantle	abnormality
tattie-bogle	gastromancy	haptotropic	many-tongued	abhorrently
rattle-brain	gastroscope	raptatorial	baby-bouncer	abortionist
battledress	xanthophyll	saltatorial	lady-trifles	obtrusively
pantheistic	Xanthochroi	jactitation	caryatidean	abbreviator
partnership	Bartholomew	partitively	calyptrogen	abusiveness
gastrectomy	gastrologer	pastourelle	razzamatazz	abstraction
castle-guard	gastronomer	pasteuriser	abracadabra	abstractive
earthenware	gastrosophy	captivating	abranchiate	abstriction
saltierwise	gastronomic	faithworthy	ablatitious	obstriction
lactoflavin	gastrostomy	hasty-witted	oblationary	abstinently
Rastafarian	Xanthoxylum	malt-extract	ablactation	obstinately
lactiferous	Zanthoxylum	east-by-north	abecedarian	obstipation
lactifluous	cartophilic	east-by-south	abactinally	obstetrical
fastigiated	earth-pillar	sapucaia-nut	abscondence	obstruction
cartography	pantophobia	natural-born	obsceneness	obstructive
pantography	earthquaked	naturalness	obscurement	obfuscation
vantageless	sartorially	manufactory	obscureness	obmutescent
castigation	Tattersall's	manufacture	obscuration	objurgation
castigatory	master-mason	carunculate	obediential	objurgatory
faith-healer	masturbator	carunculous	abbey-lubber	objurgative

ablutionary	occipitally	acknowledge	scorbutical	adscription
about-sledge	accipitrine	scholar-like	scurvy-grass	educational
above-ground	octillionth	scholarship	icosahedral	adverbially
scratch-back	schillerise	accoucheuse	icosahedron	adverseness
scratch-coat	acriflavine	accordantly	icosandrian	adversative
scratchless	schism-house	accordingly	icosandrous	advertently
scratch-work	schismatise	acromegalic	scissor-bill	adventuress
eccaleobion	actinometer	acropetally	scissor-case	adventurism
scrape-penny	schizogenic	ectogenesis	scissor-tail	adventurist
octave-flute	Echinoderma	ectogenetic	scissorwise	adventurous
octahedrons	scripophile	ectothermic	scatteredly	advertising
octahedrite	scripophily	scholiastic	scattergood	adjectively
sclate-stane	Schizophyta	schoolwards	scatterling	edification
scragginess	schizophyte	school-child	scattershot	edificatory
octachordal	acrimonious	schoolgoing	scythe-stone	admiralship
scrawlingly	schizopodal	school-point	scutch-blade	advisedness
achaenocarp	Actinomyces	school-board	Scotchwoman	advisership
octagonally	scrimpiness	schoolhouse	Scotch-Irish	addititious
scrappiness	scrimshandy	schoolcraft	Scottishman	adminicular
ocean-stream	scrimshoner	ectoblastic	Scottifying	sdeignfully
octastichon	scriptorial	ectoplasmic	scuttle-butt	adulterator
McCarthyism	scripturism	ectoplastic	acatalectic	addle-headed
McCarthyite	scripturist	accommodate	scuttle-cask	edulcorator
scabbedness	scriptorium	accountancy	acataleptic	adolescence
scaberulous	Schistosoma	accountable	Scitamineae	idempotency
acidifiable	schistosome	accountably	scotomatous	adumbration
academician	schistosity	account-book	ichthyoidal	identically
academicism	achievement	echo-sounder	ichthyology	identifying
schematical	scale-armour	ectomorphic	ichthyolite	adenomatous
screech-hawk	ochlocratic	octonocular	ichthyopsid	odontogenic
screw-driver	scoleciform	accomptable	Ichthyornis	odontoblast
accelerando	scale-insect	accompanier	ichthyosaur	odontologic
accelerator	acclamation	accompanist	accusatival	odontograph
icteritious	acclimation	schottische	scoundrelly	idiomatical
schecklaton	acclamatory	acronymania	acaulescent	idiotically
screamingly	acclimatise	scuppernong	acquiescent	idioblastic
octennially	Scolopendra	acupressure	scruffiness	idioglossia
screen-wiper	ochlophobia	scapigerous	scouthering	ideological
screencraft	scalariform	sceptically	scrutiniser	idiomorphic
sclerocauly	scalpriform	scyphistoma	octuplicate	adjournment
sclerometer	ecclesiarch	scopolamine	scout-master	ideographic
scleroderma	ecblastesis	acupuncture	scrumptious	idiographic
sclerophyll	sculpturing	scopophilia	sceuophylax	ideopraxist
sclerotioid	sculduddery	scopophilic	actuarially	adoptianism
sclerotitis	sculduggery	scopophobia	acquirement	adoptianist
acre-breadth	acolouthite	sceptreless	acquisition	Adoptionism
accessorial	acclivitous	scoriaceous	acquisitive	adoptionist
accessorily	scamblingly	scarabaeoid	acquittance	od's-pitikins
accentually	ecumenicism	scarabaeist	acoustician	odoriferous
eclecticism	acumination	schrecklich	accustomary	odorousness
eccentrical	scent-bottle	scarlet-bean	scrub-typhus	editorially
Scientology	acinaciform	scorchingly	scrub-turkey	adjudgement
screw-thread	ichnography	Scorpionida	acculturate	adjudicator
scientistic	iconography	scorpion-fly	occultation	pedal-action
acceptation	scenography	acarologist	accumulator	perambulate
acceptivity	Acanthaceae	scaremonger	schwärmerei	decarbonise
screw-wrench	scintillant	X-chromosome	advancement	decarbonate
scaffoldage	scintillate	Y-chromosome	adiathermic	decarburise
scaffolding	iconologist	achromatise	adiaphorism	rebarbative
scribacious	econometric	achromatism	adiaphorist	debauchedly
Schizar hus	scincoidian	scoring-card	adiaphorous	recalculate
scrive-board	scant-o'-grace	eccrinology	od's-bodikins	debauchment
octingenary	iconostasis	accrescence	educability	revaccinate

melancholia	metallogeny	leg-business	reed-warbler	heedfulness
melancholic	Heracleidan	verboseness	dendrachate	needfulness
debarcation	metalloidal	deobstruent	verde-antico	headhunting
defalcation	tenableness	herbivorous	readability	reed-bunting
demarcation	hexaplarian	merchandise	vendibility	meadow-grass
retardation	metallurgic	sea-crawfish	weldability	meadow-brown
retardatory	metaplastic	sea-crayfish	re-education	ready-witted
retardative	demagnetise	merchantman	needle-paper	meadow-sweet
regardfully	megalomania	merchantmen	perduellion	lese-majesty
hexateuchal	metasomatic	peach-brandy	needlewoman	leze-majesty
recalescent	petalomania	peccability	needle-point	severalfold
metagenesis	hexagonally	peacock-blue	needlecraft	telepathise
metagenetic	hepatoscopy	peacock-fish	readvertise	telepathist
sexagesimal	teratogenic	peacock-like	needle-furze	temerarious
cesarevitch	Melanochroi	beachcomber	dendritical	hemeralopia
cesarewitch	keratophyre	sea-cucumber	tendrillous	generalship
belatedness	melanophore	fetch-candle	readmission	benefaction
debasedness	nematophore	peccadillos	Kendal-green	benefactory
relatedness	demagogical	geochemical	pendulosity	remembrance
decameronic	pedagogical	rescue-grass	dead-clothes	resemblance
senate-house	megaloblast	benchership	pendulously	reverberant
hexametrise	megalopolis	teachership	mendelevium	Decemberish
hexametrist	teratologic	hercogamous	Vendémiaire	reverberate
sesame-grass	metamorphic	deictically	hebdomadary	defenceless
metacentric	senatorship	describable	seldom-times	telescopist
hepatectomy	demagoguery	perceivable	ready-monied	Telescopium
derangement	pedagoguery	perceivably	reading-book	revendicate
pelargonium	demagoguism	men-children	wedding-cake	defeudalise
cerargyrite	pedagoguish	reactionary	redding-comb	legerdemain
metaphrasis	pedagoguism	reactionist	reading-desk	dependingly
metalhedyde	depauperise	description	Heldentenor	serendipity
metachrosis	depauperate	descriptive	weeding-fork	regenerable
metaphorist	hetaerismic	peace-keeper	weeding-hook	decelerator
Megatherium	hetairismic	pencil-cedar	tendencious	regenerator
metaphysics	renaissance	Aesculapian	tendentious	never-ending
venatically	metapsychic	perchlorate	verd-antique	referendary
desalinator	hexastichal	mercilessly	redding-kame	sea-elephant
Geraniaceae	pedantocrat	pencil-stone	reading-lamp	deleterious
Pedaliaceae	pedanticise	percolation	geodynamics	téléférique
selaginella	pedanticism	sea-colewort	pendant-post	venereology
gelatiniser	semanticist	fence-lizard	wedding-ring	cerebellous
metasilicic	xeranthemum	reach-me-	reading-room	redetermine
semasiology	redactorial	down	dendrolatry	renewedness
deracialise	melanterite	peacemaking	dendrometer	decerebrise
negationist	metastasise	peace-monger	dendroglyph	decerebrate
Pelagianism	devastating	welcomeness	headborough	telemessage
relationism	decantation	beech-marten	reed-sparrow	deferential
relationist	devastation	beach-master	feldspathic	referential
legatissimo	recantation	descendable	leader-cable	reverential
reradiation	repartition	descendible	gendarmerie	reselection
retaliation	devastative	mercenarily	dead-freight	venesection
retaliatory	devaluation	mercenarism	verdureless	tenementary
retaliative	revaluation	tea-canister	pedder-coffe	pedetentous
behavioural	metal-worker	percipience	gelders-rose	never-fading
nefariously	membraneous	percipiency	fender-stool	revengeless
tenaciously	pebble-stone	perceptible	perduration	revengement
veraciously	herb-of-grace	perceptibly	reed-drawing	revengingly
vexatiously	verbigerate	peace-parted	tender-dying	level-headed
debarkation	sembling-box	mercurially	reddishness	hebephrenia
demarkation	Leibnitzian	leucorrhoea	sea-dotterel	hebephrenic
mésalliance	Verbenaceae	beach-rescue	head-station	telephonist
beta-blocker	herb-trinity	leach-trough	venditation	generically
metalliding	verberation	Neo Catholic	ready-to-wear	genetically

hereditable
heretically
beneficence
redeliverer
telekinesis
telekinetic
leze-liberty
beneficiary
beneficiate
repetitious
veneficious
heresiology
bedevilling
bedevilment
Hegelianism
deteriorism
deteriorate
deteriority
Benedictine
benediction
dereliction
remediation
benedictory
benedictive
seven-league
genealogise
genealogist
teleologism
teleologist
repellantly
repellently
repellingly
Aeneolithic
determinacy
beseemingly
determinant
determinism
determinist
determinate
perennially
sexennially
hereinafter
perennation
heterotaxis
developable
heteroscian
heteroecism
benevolence
heterocercy
werewolfish
werewolfism
hegemonical
renegotiate
ceremonious
heteroclite
development
heterotopia
heterotopic
heterospory
heterograft
heterotroph
selenograph
heterousian

heterostyly
telecontrol
Heteroptera
heterotypic
deserpidine
redemptible
betel-pepper
cerebriform
meteorogram
desegregate
telearchics
researchful
penetralian
meteorology
cerebralism
cerebralist
meteorolite
telegrammic
teleprinter
peregrinate
peregrinity
telegrapher
telegraphic
tenebrosity
meteoritics
terebratula
penetrating
celebration
cerebration
desecration
penetration
terebration
penetrative
gegenschein
reverseless
releasement
defeasanced
recessional
reversional
secessional
reversioner
necessarian
necessarily
necessitied
desensitise
necessitate
necessitous
defensative
Ceteosaurus
Teleosaurus
defensively
recessively
cement-water
fenestrated
celestially
vedette-boat
receptacula
cenesthesia
cenesthesis
telesthesia
telesthetic
seventeenth
pedestalled

repentantly
repentingly
resentingly
refectioner
mesenterial
refectorian
selectorial
sedentarily
cement-stone
cementation
delectation
detestation
cementatory
deceitfully
resentfully
deceptively
defectively
retentively
selectively
detectivist
receptivity
retentivity
selectivity
desexualise
tea-equipage
bereavement
deservingly
decemvirate
reservation
reservatory
bevel-wheels
self-harming
self-mastery
perfectible
perfectness
deification
reification
self-feeding
self-defence
self-delight
self-seeking
self-neglect
self-feeling
self-healing
self-sealing
self-devoted
self-tempted
self-despair
self-centred
self-fertile
self-service
self-serving
self-denying
self-affairs
self-offence
self-charity
self-winding
self-limited
self-figured
self-misused
self-elected
leaf-climber
self-blinded

self-planted
self-closing
perfumeless
self-imposed
deaf-and-dumb
web-fingered
self-invited
perfunctory
self-induced
self-knowing
self-conceit
self-concept
self-concern
self-loading
self-covered
self-cocking
self-locking
self-command
self-torment
self-worship
self-content
self-control
self-torture
self-opinion
performance
self-created
performable
sea-furbelow
beef-brained
self-trained
perforation
perforative
self-drawing
selfishness
self-assumed
self-assured
self-starter
self-sterile
self-subdued
leaf-cushion
reef-builder
self-support
leaf-cutting
self-culture
self-evident
self-evolved
self-excited
self-example
weigh-bridge
neighbourly
bergschrund
leaguer-lady
leaguer-lass
feignedness
seigneurial
wedge-heeled
lengthiness
hedge-hyssop
seigniorial
seigniorage
hedging-bill
begging-bowl
hedge-priest

hedge-parson
wedge-shaped
hedge-school
wedge-tailed
weightiness
hedge-writer
Rechabitism
sea-hedgehog
methodology
methodistic
dephlegmate
nephrectomy
lethiferous
meshuggenah
meshuggeneh
technically
nephritical
rechallenge
nephologist
cephalalgia
cephalalgic
methylamine
nephelinite
Cephalopoda
Cephalaspis
cephalotomy
methylation
mechanician
mechanistic
tephromancy
technocracy
netherwards
lethargical
netherlings
netherstock
lecherously
Mekhitarist
pericardiac
pericardial
pericardian
pericardium
peripatetic
pelican-fish
leviratical
semipalmate
Pedipalpida
perigastric
demi-bastion
retinacular
retinaculum
reliability
recirculate
bewitchment
heliochrome
heliochromy
desiccation
desiccative
rediscovery
periodicity
revindicate
devil-dodger
periodontal
periodontia

bewildering	deficiently	semi-monthly	tediousness	declamation
deliverance	petitioning	Lepidoptera	pediculosis	deplumation
perihepatic	petitionary	Lepidosteus	sericulture	reclamation
deliverable	religionary	helispheric	semi-tubular	declamatory
mediaevally	revisionary	hemispheric	medievalism	well-entered
deliberator	seditionary	heliophobic	medievalist	replenished
desideratum	petitionist	perispermal	believingly	replenisher
delitescent	religionise	perispermic	desilverise	Hellenistic
revivescent	religionism	menispermum	deck-passage	wellingtons
peripeteian	religionist	delinquency	deckle-edged	declination
perigenesis	revisionism	reciprocant	weak-hearted	reclination
perinephric	revisionist	reciprocate	neck-herring	declinatory
pedicellate	retinispora	demiurgeous	weak-sighted	declinature
bedizenment	semi-diurnal	demiurgical	heckelphone	sea-longworm
peridesmium	religiosity	pericranial	neckerchief	realpolitik
refinedness	defiliation	defibrinise	peckishness	well-looking
retiredness	deliciously	defibrinate	fell-walking	seal-rookery
hemihedrism	deliriously	pericranium	keelhauling	reallotment
perineurium	religiously	serigrapher	beblubbered	bell-founder
denizenship	seditiously	lexigraphic	helleborine	well-founded
desinential	revivifying	serigraphic	belly-button	well-rounded
penitential	semi-skilled	hemitropous	reflectance	bell-foundry
pericentral	semi-ellipse	demigration	neglectable	well-coupled
residential	vexillology	denigration	replaceable	Della-Robbia
pericentric	legibleness	denitration	pellucidity	well-trodden
delineation	decillionth	melioration	replacement	well-ordered
sedimentary	legislation	remigration	bellicosely	hellgramite
delineative	vexillation	meliorative	bellicosity	deploringly
delivery-man	legislature	sepiostaire	perlocution	well-groomed
delivery-van	periclitate	mediastinal	replication	well-dressed
heliography	legislative	periostitic	vellication	telluretted
meningocele	medium-dated	periostitis	well-advised	declaration
besiegement	relic-monger	mediastinum	belly-dancer	defloration
besiegingly	mediumistic	perissology	belle-de-nuit	deploration
periphrases	heliometric	peninsulate	well-behaved	declaratory
periphrasis	legionnaire	helioscopic	peelie-wally	declarative
perithecial	regionalise	registrable	well-defined	hellishness
perithecium	regionalism	hemistichal	well-derived	leglessness
delightedly	regionalist	mediatrices	well-desired	recluseness
meliphagous	benignantly	peristalsis	well-meaning	sexlessness
delightless	defiantness	peristaltic	well-beloved	perlustrate
perichylous	hemianopsia	peristalith	oeil-de-boeuf	realisation
benightment	hemianoptic	peristomial	bell-heather	well-stacked
perishingly	designation	befittingly	celliferous	zeolitiform
fetichistic	resignation	remittently	melliferous	belly-timber
fetishistic	designatory	resistingly	mellifluent	repleteness
delightsome	designative	mediateness	mellifluous	deglutinate
helichrysum	semi-annular	dexiotropic	negligeable	aeolotropic
sedigitated	peritonaeal	heliotropin	deflagrator	bellettrist
genitivally	peritonaeum	mediatorial	realignment	deglutition
levitically	retinoscopy	peristerite	negligently	deglutitory
medicinable	Perigordian	hemipterous	belligerent	deglutitive
medicinally	demigoddess	resistively	neologistic	well-judging
veridically	medico-legal	resistivity	well-thumbed	jealoushood
semicircled	Lepidosiren	geniculated	healthiness	fell-lurking
reminiscent	peritonitic	pediculated	wealthiness	fell-running
resipiscent	peritonitis	reticulated	healthfully	jealousness
reviviscent	meritorious	vesiculated	reclaimable	zealousness
medicine-man	hemimorphic	Pedicularis	reclaimably	repleviable
periwigging	perimorphic	reticularly	bell-ringing	sea-lavender
verisimilar	retinospora	semi-jubilee	seal-fishing	mellivorous
penicillate	meritocracy	deviousness	well-wishing	re-elevation
Penicillium	helicograph	seriousness	well-sinking	declivitous

yellow-earth
yellow-metal
yellow-belly
bellows-fish
yellow-ammer
reflexology
deflexional
reflexively
Wesleyanism
permeameter
vermiculate
vermiculite
vermiculous
geomedicine
Fehmgericht
Vehmgericht
gemmiferous
dermography
geomagnetic
termagantly
re-emphasise
gemmologist
gemmulation
sea-milkwort
permanganic
fermentable
segmentally
helminthoid
helminthous
seaming-lace
terminology
reamendment
permanently
germaneness
seemingness
Germanophil
Germanistic
Germanesque
germination
termination
vermination
terminatory
germinative
terminative
hermeneutic
gemmiparous
re-emergence
permissible
permissibly
permittance
hermeticity
seamstressy
helmet-shell
geometrical
Geometridae
dermatology
termitarium
permutation
vermivorous
penny-a-liner
reincarnate
teeny-bopper
re-enactment

reinterment
reinterpret
reintegrate
neanderthal
reinsertion
ferntickled
geanticline
reinflation
reanimation
pennoncelle
meaningless
teknonymous
re-endowment
re-encourage
reintroduce
tennis-match
tennis-court
fernitickle
fernytickle
reinstation
reinsurance
heinousness
pennyweight
pennywinkle
penny-wisdom
memorabilia
aeronautics
redoubtable
recombinant
debouchment
deforcement
rejoicement
rejoicingly
second-rater
seconds-hand
second-sight
second-floor
second-class
secondarily
recondition
recordation
second-guess
recoverable
merogenesis
merogenetic
xenogenesis
xenogenetic
mesocephaly
devotedness
removedness
reposedness
reposefully
oesophageal
oenophilist
xerophilous
bed-of-honour
pelotherapy
serotherapy
aerobically
denominable
denominator
Begoniaceae
demoniacism

velocipeder
Merovingian
aerobiology
genouillère
memorialise
memorialist
refocillate
demonianism
devotionist
negotiatrix
defoliation
negotiation
feloniously
ferociously
melodiously
recollected
aeroelastic
ceroplastic
meroblastic
mesoblastic
xenoglossia
xenoplastic
décolletage
decollation
reformadoes
reformulate
recommender
recommittal
deformation
leg-of-mutton
reformation
reformatory
reformative
demountable
reconnoitre
recountment
recognition
recognitory
recognitive
demonolater
demonomania
demonolatry
metoposcopy
xenodochium
aerological
gemological
oenological
pedological
penological
serological
demonologic
mesomorphic
xenomorphic
xeromorphic
demonocracy
decolourise
hero-worship
decomposite
menorrhagia
resourceful
devouringly
seborrhoeic
demographer

cerographic
demographic
xerotripsis
aerotropism
democratise
democratist
zero-grazing
belowstairs
remorseless
reconstruct
remonstrant
demonstrate
remonstrate
decorticate
Demosthenic
gerontology
reportingly
revoltingly
gerontophil
reportorial
aerostatics
aerostation
dehortation
deportation
dehortatory
dehortative
depopulator
Belorussian
devolvement
aerodynamic
metonymical
lemon-yellow
temptatious
Neoplatonic
net-practice
respectable
respectably
respectless
bespreading
resplendent
perplexedly
Hepplewhite
telpher-line
neopaganise
neopaganism
serpiginous
peep-through
Terpsichore
Delphinidae
despoilment
geopolitics
despumation
weapon-salve
weapon-schaw
despondence
despondency
respondence
respondency
reaping-hook
serpentinic
responsible
responsibly
responsions

serpentlike
weeping-rock
keeping-room
weeping-ripe
serpent-star
weeping-tree
leaping-time
deep-mouthed
reapportion
desperadoes
hesperidium
Hesperiidae
reappraisal
vespertinal
reappraiser
sempervivum
sea-purslane
temporality
temperament
pepperiness
peppercorny
temporarily
pepper-grass
temporising
desperately
temperately
desperation
respiration
respiratory
temperature
temperative
deep-drawing
leopard-wood
tempest-tost
tempestuous
perpetuance
perpetrable
perpetuable
perpetually
perpetrator
perpetuator
herpetology
sempiternal
sempiternum
helpfulness
geophysical
sesquipedal
perquisitor
sesquialter
sesquioxide
rebroadcast
merry-andrew
reproachful
tear-falling
bear-baiting
retroaction
retroactive
bear's-breech
retrobulbar
terribility
wearability
meprobamate
necrobiosis

pearl-barley	Hebraically	repressible	reassertion	sensitively
pearl-button	near-sighted	repressibly	perspective	sensitivity
reprobation	detrainment	heart's-blood	message-girl	reassurance
retribution	recruitment	wearisomely	bersaglieri	pensiveness
reprobatory	metrologist	refreshment	news-theatre	perseverant
retributory	necrologist	sea-rosemary	leaseholder	persevering
reprobative	neurologist	representer	deistically	perseverate
retributive	petrologist	bearishness	perspirable	pentlandite
refractable	neuroleptic	necroscopic	verslibrist	gentianella
retraceable	heartlessly	tetrasporic	perspicuity	neutraliser
retractable	serrulation	terrestrial	perspicuous	restraining
depreciator	merrymaking	heart-struck	tessellated	peat-casting
tetracyclic	pearl-millet	heart-strike	weasel-faced	tectibranch
retrocedent	detrimental	heart-string	sessile-eyed	vertebrated
verruciform	recremental	leprosarium	persulphate	vertebrally
tetractinal	gerrymander	regrettable	beastliness	destabilise
terricolous	jerrymander	regrettably	pensileness	petticoated
detractress	necromancer	neuroticism	ceaselessly	depth-charge
deprecation	necromantic	tetratheism	senselessly	pentacyclic
metrication	tetramerism	tear-stained	verse-making	septicaemia
deprecatory	tetramerous	deerstalker	leesome-lane	geotactical
deprecative	pearl-mussel	corratulate	leishmaniae	pentactinal
tetradrachm	terremotive	betrothment	verse-monger	Pentacrinus
tetradactyl	herring-bone	secretional	gelseminine	denticulate
regredience	herring-buss	neurotropic	pessimistic	gesticulate
rear-admiral	ferronickel	secretarial	densimetric	tentaculate
degradation	refringency	secretariat	personified	tentaculite
depredation	herring-gull	territorial	personifier	testiculate
depredatory	refrangible	territoried	geosyncline	verticality
retrievable	searing-iron	regretfully	personalise	Deutschmark
retrievably	ferronnière	secretively	personalism	penteconter
tear-jerking	retranslate	heart-urchin	personalist	geotectonic
hearse-cloth	herring-pond	defraudment	personality	leptocercal
learnedness	tetrandrian	fearfulness	seasonality	festschrift
heart-easing	tetrandrous	tearfulness	weasand-pipe	Pentecostal
reorientate	pearl-oyster	retroussage	personating	sextodecimo
retroflexed	rear-roasted	tetravalent	personation	leptodactyl
ferriferous	tetrapodous	depravement	personative	pentadactyl
pearl-fisher	tetraptoran	deprivement	pensionable	testudinary
ferrography	tetraplegia	depravingly	sessionally	death-duties
petrography	necrophilia	reprovingly	seismonasty	gentlemanly
reprography	necrophilic	sex-reversal	seismoscope	leather-back
tetragynian	necropoleis	depravation	seismometer	leather-coat
ferruginous	tetraploidy	deprivation	seismometry	weathercock
terrigenous	necrophobia	deprivative	tensiometry	feather-edge
tetragonous	negrophobia	persuadable	teaspoonful	heathenesse
tetragynous	decrepitude	felspathoid	seismologic	leatherette
refrigerant	neuropathic	persuasible	sea-scorpion	weather-fend
refrigerate	decrepitate	re-establish	seismograph	weather-gage
segregation	petropounds	sensualness	sea-scouting	weather-gall
segregative	pearl-powder	Weismannism	yeast-powder	tent-pegging
search-party	terraqueous	Messiahship	men-servants	feather-head
tetrahedral	retro-rocket	newscasting	tessaraglot	leather-head
tetrahedron	Petrarchan	feasibility	measureless	weather-helm
hearth-penny	Petrarchise	sensibility	measurement	aesthetical
searchlight	Petrarchism	tensibility	geostrophic	centre-piece
reprehender	Petrarchist	versability	mensuration	penthemimer
yeard-hunger	tetrarchate	seasickness	mensurative	nettle-cloth
searchingly	terroristic	persecution	persistence	weathermost
yeard-hungry	heart-shaped	persecutory	persistency	leather-neck
hearth-money	decrescendo	persecutive	versatilely	genteelness
hearth-brush	refreshener	Wensleydale	versatility	settledness
hearth-stone	depressible	reascension	sensational	gentlewoman

gentlewomen	death-marked	deuteration	decurionate	servant-lass
centre-board	pentamerism	reiteration	vesuvianite	servantless
feather-palm	Septembrist	restoration	Leguminosae	servant-maid
feather-pate	heptamerous	reiterative	pecuniarily	servantship
beetlebrain	pentamerous	restorative	peculiarise	leaving-shop
weather-roll	Teutonicism	nectar-guide	peculiarity	weaver-finch
feather-star	pertinacity	dexterously	repudiation	pervertible
weather-side	geitonogamy	venturously	repudiative	nervuration
weather-sign	Pelton-wheel	Kentish-fire	beautifully	peevishness
weather-ship	mentonnière	pettishness	penuriously	pervasively
weather-vane	sententious	rectiserial	reduplicate	velvet-paper
weather-worn	pertinently	death-stroke	beguilement	leave-taking
weather-wise	meltingness	pectisation	beguilingly	neovitalism
septifragal	centenarian	peptisation	republisher	neovitalist
certifiable	pentandrian	teetotaller	genuflexion	velvetiness
certifiably	septentrion	teetotalism	genuineness	servitorial
rectifiable	heptandrous	pentathlete	beaumontage	nervousness
certificate	pentandrous	restatement	resurrector	heavyweight
testificate	septenarius	gestational	requirement	between-maid
pettifogger	festinately	gestatorial	decurrently	betweenness
pestiferous	pectinately	destitution	recurrently	betweentime
septiferous	destination	restitution	sequestered	reawakening
centigramme	festination	restitutory	demulsifier	welwitschia
hectogramme	pectination	restitutive	sequestrant	re-expansion
pentagynian	pentangular	tentatively	sequestrate	deoxidation
lentiginose	rectangular	restfulness	decussately	deoxygenise
heptagynous	mentholated	zestfulness	decussation	deoxygenate
lentiginous	centrobaric	destruction	requisition	deoxyribose
pentagynous	destroyable	restructure	requisitory	re-existence
tentiginous	mentionable	destructive	decursively	dehydration
vertiginous	sectionally	pentavalent	repulsively	rehydration
dentigerous	berthon-boat	restiveness	requiteless	benzylidine
get-together	benthoscope	aestivation	requitement	off-coloured
pentahedral	oestrogenic	vestry-clerk	penultimate	afterburner
pentahedron	Neotropical	west-by-north	reluctantly	offenceless
Westphalian	section-mark	west-by-south	desultorily	after-dinner
bestridable	pentaploidy	pentazocine	degustation	after-effect
centrically	rectipetaly	ferulaceous	reluctation	aftergrowth
centripetal	perturbance	decumbently	degustatory	aftersupper
settling-day	perturbable	recumbently	resultative	offensively
restringent	centuriator	decumbiture	deductively	effectually
ventriloquy	perturbator	denunciator	reductively	affectingly
Westminster	vectorscope	pedunculate	seductively	affectional
restriction	perturbedly	sepulchrous	tenuousness	affectioned
restrictive	deuterogamy	resuscitant	beauty-sleep	affectation
centrifugal	leptorrhine	resuscitate	serviceable	affectively
ventricular	heptarchist	redundantly	serviceably	effectively
ventriculus	yesternight	fecundation	service-book	affectivity
pestologist	featureless	denumerable	pervicacity	offhandedly
rectilineal	textureless	denumerably	service-flat	efficacious
rectilinear	westernmost	recuperable	service-line	office-block
pestilently	pesteringly	remunerable	serviceless	officialdom
deathliness	venturingly	recuperator	nerve-centre	officialese
sertularian	Deuteronomy	rejuvenator	service-pipe	officialism
gentilitial	deuteranope	remunerator	service-room	officiality
gentilitian	letter-board	rejuvenesce	service-tree	efficiently
ventilation	teeter-board	oecumenical	service-wire	affiliation
ventilative	setter-forth	tegumentary	nerve-ending	officiously
sentimental	letterpress	beauteously	heavy-headed	affirmingly
testamental	lectureship	rebukefully	helve-hammer	affirmation
testamentar	venturesome	regurgitant	heavy-handed	affirmatory
testimonial	death-rattle	regurgitate	heavenwards	affirmative
vestimental	letter-stamp	delusionist	servant-girl	afforcement

affrication	chicken-wire	sheet-rubber	thalidomide	chemotactic
affricative	shock-headed	three-suited	challenging	chemotropic
affrightful	thick-headed	sheep-silver	philhellene	shameworthy
affranchise	shackle-bolt	shrew-struck	shelterless	shimmy-shake
off-scouring	shackle-bone	three-square	chalcedonic	chantarelle
effulgently	phycologist	chieftaincy	chalcedonyx	phantasiast
aguardiente	chuckle-head	chieftainry	whole-footed	phantasmata
eglandulose	thick-lipped	threatening	cheliferous	thunderbolt
agnatically	phycomycete	wheelwright	whale-fisher	thunder-clap
agrarianism	phycophaein	wheel-window	Chilognatha	thunder-dart
egregiously	thick-ribbed	chaff-cutter	philogynist	chanterelle
agriproduct	whichsoever	chaff-engine	philogynous	thunder-like
agriculture	check-string	shufflingly	whole-hogger	channelling
agglomerate	shock-troops	shiftlessly	whole-hoofed	chancellery
agglutinant	thick-witted	whiffletree	phillipsite	chancellory
agglutinate	rhododaphne	chafing-dish	shell-jacket	thunderless
egalitarian	shad-bellied	chafing-gear	philologian	chance-comer
egomaniacal	shuddersome	theftuously	philologist	change-house
agonistical	rhodium-wood	shift-worker	whole-length	thenceforth
agonisingly	shadowiness	whigmaleery	childminder	whenceforth
Ignorantine	shadowgraph	phagocytism	philomathic	thunder-peal
ignoramuses	shoe-latchet	phagocytose	philanderer	changefully
ignominious	sheet-anchor	phagedaenic	whaling-port	phonography
agrobiology	wheel-animal	shaggedness	phalanstery	phenogamous
ignobleness	wheelbarrow	phthiriasis	phyllomania	rhynchocoel
agrological	three-bottle	chain-armour	phyllotaxis	rhynchodont
agnosticism	sheep-biting	chain-bridge	Thallophyta	shanghaiing
agrostology	three-colour	chain-driven	thallophyte	chinoiserie
aggradation	sheet-copper	shrivelling	phylloclade	chanticleer
aggregately	wheel-cutter	choice-drawn	shallowness	thin-skinned
aggregation	threadmaker	chain-harrow	shell-parrot	phenologist
aggregative	thread-paper	shriekingly	cholesteric	phonologist
agoraphobia	three-decker	shrinkingly	cholesterin	rhinologist
agoraphobic	threadiness	shrink-proof	thalassemia	thingliness
aggravating	phrenetical	thrillingly	thalassemic	chandlering
aggravation	threnetical	chain-letter	cholesterol	shin-plaster
egotistical	cheesecloth	choir-master	whole-stitch	thanklessly
phrasemaker	cheese-board	chrismatory	wholesomely	phonemicise
phraseogram	cheese-wring	cheiromancy	philosopher	phonemicist
phraseology	cheese-press	cheirognomy	philosophic	phenomenise
sheath-knife	cheese-straw	cheironomer	whole-souled	phenomenism
wheat-mildew	shoe-leather	cheironomic	thelytokous	phenomenist
chiaroscuro	sheep-farmer	Cheiroptera	philatelist	shunamitism
thrasonical	three-handed	chain-plates	chalazogamy	shiningness
theatricals	Phaethontic	chairperson	rhamnaceous	phantomatic
theatricise	cheer-leader	choir-stalls	rhumb-course	chansonette
theatricism	three-leafed	chain-stitch	chamberlain	chansonnier
theatre-goer	three-leaved	chain-smoker	chambermaid	rhinoplasty
thwartships	three-legged	choir-screen	chimney-nuik	Chenopodium
chiastolite	wheedlesome	Christiania	chimney-nook	phonophobia
thwartingly	phlegmonoid	Christianly	Rhamphastos	rhinorrhoea
theanthropy	phlegmonous	Christmassy	whimsically	Chondrostei
chlamydeous	sheep-master	Christology	championess	thanksgiver
rhabdomancy	three-masted	christingle	thimble-case	rhinoscopic
Rhabdophora	three-master	christening	chameleonic	phonetician
rhabdomyoma	shoeing-horn	Christendom	shamelessly	phoneticise
chick-a-biddy	three-nooked	thriftiness	rhyme-letter	phoneticism
chock-a-block	Phaenogamae	chokecherry	thumb-marked	phoneticist
check-action	phaenogamic	choking-coil	shamanistic	thanatology
phycocyanin	phaenomenon	Shaksperian	rhombohedra	thanatopsis
thick-coming	phrenologic	shellacking	chemurgical	phonotypist
whicket-door	wheel-plough	shell-crater	rhyme-scheme	thingumajig
chicken-feed	three-parted	phylacteric	Thomistical	thankworthy

shinty-stick	whippletree	chordophone	ghastliness	photo-resist
theomachist	rhapsodical	thermotical	ghostliness	phytosterol
thrombocyte	ship-breaker	thermocline	chisel-tooth	photosphere
throbbingly	shopbreaker	tharborough	whistle-stop	whitishness
theorematic	chaperonage	theriomorph	thysanurous	phototactic
theotechnic	shop-steward	choreograph	physiolater	phytotomist
theoretical	shipbuilder	thermograph	chasmogamic	phototropic
chrome-steel	chequer-work	thermoduric	physiolatry	whitethroat
thiopentone	chequerwise	thermolysis	thesmothete	Whitsuntide
through-bolt	chars-à-bancs	thermolytic	ahistorical	Whitsun-week
throughfare	charlatanic	chiropodial	physiognomy	white-winged
through-gaun	charlatanry	chiropodist	physiologic	whitewasher
theophobist	chartaceous	chiropteran	physiologus	chitty-faced
theophagous	whereabouts	short-priced	physiocracy	what-d'ye-call
chrominance	shard-beetle	share-pusher	whist-player	rheumateese
chaotically	therebeside	Therapeutae	whosesoever	rheumatical
chronically	shirt-button	therapeutic	physitheism	rheumaticky
chlorimeter	shortchange	chirurgical	ghost-writer	Chautauquan
chlorimetry	Pherecratic	charismatic	whisky-liver	thaumatrope
shooting-box	shortcoming	short-staple	photoactive	thaumaturge
theopneusty	characinoid	wheresoever	white-billed	shrubbiness
chromoscope	charge-sheet	phariseeism	white-bonnet	shrubberied
chronoscope	charter-hand	shirt-sleeve	white-bottle	shoulder-bag
chlorometer	charge-house	pharisaical	whiteboyism	shouldering
chronometer	charge-nurse	cherishment	Whitechapel	thoughtless
chlorometry	sheriffalty	whorishness	white-collar	thought-sick
chronometry	thuriferous	short-spoken	photocopier	thought-wave
chlorophyll	sheriffship	third-stream	photochromy	thrummingly
theosophise	chirography	Thyrostraca	phytochrome	chaulmoogra
theosophism	choregraphy	theretofore	white-eyelid	thrust-plane
theosophist	chorography	charity-girl	chitterling	cheval-glass
theogonical	chiragrical	sharp-tailed	shatter-pate	shovel-board
theological	sharp-ground	thirstiness	whitleather	shaving-soap
theologiser	churchwards	thyrotropin	thitherward	shiveringly
chloroplast	church-bench	charcuterie	whitherward	showmanship
chromoplast	shareholder	thoroughwax	photo-finish	shawnee-wood
chromosomal	short-handed	short-winded	white-footed	showeriness
chronologer	churchwoman	therewithal	photography	shower-proof
chronologic	church-going	wherewithal	phytography	show-stopper
theomorphic	church-court	sharp-witted	photoglyphy	show-jumping
chloroprene	church-mouse	therewithin	white-headed	thixotropic
chronograph	thermically	cherry-stone	white-handed	chrysalides
chloroquine	thyroiditis	thirty-twomo	thatch-board	chrysalises
theobromine	thermionics	Phasmatidae	shuttlecock	chrysarobin
rheotropism	sherris-sack	Phasmatodea	phytologist	chrysoberyl
Theocritean	chirologist	physiciancy	white-listed	chrysocolla
throat-latch	chorologist	physicianer	shuttlewise	chrysocracy
throatiness	charmlessly	physicalism	rhythmicity	chrysoprase
throat-strap	whoremonger	physicalist	photometric	wheyishness
thiocyanate	chiromantic	physicality	whiting-pout	rhizocarpic
chapeau-bras	Theromorpha	whiskerando	photonastic	rhizogenous
ship-railway	whoremaster	whiskeyfied	whiting-time	rhizomatous
ship-captain	pharyngitic	chastenment	whatsomever	rhizanthous
chip-carving	pharyngitis	phosphonium	whitlow-wort	rhizosphere
Chippendale	thermotaxic	phosphorise	phytophagic	bicarbonate
shepherdess	thermotaxis	phosphorism	photophilic	Micawberish
shopkeeping	theriolatry	phosphorate	photophobia	Micawberism
ship-biscuit	thermonasty	phosphorite	photophobic	financially
whipping-boy	thermoscope	phosphorous	photophonic	vicar-choral
whipping-top	thermometer	chastisable	photoperiod	disaccustom
shop-lifting	thermogenic	thistle-down	rhetorician	bilaterally
Rhopalocera	thermometry	whistle-fish	photo-relief	disaventure
shapeliness	thermophile	whistlingly	white-rumped	filamentary

ligamentary
filamentous
ligamentous
disaffected
vicar-forane
disafforest
vinaigrette
cigar-holder
Sivatherium
rival-hating
dilapidated
piratically
dilapidator
rifacimenti
rifacimento
vivacissimo
hilariously
vicariously
vivaciously
misalliance
disablement
Cisatlantic
livable-with
disarmament
disannuller
Titanomachy
pinacotheca
disapproval
cicatricula
disassemble
disassembly
giganticide
didacticism
gigantology
didactylous
misanthrope
misanthropy
gigantesque
bipartition
itany-stool
misbecoming
kibble-chain
misbegotten
imbriation
disbeliever
misbeliever
diabolology
disbandment
ribbon-grass
imbromania
imbrophily
imber-hitch
gibberellic
gibberellin
misbestowal
gibbousness
disbowelled
gimcrackery
aircraftman
inch-backed
pitchblende
miscibility
vincibility

piscicolous
hircocervus
witch-doctor
discrepance
discrepancy
kitchenette
biochemical
circle-rider
witches'-meat
kitchen-maid
biocoenosis
biocoenotic
yince-errand
kitchen-sink
miscreation
miscreative
witch-finder
zinciferous
discography
zincography
miscegenist
miscegenate
pinch-hitter
kinchin-cove
diacritical
kinchin-mort
biscuit-root
vincristine
mischievous
miscellanea
discalceate
circularise
circularity
piacularity
circulating
circulation
circulatory
circulative
discoloured
discomycete
circumciser
discomfited
circumflect
circumpolar
circumsolar
circumvolve
circumspect
viscometric
circumlunar
circumfused
misconceive
discontinue
misconstrue
cinchoninic
disceptator
disciplinal
discipliner
discophoran
discordance
discordancy
witch-ridden
miscarriage
discernible

discernibly
air-corridor
discardment
discernment
diachronism
sincereness
diachronous
discerption
discerptive
discussable
discussible
discothèque
piscatorial
viscousness
discoursive
diacoustics
discourtesy
viscountess
piscivorous
bird-catcher
bird-fancier
bird-watcher
bird-batting
vindication
vindicatory
vindicative
middle-earth
mind-bending
mind-reading
fiddle-de-dee
riddle-me-ree
middle-sized
mind-healing
pit-dwelling
middle-class
middle-world
kind-hearted
kindredship
girdlestead
windlestrae
windlestraw
fiddlestick
bird-nesting
giddy-headed
windcheater
diadelphous
mind-blowing
misdemeanor
wisdom-tooth
sindonology
biodynamics
middenstead
wild-fowling
Windsor-soap
hinderlands
Biedermeier
widdershins
bird-brained
hinderlings
kinderspiel
cinder-track
windsurfing

wind-furnace
mindfulness
misdoubtful
misdevotion
window-barne
window-ledge
window-blind
window-glass
kiddywinkie
window-frame
fire-watcher
wire-dancing
CinemaScope®
wide-watered
witenagemot
piperaceous
time-bargain
wide-ranging
time-machine
kinematical
literaliser
mineraliser
tire-valiant
fire-walking
fire-balloon
kite-balloon
bimetallism
bimetallist
literalness
cinema-organ
fire-marshal
vice-marshal
lifemanship
fire-raising
mine-captain
wine-tasting
literatured
literaryism
disembodied
tiger-beetle
disemburden
disembitter
riverbottom
liver-colour
disencumber
linen-draper
river-dragon
aides-de-camp
vice-admiral
river-driver
vicegerency
wise-hearted
life-peerage
life-peeress
wine-measure
life-rentrix
wire-netting
time-service
time-serving
tiger-flower
tiger-footed
divergement
divergently

divergingly
rivet-hearth
dicephalous
nikethamide
line-shooter
mine-thrower
wide-chapped
time-sharing
kinesipathy
eidetically
mimetically
wine-bibbing
Ribesiaceae
rice-biscuit
wine-biscuit
vine-disease
Kimeridgian
fivefingers
fire-fighter
firelighter
pipe-lighter
line-fishing
cineritious
cine-biology
kinesiology
time-killing
misericorde
kinesiatric
life-history
time-pleaser
divellicate
miserliness
fire-flaught
libellously
river-mussel
hibernacula
mise-en-scène
hibernicise
Hibernicism
pigeon-berry
pigeon-flier
pigeon-flyer
pigeon-house
hide-and-seek
hibernation
life-annuity
viceroyalty
dive-bombing
kinetoscope
sideropenia
wireworking
kinetograph
fire-worship
viceroyship
fire-control
disemployed
pipe-dreamer
fire-cracker
fire-brigade
line-printer
vine-dresser
vine-fretter
wine-growing

wire-drawing	pilgrimager	dichogamous	highwrought	visiting-day
diversified	ring-winding	lithogenous	highbrowism	divining-rod
dimensional	disguisedly	light-headed	night-season	diminishing
dimensioned	misguidedly	light-heeled	sightseeing	divisionary
linen-scroll	linguistics	diphthongal	night-school	divisionism
disenshroud	singularise	light-handed	lithosphere	digitigrade
disentrance	singularism	night-hunter	sight-singer	dimidiation
liberty-boat	singularist	right-handed	vichyssoise	lixiviation
liberticide	singularity	right-hander	night-shriek	litigiously
directrices	singing-bird	diphthongic	sight-screen	bimillenary
misestimate	rigging-loft	diphtheroid	diphysitism	visibleness
libertinage	rigging-tree	Mithridatic	eight-square	sigillarian
disentangle	wing-and-wing	high-pitched	lithotritic	limitlessly
divertingly	wing-loading	nightingale	lithotritor	disillusion
bicentenary	diagnostics	high-sighted	lithotripsy	disillusive
libertinism	finger-paint	lightkeeper	dichotomise	sigillation
directional	pilgarlicky	tight-lacing	dichotomist	titillation
pipe-stapple	disgarrison	light-legged	lithotomist	pig-ignorant
pipe-stopple	finger-glass	lithologist	dichotomous	Titianesque
directorial	fingerplate	tightly-knit	lithotomous	disimprison
libertarian	lingeringly	sightliness	withstander	sitiophobia
disenthrall	fingerboard	high-blooded	high-stepper	civil-suited
disenthrone	gingerbread	mishallowed	without-door	misinstruct
directorate	fingerprint	tight-lipped	wishfulness	vicissitude
divestiture	finger-grass	litholapaxy	fish-gutting	sinistrally
digestively	fingerstall	sightlessly	dishevelled	pipistrelle
directivity	fingerguard	ditheletism	lightweight	sinistrorse
rice-pudding	disgustedly	dithelitism	night-waking	ministerial
wire-pulling	piggishness	light-minded	night-walker	ministering
direfulness	ring-straked	right-minded	light-winged	disinterest
hideousness	fidgetiness	nightmarish	right-winger	miniaturise
piteousness	ring-stopper	wishing-bone	nightworker	miniaturist
side-cutting	disgruntled	fishing-frog	sightworthy	sinisterity
mine-sweeper	king-vulture	siphonogamy	highly-sexed	ministerium
time-expired	misgovernor	lichenology	finicalness	tibiotarsus
misfeasance	king's-yellow	dishonorary	vigilantism	biliousness
diffraction	Mithradatic	dishonestly	disinclined	pitifulness
diffractive	Mithraicism	wishing-tree	viridescent	viciousness
misfeatured	Highlandman	dishonourer	virilescent	viniculture
difficultly	pigheadedly	wishing-well	limitedness	viticulture
diffidently	right-angled	dichromatic	citizenship	misjudgment
biofeedback	fish-packing	dichroscope	vivisection	disjunction
sinfonietta	high-ranking	high-powered	vivisective	disjuncture
rinforzando	fish-farming	high-rolling	disinfector	disjunctive
differentia	high-battled	fish-torpedo	misinformer	tick-tack-toe
differently	night-attire	high-voltage	riding-habit	nick-nackery
pilferingly	high-falutin	wishtonwish	dining-table	sick-benefit
misfortuned	night-cellar	sight-player	riding-rhyme	tickle-brain
zip-fastener	diphycercal	xiphopagous	riding-light	kirk-session
diffuseness	lithochromy	night-porter	riding-skirt	sick-service
diffusively	lithodomous	lithophysae	riding-cloak	zinkiferous
diffusivity	high-feeding	lithophytic	hiding-place	sick-chamber
disfavourer	fish-bellied	tithe-paying	tiring-glass	silk-thrower
disgraceful	high-hearted	hitherwards	riding-glove	milk-thistle
disgracious	high-tension	sight-reader	tiring-woman	milk-livered
ring-carrier	high-mettled	tichorrhine	diving-board	Pickwickian
siege-basket	righteously	withershins	biting-louse	milk-kinship
king-penguin	light-footed	dithyrambic	riding-horse	pickelhaube
single-phase	night-flower	witheringly	tiring-house	nickel-ochre
single-entry	night-faring	Michurinism	diving-dress	nickelodeon
single-soled	tight-fisted	disharmonic	civilisable	nickel-bloom
singlestick	night-flying	wither-wrung	mirifically	lick-platter
misguidance	lithography	citharistic	vinificator	nickel-steel

sinking-fund	pillar-saint	kidney-stone	jimpson-weed	mirror-image
pinking-iron	sialorrhoea	mimosaceous	hippopotami	microsecond
sickeningly	tiller-chain	bivouacking	diapophyses	nigrescence
pick-and-pick	aimlessness	lipomatosis	diapophysis	vitrescence
sinking-ripe	girlishness	pilocarpine	dispersedly	dioristical
milking-time	sinlessness	pivot-bridge	diaphragmal	vitrescible
silkworm-gut	witlessness	divorceable	disportment	nitrosamine
lickspittle	billsticker	divorcement	simperingly	microscopic
lickerishly	billets-doux	disordinate	disparately	nitrosation
pinkishness	millet-grass	widowerhood	dispiriting	microtubule
sickishness	pillow-fight	disobedient	mispersuade	diprotodont
picket-fence	pillow-block	Tironensian	disposingly	Niersteiner
ricketiness	fieldworker	misoneistic	disposition	vibratility
rickettsiae	air-mechanic	sin-offering	diapositive	microtomist
rickettsial	biomedicine	disorganise	dispositive	librational
ticket-punch	filmsetting	Sinophilism	dispatch-box	vibrational
picket-guard	filmography	Dinotherium	dispatchful	lip-rounding
tickettyboo	diamagnetic	ricochetted	disputation	dissociable
milk-pudding	sigmoidally	ricocheting	disputative	dissociably
sick-nursing	dismembered	bifoliolate	Lippizzaner	Dipsacaceae
gillravitch	firmamental	bisociation	cinquecento	dissectible
milliampere	diamond-dust	bisociative	disquietude	tissue-paper
hill-pasture	diamorphine	pilot-jacket	disquieting	diastematic
dialectally	mismarriage	disobliging	disquietful	linseed-cake
dialectical	dismissible	Sinological	disquietous	misspelling
field-cornet	dismastment	virological	disquietive	linseed-meal
dislocation	diametrally	bicorporate	microampere	einsteinium
villication	diametrical	ritournelle	rib-roasting	missheathed
digladiator	dismutation	mimographer	hierocratic	kiss-me-quick
dislodgment	dismayfully	mixotrophic	micrococcal	first-footer
millefleurs	fiançailles	lipoprotein	micrococcus	first-fruits
gillyflower	sign-painter	widow's-bench	microcephal	pig's-whisper
sialography	cinnabarine	binocularly	jinrickshaw	pig-sticking
dialogistic	pilniewinks	ribonucleic	microcosmic	midshipmate
title-holder	lion-hearted	dicotyledon	nitrocotton	dissolvable
bill-chamber	signifiable	diaphaneity	vitrifiable	dissilience
dislikeable	significant	hippiatrics	hierography	dissolutely
killikinick	significate	hippiatrist	micrography	dissolution
sillimanite	ninny-hammer	Diophantine	microgamete	dissolutive
diplomatese	giant-killer	hippeastrum	nitrogenise	dissymmetry
diplomatise	kinnikinick	Hippocratic	nitrogenous	dissembling
diplomatist	limnologist	hippocampus	microgroove	dissimilate
violoncello	simnel-bread	hippodamist	diarthrosis	dissimulate
willingness	lignum-scrub	hippodamous	Cirrhipedia	dipsomaniac
millenarian	lignum-vitae	hippodromic	vitraillist	disseminule
millenarism	lignum-swamp	mispleading	mitrailleur	lissomeness
villanously	winningness	fipple-flute	fibrillated	winsomeness
bibliomancy	winning-post	displeasant	hierologist	disseminate
bibliolater	piano-player	displeasing	micrologist	dissentient
bibliomania	giant-powder	displeasure	microlithic	dissentious
bibliolatry	dinner-dance	simpliciter	misrelation	dissonantly
billionaire	dinner-table	oil-painting	disremember	fissionable
millionaire	dinner-wagon	simplifying	misremember	diascordium
bibliopegic	sign-writing	hippologist	micrometric	ripsnorting
millionfold	pignoration	dispensable	microneedle	dissepiment
bibliotheca	piano-school	dispensably	nitraniline	fissiparism
bibliophile	minnesinger	dispensator	Hieronymian	fissiparity
bibliophily	giant-stride	hispanicise	Hieronymite	fissiparous
bibliogical	pinnatisect	hispanicism	Micronesian	dissipation
bibliopolic	Finno-Ugrian	disprovable	microphonic	dissipative
pillion-seat	lignivorous	diaphoresis	microphytic	tin-streamer
will-worship	pinnywinkle	diaphoretic	hierarchism	dissertator
lilliputian	kidney-vetch	disproperty	hierurgical	diastrophic

bias-drawing
pissasphalt
missishness
hirsuteness
victuallage
victualling
victualless
distracting
distraction
distractive
mistreading
diotheletic
rinthereout
diothelitic
diathermacy
diathermous
littleworth
virtue-proof
distressing
distressful
dittography
pictography
nitty-gritty
histrionics
histrionism
distributer
distribuend
distributor
distillable
histologist
mirthlessly
distempered
mistempered
victimology
histaminase
distensible
listening-in
distantness
listeners-in
sitting-room
fitting-shop
distinction
distincture
distinctive
distinguish
disturbance
filter-paper
historiated
pictorially
bitter-earth
picture-book
winter's-bark
dipterocarp
picture-card
picture-cord
historicise
historicism
historicist
historicity
winter-berry
historiette
picture-goer
air-terminal

winter-bloom
victoryless
sister-in-law
picture-play
bitter-apple
winter-apple
wintergreen
picture-rail
bitter-cress
winter-cress
picturesque
Pinteresque
micturition
littérateur
bittersweet
winter-sweet
picture-wire
diatessaron
distasteful
Nietzschean
pietistical
dictatorial
nictitation
riotousness
wistfulness
distrustful
mistrustful
tittivation
sinupallial
air-umbrella
sipunculoid
bifurcation
biquadratic
Liquidambar
liquidation
figure-dance
lieutenancy
minute-watch
vituperable
vituperator
minute-while
minute-glass
liquefiable
divulgation
diluvialist
dilutionary
disunionist
aiguillette
ritualistic
ailurophobe
ailurophile
bicuspidate
disulphuret
disulphuric
liquescence
liquescency
situational
sinuousness
silver-paper
silver-white
silver-plate
silversmith
silveriness

silver-point
silver-grain
silver-stick
silvestrian
rib-vaulting
lily-livered
disyllabify
disyllabism
city-slicker
ejectamenta
ejaculation
ejaculatory
ejaculative
ejector-seat
sky-aspiring
sky-coloured
Skillcentre
skilligalee
skilligolee
skeletonise
skulduddery
skulduggery
skilfulness
skimmington
skirmishing
sketchiness
skittle-ball
skating-rink
plea-bargain
alkalescent
all-American
ill-affected
clear-headed
bleach-field
alkalimeter
alkalimetry
clearing-nut
clean-limbed
cleanliness
pliableness
clean-living
olla-podrida
clean-shaven
ill-assorted
olfactology
illaqueable
pleasurable
pleasurably
pleasureful
ill-breeding
flabbergast
globe-flower
globigerina
plebeianise
plebeianism
globularity
elaborately
elaboration
elaboratory
elaborative
black-and-tan
black-a-vised
black-boding

black-beetle
click-beetle
placability
black-browed
blackbirder
blockbuster
black-coated
elucidation
elucidatory
elucidative
placket-hole
all-cheering
slickenside
flickertail
blackfellow
black-fisher
blackgrouse
blackheaded
place-hunter
slack-handed
electioneer
flaccidness
alycompaine
blackmailer
place-monger
black-market
flock-master
Placentalia
electorship
Plectoptera
electrician
electricity
electrocute
electrified
electrolier
electrology
electrolyse
electrolyte
electronics
electrotint
electrotype
electrotypy
block-system
elicitation
flocculence
fluctuating
fluctuation
sledge-chair
fly-dressing
bladder-worm
bladderwort
sliding-keel
sliding-rule
clodhopping
gladioluses
ill-disposed
Gladstonian
gladfulness
altercation
altercative
sleeve-board
all-electric
elder-flower

sleek-headed
elsewhither
sleeping-bag
sleeping-car
alleviation
alleviatory
alleviative
alder-leaved
elderliness
blue-blooded
sleeplessly
aldermanity
glue-sniffer
alternately
alternating
alternation
alternative
allegorical
allegoriser
allelomorph
algebraical
sleep-walker
cliffhanger
ill-favoured
sluggardise
flag-wagging
flag-captain
eligibility
Oligochaeta
oligochaete
oligochrome
flag-officer
clog-almanac
flagellated
flagellator
oligomerous
sloganising
plagioclase
plagiostome
Plagiostomi
blightingly
slightingly
flightiness
flagitation
alphabetise
ill-humoured
plein-airist
plain-dealer
illiberally
plaice-mouth
Albigensian
allineation
ill-informed
illimitable
illimitably
glaikitness
illicitness
claim-jumper
pleiomerous
cloisonnage
plainstanes
clairschach
ellipsoidal

plain-spoken
plainstones
Pleistocene
ellipticity
cleistogamy
pleiotropic
plaintively
illiquidity
altitudinal
illiquation
clairvoyant
climacteric
climactical
glimmer-gowk
slumberland
slumberless
slumbersome
plumber-work
slime-fungus
Glumiflorae
glumiferous
plumigerous
clam-chowder
alembicated
old-maidhood
plumularian
blamelessly
plum-blossom
elementally
ill-mannered
elimination
eliminatory
eliminative
flamboyance
flamboyancy
flamboyante
plume-pluckt
glomerulate
glomeration
clamorously
glamorously
slumbrously
blemishment
climatology
flammulated
plum-pudding
Plymouthism
Plymouthist
Plymouthite
blameworthy
clanjamfray
sling-backed
clinochlore
plano-convex
blunderbuss
flannelette
slenderness
clandestine
plenteously
blind-felled
planogamete
flinchingly
plantigrade

plentifully
planuliform
clinometric
planimetric
plantocracy
plenipotent
planisphere
blind-storey
planetoidal
planetology
planetarium
blunt-witted
allopathist
gliomatosis
blood-bought
fluorescein
fluorescent
alto-relievo
cliometrics
blood-flower
blood-frozen
elbow-grease
blood-guilty
allocheiria
pleochroism
illogically
fluorimeter
algorithmic
alto-rilievo
alloplastic
bloodletter
fluoroscope
fluoroscopy
fluorometer
algological
pleomorphic
allotropism
allotropous
blood-spavin
bloodsucker
bloodstream
bloodsprent
blood-vessel
floorwalker
bloody-faced
bloody-bones
bloody-sweat
blepharitis
elephantoid
elephantine
clapperclaw
flapperhood
slipperwort
kleptomania
glyptotheca
glyphograph
flap-mouthed
all-powerful
flirtatious
clericalism
clericalist
blarney-land
floriferous

florilegium
pluralistic
ultra-modern
ultramarine
Clarencieux
glaringness
plerophoria
florescence
ultrasonics
pluriserial
ultraviolet
clergy-woman
alismaceous
plasmatical
close-bodied
close-banded
glass-blower
close-barred
flesh-colour
glass-cutter
closed-chain
cluster-bomb
flusterment
blessedness
cluster-pine
clyster-pipe
glossectomy
plaster-work
class-fellow
close-fisted
glass-gazing
blasphemous
close-handed
close-hauled
elasticated
classically
elastically
plessimeter
plessimetry
plasticiser
elasticness
classifying
class-leader
fleshliness
close-lipped
blushlessly
flesh-monger
flesh-market
closing-time
glossolalia
blastogenic
elastomeric
Elastoplast®
glossodynia
plasmolysis
plasmolytic
clostridial
clostridium
close-reefed
elusoriness
flustration
closet-drama
glassworker

slot-machine
plate-armour
plate-basket
plutocratic
clothes-line
clothes-moth
clothes-pole
clothes-prop
blotchiness
blotting-pad
ulotrichous
elutriation
plutologist
flatulently
ill-tempered
glutaminase
Platanaceae
Platonicism
plutonomist
platinotype
glutinously
plethorical
platforming
slate-pencil
plate-powder
platyrrhine
plateresque
slate-writer
plate-warmer
cloud-castle
glaucescent
slaughterer
ploughshare
sleuth-hound
eleutherian
plough-staff
plough-stilt
illuminance
illuminable
illuminator
illuminatus
albugineous
flourishing
pleuritical
illusionism
illusionist
albuminuria
cloudlessly
glauconitic
pleurodynia
fleurs-de-lis
fleurs-de-lys
illustrated
illustrator
illustrious
flauntingly
cloud-topped
clavecinist
Clavicornia
slave-driver
clavigerous
slave-holder
slave-labour

Slavonicise
olivine-rock
pluviometer
slave-owning
cleverality
slaveringly
clover-grass
glove-shield
slavishness
slave-trader
flavourless
flavoursome
ill-wresting
slow-sighted
old-womanish
claw-and-ball
flowingness
flower-clock
floweriness
flower-stalk
flexibility
pleximetric
Alexandrian
alexandrine
alexandrite
flax-dresser
play-actress
playing-card
alcyonarian
clay-brained
player-piano
playfulness
blizzardous
Elizabethan
embarcation
empanelling
empanelment
immanentism
immanentist
immarginate
impatiently
embarkation
imparkation
amiableness
ommatophore
embarrassed
impassioned
impassively
impassivity
impartially
impartation
impastation
amicability
emmenagogic
emmenagogue
impeachable
imperceable
impeachment
impenetrate
imperfectly
imperforate
immedicable
impenitence

impenitency
impedimenta
impetigines
imperialise
imperialism
imperialist
imperiality
imperilment
immediately
immediatism
imperiously
embellisher
umbellately
impermeable
impermeably
impermanent
emperorship
impetration
impetratory
impetrative
immenseness
impersonate
Emmenthaler
impertinent
impecunious
impetuosity
impetuously
imperviable
imagination
imaginative
amphibology
amphibolite
amphibolous
Amphictyony
amphimictic
amphipodous
amphisbaena
amphetamine
emphyteusis
emphyteutic
ambivalence
ambivalency
omnipatient
omnifarious
omniscience
empiecement
ambiversion
impingement
empirically
immitigable
immitigably
empiricutic
ambitiously
impignorate
omnipotence
omnipotency
omniformity
omnipresent
immigration
embittering
ambiguously
smoke-helmet
smokelessly

smokescreen
emplacement
implacental
implication
implicative
smallholder
emulsionise
emolumental
implemental
small-minded
emblematise
emblematist
Amelanchier
smilingness
imploringly
imploration
imploratory
small-screen
implausible
emulousness
amplexicaul
amino-acetic
amentaceous
amenability
aminobutene
emancipator
amontillado
amenorrhoea
emanational
ominousness
imponderous
immoveables
embowelling
embowelment
embowerment
smooth-faced
smooth-paced
ammophilous
smooth-bored
impolitical
impoliticly
impoundable
impoundment
amboina-wood
amboyna-wood
immortalise
immortality
emboîtement
impostumate
importunacy
importantly
importunely
importuning
importunate
importunity
importation
imposthumed
smörgåsbord
improbation
improbatory
improbative
impractical
umbraculate

embracement
embracingly
Americanise
Americanism
Americanist
imprecision
embrocation
imbrication
imprecation
imprecatory
imprudently
umbriferous
impregnable
impregnably
embroiderer
amerciament
embroilment
umbrella-fir
umbrella-ant
amaranthine
embryonated
embryologic
impropriate
impropriety
emery-powder
ambrosially
impressible
impressment
smart-ticket
umbratilous
amorousness
improvident
improvement
improvingly
improvisate
smartypants
emasculator
amusiveness
ametabolism
imitability
ametabolous
smithereens
empty-headed
empty-handed
emotionable
emotionally
emotionless
amatorially
Smithsonian
smithsonite
imitatively
amateurship
amativeness
amethystine
ambuscadoes
smouldering
ampullosity
amour-propre
impuissance
impulsively
impulsivity
empyreumata
amazon-stone

unpalatable
unpalatably
unhazardous
incapacious
unparagoned
enjambement
unharboured
unmatchable
unmasculine
enhancement
incarcerate
unhandseled
unsandalled
unpardoning
unhandiness
incardinate
unwandering
incalescent
annabergite
unravelling
unravelment
untamedness
ungazed-upon
infangthief
ensanguined
enlargement
unpathwayed
unfashioned
ingathering
inhabitance
inhabitancy
unnavigated
inhabitable
innavigable
innavigably
unhabitable
unnavigable
unsatisfied
invalidhood
unsatirical
unmalicious
invalidness
inhabitress
insatiately
unsatiating
unhackneyed
intagliated
unmalleable
uncalled-for
entablement
unfailingly
ungallantly
unmanliness
unballasted
entablature
ungarmented
unharmfully
unpaintable
incarnadine
undauntedly
untaintedly
unjaundiced
encarnalise

uncanniness
ungarnished
unharnessed
untarnished
unvarnished
incarnation
uncanonical
uncanonised
unlaborious
unsavourily
unlabouring
unhappiness
unmarriable
unbarricade
unwarranted
unpatriotic
encapsulate
incapsulate
unpassioned
infanticide
infantilism
unpatterned
unfaltering
incantation
incantatory
infantryman
unsaturated
unnaturally
insalubrity
infatuation
unharvested
inobedience
inobservant
unobservant
unobserving
snobography
inebriation
unabolished
unabrogated
unobnoxious
inobtrusive
unobtrusive
unscratched
sneck-drawer
Anacreontic
snickersnee
enucleation
unscheduled
inscribable
inscription
inscriptive
knick-knacky
knuckle-bone
knuckle-head
unicolorate
unicolorous
anacoluthia
anacoluthon
inoculation
inoculatory
insculpture
inoculative
unicellular

unicoloured	undescended	underground	intelligent	intemperant
onychomancy	unrescinded	Interglossa	unhealthily	untempering
anecdotally	unmercenary	intergrowth	unhealthful	intemperate
unscholarly	underclothe	undergrowth	unreclaimed	unweariable
anecdotical	intercepter	intergatory	interlinear	unweariably
unaccounted	interceptor	enneahedral	index-linked	knee-tribute
unicorn-moth	intercostal	enneahedron	unfeelingly	interracial
anachronism	intercessor	untechnical	interlining	unrefracted
anachronous	intercrural	encephaloid	undeclining	interradial
knock-rating	intercourse	encephaline	interlunary	interradius
unscissored	undercovert	enkephaline	interlingua	unreprieved
inscrutable	interdealer	encephalous	underlooker	unlearnedly
inscrutably	under-driven	antechamber	unrealistic	unweariedly
unaccusable	unteudalise	underhanded	underletter	unterrified
unaccusably	intendiment	underhonest	intermedial	interrogant
inedibility	interdental	unmechanise	intermeddle	interrogate
inadvertent	unbendingly	inheritance	intermedium	interregnum
inadvisable	unheedingly	unmeditated	undermanned	anteorbital
unadvisable	unreadiness	angelically	unfermented	integrality
unadvisably	infeudation	endemically	unsegmented	endearingly
unadvisedly	unheedfully	indefinable	intermingle	interrupted
unidiomatic	unneedfully	indefinably	undermining	interrupter
inadaptable	incendivity	inheritable	interminate	interruptor
unadaptable	undelegated	undecidable	undermasted	undepressed
anadiplosis	inseverable	undefinable	internecine	unredressed
unaddressed	unvenerable	undesirable	internecive	unrefreshed
inodorously	independent	undesirably	internodial	integration
unseparated	undepending	unmeritable	indemnified	integrative
inseparable	antependium	inseminator	antenniform	unfearfully
inseparably	antecedence	indehiscent	internalise	unreproving
ungetatable	unbeneficed	undelivered	infernality	undershapen
unseparable	unbenefited	undecidedly	internality	understated
undebauched	unrevealing	unmeritedly	internuncio	unpersuaded
undemanding	unbeseeming	unbenighted	unmeaningly	incense-boat
unregarding	undeveloped	undelighted	enneandrian	intersperse
unrewarding	under-espial	unperishing	enneandrous	undersleeve
unveracious	unreceipted	unreligious	interneural	intensified
interallied	unrehearsed	endemiology	unbeknownst	intensifier
unrecalling	anteversion	unbeginning	unmemorable	undersigned
unremaining	unnecessary	unbenignant	unremovable	under-school
knee-capping	inferential	undesigning	angelolatry	interspinal
interactant	enterectomy	indesignate	unretouched	underseller
interaction	interesting	unpedigreed	unrejoicing	incensement
underaction	unrelenting	inheritress	unrecovered	incessantly
interactive	unrepentant	anteriority	unreposeful	unceasingly
underbearer	unrepenting	inferiority	angelophany	unreasoning
interbedded	unresenting	interiority	anaerobiont	intenseness
underbidder	unresentful	unbefitting	enterovirus	unpensioned
underbreath	unreceptive	undeviating	unmelodious	undershorts
underbridge	unretentive	unremittent	envelopment	interseptal
underbitten	undeserving	unremitting	unrecounted	insessorial
interchange	interfacial	unresisting	enterotoxin	intersertal
undercharge	unperfectly	ungenitured	interosseal	interscribe
unpeaceable	interfacing	ingeniously	enterostomy	unleisurely
unreachable	enfeoffment	indeciduate	interocular	understrata
unteachable	index-finger	indeciduous	underpraise	insensately
intercedent	unperformed	unbelieving	unrespected	insensitive
undescribed	unselfishly	interjacent	interpreter	intensative
unperceived	interfusion	under-keeper	unperplexed	intensitive
intercalary	interfluent	interleaves	enterpriser	unsensitive
intercalate	interfluous	intellected	underpriced	intensively
unwelcomely	unwedgeable	unreflected	undespoiled	under-sawyer
intercensal	unfeignedly	interludial	interpolate	intersexual

unrestraint	interviewee	enchiridion	unvisitable	antiquation
insecticide	interviewer	antheridium	annihilator	insinuation
insentience	underviewer	unchartered	anticipator	insinuatory
insentiency	undervaluer	unsharpened	invigilator	insinuative
unfeathered	intervallic	inkhorn-mate	undividedly	antipyretic
unweathered	intervallum	anchor-stock	unlimitedly	antitypical
anaesthesia	interventor	antherozoid	unfinishing	anticyclone
anaesthesis	unperverted	unchastened	infinitival	unpityingly
anaesthetic	innervation	Anthesteria	uncivilised	unskilfully
ungenteelly	underwriter	unchastised	indivisible	snakishness
unsettledly	underweight	unthought-of	indivisibly	uncleanness
uncertified	underworker	anchovy-pear	antibilious	unclearness
unrectified	unseaworthy	anticathode	incipiently	unclubbable
insectifuge	snuff-colour	antipathist	insipiently	inelaborate
insectiform	unification	anti-Jacobin	insipidness	unelaborate
investigate	snuff-dipper	antijacobin	insidiously	ineluctable
intertribal	unoffending	inviability	invidiously	Anglicanism
entertainer	inoffensive	undisclosed	unpitifully	inalienable
uncertainly	unoffensive	undiscerned	individuate	inalienably
underthirst	ineffectual	insincerely	unwinkingly	inalterable
uncertainty	unaffecting	insincerity	entitlement	unalienable
undertaking	ineffective	undiscussed	unwillingly	unalienably
insectology	unofficered	untinctured	inviolately	unalterable
infertility	inefficient	unmindfully	infirmarian	unalterably
ungentility	inofficious	incinerator	undignified	influential
unsentenced	unofficious	anti-federal	indignantly	Anglo-French
intertangle	snaffle-rein	antihelices	ancientness	inelegantly
unrestingly	uniformness	anti-Semitic	unwitnessed	analogously
unweetingly	knife-switch	enlivenment	indignation	analphabete
undertenant	snuff-taking	unfixedness	oneiromancy	Anglo-Indian
insertional	onagraceous	anti-heroine	invigorator	inflammable
intentional	enigmatical	unhidebound	oneiroscopy	inflammably
intentioned	unagreeable	engineering	antinomical	unblameable
undestroyed	unigeniture	anniversary	antimoniate	unblameably
ancestorial	anagnorisis	undiverting	antimonious	anglomaniac
intertarsal	anthracitic	antineutron	antifouling	inclemently
inventorial	enthralling	indigestion	environment	unslumbrous
unsectarian	enthralment	indirection	oneirodynia	unblemished
unperturbed	anthracnose	indigestive	undispensed	unblindfold
underthrust	anthracosis	untimeously	antispastic	unblenching
indexterity	anthocyanin	snail-flower	india-rubber	unflinching
insectarium	uncheckable	indifferent	unvitrified	Anglo-Norman
incertitude	unshockable	angiography	antirrhinum	inclination
indentation	unthickened	inking-table	unbiassedly	inclinatory
infestation	anthochlore	undisguised	undissolved	unallowable
investiture	unshrinking	unhingement	unfiltrable	unflappable
investitive	enchainment	undiagnosed	infiltrator	anglophilia
invectively	unchristian	antiphrasis	undistilled	anglophilic
inventively	unshakeable	unsighed-for	insistently	anglophobia
Insectivora	unshakeably	unwished-for	unfittingly	anglophobic
insectivore	unsheltered	unlightened	unwittingly	anglophonic
unregulated	anthologise	unrighteous	unlistening	ineloquence
ensepulchre	anthologist	antithalian	antistrophe	unflustered
antemundane	Enghalskrug	antiphonary	undistorted	unplastered
infecundity	unchildlike	unwithering	undisturbed	unclassical
unreducible	unwholesome	unlightsome	unliquefied	endlessness
unbeautiful	anthomaniac	unwithstood	Antiburgher	inclusively
unrepugnant	unshunnable	unmitigated	antiqueness	uncluttered
unreturning	unthinkable	anti-vitamin	anxiousness	inflatingly
unrequisite	enchantment	individable	enviousness	unillumined
antenuptial	enchondroma	undividable	antiquarian	unplausible
unreluctant	enchantress	unmitigable	antitussive	unplausibly
ingenuously	anthropical	unmitigably	insinuating	enslavement

unflavoured	insouciance	information	unpopularly	incredulity
inflexional	unconcealed	informatory	involucrate	incredulous
inimicality	enforceable	informative	involuntary	energetical
unimpeached	untouchable	uncountable	innocuously	snorkelling
unimpededly	unconcocted	unsoundable	unconvicted	engraftment
unambitious	unconceived	unwoundable	involvement	unpreferred
unambiguous	enforcement	unconnected	unconvinced	unprofessed
unsmilingly	unconcerned	unboundedly	unconverted	unprofiting
anomalistic	unconcerted	unfoundedly	unspeakable	intriguante
animalcular	unsoldierly	unsoundness	unspeakably	unoriginate
animalcules	intolerance	incognisant	unspecified	androgynous
anemometric	intolerable	unconniving	inspectress	unorthodoxy
unamendable	intolerably	incoronated	inappetence	enarthrosis
gnomonology	incoherence	antonomasia	inappetency	anarchistic
unimportant	incoherency	entomophagy	anaplerosis	undrainable
anamorphous	ontogenesis	entomophily	anaplerotic	engrailment
unimpressed	ontogenetic	ontological	snapshooter	entrainment
enumeration	unloverlike	endomorphic	unsprinkled	unprojected
enumerative	unforeknown	uncompacted	unipolarity	engrammatic
onomasticon	endometrial	Incompletae	anaphorical	ungrammatic
unamusingly	endometrium	uncompleted	unappointed	untrembling
animatingly	unhopefully	incompliant	inopportune	untremulous
unemotional	unforfeited	uncompliant	inspiringly	incremental
unemotioned	uncomforted	uncompelled	unsparingly	incriminate
uninhabited	unconfirmed	uncompanied	unipersonal	encrimsoned
uninucleate	unconfessed	incorporeal	unspiritual	unpromising
uninscribed	engorgement	endospermic	inspiriting	intromitted
anencephaly	uncongenial	incorporall	inspiration	intromitter
uninventive	unforgotten	incorporate	inspiratory	incremation
unenchanted	incongruent	incomposite	inoperative	undrinkable
uninhibited	incongruity	incompetent	inspirative	unprintable
uninvidious	incongruous	uncomplying	unoperative	intrenchant
enunciation	unforgiving	unconquered	unapproving	entranchise
enunciatory	endophagous	uncorrected	inspissator	intrinsical
enunciative	endochylous	incorrectly	unapostolic	infrangible
uninflected	Indo-Chinese	uncourteous	anaphylaxis	intrepidity
un-Englished	endothermic	encouraging	inequitable	unprophetic
inanimation	entophytous	incoercible	inequitably	infrequence
anonymously	incogitancy	uncorrupted	unequitable	infrequency
unanimously	unmotivated	endotrophic	unequivocal	incrassated
unannotated	incogitable	incorruptly	entreatable	uncrushable
uninforming	indomitable	unnourished	increasable	encrustment
unannounced	indomitably	inconstancy	unbreakable	engrossment
uninspiring	innominable	unmoistened	untreatable	entrustment
inenarrable	unpolitical	inconscient	increaseful	unpresuming
uninitiated	unsolicited	inconscious	unbreathing	intrusively
unendurable	unsocialism	unconscious	unpreaching	unprotected
unendurably	unsociality	endorsement	inorganised	intrathecal
unenquiring	encomiastic	inconsonant	unorganised	unbrotherly
uninquiring	innoxiously	unpossessed	entreatment	ungratified
unknowingly	unlooked-for	unmortgaged	intractable	unprotested
unknownness	uncollected	unfortified	intractably	ingratitude
uncomatable	enfouldered	unmortified	untraceable	onerousness
endocardiac	ennoblement	uncontrived	untractable	unprovident
endocardial	ungodliness	uncontemned	unpractical	unprovoking
endocardium	endoplasmic	incontinent	unpractised	untravelled
unmoralised	endoplastic	unsoftening	onirocritic	unprevented
unpolarised	incommodity	uncouthness	infracostal	intravenous
unromanised	informality	unfortunate	unprocessed	untraversed
unvocalised	uncommended	unportioned	intricately	inescapable
undoubtable	untormented	uncontested	anfractuous	unescapable
unforbidden	informatics	unmodulated	infructuous	unashamedly
undoubtedly	uncommitted	unpopulated	unfructuous	unusualness

anisocercal
inessential
unessential
unassertive
unaspirated
gnostically
inestimable
inestimably
unassisting
anisomerous
anastomoses
anastomosis
anastomotic
uniserially
angst-ridden
anisotropic
inusitation
unisexually
gnatcatcher
unsteadfast
initialling
unattainted
instability
gnotobiosis
inutterable
unutterable
unutterably
unattending
instreaming
unattempted
inattention
inattentive
unattentive
instigation
instigative
snatch-thief
snatch-block
snatchingly
snatch-purse
unstainable
unstaidness
installment
instantiate
instinctual
instinctive
gnathonical
unstoppable
unstoppably
unit-pricing
unitisation
instatement
institorial
institution
institutist
institutive
instaurator
unstaunched
instruction
instructive
snotty-nosed
pneumathode
pneumatical

incunabular
incunabulum
encumbrance
inturbidate
unhusbanded
incumbently
unpurchased
annunciator
unquickened
unsucceeded
unguiculate
inculcation
inculcatory
inculcative
unsuccoured
unsubduable
innumerable
innumerably
insuperable
insuperably
intumescent
unqueenlike
unquietness
untunefully
insufflator
unfulfilled
indulgently
unvulgarise
ingurgitate
unauthentic
unmutilated
indubitable
indubitably
unmusically
injudicious
unguligrade
incuriosity
incuriously
injuriously
undutifully
unsubjected
uncuckolded
unluckiness
induplicate
unqualified
inquilinism
inquilinity
inquilinous
unpublished
unqualitied
unaugmented
unsubmerged
unmurmuring
unquantised
unburnished
unfurnished
inquination
pneumonitis
unsuspected
unsuspicion
unsurprised
unsuspended
unsupported

unsurpassed
inculpation
inculpatory
unguardedly
unhurriedly
inquiringly
unguerdoned
enquiration
innutrition
inquiration
inquisition
inquisitive
unburthened
unjustified
uncurtailed
uncurtained
unsustained
industrious
inductility
insultingly
inductional
intuitional
unhurtfully
inductively
intuitively
intuitivism
inductivity
inaugurator
unluxuriant
unluxurious
incurvation
incurvature
unevidenced
unavailable
unavailably
unavoidable
unavoidably
univalvular
unavertable
universally
knavishness
unsweetened
snow-leopard
unawakening
unswallowed
knowingness
snow-goggles
know-nothing
unawareness
snow-dropper
snow-bunting
unexcavated
inexhausted
unexhausted
inexecrable
inexactness
inexecution
inexpedient
unexperient
inextension
inexpensive
unexpensive
inexpectant

unexpectant
inexcitable
unexcitable
unexplained
unexclusive
unexercised
unexpressed
inexistence
inexcusable
inexcusably
unsyllabled
undyingness
encystation
solanaceous
Bonapartean
Bonapartism
Bonapartist
monarchical
coparcenary
coparcenery
tobacconist
tobacco-pipe
Tom-and-Jerry
nonagesimal
Monadelphia
potash-water
notaphilism
notaphilist
foraminated
botanically
nomadically
somatically
totalisator
Loganiaceae
polariscope
polarimeter
solarimeter
polarimetry
logarithmic
foraminifer
coral-island
Moravianism
Novatianism
Novatianist
Rotarianism
voraciously
coralliform
coralloidal
movableness
notableness
womanliness
Mohammedism
botanomancy
somatogenic
potamogeton
potato-chips
moratoriums
somatoplasm
somatologic
somatotonia
somatotonic
potato-bogle
potato-apple

bog-asphodel
dolabriform
potass-water
monasticism
romanticise
romanticism
romanticist
monasterial
woman-vested
forbearance
Bombacaceae
corbiculate
forbiddance
forbiddenly
double-faced
double-eagle
double-fault
double-edged
hobbledehoy
double-agent
double-check
double-shade
double-think
double-sharp
double-lived
double-mined
double-digit
double-blind
double-ender
double-entry
double-form'd
wobble-board
double-space
double-cross
cobblestone
corbie-steps
double-stout
double-dutch
double-quick
morbiferous
corbel-table
doubtlessly
bombilation
lobby-member
Sorbonnical
bonbonnière
bombination
combination
combinatory
combinative
borborygmic
borborygmus
bombardment
Dogberrydom
Dogberryism
Hobbistical
combustible
combustious
tolbutamide
nonchalance
concealable
concealment
torch-bearer

forcibility	soldier-crab	conditional	non-existent	conflagrate
concubinage	cold-welding	conditioned	hotel-keeper	confabulate
concubinary	road-mending	conditioner	honey-locust	forficulate
concubitant	word-perfect	soldatesque	money-lender	confidently
coccidiosis	goods-engine	goddaughter	powerlessly	confidingly
concrescent	bowdleriser	coadjutress	foreclosure	confederacy
zoochemical	soldierlike	wood-cutting	role-playing	confederate
conceivable	cold-hearted	good-evening	money-making	coffee-table
conceivably	load-bearing	wood-swallow	sober-minded	pomfret-cake
conceitedly	soldiership	molecatcher	honeymooner	coffee-berry
conceitless	top-dressing	bower-anchor	money-market	toffee-nosed
monchiquite	gold-beating	Dodecandria	homeomorphy	coffee-house
conciliable	bond-service	dodecaphony	homeomerous	toffee-apple
conciliator	bondservant	rope-machine	home-and-	coffee-stall
concolorate	word-of-mouth	pole-vaulter	away	configurate
concolorous	condignness	dovetailing	home-and-	wolf-whistle
coxcombical	wood-vinegar	forepayment	home	forfeitable
concomitant	gold-digging	forewarning	love-in-a-mist	coefficient
volcanicity	cold-without	rose-campion	modernistic	conflicting
concentered	word-picture	foremastman	foreknowing	confliction
volcanology	condolement	dodecastyle	vomeronasal	conflictive
forcing-pump	condylomata	Dodecagynia	forevouched	gonfalonier
concentring	cold-blooded	honey-badger	rosewood-oil	confineless
concentrate	wood-alcohol	moveability	foretopmast	confinement
coach-office	condolatory	money-broker	come-uppance	god-forsaken
conceptacle	non-delivery	hoverbarrow	comeuppance	comfortable
concipiency	condemnable	ion-exchange	coleopteral	comfortably
conceptious	condominium	nomenclator	forespurrer	conferrable
forcipation	goldsmithry	honeycombed	none-sparing	confirmable
concernancy	condensable	power-driven	code-breaker	conformable
concordance	folding-door	Poseidonian	mole-cricket	conformably
concertante	goldenberry	molendinary	bone-breccia	confirmator
concurrence	wood-anemone	power-diving	home-crofter	confarreate
concurrency	zoodendrium	foreseeable	coleorrhiza	comfortless
concernedly	coadunation	forereading	pomegranate	confiscable
concert-goer	condonation	home-defence	voyeuristic	confiscator
concert-hall	coadunative	sovereignly	homeostatic	pop-fastener
concernment	roadholding	sovereignty	honey-sucker	confessedly
torch-staves	cold-forging	fore-recited	honeysuckle	pop-festival
vouchsafing	road-hoggish	forevermore	money-spider	toffishness
concessible	good-looking	home-keeping	sober-suited	confutement
torch-singer	good-morning	non-electric	money's-worth	confutation
conciseness	voodooistic	non-election	homesteader	confutative
concatenate	loud-mouthed	novelettish	potentially	forfoughten
touch-typist	loudspeaker	novelettist	rodenticide	confluently
wood-warbler	toad-spotted	non-elective	domesticise	congealable
coadjacency	powder-flask	comet-finder	domesticate	zoographist
wood-naphtha	ponderingly	foreignness	domesticity	congealment
bond-washing	wonderingly	rose-cheeked	home-stretch	long-waisted
word-painter	ponderosity	nonetheless	forestaller	zoografting
cordwainery	good-brother	forethinker	honest-to-God	hobgoblinry
cordialness	wood-fretter	foreshorten	momentarily	rough-coated
bondmanship	ponderation	somewhither	fomentation	congregated
cold-casting	ponderously	forethought	forestation	rouge-et-noir
good-natured	wonderfully	polemically	molestation	toggle-joint
wood-carving	condisciple	tonetically	momentously	congressman
conductance	wordishness	Lobeliaceae	molecularly	long-measure
road-scraper	nondescript	foresighted	dolefulness	rough-footed
conductible	goddess-ship	soteriology	hopefulness	long-visaged
conducement	rood-steeple	rose-diamond	honey-waggon	long-sighted
conductress	condottiere	foresignify	lonely-heart	lodge-keeper
coeducation	condottieri	Bohemianism	non-feasance	rough-legged
poodle-faker	woody-tongue	nose-nippers	conflagrant	long-clothes

coagulation
congelation
coagulatory
coagulative
long-playing
tough-minded
congenially
zoogonidium
longanimity
longanimous
congenerous
loggan-stone
morgenstern
longinquity
long-tongued
doggy-paddle
song-sparrow
Gongoristic
congestible
doggishness
hoggishness
rough-spoken
rough-string
forgettable
forget-me-not
doughtiness
forgetfully
songfulness
long-purples
congruously
forgiveness
lophobranch
Lochaber-axe
Nothofagust
nothing-gift
Cochin-China
nothingness
doch-an-doris
mother-naked
mother-water
rother-beast
mother-right
fothergilla
mother's-mark
mother-in-law
nonharmonic
mothercraft
botheration
sophistical
Bodhisattva
nominatival
comicalness
logicalness
co-rivalship
sociability
Politbureau
vociferance
vociferator
homiletical
policewoman
police-force
notice-board
police-court

domineering
police-state
police-judge
Moringaceae
doting-piece
towing-bitts
boxing-glove
poking-stick
poting-stick
coping-stone
toxiphobiac
toxiphagous
solid-hoofed
politically
Loliginidae
domiciliary
domiciliate
politicking
codicillary
volitionary
Socinianise
Socinianism
solidifying
sociologism
sociologist
docibleness
nonillionth
socialistic
solifluxion
goniometric
sociometric
notionalist
co-signatory
toxicomania
gonimoblast
monitorship
conirostral
soliloquise
sociopathic
Louis-Quinze
Rosicrucian
non-issuable
solipsistic
logistician
Louis-Treize
societarian
goniatitoid
moribundity
copiousness
noxiousness
moxibustion
pomiculture
conjectural
conjugality
conjugating
conjugation
conjugative
box-junction
conjunction
conjuncture
conjunctiva
conjunctive
conjurement

conjuration
cork-cambium
workmanlike
dock-warrant
workmanship
workability
book-account
cock-a-doodle
cook-general
cockleshell
cookie-shine
bookselling
bookkeeping
book-learned
rock-leather
nook-shotten
bookbinding
poikilocyte
cockaleekie
hook-climber
rock-climber
working-beam
cock-and-bull
mockingbird
mocking-bird
working-edge
working-face
booking-hall
working-over
rock-and-roll
rocking-tool
sockdolager
mock-modesty
sockdoliger
rock-forming
sockdologer
you-know-what
lock-forward
cock-sparrow
rock-sparrow
rock-breaker
cookery-book
rock-crystal
cock-crowing
bookishness
dockisation
rocket-range
pocket-piece
pocket-sized
rocket-plane
pocket-glass
pocket-knife
pocket-money
rocket-motor
pork-butcher
pock-pudding
monkey-wheel
monkey-shine
monkey-block
monkey-gland
monkey-board
monkey-bread
monkey-trick

monkey-grass
wool-carding
cool-tankard
colleaguing
world-beater
collaborate
collectanea
collectable
mollycoddle
collectedly
collectible
folliculose
folliculous
mould-candle
coal-scuttle
collocation
collocutory
boulder-clay
goal-tending
woollen-mill
soul-fearing
wool-bearing
mould-facing
toploftical
collegianer
hooliganism
colligation
colligative
coal-whipper
soul-killing
soul-sleeper
hoplologist
worldliness
worldly-wise
loblolly-bay
loblolly-boy
Coulommiers
noble-minded
coulometric
collimation
collenchyma
rolling-mill
pollen-grain
pollination
wool-combing
foul-mouthed
collapsable
collapsible
colliquable
colloquiums
forlorn-hope
roller-skate
coal-trimmer
forlornness
roller-towel
wool-growing
coalescence
dollishness
foolishness
godlessness
joylessness
toplessness
collusively

toilet-paper
toilet-table
toilet-glass
toilet-cloth
coalitional
coalitioner
toilet-cover
wool-stapler
soulfulness
follow-board
doomwatcher
cosmocratic
formicarium
formication
worm-gearing
cosmography
zoomagnetic
cosmogonist
cosmologist
formularise
formulation
commemorate
commendable
commendably
commensally
commendator
commentator
communicant
communicate
tormentedly
commonsense
common-shore
gormandiser
commonplace
communalise
communalism
communalist
commonality
commandment
communistic
commination
comminution
comminatory
comminative
cosmopolicy
cosmopolite
cormophytic
Kommersbuch
zoomorphism
non-marrying
cosmosphere
commiserate
solmisation
commissural
cosmetician
cosmeticise
cosmeticism
cosmothetic
cosmotheism
cosmetology
dogmatology
non-metallic
commotional

commutation	countersink	countryside	tobogganing	colour-blind
commutative	counter-time	corner-stone	tobogganist	loxodromics
round-arched	down-setting	down-draught	monothecous	sojournment
mountain-cat	town-meeting	countrywide	monophagous	Monotremata
fountain-pen	counter-turn	sound-shadow	monophthong	gonorrhoeal
mountain-dew	bounteously	connascence	homothallic	gonorrhoeic
mountaineer	counter-view	connascency	podophyllin	honour-bound
mountain-tea	countervail	hounds-berry	monothelism	honour-point
mountain-top	counter-vote	cognoscente	monothelete	doxographer
horn-madness	counter-work	cognoscenti	monothelite	horographer
moon-madness	corniferous	cognoscible	toxophilite	logographer
mountain-ash	somniferous	tonnishness	Podophyllum	monographer
mountainous	pornography	hound's-tooth	homophonous	nomographer
connubially	cornigerous	point-source	monochromat	nosographer
round-backed	round-headed	bonnet-laird	holothurian	topographer
coenobitism	down-the-line	bonnet-piece	homothermal	holographic
bonne-bouche	horny-handed	joint-tenant	notochordal	logographic
connectable	zoanthropic	cognateness	homothermic	monographic
connectedly	Eoanthropus	cognitional	Nototherium	nosographic
cornice-hook	zoantharian	bonnet-rouge	monochasial	tomographic
connectible	coincidence	connotation	monophysite	topographic
corniculate	coincidency	connotative	monochasium	monocrystal
somniculous	sounding-rod	cognitively	holophytism	colouration
cornucopian	counting-out	cognitivity	colorimeter	homoerotism
cornice-pole	moonlighter	co-insurance	colorimetry	rotogravure
townscaping	pointillism	cornhusking	monolingual	coconscious
cornice-rail	pointillist	somnivolent	honorifical	monopsonist
cornice-ring	connoisseur	hornswoggle	sodomitical	Zoroastrian
fornication	down-sitting	pound-weight	colonialism	Soroptimist
John-a-dreams	bountifully	town-dweller	colonialist	homopterous
point-device	pound-keeper	round-winged	notoriously	cohortative
point-devise	round-leaved	monocardian	corolliform	pococurante
countenance	poenologist	logodaedaly	monoclinous	mononuclear
mountenance	somnolently	monovalence	monoblepsis	coconut-milk
counter-buff	pointlessly	monovalency	holoblastic	coconut-palm
counter-bond	soundlessly	logomachist	homoblastic	monoculture
counter-blow	cognominate	sonofabitch	homoplastic	hop-o'-my-
counterbase	connumerate	monocarpous	motor-launch	thumb
counter-cast	pound-master	coronagraph	homoeopathy	toponymical
counterdraw	somnambular	monolatrous	gonococcoid	homozygosis
co-inherence	somnambulic	holocaustal	homoeomeric	monozygotic
counterfeit	morning-gift	holocaustic	homological	monomyarian
counterfoil	morning-gown	motor-bandit	horological	compearance
counter-fort	coenenchyma	cocoa-butter	monological	complacence
counter-glow	morning-land	horoscopist	nomological	complacency
co-inheritor	morning-room	motor-driven	nosological	zooplankton
counselling	morning-star	homogenesis	pomological	complainant
countermand	morning-tide	homogenetic	posological	complaining
countermine	down-to-earth	monogenesis	topological	complaisant
countermark	moon-goddess	monogenetic	monopoliser	compactedly
countermure	Johnsoniana	homogeneity	Mohorovicic	compactness
counter-move	loan-society	homogeneous	homoeomorph	torpedo-boat
pointedness	town-council	homogeniser	homomorphic	torpedo-boom
roundedness	point-of-sale	jocoserious	monomorphic	torpedinous
counter-pace	townspeople	colonelling	coronograph	torpedo-tube
counterplea	corn-cracker	Monodelphia	homoiousian	completable
counterpane	downtrodden	monodelphic	rodomontade	complexness
counter-plot	corner-teeth	holohedrism	monologuise	copple-crown
counterpart	countrified	cotoneaster	monologuist	compression
down-hearted	countryfied	colonelship	Monocotylae	compressure
counter-roll	country-folk	homocentric	ionospheric	low-pressure
counterseal	country-rock	go-to-meeting	homosporous	compressive
countersign	country-seat	locorestive	Zonotrichia	copple-stone

compaginate	composition	corruptness	Monseigneur	monstrosity
loup-the-dyke	compositive	bourtree-gun	worshipping	monstrously
complicated	corpuscular	voortrekker	consciously	consistence
comprimario	poppet-valve	morris-dance	constituent	consistency
dolphinaria	hospitaller	nourishable	conspicuity	loose-strife
comprisable	hospitalise	non-resident	conspicuous	moisturiser
soup-kitchen	hospitality	coprosterol	housekeeper	constuprate
dolphin-fish	competently	board-school	consultancy	housewifely
coupling-box	computerise	nourishment	consolidate	housewifery
Pompeian-red	competition	horrisonant	consilience	coast-waiter
compliantly	compotation	boorishness	mossbluiter	goose-winged
non-priority	computation	horrisonous	tonsillitic	contra-dance
top-priority	compotatory	corrosively	tonsillitis	nostradamic
compellable	competitive	doorstepper	dorsolumbar	contrabasso
compulsitor	computative	coarctation	loose-limbed	Nostradamus
compilement	pompousness	douroucouli	consolement	foot-lambert
corpulently	nonplussing	moor-buzzard	noiselessly	boot-catcher
pompelmoose	zoophytical	sorrowfully	horse-litter	Portlandian
pompelmouse	porphyritic	moustachial	consolatrix	contra-tenor
compilation	conquerable	Podsnappery	tonsilotomy	contrayerva
compilatory	torque-meter	house-arrest	consolation	contrariety
companiable	bouquetière	loose-bodied	consolatory	contrarious
compensator	tonquin-bean	possibilism	consummator	footballist
compendiums	gourmandise	possibilist	howsomdever	contractual
compendious	gourmandism	possibility	consimility	portmanteau
componental	corroborant	torsibility	noisomeness	post-captain
companioned	corroborate	house-broken	consumerism	contractile
compunction	correctable	consociated	consumerist	contraction
rouping-wife	correctible	consecrator	housemaster	contraption
Comptometer®	correctness	horse-collar	toastmaster	contracture
non-provided	Torridonian	mouse-colour	housemother	portraiture
soap-boiling	Corrodentia	consecution	consumption	portraitist
morphologic	comradeship	consecutive	consumptive	contractive
complotting	bourgeoisie	horse-couper	boysenberry	contrastive
copper-faced	courteously	horse-dealer	morsing-horn	portability
corporeally	journey-work	horse-doctor	nonsensical	contubernal
compurgator	courtesying	horse-drench	consentient	mortice-lock
copper-beech	corrigendum	considering	poison-gland	torticollis
non-partisan	porriginous	considerate	consonantal	monticulate
comptroller	corrugation	dog's-mercury	consonantly	monticolour
copperplate	four-wheeled	conspecific	poison-sumac	monticulous
corporality	four-wheeler	non-specific	poisonously	forthcoming
compartment	coordinance	constellate	consanguine	zootechnics
comportment	co-ordinance	tous-les-mois	comstockery	postscenium
coppersmith	tourbillion	zoospermium	comstockism	cost-account
copper-works	coercionist	consternate	hog-shoulder	tostication
corporately	courtierism	co-essential	torsiograph	tooth-drawer
co-operation	coprolaliac	worsted-work	houseparent	port-admiral
cooperation	courtliness	house-factor	consequence	mottle-faced
corporation	four-flusher	goose-flower	non-sequitur	bottle-party
corporatism	correlation	dorsiferous	conservancy	contretemps
corporatist	correlative	housefather	conservable	bootlegging
comparative	door-knocker	consignable	construable	bottle-chart
cooperative	mooring-mast	consignment	conservator	bottle-glass
co-operative	torrentuous	Moeso-gothic	constricted	northermost
corporative	four-pounder	moss-cheeper	constructer	southermost
compassable	coprophagan	householder	constrictor	loathedness
compass-card	coprophagic	constipated	constructor	northernise
torpescence	coprophilia	worshipable	horse-riding	northernism
compost-heap	corruptible	conspirator	horseradish	southernise
compossible	corruptibly	hot-spirited	constrained	southernism
foppishness	horripilant	low-spirited	bowstringed	bottle-nosed
rompishness	horripilate	worshipless	moss-trooper	bottle-gourd

bottle-green	contenement	populariser	polygenesis	speculative
soft-hearted	contentment	columbarium	polygenetic	epoch-making
bottle-brush	continental	conurbation	polytechnic	Apocynaceae
north-easter	continently	coruscation	polypeptide	apocopation
south-easter	contango-day	documentary	body-servant	spectre-crab
zootheistic	cottonmouth	lotus-eaters	rosy-cheeked	spectrogram
soft-centred	cotton-grass	loculicidal	polyphagous	spectrology
fortifiable	cotton-press	locutionary	Polyphemian	spectrality
pontificals	potting-shed	non-unionist	polyphonist	space-travel
pontificate	Montanistic	solutionist	polychromic	epidiascope
mouth-friend	fortunately	volubleness	polychroism	spud-bashing
mortiferous	fortune-tell	columniated	polyhistory	apodictical
soothfastly	rottenstone	columnarity	polyglottal	spade-guinea
vortiginous	foot-soldier	volumometer	polyglottic	spodomantic
soft-shelled	postponence	colubriform	polyonymous	spider-wheel
mouth-honour	controversy	roguishness	polyandrous	apodyterium
port-charges	montgolfier	voluntarily	polygonally	appeachment
contrivance	controlling	voluntarism	polygonatum	spread-eagle
containable	portionless	voluntarist	Cotylophora	splendidous
contrivable	controlment	voluntative	body-politic	spreadingly
doctrinally	poltroonery	nocuousness	rosy-bosomed	splendorous
doctrinaire	boot-topping	solvability	polymorphic	Ephemeridae
fortnightly	bogtrotting	convicinity	polyzoarial	splenetical
Tortricidae	tooth-picker	convocation	polyzoarium	ephemerides
bootlicking	tooth-powder	voivodeship	Polytrichum	splenectomy
post-village	co-eternally	louvre-board	polygraphic	speech-maker
containment	nocturnally	Convallaria	polycrystal	speechifier
contributor	footbreadth	convulsible	polycrotism	speech-crier
postillator	Fontarabian	pot-valorous	Polystichum	speechcraft
post-glacial	poltergeist	convolution	polystyrene	spherically
noctilucent	foster-child	Convolvulus	body-builder	appealingly
noctilucous	conterminal	convenience	apparatchik	appellation
footslogger	contorniate	conveniency	apparatuses	appellative
root-climber	lolteringly	conventicle	sphacelated	spleen-stone
southlander	potteringly	convincible	apparelling	spheroidise
loathliness	torturingly	non-violence	apparelment	speedometer
worthlessly	totteringly	conversance	speakership	spherometer
hostilities	root-pruning	conversancy	splay-footed	appeasement
postulation	posteriorly	conversable	splash-board	appeasingly
postulatory	mortar-board	conversably	splashproof	appertinent
contumacity	porterhouse	gouvernante	Aphaniptera	spherulitic
hot-tempered	porter-house	convergence	appallingly	spifflicate
bottom-glade	foster-nurse	convergency	Sphagnaceae	epigraphist
contemplant	contestable	convertible	sphagnology	apogamously
contemplate	mortise-lock	convertibly	aplanospore	epigenesist
contaminant	loathsomely	louver-board	sphaeridium	epigenetics
contaminate	doltishness	convivially	upcast-shaft	epigastrium
bottom-grass	goatishness	conveyancer	upvaluation	ophicalcite
continuance	loutishness	pot-walloner	specialiser	ipsilateral
continuable	sottishness	pot-walloper	spectatress	sphincteral
continually	hostess-ship	forwandered	spectacular	sphincteric
continuator	soothsaying	bow-windowed	ipecacuanha	spring-water
cotton-waste	footstooled	forwardness	epicheirema	spring-wheat
fortune-book	boat-builder	co-extension	specifiable	spring-clean
contingence	post-nuptial	co-extensive	specificate	upping-block
contingency	noctivagant	co-existence	specificity	springiness
contentedly	noctivagous	cony-catcher	spacefaring	springboard
continuedly	costiveness	polycarpous	space-heater	spring-house
boutonnière	northwardly	polydactyly	apocalyptic	upping-stock
contentious	southwardly	corybantism	speculatrix	upping-stone
cotton-plant	north-wester	polymastism	speculation	sprightless
contentless	south-wester	polyactinal	speculatory	uprightness
fortuneless	post-exilian	molybdenite	speculatist	ophidiarium

ophiologist
oppignerate
oppignorate
opeidoscope
epeirogenic
Ophiuroidea
split-second
split-screen
upliftingly
splinter-bar
spokeswoman
apple-blight
spellbinder
application
applicatory
applicative
spelaeology
epilogistic
apologetics
Apollinaris
spelling-bee
apollonicon
epileptical
appleringie
opalescence
spill-stream
apple-squire
apoliticism
apomictical
apomorphine
spumescence
spontaneity
spontaneous
spinach-beet
spang-cockle
up-and-coming
spinnerette
spaniel-like
sponge-cloth
open-hearted
spiniferous
spinigerous
open-circuit
spindle-legs
epanalepsis
spindle-side
spinelessly
spindle-tree
open-and-shut
opinionated
spin-bowling
span-counter
sponsorship
open-mouthed
epinephrine
spinescence
spinsterial
spinsterian
spendthrift
spinsterdom
spinsterish
spondulicks
aponeurosis

aponeurotic
spondylitis
Spinozistic
optometrist
appointment
upholsterer
apron-string
upholstress
opportunely
opportunism
opportunist
opportunity
epiplastral
epiplastron
epipetalous
epiphytical
apophyllite
epiphyllous
spermatheca
Spermaphyta
spermaphyte
spermatical
spermatozoa
opprobrious
approbation
approbatory
approbative
appreciable
appreciably
appreciator
Spirochaeta
spirochaete
spiraculate
sperm-candle
sporocystic
opera-dancer
aphrodisiac
Aphrodisian
upgradation
spur-gearing
spur-leather
sporogenous
sporogonium
sphragistic
appraisable
spermicidal
sparklingly
spirillosis
sparklessly
sporulation
apartmental
spirometric
sporangiole
sparingness
sparrow-bill
spermophile
Spermophyta
spermophyte
sparrow-hawk
appropriate
appropinque
sporophoric
sporophytic

opera-singer
operoseness
sportswoman
spiritually
spiritualty
spirit-level
spirituelle
operational
spirit-world
spiritistic
operatively
operculated
Spergularia
approvingly
approximate
apostatical
spasmatical
spessartite
spastically
epistilbite
apostleship
episcopally
aposiopesis
apostolical
epistolical
spasmodical
episepalous
apostrophic
apostrophus
epithalamia
epithalamic
spathaceous
ophthalmist
spatter-dock
spatterdash
apathetical
epithelioma
spottedness
apotheosise
spatter-work
epitrochoid
Apatosaurus
epithymetic
opium-smoker
appurtenant
spluttering
spawning-bed
sphygmogram
sphygmology
aquanautics
squandering
square-dance
aquarellist
square-built
squashiness
squalidness
aquaplaning
equableness
aquafortist
squarsonage
squattiness
aquaculture
squeakingly

squeakiness
squeamishly
equibalance
squirarchal
equilateral
equivalence
equivalency
Equisetales
Equisetinae
squirearchy
equilibrist
equilibrate
equilibrity
equilibrium
equidistant
equiangular
equivocally
equivocator
equipollent
equinoctial
squintingly
aquiculture
pre-adamical
pre-adamitic
preambulary
preambulate
bread-basket
cream-cheese
broadcasted
broadcaster
preaudience
grease-heels
grease-proof
ornamentist
triangulate
arraignment
arrangement
Argathelian
breathalyse
breathiness
preachiness
broach-spire
treacherous
treachetour
erratically
organically
organisable
Arcadianism
creatianism
creationism
creationist
irradiation
irradiative
friableness
treacliness
dreadlessly
dreamlessly
broad-minded
preadmonish
great-nephew
preannounce
dreadnaught
dreadnought

treasonable
treasonably
ergatomorph
ergatocracy
creatorship
preacquaint
groatsworth
organ-screen
breast-wheel
breastplate
breadthwise
breadthways
breadwinner
probabilism
probabilist
probability
trabeculate
treble-dated
problematic
crabbedness
Brobdingnag
tribologist
brabblement
tribalistic
tribulation
tribuneship
tribunitial
tribunitian
bribery-oath
erubescence
erubescency
Proboscidea
proboscides
proboscises
tribeswoman
arabisation
probational
probationer
tributarily
proclaimant
crocodilian
crocidolite
crocodilite
precedented
precedently
crackerjack
bracteolate
druckenness
trachearian
tracheotomy
procreation
procreative
truck-farmer
cruciferous
price-fixing
crucifixion
precognosce
crucigerous
crack-halter
practicable
practicably
practically
trichinella

Trachinidae	procaryotic	true-devoted	proficience	prohibitive
Trochilidae	procuration	free-hearted	proficiency	orthocentre
trichinised	triceratops	true-hearted	prefectship	Orchidaceae
fractionlet	procuratory	irretention	prefectural	orchidology
fractionary	brickshaped	pre-election	draft-dodger	orthodontia
fractionise	preciseness	irredentism	prefigurate	orthodontic
fractionate	tricksiness	irredentist	trafficator	orthodromic
trichinosed	precautious	irreceptive	trafficking	orchid-house
trichinosis	Procrustean	irretentive	trafficless	arch-heretic
trichinotic	fructuation	greengrocer	drift-mining	orthoepical
Brachiopoda	cracovienne	free-thinker	profaneness	archaeology
brachiation	track-walker	free-thought	profanation	orchiectomy
fractiously	brachyprism	pre-eminence	profanatory	orthography
Procellaria	brachyurous	irreligious	trifurcated	archegonial
prickle-back	credibility	arse-licking	preferrable	orthogenics
prickly-heat	predeceased	arterialise	professedly	archegonium
tracklement	predictable	irremission	profuseness	archaically
truculently	predicament	irremissive	prefatorial	archdiocese
prickliness	producement	arteriotomy	prefatorily	Brahminical
brucellosis	traducement	pre-existent	profiterole	arch-villain
prickly-pear	traducingly	green-keeper	prognathism	Archimedean
oracularity	bradycardia	orderliness	prognathous	archangelic
gracelessly	predecessor	irreflexion	pragmatical	archenteron
pricelessly	eradication	araeometric	pragmatiser	urchin-shows
tracelessly	predication	triennially	programming	prehensible
tracklessly	predicatory	free-and-easy	braggadocio	arrhenotoky
tricoloured	eradicative	irremovable	braggartism	arthropodal
oraculously	predicative	irremovably	tragi-comedy	arthrospore
bricklaying	bridgeboard	irrevocable	tragedienne	orthopraxis
track-laying	bridge-house	irrevocably	frigidarium	orthopedics
brickmaking	bridge-drive	praecordial	craggedness	orthopedist
Pre-Cambrian	trade-fallen	freeloading	progression	orthopteran
wreck-master	prodigalise	free-tongued	progressism	orthopaedic
fricandeaux	prodigality	greenockite	progressist	orthopteron
preconceive	dredging-box	Graeco-Roman	progressive	archipelago
arachnoidal	predilected	praetorship	fragmentary	orthophyric
arachnology	credulously	tree-worship	frugiferous	arch-traitor
precontract	bridemaiden	freebooting	fragileness	arch-prelate
precentress	predominant	freebootery	Tragelaphus	orthostatic
proconsular	predominate	irresoluble	grog-blossom	orthostichy
pre-conquest	tridominium	irresolubly	draggle-tail	orthoscopic
dracunculus	gradiometer	pre-emptible	dragon's-head	prehistoric
proctodaeal	urediospore	tree-creeper	originality	orchestrina
proctodaeum	bradypeptic	kriegsspiel	Origenistic	orchestrion
proctoscope	iridescence	orientalise	crag-and-tail	orchestrate
proctoscopy	prudishness	Orientalism	progenitrix	architraved
urochordate	tradeswoman	Orientalist	origination	orthotropic
trochometer	iridisation	orientality	progeniture	archdukedom
Procyonidae	gradational	priestcraft	originative	archduchess
trichomonad	traditional	arrestation	dragoon-bird	urticaceous
Trichomonas	gradationed	orientation	troglodytes	urticarious
proctorship	traditioner	irrecusable	troglodytic	trail-blazer
Trichoptera	predatorily	irrecusably	frigorifico	train-bearer
procephalic	irreparable	irrefutable	Gregarinida	argie-bargie
preceptress	irreparably	irrefutably	progestogen	artiodactyl
precipitant	trierarchal	irregularly	frightening	traineeship
precipitate	freemasonic	tree-surgeon	frighteners	Ornithogaea
precipitous	freemasonry	tree-surgery	frightfully	ornithology
procerebral	greenbottle	irreducible	frugivorous	Ornithopoda
procerebrum	irrelevance	irreducibly	Brahmanical	ornithopter
procurement	irrelevancy	irreduction	orthoborate	freight-shed
prochronism	irreverence	oriel-window	prohibition	ornithosaur
trichronous	true-seeming	drift-anchor	prohibitory	Arminianism

prairie-wolf
artillerist
fruitlessly
pre-ignition
traitorhood
traitorship
arbitrageur
arbitrament
arbitrement
arbitrarily
arbitratrix
arbitration
brainsickly
brains-trust
brain-teaser
articulated
orbiculares
orbicularis
articulable
orbicularly
articulator
projectment
prejudicial
prejudicant
prejudicate
prejudgment
araliaceous
Grallatores
argle-bargle
drill-barrow
prelibation
prolocutrix
prolocution
prolificacy
prolificity
proliferate
proliferous
prolegomena
drill-harrow
brilliantly
trellis-work
troll-my-dame
preliminary
drill-master
prolongable
proleptical
drill-plough
artlessness
prelusorily
prelusively
prolateness
proletarian
proletariat
prelateship
grammatical
grammalogue
promycelium
eremacausis
premedicate
bromidrosis
premeditate
trumpet-call
trumpet-fish

grummet-hole
trammelling
premiership
trumpet-tree
trumpet-tone
trumpet-wood
primigenial
bramah-press
crémaillère
promulgator
bramble-bush
Primulaceae
tremblement
grumblingly
tremblingly
tremulously
tromometric
priming-iron
criminology
criminalise
criminalist
criminality
prominently
crimination
premonition
criminatory
premonitory
criminative
premonitive
priming-wire
crambo-clink
dromophobia
gramophonic
primiparity
primiparous
trimorphism
trimorphous
dram-drinker
primariness
fremescence
promiseless
promisingly
trimestrial
promiscuity
promiscuous
dramaticism
trimetrical
primatology
crematorial
dramaturgic
prematurely
prematurity
crematorium
primateship
promptitude
primitively
primitivism
primitivist
brimfulness
premovement
premaxillae
transandine
transalpine

transaction
transceiver
transcriber
transcalent
arenicolous
transductor
orange-tawny
frondescent
drunkenness
iron-hearted
orange-grass
grandeeship
orange-stick
craniectomy
transeptate
transfigure
transfer-day
frankfurter
transferred
transferrer
transformed
transformer
uriniferous
transfusion
transfusive
grandfather
transfixion
uranography
Grenzgänger
crinigerous
wrong-headed
trench-fever
branch-pilot
transhumant
trenchantly
crunchiness
Frenchiness
truncheoned
truncheoner
branchiopod
transhipper
trencher-cap
trencher-man
prong-horned
trencher-fed
frantically
principally
transit-duty
wringing-wet
transilient
fringilline
transiently
franticness
grandiosely
grandiosity
crenellated
translucent
granulocyte
translocate
granuliform
translunary
franklinite
granularity

frontlessly
wranglesome
granolithic
trendle-tail
trindle-tail
trundle-tail
granulation
translation
translatory
granulative
wrong-minded
prenominate
transmarine
grandmaster
transmittal
grandmother
transmitted
transmitter
pruning-bill
crane-necked
pruning-hook
grandnephew
francomania
cranioscopy
craniometer
craniometry
ironmongery
francophobe
francophile
francophone
iron-founder
craniognomy
iron-foundry
orang-outang
uranoplasty
transpadane
transpierce
frank-pledge
transponder
transportal
transported
transporter
grandparent
transparent
uriniparous
transposing
granophyric
front-ranker
front-runner
wring-staves
trunksleeve
print-seller
transsonics
dronishness
Uranoscopus
brine-shrimp
trend-setter
transsexual
granitiform
Trinitarian
franc-tireur
graniteware
transuranic

pronouncing
branfulness
brankursine
transversal
granivorous
transvestic
brandy-glass
arboraceous
Areopagitic
crookbacked
proof-charge
preoccupied
preoccupant
preoccupate
arborescent
Eriodendron
crookedness
erroneously
arrow-headed
creophagous
cryotherapy
Eriophorous
cryophysics
cryobiology
bryological
oreological
arrow-poison
proof-puller
proof-reader
armoured-car
armour-plate
oreographic
proof-spirit
cryosurgery
areosystile
trepidation
trepidatory
drap-de-berry
prophethood
prophetical
prophetship
prophesying
propagation
propagative
crapehanger
crepehanger
cryptically
graphically
dripping-pan
crappit-head
crappit-heid
triphibious
graphicness
proprietrix
Trappistine
proprietary
prepollence
prepollency
propylamine
crapulosity
propylitise
trypanocide
treponemata

Trypanosoma	prosecution	aristocracy	protonotary	triumvirate
trypanosome	cross-cousin	prosopopeia	crithomancy	trivialness
prepunctual	brissel-cock	preservable	prothoraces	provocation
trepanation	trusteeship	brass-rubber	prothoracic	provocatory
propinquity	crescentade	Droseraceae	proteolysis	provocateur
Cryptogamia	prospecting	dress-reform	proteolytic	provocative
cryptogamic	prospection	pre-stressed	troth-plight	grave-digger
trophotaxis	trust-estate	frustration	prêt-à-porter	providently
Cryptomeria	prospective	prostration	protopathic	prevailment
drop-forging	crestfallen	cross-stitch	protophytic	travail-pain
tryptophane	presagement	dress-shield	fraternally	travail-pang
graptolitic	cross-garnet	cross-tining	erythrocyte	provokement
trophoblast	crash-helmet	brush-turkey	crateriform	provokingly
trophoplasm	preschooler	brusqueness	proterogyny	gravel-blind
graphologic	grasshopper	prose-writer	fraterniser	prevalently
trophozoite	prosthetics	trustworthy	Craterellus	trivalvular
cryptograph	prosthetist	presbyteral	prothrombin	frivolously
propforward	drastically	prothalamia	proterandry	gravimetric
prop-forward	prosaically	proteaceous	frater-house	preventable
tropophytic	prescindent	prothallial	preterition	driving-band
proper-false	trysting-day	prothalloid	trituration	graving-dock
tripersonal	crisping-pin	prothallium	preteritive	prevenience
preparation	tristichous	protractile	preterhuman	provenience
preparatory	prestigious	protraction	proterozoic	driving-gear
preparative	presciently	protractive	brutishness	preventible
property-man	Erastianism	froth-blower	grotesquely	traversable
troposphere	Priscianist	protuberant	grotesquery	prevaricate
preposition	prosaicness	protuberate	Brotstudien	previsional
proposition	Prussianise	protococcal	Prototheria	provisional
prepositive	Prussianism	Protococcus	truth-teller	provisorily
crepuscular	prestissimo	protocolled	protrudable	provostship
propitiable	prescission	protocolise	protrusible	privateness
propitiator	prostitutor	protocolist	fretfulness	gravitation
tripetalous	cross-leaved	criticality	arquebusade	gravitative
crepitation	trisyllabic	protectoral	arquebusier	privatively
crepitative	trisyllable	protectress	trout-basket	crown-antler
drop-curtain	preselector	criticaster	ground-water	crown-lawyer
crop-dusting	prosiliency	erythematic	groundsheet	drawing-room
tripe-visag'd	bristle-fern	brotherhood	ground-elder	frowardness
prophylaxis	cross-legged	brotherlike	ground-sloth	frowstiness
triphyllous	trisulphine	tritheistic	trous-de-loup	proximately
trapezoidal	bristliness	protagonist	ground-robin	proximation
triquetrous	dress-length	tritagonist	groundspeed	proxy-wedded
pruriginous	bristle-tail	erotogenous	ground-state	prayer-wheel
prorogation	proselytise	protogynous	groundburst	prayerfully
prerogative	proselytism	froth-hopper	trouser-clip	brazen-faced
crustaceous	bristle-worm	crotcheteer	trouser-suit	prize-winner
prismatical	trestle-work	brattishing	trough-fault	ashamedness
prostatitis	dressmaking	fratricidal	trough-shell	established
crystalloid	presumingly	trithionate	wrought-iron	establisher
crystalline	irksomeness	prattlement	drouthiness	Israelitish
crystallise	presumption	brittleness	grouchiness	assay-master
crystallite	presumptive	brittle-star	draughtsman	assafoetida
crossbearer	presentable	gratulation	troublesome	assassinate
crossbanded	presentably	gratulatory	trouble-town	psychagogue
crossbarred	prosenchyma	erotomaniac	troublously	psychedelia
trust-buster	presentient	protomartyr	trouble-word	psychedelic
frostbitten	presentment	writing-book	proud-minded	psychically
press-button	presentness	writing-case	trout-stream	psychiatric
crossbowman	prison-house	writing-desk	irruptively	psychopathy
dress-circle	presanctify	pretendedly	fraudulence	psychometer
grass-cutter	gressorious	pretentious	fraudulency	psychodelic
prosecutrix	Bristol-milk	protandrous	arduousness	psychogenic

psychometry	Asclepiadic	atramentous	steel-headed	stalactited
psychologic	Psilophyton	steadfastly	Atherinidae	stalactitic
psychonomic	uselessness	strangulate	streakiness	stiltedness
psychomotor	Psilotaceae	strangeness	steeple-bush	stilbestrol
psychodrama	isomagnetic	straightway	steeple-fair	styliferous
psychograph	esemplastic	straight-jet	steeplejack	stylography
usucaptible	psammophile	straight-arm	streamlined	stalagmitic
isochronise	psammophyte	straightish	streamingly	still-hunter
isochronism	isomorphism	straight-cut	streaminess	stalling-ken
isochronous	isomorphous	straight-out	athermanous	stellionate
Esperantist	isometrical	attaché-case	etheromania	stultiloquy
assemblance	asynartetic	steam-hammer	steel-plated	stellifying
assemblyman	osmotically	strap-hanger	attemptable	stultifying
osteoclasis	astonishing	stramineous	atheistical	stall-master
osteodermal	association	atrabilious	streetwards	stylopodium
osteodermic	associative	stratifying	streetlight	stilt-plover
isoelectric	astoundment	steam-jacket	attestation	stall-reader
osteography	asportation	steam-launch	attestative	stylishness
aspergillum	assortative	attaintment	attentively	stylisation
aspergillus	ascomycetes	stratopause	strenuosity	utilisation
osteogenous	isapostolic	strabometer	attenuation	athleticism
aspergation	ostreaceous	stratocracy	strenuously	stilettoing
ascetically	ostracoderm	steatopygia	otherwhiles	utilitarian
osteologist	ostrich-farm	steam-packet	steelworker	stilt-walker
osteoplasty	ostrich-like	steam-plough	stifle-joint	stomach-ache
osteopathic	Ostrogothic	steam-roller	stuffing-box	stomachical
osteophytic	estramazone	strap-shaped	stiff-necked	stomachless
ascensional	astringency	steam-shovel	stiff-rumped	stomach-pump
assessorial	estranghelo	strait-laced	staff-system	etymologise
aspersorium	astronomise	strait-lacer	stigmatical	etymologist
ostensively	ostreophage	Atlanticism	stage-driver	stumblingly
essentially	ostreophagy	Atlanticist	stage-effect	stimulating
asbestiform	estrepement	Straduarius	stage-fright	stimulation
assentingly	astraphobia	steam-vessel	stage-flower	stimulative
assentation	escritorial	Atharvaveda	stagflation	staminodium
ostentation	isorhythmic	steady-going	stage-manage	stump-orator
assertively	tsesarevich	stubble-rake	staging-area	stamp-office
isogeotherm	psittacosis	stockbroker	staging-base	stump-speech
escheatable	isotonicity	stock-feeder	steganogram	atomisation
asthmatical	esotericism	stock-farmer	staging-post	stomatology
escheatment	Osmundaceae	stock-holder	stage-player	Stomatopoda
Escherichia	assuredness	stockinette	stage-struck	standardise
eschatology	assuagement	stick-insect	Stegosaurus	stone-bruise
aspheterise	astuciously	stock-jobber	Stahlhelmer	stone-colour
aspheterism	assubjugate	stickleader	Stahlianism	stone-curlew
asphyxiated	pseudoscope	stickleback	itchy-palmed	stenochrome
asphyxiator	pseudomonad	itacolumite	stoicalness	stenochromy
espièglerie	pseudomonas	stock-market	Steinberger	stone-cutter
assimilable	pseudopodia	stactometer	stair-carpet	stintedness
ascititious	pseudomorph	stichometry	strike-fault	stuntedness
oscillogram	pseudograph	ptochocracy	strike-bound	stone-falcon
oscillating	pseudocubic	stockpiling	stringy-bark	ethnography
oscillation	Assyriology	stock-saddle	string-piece	stenography
oscillatory	ptyalagogic	stocktaking	stringently	stoneground
oscillative	ptyalagogue	studiedness	stringiness	stone-hammer
astigmatism	steam-boiler	stadtholder	string-board	stanchioned
Ossianesque	straw-colour	studentship	stainlessly	standing-bed
assignation	straw-cutter	steerage-way	stair-turret	standing-cup
Istiophorus	steam-digger	stretchless	Utricularia	stencilling
assiduously	steam-driven	etherealise	stridulator	ethnologist
isolability	strategetic	ethereality	attitudinal	stone-marten
isolecithal	steam-engine	steepe-downe	stalactical	stentmaster
psilomelane	strategical	strengthful	stalactital	stand-offish

ctenophoran	storm-petrel	subaerially	muscularity	lukewarmish
stone-plover	star-crossed	subarration	musculation	superabound
stand-patter	storm-stayed	Judaisation	musculature	rubefaction
itinerantly	sternsheets	eubacterium	subcultural	tumefaction
stone's-throw	storm-signal	Judas-window	vulcanicity	queer-basher
stenotypist	Pterosauria	eucalyptole	vulcanology	supercharge
stonewaller	star-studded	outbreeding	subcontract	supercherie
strongyloid	story-teller	bubble-shell	subcontrary	tuberculoma
strongpoint	attritional	tumble-drier	buccinatory	tuberculise
atrociously	storm-troops	rubble-stone	succinctory	tuberculose
attorneydom	storm-tossed	bumble-puppy	outcrossing	tuberculate
attorneyism	iteratively	bulbiferous	susceptance	tuberculous
stroboscope	sternutator	humbuggable	susceptible	quiescently
ethological	stirrup-bonc	lumbaginous	susceptibly	superdainty
atmospheric	stirrup-dram	lumbricalis	turcopolier	juvenescent
stool-pigeon	stirrup-iron	outbuilding	nuncupation	queene-apple
step-dancing	stirrup-pump	tumbling-box	nuncupatory	superficial
utopianiser	storm-window	Lumbricidae	nuncupative	superficies
stephanotis	stasimorphy	Turbellaria	subcortical	rule-of-thumb
stopping-out	stitchcraft	quibblingly	pulchritude	superfamily
stipulation	stateliness	turbulently	quacksalver	superfusion
stipulatory	state-monger	nubbing-cove	quicksilver	superfatted
stipendlary	stethoscope	husbandlike	successless	superfetate
stipendiate	stethoscopy	husbandland	subcategory	superfluity
stupendious	station-hand	husbandless	muscatorium	superfluous
stepbrother	state-prison	turbine-pump	suscitation	superheater
staphylitis	statesmanly	rubbing-post	punctulated	Rüdesheimer
storm-beaten	statistical	dumbfounder	succourable	fume-chamber
attribution	stateswoman	turbo-ram-jet	punctualist	eugenically
attributive	statute-book	rubber-cored	succourless	numerically
stern-chaser	statutorily	rubber-stamp	punctuality	superinduce
attractable	Etruscology	mulberry-fig	punctuation	superimpose
Styracaceae	staunchness	rubbish-heap	punctuative	superioress
storm-centre	Struthiones	rumbustical	muscovy-duck	superiority
yttro-cerite	staurolitic	rumbustious	quick-witted	superintend
store-cattle	struttingly	subbasement	quadraphony	superjacent
Pterichthys	attuitional	surbasement	quadratical	museologist
pterodactyl	attuitively	purchasable	subdiaconal	superlunary
pteridology	stave-church	cunctatious	subdeaconry	queenliness
store-farmer	Stevengraph	bunch-backed	auld-farrant	pure-blooded
yttriferous	stewardship	hunchbacked	fund-raising	cupellation
starch-paper	ithyphallic	Mulciberian	hurdle-racer	superlative
starchiness	ithyphallus	quick-change	hundredfold	queez-maddam
starch-grain	funambulist	succedaneum	subduedness	museum-piece
star-thistle	funambulate	butcher-bird	quadrennium	supermarket
storekeeper	sugar-coated	Muschelkalk	muddy-headed	queen-mother
startlingly	autarchical	luncheon-bar	quadrillion	supernormal
stereobatic	subaudition	muscle-bound	quadriennia	supernatant
stereotaxia	suraddition	quicken-tree	subdelirium	gubernation
stereotaxic	out-and-outer	quick-freeze	fundamental	supernature
stereotaxis	Fumariaceae	quick-frozen	subdominant	autecologic
stereoscope	subaxillary	quick-firing	pudding-pipe	subeconomic
stereoscopy	mutationist	furciferous	pudding-time	superoctave
stereometer	audaciously	dulcifluous	quadrophony	superpraise
stereometry	curableness	Munchhausen	murderously	queen-regent
stereophony	durableness	Punchinello	outdistance	supersubtle
stereosonic	mutableness	subclinical	subdistrict	supersedeas
sternotribe	tunableness	subcritical	quadrupedal	supersedere
stereograph	eudaemonics	punctilious	subdivision	supersedure
stereoptics	eudaemonism	functionary	subdivisive	queen-stitch
stereotyped	eudaemonist	functionate	tuberaceous	superscribe
stereotyper	auxanometer	auscultator	rubefacient	superstruct
stereotypic	curatorship	succulently	tumefacient	superscript

eupepticity	Lutheranism	subjugation	bullfronted	quinquereme
supertanker	authorcraft	subjunctive	full-fraught	quinsy-berry
quaestorial	eucharistic	buck-washing	publishable	automatical
humectation	eurhythmics	bulk-carrier	bullishness	subordinary
duteousness	pushfulness	buck-passing	sunlessness	subordinate
hugeousness	nudicaudate	huckleberry	sublittoral	autogenesis
tunefulness	punicaceous	musk-thistle	pullet-sperm	autocephaly
bureaucracy	subitaneous	muskellunge	bullet-proof	europeanise
supervolute	puritanical	sucking-fish	qualitative	Europeanism
supervision	subimagines	tucking-mill	dual-purpose	Europeanist
supervisory	nudicaulous	luckengowan	curlew-berry	Eurocentric
suffragette	cubicalness	luckenbooth	subluxation	autophagous
tufftaffeta	musicalness	ducking-pond	hurley-house	autochthons
tufftaffety	subincision	cuckoo-clock	pulmobranch	autochthony
surf-bathing	subindicate	duskishness	tummy-button	autochanger
ruffian-like	ruridecanal	luskishness	culmiferous	autophanous
sufficience	luminescent	bucket-wheel	gummiferous	autokinesis
sufficiency	businessman	hucksterage	submultiple	autokinetic
surface-mail	pumice-stone	musket-proof	nummulation	tumorigenic
suffocating	rudimentary	hucksteress	augmentable	autoplastic
suffocation	fusing-point	gull-catcher	humming-bird	Yugoslavian
suffocative	music-holder	bull-mastiff	fulminating	subornation
buff-leather	juridically	bull-baiting	culmination	autonomical
buffalo-bird	municipally	gullibility	fulmination	eurodollars
buffalo-robe	purificator	full-acorned	fulminatory	automorphic
suffumigate	munificence	duplication	submergence	out-of-pocket
muffin-fight	munitioneer	publication	bur-marigold	autographic
turfing-iron	pugilistial	duplicature	submarginal	autotrophic
muffin-worry	humiliating	duplicitous	submergible	autoerotism
luffer-board	humiliation	duplicative	submersible	autogravure
buffer-state	humiliatory	quill-driver	murmuringly	out-of-the-way
huffishness	humiliative	bull-terrier	summariness	culpability
burglarious	judiciously	full-hearted	summer-house	suspectable
jungle-green	audiologist	guelder-rose	murmuration	suspectedly
judgment-day	burial-place	qualifiable	murmurously	suspectless
cudgel-proof	audibleness	nullifidian	submissible	suppressant
burgomaster	pupillarity	qualifiedly	submissness	suppression
rumgumption	tubiflorous	curly-greens	summit-level	suppressive
surgeon-fish	curialistic	curly-headed	summational	purpresture
surgeonship	fusillation	hurly-hacket	surmounting	puppy-headed
subglobular	music-master	gully-hunter	guinea-grass	supplicavit
fulguration	numismatics	pull-through	guaniferous	surprisedly
turgescence	audiometric	full-charged	burn-the-wind	suppliantly
turgescency	numismatist	quilting-bee	turnpike-man	bumptiously
suggestible	Aurignacian	bullfighter	quintillion	jumping-bean
purgatorial	tulipomania	dull-sighted	cunnilingus	jumping-deer
purgatorian	auditorship	full-fledged	running-gear	suspenseful
gurgitation	Hudibrastic	full-blooded	running-hand	jumping-hare
purgatively	ludicrously	guilelessly	running-knot	suspensible
humgruffian	music-seller	guiltlessly	cunningness	jumping-jack
bushmanship	audiotyping	pullulation	quantometer	subpanation
Dukhobortsy	audio-typist	sublimeness	quandong-nut	supportance
rush-bearing	auriculated	sublimation	curnaptious	supportable
bushwhacker	auricularly	burling-iron	Turneresque	supportably
push-bicycle	pudibundity	curling-pond	vulneration	purportedly
euchologion	rubicundity	nucleolated	burnt-sienna	purportless
bushel-woman	curiousness	full-mouthed	furnishings	supportless
euphemistic	dubiousness	dual-control	burnishment	supportment
authentical	dutifulness	nulliparity	furnishment	out-paramour
such-and-such	furiousness	nulliparous	nunnishness	supportress
fushionless	audio-visual	fuller's-herb	quincuncial	suppuration
cushion-tire	duniewassal	dull-brained	quinquennia	suspiration
cushion-tyre	subjectship	full-frontal	ruinousness	suppurative

surpassable	currentness	tufttaffety	hunting-whip	Augustinian
purpose-like	currant-wine	subtraction	subtropical	luxulyanite
purposeless	cuir-bouilli	subtractive	hunt-counter	surveillant
dumpishness	cuir-bouilly	quotability	multiplexer	curvilineal
lumpishness	curry-powder	suitability	gutta-percha	curvilinear
mumpishness	putrescence	justiciable	multiparity	subvertical
supposition	Buprestidae	mustachioed	multiparous	pulverulent
suppository	putrescible	multicolour	multipotent	culverineer
suppositive	currishness	buttock-mail	putty-powder	quaveringly
puppet-valve	hurry-scurry	subtacksman	multiplying	quiveringly
sulphurator	hurry-skurry	justiceship	butter-paper	pulveration
sulphureous	turret-clock	multicuspid	Kulturkampf	subvitreous
sulphur-root	nutritional	rustication	muster-party	outwardness
sumptuosity	lucratively	furtherance	multiracial	butyraceous
sumptuously	nutritively	butt-welding	subterminal	eurythermal
sulphurwort	surrounding	hurtleberry	quaternion'd	eurythermic
puppy-walker	burrowstown	turtle-shell	butterflies	Eurypharynx
outquarters	quarry-water	furthermore	gutter-blood	buoyantness
surrebuttal	outstanding	furthermost	cultureless	Runyonesque
surrebutter	substandard	furthersome	gutturalise	jury-process
turriculate	substantial	subtreasury	butter-cloth	Eurypterida
supracostal	substantive	turtle-stone	butter-plate	eurypteroid
lubrication	subscapular	justifiable	hunter's-moon	quizzically
rubrication	purse-bearer	justifiably	butter-knife	evidentiary
lubricative	bursiculate	multifidous	mutteringly	evagination
puerperally	tussock-moth	guttiferous	guttersnipe	avoirdupois
quarter-back	tussac-grass	tutti-frutti	austereness	ovuliferous
quarter-bred	subspecific	fustigation	butter-woman	evolutional
quarter-deck	nun's-veiling	hunt-the-gowk	Kulturkreis	evil-starred
quarter-evil	pussyfooter	quitch-grass	butter-print	evangelical
quarter-jack	Burschenism	sustainable	surtarbrand	evangeliary
quarrelling	mud-slinging	rumti-iddity	surturbrand	evening-star
quarrellous	questioning	sustainedly	mustard-tree	eventration
guardedness	questionary	curtain-fire	mutteration	evanescence
hurriedness	questionist	punt-fishing	subterhuman	evanishment
quarter-note	substituted	curtailment	rupturewort	eventualise
quarrel-pane	substituent	sustainment	multispiral	eventuality
quarter-road	mussel-scalp	curtail-step	multisonant	evaporation
quarter-rail	mussel-scaup	multijugate	multistorey	evaporative
quarter-seal	mussel-shell	multijugous	multiserial	oviparously
quarrelsome	Mussulwoman	multilobate	hurtfulness	oviposition
quarter-tone	fulsomeness	multilineal	lustfulness	overbalance
quarter-wind	subsumption	multilinear	tub-thumping	overhandled
putrefiable	subsumptive	ductileness	tuft-hunting	overcareful
cupriferous	subsensible	subtileness	multivalent	overgarment
subregional	Russophobia	curtal-friar	furtiveness	overpayment
subrogation	subsequence	fustilarian	cultivation	overearnest
surrogation	subscribing	fustilirian	quoteworthy	overhastily
quarrington	Burseraceae	pustulation	subumbrella	everlasting
guerrillero	substractor	dusty-miller	suburbanise	overcasting
querulously	subservient	custom-house	suburbanism	svarabhakti
supremacism	nurserymaid	customarily	suburbanite	overachieve
supremacist	cursoriness	custom-built	suburbanity	overreached
nutrimental	substrative	sustentator	furunculous	overdevelop
supremeness	subsistence	hunting-crop	Subungulata	overtedious
suprematism	purse-seiner	hunting-horn	subungulate	overweening
suprematist	purse-taking	multinomial	Cupuliferae	overbearing
cupro-nickel	guesstimate	hunting-mass	luxuriantly	overmeasure
currant-cake	nurse-tender	multanimous	luxulianite	overleather
surrenderee	mussitation	hunting-seat	luxuriation	overweather
surrenderer	suasiveness	hunting-song	luxuriously	overthrower
surrenderor	pussywillow	hunting-tide	lucubration	overpitched
currant-loaf	tufttaffeta	multangular	susurration	overbidding

overviolent	twanglingly	expectantly	expostulate	lycanthrope
overpicture	swingletree	expectingly	extortioner	lycanthropy
overblanket	swingometer	exceptional	exhortation	symbolology
overflowing	swan-hopping	expectorant	exportation	symbolistic
over-anxiety	swing-plough	expectorate	exhortatory	eyebrowless
over-anxious	twin-brother	expectation	exhortative	hyacinthine
overindulge	swinishness	expectative	exorability	synchoresis
overcorrect	swine's-cress	extenuating	extractable	syncopation
overcoating	twopenn'orth	extenuation	extractible	myocarditis
overforward	sword-bearer	extenuatory	extrication	synchromesh
over-precise	sword-dollar	extenuative	extradition	synchronise
overproduce	swarthiness	oxy-fluoride	extra-floral	synchronism
overtrading	swordplayer	exaggerator	exorbitance	synchronous
overfreedom	sword-shaped	oxygenation	exorbitancy	synchrotron
overgrainer	kwashiorkor	oxy-hydrogen	exercisable	eye-catching
overfreight	awesomeness	expiscation	excremental	syndyasmian
overbrimmed	two-storeyed	exsiccation	excrementum	syndicalism
overwrestle	awe-stricken	expiscatory	expromissor	syndicalist
overdraught	twitter-bone	exsiccative	extrinsical	syndication
overfraught	switchblade	ex-directory	expropriate	syndesmosis
overwrought	switch-plant	extirpation	extrapolate	syndesmotic
overdrowsed	switchboard	extirpatory	axerophthol	cyperaceous
overgrazing	twitch-grass	extirpative	excrescence	gyre-carline
overstretch	swivel-chair	explication	excrescency	hyperactive
overstuffed	swivel-block	explicatory	expressible	hyperacusis
averruncate	awkwardness	explicative	expressness	hyperboloid
overrunning	exsanguined	Oxalidaceae	extravagant	hyperbolise
overfulness	expatiation	exaltedness	extravagate	hyperbolism
overburthen	expatiatory	explainable	extravasate	hyperborean
everywhence	expatiative	exploitable	oxyrhynchus	hypercharge
evasiveness	exhaustible	exclamation	exasperator	hypercritic
eviternally	exhaustless	exclamatory	exoskeletal	synecdochic
sweater-girl	expansional	exclamative	exoskeleton	hyperdactyl
sweet-cicely	exhaust-pipe	explanation	existential	hyperdorian
owner-driver	expansively	explanatory	exstipulate	hyperemesis
tweezer-case	expansivity	explanative	exotericism	hyperemetic
sweet-potato	exuberantly	exploration	expurgation	myoelectric
sweepstakes	oxy-chloride	exploratory	expurgatory	type-setting
sweet-willow	oxy-compound	explorative	expugnation	hypergamous
sweep-washer	executrices	exclusively	exculpation	synergistic
swift-footed	executrixes	explosively	exculpatory	hyperinosis
twofoldness	executioner	exclusivism	exquisitely	hyperinotic
swift-winged	executorial	exclusivist	excursively	hyperlydian
swagger-coat	executively	exemplified	cycadaceous	hypermarket
swagger-cane	exceedingly	exemplarily	gynaecology	cybernetics
swag-bellied	expenditure	exemplarity	gynaecomast	type-founder
twelve-penny	expeditious	examination	pyrargyrite	type-foundry
twalpennies	experienced	exanthemata	dynamically	synecologic
twelvemonth	expediently	axonometric	pyramidally	Hymenoptera
swell-headed	exteriorise	exanimation	pyramidical	hyperphagia
swallow-dive	exteriority	exoneration	sybaritical	hyperplasia
swallow-hole	excellently	exonerative	hypallactic	type-species
swallow-tail	exterminate	axiomatical	tyrannicide	typewritten
swallow-wort	externalise	exposedness	tyrannosaur	typewriting
awelessness	externalism	exponential	tyrannously	hypersthene
Twelfth-cake	externalist	expositress	dynamometer	hypersonics
Twelfth-tide	externality	excoriation	dynamometry	hypertrophy
swim-bladder	extemporary	exfoliation	synagogical	dysfunction
swing-bridge	extemporise	exfoliative	dynamograph	myographist
swingeingly	extensional	excommunion	synanthesis	syngnathous
swing-handle	excessively	axiological	synanthetic	mythography
swingle-hand	expensively	extorsively	Byzantinism	Pythagorean
dwindlement	extensively	excorticate	Byzantinist	Pythagorism

mythologian	hypotension	hypocycloid	cysticercus
mythologise	hypotensive	hypotyposis	Cyatheaceae
mythologist	Myxophyceae	lymphangial	dyotheletic
syphilology	hypothecary	Nymphalidae	synthetical
mythomaniac	hypothecate	hyoplastral	synthesiser
hyphenation	mycophagist	hyoplastron	dyothelitic
lychnoscope	hylophagous	sympodially	hyetography
mythopoetic	xylophagous	tympaniform	system-maker
mythopoeist	xylophilous	nymphomania	systematics
dysharmonic	Zygophyllum	symptomatic	systematise
xyridaceous	sycophantic	nympholepsy	systematism
cynicalness	sycophantry	symphonious	systematist
typicalness	hypothenuse	dyspeptical	system-built
cylindrical	xylophonist	symposiarch	nyctinastic
lysigenetic	cymophanous	dyspathetic	nyctophobia
myringotomy	hypothermal	sympathetic	oyster-patty
syringotomy	hypothermia	sympathiser	oyster-wench
pyritohedra	hypothyroid	sympetalous	hysterogeny
syllabicity	pyrophorous	hydrobromic	oyster-shell
syllabarium	hypothesise	Hydrocharis	hysteroidal
cyclicality	hypothetise	hydrocyanic	oyster-field
pyelography	Byronically	hydrochoric	oyster-plant
dyslogistic	synodically	hydrocarbon	oyster-knife
syllogistic	zymosimeter	hydrography	oyster-woman
cyclohexane	synonimical	hydrogenate	oyster-tongs
hyalomelane	hypolimnion	hydrogenous	mystery-play
cyclopaedia	tyroglyphid	hydra-headed	hysteresial
cyclopaedic	Tyroglyphus	hydrologist	mystery-ship
sylleptical	hypoglossal	hydrolysate	hysterotomy
cycloserine	hypoblastic	hydromedusa	mystery-tour
cyclothymia	pyroclastic	Cypro-Minoan	nyctitropic
cyclothymic	zygopleural	hydromantic	sylvestrian
myrmecology	pyrognostic	hydrometric	azocompound
myrmidonian	mycodomatia	hygrometric	ozoniferous
symmetrical	cytological	hydrometeor	ozonosphere
Hydnocarpus	Lycopodinae	cypripedium	ozonisation
hymnography	mycological	Hydrophidae	Azotobacter
Pycnogonida	typological	hydrophilic	
pycnogonoid	zymological	hydroponics	
hypnogenous	hypocorisma	hydrophobia	
hymnologist	hylomorphic	hydrophobic	
hypnopaedia	zygomorphic	hydropathic	
hypnopompic	gyrocompass	hydrophytic	
gymnorhinal	hylozoistic	hygrophytic	
gymnasiarch	mycorrhizal	hydrophyton	
gymnastical	typographer	dyer's-rocket	
hypnotistic	xylographer	hydrargyral	
zygocardiac	kymographic	hydrargyrum	
hylopathism	mycotrophic	hydrostatic	
hylopathist	typographia	hydrosphere	
pyroballogy	typographic	cypress-knee	
myxomatosis	xylographic	hydrosomata	
xylocarpous	pyrogravure	hygroscopic	
hypogastric	gynostemium	hydrotactic	
synoecology	hypostrophe	hydrothorax	
synoeciosis	synoptistic	hydrotropic	
cytogenesis	hypostasise	hypsography	
hylogenesis	gyrostatics	hypsometric	
pyrogenetic	hypostatise	hypsophobia	
pyrotechnic	synonymatic	syssarcosis	
zymotechnic	Myxomycetes	hyoscyamine	
hypoaeolian	Zygomycetes	syntactical	
Tyronensian	synonymicon	syntectical	

taramasalata
salamandrine
salamandrian
salamandroid
paralanguage
palatability
paramagnetic
caravansarai
caravanserai
paratactical
zalambdodont
parascending
balance-sheet
balance-wheel
Papaveraceae
macaberesque
parametrical
parade-ground
malapertness
paracentesis
cataphractic
paraphrastic
catachrestic
cataphyllary
paraphimosis
Panathenaean
parachronism
cataphoresis
cataphysical
Zarathustric
paradisaical
Tamaricaceae
Samaritanism
canalisation
capacitation
faradisation
nasalisation
Paradiseidae
laxativeness
paradise-fish
paramilitary
paradisiacal
parasiticide
paradigmatic
vacationless
paralipomena
parasitology
calamitously
catadioptric
cabalistical
canaliculate
catallactics
parallelwise
paraglossate
Balaam-basket
Balaamitical
paraenetical
paragnathism
paragnathous
labanotation
satanophobia
parapophyses
parapophysis

palaeolithic
paradoxidian
catamountain
palaeobotany
paraboloidal
malacologist
paradoxology
paramorphism
para-compound
palaeography
catacoustics
Malacostraca
man-about-town
paradoxurine
parasphenoid
paragraphist
parapsychism
panaesthesia
paraesthesia
palaestrical
Marattiaceae
wag-at-the-wall
paranthelion
galactagogue
galactometer
catastrophic
hamartiology
hamarthritis
panarthritis
paraquadrate
paracyanogen
parasyntheta
pay-as-you-earn
rabble-rouser
marble-cutter
marbled-white
iambographer
cabbage-white
carbohydrate
day-blindness
gambling-hell
lamb's-lettuce
carbon-dating
rabbinically
carbonaceous
rambunctious
namby-pambies
barber-monger
rabbit-warren
wag-by-the-wall
rabbeting-saw
rabbit-sucker
harbour-light
bacchanalian
Panchatantra
calceamentum
saccharinity
saccharoidal
Marcobrunner
fasciculated
watch-crystal
hatchet-faced
pancreatitis

ratchet-wheel
fancifulness
watchfulness
sanctifiedly
cancellarial
cancellarian
cancellation
tax-collector
baccalaurean
parchmentise
sarcomatosis
Vacciniaceae
gas-condenser
malcontented
falcon-gentle
falcon-gentil
marconigraph
carcinogenic
Vaccinoideae
lanceolately
raccoon-berry
watch-officer
Marcionitism
sarcoplasmic
sarcophagous
saucepan-fish
panchromatic
Lancasterian
narcissistic
narcotically
narcotherapy
march-treason
marcatissimo
lasciviously
land-yachting
sand-yachting
hard-favoured
card-carrying
hand's-breadth
laudableness
mandibulated
paedobaptism
paedobaptist
Laodiceanism
paddock-stool
paedodontics
saddlebacked
saddle-hackle
candle-waster
handkerchief
saddle-shaped
saddle-pillar
candle-holder
pandaemonium
saddle-spring
hard-featured
paedogenesis
paedogenetic
paedological
sand-blasting
paedomorphic
landing-craft
sardonically

pandanaceous
landing-field
maidenliness
Tardenoisian
cardinalship
cardinal-bird
landing-place
landing-stage
landing-speed
landing-strip
handsomeness
cardiologist
cardiography
paedophiliac
land-grabbing
banderillero
bandersnatch
gander-mooner
landgraviate
gas-discharge
land-lubberly
land-surveyor
vaudevillian
vaudevillist
vase-painting
water-boatman
saleableness
water-buffalo
water-bailiff
water-blister
water-ballast
water-bellows
water-biscuit
water-battery
Valenciennes
capercaillie
capercailzie
water-culture
water-cooling
water-carrier
water-drinker
eavesdropper
kaleidophone
calendar-line
haberdashery
kaleidoscope
sacerdotally
water-diviner
tape-recorder
baselessness
carelessness
hatelessness
namelessness
tamelessness
wave-offering
water-flowers
water-flowing
water-gilding
sage-thrasher
water-hemlock
café-chantant
catechetical
laterisation

maderisation
racemisation
watering-call
waveringness
watering-hole
waterishness
materialness
Sabellianism
water-measure
water-milfoil
gamesmanship
salesmanship
watermanship
paper-marbler
make-and-break
tabernacular
gamesomeness
malevolently
categorially
water-opossum
ravenousness
mademoiselle
warehouseman
cane-bottomed
water-parting
water-parsnip
base-spirited
bare-breached
safe-breaking
water-reactor
safe-cracking
bate-breeding
name-dropping
water-spaniel
paper-stainer
water-soldier
habeas-corpus
water-strider
majesticness
majestically
parenthesise
gazetteerish
palette-knife
water-turbine
parenterally
valetudinary
safeguarding
water-wagtail
lake-dwelling
paper-washing
caterwauling
half-seas-over
half-timbered
half-mourning
malformation
languageless
tangibleness
raggle-taggle
baggage-train
large-hearted
gang-there-out
sanguinarily
sanguineness

sanguiferous
languishment
sanguinolent
sanguivorous
mangel-wurzel
tangentially
Pan-Germanism
badger-legged
gangsterland
daughterling
machicolated
pachycarpous
pachydacious
cathodograph
Pachydermata
pachydermous
cash-register
tachygraphic
tachygrapher
pathogenesis
pathogenetic
machairodont
Panhellenism
panhellenium
panhellenion
Panhellenist
pathological
bachelorship
bachelor-girl
bachelorhood
mathematical
mathematised
cachinnation
cachinnatory
washing-board
cash-and-carry
bathing-dress
washing-house
machine-ruler
washingtonia
fashion-plate
fashiousness
lath-splitter
bathypelagic
Machtpolitik
father-lasher
oath-breaking
fatherliness
fathers-in-law
father-figure
gathering-cry
pathetically
cathetometer
cashew-apples
lachrymation
lachrymatory
lachrymosely
habitability
navigability
navigational
capitalistic
caricaturist
variableness

radiobiology
radio-compass
sapindaceous
palindromist
lapidescence
radio-element
cabinetmaker
manifestable
manifestible
manifestness
satisfaction
satisfactory
satisfyingly
habit-forming
hagiographic
radiographic
hagiographer
radiographer
taxing-master
palingenesia
palingenesis
baking-powder
babingtonite
Manicheanism
facilitative
catilinarian
facilitation
gasification
habilitation
pacification
palification
panification
ramification
ratification
salification
sanitisation
vaticination
pacificatory
laticiferous
Papilionidae
pavilion-roof
vaginicoline
caliginosity
radio-isotope
lapidicolous
radicicolous
radicivorous
vaginicolous
basidiospore
capillaceous
hagiological
radiological
carillonneur
Mariolatrous
talismanical
camiknickers
radionuclide
patience-dock
manifoldness
calico-flower
varicoloured
latirostrate
radiophonics

radiesthesia
magistrature
kakistocracy
papistically
radiotherapy
calisthenics
radio-thorium
variationist
canister-shot
paniculately
manipulative
capitulation
manipulation
capitulatory
manipulatory
fatigue-dress
latitudinous
fatigue-party
parisyllabic
backwardness
talkee-talkee
walkie-talkie
yankee-doodle
taskmistress
Jack-a-lantern
Jack-o'-lantern
Jack-in-office
larking-glass
Jack-in-the-box
Parkinsonism
parking-place
packing-press
talking point
packing-paper
walking-staff
packing-sheet
walking-stick
walking-straw
sack-doudling
backwoodsman
backboneless
backwounding
backbreaking
back-tracking
cankeredness
marker-beacon
market-garden
basket-making
racket-tailed
racketeering
market-square
backstarting
racket-ground
basket-stitch
backswordman
malleability
wall-painting
Tagliacotian
mail-carriage
hallucinogen
hallucinosis
fallaciously
nail-scissors

wallydraigle
palladianism
balladmonger
nail-head-spar
gaol-delivery
jail-delivery
ball-bearings
fault-finding
calligrapher
galligaskins
caulking-iron
gall-sickness
gallinaceous
hallan-shaker
ballanwrasse
marlinespike
Darlingtonia
wallcovering
sailboarding
mallophagous
rail-splitter
harlequinade
cable-railway
cable's-length
Naples-yellow
eagle-sighted
callisthenic
ballet-dancer
ballet-master
cable-tramway
balletically
balletomania
table-turning
Carlovingian
tallow-candle
sallow-kitten
gallows-maker
farm-labourer
barmy-brained
mammee-sapota
harmlessness
Macmillanite
mammalogical
salmon-ladder
salmon-tackle
harmonically
harmonichord
warmongering
harmonograph
salmon-fisher
harmonometer
salmon-colour
harmoniously
harmoniphone
harmoniumist
haemophiliac
hammer-headed
haemorrhagic
haematoblast
haematolysis
haematemesis
haematoxylin
haematoxylon

maintainable
damnableness
wainscotting
vaunt-courier
saunteringly
gainlessness
painlessness
magnifically
magnificence
faint-hearted
launching-pad
faintishness
Magnoliaceae
carnal-minded
magniloquent
vainglorious
cannon-fodder
balneologist
Cain-coloured
rainbow-trout
Wagnerianism
mannerliness
laundry-woman
harness-maker
earnest-money
earnest-penny
magnetically
magnetograph
malnutrition
magnetometer
magnetisable
nasolacrymal
paroccipital
gamopetalous
gamosepalous
calorescence
barometrical
gasometrical
manometrical
major-general
parochialise
parochialism
parochiality
gamophyllous
cacophonical
cacophonious
canonisation
valorisation
vaporisation
vasodilatory
saponifiable
nanoplankton
paroemiology
saloon-keeper
saloon-pistol
paronomastic
baron-officer
lagomorphous
canorousness
vaporousness
labour-saving
favouredness
Jacob's-ladder

raconteuring
manoeuvrable
man-of-war's-man
panpharmacon
palpableness
lampadedromy
campodeiform
lampadomancy
Cappagh-brown
happy-go-lucky
camp-shedding
camp-sheeting
sapphire-wing
carpenter-ant
carpenter-bee
Campanularia
happenstance
lamprophyric
camp-follower
carpophagous
camp-preacher
pamperedness
lappered-milk
way-passenger
carpetbagger
lamp-standard
carpet-knight
carpetmonger
tappet-motion
Jacquard-loom
pasque-flower
vanquishable
vanquishment
matriarchate
patriarchate
patriarchism
carriage-paid
carriageable
marriageable
laureateship
marriage-ring
marriage-bone
carriage-free
hair's-breadth
macrobiotics
iatrochemist
matriclinous
matroclinous
patriclinous
patroclinous
matriculator
capriciously
macrocephaly
macrodactyly
barrier-cream
hair-restorer
Saurognathae
carragheenin
fairnitickle
sacrilegious
patrilineage
sacramentary
saprophagous

macropterous
hair-splitter
Patripassian
saprophytism
hairdressing
sabre-rattler
barristerial
patristicism
sarrusophone
garret-master
barratrously
parrot-wrasse
narrow-minded
marrow-squash
carriwitchet
fairnytickle
manslaughter
law-stationer
passableness
passibleness
waistcoateer
waistcoating
laisser-aller
laissez-aller
tapsieteerie
laisser-faire
laissez-faire
panspermatic
parsley-piert
tax-sheltered
passage-money
false-hearted
marsh-harrier
Marseillaise
Marsileaceae
salsolaceous
tapsalteerie
tassel-gentle
ear-splitting
passemeasure
passy-measure
haussmannise
parsimonious
passionately
passion-fruit
mansion-house
passion-music
nauseousness
sarsaparilla
passe-partout
mass-produced
basso-relievo
basso-rilievo
massaranduba
masseranduba
causationism
causationist
sansculottic
pansexualism
pansexualist
cantharidine
cantharidian
carte-blanche

Cantabrigian	pantophagist	galvanoscope	absoluteness
earth-created	pantophagous	malversation	absquatulate
particularly	cartophilist	salver-shaped	ubiquitarian
pantechnicon	Dantophilist	canvas-length	ubiquitously
participable	lactoprotein	harvest-feast	aboriginally
party-capital	earthquaking	harvest-field	abortiveness
participator	masturbation	harvest-goose	abbreviation
fastidiously	bactericidal	harvest-louse	abbreviatory
Zantedeschia	halter-necked	harvest-mouse	abbreviature
rattle-headed	Gastarbeiter	salvationism	abstractedly
battlemented	matter-of-fact	salvationist	abstractness
cattle-lifter	masterliness	calycanthemy	obstreperate
cattle-plague	mastersinger	baby-batterer	obstreperous
saltpetreman	lantern-jawed	lady's-cushion	abstemiously
battleground	pattern-maker	lady's-fingers	obstetrician
tactlessness	battering-ram	laryngectomy	abstruseness
maltreatment	bacteriology	laryngophony	obdurateness
faithfulness	bacteriostat	laryngospasm	obmutescence
tastefulness	masterstroke	laryngoscope	obtuse-angled
wastefulness	master-at-arms	laryngoscopy	obnubilation
cartographic	bastard-title	dasyphyllous	scramblingly
pantographic	garter-stitch	Calyciflorae	scratch-brush
cartographer	pattern-wheel	labyrinthine	scratchiness
pantographer	master-switch	labyrinthian	scratchingly
vantage-point	Cartesianism	karyokinesis	scraper-board
Mastigophora	pantisocracy	Maryolatrous	scraggedness
faith-healing	fantasticate	baby-snatcher	occasionally
farthingland	fantasticism	calycoideous	oceanologist
farthingless	partisanship	palynologist	oceanography
cantillation	haptotropism	papyrologist	octastichous
cantillatory	partitionist	many-coloured	octastrophic
dactylically	factitiously	lady's-slipper	scabbardless
santalaceous	saltatorious	lady's-thistle	scabbard-fish
battological	gastrulation	razzle-dazzle	scabrousness
cartological	party-verdict	katzenjammer	academically
tautological	part-exchange	oblanceolate	acre's-breadth
tantalum-lamp	paludamentum	ebracteolate	accelerative
pantaloonery	salutariness	obscurantism	acceleration
dactyliology	maturational	obscurantist	acceleratory
dactyloscopy	salutational	obedientiary	sclerenchyma
bantam-weight	naturalistic	abbey-counter	screen-writer
pantomimical	salutatorian	obsessionist	sclerodermia
bastinadoing	salutatorily	object-lesson	sclerodermic
cantankerous	manufactural	absent-minded	sclerophylly
East-Indiaman	manufacturer	object-finder	screw-steamer
carton-pierre	valuableness	obreptitious	accentuation
fast-and-loose	ranunculuses	obsequiously	accentuality
canting-wheel	papuliferous	Observantine	eclectically
waiting-woman	salutiferous	obligatorily	scientifical
factionalism	paludicolous	obliterative	eccentricity
factionalist	vacuum-packed	obliteration	Schizaeaceae
xanthomatous	calumniation	obliviscence	scribblement
xanthochroia	calumniatory	obligingness	scribblingly
xanthochroic	calumniously	absinthiated	acciaccatura
xanthochroid	naturopathic	ebullioscope	schindylesis
gastrocnemii	fabulousness	ebullioscopy	schindyletic
gastrosopher	salubriously	abolitionary	accidentally
gastronomist	salvifically	abolitionism	occidentally
gastropodous	marvellously	abolitionist	schiller-spar
captiousness	Salviniaceae	obsolescence	schismatical
cautiousness	carving-knife	obsoleteness	action-taking
factiousness	galvanometer	obcompressed	schizocarpic
xanthopterin	galvanometry	absorptivity	Echinocactus

echinodermal
schizogenous
schizophrene
schizothymia
schizothymic
schizophytic
echinococcus
schizogonous
schizopodous
schizomycete
scrimshander
scripturally
script-writer
scullery-maid
ecologically
sculling-boat
scalping-tuft
achlamydeous
scallop-shell
Scolopacidae
scolopaceous
ecclesiastic
Ecclesiastes
ecclesiology
sculpturally
scampishness
ecumenically
scandalously
iconoclastic
ichnographic
scenographic
acanthaceous
Scandinavian
Schneiderian
scanning-disc
scintillator
scintigraphy
iconomachist
economically
econometrics
econometrist
iconophilism
iconophilist
scene-painter
scene-shifter
ichneumon-fly
ectoparasite
scholastical
accouchement
accordionist
octogenarian
octopetalous
octosepalous
scrophularia
acrophonetic
scrobiculate
school-taught
schoolmaster
schorlaceous
schoolfellow
school-leaver
school-divine
schoolboyish

school-doctor
school-friend
accommodable
accommodator
acroamatical
echo-sounding
accomplished
accomplisher
accompanyist
octostichous
accoutrement
acronychally
octosyllabic
octosyllable
scapegallows
scapulimancy
scoptophilia
scopophiliac
Scorpaenidae
Scarabaeidae
acaridomatia
acarodomatia
scarificator
scornfulness
scare-heading
Scorpionidea
scorpion-fish
scurrilously
ochroleucous
scoring-board
scissiparity
scissor-blade
scissor-tooth
scatter-brain
scatteringly
scattermouch
Scottishness
scutellation
acetaldehyde
scatological
scitamineous
scatophagous
ecstatically
ichthyocolla
ichthyolitic
ichthyolatry
ichthyophagy
ichthyopsida
accurateness
occupational
accusatorial
scoundreldom
scoundrelism
acquiescence
scouring-rush
scrutinising
scrutinously
acquaintance
Sciuropterus
acoustically
accumulative
accumulation
scrupulosity

scrupulously
scavengering
ectypography
Edwardianism
idealisation
ideationally
advantageous
odd-come-short
edaciousness
educationist
adscititious
adverbialise
adhesiveness
adder's-tongue
adventitious
adjectivally
advisability
additionally
administrate
administrant
adminiculate
addictedness
addle-brained
adulteration
adulterously
edulcorative
edulcoration
idolatrously
identifiable
odontomatous
odontophoral
odontophoran
odontologist
odontography
idiothermous
idiorhythmic
admonishment
idiosyncrasy
adaptability
adaptiveness
adequateness
adorableness
editorialise
adjunctively
adjudication
metagalactic
separateness
metalanguage
reparability
separability
defamatorily
hexadactylic
perambulator
pedal-clavier
melancholiac
recalcitrate
recalcitrant
heraldically
regardlessly
sexagenarian
decalescence
recalescence
metaleptical

decaffeinate
Penang-lawyer
metaphrastic
seraphically
detachedness
metachronism
metathoracic
metaphorical
metaphysical
metathetical
decapitalise
recapitalise
decapitation
delamination
deracination
desalination
gelatination
hepatisation
legalisation
penalisation
tetanisation
velarisation
negativeness
relativeness
petaliferous
metasilicate
rehabilitate
relativitist
relativistic
relationless
relationship
relationally
hepaticology
recapitulate
behaviourism
behaviourist
seraskierate
metallically
metallophone
metallurgist
remainder-man
keraunograph
retainership
metagnathous
demagnetiser
megalomaniac
metasomatism
teratomatous
megalosaurus
keratogenous
melanochroic
senatorially
keratoplasty
hepatologist
nematologist
teratologist
Nematomorpha
metamorphism
metamorphist
metamorphose
ceramography
pedal-pushers
repatriation

metapsychics	Neo-Christian	gem-engraving	level-pegging
telaesthesia	Neoceratodus	telergically	redemptioner
telaesthetic	percussively	revengefully	redemptorist
pedantocracy	percussional	hebephreniac	peremptorily
pedantically	percutaneous	genethliacal	meteorically
semantically	reoccupation	genethliacon	meretricious
departmental	bench-warrant	hereditament	meteorograph
Telautograph®	peace-warrant	veterinarian	meteorologic
tenant-at-will	peach-yellows	hereditarily	teleprompter
denaturalise	readableness	remedilessly	peregrinator
peradventure	vendibleness	beneficently	telegraphese
metal-working	hendecagonal	feverishness	telegraphist
decasyllabic	mendaciously	repetitively	terebratulae
decasyllable	needlessness	beneficially	cerebrotonia
legacy-hunter	reed-pheasant	repetitional	cerebrotonic
bedazzlement	headshrinker	televisional	reversionary
Rembrandtish	bend-sinister	terebinthine	secessionism
Rembrandtism	headmistress	Gesellschaft	retensionist
sea-buckthorn	readmittance	genealogical	secessionist
kerb-merchant	hebdomadally	teleological	teleostomous
feeble-minded	hebdomadarer	levelling-rod	teleosaurian
pebble-powder	ready-moneyed	rebelliously	Nepenthaceae
heeby-jeebies	dead-and-alive	redeployment	decentralise
verbenaceous	wedding-cards	determinable	fenestration
reabsorption	wedding-dress	determinably	receptaculum
kerb-crawling	wedding-dower	determinedly	receptacular
sea-butterfly	geodynamical	telesmatical	dejectedness
deuch-an-doris	wedding-march	perenniality	dementedness
teachability	weeding-tongs	Gemeinschaft	nevertheless
neoclassical	herd-instinct	hereinbefore	resettlement
merchantable	dendrologist	Hemerocallis	seventy-eight
merchantlike	dendrologous	heterotactic	neverthemore
peace-breaker	readaptation	heterodactyl	relentlessly
peach-blossom	feldspathoid	heteroecious	defectionist
beachcombing	tender-hefted	heterocercal	receptionist
peacock-stone	Neo-Darwinism	heteromerous	cement-copper
leucocytosis	Neo-Darwinian	benevolently	detectophone
peccadilloes	Neo-Darwinist	heterosexual	teleutospore
geochemistry	geodetically	heterophylly	cementitious
mercifulness	headquarters	heterothally	lese-humanity
peacefulness	readjustment	heterochrony	venepuncture
henceforward	vegetatively	renegotiable	hebetudinous
deactivation	revelational	ceremonially	reservedness
reactivation	generatrices	heteroplasia	receiving-set
reactiveness	benefactress	heteroblasty	heresy-hunter
peace-keeping	heterauxesis	heteroplasty	self-balanced
tercel-jerkin	remembrancer	heteroclitic	self-catering
tercel-gentle	rememberable	Heterosomata	pen-feathered
pencil-sketch	rememberably	selenologist	self-absorbed
fence-mending	reverberator	heterogonous	perfectation
sexcentenary	beseechingly	heterologous	perfectively
tercentenary	telescopical	heteronomous	self-activity
mercantilism	repercussive	heteromorphy	self-schooled
mercantilist	repercussion	Heterocontae	self-occupied
descensional	degenerately	heterokontan	self-educated
geocentrical	degenerative	heterotrophy	self-adhesive
peace-officer	regenerative	selenography	self-identity
leucoplastid	degenerating	generousness	perfidiously
perceptivity	deceleration	heterostyled	self-deceived
perceptional	degeneration	heteroousian	self-deceiver
mercurialise	regeneration	heterocyclic	self-devotion
mercurialism	regeneratory	heterozygote	self-begotten
mercurialist	never-failing	heterozygous	self-depraved

self-betrayal	hedge-mustard	desiderative	seminiferous
selflessness	Zeuglodontia	mediaevalism	retiringness
self-destruct	geognostical	deliberation	reciting-note
self-delusion	hedge-parsley	desideration	definitively
self-effacing	ledger-tackle	Semi-Pelagian	verisimility
self-affected	beggarliness	mediaevalist	verisimilous
self-thinking	hedge-sparrow	delitescence	semi-diameter
self-directed	weight-lifter	revivescence	religionless
self-director	tergiversate	revivescency	meridionally
self-lighting	hedge-warbler	perinephrium	felicitously
self-disliked	sedge-warbler	semipellucid	periwig-pated
self-violence	methodically	pedicellaria	aecidiospore
self-distrust	dephlegmator	semideponent	demi-distance
self-cleaning	hephthemimer	perineuritis	semiglobular
self-pleasing	technicality	penitentiary	aetiological
perfoliation	technicolour	residentiary	legislatress
self-elective	aethrioscope	residentship	heliolatrous
self-electing	Neohellenism	delivery-pipe	semi-imbecile
self-election	nephological	delivery-tube	devil-may-care
self-glorious	nephelometer	semi-official	perionychium
self-flattery	nephelometry	heliographic	resignedness
self-employed	mechanically	heliographer	Helianthemum
self-interest	dethronement	feeing-market	semi-annually
self-endeared	nephrologist	heliogravure	semicomatose
self-indeared	technologist	teeing-ground	demi-mondaine
self-anointed	technocratic	periphrastic	lepidomelane
newfangledly	nephroptosis	benightening	lexicologist
self-analysis	Netherlandic	perichaetial	hemimorphite
self-involved	Netherlander	perichaetium	hemimorphism
self-coloured	Mechitharist	zenith-sector	perimorphous
self-consumed	hemiparasite	delightfully	lexicography
self-portrait	semiparasite	Hemichordata	meritocratic
self-contempt	celibatarian	decipherable	desirousness
self-focusing	pericarditis	peripherical	perilousness
self-applause	delicateness	decipherment	hemispheroid
self-approval	semiwater-gas	legitimately	heliophilous
performative	delicatessen	debilitative	perispomenon
self-creation	medicamental	delimitative	delinquently
self-ordained	derivatively	demilitarise	semi-Arianism
self-gracious	meditatively	debilitation	reciprocally
self-produced	hesitatingly	delimitation	semi-precious
perfervidity	definability	felicitation	reciprocator
Jeffersonian	desirability	legitimation	semitropical
self-critical	heritability	revisitation	periostracum
new-fashioned	revivability	Semitisation	semi-attached
Newfoundland	dedicational	verification	registration
self-murderer	derivational	semifinalist	revictualled
self-judgment	revivalistic	veridicality	heliotherapy
self-luminous	dedicatorial	verificatory	belittlement
self-evidence	pelican's-foot	devil-in-a-bush	peristrephic
self-exciting	reliableness	semicircular	resistlessly
self-exertion	bewitchingly	reminiscence	redintegrate
self-existent	seriocomical	resipiscence	geriatrician
self-hypnosis	heliocentric	reviviscence	redistribute
geographical	heliochromic	resipiscency	meristematic
sergeantship	rediscoverer	reviviscency	peristomatic
sergeant-fish	periodically	medicine-ball	deviationism
neighbouring	periodontics	decisiveness	heliotropism
hedge-creeper	periodontist	definiteness	deviationist
vengefulness	bewilderment	derisiveness	mediatorship
seigniorship	deliberately	feminineness	peristeronic
seignioralty	semi-detached	decitizenise	reticulately
pergameneous	deliberative	resiniferous	geniculation

pediculation	belletristic	tennis-racket	recommitment
reticulation	deflationary	Jenny-spinner	refoundation
vesiculation	reflationary	tennis-player	denouncement
venipuncture	deflationist	Deinotherium	renouncement
meticulously	replevisable	reinstalment	resoundingly
deliquescent	yellow-backed	penny-wedding	reconnoitrer
demi-culverin	yellow-hammer	penny-whistle	recognisable
devil-worship	yellow-rattle	resonance-box	recognisably
semicylinder	fellow-member	desolateness	recognisance
pericynthion	yellow-headed	decoratively	decoloration
serjeantship	yellow-legged	denotatively	levorotatory
benjamin-tree	yellow-necked	derogatively	metoposcopic
fecklessness	yellow-ringed	pejoratively	demonologist
recklessness	yellow-billed	demoralising	mesomorphous
Pecksniffian	yellow-yowley	memorability	xeromorphous
keeking-glass	yellow-horned	removability	decorousness
neck-moulding	yellow-footed	revocability	venomousness
weak-spirited	yellow-rumped	derogatorily	decompressor
weal-balanced	seal-cylinder	debonairness	decomposable
well-balanced	Velloziaceae	aeronautical	leiotrichous
well-mannered	permeability	redoublement	resourceless
well-favoured	vermiculated	deforciation	melodramatic
pellucidness	Fehmgerichte	reconcilable	cerographist
neglectfully	Vehmgerichte	reconcilably	democratical
reflectively	geomagnetism	heroicalness	deconsecrate
neglectingly	gemmological	heroi-comical	reconsecrate
reflectingly	permanganate	second-to-none	remorsefully
reflectivity	fermentative	recordership	reconstitute
deflectional	fermentation	second-strike	demonstrable
Della-Cruscan	segmentation	mesocephalic	demonstrably
oeils-de-boeuf	Germanically	xerodermatic	remonstrance
well-educated	vermin-killer	aeroneurosis	demonstrator
re-alteration	Germanophile	recomforture	remonstrator
well-becoming	Germanophobe	decongestant	repossession
well-tempered	hermeneutics	decongestive	reconsituent
mellifluence	hermeneutist	decongestion	gerontocracy
deflagration	re-embodiment	henothelstic	besottedness
geologically	reimposition	mesothelioma	gerontophile
ncologically	permissively	mesothoracic	depopulation
belligerence	hermetically	denominative	resoluteness
belligerency	geometrician	denomination	revolutional
well-timbered	permittivity	deposition	resolutioner
well-directed	dermatophyte	detoxication	revolutioner
cell-division	deambulatory	memorisation	resolvedness
well-disposed	re-engagement	peroxidation	reconversion
well-pleasing	pernoctation	demoniacally	reconveyance
well-plighted	vernacularly	velocipedean	aerodynamics
belly-landing	perniciously	aerosiderite	genotypicity
mealy-mouthed	re-annexation	velocipedian	temptability
replantation	reinvestment	velocipedist	Neoplatonism
declensional	seine-fishing	becomingness	neoplatonist
declinometer	geanticlinal	demolishment	bespectacled
well-informed	reinvigorate	depoliticise	respectfully
selling-price	re-enlistment	devotionally	respectively
Wellingtonia	fennel-flower	negotiatress	resplendence
reallocation	neonomianism	bed-of-justice	resplendency
bell-bottomed	weaning-brash	recollective	perplexingly
well-breathed	reunionistic	recollection	reappearance
hellgrammite	deontologist	aeroplankton	helplessness
tellurometer	reinspection	ceroplastics	hemp-agrimony
well-dressing	mean-spirited	deformedness	deoppilative
well-grounded	Gesneriaceae	aeroembolism	deoppilation
seclusionist	Keynesianism	recommission	temptingness

despairingly
despoliation
geopolitical
weeping-birch
weeping-cross
responseless
respondentia
serpent-eater
despondently
leaping-house
responsively
serpentinely
despondingly
serpentinise
serpentining
serpentiform
serpentinous
responsorial
serpent-stone
jet-propelled
pepper-caster
pepper-castor
leap-frogging
temperalitie
temporaneous
jeopardously
leopard's-bane
sea-porcupine
despisedness
perpetualism
perpetration
perpetuation
perpetualist
perpetuality
despotocracy
despotically
despitefully
herpetofauna
herpetologic
sempiternity
geophysicist
desquamative
desquamation
desquamatory
sesquitertia
perquisition
sesquialtera
neuroanatomy
reproachable
reproachless
decreasingly
recreational
bearableness
terribleness
heartbreaker
jerry-builder
neurobiology
heartburning
depreciative
ferricyanide
ferrocyanide
depreciation
depreciatory

tetracycline
retractively
detractingly
refractivity
retractility
tetrachordal
refractorily
tetrachotomy
get-rich-quick
retrocessive
retrocession
reproducible
reproductive
reproduction
tetradactyly
petrodollars
tetradynamia
recrudescent
retrievement
fearlessness
peerlessness
pearl-essence
febrifacient
petrifactive
petrifaction
terrifically
retroflexion
retroflected
heart-failure
pearl-fishery
pearl-fishing
retrofitting
petrographic
reprographic
necrographer
petrographer
reprographer
ferrugineous
petrogenesis
petrogenetic
refrigerator
merry-go-round
petroglyphic
tetrahedrite
reprehensive
reprehension
reordination
dearticulate
retrojection
cedrelaceous
necrological
neurological
petrological
retromingent
recriminator
tetramorphic
Febronianism
detruncation
retrenchment
heir-apparent
necrophagous
neuropterist
neuropterous

tetrapterous
necrophiliac
necrophilism
negrophilism
negrophilist
necrophilous
retropulsive
retropulsion
metropolises
necropolises
metropolitan
tetrapolitan
necrophorous
neurypnology
decrepitness
neuropathist
tetrarchical
metrorrhagia
heart-rending
decrustation
pearl-sheller
refreshfully
neurasthenia
neurasthenic
regressively
repressively
depressingly
refreshingly
tetrastichic
tetrastichal
regressivity
representant
tetrasporous
neurosurgeon
neurosurgery
heart-service
depressurise
heart-to-heart
deerstalking
merry-thought
pearl-tapioca
secretariate
defraudation
depravedness
heart-warming
heir-by-custom
newspaperdom
newspaperism
newspaperman
persuasively
sensualistic
feasibleness
sensibleness
pease-bannock
pease-blossom
seaside-grape
reassemblage
reassessment
perspectival
versificator
message-stick
deaspiration
perspiration

perspicacity
perspiratory
reassignment
messeigneurs
tessellation
persulphuric
personifying
geosynclinal
leasing-maker
seasoning-tub
seismonastic
session-clerk
seismoscopic
seismometric
session-house
seismologist
seismography
sensuousness
pease-pudding
menstruation
Besserwisser
measuring-rod
censoriously
dessertspoon
persistently
persistingly
densitometer
sensitometer
densitometry
sensationism
sensationist
reassuringly
reassumption
perseverance
perseverator
Gentianaceae
left-handedly
septuagenary
Septuagesima
meat-salesman
reattachment
Septuagintal
restrainable
restrainedly
vertebration
pentacrinoid
lenticellate
verticillate
nectocalyces
verticalness
lenticularly
denticulated
testiculated
gesticulator
geotectonics
death-dealing
pentadactyle
pentadactyly
testudineous
weather-board
feather-brain
heather-bleat
weather-bound

fent-merchant
weather-chart
leather-cloth
weather-cloth
beetle-headed
feather-grass
weather-glass
weather-gleam
weather-gauge
weather-house
featheriness
aesthesiogen
heathenishly
aestheticise
aestheticism
aesthetician
aestheticist
leather-knife
kettleholder
weather-proof
beetle-browed
weather-stain
restlessness
weather-strip
Zeitvertreib
beatifically
certificated
testificator
meat-offering
pettifoggery
pettifogging
hectographic
pentagonally
ventripotent
restrictedly
pestological
centillionth
pestilential
dentilingual
bertillonage
gentilitious
septilateral
Pestalozzian
Septemberish
centumvirate
septemvirate
testamentary
vestimentary
Septembriser
tectonically
pectinaceous
pertinacious
sexton-beetle
meeting-house
sententially
septennially
nesting-place
resting-place
melting-point
septentrions
resting-stage
resting-spore
jesting-stock

dextrocardia
sectionalism
festoon-blind
centroclinal
Bertholletia
deltiologist
centrosphere
dextrousness
dextrogyrate
deutoplasmic
centuplicate
pentapolitan
heat-apoplexy
perturbative
sectarianise
Nestorianism
sectarianism
centuriation
perturbation
perturbatory
neoterically
letter-weight
welter-weight
heater-shield
pectoriloquy
Deuteronomic
deuteranopia
deuteranopic
teeter-totter
deuteroplasm
letter-writer
deuteroscopy
dentirostral
rectirostral
reiteratedly
welter-stakes
testosterone
centesimally
leptosomatic
pentateuchal
restaurateur
destructible
death-warrant
bequeathable
bequeathment
reputatively
secularistic
benumbedness
renunciative
denunciation
renunciation
denunciatory
renunciatory
pedunculated
resuscitable
resuscitator
recuperative
remunerative
recuperation
rejuvenation
remuneration
recuperatory
remuneratory

detumescence
oecumenicism
nebulisation
resupination
delusiveness
dehumidifier
deducibility
reducibility
genuflection
sequentially
nebulousness
sedulousness
beaumontague
resumptively
desulphurate
desulphurise
resurrective
resurrection
tenuirostral
Berufsverbot
revulsionary
sequestrator
Jesuitically
serum-therapy
reductionism
reductionist
service-berry
pervicacious
service-court
servo-control
servicewoman
heavy-hearted
heaven-fallen
heavenliness
heaven-gifted
perviousness
nerve-racking
perverseness
velvet-scoter
servitorship
velvet-guards
between-decks
betweentimes
benzaldehyde
mezzo-rilievo
mezzo-soprano
afterburning
effeminately
effectuality
affectedness
affectionate
afterthought
effecutation
effervescent
office-seeker
office-bearer
office-holder
office-hunter
effiguration
affluentness
efflorescent
afforestable
Afro-American

off-reckoning
affrightedly
affrightment
affrightened
affrontingly
aforethought
effusiveness
effusiometer
egg-and-tongue
egg-apparatus
agreeability
ignitability
uglification
ignitibility
egoistically
agribusiness
agricultural
agalmatolite
agglomerated
agglutinable
agglutinogen
agamogenesis
agent-general
agrochemical
agroindustry
agrobusiness
Egyptologist
aggressively
pheasant's-eye
phraseograph
phraseologic
phrasemonger
sheath-winged
shealing-hill
theatrically
theatromania
theatrophone
theanthropic
rhabdosphere
thick-and-thin
chick-a-diddle
checker-board
checker-berry
shockingness
checking-room
chuckie-stane
chuckie-stone
phycological
chocolate-box
Phycomycetes
thick-sighted
thick-skinned
thick-skulled
check-weigher
phycoxanthin
rhododendron
shudderingly
rhodomontade
Rhodophyceae
shadow-figure
shadow-flight
shadow-boxing
chrematistic

three-centred
thief-catcher
shield-maiden
shield-bearer
shield-shaped
cheese-paring
cheese-taster
cheese-rennet
cheese-monger
cheese-hopper
cheeseburger
cheese-cutter
cheerfulness
three-ha'porth
sheeling-hill
shieling-hill
cheerishness
sheepishness
shrewishness
thievishness
chief-justice
phlegmagogic
phlegmagogue
phaeomelanin
three-monthly
shoeing-smith
phaenogamous
phlebotomise
phrenologise
phlebotomist
phrenologist
three-pricker
three-pounder
Phaeophyceae
three-quarter
sheep-stealer
sheep-shearer
sheep-scoring
chieftainess
chrestomathy
phreatophyte
shuffle-board
shift-working
whigmaleerie
phagocytical
phagocytosis
Whiggishness
thigmotropic
chaise-longue
chain-gearing
thrivingness
shriving-time
shrill-voiced
shrill-gorged
chairmanship
cheiromantic
chrisom-cloth
cheirologist
cheirography
cheiropteran
christianise
Christianism
Christianity

thriftlessly
Christliness
Christolatry
christophany
Christ's-thorn
Shaksperiana
chiliahedron
philharmonic
childbearing
childcrowing
philadelphus
philodendron
philhellenic
whale-fishery
whale-fishing
phylogenesis
phylogenetic
whole-hearted
shilling-mark
shillingless
childishness
philological
philanthrope
philanthropy
phyllotactic
chalcolithic
chalcography
chalcopyrite
cholerically
thalassaemia
thalassaemic
Philistinise
philistinism
whole-skinned
shellshocked
philosophess
philosophise
philosophism
philosophist
phillumenist
shilly-shally
chalazogamic
chimney-board
whimperingly
chimney-piece
chimney-stack
chimney-stalk
chimney-shaft
chimney-sweep
shamefacedly
shamefulness
rhamphotheca
whimsicality
championship
rhombohedral
rhombohedron
chimerically
rhumb-sailing
thematically
chemotherapy
chemotropism
shamateurism
phantasmical

phantasmally
phonocamptic
rhinocerical
rhinoceroses
rhinocerotic
thunder-cloud
thunder-drive
chance-medley
thunderingly
thunderously
whencesoever
thunder-plump
channel-stane
thunder-sheet
channel-stone
thunder-stone
thunder-storm
thankfulness
phonographic
phonographer
Rhinegravine
Rhynchonella
Rhynchophora
phenological
phonological
rhinological
phenylalanin
phonemically
phenomenally
rhinoplastic
Phanerogamia
phanerogamic
Phanerogamae
rhinorrhoeal
rhinorrhagia
chondriosome
phanerophyte
phonasthenia
thanksgiving
phonotactics
phonetically
phenotypical
phonotypical
thank-you-ma'am
Theopaschite
theopathetic
chromaticism
chromaticity
chromatogram
chromatopsia
theorematist
chrome-yellow
theoretician
chrome-spinel
rheometrical
through-going
through-other
through-stane
through-stone
through-train
theophylline
chlorination
chlorimetric

shooting-iron
shooting-star
whooping-swan
theologaster
chlorometric
chronometric
theosophical
chronologist
chloroformer
chromosphere
theomorphism
chronography
theocratical
throttle-pipe
throstle-cock
phrontistery
chaplainship
whip-scorpion
Rhipidoptera
shepherdless
shepherdling
chapter-house
ship-chandler
whipping-post
chapelmaster
rhopaloceral
whip-and-derry
whip-poor-will
shopbreaking
whip-grafting
shipbuilding
chiquichiqui
charlatanism
thereagainst
whereagainst
pharmaceutic
pharmacology
cherubically
thirdborough
shortchanger
characterise
characterism
Characinidae
short-clothes
share-cropper
share-capital
short-circuit
Charadriidae
charter-chest
Thurberesque
charnel-house
Charterhouse
charter-mayor
thirteenthly
charterparty
sheriff-clerk
sheriff-court
sheriff's-post
chorographic
chirographer
church-parade
church-warden
churchianity

churchpeople
shareholding
thereinafter
churlishness
Thermidorian
whortleberry
chorological
sharp-looking
Chironomidae
pharyngology
pharyngotomy
thermolabile
thermotactic
thermoscopic
thermometric
thermophilic
chordophonic
choreologist
Theriomorpha
thermo-couple
Theriodontia
thermosphere
thermotropic
chartography
choreography
thermography
thermostable
thermostatic
chiropractic
chiropractor
chiropterous
sharp-pointed
choripetalae
therapeutics
therapeutist
chirurgeonly
sharp-sighted
short-sighted
sharpshooter
sharp tongued
sharp-toothed
thyrotrophin
therethrough
wherethrough
thoroughfare
thorough-bass
thoroughness
thoroughbred
sharp-visaged
shirtwaister
cherry-laurel
cherry-pepper
cherry-bounce
chorizontist
chesterfield
whisperingly
whisperously
chassé-croisé
phosphoresce
phosphaturia
chastisement
whistle-drunk
Thysanoptera

Thesmophoria
physiognomic
physiologist
physiography
physiocratic
whisky-frisky
white-bearded
white-bellied
phytobenthos
photobiology
white-crested
white-crowned
photocopying
photochromic
rhytidectomy
photoelastic
shatter-brain
photo-etching
shatter-proof
thitherwards
whitherwards
white-fronted
photo-fission
photographic
phytographic
photographer
phytographer
photogravure
phytogenesis
phytogenetic
photogeology
photoglyphic
what's-her-name
white-herring
what's-his-name
what's-its-name
photokinesis
phytological
shot-blasting
white-livered
rhythmically
rhythmometer
photomontage
rhythmopoeia
phytonadione
whitlow-grass
phytophagous
white-pudding
photophilous
photo-process
rhetorically
photospheric
photosetting
phototherapy
phototropism
photovoltaic
thousand-year
thousand-legs
thousandfold
rheumatismal
thaumatogeny
rheumatology
thaumaturgic

thaumaturgus
shoulder-mark
shoulder-belt
shoulder-high
shoulder-slip
shoulder-knot
shoulder-bone
shoulder-note
thoughtfully
ghoulishness
chauvinistic
chivalrously
shaving-brush
shaving-stick
shawl-pattern
show-business
chrysophanic
Rhizocephala
rhizocarpous
rhizogenetic
rhizophagous
rhizophilous
dilatability
air-ambulance
disaccharide
financialist
disaccordant
lizard-hipped
bilateralism
dilaceration
bicameralist
cigarette-end
disaventrous
disaffection
disaffiliate
vicar-general
dilapidation
divarication
vitalisation
vitativeness
titaniferous
Sivapithecus
misallotment
disallowable
disallowance
disannulment
disannulling
Titanosaurus
dilatoriness
misapprehend
disappointed
dicarpellary
disagreeable
disagreeably
disagreement
disassociate
kinaesthesia
kinaesthesis
kinaesthetic
didactically
gigantically
gigantomachy
disauthorise

disastrously
misanthropic
misanthropos
Sinanthropus
Simarubaceae
miraculously
disadvantage
disadventure
misadventure
misadvisedly
bibble-babble
gibble-gabble
ribble-rabble
nimble-witted
nimble-footed
misbehaviour
diabolically
misbelieving
timbromaniac
timbrologist
disbursement
nimbustratus
disbowelling
disclamation
mischanceful
pitch-and-toss
mischallenge
aircraftsman
pisciculture
pinchcommons
viscoelastic
witches'-broom
discreteness
discretively
circle-riding
discretional
biochemistry
kitchen-knave
pitcher-plant
kitchen-range
kitchen-stuff
discreetness
kitchen-wench
zincographic
discographer
zincographer
miscegenator
discriminate
discriminant
circuitously
circuit-rider
miscellanist
Lincoln-green
miscalculate
circumjacent
circumscribe
Discomycetes
Discomedusae
discomedusan
circumcentre
discomfiting
circumcision
discomfiture

circumfluent
circumfluous
discommodity
air-commodore
circumlocute
discomposure
circumstance
circumnutate
circumfusile
circumfusion
discommunity
circumgyrate
disconnexion
disconnected
discontented
miscontented
air-condition
disconsolate
misconstruct
disceptation
discipleship
disciplinant
disciplinary
discophorous
discordantly
discursively
discorporate
discerptible
viscerotonia
viscerotonic
circassienne
viscosimeter
viscosimetry
discouraging
discountable
viscountship
discourteous
discoverable
discoverture
bird-catching
bird-watching
Hildebrandic
vindictively
vindicatress
fiddle-faddle
middleweight
kiddiewinkie
middle-income
niddle-noddle
mindlessness
fiddlesticks
fiddle-string
wind-changing
disdainfully
wild-williams
misdemeanant
misdemeanour
sindonophany
birding-piece
winding-stair
winding-sheet
bird's-nesting
Windsor-chair

hindforemost
mind-boggling
Hindoostanee
kindergarten
misdirection
hindquarters
window-screen
fire-watching
cinemathèque
literariness
mixed-ability
liberalistic
mineralogise
mineralogist
vinegar-plant
vinegarrette
disembrangle
disembellish
disembarrass
disenchanter
disendowment
time-bewasted
wine-merchant
mine-detector
nineteenthly
lifelessness
timelessness
tirelessness
live-feathers
vice-chairman
side-whiskers
kinesipathic
dimerisation
fire-fighting
wine-glassful
Hibernianism
pigeon's-blood
hibernaculum
Hibernically
life-and-death
life-interest
pigeon-flying
line-engraver
tiresomeness
vice-governor
time-honoured
wine-coloured
wide-spectrum
Liverpudlian
fixed-penalty
Didelphyidae
wisecracking
birefringent
fireproofing
diseasedness
diversifying
diversionary
diversionist
disestablish
diverticulum
diverticular
wire-stringed
divertimento

dilettantish
bicentennial
dilettantism
licentiously
river-terrace
directorship
wire-stitched
miseducation
hire-purchase
pile-dwelling
wife-swapping
time-exposure
timely-parted
livery-stable
disfranchise
diffrangible
pin-feathered
bioflavonoid
misfeaturing
kilfud-yoking
diffareation
misformation
differentiae
differential
diffusedness
diffusionism
diffusionist
disgradation
biographical
diagrammatic
singableness
king's-cushion
single-handed
dingle-dangle
higgle-haggle
jingle-jangle
mingle-mangle
wiggle-waggle
disgregation
single-acting
single-decker
single-seater
single-minded
single-wicket
single-figure
wing-shooting
disguiseless
disguisement
linguistical
virgin's-bower
singing-hinny
ring-compound
diageotropic
biogeography
ring-dotterel
ring-armature
disgorgement
finger-and-toe
ring-dropping
disgustfully
disgustingly
ring-streaked
gingivectomy

fish-hatchery
right-and-left
fish-salesman
disheartened
high-faluting
night-brawler
night-crawler
night-clothes
high-reaching
eighteenthly
eighteen-hole
high-velocity
high-seasoned
rightfulness
night-fishery
lithographic
lithographer
light-hearted
diphthongise
diphtheritic
diphtheritis
mithridatism
high-fidelity
ditheistical
lithological
ditheletical
litholatrous
lightning-bug
lightning-rod
Siphonaptera
Siphonophora
siphonophore
siphonostele
wishing-stone
dichromatism
dichroscopic
withholdment
high-sounding
high-coloured
dichrooscope
sight-playing
lithophagous
lithophilous
tithe-proctor
high-spirited
hip-hip-hurrah
xiphophyllus
sight-reading
cichoraceous
witheredness
high-priestly
bilharziasis
bilharziosis
dithyrambist
disharmonise
high-pressure
withdrawment
Lithospermum
xiphisternum
lithospheric
sight-singing
lithotritise
lithotritist

lithotriptic
lithotriptor
lithotomical
high-stepping
night-terrors
dishevelment
dishevelling
highty-tighty
highly-strung
visitational
militaristic
divinatorial
visitatorial
viviparously
pitiableness
disincentive
Cicindelidae
liriodendron
viridescence
virilescence
pitilessness
disinflation
disinfectant
disinfection
misinformant
bilingualism
riding-master
riding-school
disingenuity
disingenuous
disinherison
civilisation
minification
minimisation
nidification
vilification
vinification
vivification
divisiveness
siliciferous
visiting-card
visiting-book
diminishable
diminishment
divisibility
libidinosity
silicicolous
libidinously
bimillennium
minimotorway
ministrative
ministration
sinistrality
disintegrate
disintricate
sinistrorsal
sinistrously
disinterment
sinisterwise
misinterpret
diminutively
ridiculously
vinicultural

filibusterer
niminy-piminy
misjudgement
disjointedly
sick-headache
sickle-celled
sickle-shaped
kickie-wickie
ticklishness
nickel-silver
milking-stool
kicking-strap
milk-and-water
misknowledge
milk-porridge
pickerel-weed
lick-trencher
wicket-keeper
ticket-office
ticket-holder
ticket-porter
ticket-writer
lickety-split
mickey-taking
kicksy-wicksy
billiard-ball
misleadingly
Lillibullero
Lilliburlero
dialecticism
dialectician
dialectology
dislocatedly
digladiation
dislodgement
williewaught
tirlie-wirlie
biologically
rifle-grenade
diplogenesis
yieldingness
villainously
mill-sixpence
rifleman-bird
diplomatical
billingsgate
violin-string
bibliomaniac
bibliopegist
bibliophobia
mill-mountain
bibliologist
bibliopolist
pillion-rider
kill-courtesy
bibliography
Bible-pounder
miller's-thumb
field-spaniel
millesimally
will-o'-the-wisp
Bible-thumper
willow-grouse

tilley-valley
biomechanics
diamagnetism
pigmentation
diamond-drill
diamond-field
Simmenthaler
diamond-hitch
diamond-wheel
Kimmeridgian
mismatchment
biometrician
dismayedness
dlencephalon
pinniewinkle
significance
significancy
significator
fiendishness
limnological
cinnamon-bear
Bignoniaceae
limnophilous
ligniperdous
dinner-jacket
giant's-kettle
giant's-stride
winnowing-fan
kidney-potato
mixobarbaric
kilowatt-hour
pilot-balloon
disoperation
disobedience
risorgimento
timothy-grass
mitochondria
ricochetting
nicotinamide
simoniacally
disorientate
rigorousness
timorousness
vigorousness
ailourophile
ailourophobe
timocratical
ribonuclease
displaceable
displacement
misplacement
diaphanously
Hippocratise
Hippocratism
hippocrepian
hippocentaur
ripple-marked
nipple-shield
simple-minded
displeasedly
disprivacied
disprivilege
dispensative

dispensation
dispensatory
Hispanically
Hispaniolise
mispunctuate
mispronounce
dispropriate
hippophagist
hippophagous
hippopotamic
hippopotamus
diapophysial
dispersonate
dispiritedly
dispiritment
dispossessed
dispossessor
dispatch-boat
dispiteously
disputatious
dispauperise
disqualitier
disquisitive
disquisition
disquisitory
disquietness
misquotation
nitroaniline
microbalance
nitrobenzene
microbiology
microclimate
cirro-cumulus
misreckoning
microcephaly
microcopying
microcapsule
picrocarmine
microcircuit
vitro-di-trina
vitrifaction
vitrifacture
hierographic
micrographic
hierographer
micrographer
microgranite
hierogrammat
disregardful
ditriglyphic
hieroglyphic
piercingness
mitrailleuse
fibrillation
Gibraltarian
micrological
disrelishing
nitromethane
Dibranchiata
dibranchiate
fibrinolysin
vitriolation
diprionidian

vitreousness
hierophantic
misrepresent
micropterous
disruptively
microprinted
vibraphonist
micropipette
disreputable
disreputably
microphysics
hierarchical
mirror-writer
nitroso-group
digressively
microseismic
digressional
microscopist
microsurgeon
microsurgery
cirro-stratus
microtubular
nitrotoluene
microtomical
migrationist
vibratiuncle
sir-reverence
biorhythmics
misstatement
dissuasively
dissocialise
dissociative
dissociation
dissociality
fissicostate
tissue-typing
kirschwasser
bioscientist
missel-thrush
fissilingual
missummation
dissymmetric
dissemblance
dissimilarly
dissimulator
disseminated
disseminator
kissing-crust
dissenterish
dissenterism
first-nighter
biosynthesis
biosynthetic
dissentingly
missionarise
dissipatedly
dissertative
tin-streaming
dissertation
diastrophism
fissirostral
biosatellite
dissatisfied

disseverment
disseverance
filtrability
distrainable
distrainment
mistranslate
distractible
distractedly
birthday-book
birthday-suit
mixtie-maxtie
tittle-tattle
diathermancy
Little-endian
listlessness
mistressless
mistress-ship
mistreatment
mirthfulness
pictographic
histogenesis
histogenetic
histrionical
distributary
distributive
distribution
mistakenness
distillation
distillatory
histological
diatomaceous
distemperate
tintinnabula
diatonically
distanceless
distinctness
fictionalise
Histiophorus
virtuosoship
virtuousness
winter-garden
disturbative
Victorianism
filter-passer
mixter-maxter
pitter-patter
historically
pictorically
winter-weight
winter-beaten
picture-frame
winter-cherry
picture-house
sisterliness
winter-clover
historiology
winter-bourne
victoriously
Picturephone®
winter-ground
dietetically
Uintatherium
fictitiously

dictatorship
distrustless
mistrustless
diethylamine
figuratively
figurability
sinupalliate
Sipunculacea
vituperative
vituperation
vituperatory
figure-caster
lieutenantry
liquefacient
liquefaction
liturgically
liturgiology
dijudication
dilucidation
Liguliflorae
ligulifloral
sinusoidally
ailurophobia
ailurophilia
simultaneity
simultaneous
liqueur-glass
silviculture
mid-Victorian
misventurous
silver-beater
silver-glance
silver-plated
silver-voiced
silver-footed
mizzen-course
skrimshanker
skunk-cabbage
skipping-rope
skirt-dancing
skateboarder
skutterudite
skittishness
skittle-alley
sky-tinctured
pleasantness
pleasantries
Alhambresque
alkalescence
alkalescency
clearing-bank
pleasingness
clear-obscure
clear-sighted
altaltissimo
illaqueation
pleasureless
pleasure-boat
pleasure-trip
slubberingly
blabbermouth
globigerinae
flabellation

flabelliform
ill-beseeming
plebiscitary
globe-thistle
globe-trotter
black-and-blue
elucubration
placableness
blackballing
blackbirding
blockbusting
blackcurrant
slockdolager
cliché-ridden
flickeringly
slickensided
glockenspiel
black-fishing
blackguardly
black-hearted
blacklisting
placentation
placentiform
Plectognathi
glaciologist
blackpudding
plecopterous
glucoprotein
glycoprotein
black-quarter
electrically
electrifying
electrograph
electrogenic
electrolysis
electrolytic
electromeric
electrometer
electromotor
electrometry
electron-volt
electroplate
electropolar
electrosonde
electroscope
electroshock
electrotonic
electrotonus
electrotypic
electrotyper
elocutionary
elocutionist
flocculation
black-visaged
clock-watcher
gladiatorial
gladiatorian
sledge-hammer
bladder-wrack
cloddishness
gladsomeness
alienability
alterability

sleeve-button	alimentation	plurilocular	slaughterous
sleeping-pill	flamboyantly	pluriliteral	plough-jogger
illegitimate	plum-porridge	ultramontane	ploughwright
illegitimacy	flame-thrower	ultramundane	eleutherarch
illegibility	flammulation	ultroneously	illuminative
alder-liefest	slink-butcher	clarinettist	claudication
aldermanship	plano-concave	gloriousness	illumination
aldermanlike	plano-conical	clare-obscure	allusiveness
glue-sniffing	blanc-de-Chine	ultrasensual	illusiveness
ulcerousness	flannelboard	pluriseriate	plausibility
eleemosynary	clinker-built	all-roundness	pleurisy-root
bluestocking	clinker-block	glass-blowing	cloud-kissing
sleep-walking	flannelgraph	glass-cutting	glaucomatous
cliffhanging	blunderingly	plasterboard	Pleuronectes
old-fashioned	slanderously	plasteriness	cloud-seeding
sluggishness	flint-hearted	blusteringly	illustrative
flagellation	clincher-work	blister-steel	claustration
flagellatory	glandiferous	plasterstone	illustration
flagelliform	slantingways	blissfulness	illustratory
plagiotropic	clannishness	flash-forward	clavicembalo
oligarchical	blandishment	blast-furnace	slave-holding
oligotrophic	flint-knapper	close-fitting	eleventh-hour
flagitiously	clangorously	close-grained	slovenliness
alpha-blocker	blennorrhoea	classicality	cloven-hoofed
alphabetical	plenipotence	plessimetric	cloven-footed
alphamerical	plenipotency	classifiable	pluviometric
alphanumeric	planispheric	close-mouthed	slave-traffic
clairaudient	ill-naturedly	Plesiosaurus	clownishness
pleiochasium	planetesimal	glossologist	blow-moulding
plain-clothes	planet-struck	blastosphere	flower-garden
plain-dealing	slang-whanger	elasmobranch	flower-delice
illiterately	pleonastical	glossography	flower-deluce
alliterative	blood-brother	flesh-pottery	flexibleness
liberalise	fluorescence	close-tongued	alexipharmic
alliteration	fluoridation	blastulation	playing-field
liberality	fluorination	glassy-headed	immaterially
plain-hearted	fluorimetric	Platt-Deutsch	embarquement
fluidisation	floodlighted	bletheration	ambassadress
limitation	bloodletting	clothes-brush	impassionate
clair-obscure	all-or-nothing	clothes-horse	impartiality
all-important	fluorocarbon	clatteringly	embattlement
ellipsograph	fluorometric	flatteringly	immaculately
elliptically	pleomorphism	glitteringly	immatureness
cleistogamic	pleomorphous	flitter-mouse	amicableness
pleiotropism	blood-pudding	blithesomely	imperatively
altitudinous	bloodstained	clothes-press	imperatorial
clairvoyance	bloodsucking	bletherskate	imperceptive
flammability	bloodthirsty	blatherskite	impenetrable
plumbaginous	bloody-minded	ill-treatment	impenetrably
clamjamphrie	slip-carriage	slothfulness	imperfective
plamableness	elephant's-ear	elytrigerous	imperfection
plumber-block	flippantness	sluttishness	imperforable
plummer-block	clip-fastener	Ulotrichales	imperforated
glimmeringly	clapperboard	plate-leather	immethodical
slumberingly	slipperiness	platonically	impedimental
slumberously	slop-clothing	platanaceous	impenitently
slumpflation	kleptomaniac	alstroemeria	imperishable
plamefulness	glyphography	gluttonously	imperishably
flammiferous	glyptography	slate-writing	impetiginous
plumbiferous	klipspringer	cloud-chamber	Umbelliferae
plumulaceous	claptrappery	glaucescence	impermanence
alimentative	cliquishness	slouch-hatted	impermanency
elementalism	floriculture	slaughterman	immemorially

ampelography
impersonally
impersonator
immersionism
immersionist
immeasurable
immensurable
immeasurably
impersistent
impertinence
impertinency
imperviously
embezzlement
emigrational
amygdaloidal
image-breaker
image-worship
amphibrachic
amphictyonic
amphigastria
omphalomancy
amphisbaenic
amphistomous
emphatically
amphitheatre
amphitropous
omnisciently
ambidextrous
ambitionless
omnipotently
impierceable
omnipresence
embitterment
amalgamative
amalgamation
small-clothes
implicitness
emollescence
smallholding
emolumentary
emblematical
implantation
ameliorative
amelioration
emblazonment
amenableness
emancipation
amentiferous
immovability
imponderable
immoderately
immoderation
smooth-leaved
smooth-coated
smooth-spoken
smooth-browed
impoliteness
imposingness
embourgeoise
empoisonment
imposthumate
impregnation
umbrageously

amortisation
emargination
umbrella-bird
umbrella-tree
Amarantaceae
embranchment
embryologist
ombrophilous
impropriator
ombrophobous
impressively
imprisonment
improvidence
improvisator
smash-and-grab
amissibility
emasculation
emasculatory
smotheriness
smatteringly
smotheringly
emotionalism
emotionality
amitotically
amateurishly
imputatively
immutability
imputability
immunisation
immunologist
empyreumatic
unmanageable
unmanageably
endamagement
incapacitate
incapability
unsalability
unparalleled
inhalatorium
uncatalogued
unwatchfully
unsanctified
unsanctioned
incalculable
incalculably
uncalculated
unvaccinated
uncandidness
one-and-thirty
unpardonable
unpardonably
unhandsomely
incandescent
incatenation
incalescence
unwaveringly
unlawfulness
enlargedness
entanglement
endangerment
unfathomable
unfathomably
inhabitation

insalivation
insanitation
invagination
invalidation
unsatisfying
engagingness
unfadingness
unvariegated
sneakishness
unpavilioned
unfamiliarly
unhabituated
unmarketable
unsailorlike
enharmonical
inharmonical
inharmonious
unharmonious
unmaintained
ungainliness
antagonistic
unfavourable
unfavourably
unvanquished
unpatronised
unpassionate
uncapsizable
infanticidal
unfastidious
unfaithfully
antasthmatic
incautiously
antarthritic
unnaturalise
insalubrious
unobtainable
inobediently
inobservable
unobservable
unobservedly
inobservance
unobservance
snobographer
snubbing-post
snobbishness
anabaptistic
inabstinence
unobstructed
snack-counter
sneck-drawing
inaccessible
inaccessibly
unacceptable
unscientific
unacceptance
inactivation
knocking-shop
unscriptural
unachievable
knick-knacket
knuckle-joint
unsculptured
uneconomical

unaccredited
unicorn-shell
unicorn-whale
anacatharsis
anacathartic
unscottified
inaccurately
inoccupation
unacquainted
unaccustomed
unscrupulous
unidealistic
inadvertence
inadvertency
inadmissible
inadmissibly
unadulterate
unidentified
unadmonished
inadaptation
inadequately
unrewardedly
underachieve
untenability
unremarkable
unrecallable
unrepairable
untenantable
underbearing
underblanket
interbedding
enfeeblement
underbuilder
interchanger
interchapter
unmercifully
unpeacefully
intercolline
intercommune
interconnect
underclothed
underclothes
intercropped
intercipient
interceptive
unperceptive
interception
intercurrent
undercurrent
intercession
intercessory
interclusion
underdrawing
incendiarism
interdictive
interdiction
interdictory
underdressed
interdigital
underdevelop
intemerately
inveterately
inteneration

unremembered
undependable
independence
independency
unregenerate
unregeneracy
antecedently
unrevengeful
unbeneficial
antemeridian
unrepealable
unrevealable
unredeemable
ndetermined
undetermined
ungenerously
uncelebrated
indefeasible
ndefensible
indefeasibly
ndefensibly
ndefectible
indetectable
ndetectible
undelectable
unrepeatable
nterestedly
unrepentance
undeceivable
undeservedly
unreservedly
unperfection
nterfretted
nterfollate
nterfemoral
underfunding
nterfrontal
nterfertile
unperforming
nterference
unperforated
nterfluence
nterglacial
nveiglement
undergarment
unmethodical
unmethodised
encephalitic
encephalitis
unmechanical
under-hangman
unmechanised
sneeshin-mull
ndelicately
unseminaried
unhesitating
ngemination
nsemination
angelica-tree
ndehiscence
undeliberate
unregimented
unperishable

undelightful
unverifiable
indecisively
indefinitely
unrepiningly
indelibility
infelicitous
undesignedly
unresistible
unremittedly
unregistered
antediluvial
antediluvian
unbelievable
unrelievable
unbelievably
unrelievedly
interjection
interjacency
underkingdom
interlobular
intellective
unreflective
unreflecting
intellection
interlocutor
intellectual
intelligible
intelligibly
intelligence
interlaminar
indeclinable
indeclinably
index-linking
interlingual
underletting
intermediate
intermediacy
intermediary
intermeddler
unseemliness
intermundane
interminable
interminably
unterminated
intermissive
intermission
intermittent
intermaxilla
intermixture
indemnifying
internalised
internuncial
interorbital
unreconciled
unheroically
interoceanic
interoceptor
unbecomingly
anaerobiosis
anaerobiotic
unreformable
unrecognised

enteropneust
Enteromorpha
indecorously
undecomposed
undemocratic
unremorseful
interosseous
unreportable
enteroptosis
unresolvable
unrespective
interpretate
interpleader
interpretess
interpretive
interpleural
enterprising
undespairing
interpellate
interpellant
interpolable
interpolator
unresponsive
underpinning
underpeopled
under-produce
intemperance
underperform
intempestive
underpassion
underpowered
underpayment
unreproached
unbefriended
knee-breeches
unterrifying
interrogable
unsegregated
interrogatee
interrogator
unsearchable
unsearchably
unwearyingly
underrunning
anteprandial
knee-crooking
interruptive
interruption
unrefreshing
unreprovable
understanded
understander
understaffed
unpersuasive
unsensualise
undersealing
interspatial
intersection
unpersecuted
under-sheriff
interstellar
interspersal
intensifying

interstitial
underskinker
inter-science
interspinous
unreasonable
unseasonable
unreasonably
unseasonably
unmeasurable
unmeasurably
interservice
uncensorious
understratum
unsensitised
intertraffic
unrestrained
Invertebrata
invertebrate
indebtedness
ungentleness
unsettlement
anaesthetise
anaesthetist
investigable
investigator
entertaining
intertwining
unrestricted
undertakable
unfertilised
unventilated
undertenancy
insect-powder
incestuously
infectiously
unbetterable
under-turnkey
intertissued
intertexture
unsepulchred
underutilise
unreturnable
unrepulsable
unrequitedly
intervocalic
intervenient
intervention
interwreathe
underwriting
interwrought
underwrought
underworkman
knife-and-fork
ineffaceable
ineffaceably
snuff-dipping
unaffectedly
knife-grinder
unofficially
inefficiency
snaffling-lay
unifoliolate
anagrammatic

sniggeringly
anagogically
knightliness
knight-errant
anthocarpous
unshadowable
uncheerfully
unthreatened
encheiridion
unshrinkable
unchristened
unchallenged
anthelmintic
unchangeable
unchangeably
unthankfully
enchantingly
unchangingly
unthinkingly
enthronement
unchronicled
anthropoidal
anthropogeny
anthropogony
anthropology
anthropotomy
anthophilous
unchaperoned
uncharitable
uncharitably
anchoretical
anchoritical
antherozooid
enthusiastic
unchasteness
unrhythmical
unthoughtful
unchivalrous
anthoxanthin
antimalarial
antihalation
antiparallel
antimacassar
antibarbarus
antibacchius
envisagement
anticatholic
antipathetic
antirachitic
indicatively
anti-national
anti-Gallican
antiparticle
unmiraculous
enviableness
undischarged
encirclement
indiscretely
indiscretion
indiscreetly
indiscipline
undiscipline
undiscordant

undiscerning
undiscording
angiocarpous
undiscovered
unriddleable
unkindliness
incineration
antimetabole
antipetalous
antisepalous
antiperiodic
unlikeliness
unliveliness
untimeliness
anti-Semitism
unlikelihood
engine-fitter
antilegomena
indigenously
engine-driver
indigestible
indivertible
indigestibly
undivestedly
indirectness
antineutrino
incidentally
indifference
indifferency
inking-roller
antiphrastic
unrightfully
antichthones
antitheistic
antiphonical
antiphonally
antithrombin
unwithholden
antithetical
annihilative
anticipative
annihilation
anticipation
intimidation
invigilation
anticipatory
intimidatory
anti-aircraft
incisiveness
infiniteness
invitingness
infinitively
undiminished
incivilities
invisibility
unlibidinous
individually
unwieldiness
unyieldingly
undiplomatic
anticlerical
undismantled
antimnemonic

oneiromancer
invigoration
undisordered
antisocially
oneirocritic
indisputable
indisputably
undisputedly
undispatched
antifriction
antigropelos
antipruritic
unbiasedness
Angiospermae
angiospermal
indissoluble
indissolubly
undissolving
undissembled
angiostomous
infiltration
undistracted
unfittedness
unmistakable
unmistakably
unlistened-to
indistinctly
antistrophic
antistrophon
unvirtuously
unfilterable
unhistorical
undisturbing
infibulation
unliquidated
anticyclonic
snake-charmer
unpleasantly
unpleasantry
unpleasingly
unelaborated
inflectional
analogically
unflaggingly
analphabetic
uncloistered
inflammation
inflammatory
unslumbering
unblinkingly
inclinometer
Anglophabiac
ingloriously
unblushingly
unclassified
inelasticity
Englishwoman
analytically
enclitically
unflattering
inflationary
inflationism
inflationist

unilaterally
unamiability
inimicalness
inimicitious
animadverter
anemographic
unimaginable
unimaginably
unembittered
animalculist
unemployable
unemployment
gnomonically
unimportuned
unimportance
anemophilous
anamorphosis
unimpressive
unimprisoned
mnemotechnic
onomatopoeia
onomatopoeic
unimpugnable
unendangered
uninterested
anencephalia
anencephalic
unintegrated
unenthralled
unendingness
enantiomorph
enantiopathy
enantiostyly
enantiotropy
uninfluenced
unanalysable
unanalytical
unintroduced
uninstructed
unencumbered
unincumbered
unanswerable
unanswerably
endoparasite
untowardness
endocarditis
unvoyageable
unmoralising
unromantical
undoubtingly
unconcealing
insouciantly
inconcinnity
inconcinnous
unconcerning
inconclusive
unconclusive
inconclusion
intoleration
unforewarned
uncovenanted
intolerantly
unforeseeing

incoherently
uncomeliness
unloveliness
Indo-Germanic
ungovernable
ungovernably
unmodernised
unforeboding
endometritis
uncomeatable
unconfinable
unconfinedly
unconforming
unconformity
unconfusedly
incoagulable
endophyllous
oncorhynchus
incogitative
intoxicating
intoxication
unionisation
unnoticeable
unpoliteness
unlovingness
unpolishable
unmodifiable
antoninianus
unsolicitous
unsocialised
endoskeletal
endoskeleton
entoplastral
entoplastron
ntormidable
unformidable
ncommodious
unformalised
unformulated
endosmometer
uncommonness
uncommercial
ncommutable
ncommutably
announcement
uncounselled
nsomnolence
ncognisable
ncognisance
ncoronation
entomologise
entomologist
Entomostraca
ncompletely
ncompletion
ncompliance
ncomparable
ncomparably
ncorporeity
ncorporator
uncomposable
ncompatible
ncomputable

inhospitable
unhospitable
incompatibly
inhospitably
incompetence
incompetency
uncompounded
incorrodible
incorrigible
incorrigibly
incoordinate
incorruptive
incorruption
incorrosible
unnourishing
inconstantly
unconsecrate
unconsidered
unworshipful
unworshipped
inconsolable
inconsolably
unfossilised
inconsumable
inconsumably
unconsenting
inconsonance
inconsequent
unconstraint
inconsistent
unpossessing
unpoetically
unwontedness
incontiguous
indoctrinate
unworthiness
incontinence
incontinency
uncontrolled
unpopularity
undocumented
incomunicado
insolubilise
insolubility
involutional
Indo-European
uncoquettish
inconvenient
unconvincing
inconversant
unconversant
unapparelled
unspectacled
inspectingly
inspectional
inspectorate
inspectorial
snippetiness
unappetising
inappellable
unappealable
inappeasable
unappeasable

anapaestical
snapshooting
snappishness
inapplicable
unapplicable
unapplausive
inappositely
unapproached
unoppressive
inoperculate
inspissation
anaphylactic
iniquitously
unornamented
unornamental
unbreachable
unbreathable
unbreathed-on
encroachment
entreatingly
increasingly
intracranial
unproclaimed
unprocedural
ungracefully
ungraciously
unprocurable
intracardiac
ineradicable
introducible
ineradicably
introductive
unproductive
introduction
introductory
ungrudgingly
uncreditable
unfriendship
engraftation
unprofitable
unprofitably
intriguingly
unoriginated
unfrightened
unprohibited
anarchically
enarthrodial
anarthrously
inordinately
inordination
unfruitfully
unerringness
snarling-tool
snarling-iron
inartificial
unartificial
inartistical
unartistlike
inarticulate
unarticulate
inarticulacy
introjection
unprejudiced

unbrokenness
unprelatical
untrammelled
intramundane
untremendous
intromissive
intromission
intromittent
intromitting
entrancement
infringement
entrenchment
intrenchment
unfranchised
intrinsicate
intransigent
intransitive
unprincipled
untranslated
untransmuted
unpronounced
infraorbital
enormousness
entrepreneur
unpreparedly
unpropertied
unpropitious
unfrequented
infrequently
unfrequently
incrassative
encrustation
incrassation
incrustation
androsterone
unprosperous
untrustiness
intrusionist
oniroscopist
unprescribed
ingratiating
uncritically
ungratefully
untruthfully
unprettiness
unpretending
unprotesting
ungroundedly
intra-uterine
unprovidedly
unprevailing
unprovokedly
unprivileged
introversive
introvertive
introversion
ingravescent
unassailable
one-sidedness
unascendable
unascendible
unusefulness
unaspiringly

anastigmatic
unassignable
unassistedly
unassociated
uniseriately
inosculation
inescutcheon
unassuagable
unassumingly
unisexuality
unsteadiness
unstratified
unattainable
unattainably
unstableness
gnotobiotics
gnotobiology
unstockinged
anathematise
anotherguess
installation
instillation
anatomically
unstimulated
unstanchable
unctuousness
instep-raiser
unitarianism
unattractive
unsterilised
unstatutable
unstatutably
instauration
instrumented
instrumental
instructible
instructress
unstructured
undulatingly
incurability
insurability
pneumaticity
pneumatology
incunabulist
encumbrancer
encumberment
annunciative
annunciation
injunctively
unguiculated
insusceptive
unsuccessful
unsuccessive
unpunctuated
infundibular
intumescence
unsupervised
insufflation
insufficient
unsufficient
insufferable
unsufferable
insufferably

unauthorised
unpunishable
unpunishably
inaudibility
infusibility
injudicially
unmunitioned
insubjection
anguilliform
unsublimated
one-upmanship
unsubmissive
unsubmitting
unguentarium
unquenchable
unquenchably
unquantified
invulnerable
unvulnerable
invulnerably
pneumothorax
pneumococcus
unsuspecting
inauspicious
unauspicious
unsuspicious
unsuppressed
unsupposable
insurrection
innutritious
unsubsidised
unquestioned
unsubscribed
intussuscept
inquisitress
invultuation
unsustaining
industrially
intuitionism
intuitionist
uncultivable
uncultivated
inauguration
inauguratory
untumultuous
uneventfully
universalise
universalism
universalist
universality
unoverthrown
snowball-tree
knowableness
snow-in-summer
unswervingly
snowdrop-tree
enswathement
inexpansible
inexhaustive
inexactitude
inexecutable
inexpedience
inexperience

inexpediency
inextensible
unexpectedly
inexpertness
inexpectancy
unextenuated
inextirpable
inexplicable
inexplicably
inextricable
inextricably
inexpressive
unexpressive
inexpungible
unexpurgated
inexpugnable
unexpugnable
inexpugnably
unhyphenated
encyclopedia
Ankylosauria
Ankylosaurus
enzymologist
enhypostasia
enhypostatic
unsystematic
tobacco-heart
non-alcoholic
monarchistic
tobacco-plant
tobacco-pouch
cowardliness
towardliness
nonagenarian
monadelphous
Boraginaceae
cohabitation
localisation
moralisation
nomadisation
polarisation
Romanisation
solarisation
totalisation
totalitarian
vocalisation
volatileness
polarimetric
womanishness
Foraminifera
non-alignment
vocationally
donatistical
morality-play
corallaceous
non-admission
potato-finger
potato-blight
somatopleure
soda-fountain
potamologist
potato-spirit
gonadotropic

gonadotropin
polarography
solar-powered
woman-queller
noradrenalin
monastically
romantically
non-attention
vocabularied
vocabularian
forbearingly
roebuck-berry
bombacaceous
forbiddingly
bobby-dazzler
double-handed
Combretaceae
double-dagger
double-banked
double-manned
double-acting
double-headed
double-decked
double-decker
double-dealer
gobbledegook
double-charge
double-biting
double-figure
double-glazed
double-locked
double-bottom
double-storey
gobbledygook
sorbefacient
doubtfulness
bomb-disposal
morbilliform
combinations
Hobbesianism
conclamation
nonchalantly
forcibleness
coachbuilder
concubitancy
coccidiostat
concremation
concrescence
concreteness
zoochemistry
force-feeding
voicefulness
conchiferous
moschiferous
touchingness
conciliative
porcellanise
porcellanite
conciliation
porcellanous
conciliatory
concelebrate
concelebrant

porcelainise
porcelainous
non-combatant
pot-companion
bow-compasses
non-committal
non-complying
concomitance
concomitancy
non-communion
volcanically
concentering
forcing-house
coscinomancy
concentrical
concentrator
hog-constable
non-conductor
conchologist
concupiscent
coacervation
concordantly
concurrently
concert-grand
concorporate
non-Christian
torch-thistle
Low-Churchism
Low-Churchman
conclusively
Gondwanaland
hoodman-blind
word-painting
conductivity
mordaciously
good-tempered
woodlessness
wood-offering
cold-shoulder
Cordaltaceae
condemnation
condemnatory
condensation
wooden-headed
sodden-witted
voiding-lobby
wooden-tongue
wood-engraver
cold-moulding
hood-moulding
wondrousness
conduplicate
good-breeding
powder-closet
powdering-tub
wonder-monger
wonder-worker
powder-monkey
wonder-struck
conditionate
conditioning
lord-superior
word-building

good-humoured
road-surveyor
woodburytype
wood-hyacinth
dodecandrous
moderateness
dodecahedral
dodecahedron
dodecaphonic
tolerability
nose-painting
forecarriage
dodecagynian
dodecagynous
lower-bracket
moveableness
sober-blooded
honey-buzzard
money-changer
nomenclative
nomenclature
non-Euclidean
fore-admonish
Domesday-book
foreseeingly
homelessness
hopelessness
movelessness
tonelessness
non-efficient
non-effective
powerfulness
foreign-built
money-grubber
togetherness
monetisation
novelisation
cohesiveness
covetiveness
foresightful
cohesibility
homesickness
cole-titmouse
solecistical
non-existence
nose-bleeding
money-lending
homeomorphic
honey-mouthed
fore-and-after
governmental
governorship
solenoidally
foregoneness
lonesomeness
forebodement
foretokening
forebodingly
lovelornness
rose-coloured
cometography
none-so-pretty
covetousness

coleopterist
coleopterous
co-respondent
homeopathist
code-breaking
home-produced
home-crofting
rope-drilling
power-station
money-spinner
non-essential
homesteading
potentiality
domesticable
domestically
lomentaceous
domesticated
domesticator
homeothermic
homeothermal
forestalment
forestalling
momentaneous
honey-tongued
molecularity
forejudgment
come-by-chance
non-flammable
confabulator
Confucianism
Confucianist
non-fictional
confectioner
confidential
low-frequency
confrontment
confirmative
confirmation
conformation
confirmatory
conferential
god-forgotten
confiscation
confiscatory
confusedness
confessional
confessoress
confoundedly
zoographical
congratulate
congratulant
hobgoblinism
Volga-Baltaic
longicaudate
congregation
tongue-tacked
boogie-woogie
toggle-switch
rough-grained
longshoreman
soughing-tile
long-division
long-distance

bougainvilia
dough-kneaded
cough-lozenge
cough-mixture
congeniality
lodging-house
congenerical
logging-stone
congenitally
conglobation
conglomerate
zoogeography
gorgeousness
conglobulate
hodge-pudding
longipennate
rough-perfect
long-breathed
loggerheaded
long-drawn-out
longitudinal
forgettingly
long-standing
conglutinate
conglutinant
rough-wrought
Rochelle-salt
nothingarian
doch-an-dorach
oophorectomy
mother-church
motherliness
mothers-in-law
mother-figure
mother-liquor
mother-tongue
mother-fucker
sophisticate
solitariness
nominatively
motivational
volitational
nominalistic
holidaymaker
sociableness
sociobiology
morigeration
vociferation
police-manure
police-office
bodice-ripper
vociferosity
vociferously
Cominformist
potichomania
modificative
codification
mobilisation
modification
nobilitation
notification
solicitation
modificatory

politicaster
positiveness
solidifiable
positivistic
volitionless
volitionally
solicitously
conidiophore
conidiospore
solifluction
sociological
porismatical
toxicophobia
monitorially
toxicologist
horizontally
non-intrusion
vomiturition
solitudinous
vocicultural
policy-holder
conjunctival
dock-labourer
workableness
book-scorpion
rock-scorpion
cockieleekie
folk-medicine
mock-heroical
book-learning
cock-throwing
cockfighting
cork-linoleum
workmistress
rock-climbing
cooking-apple
rocking-chair
working-class
booking-clerk
looking-glass
rocking-horse
working-house
working-model
cooking-range
rocking-stone
lock-hospital
pocket-pistol
pocket-gopher
monkey-jacket
monkey-hammer
monkey-flower
donkey-engine
monkey-engine
monkey-wrench
monkey-puzzle
toll-gatherer
world-beating
collaborator
colluctation
collectively
collectivise
collectivism
collectivist

collectivity
folliculated
collectorate
coal-merchant
Woulfe-bottle
soullessness
toploftiness
collegialism
collegiality
zoologically
coal-titmouse
loblolly-tree
coulombmeter
pollen-basket
bowling-alley
polling-booth
Coelenterata
coelenterate
bowling-green
fowling-piece
boiling-point
rolling-stock
toilsomeness
colliquative
colliquation
colloquially
dollarocracy
roller-skater
roller-skates
molluscicide
Molluscoidea
wollastonite
collision-mat
foolish-witty
pollutedness
coalitionism
coalitionist
soul-stirring
collaterally
boulevardier
world-wearied
collywobbles
hollow-ground
woolly-haired
woolly-headed
motley-minded
doomwatching
commodiously
Doomsday-book
formlessness
cosmographic
cosmographer
zoomagnetism
cosmogonical
formaldehyde
cosmological
commemorable
commemorator
commensalism
Rosminianism
commendation
commentation
commensality

commendatory
communicable
communicably
communicator
commencement
commonwealth
rooming-house
commandingly
tormentingly
common-riding
gormandising
Norman-French
commensurate
cosmonautics
cosmoplastic
cosmopolitic
cosmopolitan
dormer-window
commercially
commissarial
commissariat
commissioned
commissioner
commiserable
commiserator
cosmetically
dogmatically
noematically
dormitory-car
downwardness
foundationer
corn-marigold
mountain-hare
fountain-head
mountain-meal
fountainless
mountain-high
mountain-lion
mountain-blue
mountain-flax
mountain-wood
mountain-cork
mountain-soap
roundaboutly
connubiality
mound-builder
bound-bailiff
coenobitical
bonny-clabber
non-nucleated
connectively
fornicatress
countenancer
counter-agent
mountenaunce
counter-brace
counter-blast
counter-charm
counter-claim
corn-merchant
countercheck
counter-drain
counter-flory

counter-force
counter-guard
counter-gauge
lounge-lizard
counsellable
counterlight
countermarch
counterplead
counterpoise
counterpoint
counter-paled
counterproof
counter-round
counter-stand
counterscarp
countershaft
counter-sense
counter-tally
counter-tenor
counter-wheel
counter-weigh
pound-foolish
pornographic
pornographer
corn-shucking
corn-chandler
council-board
coincidental
coincidently
sounding-lead
sounding-line
counting-room
jointing-rule
moonlighting
council-house
pointillisme
pointilliste
councilmanic
poenological
town-planning
somniloquise
somniloquism
somniloquist
somnolescent
somnambulate
somnambulant
somnambulary
round-mouthed
somnambulism
somnambulist
morning-dress
morning-glory
corning-house
down-and-outer
conning-tower
morning-watch
country-dance
country-house
sound-ranging
countrywoman
coenesthesia
hound's-tongue
sonneteering

moonstricken	mono-compound	copper-nickel	horse-breaker
joint-tenancy	Solomon's-seal	corporalship	house-breaker
bonnet-monkey	dolorousness	copper-glance	mouse-buttock
point-to-point	sonorousness	copper-bottom	consecration
connaturally	Notodontidae	composedness	consociation
corn-exchange	rodomontader	compass-plane	consecratory
logodaedalic	homoeostatic	compass-plant	horse-courser
logodaedalus	homologumena	compatriotic	considerable
monomaniacal	loxodromical	hospital-ship	considerably
toxocariasis	monodramatic	zoopathology	topside-turvy
motor-bicycle	monographist	zoophytology	loss-adjuster
motor-cycling	rotor-station	conqueringly	zoospermatic
motor-cyclist	motor-scooter	conquistador	boisterously
monometallic	colossus-wise	journalistic	conspectuity
monopetalous	colostration	horribleness	dorsiflexion
monosepalous	motor-tractor	corroborable	boastfulness
monogenistic	monostichous	corroborator	consignation
monodelphian	monostrophic	correctional	consignatory
monodelphous	coloquintida	correctioner	non-scheduled
horometrical	co-polymerise	correctitude	house-husband
Notonectidae	monosyllabic	Torricellian	conspiration
borough-reeve	monosyllable	court-dresser	constipation
holophrastic	homonymously	journey-bated	worshipfully
monotheistic	complanation	Fourieristic	roasting-jack
homothallism	complacently	fourteenthly	toasting-fork
monothalamic	morphallaxis	torrefaction	toasting-iron
monophyletic	complaisance	horrifically	conspiringly
monotheletic	Torpedinidae	horrifyingly	conscionable
toxophilitic	corpse-candle	mournfulness	conscionably
do-nothingism	completeness	courageously	constitutive
monochromate	complemental	lorry-hopping	constitution
monochromasy	complexioned	coordinately	constituency
monochromist	complexional	co-ordinately	horse-knacker
homochromous	compressible	coordinative	housekeeping
monophyodont	complicative	co-ordinative	forsakenness
homothermous	dolphinarium	co-ordination	consultative
ionophoresis	complication	coordination	consultation
monophysitic	complimental	coerciveness	consultatory
nomothetical	complimenter	mourning-band	tonsilectomy
monofilament	doppel-ganger	boarding-pike	consolidated
colonisation	compellative	mourning-ring	consolidator
motorisation	compulsative	mourning-dove	tonsillotomy
Polonisation	compellation	courtierlike	console-table
doloriferous	compulsatory	correlatable	consummately
soboliferous	compulsively	board-measure	consummative
soporiferous	compulsorily	court-martial	consummation
monolinguist	compensation	torrentially	consummatory
non-objective	compensatory	horrendously	horsemanship
corollaceous	hooping-cough	fourfoldness	cousin-german
Cologne-earth	componential	coprophagist	consentingly
homoeopathic	companionate	coprophagous	consentience
homologation	companion-way	court-plaster	Hobson-Jobson
homopolarity	compunctious	coprophilous	poison-sumach
homoeomerous	morphologist	poor-spirited	consensually
homoiomerous	morphotropic	horror-struck	forsworness
locomotivity	morphography	morris-dancer	goose-pimples
monopodially	pompholygous	non-residence	gossip-monger
monopolistic	corporealise	non-resistant	gossip-writer
homoeomorphy	corporealism	non-resisting	consequently
monotonously	corporealist	Socratically	conservative
homomorphism	corporeality	constatation	conservatism
homomorphous	compurgation	moustache-cup	conservation
monomorphous	compurgatory	constabulary	conservatory

conservatrix
constrictive
constructive
constriction
construction
constructure
constringent
moss-trooping
conscription
house-steward
consistently
possessively
possessioned
horseshoeing
consistorial
consistorian
house-surgeon
horse-trading
house-trained
horse-trainer
forset-seller
fosset-seller
house-to-house
topsyturvily
moistureless
mousquetaire
dorsiventral
house-warming
housey-housey
contranatant
root-parasite
contrariness
contrariwise
contradictor
contrapposto
portmanteaus
portmanteaux
contractable
contractible
contractedly
portrait-bust
contrapuntal
mouth-breeder
contabescent
porte-cochère
monticellite
horticulture
Southcottian
north-country
south-country
tooth-drawing
bottle-washer
post-meridian
bottle-slider
southernwood
northernmost
southernmost
bottle-holder
pottle-bodied
röntgenology
röntgenogram
bottle-opener
north-eastern

south-eastern
bootlessness
Post-Tertiary
pontifically
loathfulness
youthfulness
mouth-filling
contignation
contagionist
contagiously
contiguously
postage-stamp
doctrinarian
contriteness
contrivement
containerise
postliminary
postliminous
fortuitously
postmistress
contriturate
contributive
post-diluvial
contribution
post-diluvian
contributory
postillation
noctilucence
nostological
footslogging
footplatemen
bottom-sawyer
zootomically
contumacious
contemplable
contumelious
contemplator
contaminable
contemporary
contemporise
contemptible
contemptibly
contemptuous
noctambulism
noctambulist
continuative
continuation
cottonocracy
goat-antelope
contingently
bolting-hutch
foot-and-mouth
continuously
portentously
doating-piece
postponement
low-thoughted
dogtooth-spar
postpositive
postposition
controllable
do-it-yourself
tortuousness

post-doctoral
route-proving
forth-putting
foster-parent
foster-father
post-graduate
forthrightly
conterminate
conterminant
coat-trailing
contortional
conterminous
foster-sister
posture-maker
post-prandial
costermonger
foster-mother
posteriority
root-pressure
contestation
north-seeking
poetastering
south-seeking
contestingly
Montessorian
mouth-to-mouth
Northumbrian
root-tubercle
posthumously
north-western
south-western
contextually
post-hypnotic
softly-softly
tootsy-wootsy
loquaciously
volumetrical
monumentally
voluminosity
voluminously
columniation
populousness
coquettishly
locum-tenency
voluptuosity
robustiously
voluptuously
voluntaryism
voluntaryist
convectional
louvre-window
convulsively
convulsional
convalescent
convincement
conveniently
convincingly
conventicler
conventional
conventioner
conversation
louver-window
convivialist

conviviality
conveyancing
conveyor-belt
pot-walloping
low-watermark
soixante-neuf
Polygalaceae
polygamously
pony-carriage
Polyadelphia
polypetalous
polysepalous
cotyledonary
cotyledonous
polyneuritis
polytheistic
polyphyllous
polyphyletic
polyphyodont
polypharmacy
polyrhythmic
rosy-fingered
polysiloxane
polyhistoric
polyglottous
polyembryony
polyanthuses
copying-press
body-snatcher
Polygonaceae
polytonality
rosy-coloured
polymorphism
polymorphous
pony-trekking
polyurethane
polyisoprene
polyethylene
body-building
polysyndeton
polysyllabic
polysyllable
sphacelation
speakerphone
apparentness
speaking-tube
apparitional
splay-mouthed
aplanogamete
spear-running
spear-thistle
spear-thrower
sprat-weather
specialistic
spectatorial
epicycloidal
specifically
space-heating
Epacridaceae
speckledness
space-lattice
apiculturist
epoch-marking

apocynaceous
spaciousness
speciousness
Epicureanism
spectrograph
spectre-lemur
apochromatic
spectrometic
spectrometry
spectroscope
spectroscopy
space-station
specktioneer
epididymides
apodeictical
epideictical
epidemically
epidemiology
spider-legged
spider-monkey
spider-stitch
speed-boating
upper-bracket
appercipient
apperceptive
apperception
appendicular
appendectomy
appendicitis
splendidness
splendidious
ephemerality
spiegeleisen
ephemeridian
speech-making
sprechgesang
speechlessly
sprechstimme
splenisation
sphericality
appetisement
appetisingly
splenomegaly
ephebophilia
apfelstrudel
appertaining
Speedwriting®
spiflication
epigrammatic
apagogically
apogeotropic
sphincterial
spring-headed
spring-heeled
spring-keeper
spring-beetle
spring-beauty
spring-bladed
spring-loaded
Ophioglossum
sprightfully
optimisation
ophiological

ophiolatrous
ophiomorphic
ophiophagous
ophiophilist
speiss-cobalt
splinter-bone
splint-armour
spokesperson
apple-blossom
apologetical
Apollinarian
spilling-line
spelling-book
apolitically
applausively
applaudingly
span-farthing
spine-chiller
epencephalic
epencephalon
sponge-finger
sponge-fisher
sponge-rubber
spinning-mill
spongicolous
spindle-shell
spinulescent
spindle-whorl
opinionately
opinionative
spongologist
epanorthosis
spinstership
spinsterhood
opposability
appoggiatura
appositeness
oppositeness
appositional
oppositional
uproariously
apron-strings
epiphenomena
apoplectical
approachable
spermathecal
approach-shot
spermaphytic
sportability
spermatocele
spermatogeny
spermatozoic
spermatozoid
spermatozoal
spermatozoan
spermatozoon
spermatocyte
appreciative
appreciation
appreciatory
sporadically
spurge-laurel
sportfulness

opera-glasses
sporogenesis
sphragistics
epirrhematic
apprehensive
apprehension
sportiveness
appraisement
sparking-plug
spurtle-blade
sporangiolum
sparrow-grass
spermophytic
aperiodicity
spermogonium
spuriousness
appropriator
sporophorous
spire-steeple
oppressively
spiritualise
spiritualism
spiritualist
spirituality
spirit-rapper
operatically
spiritedness
spiritlessly
spirituosity
episodically
epistemology
opisthodomos
opisthograph
opisthotonic
opisthotonos
episcopalism
episcopalian
epistolarian
epistolatory
apostolicism
apostolicity
apostrophise
epithalamium
epithalamion
ophthalmitis
sputteringly
apothegmatic
spotlessness
spitefulness
spittle-house
Spatangoidea
appurtenance
epexegetical
sphygmograph
sphygmometer
sphygmophone
sphygmoscope
square-rigged
square-rigger
equalisation
equalitarian
equanimously
equatorially

squattocracy
equestrienne
equivalently
Equisetaceae
equisetiform
squirearchal
equilibrator
equidistance
equivocation
equivocatory
equipollence
equipollency
equiprobable
squirrel-cage
squirrel-tail
equimultiple
organ-builder
great-bellied
bread-chipper
broadcasting
pro-and-conned
grease-monkey
triadelphous
ornamentally
dreadfulness
breakfast-set
organ-grinder
organ-gallery
triangularly
breathtaking
great-hearted
breathlessly
breathalyser
preachership
organisation
urbanisation
creativeness
freakishness
irrationally
organoleptic
urbanologist
organography
break-promise
preassurance
breast-girdle
breastplough
breakthrough
breaststroke
breastsummer
creatureship
treasure-city
trabeculated
problematics
tribespeople
proboscidean
proboscidian
tribute-money
probationary
probouleutic
proclamation
proclamatory
orichalceous
traceability

tractability
preclassical
trochanteric
crackbrained
truce-breaker
precociously
price-current
price-cutting
precedential
trocheameter
tracheoscopy
tracheostomy
brickfielder
gracefulness
precognitive
precognition
practicalism
practicalist
practicality
trichinellae
fructiferous
brackishness
trickishness
practitioner
trichiniasis
frictionless
fractionally
fractionator
fructivorous
Trichiuridae
procellarian
oracularness
precancerous
brick-nogging
precondition
dracontiasis
tracing-paper
preconstruct
proconsulate
iracundulous
tractoration
trichophyton
proctorially
trichotomise
trichologist
trichotomous
graciousness
preciousness
tricephalous
preceptorial
precipitable
precipitance
precipitancy
precipitator
price-rigging
trichromatic
tricorporate
precariously
prechristian
precisianism
precisianist
process-block
fricasseeing

trickstering
precessional
processional
processioner
precisionist
procathedral
preclusively
precautional
brachydactyl
brachycephal
brachygraphy
Trachypterus
Pre-Dravidian
credibleness
bride-chamber
Traducianism
Traducianist
productively
productivity
productional
tridactylous
cradle-scythe
pridefulness
prodigiosity
prodigiously
predigestion
predilection
predominance
predominancy
prudentially
tradescantia
tradespeople
iridescently
predesignate
predestinate
predisposing
traditionary
traditionist
creditworthy
predetermine
proditorious
tree-kangaroo
irrelatively
irrepairable
friendliness
irrelevantly
free-selector
irreverently
irremediable
irremediably
irrepealable
irrepealably
irredeemable
irredeemably
freeze-drying
irreversible
irreversibly
arpeggiation
cruel-hearted
free-wheeling
free-thinking
breech-loader
breeches-buoy

pre-eminently
freezing-down
greenishness
irreciprocal
irremissible
irresistible
irresistibly
irresistance
pre-existence
irreflective
irreflection
pre-eclampsia
irrealisable
irreconciled
gruesomeness
true-love-knot
irreformable
irresolutely
irresolution
irresolvable
irresolvably
irrespective
irresponsive
irrespirable
irrefragable
irrefragably
irreprovable
irreprovably
araeosystyle
pre-establish
orienteering
priest-ridden
priestliness
free-standing
irregularity
irrebuttable
free-swimming
creepy-crawly
prefabricate
craft-brother
proficiently
prefectorial
draft-dodging
profligately
triflingness
prefoliation
craftmanship
prefloration
preformative
preformation
trifurcation
preferential
craftsmaster
professional
professorate
professoress
professorial
profiteering
profitlessly
profoundness
orographical
programmable
programmatic

trigrammatic
fragrantness
tragicalness
tragi-comical
brigade-major
trigger-happy
priggishness
tragelaphine
progymnasium
dragon's-blood
trigonometer
trigonometry
progenitress
proglottides
troglodytism
gregarianism
gregariously
pregustation
progesterone
triglyceride
orthoboracic
orthocousins
orchidaceous
orchidectomy
orchidomania
orthodontics
orthodontist
orthodromics
archdeaconry
orthognathic
orthographic
orthographer
archegoniate
orthogonally
orthogenesis
orthogenetic
orchilla-weed
Archilochian
prehensility
prehensorial
orphan-asylum
orthopedical
orthopaedics
orthopaedist
orthopterist
orthopteroid
orthopterous
archipelagic
orchard-grass
orchard-house
orthorhombic
orthosilicic
prehistorian
orchestrator
architecture
orthotonesis
orthotropism
orthotropous
archetypical
drainage-tube
irritability
irrigational
trail-blazing

Artiodactyla	primulaceous	transitional	brandy-pawnee
praiseworthy	bramble-finch	transiliency	brandy-bottle
fruitfulness	frumentation	Fringillidae	preoccupancy
ornithogalum	graminaceous	Grandisonian	proof-correct
freight-liner	tremendously	transitorily	troop-carrier
ornithomancy	Premonstrant	frontispiece	preordinance
ornithomorph	premenstrual	frontiersman	arborescence
ornithophily	gram-molecule	transit-trade	arborisation
Ornithischia	crambo-jingle	crenellation	Oreopithecus
ornithoscopy	gram-positive	translucence	proof-reading
freight-train	trampolinist	translucency	armour-bearer
training-ship	gramophonist	granulocytic	armour-plated
artificially	Krameriaceae	transleithan	cryptanalyst
argillaceous	pro-marketeer	wranglership	trophallaxis
artillery-man	primordially	translatable	tripudiation
fruit-machine	promuscidate	trinomialism	crêpe-de-chine
traitorously	promissorily	trinomialist	triple-headed
arrière-garde	dramatically	transmigrate	propaedeutic
train-spotter	cremationist	transmigrant	dropped-scone
artistically	dramaturgist	transmogrify	triple-turned
articulately	dramatisable	transmontane	trypaflavine
articulation	trimethylene	brinkmanship	propugnation
articulatory	brimfullness	pronominally	propagandise
brainwashing	premaxillary	transmissive	propagandism
projectivity	frankalmoign	transmission	propagandist
projectional	front-bencher	transmutable	trap-shooting
prejudgement	transcendent	transmutably	triplication
broken-backed	transduction	transmitting	eruptiveness
broken-winded	granodiorite	ironing-board	dropping-well
grallatorial	frondescence	pruning-knife	proprietress
frolicsomely	bronze-pigeon	brontosaurus	tropological
Grolieresque	princeliness	Franco-German	grapple-plant
trolley-table	prince-bishop	transoceanic	trypanocidal
trolley-wheel	orange-flower	drongo-shrike	preponderate
prolificness	Frankenstein	front-of-house	preponderant
prolifically	wrongfulness	craniologist	propenseness
prolegomenon	transferable	drongo-cuckoo	cryptogamian
trolling-bait	transferring	bronco-buster	cryptogamist
brilliant-cut	transforming	transplanter	cryptogamous
brilliantine	transformism	transpicuous	trophotactic
troll-my-dames	transformist	transpontine	trophobiosis
prolongation	transference	transpirable	trophobiotic
prelatically	transfer-book	transportive	cryptomnesia
tralaticious	transfusible	transporting	cryptomnesic
Pralltriller	transgressor	transparence	cryptologist
urolithiasis	urinogenital	transparency	graphologist
proletariate	trench-plough	transposable	trophotropic
tralatitious	transhumance	transshipper	cryptography
grammaticise	French-polish	trend-setting	cryptonymous
grammaticism	Branchiopoda	frenetically	tropophilous
frame-breaker	trench-mortar	transuranium	preparedness
gram-negative	transhipping	transudation	tripartition
trumpet-major	bronchoscope	transuranian	proportioned
trumpet-shell	bronchoscopy	transudatory	proportional
primigravida	principality	pronouncedly	property-room
primogenital	frankincense	tranquillise	grapeseed-oil
primogenitor	prenticeship	tranquillity	preposterous
crimping-iron	frondiferous	transumptive	prepossessed
Kremlinology	drinking-horn	transumption	tropospheric
bromhidrosis	drinking-bout	transversely	crepusculous
Bromeliaceae	branding-iron	transversion	propitiative
promulgation	transitively	transvestite	propitiation
bramble-berry	frangibility	transvestism	propitiatory

triphthongal
propitiously
prophylactic
frequentness
prerogatived
prerequisite
ororotundity
crystal-clear
cross-and-pile
crassamentum
crystal-gazer
crystallitis
cross-bedding
crossbencher
crossbanding
crush-barrier
cross-buttock
brass-bounder
prosectorial
cross-current
prosecutable
crosscutting
press-cutting
cross-country
prosodically
presidentess
presidential
cross-examine
Trismegistus
prosperously
prospectuses
trustfulness
brassfounder
cross-grained
press-gallery
dressing-case
dressing-sack
graspingness
dressing-room
dressing-down
dressing-gown
trysting-tree
crisping-iron
crossing-over
irascibility
prestigiator
Prussianiser
prostitution
preselection
cross-lighted
crash-landing
prosyllogism
trestle-table
cross-lateral
proselytiser
freshmanship
presumptuous
presentative
presentation
presentiment
presentially
cristobalite
Bristol-board

Bristol-brick
Aristotelean
Aristotelism
Aristotelian
Aristophanic
Aristolochia
aristocratic
griseofulvin
praseodymium
prosopopoeia
prosopopeial
cross-purpose
preservative
preservation
preservatory
brass-rubbing
prestriction
droseraceous
prescriptive
proscriptive
prescription
proscription
cross-section
Crassulaceae
grossularite
pressure-cook
pressure-suit
grass-widower
presbyterate
presbyterial
Presbyterian
prothalamion
protractible
protractedly
protuberance
trituberculy
protectively
protectingly
protactinium
criticalness
triticalness
protocolling
protectorate
protectorial
criticisable
erythematous
brother-in-law
protreptical
gratifyingly
gratefulness
truthfulness
wrathfulness
wretchedness
proto-history
gratuitously
arithmometer
protomorphic
arithmetical
pretenceless
pretendingly
protonematal
writing-paper
writing-table

prothonotary
protoplasmic
protoplasmal
protoplastic
erythroblast
writer's-cramp
oratorically
pretermitted
erythromycin
protestation
protestingly
protistology
grotesquerie
prototherian
truth-telling
prototypical
protrusively
pretty-spoken
pretty-pretty
protozoology
traumatology
group-captain
ground-feeder
groundlessly
ground-beetle
ground-cherry
ground-pigeon
ground-cuckoo
proud-hearted
draughtboard
draught-hooks
draught-horse
draught-house
draughtiness
droughtiness
trouble-house
troublemaker
trouble-mirth
trouble-state
trouble-world
Frauendienst
triumphantly
fraudulently
grave-clothes
providential
arfvedsonite
prevailingly
gravel-voiced
travel-soiled
preventative
preventively
provincially
driving-shaft
driving-wheel
greviousness
previousness
brevipennate
prevaricator
proverbially
provisionary
privateering
privat-docent
privat-dozent

drawlingness
drawing-board
drawing-frame
drawing-knife
growing-pains
growing-point
drawing-paper
drawing-table
praxinoscope
prayerlessly
prayer-monger
prize-fighter
asparaginase
Islamisation
espagnolette
escapologist
assassinator
isobilateral
isocheimenal
psychiatrist
psychopathic
psychoactive
psychometric
psychosexual
psychoticism
psychosocial
psychologism
psychonomics
psychologist
psychotropic
psychography
isochromatic
psychrometer
psychrometry
isochronally
isodiametric
isodimorphic
osteodermous
asseverating
asseveration
osteogenesis
osteogenetic
osteological
osteomalacia
osteoplastic
osteoporosis
osteopathist
Ascension-day
assessorship
essentialism
essentialist
essentiality
assentaneous
ostentatious
usufructuary
eschatologic
asphyxiation
Ustilagineae
ustilaginous
assimilative
assibilation
assimilation
ossification

aspiringness	stealthiness	stage-thunder	atmospherics
oscillograph	steam-turbine	stage-whisper	strontianite
oscilloscope	steam-whistle	Stahlhelmist	stepdaughter
psilanthropy	stablishment	stridelegged	stapedectomy
Asclepiadean	stubble-field	string-course	stupefacient
isolationism	stubble-goose	stoichiology	stupefactive
isolationist	stabilisator	strikingness	stupefaction
Ishmaelitish	stubbornness	Strigiformes	stipulaceous
asymmetrical	stock-and-horn	stridulation	etepimeletic
psammophytic	stock-breeder	stridulatory	stupendously
asymptotical	stockbroking	stridulantly	stepmotherly
asynchronism	stocking-mask	attitudinise	attributable
asynchronous	stockingless	stakhanovite	attractively
astonishment	stocking-sole	Stakhanovism	attractingly
astoundingly	stocking-foot	stalwartness	pterodactyle
assortedness	stockingette	stalactiform	pteridomania
psephologist	stockishness	Stellenbosch	Pteridophyta
isoperimeter	stock-in-trade	stylographic	pteridophyte
isoperimetry	stock-jobbery	still-hunting	pteridosperm
astrogeology	stock-jobbing	stelliferous	stormfulness
astrological	stickler-like	stilboestrol	starchedness
estrangement	etiohometric	still-peering	starting-hole
astringently	stichomythia	still-piecing	starting-post
astronomical	stichomythic	athletically	eternity-ring
astronautics	stock-raising	stammeringly	storm-lantern
usuriousness	studding-sail	stamping-mill	star-blasting
astrophysics	staddle-stone	etymological	stercoranism
isostemonous	studiousness	etymologicum	stercoranist
tsesarevitch	strengthless	etymologicon	stereotactic
isothermally	strengthener	stump-oratory	stereometric
esoterically	otter-hunting	stomatodaeum	stereophonic
escutcheoned	stoechiology	standard-wing	stereochrome
assuefaction	etherisation	standardiser	stereochromy
pseudomartyr	strepitation	stone-bramble	storiologist
pseudo-Gothic	steering-gear	stone-breaker	stertorously
pseudopodium	steeplechase	stone-boiling	stereotropic
pseudography	steeple-crown	stone-chatter	stereography
pseudonymity	atheological	ethnocentric	stereoisomer
pseudonymous	steeple-house	stone-cutting	stereopticon
pseudocyesis	stream-anchor	stone-dresser	stereotyping
straw-breadth	etheromaniac	ethnographic	star-spangled
steam-chamber	atheromatous	stenographic	pterosaurian
straddle-back	etheostomine	ethnographer	storm-shutter
strangle-weed	Strepsiptera	stenographer	story-telling
stranglement	street-raking	stony-hearted	storm-trooper
stranglehold	street-walker	stanniferous	sternutative
stragglingly	streptococci	standing-bowl	sternutation
strangulated	street-keeper	standing-room	sternutatory
straightways	streptomycin	stencil-plate	stirrup-strap
straight-edge	streptoneura	ethnological	stern-wheeler
straightness	otherworldly	stentorphone	storm-warning
straightener	staff-college	stand-pattism	stormy-petrel
straightaway	stiff-hearted	stonewalling	otosclerosis
Stradivarius	staff-officer	strong-minded	stutteringly
strabismical	staff-surgeon	stoop-gallant	statuesquely
stratigraphy	stegocarpous	strongylosis	stethoscopic
stratotanker	staggeringly	strophanthin	station-house
steatomatous	stage-manager	strophanthus	station-wagon
stratosphere	steganograph	strophiolate	statistician
stratocratic	Steganopodes	strobilation	strugglingly
steatopygous	staghorn-fern	strobiliform	stout-hearted
strait-lacing	stegophilist	attorneyship	structurally
strait-jacket	stegosaurian	stroboscopic	strychninism

staying-power
subarachnoid
funambulator
subarcuation
cut-and-thrust
sun-and-planet
subabdominal
ourang-outang
humanisation
humanitarian
ruralisation
subacidulous
turacoverdin
nugatoriness
subapostolic
subarrhation
sugar-refiner
subalternate
subalternant
subantarctic
duraluminium
eucalyptuses
cupboard-love
turbocharged
turbocharger
turbidimiter
curb-merchant
tumbler-drier
hubble-bubble
rumble-tumble
purblindness
lumbriciform
turbellarian
nubbing-cheat
turbinacious
rubbing-stone
cumbrousness
lumber-jacket
cumber-ground
curb-crawling
kurchatovium
succedaneous
luncheon-meat
functionless
functionally
auscultation
auscultatory
subcelestial
subcommittee
subconscious
buccaneering
buccaneerish
subcontinent
vulcanisable
succinctness
lusciousness
Turcophilism
susceptivity
succussation
successantly
quick-scented
successfully
quick-sighted

successively
successional
quicksilvery
quacksalving
quick-selling
subcutaneous
punctulation
puncturation
Quadragesima
quadrangular
quadraphonic
quadraplegia
quadraplegic
subdiaconate
duodecennial
hurdle-racing
muddleheaded
hundred-gated
quadrivalent
quidditative
quadriplegia
quadriplegic
quadriennial
quadriennium
subdelirious
muddy-mettled
duodenectomy
pudding-faced
pudding-plate
pudding-stone
quadrophonic
subduplicate
dunderheaded
quadrumanous
subdivisible
numerability
lukewarmness
superannuate
queer-bashing
supercharger
superciliary
supercilious
tuberculosed
tuberculosis
tuberculated
queen-consort
supercargoes
supercluster
queen-dowager
juvenescence
supereminent
euhemeristic
supererogate
supererogant
superfrontal
superhighway
superhumanly
superhumeral
suberisation
juvenileness
tuberiferous
subeditorial
superimposed

superiorship
Puseyistical
supermundane
supernaculum
supernacular
supernatural
superordinal
superorganic
numerousness
sure-footedly
superplastic
sun-expelling
superposable
superrealism
superrealist
queen-regnant
supersubtile
supersedence
superstition
supersensory
supersensual
mutessarifat
superstratum
supersession
quaestionary
quaestorship
fume-cupboard
bureaucratic
supervenient
supervention
surface-craft
sufficiently
surface-to-air
surface-water
buffalo-berry
buffalo-grass
surfing-board
outfangthief
surf-boarding
furfuraceous
subfertility
subfeudation
subfeudatory
suffruticose
Muggletonian
judgment-hall
judgment-debt
judgment-seat
hunger-bitten
hunger-strike
hugger-mugger
suggestively
ruthlessness
rushy-fringed
bushwhacking
authenticate
authenticity
euphoniously
cushion-plant
rush-bottomed
authorisable
subhastation
tu-whit-tu-whoo

oughly-headed
dubitatively
ruminatively
ruminatingly
pupilability
mucilaginous
jurisconsult
jurisdictive
jurisdiction
luminescence
lucifer-match
business-like
business-wise
subinfeudate
tuning-hammer
municipalise
purificative
municipalism
cutinisation
futilitarian
humification
purification
municipality
purificatory
fugitiveness
luminiferous
munificently
musicianship
munitionette
fuliginosity
fuliginously
audiological
burial-ground
musicologist
luminousness
mutinousness
numinousness
jurisprudent
Hudibrastics
subinspector
music-teacher
autistically
juristically
curietherapy
subintroduce
fugie-warrant
subjectively
subjectivise
subjectivism
subjectivist
subjectivity
huckle-backed
buckle-beggar
lucklessness
cuckold-maker
quaking-grass
lurking-place
cucking-stool
ducking-stool
cuckoo-flower
Quaker-colour
bunko-steerer
sublibrarian

guild-brother	sudoriferous	surrejoinder	multifoliate
public-school	Euro-American	supramundane	multiflorous
quill-driving	auto-immunity	querimonious	multiformity
curliewurlie	automobilism	cuprammonium	multifarious
quill-feather	automobilist	currant-bread	multilobular
qualificator	automorphism	guaranteeing	multilocular
fully-fledged	humorousness	currant-jelly	fustillirian
bull-of-the-bog	autoptically	supra-orbital	multilingual
guilefulness	run-of-the-mill	nutritionist	multiloquent
mulligatawny	Eurocurrency	nutritiously	multiloquous
full-throated	mucopurulent	burrowing-owl	multilateral
qualmishness	autohypnosis	quarrymaster	subtemperate
bullfighting	pulp-magazine	quartz-schist	custom-shrunk
Juglandaceae	culpableness	substantiate	huntsmanship
sublineation	auspiciously	substantials	sustentative
outlandishly	suspiciously	substantival	sustentation
Euglenoidina	supplemental	guest-chamber	putting-cleek
curling-irons	supplementer	tussock-grass	multinuclear
curling-stone	sumpter-horse	subsidiarily	mutton-headed
curling-tongs	suppressible	cuisse-madame	hunting-field
full-bottomed	suppressedly	sunshine-roof	putting-green
Sublapsarian	supplicating	question-mark	hunting-knife
bullet-headed	supplication	questionable	hunting-lodge
curmudgeonly	supplicatory	questionably	hunting-sword
augmentative	subprincipal	questionless	putting-stone
augmentation	rumpti-iddity	substitutive	multungulate
subminiature	sumphishness	substitution	mutton-cutlet
outmanoeuvre	surprisingly	subsultorily	Austronesian
submergement	cupping-glass	nursing-chair	rust-coloured
summer-weight	suspensively	Russophilism	multipresent
submissively	out-pensioner	Russophilist	multiplicand
surmountable	jumping-mouse	Russophobist	multiplicate
submaxillary	suspensorial	subsequently	multipliable
burnt-almonds	suspensorium	outspreading	multiplicity
pugnaciously	sulphonamide	subscribable	multipartite
dunniewassal	pumpernickel	substraction	multipurpose
quintessence	purpose-built	substruction	subterranean
quenchlessly	purposefully	burseraceous	subterjacent
quantivalent	surpassingly	substructure	lust-breathed
quantitative	suppositious	subservience	custard-apple
quantisation	sulphuration	subserviency	muster-master
turnpike-road	sulphuretted	subscriptive	quattrocento
quantifiable	Humpty-dumpty	subscription	butterscotch
running-board	quaquaversal	nursery-rhyme	buttery-hatch
burning-glass	surrealistic	quasi-stellar	butterfly-bow
burning-house	supraciliary	purse-strings	butterfly-nut
turning-lathe	turriculated	nurse-tending	butter-cooler
burning-point	quarter-blood	Australasian	subthreshold
turning-point	quarter-bound	quotableness	butter-muslin
subnormality	quarter-final	suitableness	multiscience
burnet-leaved	quarter-guard	butty-collier	multisulcate
quinquenniad	quarter-horse	multicentral	multiseptate
quinquennial	quarter-miler	futtock-plate	multiseriate
quinquennium	quartern-loaf	multicipital	multivoltine
autocatalyse	quarter-plate	multicostate	multivalence
automaticity	quarter-round	multicauline	multivalency
suboccipital	quarter-staff	multidentate	multivariate
subordinancy	putrefacient	turtle-necked	multiversity
suboperculum	putrefactive	hurtlessness	multivarious
subopercular	putrefaction	buttress-root	cultivatable
autochthones	subreference	subtreasurer	cumulatively
sudoriparous	outrageously	multifaceted	subumbrellar
autodidactic	guardianship	justificator	cucumber-tree

furunculosis
eunuchoidism
cupuliferous
Tubuliflorae
tubulifloral
queue-jumping
luxullianite
cumulo-nimbus
cumulo-cirrus
futurologist
lugubriously
tumultuation
tumultuously
curvicostate
curvicaudate
curvifoliate
surveillance
pulvilliform
culvertailed
subvertebral
pulverulence
pulverisable
curvirostral
vulvo-uterine
survivorship
surveyorship
outward-bound
quixotically
ruby-throated
eurythermous
burying-place
ruby-coloured
puzzle-headed
muzzle-loader
puzzle-monkey
quizzicality
buzzard-clock
evidentially
availability
evil-favoured
evil-tempered
evil-speaking
evolutionary
evolutionism
evolutionist
evangelicism
evangelistic
avant-gardism
avant-gardist
evening-dress
evanescently
evaporograph
evaporimeter
overrashness
overcanopied
avariciously
overscutched
everydayness
overreaction
overweighted
overpersuade
overwhelming
overkindness

overfineness
overniceness
overripeness
oversimplify
overflourish
overfondness
overlordship
overpowering
ovariotomist
overpopulate
overpraising
overpressure
overestimate
overstrained
averruncator
overfullness
oversubtlety
overmultiply
everywhither
overexposure
overexertion
evisceration
avitaminosis
avowableness
sweet-and-sour
sweepingness
sweetishness
sweet-scented
sweet-toothed
sweet-william
swaggeringly
swagger-stick
swainishness
awe-inspiring
swell-mobsman
twelfth-night
swimming-bath
swimming-bell
swimmingness
swimming-pond
swimming-pool
swinging-boom
swinging-post
swine-keeping
Zwinglianism
Zwinglianist
swindle-sheet
twenty-four-mo
twenty-twenty
sword-breaker
sword-bayonet
dwarfishness
swashbuckler
two-sidedness
twitterboned
twitteringly
swizzle-stick
oxy-acetylene
exsanguinate
exsanguinity
exsanguinous
expatriation
expansionary

expansionism
expansionist
exhaust-steam
exhaust-value
exobiologist
execratively
exacerbation
executorship
exheredation
expeditation
experimented
experimental
experimenter
expediential
experiential
exterminable
exterminator
exteroceptor
extensimeter
extensometer
extensionist
ex-serviceman
exaggerative
exaggeration
exaggeratory
exiguousness
exegetically
exchangeable
exhilarative
exhilarating
exhilaration
exhilaratory
excitability
extinguisher
exhibitioner
explicitness
exulceration
exploitative
exploitation
explantation
exclusionism
exclusionist
exalbuminous
exemplifying
exenteration
exanthematic
excogitative
excogitation
expostulator
extortionate
extortionary
extortionist
exophthalmia
exophthalmic
exophthalmos
exophthalmus
exprobrative
exprobration
exprobratory
excruciating
excruciation
extraditable
exercitation

exorbitantly
exercise-book
extra-limital
extra-mundane
extra-marital
expromission
extranuclear
extraneously
uxoriousness
expropriable
extrapolator
extra-regular
extra-special
expressively
expressivity
expressional
extra-sensory
extra-uterine
extravaganza
extravagance
extravagancy
extraversion
extroversion
exasperative
exasperating
exasperation
exospherical
exoterically
exsufflation
exsufflicate
excursionise
excursionist
pyjama-jacket
gynaecocracy
gynaecomasty
synadelphite
hydatidiform
tyrannicidal
tyrannically
dynamometric
zygapophyses
zygapophysis
dysaesthesia
synaesthesia
dysaesthetic
synaesthetic
dynastically
synantherous
Lymantriidae
lycanthropic
synarthrosis
symbolically
symbololatry
syncretistic
synclinorium
synchroflash
synchronical
synchroniser
syndactylism
syndactylous
syndetically
hyperalgesia
hyperalgesic

hyperacidity
hyperbolical
synecdochism
hyperdactyly
Hypericaceae
hyperidrosis
type-founding
hymenopteran
hyperplastic
hyperpyretic
hyperpyrexia
hypersthenia
hypersthenic
hypersensual
hypersarcoma
hyperthermia
hyperthermal
hypertensive
hypertension
hypertrophic
type-cylinder
myographical
Syngnathidae
syngenesious
mythographer
mythogenesis
nychthemeral
nychthemeron
mythological
mythologiser
pythonomorph
cylindricity
cylindriform
cylinder-head
cylinder-seal
myringoscope
pyrithiamine
typification
pyritiferous
hygienically
pyritohedral
pyritohedron
syllabically
cyclopropane
Byelorussian
Cyclostomata
cyclostomous
myrmecologic
Myrmecophaga
myrmecophile
myrmecophily
dysmenorrhea
ayuntamiento
hymnographer
hypnogenesis
hypnogenetic
Cyanophyceae
gymnosophist
hypnotically
hypnotherapy
hypnotisable
pyromaniacal
gyromagnetic

xylobalsamum
pyrotartrate
hypogastrium
zygodactylic
pyrotartaric
cytogenetics
pyrotechnics
pyrotechnist
Cynocephalus
pyrometrical
hypothecator
pyrophyllite
hypothalamic
hypothalamus
pyrochemical
sycophantise
sycophantish
hypochondria
hypochlorite
hypothetical
hypophrygian
gynodioecism
pyroligneous
hypoglycemia
pyro-electric
mycoplasmata
hypognathism
hypognathous
mycodomatium
Lycopodineae
cytotoxicity
Lycopodiales
hypocoristic
pyromorphite
hylomorphism
zygomorphism
zygomorphous
hypotrochoid
cymotrichous
typographist
hypocritical
synoptically
hypostatical
hyposulphate
hyposulphite
zygomycetous
synonymously
Nymphaeaceae
lymphangitis
dysphemistic
nymphomaniac
symptomatise
nympholeptic
lymphography
hydrobiology
hygrochastic
hydrochloric
hydrodynamic
hybridisable
hydroelastic
hydrofluoric
hydrographic
hygrographic

hydrographer
hydrogeology
hydrological
Hydromedusae
hydromedusan
aye-remaining
hydrophanous
hydrophilite
hydrophilous
hygrophilous
hydrophobous
hydropathist
hydrophytous
hydroquinone
hydrargyrism
hydrostatics
cypress-swamp
hydrotherapy
hydrothermal
hydrotropism
hydraulicked
hydrozincite
mysticalness
dyotheletism
syntheticism
hyetographic
syntagmatite
mystagogical
dysteleology
system-monger
systematical
systematiser
hysterically
hysterectomy
hysterogenic
hysteromania
mysteriously
nyctitropism
Tyburn-ticket
Tyburn-tippet
sylviculture
Czechoslovak

palatableness
paramagnetism
maladaptation
Lamarckianism
rag-and-bone-man
hazardousness
papaveraceous
manageability
paraleipomena
Saracen's-stone
paraffin-scale
paraphernalia
Zarathustrian
Zarathustrism
satanicalness
magazine-rifle
parasitically
malariologist
paralipomenon
canaliculated
capaciousness
rapaciousness
sagaciousness
salaciousness
maladjustment
parallactical
parallelogram
parallelistic
maladminister
savanna-forest
savanna-wattle
malacophilous
Palaeotherium
parapophysial
macaronically
parabolically
paradoxically
Balanoglossus
malacological
palaeozoology
palaeographer
palaeographic
palaeocrystic
malacostracan
palaeontology
Pan-Africanism
maladroitness
papaprelatist
paragraphical
parapsychical
parapsychosis
panaesthetism
catastrophism
catastrophist
galactorrhoea
galactosaemia
catalytically
canary-creeper
parasynthesis
parasynthetic
parasyntheton
marble-hearted
rabble-rousing

wamble-cropped
gambling-house
cabbalistical
carboniferous
carbonylation
carbonisation
bamboozlement
namby-pambical
namby-pambyish
namby-pambyism
barbarisation
carburisation
barber-surgeon
barbarousness
Sabbath-breach
harbour-master
narco-analysis
paschal-candle
paschal-flower
saccharimeter
saccharimetry
saccharometer
Saccharomyces
matchboarding
lance-corporal
calcification
narcohypnosis
sanctimonious
sanctifyingly
cancellariate
masculineness
matchlessness
calculational
baccalaureate
carcinologist
dancing-master
carcinomatous
gas-centrifuge
sarcophaguses
panchromatism
sarcastically
lance-sergeant
card-catalogue
paediatrician
pandiculation
tax-deductible
candidateship
saddle-feather
candle-lighter
candle-dipping
Gaidhealtachd
saddle-blanket
candle-snuffer
hard-heartedly
land-measuring
paddle-steamer
maid-of-all-work
daddy-long-legs
sandy-laverock
pandemoniacal
paedomorphism
randomisation
landing-ground

maiden-widowed
cardinalatial
cardinalitial
maiden-tongued
cardiographer
land-surveying
land-ownership
sale-catalogue
case-hardening
barefacedness
labefactation
water-breather
water-chestnut
capercaillzie
parencephalon
catercornered
water-carriage
eavesdropping
water-dropwort
lavender-water
kaleidoscopic
sacerdotalise
sacerdotalism
sacerdotalist
tape-recording
casement-cloth
materfamilias
paterfamilias
paper-fastener
water-hyacinth
catechumenism
catechumenate
paper-hangings
catechistical
watering-place
watering-house
materialistic
Valerianaceae
valedictorian
facetiousness
lamellibranch
Lamellicornia
capellmeister
kapellmeister
water-mocassin
paper-mulberry
hare-and-hounds
cayenne-pepper
categorematic
gametogenesis
categorically
water-plantain
waterproofing
Galeopithecus
water-standing
water-softener
water-sapphire
water-sprinkle
parenthetical
Jamestown-weed
water-vascular
safety-deposit
panegyrically

Rafflesiaceae
half-heartedly
half-sovereign
wayfaring-tree
half-evergreen
laughableness
pangrammatist
baggage-animal
laughing-stock
bargain-hunter
languishingly
mangold-wurzel
manganiferous
tangentiality
jargonisation
badger-baiting
kangaroo-thorn
kangaroo-apple
kangaroo-grass
badger-drawing
dangerousness
daughter-in-law
washhand-basin
washhand-stand
Machiavellian
Machiavellism
machicolation
cathodography
mashie-niblick
tachygraphist
pathogenicity
pathognomonic
naphthylamine
mathematician
mathematicise
mathematicism
bathymetrical
tachometrical
tachymetrical
washing-bottle
machine-gunner
washing-powder
gathering-coal
gathering-peat
panharmonicon
yachtsmanship
tachistoscope
haphazardness
Latin-American
sanitarianism
sanitationist
fatigableness
habitableness
navigableness
radio-actinium
radioactivity
variable-sweep
Lasiocampidae
ratiocination
ratiocinatory
ratiocinative
palindromical
cabinet-making

manifestation	mallemaroking	raspberry-bush	Balsaminaceae
manifestative	cable-moulding	Malpighiaceae	passementerie
hagiographist	sailing-master	camp-sheathing	marsh-marigold
palingenesist	ballast-heaver	salpingectomy	passenger-mile
Manichaeanism	callisthenics	wappenshawing	passion-flower
satiricalness	table-skittles	Campanulaceae	Passion-Sunday
Papilionaceae	tablespoonful	campanologist	marsipobranch
maliciousness	ballet-dancing	camphoraceous	Passeriformes
radiolocation	palletisation	rapprochement	caesaropapism
papilliferous	haemodialysis	Capparidaceae	marsh-samphire
papillomatous	palmification	pauperisation	Vansittartism
radialisation	mammaliferous	waspish-headed	saussuritised
vacillatingly	sarmentaceous	carpet-bedding	sansculottism
nationalistic	salmon-leister	carpet-beating	sansculottist
rationalistic	salmon-disease	carpet-slipper	lactobacillus
manifold-paper	salmon-fishing	carpet-bombing	lattice-bridge
Maginot-minded	salmon-fishery	carpet-sweeper	lattice-girder
calico-printer	salmonellosis	panpsychistic	particularise
Saxifragaceae	harmonisation	marriage-lines	particularism
pasigraphical	haemorrhoidal	carriage-drive	particularist
satin-sheeting	Hammerklavier	sabre-battling	particularity
panic-stricken	haematologist	iatrochemical	parti-coloured
magistratical	cannibalistic	matriculation	party-coloured
radiotelegram	barnacle-goose	matriculatory	participially
magisterially	magnificently	macrocephalic	participantly
caliature-wood	damnification	macrodiagonal	participating
manipulatable	magnification	macrodactylic	participation
backwardation	launching-site	macroeconomic	participative
backscratcher	launching-ways	carrier-pigeon	tautochronism
lackadaisical	magnoliaceous	sacrificially	tautochronous
back-pedalling	magniloquence	matrifocality	carte-de-visite
hacking-jacket	dauntlessness	patrifocality	battle-scarred
packing-needle	gauntlet guard	caprification	cattle-lifting
walking-orders	magnanimously	tarry-fingered	tattie-lifting
walking-papers	darning-needle	saurognathous	pantheologist
Balkanisation	rainbow-chaser	iatrogenicity	parthenocarpy
parking-ticket	balneotherapy	barrel-vaulted	battle-cruiser
walking-ticket	rainbow-tinted	barrel-chested	rattle-brained
back-formation	lawn-sprinkler	matrilineally	pantheistical
mackerel-shark	garnisheement	garrulousness	vantage-ground
mackerel-midge	varnishing-day	macromolecule	mastigophoran
mackerel-guide	Parnassianism	matrimonially	mastigophoric
jack-crosstree	Saint-Simonian	patrimonially	Pantagruelian
marketability	Saint-Simonism	sacramentally	Pantagruelion
talkativeness	Saint-Simonist	tauromorphous	Pantagruelism
parliament-man	garnetiferous	patronisingly	Pantagruelist
parliamenting	magnetomotive	fair-and-square	cartridge-belt
parliamentary	magneto-optics	carrion-flower	partridge-wood
malleableness	magnetosphere	patriotically	dactylography
railway-stitch	magnetisation	Sauropterygia	cartilaginous
ball-cartridge	carnivorously	hair-splitting	earthly-minded
sable-coloured	sado-masochism	macropinakoid	dactyliomancy
hallucination	sado-masochist	barristership	tantalisingly
hallucinatory	panophthalmia	sacrosanctity	faithlessness
hallucinative	cat-o'-nine-tails	parrot-fashion	tastelessness
garlic-mustard	laboriousness	parrot-disease	cartelisation
cable-drilling	taxonomically	narrowcasting	tantalisation
eagle-flighted	cacographical	panspermatism	tautometrical
calligraphist	vapourishness	panspermatist	earth-movement
rallying-point	baton-sinister	laissez-passer	waiting-vassal
vaulting-horse	campeachy-wood	falsification	casting-weight
vaulting-house	palpable-gross	causelessness	xanthochromia
faultlessness	lampadephoria	balsamiferous	xanthochroism

xanthochroous
gastroenteric
gastrocnemius
gastrological
east-north-east
east-south-east
xanthopterine
party-politics
tautophonical
master-mariner
master-passion
factorability
martyrologist
dastardliness
bacteriophage
bacteriolysin
bacteriolysis
bacteriolytic
gasteropodous
cauterisation
factorisation
master-builder
masterfulness
wasterfulness
Baltoslavonic
pantisocratic
fantastically
party-spirited
partitionment
partition-wall
Malthusianism
manufacturing
Ranunculaceae
nature-worship
casualisation
vacuolisation
vacuum-cleaner
haruspication
daguerreotype
daguerreotypy
Casuarinaceae
casuistically
facultatively
salviniaceous
galvanoplasty
Calvinistical
galvanisation
laevorotation
laevorotatory
canvas-climber
baby-battering
Caryocaraceae
laryngologist
laryngoscopic
many-sidedness
labyrinthical
labyrinthitis
lady-in-waiting
baby-snatching
palynological
ranz-des-vaches
objectionable
objectionably

objectiveness
objectivistic
objectivation
observational
obliviousness
ebullioscopic
absorbability
obnoxiousness
aboriginalism
aboriginality
abortifacient
obtrusiveness
abstractional
obstinateness
obstructively
obtuse-angular
schadenfreude
occasionalism
occasionalist
occasionality
scrap-merchant
oceanological
oceanographer
oceanographic
acidification
academicalism
schematically
screech-martin
screech-thrush
accelerometer
sclerocaulous
sclerodermite
sclerodermous
scleroprotein
accessibility
acceptability
eccentrically
acceptilation
scribbling-pad
scrivenership
accidentalism
occidentalise
Occidentalism
Occidentalist
accidentality
accident-prone
actinobacilli
schizocarpous
schizogenesis
schizogenetic
Echinodermata
Schizophyceae
schizophrenia
schizophrenic
scripophilist
actinotherapy
acrimoniously
actinomorphic
Schizomycetes
schizomycetic
actinomycosis
scripturalism
scripturalist

ochlocratical
scoleciformia
scalpelliform
scalping-knife
acclimatation
scalenohedron
scaling-ladder
scolopendrine
Scolopendrium
ecclesiolater
ecclesiolatry
sculpturesque
scambling-days
ecumenicalism
scandal-bearer
scandalmonger
scintillation
economisation
iconomaticism
scenarisation
scholarliness
scholasticism
octocentenary
school-marmish
school-teacher
school-leaving
schoolgirlish
school-trained
accommodating
accommodation
accommodative
accompaniment
scapulimantic
scaphocephaly
Scyphomedusae
acaridomatium
acarodomatium
accreditation
scarlet-runner
scarification
scorification
scorchingness
scorpion-grass
achromatopsia
scathefulness
acetification
Scotification
acotyledonous
ichthyography
ichthyologist
ichthyopsidan
Ichthyosauria
Ichthyosaurus
acquiescently
acquiescingly
scouring-stick
actualisation
scrumptiously
acquirability
acculturation
schutzstaffel
Schwenkfelder
acrylonitrile

adiabatically
advantageable
educatability
educationally
admeasurement
adventuresome
adventurously
advertisement
admirableness
advisableness
administrable
administrator
admissibility
identicalness
adenoidectomy
odontophorous
odontoglossum
odontornithes
odontological
idiomatically
ideographical
idiorrhythmic
idiosyncratic
odoriferously
Addressograph®
separationist
separableness
hexadactylous
perambulation
perambulatory
decarbonation
debauchedness
revaccination
melancholious
recalcitrance
regardfulness
megacephalous
sexagesimally
dematerialise
nemathelminth
refashionment
metaphysician
metaphosphate
mesaticephaly
denationalise
nefariousness
tenaciousness
vexatiousness
metalliferous
metallography
metallurgical
metallisation
megalosaurian
melanochroous
pedagogically
teratological
metamorphoses
metamorphosis
megasporangia
metagrabolise
metagrobolise
metapsychical
metastability

pedantocratic	tender-hearted	heterothermal	receiving-room
telautography	deodorisation	ceremonialism	receiving-ship
tetartohedral	perditionable	renegotiation	defervescence
Melastomaceae	headquartered	ceremoniously	defervescency
tenant-in-chief	meadow-saffron	heteroblastic	self-satisfied
hexactinellid	generalisable	heteroplastic	self-abasement
devastatingly	generationism	heteroclitous	perfectionism
membranaceous	revelationist	developmental	perfectionist
Serbo-Croatian	vegetarianism	selenological	perfectionate
heebie-jeebies	generalissimo	heteromorphic	self-admission
verbigeration	temerariously	heterosporous	self-addressed
Leibnizianism	venerableness	selenographer	self-dependent
verbalisation	reverberation	heterotrophic	self-levelling
Berberidaceae	reverberatory	selenographic	self-revealing
herborisation	reverberative	heterostylism	self-defeating
deoch-an-doruis	seneschalship	heterostylous	self-deception
merchandising	rebecca-eureka	heterostrophy	self-deceitful
peaceableness	defencelessly	heteropterous	self-fertility
teachableness	level-crossing	level-peggings	self-denyingly
neoclassicism	mesencephalic	redemptionist	self-shielding
neoclassicist	mesencephalon	metempiricism	self-financing
peacock-copper	telescopiform	metempiricist	self-directing
peacock-flower	revendication	penetrability	self-direction
peach-coloured	serendipitous	desegregation	reaffirmation
leuco-compound	reference-mark	meteorologist	self-dispraise
peacock-throne	deleteriously	telegrammatic	self-slaughter
geochemically	venereologist	peregrination	self-important
reactionarism	telerecording	Tenebrionidae	self-annealing
reactionarist	decelerometer	telegraph-pole	self-infection
descriptively	redevelopment	telegraph-wire	self-injection
descriptivism	decerebration	cerebrospinal	reefing-jacket
reacclimatise	deferentially	penetratingly	self-inflicted
pencil-compass	referentially	penetratively	newfangleness
mercilessness	reverentially	defeasibility	self-enjoyment
peacelessness	beleaguerment	defensibility	perfunctorily
tercentennial	genethlialogy	reversibility	self-insurance
fencing-master	redeliverance	depersonalise	self-indulgent
geocentrism	beneficential	reversionally	self-induction
peace offering	heresiography	remeasurement	self knowledge
Cercopithecus	repetitionary	necessariness	self-conceited
sex-chromosome	televisionary	necessitarian	self-condemned
geochronology	dereligionise	necessitation	self-governing
mercerisation	beneficiation	necessitously	self-confident
percussion-cap	repetitiously	recessiveness	self-confiding
percussionist	heresiologist	deceptibility	self-confessed
leucitohedron	deterioration	defectibility	self-forgetful
pendragonship	deteriorative	delectability	self-conjugate
dead-reckoning	benedictional	detestability	self-collected
needle-pointed	redeemability	receptibility	self-pollution
re-edification	beseemingness	seventeenthly	self-communion
feudalisation	deterministic	pedestrianise	self-tormentor
pendulousness	determinately	pedestrianism	self-conscious
feeding-bottle	determination	reception-room	self-consuming
weeding-chisel	determinative	sedentariness	self-contained
wedding-finger	perennibranch	desertisation	self-convicted
wedding-favour	heterocarpous	deceitfulness	self-opinioned
tendentiously	Hemerobaptist	deceptiveness	self-appointed
redding-straik	heterogenesis	defectiveness	self-operating
Dendrocalamus	heterogenetic	receptiveness	self-approving
dendrological	heterogeneity	retentiveness	self-treatment
dead-colouring	heterogeneous	revenue-cutter	self-professed
lead-poisoning	heterothallic	deceivability	perfervidness
perdurability	heterochronic	receivability	self-propelled

self-criticism	semimenstrual	mediatorially	reflexibility
self-asserting	penitentially	register-plate	re-embarkation
self-assertion	sedimentology	sex-intergrade	vermiculation
self-assertive	regimentation	mediatisation	mermaid's-glove
self-assurance	sedimentation	semi-automatic	mermaid's-purse
self-sterility	sewing-machine	deliquescence	Neo-Melanesian
self-murdering	meningococcal	sericulturist	terminability
self-sufficing	meningococcic	deciduousness	helminthiasis
self-supported	meningococcus	semioviparous	helminthology
self-surrender	perishability	perityphlitis	fermentitious
self-sustained	delightedness	serjeant-at-law	Germanophilia
self-surviving	perichondrium	deck-passenger	seeming-simple
self-awareness	delirifacient	Berkeleianism	Germanisation
self-executing	verifiability	Neo-Kantianism	terminational
self-existence	reminiscently	seek-no-further	terminatively
self-hypnotism	medicine-chest	well-warranted	hermeneutical
hedge-accentor	verisimilarly	neglectedness	hermaphrodite
neogrammarian	penicilliform	well-beseeming	geomorphology
sergeant-major	meridionality	well-developed	mesmerisation
neighbourhood	deficientness	well-respected	permutability
hedge-marriage	deliciousness	well-regulated	dermatography
begging-letter	deliriousness	mellification	geometrically
sea-gooseberry	religiousness	mellifluently	dermatologist
weight-watcher	seditiousness	mellifluously	reimbursement
weight-lifting	sericiculture	negligibility	reincarnation
tergiversator	vexillologist	re-eligibility	bernicle-goose
methodistical	serialisation	belligerently	vernacularise
dephlegmation	feuilletonism	neologistical	vernacularism
technicalness	feuilletonist	well-thought-of	vernacularist
Cephalochorda	legislatorial	healthfulness	vernacularity
keyhole-limpet	legislatively	celluliferous	reinterrogate
nephelometric	beginningless	Neo-Lamarckian	reintegration
cephalothorax	semilogarithm	Neo-Lamarckism	neanderthaler
mechanisation	semiporcelain	declamatorily	reunification
nephrological	retinoscopist	selling-plater	penny-farthing
technological	semiconductor	seal-engraving	Jenny-long-legs
Netherlandish	Lepidodendron	Hellenistical	pennilessness
lethargically	meritoriously	replenishment	vernalisation
lecherousness	genito-urinary	well-conducted	re-enforcement
hemiparasitic	lexicographer	well-worked-out	reinforcement
semiparasitic	lexicographic	well-connected	deontological
semi-barbarian	semiconscious	meals-on-wheels	penny-pinching
semi-barbarism	Lepidostrobus	well-appointed	Semnopithecus
semicarbazide	lepidopterist	deplorability	seine-shooting
peripatetical	lepidopterous	well-preserved	reinstatement
medicamentary	helispherical	declaratorily	memorableness
pelican-flower	hemispherical	declaratively	revocableness
derivationist	reciprocality	belles-lettres	recombination
recitationist	reciprocation	realistically	reconcilement
semi-sagittate	reciprocative	perlustration	lemon-coloured
desirableness	demiurgically	deglutination	secondariness
semipalmation	defibrillator	pelletisation	aerogenerator
perigastritis	defibrination	yellow-bellied	mesocephalism
periodicalist	lexigraphical	fellow-feeling	mesocephalous
revindication	remissibility	fellow-servant	xerodermatous
bewilderingly	perissodactyl	fellow-citizen	deforestation
periodisation	peninsularity	yellow-covered	recomfortless
perihepatitis	redissolution	yellow-yorling	xerophthalmia
perinephritis	revictualling	yellow-spotted	negotiability
semiperimeter	registrarship	yellow-fronted	aerolithology
Pedicellariae	resistibility	yellow-crowned	demolitionist
semipermeable	remittance-man	yellowishness	refocillation
mediterranean	resistance-box	yellow-bunting	devotionalist

feloniousness	deipnosophist	heir-portioner	gentianaceous
ferociousness	sexploitation	zebra-parakeet	left-handiness
melodiousness	jet-propulsion	neuropathical	velt-mareschal
recollectedly	temperamental	decrepitation	geotactically
désobligeante	pepper-and-salt	terrorisation	verticillated
deformability	temporariness	recrystallise	denticulation
reformability	temporisingly	heart-sickness	gesticulation
recommendable	temporisation	pearl-shelling	gesticulatory
recommendably	desperateness	retrospection	leptocephalic
metoposcopist	temperateness	retrospective	leptocephalus
serologically	tempest-beaten	ferrosoferric	Testicardines
Peloponnesian	tempest-tossed	neurastheniac	pentadactylic
demonological	tempestuously	heuristically	pentadelphous
decompression	bespottedness	peirastically	weather-anchor
recompression	sempstressing	tetrastichous	gentlemanhood
decompressive	herpetologist	heart-stirring	gentlemanlike
decomposition	sesquiplicate	tetrasyllabic	gentlemanship
recomposition	rearrangement	tetrasyllable	weather-beaten
melodramatist	reproachfully	wearisomeness	feather-bonnet
cerographical	retroactively	representamen	weather-bitten
reconsolidate	retroactivity	representable	weather-driven
remorselessly	Tetrabranchia	representment	feather-duster
reconstructor	heartbreaking	necroscopical	gentle-hearted
remonstrantly	jerry-building	terrestrially	weather-headed
demonstration	retributively	heart-stricken	aesthetically
remonstration	ferricyanogen	territorially	penthemimeral
demonstratory	ferrocyanogen	secretary-bird	heat-resistant
remonstratory	petrochemical	secretaryship	leather-jacket
demonstrative	tetrachloride	secretiveness	leather-lunged
remonstrative	ferroconcrete	neurovascular	gentlewomanly
gerontocratic	refractometer	geostationary	weatherometer
decortication	petrocurrency	versicoloured	centre-forward
gerontologist	ferrochromium	rensselaerite	beetlebrained
decontaminant	deprecatingly	Meistersinger	kettledrummer
decontaminate	tetradynamous	perspectively	beetle-crusher
gerontophilia	recrudescence	perspectivism	feather-stitch
devolutionary	recrudescency	versification	weather-symbol
revolutionary	ferroelectric	perspicacious	feather-weight
devolutionist	reorientation	perspicuously	leather-winged
revolutionise	metrification	senselessness	beatification
revolutionism	petrification	leishmaniasis	certification
revolutionist	retroflection	leishmaniosis	rectification
resolvability	retrogression	pessimistical	testification
aerodynamical	retrogressive	messenger-wire	certificatory
genotypically	refrigeration	leasing-making	testificatory
metonymically	refrigeratory	sea-shouldring	pestiferously
temptableness	refrigerative	seismological	vertiginously
Neo-Plasticism	search-warrant	seismographer	centricalness
neoplasticism	reprehensible	seismographic	ventriloquial
tea-plantation	reprehensibly	sessions-house	ventriloquise
despicability	searchingness	pease-porridge	ventriloquism
resplendently	terra-japonica	mensurability	ventriloquist
perplexedness	petroliferous	Messerschmitt	ventriloquous
terpsichorean	heartlessness	measuring-tape	restrictively
reapplication	ferromagnetic	measuring-worm	centrifugally
geopolitician	detrimentally	perscrutation	centrifugence
weaponshawing	retromingency	versatileness	reptiliferous
perpendicular	necromantical	densitometric	rectilinearly
serpent-lizard	decriminalise	sensationally	deathlessness
weeping-spring	recrimination	sensitisation	fertilisation
weeping-willow	recriminatory	sensitiveness	sentimentally
tenpenny-piece	recriminative	perseveringly	geitonogamous
reappointment	retranslation	perseveration	sententiously

netting-needle
septentrional
septentriones
peptonisation
Teutonisation
rectangularly
dextrocardiac
section-cutter
geotropically
rent-collector
rectipetality
leptophyllous
tent-preaching
letter-carrier
Heath-Robinson
letter-perfect
nectariferous
deuterogamist
helter-skelter
Deuteronomist
letter-founder
yestermorning
letters-patent
venturesomely
deuteroscopic
restoratively
dexterousness
venturousness
yesterevening
lectisternium
pentastichous
leptospirosis
heptasyllabic
pentasyllabic
restaurant-car
destructional
destructively
destructivist
destructivity
resuscitation
resuscitative
gerund-grinder
rejuvenescent
beauteousness
regurgitation
deducibleness
reducibleness
penuriousness
Gemütlichkeit
republicanise
republicanism
reduplication
republication
reduplicative
sequentiality
desulphuriser
sequestration
requisiteness
repulsiveness
deductibility
desultoriness
seductiveness
nervelessness

heaven-kissing
serving-mallet
heave-offering
heave-shoulder
pervasiveness
velvet-fiddler
nerve-wracking
betweenwhiles
seaworthiness
sea-water-green
deoxidisation
re-examination
re-exportation
Lecythidaceae
demythologise
affenpinscher
offensiveness
effectualness
effectiveness
effervescence
effervescency
effervescible
offhandedness
efficaciously
officiousness
affirmatively
efflorescence
afforestation
affreightment
egocentricity
agreeableness
egregiousness
agriculturist
agglomeration
agglomerative
agglutination
agglutinative
agonistically
ignominiously
agrobiologist
agrostologist
Egyptological
aggravatingly
egotistically
phraseologist
thrashing-mill
thrasonically
theatricalise
theatricalism
theatricality
theanthropism
theanthropist
Chlamydomonas
chlamydospore
rhabdomantist
shabby-genteel
shock-absorber
chicken-hazard
phycoerythrin
chuck-farthing
thick-pleached
check-weighman
rhodochrosite

rhadamanthine
shadowcasting
chrematistics
three-cornered
wheel-carriage
wheeler-dealer
Phlegethontic
phrenetically
threefoldness
three-farthing
threshing-mill
thresher-whale
thresher-shark
thremmatology
Rhaeto-Romance
Rhaeto-Romanic
phaenological
phrenological
threepenn'orth
three-per-cents
sheep-stealing
sheep-shearing
chieftainship
chrestomathic
threateningly
phreatophytic
shiftlessness
thigmotropism
phthalocyanin
thrillingness
shrill-tongued
chain-moulding
Cheirotherium
cheirographer
cheiropterous
Christianlike
Christianness
Christmas-tide
Christmas-tree
Christmas-time
Christologist
Shakespearean
Shakespearian
phylacterical
whole-coloured
cholecystitis
Philadelphian
challengeable
challengingly
philhellenism
philhellenist
Thalamiflorae
thalamifloral
philomathical
philanthropic
whaling-master
phalansterian
phalansterism
phalansterist
phellogenetic
phyllophagous
phelloplastic
shell-ornament

chalcographer
phylloquinone
shell-parakeet
wholesomeness
thalassocracy
philosophical
philosophiser
thalattocracy
chimney-breast
chimney-corner
chamber-fellow
chymification
shamefastness
whimsicalness
Thymelaeaceae
chameleonlike
thimble-rigger
shamelessness
rhombporphyry
chemoreceptor
shammy-leather
phantasmalian
phantasmality
phonocamptics
thunder-bearer
changeability
thunder-darter
chinkerinchee
change-ringing
thunder-master
thenceforward
thunder-shower
thunder-struck
thunder-strike
thunder-stroke
changefulness
phonographist
changing-piece
thing-in-itself
phenylalanine
shingle-roofed
thanklessness
phenomenology
phenomenalise
phenomenalism
phenomenalist
phenomenality
phonendoscope
thank-offering
phanerogamous
rhinoscleroma
thanatography
thanatophobia
phonautograph
thankworthily
theopaschitic
chlorargyrite
chromatically
chromatophore
chromatograph
thrombokinase
theorematical
chrome-tanning

chrome-leather
theoretically
chrome-plating
through-ticket
shooting-range
throwing-table
shooting-lodge
whooping-cough
shooting-board
shooting-brake
shooting-stick
throwing-stick
phlogisticate
Chlorophyceae
theologically
chronobiology
chronological
chloroformist
chlorobromide
chlorocruorin
chronographer
Chloromycetin®
throttle-valve
throttle-lever
ship-carpenter
ship-of-the-line
ship-chandlery
whipping-cheer
chopping-block
chopping-knife
chopping-board
whipping-cream
rhopalocerous
shapelessness
rhapsodically
rhyparography
shop-assistant
charlatanical
pharmaceutics
pharmaceutist
pharmacognosy
pharmacopoeia
Pherecrataean
characterless
short-division
charter-member
thurification
sheriff-depute
chirographist
church-service
church-officer
thereinbefore
whirling-table
whereinsoever
chiromantical
whoremasterly
pharyngoscope
pharyngoscopy
thermobalance
thermogenesis
thermogenetic
thermosetting
thermophilous

thermochemist
thermoplastic
theriomorphic
choreographer
choreographic
thermographic
thermotropism
thermonuclear
thermodynamic
chorepiscopal
pharisaically
sharpshooting
short-tempered
charity-school
thorough-paced
thorough-going
thoroughbrace
sherry-cobbler
physharmonica
physicianship
phase-contrast
whiskerandoed
phosphorylase
phosphoretted
phosphuretted
whistle-blower
whistled-drunk
whistling-shop
physiotherapy
physiognomist
physiological
physiographer
physiographic
chest-register
physitheistic
Chateaubriand
white-breasted
photochemical
photochromics
photochromism
photoelectric
photoelectron
photo-emission
whithersoever
white-favoured
photographist
phytoplankton
photophoresis
photoperiodic
photo-receptor
phytotoxicity
photovoltaics
what-d'ye-call-'em
what-d'ye-call-it
thousand-pound
rheumatically
thaumatolatry
thaumaturgics
thaumaturgism
thaumaturgist
shoulder-blade
shoulder-joint
shoulder-strap

thoughtlessly
thought-reader
cheval-de-frise
chrysanthemum
chrysophilite
rhizomorphous
cigarette-butt
cigarette-card
disaffectedly
disaffirmance
vicariousness
vivaciousness
miracle-monger
Titanotherium
disappearance
misappreciate
disappointing
disagreeables
cicatrisation
disassimilate
disarticulate
gigantomachia
misanthropist
disadvantaged
misadventured
misadventurer
misadvertence
timbrophilist
discharge-tube
piscicultural
witches-butter
kitchen-garden
discreditable
discreditably
discretionary
kitchen-midden
zincification
pitch-farthing
miscegenation
mischief-maker
discriminator
mischievously
miscellaneous
discoloration
circumjacency
circumvallate
circumscriber
discomycetous
circumference
circumvention
circumventive
discommission
circumfluence
circumflexion
circumambages
circumambient
discommodious
circumspectly
miscomprehend
air-compressor
viscometrical
circumduction
circumductory

discontenting
disconcertion
disconnection
misconception
misconjecture
discontentful
discontinuity
discontinuous
disconformity
cinchonaceous
disceptatious
discapacitate
disciplinable
miscorrection
diachronistic
visceroptosis
viscosimetric
diacatholicon
Hildebrandism
vindicability
vindicatorily
fiddle-faddler
fiddle-pattern
Middle-Eastern
middle-bracket
tiddledywinks
biodegradable
findon-haddock
winding-engine
sindonologist
bidding-prayer
Bildungsroman
kindergartner
Kidderminster
tic-douloureux
window-curtain
kindly-natured
liberationism
liberationist
miserableness
mineralogical
cinematograph
kinematograph
disembodiment
disembarkment
liver-coloured
vice-admiralty
life-rendering
mine-detection
fire-resistant
fire-resisting
time-bettering
time-beguiling
disengagement
dimethylamine
kinesipathist
line-fisherman
kinesitherapy
kinesiologist
time-signature
vitelligenous
pigeon-fancier
pigeon-hearted

hide-and-go-seek
pigeon-chested
pigeon-livered
line-engraving
hibernisation
fire-insurance
life-insurance
Ciceronianism
vice-consulate
time-consuming
side-splitting
pineapple-weed
disemployment
misemployment
cine-projector
birefringence
vice-principal
vice-president
life-preserver
diversifiable
dimensionless
life-assurance
digestibility
divertibility
diverticulate
wide-stretched
disestimation
dilettanteism
divertisement
disequilibria
wide-awakeness
livery-servant
livery-company
disfigurement
disfiguration
disfellowship
differentiate
diffusibility
diffusion-tube
diffusiveness
disgracefully
Zingiberaceae
single-hearted
single-chamber
pilgrim-bottle
disguisedness
linguistician
singing-master
wing-commander
biogeographer
diageotropism
diagnostician
niggardliness
finger-pointer
jiggery-pokery
finger-breadth
disgospelling
misgovernment
pigheadedness
disheartening
dichlamydeous
dishabilitate
eighteen-pence

eighteen-penny
righteousness
light-fingered
tithe-gatherer
diphthongally
light-horseman
High-Churchman
High-Churchism
lighthouseman
might-have-been
light-infantry
sightlessness
lichenologist
lightning-tube
lithontriptic
lithontriptor
fishing-tackle
dishonourable
dishonourably
dichrooscopic
xiphiplastral
xiphiplastron
disharmonious
light-spirited
lightsomeness
lithesomeness
right-thinking
night-tripping
lithotriptist
high-stomached
dichotomously
night-wanderer
night-warbling
night-watchman
high-explosive
filipendulous
vivisectional
vivisectorium
vivisepulture
riding-clothes
disinhibition
disinhibitory
diminishingly
division-lobby
litigiousness
disilluminate
limitlessness
disillusioned
visionariness
disintegrable
disintegrator
ministerially
disinterested
minisubmarine
filibustering
filibusterism
viniculturist
viticulturist
filibusterous
disinvigorate
disinvestment
Zinjanthropus
disjunctively

nick-nackatory
pickle-herring
sickle-feather
winkle-pickers
sick-feathered
milk-dentition
zinkification
silk-throwster
sick-thoughted
nickeliferous
nickel-plating
pinking-shears
lickerishness
ticket-of-leave
ticket-writing
Rickettsiales
tickly-benders
billiard-table
billiard-cloth
yieldableness
dialectically
viol-de-gamboys
gillie-wetfoot
millefeuilles
villeggiatura
dialogistical
villagisation
dipleidoscope
diplomatology
violoncellist
millennialist
millennianism
millenniarism
bibliolatrist
millionairess
bibliolatrous
bibliothecary
bibliophagist
bibliophilism
bibliophilist
wills-o'-the-wisp
bibliopolical
bibliographer
bibliographic
dialypetalous
will-o'-the-wisps
millstone-grit
willow-warbler
sigmoidoscope
dismemberment
diamond-beetle
mismanagement
Birminghamise
diamond-powder
diametrically
significantly
dignification
lignification
signification
significatory
significative
cinnamon-stone
finnan-haddock

bignoniaceous
dinner-service
pianistically
disnaturalise
signature-tune
disordinately
disobediently
mitochondrial
mitochondrion
disobligement
disobligingly
disobligation
disobligatory
lipogrammatic
ailourophilia
ailourophobia
widow's-chamber
misobservance
Dicotyledones
diaphanometer
dispraisingly
displantation
simple-hearted
displeasingly
tippling-house
simplificator
dipping-needle
diaphototropy
disproportion
misproportion
hippopotamian
dispurveyance
dispersedness
diaphragmatic
disparagement
disparagingly
dispiritingly
disparateness
mispersuasion
dispossession
dispassionate
dispositional
dispositioned
dispositively
disputability
dispatch-rider
disputatively
cinque-spotted
disquietingly
microanalysis
nitrobacteria
vibracularium
nitro-compound
microcomputer
microcephalic
microcosmical
microdetector
microeconomic
nitrification
vitrification
microfelsitic
microgranitic
hierogrammate

hieroglyphist	fictionalised	electrography	clincher-built
micrometrical	histiophoroid	electromagnet	plantie-cruive
citronella-oil	Winter-gardens	electromerism	plentifulness
micronutrient	filterability	electrometric	flint-knapping
micro-organism	winter-aconite	electromotive	blindman's-buff
microprinting	Dipterocarpus	electrophorus	planimetrical
disreputation	picture-palace	electrostatic	clinopinacoid
microphyllous	picturesquely	electroscopic	clinopinakoid
librarianship	picture-window	electrisation	alongshoreman
mirror-writing	distastefully	electrothermy	plenitudinous
disrespectful	dictatorially	electrotypist	planetologist
dioristically	mistrustingly	electrovalent	oleomargarine
microscopical	distrustfully	clock-watching	allowableness
Diprotodontia	mistrustfully	gladiatorshlp	blood-boltered
microtonality	kittly-benders	bladder-cherry	blood-curdling
vibrationless	Sipunculoidea	Illecebraceae	almond-blossom
fibrovascular	misunderstand	bleeding-heart	illogicalness
misshapenness	misunderstood	sleeping-berth	floodlighting
first-begotten	figure-casting	illegibleness	bloodlessness
bioscientific	figure-weaving	sleep-learning	alcoholometer
dissolubility	figure-skating	sleeplessness	alcoholometry
dieselisation	ritualisation	alternatively	blood-relation
dissoluteness	visualisation	allegorically	Bloomsburyite
dissemblingly	silver-shafted	allelomorphic	illocutionary
dissimilarity	silver-tongued	algebraically	elephantiasis
dissimilitude	silver-mounted	ill-favouredly	elephant's-ears
dissimilation	airworthlness	flagellantism	elephant's-foot
dissimulation	piezoelectric	plagiotropism	clapperboards
dissimulative	piezomagnetic	plagiostomata	clapperclawer
dissemination	skulking-place	plagiostomous	glyphographer
disseminative	skeletogenous	oligopolistic	glyphographic
kissing-comfit	skirting-board	flight-feather	glyptographic
kiss-in-the-ring	skirl-in-the-pan	alphabetiform	floricultural
Dioscoreaceae	skateboarding	alphabetarian	clarification
first-offender	sketchability	All-hallowmass	glorification
dissepimental	skittle-ground	All-hallowtide	pluralisation
fissiparously	cloak-and-sword	clairaudience	pluripresence
lissotrichous	cleavableness	sleight-of-hand	floristically
disseveration	clearing-house	plaigotropous	ultra tropical
linsey-woolsey	clear-starcher	plain-speaking	ultra-virtuous
distractingly	olfactologist	cleistogamous	blister-beetle
distractively	clean-timbered	cloister-garth	glass-grinding
biotechnology	pleasure-house	plaintiveness	blasphemously
tittle-tattler	plebification	climacterical	classicalness
diotheletical	globuliferous	climactically	clishmaclaver
diothelitical	globalisation	flame-coloured	plesiosaurian
diathermanous	elaborateness	Flammenwerfer	blastogenesis
distressingly	globe-trotting	climbing-frame	glossological
distressfully	black-and-white	plumbisolvent	glossographer
histrionicism	clickety-clack	aluminiferous	glass-painting
distributable	clickety-click	plumbosolvent	slate-coloured
mirthlessness	blackguardism	glamorisation	platycephalic
victimologist	floccillation	clamorousness	clothes-basket
fifth-monarchy	electioneerer	climatography	Kletterschuhe
victimisation	ill-considered	climatologist	clothes-screen
tintinnabular	old-clothesman	plantain-eater	blotting-paper
tintinnabulum	plectognathic	clinodiagonal	plotting-paper
lifting-bridge	glaciological	flannel-flower	platiniferous
listening-post	plectopterous	blanket-stitch	plethorically
distant-signal	electrochemic	clandestinely	plate-printing
distinctively	electrocement	clandestinity	platyrrhinian
distinguished	electrocution	plenteousness	platitudinise
distinguisher	electrifiable	blankety-blank	platitudinous

floutingstock
flourishingly
plausibleness
illustriously
fluvioglacial
flower-service
clay-ironstone
immarcescible
immarcessible
immaterialise
immaterialism
immaterialist
immateriality
imparipinnate
impalpability
embarrassment
impassability
impassibility
ambassadorial
impassiveness
impartialness
impartibility
impeccability
imperceptible
imperceptibly
impenetration
imperfectible
imperfectness
imperforation
imperialistic
immediateness
imperiousness
umbelliferous
embellishment
impermissible
impermissibly
impersonalise
impersonality
impersonation
imperseverant
impertinently
imperturbable
imperturbably
impecuniosity
impetuousness
amygdalaceous
emigrationist
amphigastrium
emphysematous
amphitheatral
immiscibility
amniocentesis
ambidexterity
ambidexterous
ambitiousness
impignoration
omnicompetent
ambiguousness
smoke-consumer
smokelessness
small-and-early
implacability
implicatively

amplification
smelling-salts
smelting-works
smelting-house
immovableness
imponderables
smooth-chinned
smooth-dittied
smooth-tongued
impolitically
impossibilism
impossibilist
impossibility
impostumation
importunately
omoplatoscopy
improbability
impracticable
impracticably
umbraculiform
embracingness
umbrella-stand
emerald-copper
amarantaceous
Amaranthaceae
embranglement
embryogenesis
embryological
impropriation
impressionism
impressionist
improvability
improvidently
improvisatrix
improvisation
improvisatory
imitativeness
immutableness
imputableness
immunotherapy
immunological
impulsiveness
empyreumatise
unmacadamised
uneatableness
untamableness
uncalculating
incarceration
incandescence
unsaleability
intangibility
ensanguinated
unfashionable
unfashionably
insatiability
invariability
unsatisfiable
unfamiliarity
insatiateness
infallibilism
infallibilist
infallibility
ungainsayable

undauntedness
untaintedness
unsaintliness
unsavouriness
unwarrantable
unwarrantably
unwarrantedly
encapsulation
unearthliness
unfalteringly
unpasteurised
unnaturalised
unnaturalness
inobservation
inobtrusively
unobtrusively
unabbreviated
unobstructive
knickerbocker
unaccentuated
inscriptional
inscriptively
knick-knackery
inoculability
knuckleduster
unicameralism
unicameralist
unscholarlike
onychophagist
unaccountable
unaccountably
unaccompanied
Anacardiaceae
anachronistic
anachronously
unscrutinised
unscavengered
ineducability
inadvertently
unadventurous
unadvisedness
unadulterated
inodorousness
underachiever
indefatigable
indefatigably
annexationist
untenableness
interbreeding
underclassman
indescribable
indescribably
undescribable
unperceivable
unperceivably
unperceivedly
intercolumnar
intercolonial
intercalation
intercalative
intercellular
unwelcomeness
intercommunal

undescendable
undescendible
underclothing
intercropping
intercurrence
undercarriage
invendibility
interdigitate
interdentally
unbendingness
unremembering
independently
unregenerated
indeterminacy
unbeseemingly
indeterminism
indeterminist
indeterminate
undeterminate
unceremonious
underexposure
unnecessarily
inferentially
underestimate
interestingly
unrelentingly
unrepentingly
undeservingly
unperfectness
interferingly
unselfishness
undergraduate
unneighboured
unneighbourly
unfeignedness
intergalactic
encephalocele
encephalogram
Encephalartos
encephalotomy
underhandedly
unreliability
unmedicinable
indelibleness
undeviatingly
unremittently
unremittingly
unresistingly
ingeniousness
unbelievingly
interjaculate
interjectural
index-learning
unreplaceable
interlacement
interlocutrix
interlocation
interlocution
interlocutory
intelligencer
intelligently
unhealthiness
unhealthfully

unreclaimable
unreclaimably
interlaminate
unfeelingness
unreplenished
interlunation
intermediator
intermarriage
intermittence
intermittency
underniceness
antenniferous
unmeaningness
international
interosculant
interosculate
unrecoverable
unrecoverably
interoceptive
anaerobically
unrecollected
unrecommended
unrecognising
Enteropneusta
unrecompensed
unremorseless
underprepared
interpretable
interpretress
interpilaster
interpolation
interpolative
interpunction
interparietal
interpersonal
intemperately
interposition
unperpetrated
interpetiolar
unreproaching
unreproachful
undepreciated
interradially
unreprievable
unlearnedness
interrogation
interrogatory
interrogative
interrelation
unreprimanded
endearingness
interruptedly
unrepresented
unterrestrial
unpersuadable
understanding
interscapular
infeasibility
insensibility
incense-burner
intersidereal
under-shepherd
interspecific

interstellary
interspersion
unreasoningly
understrapper
interstratify
insensateness
unsensational
insensitively
insensitivity
intensiveness
ungentlemanly
unsettledness
investigation
investigatory
investigative
entertainment
uncertainness
insectologist
unsentimental
unrestingness
intentionally
unmentionable
intertropical
inventorially
unrestfulness
infectiveness
inventiveness
insectivorous
integumentary
unreturningly
ungenuineness
ingenuousness
unserviceable
ineffableness
snuff-coloured
inoffensively
ineffectually
ineffectively
inefficacious
snifting-valve
inefficiently
inofficiously
snaffle-bridle
enigmatically
anagrammatise
anagrammatism
anagrammatist
knight-marshal
knights-errant
knight-service
unshrinkingly
unchristianly
unthriftiness
anthelminthic
unwholesomely
unphilosophic
enchondromata
anthropolatry
anthropogenic
anthropometry
anthropophagi
anthropophagy

untheological
anthroposophy
anthropomorph
anthophyllite
unchastisable
anti-marketeer
antiballistic
invincibility
antiochianism
uncircumcised
undiscomfited
undisciplined
undiscernedly
indiscernible
indiscernibly
undiscernible
undiscernibly
antiscorbutic
undiscussable
undiscussible
undiscouraged
unmindfulness
antinephritic
antigenically
undiversified
anti-personnel
antisepticise
antisepticism
engine-turning
undifferenced
indifferently
undisguisable
undisguisedly
enlightenment
unrighteously
antichristian
unsightliness
undishonoured
unwithholding
unwithdrawing
unmitigatedly
infinitesimal
undividedness
unlimitedness
invisibleness
antihistamine
unministerial
individualise
individualism
individualist
individuality
insidiousness
invidiousness
unpitifulness
individuation
inviolability
anticlockwise
anticlimactic
unwillingness
anticlinorium
inviolateness
insignificant
antilogarithm

oneiroscopist
anticoagulant
antisocialism
antisocialist
antisociality
antinomianism
environmental
indispensable
indispensably
antispasmodic
indisposition
unvitrifiable
antigropeloes
indissuadable
indissuadably
indissociable
angiospermous
unbiassedness
indissolvable
undistracting
undistributed
undistempered
unwittingness
indistinction
indistinctive
undistinctive
undisturbedly
unmistrustful
insinuatingly
antiquitarian
unskilfulness
Anglo-American
uncleanliness
unpleasurable
unpleasurably
inelaborately
unelectrified
Anglo-Catholic
influentially
ineligibility
analogousness
unflinchingly
inclinational
inclinatorium
inflorescence
unblessedness
Anglo-Saxondom
unilateralism
unilateralist
unilaterality
uncloudedness
unilluminated
unillustrated
inflexibility
inflexionless
unamiableness
unembarrassed
unimpassioned
animadversion
unimpeachable
unembellished
unimaginative
unambitiously

13 ənəməi

unambiguously
animal-worship
anomalistical
animalisation
un-Americanise
unimpregnated
unimpressible
inimitability
mnemotechnics
mnemotechnist
unsmotherable
unemotionally
onomatopoesis
onomatopoetic
uninhabitable
uninteresting
unintelligent
unintermitted
uninterrupted
unentertained
unintentional
enantiodromia
enantiodromic
unenlightened
unanticipated
enantiomorphy
enantiotropic
uninfluential
uninflammable
inanimateness
uninformative
uninstructive
uninquisitive
uninaugurated
unknowingness
unpolarisable
innovationist
enjoyableness
unwomanliness
incombustible
incombustibly
unconcealable
inconceivable
inconceivably
unconceivable
unconceivably
unconcernedly
unconcernment
unsoldierlike
incondensable
unconditional
unconditioned
unforeseeable
ontogenically
unforeskinned
endometriosis
undomesticate
uncomfortable
uncomfortably
unconformable
unconformably
unforgettable
unforgettably

incongruously
unforgiveable
unforgiveness
insociability
unsociability
encomiastical
innoxiousness
unconjectured
unconjunctive
unworkmanlike
unworldliness
endosmometric
uncommendable
uncommendably
incommunicado
incommiscible
informatician
informational
unboundedness
incognoscible
inhomogeneity
inhomogeneous
entomophagous
entomophilous
ontologically
entomological
entomostracan
uncomplaining
uncomplaisant
uncomplicated
uncompensated
uncompanioned
incorporeally
incorporating
incorporation
incorporative
unco-operative
uncooperative
incompossible
encompassment
inhospitality
incompetently
uncompetitive
unconquerable
unconquerably
incorrectness
encouragement
encouragingly
unco-ordinated
uncoordinated
uncourtliness
endocrinology
incorruptible
incorruptibly
incorruptness
unconsecrated
inconsecutive
unconsidering
inconsiderate
inconsciently
unconsciously
inconspicuous
unconsummated

inconsonantly
inconsequence
unconstrained
inconsistence
inconsistency
unforthcoming
indoctrinator
uncontentious
incontinently
unfortunately
incontestable
incontestably
uncontestable
involucellate
insolubleness
involuntarily
innocuousness
insolvability
inconvenience
inconveniency
inconvincible
inconversable
unconversable
inconvertible
inconvertibly
unconvertible
unspecialised
unspectacular
unspeculative
inspectorship
anaphorically
inopportunely
inopportunist
inopportunity
inoperability
unappreciated
inappreciable
anaphrodisiac
unapprehended
unsparingness
inappropriate
unappropriate
unspiritually
inspiritingly
inspirational
unapprovingly
unapostolical
unspottedness
unequivocally
uncreatedness
encroachingly
inorganically
intra-arterial
unprecedented
unpracticable
unpractically
onirocritical
intracellular
intracapsular
intricateness
anfractuosity
infructuously
incredibility

unpredictable
unbridledness
incredulously
androdioecism
energetically
introgression
unprogressive
unoriginality
unarticulated
ungrammatical
untremblingly
incriminatory
unpromisingly
intramuscular
untransformed
intrinsically
intransigence
intransigency
untransmitted
untransparent
unpreoccupied
unprophetical
intraparietal
intrapetiolar
untrespassing
introspection
introspective
unpresentable
intrusiveness
untrustworthy
unbrotherlike
unpretentious
intratropical
unprovocative
unprovided-for
unpreventable
untraversable
introversible
unprovisioned
intravasation
unestablished
unascertained
unassimilated
unassimilable
anastigmatism
anisophyllous
unsteadfastly
unit-packaging
anathematical
inattentively
unstigmatised
instigatingly
anythingarian
instantaneity
instantaneous
instantiation
instinctually
instinctively
instinctivity
unstercorated
institutional
institutively
unstaunchable

instructional	answerability	double-or-quits	powdering-gown
instructively	inexhaustible	hobby-horsical	soldering-iron
pneumatically	inexhaustibly	combinatorial	powdering-room
undulationist	inexperienced	bombastically	wonder-working
endurableness	unexperienced	combativeness	wonder-wounded
incurableness	inexpediently	touchableness	ponderousness
untunableness	inexpensively	coachbuilding	wonderfulness
pneumatometer	unexpensively	concyclically	condescending
pneumatophore	unexceptional	concretionary	condescension
pneumatolysis	unexaggerated	non-cognisable	conditionally
pneumatolytic	unexplainable	conceitedness	coadjutorship
unpurchasable	unexclusively	porcellaneous	Wordsworthian
insusceptible	unexemplified	non-collegiate	homeward-bound
insusceptibly	inexorability	porcelain-clay	dodecaphonist
unsusceptible	inexpressible	porcelaineous	tolerationist
unpunctuality	inexpressibly	voicelessness	moderatorship
infundibulate	unexpressible	coxcombically	power-assisted
unputdownable	encyclopaedia	non-compliance	nomenclatural
unsuperfluous	encyclopaedic	non-compounder	women-children
untunefulness	unsymmetrical	concomitantly	honeycomb-moth
insufficience	unsymmetrised	volcanologist	robe-de-chambre
insufficiency	enhypostatise	nonconforming	forefeelingly
ingurgitation	unsympathetic	nonconformist	forementioned
injudiciously	monarchianism	nonconformity	lozenge-shaped
inaudibleness	tobaccanalian	concentricity	foreshadowing
incuriousness	non-acceptance	concentration	foresightless
injuriousness	non-aggression	concentrative	co-religionist
undutifulness	boraginaceous	volcanisation	co-belligerent
induplication	logarithmical	non-conducting	powerlessness
unqualifiedly	volatilisable	conchological	homeomorphism
unmurmuringly	foraminiferal	conceptionist	homeomorphous
pneumogastric	vocationalism	porcupine-wood	hole-and-corner
insubordinate	voraciousness	concupiscence	hole-in-the-wall
pneumonectomy	coralliferous	concupiscible	modernisation
unsuspectedly	coralligenous	conceptualise	solemnisation
insuppressive	Mohammedanise	conceptualism	foreknowledge
insupportable	Mohammedanism	conceptualist	foreknowingly
insupportably	cocainisation	concernedness	Polemoniaceae
unsupportable	potato-disease	concert-master	vote-splitting
unsupportedly	potamological	vouchsafement	power-politics
unsurpassable	somatological	concessionary	domestication
unsurpassably	gonadotrophic	concessionist	homeothermous
unguardedness	gonadotrophin	concatenation	homeoteleuton
insubstantial	Romano-British	concavo-convex	potentiometer
unsubstantial	non-appearance	coachwhip-bird	momentariness
unquestioning	noradrenaline	wood-sandpiper	momentousness
inquisitional	woman-suffrage	good-naturedly	forejudgement
inquisitorial	romanticality	conductorship	bone-turquoise
inquisitively	copartnership	coeducational	confraternity
unsuitability	cobaltiferous	road-metalling	conflagration
unjustifiable	non-attendance	soldierliness	confabulation
unjustifiably	roe-blackberry	wood-germander	confabulatory
unsustainable	double-natured	good-King-Henry	confectionary
industrialise	double-dealing	condylomatous	confectionery
industrialism	double-hearted	word-blindness	confidingness
industrialist	double-shuffle	cold-bloodedly	confederation
industriously	double-shotted	toad-in-the-hole	confederative
unhurtfulness	double-glazing	golden-crested	coffee-disease
unevangelical	double-concave	wood-engraving	configuration
inevitability	double-tongued	woodcock's-head	non-fulfilment
knowledgeable	double-founted	word-splitting	confrontation
knowledgeably	double-jointed	ponderability	non-forfeiting
snow-blindness	double-crosser	soldering-bolt	confarreation

confessionary
confessorship
confoundingly
rough-and-ready
congratulable
congratulator
tongue-lashing
long-descended
Congreve-match
tongue-in-cheek
tongue-doubtie
congressional
Congresswoman
tongue-twister
coagulability
conglomeratic
zoogeographer
zoogeographic
forgottenness
forgetfulness
long-suffering
conglutinator
congruousness
cochleariform
mother-of-pearl
mother-country
sophisticated
sophistically
sophisticator
bonheur-du-jour
nominatively
noli-me-tangere
police-officer
police-station
mowing-machine
sowing-machine
dolichocephal
Dolichosauria
Dolichosaurus
solifidianism
domiciliation
solicitorship
bouillabaisse
sociologistic
sociolinguist
socialisation
poliomyelitis
goniometrical
coriander-seed
motion-picture
toxicophagous
Morisonianism
codicological
toxicological
horizontality
Louis-Quatorze
corinthianise
Sovietologist
solidungulate
solidungulous
conjecturable
conjecturally
conjugational

conjunctional
conjunctively
book-canvasser
cockle-brained
cock-of-the-rock
cock-thrappled
cock-throppled
poikilothermy
booking-office
mocking-thrush
cook-housemaid
pocket-picking
folk-etymology
pocket-borough
sock-suspender
foolhardiness
wool-gathering
colleagueship
collaboration
collaborative
collectedness
collecting-box
collectorship
pollicitation
woollen-draper
collieshangie
soul-searching
jollification
mollification
moulding-board
boulting-hutch
worldly-minded
bowling-crease
polliniferous
roll-on-roll-off
colloquialism
colloquialist
roller-bandage
roller-bearing
roller-skating
roller-coaster
molluscicidal
toilet-service
follow-through
commeasurable
formidability
Commelinaceae
formularistic
formalisation
normalisation
commemoration
commemoratory
commemorative
communication
communicatory
communicative
commandership
communitarian
commensurable
commensurably
cosmopolitics
cosmopolitism
commercialese

commercialise
commercialism
commercialist
commerciality
commiseration
commiserative
commutability
cosmothetical
committeeship
commutatively
foundation-net
mountain-sheep
mountains-high
mountain-chain
downcast-shaft
boundary-layer
boundary-rider
sound-boarding
connecting-rod
mountebanking
mountebankery
mountebankism
counter-attack
counteraction
counteractive
counterchange
countercharge
counter-caster
counter-fleury
counterfeiter
counterfeitly
co-inheritance
counter-jumper
counsel-keeper
founder-member
counter-motion
counter-poison
counter-parole
counter-signal
counterstroke
counter-spying
coenaesthesis
bounteousness
counter-weight
cornification
mounting-block
sounding-board
counting-house
pointing-stock
downrightness
bountifulness
cornelian-tree
somniloquence
boundlessness
pointlessness
cognomination
connumeration
somnambulance
somnambulator
morning-prayer
Johnsonianism
soundproofing
hound-trailing

round-the-clock
round-tripping
cornet-à-piston
connaturalise
connaturality
monodactylous
no-holds-barred
monometallism
monometallist
holometabolic
monotelephone
homogenetical
novocentenary
homosexualist
homosexuality
borough-monger
podophthalmus
monophthongal
monothalamous
monotheletism
monothelitism
do-nothingness
monochromatic
monochromator
Holothuroidea
monophysitism
honorifically
sodomitically
notoriousness
Corolliflorae
corollifloral
toxoplasmosis
homoeopathist
homoeothermal
homoiothermal
homoeothermic
homoiothermic
homologically
topologically
homologoumena
homoeomorphic
homomorphosis
monocotyledon
monogrammatic
monotrematous
logographical
monographical
topographical
homoeroticism
monopsonistic
non-observance
motor-traction
Podostemaceae
monostrophics
pococurantism
pococurantist
coconut-butter
mononucleosis
monosyllabism
monosymmetric
complainingly
complaisantly
compactedness

complexedness
comprehension
comprehensive
complementary
pompier-ladder
copple-crowned
compressional
compagination
complimentary
morphinomania
compulsionist
popping-crease
compendiously
companionable
companionably
companionhood
companionless
companionship
morphogenesis
morphogenetic
morphophoneme
comprovincial
non-proficient
morphological
morphographer
non-production
non-productive
copper-captain
comparability
corporateness
comparatively
dog-periwinkle
copper-pyrites
compassionate
colposcopical
compass-signal
compass-timber
compositeness
compositional
compass-window
compatibility
compatriotism
computational
zoopsychology
conquistadors
corroboration
corroboratory
corroborative
court-cupboard
porridge-stick
corridor-train
coarse-grained
courteousness
journey-weight
corrigibility
non-regardance
mourning-piece
mourning-cloak
mourning-coach
coursing-joint
boarding-house
mourning-bride
mourning-stuff

correlatively
correlativity
torrentiality
corruptionist
horripilation
courts-martial
corrosibility
correspondent
corresponding
corresponsive
non-resistance
corrosiveness
non-returnable
sorrowfulness
horse-and-buggy
dog's-tail-grass
constableship
constablewick
Constantinian
house-breaking
consectaneous
horse-chestnut
mouse-coloured
consecutively
consideringly
considerately
consideration
considerative
topside-turvey
non-specialist
constellation
constellatory
consternation
coastguardman
conspiratress
conscientious
consciousness
conspicuously
consolidation
consolidative
tonsillectomy
fossiliferous
noiselessness
fossilisation
consimilarity
consimilitude
housemistress
toastmistress
consumptively
consumptivity
consentaneity
consentaneous
nonsensically
consenescence
consenescency
poisonousness
consanguinity
zoosporangium
go-as-you-please
consequential
conservatoire
constructable
constructible

constrainable
constrainedly
constringency
bowstring-hemp
boustrophedon
monstrousness
horse-sickness
possessionary
possessionate
possessorship
topsyturvydom
conspurcation
constupration
housewifeskep
housewifeship
contrabandism
contrabandist
contrafagotto
contrabassoon
foot-land-raker
contraterrine
contraception
contravention
contraceptive
toothache-tree
contradiction
contradictory
contradictive
contrariously
foot-passenger
contractility
contractional
contrapuntist
mouth-breather
contabescence
horticultural
volta-electric
northerliness
southerliness
röntgenoscopy
bottle-coaster
north-easterly
south-easterly
north-eastward
south-eastward
pontificality
fortification
mortification
cost-effective
soothfastness
doctrinairism
tortoise-shell
tortoise-plant
Voltaireanism
postliminiary
Voltairianism
contristation
contributable
Portulacaceae
nostalgically
worthlessness
postulational
mortal-staring

contemplation
contemplatist
contemplative
contamination
contaminative
root-and-branch
contentedness
continuedness
fortune-hunter
cotton-thistle
cotton-picking
contentiously
cotton-spinner
fortune-teller
fortunateness
pontoon-bridge
controversial
controvertist
post-communion
tooth-ornament
iontophoresis
iontophoretic
post-operative
contortionism
contortionist
contortionate
costardmonger
posture-master
foster-brother
fortississimo
loathsomeness
toothsomeness
fortitudinous
noctivagation
boatswain-bird
north-westerly
south-westerly
north-westward
south-westward
mouthwatering
post-existence
contextualise
rogue-elephant
volumenometer
documentalist
documentation
voluntariness
voluntaristic
convocational
convulsionary
convulsionist
convalescence
convalescency
conventionary
conventionist
conversazione
conversazioni
convertiplane
convexo-convex
polygalaceous
polycarbonate
polydactylism
polydactylous

polyadelphous	sprightliness	epitrachelion	cribbage-board
polytechnical	ophiomorphous	ophthalmology	probabilistic
polythalamous	oppignoration	apathetically	probabilities
polychromatic	epeirogenesis	apothegmatise	problematical
polyphloisbic	epeirogenetic	apothegmatist	Brobdignagian
copyrightable	splinter-proof	splutteringly	Orobanchaceae
polyhistorian	spike-lavender	sphygmography	tribunitial
polyembryonic	applicability	squandermania	tribunitician
copying-pencil	spelaeologist	squanderingly	probe-scissors
polygonaceous	apomictically	square-dancing	tributariness
Polypodiaceae	spontaneously	square-bashing	tractarianism
polynomialism	spine-chilling	square-measure	traceableness
polypropylene	epanadiplosis	square-pierced	tractableness
polyprotodont	sponge-fishing	aqua-mirabilis	procrastinate
polycythaemia	Spencerianism	squeamishness	cracker-barrel
polysyllabism	spinning-jenny	equestrianism	practicalness
polysyllogism	spinning-wheel	squeezability	fractionalise
polysynthesis	spinning-house	squirarchical	fractionalism
polysynthetic	sponging-house	squinancy-wort	fractionalist
splanchnocele	spunging-house	equitableness	fractionation
speaking-voice	spinuliferous	equisetaceous	brachiosaurus
aphanipterous	spindle-legged	equidifferent	fractiousness
sphagnicolous	spindle-shaped	equilibration	gracelessness
sphagnologist	spindle-shanks	equidistantly	pricelessness
spectatorship	spinelessness	equivocalness	tracklessness
spectacularly	epinastically	equiponderant	oraculousness
species-monger	up-to-the-moment	equiponderate	prick-me-dainty
specification	up-to-the-minute	equipotential	preconception
apocalyptical	oppositionist	Aquifoliaceae	arachnologist
speculatively	sprocket-wheel	equinoctially	precentorship
space-platform	opportuneness	squirrel-shrew	preconisation
spectrography	apportionment	pre-adamitical	proconsulship
spectre-insect	epiphenomenon	breakableness	trichological
apochromatism	apophlegmatic	preadaptation	trichopterist
spectroscopic	Sparganiaceae	preambulatory	trichopterous
spectre-shrimp	spermatogenic	cream-coloured	precipitantly
apocatastasis	spermatotheca	pro-and-conning	precipitately
spadicifloral	spermatophore	armamentarium	precipitation
apodictically	Spermatophyta	ornamentation	precipitative
epidotisation	spermatophyte	breakfast-room	precipitously
appendiculate	spermatoblast	great-grandson	tricarpellary
splendiferous	opprobriously	triangularity	trichromatism
splenetically	apprehensible	triangulately	procuratorial
Ephemeroptera	appropriately	triangulation	processioning
speech-reading	appropriation	breathing-time	processionary
speechfulness	appropriative	treacherously	process-server
sphericalness	appropinquate	breaking-point	prices-current
apheliotropic	appropinquity	irrationalise	prick-the-louse
spheristerion	sportsmanlike	irrationalism	precautionary
appealingness	sportsmanship	irrationalist	brachydactyly
appellational	spiritualiser	irrationality	brachycephaly
appellatively	spiritualness	dreadlessness	brachypterous
spheroidicity	spirit-varnish	dreamlessness	predicability
appertainance	spirit-rapping	preadmonition	producibility
appertainment	spiritousness	organogenesis	predicamental
spifflication	operativeness	organotherapy	predicatively
epigrammatise	approximately	ergatomorphic	bridge-of-boats
epigrammatist	approximation	broad-spectrum	bridge-builder
epigeneticist	approximative	breast-feeding	predefinition
apogeotropism	opisthobranch	treasure-chest	credulousness
spring-balance	opisthography	treasure-house	predominantly
spring-cleaner	apostolically	treasure-trove	predomination
uprighteously	spasmodically	treasurership	prudentialism

prudentialist
prudentiality
urediniospore
tradesmanlike
predestinator
traditionally
predatoriness
trade-unionism
trade-unionist
irreverential
free-selection
irredeemables
pre-engagement
triethylamine
breechloading
freezing-point
irreligiously
true-disposing
irreciprocity
irreplaceable
irreplaceably
irreclaimable
irreclaimably
araeometrical
irrecoverable
irrecoverably
irrecognition
arseno-pyrites
irresponsible
irresponsibly
irretrievable
irretrievably
irrefrangible
irrefrangibly
irrepressible
irrepressibly
grief-stricken
argentiferous
prefabricated
prefabricator
profectitious
prefigurement
prefiguration
prefigurative
traffic-lights
preferability
craftsmanship
draftsmanship
professoriate
professorship
profitability
profit-sharing
prefatorially
pragmatically
progressional
progressively
progressivism
progressivist
fragmentarily
fragmentation
draggle-tailed
trigonometric
progenitorial

prognosticate
troglodytical
frighteningly
frightfulness
prohibitively
ortho-compound
archidiaconal
orthodiagonal
orchidologist
orchidomaniac
archaeologist
archaeopteryx
orthognathism
orthographist
orthognathous
Archegoniatae
archbishopric
archimandrite
urchin-snouted
orthopaedical
orthopinakoid
orchesography
orthostichous
orthosilicate
prehistorical
orchestralist
orchestration
architectonic
architectural
drainage-basin
drainage-board
irritableness
groin-centring
vraisemblance
cruiser-weight
ornithichnite
ornithologist
ornithomantic
ornithischian
artificialise
artificiality
prairie-oyster
prairie-turnip
fruitlessness
arbitrariness
brainsickness
train-spotting
projectionist
prejudicially
prejudication
prejudicative
broken-hearted
prolification
proliferation
proliferative
proliferously
prolegomenary
prolegomenous
drilling-lathe
trolling-spoon
brilliantness
preliminaries
preliminarily

proleptically
drill-sergeant
triliteralism
uralitisation
grammatically
premedication
premeditation
premeditative
trumpet-flower
trumpet-shaped
primigravidae
primogenitrix
primogenitary
primogeniture
primogenitive
bromeliaceous
premillennial
Grumbletonian
tremulousness
frumentaceous
frumentarious
premandibular
criminologist
priming-powder
premonitorily
criminousness
graminivorous
tram-conductor
primordialism
primordiality
promise-breach
promiscuously
primatologist
prematureness
dramatisation
primitiveness
transatlantic
drinkableness
trunk-breeches
transcription
transcriptive
crinicultural
transcendence
transcendency
granddaughter
Frankeniaceae
orange-blossom
prince-consort
cranberry-tree
princess-skirt
princess-royal
princess-dress
transfer-paper
transferrable
transformable
transferrible
transfusively
grandfatherly
transgression
transgressive
wrong-headedly
branch-officer
franchisement

bronchoscopic
arundinaceous
principalness
principalship
transit-circle
printing-house
printing-press
transitionary
fringilliform
transientness
grandiloquent
grandiloquous
translsthmian
transistorise
translucidity
translucently
translocation
granuliferous
granulomatous
translational
transliterate
transmigrator
transmissible
transmittable
grandmotherly
transmutation
transmutative
pronunciation
pruning-shears
transnational
cranioscopist
drink-offering
craniological
Franco-Russian
transplanting
transportance
transportable
transportedly
transparently
transport-ship
transpiration
transpiratory
transposition
transpositive
transshipping
frank-tenement
granitisation
pronounceable
pronouncement
tranquilliser
transversally
Eriocaulaceae
preoccupation
preordainment
preordination
erroneousness
cryobiologist
arboriculture
creosote-plant
armoured-train
oreographical
cryptanalysis
trophallactic

propraetorial
propraetorian
graphemically
prophetically
Tropaeolaceae
triple-crowned
proprioceptor
wrapping-paper
proprietorial
grappling-hook
grappling-iron
preponderance
preponderancy
trophoblastic
cryptological
graphological
cryptographer
cryptographic
trophotropism
proportioning
proportionate
preparatorily
preparatively
proparoxytone
prepossessing
prepossession
prepositional
propositional
trapezohedron
triquetrously
frequentation
frequentative
prerogatively
Pre-Raphaelism
Pre-Raphaelite
prostatectomy
crystal-gazing
prismatically
crystallinity
crossbreeding
trisoctahedra
trisaccharide
cross-crosslet
prosectorship
criss-cross-row
prosecutrices
prosecutrixes
presidentship
cross-division
prospect-glass
prospectively
press-fastener
brassfounding
cross-gartered
prosthodontia
cross-hatching
prosaicalness
dressing-table
trysting-place
trysting-stile
prescientific
dress-improver
trisyllabical

trestle-bridge
trustlessness
wristlet-watch
presumptively
presentiality
prison-breaker
prisoners'-base
aristocratism
prosopography
erysipelatous
prosopopoeial
cross-quarters
cross-question
preserving-pan
prescriptible
cross-springer
pressure-cabin
cross-vaulting
trustworthily
presbytership
protoactinium
protuberantly
protuberation
tritubercular
Protococcales
protectionism
protectionist
graticulation
Protochordata
protectorless
protectorship
brother-german
brotherliness
tritheistical
gratification
proto-historic
proteinaceous
brattice-cloth
protolanguage
truthlessness
brutalisation
arithmetician
pretendership
pretentiously
writing-master
writing-school
protonotarial
protonotariat
troth-plighted
preternatural
preterperfect
proterogynous
pretermission
pretermitting
proterandrous
preteriteness
protospataire
Protestantise
Protestantism
grotesqueness
traumatically
traumatonasty
trout-coloured

ground-officer
ground-angling
ground-control
trouser-button
grouse-disease
trouser-pocket
argumentation
argumentative
draught-animal
draught-engine
draught-screen
troublesomely
troublousness
provocatively
travel-tainted
traveller's-joy
travel-stained
frivolousness
gravimetrical
provincialise
provincialism
provinciality
driving-mirror
prevarication
proverbialise
proverbialism
proverbialist
provisionally
privateersman
privatisation
gravitational
crown-imperial
drawing-master
drawing-pencil
prayer-meeting
prayerfulness
prize-fighting
island-hopping
estate-bottled
isoagglutinin
ismaticalness
establishment
assassination
isobarometric
psychasthenia
psychiatrical
psychopathist
psychogenesis
psychogenetic
psychometrics
psychometrist
psychotherapy
psychophysics
psychokinesis
psychokinetic
psychobiology
psychohistory
psychoanalyse
psychoanalyst
psychosomatic
psychological
psychographic
psychosurgery

psychodynamic
psychrometric
isochronously
psychrophilic
isodimorphism
isodimorphous
isoelectronic
aspergillosis
osteomyelitis
ostensibility
Ascensiontide
asset-stripper
essentialness
ascertainable
ascertainment
assentiveness
assertiveness
isogeothermal
isogeothermic
asthmatically
eschscholtzia
asthenosphere
eschatologist
Ustilaginales
ustilagineous
assiduousness
psilanthropic
Psilophytales
psammophilous
isomerisation
isometrically
ostodermatous
associability
astonishingly
associateship
associativity
psephological
astrodynamics
ostreiculture
estrangedness
ostreophagous
astrapophobia
astrophysical
isostatically
pseudomonades
pseudomorphic
pseudo-archaic
assumptionist
Assyriologist
straw-coloured
steam-carriage
strategetical
strategically
steadfastness
strangulation
straight-pight
straightforth
steam-governor
stratigraphic
stratigraphic
attainability
straining-beam
ethanolamines

stratospheric	stenographist	surchargement	superdominant
stratocruiser	standing-place	subclavicular	supereminence
strato-cumulus	standing-stone	quick-answered	superficially
Atlantosaurus	strombuliform	muscle-reading	superfineness
stabilisation	strophiolated	butcher's-broom	superfetation
staccatissimo	strobilaceous	dulcification	superfluidity
stock-breeding	atrociousness	punctiliously	superfluously
sticking-place	atmospherical	functionalism	rumelgumption
sticking-point	stopping-place	functionalist	superhumanise
stocking-frame	stepping-stone	Hutchinsonian	superhumanity
stick-in-the-mud	stop-consonant	subcommission	subeditorship
athematically	Staphyleaceae	pucciniaceous	superlatively
utterableness	Staphylindiae	subcontiguous	supernumerary
stretcher-bond	star-catalogue	subcontinuous	luteinisation
strengthening	attributively	vulcanologist	supernational
stoechiometry	pteridologist	subcontractor	gubernatorial
steering-wheel	stern-foremost	vulcanisation	superordinary
steeplechaser	starch-reduced	succinctorium	superordinate
atheistically	storming-party	quick-scenting	autecological
street-walking	starting-point	successionist	superposition
street-railway	starting-price	quicksilvered	superphysical
otter-trawling	stirpiculture	successlessly	Queensland-nut
streptococcal	pterylography	successorship	superstitious
streptococcic	sterilisation	quick-tempered	supersensible
streptococcus	stercoraceous	quadragesimal	supersensibly
street-orderly	stercorarious	quadraphonics	supersaturate
attentiveness	stereoscopist	subdeaconship	bureaucratise
street-sweeper	stereographic	quadrennially	bureaucratist
strenuousness	stereotropism	hundredweight	subequatorial
otherworldish	Sterculiaceae	mundification	supervenience
staff-notation	statelessness	mundificative	suffraganship
staff-sergeant	stethoscopist	quadrilateral	surface-active
stigmatically	station-master	quadrivalence	sufficingness
stagecoachman	state-of-the-art	quadrifarious	suffocatingly
stagecoaching	state-religion	quadripartite	surface-vessel
Stegocephalia	statesmanlike	quadrigeminal	suffumigation
steganography	statesmanship	quodlibetical	burglariously
steganopodous	states-general	quadrisection	judge-advocate
strike-breaker	statistically	quadringenary	hunger-marcher
stringentness	statute-labour	quadriliteral	vulgarisation
string-pulling	Etruscologist	quadrilingual	hunger-striker
stoicheiology	structuralism	quadricipital	suggestionise
stoichiometry	structuralist	quadrillionth	suggestionism
stainlessness	structureless	quadrinominal	suggestionist
attitudiniser	funambulation	quadrifoliate	authentically
stalactitical	funambulatory	quadrilocular	authenticator
stalactitious	Judas-coloured	fundamentally	Euphorbiaceae
italicisation	sun-animalcule	pudding-headed	rutherfordium
stalagmitical	audaciousness	pudding-sleeve	eucharistical
stalagmometer	fugaciousness	quadrophonics	authorisation
stalagmometry	furaciousness	dunderheadism	authoritarian
stalking-horse	subappearance	quadruplicate	authoritative
stultiloquent	sugar-refining	quadruplicity	puritanically
stoloniferous	sugar-refinery	quadrumvirate	subindication
still-piercing	Judaistically	subdivisional	subindicative
still-room-maid	Eubacteriales	superaddition	audio-engineer
stylistically	cupboard-faith	superannuated	rudimentarily
staminiferous	turbocharging	superannuable	punishability
atomistically	turbo-electric	superabundant	judiciousness
stomatoplasty	bubble-chamber	supercritical	audio-location
stone-coloured	humble-mouthed	supercolumnar	pusillanimity
ethnocentrism	tumbler-switch	supercalender	pusillanimous
ethnographica	mulberry-faced	tuberculation	music-mistress

numismatology
musicotherapy
musicological
jurisprudence
subirrigation
ludicrousness
subject-matter
subject-object
subjunctively
sucking-bottle
cuckoo-spittle
Quaker-buttons
turkey-buzzard
full-fashioned
bullock's-heart
sublieutenant
nullification
qualification
qualificatory
qualificative
rumlegumption
building-block
building-board
quilting-frame
guilelessness
guiltlessness
juglandaceous
sublanceolate
nucleo-protein
dualistically
qualitatively
submachine-gun
mummification
summer-seeming
quincentenary
quingentenary
quantivalence
quintillionth
burning-mirror
burnt-offering
turnip-lantern
vulnerability
quincuncially
Quinquagesima
quintuplicate
quinquevalent
autocatalysis
autocatalytic
automatically
autoschediasm
autoschediaze
subordinately
subordination
subordinative
autocephalous
tumorgenicity
autochthonism
autochthonous
autodigestion
autobiography
Europocentric
Eurocommunism
Eurocommunist

autoeroticism
sulphadiazine
supplantation
suspectedness
suspicionless
subprefecture
supplementary
purple-in-grain
gumple-foisted
bumptiousness
suspender-belt
subpopulation
eusporangiate
suspercollate
purposelessly
suppositional
purposiveness
sulphur-bottom
sulphureously
sumptuousness
sulphur-yellow
turquoise-blue
supra-axillary
outrecuidance
hurricane-deck
hurricane-lamp
quarter-decker
quarter-gunner
quarter-hourly
quartermaster
quarrelsomely
surrogateship
querulousness
supranational
quartodeciman
subreptitious
surreptitious
hubristically
suprasensible
supratemporal
quartz-halogen
quartziferous
quartz-crystal
outstandingly
substantially
substantively
substantivise
substantivity
puss-gentleman
Russification
questionnaire
questioningly
pulselessness
nursing-father
outspokenness
subsequential
substructural
subserviently
purse-snatcher
subsistential
out-settlement
Australianism
multicellular

multicoloured
putty-coloured
rusty-coloured
multicamerate
multicapitate
custodianship
multidigitate
quatrefeuille
rust-resistant
justification
justificatory
justificative
multifilament
quatch-buttock
subtriplicate
subtriangular
curtain-raiser
multilobulate
multiloculate
multiloquence
subtilisation
subtile-witted
customariness
sustentacular
sustentaculum
multinucleate
Huntingdonian
hunting-ground
mutton-thumper
button-through
multinational
mutton-dummies
Austroasiatic
multipresence
multiplicable
multiplicator
juxtaposition
subterraneous
subternatural
custard-coffin
butter-biscuit
butter-fingers
quaternionist
butterfly-fish
butterfly-weed
multiramified
multitudinary
multitudinous
quotation-mark
multivibrator
suburbicarian
Cucurbitaceae
future-perfect
tubuliflorous
luxuriousness
mutualisation
futurological
subventionary
subversionary
pulverisation
suovetaurilia
sun-worshipper
burying-beetle

burying-ground
muzzle-loading
quizzing-glass
Aviculariidae
evocativeness
availableness
evangelically
evangeliarion
evangeliarium
evangelistary
avant-gardiste
even-Christian
everlastingly
overhastiness
overvaluation
overabundance
overabounding
overbearingly
overflowingly
over-anxiously
overinsurance
overindulgent
over-confident
overcredulity
overcredulous
overstatement
averruncation
oversubscribe
overmultitude
overexcitable
over-exquisite
ovoviviparous
swaddling-band
twiddling-line
Swedenborgian
owner-occupied
owner-occupier
sweet-savoured
sweet-tempered
swelled-headed
swollen-headed
dwelling-place
dwelling-house
swallow-tailed
swingebuckler
swinging-block
swine's-succory
twopenceworth
twopennyworth
swordsmanship
swashbuckling
exsanguineous
expansibility
expansiveness
expendability
extendability
extendibility
experimentist
expeditionary
expeditiously
extermination
exterminatory
exterminative

extemporarily
exterritorial
extensibility
extensionally
excessiveness
expensiveness
extensiveness
exceptionable
exceptionably
exceptionally
expectoration
expectorative
extenuatingly
excitableness
extinguishant
exhibitionism
exhibitionist
explanatorily
exclusiveness
explosiveness
exemplifiable
exemplariness
exanthematous
axiomatically
exponentially
excommunicate
excortication
expostulation
expostulatory
expostulative
extra-axillary
extra-cellular
extra-galactic
extra-judicial
extra-limitary
extra-metrical
extrinsically
extraordinary
expropriation
extrapolation
extrapolatory
extrapolative
extra-physical
excrescential
expressionism
expressionist
extra-tropical
extravagantly
extravasation
extra-vascular
exothermicity
excusableness
expurgatorial
exquisiteness
excursiveness
gynaecocratic
gynaecologist
gynaecomastia
gynandromorph
pyramidically
synallagmatic
tyrannosaurus
synaposematic

dynamogenesis
zygapophyseal
zygapophysial
synarthrodial
lycanthropist
symbolography
symbolistical
symbolisation
symbiotically
synchondrosis
synchronicity
synchronology
synchronistic
synchronously
syndicalistic
dyed-in-the-wool
hyperactivity
hypercritical
hypercalcemia
synecdochical
hyperglycemia
hyperhidrosis
hypermetrical
hypermetropia
hypermetropic
cyberneticist
pyretotherapy
synecological
hymenopterous
Hymenomycetes
Pyrenomycetes
synecphonesis
hyperphrygian
hyperphysical
hypersthenite
hypersarcosis
hypertrophied
hypertrophous
hypervelocity
dysfunctional
syphilologist
pyrheliometer
syphilophobia
syphilisation
hyphenisation
cylindraceous
cylindrically
cylinder-block
pyrimethamine
syringomyelia
Myristicaceae
syllabication
syllogistical
syllogisation
Cyclanthaceae
hyalinisation
sylleptically
cyclospermous
myrmecologist
dysmenorrheal
dysmenorrhoea
dysmenorrheic
symmetrically

hypno-analysis
pycnoconidium
pycnidiospore
gymnospermous
gymnastically
hypnotisation
gyromagnetism
zygodactylism
zygodactylous
pyrotechnical
hypothecation
Syrophoenicia
sycophantical
hypochondriac
hypochondrium
hypophosphite
pyrophosphate
gynodioecious
cytodiagnosis
Lycopodiaceae
mycotoxicosis
gynomonoecism
typographical
xylographical
hyposulphuric
pyrosulphuric
hypogylcaemia
hypocycloidal
lymphatically
sympiesometer
symptomatical
dyspeptically
sympathetical
sympathectomy
sympatholytic
symphyseotomy
symphysiotomy
hydro-airplane
hydrocracking
hydrochloride
hydrocephalic
hydrocephalus
hydrodynamics
hybridisation
hydroelectric
hydrogenation
hydrokinetics
hydromedusoid
hydromagnetic
hydrometrical
hygrometrical
hydropathical
hydrostatical
hydrosulphide
hydrosulphite
hydrosomatous
hygroscopical
hydraulically
hydraulicking
hydroxylamine
hypsophyllary
syntactically
dyotheletical

synthetically
dyothelitical
mystification
nyctaginaceae
systemisation
systematician
systematology
Cyathophyllum
oyster-catcher
oyster-fishery
mystery-monger
hysteranthous

salamander-like
macadamisation
paratactically
palaeanthropic
Palaeanthropus
manageableness
palaeethnology
Hamamelidaceae
Pan-Americanism
caramelisation
cadaverousness
paraleipomenon
palaegeography
paraphrastical
catachrestical
paralinguistic
paradigmatical
parasitologist
calamitousness
catadioptrical
parallel-veined
parallelepiped
parallelopiped
savanna-sparrow
pararosaniline
palaeopedology
palagonite-tuff
palato-alveolar
palaeobotanist
palaeographist
malacostracous
Malacopterygii
malappropriate
paragrammatist
parapsychology
galactopoietic
galactophorous
marble-constant
marble-breasted
cabbage-lettuce
rambunctiously
namby-pambiness
Sabbath-breaker
rabbeting-plane
rabbit-squirrel
Sabbatarianism
sacchariferous
Marchantiaceae
watch-committee
narcocatharsis
sanctification
malcontentedly
carcinogenesis
carcinological
carcinomatosis
Marcgraviaceae
narcosynthesis
lasciviousness
handicraftsman
handkerchieves
sandwich-boards
paedomorphosis
maidenhair-tree

pardonableness
cardinal-deacon
cardinal-bishop
cardinal-flower
cardinal-priest
cardiovascular
cardiomyopathy
Rabelaisianism
water-breathing
water-barometer
water-colourist
parenchymatous
lavender-cotton
casement-window
catechumenical
catechumenship
catechetically
watering-trough
valerianaceous
lamellirostral
tabernacle-work
Camelopardalis
water-privilege
davenport-trick
galeopithecine
galeopithecoid
water-repellent
water-resistant
majesticalness
watertightness
Valentinianism
valetudinarian
daffadowndilly
half-pennyworth
malfunctioning
half-a-sovereign
sanguinariness
bargain-counter
sanguification
sanguinivorous
daughterliness
daughters-in-law
bashi-bazoukery
cathodographer
pachydermatous
bathygraphical
tachygraphical
pathologically
mathematically
mathematicised
bathing-costume
bathing-machine
washing-machine
tacheometrical
fashionmonging
fatherlessness
Catherine-wheel
tachistoscopic
capitalisation
radicalisation
radioautograph
radioastronomy
radiochemistry

cabinet-edition
cabinet-pudding
satisfactorily
tariff-reformer
hagiographical
palingenetical
lapidification
Basidiomycetes
papilionaceous
manifold-writer
facinorousness
saxifragaceous
radiosensitise
radiosensitive
radio-strontium
radiotelegraph
radiotelemeter
radiotelephone
radiotelephony
fatiguableness
latitudinarian
backscratching
Jack-in-the-green
talking-machine
mackerel-breeze
market-gardener
marketableness
Jack-by-the-hedge
parliament-cake
parliament-heel
hallucinogenic
fallaciousness
calligraphical
daylight-saving
haplostemonous
ballet-mistress
parlour-boarder
early-Victorian
tallow-chandler
salmon-coloured
harmoniousness
haematogenesis
palmatipartite
maintenance-man
painter-stainer
faint-heartedly
magniloquently
vaingloriously
cannonball-tree
Haloragidaceae
barometrically
major-generalcy
vasodilatation
vasodilatatory
calorification
saponification
paroemiography
saloon-carriage
paronomastical
malodorousness
favourableness
rampageousness
sapphire-quartz

pamphleteering
campylotropous
wappenschawing
campanulaceous
campanological
capparidaceous
banqueting-hall
matriarchalism
patriarchalism
marriage-favour
marriage-broker
patrialisation
iatrochemistry
Sarraceniaceae
capriciousness
macrocephalous
macrodactylous
macroeconomics
Caprifoliaceae
barrage-balloon
fairy-godmother
cairngorm-stone
sacrilegiously
sacramentalism
sacramentarian
sacramentalist
sacrament-house
warrant-officer
sauropterygian
patresfamilias
macrosporangia
falsifiability
Passifloraceae
sausage-bassoon
parsimoniously
passionateness
mass-production
sansculottides
sansculotterie
castrametation
particularness
fastidiousness
parthenocarpic
saltpetre-paper
castle-building
cartographical
pantographical
mastigophorous
partridge-berry
captain-general
cartridge-paper
farthingsworth
tautologically
dactyliography
pantomimically
cantankerously
Castanospermum
xanthomelanous
pantopragmatic
tatterdemalion
bastardisation
martyrological
Gasteromycetes

bacteriologist
bacteriostasis
bacteriostatic
fantasticality
factitiousness
pasteurisation
naturalisation
tabularisation
ranunculaceous
nature-printing
Baluchitherium
daguerreotyper
salubriousness
marvellousness
galvanoplastic
Calycanthaceae
laryngological
laryngoscopist
labyrinthodont
dazzle-painting
absent-mindedly
obsequiousness
observableness
obligatoriness
abominableness
absorbefacient
absorptiveness
absorptiometer
eburnification
abstractedness
abstractionist
obstreperously
abstemiousness
obstructionist
above-mentioned
ocean-greyhound
schematisation
sclerophyllous
screw-propeller
acceptableness
scientifically
scribbling-book
octingentenary
schismatically
actinobacillus
schizophyceous
schizognathous
schizomycetous
scale-staircase
ecclesiastical
Ecclesiasticus
ecclesiologist
Scombresocidae
scandalisation
scandalmonging
scandalousness
ichnographical
Acanthocephala
scintillometer
scintilloscope
econometrician
acknowledgment
achondroplasia

schoolmasterly
school-teaching
school-divinity
schoolmistress
accountability
accountantship
schooner-rigged
accomplishable
accomplishment
across-the-board
scaphocephalic
scaphocephalus
scorpion-spider
scurrilousness
scaremongering
achromatically
scatter-brained
Scottification
ichthyological
ichthyolatrous
ichthyophagist
ichthyophagous
ichthyosaurian
scrubbing-board
scrubbing-brush
scrutinisingly
sceuophylacium
accustomedness
scrupulousness
Schwenkfeldian
idealistically
advantageously
odd-come-shortly
educationalist
adventitiously
administrative
administration
administratrix
edriophthalmic
identification
idiopathically
recalcitration
rewardableness
regardlessness
hen-and-chickens
telangiectasis
telangiectatic
metaphorically
semaphorically
metaphysically
metaphosphoric
mesaticephalic
metalinguistic
rehabilitative
gelatinisation
keratinisation
rehabilitation
hepaticologist
legalistically
retaliationist
recapitulative
recapitulation
recapitulatory

remarkableness
metallographic
metallographer
devalorisation
revalorisation
megasporangium
megasporophyll
metapsychology
departmentally
telautographic
melastomaceous
Hexactinellida
Rembrandtesque
feeble-mindedly
Leibnitzianism
berberidaceous
leucocythaemia
leucocytolysis
leucocytopenia
neocolonialism
geocentrically
perceptiveness
perceptibility
percussion-lock
percussion-fuse
percutaneously
reacquaintance
meddlesomeness
mesdemoiselles
weeding-forceps
wedding-garment
leading-strings
leaden-stepping
reed-instrument
telepathically
federalisation
generalisation
vegetativeness
general-purpose
beseechingness
telescopically
aerenchymatous
degenerateness
regeneratively
defenestration
revengefulness
genethliacally
genethlialogic
telephonically
telephotograph
hereditariness
hereditability
remedilessness
heresiographer
repetitiveness
beneficialness
genealogically
teleologically
levelling-staff
rebelliousness
telesmatically
never-never-land
heterothallism

heterophyllous
heterochronism
heterochromous
heterochronous
heterosomatous
heteromorphism
heteromorphous
heterostrophic
peremptoriness
metempsychoses
metempsychosis
penetrableness
meretriciously
teleprocessing
meteorological
telegraph-board
telegraph-cable
telegraph-plant
defeasibleness
necessarianism
delectableness
detestableness
relentlessness
reception-order
hebetudinosity
deceivableness
receivableness
receiving-house
receiving-order
teletypewriter
self-management
self-satisfying
self-abnegation
self-absorption
perfectibilism
perfectibilian
perfectibilist
perfectibility
self-accusation
self-accusatory
self-advertiser
self-admiration
perfidiousness
self-generating
self-revelation
self-dependence
self-determined
self-heterodyne
self-neglecting
self-destroying
self-effacement
self-affrighted
self-discipline
self-displeased
self-flattering
self-employment
self-immolation
self-importance
self-interested
self-enrichment
newfangledness
self-indulgence
self-inductance

self-condemning
self-government
self-confidence
self-tormenting
self-commitment
self-complacent
self-comparison
self-correcting
self-consequent
self-consistent
self-controlled
self-torturable
self-conviction
self-proclaimed
self-propulsion
self-protective
self-protecting
self-assumption
self-sufficient
self-fulfilment
self-fulfilling
self-suggestion
self-punishment
self-supporting
self-justifying
self-sustaining
self-sustenance
self-explaining
self-expression
geographically
sergeant-at-arms
sea-gilliflower
sea-gillyflower
geognostically
weightlessness
tergiversation
methodicalness
hephthemimeral
dechristianise
Mephistophelic
Mephistopheles
Mephistophilis
Mephostophilus
semicarbazones
peripateticism
medicamentally
decimalisation
devitalisation
meditativeness
recitation-room
semi-occasional
periodontology
deliberateness
deliberatively
deliverability
demi-semiquaver
semi-centennial
semi-officially
periphrastical
perishableness
delightfulness
zenith-distance
legitimateness

semicircularly
reminiscential
medicine-bottle
resinification
revivification
sericitisation
definitiveness
verisimilitude
semi-elliptical
legislatorship
semiconducting
lepidodendroid
lexicographist
devil-on-the-neck
hemispheroidal
Menispermaceae
periophthalmus
relinquishment
denitrificator
Perissodactyla
heliosciophyte
resistlessness
redintegration
redistribution
redistillation
resistance-coil
meticulousness
serjeant-at-arms
weak-mindedness
neck-sweetbread
neglectfulness
reflectiveness
reflectionless
perlocutionary
well-acquainted
deflagrability
healthlessness
well-thought-out
deplorableness
belletristical
yellow-centaury
yellow-yoldring
fellow-commoner
fellow-townsman
yellow-breasted
fellow-creature
reflexological
fermentability
terminableness
fermentescible
helminthologic
terminological
hermaphroditic
geomorphologic
permissiveness
permissibility
dermatological
penny-a-linerism
pernicketiness
perniciousness
neanderthaloid
reinvigoration
penny-in-the-slot

reintroduction
pennystone-cast
pennatulaceous
demoralisation
depolarisation
decorativeness
derogatoriness
reconciliation
reconciliatory
recondensation
recoverability
terotechnology
remonetisation
denominatively
denominational
demobilisation
detoxification
aerobiological
deposit-receipt
aerobiotically
aeroelastician
recommendation
recommendatory
recommencement
reformationist
reconnaissance
metoposcopical
decolonisation
decolorisation
recolonisation
decompoundable
democratically
deconsecration
reconsecration
remorsefulness
reconstitution
reconstructive
reconstruction
gerontological
decontaminator
aerodynamicist
aerohydroplane
respectability
despicableness
respectfulness
weapon-schawing
serpent-goddess
responsiveness
serpentine-rock
serpentiningly
responsibility
reaping-machine
serpent-worship
reappraisement
peppermint-drop
temperamentful
Neopythagorean
despoticalness
sempstress-ship
despitefulness
herpetological
sesquipedalian
sesquipedality

sesquisulphide
neuroanatomist
reorganisation
retrocognition
refractoriness
tetrachotomous
reproductively
reproductivity
tetradactylous
retrogradation
petrographical
tetragrammaton
segregationist
heart-heaviness
reprehensively
neurohypnology
hebraistically
rear-view-mirror
petrologically
ferromagnesian
ferro-manganese
wearing-apparel
herring-fishery
refrangibility
bear-animalcule
retransmission
retro-operative
Neuropteroidea
metropolitical
zebra-parrakeet
neuropathology
ferroprussiate
neuroradiology
Petrarchianism
Petrarchianist
terror-stricken
heart-searching
regressiveness
representative
representation
tetrasporangia
territorialise
territorialism
territorialist
territoriality
serratirostral
newspaper-woman
sensualisation
persuasiveness
persuasibility
verse-mongering
personableness
reasonableness
seasonableness
geosynchronous
person-to-person
seismometrical
newsworthiness
censurableness
measurableness
censoriousness
dessert-service
bed-sitting-room

sensationalism
sensationalist
left-handedness
septuagenarian
centralisation
neutralisation
restrainedness
petticoat-tails
verticillaster
Pentecostalist
pentadactylism
leptodactylous
pentadactylous
gentleman-cadet
heather-bleater
heather-bluiter
heather-blutter
aesthesiogenic
heathenishness
geothermometer
leather-mouthed
heather-mixture
mettlesomeness
weather-prophet
weather-station
centripetalism
gentrification
restrictionist
centrifugalise
centrifugation
rectilinearity
pestilentially
sentimentalise
testimonialise
sentimentalism
sentimentalist
sentimentality
testamentarily
centimetre-gram
pertinaciously
centenarianism
rectangularity
dextrorotation
dextrorotatory
death-practised
centuplication
perturbational
restorableness
westernisation
Deuteronomical
nectareousness
restorationism
restorationist
restitutionism
restitutionist
destructionist
regularisation
secularisation
sequaciousness
rejuvenescence
oecumenicalism
nebuchadnezzar
beautification

repudiationist
desulphuration
resurrectional
requisitionary
requisitionist
resultlessness
recurvirostral
serviceability
heavier-than-air
servo-mechanism
heaven-directed
heavenly-minded
lecythidaceous
benzodiazepine
effeminateness
affectionately
effervescingly
Africanisation
aforementioned
egalitarianism
agrobiological
agrostological
aggrandisement
aggressiveness
phraseological
thrashing-floor
theatricalness
chicken-hearted
chicken-livered
threadbareness
wheeler-dealing
three-farthings
three-halfpence
three-halfpenny
threshing-floor
sheet-lightning
phlegmatically
Chaetodontidae
sheep-whistling
shifting-boards
phthalocyanine
chain-lightning
shrill-shriking
cheiromantical
cheirographist
thriftlessness
Christological
Christ-cross-row
Shakespeariana
cholecystotomy
shelf-catalogue
whole-heartedly
shillingsworth
philologically
shell-limestone
cholelithiasis
philanthropist
phyllotactical
phelloplastics
chalcographist
child-resistant
thalassography
philosophaster

philosopheress
philosophistic
shilly-shallier
chamber-counsel
rhombenporphyr
chimney-swallow
chimney-sweeper
shamefacedness
thymelaeaceous
thimble-rigging
chemoreceptive
chemoreception
chemosynthesis
phantasmagoria
phantasmagoric
phenobarbitone
rhinoceros-bird
Rhinocerotidae
changeableness
chancellorship
rhynchophorous
chincherinchee
phenylbutazone
phonematically
rhinencephalic
rhinencephalon
Chenopodiaceae
chondrocranium
chondrogenesis
Theopaschitism
chromatosphere
chromatography
thromboplastin
through-ganging
through-traffic
chlorite-schist
shooting-jacket
chloritisation
chronometrical
theosophically
chlorpromazine
theocratically
chaptalisation
ship's-carpenter
whippersnapper
rhyparographic
rhyparographer
pharmaceutical
pharmacopoeial
pharmacopoeian
pharmacologist
pharmacopolist
therianthropic
characteristic
chargeableness
Charley-pitcher
sheriff-officer
chorographical
thermometrical
thermochemical
thermo-electric
theriomorphism
theriomorphous

thermodynamics
third-programme
short-sightedly
charitableness
thyrotoxicosis
whispering-dome
phosphoprotein
phosphor-bronze
phosphorescent
whistle-blowing
thysanopterous
physiognomical
chest-protector
chittagong-wood
photobiologist
photochemistry
shatter-brained
photo-engraving
photographical
photogrammetry
phytogenetical
phytogeography
whittie-whattie
Phytolaccaceae
photoperiodism
phytopathology
photosynthesis
photosynthetic
photosensitise
photosensitive
phototelegraph
what-d'you-call-'em
what-d'you-call-it
rheumatologist
thaumatography
thaumaturgical
shoulder-height
shoulder-girdle
thoughtfulness
thought-process
thought-reading
shove-halfpenny
chivalrousness
chevaux-de-frise
shawl-waistcoat
Rhizophoraceae
vicar-apostalic
disaccommodate
misacceptation
cigarette-paper
disaffiliation
disaffirmation
vitalistically
disacknowledge
disapplication
misapplication
disappointment
disapprobative
disapprobation
disapprobatory
disapprovingly
disappropriate
misappropriate

disarrangement
misarrangement
disassociation
misanthropical
miraculousness
disadventurous
misadventurous
misadvisedness
nimble-fingered
ribbon-building
aircraftswoman
pisciculturist
discretionally
witches'-thimble
zincographical
circuit-breaker
mischief-making
discriminately
discriminative
discriminating
discrimination
zinckification
discriminatory
circuitousness
miscellanarian
discolouration
miscalculation
circumnavigate
circumscissile
discommendable
circumbendibus
circumferentor
circumlittoral
circumambience
circumambiency
circumambulate
circumforanean
discomboberate
circumposition
discomfortable
discombobulate
circumlocution
circumvolution
circumlocutory
circumspective
circumspection
circumstantial
circumnutation
miscomputation
circumnutatory
circumgyration
circumgyratory
disconnectedly
discontentedly
disconcertment
discontentment
miscontentment
air-conditioned
discontinuance
disconsolately
disconsolation
disconformable
cinchonisation

disceptatorial
disciplinarium
disciplinarian
discursiveness
discerpibility
diachronically
pincer-movement
discouragement
discouragingly
discountenance
discourteously
discount-broker
vindictiveness
fiddle-faddling
middle-distance
Middle-American
bird-of-paradise
biodegradation
disdainfulness
wind-instrument
kindergartener
window-shopping
window-dressing
liberalisation
mineralisation
cinematography
tide-waitership
disemboguement
disembarkation
disembowelment
disenchantress
disenchantment
disencumbrance
fivepenny-piece
bioelectricity
disenfranchise
eigen-frequency
disengagedness
bioengineering
vice-chancellor
kinetheodolite
vicesimo-quarto
vigesimo-quarto
pigeon-fancying
pigeon-breasted
rice-polishings
fire-worshipper
vice-consulship
vice-presidency
disentrainment
diverticulosis
diverticulated
diverticulitis
videotelephone
licentiousness
libertarianism
disenthralment
divertissement
disequilibrium
diffractometer
disfurnishment
differentially
differentiator

biographically
siege-artillery
zingiberaceous
single-breasted
jingoistically
linguistically
singing-gallery
finger-painting
finger's-breadth
finger-alphabet
finger-pointing
fingerprinting
disgustfulness
disgustingness
high-handedness
night-blindness
lithochromatic
lighter-than-air
night-flowering
night-fossicker
night-foundered
lithographical
light-heartedly
xiphihumeralis
high-mindedness
diaheliotropic
Wilhelmstrasse
lithonthryptic
lithontriptist
high-priesthood
withering-floor
high-principled
night-wandering
highly-seasoned
militarisation
viviparousness
disinclination
disincarcerate
disincorporate
vivisectionist
disinformation
misinformation
disinfestation
riding-interest
disingenuously
riding-breeches
disinheritance
dividing-engine
silicification
vitilitigation
libidinousness
Sigillariaceae
disillusionary
disillusionise
filiopietistic
misimprovement
disimpassioned
dinitrobenzene
misinstruction
disintegrative
disintegration
sinistrorsally
ministerialist

misinterpreter
diminutiveness
ridiculousness
disinvestiture
disjointedness
milking-parlour
hickery-pickery
Rickettsiaceae
billiard-marker
dialectologist
bill-discounter
diplomatically
willing-hearted
Finlandisation
millenarianism
bibliomaniacal
diplostemonous
pillow-fighting
mismeasurement
diamantiferous
diamondiferous
diamond-wedding
biomathematics
piano-accordion
pinnatipartite
widow-bewitched
disorderliness
disorientation
dinoflagellate
lipogrammatism
lipogrammatist
dicotyledonous
misogynistical
diaphanousness
displenishment
displeasedness
simplificative
simplification
simplistically
dispensatively
dispensability
dispensational
dispensatorily
mispunctuation
diaphototropic
hippopotamuses
dispiritedness
hippety-hoppety
dispiteousness
disputatiously
disqualifiable
disquisitional
microbiologist
microchemistry
nitrocellulose
microcomponent
microcephalous
fibrocartilage
microdetection
microeconomics
vibroflotation
hierographical

hierogrammatic
disregardfully
nitroglycerine
hieroglyphical
micrologically
microminiature
micro-meteorite
vitriolisation
micropegmatite
microprocessor
hierarchically
disrespectable
vitrescibility
microseismical
Hierosolymitan
microsporangia
microstructure
dissociability
dissolvability
dissolubleness
diesel-electric
dissolutionism
dissolutionist
dissymmetrical
kissing-strings
dioscoreaceous
dissertational
disserviceable
biosystematics
mistranslation
distractedness
histochemistry
tittle-tattling
diathermaneity
histogenically
histrionically
distributively
distributional
distemperature
tintinnabulate
tintinnabulant
tintinnabulary
tintinnabulous
distensibility
distinguishing
histopathology
dipterocarpous
picture-gallery
historiography
victoriousness
picture-writing
Nietzscheanism
figurativeness
vituperatively
lieutenantship
liturgiologist
bituminisation
simultaneously
air-vice-marshal
silver-shedding
silversmithing
zinziberaceous
piezochemistry

piezomagnetism
skeleton-shrimp
skimble-skamble
skunk-blackbird
cloak-and-dagger
plea-bargaining
oleaginousness
clear-starching
pleasure-seeker
pleasure-giving
pleasure-ground
blockade-runner
electioneering
black-marketeer
ill-conditioned
plectognathous
electrobiology
electrochemist
electroculture
electrogilding
electrogenesis
electronically
electroplating
electrostatics
electrotherapy
electrothermic
electrothermal
electrovalency
electrowinning
bladder-campion
alder-buckthorn
illegitimately
illegitimation
allegorisation
allelomorphism
old-established
sleepy-sickness
oligocythaemia
plague-stricken
flag-lieutenant
flagelliferous
old-gentlemanly
slug-foot-second
oligopsonistic
flight-recorder
flagitiousness
alphabetically
alphamerically
alphanumerical
illiterateness
Albigensianism
ultimogeniture
altitudinarian
Plumbaginaceae
alimentiveness
flamboyant-tree
climatological
Plantaginaceae
blank-cartridge
slantendicular
slanderousness
plant-formation
slantindicular

planing-machine
plane-polarised
plenipotential
ill-naturedness
planet-stricken
glanduliferous
pleonastically
blood-bespotted
blood-consuming
all-overishness
alcoholisation
alloiostrophos
blood-poisoning
blood-sacrifice
ultracrepidate
floriculturist
altruistically
ultramicrotome
ultramicrotomy
ultramontanism
ultramontanist
ultroneousness
ultra-Neptunian
ultrastructure
plasmapheresis
class-conscious
blistered-steel
blister-plaster
classification
classificatory
Elasmobranchii
platycephalous
plutodemocracy
bletheranskate
clitter-clatter
slatternliness
blithesomeness
flat-footedness
plethysmograph
pleurapophyses
pleurapophysis
slaughter-house
slaughterously
Pleuronectidae
illustratively
illustrational
claustrophobia
claustrophobic
clavicytherium
pluviometrical
glove-stretcher
claw-hammer-coat
flowery-kirtled
alexipharmakon
Elizabethanism
imparisyllabic
impassableness
impassibleness
ambassadorship
immaculateness
imperfectively
immethodically
embellishingly

impermeability
imperturbation
imperviability
imperviousness
imaginableness
amphibological
emphaticalness
omnibenevolent
empire-building
omnium-gatherum
omnicompetence
smoking-concert
implacableness
smelling-bottle
emulsification
implementation
emblematically
implausibility
imponderabilia
immoderateness
impoverishment
immobilisation
imposthumation
impracticality
impregnability
umbrageousness
Amaryllidaceae
amaranthaceous
impressiveness
impressibility
impressionable
improvableness
amateurishness
immunosuppress
empyreumatical
incapacitation
unwatchfulness
unhandsomeness
untameableness
engagement-ring
unmaterialised
intangibleness
unmathematical
antaphrodisiac
insanitariness
insatiableness
invariableness
unsatisfaction
unsatisfactory
kneading-trough
inhabitiveness
unmalleability
enharmonically
inharmoniously
unmannerliness
antagonisation
unvanquishable
unmarriageable
unmatriculated
unpassableness
unfaithfulness
incautiousness
unmanufactured

insalubriously
unscripturally
unacknowledged
unaccommodated
unaccounted-for
unaccomplished
anacardiaceous
anachronically
inscrutability
unacquaintance
unscrupulously
inadvisability
unidentifiable
inadequateness
unidirectional
inseparability
interambulacra
unmetaphorical
unmetaphysical
interactionism
interactionist
unrecapturable
unmerchantable
under-clerkship
unmercifulness
indescribables
intercommunion
intercommunity
interconnexion
under-constable
intercessional
intercessorial
unreadableness
interdependent
underdeveloped
inveterateness
indeterminable
undeterminable
indeterminably
interestedness
undeservedness
unreservedness
interferometer
interferometry
interferential
intergradation
undergraduette
encephalograph
unhesitatingly
undesirability
undeniableness
unreliableness
indecipherable
undecipherable
indecisiveness
indefiniteness
undesignedness
unreciprocated
interior-sprung
antediluvially
interjec ional
unreflectingly
interlocutress

interlocutrice
intellectually
intelligential
intelligentsia
intelligentzia
interlineation
interlingually
intermediately
intermediation
intermediatory
intermigration
intermolecular
undermentioned
intermittently
intermittingly
intermaxillary
Internationale
undernourished
unreconcilable
unreconcilably
enterocentesis
unbecomingness
unrecognisable
unrecognisably
indecorousness
indecomposable
undecomposable
unremorsefully
indemonstrable
undemonstrable
unresolvedness
interplanetary
interpretative
interpretation
enterprisingly
undespairingly
interpellation
unresponsively
interpenetrate
interpunctuate
interpenetrant
under-populated
intempestivity
unbearableness
unreproducible
interruptively
integrationist
understandable
understatement
interspatially
insensibleness
under-secretary
intersectional
understrapping
intersexuality
unrestrainable
unrestrainedly
uncertificated
intertwinement
entertainingly
intertwiningly
unrestrictedly
intentionality

unmentionables
incestuousness
infectiousness
unsectarianism
indestructible
indestructibly
unremunerative
undervaluation
ineffectuality
unaffectedness
uniformitarian
anagrammatical
enigmatography
knight-bachelor
knight-banneret
knight-errantry
onchocerciasis
uncheerfulness
unchristianise
enthymematical
unthinkability
unthankfulness
unthinkingness
enthronisation
anthropopathic
anthropometric
anthropophuism
anthropologist
anthropography
enthusiastical
unrhythmically
unthoughtfully
antipathetical
anti-Jacobinism
invincibleness
indiscreteness
indiscreetness
indiscriminate
antiscriptural
uncircumcision
indiscerptible
indiscoverable
undiscoverable
undiscoverably
antiodontalgic
antimetathesis
anti-federalism
anti-federalist
indigenisation
antiperistasis
antidepressant
antiperspirant
antiseptically
incidentalness
indifferentism
indifferentist
antiphrastical
unrightfulness
antiphonically
antiphlogistic
antithetically
anticipatively
anticipatorily

undiminishable
indivisibility
inviolableness
unyieldingness
insignificance
insignificancy
antimonarchist
oneirocritical
anticonvulsant
indisposedness
angiostomatous
undistractedly
indistinctness
unsisterliness
antiquarianism
unpleasantness
inflectionless
inalienability
inalterability
Anglo-Israelite
inflammability
unblamableness
inclinableness
unflappability
ingloriousness
unflatteringly
inflation-proof
unilluminating
inflexibleness
anamnestically
inimitableness
onomatopoiesis
unintellectual
unintelligible
unintelligibly
unintermitting
unenterprising
unentertaining
unknightliness
unenthusiastic
enantiomorphic
enantiostylous
unintoxicating
unincorporated
unknowableness
untowardliness
endoradiosonde
unromantically
unconceiveable
unconciliatory
inconclusively
intolerability
unforeknowable
undomesticated
unconfederated
uncongeniality
unsophisticate
incogitability
unsociableness
incommodiously
incommunicable
uncommunicable
incommunicably

uncommunicated
incommensurate
endosmotically
entomostracous
uncomprehended
incompleteness
incompressible
uncompromising
incorporealism
incorporeality
uncorroborated
incoordination
inconsiderable
inconsiderably
inconscionable
unconscionable
unconscionably
unconsolidated
inconsequently
inconsistently
uncontradicted
unpoeticalness
incontiguously
indoctrination
uncontemplated
uncontaminated
uncontroverted
incontrollable
uncontrollable
incontrollably
uncontrollably
uncontrolledly
inconveniently
unconventional
snipper-snapper
knapping-hammer
snapping-turtle
unsplinterable
snip-snap-snorum
inappositeness
inapproachable
unapproachable
inapproachably
unapproachably
inoperableness
inappreciative
unappreciative
inappreciation
inapprehensive
unapprehensive
inapprehension
unappropriated
unspiritualise
inspirationism
inspirationist
iniquitousness
intra-abdominal
inorganisation
intractability
ungracefulness
unpracticality
onirocriticism
ungraciousness

androcephalous
incredibleness
unproductively
unproductivity
introductorily
androdioecious
unfriendedness
unfriendliness
unprofessional
inordinateness
unpraiseworthy
unfruitfulness
inartificially
unartificially
inartistically
inarticulately
inarticulation
infralapsarian
unpremeditable
unpremeditated
andromedotoxin
intramolecular
andromonoecism
intramercurial
inframaxillary
untransferable
intrinsicality
intransitively
infrangibility
untranslatable
untranslatably
intransmutable
untransmutable
unpreparedness
unproportioned
unprepossessed
unpropitiously
uncrystallised
unprosperously
unpresumptuous
infrastructure
ungratefulness
untruthfulness
unpretendingly
ungroundedness
anisodactylous
unostentatious
unaspiringness
unassumingness
unstrengthened
knitting-needle
Gnathobdellida
unattractively
institutionary
instrumentally
pneumatologist
unpurchaseable
insusceptively
unsuccessfully
innumerability
insuperability
insufficiently
unauthenticity

indubitability
unbusinesslike
insurmountable
unsurmountable
insurmountably
pneumoconiosis
pneumokoniosis
pneumoconiotic
pneumodynamics
unsuspectingly
inauspiciously
unsuspiciously
insuppressible
insuppressibly
insurrectional
unquestionable
unquestionably
intussuscepted
inquisiturient
unsuitableness
angustifoliate
intuitionalism
intuitionalist
unavoidability
universalistic
universitarian
inevitableness
know-nothingism
snow-spectacles
unexpectedness
inexpiableness
unextinguished
inexorableness
inexpressibles
inexcusability
encyclopaedism
encyclopaedian
encyclopaedist
unsympathising
unsystematical
unsystematised
tobacco-stopper
volatilisation
foraminiferous
Johannisberger
potassium-argon
forbiddingness
double-declutch
hobbledehoydom
hobbledehoyish
hobbledehoyism
double-flowered
double-breasted
double-stopping
combustibility
conceivability
concelebration
non-compearance
coxcombicality
non-communicant
non-contentious
volcanological
concentrically

boa-constrictor
non-concurrence
non-cooperation
porcupine-grass
worcesterberry
worcester-sauce
concessionaire
moccasin-flower
conclusiveness
concavo-concave
conductibility
bowdlerisation
good-fellowship
gold-of-pleasure
wood-nightshade
condensability
folding-machine
good-for-nothing
road-worthiness
food-controller
powder-magazine
wonder-stricken
condescendence
conditionality
good-humouredly
dodecasyllabic
dodecasyllable
nomenclatorial
non-electrolyte
foreshortening
forethoughtful
norepinephrine
soteriological
solecistically
love-in-idleness
polemoniaceous
noteworthiness
foreordination
money-scrivener
potentiometric
confidentially
conformability
longs-and-shorts
rough-and-tumble
congratulative
congratulation
congratulatory
congregational
long-headedness
long-windedness
bougainvillaea
morganatically
conglomeration
conglobulation
longitudinally
conglutinative
conglutination
Rochelle-powder
sophistication
solitaire-board
sociobiologist
motivelessness
vociferousness

forisfamiliate
loving-kindness
dolichocephaly
polishing-paste
polishing-slate
politicisation
solidification
solicitousness
Rosicrucianism
holier-than-thou
Sovietological
solitudinarian
non-involvement
conjunctivitis
cock-a-doodle-doo
mock-heroically
book-mindedness
poikilothermic
poikilothermal
working-drawing
joukery-pawkery
woollen-drapery
soul-destroying
coelanaglyphic
soul-confirming
collapsability
collapsibility
colliquescence
bouleversement
follow-my-leader
formidableness
commodiousness
cosmographical
commentatorial
commandantship
cornmonsensical
common-or-garden
commensurately
commensuration
cosmopolitical
commissaryship
commissionaire
foundation-stop
mountain-tallow
mountain-laurel
mountain-marrow
mountaineering
mountain-beaver
roundaboutedly
roundaboutness
counterbalance
counter-battery
counter-changed
counter-current
counsel-keeping
counsellorship
counter-measure
counter-opening
counter-passant
counter-subject
counter-skipper
counter-salient
counter-trading

counter-wrought
council-chamber
coincidentally
somnambulation
somnambulistic
town-councillor
country-dancing
sonnet-sequence
cornet-à-pistons
connaturalness
monosaccharide
monocarpellary
non-operational
holometabolism
homogenisation
colonel-in-chief
borough-English
Monochlamydeae
monophthongise
monotheistical
monotheletical
monochromatism
soporiferously
monolingualism
dolomitisation
Monoplacophora
corolliflorous
homoeoteleuton
homoeothermous
homoiothermous
Mohorovicician
homoeomorphism
homoeomorphous
monotonousness
honourableness
colour-sergeant
monoprionidian
Zoroastrianism
pococuranteism
coconut-matting
comprehensible
comprehensibly
complexionless
morphinomaniac
compensational
companion-hatch
louping-on-stane
compunctiously
morphophonemic
compurgatorial
copper-fastened
comparableness
non-performance
copper-bottomed
compossibility
compassionable
composing-stick
corpuscularian
compatibleness
hospitableness
Porphyrogenite
zoophytologist
mosquito-weight

conquistadores
courageousness
co-ordinateness
coordinateness
boarding-school
mourning-border
corruptibility
horror-stricken
correspondence
correspondency
non-restrictive
gooseberry-wine
gooseberry-moth
gooseberry-fool
gooseberry-bush
consubstantial
consociational
boisterousness
co-essentiality
consuetudinary
coastguardsman
horse-godmother
conspiratorial
worshipfulness
constitutional
consulting-room
nonsensicality
consanguineous
torsion-balance
dog's-tooth-grass
house-physician
construability
conservational
conservatorium
constructively
constructivism
constructional
conscriptional
possessiveness
topsyturviness
contradictable
contradictious
contraindicate
contraindicant
contrarotating
contrapositive
contraposition
contractedness
contractionary
postmastership
contracyclical
horticulturist
cost-accountant
cost-accounting
corticosteroid
Pontederiaceae
röntgenography
north-eastwards
south-eastwards
Pontefract-cake
contagiousness
contiguousness
post-millennial

fortuitousness
contumaciously
contemperation
contemperature
contumeliously
contemporanean
contemptuously
noctambulation
continentalism
continentalist
continuousness
portentousness
north-north-east
north-north-west
fortune-telling
rostrocarinate
controvertible
controvertibly
dogtooth-violet
postpositively
postpositional
controllership
foster-daughter
forthrightness
contesseration
south-south-east
south-south-west
north-westwards
south-westwards
popularisation
loquaciousness
volumetrically
solubilisation
voluminousness
coquettishness
robustiousness
voluptuousness
convocationist
convulsiveness
Convolvulaceae
conventionally
conversational
conversaziones
convertibility
convexo-concave
forward-looking
polysaccharide
polymerisation
polytheistical
Polyplacophora
polyembryonate
polysyllabical
polysynthetism
sphaerocrystal
specialisation
spectacularity
spectrographic
spectrological
spectroscopist
space-traveller
spade-husbandry
apodeictically
epidemiologist

spread-eagleism
appendicectomy
Appendicularia
speechlessness
speech-training
apheliotropism
epigrammatical
optimalisation
spring-carriage
spring-mattress
spring-ligament
spring-cleaning
sprightfulness
optimistically
spelaeological
apologetically
open-handedness
spinthariscope
open-mindedness
spindle-shanked
opinionatively
aphoristically
optoelectronic
uproariousness
apoplectically
apophthegmatic
approach-stroke
spermatogenous
spermatophytic
spermatogonium
spermatorrhoea
appreciatively
spirochaetosis
apprehensively
apprenticement
apprenticeship
apprenticehood
sporangiophore
sporangiospore
sparrow-blasted
oppressiveness
spiritualistic
spiritlessness
spirituousness
spirit-stirring
epistemologist
opisthocoelian
opisthocoelous
opisthographic
opisthoglossal
epistolography
ophthalmometer
ophthalmometry
ophthalmoscope
ophthalmoscopy
apothegmatical
spatiotemporal
spawning-ground
epexegetically
sphygmographic
squadron-leader
squirearchical
equiangularity

equiponderance
aquifoliaceous
squirrel-monkey
bread-and-butter
breakfast-table
breathlessness
wreath-filament
preaching-cross
preaching-friar
preaching-house
breathing-space
breathing-while
organ-harmonium
organisability
organisational
treacle-mustard
organometallic
prearrangement
probabiliorism
probabiliorist
brobdingnagian
pribble-prabble
orobanchaceous
grace-and-favour
procrastinator
precociousness
Trochelminthes
practicability
fructification
trichinisation
traction-engine
proceleusmatic
preconcertedly
arachnological
triconsonantic
triconsonantal
trichobacteria
trichophytosis
trichomoniasis
trichotomously
precariousness
procuratorship
prick-the-garter
brachydactylic
brachycephalic
brachypinakoid
brachydiagonal
procryptically
Trachypteridae
predictability
productiveness
productibility
predaciousness
prodigiousness
tridimensional
predesignation
predesignatory
predestinative
predestinarian
predestination
predisposition
creditableness
traditionalism

traditionalist
traditionality
traditionarily
predeterminate
predeterminism
predevelopment
irreparability
Praeraphaelite
irrelativeness
friendlessness
breeding-ground
irremovability
irrevocability
irreconcilable
irreconcilably
true-lover's-knot
irrecognisable
tree-worshipper
irresoluteness
irresolubility
irrespectively
free-spokenness
irresponsively
irreproachable
irreproachably
irreproducible
irrestrainable
irrefutability
irresuscitable
irresuscitably
irreducibility
prefabrication
traffic-manager
traffic-returns
traffic-signals
preferentially
professionally
professorially
profitableness
pragmaticality
tragi-comically
progressionary
progressionism
progressionist
dragon-standard
progenitorship
prognosticator
gregariousness
prohibitionary
prohibitionism
prohibitionist
orthochromatic
archgenethliac
archiepiscopal
archaeological
Archaeornithes
orthographical
orthopterology
orthophosphate
greisenisation
praiseworthily
Ornithodelphia
ornithodelphic

ornithological
ornithomorphic
ornithophilous
prairie-chicken
artificialness
artillery-plant
traitorousness
articulateness
frolicsomeness
prolocutorship
drill-husbandry
proletarianise
proletarianism
grammaticaster
premeditatedly
trumpet-tongued
Kremlinologist
premillenarian
tremendousness
gram-equivalent
promise-breaker
promise-crammed
promise-keeping
bremsstrahlung
trimethylamine
transcendental
transcendently
grangerisation
prince-imperial
orange-coloured
orange-squeezer
princesse-dress
princesse-skirt
transformative
transformation
transfer-ticket
transformistic
transfusionist
French-Canadian
broncho-dilator
bronchiectasis
French-polisher
trencher-knight
trencher-friend
printing-office
transitiveness
transitionally
fringillaceous
transitoriness
grandiloquence
transliterator
transmigrative
transmigration
transmigratory
transmogrified
transmissivity
transmissional
pronunciamento
transplantable
transportation
transportingly
transport-rider
transsexualism

trinitrophenol
trinitrotoluol
Trinitarianism
crinkum-crankum
trinkum-trankum
transvaluation
transversality
transvestitism
arrondissement
cryobiological
arboricultural
cryptaesthesia
cryptaesthetic
propaedeutical
triphenylamine
proprioceptive
graphitisation
proprietorship
propeller-shaft
tropologically
preponderantly
trophoneurosis
cryptographist
proportionable
proportionably
proportionless
proportionment
proportionally
tripersonalism
tripersonalist
tripersonality
property-master
preposterously
propitiatorily
propitiousness
pre-Reformation
crystallomancy
prostaglandins
crystallisable
trisoctahedron
prosperousness
prosthodontics
prosthodontist
cross-infection
dressing-jacket
Prussification
presumptuously
presentability
presentational
prosencephalic
prosencephalon
presentiveness
presentimental
prison-breaking
Bristol-diamond
aristocratical
Crossopterygii
presupposition
preservability
cross-reference
dress-rehearsal
prescriptively
proscriptively

cross-sectional
pressure-helmet
presbyterially
trituberculate
trituberculism
protectiveness
Crutched-friars
prettification
prittle-prattle
arithmetically
prothonotarial
prothonotariat
protoplasmatic
fraternisation
erythropoiesis
Protospathaire
Arctostaphylos
protistologist
Prototracheata
protrusiveness
Protevangelium
protozoologist
groundlessness
ground-squirrel
Crouched-friars
troubleshooter
proud-stomached
trivialisation
providentially
traveller's-tree
preventability
preventiveness
provincial-rose
proventriculus
provost-marshal
greywacke-slate
prayerlessness
asparagus-stone
psychometrical
psychoneurosis
psychoneurotic
psychochemical
psychophysical
psycholinguist
psychoanalysis
psychoanalytic
psychosomatics
psychodramatic
psychodynamics
isodiametrical
osteoarthrosis
osteo-arthritis
asseveratingly
osteoglossidae
esterification
asset-stripping
ostentatiously
eschatological
Ustilaginaceae
astigmatically
psilanthropism
psilanthropist
Asclepiadaceae

asymmetrically
asymptotically
psephoanalysis
ostrich-feather
astrogeologist
astrologically
astronomically
astrophysicist
pseudaesthesia
pseudepigrapha
pseudepigraphy
pseudomembrane
pseudomorphism
pseudomorphous
pseudosolution
pseudo-archaism
pseudosymmetry
pseudonymously
strawberry-mark
strawberry-leaf
strawberry-tree
strand-scouring
straddle-legged
stratification
strabismometer
stratigraphist
attainableness
straining-piece
stocking-filler
stocking-stitch
stichometrical
sticky-fingered
stretching-bond
stretching-iron
steel-engraving
stoechiometric
etherification
steeplechasing
steeple-crowned
attemptability
strepsipterous
street-railroad
stigmatisation
stigmatiferous
stegocephalian
stegocephalous
stage-direction
steganographic
steganographer
strike-breaking
stoicheiometry
stoichiometric
striking-circle
attitudinarian
attitudinising
Italianisation
stalactitiform
stultification
stultiloquence
otolaryngology
stiletto-heeled
utilitarianise
utilitarianism

stomachfulness
stamp-collector
stamping-ground
stomping-ground
etymologically
stumbling-block
stumbling-stone
stomatogastric
standard-bearer
stenographical
standing-ground
ethnologically
stentorophonic
stoope-gallaunt
strobilisation
stupendousness
staphylococcal
Staphylococcus
Sturmabteilung
attractiveness
yttro-columbite
pteridophilist
star-of-the-earth
star-of-the-night
uterogestation
starch-hyacinth
pterylographic
ottrelite-slate
stereotactical
stereoscopical
stereometrical
stertorousness
stereospecific
stereoisomeric
yttro-tantalite
stirrup-leather
statuesqueness
stationariness
stethoscopical
station-manager
stout-heartedly
subarborescent
subalternation
rumblegumption
turbo-generator
tumbling-barrel
turbine-steamer
lumbersomeness
rubber-solution
luncheon-basket
durchkomponirt
succulent-house
Durchmusterung
subconsciously
subcontinental
vulcanological
subcontrariety
susceptibility
successfulness
successiveness
successionless
successionally
quicksilvering

quicksilverish
subcutaneously
quadragenarian
quadrangularly
muddleheadedly
hundred-per-cent
quadrigeminate
quadrigeminous
quadriennially
quadrisyllabic
quadrisyllable
fundamentalism
fundamentalist
fundamentality
murdering-piece
superannuation
superabundance
superciliously
supercelestial
supercontinent
superconductor
supercargoship
superexcellent
superelevation
supereminently
supererogative
supererogation
supererogatory
superessential
superficialise
superficiality
superfoetation
superincumbent
superinduction
superintendent
supernaturally
sure-footedness
superovulation
superphosphate
supersensitive
superstructive
superstruction
superstructure
superscription
superterranean
supervisorship
turf-accountant
sufferableness
Kupferschiefer
furfuraldehyde
luggage-carrier
subgenerically
suggestiveness
suggestibility
euphuistically
authentication
mushroom-anchor
euphorbiaceous
jurisdictional
audio-frequency
subinfeudation
subinfeudatory
humidification

munition-worker
pugilistically
audiometrician
Nudibranchiata
nudibranchiate
subinsinuation
subject-heading
subjectiveness
subjectivistic
huckleberrying
nuclear-powered
public-spirited
bull-headedness
quilting-cotton
outlandishness
burling-machine
submicroscopic
rummlegumption
rummelgumption
subminiaturise
submergibility
submersibility
submissiveness
pugnaciousness
quintessential
quantitatively
quantification
running-banquet
vulnerableness
quinquecostate
quinquefoliate
quinquefarious
quinquagesimal
quinquennially
quinquevalence
autoradiograph
mucoviscidosis
tumorigenicity
autobiographer
eulogistically
auto-intoxicant
humoursomeness
autocratically
auto-suggestion
autotypography
sulphathiazole
sulphanilamide
sulphapyridine
auspiciousness
suspiciousness
supplementally
purple-coloured
supplicatingly
surprisingness
turpentine-tree
suspensibility
purposefulness
surpassingness
suppositionary
supposititious
quaquaversally
turquoise-green
quarter-gallery

outrageousness
Supralapsarian
querimoniously
current-bedding
eutrophication
suprasegmental
nutritiousness
quartz-porphyry
Russianisation
substantialise
substantialism
substantiation
substantialist
substantiality
substantivally
Russo-Byzantine
Burschenschaft
question-master
substitutively
substitutional
purse-snatching
multicuspidale
futtock-shrouds
multifoliate
multifariously
hunt-the-slipper
multinucleated
hunting-leopard
multi-ownership
multiple-choice
multiplicative
multiplication
multiracialism
quattrocentism
quattrocentist
gutter-merchant
subtersensuous
subterrestrial
butter-fingered
multarticulate
butterfly-screw
subterposition
mustard-plaster
cucurbitaceous
Augustinianism
tumultuousness
curvilinearity
outward-sainted
muzzle-velocity
quizzification
evangelicalism
evangelisation
overcapitalise
avariciousness
overscrupulous
over-determined
over-refinement
over-the-counter
overwhelmingly
overindulgence
overpoweringly
over-confidence
overcompensate

overcorrection
overpopulation
overspecialise
ivory-porcelain
overproduction
overprotective
overestimation
overburdensome
swaddling-cloth
two-dimensional
sweet-and-twenty
two-for-his-heels
swindge-buckler
swingling-stock
swoopstake-like
sword-swallower
swathing-clouts
exacerbescence
experimentally
experienceless
extemporaneity
extemporaneous
extensionalism
extensionality
oxy-haemoglobin
exhilaratingly
extinguishable
extinguishment
exclaustration
examine-in-chief
excommunicable
extortionately
excruciatingly
extractability
extra-condensed
extracanonical
extracorporeal
extraforaneous
excrementitial
extrinsicality
extraneousness
extra-parochial
expressiveness
expressionless
extravehicular
existentialism
existentialist
pyjama-trousers
gynaecological
gynandromorphy
tyrannicalness
synaposematism
dynamometrical
dynamo-electric
symbolicalness
myocardiopathy
synchronically
hyperaesthesia
hyperaesthesic
hyperaesthetic
hyperacuteness
hyperbolically
hyperbatically

hypercriticise
hypercriticism
hypercalcaemia
hyperconscious
hypercatalexis
hyperglycaemia
hyperinflation
hypernatraemia
pyrenomycetous
hypersensitise
hypersensitive
hypertrophical
Pythagoreanism
mythologically
pyrheliometric
cyclanthaceous
pyelonephritic
pyelonephritis
myrmecological
myrmecophagous
myrmecophilous
dysmenorrhoeic
dysmenorrhoeal
symmetrisation
symmetrophobia
cyanocobalamin
hypodermically
Syrophoenician
sycophantishly
hypochondriasm
hypochondriast
hypothyroidism
pyrophosphoric
hypothetically
pyrophotograph
mylonitisation
hypomixolydian
hypocoristical
gynomonoecious
Zygobranchiata
zygobranchiate
hypocritically
gyrostabiliser
hypostatically
hyposulphurous
xylopyrography
xylotypography
synonymousness
lyophilisation
symptomatology
hydro-aeroplane
hydrobiologist
hydrocellulose
hydrocephalous
hydrocortisone
hydrocoralline
hydrodynamical
hydroextractor
hydrographical
hygrographical
dyer's-greenweed
hydrogeologist
hydromechanics

hydromagnetics
hydronephrosis
hydronephrotic
Hydropterideae
hydropneumatic
hydrosulphuric
hygroscopicity
hyetographical
nyctaginaceous
dysteleologist
systematically
hysterectomise
mysteriousness

araheliotropic
atathermometer
aralinguistics
arasiticalness
atallactically
ataclysmically
alaeomagnetism
alaeogeography
alaeophytology
aradoxicalness
alaeolimnology
alaeobotanical
alaeozoologist
alaeographical
alaeontography
alaeontologist
1alacopterygian
aragraphically
1alassimilation
arasympathetic
abbath-breaking
acchanalianism
atch-as-catch-can
anctimoniously
ascularisation
arcenchymatous
1alconformation
1ndscape-marble
addler-corporal
ard-heartedness
addler-sergeant
1nding-carriage
ard-and-fastness
andwort-spurrey
1aldistribution
asement-curtain
/ater-equivalent
1aterialvalent
1aterialisation
:apernaitically
ategoricalness
arenthetically
alf-wellingtons
alf-heartedness
argain-basement
aughing-jackass
1argaritiferous
1achine-readable
ashionableness
athering-ground
1anic-depressive
adiogramophone
adiogoniometer
asidiomycetous
ationalisation
ationalisation
adiotelegraphy
1agisterialness
anisterisation
ackney-coachman
ackney-carriage
ack-of-all-trades
ack-in-the-pulpit

market-gardening
packet-switching
railway-crossing
railway-carriage
parliament-hinge
parliament-house
parliamentarian
parliamentarily
parliamentarism
wall-gillyflower
paulo-post-future
Callitrichaceae
warm-heartedness
rainbow-coloured
manneristically
magneto-electric
carnivorousness
sado-masochistic
panophthalmitis
paroemiographer
saloon-passenger
vasoconstrictor
manoeuvrability
malpractitioner
Pan-Presbyterian
malpresentation
carpometacarpus
banqueting-house
marriage-licence
marriage-portion
carriage-forward
macrocosmically
caprifoliaceous
warrantableness
Patripassianism
macrosporangium
macroscopically
marsh-cinquefoil
Caesalpiniaceae
tarsometatarsal
tarsometatarsus
passenger-pigeon
Marsipobranchii
particularistic
pantechnicon-van
parthenogenesis
parthenogenetic
party-government
gastroenteritis
Bartholomew-tide
pantopragmatics
bacteriological
fantasticalness
faithworthiness
nature-knowledge
daguerreotypist
harvest-festival
canvas-stretcher
Caryophyllaceae
objectification
observationally
ebullioscopical
abiogenetically

oceanographical
éclaircissement
sclerodermatous
scribaciousness
scribbling-paper
schillerisation
echinodermatous
schizophrenetic
scripture-reader
schistosomiasis
ochlocratically
acclimatisation
scolopendriform
ecclesiological
acknowledgeable
acknowledgeably
acknowledgement
achondroplastic
schoolmastering
schoolmasterish
school-inspector
accountableness
scaphocephalous
Schrecklichkeit
icositetrahedra
ichthyodorulite
ichthyodorylite
Ichthyopterygia
acquisitiveness
adventurousness
edriophthalmian
edriophthalmous
odontostomatous
ideographically
idiosyncratical
odoriferousness
adjutant-general
metamathematics
decarbonisation
decarburisation
decalcification
bed-and-breakfast
Megacheiroptera
Nemathelminthes
nemathelminthic
hexachlorophane
hexachlorophene
mesaticephalous
Selaginellaceae
metalinguistics
hepaticological
demagnetisation
pedagoguishness
departmentalise
departmentalism
herb-Christopher
peacock-pheasant
descriptiveness
pencil-sharpener
new-Common-
wealth
geochronologist
Neo-Christianity

hendecasyllabic
hendecasyllable
readvertisement
tendentiousness
tender-heartedly
meadow-saxifrage
defencelessness
degenerationist
deleteriousness
redetermination
telephotography
repetitiousness
determinability
heterodactylous
heterocercality
heterogeneously
heterosexuality
ceremoniousness
developmentally
selenographical
telegraphically
penetrativeness
cerebrovascular
necessitousness
seventeen-hunder
desertification
desexualisation
receiving-office
receiver-general
self-capacitance
self-observation
self abandonment
self-advancement
self-determining
self-degradation
self-destruction
self-destructive
self-affirmation
self-vindication
self-liquidating
self-slaughtered
self-improvement
perfunctoriness
self-sovereignty
reafforestation
self-confidently
self-forgetfully
self-pollination
self-complacence
self-considering
self-constituted
self-consequence
self-consistency
self-portraiture
self-opinionated
self-approbation
self-sufficiency
self-humiliation
self-substantial
self-sustainment
self-explication
self-explanatory
self-examination

sergeant-drummer
neighbourliness
weighing-machine
pergamentaceous
methodistically
nepheline-basalt
mechanistically
dephlogisticate
technologically
Mephistophelean
Mephistophelian
semimanufacture
Semi-Pelagianism
sedimentologist
decipherability
medicine-dropper
sericiculturist
vehicle-actuated
semi-independent
regionalisation
meritoriousness
lexicographical
lepidopterology
semi-documentary
menispermaceous
denitrification
devitrification
semitransparent
hemicrystalline
perissodactylic
perissosyllabic
peristaltically
heliotropically
desilverisation
devil-worshipper
well-accomplisht
well-intentioned
hellenistically
well-conditioned
well-upholstered
fellow-traveller
helminthologist
hermeneutically
seeming-virtuous
hermaphroditism
geomorphologist
dermatoglyphics
reinterrogation
deindustrialise
xeroradiography
reconcilability
Second-adventist
second-in-
command
seconds-pendulum
recoverableness
before-mentioned
recollectedness
meroblastically
decolourisation
decomposability
resourcefulness
democratifiable

democratisation
reconsideration
reconsolidation
remorselessness
demonstrability
remonstratingly
demonstratively
refortification
decontamination
decontaminative
reconvalescence
seaplane-carrier
respectableness
perpendicularly
reapportionment
temperamentally
tempestuousness
sesquicentenary
reproachfulness
Tetrabranchiata
tetrabranchiate
Tetractinellida
jerry-come-tumble
retrievableness
retrogressional
retrogressively
near-sightedness
ferro-molybdenum
necromantically
recrementitious
refrangibleness
metropolitanate
neuropsychiatry
neurophysiology
heir-presumptive
retrospectively
tetrasyllabical
refreshment-room
tetrasporangium
re-establishment
peasecod-bellied
peasecod-cuirass
perspicaciously
perspicuousness
pessimistically
messenger-at-arms
personification
personalisation
seismographical
sense-perception
dessertspoonful
sensation-monger
Tectibranchiata
tectibranchiate
tentaculiferous
gentleman-at-arms
gentlemanliness
feather-boarding
weather-boarding
weather-notation
rent-restriction
vertiginousness
ventriloquially

ventriloquistic
testament-dative
sententiousness
septentrionally
venturesomeness
destructibility
destructiveness
secundogeniture
resurrection-man
resurrection-pie
resurrectionary
resurrectionise
resurrectionism
resurrectionist
demulsification
serviceableness
efficaciousness
affranchisement
agriculturalist
shabby-gentility
shadow-pantomime
wheel-animalcule
phrenologically
threepenceworth
threepennyworth
chrestomathical
shrink-resistant
Christadelphian
Christy-minstrel
cholecystectomy
cholecystostomy
philanthropical
cholangiography
thalassographer
thalassographic
philosophically
rhombencephalon
chamber-hangings
chamberlainship
rhombenporphyry
Rhamphorhynchus
chemopsychiatry
phantasmagorial
Rhynchobdellida
Rhynchocephalia
thin-skinnedness
phenakistoscope
phenylketonuria
phenylketonuric
phenolphthalein
phonemicisation
phenomenologist
phenomenalistic
chenopodiaceous
chondrification
chondropterygii
thanatognomonic
phonautographic
thankworthiness
chromatographic
chloramphenicol
thrombo-embolism
theorematically

shooting-gallery
theosophistical
chronologically
chromoxylograph
pharmacognostic
pharmacognosist
therianthropism
chargé-d'affaires
whirling-machine
whirling-dervish
thermochemistry
theriomorphosis
therapeutically
pharisaicalness
physicochemical
phase-difference
phosphorylation
phosphorescence
physiotherapist
physiologically
physiographical
photoconducting
photoconductive
photoelasticity
photogrammetric
phytogeographer
phytogeographic
photolithograph
photomechanical
photomicrograph
photosensitiser
phototelegraphy
photoxylography
photozincograph
rheumatological
shoulder-shotten
shoulder-clapper
shoulder-slipped
thoughtlessness
cigarette-holder
disaffectedness
disaffectionate
disafforestment
misapprehension
misapprehensive
misappreciation
misappreciative
disagreeability
disassimilative
disarticulation
bioastronautics
disadvantageous
misbecomingness
aircraft-carrier
kitchen-gardener
discretionarily
air-chief-marshal
mischievousness
miscellaneously
circumnavigable
circumnavigator
circumvallation
circumscribable

ircumscription	misintelligence	distastefulness	amphitheatrical
ircumscriptive	disinterestedly	distrustfulness	omnibenevolence
iscommendation	miniaturisation	mistrustfulness	omnidirectional
ircumferential	ticket-collector	ritualistically	smelting-furnace
ircumambagious	gillie-whitefoot	clearing-station	emancipationist
ircumincession	bioluminescence	pleasurableness	imponderability
ircuminsession	bibliographical	pleasure-seeking	immortalisation
ircumforaneous	field-sequential	flibbertigibbet	importunateness
iscommodiously	pillow-structure	all-changing-word	impracticalness
ircumspectness	diamagnetically	electroanalysis	amaryllidaceous
ircumstantials	significatively	electrochemical	impressionistic
ircumstantiate	disorganisation	electrodynamics	imprescriptible
ir-conditioning	disobligingness	electrification	improvisatorial
iscontinuation	kilogram-calorie	electrokinetics	ambulance-chaser
iscontinuously	displeasingness	electromagnetic	immunochemistry
isconstruction	dispensableness	electromyograph	incapaciousness
iscosimetrical	diaphototropism	electrometrical	incalculability
indicativeness	disproportional	electronegative	unsatisfiedness
Middle-Easterner	misproportioned	electrophoresis	unparliamentary
niddle-of-the-road	diaphragmatitis	electrophoretic	uncanonicalness
Ind-heartedness	dispassionately	electropositive	unpatriotically
niddle-stitching	disputativeness	electrotechnics	unobjectionable
Cinderella-dance	disquisitionary	electrothermics	unobjectionably
iodestructible	microanalytical	sleeping-partner	inobtrusiveness
vindow-gardening	Microchiroptera	sleeping-draught	unobtrusiveness
nineralogically	nitro-derivative	ill-favouredness	anacreontically
inematographer	microdissection	plagiostomatous	inaccessibility
inematographic	microelectronic	Gleichschaltung	knick-knackatory
imethylaniline	hierogrammatist	illimitableness	unaccommodating
ice-chamberlain	micromicrofarad	plumbaginaceous	onychocryptosis
inemicrography	micromicrocurie	slumpflationary	inscrutableness
Iversification	micromillimetre	flamboyante-tree	inadvisableness
isentrancement	citronella-grass	plantaginaceous	unadvisableness
isentanglement	micropegmatitic	clandestineness	inadmissibility
lirection-finder	microphotograph	slantingdicular	unidiomatically
lirector-general	disreputability	plenipotentiary	interambulacral
liffrangibility	disrespectfully	blood-and-thunder	interambulacrum
litterentiation	microsporanglum	blood-guiltiness	interchangeable
lisgracefulness	microscopically	allotriomorphic	interchangeably
ingle-heartedly	microsporophyll	ultracentrifuge	interchangement
ingularisation	microtechnology	ultramicroscope	interclavicular
iogeochemistry	dissociableness	ultramicroscopy	unpeaceableness
iogeographical	dissolvableness	ultra-Protestant	unteachableness
lishearteningly	dieselhydraulic	ultrasonography	intercollegiate
lishabilitation	lissencephalous	blast-furnaceman	intercolonially
'ithecanthropus	dissatisfaction	glossographical	interconnection
ithochromatics	dissatisfactory	flutter-tonguing	interdigitation
Michaelmas-daisy	victualling-bill	Platyhelminthes	interdependence
ight-headedness	victualling-ship	slotting-machine	inseperableness
ight-handedness	victualling-yard	platitudinarian	indeterminately
liaheliotropism	distractibility	cloud-cuckoo-land	indetermination
ight-mindedness	distressfulness	cloud-cuckoo-town	undetermination
ight-mindedness	fifth-monarchism	cloud-compelling	unceremoniously
lithyrambically	fifth-monarchist	eleutherodactyl	under-employment
lisharmoniously	distinctiveness	pleuro-pneumonia	indefeasibility
igh-gravel-blind	distinguishable	illustriousness	indefensibility
vithdrawing-room	distinguishably	slave-trafficker	unnecessariness
lividend-warrant	distinguishment	impenetrability	underestimation
lisinflationary	picture-moulding	imperishability	interestingness
iding-committee	historiographer	impermeableness	unrelentingness
lisillusionment	historiographic	immensurability	antepenultimate
lisimprisonment	picture-restorer	imperviableness	unselfconscious
icissitudinous	picturesqueness	imaginativeness	interferometric

interfascicular
encephalography
underhandedness
undesirableness
unverifiability
unremittingness
interjectionary
interjaculatory
intellectualise
intellectualism
intellectualist
intellectuality
intelligibility
unhealthfulness
interlamination
indemnification
internationally
unreconciliable
interosculation
unrecommendable
unreconstructed
undemonstrative
interpretership
under-privileged
interpenetrable
interprovincial
under-production
interpersonally
intemperateness
interrogatively
understandingly
intersubjective
intensification
interscholastic
interstratified
insensitiveness
ungentlemanlike
anaesthetically
anaesthesiology
under-the-counter
intertwistingly
intertentacular
intertanglement
ancestor-worship
interventionism
interventionist
unseaworthiness
inoffensiveness
ineffectualness
ineffectiveness
inefficaciously
inofficiousness
unchristianlike
unchallengeable
unchallengeably
unwholesomeness
unphilosophical
unchangeability
anthropopathism
anthropogenesis
anthropocentric
anthropophagite
anthropophagous

anthropobiology
anthroposophist
anthropological
anthropomorphic
anthropopsychic
anti-Gallicanism
uncircumscribed
indisciplinable
undisciplinable
antiperistaltic
indigestibility
unrighteousness
antichristianly
anticholinergic
annihilationism
infinitesimally
antivivisection
indivisibleness
individualistic
anticlericalism
insignificantly
insignificative
antimonarchical
oneirocriticism
antitrinitarian
indissolubility
indistributable
indistinctively
undistinguished
unalterableness
inflammableness
unblameableness
unimaginatively
anomalistically
uninterestingly
unintermittedly
uninterpretable
uninterruptedly
unintentionally
enantiomorphism
enantiomorphous
unconcernedness
unconditionally
intolerableness
ontogenetically
incongruousness
unforgivingness
unsophisticated
encomiastically
incommunicative
uncommunicative
incommensurable
incommensurably
incommutability
entomologically
uncomplainingly
uncomplaisantly
uncomprehending
incomprehension
incomprehensive
uncomprehensive
uncomplimentary
uncompanionable

incomparability
uncooperatively
unco-operatively
uncompassionate
incompatibility
incorrigibility
inconsiderately
inconsideration
unconscientious
unconsciousness
inconspicuously
unfossiliferous
unconsentaneous
inconsequential
unconstrainable
unconstrainedly
unfortunateness
uncontroversial
involuntariness
inapplicability
inopportuneness
inapprehensible
unapprehensible
inappropriately
unsportsmanlike
inspirationally
inoperativeness
unapostolically
intractableness
untractableness
unprecedentedly
unpractisedness
incredulousness
unprogressively
ungrammatically
unpremeditation
andromonoecious
enfranchisement
intrinsicalness
intransigentism
intransigentist
infrangibleness
untransmigrated
intransmissible
untransmissible
unpronounceable
entrepreneurial
unproportionate
unprepossessing
introsusception
untrustworthily
unprotectedness
unprotestantise
unascertainable
unsteadfastness
gnotobiotically
gnotobiological
inattentiveness
knitting-machine
instantaneously
unstatesmanlike
institutionally
instrumentalism

instrumentalist
instrumentality
instrumentation
instructiveness
pneumatological
Annunciation-day
infundibuliform
innumerableness
insuperableness
unauthenticated
unauthoritative
indubitableness
injudiciousness
unqualifiedness
invulnerability
insubordinately
insubordination
unsuspectedness
insurrectionary
insurrectionism
insurrectionist
unsubstantiated
insubstantially
intussusception
intussusceptive
inquisitorially
inquisitiveness
angustirostrate
unavailableness
unavoidableness
inextensibility
inexpensiveness
unexceptionable
unexceptionably
unexceptionally
inexplicability
inexcusableness
encyclopaedical
unsymmetrically
ankylostomiasis
monarchianistic
totalitarianism
logarithmically
romanticisation
bomb-calorimeter
double-facedness
double-barrelled
hobbledehoyhood
combustibleness
conceivableness
porcelain-cement
non-commissioned
non-contributory
conceptualistic
good-naturedness
cold-bloodedness
woody-nightshade
good-conditioned
powdering-closet
wonder-mongering
condescendingly
mole-electronics
sober-mindedness

governor-general
homeopathically
poverty-stricken
confidentiality
configurational
confrontational
comfortlessness
confessionalism
confessionalist
congealableness
long-sightedness
zoogeographical
lophobranchiate
nothingarianism
sociobiological
police-inspector
police-constable
boning-telescope
dolichocephalic
polishing-powder
sociolinguistic
socialistically
goniometrically
co-significative
non-intervention
non-intrusionist
conjunctionally
conjunctiveness
cockneyfication
lob-lie-by-the-fire
noble-mindedness
collenchymatous
foul-mouthedness
world-without-end
formularisation
commendableness
communicability
communicatively
communalisation
cosmopolitanism
commission-agent
foundation-stone
mountain-railway
mountain-leather
mountain-bramble
roundaboutility
roundaboutation
counter-approach
counteractively
counter-evidence
counterfeisance
counter-flowered
counter-irritant
countermandable
counter-movement
counter-pressure
counter-proposal
counter-security
countervailable
connoisseurship
morning-sickness
round-shouldered
co-instantaneity

co-instantaneous
Johnny-head-in-air
homogeneousness
homochlamydeous
monochlamydeous
Monocotyledones
logographically
topographically
holocrystalline
monocrystalline
coconsciousness
monosymmetrical
comprehensively
comprehensivise
complementarily
complementarity
compressibility
compendiousness
companion-ladder
non-professional
morphophonemics
non-profit-making
corporification
compartmentally
compassionately
colposcopically
hospitalisation
computerisation
compotationship
competitiveness
zoophytological
conquerableness
torque-converter
correlativeness
corruptibleness
correspondently
correspondingly
dorsibranchiate
gooseberry-stone
consubstantiate
consecratedness
consecutiveness
considerateness
consideratively
low-spiritedness
conscience-proof
conscientiously
constitutionist
conspicuousness
consolation-race
consumptiveness
consentaneously
nonsensicalness
consequentially
conservationist
conservatorship
constructionism
conscriptionist
dorsiventrality
contravallation
contradictorily
contradictively
contrapropeller

portrait-gallery
portrait-painter
portmanteau-word
contractability
contractibility
north-countryman
röntgenotherapy
north-eastwardly
south-eastwardly
mortiferousness
doctrinarianism
post-millenarian
postulationally
contemplatively
contemporaneity
contemporaneous
contemptibility
continuation-day
contentiousness
controversially
montmorillonite
controllability
Götterdämmerung
north-westwardly
south-westwardly
softly-sprighted
conventionalise
conventionalism
conventionalist
conventionality
conversationism
conversationist
notwithstanding
polychloroprene
polyphloesboean
polyunsaturated
polycrystalline
Polyprotodontia
polysyllabicism
polysynthetical
speaking-trumpet
sphaerosiderite
apocalyptically
speculativeness
spectroscopical
space-travelling
epidemiological
spread-eaglewise
speechification
Sphenisciformes
spheroidisation
Ophioglossaceae
Apollinarianism
spontaneousness
open-heartedness
optoelectronics
apophthegmatise
apophthegmatist
approachability
spermatogenesis
spermatogenetic
spermatoblastic
opprobriousness

appropriateness
appropinquation
epistemological
Opisthobranchia
opisthognathous
episcopalianism
ophthalmologist
ophthalmoplegia
ophthalmoscopic
epitheliomatous
equalitarianism
equiprobability
ergatandromorph
crease-resistant
crease-resisting
great-grandchild
treacherousness
irrationalistic
treasonableness
preacquaintance
problematically
probationership
procrastinating
procrastination
procrastinatory
procrastinative
procreativeness
practicableness
fractionisation
brachistochrone
preconstruction
precipitability
precipitousness
processionalist
brachydactylous
brachycephalous
predictableness
predeterminable
irreparableness
irrepealability
irredeemability
free-heartedness
true-heartedness
irreversibility
irretentiveness
greenery-yallery
freezing-mixture
irreligiousness
arterialisation
irremissibility
irresistibility
irremovableness
irrevocableness
irreconcilement
irresolvability
irrefragability
irreprehensible
irreprehensibly
irrefutableness
irreducibleness
irreductibility
preformationism
preformationist

preferentialism
preferentialist
professionalise
professionalism
pragmaticalness
programmability
progressiveness
fragmentariness
trigonometrical
prognostication
prognosticative
prohibitiveness
Archichlamydeae
archiepiscopacy
archiepiscopate
orthophosphoric
orthopsychiatry
prehistorically
architectonical
ornithodelphian
ornithodelphous
Erziehungsroman
ornithorhynchus
training-college
prairie-schooner
drilling-machine
crimping-machine
criminalisation
gramophonically
transcriptional
transcriptively
transfigurement
transfiguration
transferribilty
transgressional
transgressively
wrong-headedness
Frenchification
French-polishing
bronchoscopical
franking-machine
printing-machine
wringing-machine
transilluminate
grandiloquently
transliteration
granulitisation
transmogrifying
transmutability
transplantation
transportedness
transparentness
transpositional
granitification
trinitrobenzene
trinitrotoluene
Eriocaulonaceae
proof-correcting
proof-correction
arboriculturist
armoured-cruiser
crook-shouldered
proprietorially

propylitisation
trypanosomiasis
crypto-Christian
crypto-communist
proportionality
proportionately
properispomenon
prepossessingly
prepositionally
Pre-Raphaelistic
Pre-Raphaelitish
Pre-Raphaelitism
crystallography
crystallisation
prospectiveness
dressing-station
crossing-sweeper
prestidigitator
trisyllabically
cross-laterality
presentationism
presentationist
presentableness
presence-chamber
prosenchymatous
Aristotelianism
crossopterygian
preservationist
trustworthiness
Presbyterianise
Presbyterianism
pretentiousness
preternaturally
protospatharius
protozoological
traumatological
argumentatively
troublesomeness
troubleshooting
provocativeness
provost-sergeant
gravitationally
drawn-threadwork
psychopathology
psychogenetical
psychogeriatric
psychometrician
psychochemistry
psychotherapist
psychophysicist
psychobiography
psychobiologist
psychohistorian
psychosomimetic
psychotomimetic
psychographical
psychrometrical
asclepiadaceous
isoperimetrical
astrodynamicist
ostreiculturist
astronavigation
pseudepigraphic

pseudohexagonal
strawberry-shrub
straightforward
stratigraphical
steam-navigation
strait-waistcoat
sticking-plaster
stretcher-bearer
stretching-frame
etherealisation
stoechiological
atherosclerosis
stiff-neckedness
steganographist
stoicheiometric
stoichiological
stalactitically
stalagmitically
stilpnosiderite
stamping-machine
standardisation
standing-rigging
ethnomusicology
stand-offishness
strombuliferous
attorney-general
atmospherically
stapling-machine
staphylorrhaphy
star-of-Bethlehem
stereochemistry
stereographical
stereoisomerism
humanitarianism
bubble-and-squeak
quick-conceiving
punctiliousness
durchkomponiert
subcommissioner
susceptibleness
pulchritudinous
successlessness
quick-wittedness
quadripartition
quadruplication
superabundantly
supercalendered
tuberculisation
superconducting
superconductive
superexaltation
superexcellence
superficialness
superfluousness
superheterodyne
superincumbence
superinducement
superimposition
superintendence
superintendency
superlativeness
supernaturalise
supernaturalism

supernaturalist
superordination
superplasticity
superstitiously
superstructural
supersaturation
Jungermanniales
euphemistically
authoritatively
rudimentariness
pusillanimously
numismatologist
jurisprudential
subintellection
subintelligence
subintelligitur
subject-superior
sublapsarianism
pulmobranchiate
quinquagenarian
quintuplication
autoradiography
autoschediastic
subordinateness
automorphically
autographically
sulphaguanidine
supplementarily
supplementation
supportableness
purposelessness
suppositionally
sulphur-bacteria
sulphureousness
quartermistress
quarrelsomeness
quarter-sessions
surreptitiously
substantialness
substantiveness
subspecifically
quasihistorical
questionability
question-begging
substitutionary
substratosphere
multiarticulate
justifiableness
multinucleolate
juxtapositional
subterraneously
quatercentenary
butterfly-flower
butterfly-orchis
multitudinously
suburbanisation
evangelicalness
evangelistarion
evening-primrose
everlastingness
overdevelopment
overbearingness
overforwardness

wner-occupation
wo-pair-of-stairs
word-and-buckler
wathing-clothes
xperimentalise
xperimentalism
xperimentalist
xperimentation
xperimentative
xpeditiousness
xperientialism
xperientialist
xteriorisation
xternalisation
xtemporariness
xtemporisation
xchangeability
xhibitionistic
xemplification
xcommunication
xcommunicatory
xtra-curricular
xtra-illustrate
xtra-judicially
xcrementitious
xtraordinaries
xtraordinarily
xtra-provincial
xpressionistic
ynandromorphic
ynarthrodially
synchronistical
synchronisation
synchronousness
yperadrenalism
ypercritically
ypercatalectic
synecdochically
synecologically
yperthyroidism
nyristicivorous
syllabification
dyslogistically
syllogistically
dysmenorrhealic
symmetricalness
ypnotisability
cytomegalovirus
pyrotechnically
sycophantically
ypochondriacal
ypochondriasis
ypophosphorous
pyrophotography
pyro-electricity
ypographically
xylotypographic
symptomatically
sympathetically
sympathomimetic
ydrobiological
Hydrocorallinae
ydrodynamicist

hydrometallurgy
hydropathically
hydrostatically
dyer's-yellowweed
dysteleological
hyetometrograph
systematisation
Czechoslovakian